CONTENTS OF MOTOR IMPORTED CAR TIME GUIDE

EACH CAR SECTION INCLUDES THE FOLLOWING:

1. Detailed Index
2. Vehicle Identification
3. Illustrations
4. Operation Times

Each car operation time section has been divided into a number of smaller sections. At the start of each section is an Operation Index. A partial example of the Ignition, Starting & Charging section index follows.

OPERATION INDEX

Tune-Up, Minor 1
Tune-Up, Major 2
Compression Test 3
Distributor, R & R Or Renew 4
Distributor, R & R & Overhaul 5
Distributor Cap, Renew 6
Ignition Cable Set, Renew 7
Vacuum Control Unit, Renew 8
Ignition Coil, Renew 9
Starter & Ignition Switch, Renew 10
Starter, R & R Or Renew 11
Starter Solenoid, Renew 12
Starter Bendix Drive, Renew 13
Starter, R & R & Overhaul 14
Starter Brushes, Renew 15

Each operation in a given section is numbered. Locate the desired operation in the index and its number. Thus, instead of reading through the operations until the desired one is reached, merely find the operation in the index and follow through to the assigned number.

The operation times reported in this publication are to be used as a guide only. They are based on data supplied by the vehicle manufacturer, who has arrived at them by repeated performance of each operation a sufficient number of times under normal shop conditions to establish the requirements of the average mechanic, working under average conditions and following procedures outlined in their service manuals.

The times shown apply only to standard stock models. The times do not apply to cars with equipment other than that supplied by the car manufacturer as standard or regular production options. If other equipment is used, the time may be adjusted to compensate for the variables. Also, additional time may be encountered when difficulties arise due to corrosion, rust, carbon build-up, varnish, broken studs, etc. The time is listed in hours and tenths of an hour. A computation table for converting time into dollars to fit local rates per hour is located on the inside rear cover.

DEFINITIONS

R & R means remove and replace the same part.
RENEW means remove the old part and install a new one.
OVERHAUL means to remove an assembly from the car, inspect, disassemble, repair, re-assemble, install and adjust.

MOTOR

IMPORTED CAR TIME GUIDE

2nd Edition

USE THE INDEX on the first page of each car chapter to locate
VEHICLE IDENTIFICATION – ILLUSTRATIONS – OPERATION TIMES

CONTENTS

ALFA ROMEO 2
ARROW 66
AUDI 15
AUSTIN 26
BMW 39
CAPRI 52
COLT 66
CORTINA 81
COURIER 91
CRICKET 114
DATSUN 125
FIAT 140
FIESTA 156
HONDA 178
JAGUAR 195
LANCIA 209
LUV 216
MAZDA 240
MERCEDES 262
MG (Except Midget) 280
MG MIDGET 26
OPEL (1966-75) 292
OPEL (1976-78) 304
PEUGEOT 327
PORSCHE 337
RENAULT 353
SAAB 368
SIMCA 381
SUBARU 394
TOYOTA 409
TRIUMPH 426
VOLKSWAGEN 438
VOLVO 458

CONVERSION TABLES
Time/Dollar 480
Inch Fractions, Decimals, Metric .. 472
JACK & LIFT POINTS 470

Published by
MOTOR
1790 Broadway, New York, N.Y. 10019
The Automotive Business Magazine

Printed in the U. S. A.

ISBN 0-910992-92-4

IDENTIFICATION

ALL MODELS.................................3

ILLUSTRATIONS

FIG 1 – ENGINE BLOCK & MOUNTINGS
FIG 2 – CYLINDER HEAD
FIG 3 – CYLINDER HEAD DETAILS
FIG 4 – OIL PAN
FIG 5 – CRANKSHAFT, PISTONS & RODS
FIG 6 – TRANSMISSION
FIG 7 – FRONT SUSPENSION
FIG 8 – STEERING
FIG 9 – REAR SUSPENSION
FIG 10 – REAR AXLE
FIG 11 – DIFFERNTIAL GEARS
FIG 12 – DIFFERNTIAL CASE

OPERATION TIMES

A

Air Pump.................. 10
Alternator.................. 10
Altitude Compensator.................. 10
Axle Shaft.................. 13

B

Ball Joints.................. 13
Back-Up Lamp Switch.................. 14
Brakes.................. 12

C

Cables (Ignition).................. 10
Calipers.................. 12
Camshaft.................. 11
Catalytic Converter.................. 11
Clutch.................. 12
Coil Ignition.................. 10
Compression Test.................. 10
Connecting Rods.................. 11
Cooling System.................. 11
Crankshaft.................. 11
Cylinder Head.................. 11

D

Dash Gauges.................. 14
Differential.................. 13
Disc Brakes.................. 12
Distributor.................. 10

E

Emission Controls.................. 10
Engine Assembly.................. 11
Engine Oiling.................. 11
Engine Tune-Up.................. 10
Exhaust System.................. 10

F

Flywheel.................. 12
Front Suspension.................. 13
Fuel Gauges.................. 14
Fuel Pump.................. 10
Fuel Tank.................. 10

H

Hand Brake.................. 13
Hazard Light Switch.................. 14
Heat Gauge.................. 14
Heated Rear Window Switch.................. 14
Heater Core.................. 11
Hose (Brake).................. 12
Hose (Radiator).................. 11
Hydraulic Brakes.................. 12

I

I Beam Axle.................. 14
Idle Equalizer.................. 10
Ignition.................. 10
Ignition Coil.................. 10
Ignition Switch.................. 10
Injector.................. 10

L

Light Switches.................. 14

M

Master Cylinder.................. 12

O

Oil Gauge.................. 14
Oiling, Engine.................. 11
Oil Pan.................. 11
Oil Pump.................. 11

P

Parking Brake.................. 13
Pistons.................. 11
Power Brake.................. 12

R

Radiator.................. 11
Radiator Hose.................. 11
Rear Axle.................. 13
Regulator (Alternator).................. 10
Rod Bearings.................. 11

S

Shocks (Front).................. 13
Shocks (Rear).................. 13
Speedometer.................. 14
Springs (Front).................. 13
Springs (Rear).................. 14
Stabilizer.................. 13
Starting Motor.................. 10
Steering Gear.................. 13
Steering Linkage.................. 13
Stop Light Switch.................. 14
Switches (light).................. 14

T

Tachometer.................. 14
Temperature Gauge.................. 14
Timing Case Cover.................. 11
Timing Chain.................. 11
Timing Gears.................. 11
Torsion Bar.................. 13
Track Rod.................. 13
Transmission.................. 12
Transverse Bar.................. 14
Tune-Up, Engine.................. 10

V

Valve System.................. 11

W

Water Pump.................. 11
Windshield Wiper.................. 14

MODEL IDENTIFICATION

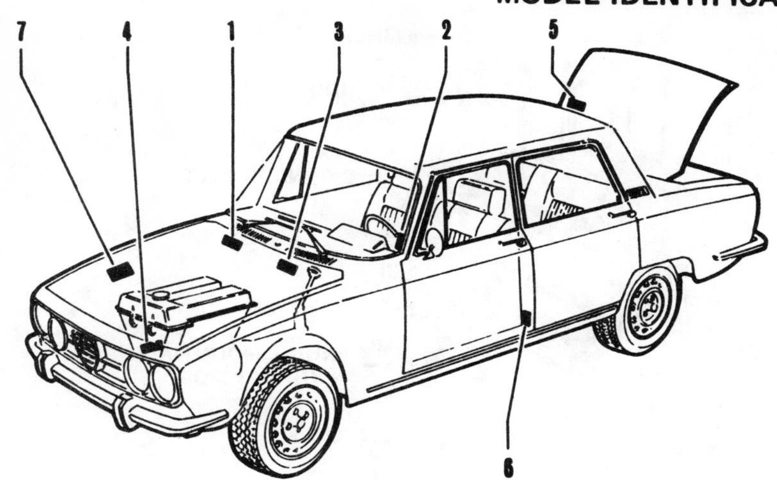

2000 BERLINA

1 – Chassis No. On Firewall
2 – Chassis No. On Windshield Post
3 – Car Model Number
4 – Engine Number
5 – Finish Paint Plate
6 – D.O.T. Certification Label
7 – Emission Data Label

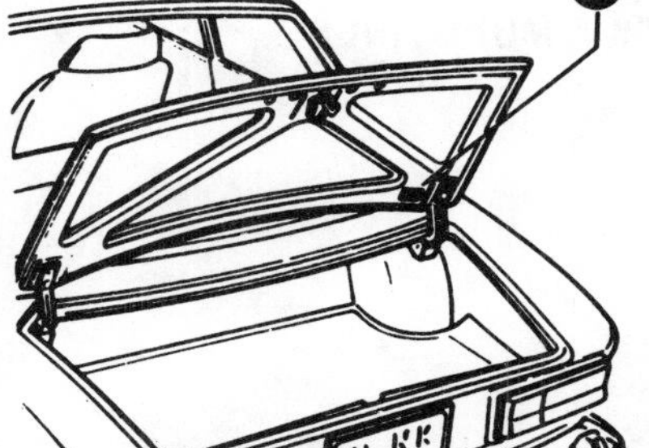

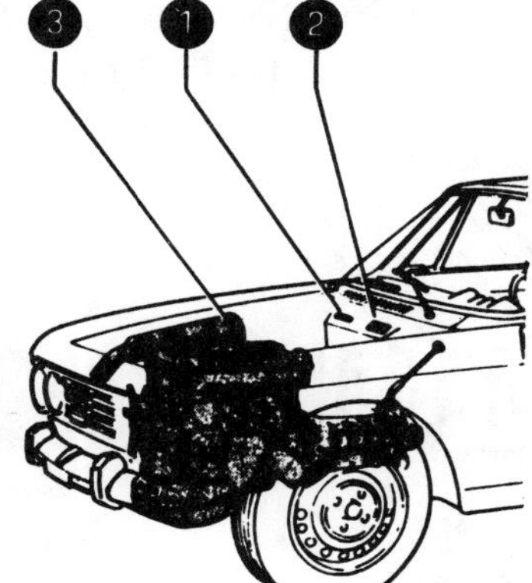

2000 G.T.V. & SPIDER

1 – Chassis No. On Firewall
2 – Car Model & Type Approval Plate
3 – Engine Number
4 – Finish Paint Plate

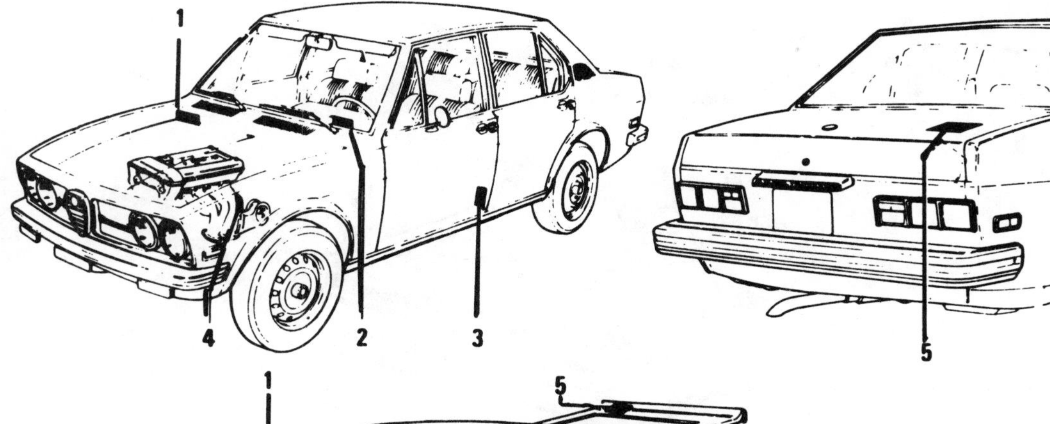

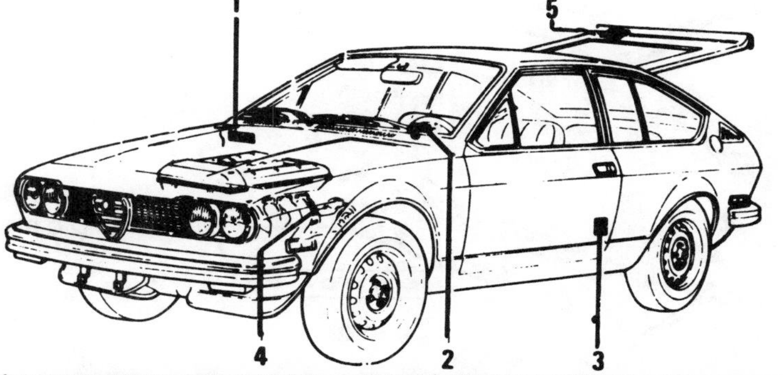

ALFETTA

1,2,3 – Vehicle, Chassis & Serial Numbers
3 – Production Date (Month)
4 – Engine Type & Serial Number
5 – Paint Code

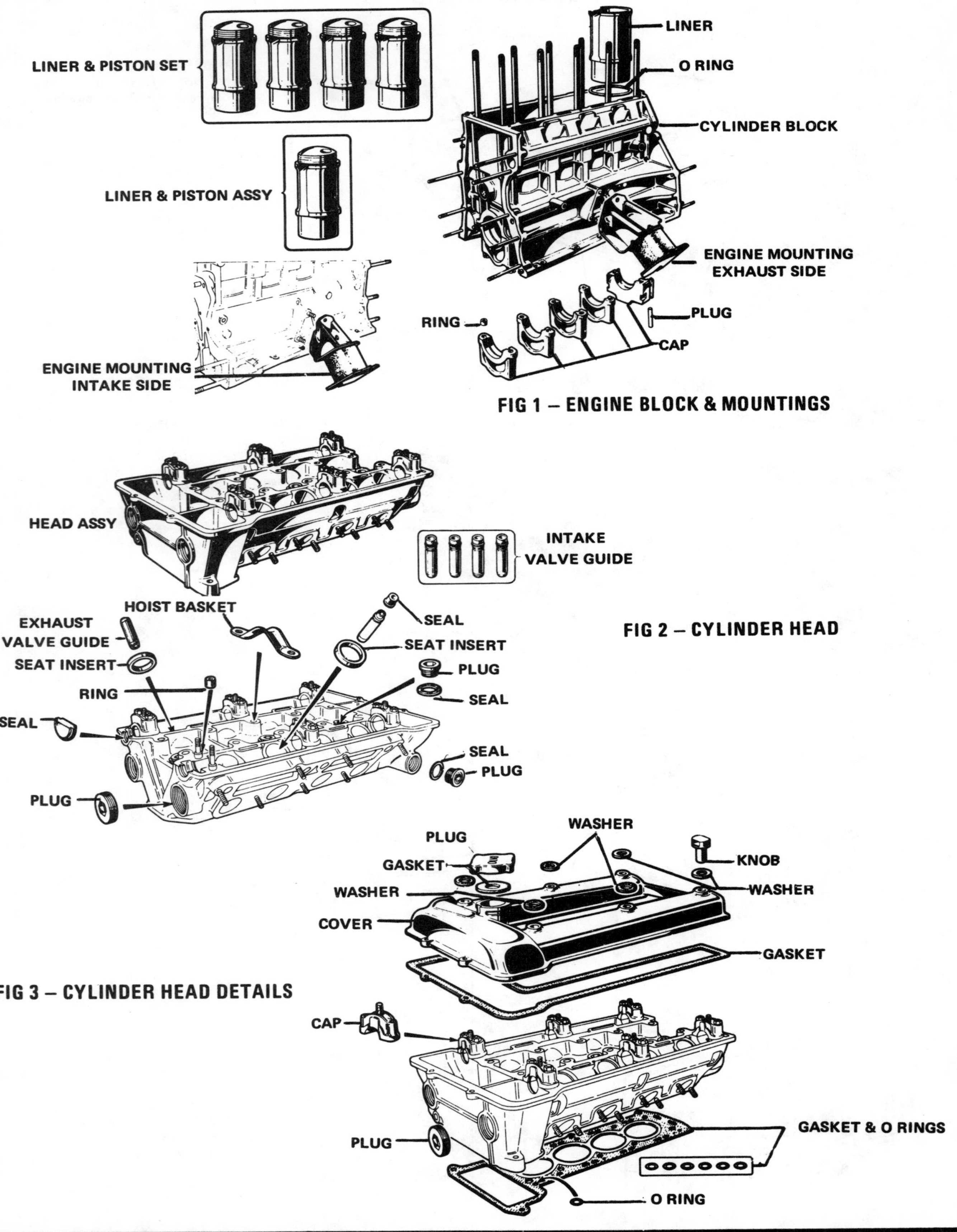

FIG 1 – ENGINE BLOCK & MOUNTINGS

FIG 2 – CYLINDER HEAD

FIG 3 – CYLINDER HEAD DETAILS

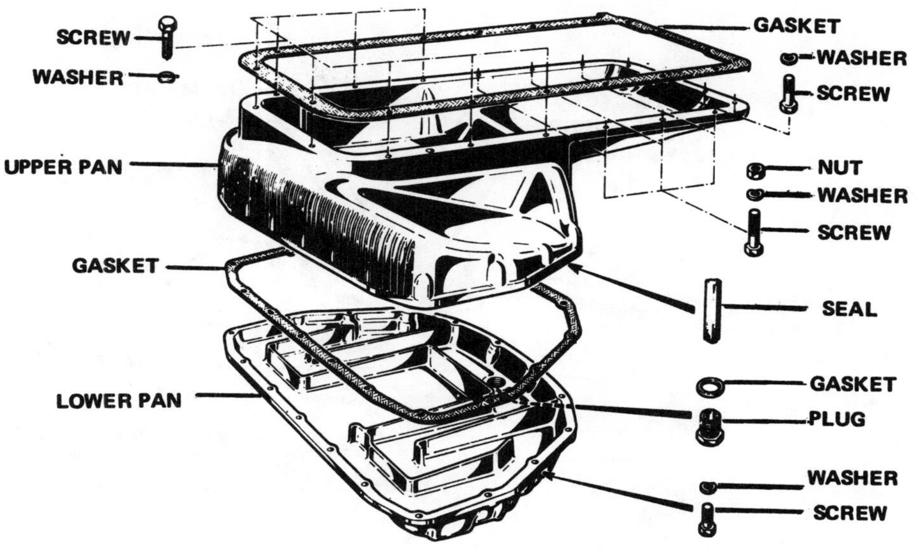

FIG 4 – OIL PAN

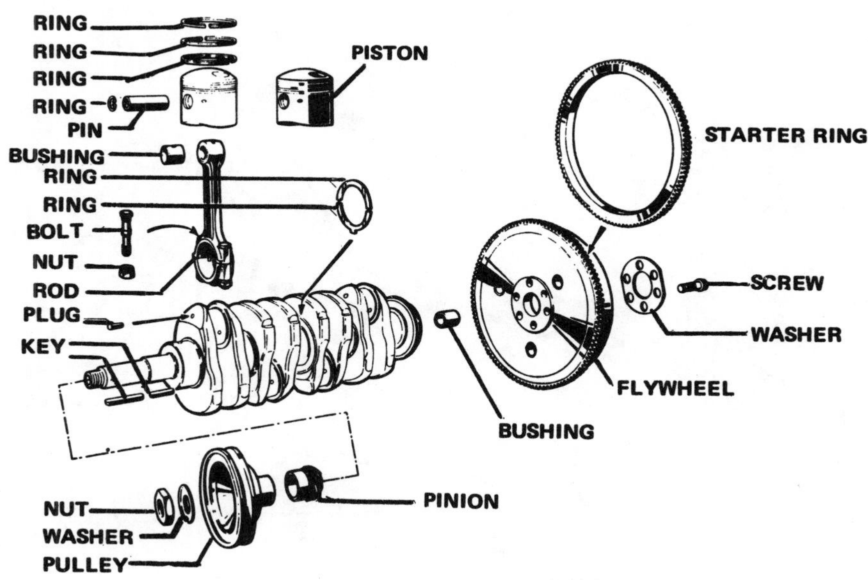

FIG 5 – CRANKSHAFT, PISTONS & RODS

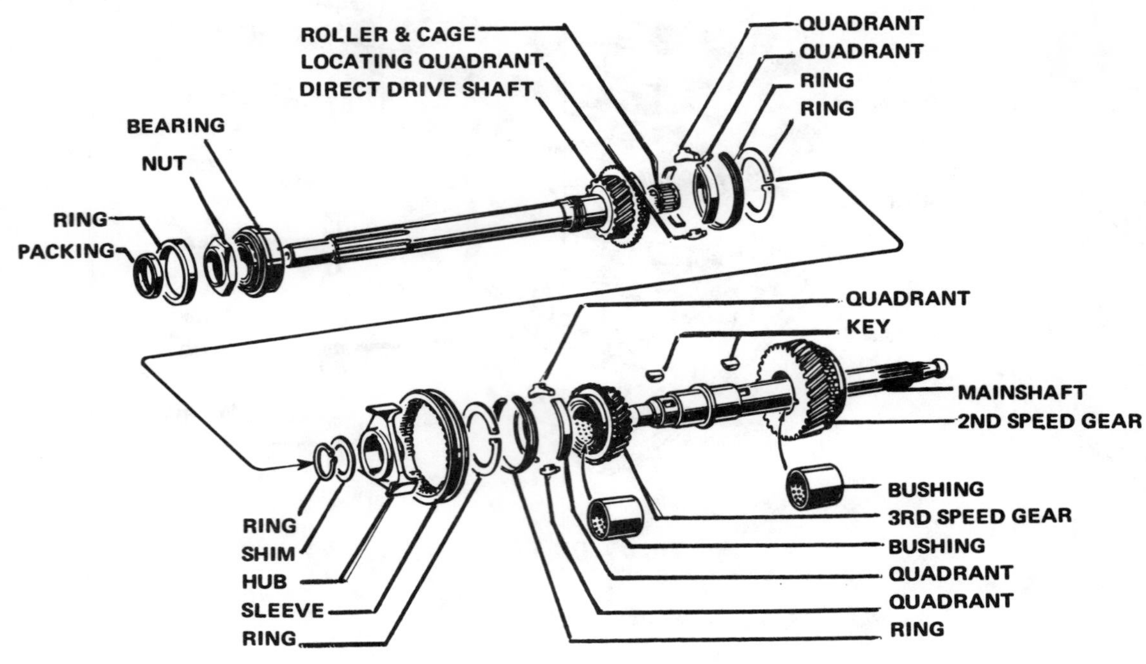

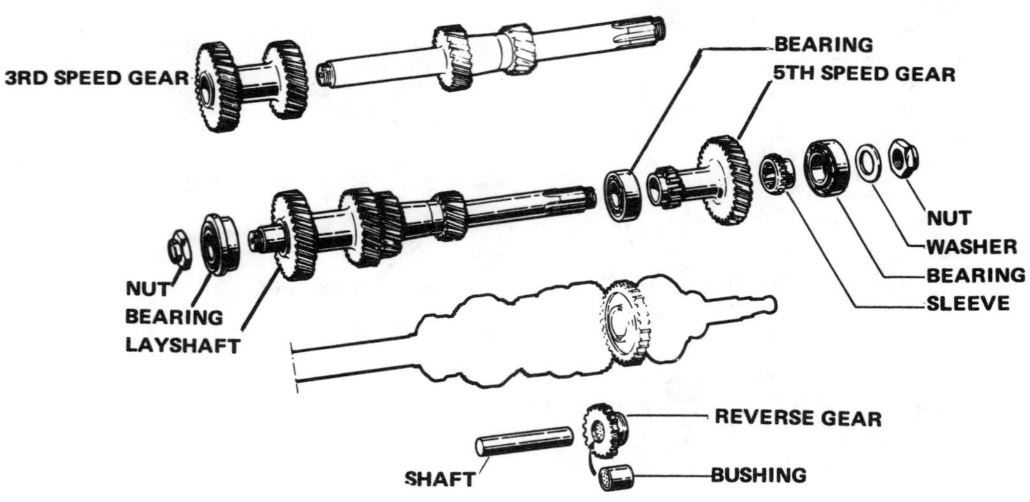

FIG 6 – TRANSMISSION

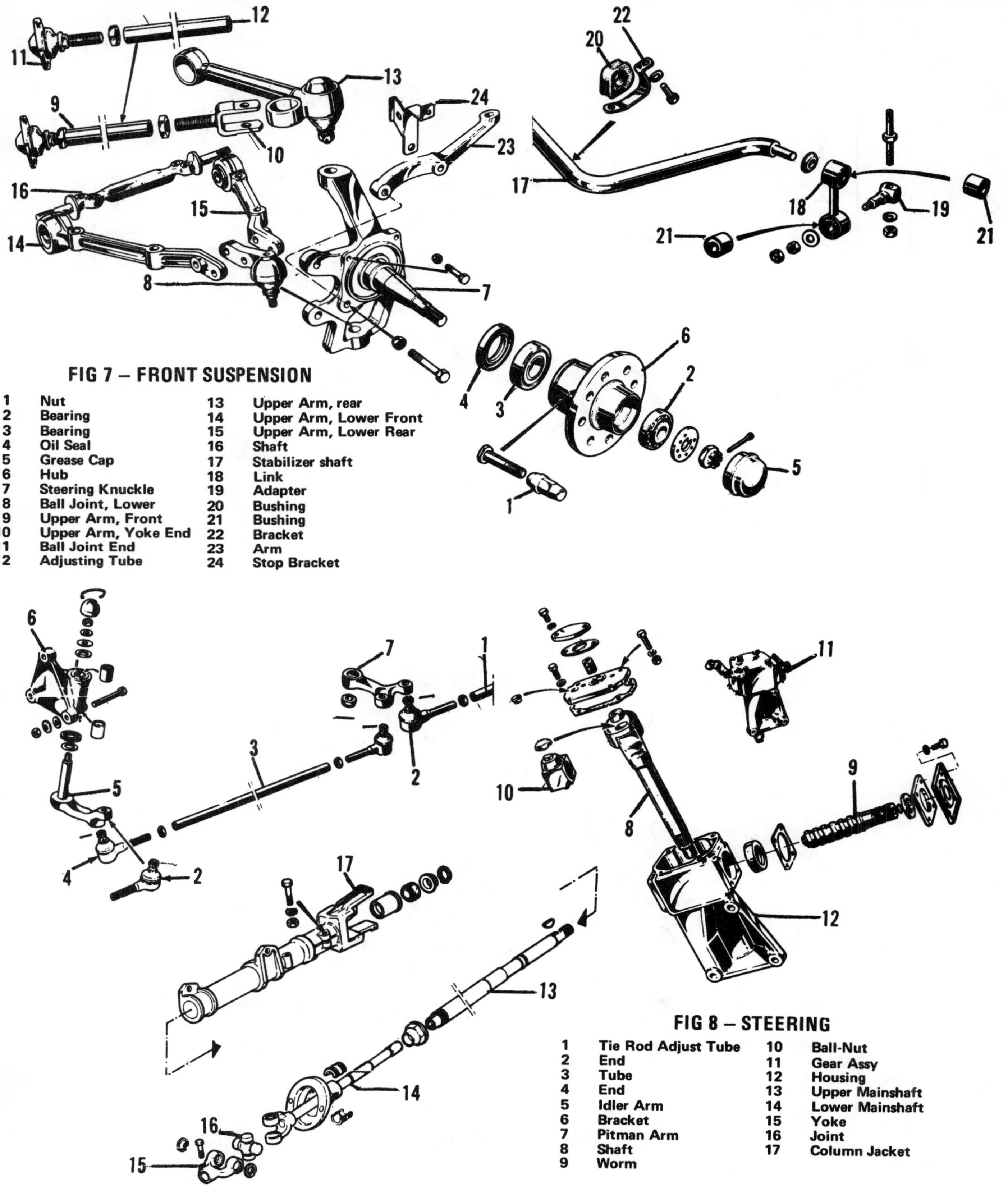

FIG 7 – FRONT SUSPENSION

1	Nut	13	Upper Arm, rear
2	Bearing	14	Upper Arm, Lower Front
3	Bearing	15	Upper Arm, Lower Rear
4	Oil Seal	16	Shaft
5	Grease Cap	17	Stabilizer shaft
6	Hub	18	Link
7	Steering Knuckle	19	Adapter
8	Ball Joint, Lower	20	Bushing
9	Upper Arm, Front	21	Bushing
10	Upper Arm, Yoke End	22	Bracket
11	Ball Joint End	23	Arm
12	Adjusting Tube	24	Stop Bracket

FIG 8 – STEERING

1	Tie Rod Adjust Tube	10	Ball-Nut
2	End	11	Gear Assy
3	Tube	12	Housing
4	End	13	Upper Mainshaft
5	Idler Arm	14	Lower Mainshaft
6	Bracket	15	Yoke
7	Pitman Arm	16	Joint
8	Shaft	17	Column Jacket
9	Worm		

1 T-Arm
2 Bushing
3 Pad
4 Strap
5 Trailing Arm
6 Bushing
7 Bushing
8 Stabilizer Rod
9 Link
10 Bushing
11 Bracket
12 Bushing
13 Bushing
14 Spring
15 Sheath, Lower
16 Seat, Upper
17 Pad

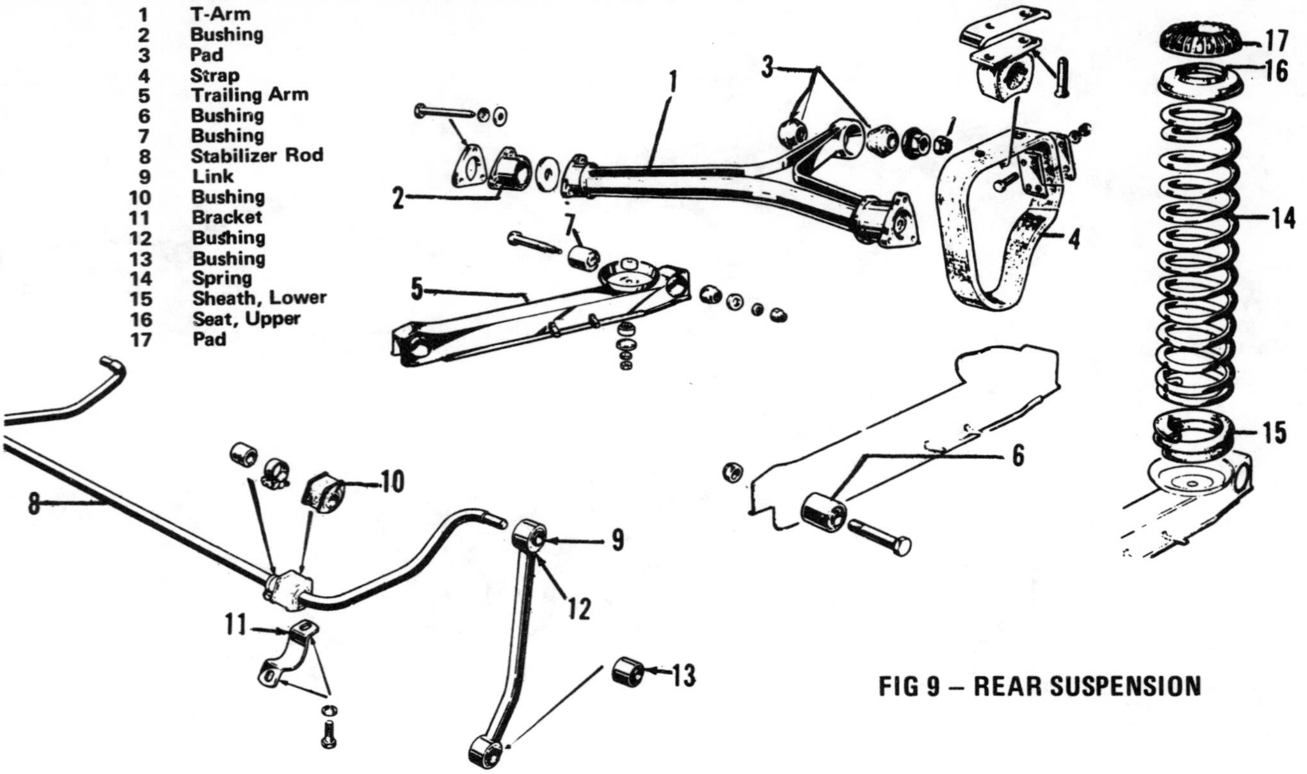

FIG 9 – REAR SUSPENSION

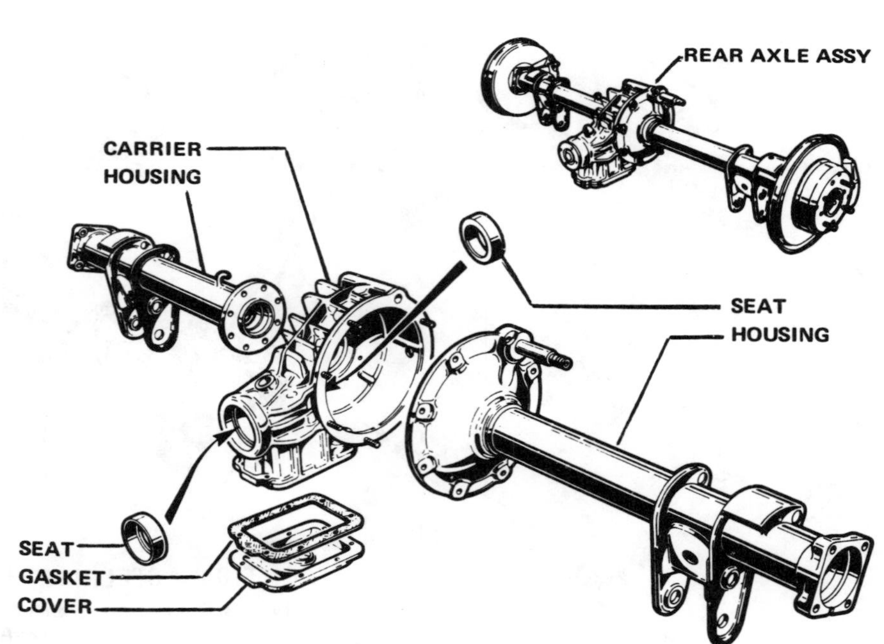

FIG 10 – REAR AXLE

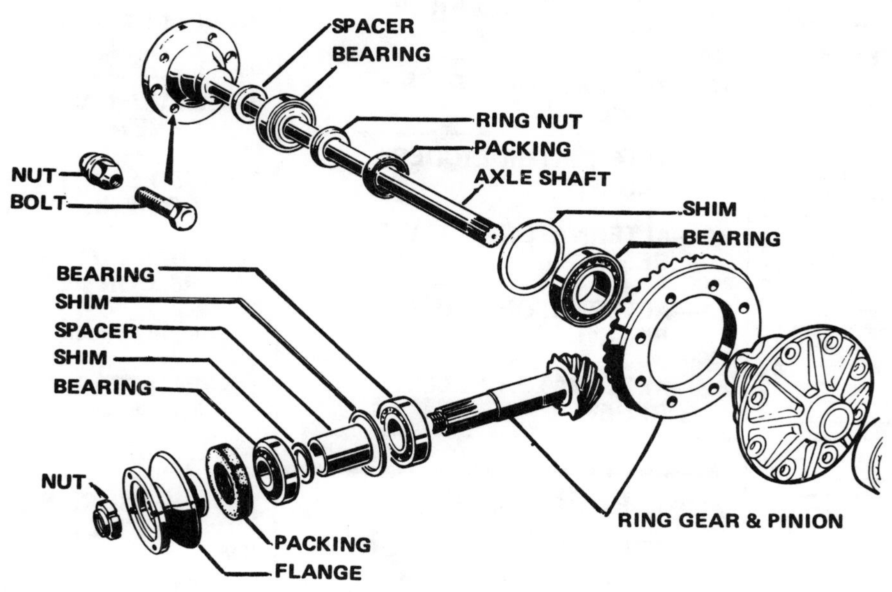

FIG 11 – DIFFERENTIAL GEARS

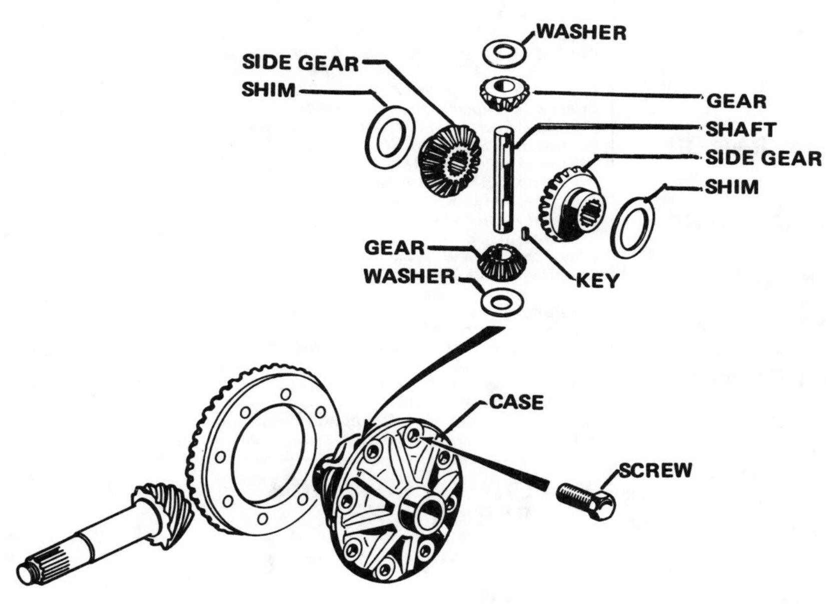

FIG 12 – DIFFERENTIAL CASE

Ignition, Starting & Charging—TIME

OPERATION INDEX

Tune-Up, Minor 1
Tune-Up, Major 2
Compression Test 3
Distributor, R&R Or Renew 4
Distributor Cap, R&R Or Renew 5
Ignition Cable Set, Renew 6
Ignition Coil, Renew 7
Ignition Points, Renew 8
Starter & Ignition Switch, Renew 9
Starter, R&R Or Renew 10
Starter Solenoid, R&R Or Renew 11
Starter Bendix Drive, Renew 12
Starter, R&R & Overhaul 13
Starter Brushes, Renew 14
Starter Armature, Renew 15
Alternator Regulator, Renew 16
Alternator, R&R Or Renew 17
Alternator, R&R & Overhaul 18
Alternator Diodes, Renew 19
Alternator Bearings, Renew 20
Alternator Brushes, Renew 21
Alternator Pulley, Renew 22

1—TUNE-UP, MINOR
Includes clean plugs & bench test, set distributor points and advance, clean air filter & test exhaust emissions.
2000 ....1.5

2—TUNE-UP, MAJOR
Includes check compression, clean or renew & adjust plugs. R&R distributor, renew points and condenser. Adjust ignition timing, engine idle and fan belts. Clean battery terminals and service air cleaner. Check coil & clean or replace fuel filter.
2000, Exc 4.8
Alfetta 4.4

3—COMPRESSION TEST
2000 ....0.5

4—DISTRIBUTOR, R&R OR RENEW
2000, Exc 0.6
Alfetta 0.7

5—DISTRIBUTOR CAP, R&R OR RENEW
2000 ....0.3

6—IGNITION CABLE SET, RENEW
2000 ....0.3

7—IGNITION COIL, RENEW
2000 ....0.2

8—IGNITION POINTS, RENEW
2000 ....0.8

9—STARTER & IGNITION SWITCH, RENEW
2000, Exc 1.4
Alfetta 0.6

10—STARTER, R&R OR RENEW
2000 ....0.8

11—STARTER SOLENOID, R&R OR RENEW
2000 ....1.0

12—STARTER BENDIX DRIVE, RENEW
2000 ....1.5

13—STARTER, R&R & OVERHAUL
Includes true up commutator.
2000 ....3.0

14—STARTER BRUSHES, RENEW
Includes true up commutator.
2000 ....2.5

15—STARTER ARMATURE, RENEW
2000 ....1.5

16—ALTERNATOR REGULATOR, RENEW
2000 ....0.3

17—ALTERNATOR, R&R OR RENEW
2000 ....0.6

18—ALTERNATOR, R&R & OVERHAUL
2000 ....1.9

19—ALTERNATOR DIODES, RENEW
2000 ....1.7

20—ALTERNATOR BEARINGS, RENEW
2000 ....1.6

21—ALTERNATOR BRUSHES, RENEW
2000 ....1.6

22—ALTERNATOR PULLEY, RENEW
2000 ....0.7

Fuel, Emission Controls, Intake & Exhaust Systems—TIME

OPERATION INDEX

Altitude Compensator, R&R Or Renew 1
Idle Equalizer, R&R Or Renew 2
Main Fuel Filter, Renew 3
Main Fuel Filter Element, Renew 4
Injection Pump Oil Filter Element, Renew 5
Injection Pump Drive Belt, Renew 6
Air Pump Drive Belt, Renew 7
Vacuum Actuator & Valve, Renew 8
Cold Start Solenoid, R&R Or Renew 9
Fuel Cut Off Solenoid, R&R Or Renew 10
Fuel Tank Filter, Renew 11
Injector, Complete, R&R Or Renew 12
Pressure Switch On Main Fuel Filter, Renew 13
Evaporative Reservoir, Renew 14
Electric Fuel Pump, R&R Or Renew 15
Air Pump, R&R Or Renew 16
Injection Pump, R&R Or Renew 17
Vacuum Actuator Thermal Sensor, R&R Or Renew 18
Fuel Tank, Renew 19
Injection Pump Thermostatic Actuator Assy, Renew 20
Air Pump Check Valve, Renew 21
Pump To Injector Pipe (S), Renew 22
Exhaust Manifold Or Gaskets, R&R Or Renew 23
Exhaust Pipe, Front, R&R 24
Exhaust Pipe, Rear, R&R 25
Silencer Or Expansion Chamber, R&R 26
Catalytic Converter, R&R 27

1—ALTITUDE COMPENSATOR, R&R OR RENEW
2000 ....1.8

2—IDLE EQUALIZER, R&R OR RENEW
Alfetta 0.2

3—MAIN FUEL FILTER, RENEW
2000, Exc 1.0
Alfetta 0.5

4—MAIN FUEL FILTER ELEMENT, RENEW
2000, Exc 0.8
Alfetta 0.6

5—INJECTION PUMP OIL FILTER ELEMENT, RENEW
2000, Exc 0.5
Alfetta 3.5

6—INJECTION PUMP DRIVE BELT, RENEW
2000, Exc 2.0
Alfetta 4.6

7—AIR PUMP DRIVE BELT, RENEW
Alfetta 2.0

8—VACUUM ACTUATOR & VALVE, RENEW
Alfetta 0.3

9—COLD START SOLENOID, R&R OR RENEW
2000 ....3.4

10—FUEL CUT OFF SOLENOID, R&R OR RENEW
2000 ....1.3

11—FUEL TANK FILTER, RENEW
2000 ....0.4

12—INJECTOR, COMPLETE, R&R OR RENEW
Includes: Adjust linkage.
One 0.9
All 1.8

13—PRESSURE SWITCH ON MAIN FUEL FILTER, RENEW
2000 ....0.8

14—EVAPORATIVE RESERVOIR, RENEW
Alfetta, Exc 0.2
GT 0.5

15—ELECTRIC FUEL PUMP, R&R OR RENEW
2000, Exc 0.5
Alfetta 0.8

16—AIR PUMP ASSY, R&R OR RENEW
Alfetta 2.8

17—INJECTION PUMP, R&R OR RENEW
2000, Exc 2.9
Alfetta 5.9

18—VACUUM ACTUATOR THERMAL SENSOR, R&R OR RENEW
Alfetta 0.7

19—FUEL TANK, RENEW
2000, Exc 0.8
Alfetta 1.2

20—INJECTION PUMP THERMOSTATIC ACTUATOR, RENEW
2000 ....1.0

21—AIR PUMP CHECK VALVE, RENEW
2000 ....0.6

22—PUMP TO INJECTOR PIPE(S), RENEW
One 0.5
All 1.5

23—EXHAUST MANIFOLD OR GASKETS, R&R OR RENEW
2000, Exc 1.3
Alfetta 1.8

24—EXHAUST PIPE, FRONT, R&R
2000, Exc 0.9
Alfetta 1.1

25—EXHAUST PIPE, REAR, R&R
2000, Exc 0.7
Alfetta 0.5

(Continued)

Fuel, Emission Controls, Intake & Exhaust Systems—TIME Cont'd

26—SILENCER OR EXPANSION CHAMBER, R&R
After pipe is removed.
2000 .... 0.5

27—CATALYTIC CONVERTER, R&R
Alfetta 0.5

Engine Cooling & Heater System—TIME

OPERATION INDEX

Electric Fan, R&R Or Renew 1
Water Pump, R&R Or Renew 2
Radiator, R&R Or Renew 3
Expansion Tank, Renew 4
Radiator Thermostatic Switch, R&R Or Renew 5
Water Temperature Transmitter, Renew 6
Radiator Hose, Renew 7
Fan, R&R Or Renew 8
Heater Water Valve, Renew 9
Heater Core, R&R Or Renew 10
Heater Motor, R&R Or Renew 11
Heater Controls, Renew 12
Heater Pipe, Renew 13

1—ELECTRIC FAN, R&R OR RENEW
Alfetta 0.6

2—WATER PUMP, R&R OR RENEW
2000, Exc 2.3
Alfetta 3.5

3—RADIATOR, R&R OR RENEW
2000, Exc 0.8
Alfetta 0.9

4—EXPANSION TANK, RENEW
2000 .... 0.3

5—RADIATOR FAN THERMOSTATIC SWITCH, R&R OR RENEW
Alfetta 0.2

6—WATER TEMPERATURE TRANSMITTER, RENEW
2000 .... 0.1

7—RADIATOR HOSE, RENEW
Upper—
2000 Exc 0.6
Alfetta 0.7
Lower—
2000, Exc 0.6
Alfetta 0.8

8—FAN, R&R OR RENEW
2000, Exc 1.0
Alfetta 0.6

9—HEATER WATER VALVE, RENEW
2000, Exc 1.0
Alfetta 1.3

10—HEATER CORE, R&R OR RENEW
Includes R&R heater assy.
2000, Exc 2.5
Alfetta 1.7

11—HEATER MOTOR, R&R OR RENEW
2000, Exc 2.4
Alfetta 1.6

12—HEATER CONTROLS, RENEW
2000, Exc 1.2
Alfetta 0.9

13—HEATER PIPE, RENEW
2000, Exc 0.9
Alfetta 1.2

Engine—TIME

OPERATION INDEX

Engine, R&R Or Renew 1
Eng, R&R & Overhaul (Major) 2
Eng, R&R & Overhaul (Minor) 3
Cylinder Head, R&R Or Gasket, Renew 4
Cyl Head, R&R & Overhaul 5
Valves, Grind 6
Camshaft &/Or Driving Gears, Renew 7
Valves, Adjust 8
Timing Chain & Or Gears, R&R Or Renew 9
Engine Front Cover Or Gasket, Renew 10
Timing And Chain Tension, Adjust 11
Oil Pan Gasket, Renew 12
Oil Pump, R&R Or Renew 13
Pistons & Cylinder Liners, R&R Or Renew 14
Front Crankshaft Oil Seal, Renew 15
Rear Crankshaft Oil Seal, Renew 16
Connecting Rod Bearing, R&R 17
Rear Crankshaft Bearing, Renew 18
Crankshaft Pulley, Renew 19
Valve Guide Oil Seals, Renew 20
Oil Pressure Transmitter, Renew 21

1—ENGINE, R&R OR RENEW
Does not include transfer of any part of engine or replacement of special equipment.
2000, Exc 7.3
Alfetta 6.3

2—ENGINE, R&R & OVERHAUL (MAJOR)
Includes complete dismantling and re-assembling, inspect & replace necessary parts, oil pump, cyl head, dist injection pump setting.
2000, Exc 30.0
Alfetta 29.0

3—ENGINE, R&R & OVERHAUL (MINOR)
Includes dismantle & reassemble, inspect, replace any parts as required of crankshaft & timing system. (If required, replace big end bearings & timing chain idle gear bushings separately).
2000, Exc 20.8
Alfetta 19.8

4—CYLINDER HEAD, R&R OR GASKET RENEW
2000, Exc 4.3
Alfetta 4.8

5—CYLINDER HEAD, R&R & OVERHAUL
Includes: Bore valve guides & re-cut seats, grind valves and seats, grind cylinder head face.
2000, Exc 12.3
Alfetta 12.8

6—VALVES, GRIND
After head is removed
One 0.3
Each Additional 0.2

7—CAMSHAFT &/OR DRIVING GEARS, RENEW
Includes: Valve adjustment.
2000, Exc 1.4
Alfetta 1.6

8—VALVES, ADJUST
2000, Exc 1.2
Alfetta 1.4

9—TIMING CHAIN & OR GEAR, R&R OR RENEW
2000, Exc 9.3
Alfetta 12.0

10—ENGINE FRONT COVER OR GASKET, RENEW
2000, Exc 8.8
Alfetta 11.5

11—TIMING & CHAIN TENSION, ADJUST
With camshaft cover removed.
2000 .... 0.3

12—OIL PAN GASKET, RENEW
2000, Exc 2.5
Alfetta 3.2

13—OIL PUMP ASSY, R&R OR RENEW
2000, Exc 3.1
Alfetta 4.0

14—PISTONS & CYLINDER LINERS, R&R OR RENEW
One—
2000, Exc 7.4
Alfetta 8.5
Each Additional—
2000, Exc 0.9
Alfetta 0.9

15—FRONT CRANKSHAFT OIL SEAL, RENEW
2000, Exc 2.1
Alfetta 3.3

16—REAR CRANKSHAFT OIL SEAL, RENEW
2000, Exc 4.3
Alfetta 4.4

17—CONNECTING ROD BEARING, R&R
After rod is removed. Includes boring.
One 0.2
Each Additional 0.2

18—REAR CRANKSHAFT BEARING, RENEW
With flywheel or clutch removed.
2000 .... 0.3

19—CRANKSHAFT PULLEY, RENEW
2000, Exc 1.8
Alfetta 3.0

20—VALVE GUIDE OIL SEALS, RENEW
With head removed.
2000 .... 1.3

21—OIL PRESSURE TRANSMITTER, RENEW
2000, Exc 0.4
Alfetta 0.2

Clutch, Mounts & Transmission—TIME

OPERATION INDEX

Flywheel, R&R Or Renew 1
Clutch Or Disc, Renew 2
Clutch Assy, Overhaul 3
Release Fork Or Lever, R&R Or Renew 4
Clutch Pedal, Adjust 5
Clutch Master Cylinder, R&R Or Renew 6
Slave Cylinder, R&R Or Renew 7
Clutch Fluid Reservoir, Renew 8
Clutch Hydraulic System Bleed 9
Trans Assy, R&R Or Renew 10
Transmission, Overhaul 11
Oil Seal, Primary Gearshaft, Renew 12
Oil Seal, Selector Rod, Renew 13
Oil Seal, Rear, Renew 14
Selector Rod Muff, Renew 15
Gear Selection Swivel & Trunnion, Renew 16
Gear Lever, R&R Or Renew 17
Rubber Bushing, Gear Box Rear Mounting, Renew 18
Speedometer Drive, Complete, R&R Or Renew 19
Drive Shafts, R&R Or Renew 20

(Continued)

Clutch, Mounts & Transmission—TIME Cont'd

1—FLYWHEEL, R&R OR RENEW
2000, Exc 4.2
Alfetta 4.3

2—CLUTCH OR DISC, RENEW
2000, Exc 3.9
Alfetta 2.4

3—CLUTCH ASSY, OVERHAUL
2000, Exc 4.4
Alfetta 3.7

4—RELEASE FORK OR LEVER, R&R OR RENEW
2000, Exc 3.6
Alfetta 2.3

5—CLUTCH PEDAL, ADJUST
2000 ....0.4

6—CLUTCH MASTER CYLINDER, R&R OR RENEW
2000, Exc 1.1
Alfetta 1.0

7—SLAVE CYLINDER, R&R OR RENEW
2000, Exc 0.3
Alfetta 0.4

—NOTE—
To Bleed Cylinder, Add 0.3

8—CLUTCH FLUID RESERVOIR, RENEW
2000 ....0.2

9—CLUTCH HYDRAULIC SYSTEM, BLEED
2000, Exc 0.4
Alfetta 0.3

10—TRANSMISSION ASSY, R&R OR RENEW
2000, Exc 3.8
Alfetta 3.3

11—TRANSMISSION ASSY, R&R & OVERHAUL
2000, Exc 8.3
Alfetta 5.1

12—OIL SEAL, PRIMARY GEARSHAFT, RENEW
Includes: R&R assembly.
2000, Exc 4.8
Alfetta 3.0

13—OIL SEAL, SELECTOR ROD, RENEW
Alfetta 2.9

14—OIL SEAL, REAR, RENEW
Berlina & Veloce 1.4

15—SELECTOR ROD MUFF, RENEW
Alfetta 1.4

16—GEAR SELECTION SWIVEL & TRUNION, RENEW
Berlina & Veloce 1.3

17—GEAR LEVER, R&R OR RENEW
2000 ....1.1

18—RUBBER BUSHING, GEARBOX REAR MOUNTING, RENEW
2000, Exc 0.7
Alfetta 1.0

19—SPEEDOMETER DRIVE, COMPLETE, R&R OR RENEW
2000, Exc 0.3
Alfetta 0.2

20—DRIVE SHAFTS, R&R OR RENEW
Alfetta—
One 1.1
All 2.0

Brakes, Steering, Suspension, Universals & Rear Axle—TIME

OPERATION INDEX

Brake Friction Pads, Renew 1
Master Cylinder, Renew 2
Master Cylinder With Servo Brake, Renew 3
Master Cyl, R&R & Overhaul 4
Brake Fluid Reservoir, R&R Or Renew 5
Caliper Assy, R&R Or Renew 6
Bleed Brakes 7
Complete Brake Overhaul 8
Hub Or Disc, Renew 9
Brake Anti-Lock Valve, Renew 10
Brake Pressure Valve, Renew 11
Brake Servo, Renew 12
Servo Vacuum Hose, Renew 13
Brake Hose, Front, Renew 14
Brake Hose, Rear, Renew 15
Pressure Switch (Warning Light), Renew 16
Servo Check Valve, Renew 17
Handbrake Control Cable, Renew 18
Handbrake Lever Assy, Renew 19
Handbrake Warning Light Switch, Renew 20
Handbrake, Adjust 21
Steering Gear Assy, R&R Or Renew 22
Steering Rack Assy, R&R Or Renew 23
Steering Gear Assy, R&R & Overhaul 24
Steering Rack Assy, R&R & Overhaul 25
Steering Gear Box Oil Seal, R&R Or Renew 26
Track Rod Joint, R&R Or Renew 27
Track Rods, R&R Or Renew 28
Steering Link, W/Idler Arm & Brkt, R&R Or Renew 29
Idler Arm & Brkt, R&R Or Renew 30
Steering Shaft (Spindle) Intermediate, R&R Or Renew 31
Steering Gear Shaft, Adjust End Play 32
Steering Rack & Pinion, Adjust Backlash 33
Front Suspension Alignment 34
Front Suspension Height, Adjust 35
Front Wheel Hub, Renew 36
Front Suspension, Overhaul 37
Front Shock Absorber, R&R Or Renew 38
Front Stabilizer Bar Assy, R&R Or Renew 39
Front Stabalizer Bar Link, R&R Or Renew 40
Front Upper Wishbone, R&R Or Renew 41
Rear Upper Wishbone (S), R&R Or Renew 42
Lower Wishbone & Shaft, R&R Or Renew 43
Torsion Bar Support Beam, R&R Or Renew 44
Front Torsion Bar, R&R Or Renew 45
Front Spring(S), R&R Or Renew 46
Front Suspension Lwr Ball Joint(S), Renew 47
Front Suspension Upr Ball Joint(S), Renew 48
Steering Knuckle, R&R Or Renew 49
Height Adjustment, Rear Suspension 50
Height Adjustment, Front & Rear Suspension 51
Axle Shaft(S), Rear, Renew 52
Rear Axle & Housing, R&R 53
Rear Axle & Housing Assy, R&R & Overhaul 54
Rear Axle Bearing(S), R&R Or Renew 55
Differential, R&R & Overhaul 56
Differential, R&R Or Renew 57
Axle Shaft Oil Seals, Renew 58
Rear Stabilizer Bar, R&R Or Renew 59
Rear Shock Absorber(S), R&R Or Renew 60
Rear Suspension Trailing Arm(S), R&R Or Renew 61
Rear Suspension Spring(S), R&R Or Renew 62
T-Arm, R&R Or Renew 63
I-Beam (Didion) Axle, R&R Assy 64
I-Beam (Didion) Axle, Renew 65
I-Beam (Didion) Axle Cross Member, R&R Or Renew 66
Transverse Bar & Bell Crank Bushings, Renew 67
Transverse Bar, R&R Or Renew 68

1—BRAKE FRICTION PADS, RENEW
Front—
2000, Exc 0.5
Alfetta 0.5
Rear—.
2000, Exc 0.5
Alfetta 1.2
Both Front & Rear—
2000, Exc 0.9
Alfetta 1.6

2—MASTER CYLINDER, RENEW
2000, Exc 1.1
Alfetta 1.1

3—MASTER CYLINDER WITH SERVO BRAKE, RENEW
2000, Exc 2.6
Alfetta 2.8

4—MASTER CYLINDER, R & R & OVERHAUL
2000, Exc 1.6
Alfetta 1.6

5—BRAKE FLUID RESERVOIR, R & R OR RENEW
2000 ....0.8

6—CALIPER ASSY, R & R OR RENEW
Front—
2000, Exc 0.6
Alfetta 0.6
Rear—
2000, Exc 0.6
Alfetta 1.7

—NOTE—
Add To Bleed System

7—BLEED BRAKES
2000, Exc 0.6
Alfetta 0.4

8—COMPLETE BRAKE OVERHAUL
Includes: Replace all pads, discs, master cylinder, anti-lock valve, pressure valve, change fluid & bleed system, grind discs.
2000, Exc 9.7
Alfetta 9.5

9—HUB OR DISC, RENEW
2000, Exc Alfetta—
Front, One 1.2
Both 1.8
Rear, One 0.6
Both 1.0
Alfetta—
Front, One 0.8
Both 1.4
Rear, One 1.8
Both 2.8

10—BRAKE ANTI-LOCK VALVE, RENEW
Includes: Bleed system
2000 ....0.9

11—BRAKE PRESSURE VALVE, RENEW
Alfetta 0.7

12—BRAKE SERVO, RENEW
Includes: Bleed system
2000, Exc 2.7
Alfetta 2.8

13—SERVO VACUUM HOSE, RENEW
2000 ....0.2

14—BRAKE HOSE, FRONT, RENEW
Includes: Bleed system
2000, Exc 0.9
Alfetta 0.7

15—BRAKE HOSE, REAR, RENEW
Includes: Bleed system
2000, Exc 0.9
Alfetta 0.7

16—PRESSURE SWITCH (WARNING LIGHT), RENEW
Alfetta 0.8

17—SERVO CHECK VALVE, RENEW
2000, Exc 0.2
Alfetta 0.3

(Continued)

Brakes, Steering, Suspension, Universals & Rear Axle—TIME Cont'd

18—HANDBRAKE CONTROL CABLE, RENEW
2000, Exc Alfetta—
One 1.3
Both 2.4
Alfetta 1.5

19—HANDBRAKE LEVER ASSY, RENEW
2000, Exc Alfetta 0.8
Alfetta, Exc 1.1
GT 0.6

20—HANDBRAKE WARNING LIGHT SWITCH, RENEW
2000—
Berlina 0.3
Veloce—
GT 0.5
Spider 0.4
Alfetta, Exc 1.0
GT 0.5

21—HANDBRAKE, ADJUST
2000, Exc 0.4
GT 0.3

22—STEERING GEAR ASSY, R & R OR RENEW
Berlina & Veloce 4.0

23—STEERING RACK ASSY, R & R OR RENEW
Includes: Adjust toe-in
Alfetta 2.3

24—STEERING GEAR ASSY, R & R & OVERHAUL
Berlina & Veloce 7.3

25—STEERING RACK ASSY, R & R & OVERHAUL
Includes: Adjust toe-in
Alfetta 3.5

26—STEERING GEAR BOX OIL SEAL, R & R OR RENEW
Berlina & Veloce 1.7

27—TRACK ROD JOINT, R & R OR RENEW
2000, Exc 0.3
Alfetta 0.3
—NOTE—
For Toe-In Adjust, Add. 0.5

28—TRACK RODS, R & R OR RENEW
Berlina & Veloce—
Center, W/Joints 0.4
Side, W/Joint 0.4
Alfetta—
Rod, W/Joint 0.4
Joint Only 0.3
—NOTE—
For Toe-In Adjust, Add. 0.5

29—STRG LINK W/IDLER ARM & BRKT, R & R OR RENEW
Berlina & Veloce 1.0
—NOTE—
For Toe-In Adjust, Add. 0.5

30—IDLER ARM & BRKT, R & R OR RENEW
Berlina & Veloce 0.5
—NOTE—
For Toe-In Adjust, Add. 0.5

31—STRG SHAFT (SPINDLE), INTERMEDIATE, R & R OR RENEW
Alfetta 0.9

32—STEERING GEAR SHAFT, ADJUST END PLAY
Berlina & Veloce 0.5

33—STEERING RACK & PINION, ADJUST BACKLASH
Alfetta 2.2

34—FRONT SUSPENSION ALIGNMENT
2000, Exc 2.0
Alfetta 3.2

35—FRONT SUSPENSION HEIGHT, ADJUST
2000, Exc 1.8
Alfetta 2.5

36—FRONT WHEEL HUB, RENEW
One—
2000, Exc 1.5
Alfetta 1.1
Both—
2000, Exc 2.4
Alfetta 2.0

37—FRONT SUSPENSION, OVERHAUL
One Side—
2000, Exc 3.0
Alfetta 4.9
Both Sides—
2000, Exc 4.9
Alfetta 8.9
—NOTE—
Add For Alignment.

38—FRONT SHOCK ABSORBER, R & R OR RENEW
2000, Exc Alfetta—
One 0.5
Both 0.9
Alfetta—
One 0.4
Both 0.8

39—FRONT STABILIZER BAR ASSY, R & R OR RENEW
2000, Exc 0.3
Alfetta 0.4

40—FRONT STABILIZER BAR LINK, R & R OR RENEW
All Models 0.6
—NOTE—
Includes R & R Stabilizer.

41—FRONT UPPER WISHBONE, R & R OR RENEW
One—
2000, Exc ①0.5
Alfetta ②1.8
Both—
2000, Exc ①0.8
Alfetta ②3.0
①*To Adjust Toe-In, Add. 0.5*
②*To Change Bushings & Bleed Brakes, Add. 0.7*

42—REAR UPPER WISHBONES, R & R OR RENEW
Berlina & Veloce 0.6

43—LOWER WISHBONE & SHAFT, R & R OR RENEW
One—
2000, Exc 1.3
Alfetta 1.5
Both—
2000, Exc 2.3
Alfetta 2.5

44—TORSION BAR SUPPORT BEAM, R & R OR RENEW
Alfetta 2.8

45—FRONT TORSION BAR, R & R OR RENEW
Alfetta—
One 1.5
Both 2.5

46—FRONT SPRING(S), R & R OR RENEW
Berlina & Veloce—
One 0.8
Both 1.4

47—FRONT SUSPENSION LWR BALL JOINT(S), RENEW
One—
2000, Exc 1.0
Alfetta 1.1
Both—
2000, Exc 1.8
Alfetta 1.5

48—FRONT SUSPENSION UPR BALL JOINT(S), RENEW
Includes: R & R wishbone.
Berlina & Veloce 1.6

49—STEERING KNUCKLE, R & R OR RENEW
Includes bleed brakes on alfetta.
2000, Exc 2.5
Alfetta 2.0

50—HEIGHT ADJUSTMENT, REAR SUSPENSION
2000, Exc 1.8
Alfetta 2.3

51—HEIGHT ADJUSTMENT, FRONT & REAR SUSPENSION
2000, Exc 3.3
Alfetta 3.8

52—AXLE SHAFT(S), REAR, RENEW
One—
2000, Exc 1.4
Alfetta 1.1
Both—
2000, Exc 2.6
Alfetta 2.2

53—REAR AXLE & HOUSING ASSY, R & R
Includes: Bleed brakes.
Berlina & Veloce 2.9

54—REAR AXLE & HOUSING ASSY, R & R & OVERHAUL
Includes: Bleed brakes.
Berlina & Veloce 9.6

55—REAR AXLE BEARING(S), R & R OR RENEW
Berlina & Veloce—
One 1.1
Both 2.1

56—DIFFERENTIAL, R & R & OVERHAUL
Alfetta 12.0

57—DIFFERENTIAL ASSY, R & R OR RENEW
Alfetta 3.8

58—AXLE SHAFT OIL SEALS, RENEW
Berlina & Veloce—
One 1.0
Both 1.9

59—REAR STABILIZER BAR, R & R OR RENEW
2000, Exc 1.0
Alfetta 1.2

60—REAR SHOCK ABSORBER(S), R & R OR RENEW
One—
2000, Exc 0.7
Alfetta 0.4
Both—
2000, Exc 1.1
Alfetta 0.7

61—REAR SUSP TRAILING ARMS, R & R OR RENEW
Berlina & Veloce—
One 0.9
Both 1.4

(Continued)

Brakes, Steering, Suspension, Universals & Rear Axle—TIME Cont'd

62—REAR SPRING, R & R OR RENEW

One—
- 2000, Exc 0.9
- Alfetta 1.4

Both—
- 2000, Exc 1.6
- Alfetta 1.5

63—T-ARM, R & R OR RENEW

Berlina & Veloce 1.7

64—I-BEAM (DIDION) AXLE, R & R ASSY

Alfetta 3.3

65—I-BEAM (DIDION) AXLE, RENEW

Alfetta 5.0

66—I-BEAM (DIDION) AXLE C'MEMBER, R & R

Alfetta 1.7

67—TRANSVERSE BAR & BELLCRANK BUSHINGS, RENEW

Alfetta 0.7

68—TRANSVERSE BAR, R & R OR RENEW

Alfetta 0.3

Speedometer, W/S Wipers, Switches & Instruments—TIME

OPERATION INDEX

Speedometer Cable, Renew 1
Speedometer Head, Renew 2
Tachometer Cable, Renew 3
Tachometer Head, Renew 4
Tripmeter Reset Cable, Renew 5
Fuel Gauge, Renew 6
Oil Pressure Gauge, Renew 7
Heat Gauge, Renew 8
W/S Wiper Motor, Renew 9
W/S Wiper Arm, Renew 10
W/S Wiper Motor, R & R Or Renew 11
W/S Washer Pump, Renew 12
Safety &/Or Turn Signal Flasher Unit, Renew 13
Back-Up Lamp Switch, Renew 14
Stop Light Switch, Renew 15
Road Hazard Light Switch, Renew 16
Heated Rear Window Switch, Renew 17

1—SPEEDOMETER CABLE, RENEW

2000, Exc 0.8
- Alfetta 0.6

2—SPEEDOMETER HEAD, RENEW

Berlina & Veloce 0.5
Alfetta, Exc 0.8
- GT 0.5

3—TACHOMETER CABLE, RENEW

2000, Exc 0.8
- Alfetta 0.4

4—TACHOMETER HEAD, RENEW

2000, Exc 0.5
- Alfetta 0.2

5—TRIPMETER RESET CABLE, RENEW

2000, Exc 0.5
- Alfetta 0.7

6—FUEL GAUGE, RENEW

2000, Exc 0.5
- Alfetta 0.9
- Berlina 0.2

7—OIL PRESSURE GAUGE, RENEW

2000, Exc 0.5
- Alfetta 0.9

8—HEAT GAUGE, RENEW

Berlina 1.5
Veloce 0.5
Alfetta, Exc 0.9
- GT 0.5

9—W/S WIPER MOTOR, RENEW

2000, Exc 1.0
- Alfetta 0.5

10—W/S WIPER ARM, RENEW

2000 ....0.1

11—W/S WIPER MOTOR, R & R OR RENEW

2000, Exc 0.2
- Alfetta 0.4

12—W/S WASHER PUMP, RENEW

2000, Exc 0.2
- Alfetta 0.4

13—SAFETY &/OR TURN SIGNAL FLASHER UNIT, RENEW

2000 ....0.2

14—BACK-UP LAMP SWITCH, RENEW

2000, Exc 0.2
- Berlina 0.3
- Veloce 0.5

15—STOP LIGHT SWITCH, RENEW

2000, Exc 0.4
- Alfetta 0.3

16—ROAD HAZARD LIGHT SWITCH, RENEW

Alfetta 0.2

17—HEATED REAR WINDOW SWITCH, RENEW

2000 ....0.2

IDENTIFICATION

ALL MODELS....................................16

ILLUSTRATIONS

FIG 1 – ENGINE – CRANKSHAFT & PISTONS
FIG 2 – ENGINE – CYLINDER HEAD & VALVE DRIVE
FIG 3 – MANUAL TRANSMISSION CASE & CONTROLS
FIG 4 – MANUAL TRANSMISSION GEARS & SHAFTS
FIG 5 – AUTOMATIC TRANSMISSION CASE & CONTROLS
FIG 6 – AUTOMATIC TRANSMISSION GEARS & SHAFTS
FIG 7 – FRONT SUSPENSION
FIG 8 – STEERING
FIG 9 – REAR SUSPENSION

OPERATION TIMES

A

Alternator.. 22
Automatic Transmission.................... 23

B

Brake Drums.. 24
Brakes... 24

C

Cables (Ignition).................................. 22
Calipers... 24
Camshaft.. 23
Carburetor.. 22
Clutch.. 23
Coil, Ignition....................................... 22
Compression Test................................ 22
Connecting Rods.................................. 23
Cooling System.................................... 22
Crankshaft... 23
Cylinder Block..................................... 23
Cylinder Head...................................... 23

D

Dash Gauges....................................... 25
Disc Brakes... 24
Distributor... 22

E

Emission Controls............................... 22
Engine Assembly................................. 23
Engine Mountings................................ 23
Engine Oiling....................................... 23
Engine Tune-Up................................... 22
Exhaust System................................... 22

F

Flywheel.. 23
Front Suspension................................. 24
Fuel Guages... 25
Fuel Pump... 22
Fuel Tank... 22

H

Hand Brake.. 24
Hazard Flasher Switch......................... 25
Headlight Switch.................................. 25
Heater Motor....................................... 22
Hose (Brake).. 24
Hose (Radiator).................................... 22
Hydraulic Brakes.................................. 24

I

Ignition.. 22
Ignition Coil... 22
Ignition Switch..................................... 22
Intake Manifold.................................... 22

L

Light Switches...................................... 25

M

Main Bearings...................................... 23
Master Cylinder.................................... 24
Muffler... 22

O

Oil Gauge... 25
Oiling, Engine...................................... 23
Oil Pan... 23
Oil Pump.. 23

P

Parking Brake....................................... 24
Piston Rings... 23
Pistons... 23
Power Brake... 24

R

Radiator... 22
Radiator Hose...................................... 22
Rear Axle... 25
Regulator (Alternator)......................... 22
Rocker Levers...................................... 23
Rod Bearings....................................... 23

S

Shocks (Front)..................................... 24
Shocks (Rear)...................................... 24
Speedometer.. 25
Springs (Rear)...................................... 25
Spur Belt.. 23
Stabilizer... 25
Starting Motor..................................... 22
Steering.. 24
Switches (Light)................................... 25
Synchro-Mesh Trans............................ 23

T

Tachometer.. 25
Temperature Gauge............................. 25
Thermostat.. 22
Timing Case Cover.............................. 23
Timing Chain....................................... 23
Timing Gears....................................... 23
Torsion Bar.. 24
Track Rods... 24
Transmission, Manual.......................... 23
Transmission, Automatic..................... 23
Tune-Up, Engine.................................. 22

V

Vacuum Control Unit.......................... 22
Valve Lifters.. 23
Valve System....................................... 23

W

Water Pump... 22
Wheel Cylinders................................... 24
Windshield Wiper................................ 25

CHASSIS NUMBER LOCATION

AUDI (EXC FOX) – In engine compartment on right front wheelhouse.

AUDI FOX – In engine compartment on upper center part of firewall.

STARTING CHASSIS NUMBERS

1970	Super 90	2-Door Sedan	0201000001
		4-Door Sedan	0301000001
		Station Wagon	0401000001
	100 LS	2-Door Sedan	8001000001
		4-Door Sedan	8101000001
1971	Super 90	2-Door Sedan	0211000001
		4-Door Sedan	0311000001
		Station Wagon	0411000001
	100 LS	2-Door Sedan	8011000001
		4-Door Sedan	8111000001
1972	Super 90	2-Door Sedan	0221000001
		4-Door Sedan	0321000001
		Station Wagon	0421000001
	100 LS	2-Door Sedan	8021000001
		4-Door Sedan	8121000001
	100	2 & 4-Door	8521000001
	100 GL	2 & 4-Door	8521050992
1973	100 LS	2-Door Sedan	8031000001
		4-Door Sedan	8131000001
	100	2 & 4-Door	8531000001
	GL	2 & 4-Door	8531000001
	Fox	2-Door	8432000001
		4-Door	8532000001
1974	100LS	2-Door	8041000001
		4-Door	8141000001
	Fox	2-Door	8442000051
		4-Door	8542000051
1975	100LS	2-Door	8051000001
		4-Door	8151000001
	Fox	2-Door	8452007172
		4-Door	8552007172
		Sta. Wgn.	3352900001
1976	100LS	2-Door	8061000001
		4-Door	8161000001
	Fox	2-Door	8462000001
		4-Door	8562000001
		Sta.Wgn.	3362900001
1977	100LS	2-Door	8071000001
		4-Door	8171000001
	Fox	2-Door	8471000001
		4-Door	8572000001
		Sta. Wgn.	3372900001

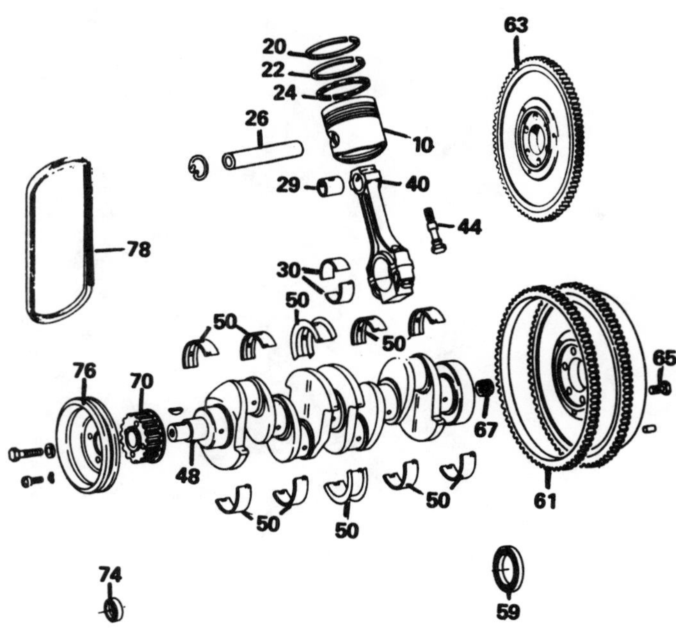

FIG 1 – ENGINE – CRANKSHAFT & PISTONS

10	Piston
20	Piston Ring
22	Piston Ring
24	Piston Ring
26	Piston Pin
29	Conn Rod Bushing
30	Conn Rod Bearings
40	Connecting Rod
44	Bolt & Nut
48	Crankshaft
50	Crankshaft Bearings
59	Oil Seal
61	Ring Gear
63	Drive Plate
65	Bolt
67	Needle Bearing
70	Sprocket
74	Oil Seal
76	Pulley
78	V Belt

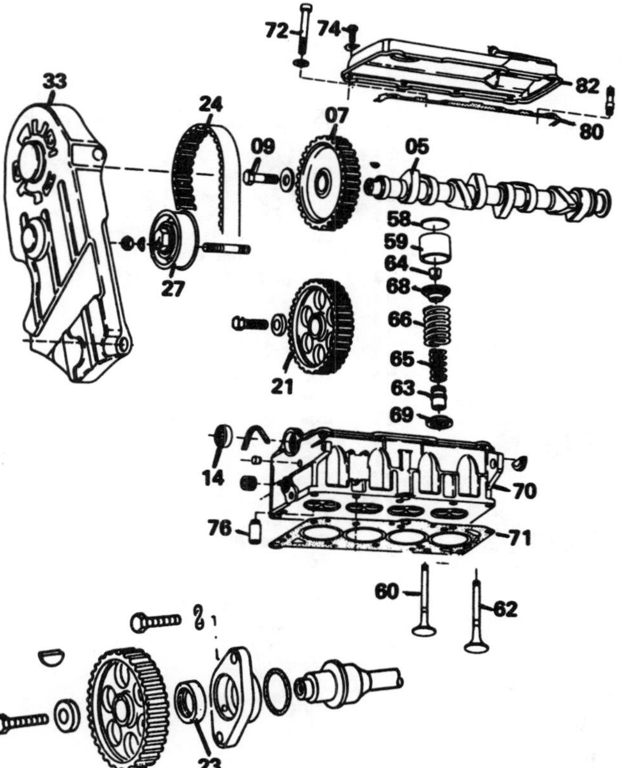

FIG 2 – EINGINE - CYLINDER HEAD & VALVE DRIVE

05	Camshaft
07	Camshaft Sprocket
09	Bolt
14	Oil Seal
21	Intermediate Sprocket
23	Oil Seal
24	Spur Belt
27	Pulley
33	Cover
58	Disc
59	Cam Follower
60	Intake Valve
62	Exhaust Valve
63	Valve Stem Seal
64	Valve Cotter
65	Spring, Inner
66	Spring, Outer
68	Retainer, Top
69	Retainer, Bottom
70	Cylinder Head
71	Gasket
72	Bolt
74	Bolt
76	Guide
80	Gasket
82	Cylinder Head Cover

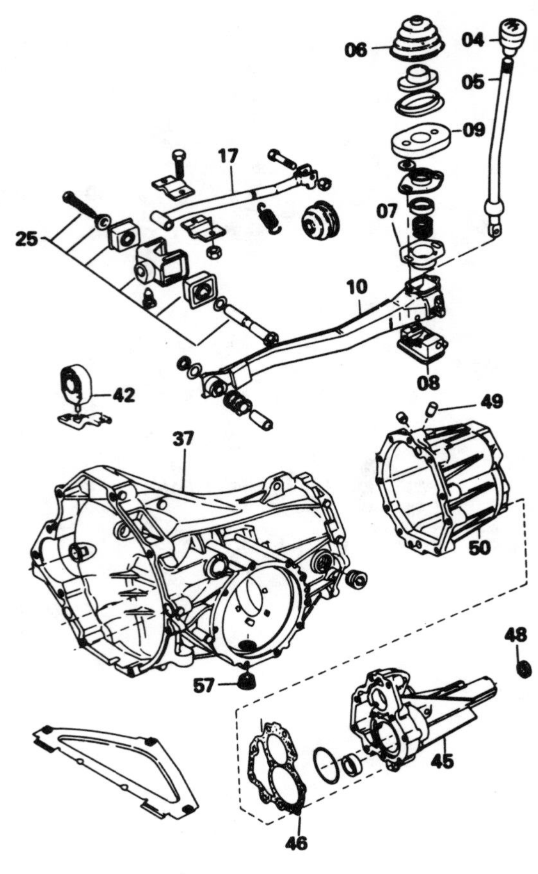

FIG 3 – MANUAL TRANSMISSION CASE & CONTROLS

04	Knob
05	Gearshift Lever
06	Boot
07	Base Plate
08	Gearshift Gate
09	Gasket
10	Lever Housing
17	Gearshift Tube
25	Coupling
37	Transmission Case
42	Rubber Mount
45	End Cover
46	Gasket
48	Seal
49	Plug
50	Intermediate Housing
57	Plug

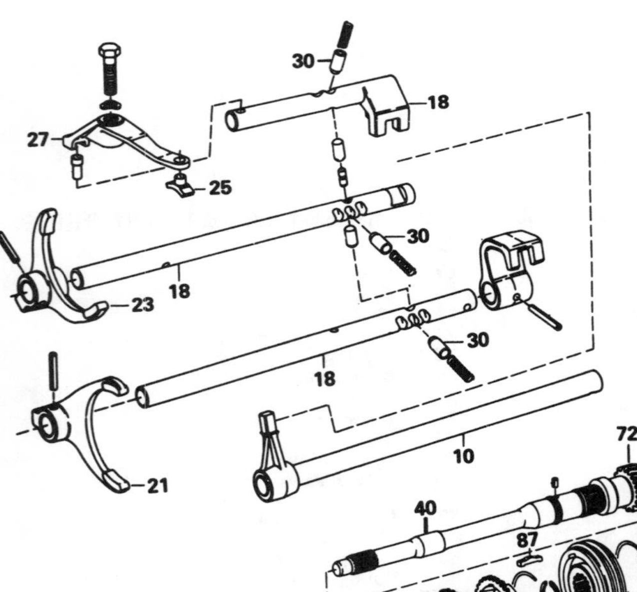

FIG 4 – MANUAL TRANSMISSION GEARS & SHAFTS

10	Shift Lever
18	Shift Rods
21	Shift Fork Gears 1 & 2
23	Shift Fork Gears 3 & 4
25	Shift Fork - Reverse Gear
27	Reverse Idler Gear
30	Plungers
40	Mainshaft
43	Shim
46	Bearing
48	Bearing
50	Oil Seal
60	Bearing
61	Bearing
65	Gear
71	Gear Set
72	Gear Set
73	Gear Set
74	Gear Set
77	Reverse Gear
79	Bushing
80	Gear Bearings
81	Clutch Gear (1 & 2)
82	Clutch Gear (3 & 4)
84	Washer
87	Stop
92	Ring
93	Ring
94	Ring

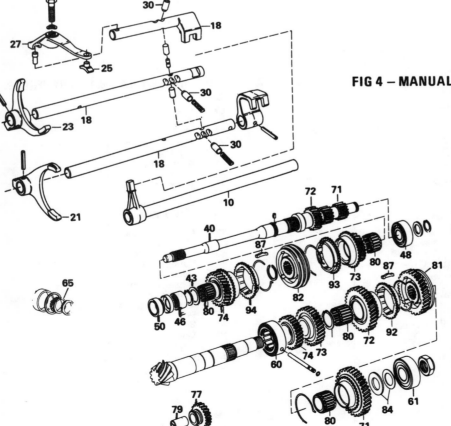

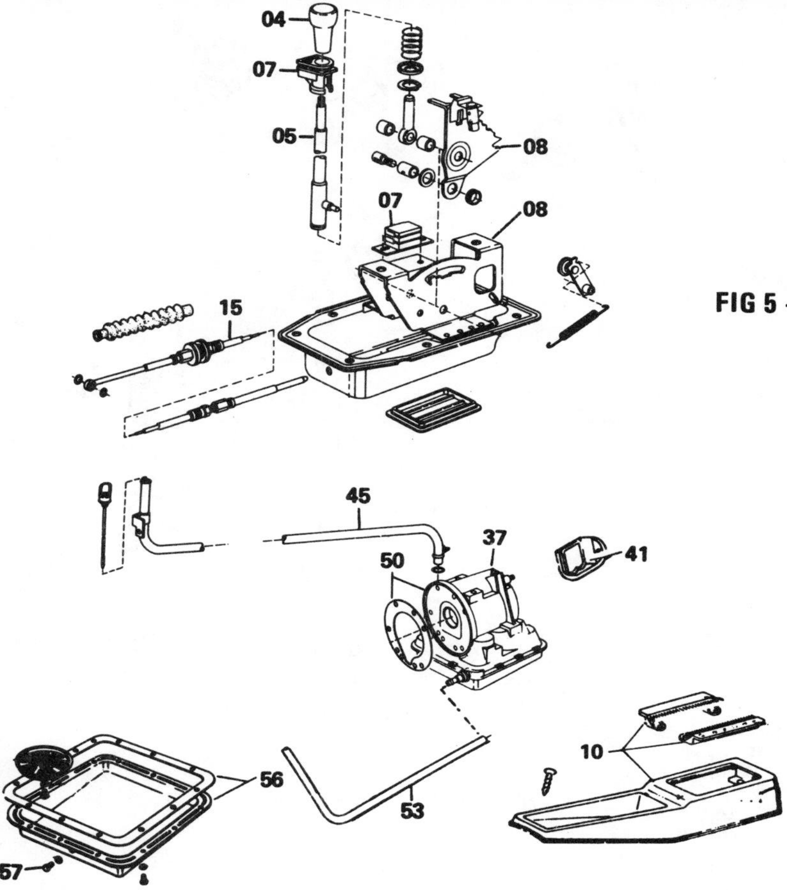

FIG 5 – AUTOMATIC TRANSMISSION CASE & CONTROLS

04	Knob
05	Selector Lever
07	Neutral Safety Switch
08	Selector Mechanism
10	Shift Lever Housing
15	Cable
37	Transmission Case
41	Rubber Mount
45	Filler Pipe
50	Bearing Flange
53	Vacuum Hose
56	Gasket
57	Drain Plug

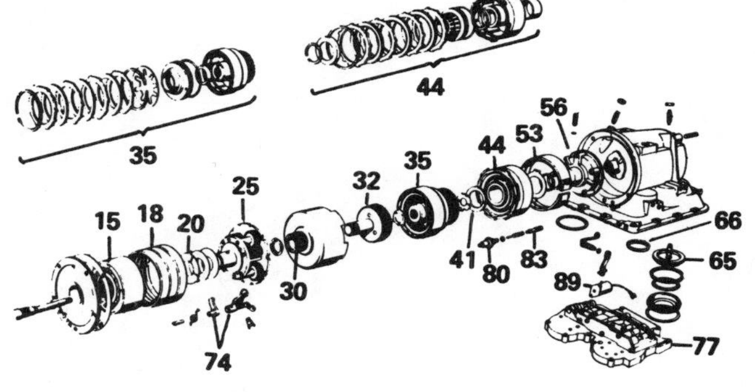

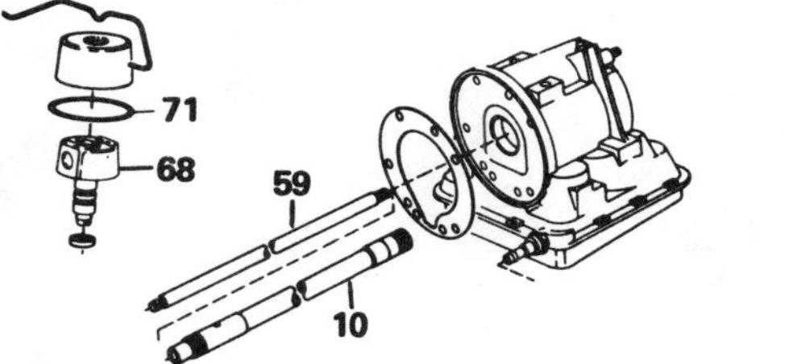

FIG 6 – AUTOMATIC TRANSMISSION GEARS & SHAFTS

10	Main Shaft
15	Annulus Gear
18	Reverse Brake Band
20	Shim
25	Planetary Gear Set
30	Sun Gear
32	Clutch Hub
35	Forward Clutch
41	Washer
44	Direct & Reverse Clutch Gear
53	Brake Band
56	Pump
59	Pump Shaft
65	Servo Piston
66	O Ring
68	Governor
71	Cover
74	Lever
77	Valve Body
80	Vacuum Unit
83	Primary Pressure Valve
89	Electro Magnet
90	Kickdown Switch

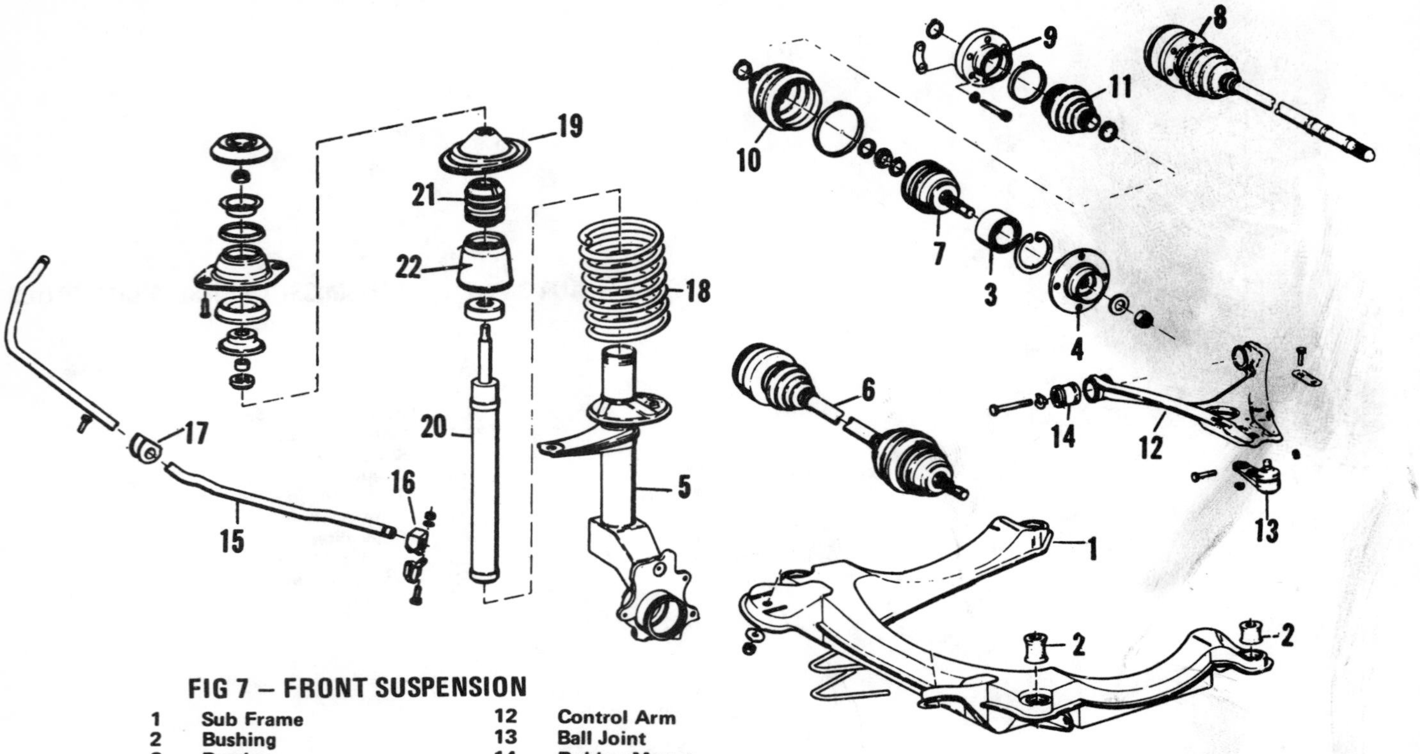

FIG 7 – FRONT SUSPENSION

1	Sub Frame	12	Control Arm
2	Bushing	13	Ball Joint
3	Bearing	14	Rubber Mount
4	Hub	15	Stabilizer Bar
5	Knuckle & Shock Housing	16	Rubber Mount, Outer
6	Drive Shaft Assy	17	Rubber Mount, Inner
7	Shaft & Joint, Outer	18	Spring
8	Shaft & Joint, Inner	19	Seat
9	Joint	20	Shock Absorber
10	Dust Sleeve, Outer	21	Stop Pad
11	Dust Sleeve, Inner	22	Dust Sleeve

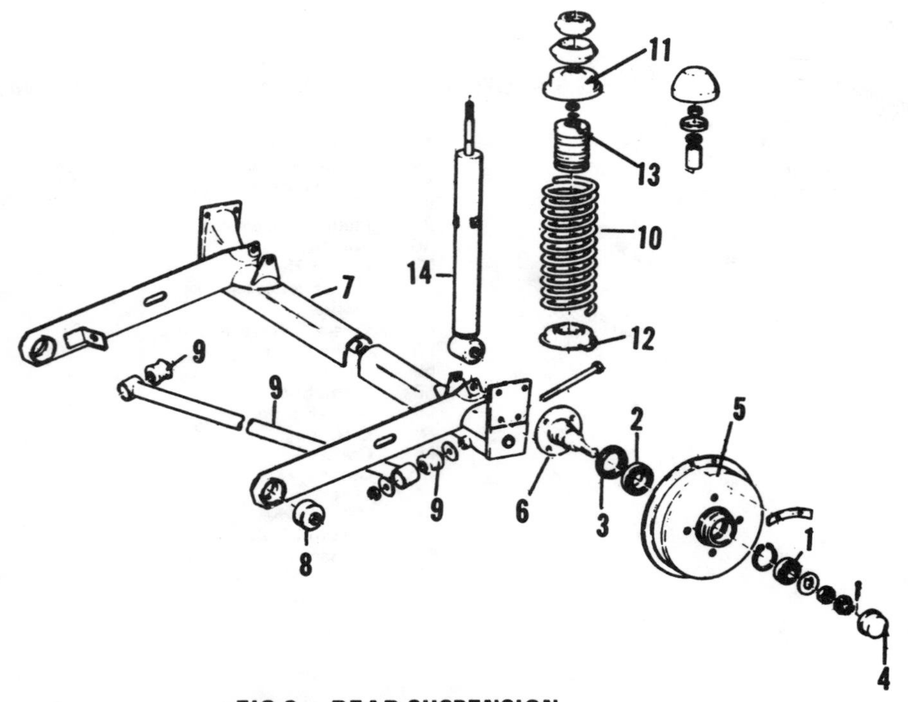

1 Bearing
2 Bearing
3 Oil Seal
4 Grease Cap
5 Hub & Drum
6 Stub Axle
7 Axle Beam
8 Rubber Mount
9 Diagonal Strut & Bush
10 Spring
11 Seat, Upper
12 Seat, Lower
13 Stop Pad
14 Shock Absorber

FIG 9 – REAR SUSPENSION

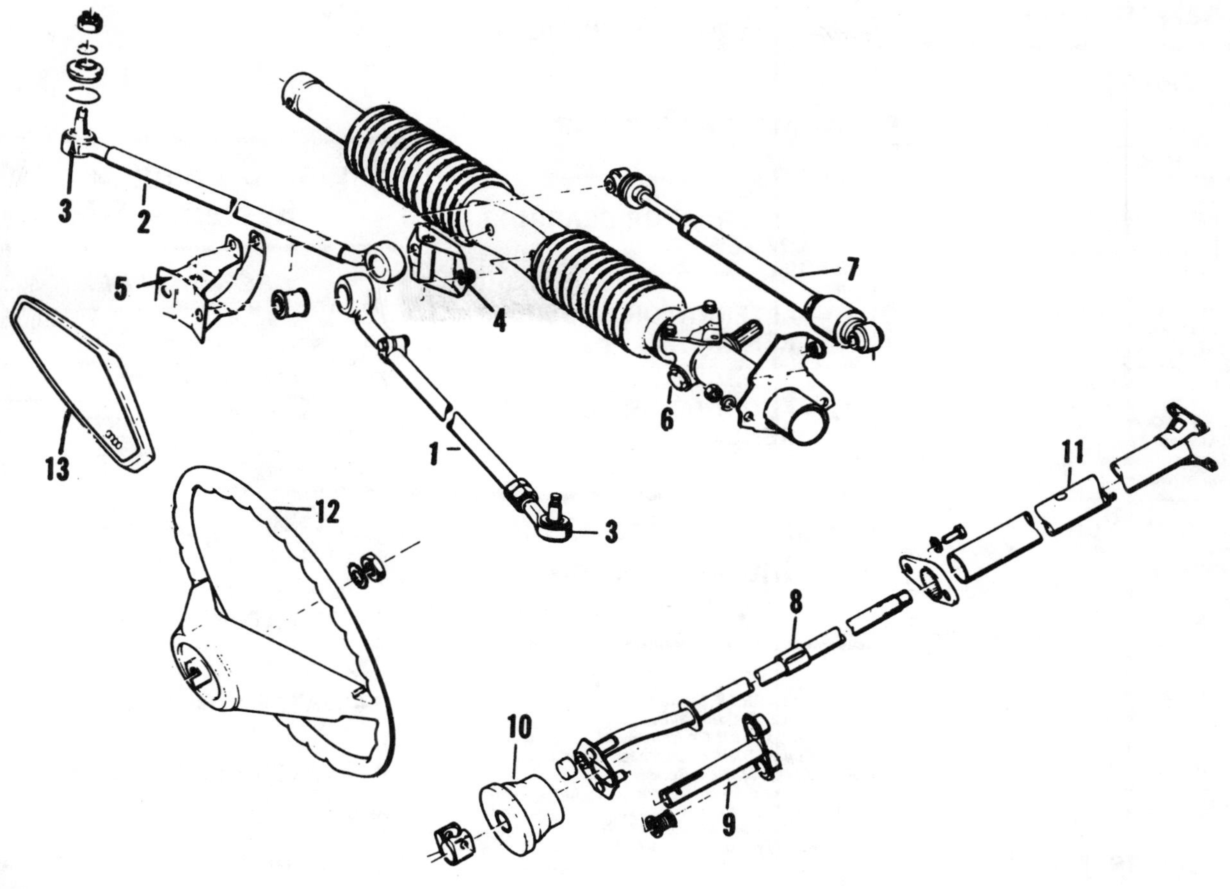

FIG 8 – STEERING

1	Tie Rod Assy, Left
2	Tie Rod Assy, Right
3	End, Outer
4	Mounting Bracket
5	Mounting Plate
6	Gear Assy
7	Damper
8	Main Shaft, Upper
9	Tube, Lower
10	Bushing
11	Column Jacket
12	Wheel
13	Horn Pad

Ignition, Starting & Charging—TIME

OPERATION INDEX

Tune-Up, Minor 1
Tune-Up, Major 2
Compression Test 3
Distributor, R&R Or Renew 4
Distributor Cap, Renew 5
Ignition Cables, Renew 6
Vacuum Control Unit, Renew 7
Ignition Coil, Renew 8
Starter & Ignition Lock, Renew 9
Ignition Lock Starter Switch, Renew 10
Starter, R&R Or Renew 11
Starter Solenoid, Renew 12
Starter Bendix Drive, Renew 13
Starter, R&R & Overhaul 14
Starter Brushes, Renew 15
Alternator Regulator, Renew 16
Alternator, R&R Or Renew 17
Alternator, R&R & Overhaul 18
Alternator Bearings, Renew 19
Alternator Brushes, Renew 20
Alternator Pulley, Renew 21

1—TUNE-UP, MINOR
Includes renew points, condenser & plugs, set spark timing and adjust carburetor idle.
All Models 2.0

2—TUNE-UP, MAJOR
Includes check compression, clean or renew & adjust spark plugs. R&R distributor, renew points & condenser. Adjust ignition timing, carburetor & fan belts. Clean battery terminals and service air cleaner. Check coil and renew fuel filter.
All Models 3.4

—NOTE—
For Oscillograph Adjustment, Add *0.6*

3—COMPRESSION TEST
All Models 0.6

4—DISTRIBUTOR, R&R OR RENEW
All Models 1.0

5—DISTRIBUTOR CAP, RENEW
All Models 0.2

6—IGNITION CABLES, RENEW
One 0.2
All 0.4

7—VACUUM CONTROL UNIT, RENEW
All Models 1.0

8—IGNITION COIL, RENEW
All Models 0.2

9—STARTER & IGNITION LOCK, RENEW
90 ....1.8
100 ....1.7
Fox 1.0

10—IGNITION LOCK STARTER SWITCH, RENEW
90 & 100 ....0.8

11—STARTER, R&R OR RENEW
90 & 100 ....0.8
Fox 0.6

12—STARTER SOLENOID, RENEW
All Models 0.9

13—STARTER BENDIX DRIVE, RENEW
All Models 1.2

14—STARTER, R&R & OVERHAUL
90 & 100 ....2.0
Fox 1.8

15—STARTER BRUSHES, RENEW
90 & 100 ....1.1
Fox 0.9

16—ALTERNATOR REGULATOR, RENEW
All Models 0.3

17—ALTERNATOR, R&R OR RENEW
90 & 100 ....0.9
Fox 0.5

18—ALTERNATOR, R&R & OVERHAUL
90 & 100 ....1.8
Fox 1.4

19—ALTERNATOR BEARINGS, RENEW
90 & 100 ....1.4
Fox 1.0

20—ALTERNATOR BRUSHES, RENEW
90 & 100 ....1.3
Fox 0.9

21—ALTERNATOR PULLEY, RENEW
All Models 0.9

Fuel, Emission Controls, Intake & Exhaust Systems—TIME

OPERATION INDEX

Carburetor, R&R Or Renew 1
Carb, R&R & Overhaul 2
Fuel Pump, R&R Or Renew 3
Fuel Pump, R&R & Overhaul 4
Fuel Tank, R&R Or Renew 5
Choke Cable Assy, Renew 6
Vacuum Unit, Renew 7
Intake Manifold Or Gasket, Renew 8
Exhaust Manifold Or Gasket, Renew 9
Exhaust Pipe, Renew 10
Muffler, Renew 11

1—CARBURETOR, R&R OR RENEW
All Models 0.6

2—CARBURETOR, R&R & OVERHAUL
All Models 1.8

3—FUEL PUMP, R&R OR RENEW
90 ....0.5
100 ....0.4
Fox 0.3

4—FUEL PUMP, R&R & OVERHAUL
90 ....1.0
100 ....0.9
Fox 0.8

5—FUEL TANK, R&R OR RENEW
90 & 100 ....1.0
Fox 0.6

6—CHOKE CABLE ASSY, RENEW
All Models 0.6

7—VACUUM UNIT, RENEW
Two Phase Carb 0.4

8—INTAKE MANIFOLD OR GASKET, RENEW
90 & 100 ....1.1
Fox 0.9

9—EXHAUST MANIFOLD OR GASKET, RENEW
All Models 1.0

10—EXHAUST PIPE, RENEW
Front 0.5
Rear 0.4

11—MUFFLER, RENEW
Primary—
90 ....1.0
100 ....1.1
Fox 0.9
Final—
90 ....0.6
100 ....0.8
Fox 0.4

Engine Cooling & Heater System—TIME

OPERATION INDEX

Radiator, R&R Or Renew 1
Radiator Hoses, Renew 2
Water Pump, R&R Or Renew 3
Water Pump, R&R & Overhaul 4
Thermostat Or Housing, Renew 5
Fresh Air Heater, Renew 6
Heat Exchanger, Renew 7
Heater Blower Motor, Renew 8
Blower Motor, R&R & Overhaul 9
Heater Control, Renew 10
Heater Hoses, Renew 11

1—RADIATOR, R&R OR RENEW
90 & 100 ....(1)0.8
Fox 0.6
(1)*Includes Renew Cowl.*

2—RADIATOR HOSES, RENEW
Upper 0.4
Lower, Exc 100 ....0.5
100 ....0.6

3—WATER PUMP, R&R OR RENEW
90 & 100 ....1.2
Fox 0.9

4—WATER PUMP, R&R & OVERHAUL
90 & 100 ....2.0
Fox 1.6

5—THERMOSTAT OR HOUSING, RENEW
All Models 0.4

6—FRESH AIR HEATER, RENEW
90 ....2.2
100 ....1.2
Fox 1.2

7—HEAT EXCHANGER, RENEW
90 ....2.6
100 ....1.8
Fox 1.4

8—HEATER BLOWER MOTOR, RENEW
90 ....3.3
100 ....1.5
Fox 1.1

9—BLOWER MOTOR, R&R & OVERHAUL
90 ....3.9
100 ....2.2

10—HEATER CONTROL, RENEW
90 ....0.7
100 ....1.0
Fox 0.3

11—HEATER HOSES, RENEW
90, Each 0.4
100 ....0.3
Fox 0.3

Engine—TIME

OPERATION INDEX

Engine, R&R 1
Engine, R&R & Overhaul 2
(Continued)

Engine—TIME Cont'd

Engine Block Assy & Crankshaft Bearing Caps, Renew 3
Cylinder Head, R&R Or Gasket, Renew 4
Valves, Grind & Overhaul Cylinder Head 5
One Valve, Renew & Grind 6
Valve Springs, Renew 7
Cylinder Head Cover Gasket, Renew 8
Push Rods & Tappets, Renew 9
Rocker Levers, Renew 10
Valve Play, Adjust 11
Oil Pan Or Gasket, R&R Or Renew 12
Timing Housing Cover Seal, Renew 13
Timing Chain & Gears, Renew 14
Hydraulic Chain Tensioner Or Guide Rail, Renew 15
Camshaft Sprocket, Renew 16
Spur Belt, Renew 17
Intermediate Sprocket, Renew 18
Camshaft, R&R Or Renew 19
Oil Pump, R&R Or Renew 20
Pistons Or Rings, Renew 21
Connecting Rods Or Bearings, Renew 22
Oil Spray Jet, Renew 23
Crankshaft, R&R Or Renew 24
Crankshaft Rear Main Oil Seal, Renew 25
Crankshaft Main Needle Bearing, Renew 26
Crankshaft Pulley, Renew 27

1—ENGINE, R&R
Does not include transfer of any part of engine or replacement of special equipment.
90 & 100 ....5.2
Fox 3.2

—NOTE—
To Renew Engine, Add *3.6*

2—ENGINE, R&R & OVERHAUL
Includes rebore cylinders with boring bar, renew pistons, rings, pins, bearings, grind valves, plastigauge bearings and perform minor tune-up.
90 & 100 ....25.1
Fox 19.0

3—ENGINE BLOCK ASSY & CRANKSHAFT BRG CAPS, RENEW
90 & 100 ....14.7

4—CYLINDER HEAD, R&R OR GASKET, RENEW
90 & 100 ....2.7
Fox 2.2

5—VALVES, GRIND & OVERHAUL CYLINDER HEAD
90 & 100 ....7.4
Fox 7.0

6—ONE VALVE, RENEW & GRIND
90 & 100 ....3.0
Fox 2.4

7—VALVE SPRINGS, RENEW
90 & 100—
Each 0.9
All ①3.7
Fox 1.8
①*Includes R&R Cylinder Head.*

8—CYLINDER HEAD COVER GASKET, RENEW
All Models 0.2

9—PUSH RODS & TAPPETS, RENEW
All Models 1.3

10—ROCKER LEVERS, RENEW
All Models—
One 0.8
All 1.1

11—VALVE PLAY, ADJUST
All Models 0.6

12—OIL PAN OR GASKET, R&R OR RENEW
90 ....1.6
100 ....①1.8
Fox 1.2

—NOTE—
To Replace Oil Safety Valve, Add *0.1*
①*Includes R&R Left Eng Supt.*

13—TIMING HOUSING COVER SEAL, RENEW
All Models 1.2

14—TIMING CHAIN & GEARS, RENEW
90 ....3.1
100 ....3.3

15—HYDRAULIC CHAIN TENSIONER OR GUIDE RAIL, RENEW
90 ....2.6
100 ....2.8

16—CAMSHAFT SPROCKET, RENEW
Fox 0.7

17—SPUR BELT, RENEW
Fox 0.8

18—INTERMEDIATE SPROCKET, RENEW
Fox 1.3

19—CAMSHAFT, R&R OR RENEW
90 & 100 ....10.2
Fox 2.5

20—OIL PUMP, R&R OR RENEW
90 ....2.0
100 ....2.2
Fox 1.4

21—PISTONS OR RINGS, RENEW
All Models—
One 4.6
Each Additional 0.5

22—CONNECTING RODS OR BEARINGS, RENEW
All Models—
One 4.6
Each Additional 0.8

23—OIL SPRAY JET, RENEW
All Models 1.0

24—CRANKSHAFT, R&R OR RENEW
90 & 100 ....7.5
Fox 2.2

25—CRANKSHAFT REAR MAIN OIL SEAL, RENEW
90 ....①6.5
100 ....①7.5
Fox ①3.1
①*Includes R&R Transmission.*

26—CRANKSHAFT MAIN NEEDLE BEARING, RENEW
90 ....5.6
100 ....7.2
Fox 3.0

—NOTE—
Includes R&R Clutch.

27—CRANKSHAFT PULLEY, RENEW
90 & 100 ....0.8
Fox 0.4

Clutch, Mounts & Transmissions—TIME

OPERATION INDEX

Flywheel, R&R Or Renew 1
Flywheel Ring Gear, Renew 2
Clutch, R&R & Overhaul 3
Clutch Cover Or Thrust Plate, Renew 4
Ball Bearing Withdrawer, Renew 5
Withdrawal Shaft, Renew 6
Clutch Pedal, Adjust 7
Engine Mounts, Renew 8
Trans Assy, R&R Or Renew 9
Gearbox Housing, Renew 10
Gearbox Cover Or Gasket, Renew 11
Mainshaft, Renew 12
Mainshaft Oil Seal, Renew 13
Shift Rods & Selector Forks, Renew 14
Gearbox, R&R & Overhaul 15
Gearbox End Cover, Renew 16
Differential Flange Gasket Or Seal, Renew 17

1—FLYWHEEL, R&R OR RENEW
90 ....5.6
100 ....7.2
Fox 4.5

2—FLYWHEEL RING GEAR, RENEW
90 ....5.8
100 ....7.4
Fox 4.7

3—CLUTCH, R&R & OVERHAUL
90 ....5.8
100 ....7.2
Fox 4.2

4—CLUTCH COVER OR THRUST PLATE, RENEW
90 ....4.9
100 ....6.5
Fox 3.5

—NOTE—
To Renew Clutch Lining, Add *0.5*

5—BALL BEARING WITHDRAWER, RENEW
90 ....4.8
100 ....6.4

6—WITHDRAWAL SHAFT, RENEW
90 ....①5.2
100 ....②6.8
①*Includes R&R Gearbox.*
②*Includes R&R Eng & Gearbox.*

7—CLUTCH PEDAL, ADJUST
All Models 0.2

8—ENGINE MOUNTS, RENEW
Front, 90 ....1.0
Front, 100—
Right Or Left 0.5
Both 0.8
Front, Fox—
Right Or Left 0.3
Both 0.5
Rear, All 0.5
All Mounts—
90 ....1.5
100 ....1.1
Fox 1.0

9—TRANSMISSION ASSY, R&R OR RENEW
90 ....4.6
100—
Std Trans ①6.2
Auto Trans 5.6
Fox—
Std Trans 2.5
Auto Trans 3.5
①*Includes R&R Engine.*

—NOTE—
To Renew Trans, Add *0.9*

10—GEARBOX HOUSING, RENEW
90 ....11.0
100 ....12.6
Fox 6.0

11—GEARBOX COVER OR GASKET, RENEW
90 ....6.8
100 ....8.4

12—MAINSHAFT, RENEW
90 ....6.5
100 ....8.1

13—MAINSHAFT OIL SEAL, RENEW
90 ....4.9
100 ....6.5

(Continued)

Clutch, Mounts & Transmissions—TIME Cont'd

Fox	3.0

14—SHIFT RODS & SELECTOR FORKS, RENEW

90	7.3
100	8.9
Fox	4.5

15—GEARBOX, R&R & OVERHAUL

90	11.0
100	12.6
Fox	7.5

16—GEARBOX END COVER, RENEW

90	5.2
100	6.8
Fox	3.0

17—DIFFERENTIAL FLANGE GASKET OR SEAL, RENEW

90 & 100—	
Std Trans	2.4
Auto Trans	2.0

Brakes, Steering, Suspension, Universals & Rear Axle—TIME

OPERATION INDEX

Brake Shoes Or Friction Pads, Renew *1*
Master Cylinder, Renew *2*
Master Cylinder, R&R & Overhaul *3*
Brake Fluid Reservoir, Renew *4*
Wheel Cylinders, Renew *5*
Wheel Cylinders, R&R & Overhaul *6*
Caliper Assy, Renew *7*
Caliper Assy, R&R & Overhaul *8*
Bleed System *9*
Brake Hose, Renew *10*
Hub Disc Or Bearings, Renew *11*
Power Brake Unit, Renew *12*
Power Brake Check Valve, Renew *13*
Brake Drum, Renew *14*
Brake Pedal, Renew *15*
Parking Brake Cable, Renew *16*
Parking Brake Lever, Renew *17*
Hardy Disc (Disc Joint) Renew *18*
Steering Gear Assy, R&R Or Renew *19*
Steering Gear, R&R & Overhaul *20*
Track Rods, Renew *21*
Track Rod Ball Joint, Renew *22*
Steering Knuckles Or Bearings & Seals, Renew *23*
Wishbone Joints, Renew *24*
Wishbones & Supports, Renew *25*
Wishbone Bearings, Renew *26*
Front Coil Spring Shock Abosrber Assy, Renew *27*
Torsion Bars, Renew *28*
Front Spring Adjusting Levers Or Pressure Pieces, Renew *29*
Shock Abosrbers, Renew *30*
Front Stabilizer, Renew *31*
Rear Spring & Suspension Arm, Renew *32*
Suspension Arms, Renew *33*
Transverse Suspension Rod, Renew *34*
Rear Suspension Cross Tube, Renew *35*
Rear Axle, R&R *36*
Rear Axle, Renew *37*
Rear Axle Cap, Renew *38*
Rear Axle Bearings & Seals, Renew *39*
Stub Axles, R&R Or Renew *40*
Stub Axle Oil Seals, Renew *41*

1—BRAKE SHOES OR FRICTION PADS, RENEW

Drum Type, Rear—	
One	0.8
Both	1.3
Disc Type Front Both—	
Exc Below	0.6
100 W/Auto Trans	0.9

2—MASTER CYLINDER, RENEW

All Models	1.0

3—MASTER CYLINDER, R&R & OVERHAUL

All Models	1.3

4—BRAKE FLUID RESERVOIR, RENEW

All Models	0.3

5—WHEEL CYLINDERS, RENEW

All Models, Rear—	
One	1.0
Both	1.6

6—WHEEL CYLINDERS, R&R & OVERHAUL

All Models, Rear—	
One	1.2
Both	2.0

7—CALIPER ASSY, RENEW

90 & 100—	
One	1.2
Both	2.0
Fox—	
One	1.0
Both	1.8

8—CALIPER ASSY, R&R & OVERHAUL

90 & 100—	
One	2.0
Both	3.5
Fox—	
One	1.6
Both	3.0

9—BLEED SYSTEM

90 & 100—	
Front	0.3
Rear	0.3
Fox	0.5

10—BRAKE HOSE, RENEW

All Models—	
Front, Each	0.6
Rear, Each	0.6
All Four	1.0

11—HUB DISC OR BEARINGS, RENEW

Disc Front—	
One	1.5
Both	2.5
Drum Rear—	
One	1.8
Both	3.0

12—POWER BRAKE UNIT, RENEW

90 & 100	1.4
Fox	1.0

13—POWER BRAKE CHECK VALVE, RENEW

All Models	0.3

14—BRAKE DRUM, RENEW

90 & 100, Rear—	
One	1.0
Both	1.8
Fox—	
One	0.6
Both	1.0

15—BRAKE PEDAL, RENEW

90	①2.5
100	②1.0
Fox	0.2

①Includes R&R Heater
Includes R&R Clutch Pedal

16—PARKING BRAKE CABLE, RENEW

90, Each	1.0
100	1.7
Fox	0.6

17—PARKING BRAKE LEVER, RENEW

90 & 100	1.1
Fox	0.6

18—HARDY DISC (DISC JOINT) RENEW

90	1.5
100	1.0

19—STEERING GEAR ASSY, R&R OR RENEW

90	3.2
100	3.5
Fox	1.2

20—STEERING GEAR, R&R & OVERHAUL

90	6.0

21—TRACK RODS, RENEW

90 & 100—	
One	1.2
Both	1.5

22—TRACK ROD BALL JOINT, RENEW

90 & 100	1.1

23—STEERING KNUCKLES OR BEARINGS & SEALS, RENEW

90 & 100—	
One	2.0
Both	3.1

24—WISHBONE JOINTS, RENEW

90—	
One	1.1
Both	1.4
100—	
One	0.4
Both	0.7
Fox, Lower	0.8

25—WISHBONES & SUPPORTS, RENEW

Upper—	
90, One	2.3
90, Both	2.9
100, One	2.8
100, Both	3.4
Lower—	
90, One	①3.1
90, Both	①4.6
100, One	①2.3
100, Both	①2.9
Fox	1.1
All Both Sides—	
90	6.0
100	4.2

①Includes R&R Thrust Rod.

26—WISHBONE BEARINGS, RENEW

Lower—	
90, One	2.5
90, Both	3.6
100, One	1.2
100, Both	1.4
Upper—	
90, One Side (Both)	2.3
90, Both Sides (All)	3.4
100, One Side, (Both)	2.7
100, Both Sides (All)	3.6

27—FRONT COIL SPRING SHOCK ABSORBER ASSY, RENEW

Model 100—	
One	0.6
Both	1.0

28—TORSION BARS, RENEW

Front—	
90, One	2.5
90, Both	4.0
100, One	1.0
100, Both	1.8
Rear—	
90, One	2.5
100, One	2.0
100, Both	2.3

29—FRONT SPRING ADJ LEVERS OR PRESSURE PIECES, RENEW

One	2.6
Both	4.1

30—SHOCK ABSORBERS, RENEW

Front—	
One Exc	0.5
Model 100	1.0
Both Exc	0.7
Model 100	1.8

(Continued)

Brakes, Steering, Suspension, Universals & Rear Axle—TIME Cont'd

Rear—
- One Exc 0.5
  - Model 100 ..... 0.8
- Both Exc 0.8
  - Model 100 ..... 1.2

31—FRONT STABILIZER, RENEW
90 ..... 1.1
100 ..... 1.3
Fox 0.9

32—REAR SPRING & SUSPENSION ARM, RENEW
One (Exc Fox) 0.6

33—SUSPENSION ARMS, REAR, RENEW
90, One 0.9
90, Both 1.4
100, One 1.8
100, Both 2.0

34— TRANSVERSE SUSPENSION ROD, RENEW
All Models 0.4

35—REAR SUSPENSION CROSS TUBE, RENEW
Exc Below 1.4
Fox 0.9

36—REAR AXLE, R&R
All Models 1.6

37—REAR AXLE, RENEW
90 & 100 ..... 3.1

38— REAR AXLE CAP, RENEW
90 & 100 ..... 0.3

39—REAR AXLE BEARINGS & SEALS, RENEW
- One Side Exc 1.0
  - Fox 0.8
- Both Sides Exc 1.8
  - Fox 1.2

40—AXLE STUBS, R&R OR RENEW
- One Side Exc 1.4
  - Fox 0.7
- Both Sides Exc 2.2
  - Fox 1.3

41—STUB AXLE OIL SEALS, RENEW
- One Side Exc 0.7
  - Fox 0.5
- Both Sides Exc 1.2
  - Fox 1.0

Speedometer, W/S Wipers, Switches & Instruments—TIME

OPERATION INDEX

Speedometer Cable, Renew 1
Speedometer Head, Renew 2
W/S Wiper Motor, Renew 3
W/S Wiper Connecting Rods, Renew 4
W/S Wiper Bearings, Renew 5
W/S Wiper Arm, Renew 6
Fuel Gauge (Dash Unit) Renew 7
Fuel Tank Gauge, Renew 8
Oil Pressure Switch, Renew 9
Temperature Gauge (Dash Unit) Renew 10
Temperature Gauge Element, Renew 11
Tachometer, Renew 12
Headlight Switch, Renew 13
Dip Beam & Turn Indicator Switch, Renew 14
Hazard Flasher Switch, Renew 15

1—SPEEDOMETER CABLE, RENEW
90 & 100 ..... 0.7
Fox 0.4

2—SPEEDOMETER HEAD, RENEW
90 ..... 1.0
100 ..... 0.6
Fox 0.6

3—W/S WIPER MOTOR, RENEW
90 ..... 3.1
100 ..... 0.9
Fox 0.7

4—W/S WIPER CONNECTING RODS, RENEW
- One—
  - 90 ..... 3.3
  - 100 ..... 0.2
  - Fox 0.4
- Both—
  - 90 ..... 3.4
  - 100 ..... 0.3
  - Fox 0.5

5—W/S WIPER BEARINGS, RENEW
- One—
  - 90 ..... 3.3
  - 100 ..... 1.5
- Both—
  - 90 ..... 3.5
  - 100 ..... 1.6

6—W/S WIPER ARM, RENEW
One 0.1
Both 0.2

7—FUEL GAUGE (DASH UNIT) RENEW
90 ..... 1.3
100 ..... 0.9
Fox 0.8

8—FUEL TANK GAUGE, RENEW
90 & 100 ..... 0.5
Fox 0.3

9—OIL PRESSURE SWITCH, RENEW
90 ..... 0.2
100 ..... 0.7
Fox 0.2

10—TEMPERATURE GAUGE (DASH UNIT) RENEW
90 ..... 1.2
100 ..... 0.9
Fox 0.9

11—TEMPERATURE GAUGE ELEMENT, RENEW
90 ..... 0.3
100 ..... 0.1
Fox 0.2

12—TACHOMETER, RENEW
90 ..... 0.7
100 ..... 0.6

13—HEADLIGHT SWITCH, RENEW
90 ..... 0.4
100 ..... 0.6
Fox 0.4

14—DIP BEAM & TURN INDICATOR SWITCH, RENEW
All Models 0.7

15—HAZARD FLASHER SWITCH, RENEW
90 ..... 0.4
100 ..... 0.6
Fox 0.4

IDENTIFICATION

ALL MODELS....27

ILLUSTRATIONS

FIG 1 – ENGINE BLOCK
FIG 2 – ENGINE CRANKSHAFT, CAMSHAFT & FLYWHEEL
FIG 3 – TRANSMISSION
FIG 4 – FRONT SUSPENSION
FIG 5 – STEERING
FIG 6 – REAR AXLE

OPERATION TIMES

A

Air Pump.... 34
Alternator.... 34
Automatic Transmission.... 36

B

Brake Drums.... 37
Brakes.... 37

C

Cables (Ignition).... 34
Calipers.... 37
Camshaft.... 35
Carburetor.... 34
Clutch.... 36
Coil, Ignition.... 34
Compression Test.... 34
Cooling System.... 34
Crankshaft.... 36
Cylinder Head.... 35

D

Dash Gauges.... 38
Differential.... 38
Disc Brakes.... 37
Distributor.... 34

E

Emission Controls.... 34
Engine Assembly.... 35
Engine Mountings.... 36
Engine Oiling.... 35
Engine Tune-Up.... 34
Exhaust System.... 34

F

Flywheel.... 36
Front Suspension.... 37
Fuel Gauges.... 38
Fuel Pump.... 34
Fuel Tank.... 34

G

Generator.... 34

H

Hand Brake.... 37
Hazard Flasher Switch.... 38
Headlight Switch.... 38
Heater.... 35
Hose (Brake).... 37
Hose (Radiator).... 35
Hydraulic Brakes.... 37

I

Ignition.... 34
Ignition Coil.... 34
Ignition Switch.... 34
Intake Manifold.... 34

L

Light Switches.... 38

M

Main Bearings.... 36
Master Cylinder.... 37
Muffler.... 34

O

Oil Gauge.... 38
Oiling, Engine.... 35
Oil Pump.... 35
Oil Sump.... 35

P

Parking Brake.... 37
Piston Rings.... 35
Pistons.... 36

R

Radiator.... 34
Radiator Hose.... 35
Regulator.... 34
Rocker Arms.... 35
Rod Bearings.... 36

S

Shocks (Front).... 38
Shocks (Rear).... 38
Speedometer.... 38
Springs.... 37
Starting Motor.... 34
Steering Gear.... 37
Steering Linkage.... 37
Stop Light Switch.... 38
Switches (Light).... 38
Synchro-Mesh Trans.... 36

T

Tachometer.... 38
Temperature Gauge.... 38
Thermostat.... 35
Timing Case Cover.... 35
Timing Chain.... 35
Timing Gears.... 35
Transmission, Manual.... 36
Transmission, Automatic.... 36
Tune-Up Engine.... 34

U

Universals.... 38

V

Vacuum Control Unit.... 34
Valve Lifters.... 35
Valve System.... 35

W

Water Pump.... 35
Wheel Cylinders.... 37
Windshield Wiper.... 38

AUSTIN IDENTIFICATION PLATE LOCATIONS

AUSTIN AMERICA

CHASSIS NUMBER – Stamped on a plate attached to the right front wheelhouse above the battery.

CAR NUMBER – Stamped on a plate on the right hand side of the hood lock platform and on a plate on the top left side of instrument panel, visible thru windshield.

BODY NUMBER – Stamped on a plate attached to the top of the right front wheelhouse.

ENGINE NUMBER – Stamped on a plate on the right hand side of the block.

TRANSMISSION NUMBER – Stamped on the housing below the starting motor.

AUSTIN MARINA

CHASSIS NUMBER – Stamped on a plate attached to the hood lock platform.

BODY NUMBER – Stamped on a plate attached to the left side of the hood platform.

ENGINE NUMBER – Stamped on the block or on a plate attached to the right side of the block.

TRANSMISSION NUMBER – Stamped on the right hand side of the housing.

AXLE NUMBER – Stamped on the outside face of the differential casting joint flanges.

AUSTIN HEALEY SPRITE & MG MIDGET IDENTIFICATION PLATE LOCATIONS

The **Car Number** is stamped on a plate secured to the left-hand inner wheel arch valance under the bonnet

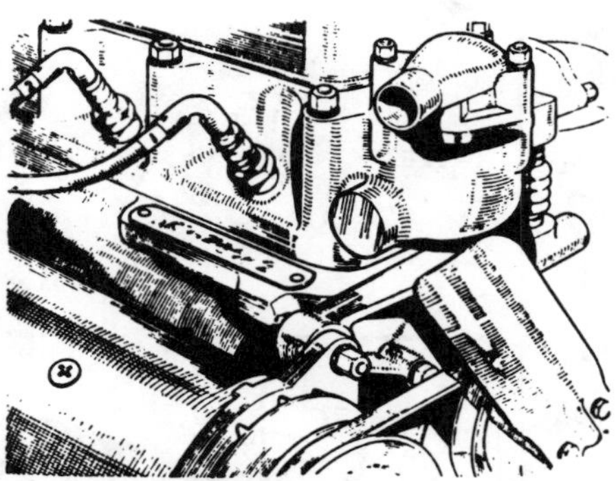

The **Engine Number** is stamped on a plate secured to the right-hand side of the cylinder block above the dynamo

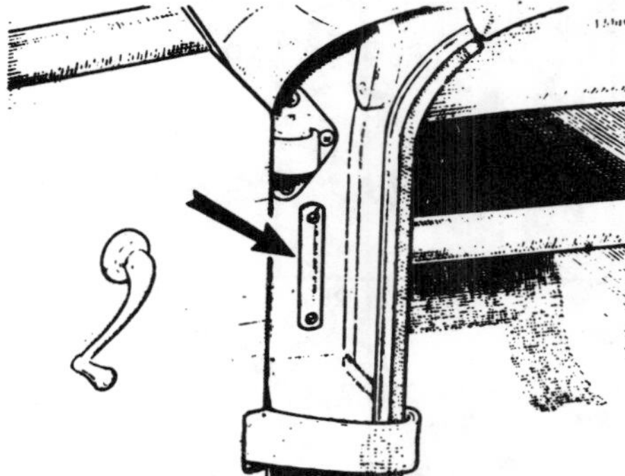

The **Body Number** is stamped on a plate secured to the left-hand front door pillar

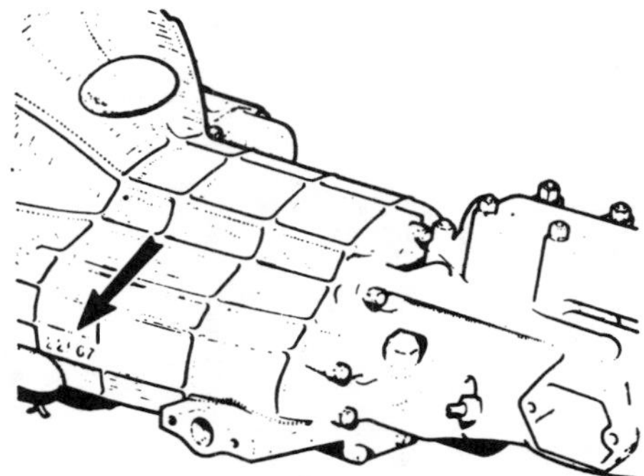

The **Gearbox Number** is stamped on the left-hand side of the gearbox casing

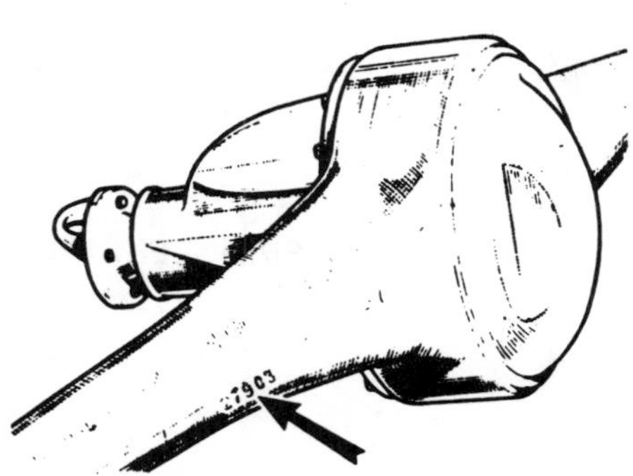

The **Rear Axle Number** is stamped on the rear of the left-hand rear axle tube adjacent to the spring anchorage

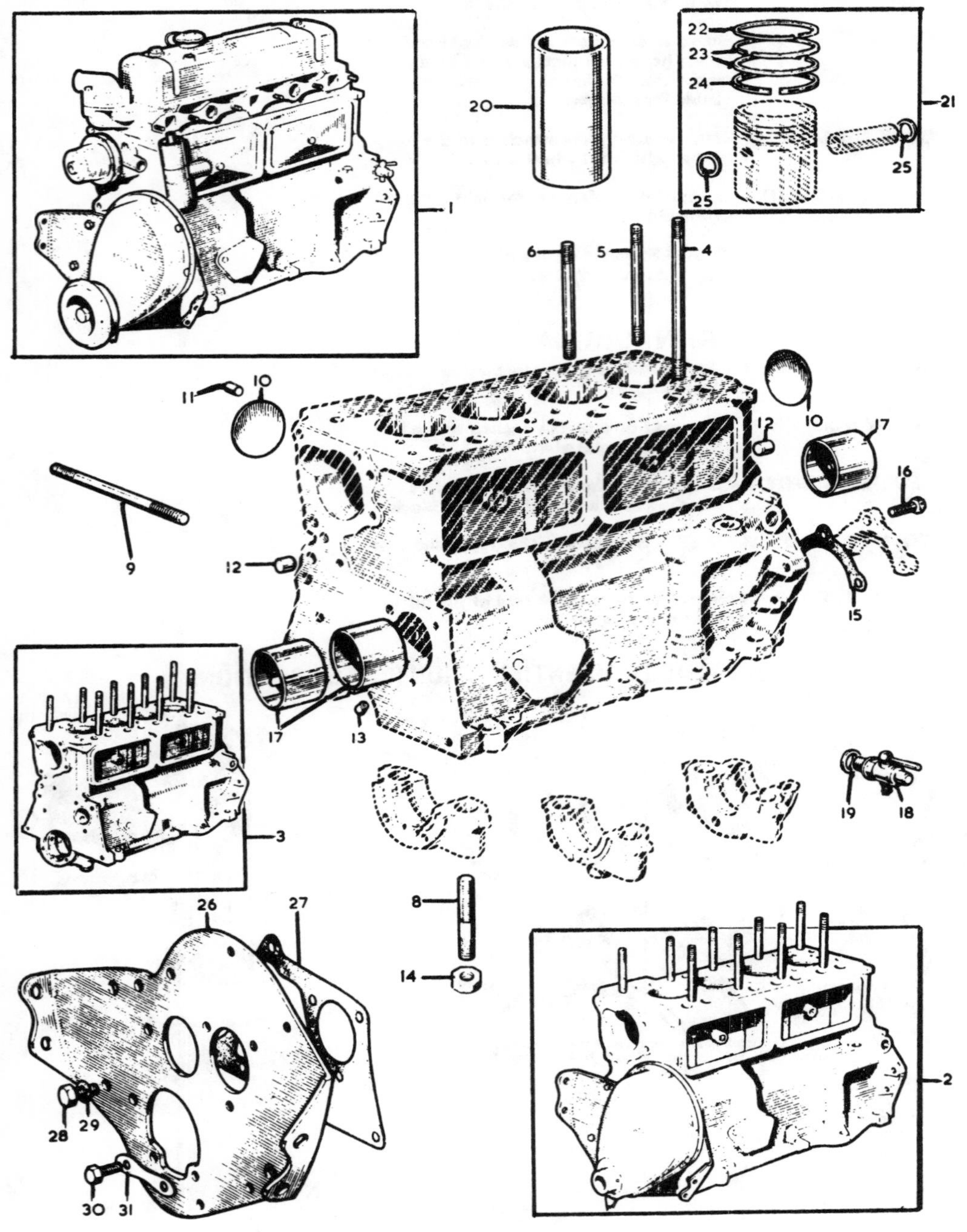

1	Engine Stripped
2	Engine Partial
3	Cylinder Block
4	Stud
5	Stud
6	Stud
8	Stud
9	Stud
10	Plug
11	Plug
12	Plug
13	Restrictor
14	Nut
15	Washer
16	Screw
17	Bearing
18	Drain Tap
19	Washer
20	Cylinder Liner
21	Pistons & Rings
22	Ring
23	Ring
24	Ring
25	Circlip
26	Plate, Front
27	Washer
28	Screw
29	Washer
30	Screw
31	Plate

FIG 1 – ENGINE BLOCK

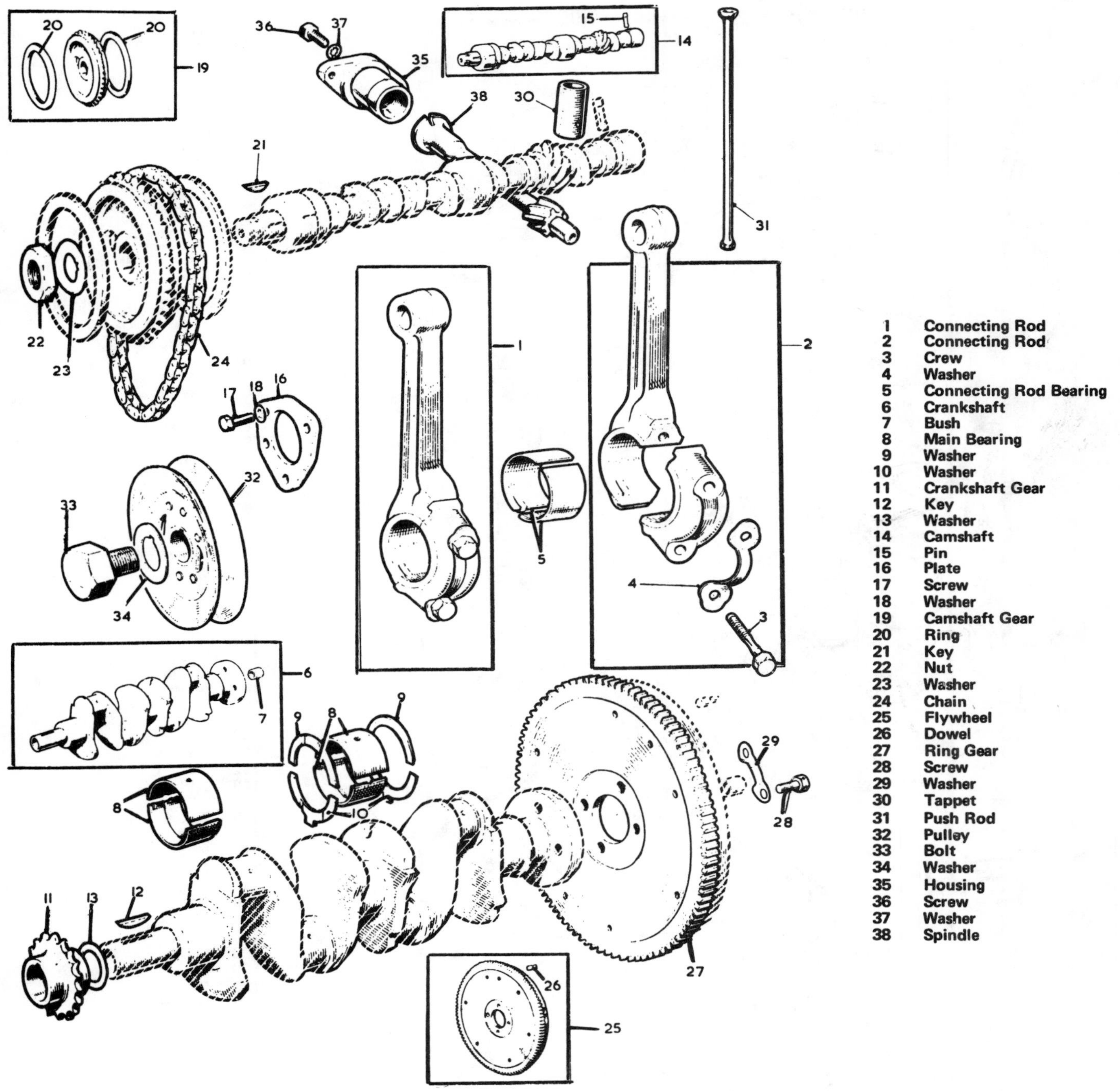
1 Connecting Rod
2 Connecting Rod
3 Crew
4 Washer
5 Connecting Rod Bearing
6 Crankshaft
7 Bush
8 Main Bearing
9 Washer
10 Washer
11 Crankshaft Gear
12 Key
13 Washer
14 Camshaft
15 Pin
16 Plate
17 Screw
18 Washer
19 Camshaft Gear
20 Ring
21 Key
22 Nut
23 Washer
24 Chain
25 Flywheel
26 Dowel
27 Ring Gear
28 Screw
29 Washer
30 Tappet
31 Push Rod
32 Pulley
33 Bolt
34 Washer
35 Housing
36 Screw
37 Washer
38 Spindle

FIG 2 – ENGINE CRANKSHAFT, CAMSHAFT & FLYWHEEL

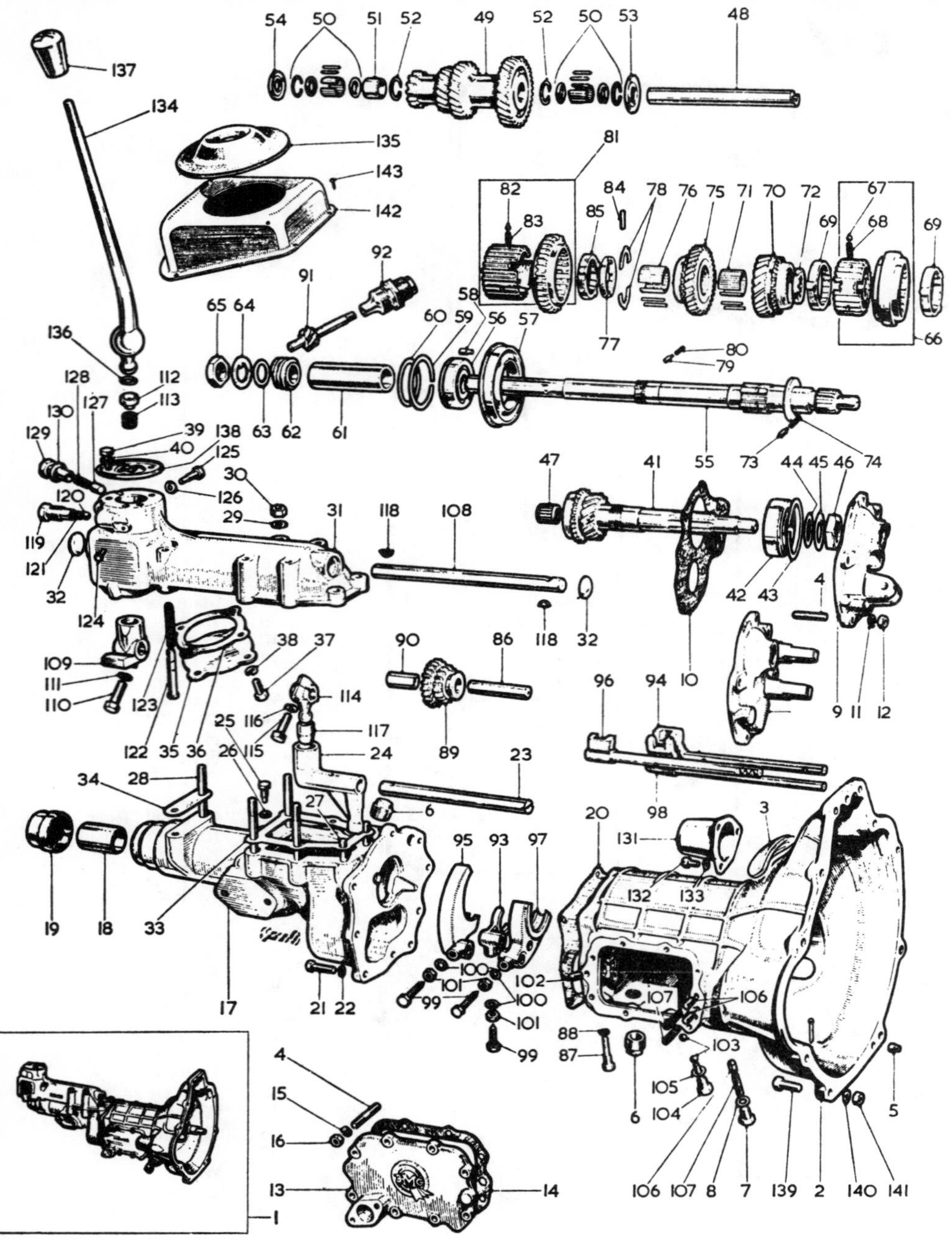

FIG 3 – TRANSMISSION

1 Transmission Assy
2 Case
3 Cover
4 Stud
5 Dowel
6 Plug
7 Plug
8 Washer
9 Front Cover
10 Washer
11 Washer
12 Nut
13 Side Cover
14 Washer
15 Washer
16 Nut
17 Rear Extension
18 Bush
19 Oil Seal
20 Washer
21 Screw
22 Washer
23 Shaft
24 Lever
25 Peg
26 Washer
27 Stud
28 Stud
29 Washer
30 Nut
31 Casing
32 Plug
33 Washer
34 Washer
35 Cover
36 Washer
37 Screw
38 Washer
39 Screw
40 Washer
41 Shaft
42 Bearing
43 Ring
44 Washer
45 Washer
46 Nut
47 Bearing
48 Layshaft
49 Laygear
50 Bearing
51 Distance Piece
52 Ring
53 Washer
54 Washer
55 Shaft
56 Bearing
57 Bearing Housing
58 Peg
59 Ring
60 Washer
61 Distance Piece
62 Speedometer Gear
63 Washer
64 Washer
65 Nut
66 Synchronizer Assy
67 Ball
68 Spring
69 Ring
70 3rd Speed Gear
71 Roller
72 Collar
73 Peg
74 Spring
75 2nd Speed Gear
76 Roller
77 Collar
78 Washer
79 Peg
80 Spring
81 Synchronizer Assy
82 Ball
83 Spring
84 Plunger
85 Ring
86 Reverse Shaft
87 Screw
88 Washer
89 Reverse Gear
90 Bush
91 Pinion
92 Bush
93 Fork
94 Rod
95 Fork
96 Rod
97 Fork
98 Rod
99 Screw
100 Washer
101 Nut
102 Plunger
103 Ball
104 Plug
105 Washer
106 Plunger
107 Spring
108 Shaft
109 Lever
110 Screw
111 Washer
112 Button
113 Spring
114 Lever
115 Screw
116 Washer
117 Bush
118 Key
119 Plug
120 Ball
121 Spring
122 Plunger
123 Spring
124 Pin
125 Pin
126 Washer
127 Plunger
128 Spring
129 Cap
130 Washer
131 Cover
132 Screw
133 Washer
134 Lever
135 Grommet
136 Ring
137 Knob
138 Cover
139 Bolt
140 Washer
141 Nut
142 Cover
143 Screw

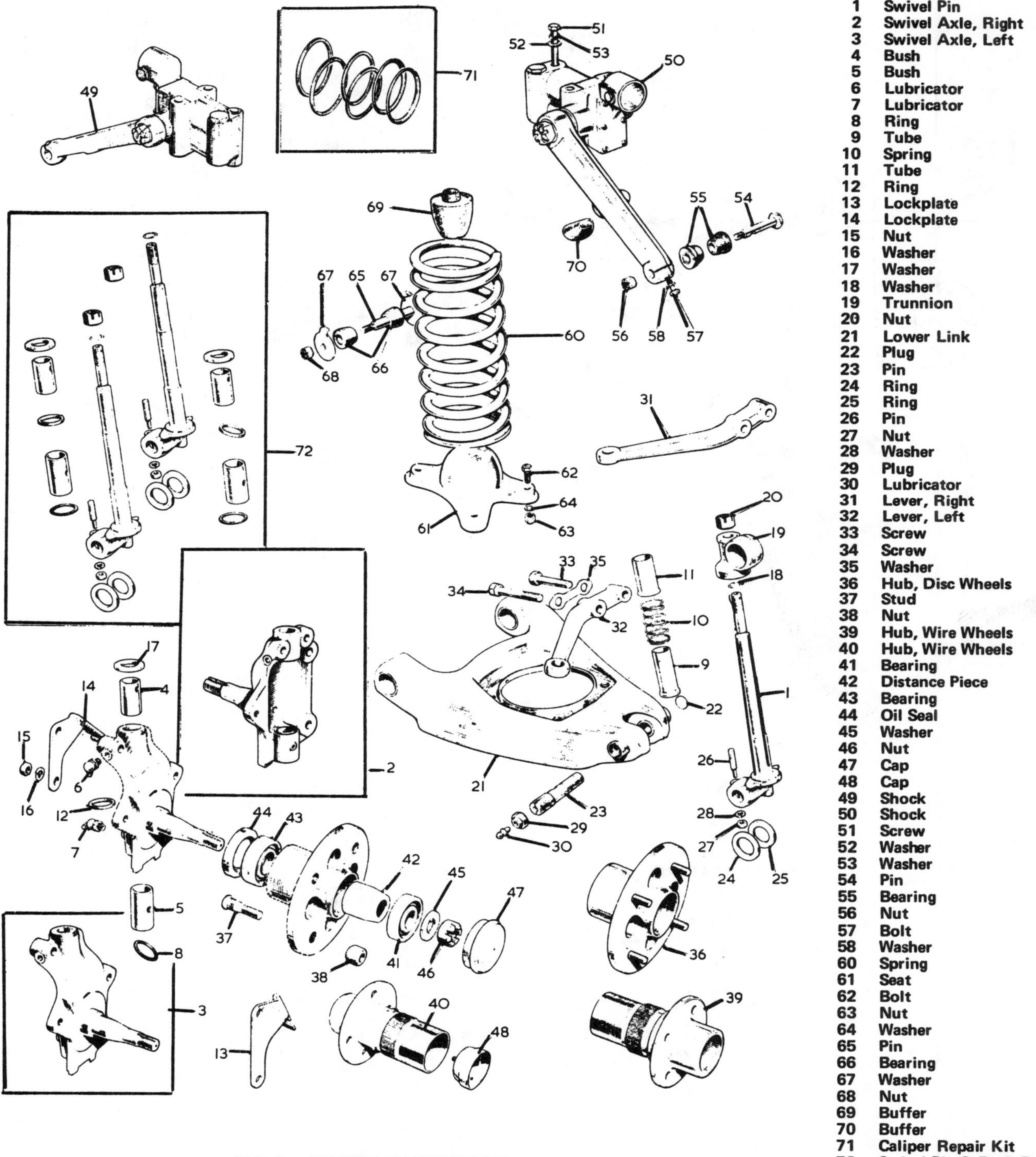

1 Swivel Pin
2 Swivel Axle, Right
3 Swivel Axle, Left
4 Bush
5 Bush
6 Lubricator
7 Lubricator
8 Ring
9 Tube
10 Spring
11 Tube
12 Ring
13 Lockplate
14 Lockplate
15 Nut
16 Washer
17 Washer
18 Washer
19 Trunnion
20 Nut
21 Lower Link
22 Plug
23 Pin
24 Ring
25 Ring
26 Pin
27 Nut
28 Washer
29 Plug
30 Lubricator
31 Lever, Right
32 Lever, Left
33 Screw
34 Screw
35 Washer
36 Hub, Disc Wheels
37 Stud
38 Nut
39 Hub, Wire Wheels
40 Hub, Wire Wheels
41 Bearing
42 Distance Piece
43 Bearing
44 Oil Seal
45 Washer
46 Nut
47 Cap
48 Cap
49 Shock
50 Shock
51 Screw
52 Washer
53 Washer
54 Pin
55 Bearing
56 Nut
57 Bolt
58 Washer
60 Spring
61 Seat
62 Bolt
63 Nut
64 Washer
65 Pin
66 Bearing
67 Washer
68 Nut
69 Buffer
70 Buffer
71 Caliper Repair Kit
72 Swivel Pin & Bush Repair Kit

FIG 4 – FRONT SUSPENSION

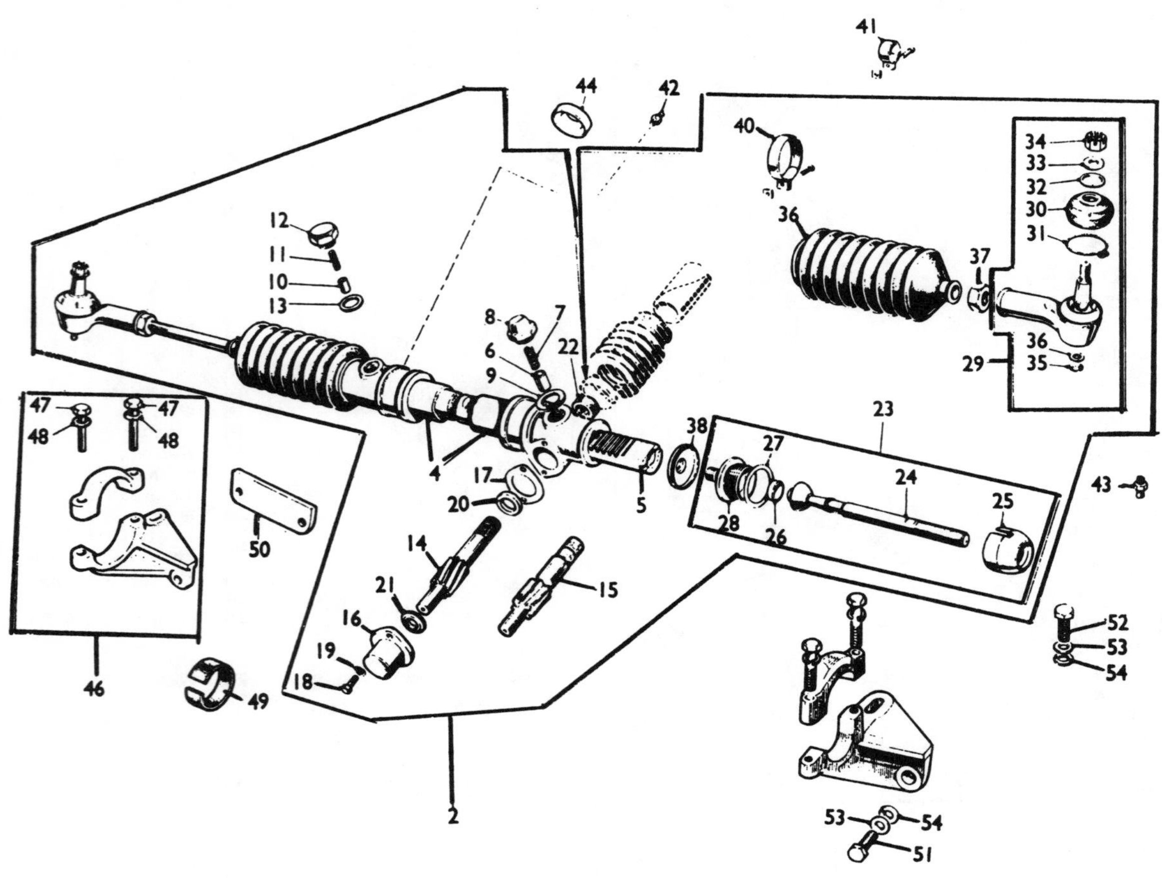

FIG 5 – STEERING

2	Rack Assy
4	Housing
5	Rack
6	Pad
7	Spring
8	Pad Housing
9	Shim
10	Pad
11	Spring
12	Damper Housing
13	Washer
14	Pinion
15	Pinion
16	Bearing
17	Shim
18	Screw
19	Washer
20	Washer
21	Washer
22	Seal
23	Tie Rod Assy
24	Tie Rod
25	Ball
26	Seat
27	Shim
28	Ball Housing
29	Socket Assy
30	Boot
31	Clip
32	Ring
33	Washer
34	Nut
35	Washer
36	Washer
37	Locknut
38	Washer
39	Seal
40	Clip
41	Clip
42	Lubricator
43	Lubricator
44	Retainer
45	Bracket & Cap
46	Bracket & Cap
47	Bolt
48	Washer
49	Seat
50	Packing
51	Screw
52	Screw
53	Washer
54	Washer

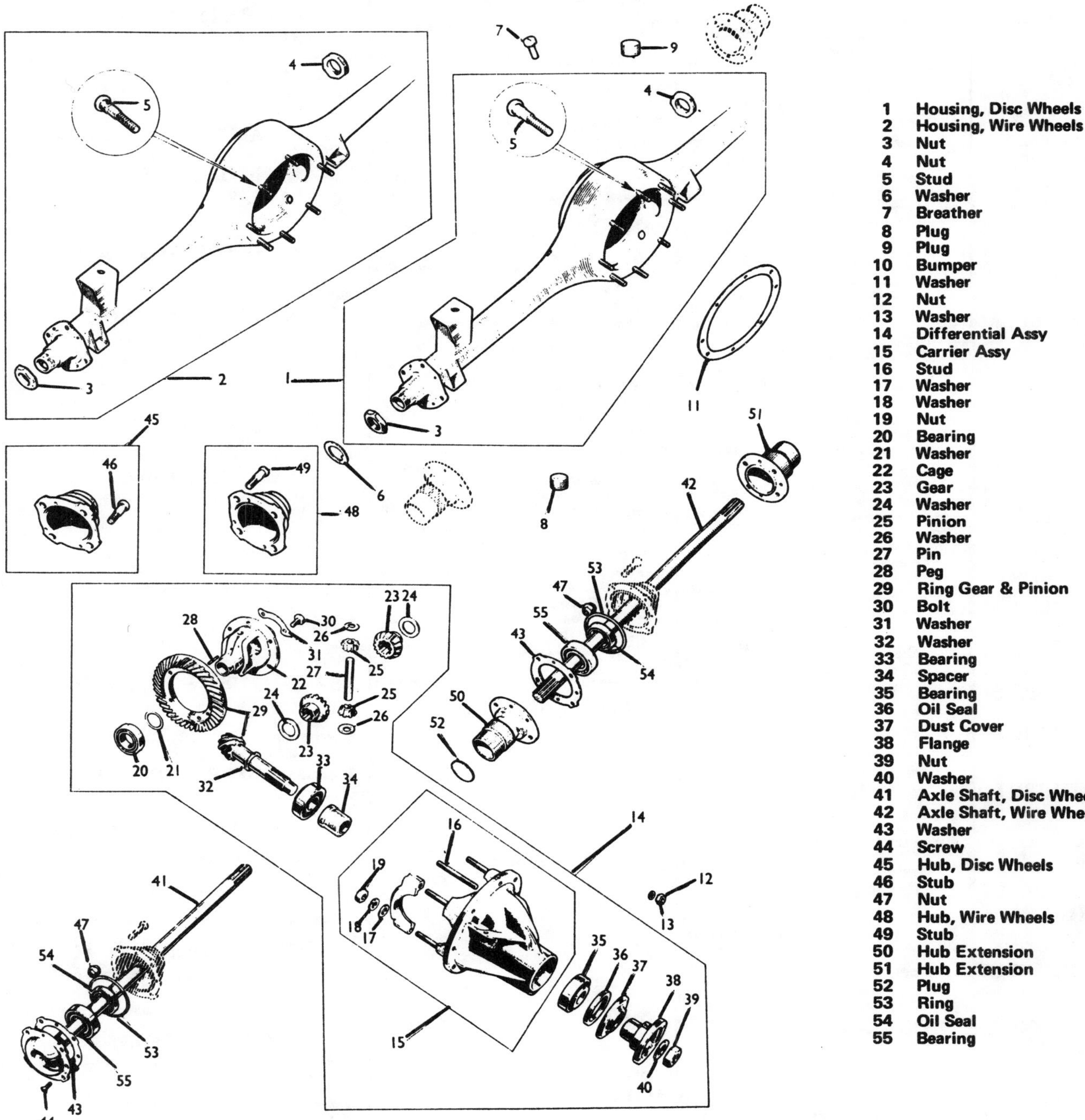

1 Housing, Disc Wheels
2 Housing, Wire Wheels
3 Nut
4 Nut
5 Stud
6 Washer
7 Breather
8 Plug
9 Plug
10 Bumper
11 Washer
12 Nut
13 Washer
14 Differential Assy
15 Carrier Assy
16 Stud
17 Washer
18 Washer
19 Nut
20 Bearing
21 Washer
22 Cage
23 Gear
24 Washer
25 Pinion
26 Washer
27 Pin
28 Peg
29 Ring Gear & Pinion
30 Bolt
31 Washer
32 Washer
33 Bearing
34 Spacer
35 Bearing
36 Oil Seal
37 Dust Cover
38 Flange
39 Nut
40 Washer
41 Axle Shaft, Disc Wheels
42 Axle Shaft, Wire Wheels
43 Washer
44 Screw
45 Hub, Disc Wheels
46 Stub
47 Nut
48 Hub, Wire Wheels
49 Stub
50 Hub Extension
51 Hub Extension
52 Plug
53 Ring
54 Oil Seal
55 Bearing

FIG 6 – REAR AXLE

Ignition, Starting & Charging—TIME

OPERATION INDEX

Tune- Up, Minor *1*
Tune-Up, Major *2*
Compression Test *3*
Distributor, R&R Or Renew *4*
Distributor Cap, Renew *5*
Ignition Cable Set, Renew *6*
Vacuum Control Unit, Renew *7*
Ignition Coil, Renew *8*
Starter & Ignition Switch, Renew *9*
Starter, R&R Or Renew *10*
Starter Solenoid, Renew *11*
Starter, R&R & Overhaul *12*
Regulator, Renew *13*
Generator, R&R Or Renew *14*
Generator, R&R & Overhaul *15*
Alternator, R&R Or Renew *16*
Alternator, R&R & Overhaul *17*

1—TUNE-UP, MINOR
Includes: Renew points, condenser and plugs, set spark timing and adjust carburetor idle. Check exhaust emissions.

Exc Below 2.6
America 2.5
Sprite & Midget 2.8
Marina—
Manual Trans 2.5
Auto Trans 3.0

2—TUNE-UP, MAJOR
Includes: Check compression, clean or renew and adjust spark plugs. R&R distributor, renew points and condenser. Adjust ignition timing, carburetor and fan belts. Clean battery terminals and service air cleaner. Check coil, exhaust emissions and clean or replace fuel filter.

Exc Below 4.0
America 3.5
Sprite & Midget 4.3
Marina—
Manual Trans 3.5
Auto Trans 4.0

3—COMPRESSION TEST
All Models 0.5

4—DISTRIBUTOR, R&R OR RENEW
Exc Below 0.4
Marina 0.6

5—DISTRIBUTOR CAP, RENEW
Exc Below 0.8
Marina 0.4

6—IGNITION CABLE SET, RENEW
All Models 0.8

7—VACUUM CONTROL UNIT, RENEW
Exc Below 0.6
America 0.5

8—IGNITION COIL, RENEW
Exc Below 0.3
America 0.2

9—STARTER & IGNITION SWITCH, RENEW
Exc Below 0.2
Sprite & Midget 1.7
America & Marina 0.5

10—STARTER, R&R OR RENEW
Exc Below 0.7
America—
Auto Trans 0.6
Std Trans 0.2
Marina 0.4

11—STARTER SOLENOID, RENEW
All Models 0.3

12—STARTER, R&R & OVERHAUL
Exc Below 1.7
America—
Auto Trans 1.5
Std Trans 1.2
Marina 1.3

13—REGULATOR, RENEW
All Models 0.2

14—GENERATOR, R&R OR RENEW
All Models 0.6

15—GENERATOR, R&R & OVERHAUL
All Models 1.5

16—ALTERNATOR, R&R OR RENEW
All Models 0.4

17—ALTERNATOR, R&R & OVERHAUL
All Models 1.3

Fuel, Emission Controls, Intake Manifold & Exhaust System—TIME

OPERATION INDEX

Carburetor, R&R Or Renew *1*
Carburetor, R&R & Overhaul *2*
Fuel Pump, R&R Or Renew *3*
Fuel Pump, R&R & Overhaul *4*
Fuel Tank, R&R Or Renew *5*
Choke Control Cable(S), Renew *6*
Air Pump, Renew *7*
Air Pump, R&R & Overhaul *8*
Pressure Relief Valve, Renew *9*
Pump Cleaner Element, Renew *10*
Air Pump Pulley, Renew *11*
Air Manifold, Renew *12*
Manifold Check Valve, Renew *13*
Emission Gulp Valve, Renew *14*
Intake Manifold Or Gasket, Renew *15*
Exhaust Manifold Or Gasket, Renew *16*
Exhaust System Assy, Renew *17*
Exhaust Pipe Front, Renew *18*
Muffler Front, Renew *19*
Exhaust Tailpipe Or Silencer, Renew *20*

1—CARBURETOR, R&R OR RENEW
Exc Below, Both 1.1
America, Each—
Auto Trans 0.8
Std Trans 0.5
Marina—
Auto Trans 1.3
Std Trans 0.8

2—CARBURETOR, R&R & OVERHAUL
Exc Below, Both 3.1
America, Each—
Auto Trans 1.8
Std Trans 1.5
Marina—
Auto Trans 2.1
Std Trans 1.5

3—FUEL PUMP, R&R OR RENEW
Exc Below 0.4
America 0.7

4—FUEL PUMP, R&R & OVERHAUL
Exc Below 1.7
America 1.9
Marina 1.0

5—FUEL TANK, R&R OR RENEW
Ecx Below 0.7
America 1.7

6—CHOKE CONTROL CABLE(S), RENEW
Exc Renew 0.3
Sprite & Midget 0.6
America 0.7

7—AIR PUMP, RENEW
All Models 0.4

8—AIR PUMP, R&R & OVERHAUL
All Models 0.9

9—PRESSURE RELIEF VALVE, RENEW
All Models 0.5

10—PUMP CLEANER ELEMENT, RENEW
All Models 0.1

11—AIR PUMP PULLEY, RENEW
Exc Below 0.3
America 1.0

12—AIR MANIFOLD, RENEW
All Models 0.3

13—MANIFOLD CHECK VALVE, RENEW
Exc Below 0.2
America 0.1

14—EMISSION GULP VALVE, RENEW
All Models 0.2

15—INTAKE MANIFOLD OR GASKET, RENEW
Exc Below 1.4
America—
Auto Trans ①1.2
Std Trans ①1.0
Marina ①0.8
①*Includes; R&R Exhaust Manifold.*

16—EXHAUST MANIFOLD OR GASKET, RENEW
Exc Below 1.5
America—
Auto Trans ①1.2
Std Trans ①1.0
Marina ①0.8
①*Includes: R&R Intake Manifold*

17—EXHAUST SYSTEM ASSY, RENEW
Exc Below 0.5
America 0.6
Marina 0.7

18—EXHAUST PIPE, FRONT, RENEW
Exc Below 0.6
America 0.5
Marina 0.9

19—MUFFLER, FRONT, RENEW
Exc Below 1.0
Marina 0.9

20—EXHAUST TAIL PIPE OR SILENCER, RENEW
Sprite & Midget 0.6
Marina 0.9

Engine Cooling & Heater System—TIME

OPERATION INDEX

Radiator, R&R Or Renew *1*
Radiator Hoses, Renew *2*
By-Pass Hose, Renew *3*
Water Pump, R&R Or Renew *4*
Water Pump, R&R & Overhaul *5*
Thermostat Or Housing, Renew *6*
Expansion Tank, Renew *7*
Heater Assy, Renew *8*
Heater Matrix, Renew *9*
Heater Blower Motor, Renew *10*
Heater Temperature Control Valve, Renew *11*
Heater Control, Renew *12*
Demister Duct, Renew *13*
Heater Hoses, Renew *14*

1—RADIATOR, R&R OR RENEW
Exc Below 1.1
Sprite & Midget 1.6

(Continued)

Engine Cooling & Heater System—TIME Cont'd

Marina 0.8

2—RADIATOR HOSES, RENEW
Upper—
All Models 0.3
Lower—
All Models 0.4
Both—
Exc Below 0.6
America—
Auto Trans 0.7
Std Trans 0.9
Marina 0.7

3—BY-PASS HOSE, RENEW
Exc Below 1.6
America 1.1

4—WATER PUMP, R&R OR RENEW
Exc Below 1.6
Sprite & Midget 2.2
America 1.1
Marina 1.3

5—WATER PUMP, R&R & OVERHAUL
Exc Below 2.4
Sprite & Midget 3.0
America 2.0
Marina 2.0

6—THERMOSTAT OR HOUSING, RENEW
Exc Below 0.7
Sprite & Midget 0.4
Marina 0.5

7—EXPANSION TANK, RENEW
Exc Below 0.5
America 0.6
Marina 0.4

8—HEATER ASSY, RENEW
Exc Below 0.7
America 1.9
Marina 1.8

9—HEATER MATRIX, RENEW
Exc Below 0.8
America 2.1

10—HEATER BLOWER MOTOR, RENEW
Exc Below 0.4
America 2.1
Marina 2.1

11—HEATER TEMPERATURE CONTROL VALVE, RENEW
All Models 0.4

12—HEATER CONTROL, RENEW
Exc Below 1.0
Sprite & Midget 0.3
America 0.2
Marina 0.6

13—DEMISTER DUCT, RENEW
Exc Below 1.0
Sprite & Midget 1.8
America 0.6
Marina 0.5

14—HEATER HOSES, RENEW
Exc Below—
One 0.2
Both 0.3
Marina—
Return Only 0.5
All 0.7
America—

Engine—TIME

OPERATION INDEX
Engine, R&R 1
Engine, Renew 2
Engine, R&R & Overhaul 3
Engine (Short), Renew & Grind Valves 4
Cylinder Head, R&R Or Gasket, Renew 5
Valves, Grind 6
One Valve, Renew & Grind 7
Rocker Arm Cover Gasket, Renew 8
Valve Rocker Arm Assy, Clean Or Renew 9
Valve Tappets, Renew 10
Valve Tappets, Adjust 11
Timing Cover Seal & Gasket, Renew 12
Timing Chain Or Gears, Renew 13
Timing Chain Tensioner, Renew 14
Oil Sump Or Gasket, Renew 15
Camshaft, R&R Or Renew 16
Camshaft Bearings, Renew 17
Oil Pump, R&R Or Renew 18
Piston Ring(S), Renew 19
Rings & Main Bearings, Renew & Grind Valves 20
Rod Bearing(S), Renew 21
Main Bearings, Renew 22
Main & Rod Bearings, Renew 23
Crankshaft, R&R Or Renew 24
Crankshaft Thrust Washer, Renew 25
Crankshaft Rear Main Oil Seal, Renew 26
Piston(S), Renew 27
Crankshaft Damper, Renew 28
Crankshaft Pulley, Renew 29

1—ENGINE, R&R
Does not include transfer of any part of engine or replacement of special equipment.
Exc Below 4.8
Sprite & Midget 5.0
America—
Auto Trans ①4.3
Std Trans ①3.4
Marina—
Auto Trans ①3.0
Std Trans ①3.3
①*Includes R&R Trans.*

2—ENGINE, RENEW
Includes: Fit replacement, change over ancillary equipment, clean & adjust carburetors.
Exc Below 7.7
Sprite & Midget 8.8
America Auto Trans 8.6
Marina—
Auto Trans 7.0
Std Trans 7.5

3—ENGINE, R&R & OVERHAUL
Includes: Rebore cylinders with boring bar, renew pistons, rings, bearings, grind valves, plastigauge bearings and perform minor tune-up.
Exc Below 22.2
Sprite & Midget 22.7
America—
Auto Trans 22.3
Std Trans 24.4
Marina—
Auto Trans 20.5
Std Trans 21.2

—NOTE—
On Transverse Engine, Includes Clutch Overhaul & Adjust Idler Gear.

4—ENGINE (SHORT), RENEW & GRIND VALVES
Includes: Minor tune-up
Exc Below 16.8
Sprite & Midget 18.2
America—
Auto Trans 20.7
Std Trans 19.5
Marina—
Auto Trans 15.5
Std Trans 16.2

5—CYLINDER HEAD, R&R OR GASKET, RENEW
Exc Below 2.4
America 2.1
Marina 1.4

6—VALVES, GRIND
Includes: Minor tune-up.
Exc Below 6.3
America 6.0
Marina 5.0

7—ONE VALVE, RENEW & GRIND
Exc Below 2.7
America 2.5
Marina 2.3

8—ROCKER ARM COVER GASKET, RENEW
All Models 0.4

9—VALVE ROCKER ARM ASSY, CLEAN OR OVERHAUL
Exc Below 0.9
America 1.3
Marina 1.0

10—VALVE TAPPETS, RENEW
Exc Below 8.0
Sprite & Midget 8.6
America—
Auto Trans 6.7
Std Trans 9.2
Marina 1.6

11—VALVE TAPPETS, ADJUST
All Models 0.7

12—TIMING COVER SEAL & GASKET, RENEW
Exc Below 1.9
Sprite & Midget 2.2
America 1.8
Marina 1.3

13—TIMING CHAIN OR GEARS, RENEW
Exc Below 2.3
Sprite & Midget 2.7
America ①2.2
Marina 1.7
①*To Remove Gears, Add 0.5*

14—TIMING CHAIN TENSIONER, RENEW
Exc Below 2.3
Sprite & Midget 2.7
America 2.2
Marina 1.5

15—OIL SUMP OR GASKET, RENEW
Exc Below 0.7
America—
Auto Trans 7.6
Std Trans 5.0
Marina 0.8

16—CAMSHAFT, R&R OR RENEW
Exc Below 7.0
Sprite & Midget 7.8
America—
Auto Trans 5.8
Std Trans 4.9
Marina 4.2

17—CAMSHAFT BEARINGS, RENEW
Exc Below 14.6
Sprite & Midget 15.2
Auto Trans 16.5
Std Trans 14.0
Marina—
Auto Trans 11.1
Std Trans 12.0

18—OIL PUMP, R&R OR RENEW
Exc Below 5.8
Sprite & Midget 6.3
America—
Auto Trans 6.6
Std Trans 5.5
Marina 1.3

—NOTE—
Includes Overhaul Clutch On Transverse Engine.

19—PISTON RING(S), RENEW
Exc Below 4.2
Sprite & Midget—
Auto Trans 9.7
Std Trans 7.2
Marina 7.6

—NOTE—
Includes Overhaul Clutch On Transverse Engine.

20—RINGS & MAIN BEARINGS, RENEW & GRIND VALVES
Exc Below 12.8
Sprite & Midget 13.6

(Continued)

Engine—TIME Cont'd

America—
Auto Trans 14.3
Std Trans 11.7
Marina 10.2

—NOTE—
Transverse Engine Includes Overhaul Clutch & Adjust Idler Gear End Float.

21—ROD BEARING(S), RENEW
Exc Below (One Pair) 0.9
America—
Auto Trans 7.9
Std Trans 5.3
Marina 4.4
Each Additional 0.4

22—MAIN BEARINGS, RENEW
Exc Below 8.0
Sprite & Midget 8.5
America—
Auto Trans 9.3
Std Trans 6.7
Marina—
Auto Trans 7.5
Std Trans 7.0

—NOTE—
Transverse Engine Includes Overhaul Clutch & Adjust Idler Gear End Float.

23—MAIN & ROD BEARINGS, RENEW
Exc Below 9.6
Sprite & Midget 10.1
America—
Auto Trans 10.9
Std Trans 8.9
Marina—
Auto Trans 8.7
Std Trans 8.2

—NOTE—
Transverse Engine Includes Overhaul Clutch & Adjust Idler Gear End Float.

24—CRANKSHAFT, R&R OR RENEW
Exc Below 8.2
Sprite & Midget 8.7
America—
Auto Trans 9.6
Std Trans 7.0
Marina—
Auto Trans 8.4
Std Trans 7.1

25—CRANKSHAFT THRUST WASHER, RENEW
Exc Below 1.0
America—
Auto Trans 7.3
Std Trans 5.2

—NOTE—
Transverse Engine Includes Overhaul Clutch & Adjust Idler Gear End Float.

26—CRANKSHAFT REAR MAIN OIL SEAL, RENEW
Exc Below 5.2
Sprite & Midget 5.4
Marina—
Auto Trans 3.5
Std Trans 3.0

27—PISTON(S), RENEW
Exc Below 4.2
Sprite & Midget—
Auto Trans 9.7
Std Trans 7.2
Marina 7.6

—NOTE—
Transverse Engine Includes Clutch Overhaul.

28—CRANKSHAFT DAMPER, RENEW
America 1.3

29—CRANKSHAFT PULLEY, RENEW
Exc Below 1.3
Sprite & Midget 1.8
Marina 0.9

Clutch, Mounts, Manual & Automatic Transmissions—TIME

OPERATION INDEX
Flywheel, R&R Or Renew *1*
Flywheel Ring Gear, Renew *2*
Oil Seal Flywheel Housing, Renew *3*
Clutch Or Disc, Renew *4*
Release Bearing, Renew *5*
Clutch Master Cylinder , Renew *6*
Clutch Master Cylinder , R&R & Overhaul *7*
Slave Cylinder, Renew *8*
Slave Cylinder, R&R & Overhaul *9*
Bleed System *10*
Engine Mounts, Renew *11*
Transmission Assy, R&R Or Renew *12*
Gearbox Front Plate, Or Gasket & Seal, Renew *13*
Gearbox Rear Extension, Gasket, Renew *14*
Extension Housing Oil Seal, Renew *15*
Gearbox Side Plate Gasket, Renew *16*
Gearbox Top Cover Gasket, Renew *17*
Shift Forks Or Rail, Renew *18*
Idler Gear End Float, Adjust *19*
Gearbox, R&R & Overhaul *20*
Front & Rear Band, Adjust *21*
Gearshift Or Selector Lever, Renew *22*
Gear Selector Cable, Renew *23*

1—FLYWHEEL, R & R OR RENEW
Exc Below 5.5
Sprite & Midget 6.0
America 2.7
Marina 2.3

2—FLYWHEEL RING GEAR, RENEW
Exc Below 6.7
Sprite & Midget 7.2
America 3.9
Marina—
Auto Trans 3.1
Std Trans 3.5

3—OIL SEAL FLYWHEEL HOUSING, RENEW
America 3.0

—NOTE—
Transverse Engine Overhaul Clutch.

4—CLUTCH OR DISC, RENEW
Exc Below 5.3
Sprite & Midget 5.8
America 2.7
Marina 2.2

5—RELEASE BEARING, RENEW
Exc Below 5.3
Sprite & Midget 5.8
America 1.8
Marina 2.0

6—CLUTCH MASTER CYLINDER, RENEW
Includes: Bleed system
Exc Below 1.1
America 0.7
Marina 0.6

7—CLUTCH MASTER CYLINDER, R & R & OVERHAUL
Includes: Bleed system
Exc Below 2.5
America 1.7
Marina 1.0

8—SLAVE SYLINDER, RENEW
Includes: Bleed system
Exc Below 0.6
America 0.4
Marina 2.0

9—SLAVE CYLINDER, R & R & OVERHAUL
Includes: Bleed system
Exc Below 1.4
America 1.1
Marina 2.5

10—BLEED SYSTEM
All Models 0.3

11—ENGINE MOUNTS, RENEW
Front—
Left—
Exc Below 0.7
America 1.4
Marina 0.4
Right—
Exc Below 0.5
America & Marina 0.4
Rear—
Center—
America, Auto Trans 2.8
America, Std Trans 0.6
Marina 0.4
Set—
Sprite & Midget 5.5

12—TRANSMISSION ASSY, R & R OR RENEW
Exc Below 5.1
Sprite & Midget 5.9
America—
Auto Trans 7.6
Std Trans 5.5
Marina—
Auto Trans 2.0
Std Trans 2.1

13—GEARBOX FRONT PLATE OR GASKET & SEAL, RENEW
Exc Below 5.5
Sprite & Midget 6.3
Marina 2.6

14—GEARBOX REAR EXTENSION GASKET, RENEW
Exc Below 5.4
Sprite & Midget 6.2
Marina 3.5

15—EXTENSION HOUSING OIL SEAL, RENEW
Exc Below 4.8
Sprite & Midget 5.3
Marina 0.8

16—GEARBOX SIDE PLATE GASKET, RENEW
Sprite & Midget—
All Models 0.8

17—GEARBOX TOP COVER GASKET, RENEW
Exc Below 4.9
Sprite & Midget 5.1

18—SHIFT FORKS OR RAILS, RENEW
Exc Below 6.0
Sprite & Midget 6.2
America 10.3

19—IDLER GEAR END FLOAT, ADJUST
America, Std Trans 5.9

—NOTE—
Includes Overhaul Clutch.

20—GEARBOX, R & R & OVERHAUL
Exc Below 8.9
Sprite & Midget 9.7
Marina 6.5

21—FRONT & REAR BANDS, ADJUST
Both 1.4

22—GEARSHIFT OR SELECTOR LEVER, RENEW
Exc Below 0.3
America, Auto Trans 1.1

Clutch, Mounts, Manual & Automatic Transmissions—TIME Cont'd

23—GEAR SELECTOR CABLE, RENEW

America, Auto Trans 1.3

Brakes, Steering, Suspension, Universals & Rear Axle—TIME

OPERATION INDEX

Brake Shoes Or Friction Pads, Renew *1*
Master Cylinder, Renew *2*
Master Cylinder, R & R & Overhaul *3*
Brake Fluid Reservoir, Renew *4*
Wheel Cylinders, Renew *5*
Wheel Cylinders, R & R & Overhaul *6*
Caliper Assy, Renew *7*
Caliper Assy, R & R & Overhaul *8*
Bleed System *9*
Brake Hose, Renew *10*
Hub Or Bearings, Renew *11*
Disc Or Shield, Renew *12*
Brake Drum, Renew *13*
Brake Pressure Regulating Valve, Renew *14*
Pedal Assy, Renew *15*
Pedal Assy, R & R & Overhaul *16*
Handbrake Assy, Renew *17*
Handbrake Lever Ratchet, Renew *18*
Rack & Pinion Assy, Renew *19*
Rack & Pinion Assy, R & R & Overhaul *20*
Swivel Axle Or Hub Pins & Bushings, Renew *21*
Steering Lever, Renew *22*
Tie Rod Ball Ends, Renew *23*
Front Suspension Assy, Renew *24*
Front Suspension Assy, Overhaul *25*
Upper Arm Or Bushings, Renew *26*
Lower Arm Or Bushings, Renew *27*
Wishbone Pivot Or Bushings, Renew *28*
Tie Rod Front Assy, Renew *29*
Spring(S), Renew *30*
Leaf Spring, Renew *31*
Leaf Spring, Overhaul *32*
Subframe Assy, Renew *33*
Subframe Assy, Overhaul *34*
Subframe Assy Mounts, Renew *35*
Anti Roll Bar (Rear), Renew *36*
Shock Absorber, Renew *37*
Hydrolastic Displacer Or Strut, Renew *38*
Evacuate & Pressurize System *39*
Connecting Pipe, Renew *40*
Radius Arm Assy, Renew *41*
Auxiliary Rear Spring Or Bracket, Renew *42*
Universal Joints, Renew *43*
Half Shaft Or Gasket Renew *44*
Final Drive Or Axle Assy, Renew *45*
Differential Gear Carrier Assy, Renew *46*
Differential Cage Bearings, Renew *47*
Differential Drive Gear & Pinion, Overhaul *48*
Differential Drive Flange, Renew *49*
Pinion Oil Seal, Renew *50*
Differential End Cover Seal, Renew *51*

1—BRAKE SHOES OR FRICTION PADS, RENEW

Exc Below 0.5
America 0.7
Marina 1.4

2—MASTER CYLINDER, RENEW

Exc Below 1.2
Sprite & Midget 1.3
America 1.4
Marina 0.7

3—MASTER CYLINDER, R & R & OVERHAUL

Exc Below 1.6
Sprite & Midget 2.3
America 2.0
Marina 1.0

4—BRAKE FLUID RESERVOIR, RENEW

Exc Below 1.4
America 1.5
Marina 0.6

5—WHEEL CYLINDERS, RENEW

Rear—
One—
Exc Below 1.0
America 1.4
Marina 1.0
Both—
Exc Below 1.6
America 2.4
Marina 1.3

6—WHEEL CYLINDER, R & R & OVERHAUL

Rear—
One—
Exc Below 1.3
America 1.9
Marina 1.1
Both—
Exc Below 2.2
America 3.4
Marina 1.5

7—CALIPER ASSY, RENEW

Each—
Exc Below 0.7
America 0.9
Marina 0.8
Both—
Exc Below 1.0
America 1.4
Marina 1.0

8—CALIPER ASSY, R & R & OVERHAUL

Each—
Exc Below 1.1
America 1.0
Marina 1.1
Both—
Exc Below 1.8
America 1.6
Marina 1.6

9—BLEED SYSTEM

All Models 0.4

10—BRAKE HOSE, RENEW

Exc Below 0.5
America 0.6
Marina 0.8

11—HUB OR BEARINGS, RENEW

Front—
All Models 0.9
Rear—
Exc Below 0.8
America 0.7
Marina 0.6

12—DISC OR SHIELD, RENEW

Each—
Exc Below 0.9
America & Marina 1.0
Both—
Exc Below 1.6
America & Marina 1.9

—NOTE—

To Replace Shield, Add. *0.1*

13—BRAKE DRUM, RENEW

Each—
Exc Below 0.3
America 0.5
Both—
Exc Below 0.5
America 1.0

14—BRAKE PRESSURE REGULATING VALVE, RENEW

America 0.6

15—PEDAL ASSY, RENEW

Exc Below 2.0
America—
Auto Trans 1.1
Std Trans 1.3
Marina 0.6

16—PEDAL ASSY, R & R & OVERHAUL

Exc Below 2.4
America—
Auto Trans 1.3
Std Trans 1.6
Marina 0.9

17—HANDBRAKE ASSY, RENEW

Exc Below 0.8
America 0.2
Marina 0.9

18—HANDBRAKE LEVER RATCHET, RENEW

Exc Below 1.0
America 0.4

19—RACK & PINION ASSY, RENEW

Exc Below 2.0
Sprite & Midget 2.8
America 1.9
Marina 2.0

20—RACK & PINION ASSY, R & R & OVERHAUL

Exc Below 3.2
Sprite & Midget 3.6
America & Marina 3.3

21—SWIVEL AXLE OR HUB PINS & BUSHINGS, RENEW

One Side—
Exc Below 2.5
America 1.0
Both Sides—
Exc Below 4.8
America 1.9

22—STEERING LEVER, RENEW

Each, Exc 0.8
Marina 0.7

23—TIE ROD BALL ENDS, RENEW

America—
Each 0.6
Both 1.0
Marina—
Each 0.6
Both 0.9

24—FRONT SUSPENSION ASSY, RENEW

One Side—
Exc Below 2.6
America 1.7
Marina 3.0
Both Sides—
Exc Below 5.0
America 3.2
Marina 5.5

25—FRONT SUSPENSION ASSY, OVERHAUL

One Side—
Exc Below 2.6
America 1.7
Marina 3.0
Both Sides—
Exc Below 5.0
America 3.2
Marina 5.5

26—UPPER ARM OR BUSHINGS, RENEW

America 1.0

27—LOWER ARM OR BUSHINGS, RENEW

America 0.6
Marina 1.4

28—WISHBONE PIVOT OR BUSHINGS, RENEW

Sprite & Midget—
All Models 1.3

29—TIE ROD FRONT ASSY, RENEW

America 0.3
Marina 0.5

30—SPRING(S), RENEW

Sprite & Midget—
Each 0.7
Both 1.4

(Continued)

Brakes, Steering, Suspension, Universals & Rear Axle—TIME Cont'd

31—LEAF SPRING, RENEW
Sprite & Midget—
Each 1.2
Both 2.3

32—LEAF SPRING, OVERHAUL
Sprite & Midget—
Each 1.7
Both 3.3

33—SUBFRAME ASSY, RENEW
America—
Front—
Auto Trans 7.8
Std Trans 7.1
Rear 3.7

34—SUBFRAME ASSY, OVERHAUL
America—
Front—
Auto Trans 7.8
Std Trans 7.1
Rear 5.5

35—SUBFRAME ASSY MOUNTS, RENEW
America—
Front—
Each 0.3
Both 0.9
Rear, Pair 0.5
Set 3.7

36—ANTI ROLL BAR (REAR), RENEW
America 4.0

37—SHOCK ABSORBERS, RENEW
Sprite & Midget—
Front, Each 0.7
Front, Both 1.3
Rear, Each 0.4
Marina—
Front, Each 0.7
Front, Both 1.1
Rear, Each 0.4

38—HYDROLASTIC DISPLACER OR STRUT, RENEW
America—
Front 0.9
Rear 1.5

39—EVACUATE & PRESSURIZE SYSTEM
Each Side 0.5

40—CONNECTING PIPE, RENEW
Each Side 6.9
Both Sides 7.1

41—RADIUS ARM ASSY, RENEW
America 4.4
—NOTE—
To Renew Bushings, Add. 0.3

42—AUXILIARY REAR SPRING OR BRACKET, RENEW
Each Side 4.0
Both Sides 7.0

43—UNIVERSAL JOINTS, RENEW
Sprite & Midget—
Each 0.9
Both 1.3
America, Each 1.4

44—HALF SHAFT OR GASKET, RENEW
Sprite & Midget—
All Models 0.4
Marina 1.3

45—FINAL DRIVE OR AXLE ASSY, RENEW
Exc Below 1.6
America 11.3
Marina 2.0

46—DIFFERENTIAL GEAR CARRIER ASSY, RENEW
Sprite & Midget—
All Models 1.3

47—DIFFERENTIAL CAGE BEARINGS, RENEW
Exc Below 2.8
America—
Auto Trans 5.6
Std Trans 4.2
Marina 3.5

48—DIFFERENTIAL DRIVE GEAR & PINION, OVERHAUL
Exc Below 4.9
America—
Auto Trans 11.3
Std Trans 6.4

49—DIFFERENTIAL DRIVE FLANGE, RENEW
Sprite & Midget—
All Models 0.6
Marina 0.7

50—PINION OIL SEAL, RENEW
Sprite & Midget—
All Models 0.8
Marina 0.7

51—DIFFERENTIAL END COVER SEAL, RENEW
America—
Auto Trans 1.9
Std Trans 1.5

Speedometer, W/S Wipers, Switches & Instruments—TIME

OPERATION INDEX
Speedometer Cable, Renew 1
Speedometer Head, Renew 2
W/S Wiper Motor, Renew 3
W/S Wiper Wheel Box Assy, Renew 4
W/S Wiper Arm, Renew 5
Fuel Gauge (Dash Unit), Renew 6
Fuel Tank Gauge, Renew 7
Oil Pressure Warning Light Switch, Renew 8
Oil Gauge (Dash Unit), Renew 9
Temperature Gauge (Dash Unit), Renew 10
Temperature Gauge Sending Unit, Renew 11
Tachometer Head, Renew 12
Instrument Cluster Voltage Limiter, Renew 13
Headlight Switch, Renew 14
Dimmer Switch, Renew 15
Headlamp Flasher Switch, Renew 16
Turn Signal Flasher Switch, Renew 17
Stop Light Switch, Renew 18
Hazard Flasher Switch, Renew 19

1—SPEEDOMETER CABLE, RENEW
Exc Below 0.3
America 0.5
Marina 0.4

2—SPEEDOMETER HEAD, RENEW
Exc Below 0.2
Sprite & Midget 0.3
Marina 0.4

3—W/S WIPER MOTOR, RENEW
Exc Below 0.5
America 0.4
Marina 0.3

4—W/S WIPER WHEEL BOX ASSY, RENEW
Exc Below 1.4
Sprite & Midget 2.0
America 2.2
Marina 1.0

5—W/S WIPER ARM, RENEW
All Models 0.3

6—FUEL GAUGE (DASH UNIT), RENEW
Exc Below 0.2
Sprite & Midget 0.5
Marina 0.5

7—FUEL TANK GAUGE, RENEW
Exc Below 0.9
America 1.8
Marina 0.5

8—OIL PRESSURE WARNING LIGHT SWITCH, RENEW
America 0.2
Marina 0.3

9—OIL GAUGE (DASH UNIT), RENEW
Sprite & Midget—
All Models 0.7

10—TEMPERATURE GAUGE (DASH UNIT), RENEW
Exc Below 0.7
America 0.6
Marina 0.5

11—TEMPERATURE GAUGE SENDING UNIT, RENEW
All Models 0.4

12—TACHOMETER HEAD, RENEW
Sprite & Midget—
All Models 0.2
Marina 0.4

13—INSTRUMENT CLUSTER VOLTAGE LIMITER, RENEW
Exc Below 0.3
America 0.6

14—HEADLIGHT SWITCH, RENEW
Exc Below 0.2
Sprite & Midget 0.6
America, Std Trans 0.3
Marina 0.7

15—DIMMER SWITCH, RENEW
Exc Below 0.2
Sprite & Midget 1.6
America 0.6

16—HEADLAMP FLASHER SWITCH, RENEW
Sprite & Midget 1.6
America 0.6
Marina 0.7

17—TURN SIGNAL FLASHER SWITCH, RENEW
Exc Below 0.4
Sprite & Midget 1.6
Marina 0.7

18—STOP LIGHT SWITCH, RENEW
Exc Below 0.2
Sprite & Midget 0.5
Marina 0.4

19—HAZARD FLASHER SWITCH, RENEW
All Models 0.3

IDENTIFICATION

ALL MODELS....40

ILLUSTRATIONS

FIG 1 – ENGINE BLOCK & OIL PAN
FIG 2 – CYLINDER HEAD & COVER
FIG 3 – CAMSHAFT HOUSING
FIG 4 – CAMSHAFT & VALVES
FIG 5 – FOUR SPEED TRANSMISSION
FIG 6 – FRONT SUSPENSION
FIG 7 – STEERING
FIG 8 – REAR SUSPENSION

OPERATION TIMES

A

Air Pump.... 48
Alternator.... 46
Automatic Transmission.... 49
Axle Shaft.... 50

B

Brake Drums.... 50
Brakes.... 49

C

Cables (Ignition).... 46
Calipers.... 49
Camshaft.... 48
Carburetor.... 46
Clutch.... 48
Coil, Ignition.... 46
Compression Test.... 46
Cooling System.... 47
Crankshaft.... 48
Cylinder Head.... 47

D

Dash Gauges.... 51
Differential.... 50
Disc Brakes.... 49
Distributor.... 46

E

Engine Assembly.... 47
Engine Mountings.... 48
Engine Oiling.... 48
Engine Tune-Up.... 46
Exhaust Gas Recirculation.... 48
Exhaust System.... 46

F

Final Drive.... 50
Flywheel.... 48
Front Suspension.... 50
Fuel Gauges.... 51
Fuel Pump.... 46
Fuel Tank.... 47

H

Hand Brake.... 50
Hazard Flasher Switch.... 51
Headlight Switch.... 51
Heater.... 47
Hose (Brake).... 49
Hose (Radiator).... 47
Hydraulic Brakes.... 49

I

Ignition.... 46
Ignition Coil.... 46
Ignition Switch.... 46
Injectors.... 46
Intake Manifold.... 46

L

Light Switches.... 51

M

Main Bearings.... 48
Master Cylinder.... 49
Muffler.... 46

O

Oiling, Engine.... 48
Oil Pump.... 48
Oil Sump.... 48

P

Parking Brake.... 50
Piston Rings.... 48
Pistons.... 48

R

Radiator.... 47
Radiator Hose.... 47
Rear Axle.... 50
Regulator (Alternator).... 46
Rocker Arms.... 47
Rod Bearings.... 48

S

Shocks (Front).... 50
Shocks (Rear).... 50
Speedometer.... 51
Springs (Front).... 50
Springs (Rear).... 50
Stabilizer.... 50
Starting Motor.... 46
Steering.... 50
Switches (Light).... 51
Synchro-Mesh Trans.... 49

T

Thermostat.... 47
Timing Case Cover.... 47
Timing Chain.... 48
Track Rod.... 50
Transmission, Manual.... 49
Transmission, Automatic.... 49
Tune-Up, Engine.... 46
Turn Indicator Switch.... 51

V

Vacuum Control Unit.... 46
Valve System.... 47

W

Water Pump.... 47
Wheel Cylinders.... 49
Windshield Wiper.... 51

VEHICLE IDENTIFICATION

MODEL	YEAR	FROM CHASSIS	TO CHASSIS
1602	1968-70	1560001	1572930
	1971	1572931	1573162
2002	1968-69	1660001	1680000
	1970	2570001	2572069
	1971-72	2572070	2593704
	1973	3660001	3700000
	1974	4220001	4250000
	1975	2360001	2380000
2002 A	1968-70	2530001	2532124
	1971-72	2532125	2534861
	1973	4250001	4270000
	1974	4280001	4290000
	1975	2380001	2400000
2002 TII	1971-72	2760001	2764521
	1973	2730001	2750000
	1974	2780001	2790000
2500	1970	2120001	2120750
	1971-72	2034258	2060000
	1973	2060001	2080000
2500A	1970	2150001	2150999
	1971-72	2145247	2150000
	1973	2450001	2460000
2800	1970	2420001	2420708
	1971-72	2330000	2340000
	1973	2340001	2350000
2800 A	1970	2460001	2460862
	1971-72	2400001	2410000
	1973	2410001	2420000
2800 BAV	1970	2130001	2130691
	1971-72	2130692	2131046
2800 ABAV	1970	2160001	2160654
	1971-72	2160655	2160866
2800 CS		2270001	2270641
2800 CS A		2280001	2280526
3.0 BAV	1971-72	3100001	3110000
3.0	1973	3020001	3050000
3.0	1974	3160001	3170000
3.0 BAV	1974	2100001	2110000
3.0 A BAV	1971-72	3130001	3140000
3.0A	1973	2110001	2120000
3.0 A	1974	3180001	3190000
3.0 A BAV	1974	3280001	3290000
3.0 SI	1975	3170001	3180000
3.0 SI-A	1975	3190001	3200000
530 I	1975	5000001	5010000
530 I-A	1975	5020001	5030000

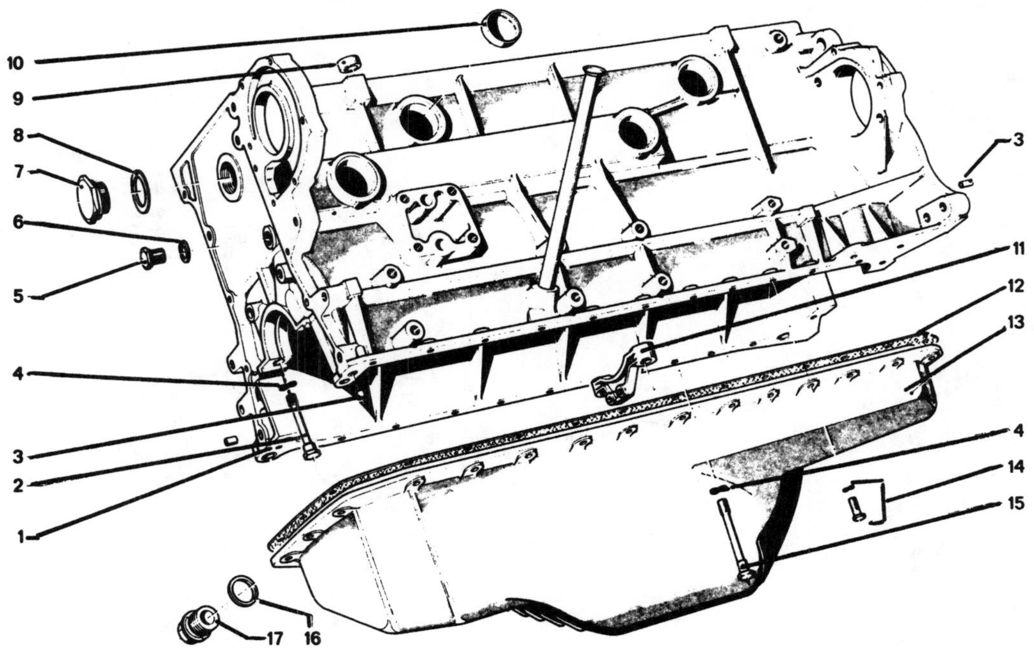

1 Cylinder Block
2 Screw
3 Sleeve
4 Washer
5 Screw
6 Seal Ring
7 Screw
8 Seal Ring
9 Sleeve
10 Cover
11 Supporting Piece
12 Gasket
13 Oil Pan
14 Screw
15 Screw
16 Seal Ring
17 Drain Screw

FIG 1 – ENGINE BLOCK & OIL PAN

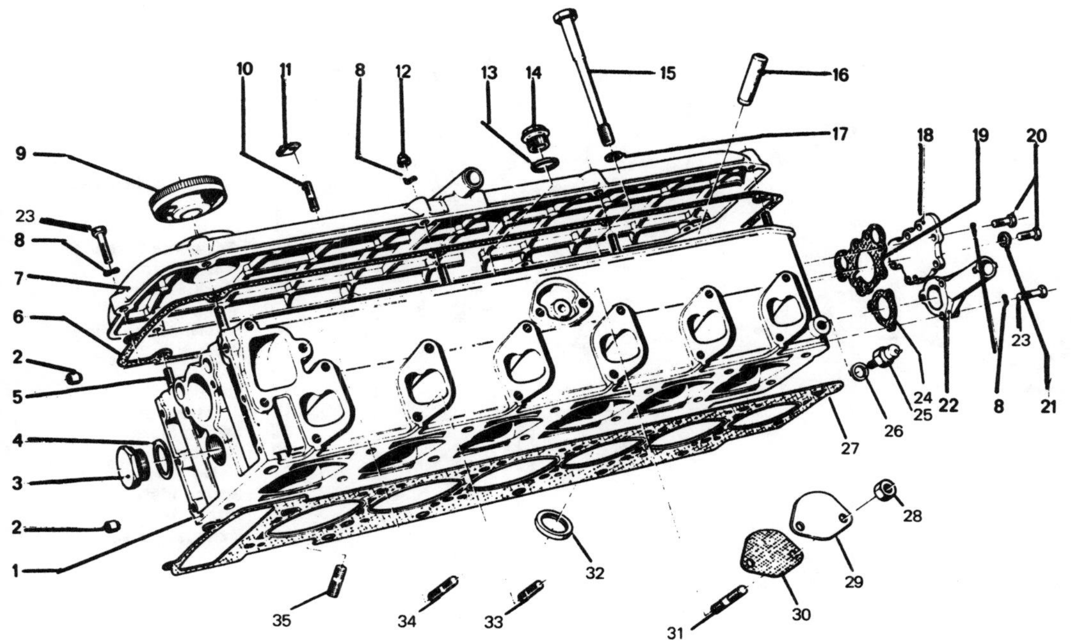

1 Cylinder Head
2 Sleeve
3 Plug
4 Seal Ring
5 Stud
6 Gasket
7 Cover
8 Washer
9 Oil Cap
10 Stud
11 Clamp
12 Nut
13 Seal Ring
14 Screw
15 Screw
16 Valve Guide
17 Washer
18 Cover
19 Gasket
20 Screw
21 Washer
22 Cover
23 Screw
24 Gasket
25 Oil Pressure Switch
26 Seal Ring
27 Gasket
28 Nut
29 Cover Plate
30 Gasket
31 Stud
32 Valve Seat Ring
33 Stud
34 Stud
35 Stud

FIG 2 – CYLINDER HEAD & COVER

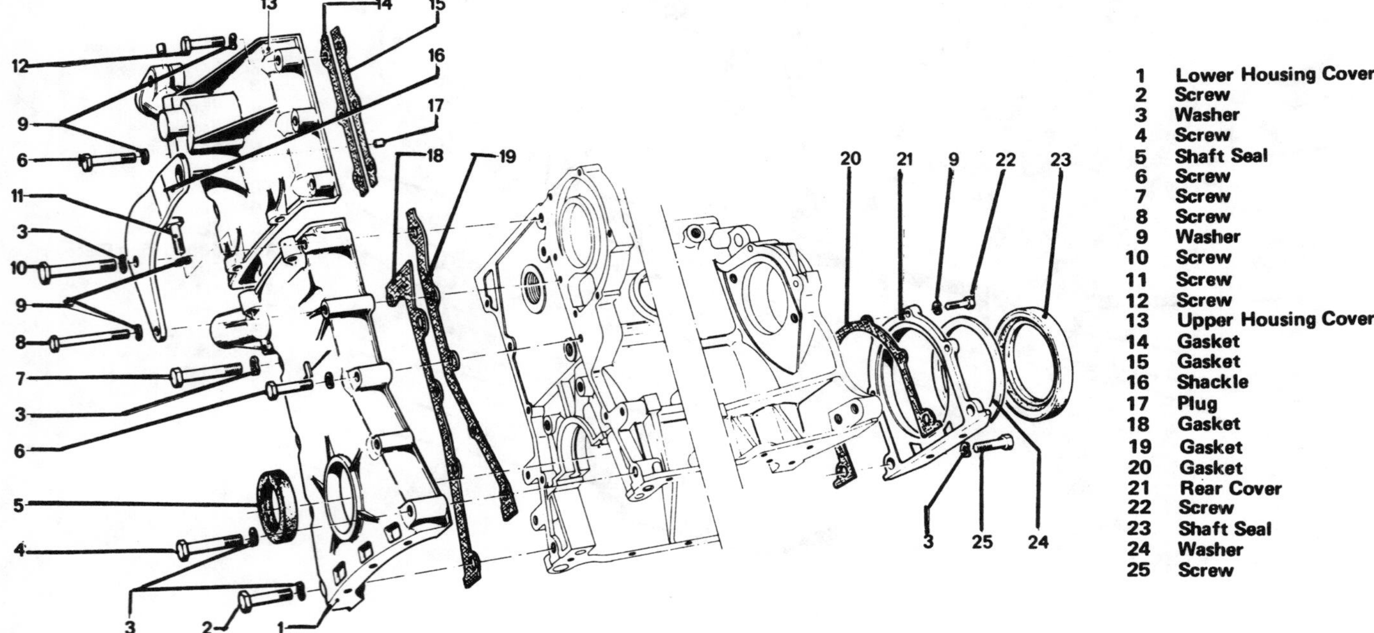
1 Lower Housing Cover
2 Screw
3 Washer
4 Screw
5 Shaft Seal
6 Screw
7 Screw
8 Screw
9 Washer
10 Screw
11 Screw
12 Screw
13 Upper Housing Cover
14 Gasket
15 Gasket
16 Shackle
17 Plug
18 Gasket
19 Gasket
20 Gasket
21 Rear Cover
22 Screw
23 Shaft Seal
24 Washer
25 Screw

FIG 3 – CAMSHAFT HOUSING

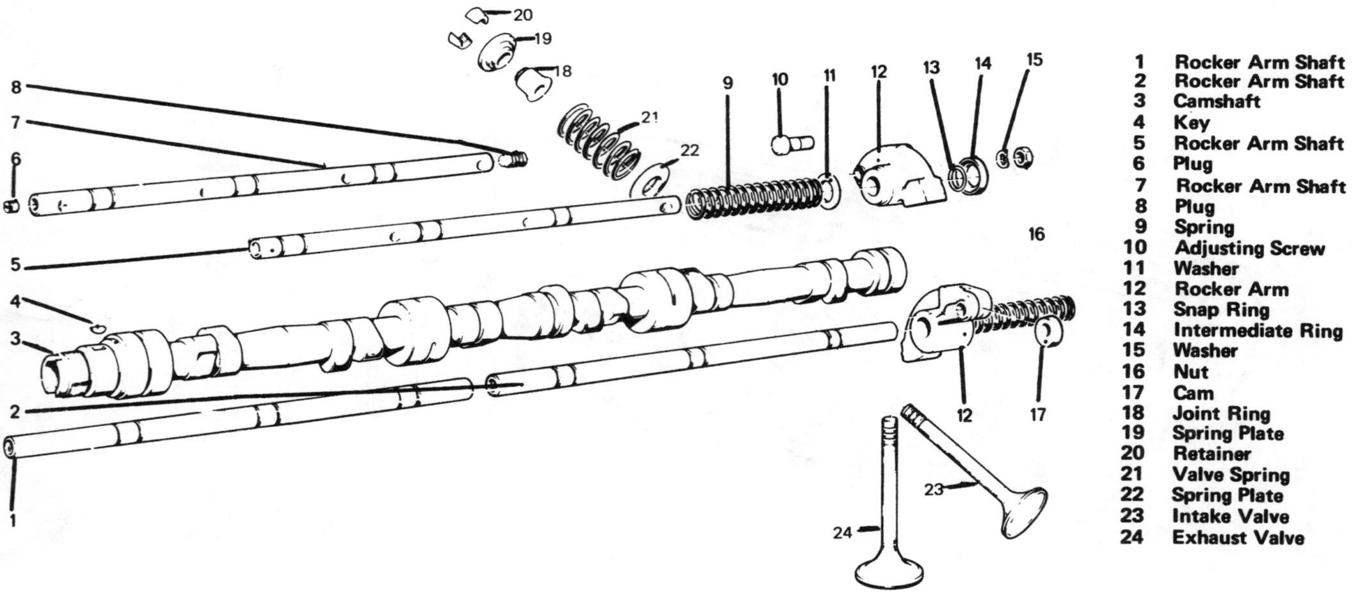
1 Rocker Arm Shaft
2 Rocker Arm Shaft
3 Camshaft
4 Key
5 Rocker Arm Shaft
6 Plug
7 Rocker Arm Shaft
8 Plug
9 Spring
10 Adjusting Screw
11 Washer
12 Rocker Arm
13 Snap Ring
14 Intermediate Ring
15 Washer
16 Nut
17 Cam
18 Joint Ring
19 Spring Plate
20 Retainer
21 Valve Spring
22 Spring Plate
23 Intake Valve
24 Exhaust Valve

FIG 4 – CAMSHAFT & VALVES

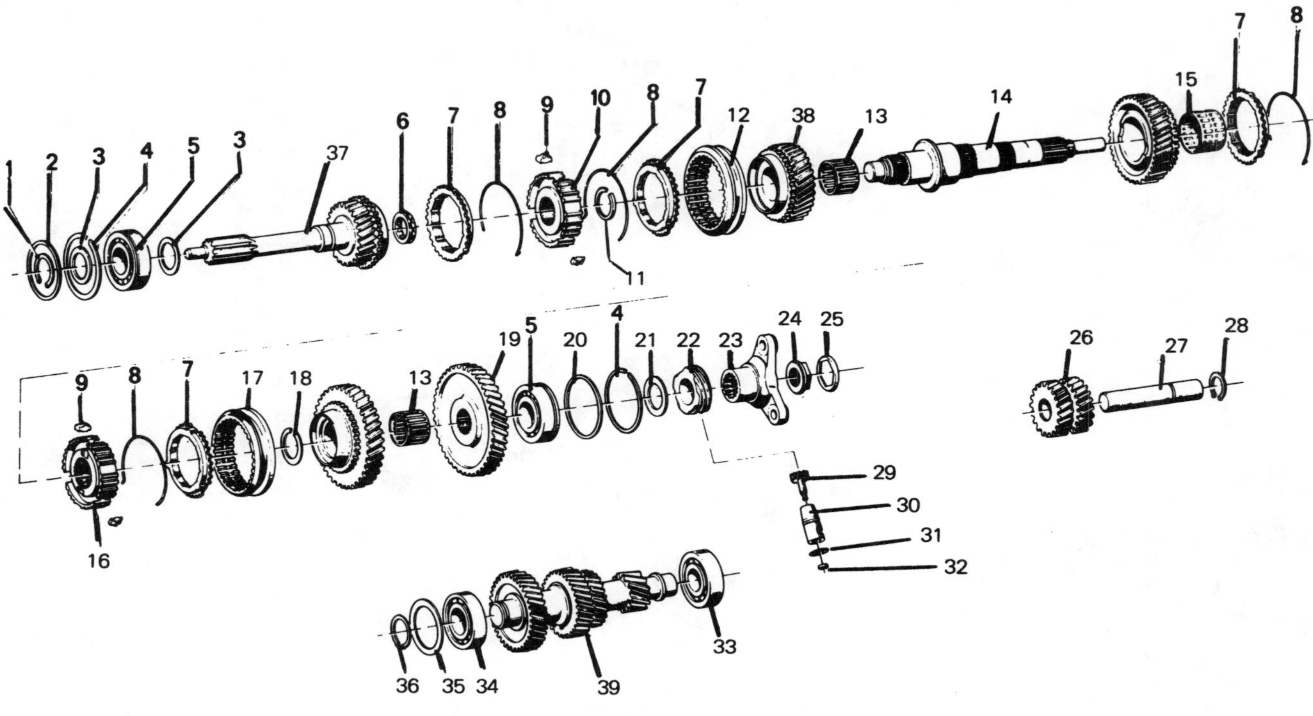

FIG 5 – FOUR SPEED TRANSMISSION

1 Lock Ring
2 Washer
3 Washer
4 Snap Ring
5 Bearing
6 Roller Ring
7 Synchronizer Ring
8 Spring
9 Thrust Piece
10 Synchronizer Body, 3rd & 4th Gear
11 Lock Ring
12 Sleeve, 3rd & 4th Gear
13 Needle Cage
14 Driven Shaft
15 Needle Cage
16 Syncronizer Body, 1st & 2nd Gear
17 Sleeve, 1st & 2nd Gear
18 Lock Ring
19 Reverse Gear
20 Shim
21 Washer
22 Speedometer Worm
23 Drive Flange
24 Nut
25 Lock Plate
26 Reverse Sliding Gear
27 Reverse Shaft
28 Ring
29 Speedometer Pinion
30 Rush
31 O Ring
32 Seal
33 Ball Bearing
34 Ball Bearing
35 Shim
36 Lock Ring
37 Gear Set
38 3rd Gear
39 Gear Set

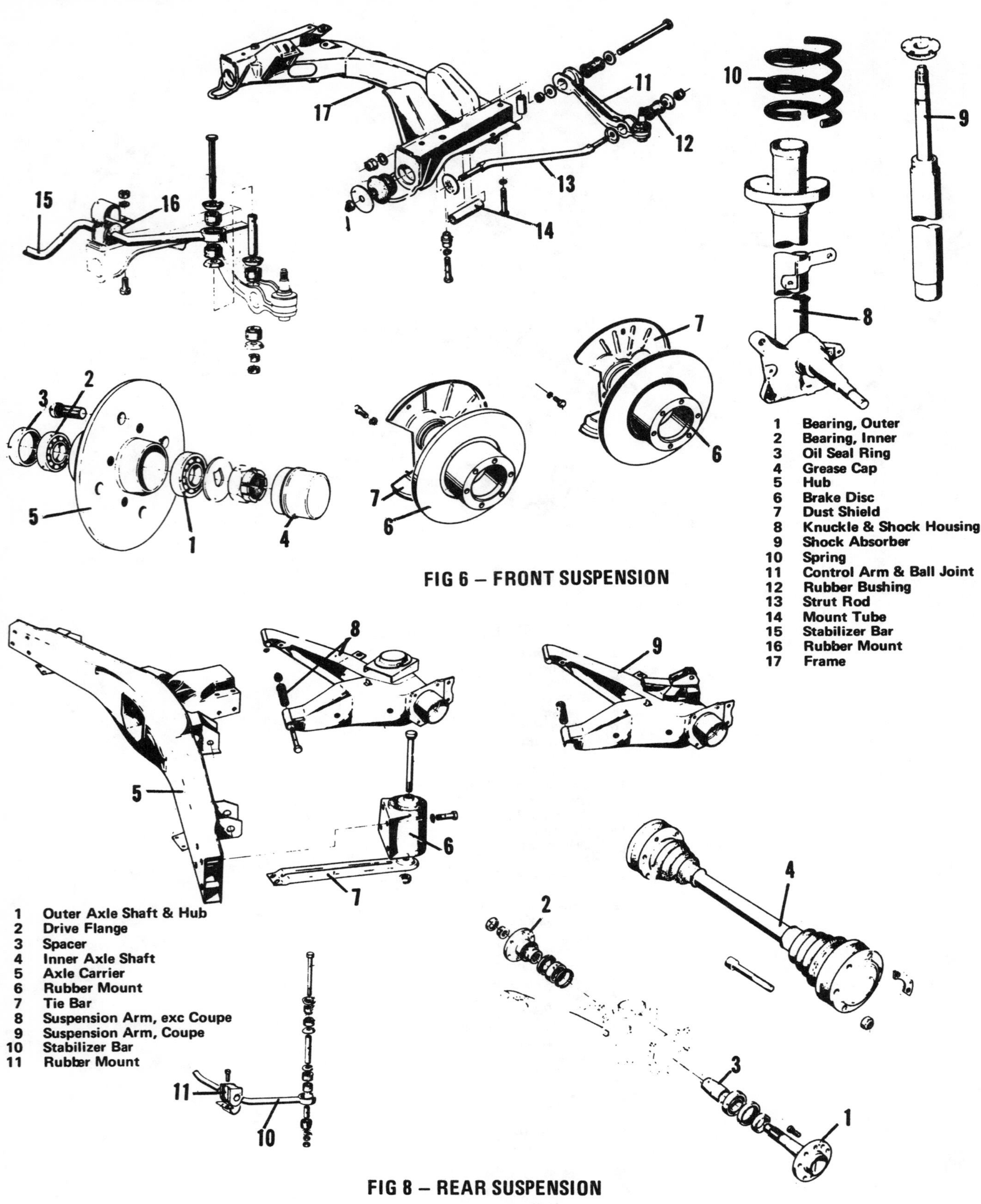

17
11
10
9
12
13
15
16
14
8
7
2
3
6
5
1
4
1 Bearing, Outer
2 Bearing, Inner
3 Oil Seal Ring
4 Grease Cap
5 Hub
6 Brake Disc
7 Dust Shield
8 Knuckle & Shock Housing
9 Shock Absorber
10 Spring
11 Control Arm & Ball Joint
12 Rubber Bushing
13 Strut Rod
14 Mount Tube
15 Stabilizer Bar
16 Rubber Mount
17 Frame

FIG 6 – FRONT SUSPENSION

8
9
5
6
7
4
2
3
1
11
10
1 Outer Axle Shaft & Hub
2 Drive Flange
3 Spacer
4 Inner Axle Shaft
5 Axle Carrier
6 Rubber Mount
7 Tie Bar
8 Suspension Arm, exc Coupe
9 Suspension Arm, Coupe
10 Stabilizer Bar
11 Rubber Mount

FIG 8 – REAR SUSPENSION

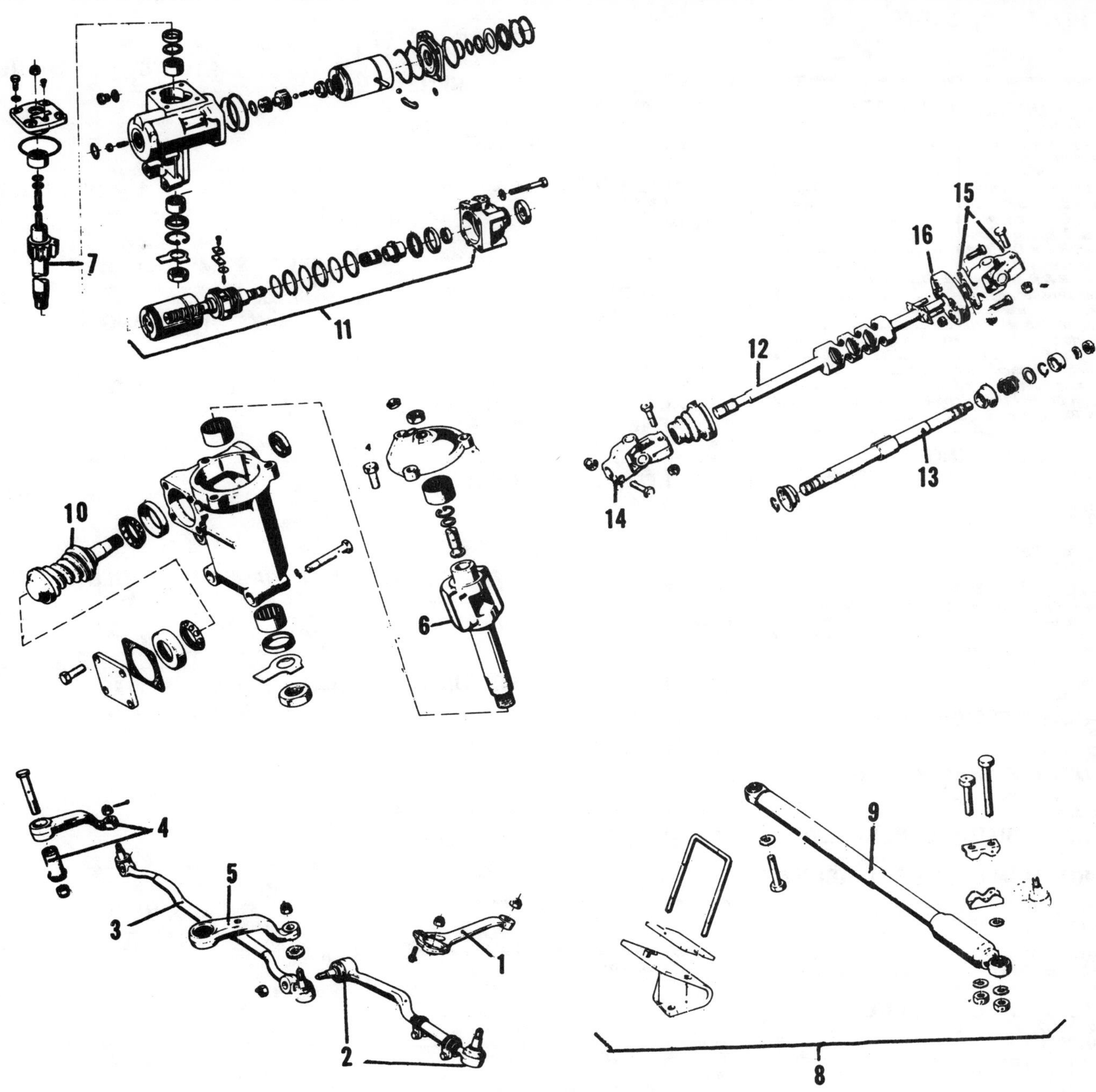

FIG 7 – STEERING

1 Arm
2 Tie Rod Assy
3 Drag Link
4 Idler Arm & Bushing
5 Pitman Arm
6 Shaft & Roller, Std Strg
7 Shaft & Roller, Pwr Strg
8 Strg Damper & Mtg Kit
9 Strg Damper
10 Worm, Std Strg
11 Worm & Piston, Pwr Strg
12 Mainshaft, Lower
13 Mainshaft, Upper
14 Coupling, Lower
15 Coupling, Upper
16 Flex Disc

Ignition, Starting & Charging—TIME

OPERATION INDEX

Tune-Up, Minor ... 1
Tune-Up, Major ... 2
Compression Test ... 3
Distributor, R & R Or Renew ... 4
Distributor Cap, Renew ... 5
Ignition Cable Set, Renew ... 6
Ignition Coil, Renew ... 7
Starter & Ignition Switch, Renew ... 8
Starter, R & R Or Renew ... 9
Starter Solenoid, Renew ... 10
Starter, R & R & Overhaul ... 11
Starter Brushes, Renew ... 12
Regulator, Renew ... 13
Alternator, R & R Or Renew ... 14
Alternator, R & R & Overhaul ... 15
Alternator Bearing, Renew ... 16
Alternator Brushes, Renew ... 17
Alternator Pulley, Renew ... 18
Vacuum Control Unit, Renew ... 19
Spark Plugs, Renew ... 20

1—TUNE-UP, MINOR
Includes: Renew points, condenser and plugs, set spark timing and adjust carburetor idle.
1602, 2002 ... 2.5
2500, 2800, 3.0 ... 3.0
530 ... ①2.0
①Includes Check Exhaust Gas Recirculation Valve.

2—TUNE-UP, MAJOR
Includes: Check compression, clean or renew and adjust spark plugs. R & R distributor, renew points and condenser. Adjust ignition timing, carburetor & fan belts. Clean battery terminals & service air cleaner. Check coil & renew filter elements.
Exc Below ... 3.1
1602, 2002 ... 2.2

3—COMPRESSION TEST
Exc Below ... 0.7
1602, 2002 ... 0.5

4—DISTRIBUTOR, R & R OR RENEW
All Models ... 0.7

5—DISTRIBUTOR CAP, RENEW
All Models ... 0.2

6—IGNITION CABLE SET, RENEW
One—
1602, 2002 ... 0.3
2500, 2800, 3.0, 530 ... 0.2
All—
1602, 2002 ... 0.8
2500, 2800, 3.0 ... 0.7
530 ... 0.6

7—IGNITION COIL, RENEW
1602, 2002, 530 ... 0.2
2500, 2800, 3.0 ... 0.3

8—STARTER & IGNITION SWITCH, RENEW
Exc Below ... 0.9
1602, 2002 ... 0.5

9—STARTER, R & R OR RENEW
1602, 2002 ... ①0.4
2500, 2800, 3.0, Exc ... ①0.7
3.0 CSI ... 1.5
530, Exc ... 0.9
530 IA ... 1.2
①With Auto Trans Or TII Models, Add. ... 0.7

10—STARTER SOLENOID, RENEW
With starter removed.
All Models ... 0.2

11—STARTER, R & R & OVERHAUL
1602 & 2002, Exc ... 2.8
2002A ... 1.5
2002TII ... 2.0
2500, 2800, Exc ... 1.6
2500A, 2800A ... 1.7
3.0, Exc ... 1.6
CSA, SA ... 1.7
CSI ... 2.4
530 ... 1.8
530IA ... 2.1

12—STARTER BRUSHES, RENEW
With starter removed.
All Models ... 0.4

13—REGULATOR, RENEW
All Models ... 0.2

14—ALTERNATOR, R & R OR RENEW
Exc Below ... 0.4
2002TII ... 1.2
2500, 2800 & 3.0 ... 0.5
530 ... 0.8

15—ALTERNATOR, R & R & OVERHAUL
Exc Below ... 1.6
2002TII ... 2.4
3.0, Exc ... 1.6
3.0SI, CSI ... 2.1

16—ALTERNATOR BEARING, RENEW
After alternator is dismantled.
All Models ... 0.2

17—ALTERNATOR BRUSHES, RENEW
Exc Below ... 1.1
2002TI ... 1.9
2500, 2800 ... 1.5
3.0CSI ... 1.7
3.0CS, CSA ... 1.5
530 ... 2.1

18—ALTERNATOR PULLEY, RENEW
All Models ... 0.3

19—VACUUM CONTROL UNIT, RENEW
All Models ... 0.6

20—SPARK PLUGS, RENEW
Exc Below ... 0.4
1602, 2002 ... 0.3

Fuel, Intake & Exhaust Systems—TIME

OPERATION INDEX

Carburetor(S) Or Gasket(S), R & R Or Renew ... 1
Carburetor(S), Overhaul ... 2
Fuel Pump, R & R Or Renew ... 3
Fuel Pump, Clean ... 4
Choke Operating Rod, Renew ... 5
Intake Manifold Or Pipes, Renew ... 6
Exhaust Manifold Or Gasket, Renew ... 7
Exhaust System (Complete), Renew ... 8
Exhaust Pipe, Renew ... 9
Primary & Main Silencers, Renew ... 10
Fuel Filter, Renew (Injection System) ... 11
Injection Pump, Renew ... 12
Suction Or Pressure Valves, Renew ... 13
Pressure Regulator, Renew ... 14
Injector(S), Renew ... 15
Fuel Ring Line (Complete), Renew ... 16
Control Unit (Fuel Injection), Renew ... 17
Starting Valve, Renew ... 18
Air Flow Meter, Renew ... 19
Starting Valve, Renew ... 20
Fuel Tank, Renew ... 21

1—CARBURETOR(S) OR GASKET(S), R & R OR RENEW
One—
Exc Below ... 0.7
2002A ... 0.9
Two—
2500 & 2800 ... 2.3
3.0, Exc ... 2.3
3.0CSA ... 2.6

—NOTE—
Where One Carburetor Is Used, Time Is For One. Where Two Are Used, Time Is For Both.

2—CARBURETOR(S), OVERHAUL
After carburetors are removed.
One—
Exc Below ... 1.1
2002A ... 1.9
Both—
All Models ... 3.4

3—FUEL PUMP, R & R OR RENEW
1602, 2002 ... 0.3
2500, 2800, 3.0 ... 0.4
530 ... 0.6

4—FUEL PUMP, CLEAN
Exc Below ... 0.2
1602 & 530 ... 0.3

5—CHOKE OPERATING ROD, RENEW
All Models ... 0.4

6—INTAKE MANIFOLD, OR PIPES, RENEW
4 Cyl—
Exc Below ... 1.6
2002A ... 1.8
6 Cyl, Front—
Exc Below ... 1.8
2500A, 3.0CSA ... 2.1
6 Cyl, Rear—
Exc Below ... 1.9
3.0CSA ... 2.2

7—EXHAUST MANIFOLD OR GASKET, RENEW
Front, Exc ... 0.9
2500, 2800, 3.0 ... 1.5
Rear ... 0.9
Both ... 1.8

8—EXHAUST SYSTEM (COMPLETE), RENEW
1602, 2002 ... 0.8
2500, 2800 ... 1.0
3.0 ... 1.6
530 ... 1.1

9—EXHAUST PIPE, RENEW
Front—
1602, 2002 ... 0.4
Rear—
All Models ... 0.5

10—PRIMARY & MAIN SILENCERS, RENEW
1602, 2002 ... 0.7
2500, 2800 ... 0.8
3.0 ... ①1.3
530 ... ②1.2
①Includes Intermediate
②Includes Both Mufflers And Front Pipe.

11—FUEL FILTER, RENEW (INJECTION SYSTEM)
Exc Below ... 0.3
3.0CSI ... 0.2

12—INJECTION PUMP, RENEW
2002TII ... 2.4

13—SUCTION OR PRESSURE VALVES, RENEW
2002TII ... 0.4

14—PRESSURE REGULATOR, RENEW
Exc Below ... 0.7
530 ... 1.0

15—INJECTOR(S), RENEW
One—
2002TII ... 0.3
530 ... 0.7
All—
2002TII ... 1.1
530 ... 2.3

(Continued)

Fuel, Intake & Exhaust Systems—TIME Cont'd

16—FUEL RING LINE (COMPLETE), RENEW
Exc Below 1.4
530 ....1.9

17—CONTROL UNIT (FUEL INJECTION), RENEW
Exc Below 0.5
530 ....0.3

18—STARTING VALVE, RENEW
2002TII 0.2
3.0CSI 0.1

19—AIR FLOW METER, RENEW
530 ....0.3

20—STARTING VALVE, RENEW
2002TII 0.2
530 ....0.4

21—FUEL TANK, RENEW
Exc Below 1.3
2500, 2800, 3.0 ....1.2
530 ....0.9

Engine Cooling & Heater System—TIME

OPERATION INDEX
Radiator, R & R Or Renew 1
Radiator Hose(S), Renew 2
Water Pump, R & R Or Renew 3
Water Pump, R & R & Overhaul 4
Thermostat, Renew 5
Heater Unit, Renew 6
Heater Water Valve Or Sealing Ring, Renew 7
Heater Controls, Renew 8
Heater Hose(S), Renew 9
Header Tank, R & R Or Renew 10

1—RADIATOR, R & R OR RENEW
Exc Below 0.6
W/Auto Trans, Exc 0.7
530 ....0.8

2—RADIATOR HOSE(S), RENEW
Rad. To Thermostat—
All Models 0.5
Connection Flange To Rad—
1602, 2002 ....0.3
2500, 2800, 3.0, 530 ....0.5
Thermo Hsg To Pump—
Exc Below 0.4
2500, 2800, 3.0, 530 ....0.5
All Hoses—
Exc Below 0.9
3.0CSI & 530 ....1.1

3—WATER PUMP, R & R OR RENEW
1602, 2002 ....1.4
530, Exc 1.5
W/Auto Trans 1.6
2500, 2800, Exc 1.8
W/Auto Trans 1.9
3.0, Exc 2.2
CSA 2.3
CSI 2.1

4—WATER PUMP, OVERHAUL
After pump is removed.
All Models 0.7

5—THERMOSTAT, RENEW
Exc Below 0.6
1602, 2002 ....0.4

6—HEATER UNIT, RENEW
Exc Below 2.7
3.0 ....3.2
530 ....3.0

7—HEATER WATER VALVE & SEALING RING, RENEW
1602, 2002 ....1.1

8—HEATER CONTROLS, RENEW
Exc Below 0.8
530 ....1.1

9—HEATER HOSE(S), RENEW
Left Or Right—
Exc Below 0.7
1602, 2002 ....0.5
530 ....0.3
Both—
Exc Below 0.9
1602, 2002 ....0.7
530 ....0.5

10—HEADER TANK, R & R OR RENEW
530 ....0.5

Engine—TIME

OPERATION INDEX
Engine, R & R Or Renew 1
Engine, Exchange Unit, Install 2
Engine, R & R & Overhaul 3
Cylinder Head, R & R Or Gasket, Renew 4
Valves, Grind 5
One Valve, Renew & Grind 5A
One Valve Spring, Renew 6
Cylinder Head Cover Gasket, Renew 7
Rocker Shaft & Rockers, R & R Or Renew 8
Valve Clearance, Adjust 9
Upper Timing Case Cover Or Seal, Renew 10
Upper & Lower Timing Case Covers Or Seals, Renew 11
Timing Chain Or Sprockets, Renew 12
Timing Chain Tensioner Piston, Renew 13
Timing Case Cover Ring Seal, Renew 14
Oil Sump Or Gasket, Renew 15
Camshaft, R & R Or Renew 16
Oil Pump, R & R Or Renew 17
Oil Pump Drive Chain, Renew 18
Piston Ring(S), Renew 19
Rings & Main Bearings, Renew & Grind Valves 20
Rod Bearing(S), Renew 21
Main Bearings, Renew 22
Main & Rod Bearings, Renew 23
Crankshaft, R & R Or Renew 24
Crankshaft Rear Main Oil Seal, Renew 25
Piston(S), Renew 26
Crankshaft Pulley, Renew 27
Injection Drive Hub, R & R Or Renew 28
EGR Valve, Renew 29
Air Pump, R & R Or Renew 30

1—ENGINE, R & R OR RENEW
Does not include transfer of any part of engine or replacement of special equipment.
1602 ....5.2
2002, Exc 5.6
2002TII 6.7
2500, 2800, 3.0, Exc 6.3
W/Auto Trans 08.4
CSI 7.0
530, Exc 6.0
W/Auto Trans 8.2

2—ENGINE, EXCHANGE UNIT, INSTALL
Includes removing & installing engine, detach & attach auxiliary assys. Adjust engine idle, check exhaust emissions.
1602 ....6.4
2002, Exc 7.1
2002TII 7.7
2500, 2800, 3.0, Exc 7.3
W/Auto Trans 10.1
CSI 7.4
530, Exc 8.2
W/Auto Trans 10.0

3—ENGINE, R & R & OVERHAUL
Includes R & R engine. Removing & installing cyl head, oil pump, connecting rods w/pistons & c'shaft. Renew all gaskets. Make all micrometer checks on shafts, bearings, cylinders & pistons.
1602, 2002, Exc 14.9
2002A 15.9
2002TII 17.6
2500, 2800, 3.0, Exc 18.1
W/Auto Trans 19.7
3.0CSI 18.8
530, Exc 18.6
W/Auto Trans 20.3

4—CYLINDER HEAD, R & R OR GASKET, RENEW
Includes: Adjust valves and timing.
1602 & 2002, Exc 3.6
2002A 3.9
2002TII 4.9
2500 & 2800 ....5.2
3.0, Exc 5.2
3.0CSA 5.5
3.0CSI 5.9
530 ....7.2

5—VALVES, GRIND
Includes: R & R, clean, inspect & change defective parts. To grind one valve seat, add 0.3 exc 530. To grind all, add 2.0 for 1602 & 2002, 3.0 for 2500, 2800, 3.0 model and 0.7 for 530.
1602 & 2002, Exc 7.8
2002A 8.1
2002TII 10.0
2500 & 2800 ....12.6
3.0, Exc 12.6
3.0CSA 12.9
3.0CSI 13.6
530 ....16.0

5A—ONE VALVE, RENEW & GRIND
1602 & 2002, Exc 3.9
2002A 4.2
2002TII 5.2
2500 & 2800 ....5.5
3.0, Exc 5.5
3.0CSA 5.8
3.0CSI 6.2
530 ....7.5

—NOTE—
To Grind Valve Seat, Add. 0.3

6—ONE VALVE SPRING, RENEW
—NOTE—
Includes Grind Valve.
For Each Additional Valve Add 0.3
1602 & 2002, Exc 4.5
2002A 4.9
2002TII 5.8
2500 & 2800 & 3.0, Exc 6.7
3.0CSA 7.0
3.0CSI 8.9

7—CYLINDER HEAD COVER GASKET, RENEW
1602, 2002 ....0.2
2500, 2800, 3.0, Exc 0.5
3.0CSI 0.7
530 ....0.6

8—ROCKER SHAFT & ROCKERS, R & R OR RENEW
1602 ....4.5
2002, Exc 4.8
2002TII 5.7
2500, 2800 & 3.0, Exc 6.9
3.0CSA 7.2
3.0CSI 7.6
530 ....9.1

—NOTE—
Time Is For One Side,
Both Sides Add 0.2

9—VALVE CLEARANCE, ADJUST
1602, 2002 ....0.5
2500, 2800, & 3.0, Exc 0.9
3.0CSI 1.1
530 ....1.0

10—UPPER TIMING CASE COVER OR SEAL, RENEW
1602, 2002, Exc 0.7
2002TII 1.4
2500, 2800, 3.0, Exc 1.9
3.0CSI 2.2
530 ....2.0

(Continued)

Engine—TIME Cont'd

11—UPPER & LOWER TIMING CASE COVERS OR SEALS, RENEW
1602, 2002, Exc 7.6
2002A 7.9
2002TII 10.2
2500, 2800, 3.0, Exc 9.3
Auto Trans 11.5
3.0CSI 10.1
530, Exc 6.9
530IA 7.0

12—TIMING CHAIN OR SPROCKETS, RENEW
1602, 2002, Exc 7.8
2002A 8.2
2002TII 10.4
2500, 2800, 3.0, Exc 9.6
3.0CSA 11.8
3.0CSI 10.3

—NOTE—

To Renew Sprockets, Add. 0.6

13—TIMING CHAIN TENSIONER PISTON, RENEW
1602, 2002, Exc 0.7
2002TII 1.5
2500, 2800, 3.0, Exc 0.8
3.0CSI 1.0

14—TIMING CASE COVER RING SEAL, RENEW
1602, 2002, Exc 1.3
2002TII 2.0
2500, 2800, 3.0, Exc 1.6
Auto Trans 1.7
530 ....0.9

15—OIL SUMP OR GASKET, RENEW
1602 ....1.6
2002, Exc 2.2
2002TII 2.6
2500, 2800 ....2.2
3.0 ....2.6
530 ....2.4

16—CAMSHAFT, R & R OR RENEW
1602 , 2002, Exc 4.3
2002TII 5.5
2500, 2800, 3.0, Exc 6.1
3.0CSA 6.4
3.0CSI 6.8
530 ....7.0

17—OIL PUMP, R & R OR RENEW
1602 ....2.0
2002, Exc 2.6
2002TII 3.0
2500, 2800 ....2.5
3.0 ....2.9
530 ....2.8

—NOTE—

To Overhaul, Add. 1.1

18—OIL PUMP DRIVE CHAIN, RENEW
1602, 2002, Exc 8.3
2002A 8.7
2002TII 10.9
2500, 2800, 3.0, Exc 10.0
W/Auto Trans 12.1
3.0CSI 10.7

19—PISTON RING(S), RENEW
1602 ....10.6
2002, Exc 11.5
2002TI 11.9
2500, 2800, 3.0, Exc 12.0
W/Auto Trans 15.0
CSI 12.3
530, Exc 13.1
W/Auto Trans 14.9

—NOTE—

For All Pistons, Add. 1.5

20—RINGS & MAIN BEARINGS, RENEW & GRIND VALVES
1602, 2002, Exc 19.1
2002A 19.6
2002TII 21.8
2500, 2800, 3.0, Exc 25.5
W/Auto Trans 27.1
3.0CSI 26.2
530, Exc 29.5
W/Auto Trans 31.2

21—ROD BEARING(S), RENEW
After piston is removed.
One 0.1
All 0.3

22—MAIN BEARINGS, RENEW
1602, 2002, Exc 16.0
2002A 16.4
2002TII 18.8
2500, 2800, 3.0, Exc 19.9
W/Auto Trans 21.6
530 ....24.0

23—MAIN & ROD BEARINGS, RENEW
1602, 2002, Exc 18.8
2002A 19.2
2002TII 21.6
2500, 2800, 3.0, Exc 24.0
W/Auto Trans 25.7
530 ....25.0

24—CRANKSHAFT, R & R OR RENEW
1602, 2002, Exc 16.0
2002A 16.4
2002TII 18.8
2500, 2800, 3.0, Exc 19.9
W/Auto Trans 21.9
3.0CSI 20.6
530 ....20.6

25—CRANKSHAFT REAR MAIN OIL SEAL, RENEW
1602, 2002, Exc 4.4
2002A, TII 4.6
2500, 2800, 3.0, Exc 4.5
W/Auto Trans 5.1
530, Exc 3.8
W/Auto Trans 4.8

26—PISTON(S), RENEW
One—
1602, 2002, Exc 9.2
2002A 10.0
2002TII 9.7
2500, 2800, 3.0, Exc 11.0
W/Auto Trans 13.1
CSI 11.7
530, Exc 10.7
W/Auto Trans 12.9
All—
1602, 2002, Exc 10.6
2002A 10.9
2002TI 12.2
2500, 2800, 3.0, Exc 13.2
W/Auto Trans 15.3
CSI 13.9
530, Exc 12.1
W/Auto Trans 14.3

27—CRANKSHAFT PULLEY, RENEW
Exc Below 1.0
2002TII 0.4

28—INJECTION DRIVE HUB, R & R OR RENEW
All Models 1.9

29—EGR VALVE, RENEW
530 ....0.2

30—AIR PUMP, R & R OR RENEW
530 ....0.6

Clutch, Mounts & Transmission—TIME

OPERATION INDEX

Flywheel, R & R Or Renew 1
Torque Converter Driving Disc, Renew 2
Clutch Or Disc, Renew 3
Release Fork (Or Lever), Renew 4
Clutch Pedal, Adjust 5
Clutch Master Cylinder, R & R Or Renew 6
Master Cylinder, R & R & Overhaul 7
Slave Cylinder, R & R Or Renew 8
Slave Cylinder, R & R & Overhaul 9
Clutch Hydraulic Fluid Reservoir, Renew 10
Engine Mounts, Renew 11
Transmission Assy, R & R Or Renew 12
Manual Trans Housing, Renew 13
Input Shaft Seal, Renew (Std Trans) 14
Output Shaft Seal, Renew (Std Trans) 15
Gear Selector Forks, Renew 16
Selector Lever, Renew 17
Gear Lever, Renew (Std Trans) 18
Gearbox, Std Trans, R & R & Overhaul 19
Oil Sump Or Seal, Renew 20
Speedometer Pinion Oil Seal, Renew 21
Gearshift Or Selector Lever, Renew 22
Automatic Transmission, Overhaul 23
Oil Pressure, Check 24
Gear Box Extn (Automatic) Seal, Renew 25
Output Shaft, Auto Trans, R & R 26
Plate Clutch & Discs, Renew 27
Plate Clutches, Strip & Assemble 28
Primary Pump, Renew 29
Centrifugal Governor, Renew 30

1—FLYWHEEL, R & R OR RENEW
1602, 2002, Exc 3.4
2002A, TII 3.6
2500, 2800, 3.0, Exc 3.3
W/Auto Trans 4.2
530 ....3.1

2—TORQUE CONVERTER DRIVING DISC, RENEW
2002 ....3.6
2500, 2800, 3.0 ....4.2
530 ....4.1

3—CLUTCH OR DISC, RENEW
1602, 2002, Exc 3.1
2002TII 3.3
2500, 2800, 3.0 ....3.2
530 ....2.8

—NOTE—

To Renew Grooved Ball Bearing In Crankshaft, Add. 0.3

4—RELEASE FORK (OR LEVER), RENEW
1602, 2002, Exc 2.9
2002TII 3.1
2500, 2800, 3.0, 530 ....1.8

5—CLUTCH PEDAL, ADJUST
All Models 0.2

6—CLUTCH MASTER CYLINDER, R & R OR RENEW
Exc Below 1.5
1602, 2002 ....1.8

7—MASTER CYLINDER, R & R & OVERHAUL
Exc Below 1.9
1602, 2002 ....2.2

8—SLAVE CYLINDER, R & R OR RENEW
Exc Below 0.7
1602, 2002 ....0.9

9—SLAVE CYLINDER, R & R & OVERHAUL
Exc Below 1.0
1602, 2002 ....1.2

10—CLUTCH HYDRAULIC FLUID RESERVOIR, RENEW
Exc Below 0.4
530 ....0.3

11—ENGINE MOUNTS, RENEW
Right—
1602, 2002 ....0.7
2500, 2800, 3.0 ....0.8
530 ....0.3
Left—
1602, 2002 ....0.5
2500, 2800, 3.0 ....0.8
530 ....0.3

(Continued)

Clutch, Mounts & Transmission—TIME Cont'd

Both—
1602, 2002 ....0.9
2500, 2800, 3.0 ....0.8
530 ....0.5
Rear, At Trans—
Manual 0.3
Auto Trans—
Exc Below 0.6
1602, 2002 ....0.5

12—TRANSMISSION ASSY, R & R OR RENEW

Std Trans—
1602, 2002, Exc 2.8
2002TI 3.0
530 ....1.9
Auto Trans—
1602, 2002 ....3.3
2500, 2800 ....3.9
3.0 ....4.0
530 ....3.9

—NOTE—

To Renew Trans, Add. 0.3

13—MANUAL TRANS HOUSING, RENEW

One Piece Housing—
1602 ....4.2
2002, Exc 4.5
2002TI 4.7
Two Piece—
Front—
2500, 2800, 3.0 ....3.5
530 ....3.2
Rear—
All Models 5.6
Both—
All Models 5.6

14—INPUT SHAFT SEAL, RENEW (STD TRANS)

1602, 2002, Exc 3.0
2002TII 3.3
All Others 2.3

15—OUTPUT SHAFT SEAL, RENEW (STD TRANS)

Exc Below 1.4
530 ....1.3

16—GEAR SELECTOR FORKS, RENEW

1602, 2002, Exc 4.9
2002TII 5.2

17—SELECTOR LEVER, RENEW

2002, 3.0 ....0.8
2500, 2800 ....0.5
530 ....0.6

18—GEAR LEVER, RENEW (STD TRANS)

All Models 0.5

19—GEARBOX, R & R & OVERHAUL (STD TRANS)

1602, 2002, Exc 5.9
2002TII 6.1
2500, 2800, 3.0 ....6.0
530 ....5.9

20—OIL SUMP OR SEAL, RENEW

Exc Below 0.8
3.0, 530 ....1.1

21—SPEEDOMETER PINION OIL SEAL, RENEW

Std Trans 0.3
Auto Trans 0.4

22—GEARSHIFT OR SELECTOR LEVER, RENEW

Std Trans 1.2
Auto Trans—
1602, 2002 ....4.0
2500, 2800 ....1.8
3.0, 530 ....0.3

23—AUTOMATIC TRANSMISSION, OVERHAUL

2002 ....8.3
2500, 2800 ....9.4
3.0 ....12.1
530 ....12.0

24—AUTO TRANS OIL PRESSURE, CHECK

2002 ....1.6
2500, 2800 ....1.3
3.0, 530 ....0.9

25—GEAR BOX EXTN (AUTOMATIC) SEAL, RENEW

Exc Below 1.7
3.0 ....2.1

26—OUTPUT SHAFT, AUTO TRANS, R & R

2002 ....6.2
2500, 2800 ....7.0
3.0, 530 ....6.9

27—PLATE CLUTCH & DISCS, RENEW

Exc Below 5.7
2500, 2800 ....6.3

28—PLATE CLUTCHES, STRIP & ASSEMBLE

3.0 & 530 ....7.0

29—PRIMARY PUMP, RENEW

2002 ....3.8
2500, 2800 ....4.4
3.0 ....5.4
530 ....5.2

30—CENTRIFUGAL GOVERNOR, RENEW

2002 ....1.7
2500, 2800 ....1.9
3.0 & 530 ....2.1

Brakes, Steering, Suspension, Universals & Rear Axle—TIME

OPERATION TIMES

Brake Shoes Or Friction Pads, Renew 1
Master Cylinder, Renew 2
Master Cylinder, R & R & Overhaul 3
Compensating Reservoir, Renew 4
Wheel Cylinders, Renew 5
Wheel Cylinders, R & R & Overhaul 6
Caliper Assy, Renew 7
Caliper Assy, R & R & Overhaul 8
Bleed System 9
Brake Hose, Renew 10
Hub Or Disc, Renew 11
Brake Drum(S), Renew 12
Non-Return Valve, Renew 13
Brake Limiter, Renew 14
Handbrake Lever, Renew 15
Handbrake Cables, Renew 16
Steering Column Joint (Hardy Disc), Renew 17
Steering Box, Renew 18
Steering Box, R & R & Overhaul 19
Track Rod Arm, Renew 20
Track Rod Joint(S), Renew 21
Track Rod, Renew 22
Centre Track Rod, Renew 23
Front Wheel Alignment 24
Front Hub Bearings, Renew 25
Front Axle Complete, R & R 26
Front Axle Carrier, Renew 27
Wishbone, Renew 28
Trailing Link, Renew 29
Track Rod End, Renew 30
Spring/Shock Absorber Strut, Renew 31
Spring Strut Support Bearing Or Sleeve, Renew 32
Spring Strut Front Coil Spring, Renew 33
Front Stabilizer Or Bushings, Renew 34
Rear Suspension Arm, Renew 35
Rear Axle Thrust Rod, Renew 36
Driving Flange At Axle Shaft, Renew 37
Rear Axle Shaft(S), Renew 38
Axle Shaft Bearings & Seals, Renew 39
Rear Shock Absorber(S), Renew 40
Rear Coil Spring(S), Renew 41
Rear Stabilizer Or Bushings, Renew 42
Propeller (Drive) Shaft, Renew 43
Final Drive, Renew 44
Final Drive, R & R & Overhaul 45
Driving Flange Or Seal On Final Drive, Renew 46
Differential Axle Housing, Renew 47
Differential Pinion, Renew 48
Differential, R & R & Overhaul 49
Half Shaft(S), Renew 50

1—BRAKE SHOES OR FRICTION PADS, RENEW

Drum Type, Both—
All Models 1.1
Disc Type—
Front, Both 0.6
Rear, Both 0.6

2—MASTER CYLINDER, RENEW

1602, 2002, Exc 1.2
2002TII 1.4
2500, 2800, 3.0, 530 ....1.3

3—MASTER CYLINDER, R & R & OVERHAUL

1602, 2002, Exc 1.6
2002TII 1.8
2500, 2800, 3.0, 530 ....1.7

4—COMPENSATING RESERVOIR, RENEW

1602, 2002, Exc 0.4
2002TII 0.6
2500, 2800, 3.0, 530 ....0.3

5—WHEEL CYLINDERS, RENEW

One—
Exc Below 0.7
1602 ....0.8
Both—
Exc Below 1.0
1602 ....1.2

6—WHEEL CYLINDER(S), R & R & OVERHAUL

One—
Exc Below 0.9
1602 ....1.0
Both—
Exc Below 1.3
1602 ....1.4

7—CALIPER ASSY, RENEW

Front—
One 0.9
Both 1.2
Rear—
One 1.0
Both 1.4

8—CALIPER ASSY, R & R & OVERHAUL

Front—
One 1.5
Both 2.4
Rear—
One 1.6
Both 2.5

9—BLEED SYSTEM

All Models 0.6

10—BRAKE HOSE, RENEW

Includes: Bleed brakes

Front, One—
1602, 2002, 530 ....0.7
2500, 2800, 3.0 ....0.8
Front, Two—
1602, 2002, 530 ....1.0
2500, 2800, 3.0 ....1.7
Rear, One—
All Models 0.8
Rear, Both—
All Models 0.9
All Hoses—
Exc Below 1.3
1602, 2002 ....1.4

11—HUB OR DISC, RENEW

Hub—
Front, One 0.6
Both 1.1

(Continued)

Brakes, Steering, Suspension, Universals & Rear Axle—TIME Cont'd

Disc—
- Front, One 0.7
  - Both 1.7
- Rear, One 0.8
  - Both 1.2

—NOTE—
To Renew Each Bushing Hub, Add. *0.2*

12—BRAKE DRUM(S), RENEW
All Models—
- One 0.4
- Both 0.5

13—NON-RETURN VALVE, RENEW
Exc Below 0.3
1602, 2002 ....0.2

14—BRAKE LIMITER, RENEW
Exc Below 0.9
2002 ....0.5

15—HANDBRAKE LEVER, RENEW
Exc Below 0.4
1602, 2002 ....0.5

16—HANDBRAKE CABLES, RENEW
One—
- All Models 1.2

Both—
- Exc Below 1.7
- 1602, 2002 ....1.8

17—STEERING COLUMN JOINT (HARDY DISC), RENEW
1602, 2002 ....0.7
2500, 2800, 3.0 ....0.6
530 ....0.4

18—STEERING BOX, RENEW
Standard Steering—
- 1602, 2002 ....1.5

Power Steering—
- All Models 1.3

29—STEERING BOX, R & R & OVERHAUL
Standard Steering—
- 1602, 2002 ....2.2

Power Steering—
- All Models 2.0

20—TRACK ROD ARM, RENEW
Includes: Adjust toe-in.
One—
- 1602, 2002 ....2.3
- 2500, 2800, 3.0 ....1.4
- 530 ....1.6

Both—
- 1602, 2002 ....3.7
- 2500, 2800, 3.0 ....1.9
- 530 ....2.4

21—TRACK ROD JOINT(S), RENEW
Includes: Adjust toe-in
One 1.0
Each Additional 0.2

22—TRACK ROD, RENEW
Includes: Adjust toe-in
One—
- Exc Below 1.1
- 530 ....1.0

Both—
- Exc Below 1.3
- 530 ....1.2

23—CENTRE TRACK ROD, RENEW
Includes: Adjust toe-in
All Models 1.3

24—FRONT WHEEL ALIGNMENT
All Models 0.8

25—FRONT HUB BEARINGS, RENEW
All Models—
- One 0.8
- Both 1.5

26—FRONT AXLE COMPLETE, R & R
Includes: Wheel alignment
1602, 2002, Exc 2.4
- 2002TII 2.6

2500, 2800, 3.0 ....3.1
530 ....2.8

27—FRONT AXLE CARRIER, RENEW
Includes: Wheel alignment
1602 ....3.4
2002, Exc 3.8
- 2002TII 4.0

2500, 2800, 3.0 ....3.9
530 ....3.6

28—WISHBONE, RENEW
One—
- Exc Below 1.4
- 530 ....1.5

Both—
- Exc Below 2.2
- 530 ....2.3

29—TRAILING LINK, RENEW
One—
- Exc Below 0.7
- 1602 ....0.6

Both—
- Exc Below 1.2
- 1602 ....1.1

30—TRACK ROD END, RENEW
All Models—
- One 0.9
- Both 1.3

31—SPRING/SHOCK ABSORBER STRUT, RENEW
Exc Below 1.6
1602, 2002 ....1.5

32—SPRING STRUT SUPPORT BEARING OR SLEEVE, RENEW
All Models—
- One 1.0
- Both 1.8

33—SPRING STRUT FRONT COIL SPRING, RENEW
One—
- Exc Below 1.4
- 1602, 2002 ....1.3

Both—
- Exc Below 2.6
- 1602, 2002 ....2.3

34—FRONT STABILIZER OR BUSHINGS, RENEW
1602, 2002 ....0.6
2500, 2800, 3.0 ....0.8
530 ....0.7

35—REAR SUSPENSION ARM, RENEW
One—
- 1602 ....3.4
- 2002 ....3.5
- 2500, 2800, 530 ....3.6
- 3.0 ....3.7

Both—
- 1602 ....5.5
- 2002 ....5.7
- 2500, 2800, 530 ....5.8
- 3.0 ....6.0

36—REAR AXLE THRUST ROD, RENEW
All Models—
- One 0.3
- Both 0.5

37—DRIVING FLANGE AT AXLE SHAFT, RENEW
One—
- 1602, 2002 ....0.4
- 2500, 2800, 3.0 ....0.5
- 530 ....0.8

Both—
- 1602, 2002 ....0.6
- 2500, 2800, 3.0 ....0.9
- 530 ....1.4

38—REAR AXLE SHAFT(S), RENEW
One—
- Exc Below 0.6
- 530 ....0.7

Both—
- Exc Below 1.0
- 530 ....1.2

39—AXLE SHAFT BEARINGS & SEALS, RENEW
One—
- Exc Below 1.3
- 1602, 2002 ....1.1

Both—
- Exc Below 2.5
- 1602, 2002 ....2.1

40—REAR SHOCK ABSORBER(S), RENEW
One—
- Exc Below 0.3
- 530 ....0.5

Both—
- Exc Below 0.4
- 530 ....0.8

—NOTE—
To Renew Each Rubber Mounting, Add. *0.1*

41—REAR COIL SPRING(S), RENEW
One—
- 1602 ....0.7
- 2002 ....0.8
- 2500, 2800 ....0.9
- 3.0 ....0.7
- 530 ....1.1

Both—
- 1602 ....1.1
- 2002 ....1.3
- 2500, 2800 ....1.7
- 3.0 ....1.1
- 530 ....2.0

42—REAR STABILIZER OR BUSHINGS, RENEW
All Models 0.5

43—PROPELLER (DRIVE) SHAFT, RENEW
Assembly—
- Exc Below 1.2
- 2500, 2800, 3.0 ....1.1
- 530, Exc 1.0
  - W/Auto Trans 0.6

Pilot Bearing—
- Exc Below 1.4
- 2500, 2800, 3.0 ....1.3
- 530, Exc 1.3
  - W/Auto Trans 0.9

Rubber Coupling—
- 2500, 2800, 3.0 ....0.9
- 1602, 2002, 530, Exc 1.0
  - 530, W/Auto Trans 0.6

44—FINAL DRIVE, RENEW
Exc Below 1.6
2500, 2800, 530 ....1.7
3.0 ....1.8

45—FINAL DRIVE, R & R & OVERHAUL
Exc Below 7.2
2500, 2800 ....8.2
3.0 ....8.3
530 ....8.0

—NOTE—
With Limited Slip, Add. *0.2*

46—DRIVING FLANGE OR SEAL ON FINAL DRIVE, RENEW
All Models—
- One 0.6
- Both 1.1

47—DIFFERENTIAL AXLE HOUSING, RENEW
Exc Below 3.2
3.0 ....3.3

(Continued)

Brakes, Steering, Suspension, Universals & Rear Axle—TIME Cont'd

48—DIFFERENTIAL PINION, RENEW

Exc Below 3.7
3.0 ....3.8

49—DIFFERENTIAL, R & R & OVERHAUL

1602, 2002 ....5.3
2500, 2800, 530 ....6.1
3.0 ....6.2

50—HALF SHAFT(S), RENEW

One—
Exc Below 0.9
1602, 2002 ....0.7
Both—
Exc Below 1.6
1602, 2002 ....1.3
530 ....1.7

Speedometer, W/S Wipers, Switches & Instruments—TIME

OPERATION INDEX

Speedometer Cable, Renew *1*
Speedometer Head, Renew *2*
W/S Wiper Motor, Renew *3*
W/S Wiper Drive Crank, Renew *4*
W/S Wiper Arm, Renew *5*
W/S Wiper Arm Pivot Bearings, Renew *6*
Combination Instrument, Renew *7*
Remote Thermometer, Renew *8*
Fuel Tank Indicator Tube, Renew *9*
Headlight Switch, Renew *10*
Dimmer Switch, Renew *11*
Stop Light Switch, Renew *12*
Turn Indicator Switch, Renew *13*
Hazard Flasher Switch, Renew *14*
Hazard Flasher Unit, Renew *15*
W/S Washer Pump, Renew *16*

1—SPEEDOMETER CABLE, RENEW

All Models 0.5

2—SPEEDOMETER HEAD, RENEW

Exc Below 0.7
530 ....0.6

3—W/S WIPER MOTOR, RENEW

Exc Below 0.6
3.0 ....0.4
530 ....0.8

4—W/S WIPER DRIVE CRANK, RENEW

1602, 2002 ....0.2

5—W/S WIPER ARM, RENEW

All Models 0.2

6—W/S WIPER ARM PIVOT BEARINGS, RENEW

Exc Below 0.5
1602 ....0.6
2002 ....0.4

7—COMBINATION INSTRUMENT, RENEW

One—
1602, 2002 ....0.7
3.0 ....0.8
Additional—
1602, 2002 ....0.1
3.0 ....0.2

8—REMOTE THERMOMETER, RENEW

1602, 2002 ....0.9
2500, 2800 ....0.5
3.0 ....0.8
530 ....0.7

9—FUEL TANK INDICATOR TUBE, RENEW

Exc Below 0.4
1602, 2002 ....0.3

10—HEADLAMP SWITCH, RENEW

All Models 0.5

11—DIMMER SWITCH, RENEW

Exc Below 0.6
1602, 2002 ....0.7
530 ....0.5

17—STOP LIGHT SWITCH, RENEW

Exc Below 0.4
1602, 2002A 0.2
530 ....0.5

13—TURN INDICATOR SWITCH, RENEW

Exc Below 0.6
1602, 2002 ....0.7
530 ....0.5

14—HAZARD FLASHER SWITCH, RENEW

Exc Below 0.3
1602, 2002 ....0.4

15—HAZARD FLASHER UNIT, RENEW

Exc Below 0.3
3.0 ....0.1

16—W/S WASHER PUMP, RENEW

All Models 0.2

IDENTIFICATION

1970-74..........53
1976..........54

ILLUSTRATIONS

FIG 1 — ENGINE — 2300cc INTERNAL PARTS (UPPER)
FIG 2 — ENGINE — 2300cc INTERNAL PARTS (LOWER)
FIG 3 — ENGINE — 2300cc EXTERNAL PARTS
FIG 4 — ENGINE — 2800cc
FIG 5 — TRANSMISSION
FIG 6 — FRONT SUSPENSION
FIG 7 — STEERING LINKAGE
FIG 8 — REAR AXLE

OPERATION TIMES

A

Air Pump.......... 61
Alternator.......... 61
Automatic Transmission.......... 63
Axle Shaft.......... 65

B

Brake Drums.......... 64
Brakes.......... 64

C

Cables (Ignition).......... 61
Calipers.......... 64
Camshaft.......... 63
Carburetor.......... 61
Catalytic Converter.......... 61
Clutch.......... 63
Coil, Ignition.......... 61
Compression Test.......... 61
Connecting Rods.......... 63
Cooling System.......... 62
Crankshaft.......... 63
Cylinder Block.......... 62
Cylinder Head.......... 62

D

Dash Gauges.......... 65
Differential.......... 65
Disc Brakes.......... 64
Distributor.......... 61

E

Emission Controls.......... 61
Engine Assembly.......... 62
Engine Mountings.......... 63
Engine Oiling.......... 62
Engine Tune-Up.......... 61
Exhaust Gas Recirculation.......... 61
Exhaust System.......... 61

F

Flywheel.......... 63
Front Suspension.......... 64
Fuel Gauges.......... 65
Fuel Pump.......... 61
Fuel Tank.......... 61

H

Hand Brake.......... 64
Headlight Switch.......... 65
Heater Core.......... 62
Hose (Brake).......... 64
Hose (Radiator).......... 62
Hydraulic Brakes.......... 64

I

Ignition.......... 61
Ignition Coil.......... 61
Ignition Switch.......... 61
Intake Manifold.......... 61

L

Light Switches.......... 65

M

Main Bearings.......... 63
Master Cyliner.......... 64
Muffler.......... 61

O

Oil Gauge.......... 65
Oiling, Engine.......... 62
Oil Pan.......... 62
Oil Pump.......... 63

P

Parking Brake.......... 64
Piston Rings.......... 63
Pistons.......... 63
Power Brake.......... 64
Power Steering.......... 64

R

Radiator.......... 62
Radiator Hose.......... 62
Rear Axle.......... 65
Regulator (Alternator).......... 61
Resonator.......... 61
Rocker Arms.......... 62
Rod Bearings.......... 63

S

Shocks (Front).......... 64
Shocks (Rear).......... 64
Speedometer.......... 65
Springs (Front).......... 64
Springs (Rear).......... 64
Starting Motor.......... 61
Steering Gear.......... 64
Steering Linkage.......... 64
Switches (Light).......... 65
Synchro-Mesh Trans.......... 63

T

Tachometer.......... 65
Temperature Gauge.......... 65
Thermostat.......... 62
Timing Case Cover.......... 62
Timing Chain.......... 62
Timing Gears.......... 62
Track Bar.......... 64
Transmission, Manual.......... 63
Transmission, Automatic.......... 63
Tune-Up,Engine.......... 61

U

Universals.......... 65

V

Vacuum Control Unit.......... 61
Valve Lifters.......... 62
Valve System.......... 62

W

Water Pump.......... 62
Wheel Cylinders.......... 64
Windshield Wiper.......... 65

IDENTIFICATION PLATE – 1970-74

LOCATION – On right hand fender apron or left hand windshield pillar.

WARRANTY PLATE

Ford

FORD-WERKE AG KÖLN
WESTERN GERMANY

Typ/Type	Version	Fahrgestell/Vehicle No.
ECL		GAECKU 78175

Zul. Gesamtgew. Gross Vehicle Wgt.	Zul. Achslast vorn Perm. Axle Ld. Front	Zul. Achslast hinten Perm. Axle Ld. Rear
Kg	Kg	Kg

Lenk Drive	Motor Engine	Getr. Trans.	Achse Axle	Farbe Colour	Polst Trim	K.D. Ref.	Bremsen Brakes
1	NB	7	Q	6A	KE		

LOCATION – On right hand fender apron in the engine compartment.

TYPE – ECL

First 2 letters indicate body code.
- EC – 2-Door Sedan

Third letter indicates Model year.
- K – 1970
- L – 1971
- M – 1972
- N – 1973
- P – 1974

VEHICLE NUMBER – GAECKU 78175

First letter indicates Country of Origin.
- G – Germany

Second letter indicates assembly plant.
- A – Cologne
- B – Genk

Third & fourth letters indicate Body Type.
- EC – 2-Door Sedan

Fifth letter indicates Model Year.
- K – 1970
- L – 1971
- M – 1972
- N – 1973
- P – 1974

Sixth letter indicates Month Code.

	1970	1971	1972	1973	1974
January	L	C	B	J	L
February	Y	K	R	U	Y
March	S	D	A	M	S
April	T	E	G	P	T
May	J	L	C	B	J
June	U	Y	K	R	U
July	M	S	D	A	M
August	P	T	E	G	P
September	B	J	L	C	B
October	R	U	Y	K	R
November	A	M	S	D	A
December	G	P	T	E	G

Last 5 digits indicate sequence code.

DRIVE
- 1 – Left Hand Drive
- 2 – Right Hand Drive

ENGINE
- LI – 98 C.I.D. (1600 CC or 1.6 Litre)
- NB – 122 C.I.D (2000CC or 2.0 Litre)
- UX – 159 C.I.D (2600cc or 2.6 Litre)

TRANSMISSION
- 5 – Manual – Floor Shift
- 7 – Automatic – Floor Shift
- C – Automatic – C4

AXLE RATIO CODE
- Q – 3.44 to 1
- V – 3.89 to 1
- B – 3.75 to 1
- C – 3.89 to 1
- R – 3.22 to 1
- S – 3.44 to 1

COLOR CODE
Single digit indicates solid color.
Two digits solid color with vinyl roof.

TRIM
First digit indicates color.
Second digit indicates type of fabric.

IDENTIFICATION PLATE – 1976

LOCATION – On right hand fender apron or left hand windshield pillar.

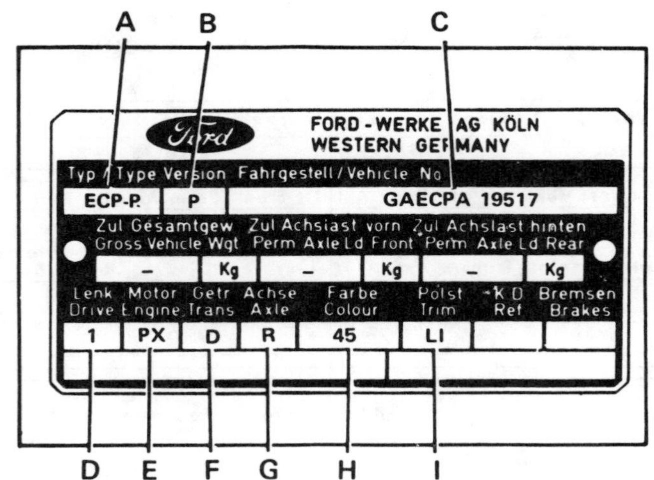

A – BODY TYPE
ECP – Three Door Hatchback

B – VERSION
D – Standard
P – Decor Option
S – S Model
T – Ghia

C – VEHICLE NUMBER (GAECPA19517)
First letter indicates country of origin
G – Germany
Second letter indicates assembly plant
A – Cologne
Third & fourth letters indicate model
EC – Capri
Fifth letter indicates calendar year built
P – 1974
R – 1975
S – 1976
Sixth letter indicates month built

	1974	1975	1976
January		C	B
February		K	R
March		D	A
April		E	G
May		L	C
June		Y	K
July		S	D
August		T	E
September		J	L
October		U	Y
November	A	M	S
December	G	P	T

Last five digits indicate sequence number

D – DRIVE CODE
1 – Left Hand Drive

E – ENGINE CODE
YA – 2300 O.H.C.
PX – 2800 V6

F – TRANSMISSION CODE
B – 4 Speed Manual
D – 3 Speed Automatic

G – REAR AXLE CODE
L – 3.09:1
R – 3.22:1
S – 3.44:1

H – PAINT CODE
A6 – Black
B5 – White
B6 – White
J5 – Orange
L6 – Bright Orange
O5 – Dark Red
O6 – Dark Red
S6 – Brown Metallic
T5 – Yellow
T6 – Yellow
U6 – Silver Metallic
15 – Medium Blue Metallic
16 – Medium Blue Metallic
35 – Silver Metallic
45 – Bronze Metallic
55 – Light Green Metallic
56 – Light Green Metallic

I – TRIM CODE
AA – Black Vinyl
AI – Black Cloth
KA – Light Tan Vinyl
KI – Light Tan Cloth
LA – Saddle Vinyl
LI – Saddle Cloth

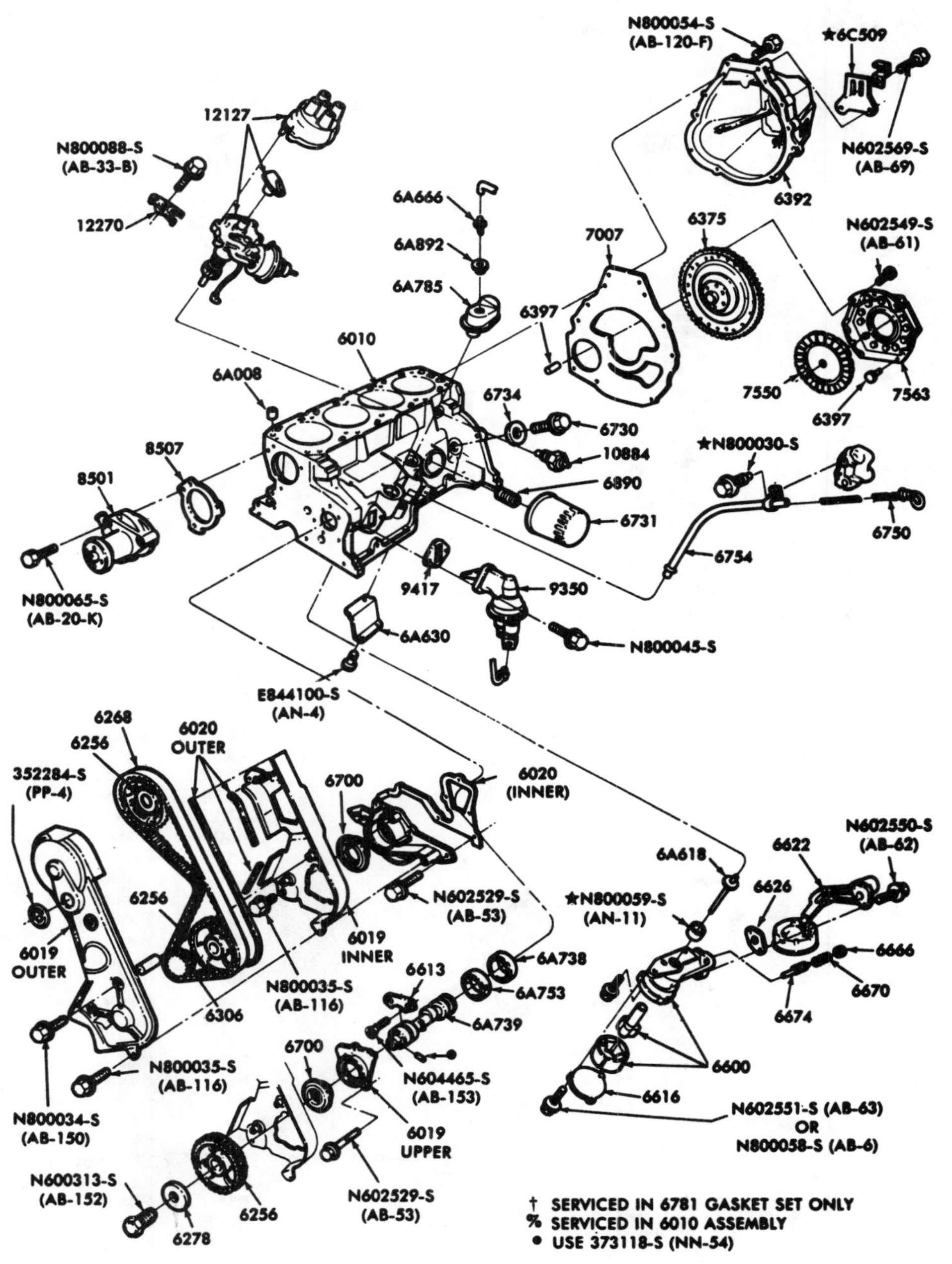

6A008	Dowel
6010	Block
6019	Cover
6020	Gasket
6256	Sprocket
6268	Chain
6278	Washer
6306	Sprocket
6375	Flywheel
6392	Housing
6397	Dowel
6600	Pump
6613	Plate
6616	Plate
6A618	Shaft
6622	Screen & Tube
6626	Gasket
6A630	Baffle
6666	Plug
6A666	Valve
6670	Spring
6674	Plunger
6700	Seal
6730	Plug
6731	Element
6734	Gasket
6A738	Bearing
6A739	Shaft
6750	Indicator
6A753	Bearing
6754	Tube
6A785	Separator
6890	Insert
6A892	Retainer
7007	Retainer
7550	Plate
7563	Plate
8501	Pump
8507	Gasket
9350	Pump
9417	Gasket
10884	Sender
12127	Distributor
12270	Clamp

FIG 1 – ENGINE – 2300CC INTERNAL PARTS (UPPER)

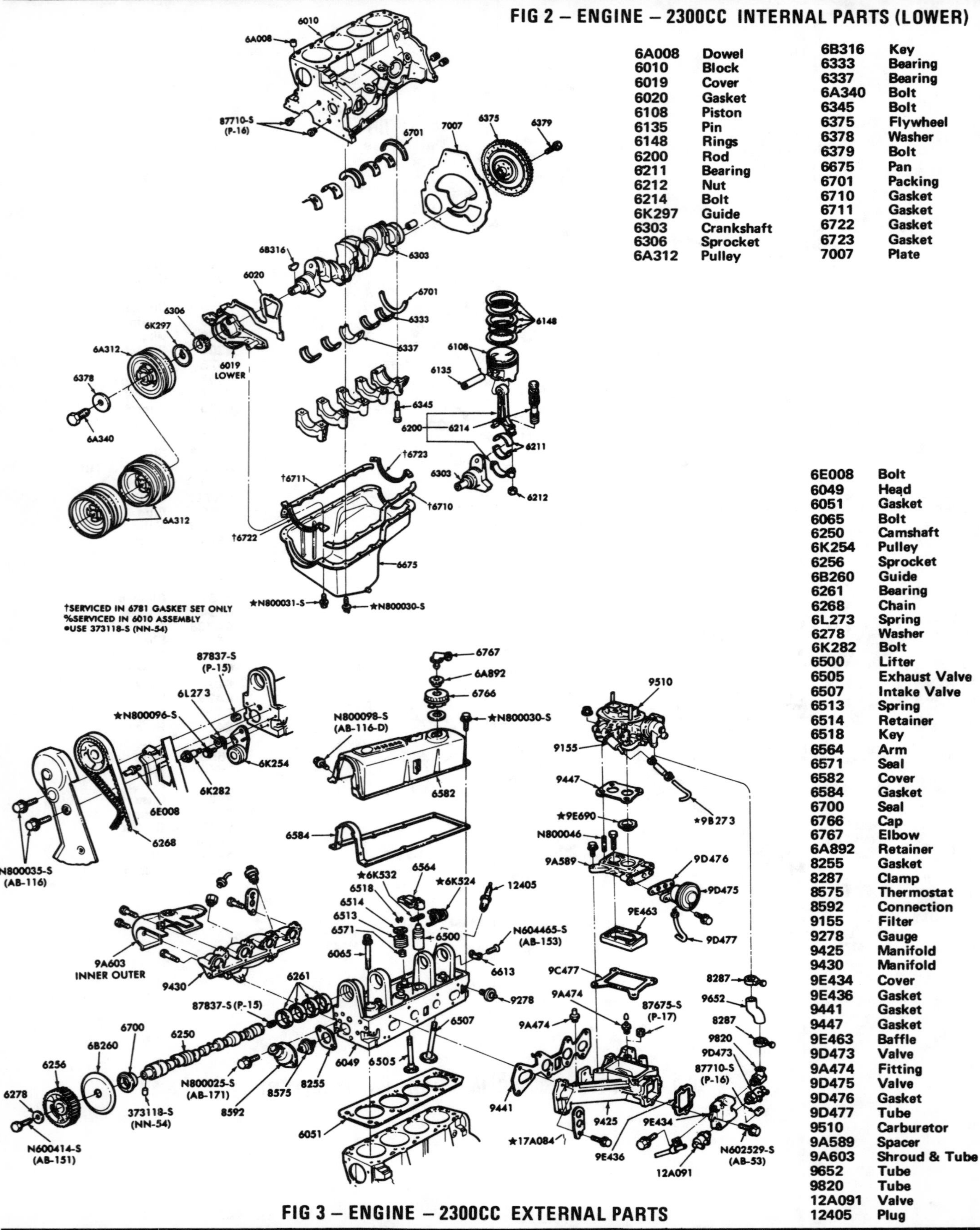

FIG 2 – ENGINE – 2300CC INTERNAL PARTS (LOWER)

6A008	Dowel	6B316	Key
6010	Block	6333	Bearing
6019	Cover	6337	Bearing
6020	Gasket	6A340	Bolt
6108	Piston	6345	Bolt
6135	Pin	6375	Flywheel
6148	Rings	6378	Washer
6200	Rod	6379	Bolt
6211	Bearing	6675	Pan
6212	Nut	6701	Packing
6214	Bolt	6710	Gasket
6K297	Guide	6711	Gasket
6303	Crankshaft	6722	Gasket
6306	Sprocket	6723	Gasket
6A312	Pulley	7007	Plate

6E008	Bolt
6049	Head
6051	Gasket
6065	Bolt
6250	Camshaft
6K254	Pulley
6256	Sprocket
6B260	Guide
6261	Bearing
6268	Chain
6L273	Spring
6278	Washer
6K282	Bolt
6500	Lifter
6505	Exhaust Valve
6507	Intake Valve
6513	Spring
6514	Retainer
6518	Key
6564	Arm
6571	Seal
6582	Cover
6584	Gasket
6700	Seal
6766	Cap
6767	Elbow
6A892	Retainer
8255	Gasket
8287	Clamp
8575	Thermostat
8592	Connection
9155	Filter
9278	Gauge
9425	Manifold
9430	Manifold
9E434	Cover
9E436	Gasket
9441	Gasket
9447	Gasket
9E463	Baffle
9D473	Valve
9A474	Fitting
9D475	Valve
9D476	Gasket
9D477	Tube
9510	Carburetor
9A589	Spacer
9A603	Shroud & Tube
9652	Tube
9820	Tube
12A091	Valve
12405	Plug

FIG 3 – ENGINE – 2300CC EXTERNAL PARTS

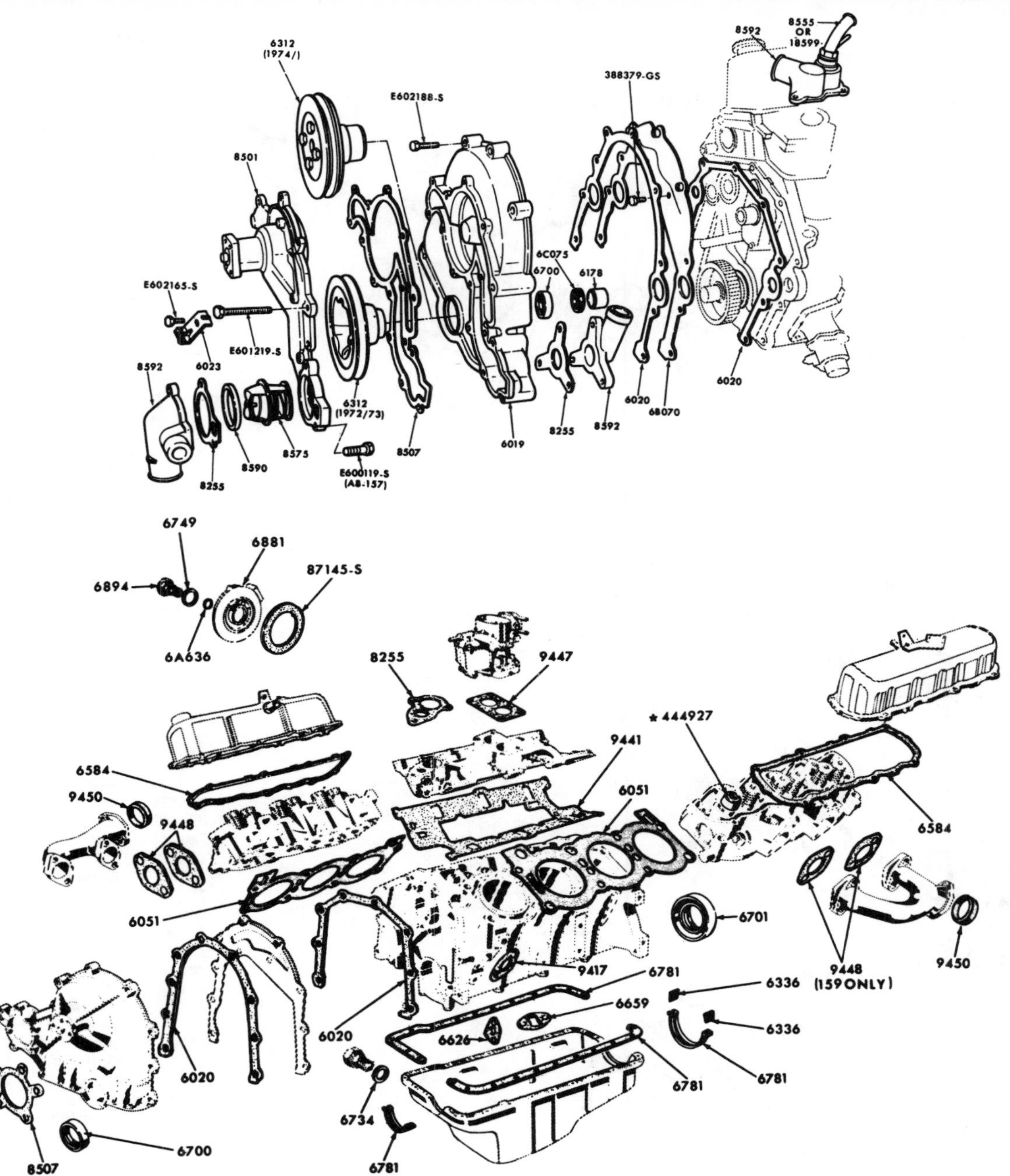

FIG 4 – ENGINE – 2800CC

6019	Cover	6749	Seal
6020	Gasket	6781	Gasket
6023	Pointer	6881	Adapter
6051	Gasket	6894	Bolt
6B070	Plate	8255	Gasket
6C075	Seal	8501	Pump
6178	Connection	8507	Gasket
6312	Pulley	8555	Tube
6336	Seal	8575	Thermostat
6584	Gasket	8590	Gasket
6626	Gasket	8592	Connection
6A636	Gasket	9417	Gasket
6659	Gasket	9441	Gasket
6700	Seal	9447	Gasket
6701	Packing	9448	Gasket
6734	Gasket	9450	Gasket

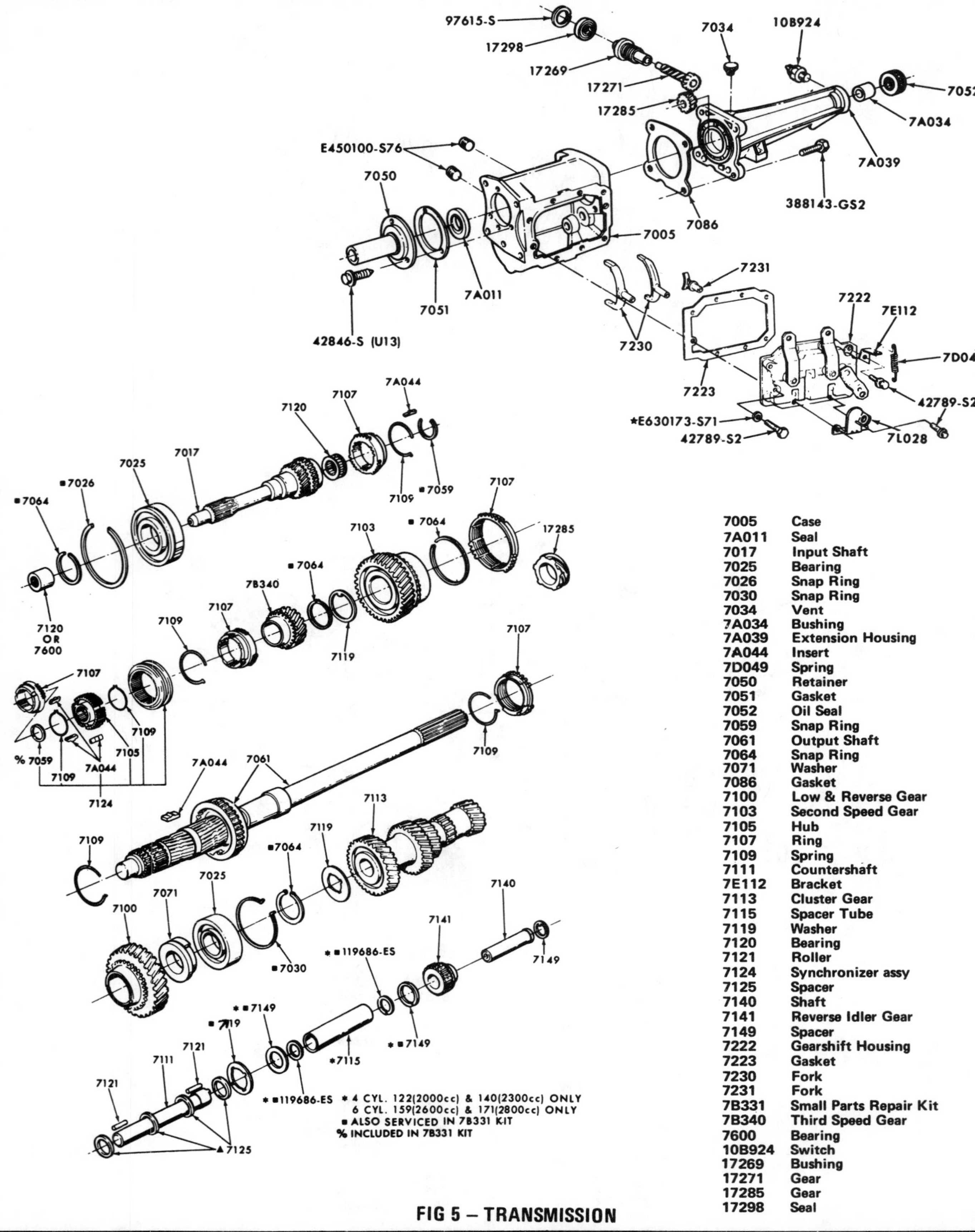

7005	Case
7A011	Seal
7017	Input Shaft
7025	Bearing
7026	Snap Ring
7030	Snap Ring
7034	Vent
7A034	Bushing
7A039	Extension Housing
7A044	Insert
7D049	Spring
7050	Retainer
7051	Gasket
7052	Oil Seal
7059	Snap Ring
7061	Output Shaft
7064	Snap Ring
7071	Washer
7086	Gasket
7100	Low & Reverse Gear
7103	Second Speed Gear
7105	Hub
7107	Ring
7109	Spring
7111	Countershaft
7E112	Bracket
7113	Cluster Gear
7115	Spacer Tube
7119	Washer
7120	Bearing
7121	Roller
7124	Synchronizer assy
7125	Spacer
7140	Shaft
7141	Reverse Idler Gear
7149	Spacer
7222	Gearshift Housing
7223	Gasket
7230	Fork
7231	Fork
7B331	Small Parts Repair Kit
7B340	Third Speed Gear
7600	Bearing
10B924	Switch
17269	Bushing
17271	Gear
17285	Gear
17298	Seal

FIG 5 – TRANSMISSION

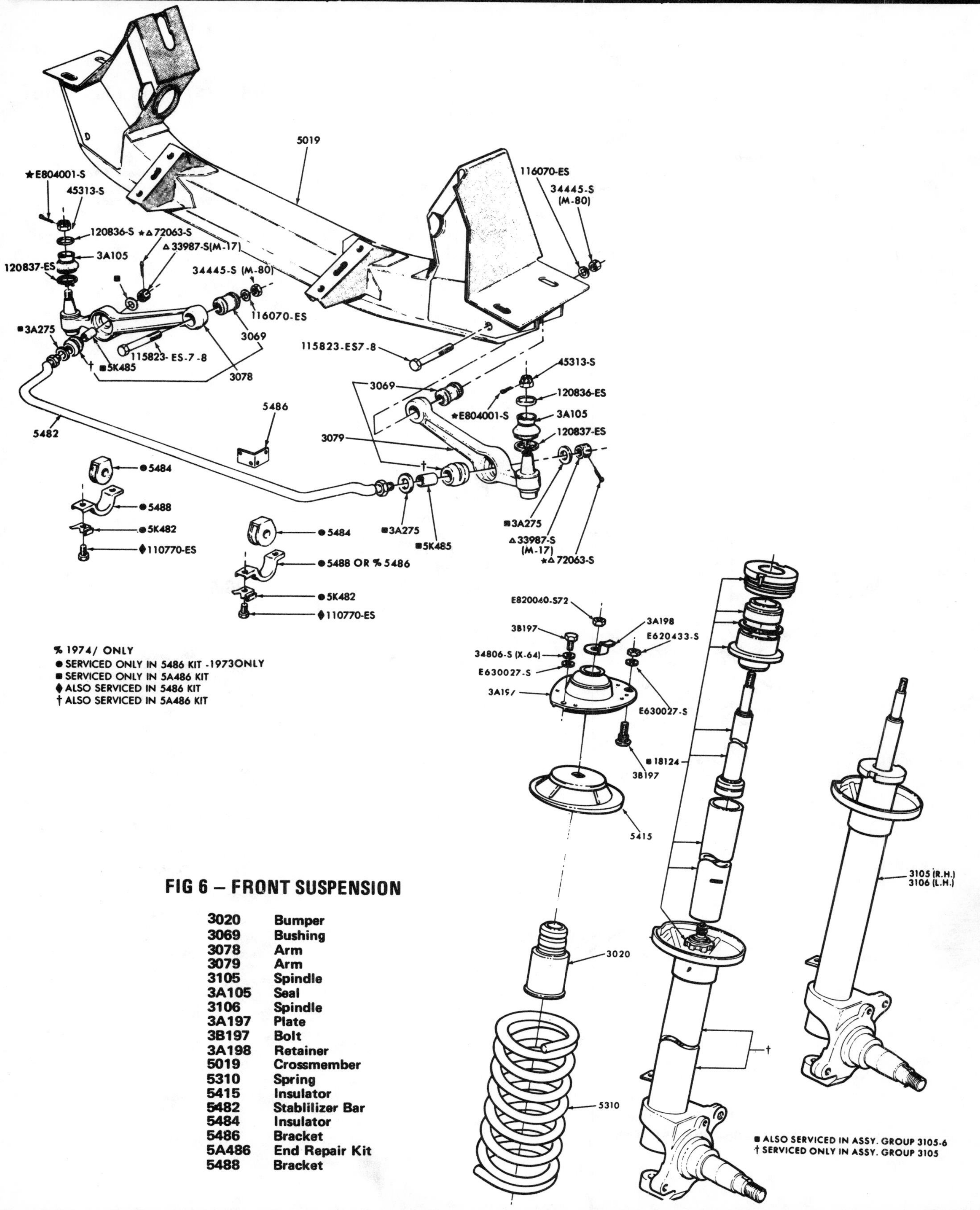

FIG 6 – FRONT SUSPENSION

3020	Bumper
3069	Bushing
3078	Arm
3079	Arm
3105	Spindle
3A105	Seal
3106	Spindle
3A197	Plate
3B197	Bolt
3A198	Retainer
5019	Crossmember
5310	Spring
5415	Insulator
5482	Stablilizer Bar
5484	Insulator
5486	Bracket
5A486	End Repair Kit
5488	Bracket

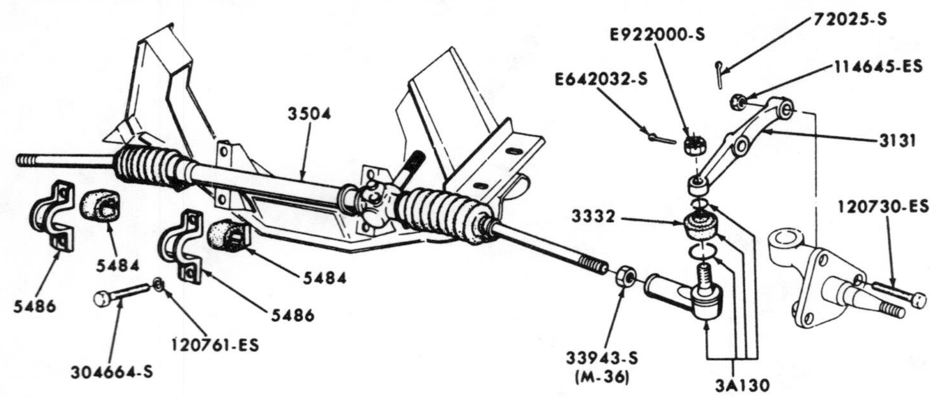

FIG 7 – STEERING LINKAGE

3A130	End
3131	Arm
3332	Seal
3504	Gear Assy
5484	Insulator
5486	Bracket

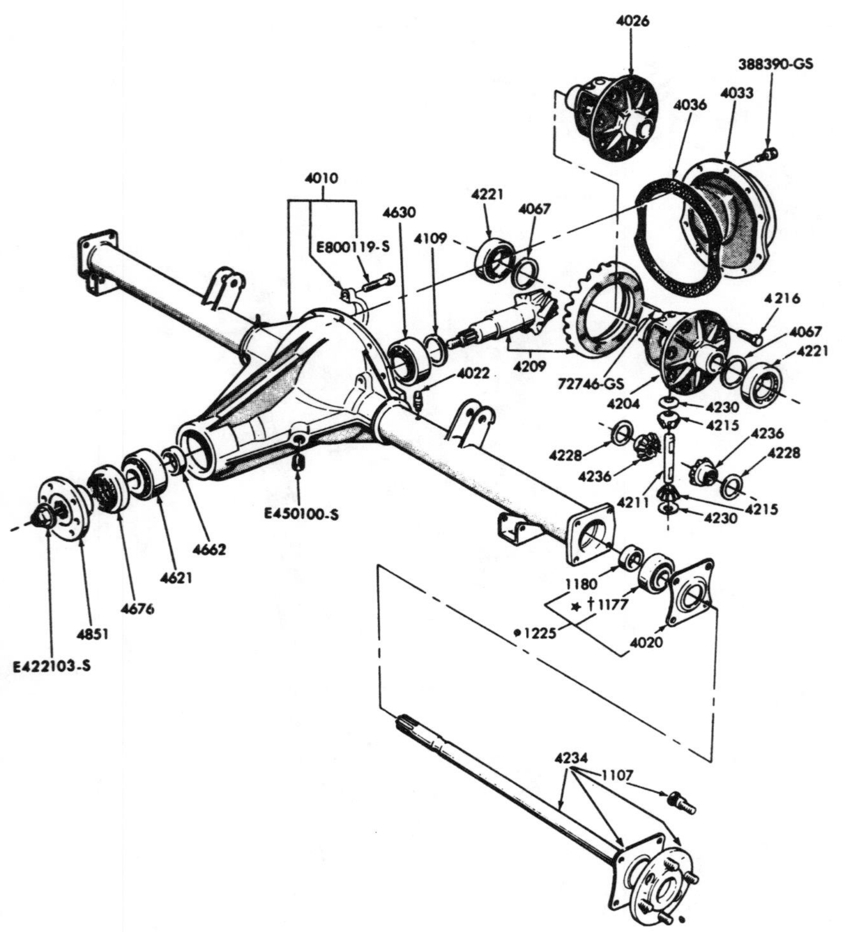

† SERVICE ONLY IN 1225 KIT

• ALSO INCLUDED ON 4234 AXLE SHAFT

FIG 8 – REAR AXLE

1107	Bolt
1177	Seal
1180	Retainer
1225	Bearing
4010	Housing
4020	Retainer
4022	Vent
4026	Differential Assy
4033	Cover
4036	Gasket
4067	Adjuster
4109	Shim
4204	Case
4209	Ring Gear & Pinion
4211	Pinion Shaft
4215	Pinion Kit
4216	Bolt
4221	Bearing
4228	Washer
4230	Washer
4234	Axle Shaft
4236	Side Gear
4621	Bearing
4630	Bearing
4662	Spacer
4676	Seal
4851	Flange

Ignition, Starting & Charging—TIME

OPERATION INDEX

Tune-Up, Minor 1
Tune-Up, Major 2
Compression Test 3
Distributor, R & R Or Renew 4
Distributor, R & R & Overhaul 5
Distributor Cap, Renew 6
Ignition Cable Set, Renew 7
Vacuum Control Unit, Renew 8
Ignition Coil, Renew 9
Starter & Ignition Switch, Renew 10
Starter, R & R Or Renew 11
Starter Solenoid, Renew 12
Starter Bendix Drive, Renew 13
Starter, R & R & Overhaul 14
Starter Brushes, Renew 15
Starter Armature, Renew 16
Alternator Regulator, Renew 17
Alternator, R & R Or Renew 18
Alternator, R & R & Overhaul 19
Alternator Diodes, Renew 20
Alternator Bearings, Renew 21
Alternator Brushes, Renew 22
Alternator Pulley, Renew 23

1—TUNE-UP, MINOR
Includes: Renew points, condenser & plugs. Set timing and adjust carburetor idle.
1971-74 ..... 1.2

2—TUNE-UP, MAJOR
Includes: Check compression, clean or renew and adjust spark plugs. R & R distributor, renew points and condenser. Adjust ignition timing, carburetor and fan belts. Clean battery terminals and service air cleaner. Check coil & clean or replace fuel filter.
1971-78 ..... 2.7

3—COMPRESSION TEST
1971-74 ..... 0.3
1975-78 ..... 0.4

4—DISTRIBUTOR, R & R OR RENEW
1971-78, Exc 0.4
2600cc 0.5

—NOTE—
For Stroboscope Adjustment, Add *0.3*

5—DISTRIBUTOR, OVERHAUL
1971-74 ..... 1.2

6—DISTRIBUTOR CAP, RENEW
1971-78 ..... 0.3

7—IGNITION CABLE SET, RENEW
1971-78—
One 0.3
All 0.4

8—VACUUM CONTROL UNIT, RENEW
1971-78, Exc 0.7
2600cc 0.8

9—IGNITION COIL, RENEW
1971-78 ..... 0.4

10—STARTER & IGNITION SWITCH, RENEW
1971-74 ..... 0.4
1976-78 ..... 0.5

11—STARTER, R & R OR RENEW
1971-78 ..... 0.4

12—STARTER SOLENOID, RENEW
1971-78 ..... 0.5

13—STARTER BENDIX DRIVE, RENEW
1971-78, Exc 0.9
2600cc 0.6

14—STARTER, R & R & OVERHAUL
Includes: Turn down commutator and replace all parts necessary.
1971-78, Exc 1.6
2600cc 1.3

15—STARTER BRUSHES, RENEW
1971-78, Exc 1.2
2600cc 1.0

16—STARTER ARMATURE, RENEW
1971-78, Exc 1.1
2600cc 0.8

17—ALTERNATOR REGULATOR, RENEW
1971-74, Exc 0.7
2600cc 0.3
1976-78 ..... 0.3

18—ALTERNATOR, R & R OR RENEW
1971-78, Exc 0.5
2600 & 2800cc—
1972 ..... 0.6
1973-78 ..... 1.3

19—ALTERNATOR, R & R & OVERHAUL
1971-78, Exc 1.1
2600 & 2800cc—
1972 ..... 1.2
1973-78 ..... 1.9

20—ALTERNATOR DIODES, RENEW
1971-78, Exc 0.8
2600 & 2800cc—
1972 ..... 0.9
1973-78 ..... 1.6

21—ALTERNATOR BEARINGS, RENEW
1971-78, Exc 0.9
2600, 1972 ..... 0.9
2600, 1973 ..... 1.6
2800 ..... 1.6

22—ALTERNATOR BRUSHES, RENEW
1971-78, Exc 0.8
2600, 1972 ..... 0.8
2600, 1973 ..... 1.5
2800 ..... 1.6

23—ALTERNATOR PULLEY, RENEW
1971-78, Exc 0.6
2600 & 2800—
1972 ..... 0.7
1973-78 ..... 1.4

Fuel, Intake & Exhaust System—TIME

OPERATION INDEX

Carburetor Or Flange Gasket, Renew 1
Carburetor, R & R & Overhaul 2
Fuel Pump, R & R Or Renew 3
Fuel Tank, R & R Or Renew 4
Thermostatic Choke, Renew 5
Intake Manifold Or Gasket, Renew 6
Air Pump (Thermactor), Renew 7
Exhaust Gas Recirculaton Valve, Renew 8
Exhaust Manifold, Renew 9
Inlet Pipe, Renew 10
Muffler, Renew 11
Catalytic Converter, Renew 12
Resonator, Renew 13

1—CARBURETOR OR FLANGE GASKET, RENEW
1600cc 0.6
2000 & 2300cc 0.6
2600 & 2800, 72-74 ..... 0.7
2800, 1976-78 ..... 0.6

2—CARBURETOR, R & R & OVERHAUL
1971-78, Exc 1.2
2800cc 1.7

3—FUEL PUMP, R & R OR RENEW
1971-78, Exc 0.3
2300 ..... 0.5
2600 ..... 0.4
2800 ..... 0.6

4—FUEL TANK, R & R OR RENEW
1971-78 ..... 1.0

—NOTE—
To Renew, Add *0.2*

5—THERMOSTATIC CHOKE, RENEW
1971-78, Exc 0.7
2000cc 0.8
2300cc 0.8
2800cc, 74 ..... 0.8
2800cc, 76-78 ..... 0.4

6—INTAKE MANIFOLD OR GASKET, RENEW
1971-78—
1600cc 0.7
2000 & 2300cc 1.0
2600cc 1.9
2800cc, 74 ..... 1.9
2800cc, 76-78 ..... 2.0

7—AIR PUMP (THERMACTOR), RENEW
1976-78—
2300cc 0.4
2800cc 0.7

8—EXHAUST GAS RECIRCULATION VALVE, RENEW
1973-78 ..... 0.3

9—EXHAUST MANIFOLD, RENEW
1971-78—
1600cc 0.5
2000cc 0.6
2300cc 0.8
2600cc, Left 0.6
Right 0.5
Both 0.9
2800cc, Left 0.9
Right 0.8
Both 1.5

10—INLET PIPE, RENEW
1600 & 2000cc 0.6
2600 & 2800cc—
One 0.5
Both 0.8

11—MUFFLER, RENEW
1971-76, Exc 0.4
2600cc 0.6
2800cc, 1974—
One 0.4
Both 0.6
2800cc, 1976-78—
One 0.5
Both 0.7

12—CATALYTIC CONVERTER, RENEW
1976-78—
Single 0.5
Dual 0.8

13—RESONATOR, RENEW
1972—
One 0.7
Both 0.9
1973-74—
One 0.4
Both 0.6
1976—
One 0.5
Both 0.7
1977-78 ..... 0.5

Engine Cooling & Heater System—TIME

OPERATION INDEX

Radiator, R & R Or Renew *1*
Radiator Hoses, Renew *2*
Water Pump, R & R Or Renew *3*
Thermostat Or Housing, Renew *4*
Heater Core, Renew *5*
Heater Blower Motor, Renew *6*
Heater Control, Renew *7*
Heater Hoses, Renew *8*

1—RADIATOR, R & R OR RENEW
1971-78—
4 Cyl, Exc 0.5
1976-78 .... 0.7
6 Cyl 0.7

2—RADIATOR HOSES, RENEW
1971-78—
Upper 0.4
Lower—
1600cc 0.4
2000 & 2300cc 0.6
2600 & 2800cc 0.5

3—WATER PUMP, R & R OR RENEW
—NOTE—
With Thermactor, Add *0.1*
1971-78—
1600 & 2000cc 0.9
2300cc 1.2
2800cc 1.7

4—THERMOSTAT OR HOUSING, RENEW
1971-78—
1600cc 0.4
2000cc 0.5
2300cc 0.8
2600 & 2800cc 0.6

5—HEATER CORE, RENEW
1971-78, Exc 1.9
W/Air Cond 2.3

6—HEATER BLOWER, RENEW
1971-78, Exc 1.9
W/Center Console 2.2

7—HEATER CONTROL, RENEW
1971-78, Exc 0.4
W/Air Cond 0.7

8—HEATER HOSE, RENEW
1971-78 .... 0.4

Engine—TIME

OPERATION INDEX

Engine, R & R *1*
Engine, R & R & Overhaul *2*
Engine (Block), Renew & Grind Valves *3*
Cylinder Head, R & R Or Gasket, Renew *4*
Valves, Grind *5*
One Valve, Renew & Gring *6*
Valve Springs, Renew *7*
Rocker Arm Cover Gasket, Renew *8*
Push Rods, Renew *9*
Valve Rocker Arm Assy, Clean Or Overhaul *10*
Oil Pan Or Gasket, R & R Or Renew *11*
Valve Tappets, Adjust *12*
Timing Case Cover, Seal & Gasket, Renew *13*
Timing Chain Or Gears, Renew *14*
Timing Chain Tensioner, Renew *15*
Camshaft, R & R Or Renew *16*
Camshaft Bearings, Renew *17*
Oil Pump, R & R Or Renew *18*
Camshaft Rear Welch Plug, Renew *19*
Piston Ring(S), Renew *20*
Rings & Main Bearings, Renew & Grind Valves *21*
Rod Bearing(S), Renew *22*
Main Bearings, Renew *23*
Main & Rod Bearings, Renew *24*
Crankshaft, R & R Or Renew *25*
Crankshaft Rear Main Oil Seal, Renew *26*
Piston(S), Renew *27*
Connecting Rod(S), Renew *28*
Crankshaft Pulley, Renew *29*

1—ENGINE, R & R
Does not include transfer of any part of engine or replacement of special equipment.
1971-78—
1600cc 2.2
2000 & 2300cc, 71-74 Exc 2.4
W/Auto Trans 2.8
2000 & 2300cc, 76-78 .... 3.4
2600 & 2800cc—
1972-74 .... 3.4
1976-78 .... 3.6
—NOTE—
To Renew Engine, For Transfer Of All Parts Not Included With New Engine, Not Including Special Equipment, Add *2.0*

2—ENGINE, R & R & OVERHAUL
Includes rebore cylinders with boring bar, renew piston, rings, pins & all bearings, grind valves, plastigauge bearings and perform minor tune-up.
1971-78—
1600cc 13.4
2000cc, Exc 13.9
W/Auto Trans 14.4
2300cc, Exc 13.8
W/Auto Trans 14.3
2600cc 12.7
2800cc 13.1

3—CYLINDER BLOCK, RENEW
Includes transfer and clean all component parts without disassembly, replace rings and bearings, adjust clearances & timing.
1971-78—
1600cc 9.7
2000cc, Exc 9.3
W/Auto Trans 9.8
2300cc, Exc 9.5
W/Auto Trans 10.0
2600cc 7.7
2800cc 8.1
—NOTE—
With Thermactor, Add. *0.3*

4—CYLINDER HEAD, R & R OR GASKET, RENEW
Includes adjust tappets.
1971-74—
1600cc 1.8
2000 & 2300cc 2.6
2600 & 2800cc—
One 2.9
Both 3.7
1976-78—
2000 & 2300cc 3.8
2600 & 2800cc—
One 3.1
Both 3.9

5—VALVES, GRIND
Includes: R & R head & adjust tappets.
1971-74—
1600cc 3.8
2000cc 5.5
2300cc 5.2
2600 & 2800cc 6.7
1976-78—
2000cc 6.7
2300cc 6.4
2800cc 6.9

6—ONE VALVE, RENEW & GRIND
Includes: R & R head & adjust valves.
1971-74—
1600cc 2.2
2000cc 3.4
2300cc 3.6
2600 & 2800cc 3.2
1976-78—
2000cc 4.6
2300cc 4.8
2800cc 3.4

7—VALVE SPRINGS, RENEW
Includes: Replace valve stem oil seals & adjust tappets.
1971-78—
1600cc—
One 0.9
All 1.6
2000 & 2300cc—
One 1.0
All 1.8
2600 & 2800cc—
One 0.9
All 2.1

8—ROCKER ARM COVER GASKET, RENEW
1971-78—
1600cc 0.4
2000 & 2300cc, Exc 0.8
1976 .... 0.7
2600 & 2800cc, 72-74—
One 0.5
Both 0.8
2600 & 2800cc, 76-78—
One 0.6
Both 1.0

9—PUSH RODS, RENEW
Includes: Adjust tappets.
1971-78—
1600cc 0.7
2600 & 2800cc 1.2

10—VALVE ROCKER ARM ASSY, CLEAN OR OVERHAUL
1971-78—
1600cc 0.9
2600 & 2800cc—
One Side 1.0
Both Sides 1.4

11—OIL PAN OR GASKET, R & R OR RENEW
1971-78—
1600cc ①3.2
2000 & 2300cc—
Std Trans 1.9
Auto Trans 2.0
2600 & 2800cc 1.9
①*Includes R & R Engine.*

12—VALVE TAPPETS, ADJUST
1971-78—
1600cc 0.6
2000cc 1.2
2600 & 2800cc 1.1

13—TIMING CASE COVER SEAL & GASKET, RENEW
1971-76—
1600cc 1.6
2000 & 2300cc—
Gasket 2.9
Seal, 71-74 .... 1.2
Seal, 76-78 .... 1.8
2600 & 2800cc—
Gasket—
72-74 Std Trans 2.9
72-74 Auto Trans 3.1
76-78 .... 4.2
Seal (All) 1.4

14—TIMING CHAIN OR GEARS, RENEW
1971-78—
1600cc 1.9
2000 & 2300cc 3.2
2600 & 2800cc—
Std Trans 3.1
Auto Trans 3.3

15—TIMING CHAIN TENSIONER, RENEW
1971-78—
1600cc ①3.3
2000 & 2300cc—
Auto Trans 2.1
Std Trans 2.0
2600 & 2800cc 2.0
①*Includes R & R Engine.*

(Continued)

Engine—TIME Cont'd

16—CAMSHAFT, R & R OR RENEW
1971-78—
1600cc ①5.1
2000 & 2300cc 3.1
2600 & 2800cc—
Auto Trans 6.5
Std Trans 6.3
①*Includes R & R Engine.*

17—CAMSHAFT BEARINGS, RENEW
1971-78—
1600cc ①5.7
2000cc 3.4
2300cc 3.6
2600cc ①8.7
2800cc ①8.8
①*Includes R & R Engine.*

18—OIL PUMP, R & R OR RENEW
1971-78—
1600cc 0.5
2000 & 2300cc—
Std Trans 2.0
Auto Trans 2.1
2600 & 2800cc 2.0
—NOTE—
For Overhaul, Add 0.3

19—CAMSHAFT REAR WELCH PLUG, RENEW
1971-78—
1600cc 1.9
2000 & 2300cc 2.0
2600 & 2800cc—
1972 ....1.8
1974-78 ....1.9

20—PISTON RING(S), RENEW
1971-78—
1600cc—
One 4.7
All 6.2
2000 & 2300cc—
One 4.7
All 6.0
2600 & 2800cc—
One 4.9
All 8.4

21—RINGS & MAIN BEARINGS, RENEW & GRIND VALVES
1971-78—
1600cc 8.1
2000cc 8.9
2600 & 2800cc 10.7

22—ROD BEARING(S), RENEW
1971-78—
1600cc ①4.2
2000 & 2300cc—
Std Trans 2.9
Auto Trans 3.0
2600 & 2800cc 3.7
①*Includes R & R Engine.*

23—MAIN BEARINGS, RENEW
Includes: Plastigauge bearings.
1971-78—
1600cc ①5.1
2000cc—
Std Trans 5.3
Auto Trans 5.8
2300cc—
Std Trans 3.8
Auto Trans 3.9
2600 & 2800cc 5.7
①*Includes R & R Engine.*

24—MAIN & ROD BEARINGS, RENEW
Includes: Plastigauge bearings.
1971-78—
1600cc ①6.1
2000cc—
Std Trans 6.3
Auto Trans 6.8
2300cc—
Std Trans 4.8
Auto Trans 4.9
2600 & 2800cc 7.1
①*Includes R & R Engine.*

25—CRANKSHAFT, R & R OR RENEW
1971-78—
1600cc 6.1
2000 & 2300cc—
Std Trans 6.0
Auto Trans 6.5
2600cc 6.9
2800cc 7.2

26—CRANKSHAFT REAR MAIN OIL SEAL, RENEW
1971-78—
1600cc 3.7
2000cc—
Std Trans 2.0
Auto Trans 2.3
2300cc—
Std Trans 2.7
Auto Trans 2.8
2600 & 2800cc—
Std Trans 1.9
Auto Trans 2.5

27—PISTON(S), RENEW
1971-78—
1600cc—
One 4.7
All 6.2
2000 & 2300cc—
One 4.7
All 6.0
2600 & 2800cc—
One 4.9
All 8.4

28—CONNECTING ROD(S), RENEW
1971-78—
1600cc—
One 4.7
All 6.2
2000 & 2300cc—
One 4.7
All 6.0
2600 & 2800cc—
One 4.9
All 8.4

29—CRANKSHAFT PULLEY, RENEW
1971-78—
1600cc 0.4
2000 & 2300cc 0.3
2600 & 2800cc—
Std Trans 0.8
Auto Trans 1.0

Clutch, Mounts & Transmission—TIME

OPERATION INDEX

Flywheel, R & R Or Renew 1
Flywheel Ring Gear, Renew 2
Clutch Or Disc, Renew 3
Release Bearing, Renew 4
Pilot Bearing, Renew 5
Clutch Pedal, Adjust 6
Engine Front Mounts, Renew 7
Engine Rear Mount, Renew 7A
Transmission Assy, R & R Or Renew 8
Extension Housing Or Gasket, Renew 9
Extension Housing Oil Seal, Renew 10
Oil Pan Gasket, Renew 11
Rear Band, Adjust 12
Manual Trans, R & R & Overhaul 13
Bands, Front Or Rear, Adjust 14
Automatic Transmission, R & R And Renew 15
Automatic Transmission, R & R And Overhaul 16
Parking Pawl, Renew 17

1—FLYWHEEL, R & R OR RENEW
1971-78—
1600cc 1.7
2000 & 2300cc 1.8
2600 & 2800cc 1.7

2—FLYWHEEL RING GEAR, RENEW
1971-78—
1600cc 2.0
2000 & 2300cc 2.1
2600 & 2800cc 2.0

3—CLUTCH OR DISC, RENEW
1971-78—
1600cc 1.6
2000 & 2300cc 1.7
2600 & 2800cc 1.6

4—RELEASE BEARING, RENEW
1971-78—
Except 1.4
2000 & 2300cc 1.5

5—PILOT BEARING, RENEW
1971-78—
Except 1.6
2000 & 2300cc 1.7

6—CLUTCH PEDAL, ADJUST
1971-78 ....0.4

7—ENGINE FRONT MOUNTS,RENEW
1971-76—
Except Below—
One 0.3
Both 0.5
2600 & 2800cc, 72-74—
One 0.7
Both 0.8
2600 & 2800cc, 76-78—
One Or Both 1.3

7A—ENGINE REAR MOUNT, RENEW
1971-74 ....0.5
1976-78 ....0.4

8—MANUAL TRANSMISSION, R & R OR RENEW
1971-78—
Except 1.4
2000 & 2300cc 1.5

9—EXTENSION HOUSING OR GASKET, RENEW
1971-78—
2000cc 0.8
All Others—
C4 Trans 1.0
C3 Trans 0.9

10—EXTENSION OIL SEAL, RENEW
1971-78—
Auto Trans 0.6
Std Trans 0.5

11—OIL PAN GASKET, RENEW
1971-78 ....0.6

12—REAR BAND, ADJUST
1971-78 ....0.5

13—MANUAL TRANS, R & R & OVERHAUL
1971-78—
1600cc 3.1
2000 & 2300cc 3.2
2600 & 2800cc 3.1
—NOTE—
For GT, Add 0.3

14—BANDS, FRONT OR REAR, ADJUST
1971-78—
Front 0.7
Rear 0.6
Both 1.1

15—AUTOMATIC TRANSMISSION, R & R OR RENEW
1971-74—
2000 & 2300cc 2.4
2600 & 2800cc 2.9
1976-78—
2000 & 2300cc 2.1
2600 & 2800cc 2.2

(Continued)

Clutch, Mounts & Transmission—TIME Cont'd

16—AUTOMATIC TRANSMISSION, R & R & OVERHAUL
1971-74—
2000 & 2300cc 6.7
2600 & 2800cc 7.1
1976-78—
2000 & 2300cc 6.1
2600 & 2800cc 6.2

17—PARKING PAWL, RENEW
1971-74—
2000 & 2300cc 3.0
2600 & 2800cc 3.5
1976-78—
2000 & 2300cc 2.7
2600 & 2800cc 2.8

Brakes, Steering, Suspension, Universal & Rear Axle—TIME

OPERATION INDEX

Brake Shoes Or Friction Pads, Renew 1
Master Cylinder, Renew 2
Master Cylinder, R & R & Overhaul 3
Wheel Cylinders, Renew 4
Wheel Cylinders, R & R & Overhaul 5
Caliper Assy, Renew 6
Caliper Assy, R & R & Overhaul 7
Disc Rotor, Renew 7A
Disc Rotor, Reface 7B
Bleed System 8
Brake Hose, Renew 9
Hub, Disc Or Shield, Renew 10
Power Brake Unit, Renew 11
Power Brake Check Valve, Renew 12
Brake Drum, Renew 13
Brake Proportioning Valve, Renew 14
Parking Brake Cable, Renew 15
Parking Brake Lever, Renew 16
Steering Gear Assy, Renew 17
Steering Gear Assy, R & R & Overhaul 18
Steering Rod Or End, Renew 19
Power Steering Pump, Renew 20
Power Strg Pump, Overhaul 21
Power Steering Reservoir Seal, Renew 22
Power Steering Pump Shaft Seal, Renew 23
Power Steering Pump Flow & Pressure Test 24
Power Steering Pump Hose, Renew 25
Spring(S), Renew 26
Track Bar Assy, Renew 27
Front Hub Bearings, Renew 28
Stabilizer End Bushings, Renew 29
Shock Absorbers, Renew 30
Wheel Alignment 30A
Toe-In, Check & Adjust 30B
Front Suspension Lower Arm, Renew 31
Front Suspension Lower Arm Bushing(S), Renew 32
Axle Housing & Differential Assy, Renew 33
Universal Joints, Renew 34
Rear Axle Housing, Renew 35
Rear Axle Housing Cover Or Gasket, Renew 36
Axle Shaft, Renew 37
Axle Shaft Bearings, Renew 38
Differential Assy, Overhaul 39
Axle Drive Pinion Oil Seal, Renew 40

1—BRAKE SHOES OR FRICTION PADS, RENEW
1971-78—
Front Disc 0.7
Rear Drum 0.9

2—MASTER CYLINDER, RENEW
Includes: Bleed system.
1971-78—
Exc Below 0.6
2600cc 0.5

3—MASTER CYLINDER, R & R & OVERHAUL
Includes: Bleed system.
1971-78 ....0.8

4—WHEEL CYLINDER, RENEW
Includes: Bleed system and adjust brakes.
1971-78—
One 1.3
Both 1.4

5—WHEEL CYLINDER, R & R & OVERHAUL
Includes: Bleed system and adjust brakes.
1971-78—
One 1.4
Both 1.6

6—CALIPER ASSY, RENEW
Includes: Bleed system.
1971-78—
One 0.7
Both 0.9

7—CALIPER ASSY, R & R & OVERHAUL
Includes: Bleed system.
1971-78—
One 1.2
Both 1.5

7A—DISC ROTOR, RENEW
1971-78—
One 0.7
Both 1.0

7B—DISC ROTOR, REFACE
1971-78, Both 1.8

8—BLEED SYSTEM
1971-78 ....0.3

9—BRAKE HOSE, RENEW
Includes: Bleed system
1971-78—
Front, One 0.6
Front, Both 0.7
Rear 0.5

10—HUB, DISC OR SHIELD, RENEW
Includes: Bleed brakes.
One 0.4
Both 0.7

11—POWER BRAKE UNIT, RENEW
1971-78—
2000cc 0.9
2300cc 0.7
2600 & 2800cc—
1972-73 ....0.7
1974-78 ....0.6

12—POWER BRAKE CHECK VALVE, RENEW
1971-78 ....0.3

13—BRAKE DRUM, RENEW
Includes: Adjust brakes.
1971-78 ....0.4

14—BRAKE PROPORTIONING VALVE, RENEW
Includes: Bleed system.
1971-78—
Except 0.6
2600cc 0.8

15—PARKING BRAKE CABLE, RENEW
1971-78 ....0.3

16—PARKING BRAKE LEVER, RENEW
1971-74 ....0.7
1976-78 ....0.8

17—STEERING GEAR ASSY, RENEW
Note: Does not include transfer tie rod ends or correct toe-in.
1971-74 ....0.8
1976-78 ....0.6

18—STEERING GEAR ASSY, R & R & OVERHAUL
1971-74 ....1.8
1976-78 ....2.2

19—STEERING ROD OR END, RENEW
Includes: Check & correct toe-in.
1971-76—
One 1.0
Both 1.1

20—POWER STEERING PUMP, RENEW
1976-78, 2300cc 0.6
2800cc, Less Air Cond 0.9
2800cc, With Air Cond 1.0

21—POWER STEERING PUMP, OVERHAUL
1976-78, 2300cc 1.2
2800cc, Less Air Cond 1.5
2800cc With Air Cond 1.6

22—POWER STEERING RESERVOIR SEAL, RENEW
1976-78 ....0.9

23—POWER STEERING PUMP SHAFT SEAL, RENEW
1976-78 ....0.7

24—POWER STEERING PUMP FLOW & PRESSURE TEST
Note: Use only with overhaul.
1976-78 ....0.4

25—POWER STEERING PUMP HOSE, RENEW
1976-78 ....0.4
Return 0.5
Cooling 0.4
Filler 0.5

26—SPRING(S), RENEW
1971-78—
Front—
One 1.0
Both 1.5
Rear—
One 0.5
Both 0.8

27—TRACK BAR ASSY, RENEW
1971-78 ....0.3

28—FRONT HUB BEARINGS, RENEW
1971-78 ....1.0

29—STABILIZER END BUSHINGS, RENEW
1971-78 ....0.8

30—SHOCK ABSORBERS, RENEW
Front—
1971-78—
One 0.4
Both 0.6
Rear—
1971-74—
One 0.4
Both 0.6
1976-78 Less Access Port—
One 0.7
Both 1.0
1976-78 With Access Port—
One 0.4
Both 0.6

30A—WHEEL ALIGNMENT
1971-78 ....1.1

30B—TOE-IN, CHECK & ADJUST
1971-78 ....0.5

31—FRONT SUSPENSION LOWER ARM, RENEW
1971-78—
One 1.0
Both 1.3

32—FRONT SUSPENSION LOWER ARM BUSHINGS, RENEW
1971-78—
One 0.6
Both 0.9

(Continued)

Brakes, Steering, Suspension, Universal & Rear Axle—TIME Cont'd

33—AXLE HOUSING & DIFFERENTIAL ASSY, RENEW
1971-78 .... 1.9

34—UNIVERSAL JOINTS, RENEW
Front—
1971-74 .... 1.3
1976-78 .... 1.2
Rear Center—
1971-74 .... 1.4
1976-78 .... 1.3
All—
1971-74 .... 3.2
1976-78 .... 2.1

35—REAR AXLE HOUSING, RENEW
1971-78 .... 3.9

36—REAR AXLE HOUSING COVER OR GASKET, RENEW
1971-78 .... 0.6

37—AXLE SHAFT, RENEW
Note: Includes replace bearing assy & oil seal.
1971-78—
One 0.4
Both 0.6

38—AXLE SHAFT BEARINGS, RENEW
1971-78—
One 0.5
Both 0.8

39—DIFFERENTIAL ASSY, OVERHAUL
1971-78 .... 3.9

40—AXLE DRIVE PINION OIL SEAL, RENEW
1971-78 .... 0.6

Speedometer, Wipers & Instruments—TIME

OPERATION INDEX
Speedometer Cable & Housing, Renew 1
Speedometer Head, Renew 2
Speedometer Driven Gear, Renew 3
Tachometer Assy, Renew 4
Windshield Wiper Motor, Renew 5
Windshield Wiper Link Set, Renew 6
Windshield Wiper Arm, Renew 7
Windshield Washer Pump, Renew 8
Ammeter, Renew 8A
Fuel Gauge (Dash Unit), Renew 9
Fuel Tank Gauge, Renew 10
Oil Gauge Sending Unit, Renew 11
Oil Gauge (Dash Unit), Renew 12
Temperature Gauge (Dash Unit), Renew 13
Temperature Gauge Sending Unit, Renew 14
Instrument Cluster Voltage Limiter, Renew 15
Headlight Switch, Renew 16
Headlamp Foot Switch, Renew 17
Stop Light Switch, Renew 18
Turn Signal Switch, Renew 19
Hazard Flasher Switch, Renew 20

1—SPEEDOMETER CABLE & HOUSING, RENEW
1972-73, Exc 0.5
GT 0.6
1974-78 .... 0.9

2—SPEEDOMETER HEAD, RENEW
1971-78—
Except 0.8
GT 0.7

3—SPEEDOMETER DRIVEN GEAR, RENEW
1971-78 .... 0.3

4—TACHOMETER ASSY, RENEW
1972 .... 0.7
1973-74 .... 0.8
1976-78 .... 0.9

5—WINDSHIELD WIPER MOTOR, RENEW
1971-73 .... 1.7
1974-78 .... 1.1

6—WINDSHIELD WIPER LINK SET, RENEW
1971-73 .... 1.7
1974-78 .... 2.0

7—WINDSHIELD WIPER ARM, RENEW
1971-78 .... 0.2

8—WINDSHIELD WASHER PUMP, RENEW
1971-78 .... 0.3

8A—AMMETER, RENEW
1972 .... 0.7
1973-78 .... 0.8

9—FUEL GAUGE (DASH UNIT), RENEW
1971-74, Exc 0.8
GT 0.7
1976-78 .... 0.9

10—FUEL TANK GAUGE, RENEW
1971-74 .... 1.1
1976-78 .... 0.4

11—OIL GAUGE SENDING UNIT, RENEW
1971-78 .... 0.3

12—OIL GAUGE (DASH UNIT), RENEW
1971-78 .... 0.8

13—TEMPERATURE GAUGE (DASH UNIT), RENEW
1971-78 .... 0.8

14—TEMPERATURE GAUGE SENDING UNIT, RENEW
1971-78 .... 0.3

15—INSTRUMENT CLUSTER VOLTAGE LIMITER, RENEW
1971-72 .... 0.3
1973-78 .... 0.7

16—HEADLIGHT SWITCH, RENEW
1971-74 .... 0.3
1976-78 .... 0.5

17—HEADLAMP FOOT SWITCH, RENEW
1971-78 .... 0.3

18—STOP LIGHT SWITCH, RENEW
1971-78 .... 0.3

19—TURN SIGNAL SWITCH, RENEW
1971-74 .... 0.4
1976-78 .... 0.5

20—HAZARD FLASHER SWITCH, RENEW
1971-78 .... 0.3

IDENTIFICATION

1971-73....67
1974-75....68
1976 Colt....69
1976 Arrow....70
1977 Colt & Arrow....71

ILLUSTRATIONS

FIG 1 – CYLINDER HEAD
FIG 2 – CYLINDER BLOCK
FIG 3 – TIMING CASE & OIL PAN
FIG 4 – PISTON & CRANKSHAFT
FIG 5 – CAMSHAFT & TIMING CHAIN
FIG 6 – MANUAL TRANSMISSION
FIG 7 – FRONT SUSPENSION
FIG 8 – STEERING LINKAGE
FIG 9 – REAR AXLE DIFFERENTIAL

OPERATION TIMES

A

Alternator.... 77
Automatic Transmission.... 78
Axle Shaft.... 80

B

Ball Joint.... 80
Brake Drums, or Disc.... 79
Brakes.... 79

C

Cables (Ignition).... 77
Calipers.... 79
Camshaft.... 78
Carburetor.... 77
Clutch.... 79
Coil, Ignition.... 77
Compression Test.... 77
Connecting Rods.... 78
Cooling System.... 77
Crankshaft.... 78
Cylinder Head.... 78

D

Dash Gauges.... 80
Differential.... 80
Disc Brakes.... 79
Distributor.... 77

E

Emission Controls.... 77
Engine Assembly.... 78
Engine Mountings.... 79
Engine Oiling.... 78
Engine Tune-Up.... 77
Exhaust System.... 77

F

Flywheel.... 78
Front Suspension.... 79
Fuel Gauges.... 80
Fuel Pump.... 77
Fuel Tank.... 77

H

Hand Brake.... 79
Headlight Switch.... 80
Heater.... 77
Hose (Brake).... 79
Hose (Radiator).... 77
Hydraulic Brakes.... 79

I

Ignition.... 77
Ignition Coil.... 77
Ignition Switch.... 77
Intake Manifold.... 77

L

Light Switches.... 80

M

Main Bearings.... 78
Master Cylinder.... 79
Muffler.... 77

O

Oiling, Engine.... 78
Oil Pan.... 78
Oil Pump.... 78

P

Parking Brake.... 79
Piston Rings.... 78
Pistons.... 78
Propeller Shaft.... 80

R

Radiator.... 77
Radiator Hose.... 77
Rear Axle.... 80
Regulator (Alternator).... 77
Rocker Arms.... 78
Rod Bearings.... 78

S

Shocks (Front).... 80
Shocks (Rear).... 80
Speedometer.... 80
Springs (Front).... 79
Springs (Rear).... 79
Stabilizer.... 80
Starting Motor.... 77
Steering Gear.... 79
Steering Linkage.... 79
Switches (Light).... 80
Synchro-Mesh, Trans.... 79

T

Temperature Gauge.... 80
Thermostat.... 77
Timing Case Cover.... 78
Timing Chain.... 78
Timing Gears.... 78
Transmission, Manual.... 79
Transmission, Automatic.... 79
Tune-Up, Engine.... 77

U

Universals.... 80

V

Vacuum Control Unit.... 77
Valve System.... 78

W

Water Pump.... 77
Wheel Cylinders.... 79
Windshield Wiper.... 80

MODEL	CODE	BODY STYLE
6L21	53	STANDARD HARDTOP
6H23	51	CUSTOM HARDTOP
6H23	91	CUSTOM HARDTOP AUTOMATIC
6P23	50	SUPER DELUXE HARDTOP
6P23	90	SUPER DELUXE HARDTOP AUTOMATIC
6P45	50	SUPER DELUXE STATION WAGON
6P45	90	SUPER DELUXE STATION WAGON AUTOMATIC
6H41	51	CUSTOM SEDAN
6H41	91	CUSTOM SEDAN AUTOMATIC
6H45	51	CUSTOM STATION WAGON
6H45	91	CUSTOM STATION WAGON AUTOMATIC

VEHICLE IDENTIFICATION PLATE

Attached to the left top side of the instrument panel, visible through the windshield.

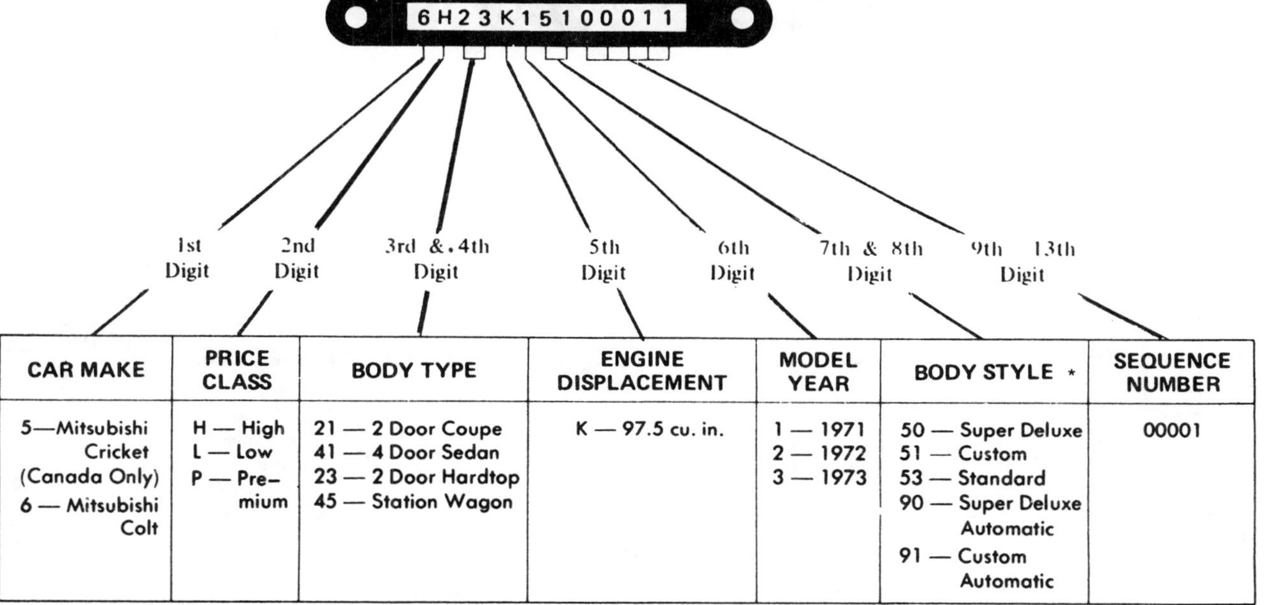

CAR MAKE	PRICE CLASS	BODY TYPE	ENGINE DISPLACEMENT	MODEL YEAR	BODY STYLE *	SEQUENCE NUMBER
5—Mitsubishi Cricket (Canada Only) 6 — Mitsubishi Colt	H — High L — Low P — Pre-mium	21 — 2 Door Coupe 41 — 4 Door Sedan 23 — 2 Door Hardtop 45 — Station Wagon	K — 97.5 cu. in.	1 — 1971 2 — 1972 3 — 1973	50 — Super Deluxe 51 — Custom 53 — Standard 90 — Super Deluxe Automatic 91 — Custom Automatic	00001

*Body Style Note: 1st Digit-5 = Manual Transmission, 9 = Automatic
2nd Digit-3 = Standard Trim, 1 = Custom, 0 = Super DeLuxe

STARTING SERIAL NUMBERS

1971 MODELS

CHASSIS:

6H41K1-5100011
6H41K1-9100011
6H23K1-5100011
6L21K1 -5300011
6H23K1-9100011
6H45K1-5100011
6H45K1-9100011

ENGINE: 00123

1972 MODELS

CHASSIS:

6H41K2-5104191
6H41K2-9103300
6H23K2-5107569
6L21K2 -5302261
6H23K2-9105753
6H45K2-5103070
6H45K2-9102409

ENGINE: 42995

1973 MODELS

CHASSIS:

6L21K3-5306092
6H23K3-5116853
6H23K3-9122836
6P23K3-5000001
6P23K3-9000001
6H41K3-5108108
6H41K3-9112852
6P45K3-5000001
6H45K3-5108601
6P45K3-9000001
6H45K3-9115300

ENGINE: 41614

VEHICLE IDENTIFICATION — 1971-73

1974 Model	1974 Codes	1975 Model	1975 Codes	Body Style	Trim Level
6L21	53,93			Coupe	Standard
		6M21	51,91	Hardtop	Medium
6H23	51,91			Hardtop	Custom
		6S23	55,95	Hardtop	Special
6P23	50,90			Hardtop	Super DeLuxe (G.T.)
		6P23	70,90	Hardtop	Premium (G.T.)
6H41	51,91			Sedan	Custom
		6H41	51,91	Sedan	High Line
6H45	51,91			Station Wagon	Custom
		6H45	51,91	Station Wagon	High Line
6P45	50,90			Station Wagon	Super DeLuxe
		6H45	50,90	Station Wagon	Premium (w/Decor Pkg.)

VEHICLE IDENTIFICATION PLATE

Attached to the left top side of the instrument panel, visible through the windshield.

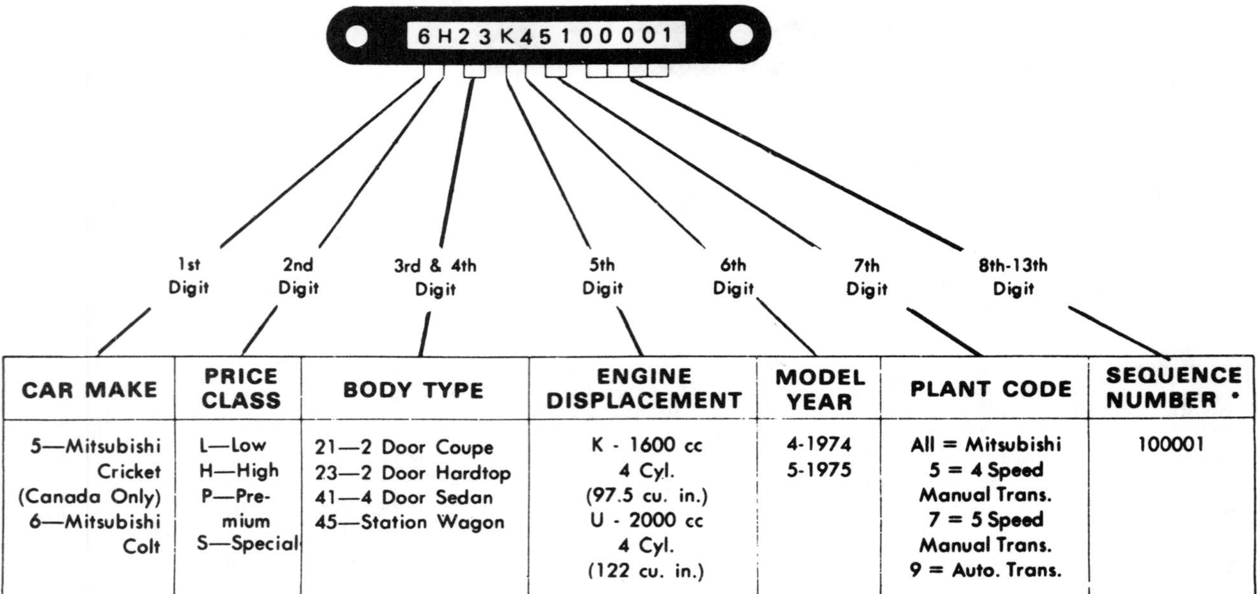

CAR MAKE	PRICE CLASS	BODY TYPE	ENGINE DISPLACEMENT	MODEL YEAR	PLANT CODE	SEQUENCE NUMBER *
5—Mitsubishi Cricket (Canada Only) 6—Mitsubishi Colt	L—Low H—High P—Premium S—Special	21—2 Door Coupe 23—2 Door Hardtop 41—4 Door Sedan 45—Station Wagon	K - 1600 cc 4 Cyl. (97.5 cu. in.) U - 2000 cc 4 Cyl. (122 cu. in.)	4-1974 5-1975	All = Mitsubishi 5 = 4 Speed Manual Trans. 7 = 5 Speed Manual Trans. 9 = Auto. Trans.	100001

* Sequence Number Note: The first character represents the Trim Level

BODY NUMBER

The Body Number is stamped on the top center of the cowl (firewall) located inside the engine compartment.

ENGINE MODEL AND SERIAL NUMBER

The Engine Model is embossed at the rear lower corner of the left side of the cylinder block; 4G32 = K Engine, 4G52 = U Engine.

The Engine Serial Number is stamped on top of the cylinder block at the right front corner.

TRANSMISSION MODEL and SERIAL NUMBER

Mitsubishi Manual Transmission Serial Numbers are stamped on the left side of the transmission case. Chrysler built Automatic Transmission identification numbers are stamped on the left oil pan side rail as follows:

TRANS. ASSY. NUMBER	CHANGE CODE	DATE CODE	SERIAL NUMBER
7 Digits	1 Digit	4 Digits	4 Digits
1234567	A	4540	0001
	(Factory use only-of no significance to the field)	(Jan. 1, 1974)	(A sequential number for each days' production)

VEHICLE IDENTIFICATION — 1974-75

VEHICLE IDENTIFICATION NUMBER LOCATION

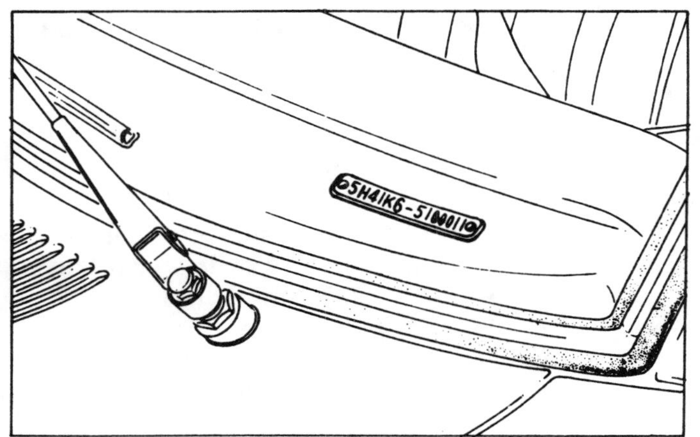

The vehicle number is located on a plate which is attached to the left top side of the instrument panel and visible through the windshield.

VEHICLE IDENTIFICATION NUMBERS

All vehicle identification numbers contain 13 digits. The vehicle number is a code which tells the line of vehicle (1st digit), price class (2nd digit), body type (3rd and 4th digits), engine displacement (5th digit), model year (6th digit), transmission code (7th digit), trim code (8th digit) and vehicle sequence number (last five digits).

Vehicle Identification Plate

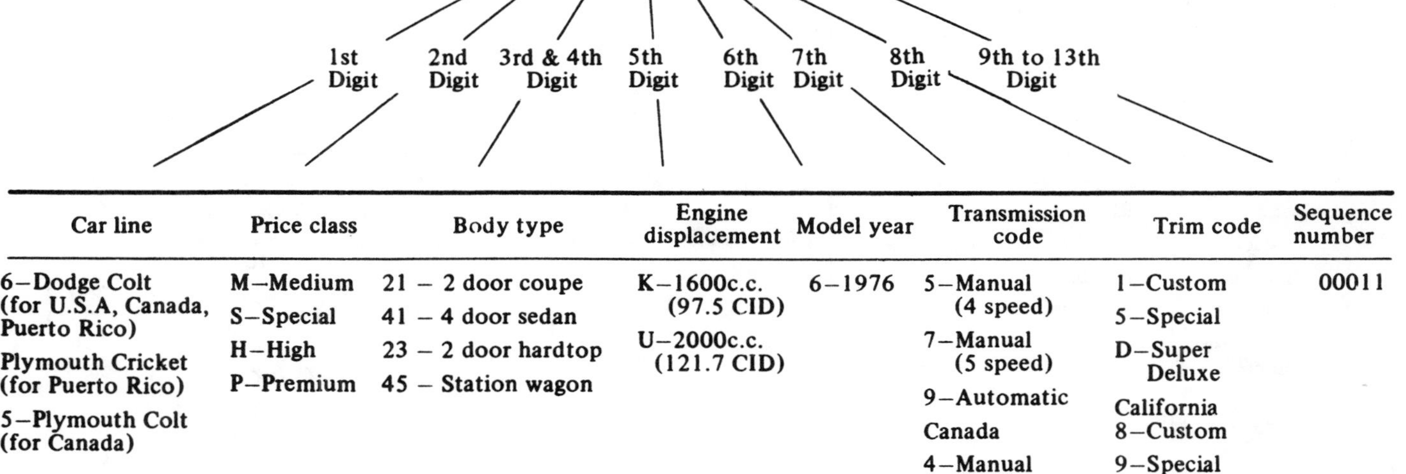

Car line	Price class	Body type	Engine displacement	Model year	Transmission code	Trim code	Sequence number
6–Dodge Colt (for U.S.A, Canada, Puerto Rico)	M–Medium	21 – 2 door coupe	K–1600c.c. (97.5 CID)	6–1976	5–Manual (4 speed)	1–Custom	00011
Plymouth Cricket (for Puerto Rico)	S–Special	41 – 4 door sedan	U–2000c.c. (121.7 CID)		7–Manual (5 speed)	5–Special	
5–Plymouth Colt (for Canada)	H–High	23 – 2 door hardtop			9–Automatic	D–Super Deluxe	
	P–Premium	45 – Station wagon			Canada	California	
					4–Manual (4 speed)	8–Custom	
					6–Manual (5 speed)	9–Special	
					8–Automatic	7–Super Deluxe	

VEHICLE IDENTIFICATION – 1976 COLT

VEHICLE IDENTIFICATION NUMBER LOCATION

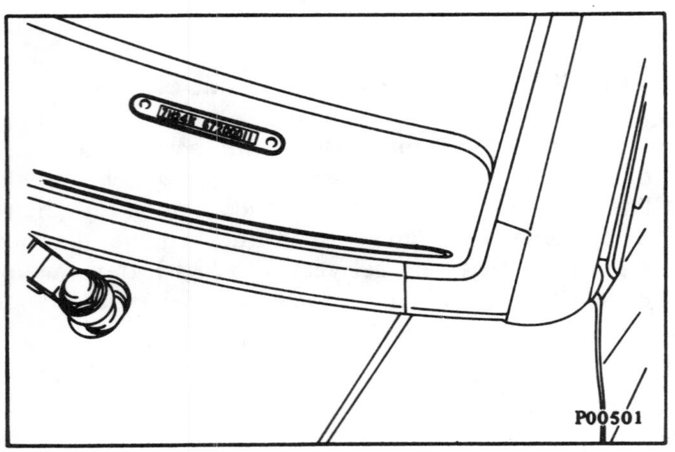

The vehicle number is located on a plate which is attached to the left top side of the instrument panel and visible through the windshield.

VEHICLE IDENTIFICATION NUMBERS

All vehicle identification numbers contain 13 digits. The vehicle number is a code which tells the line of vehicle (1st digit), price class (2nd digit), body type (3rd and 4th digits), engine displacement (5th digit), model year (6th digit), transmission code (7th digit), trim code (8th digit) and vehicle sequence number (last five digits).

Vehicle Identification Plate

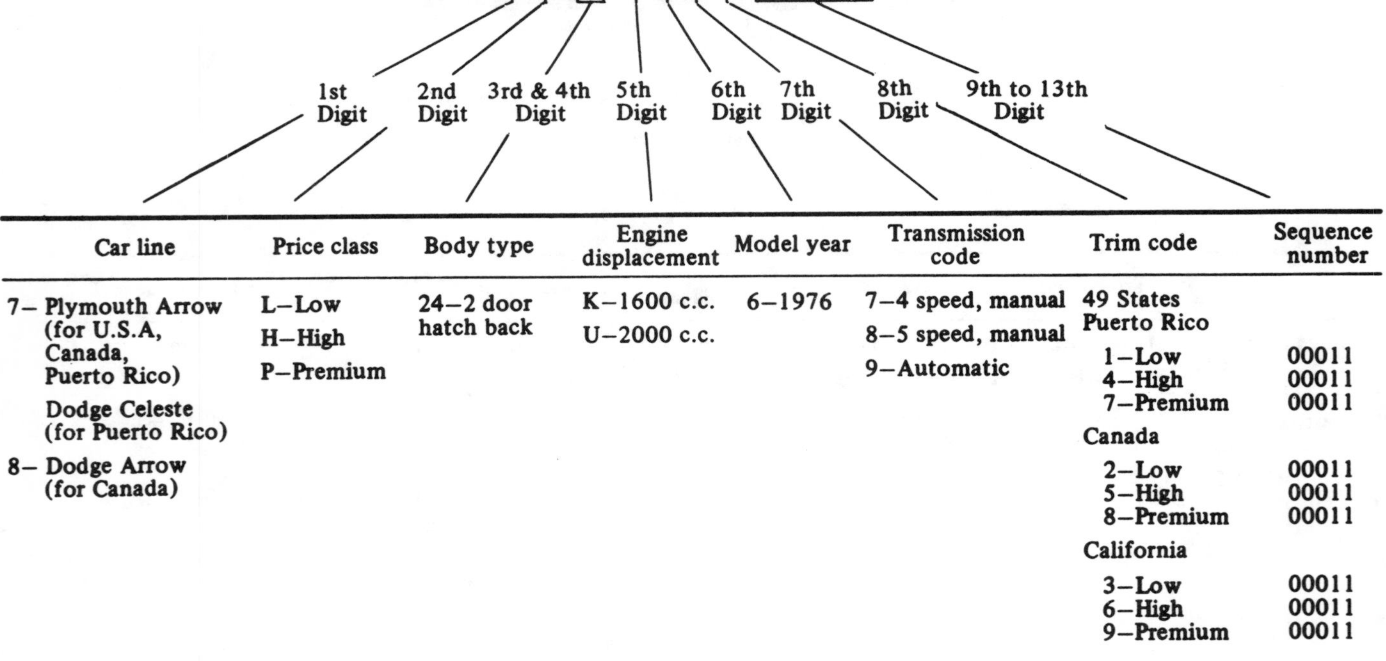

Car line	Price class	Body type	Engine displacement	Model year	Transmission code	Trim code	Sequence number
7– Plymouth Arrow (for U.S.A, Canada, Puerto Rico)	L–Low	24–2 door hatch back	K–1600 c.c.	6–1976	7–4 speed, manual	49 States Puerto Rico	
	H–High		U–2000 c.c.		8–5 speed, manual	1–Low	00011
	P–Premium				9–Automatic	4–High	00011
Dodge Celeste (for Puerto Rico)						7–Premium	00011
						Canada	
8– Dodge Arrow (for Canada)						2–Low	00011
						5–High	00011
						8–Premium	00011
						California	
						3–Low	00011
						6–High	00011
						9–Premium	00011

VEHICLE IDENTIFICATION – 1976 ARROW

VEHICLE IDENTIFICATION NUMBERS

The vehicle number is located on a plate which is attached to the left top side of the instrument panel and visible through the windshield.

All vehicle identification numbers contain 13 digits. The vehicle number is a code which tells the line of vehicle (1st digit), price class (2nd digit), body type (3rd and 4th digits), engine displacement (5th digit), model year (6th digit), transmission code (7th digit), trim code (8th digit) and vehicle sequence number (last five digits).

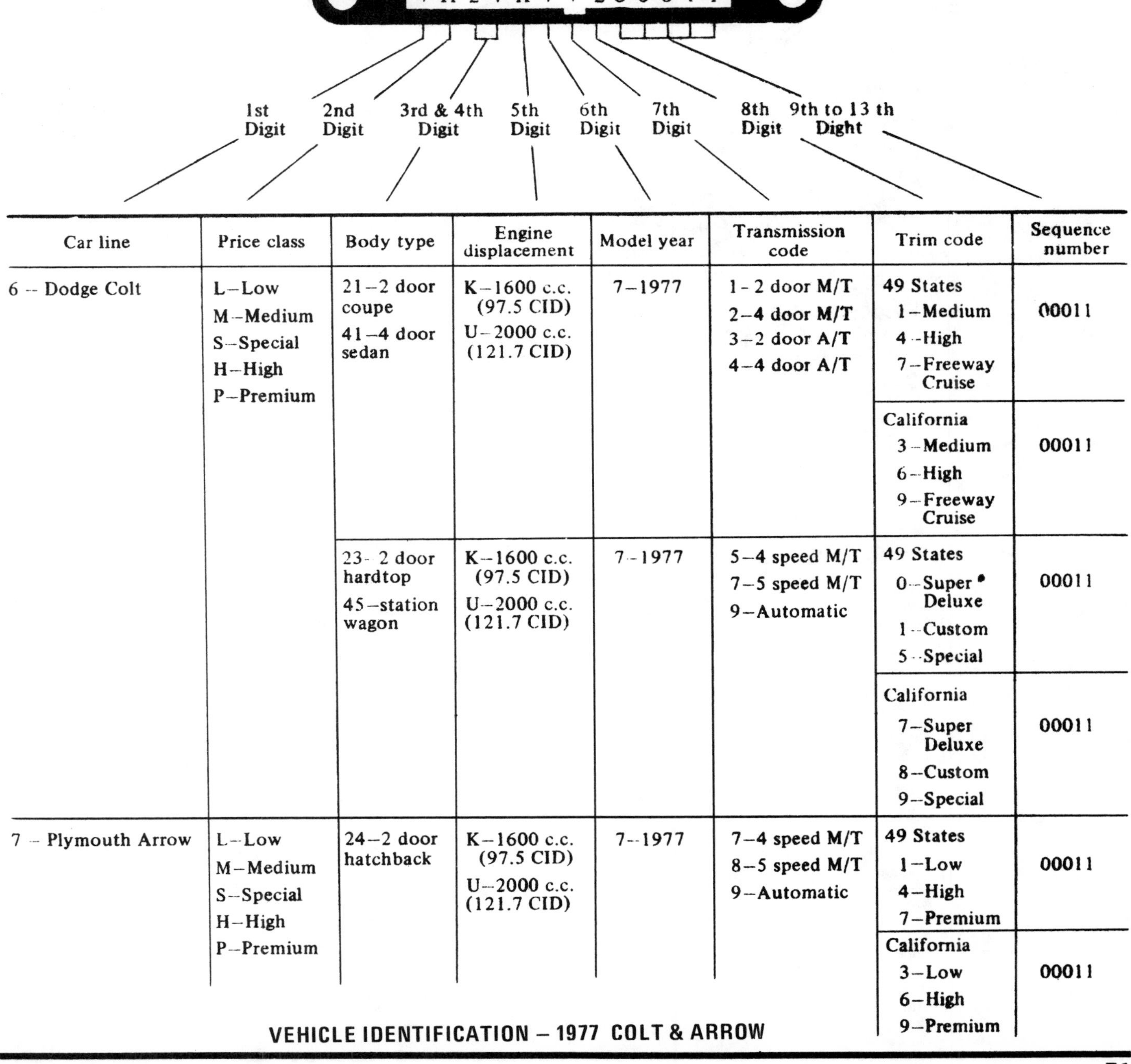

Car line	Price class	Body type	Engine displacement	Model year	Transmission code	Trim code	Sequence number
6 – Dodge Colt	L–Low M–Medium S–Special H–High P–Premium	21–2 door coupe 41–4 door sedan	K–1600 c.c. (97.5 CID) U–2000 c.c. (121.7 CID)	7–1977	1-2 door M/T 2–4 door M/T 3–2 door A/T 4–4 door A/T	49 States 1–Medium 4–High 7–Freeway Cruise	00011
						California 3–Medium 6–High 9–Freeway Cruise	00011
		23–2 door hardtop 45–station wagon	K–1600 c.c. (97.5 CID) U–2000 c.c. (121.7 CID)	7–1977	5–4 speed M/T 7–5 speed M/T 9–Automatic	49 States 0–Super* Deluxe 1–Custom 5–Special	00011
						California 7–Super Deluxe 8–Custom 9–Special	00011
7 – Plymouth Arrow	L–Low M–Medium S–Special H–High P–Premium	24–2 door hatchback	K–1600 c.c. (97.5 CID) U–2000 c.c. (121.7 CID)	7–1977	7–4 speed M/T 8–5 speed M/T 9–Automatic	49 States 1–Low 4–High 7–Premium	00011
						California 3–Low 6–High 9–Premium	00011

VEHICLE IDENTIFICATION – 1977 COLT & ARROW

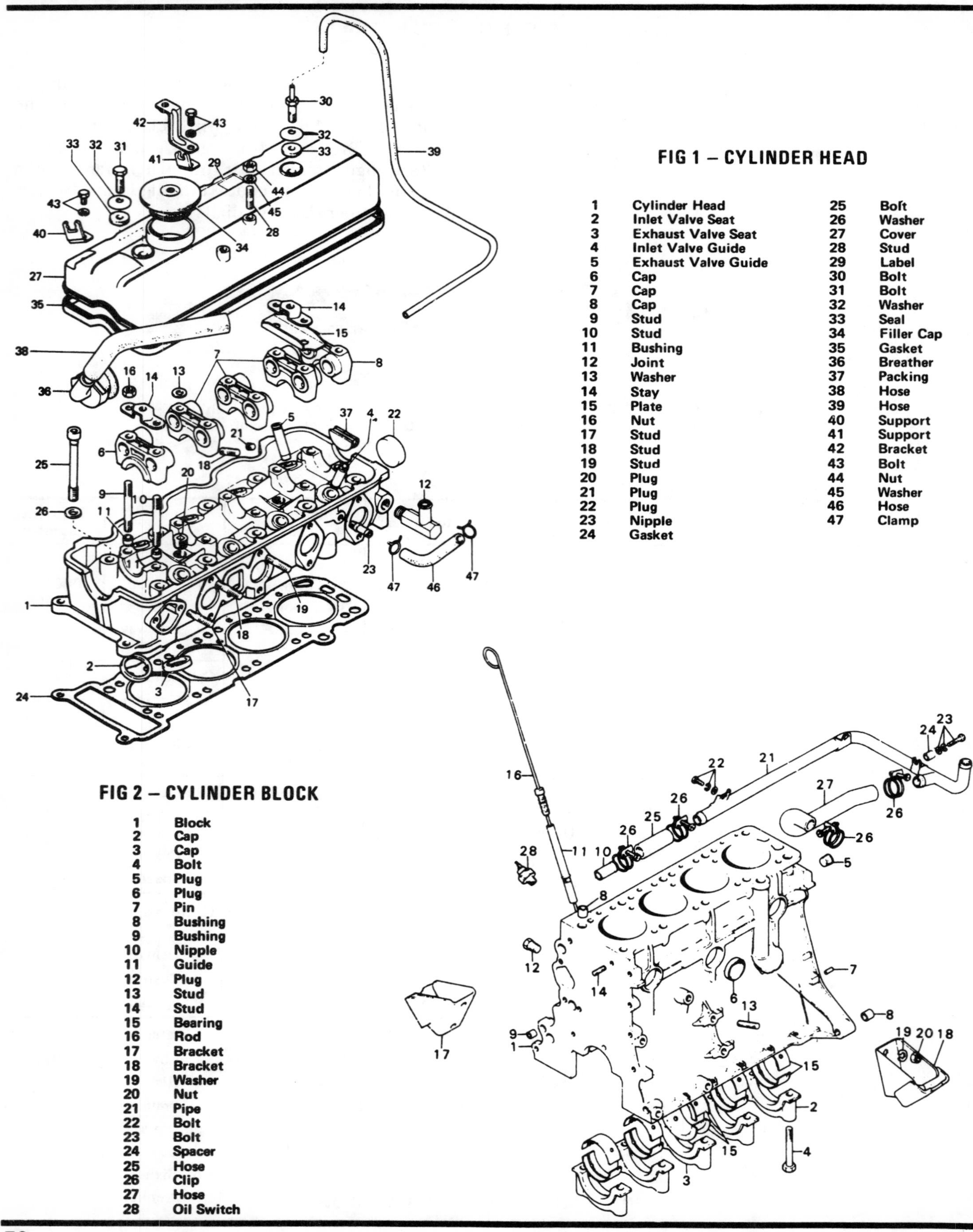

FIG 1 – CYLINDER HEAD

1	Cylinder Head	25	Bolt
2	Inlet Valve Seat	26	Washer
3	Exhaust Valve Seat	27	Cover
4	Inlet Valve Guide	28	Stud
5	Exhaust Valve Guide	29	Label
6	Cap	30	Bolt
7	Cap	31	Bolt
8	Cap	32	Washer
9	Stud	33	Seal
10	Stud	34	Filler Cap
11	Bushing	35	Gasket
12	Joint	36	Breather
13	Washer	37	Packing
14	Stay	38	Hose
15	Plate	39	Hose
16	Nut	40	Support
17	Stud	41	Support
18	Stud	42	Bracket
19	Stud	43	Bolt
20	Plug	44	Nut
21	Plug	45	Washer
22	Plug	46	Hose
23	Nipple	47	Clamp
24	Gasket		

FIG 2 – CYLINDER BLOCK

1	Block
2	Cap
3	Cap
4	Bolt
5	Plug
6	Plug
7	Pin
8	Bushing
9	Bushing
10	Nipple
11	Guide
12	Plug
13	Stud
14	Stud
15	Bearing
16	Rod
17	Bracket
18	Bracket
19	Washer
20	Nut
21	Pipe
22	Bolt
23	Bolt
24	Spacer
25	Hose
26	Clip
27	Hose
28	Oil Switch

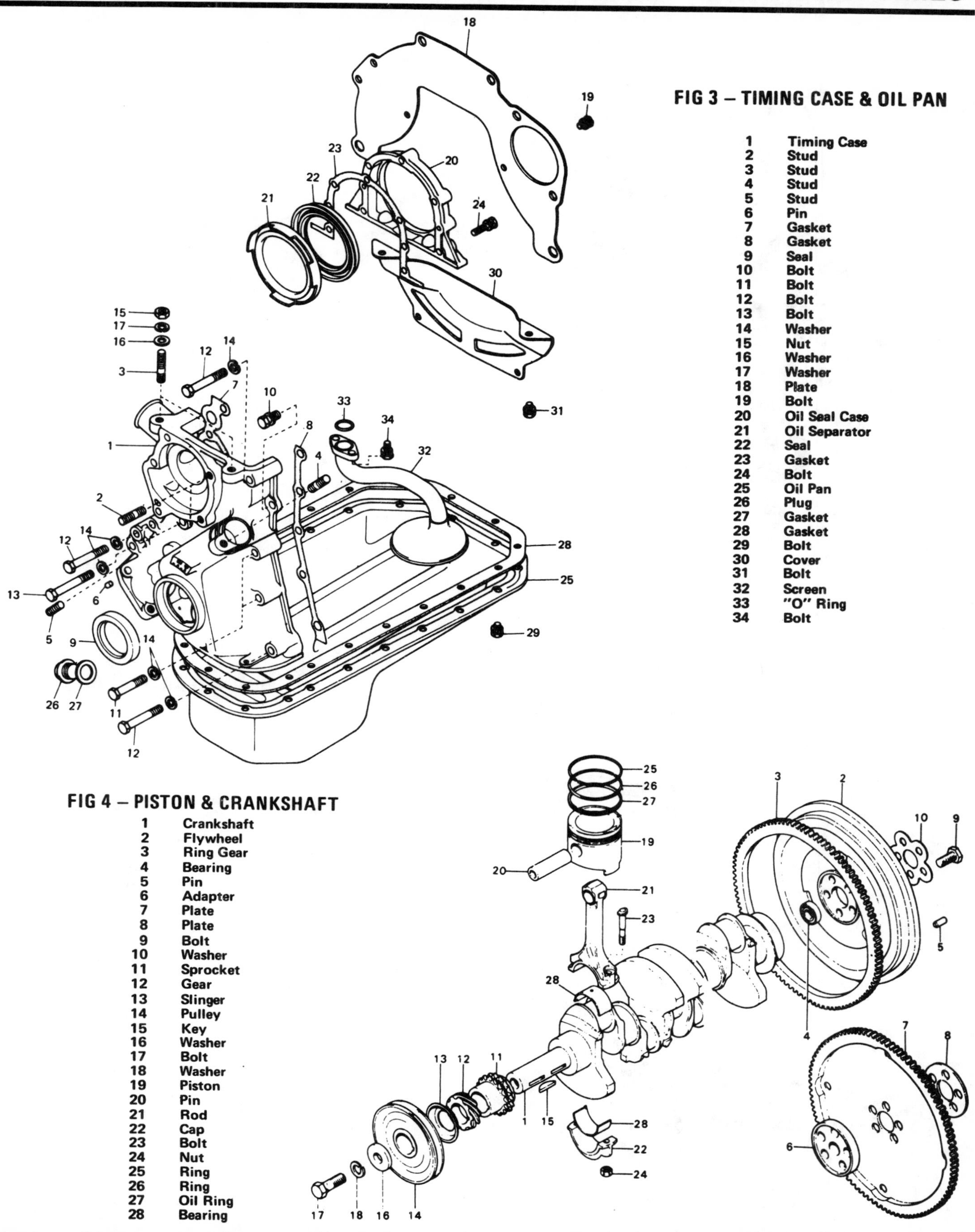
FIG 3 – TIMING CASE & OIL PAN
1 Timing Case
2 Stud
3 Stud
4 Stud
5 Stud
6 Pin
7 Gasket
8 Gasket
9 Seal
10 Bolt
11 Bolt
12 Bolt
13 Bolt
14 Washer
15 Nut
16 Washer
17 Washer
18 Plate
19 Bolt
20 Oil Seal Case
21 Oil Separator
22 Seal
23 Gasket
24 Bolt
25 Oil Pan
26 Plug
27 Gasket
28 Gasket
29 Bolt
30 Cover
31 Bolt
32 Screen
33 "O" Ring
34 Bolt
FIG 4 – PISTON & CRANKSHAFT
1 Crankshaft
2 Flywheel
3 Ring Gear
4 Bearing
5 Pin
6 Adapter
7 Plate
8 Plate
9 Bolt
10 Washer
11 Sprocket
12 Gear
13 Slinger
14 Pulley
15 Key
16 Washer
17 Bolt
18 Washer
19 Piston
20 Pin
21 Rod
22 Cap
23 Bolt
24 Nut
25 Ring
26 Ring
27 Oil Ring
28 Bearing

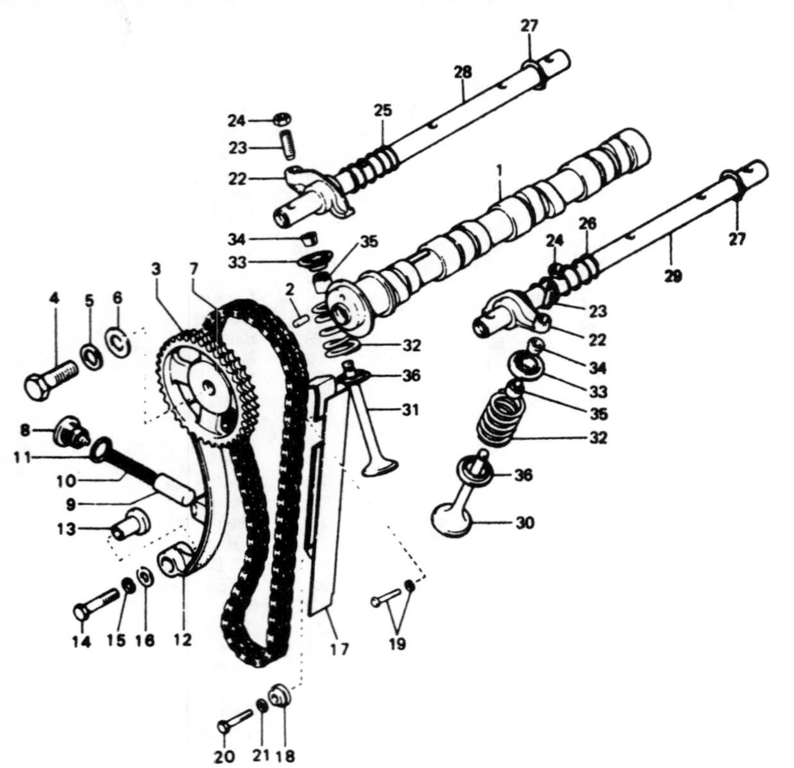

FIG 5 – CAMSHAFT & TIMING CHAIN

1	Camshaft
2	Pin
3	Sprocket
4	Bolt
5	Washer
6	Washer
7	Timing Chain
8	Holder
9	Plunger
10	Spring
11	Gasket
12	Lever
13	Shaft
14	Bolt
15	Washer
16	Washer
17	Guide
18	Jet
19	Nut
20	Bolt
21	Gasket
22	Rocker Arm
23	Screw
24	Nut
25	Spring
26	Spring
27	Washer
28	Shaft
29	Shaft
30	Inlet Valve
31	Exhaust Valve
32	Spring
33	Retainer
34	Lock
35	Seal
36	Seat

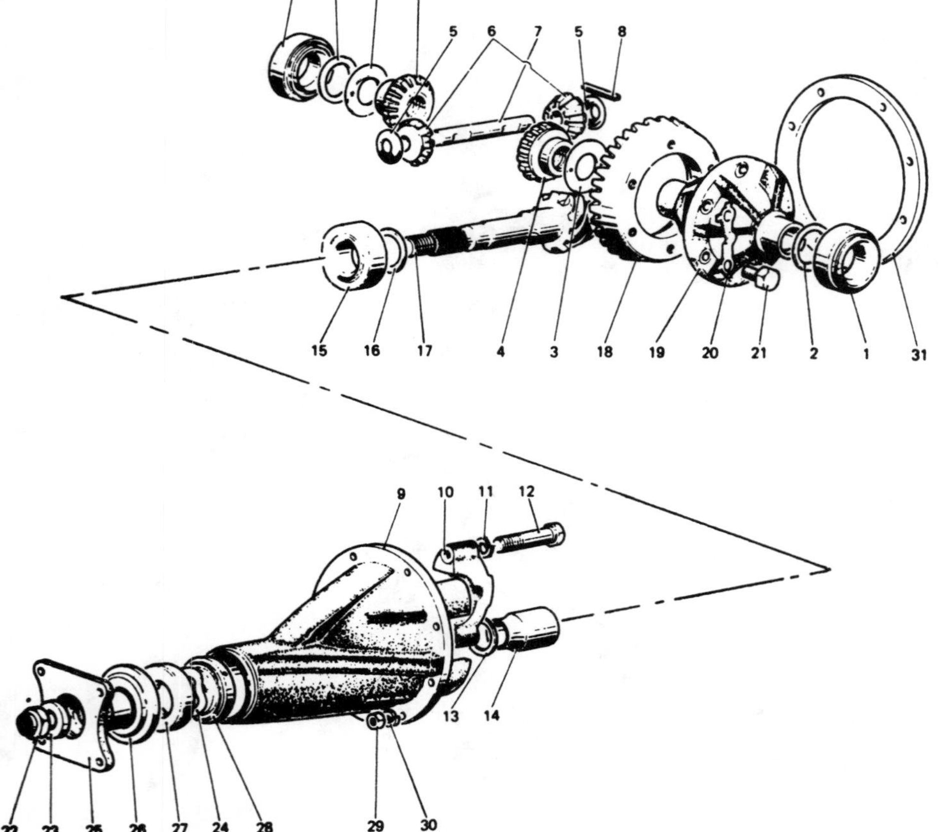

FIG 9 – REAR AXLE DIFFERENTIAL

1	Bearing
2	Shim
3	Spacer
4	Side Gear
5	Washer
6	Pinion
7	Shaft
8	Pin
9	Carrier
10	Cap
11	Washer
12	Bolt
13	Shim
14	Spacer
15	Bearing
16	Shim
17	Gear Set
18	Gear Set
19	Case
20	Washer
21	Bolt
22	Nut
23	Washer
24	Washer
25	Yoke
26	Cover
27	Oil Seal
28	Bearing
29	Nut
30	Washer
31	Packing

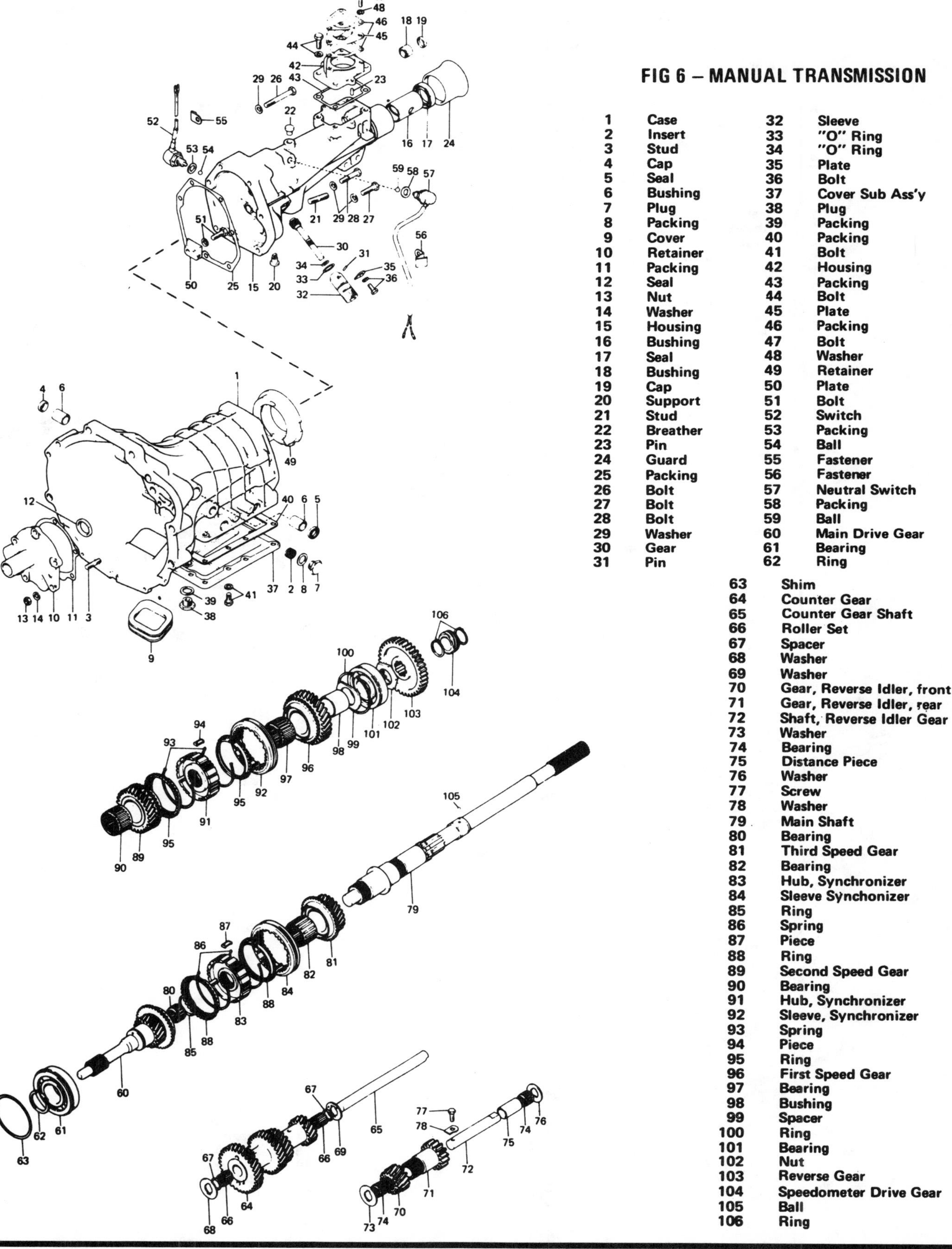

FIG 6 – MANUAL TRANSMISSION

1	Case
2	Insert
3	Stud
4	Cap
5	Seal
6	Bushing
7	Plug
8	Packing
9	Cover
10	Retainer
11	Packing
12	Seal
13	Nut
14	Washer
15	Housing
16	Bushing
17	Seal
18	Bushing
19	Cap
20	Support
21	Stud
22	Breather
23	Pin
24	Guard
25	Packing
26	Bolt
27	Bolt
28	Bolt
29	Washer
30	Gear
31	Pin
32	Sleeve
33	"O" Ring
34	"O" Ring
35	Plate
36	Bolt
37	Cover Sub Ass'y
38	Plug
39	Packing
40	Packing
41	Bolt
42	Housing
43	Packing
44	Bolt
45	Plate
46	Packing
47	Bolt
48	Washer
49	Retainer
50	Plate
51	Bolt
52	Switch
53	Packing
54	Ball
55	Fastener
56	Fastener
57	Neutral Switch
58	Packing
59	Ball
60	Main Drive Gear
61	Bearing
62	Ring
63	Shim
64	Counter Gear
65	Counter Gear Shaft
66	Roller Set
67	Spacer
68	Washer
69	Washer
70	Gear, Reverse Idler, front
71	Gear, Reverse Idler, rear
72	Shaft, Reverse Idler Gear
73	Washer
74	Bearing
75	Distance Piece
76	Washer
77	Screw
78	Washer
79	Main Shaft
80	Bearing
81	Third Speed Gear
82	Bearing
83	Hub, Synchronizer
84	Sleeve Synchonizer
85	Ring
86	Spring
87	Piece
88	Ring
89	Second Speed Gear
90	Bearing
91	Hub, Synchronizer
92	Sleeve, Synchronizer
93	Spring
94	Piece
95	Ring
96	First Speed Gear
97	Bearing
98	Bushing
99	Spacer
100	Ring
101	Bearing
102	Nut
103	Reverse Gear
104	Speedometer Drive Gear
105	Ball
106	Ring

FIG 7 – FRONT SUSPENSION

1	Cover	21	Washer
2	Nut	22	Nut
3	Washer	23	Bushing
4	Nut	24	Washer
5	Washer	25	Washer
6	Insulator	26	Bolt
7	Bearing	27	Spacer
8	Seat	28	Bolt
9	Bumper	29	Washer
10	Spring	30	Lower Shaft
11	Seal	31	Stopper
12	Seal	32	Lower Arm
13	Absorber	33	Ball Joint
14	Strut	33A	Packing
15	Knuckle Arm	33B	Washer
16	Washer	34	Bolt
17	Bolt	35	Cover
18	Crossmember	36	Nut
19	Nut	37	Ring
20	Bolt		

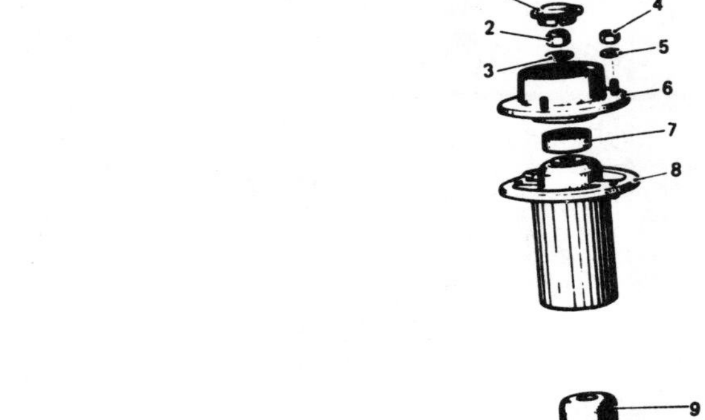

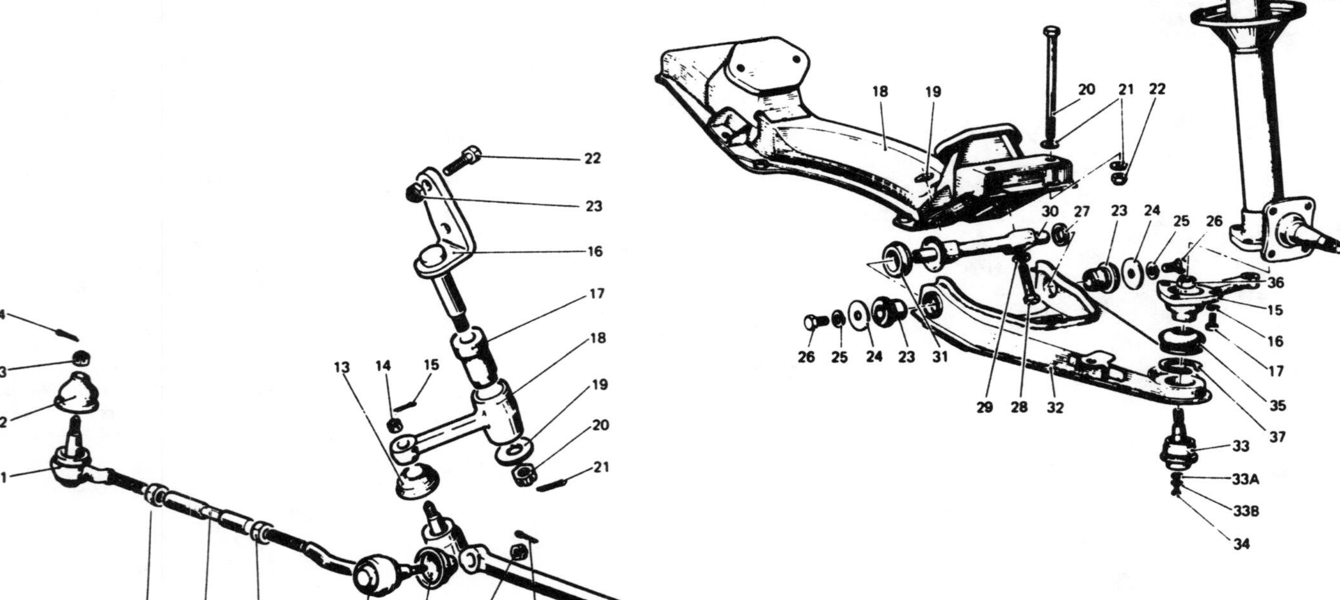

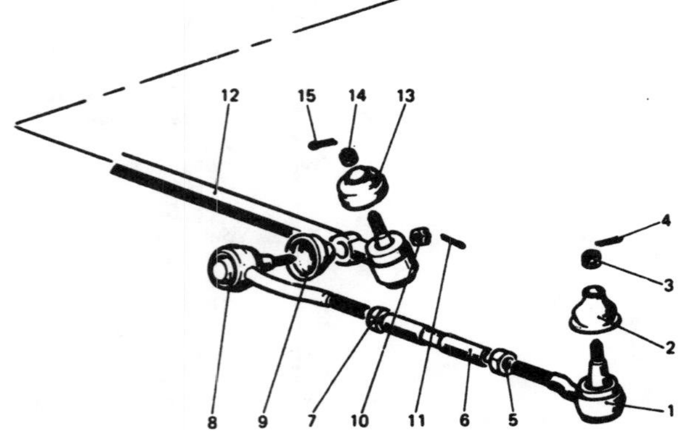

FIG 8 – STEERING LINKAGE

1	End
2	Cover
3	Nut
4	Pin
5	Nut
6	Tie Rod
7	Nut
8	End
9	Cover
10	Nut
11	Pin
12	Relay Rod
13	Cover
14	Nut
15	Pin
16	Bracket
17	Bushing
18	Idler Arm
19	Washer
20	Nut
21	Pin
22	Bolt
23	Nut

Ignition, Starting & Charging—TIME

OPERATION INDEX

Tune-Up, Minor *1*
Tune-Up, Major *2*
Compression Test *3*
Distributor, R&R Or Renew *4*
Distributor Cap, Renew *5*
Ignition Cable Set, Renew *6*
Vacuum Control Unit, Renew *7*
Ignition Coil, Renew *8*
Starter & Ignition Switch, Renew *9*
Starter, R&R Or Renew *10*
Starter Solenoid, Renew *11*
Starter Bendix Drive, Renew *12*
Starter, R&R & Overhaul *13*
Starter Brushes, Renew *14*
Starter Armature, Renew *15*
Alternator Regulator, Renew *16*
Alternator, R&R Or Renew *17*
Alternator, R&R & Overhaul *18*
Alternator Diodes, Renew *19*
Alternator Bearings, Renew *20*
Alternator Brushes, Renew *21*
Alternator Pulley, Renew *22*

1—TUNE-UP, MINOR
Includes: Renew points, condenser & plugs. Set spark timing and adjust carburetor idle.
1971-78 .... 1.7

2—TUNE-UP, MAJOR
Includes: Check compression, clean or renew and adjust spark plugs. R&R distributor, renew points and condenser. Adjust ignition timing, carburetor and fan belts. Clean battery terminals and service air cleaner. Check coil & clean or replace fuel filter.
1971-78 .... 2.6

3—COMPRESSION TEST
1971-75 .... 0.6
1976-78 .... 0.5

4—DISTRIBUTOR, R&R OR RENEW
1971-75 .... 0.4
1976-78 .... 0.5

—NOTE—
For Stroboscope Adjustment, Add *0.3*

5—DISTRIBUTOR CAP, RENEW
1971-78 .... 0.2

6—IGNITION CABLE SET, RENEW
1971-78—
One 0.3
All 0.4

7—VACUUM CONTROL UNIT, RENEW
1971-75 .... 0.5
1976-78 .... 0.7

8—IGNITION COIL, RENEW
1971-78 .... 0.3

9—STARTER & IGNITION SWITCH, RENEW
1971-78 .... 0.4

10—STARTER, R&R OR RENEW
1971-76 .... 0.5
1977-78 .... 0.8

11—STARTER SOLENOID, RENEW
1971-76 .... 0.7
1977-78 .... 0.9

12—STARTER BENDIX DRIVE, RENEW
1971-76 .... 1.4
1977-78 .... 1.7

13—STARTER, R&R & OVERHAUL
Includes: Turn down commutator and replace all necessary parts.
1971-76 .... 2.0
1977-78 .... 2.4

14—STARTER BRUSHES, RENEW
1971-76 .... 1.3
1977-78 .... 1.5

15—STARTER ARMATURE, RENEW
1971-76 .... 1.1
1977-78 .... 1.4

16—ALTERNATOR REGULATOR, RENEW
1971-78 .... 0.3

17—ALTERNATOR, R&R OR RENEW
1971-76 .... 0.4
1977-78 .... 0.5

18—ALTERNATOR, R&R & OVERHAUL
1971-76 .... 2.1
1977-78 .... 2.2

19—ALTERNATOR DIODES, RENEW
1971-78 .... 1.3

20—ALTERNATOR BEARINGS, RENEW
1971-76 .... 1.0
1977-78 .... 1.2

21—ALTERNATOR BRUSHES, RENEW
1971-76 .... 0.8
1977-78 .... 1.0

22—ALTERNATOR PULLEY, RENEW
1971-76 .... 0.5
1977-78 .... 0.6

Fuel, Emission Controls, Intake & Exhaust System—TIME

OPERATION INDEX

Carburetor Or Flange Gasket, Renew *1*
Carburetor, R&R & Overhaul *2*
Fuel Pump, R&R Or Renew *3*
Fuel Tank, R&R Or Renew *4*
Sub Tank, Renew *5*
Canister Assy, Renew *6*
Emission Purge Valve, Renew *7*
Intake Manifold Or Gasket Renew *8*
Exhaust Manifold Or Gasket, Renew *9*
Exhaust Pipe, Renew *10*
Sub Muffler Assy, Renew *11*
Muffler, Renew *12*
Tail Pipe, Renew *1313*
Catalytic Converter, Renew *1414*

1—CARBURETOR OR FLANGE GASKET, RENEW
1971-76 .... 1.1
1977-78 .... 1.0

2—CARBURETOR, R&R & OVERHAUL
1971-78 .... 2.6

3—FUEL PUMP, R&R OR RENEW
1971-76 .... 0.4
1977-78 .... 0.3

4—FUEL TANK, R&R OR RENEW
1971-76 .... 1.1
1977-78 Colt—
Exc Wagon 0.9
Wagon 1.2
1977-78 Arrow 1.1

5— SUB TANK, RENEW
1971-76 .... 0.4

6—CANISTER ASSY, RENEW
1971-76 .... 0.2

7—EMISSION PURGE VALVE, RENEW
1971-76 .... 0.2

8—INTAKE MANIFOLD OR GASKET, RENEW
1971-76—
Manifold 1.3
Gasket 0.9
1977-78—
Manifold, 1600 Eng 2.4
Manifold, 2000 Eng 3.0
Gasket, 1600 Eng 2.1
Gasket, 2000 Eng 3.0

9—EXHAUST MANIFOLD OR GASKET, RENEW
1971-76 .... 0.7
1977-78—
1600 Eng 0.6
2000 Eng 0.7

10—EXHAUST PIPE, RENEW
1971-76 .... 0.7
1977-78 .... 0.6

11—SUB MUFFLER ASSY, RENEW
1971-76 .... 0.4

12—MUFFLER, RENEW
1977-78 Colt 0.6
1977-78 Arrow 0.7

13—TAIL PIPE, RENEW
Arrow 0.4

14—CATALYTIC CONVERTER, RENEW
All Models 1.3

Engine Cooling & Heater System—TIME

OPERATION INDEX

Radiator, R&R Or Renew *1*
Radiator Hoses, Renew *2*
Water Pump, R&R Or Renew *3*
Thermostat Or Housing, Renew *4*
Heater Assy, Renew *5*
Heater Core, Renew *6*
Heater Blower Motor, Renew *7*
Heater Control, Renew *8*
Heater Hoses, Renew *9*
Air Duct Ventilator Assy, Renew *10*

1—RADIATOR, R&R OR RENEW
1971-76 .... 0.4
1977-78 Colt 0.5
1977-78 Arrow 0.7

2—RADIATOR HOSES, RENEW
1971-78—
Upper 0.3
Lower 0.4

3—WATER PUMP, R&R OR RENEW
1971-78 .... 0.7

4—THERMOSTAT OR HOUSING, RENEW
1971-78 .... 0.4

5—HEATER ASSY, RENEW
1971-78 .... 1.1

6—HEATER CORE, RENEW
1971-78 .... 1.2

7—HEATER BLOWER MOTOR, RENEW
1971-76 .... 0.4
1977-78 Colt 0.6
1977-78 Arrow 0.5

8—HEATER CONTROL, RENEW
1971-76 .... 0.8
1977-78 Colt 0.7
1977-78 Arrow 0.3

(Continued)

Engine Cooling & Heater System—TIME Cont'd

9—HEATER HOSE, RENEW
1971-78—
One 0.6
Both 0.9

10—AIR DUCT VENTILATOR ASSY, RENEW
1971-76 ....0.6

Engine—TIME

OPERATION INDEX

Engine, R&R 1
Engine, R&R & Overhaul 2
Cylinder Head, R&R Or Gasket, Renew 3
Valves, Grind 4
One Valve, Renew & Grind 5
Valve Springs, Renew 6
Rocker Arm Cover Gasket, Renew 7
Oil Pan Or Gasket, R&R Or Renew 8
Valve Clearance, Adjust 9
Timing Cover Seal & Gasket, Renew 10
Timing Chain Or Gears, Renew 11
Timing Chain Tensioner, Renew 12
Camshaft, R&R Or Renew 13
Oil Pump, R&R Or Renew 14
Piston Ring(S), Renew 15
Rings & Main Bearings, Renew & Grind Valves 16
Rod Bearing(S), Renew 17
Main Bearings, Renew 18
Main & Rod Bearings, Renew 19
Crankshaft, R&R Or Renew 20
Crankshaft Rear Main Oil Seal, Renew 21
Piston(S), Renew 22
Connecting Rod(S), Renew 23
Crankshaft Pulley, Renew 24

1—ENGINE, R&R
Does not include transfer of any part of engine or replacement of special equipment.
1971-78—
Auto Trans 5.1
Std Trans 4.4

—NOTE—
To Renew Engine, For Transfer Of All Parts Not Included With New Engine, Not Including Special Equipment, Add 2.0

2—ENGINE, R&R & OVERHAUL
Includes rebore cylinders with boring bar, renew pistons, rings, pins & all bearings, grind valves, plastigauge bearings and perform minor tune-up.
1971-78—
Auto Trans 16.7
Std Trans 16.0

3—CYLINDER HEAD, R&R OR GASKET, RENEW
Includes adjust valve clearance.
1971-76 ....3.5
1977-78—
1600 Eng 3.0
2000 Eng 3.9

—NOTE—
To Renew Head Add 1.0

4—VALVES, GRIND
Includes R&R head & adjust valve clearance.
1971-76 ....4.4
1977-78—
1600 Eng 3.8
2000 Eng 4.4

5—ONE VALVE, RENEW & GRIND
Includes R&R head & adjust valve clearance.
1971-76 ....3.7
1977-78—
1600 Eng 2.7
2000 Eng 3.8

6—VALVE SPRINGS, RENEW
Includes replace valve stem oil seals & adjust valve clearance.
1971-76—
One 1.4
All 3.7
1977-78, 1600 Eng—
One 2.6
All 3.1
1977-78, 2000 Eng—
One 3.8
All 4.4

—NOTE—
Use Air To Hold Up Valves.

7—ROCKER ARM COVER GASKET, RENEW
1971-78 ....0.5

8—OIL PAN OR GASKET, R&R OR RENEW
1971-76 ....1.1
1977-78—
1600 Eng 0.9
2000 Eng 1.1

9—VALVE CLEARANCE, ADJUST
1971-78 ....0.6

10—TIMING CASE COVER SEAL & GASKET, RENEW
1971-76—
Oil Seal 0.7
Cover Gasket 4.1
1977-78, 1600 Eng—
Oil Seal 0.5
Cover Gasket 5.0
1977-78, 2000 Eng—
Oil Seal 0.7
Cover Gasket 4.2

11—TIMING CHAIN OR GEARS, RENEW
1971-76 ....4.5
1977-78—
1600 Eng 5.2
2000 Eng 4.8

12—TIMING CHAIN TENSIONER, RENEW
1971-76 ....4.5
1977-78—
1600 Eng 5.1
2000 Eng 4.7

13—CAMSHAFT, R&R OR RENEW
1971-76 ....1.1
1977-78—
1600 Eng 1.2
2000 Eng 1.2

14—OIL PUMP, R&R OR RENEW
1971-76 ....1.0
1977-78—
1600 Eng 1.0
2000 Eng 4.7

—NOTE—
To Overhaul, Add 0.6

15—PISTON RING(S), RENEW
1971-76—
One Piston 4.7
All Pistons 5.6
1977-78, 1600 Eng—
One Piston 4.3
All Pistons 4.9
1977-78, 2000 Eng—
One Piston 5.3
All Pistons 6.3

16—RINGS & MAIN BEARINGS, RENEW & GRIND VALVES
1971-78 ....8.8

17—ROD BEARING(S), RENEW
1971-78—
One 1.7
All 2.3

18—MAIN BEARINGS, RENEW
Includes plastigauge bearings.
1971-78 ....2.6

19—MAIN & ROD BEARINGS, RENEW
Includes platigauge bearings.
1971-78 ....3.8

—NOTE—
To Renew Oil Pump, Add 0.8

20—CRANKSHAFT, R&R OR RENEW
1971-76—
Auto Trans 7.7
Std Trans 7.0
1977-78—
1600 Eng Exc 6.3
W/Air Cond 7.3
2000 Eng Exc 6.5
W/Air Cond 7.5

21—CRANKSHAFT REAR MAIN OIL SEAL, RENEW
1971-76 ....2.5
1977-78 ....1.9

22—PISTON(S), RENEW
Includes: Replace rings & rod bearings.
1971-76—
One 4.9
All 6.1
1977-78, 1600 Eng—
One 4.5
All 5.5
1977-78, 2000 Eng—
One 5.5
All 6.5

23—CONNECTING ROD(S), RENEW
Includes: Replace rod bearings.
1971-76—
One 4.8
All 5.9
1977-78, 1600 Eng—
One 4.3
All 5.3
1977-78, 2000 Eng—
One 5.1
All 6.1

24—CRANKSHAFT PULLEY, RENEW
1971-78 ....0.6

Clutch, Mounts & Transmission—TIME

OPERATION INDEX

Flywheel, R&R Or Renew 1
Flywheel Ring Gear, Renew 2
Clutch Or Disc, Renew 3
Release Bearing, Renew 4
Pilot Bearing, Renew 5
Clutch Control Shaft, Renew 6
Clutch Pedal, Adjust 7
Engine Mounts, Renew 8
Transmission Assy, R&R Or Renew 9
Manual Trans Case, Renew 10
Manual Control Shaft & Oil Seal, Renew 11
Main Drive Pinion Retainer Or Seal, Renew 12
Extension Housing Or Gasket, Renew 13
Extension Housing Oil Seal, Renew 14
Oil Pan Gasket, Renew 15
Front & Rear Bands, Adjust 16
Manual Trans, R&R & Overhaul 17
Main Drive Gear Bearing, Renew 18
Gear Selector Forks, Renew 19
Shift Lever, Renew 20
Speedometer Pinion Oil Seal, Renew 21
Downshift Cable, Renew 22
Neutral Safety Switch, Renew 23

1—FLYWHEEL, R&R OR RENEW
1971-78 ....2.5

2—FLYWHEEL RING GEAR, RENEW
1971-78 ....2.9

(Continued)

Clutch, Mounts & Transmission—TIME Cont'd

3—CLUTCH OR DISC, RENEW
Includes: Replace release bearing.
1971-78 .... 2.2

4—RELEASE BEARING, RENEW
1971-78 .... 2.0

5—PILOT BEARING, RENEW
1971-78 .... 2.5

6—CLUTCH CONTROL SHAFT, RENEW
1971-78 .... 2.2

7—CLUTCH PEDAL, ADJUST
1971-78 .... 0.4

8—ENGINE MOUNTS, RENEW
1971-78—
Front—
One 0.5
Both 0.7
Rear 0.4

9—TRANSMISSION ASSY, R&R OR RENEW
1971-78—
Auto Trans 3.1
Std Trans 2.1

10—MANUAL TRANS CASE, RENEW
1971-78 .... 6.8

11—MANUAL CONTROL SHAFT & OIL SEAL, RENEW
1971-78 .... 4.9

12—MAIN DRIVE PINION RETAINER OR SEAL, RENEW
1971-78 .... 2.5

13—EXTENSION HOUSING OR GASKET, RENEW
1971-78 Auto Trans 1.5

14—EXTENSION HOUSING OIL SEAL, RENEW
1971-78—
Auto Trans 0.6
Std Trans 0.5

15—OIL PAN GASKET, RENEW
1971-78—
Auto Trans 0.6
Std Trans 0.5

16—FRONT & REAR BANDS, ADJUST
1971-78 .... 1.6

17—MANUAL TRANS, R&R & OVERHAUL
1971-78 .... 6.9

18—MAIN DRIVE GEAR BEARING, RENEW
1971-78 .... 4.2

19—GEAR SELECTOR FORKS, RENEW
1971-78 .... 3.1

20—SHIFT LEVER, RENEW
1971-78 .... 0.5

21—SPEEDOMETER PINION OIL SEAL, RENEW
1971-78 .... 0.3

22—DOWNSHIFT CABLE, RENEW
1971-78 .... 0.7

23—NEUTRAL SAFETY SWITCH, RENEW
1971-78 .... 0.3

Brakes, Steering, Suspension, Universals & Rear Axle—TIME

OPERATION INDEX

Brake Shoes Or Friction Pads, Renew 1
Master Cylinder, Renew 2
Master Cylinder, R&R & Overhaul 3
Wheel Cylinders, Renew 4
Wheel Cylinders, R&R & Overhaul 5
Caliper Assy, Renew 6
Caliper Assy, R&R & Overhaul 7
Bleed System 8
Brake Hose, Renew 9
Hub, Disc Or Shield, Renew 10
Brake Drum, Renew 11
Brake Adjuster, Renew 12
Brake Proportioning Valve, Renew 13
Brake Pedal, Renew 14
Parking Brake Cable, Renew 15
Parking Brake Lever, Renew 16
Steering Gear Assy, Renew 17
Steering Gear Assy, Overhaul 18
Cross Shaft Oil Seal, Renew 19
Steering Knuckle Arm, Renew 20
Tie Rod Assy, Renew 21
Tie Rod End, Renew 22
Relay Rod Assy, Renew 23
Idler Arm Assy, Or Bushing, Renew 24
Spring(S), Renew 25
Rear Spring Leaf, Renew 26
Strut Insulator, Renew 27
Strut Sub Assy, Renew Or Overhaul 28
Pitman Arm, Renew 29
Front Hub Bearings, Renew 30
Stabilizer Or Link Bushing, Renew 31
Front Lower Arm, Renew 32
Front Lower Arm Shaft Or Bushing, Renew 33
Lower Ball Joint Assy, Renew 34
Crossmember Assy, Renew 35
Shock Absorbers, Renew 36
Rear Spring Front Eye Bushing Or U-Bolt, Renew 37
Universal Joints, Overhaul 38
Universal Joint Yoke, Renew 39
Propeller Shaft & U-Joint Assy, Renew 40
Rear Axle Housing, Renew 41
Axle Shaft, Renew 42
Axle Shaft Bearing, Renew 43
Differential Assy, Overhaul 44
Differential Side Bearings, Renew 45
Drive Pinion Front Or Rear Bearing, Renew 46
Differential End Yoke Or Oil Seal, Renew 47
Differential Assy Gasket, Renew 48

1—BRAKE SHOES OR FRICTION PADS, RENEW
1971-78—
Front Disc 0.5
Rear Drum 1.2

2—MASTER CYLINDER, RENEW
Includes: Bleed system
1971-78 .... 0.8

3—MASTER CYLINDER, R&R & OVERHAUL
Includes: Bleed system
1971-78 .... 1.5

4—WHEEL CYLINDER, RENEW
Includes: Bleed system& adjust brakes.
1971-78—
One 0.7
Both 1.2

5—WHEEL CYLINDER, R&R & OVERHAUL
Includes: Bleed system& adjust brakes.
1971-78—
One 1.2
Both 2.2

6—CALIPER ASSY, RENEW
Includes: Bleed system
1971-78—
One 0.7
Both 1.2

7—CALIPER ASSY, R&R & OVERHAUL
Includes: Bleed system
1971-78—
One 1.2
Both 2.2

8—BLEED SYSTEM
1971-78 .... 0.4

9—BRAKE HOSE, RENEW
Includes: Bleed system
1971-78 Each 0.6

10—HUB, DISC OR SHIELD, RENEW
1971-78 Each 0.8

11—BRAKE DRUM, RENEW
Includes: Adjust brakes
1971-78 .... 0.4

12—BRAKE ADJUSTER, RENEW
1971-78 .... 0.8

13—BRAKE PROPORTIONING VALVE, RENEW
Includes: Bleed system
1971-78 .... 0.5

14—BRAKE PEDAL, RENEW
1971-76 .... 0.8
1977-78 Colt Exc 0.8
W/Auto Trans 0.6
1977-78 Arrow Exc 1.0
W/Auto Trans 0.6

15—PARKING BRAKE CABLE, RENEW
1971-76 .... 0.6
1977-78 Colt 0.7
1977-78 Arrow 0.4

16—PARKING BRAKE LEVER, RENEW
1971-76 .... 0.3
1977-78 Colt 0.3
1977-78 Arrow 0.7

17— STEERING GEAR ASSY, RENEW
1971-76 .... 0.9
1977-78 .... 1.1

18—STEERING GEAR ASSY, OVERHAUL
1971-76 .... 1.5
1977-78 .... 1.7

19—CROSS SHAFT OIL SEAL, RENEW
1971-78 .... 0.7

20—STEERING KNUCKLE ARM, RENEW
1971-78 .... 1.0

21—TIE ROD ASSY, RENEW
1971-78 .... 0.6

22—TIE ROD END, RENEW
1971-78 .... 0.4

23—RELAY ROD ASSY, RENEW
1971-78 .... 0.5

24—IDLER ARM ASSY OR BUSHING, RENEW
1971-78 .... 0.7
—NOTE—
To Renew Bushing, Add 0.2

25—SPRING(S), RENEW
1971-78—
Front (Each) 1.4
Rear (Each) 0.8

26—REAR SPRING LEAF, RENEW
1971-78 .... 1.1

27—STRUT INSULATOR, RENEW
1971-78 .... 1.2

28—STRUT SUB ASSY, RENEW OR OVERHAUL
1971-78 .... 1.4

(Continued)

Brakes, Steering, Suspension, Universals & Rear Axle—TIME Cont'd

—NOTE—

For Overhaul, Add *0.2*

29—PITMAN ARM, RENEW

1971-78 .... 0.5

30—FRONT HUB BEARINGS, RENEW

1971-78—
One Side—
Inner & Outer 0.7
Both Sides—
Inner & Outer 1.3

31—STABILIZER OR LINK BUSHING, RENEW

1971-78 .... 0.6

32—FRONT LOWER ARM, RENEW

1971-78 .... 1.5

33—FRONT LOWER ARM SHAFT OR BUSHING, RENEW

1971-78 .... 1.7

34—LOWER BALL JOINT ASSY, RENEW

1971-78 .... 1.2

35—CROSSMEMBER ASSY, RENEW

1971-78 .... 2.2

36—SHOCK ABSORBERS, RENEW

1971-78—
Front Assy 1.5
Rear—
One 0.4
Both 0.6

37—REAR SPRING FRONT EYE BUSHING OR U-BOLT, RENEW

1971-78 .... 0.5

38—UNIVERSAL JOINTS, OVERHAUL

1971-78—
One 0.6
Both 1.0

39—UNIVERSAL JOINT YOKE, RENEW

1971-78 .... 0.6

40—PROPELLER SHAFT & U-JOINT ASSY, RENEW

1971-78 .... 0.4

41—REAR AXLE HOUSING, RENEW

1971-78 .... 3.2

42—AXLE SHAFT, RENEW

Includes: Replace bearing, inner oil seal & gasket.
1971-78 .... 0.8

43—AXLE SHAFT BEARING, RENEW

1971-78 .... 1.2

44—DIFFERENTIAL ASSY, OVERHAUL

1971-78 .... 4.3

45—DIFFERENTIAL SIDE BEARINGS, RENEW

1971-78 .... 3.8

46—DRIVE PINION FRONT OR REAR BEARING, RENEW

1971-78 .... 3.4

47—DIFFERENTIAL END YOKE OR OIL SEAL, RENEW

1971-78 .... 0.5

48—DIFFERENTIAL ASSY GASKET, RENEW

1971-78 .... 1.6

Speedometer, Wipers & Instrument—TIME

OPERATION INDEX

Speedometer Cable, Renew *1*
Speedometer Head, Renew *2*
W/S Wiper Motor, Renew *3*
W/S Wiper Link Assy, Renew *4*
W/S Wiper Arms, Renew *5*
Fuel Gauge (Dash Unit), Renew *6*
Fuel Tank Gauge, Renew *7*
Oil Pressure Switch, Renew *8*
Temperature Gauge (Dash Unit), Renew *9*
Temperature Gauge Sending Unit, Renew *10*
Headlamp Switch, Renew *11*
Stop Lamp Switch, Renew *12*
Hazard Warning & Turn Signal Switch, Renew *13*

1—SPEEDOMETER CABLE, RENEW

1971-78 .... 0.4

2—SPEEDOMETER HEAD, RENEW

1971-74 .... 0.4
1975-76 .... 1.1
1977-78 .... 0.8

3—W/S WIPER MOTOR, RENEW

1971-76 .... 0.5
1977-78 Colt 0.5
1977-78 Arrow 0.6

4—W/S WIPER LINK ASSY, RENEW

1971-78 .... 0.6

5—W/S WIPER ARM, RENEW

1971-78 .... 0.2

6—FUEL GAUGE (DASH UNIT), RENEW

1971-74 .... 0.6
1975-76 .... 1.1
1977-78 Colt 1.0
1977-78 Arrow 0.9

7—FUEL TANK GAUGE, RENEW

1971-76 .... 0.4
1977-78 Colt Exc 0.8
Wagon 0.4
1977-78 Arrow 1.1

8—OIL PRESSURE SWITCH, RENEW

1971-78 .... 0.3

9—TEMPERATURE GAUGE (DASH UNIT), RENEW

1971-74 .... 0.6
1975-76 .... 1.1
1977-78 Colt 1.1
1977-78 Arrow 0.9

10—TEMPERATURE GAUGE SENDING UNIT, RENEW

1971-78 .... 0.3

11—HEADLAMP SWITCH, RENEW

1971-78 .... 0.4

12—STOP LAMP SWITCH, RENEW

1971-78 .... 0.2

13—HAZARD WARNING & TURN SIGNAL SWITCH, RENEW

1971-78 .... 0.8

IDENTIFICATION

ALL MODELS....82

ILLUSTRATIONS

FIG 1 – ENGINE EXTERIOR
FIG 2 – CRANKSHAFT, FLYWHEEL & PISTONS
FIG 3 – VALVE MECHANISM
FIG 4 – MANUAL TRANSMISSION
FIG 5 – FRONT SUSPENSION
FIG 6 – STEERING LINKAGE
FIG 7 – REAR AXLE

OPERATION TIMES

A

Air Pump.... 87
Alternator.... 87
Ammeter.... 90
Automatic Transmission.... 88
Axle Shaft.... 89

B

Brake Drums.... 89
Brakes.... 89

C

Cables (Ignition).... 87
Calipers.... 89
Camshaft.... 88
Carburetor.... 87
Clutch.... 88
Coil, Ignition.... 87
Compression Test.... 87
Connecting Rods.... 88
Cooling System.... 87
Crankshaft.... 88
Cylinder Block.... 88
Cylinder Head.... 88

D

Dash Gauges.... 89
Differential.... 89
Disc Brakes.... 89
Distributor.... 87

E

Emission Controls.... 87
Engine Assembly.... 88
Engine Mountings.... 88
Engine Oiling.... 88
Engine Tune-Up.... 87
Exhaust System.... 87

F

Flywheel.... 88
Front Suspension.... 89
Fuel Gauges.... 89
Fuel Pump.... 87
Fuel Tank.... 87

H

Hand Brake.... 89
Headlight Switch.... 90
Heater.... 87
Hose (Brake).... 89
Hose (Radiator).... 87
Hydraulic Brakes.... 89

I

Ignition.... 87
Ignition Coil.... 87
Ignition Switch.... 87
Intake Manifold.... 87

L

Light Switches.... 90

M

Main Bearings.... 88
Master Cylinder.... 89
Muffler.... 87

O

Oil Gauge.... 89
Oiling, Engine.... 88
Oil Pan.... 88
Oil Pump.... 88

P

Parking Brake.... 89
Piston Rings.... 88
Pistons.... 88
Power Brake.... 89

R

Radiator.... 87
Radiator Hose.... 87
Rear Axle.... 89
Regulator (Alternator).... 87
Rocker Arms.... 88
Rod Bearings.... 88

S

Shocks (Front).... 89
Shocks (Rear).... 89
Speedometer.... 89
Springs (Front).... 89
Springs (Rear).... 89
Starting Motor.... 87
Steering Gear.... 89
Steering Linkage.... 89
Switches (light).... 90
Synchro-Mesh Trans.... 88

T

Tachometer.... 90
Temperature Gauge.... 90
Thermostat.... 87
Timing Case Cover.... 88
Timing Chain.... 88
Timing Gears.... 88
Transmission, Manual.... 88
Transmission, Automatic.... 88
Tune-Up, Engine.... 87

U

Universals.... 89

V

Vacuum Control Unit.... 87
Valve Lifters.... 88
Valve System.... 88

W

Water Pump.... 87
Wheel Cylinders.... 89
Windshield Wiper.... 89

IDENTIFICATION PLATE

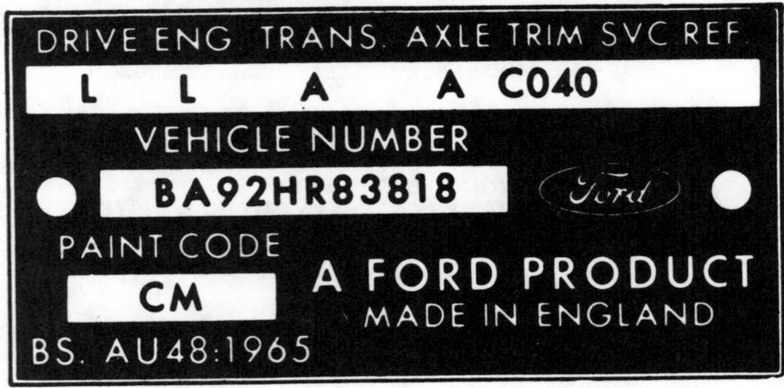

LOCATION – On right hand fender apron in the engine compartment

TOP LINE

Drive – L or 2 indicates Left Hand Drive
Eng – D – 1500 c.c. High Compression with Low Compression Distributor – 1967 Exc GT
F – 1500 c.c. High Compression with normal distributor – 1967 exc GT
G – 1500 c.c. – 1967 GT
L – 1600 c.c. High Compression – 1967-70 exc GT
N – 1600 c.c. High Compression –1967-70 GT
Trans – A – 4 Speed Manual (Floor Mounted)
C – Automatic
Axle – A – 3.9 to 1
B – 4.125 to 1
Trim – Various Trim Codes

MIDDLE LINE

First Digit (Letter B) indicates Ford of Britain.
2nd Digit (Letter A) indicates assembled at Dagenham.
3rd & 4th Digits indicates BODY TYPE –
80 – Standard 4-Door Sedan
90 – Standard 2-Door Sedan
92 – Deluxe 2-Door Sedan
93 – Deluxe 4-Door Sedan
96 – GT 2-Door Sedan
97 – GT 4-Door Sedan
98 – Deluxe 4-Door Station Wagon
5th Digit (Letter) indicates Year Code –
F – 1966
G – 1967
H – 1968
J – 1969
K – 1970
6th Digit (Letter) indicates Month Code –

	1966	1967	1968	1969	1970
January	L	C	B	J	L
February	Y	K	R	U	Y
March	S	D	A	M	S
April	T	E	G	P	T
May	J	L	C	B	J
June	U	Y	K	R	U
July	M	S	D	A	M
August	P	T	E	G	P
September	B	J	L	C	B
October	R	U	Y	K	R
November	A	M	S	D	A
December	G	P	T	E	G

Last 5 digits indicates Sequence Code.

BOTTOM LINE (PAINT CODE)

1967-68 – BA – Ermine White
CJ – Lagoon Blue
CL – Black Cherry
CM – Alpine Green
CR – Blue Mink
CU – Dragoon Red
CV – Silver Fox
1969-70 – ABP – Ermine White
BJP – Anchor Blue (Dark)
BNP – Red
B4P – Amber Gold
B5P – Fern Green
CGP – Light Blue
BVP – Beige

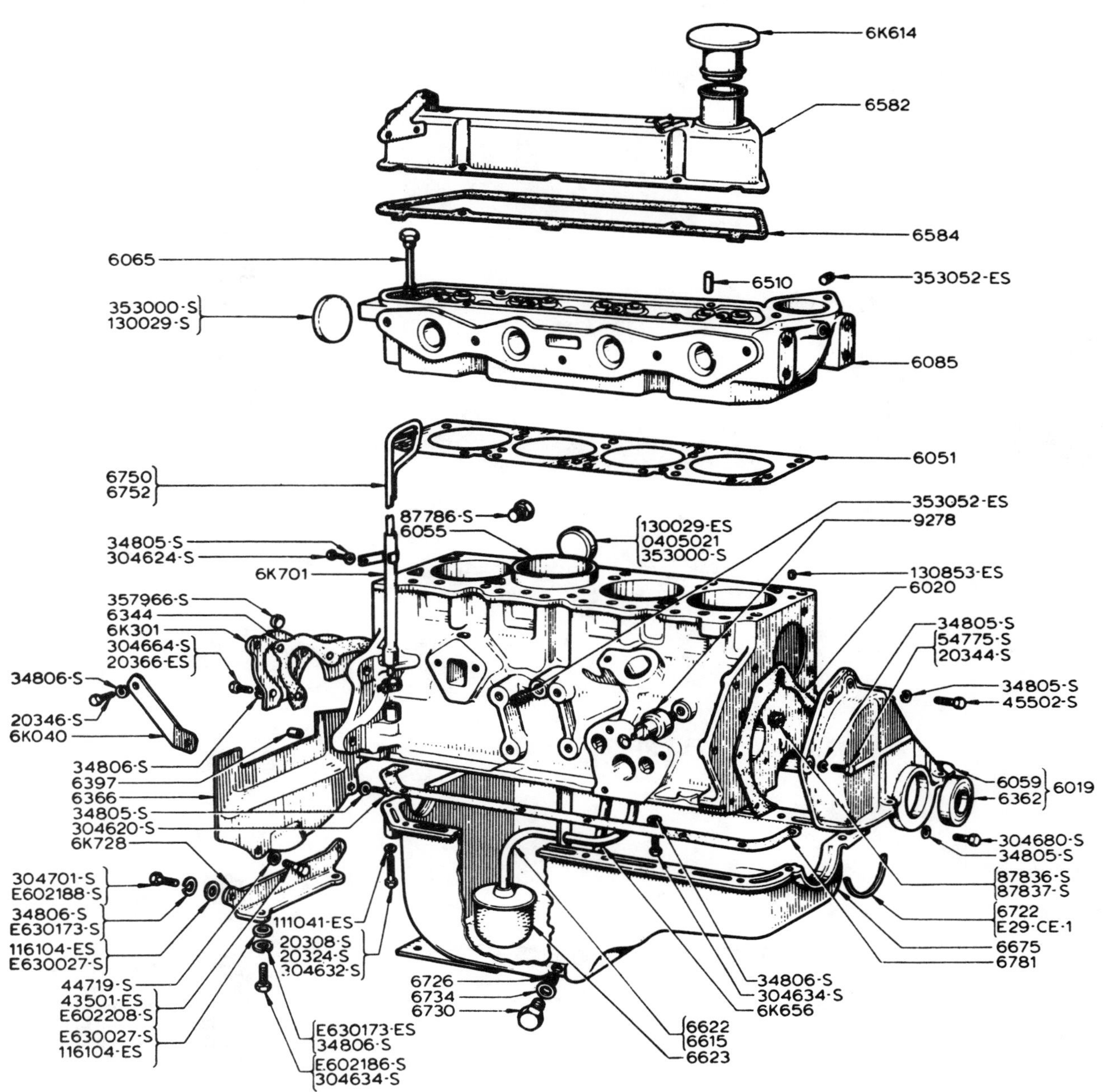

FIG 1 – ENGINE EXTERIOR

6019	**Front Cover & Seal**	**6584**	**Gasket**
6020	**Gasket**	**6K614**	**Cap**
6K040	**Bracket**	**6615**	**Cover & Tube**
6051	**Gasket**	**6622**	**See 6615**
6055	**Cylinder Liner**	**6623**	**Screen**
6059	**Front Cover**	**6675**	**Oil Pan**
6065	**Bolt**	**6K701**	**Indicator Housing**
6085	**Cylinder Head**	**6722**	**Seal**
6K301	**Retainer**	**6730**	**Plug**
6344	**Gasket**	**6734**	**Gasket**
6362	**Seal**	**6750**	**Indicator**
6366	**Cover**	**6752**	**Indicator**
6397	**Dowel**	**6781**	**Gasket**
6510	**Bushing**	**9278**	**Oil Pressure Sender**
6582	**Rocker Cover**		

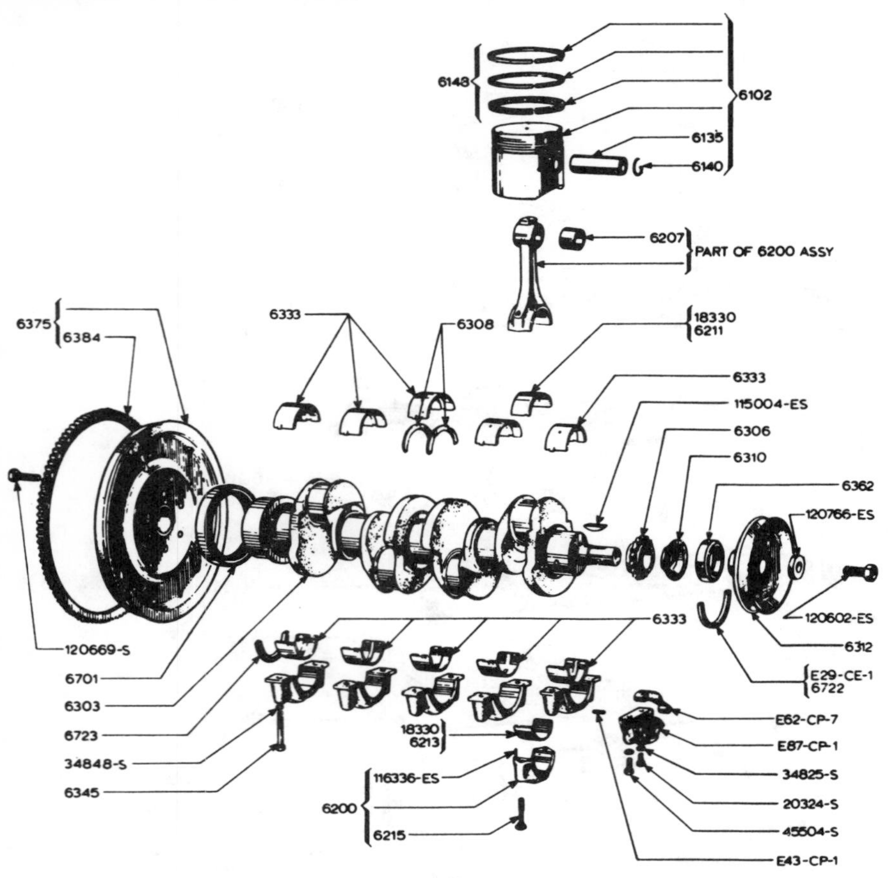

6102	Piston, Pin & Rings
6135	Pin
6140	Retainer
6148	Ring Set
6200	Connecting Rod
6207	See 6200
6211	Bearing
6213	Bearing
6215	Bolt
6303	Crankshaft
6306	Crankshaft Sprocket
6308	Washer
6310	Slinger
6312	Pulley
6333	Bearing Liner
6345	Bolt
6362	Seal
6375	Flywheel & Ring Gear
6384	Ring Gear
6701	Seal
6722	Seal
6723	Seal
18330	Bearing

FIG 2 – CRANKSHAFT, FLYWHEEL & PISTONS

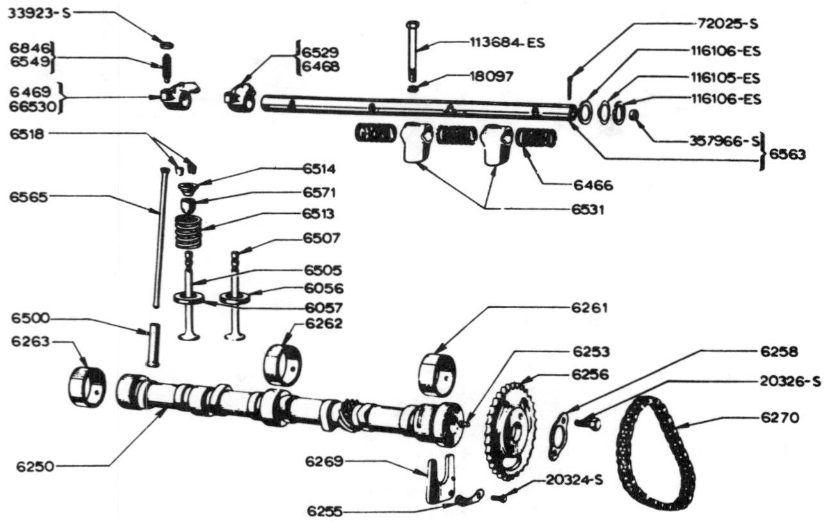

6056	Seat Insert
6057	Seat Insert
6250	Camshaft
6253	Dowel
6255	Retainer
6256	Camshaft Sprocket
6258	Retainer
6261	Bearing Liner
6262	Bearing Liner
6263	Bearing Liner
6269	Thrust Plate
6770	Timing Chain
6466	Spring
6468	Rocker Arm
6469	Rocker Arm
6486	Screw
6500	Lifter
6505	Exhaust Valve
6507	Intake Valve
6513	Spring
6514	Retainer
6518	Lock
6531	Support
6549	Screw
6563	Shaft
6565	Push Rod
6571	Seal

FIG 3 – VALVE MECHANISM

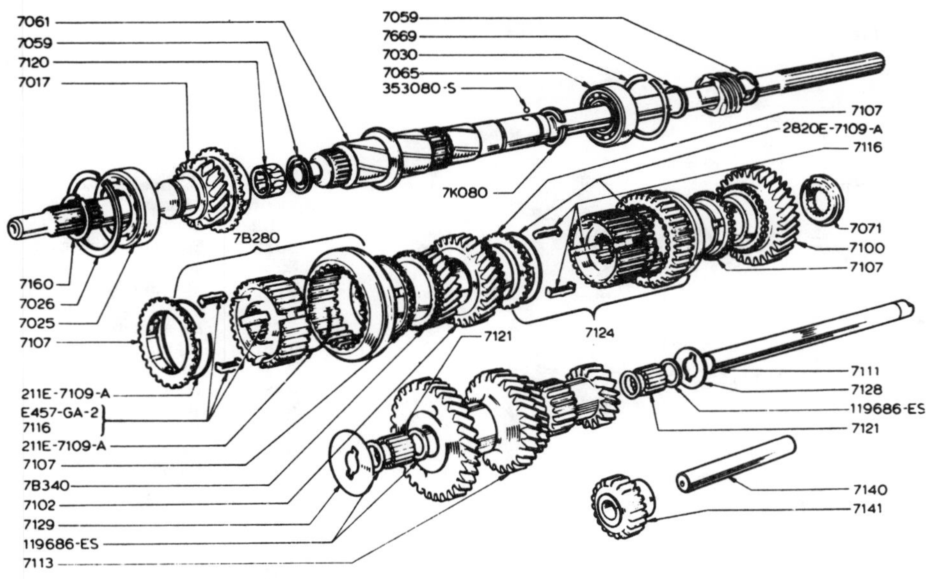

FIG 4 – MANUAL TRANSMISSION

7017	Main Drive Gear
7025	Bearing
7026	Snap Ring
7030	Snap Ring
7059	Snap Ring
7061	Main Shaft
7065	Bearing
7071	Washer
7K080	Snap Ring
7100	Low & Reverse Gear
7102	Second Speed Gear
7107	Blocking Ring
7111	Countershaft
7113	Cluster Gear
7116	Insert
7120	Bearing
7121	Roller
7124	Synchronizer
7128	Washer
7129	Washer
7140	Idler Gear Shaft
7141	Idler Gear
7160	Snap Ring
7B340	Third Speed Gear
7669	Snap Ring

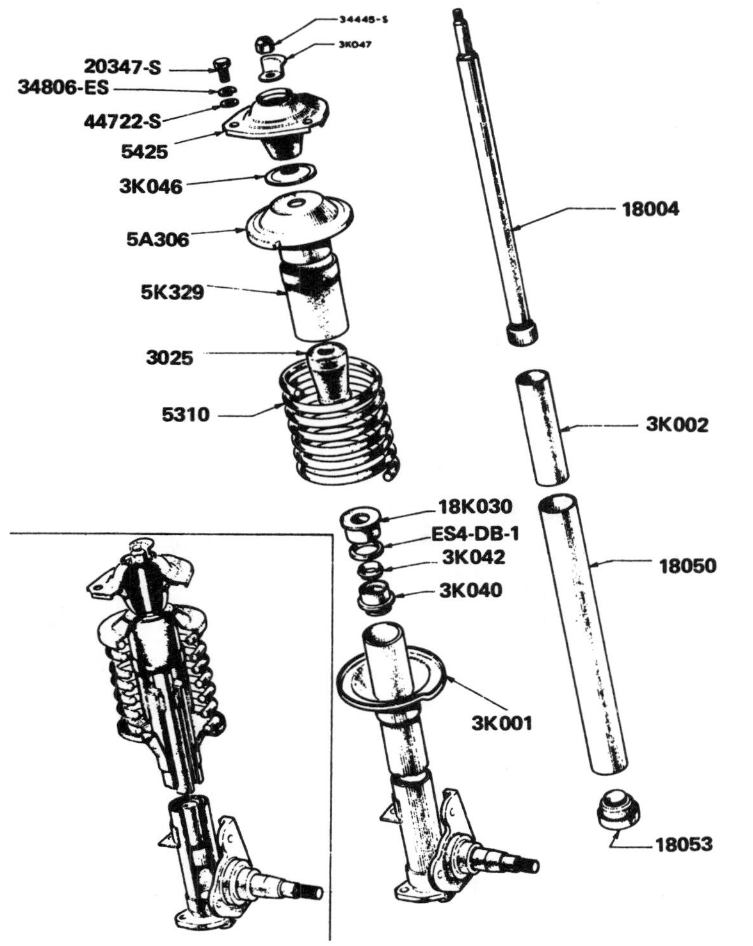

FIG 5 – FRONT SUSPENSION

3K001	Tube & Spindle
3K002	Tube
3025	Bumper
3K040	Guide & Bushing
3K042	Seal
3K046	Retainer
3K047	Bracket
5A306	Seat
5310	Spring
5K329	Seat Extension
5425	Support & Bumper
18004	Shock Piston & Rod
18K030	Cap
18050	Cylinder
18053	Valve

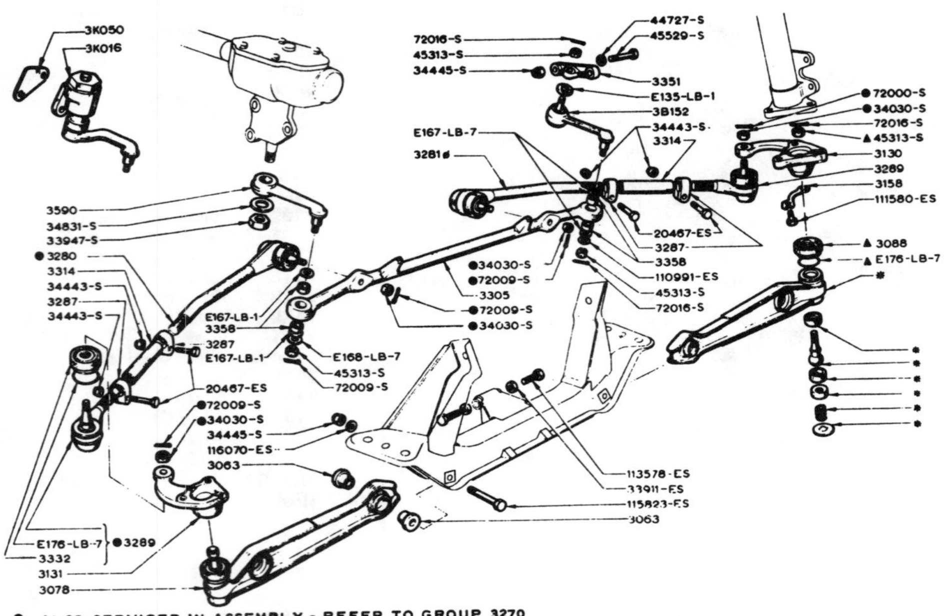

● ALSO SERVICED IN ASSEMBLY - REFER TO GROUP 3270
* SERVICED ONLY IN ASSEMBLY - REFER TO GROUP 3078
▲ ALSO SERVICED IN ASSEMBLY - REFER TO GROUP 3078

FIG 6 – STEERING LINKAGE

3K016 Damper & Arm
3K050 Spacer
3063 Bushing
3078 Suspension Arm
3088 Seal
3130 Spindle Arm
3131 Spindle Arm
3B152 Idler Arm
3158 Plate
3270 Rod
3280 Rod
3281 Rod
3287 Clamp
3289 End
3305 Rod
3314 Sleeve
3332 Seal
3351 Bracket
3358 Bushing
3590 Arm

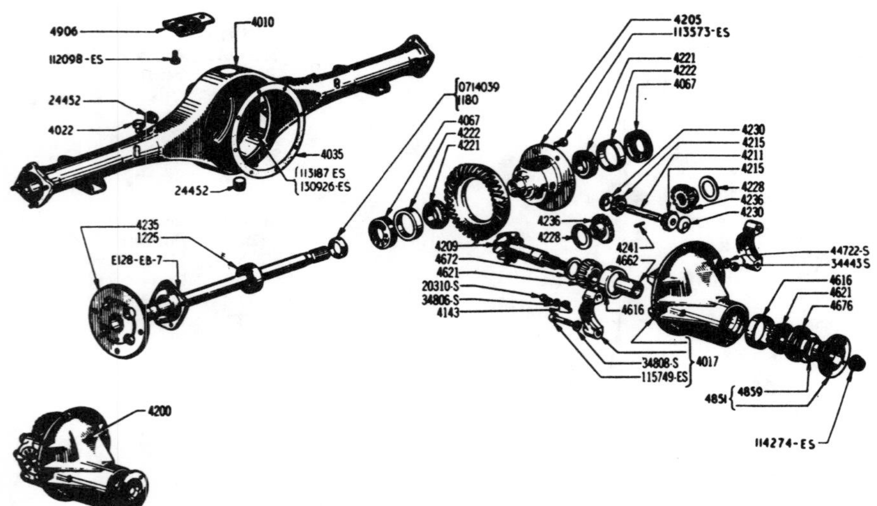

FIG 7 – REAR AXLE

1180 Bearing Retainer
1225 Bearing
4010 Housing
4017 Differntial Carrier
4035 Gasket
4067 Nut
4143 Lock
4200 Carrier & Differential
4205 Case
4209 Gear & Pinion
4211 Shaft
4215 Pinion
4221 Cone & Roller
4222 Cup
4228 Washer
4230 Washer
4235 Axle Shaft
4236 Differntial Gear
4241 Pin
4616 Cup
4621 Cone & Roller
4662 Spacer
4672 Shim
4676 Seal
4851 Flange
4859 Reflector
4906 Bumper

Ignition, Starting & Charging—TIME

OPERATION INDEX

Tune-Up, Minor *1*
Tune-Up, Major *2*
Compression, Test *3*
Distributor, R&R Or Renew *4*
Distributor, R&R & Overhaul *5*
Distributor Cap, Renew *6*
Ignition Cable Set, Renew *7*
Vacuum Control Unit, Renew *8*
Ignition Coil, Renew *9*
Starter & Ignition Switch, Renew *10*
Starter, R&R Or Renew *11*
Starter Solenoid, Renew *12*
Starter Bendix Drive, Renew *13*
Starter, R&R & Overhaul *14*
Starter Brushes, Renew *15*
Starter Armature, Renew *16*
Alternator Regulator, Renew *17*
Alternator, R&R Or Renew *18*
Alternator, R&R & Overhaul *19*
Alternator Diodes, Renew *20*
Alternator Bearings, Renew *21*
Alternator Brushes, Renew *22*
Alternator Pulley, Renew *23*

1—TUNE-UP, MINOR
Includes renew points, condenser & plugs. Set spark timing & adjust carburetor idle.
1967-70 .... 1.2

2—TUNE-UP, MAJOR
Includes: Check compression, clean or renew and adjust spark plugs. R&R dist, renew points and condenser. Adjust ignition timing, carburetor and fan belts. Clean battery terminals and service air cleaner. Check coil & clean or replace fuel filter.
1967-70 .... 2.7

3—COMPRESSION TEST
1967-70 .... 0.5

4—DISTRIBUTOR, R&R OR RENEW
1967-70 .... 0.4

—NOTE—
For Stroboscope Adjust, Add *0.3*

5—DISTRIBUTOR, R&R & OVERHAUL
1967-70 .... 1.2

6—DISTRIBUTOR CAP, RENEW
1967-70 .... 0.3

7—IGNITION CABLE SET, RENEW
1967-70—
One 0.3
All 0.4

8—VACUUM CONTROL UNIT, RENEW
1967-70 .... 0.7

9—IGNITION COIL, RENEW
1967-70 .... 0.4

10—STARTER & IGNITION SWITCH, RENEW
1967-70 .... 0.3

11—STARTER, R&R OR RENEW
1967-70 .... 0.6

12—STARTER SOLENOID, RENEW
1967-70 .... 0.3

13—STARTER BENDIX DRIVE, RENEW
1967-70 .... 1.0

14—STARTER, R&R & OVERHAUL
Includes: Turn down commutator & replace all necessary parts.
1967-70 .... 1.8

15—STARTER BRUSHES, RENEW
1967-70 .... 0.8

16—STARTER ARMATURE, RENEW
1967-70 .... 0.5

17—ALTERNATOR REGULATOR, RENEW
1967-70 .... 0.7

18—ALTERNATOR, R&R OR RENEW
1967-70 .... 0.5

19—ALTERNATOR, R&R & OVERHAUL
1967-70 .... 1.1

20—ALTERNATOR DIODES, RENEW
1967-70 .... 0.3

21—ALTERNATOR BEARINGS, RENEW
1967-70 .... 0.4

22—ALTERNATOR BRUSHES, RENEW
1967-70 .... 0.3

23—ALTERNATOR PULLEY, RENEW
1967-70 .... 0.5

Fuel, Emission Controls, Intake & Exhaust Systems—TIME

OPERATION INDEX

Carburetor Or Flange Gasket, Renew *1*
Carburetor, R&R & Overhaul *2*
Fuel Pump, R&R Or Renew *3*
Fuel Tank, R&R Or Renew *4*
Thermostatic Choke, Renew *5*
Air Pump Thermactor, Renew *6*
Intake Manifold Or Gasket, Renew *7*
Exhaust Manifold, Renew *8*
Inlet Pipe, Renew *9*
Muffler, Renew *10*

1—CARBURETOR OR FLANGE GASKET, RENEW
1967-70—
Exc Below 0.4
Auto Choke 0.7
G T 0.5

2—CARBURETOR, R&R & OVERHAUL
1967-70—
Exc Below 1.1
Auto Choke 1.4

3—FUEL PUMP, R&R OR RENEW
1967-70 .... 0.4

4—FUEL TANK, R&R OR RENEW
1967-70 .... 0.7

—NOTE—
To Renew Add *0.2*

5—THERMOSTATIC CHOKE, RENEW
1967-69 .... 0.3
1970 .... 0.5

6—AIR PUMP THERMACTOR, RENEW
1967-70 .... 0.4

7—INTAKE MANIFOLD OR GASKET, RENEW
1967-70—
Exc Below 0.8
Thermactor Equipped 0.9

8—EXHAUST MANIFOLD, RENEW
1967-70 .... 0.5

9—INLET PIPE, RENEW
Includes replace front resonator.
1967-70 .... 0.4

10—MUFFLER, RENEW
1967-70 .... 0.4

Engine Cooling & Heater System—TIME

OPERATION INDEX

Radiator, R&R Or Renew *1*
Radiator Hoses, Renew *2*
Water Pump, R&R Or Renew *3*
Thermostat Or Housing, Renew *4*
Heater Core, Renew *5*
Heater Blower Motor, Renew *6*
Heater Temperature Control Valve, Renew *7*
Heator Control, Renew *8*
Heater Hoses, Renew *9*

1—RADIATOR, R&R OR RENEW
1967-70 .... 0.5

2—RADIATOR HOSES, RENEW
1967-70, Each 0.4

3—WATER PUMP, R&R OR RENEW
1967-68 .... 0.8
1969-70 .... 0.9

4—THERMOSTAT OR HOUSING, RENEW
1967-70 .... 0.4

5—HEATER CORE, RENEW
1967-70 .... 1.5

6—HEATER BLOWER MOTOR, RENEW
1967-70 .... 1.6

7—HEATER TEMPERATURE CONTROL VALVE, RENEW
1967-70 .... 0.5

8—HEATER CONTROL, RENEW
1967-70 .... 0.6

9—HEATER HOSES, RENEW
1967-70, Each 0.4

Engine—TIME

OPERATION INDEX

Engine, R&R *1*
Engine, R&R & Overhaul *2*
Engine (Block), Renew & Grind Valves *3*
Cylinder Head, R&R Or Gasket, Renew *4*
Valves, Grind *5*
One Valve, Renew & Grind *6*
Valve Springs, Renew *7*
Rocker Arm Cover Gasket, Renew *8*
Push Rods, Renew *9*
Valve Rocker Arm Assy, Clean Or Overhaul *10*
Oil Pan Or Gasket, R&R Or Renew *11*
Valve Tappets, Adjust *12*
Timing Case Cover Seal & Gasket, Renew *13*
Timing Chain Or Gears, Renew *14*
Timing Chain Tensioner, Renew *15*
Camshaft, R&R Or Renew *16*
Camshaft Bearings, Renew *17*
Oil Pump, R&R Or Renew *18*
Camshaft Rear Welch Plug, Renew *19*
Piston Ring(S), Renew *20*
Rings & Main Bearings, Renew & Grind Valves *21*
Rod Bearing(S), Renew *22*
Main Bearings, Renew *23*
Main & Rod Bearings, Renew *24*
Crankshaft, R&R Or Renew *25*
Crankshaft Rear Main Oil Seal, Renew *26*
Piston(S), Renew *27*
Connecting Rod(S), Renew *28*
Crankshaft Pulley, Renew *29*

(Continued)

Engine—TIME Cont'd

1—ENGINE, R&R
Does not include transfer of any part of engine or replacement of special equipment.
1967-70—
Auto Trans. 2.3
Std Trans. 2.0

—NOTE—
To Renew Engine: For Transfer Of All Parts Not Included With Engine & Not Including Special Equipment, Add 2.0

2—ENGINE, R&R & OVERHAUL
Includes rebore cylinders with boring bar, renew pistons, rings, pins & all bearings, grind valves, plastigauge bearings and perform minor tune-up.
1967-70—
Auto Trans 16.6
Std Trans 16.3

3—ENGINE (BLOCK), RENEW & GRIND VALVES
1967-70—
Thermactor Equipped 11.5
Imco Equipped 11.4

—NOTE—
For Auto Trans, Add 0.3

4—CYLINDER HEAD, R&R OR GASKET, RENEW
Includes adjust tappets
1967-70—
Thermactor Equipped 1.9
Imco Equipped 1.8
Includes R&R head & adjust tappets.
1967-70—
Thermactor Equipped 3.9
Imco Equipped 3.8

6—ONE VALVE, RENEW & GRIND
Includes R&R head & adjust tappets.
1967-70—
Thermactor Equipped 2.3
Imco Equipped 2.2

7—VALVE SPRINGS, RENEW
Includes replace valve stem oil seals & adjust tappets.
1967-70—
One 0.9
All 1.6

8—ROCKER ARM COVER GASKET, RENEW
1967-70 ....0.4

9—PUSH RODS, RENEW
Includes adjust tappets.
1967-70, All 0.7

10—VALVE ROCKER ARM ASSY, CLEAN OR OVERHAUL
1967-70 ....0.5

11—OIL PAN OR GASKET, R&R OR RENEW
1967-70 ....1.6

12—VALVE TAPPETS, ADJUST
1967-70 ....0.6

13—TIMING CASE COVER SEAL & GASKET, RENEW
1967-70—
Thermactor Equipped 1.7
Imco Equipped 1.6

14—TIMING CHAIN OR GEARS, RENEW
1967-70—
Thermactor Equipped 2.0
Imco Equipped 1.9

15—TIMING CHAIN TENSIONER, RENEW
1967-70 ....1.7

16—CAMSHAFT, R&R OR RENEW
Includes R&R engine.
1967-70—
Std Trans 4.8
Auto Trans—
Thermactor 5.2
Imco 5.1

17—CAMSHAFT BEARINGS, RENEW
Includes R&R engine.
1967-70—
Auto Trans 5.8
Std Trans 5.5

18—OIL PUMP, R&R OR RENEW
1967-70 ....0.4

—NOTE—
For Overhaul, Add 0.4

19—CAMSHAFT REAR WELCH PLUG, RENEW
1967-70 ....1.9

20—PISTON RING(S), RENEW
1967-70—
Thermactor Equipped—
One 3.8
All 5.4
Imco Equipped—
One 3.7
All 5.2

21—RINGS & MAIN BEARINGS, RENEW & GRIND VALVES
1967-70—
Thermactor Equipped 7.2
Imco Equipped 7.0

22—ROD BEARING(S), RENEW
1967-70—
One 2.6
All 3.2

23—MAIN BEARINGS, RENEW
Includes plastigauge bearings.
1967-70 ....3.4

24—MAIN & ROD BEARINGS, RENEW
Includes plastigauge bearings.
1967-70 ....4.4

25—CRANKSHAFT, R&R OR RENEW
1967-70—
Auto Trans 6.2
Std Trans 5.9

26—CRANKSHAFT REAR MAIN OIL SEAL, RENEW
1967-70—
Auto Trans 7.7
Std Trans 7.4

27—PISTON(S), RENEW
1967-70—
Thermactor Equipped—
One 4.0
All 6.2
Imco Equipped—
One 3.9
All 6.0

28—CONNECTING ROD(S), RENEW
1967-70—
Thermactor Equipped—
One 4.0
All 6.2
Imco Equipped—
One 3.9
All 6.0

29—CRANKSHAFT PULLEY, RENEW
1967-70—
Thermactor Equipped 0.5
Imco Equipped 0.4

5—VALVES, GRIND
26-FRONT SUSPENSION LWER ARM, RENW

Clutch, Mounts & Transmission—TIME

OPERATION INDEX

Flywheel, R&R Or Renew 1
Flywheel Ring Gear, Renew 2
Clutch Or Disc, Renew 3
Release Bearing, Renew 4
Pilot Bearing, Renew 5
Clutch Pedal, Adjust 6
Clutch Master Cylinder, Renew 7
Clutch Master Cylinder, Overhaul 8
Clutch Slave Cyl, Renew 9
Clutch Slave Cyl, Overhaul 10
Engine Mounts, Renew 11
Transmission Assy, R&R Or Renew 12
Extension Housing Or Gasket Renew 13
Extension Housing Oil Seal, Renew 14
Oil Pan Gasket, Renew 15
Front & Rear Bands, Adjust 16
Manual Trans, R&R & Overhaul 17

1—FLYWHEEL, R&R OR RENEW
1967-70 ....1.7

2—FLYWHEEL RING GEAR, RENEW
1967-70 ....2.0

3—CLUTCH OR DISC, RENEW
1967-70 ....1.7

4—RELEASE BEARING, RENEW
1967-70 ....1.4

5—PILOT BEARING, RENEW
1967-70 ....1.8

6—CLUTCH PEDAL, ADJUST
1967-70 ....0.3

7—CLUTCH MASTER CYL, RENEW
1967-70—
L/Power Bbrakes 0.4
W/Power Brakes 0.5

8—CLUTCH MASTER CYL, OVERHAUL
1967-70—
L/Power Brakes 0.6
W/Power Brakes 0.7

9—CLUTCH SLAVE CYL, RENEW
1967-70 ....0.4

10—CLUTCH SLAVE CYL, OVERHAUL
1967-70 ....0.5

11—ENGINE MOUNTS, RENEW
1967-70—
Front—
Right 0.6
Left 0.5
Both 0.9
Rear 00.5

12—TRANSMISSION ASSY, R&R OR RENEW
1967-70—
Auto Trans 2.3
Std Trans 1.4

13—EXTENSION HOUSING OR GASKET, RENEW
1967-70 ....0.7

14—EXTENSION HOUSING OIL SEAL, RENEW
1967-70—
Auto Trans 0.5
Std Trans 0.6

15—OIL PAN GASKET, RENEW
1967-70 ....0.6

16—FRONT & REAR BANDS, ADJUST
1967-70—
Front 0.7
Rear 0.3

Clutch, Mounts & Transmission—TIME Cont'd

17—MANUAL TRANS, R&R & OVERHAUL
1967-70 ....3.1

Brakes, Steering, Suspension, Universals & Rear Axle—TIME

OPERATION INDEX

Brake Shoes, Or Friction Pads, Renew 1
Master Cylinder, Renew 2
Master Cylinder, R&R & Overhaul 3
Wheel Cylinders, Renew 4
Wheel Cylinders, R&R & Overhaul 5
Caliper Assy, Renew 6
Caliper Assy, R&R & Overhaul 7
Bleed System 8
Brake Hose, Renew 9
Hub, Disc Or Shield, Renew 10
Power Brake Unit, Renew 11
Power Brake Check Valve, Renew 12
Brake Drum, Renew 13
Brake Proportioning Valve, Renew 14
Parking Brake Cable, Renew 15
Parking Brake Lever, Renew 16
Steering Gear Assy, Renew 17
Steering Gear Assy, R&R & Overhaul 18
Steering Rod Or End, Renew 19
Idler Arm, Renew 20
Sector Arm, Renew 21
Spring(S), Renew 22
Front Hub Bearings, Renew 23
Stabilizer End Bushings, Renew 24
Shock Absorbers, Renew 25
Front Suspension Lower Arm, Renew 26
Front Suspension Lower & Upper Arm Bushings, Renew 27
Rear Suspension Unit, Overhaul 28
Universal Joints, Renew 29
Differential Axle Housing, Renew 30
Axle Shaft, Renew 31
Axle Shaft Bearings, Renew 32
Differential Assy, Overhaul 33
Axle Drive Pinion Oil Seal, Renew 34

1—BRAKE SHOES OR FRICTION PADS, RENEW
1967-70—
Front Disc 0.8
Rear Drum 0.9

2—MASTER CYLINDER, RENEW
Includes bleed system.
1967-70 ....0.6

3—MASTER CYLINDER, R&R & OVERHAUL
Includes bleed system.
1967-70 ....0.9

4—WHEEL CYLINDER, RENEW
Includes bleed system & adjust brakes.
1967-70—
One 1.2
Both 1.4

5—WHEEL CYLINDERS, R&R & OVERHAUL
Includes bleed system & adjust brakes.
1967-70—
One 1.3
Both 1.6

6—CALIPER ASSY, RENEW
Includes bleed system.
1967-70—
One 0.7
Both 0.9

6—CALIPER ASSY, R&R & OVERHAUL
Includes bleed system.
1967-70—
One 1.3
Both 1.7

8—BLEED SYSTEM
1967-70 ....0.3

9—BRAKE HOSE, RENEW
Includes bleed system.
1967-70—
One 0.5
Both 0.7

10—HUB, DISC OR SHIELD, RENEW
1967-70—
One 1.0
Both 1.6

11—POWER BRAKE UNIT, RENEW
1967-70 ....0.6

12—POWER BRAKE CHECK VALVE, RENEW
1967-70 ....0.3

13—BRAKE DRUM, RENEW
Includes adjust brakes.
1967-70 ....0.4

14—BRAKE PROPORTIONING VALVE, RENEW
Includes adjust brakes.
1967-70 ....0.7

15—PARKING BRAKE CABLE, RENEW
1967-70—
Floor Mounted 0.3
Dash Mounted 0.6

16—PARKING BRAKE LEVER, RENEW
1967-70 ....0.7

17—STEERING GEAR ASSY, RENEW
1967-70 ....1.2

18—STEERING GEAR ASSY, R&R & OVERHAUL
1967-70 ....2.3

19—STEERING ROD OR END, RENEW
1967-70—
One 0.8
Each Additional 0.2

20—ILDER ARM, RENEW
1967-70 ....0.7

21—SECTOR ARM, RENEW
1967-70 ....0.4

22—SPRING(S), RENEW
1967-70—
Front—
One 0.8
Both 1.2
Rear—
One ①0.6
Both—
Exc. Below ①0.8
Sta Wagon ①1.0
①*To Renew Spring Leaf, Add 0.5*

23—FRONT HUB BEARINGS, RENEW
1967-70, Each 1.0

24—STABILIZER END BUSHINGS, RENEW
1967-70 ....0.8

25—SHOCK ABSORBERS, RENEW
1967-70—
Front—
One 0.4
Both 0.6
Rear—
One 0.4
Both—
Exc Below 0.5

26—FRONT SUSPENSION LOWER ARM, RENEW
1967-70—
One 1.3
Both 1.8

27—FRONT SUSPENSION LOWER ARM BUSHINGS, RENEW
1967-70, Both 0.4

28—REAR SUSPENSION UNIT, OVERHAUL
1967-70, Each 1.4

29—UNIVERSAL JOINTS, RENEW
1967-70—
Each 0.3
All 0.6

30—DIFFERENTIAL AXLE HOUSING, RENEW
1967-70 ....2.3

31—AXLE SHAFT, RENEW
Includes replace bearing & retainer gasket.
1967-70—
One 0.4
Both 0.6

32—AXLE SHAFT BEARINGS, RENEW
1967-70, Each 0.3

33—DIFFERENTIAL ASSY, OVERHAUL
1967-70 ....3.3

34—AXLE DRIVE PINION OIL SEAL, RENEW
1967-70 ....0.6

Speedometer, Wipers & Instruments—TIME

OPERATION INDEX

Speedometer Cable & Housing, Renew 1
Speedometer Head, Renew 2
W/S Wiper Motor, Renew 3
W/S Wiper Link Set, Renew 4
W/S Wiper Arm, Renew 5
Fuel Gauge (Dash Unit), Renew 6
Fuel Tank Gauge, Renew 7
Oil Gauge Sending Unit, Renew 8
Temperature Gauge (Dash Unit), Renew 9
Temperature Gauge Sending Unit, Renew 10
Ammeter, Renew 11
Tachometer, Renew 12
Instrument Cluster Voltage Limiter, Renew 13
Headlight Switch, Renew 14
Headlamp Foot Dimmer Switch, Renew 15
Stop Light Switch, Renew 16
Turn Signal Switch, Renew 17
Hazard Flasher Switch, Renew 18

1—SPEEDOMETER CABLE & HOUSING, RENEW
1967-70 ....0.4

2—SPEEDOMETER HEAD, RENEW
1967-70 ....0.4

3—W/S WIPER MOTOR, RENEW
1967-70 ....0.7

4—W/S WIPER LINK SET, RENEW
1967-70 ....0.7

5—W/S WIPER ARM, RENEW
1967-70 ....0.2

6—FUEL GAUGE (DASH UNIT), RENEW
1967-70 ....0.3

7—FUEL TANK GAUGE, RENEW
1967-70—
Exc Below 0.4
Sta Wagon 0.7

8—OIL GAUGE SENDING UNIT, RENEW
1967-70 ....0.3

(Continued)

Speedometer, Wipers & Instruments—TIME Cont'd

9—TEMPERATURE GAUGE (DASH UNIT), RENEW
1967-70—
Ecx Below 0.4
G. T. 0.3

10—TEMPERATURE GAUGE SENDING UNIT, RENEW
1967-70 .... 0.3

11—TACHOMETER, RENEW
1967-70 .... 0.3

12—AMMETER, RENEW
1967-70 .... 0.3

13—INSTRUMENT CLUSTER VOLTAGE LIMITER, RENEW
1967-70 .... 0.4

14—HEADLIGHT SWITCH, RENEW
1967-70 .... 0.3

15—HEADLIGHT FOOT DIMMER SWITCH, RENEW
1967-70 .... 0.3

16—STOP LIGHT SWITCH, RENEW
1967-70 .... 0.3

17—TURN SIGNAL SWITCH, RENEW
1967-70 .... 0.4

18—HAZARD FLASHER SWITCH, RENEW
1967-70 .... 0.3

IDENTIFICATION

ALL MODELS....92

ILLUSTRATIONS

FIG 1 – ENGINE – 1800cc CYLINDER BLOCK – EXTERNAL
FIG 2 – ENGINE – 1800 cc CYLINDER BLOCK – INTERNAL
FIG 3 – ENGINE – 1800cc CRANKSHAFT, FLYWHEEL & PISTONS
FIG 4 – ENGINE – 1800cc CAMSHAFT, GEARS & BEARINGS
FIG 5 – ENGINE – 2300cc INTERNAL PARTS (UPPER)
FIG 6 – ENGINE – 2300cc INTERNAL PARTS (LOWER)
FIG 7 – ENGINE – 2300cc EXTERNAL PARTS
FIG 8 – MANUAL TRANSMISSION – 4 SPEED
FIG 9 – MANUAL TRANSMISSION – 5 SPEED
FIG 10 – AUTOMATIC TRANSMISSION CASE, OIL PAN, EXTN HOUSING & SERVO
FIG 11 – AUTOMATIC TRANSMISSION CONVERTER, OIL PUMP & OIL COOLER
FIG 12 – AUTOMATIC TRANSMISSION CLUTCH & PLANETARY GEARS
FIG 13 – AUTOMATIC TRANSMISSION LOW & REVERSE GEARS & GOVERNOR
FIG 14 – FRONT SUSPENSION
FIG 15 – STEERING LINKAGE – 1972-76
FIG 16 – STEERING LINKAGE – 1977-78
FIG 17 – STEERING COLUMN, GEAR & WHEEL
FIG 18 – REAR AXLE & DIFFERENTIAL GEARS

A

Alternator.... 129
Alternator Regulator.... 109
Ammeter.... 109
Automatic Trans.... 111
Axle Shaft.... 112

B

Back-Up Lamp Switch.... 110
Ball Joints, Front.... 112
Battery Cables.... 110
Brakes.... 112
Brake Drum.... 112
Brake Hose.... 112

C

Cables, Battery.... 110
Cables, Ignition.... 109
Camshaft.... 110
Carburetor.... 109
Clutch.... 111
Coil, Ignition.... 109
Compression, Test.... 109
Condenser, Distributor.... 109
Control Arms, Front.... 112
Cooling System.... 110
Crankshaft.... 110
Cylinder Block.... 111
Cylinder Head.... 110

D

Dash Gauges.... 109
Differential.... 112
Directional Flasher.... 110
Directional Switch.... 110
Distributor.... 109

E

Engine Assy.... 110
Engine Mounting.... 111
Engine Oiling.... 111
Engine Tune-Up.... 109
Exhaust System.... 109

F

Fan.... 110
Flywheel.... 111
Front End Adjustments.... 112
Front Suspension.... 112
Front Wheel Bearings.... 112
Fuel Gauge.... 109
Fuel Pump.... 109
Fuel Tank.... 109

H

Handbrake.... 112
Headlamp.... 110
Heater Core.... 110
Horn.... 110
Hose, Brake.... 112
Hose, Radiator.... 110
Hydraulic Brake System.... 112

I

Idler Arm.... 112
Ignition System.... 109
Intake Manifold Gasket.... 109

L

Lamps.... 110
Lens, Lamp.... 110
Light Switch.... 110

M

Manual Transmission.... 111
Main Bearings.... 110
Master Cylinder.... 112
Muffler.... 109

O

Oiling, Engine.... 111
Oil Gauge.... 109
Oil Pan.... 111
Oil Pump.... 111

P

Parking Brake.... 112
Piston.... 110
Piston Rings.... 110
Pitman Arm.... 112
Propeller Shaft.... 112

R

Radiator.... 110
Radiator Hose.... 110
Rear Suspension.... 112
Regulator (Alternator).... 109
Rings (Piston).... 110
Rod Bearings.... 110

S

Shocks, Front.... 112
Shocks, Rear.... 112
Spark Plugs.... 109
Speedometer.... 109
Spring, Front.... 112
Spring, Rear.... 112
Starting Motor.... 109
Steering Gear.... 113
Steering Knuckle.... 112
Steering Linkage.... 112
Stop Light Switch.... 110
Switches –
Back-Up Lamp.... 110
Ignition.... 109
Light.... 110
Stop Light.... 110
Turn Signal.... 110

T

Tail Pipe.... 109
Temperature Gauge.... 109
Thermostat.... 110
Tie Rod.... 112
Timing Case.... 110
Timing Chain.... 110
Transmission.... 111
Tune-Up, Engine.... 109
Turn Signal Switch.... 110

U

Universal Joint.... 111

V

Valve System.... 110
Vibration Damper.... 111

W

Water Pump.... 110
Wheel Alignment.... 112
Wheel Bearing, Front.... 112
Wheel Bearing, Rear.... 112
Windshield Wiper.... 109
Wiring Harness.... 110

IDENTIFICATION PLATE

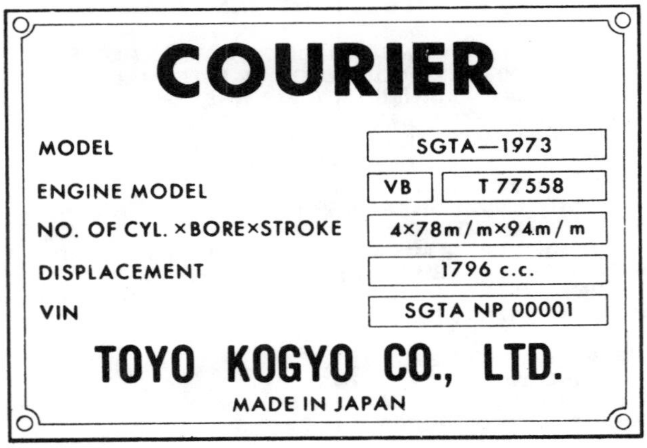

COURIER

MODEL	SGTA—1973
ENGINE MODEL	VB | T 77558
NO. OF CYL. ×BORE×STROKE	4×78m/m×94m/m
DISPLACEMENT	1796 c.c.
VIN	SGTA NP 00001

TOYO KOGYO CO., LTD.
MADE IN JAPAN

LOCATION — On top right hand side of the cowl panel in the engine compartment.

TOP LINE — SGTA — 1973

S — Source Company — Toyo Kogyo
G — Assembly Plant — Hiroshima
TA — Series — 2-Door Pick-up
1973 — Model Year

SECOND LINE — Engine Model & Number

THIRD LINE — Engine Cylinder Bore & Stroke

FOURTH LINE — Engine Cubic Centimeters

BOTTOM LINE — SGTA NP 00001

S — Source Company — Toyo Kogyo
G — Assembly Plant — Hiroshima
TA — Series — 2-Door Pick-up
N — Year Model —

L — 1971
M — 1972
N — 1973
P — 1974
R — 1975
S — 1976
T — 1977
U — 1978

P — Month Code —

	1971	1972	1973	1974	1975	1976	1977	1978
January		B	J	L	C	B	J	L
February		R	U	Y	K	R	U	Y
March		A	M	S	D	A	M	S
April		G	P	T	E	G	P	T
May		C	B	J	L	C	B	J
June.		K	R	U	Y	K	R	U
July.		D	A	M	S	D	A	M
August.		E	G	P	T	E	G	P
September.		L	C	B	J	L	C	B
October.		Y	K	R	U	Y	K	R
November		S	D	A	M	S	D	A
December	P	T	E	G	P	T	E	G

Last 5 digits indicate sequence number.

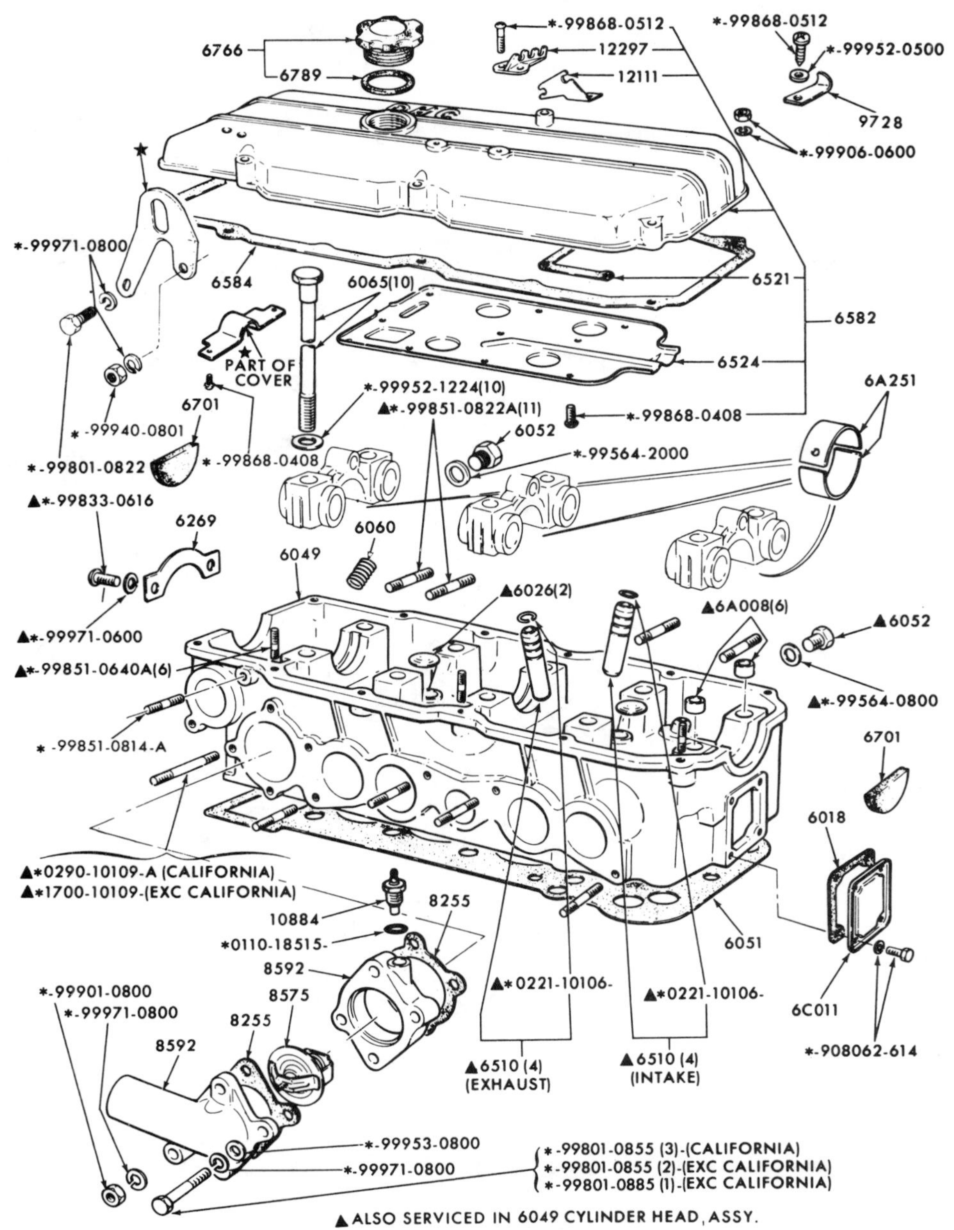

▲ALSO SERVICED IN 6049 CYLINDER HEAD, ASSY.

FIG 1 – ENGINE – 1800 CC CYLINDER BLOCK & RELATED PARTS – EXTERNAL

6A008	**Dowel**
6C011	**Plate**
6018	**Gasket**
6026	**Plug**
6049	**Cylinder Head**
6051	**Gasket**
6052	**Plug**
6060	**Insert**
6065	**Bolt**
6A251	**Bearing**
6269	**Thrust Plate**
6510	**Valve Guides**
6521	**Gasket**
6524	**Baffle**
6582	**Rocker Cover**
6584	**Gasket**
6701	**Seal**
6766	**Cap**
6789	**Gasket**
8255	**Gasket**
8575	**Thermostat**
8592	**Housing**
9728	**Bracket**
10884	**Temperature Sender**
12111	**Bracket**
12297	**Grommet**

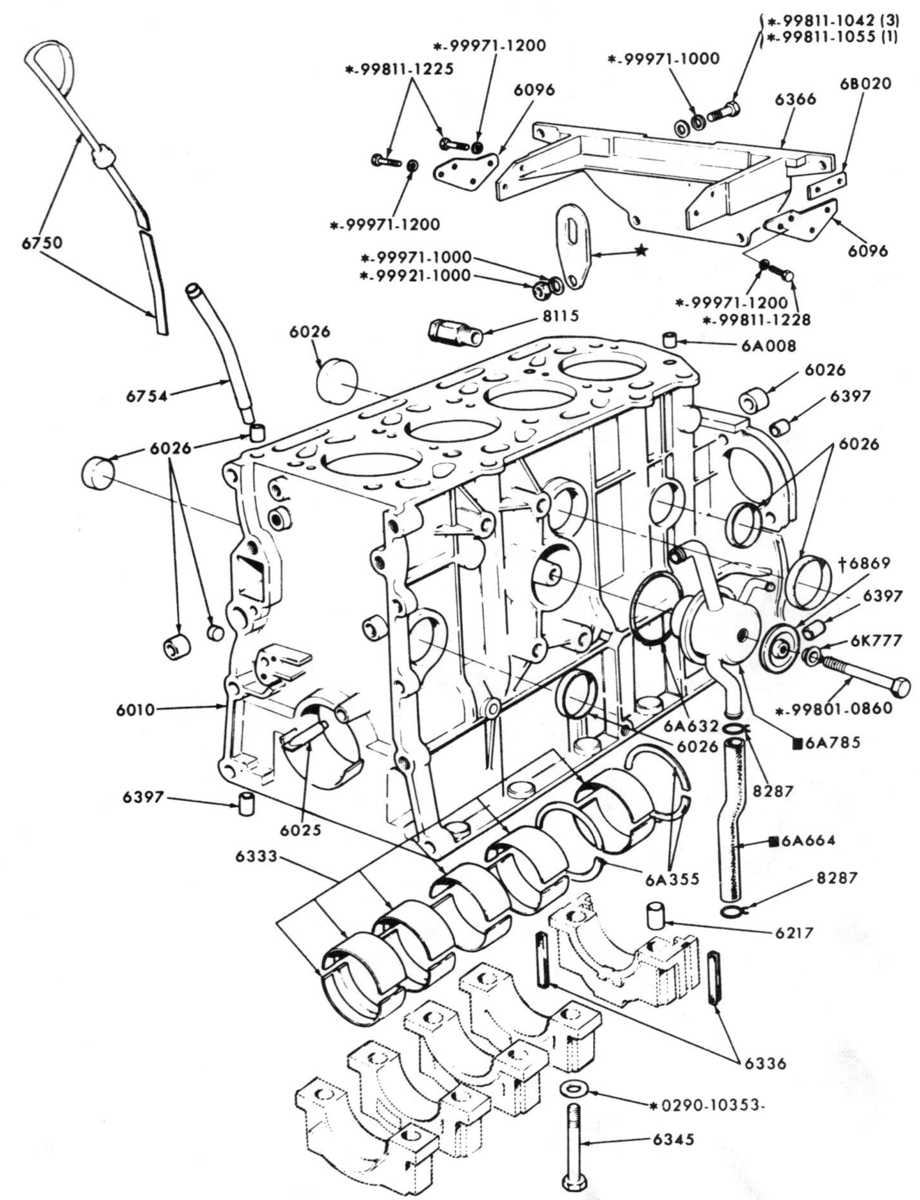

FIG 2 – ENGINE – 1800 CC CYLINDER BLOCK & RELATED PARTS – INTERNAL

6A008	Dowel	6366	Cover
6010	Cylinder Block	6397	Dowel
6B020	Spacer	6A632	Gasket
6025	Tube	6A664	Hose
6026	Plug	6750	Dipstick
6096	Bracket	6754	Tube
6217	Dowel	6K777	Seal
6333	Bearings	6A785	Oil Separator
6336	Seal	6869	Cover
6345	Bolt	8115	Drain Cock
6A355	Washer	8287	Clamp

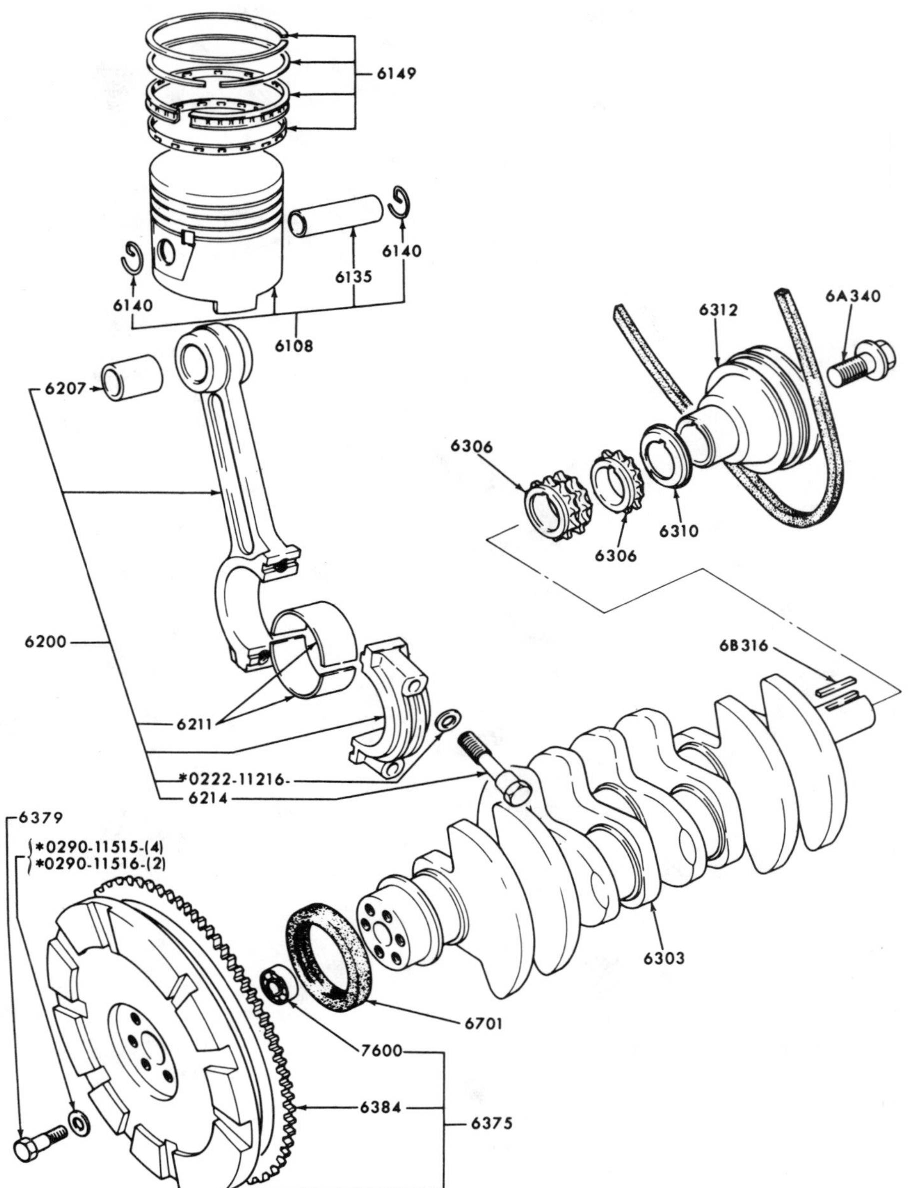

FIG 3 – ENGINE – 1800 CC CRANKSHAFT, FLYWHEEL & PISTONS

6108	Piston
6135	Pin
6140	Retainer
6149	Ring Set
6200	Connecting Rod
6207	Bushing
6211	Bearing
6214	Bolt
6303	Crankshaft
6306	Sprockets
6310	Slinger
6312	Pulley
6B316	Key
6A340	Bolt
6375	Flywheel
6379	Bolt
6384	Flywheel Ring Gear
6701	Gear
7600	Pilot Bearing

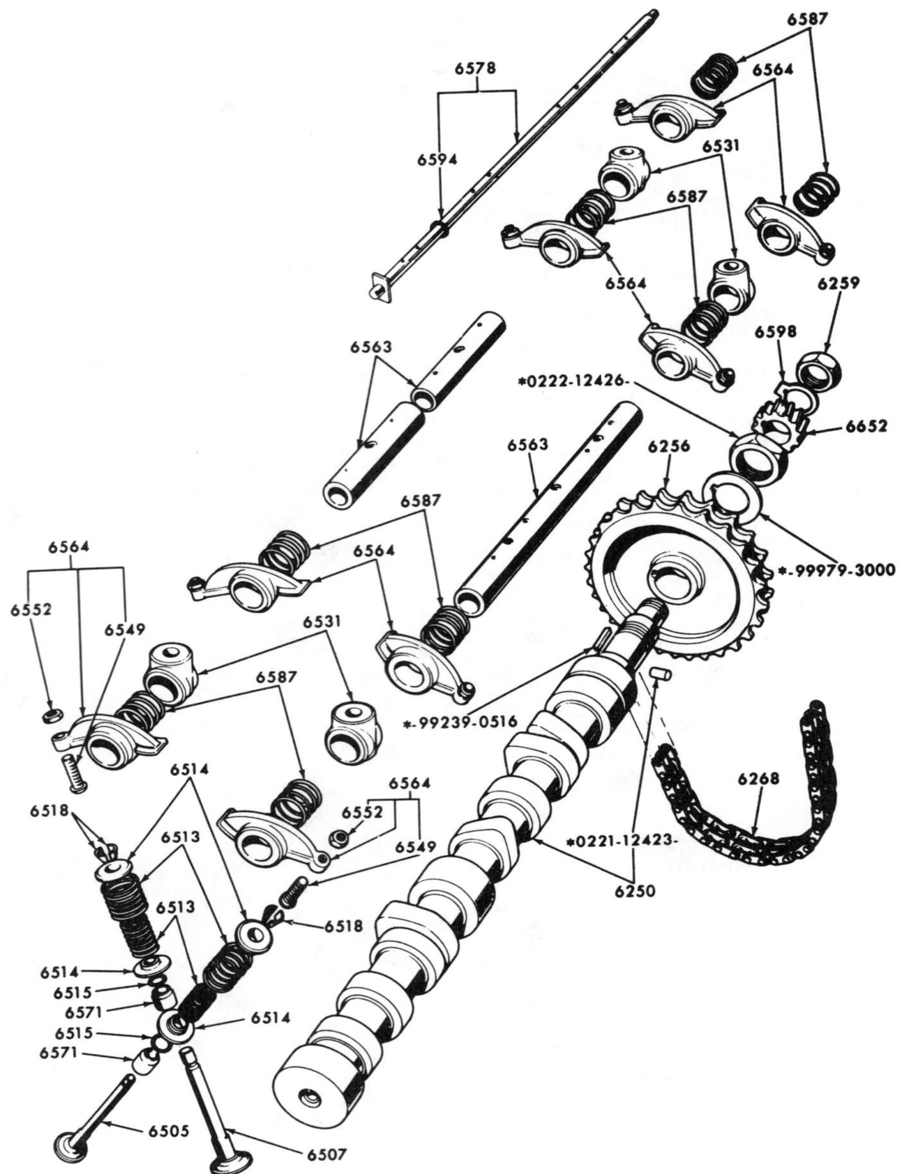

FIG 4 – ENGINE – 1800 CC CAMSHAFT, GEARS & BEARINGS

6250	Camshaft
6256	Sprocket
6259	Nut
6268	Chain
6505	Exhaust Valves
6507	Intake Valve
6513	Spring
6514	Retainer
6515	Spacer
6518	Key
6531	Support
6549	Screw
6552	Nut
6563	Shaft
6564	Arm
6571	Seal
6578	Tube
6587	Spring
6594	Seal
6598	Washer
6652	Gear

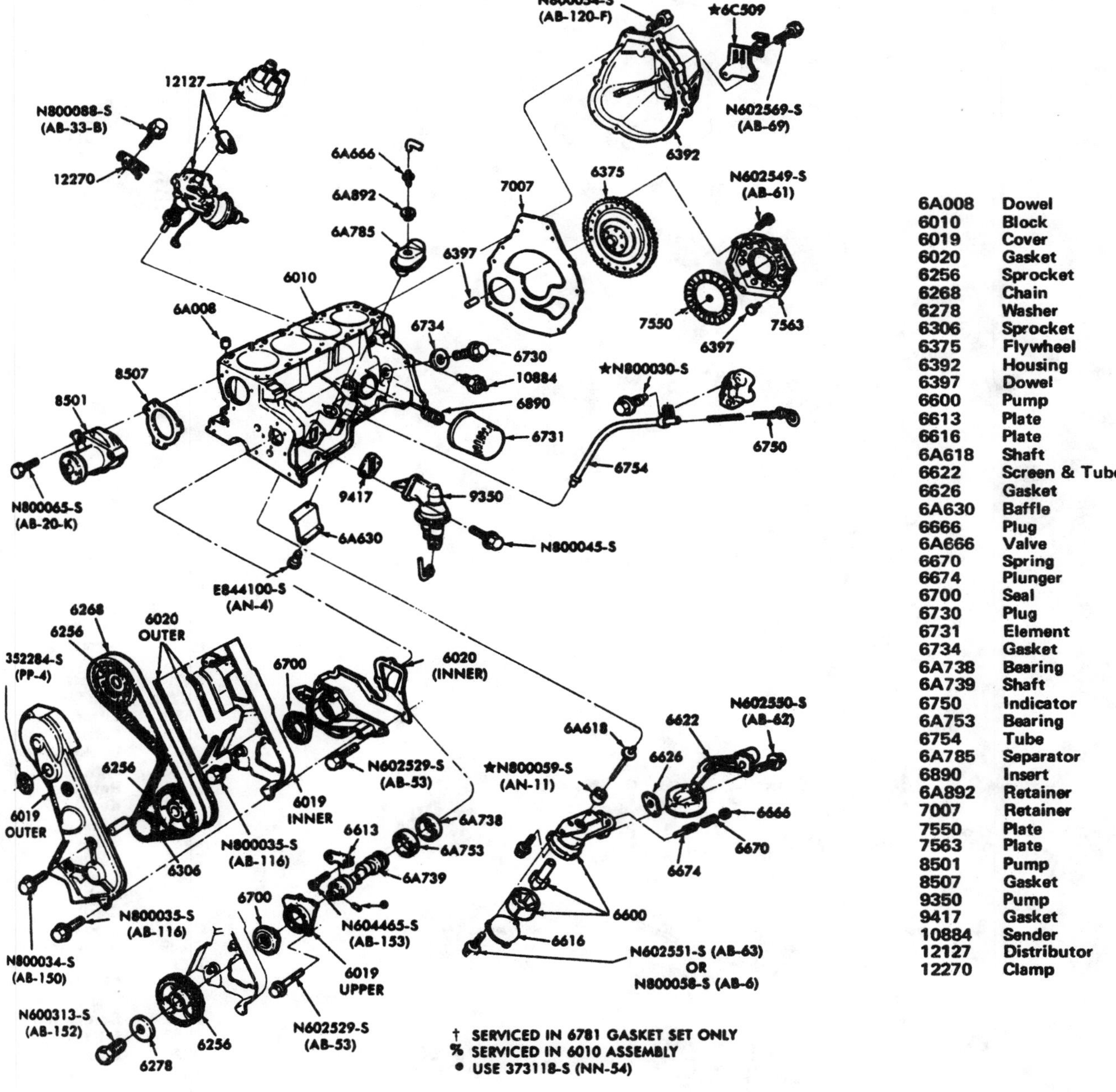

6A008	Dowel
6010	Block
6019	Cover
6020	Gasket
6256	Sprocket
6268	Chain
6278	Washer
6306	Sprocket
6375	Flywheel
6392	Housing
6397	Dowel
6600	Pump
6613	Plate
6616	Plate
6A618	Shaft
6622	Screen & Tube
6626	Gasket
6A630	Baffle
6666	Plug
6A666	Valve
6670	Spring
6674	Plunger
6700	Seal
6730	Plug
6731	Element
6734	Gasket
6A738	Bearing
6A739	Shaft
6750	Indicator
6A753	Bearing
6754	Tube
6A785	Separator
6890	Insert
6A892	Retainer
7007	Retainer
7550	Plate
7563	Plate
8501	Pump
8507	Gasket
9350	Pump
9417	Gasket
10884	Sender
12127	Distributor
12270	Clamp

FIG 5 – ENGINE – 2300 CC INTERNAL PARTS (UPPER)

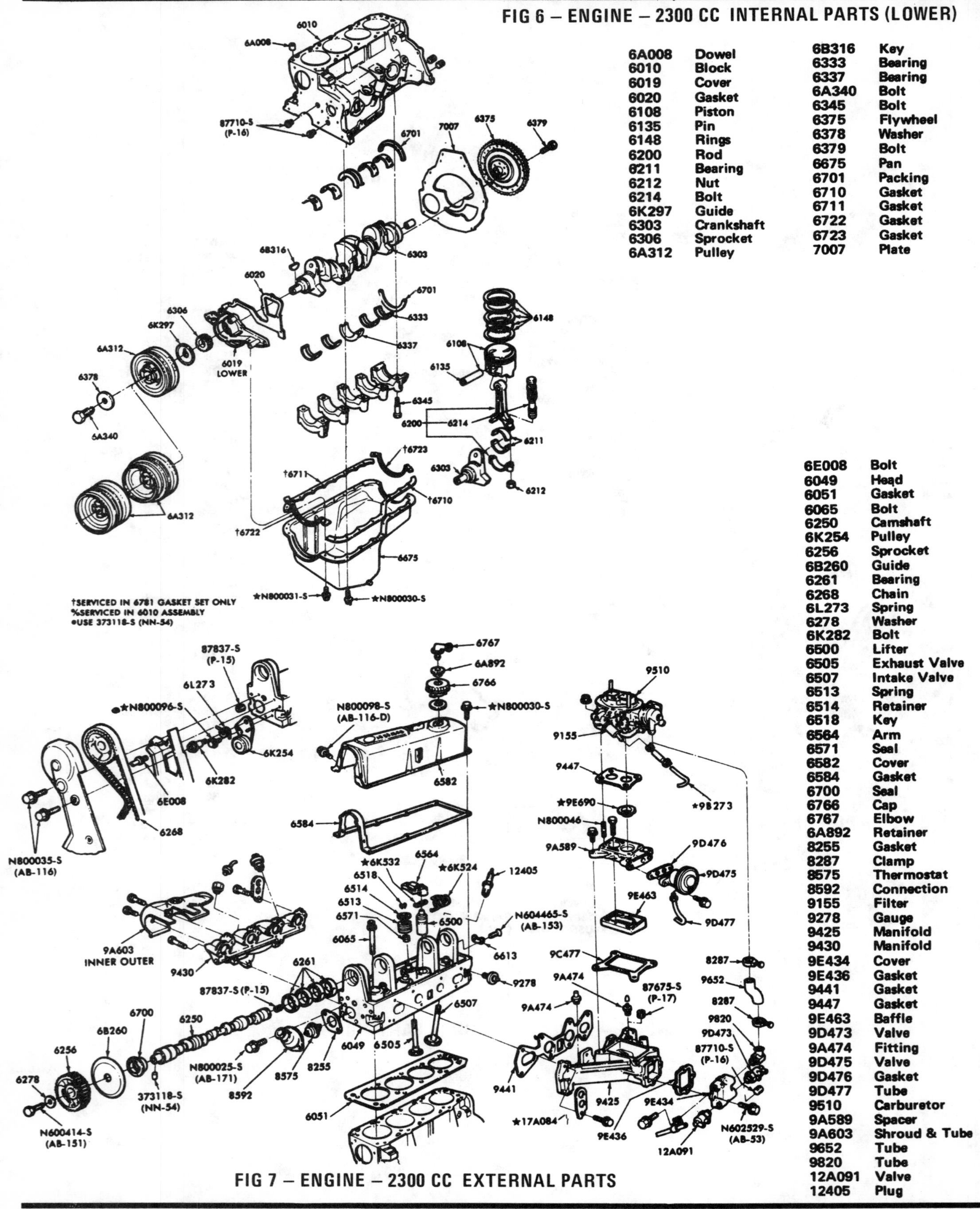

FIG 6 – ENGINE – 2300 CC INTERNAL PARTS (LOWER)

FIG 7 – ENGINE – 2300 CC EXTERNAL PARTS

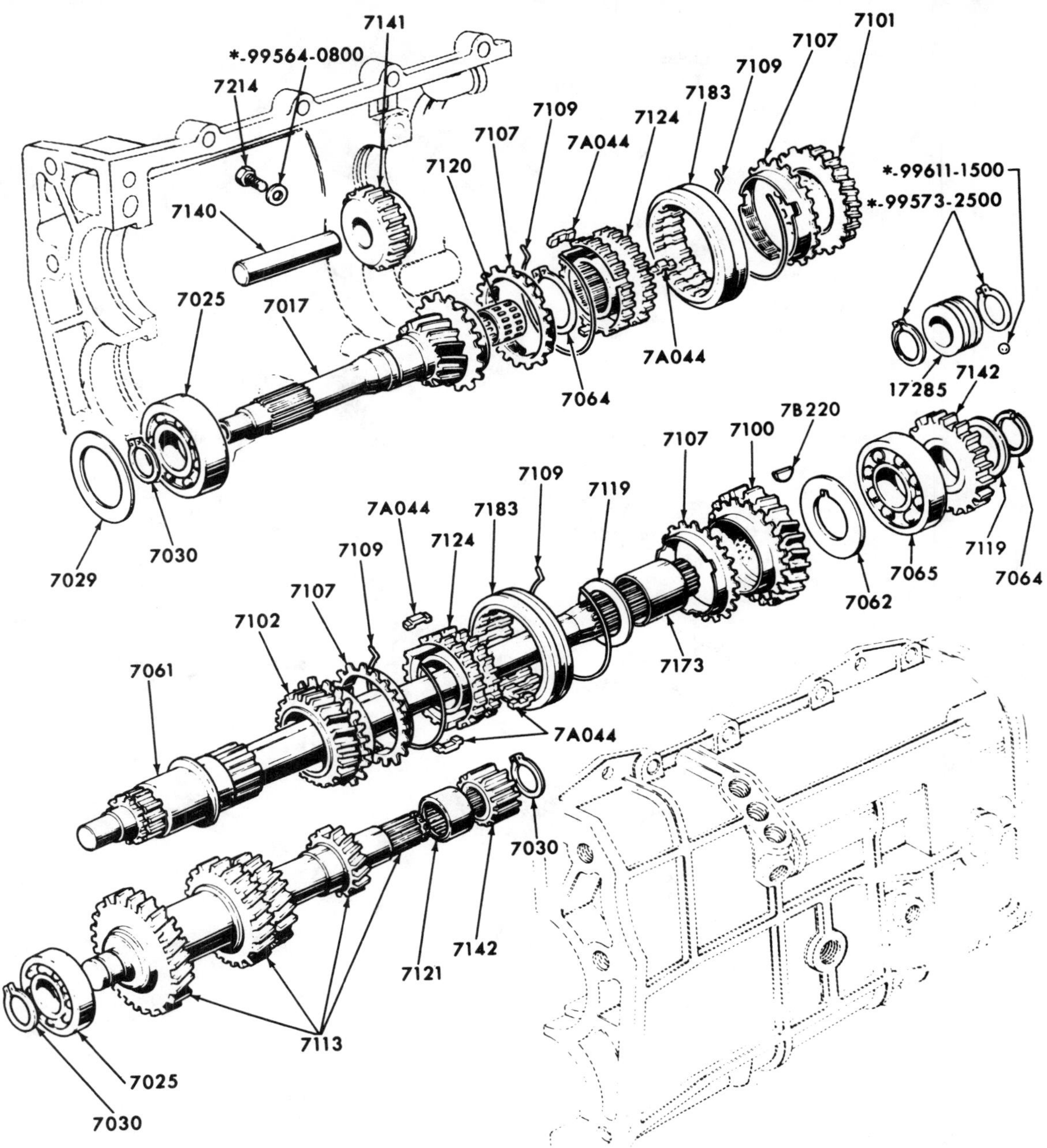

FIG 8 – MANUAL TRANSMISSION – 4-SPEED

7017	Input Shaft
7025	Bearing
7029	Shim
7030	Ring
7A044	Insert
7061	Output Shaft
7062	Washer
7064	Ring
7065	Bearing
7100	First Speed Gear
7101	Third Speed Gear
7102	Second Speed Gear
7107	Ring
7109	Spring

7113	Cluster Gear
7119	Washer
7120	Bearing
7121	Roller
7124	Synchronizer
7140	Reverse Idler Gear Shaft
7141	Reverse Idler Gear
7146	Reverse Gear
7173	Sleeve
7183	Hub
7214	Screw
7B220	Key
17285	Gear

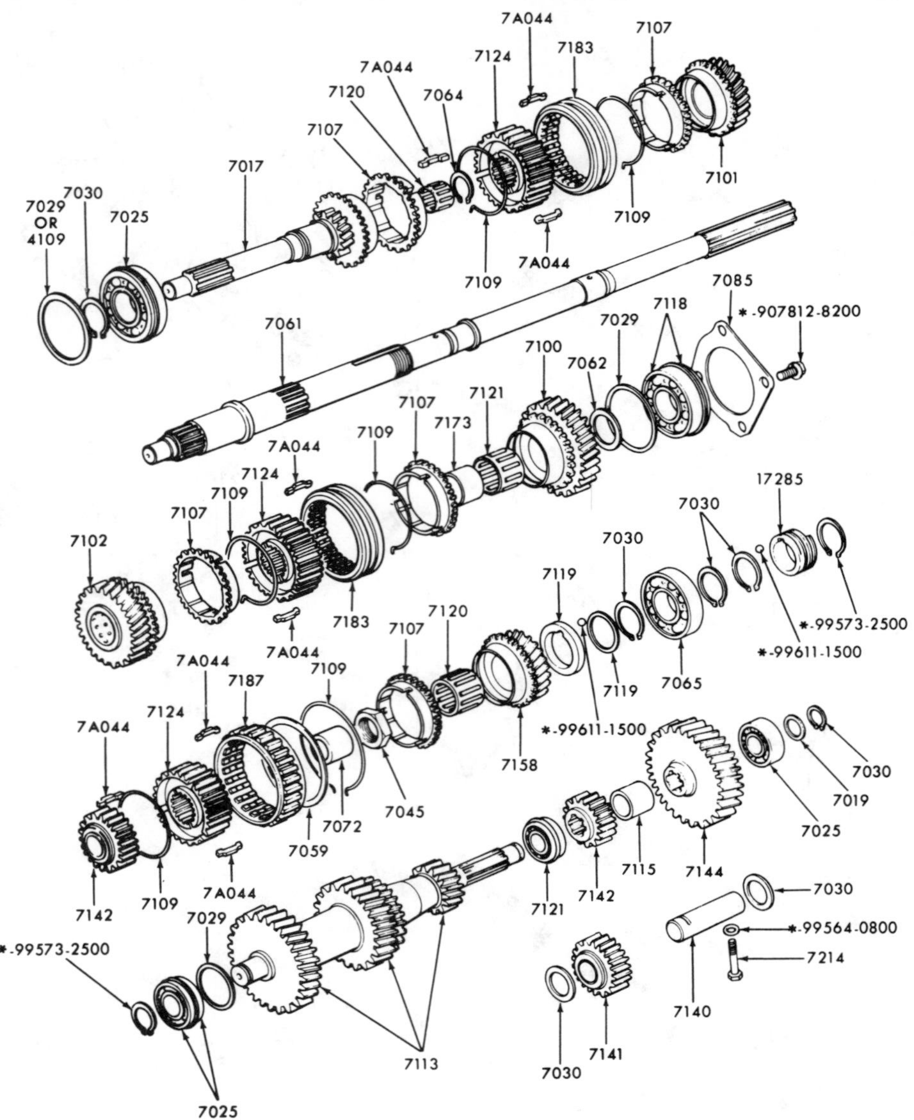

FIG 9 – MANUAL TRANSMISSION – 5-SPEED

4109 Shim
7017 Input Shaft
7019 Shim
7025 Bearing
7029 Shim
7030 Ring
7A044 Insert
7045 Nut
7059 Ring
7061 Output Shaft
7062 Washer
7064 Ring
7065 Bearing
7072 Spacer
7085 Retainer
7100 First Speed Gear
7101 Third Speed Gear
7102 Second Speed Gear
7107 Ring
7109 Spring
7113 Cluster Gear
7115 Spacer
7118 Bearing
7119 Washer
7120 Bearing
7121 Roller
7124 Synchronizer
7140 Reverse Idler Gear Shaft
7141 Reverse Idler Gear
7142 Reverse Gear
7144 Fifth Counter Gear
7158 Overdrive Gear
7173 Sleeve
7183 Hub
7187 Sleeve
7214 Screw
17285 Gear

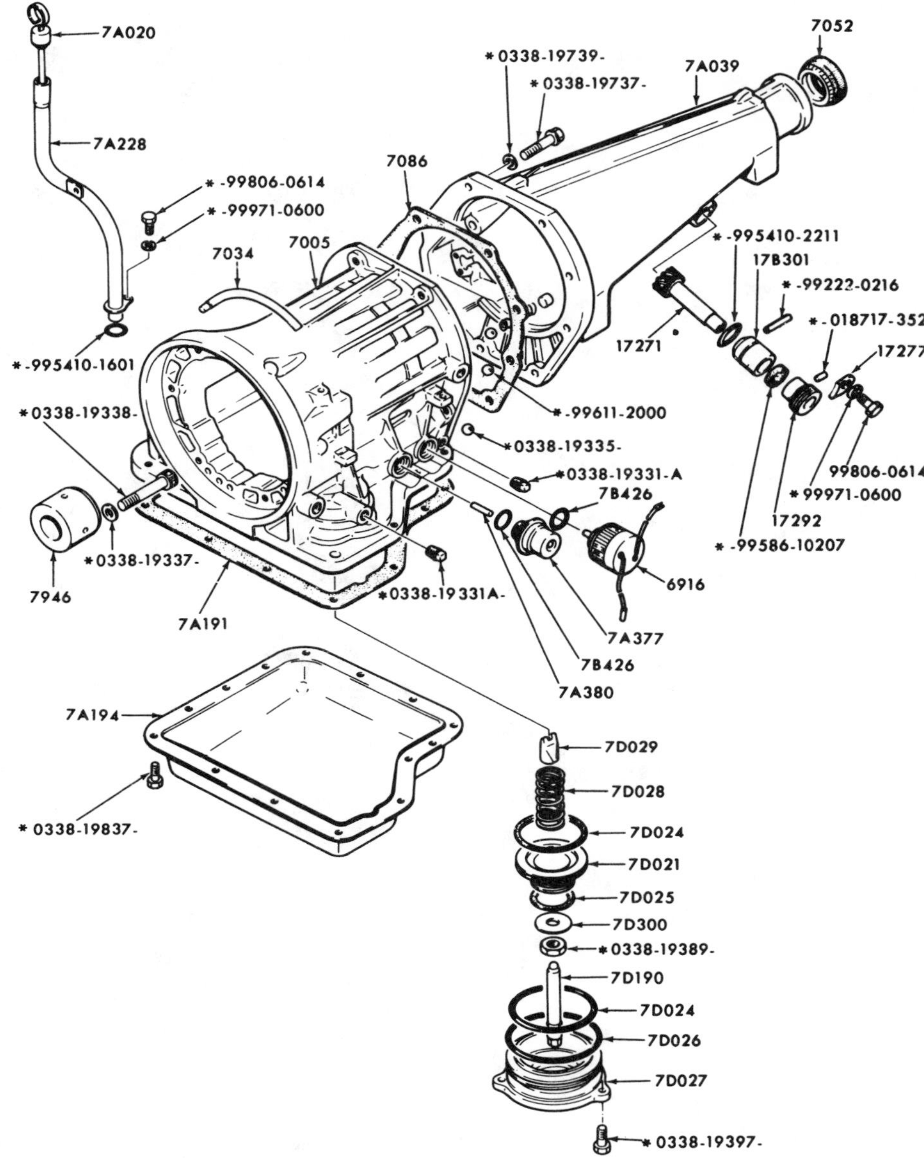

FIG 10 – AUTOMATIC TRANSMISSION CASE, OIL PAN, EXTENSION HOUSING & SERVO PARTS

6916	Solenoid	7A191	Gasket
7005	Transmission Case	7A194	Oil Pan
7A020	Oil Indicator	7A228	Tube
7D021	Servo Band Piston	7D300	Spacer
7D024	Seal	7A377	Diaphragm
7D025	Seal	7A380	Rod
7D026	Gasket	7B426	Gasket
7D027	Cover	7946	Race
7D028	Spring	17271	Gear
7D029	Strut	17277	Lock Plate
7034	Vent	17292	Retainer
7A039	Extension Housing	17B301	Sleeve
7052	Seal		
7086	Gasket		
7D190	Piston Rod Stem		

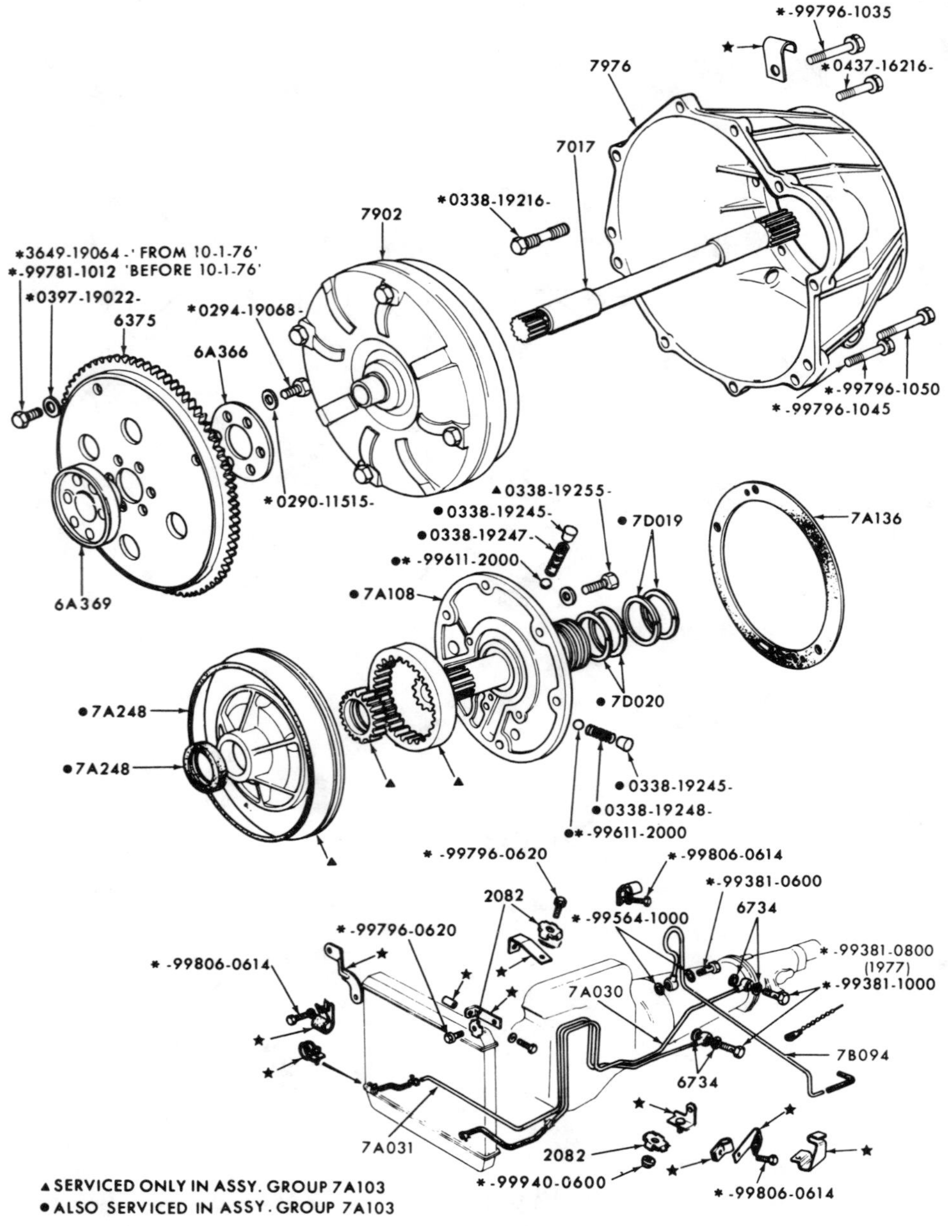

FIG 11 – AUTOMATIC TRANSMISSION CONVERTER, OIL PUMP & OIL COOLER SYSTEM

2082	Bracket
6A366	Plate
6A369	Adapter
6375	Flywheel
6734	Gasket
7017	Input Shaft
7D019	Ring
7D020	Seal
7A031	Tube
7B094	Tube
7A103	Oil Pump
7A108	Support
7A136	Gasket
7A248	Seal
7902	Converter
7976	Converter Housing

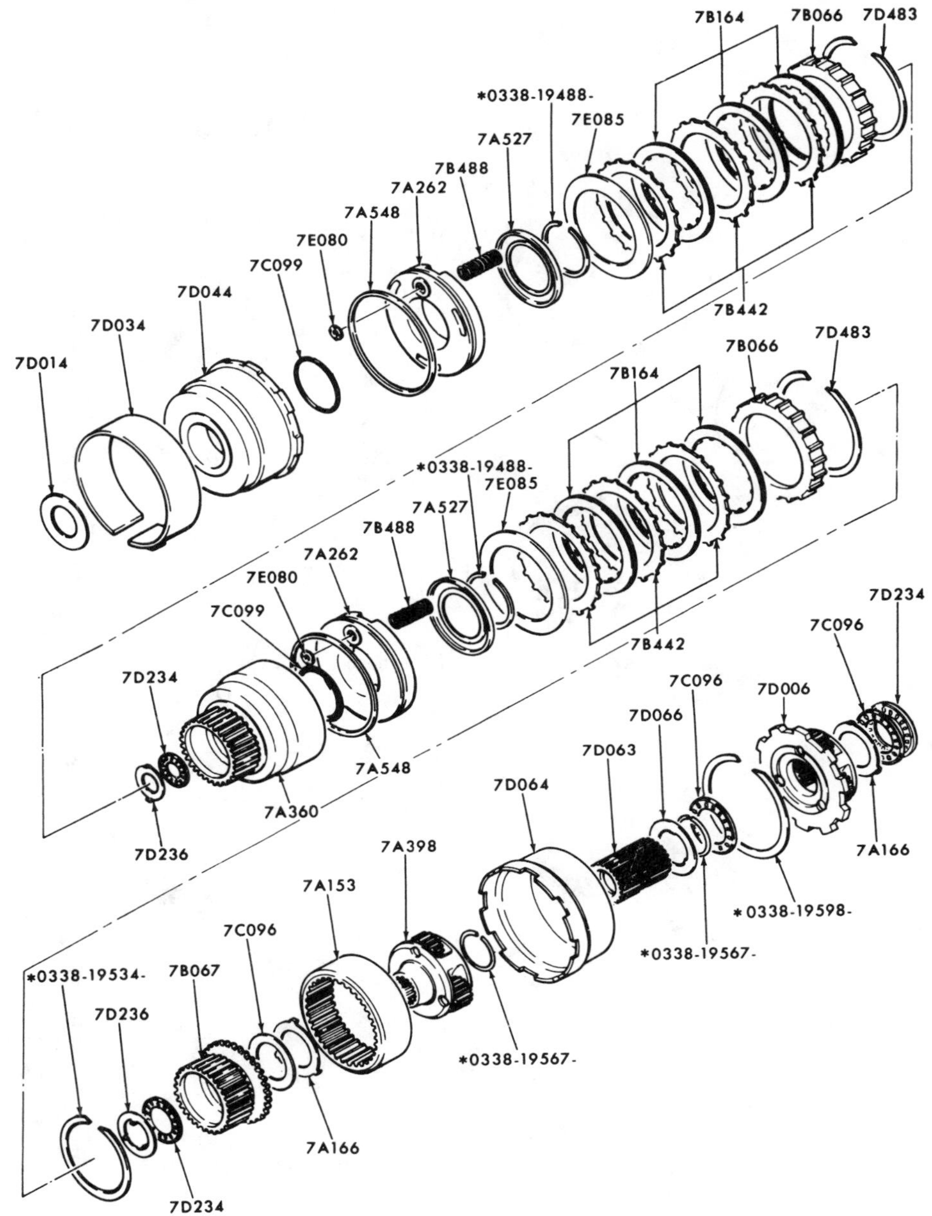

FIG 12 – AUTOMATIC TRANSMISSION CLUTCH & PLANETARY GEARS

7D006	Reverse Planet Assy	**7A153**	Gear
7D014	Washer	**7B164**	Plate
7D034	Band Assy	**7A166**	Bearing Race
7D044	Intermediate Drum	**7D234**	Bearing
7D063	Sun Gear	**7D236**	Race
7D064	Input Shell	**7A262**	Clutch Piston
7B066	Pressure Plate	**7A360**	Forward Clutch Cylinder
7D066	Washer	**7A398**	Forward Planet Assy
7B067	Forward Clutch Hub	**7B442**	Plate
7E080	Retainer	**7D483**	Ring
7E085	Spring	**7B488**	Spring
7C096	Bearing	**7A527**	Retainer
7C099	Seal	**7A548**	Seal

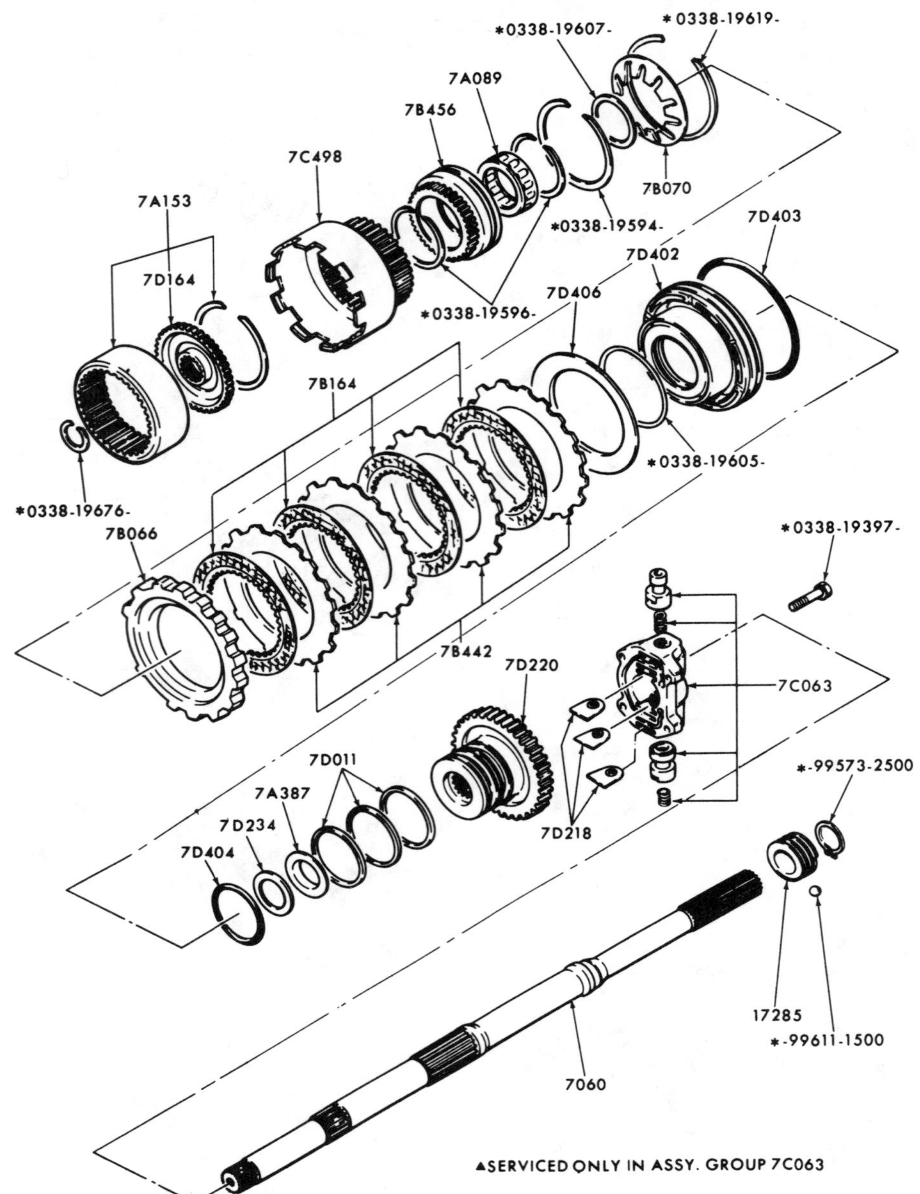

FIG 13 – AUTOMATIC TRANSMISSION LOW & REVERSE GEARS & GOVERNOR

7D011	Ring
7060	Output Shaft
7C063	Governor
7B066	Pressure Plate
7B070	Spring
7A089	Over-Running Clutch
7A153	Gear
7B164	Plate
7D164	Output Shaft Hub
7D218	Retainer
7D220	Oil Collector Body
7D234	Bearing
7A387	Race
7D402	Reverse Clutch Piston
7D403	Seal
7D404	Seal
7D406	Retainer
7B442	Plate
7B456	Race
7C498	Reverse Brake Drum
17285	Gear

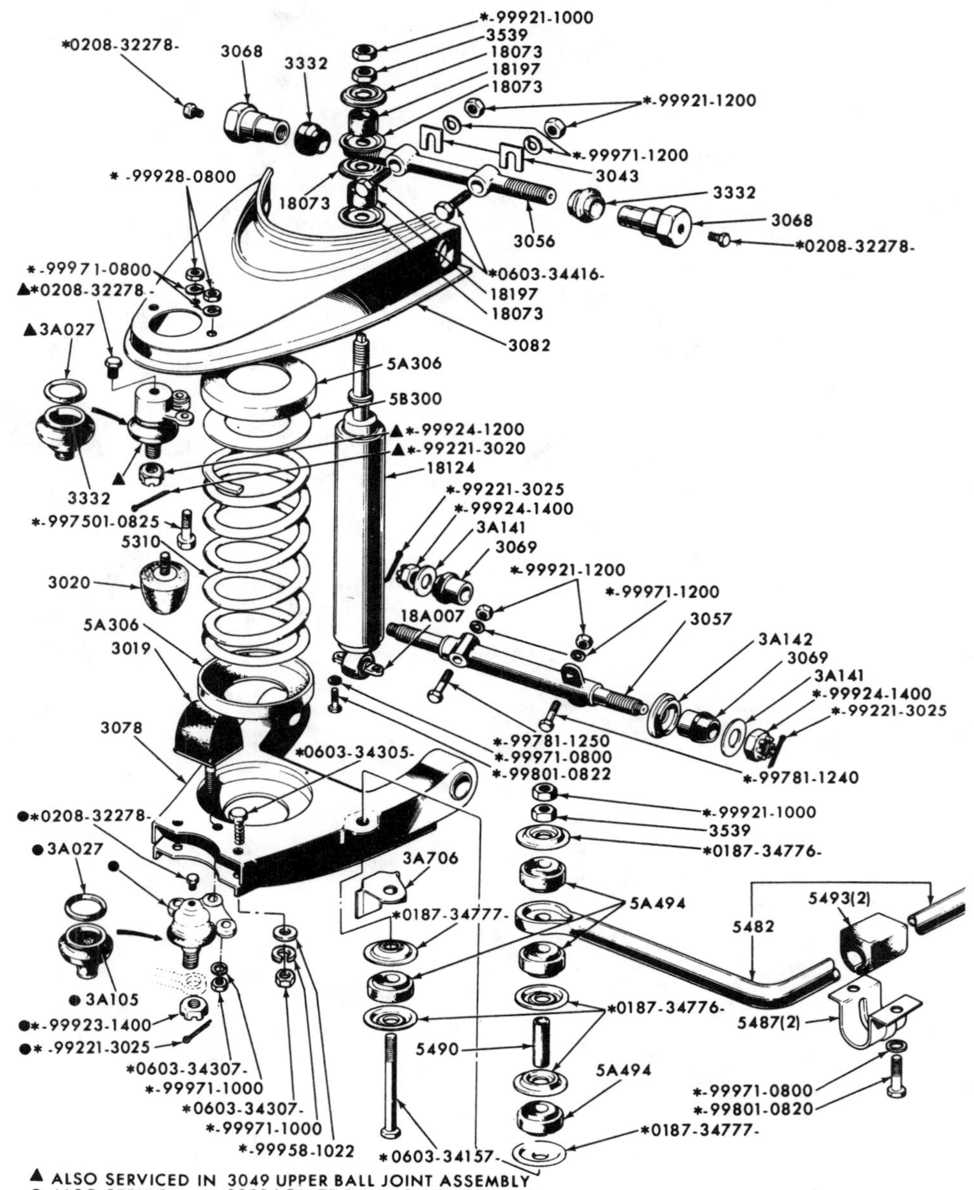

FIG 14 – FRONT SUSPENSION

3019	Bumper
3020	Bumper
3A027	Retainer
3043	Shim
3056	Upper Shaft
3057	Lower Shaft
3068	Bushing
3069	Bushing
3078	Lower Arm
3A105	Seal
3A141	Washer
3A142	Retainer
3332	Seal
3539	Nut
3A706	Stop
5B300	Retainer
5A306	Seal
5310	Spring
5482	Stabilizer
5487	Clamp
5490	Spacer
5493	Insulation
5A494	Insulation
18A007	Bushing
18073	Washer
18124	Shock Absorber
18197	Bushing

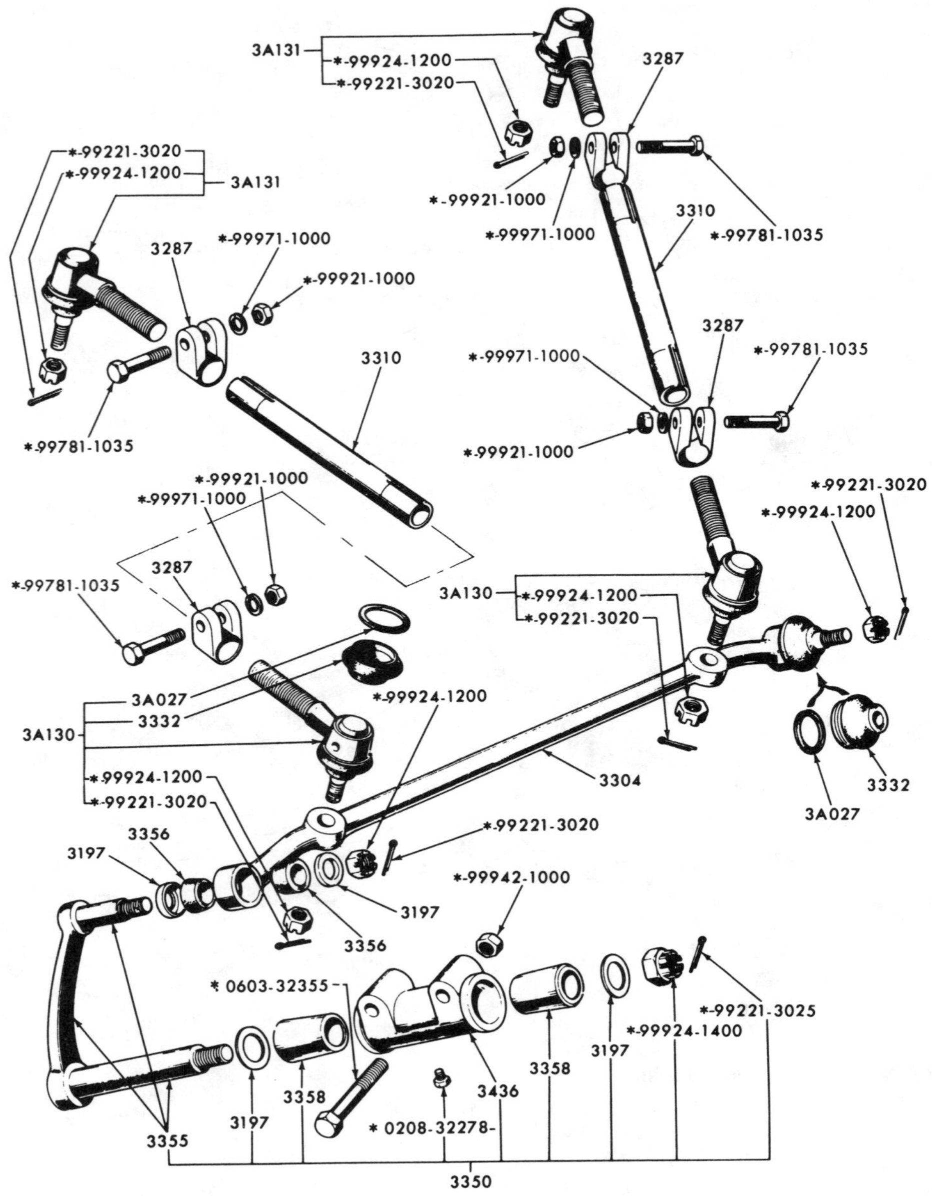

FIG 15 – STEERING LINKAGE – 1972-76

3A027	Retainer
3A130	End, Outer
3A131	End, Inner
3197	Seal
3287	Clamp
3304	Drag Link
3310	Adjusting Sleeve
3332	Seal
3350	Idler Arm W/Bracket
3355	Idler Arm WO/Bracket
3356	Bushing
3358	Bushing
3436	Idler Arm Support

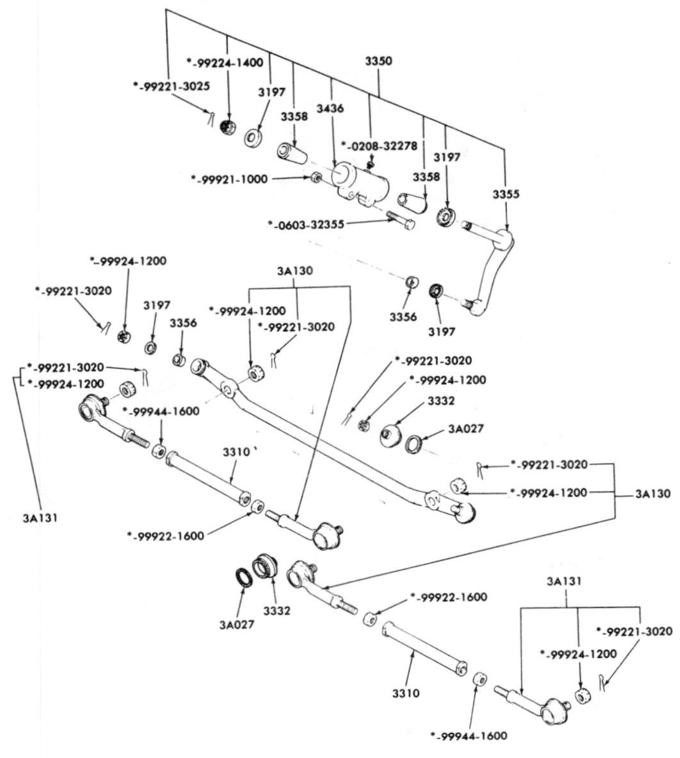

FIG 16 – STEERING LINKAGE – 1977-78

3A027	Retainer
3A130	End, Outer
3A131	end, Inner
3197	Seal
3310	Adjusting Sleeve
3332	Seal
3350	Idler Arm w/Bracket
3355	Idler Arm wo/Bracket
3356	Bushing
3358	Bushing
3436	Idler Arm Support

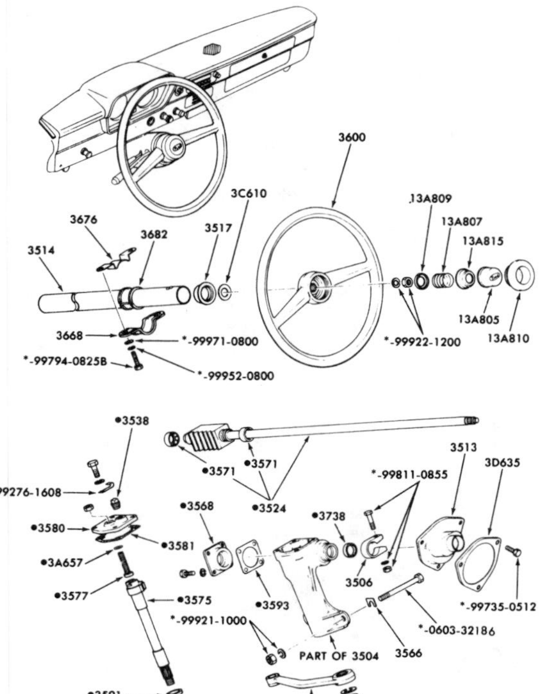

FIG 17 – STEERING COLUMN, GEAR & WHEEL

3504	Gear Assy
3506	Clamp
3513	Seal
3514	Column Tube
3517	Bushing
3524	Rack & WormInput Shaft
3538	Plug
3566	Spacer
3568	Cover
3571	Bearing
3575	Sector Shaft
3577	Screw
3580	Cover
3581	Gasket
3590	Sector Arm
3591	Seal
3593	Gasket
3600	Wheel
3C610	Retainer
3D635	Retainer
3A657	Shim
3668	Clamp
3676	Bracket
3682	Insulator
3738	Seal
13A805	Button
13A807	Spring
13A809	Plate
13A810	Retainer
13A815	Cup

•ALSO SERVICED IN 3504 STEERING GEAR ASSY.

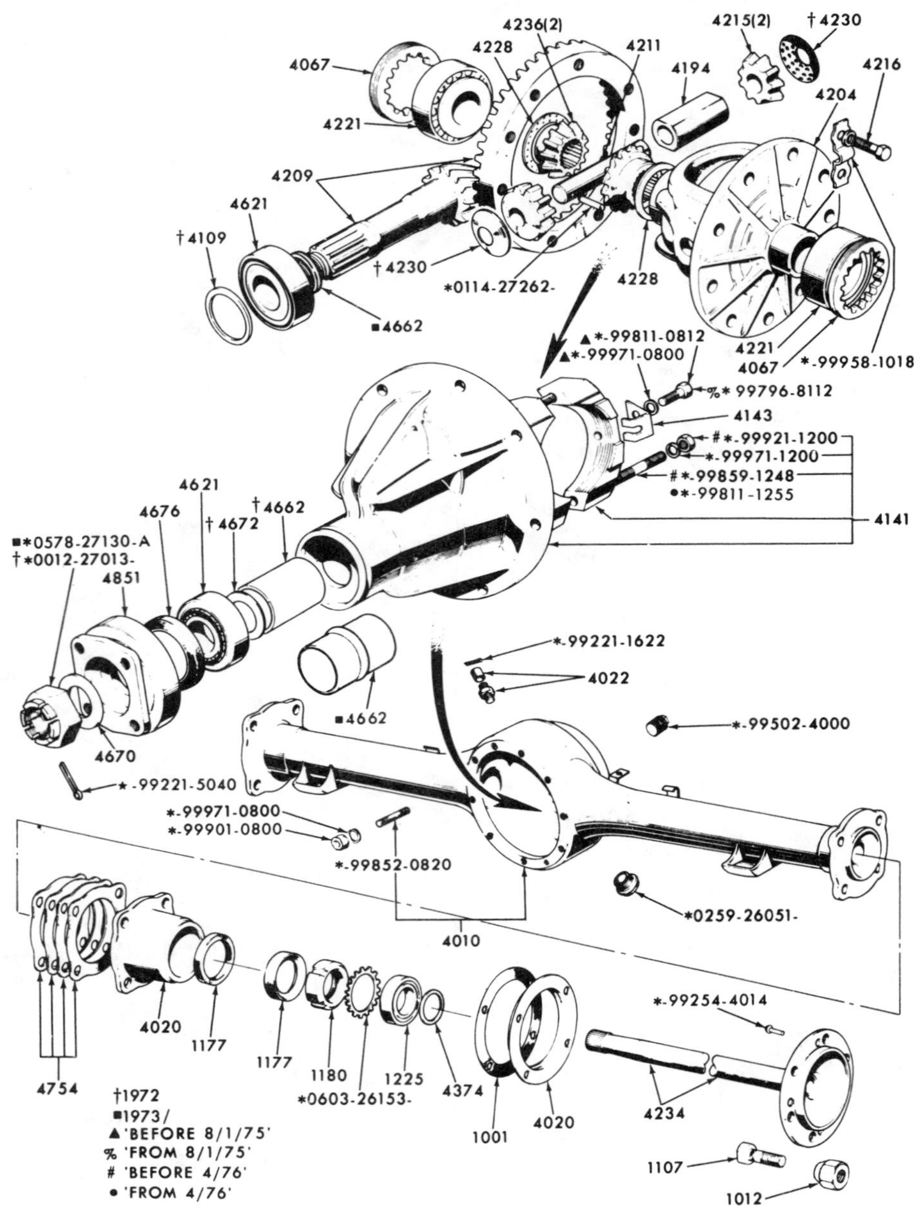

FIG 18 – REAR AXLE & DIFFERENTIAL GEARS

1001	Gasket	4211	Pinion Shaft
1012	Nut	4215	Pinion
1107	Bolt	4216	Bolt
1177	Seal	4221	Cone & Roller
1180	Retainer	4228	Washer
1225	Bearing	4230	Washer
4010	Housing	4234	Axle Shaft
4020	Retainer	4236	Side Gear
4022	Body	4374	Spacer
4067	Adjuster	4621	Cone & Roller
4109	Shim	4662	Spacer
4141	Differential Carrier	4670	Slinger
4143	Lock	4672	Shim
4194	Block	4676	Seal
4204	Case Assy	4754	Spacer
4209	Ring Gear & Pinion	4851	Flange

Tune-Up & Ignition—TIME

OPERATION INDEX

Tune-Up, Minor 1
Tune-Up, Major 2
Compression, Test 3
Points & Condenser, Renew 4
Spark Plugs, Clean Or Renew 5
Distributor, Renew 6
Distributor, Overhaul 7
Distributor Cap, Renew 8
Distributor, Adj On Strobescope 9
Ignition Coil, Renew 10
Ignition Switch, Renew 11
Ignition Cable Set, Renew 12

1—TUNE-UP, MINOR
Includes renew points, condenser & plugs, set spark timing & adjust carburetor idle.
All Models 1.2

2—TUNE-UP, MAJOR
Includes check compression, clean or renew & adjust spark plugs. R & R distributor, renew points & condenser. Adjust ignition timing, carburetor & fan belts. Clean battery terminals & service air cleaner, check coil & service manifold heat control valve, clean fuel pump sediment bowl & replace or clean fuel filter.
All Models 2.8

3—COMPRESSION, TEST
All Models 0.4

4—POINTS & CONDENDER, RENEW
Distributor on car
All Models 0.7

5—SPARK PLUGS, CLEAN & ADJUST OR RENEW
All Models 0.6

6—DISTRIBUTOR, R & R OR RENEW
All Models 0.6

7—DISTRIBUTOR, R & R & OVERHAUL
All Models 1.4

8—DISTRIBUTOR CAP, RENEW
All Models 0.5

9—DISTRIBUTOR, ADJUST ON STROBOSCOPE (DIST OFF)
All Models 0.5

10—IGNITION COIL, RENEW
All Models 0.6

11—IGNITION SWITCH, RENEW
All Models 0.4

12—IGNITION CABLE SET, RENEW
Time allowance covers installation of factory supplied sets.
All Models 0.6

Fuel System & Intake Manifold—TIME

OPERATION INDEX

Carburetor, Renew 1
Carburetor, Overhaul 2
Float Needle & Seat, Renew 3
Manual Choke Cable, Renew 4
Fuel Pump, R & R Or Renew 5
Fuel Tank, R & R Or Renew 6
Fuel System, Clean 7
Intake Manifold Gasket, Renew 8

1—CARBURETOR, R & R OR RENEW
All Models 0.6

2—CARBURETOR, R & R & OVERHAUL
All Models 1.9

3—FLOAT NEEDLE & SEAT, RENEW
All Models 0.6

4—MANUAL CHOKE CABLE, RENEW
All Models 0.4

5—FUEL PUMP, R & R OR RENEW
All Models 0.6

6—FUEL TANK, R & R OR RENEW
All Models 0.7

7—FUEL SYSTEM, CLEAN
Includes R & R tank, blow out lines & renew fuel filter.
All Models 1.4

8—INTAKE MANIFOLD GASKET, RENEW
All Models 1.3

Exhaust System—TIME

OPERATION INDEX

Exhaust Manifold, Renew 1
Exhaust Pipe & Resonator, Renew 2
Muffler & Tail Pipe, Renew 3
Exhaust System, Renew 4

1—EXHAUST MANIFOLD, RENEW
All Models 0.7

2—EXHAUST PIPE & RESONATOR, RENEW
All Models 0.5

3—MUFFLER & TAIL PIPE, RENEW
All Models 0.4

4—EXHAUST SYSTEM (EXC MANIFOLDS), RENEW
All Models 0.7

Starting Motor—TIME

OPERATION INDEX

Starter, R & R Or Renew 1
Starter, R & R & Overhaul 2
Starter Drive, Renew 3
Brushes, Renew & Turn Down Commutator 4
Armature & Brushes, Renew 5
Starter Switch, Renew 6

1—STARTER, R & R OR RENEW
All Models 0.7

2—STARTER, R & R & OVERHAUL
Includes turn down armature and replace all necessary parts.
All Models 1.5

3—STARTER DRIVE, RENEW
All Models 0.9

4—BRUSHES, RENEW & TURN DOWN COMMUTATOR
Includes R & R starter
All Models 1.3

5—ARMATURE & BRUSHES, RENEW
Includes R & R starter.
All Models 1.0

6—STARTER SWITCH, RENEW
All Models 0.4

Alternator—TIME

OPERATION INDEX

Regulator, Check & Adjust 1
Regulator, Renew 2
Alternator, R & R Or Renew 3
Alternator, R & R & Overhaul 4
Alternator Bearings, Renew 5
Alternator Brushes, Renew 6

1—ALTERNATOR REGULATOR, CHECK & ADJUST
All Models 0.3

2—ALTERNATOR REGULATOR, RENEW
Includes check & adjust
All Models 0.4

3—ALTERNATOR, R & R OR RENEW
All Models 0.7

4—ALTERNATOR, R & R & OVERHAUL
All Models 1.3

5—ALTERNATOR BEARINGS, RENEW
Front 0.8
Rear 0.9

6—ALTERNATOR BRUSHES, RENEW
All Models 1.1

Dash Gauges, Speedometer & Windshield Wiper—TIME

OPERATION INDEX

Fuel Gauge Dash Unit, Renew 1
Fuel Gauge Tank Unit, Renew 2
Oil Gauge Sending Unit, Renew 3
Temp Gauge Sending Unit, Renew 4
Temp Gauge Dash Unit, Renew 5
Ammeter, Renew 6
Speedometer Head, R & R Or Renew 7
Speedometer Cable, Renew 8
Speedometer Cable, Lubricate 9
W/S Wiper Motor, Renew 10
W/S Wiper Switch, Renew 11

1—FUEL GAUGE DASH UNIT, RENEW
All Models 0.7

2—FUEL GAUGE TANK UNIT, RENEW
All Models 0.5

3—OIL GAUGE SENDING UNIT, RENEW
All Models 0.5

4—TEMPERATURE GAUGE SENDING UNIT, RENEW
All Models 0.4

5—TEMPERATURE GAUGE DASH UNIT, RENEW
All Models 0.6

6—AMMETER, RENEW
All Models 0.5

7—SPEEDOMETER HEAD, R & R OR RENEW
All Models 0.7

8—SPEEDOMETER CABLE, RENEW
All Models 0.5

(Continued)

Dash Gauges, Speedometer & Windshield Wiper—TIME Cont'd

9—SPEEDOMETER CABLE, LUBRICATE
All Models 0.2

10—W/S WIPER MOTOR, RENEW
All Models 0.6

11—W/S WIPER SWITCH, RENEW
All Models 0.6

Battery Cables, Wiring Harness & Horn—TIME

OPERATION INDEX

Battery Cables, Renew 1
Horn, Renew 2
Horn Relay, Renew 3
Wiring Harness, Renew 4

1—BATTERY CABLES, RENEW
Starter To Relay 0.4
Battery To Relay 0.4
Ground 0.2

2—HORN, RENEW
All Models 0.2

3—HORN RELAY, RENEW
All Models 0.4

4—WIRING HARNESS, RENEW
Instrument Panel To Dash 1.7

Lamps & Light Switches—TIME

OPERATION INDEX

Headlamps, Aim 1
Lamp Lens Or Bulb, Renew 2
Light Switch, Renew 3
Stop Light Switch, Renew 4
Back-Up Lamp Switch, Renew 5
Direction Signal Flasher, Renew 6
Headlamp Dimmer Switch, Renew 7
Turn Signal Switch, Renew 8

1—HEADLAMPS, AIM
All Models 0.3

2—LAMP LENS OR BULB, RENEW
Each 0.4

3—LIGHT SWITCH, RENEW
All Models 0.5

4—STOP LIGHT SWITCH, RENEW
All Models 0.4

5—BACK-UP LAMP SWITCH, RENEW
All Models 0.4

6—DIRECTION SIGNAL FLASHER, RENEW
All Models 0.4

7—HEADLAMP DIMMER SWITCH, RENEW
All Models 0.6

8—TURN SIGNAL SWITCH, RENEW
All Models 0.6

Cooling System—TIME

OPERATION INDEX

Radiator, R & R Or Renew 1
Radiator Hoses, Renew 2
Fan, Renew 3
Fan Belt, Renew 4
Water Pump, R & R Or Renew 5
Thermostat, Renew 6
Heater Core, R & R Or Renew 7

1—RADIATOR, R & R OR RENEW
All Models 0.8

2—RADIATOR HOSES, RENEW
Upper 0.4
Lower 0.7
Both 0.8

3—FAN, RENEW
All Models 0.5

4—FAN BELT, RENEW
All Models 0.4

5—WATER PUMP, R & R OR RENEW
All Models Exc 1.5
With Thermactor 1.7

6—THERMOSTAT, RENEW
All Models 0.6

7—HEATER CORE, R & R OR RENEW
All Models 1.4

Cylinder Head & Valves—TIME

OPERATION INDEX

Cylinder Head, R & R 1
Cylinder Head, Renew 2
Cylinder Head Gasket, Renew 3
Cylinder Head, Tighten 4
Valves, Grind 5
Valves, Grind (Head Off) 6
Rocker Arm Cover Gasket, Renew 7
Valve Tappets, Adjust 8

1—CYLINDER HEAD, R & R
Use Cylinder Head Gasket, Renew

2—CYLINDER HEAD, RENEW
Include transfer all parts & grind valves.
All Models Exc 4.8
With Thermactor 5.3

3—CYLINDER HEAD GASKET, RENEW
Includes check head & block flatness, adjust carburetor, ignition timing (when distributor is removed) and valves.
All Models Exc 4.0
With Thermactor 4.4

4—CYLINDER HEAD, TIGHTEN
All Models 0.5

5—VALVES, GRIND & TUNE-UP, MINOR
All Models Exc 6.6
With Thermactor 7.2

6—VALVES, GRIND (HEAD OFF)
All Models Exc 2.6
With Thermactor 2.8

7—ROCKER ARM COVER GASKET, RENEW
All Models 0.6

8—VALVE TAPPETS, ADJUST
All Models 0.9

Timing Case & Camshaft—TIME

OPERATION INDEX

Timing Cover Or Gasket, Renew 1
Timing Chain Or Sprockets, Renew 2
Camshaft, Renew 3

1—TIMING CASE COVER OR GASKET, RENEW
All Models Exc 3.3
With Thermactor 3.5

2—TIMING CHAIN OR SPROCKETS, RENEW (COVER OFF)
Includes adjust timing
All Models Exc 2.7
With Thermactor 2.8

3—CAMSHAFT, RENEW
All Models Exc 3.5
With Thermactor 3.7

Engine/Pistons, Rings, Bearings & Crankshaft—TIME

OPERATION INDEX

Pistons Or Rings, Renew 1
Rings, Renew & Grind Valves 2
Rings & Main Bearings, Renew & Grind Valves 3
Rod Bearings, Renew 4
Main Bearings, Renew 5
Main & Rod Bearings, Renew 6
Crankshaft, Renew 7
Rear Main Bearing Oil Seal, Renew 8
Engine, R & R 9
Cylinder Assy, Renew 10
Cylinder Block, Renew 11

1—PISTONS OR RINGS, RENEW
Includes check rod bearing clearances, replace necessary bearings, adjust carburetor, ignition timing & valves, replace oil filter, clean carbon & hone cylinder walls.
One Exc 6.8
With Thermactor 7.1
All Exc 7.9
With Thermactor 8.3

2—RINGS, RENEW & GRIND VALVES
All Models Exc 10.5
With Thermactor 11.1

3—RINGS & MAIN BEARINGS, RENEW & GRIND VALVES
All Models Exc 12.8
With Thermactor 13.3

4—ROD BEARINGS (ALL), RENEW
Includes plastigage
All Models 2.5

5—MAIN BEARINGS, RENEW
Includes R & R engine & plastigage bearings
All Models Exc 5.4
With Thermactor 5.8

6—MAIN & ROD BEARINGS, RENEW
Includes R & R engine & plastigage bearings.
All Models Exc 6.4
With Thermactor 6.8

7—CRANKSHAFT, RENEW
Includes R & R engine, check all bearings and adjust ignition timing
All Models Exc 6.5
With Thermactor 6.9

(Continued)

Engine/Pistons, Rings, Bearings & Crankshaft—TIME Cont'd

8—REAR BEARING OIL SEAL, RENEW
All Models 2.1

9—ENGINE, R & R
Includes remove hood & radiator & adjust carburetor linkage.
All Models Exc 3.1
With Thermactor 3.5

10—CYLINDER ASSY, RENEW
Includes R & R engine, transfer & clean all component parts without disassembly, adjust valves & ignition timing.
All Models Exc 7.0
With Thermactor 7.4

11—CYLINDER BLOCK, RENEW
Includes R & R engine, transfer & clean all component parts without disassembly, replace rings & bearings, adjust clearances, valves & ignition timing.
All Models Exc 9.8
With Thermactor 10.2

Vibration Damper, Flywheel & Engine Mounts—TIME

OPERATION INDEX

Vibration Damper, Renew 1
Flywheel Renew (Trans Out) 2
Engine Front Mount, Renew 3

1—VIBRATION DAMPER, RENEW
All Models 1.1

2—FLYWHEEL, RENEW (TRANSMISSION OUT)
All Models 0.6

3—ENGINE MOUNT, FRONT, RENEW
One 1.4
Both 1.7

Engine Oiling—TIME

OPERATION INDEX

Oil Pan, R & R Or Renew Gasket 1
Oil Pump, Renew 2
Oil Pump, Overhaul 3

1—OIL PAN, R & R OR RENEW GASKET
All Models 1.5

2—OIL PUMP, RENEW
All Models 1.9

3—OIL PUMP, OVERHAUL (PUMP REMOVED)
All Models 0.3

Clutch—TIME

OPERATION INDEX

Pedal Free Travel, Adjust 1
System, Bleed 2
Master Cylinder, Renew 3
Master Cylinder, R & R & Overhaul 4
Slave Cylinder, Renew 5
Slave Cylinder, Overhaul 6
Clutch (Or Disc), R & R Or Renew 7
Clutch Release Bearing, Renew 8
Pilot Bearing, Renew (Clutch Out) 9

1—CLUTCH PEDAL FREE TRAVEL, ADJUST
All Models 0.4

2—CLUTCH SYSTEM, BLEED
All Models 0.4

3—CLUTCH MASTER CYLINDER, RENEW
All Models 0.4

4—CLUTCH MASTER CYLINDER, R & R & OVERHAUL
All Models 0.6

5—CLUTCH SLAVE CYLINDER, RENEW
All Models 0.4

6—CLUTCH SLAVE CYLINDER, OVERHAUL
All Models 0.5

7—CLUTCH (OR DISC), R & R OR RENEW
All Models 1.6

8—CLUTCH RELEASE BEARING, RENEW
Includes R & R transmission.
All Models 1.4

9—CLUTCH PILOT BEARING, RENEW (CLUTCH OUT)
All Models 0.2

Manual Transmission—TIME

OPERATION INDEX

Trans, R & R Or Renew 1
Trans, R & R & Overhaul 2
Extn Housing Or Seal, Renew 3
Gear Selector Lever, Renew 4

1—TRANSMISSION, R & R OR RENEW
All Models 1.4

2—TRANSMISSION, R & R & OVERHAUL
All Models 3.2

3—EXTENSION HOUSING OR OIL SEAL, RENEW
All Models 1.5

4—GEAR SELECTOR LEVER, RENEW
All Models 0.4

Automatic Transmission—TIME

OPERATION INDEX

Trans, R & R Or Renew 1
Trans, R & R & Overhaul 2
Converter, Check & Clean 3
Front Pump, Overhaul 4
Front Pump Seal, Renew 5
Case, Renew 6
Oil Cooler & Lines, Renew 7
Governor, Renew 8
Oil Pan Or Gasket, Renew 9
Main Valve Body, Renew 10
Main Valve Body, Clean 11
Servo, Overhaul 12
Vacuum Diaphragm, Renew 13
Manual Linkage, Adjust 14
Throttle Linkage, Adjust 15
Band, Adjust 16

1—TRANSMISSION, R & R OR RENEW
Includes remove trans & converter assy, drain, refill & linkage adjustment.
All Models 2.1

2—TRANSMISSION, R & R & OVERHAUL
All Models 6.0

3—CONVERTER, CHECK & CLEAN
Transmission removed.
All Models 0.4

4—FRONT PUMP, OVERHAUL
Transmission removed.
All Models 0.9

5—FRONT PUMP SEAL, RENEW
Transmission removed.
All Models 0.2

6—TRANSMISSION CASE, RENEW
Transmission removed, includes transfer & clean all parts & make necessary adjustments.
All Models 2.3

7—OIL COOLER & LINES, RENEW
Transmission removed.
All Models 0.2

8—GOVERNOR ASSY, RENEW
Transmission removed.
All Models 0.7

9—OIL PAN OR GASKET, RENEW
All Models 0.5

10—MAIN CONTROL VALVE BODY, RENEW
Oil pan removed.
All Models 0.7

11—MAIN CONTROL VALVE BODY, CLEAN
Oil pan removed.
All Models 1.2

12—SERVO, OVERHAUL
Oil pan removed.
All Models 0.6

13—VACUUM DIAPHRAGM, RENEW
Oil pan removed.
All Models 0.6

14—MANUAL LINKAGE, ADJUST
All Models 0.4

15—THROTTLE LINKAGE, ADJUST
All Models 0.3

16—BAND, ADJUST
Includes replace pan gasket.
All Models 1.0

Universals, Propeller Shaft & Rear Axle—TIME

OPERATION INDEX

Universal Joint, Renew 1
Propeller Shaft, R & R Or Renew 2
Differential, R & R Or Renew 3
Differential, R & R & Overhaul 4
Pinnion Shaft Oil Seal, Renew 5
Axle Shaft, Renew 6
Axle Shaft Bearing, Renew 7

1—UNIVERSAL JOINT, RENEW OR OVERHAUL
One 0.8
Both 1.4

(Continued)

Universals, Propeller Shaft & Rear Axle—TIME Cont'd

2—PROPELLER SHAFT, R & R OR RENEW
All Models 0.5

3—DIFFERENTIAL CASE & CARRIER ASSY, R & R OR RENEW
All Models 1.9

4—DIFFERENTIAL CASE & CARRIER, R & R & OVERHAUL
All Models 4.5

5—PINION SHAFT FLANGE OR OIL SEAL, RENEW
All Models 0.5

6—AXLE SHAFT, RENEW
One Side 1.4
Both Sides 2.3

7—AXLE SHAFT BEARINGS, RENEW
One Side 1.7
Both Sides 2.6

Rear Suspension—TIME

OPERATION INDEX

Rear Spring, Renew 1
Shackle & Bushings, Renew 2
Rear Shock Absorber, Renew 3

1—REAR SPRING, RENEW
One Side 0.9
Both Sides 1.4

2—REAR SPRING SHACKLES & BUSHINGS, RENEW
One Side 0.4
Both Sides 0.5

3—REAR SHOCK ABSORBER, RENEW
One Side 0.4
Both Sides 0.5

Brakes—TIME

OPERATION INDEX

Brakes, Adjust 1
Brake Shoes (All), Renew 2
Brake Shoes (Front, Renew 3
Brake Shoes (Rear), Renew 4
Parking Brake, Adjust 5
Parking Brake Cable, Renew 6
Parking Brake Control, Renew 7
Master Cylinder, Renew 8
Master Cylinder, Overhaul 9
Wheel Cylinder, Renew 10
Wheel Cylinder, Overhaul 11
Flush & Refill System 12
Bleed System 13
Front Wheel Hub, Renew 14
Front Brake Drum, Renew 15
Rear Brake Drum, Renew 16
Front Brake Hose, Renew 17
Rear Brake Hose, Renew 18

1—BRAKES, ADJUST
All Models 0.4

2—BRAKE SHOES (ALL WHEELS), RENEW & BLEED SYSTEM
All Models 2.1

3—BRAKE SHOES (FRONT WHEELS), RENEW & BLEED SYSTEM
All Models 1.5

4—BRAKE SHOES (REAR WHEELS), RENEW & BLEED SYSTEM
All Models 1.5

5—PARKING BRAKE, ADJUST
All Models 0.4

6—PARKING BRAKE CABLE, RENEW
Front 0.7
Rear, One 0.7
Both 1.1

7—PARKING BRAKE CONTROL, RENEW
All Models 0.6

8—MASTER CYLINDER, R & R OR RENEW
Includes bleed
All Models 1.0

9—MASTER CYLINDER, R & R & OVERHAUL
Includes bleed
All Models 1.5

10—WHEEL CYLINDER, RENEW
Includes bleed brakes.
Front (One Wheel)—
One Cylinder 1.1
Both Cylinders 1.3
Rear (One Wheel)—
One Cylinder 1.1
Both Cylinders 1.3

11—WHEEL CYLINDER, OVERHAUL
Includes bleed brakes.
Front (One Wheel)—
One Cylinder 1.2
Both Cylinders 1.4
Rear (One Wheel)—
One Cylinder 1.2
Both Cylinders 1.4

12—FLUSH & REFILL SYSTEM
All Models 0.9

13—BLEED SYSTEM
All Models 1.0

14—FRONT WHEEL HUB, RENEW
One Side 0.5
Both Sides 0.9

15—FRONT BRAKE DRUM, R & R OR RENEW
All Models ①0.4
①To Reface Drum, Add 0.3

16—REAR BRAKE DRUM, R & R OR RENEW
All Models ①0.3
①To Reface Drum, Add 0.3

17— FRONT BRAKE HOSE, RENEW
Includes bleed system.
One Side 0.5
Both Sides 0.6

18—REAR BRAKE HOSE, RENEW
All Models 0.6

Front Suspension—TIME

OPERATION INDEX

Toe-In, Adjust 1
Caster, Camber & Toe-In, Adjust 2
Steering Knuckle, Renew 3
Upper Control Arm, Renew 4
Lower Control Arm, Renew 5
Upper Ball Joint, Renew 6
Lower Ball Joint, Renew 7
Spring, Renew 8
Shock Absorber, Renew 9
Wheel Bearing, Renew 10

1—TOE-IN, ADJUST
All Models 0.5

2—CASTER, CAMBER & TOE-IN, ADJUST
All Models 1.5

3—STEERING KNUCKLES, RENEW
Does not include wheel alignment.
One Side 1.2
Both Sides 1.7

4—UPPER CONTROL ARM, RENEW
Does not include wheel alignment.
One Side 1.1
Both Sides 1.4

5—LOWER CONTROL ARM, RENEW
Does not include wheel alignment. One side
Both Sides 2.1

6—UPPER BALL JOINT, RENEW
Does not include wheel alignment.
One Side 0.9
Both Sides 1.1

7—LOWER BALL JOINT, RENEW
Does not include wheel alignment.
One Side 0.9
Both Sides 1.2

8—SPRING, RENEW
One Side 1.3
Both Sides 2.0

9—SHOCK ABOSRBER, RENEW
One Side 0.4
Both Sides 0.6

10—FRONT WHEEL BEARING, RENEW
One Side 0.8
Both Sides 1.1

Steering Linkage—TIME

OPERATION INDEX

Tie Rod Or Ends, Renew 1
Relay Rod, Renew 2
Idler Arm, Renew 3
Pitman Arm, Renew 4

1—TIE ROD OR ENDS, RENEW
One Side 0.9
Both Sides 1.1

2—STEERING RELAY ROD, RENEW
Includes adjust toe-in.
All Models 0.9

3—IDLER ARM, RENEW
All Models 0.8

4—PITMAN ARM, RENEW
All Models 0.4

Steering Gear—TIME

OPERATION INDEX

Steering Gear, Adjust 1
Steering Gear, Renew 2
Steering Gear, Overhaul 3
Column Upper Bearing, Renew 4

1—STEERING GEAR, ADJUST (ON CAR)
All Models 0.9

2—STEERING GEAR, RENEW
All Models 2.0

(Continued)

Steering Gear—TIME Cont'd

3—STEERING GEAR, R & R & OVERHAUL

All Models 2.6

4—COLUMN UPPER BEARING, RENEW

All Models 0.4

IDENTIFICATION

ALL MODELS.................................. 115

ILLUSTRATIONS

FIG 1 – CYLINDER HEAD
FIG 2 – CYLINDER BLOCK
FIG 3 – TIMING CASE & OIL PAN
FIG 4 – PISTON & CRANKSHAFT
FIG 5 – CAMSHAFT & TIMING CHAIN
FIG 6 – MANUAL TRANSMISSION
FIG 7 – FRONT SUSPENSION
FIG 8 – STEERING LINKAGE
FIG 9 – REAR AXLE DIFFERENTIAL

OPERATION TIMES

A

Alternator.. 121
Ammeter.. 124
Automatic Transmission.................. 122
Axle Shaft.. 123

B

Brake Drums.................................. 123
Brakes.. 123

C

Cables (Ignition).............................. 121
Calipers.. 123
Camshaft.. 122
Carburetor.. 121
Clutch.. 122
Coil, Ignition.................................. 121
Compression Test.......................... 121
Connecting Rods.............................. 122
Cooling System.............................. 121
Crankshaft.. 122
Cylinder Head.................................. 122

D

Dash Gauges.................................. 124
Differntial.. 123
Disc Brakes.................................. 123
Distributor.. 121

E

Emission Controls.......................... 121
Engine Assembly.............................. 122
Engine Mountings.......................... 122
Engine Oiling.................................. 122
Engine Tune-Up.............................. 121
Exhaust System.............................. 121

F

Flywheel.. 122
Front Suspension.......................... 123
Fuel Gauges.................................. 124
Fuel Pump.. 121
Fuel Tank.. 121

H

Hand Brake.................................. 123
Headlight Switch.............................. 124
Heater.. 121
Hose (Brake).................................. 123
Hose (Radiator).............................. 121
Hydraulic Brakes.............................. 123

I

Ignition.. 121
Ignition Coil.................................. 121
Ignition Switch.............................. 121
Intake Manifold.............................. 121

L

Light Switches.............................. 124

M

Main Bearings.............................. 122
Master Cylinder.............................. 123
Muffler.. 121

O

Oil Gauge.. 124
Oiling, Engine.............................. 122
Oil Pan.. 122
Oil Pump.. 122

P

Parking Brake.............................. 123
Piston Rings.................................. 122
Pistons.. 122
Power Brake.................................. 123

R

Radiator.. 121
Radiator Hose.............................. 121
Rear Axle.. 123
Regulator (Alternator).................. 121
Rocker Arms.................................. 122
Rod Bearings.................................. 122

S

Shocks.. 123
Speedometer.................................. 124
Springs (Front).............................. 123
Springs (Rear).............................. 123
Starting Motor.............................. 121
Steering Gear.................................. 123
Steering Linkage.............................. 123
Switches (light).............................. 124
Synchro-Mesh Trans...................... 122

T

Temperature Gauge.......................... 124
Thermostat.................................. 121
Timing Case Cover.......................... 122
Timing Chain.................................. 122
Timing Gears.................................. 122
Transmission, Manual...................... 122
Transmission, Automatic.................. 122
Tune-Up, Engine.............................. 121

U

Universals.. 123

V

Vacuum Control Unit...................... 121
Valve Lifters.................................. 122
Valve System.................................. 122

W

Water Pump.................................. 121
Wheel Cylinders.............................. 123
Windshield Wiper.............................. 124

VEHICLE SERIAL NUMBER PLATE

4B41 J1 R000000

LOCATION: On top of instrument panel, viewed through windshield.

1st Digit – Car Line – 4 is Cricket.
2nd Digit – (Letter) Indicates Price Class.
- B – Low Line
- C – High Line

3rd & 4th Digits Indicate Body Style.
- 41 – Sedan
- 45 – Station Wagon

5th Digit (Letter) Indicates Engine.
- J – Single Carb, Manual Choke
- G – Single Carb, Automatic Choke
- L – Dual Carb, Manual Choke

6th Digit Indicates Model Year.
- 1 – 1971
- 2 – 1972
- 3 – 1973

7th Digit (Letter) indicates Assembly plant
- R – Ryton

Last 6 digits indicates sequence number.

VEHICLE IDENTIFICATION PLATE

Service Code		Paint Code	CHRYSLER UNITED KINGDOM LTD.
		Trim Code	
Serial No.		Type	
Type Approval		Max. Gross Vehicle Weight	
		Max. Load With Trailer	
Max. Allowable Axle Load Frt.		Rr.	

LOCATION: On Hood Lock Platform.

The Serial Number is comprised of nine numbers.

The first three numbers Indicate Model:
- 219 – Model B Lowline Sedan
- 239 – Model C Highline Sedan
- 289 – Station Wagon

The last six digits is the sequence number and is the same as the sequence number portion of the vehicle serial number.

PAINT CODES

108	Polar White
133	Tangerine Metallic
135	Oasis Green
137	Firebrand Red
138	Safari Beige
142	Sunset Metallic
143	Aztec Gold Metallic
144	Golden Olive Metallic
145	Electric Blue Metallic
146	Mood Indigo
147	Ginger Poly
148	Cedar Green Poly
149	Phantom Mist Poly
154	Carib Blue
155	Sunfire Yellow

TRIM CODES

701	Black
714	Vellum
717	Tan
718	Blue
719	Olive

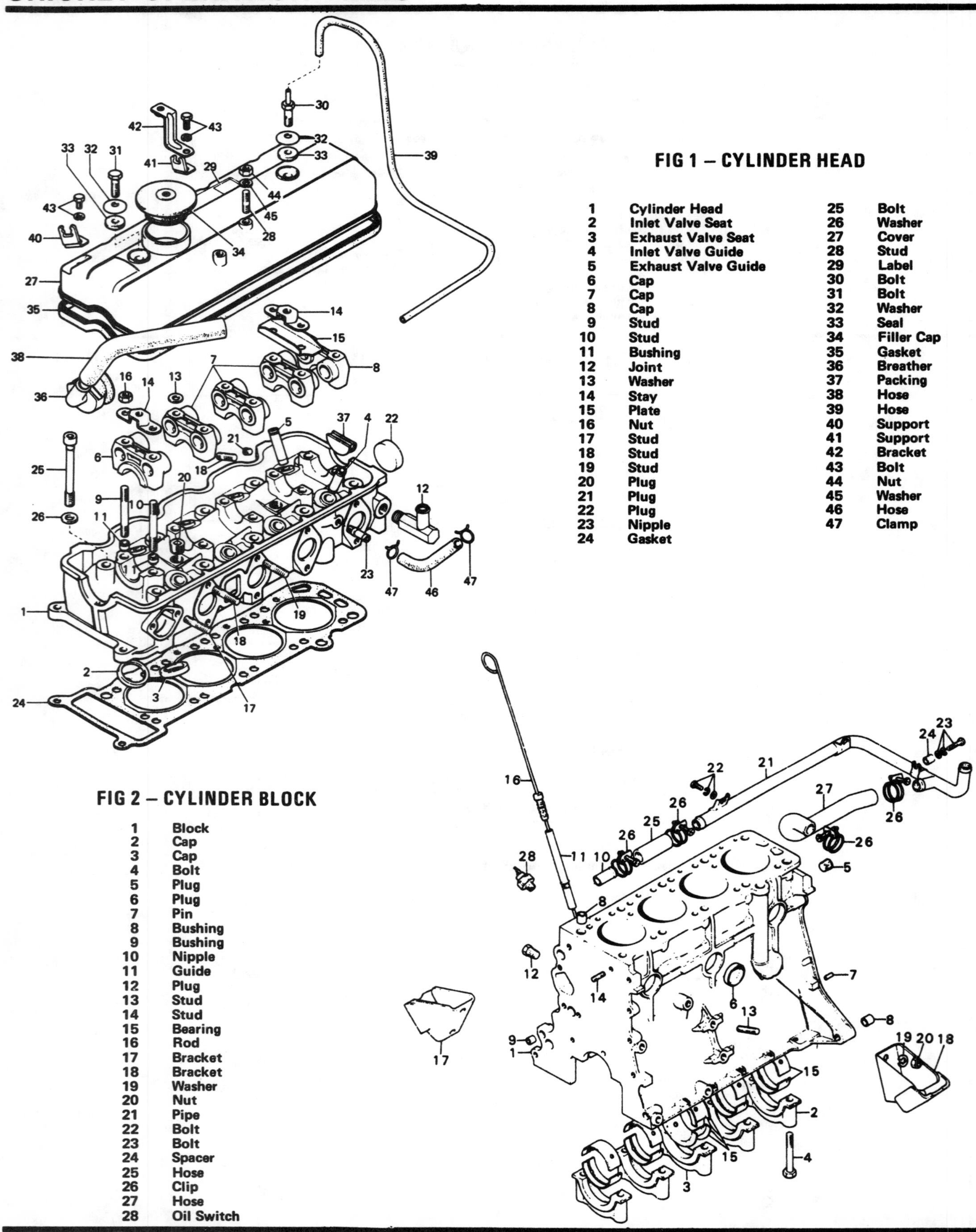

FIG 1 – CYLINDER HEAD

1	Cylinder Head	25	Bolt
2	Inlet Valve Seat	26	Washer
3	Exhaust Valve Seat	27	Cover
4	Inlet Valve Guide	28	Stud
5	Exhaust Valve Guide	29	Label
6	Cap	30	Bolt
7	Cap	31	Bolt
8	Cap	32	Washer
9	Stud	33	Seal
10	Stud	34	Filler Cap
11	Bushing	35	Gasket
12	Joint	36	Breather
13	Washer	37	Packing
14	Stay	38	Hose
15	Plate	39	Hose
16	Nut	40	Support
17	Stud	41	Support
18	Stud	42	Bracket
19	Stud	43	Bolt
20	Plug	44	Nut
21	Plug	45	Washer
22	Plug	46	Hose
23	Nipple	47	Clamp
24	Gasket		

FIG 2 – CYLINDER BLOCK

1	Block
2	Cap
3	Cap
4	Bolt
5	Plug
6	Plug
7	Pin
8	Bushing
9	Bushing
10	Nipple
11	Guide
12	Plug
13	Stud
14	Stud
15	Bearing
16	Rod
17	Bracket
18	Bracket
19	Washer
20	Nut
21	Pipe
22	Bolt
23	Bolt
24	Spacer
25	Hose
26	Clip
27	Hose
28	Oil Switch

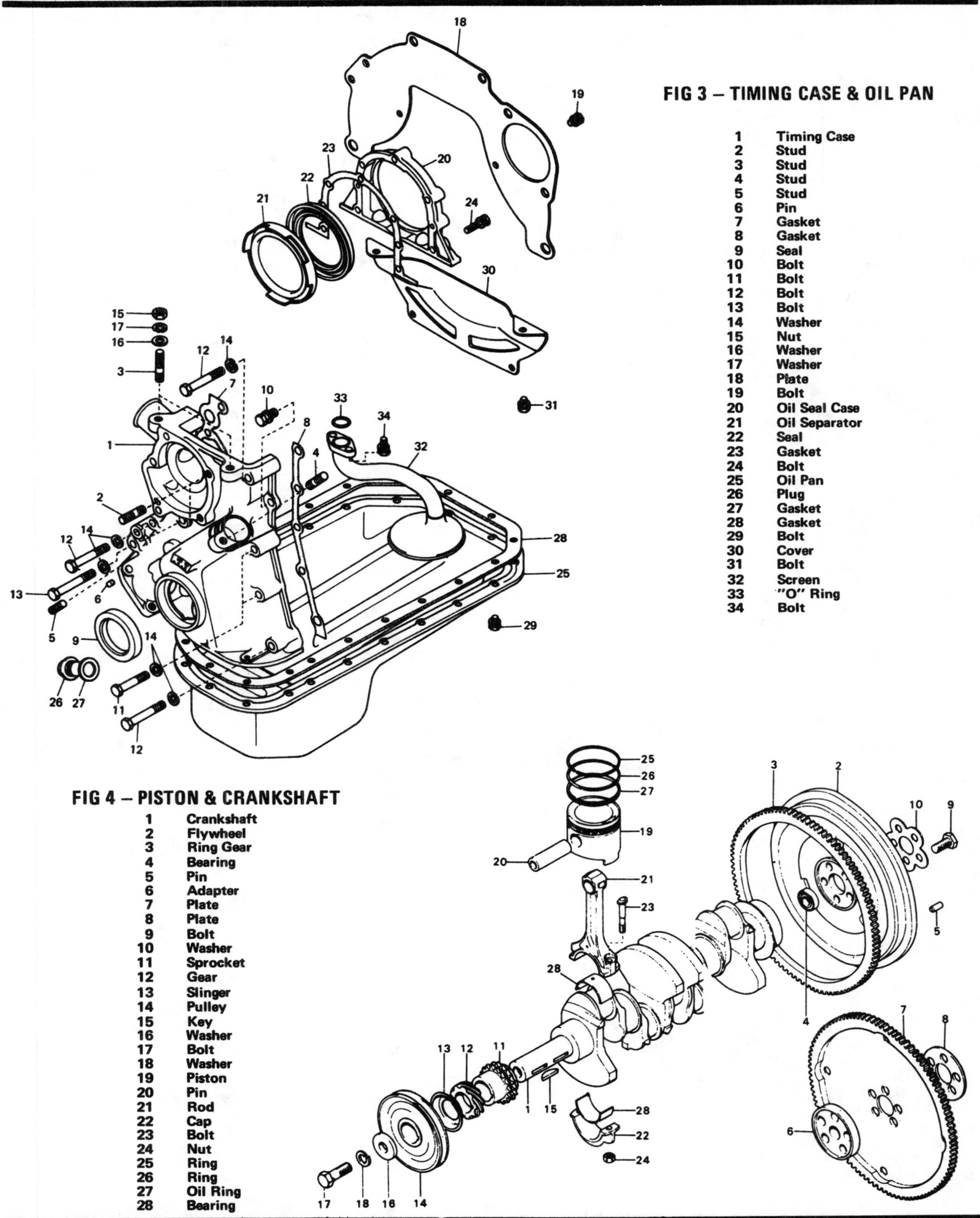
FIG 3 – TIMING CASE & OIL PAN
1 Timing Case
2 Stud
3 Stud
4 Stud
5 Stud
6 Pin
7 Gasket
8 Gasket
9 Seal
10 Bolt
11 Bolt
12 Bolt
13 Bolt
14 Washer
15 Nut
16 Washer
17 Washer
18 Plate
19 Bolt
20 Oil Seal Case
21 Oil Separator
22 Seal
23 Gasket
24 Bolt
25 Oil Pan
26 Plug
27 Gasket
28 Gasket
29 Bolt
30 Cover
31 Bolt
32 Screen
33 "O" Ring
34 Bolt
FIG 4 – PISTON & CRANKSHAFT
1 Crankshaft
2 Flywheel
3 Ring Gear
4 Bearing
5 Pin
6 Adapter
7 Plate
8 Plate
9 Bolt
10 Washer
11 Sprocket
12 Gear
13 Slinger
14 Pulley
15 Key
16 Washer
17 Bolt
18 Washer
19 Piston
20 Pin
21 Rod
22 Cap
23 Bolt
24 Nut
25 Ring
26 Ring
27 Oil Ring
28 Bearing

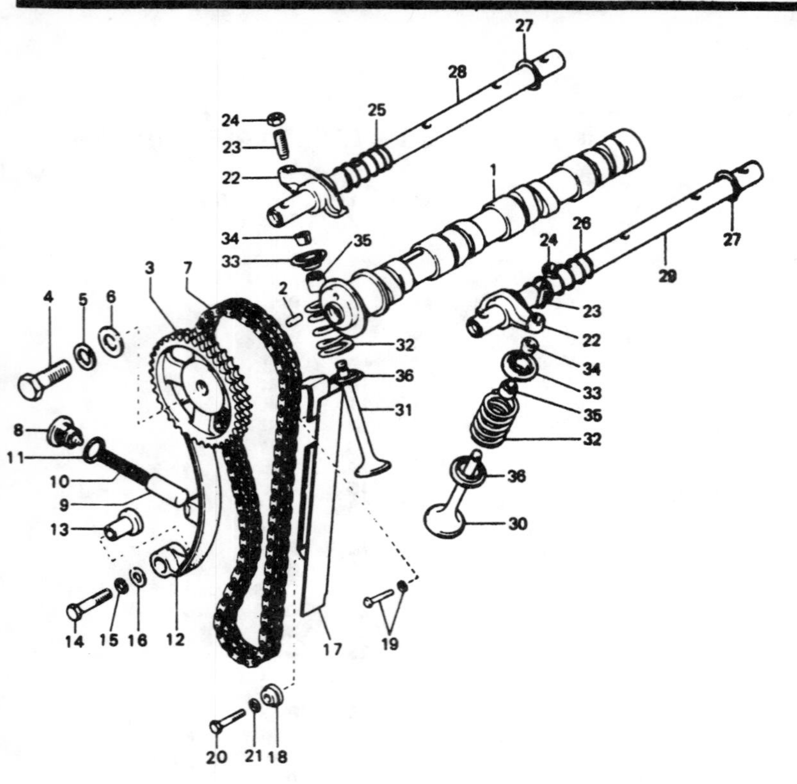

FIG 5 – CAMSHAFT & TIMING CHAIN

1	Camshaft
2	Pin
3	Sprocket
4	Bolt
5	Washer
6	Washer
7	Timing Chain
8	Holder
9	Plunger
10	Spring
11	Gasket
12	Lever
13	Shaft
14	Bolt
15	Washer
16	Washer
17	Guide
18	Jet
19	Nut
20	Bolt
21	Gasket
22	Rocker Arm
23	Screw
24	Nut
25	Spring
26	Spring
27	Washer
28	Shaft
29	Shaft
30	Inlet Valve
31	Exhaust Valve
32	Spring
33	Retainer
34	Lock
35	Seal
36	Seat

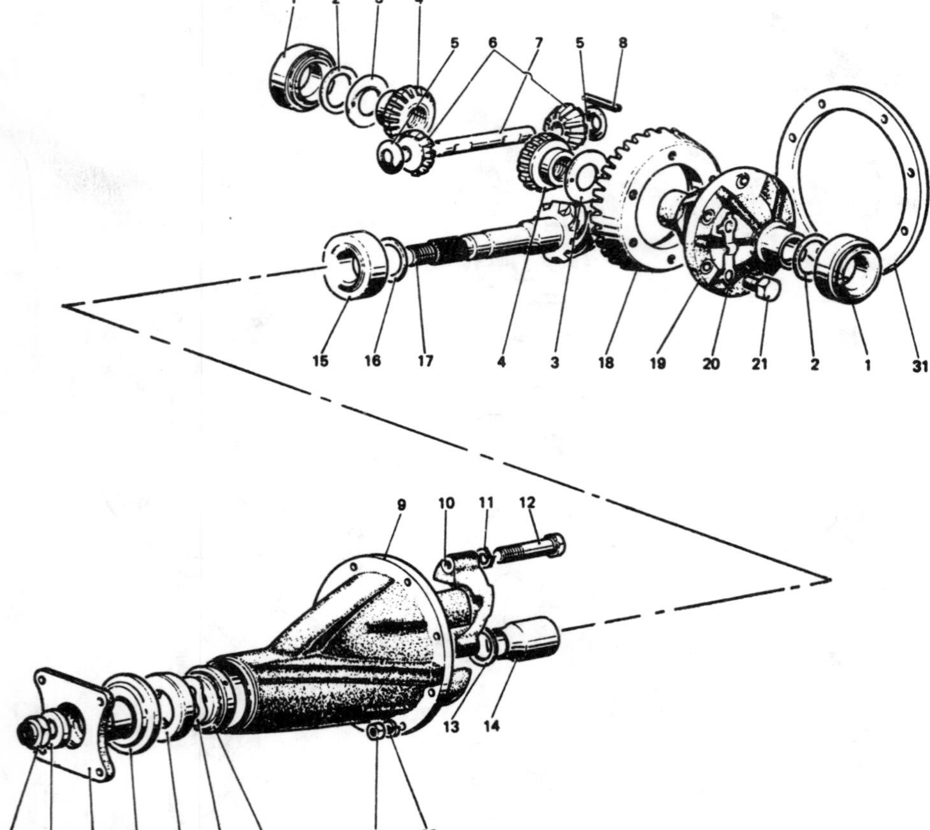

FIG 9 – REAR AXLE DIFFERENTIAL

1	Bearing
2	Shim
3	Spacer
4	Side Gear
5	Washer
6	Pinion
7	Shaft
8	Pin
9	Carrier
10	Cap
11	Washer
12	Bolt
13	Shim
14	Spacer
15	Bearing
16	Shim
17	Gear Set
18	Gear Set
19	Case
20	Washer
21	Bolt
22	Nut
23	Washer
24	Washer
25	Yoke
26	Cover
27	Oil Seal
28	Bearing
29	Nut
30	Washer
31	Packing

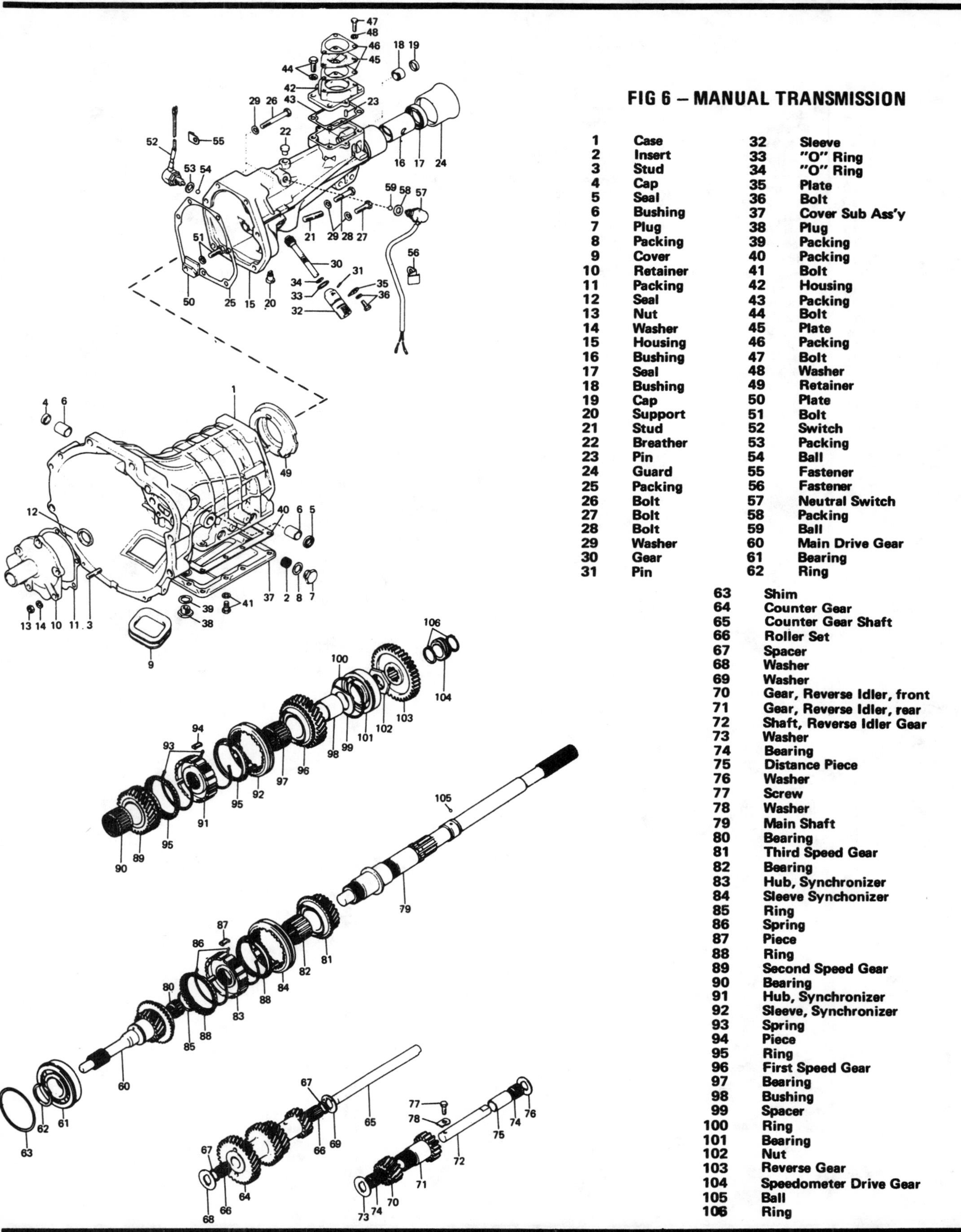

FIG 6 – MANUAL TRANSMISSION

1	Case	32	Sleeve
2	Insert	33	"O" Ring
3	Stud	34	"O" Ring
4	Cap	35	Plate
5	Seal	36	Bolt
6	Bushing	37	Cover Sub Ass'y
7	Plug	38	Plug
8	Packing	39	Packing
9	Cover	40	Packing
10	Retainer	41	Bolt
11	Packing	42	Housing
12	Seal	43	Packing
13	Nut	44	Bolt
14	Washer	45	Plate
15	Housing	46	Packing
16	Bushing	47	Bolt
17	Seal	48	Washer
18	Bushing	49	Retainer
19	Cap	50	Plate
20	Support	51	Bolt
21	Stud	52	Switch
22	Breather	53	Packing
23	Pin	54	Ball
24	Guard	55	Fastener
25	Packing	56	Fastener
26	Bolt	57	Neutral Switch
27	Bolt	58	Packing
28	Bolt	59	Ball
29	Washer	60	Main Drive Gear
30	Gear	61	Bearing
31	Pin	62	Ring

63	Shim
64	Counter Gear
65	Counter Gear Shaft
66	Roller Set
67	Spacer
68	Washer
69	Washer
70	Gear, Reverse Idler, front
71	Gear, Reverse Idler, rear
72	Shaft, Reverse Idler Gear
73	Washer
74	Bearing
75	Distance Piece
76	Washer
77	Screw
78	Washer
79	Main Shaft
80	Bearing
81	Third Speed Gear
82	Bearing
83	Hub, Synchronizer
84	Sleeve Synchonizer
85	Ring
86	Spring
87	Piece
88	Ring
89	Second Speed Gear
90	Bearing
91	Hub, Synchronizer
92	Sleeve, Synchronizer
93	Spring
94	Piece
95	Ring
96	First Speed Gear
97	Bearing
98	Bushing
99	Spacer
100	Ring
101	Bearing
102	Nut
103	Reverse Gear
104	Speedometer Drive Gear
105	Ball
106	Ring

FIG 7 – FRONT SUSPENSION

1 Cover
2 Nut
3 Washer
4 Nut
5 Washer
6 Insulator
7 Bearing
8 Seat
9 Bumper
10 Spring
11 Seal
12 Seal
13 Absorber
14 Strut
15 Knuckle Arm
16 Washer
17 Bolt
18 Crossmember
19 Nut
20 Bolt
21 Washer
22 Nut
23 Bushing
24 Washer
25 Washer
26 Bolt
27 Spacer
28 Bolt
29 Washer
30 Lower Shaft
31 Stopper
32 Lower Arm
33 Ball Joint
33A Packing
33B Washer
34 Bolt
35 Cover
36 Nut
37 Ring

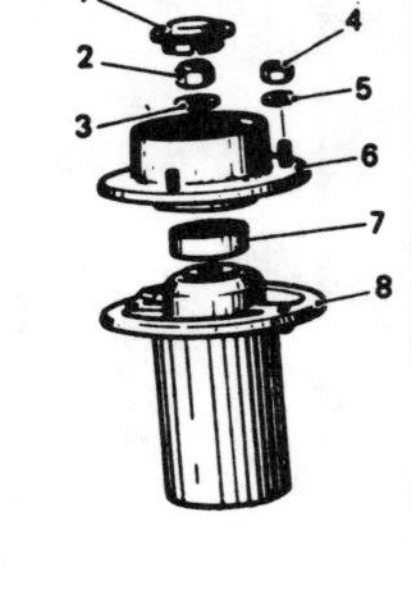

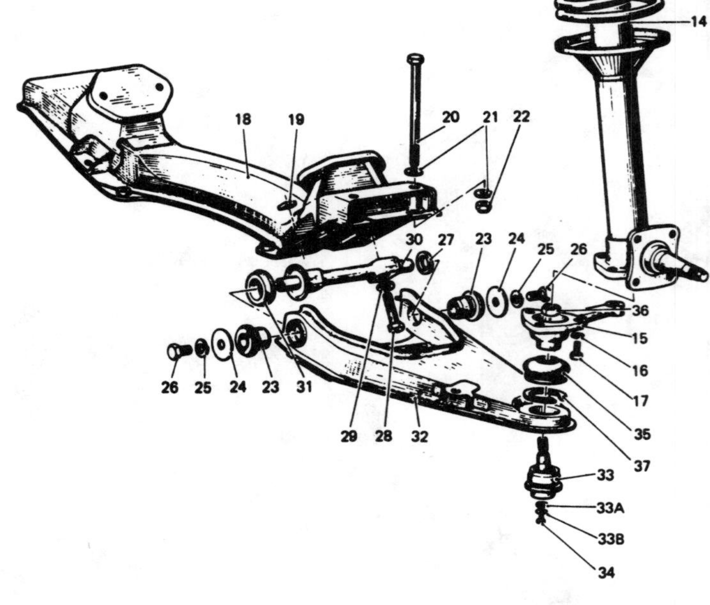

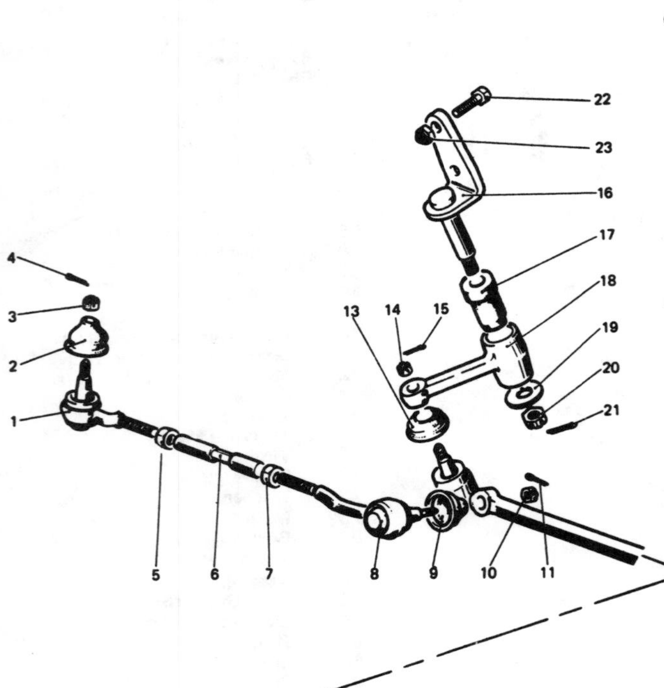

FIG 8 – STEERING LINKAGE

1 End
2 Cover
3 Nut
4 Pin
5 Nut
6 Tie Rod
7 Nut
8 End
9 Cover
10 Nut
11 Pin
12 Relay Rod
13 Cover
14 Nut
15 Pin
16 Bracket
17 Bushing
18 Idler Arm
19 Washer
20 Nut
21 Pin
22 Bolt
23 Nut

Ignition, Starting & Charging—TIME

OPERATION INDEX

Tune-Up, Minor 1
Tune-Up, Major 2
Compression Test 3
Distributor, R&R Or Renew 4
Distributor Cap, Renew 5
Ignition Cable Set, Renew 6
Vacuum Control Unit, Renew 7
Ignition Coil, Renew 8
Starter & Ignition Switch, Renew 9
Starter, R&R Or Renew 10
Starter Solenoid, Renew 11
Starter Bendix Drive, Renew 12
Starter, R&R & Overhaul 13
Starter Brushes, Renew 14
Starter Armature, Renew 15
Alternator Regulator, Renew 16
Alternator, R&R Or Renew 17
Alternator, R&R & Overhaul 18
Alternator Diodes, Renew 19
Alternator Bearings, Renew 20
Alternator Brushes, Renew 21
Alternator Pulley, Renew 22

1—TUNE-UP, MINOR
Includes renew points, condenser & plugs. Set spark timing and adjust carburetor idle
1971-73 ....1.5

2—TUNE-UP, MAJOR
Includes check compression, clean or renew and adjust spark plugs. R&R distributor, renew points and condenser. Adjust ignition timing, carburetor and fan belts. Clean battery terminals and service air cleaner. Check coil & clean or replace fuel filter.
1971-73 ....2.7

3—COMPRESSION TEST
1971-73 ....0.6

4—DISTRIBUTOR, R&R OR RENEW
1971-73 ....0.5

—NOTE—
For Stroboscope Adjustment Add 0.3

5—DISTRIBUTOR CAP, RENEW
1971-73 ....0.3

6—IGNITION CABLE SET, RENEW
1971-73—
One 0.3
All 0.4

7—VACUUM CONTROL UNIT, RENEW
1971-73 ....0.5

8—IGNITION COIL, RENEW
1971-73 ....0.3

9—STARTER & IGNITION SWITCH, RENEW
1971-73 ....0.8

10—STARTER, R&R OR RENEW
1971-73 ....0.4

11—STARTER SOLENOID, RENEW
1971-73 ....0.3

12—STARTER BENDIX DRIVE, RENEW
1971-73 ....1.4

13—STARTER, R&R & OVERHAUL
Includes: Turn down commutator and replace all necessary parts.
1971-73 ....2.0

14—STARTER BRUSHES, RENEW
1971-73 ....1.2

15—STARTER ARMATURE, RENEW
1971-73 ....1.2

16—ALTERNATOR REGULATOR, RENEW
1971-73 ....0.7

17—ALTERNATOR, R&R OR RENEW
1971-73 ....0.5

18—ALTERNATOR, R&R & OVERHAUL
1971-73 ....2.0

19—ALTERNATOR DIODES, RENEW
1971-73 ....1.3

20—ALTERNATOR BEARINGS, RENEW
1971-73 ....1.1

21—ALTERNATOR BRUSHES, RENEW
1971-73 ....0.8

22—ALTERNATOR PULLEY, RENEW
1971-73 ....0.6

Fuel, Emission Controls, Intake & Exhaust Systems—TIME

OPERATION INDEX

Carburetor Or Flange Gasket, Renew 1
Carburetor, R&R & Overhaul 2
Fuel Pump, R&R Or Renew 3
Fuel Tank, R&R Or Renew 4
Choke Cable Assy, Renew 5
Canister Assy, Renew 6
Emission Control Valve, Renew 7
Intake Manifold, Renew 8
Exhaust Manifold Or Gasket, Renew 9
Exhaust Pipe, Renew 10
Exhaust Tail Pipe, Renew 11
Muffler, Renew 12

1—CARBURETOR OR FLANGE GASKET, RENEW
1971-73 ....0.6

2—CARBURETOR, R&R & OVERHAUL

3—FUEL PUMP, R&R OR RENEW
1971-73 ....0.4

4—FUEL TANK, R&R OR RENEW
1971-73 ....0.8

5—CHOKE CABLE ASSY, RENEW
1971-73 ....0.5

6—CANISTER ASSY, RENEW
1971-73 ....0.3

7—EMISSION CONTROL VALVE, RENEW
1971-73 ....0.3

8—INTAKE MANIFOLD, RENEW
1971-73 ....1.1

9—EXHAUST MANIFOLD OR GASKET, RENEW
1971-73 ....1.0

10—EXHAUST PIPE, RENEW
1971-73 ....0.6

11—EXHAUST TAIL PIPE, RENEW
1971-73 ....0.4

12—MUFFLER, RENEW
1971-73 ....0.7
1971-73 ....2.0

Engine Cooling & Heater System—TIME

OPERATION INDEX

Radiator, R&R Or Renew 1
Radiator Hoses, Renew 2
Water Pump, R&R Or Renew 3
Thermostat Or Housing, Renew 4
Heater Assy, Renew 5
Heater Core, Renew 6
Heater Blower Motor, Renew 7
Heater Temperature Control Valve, Renew 8
Heater Control, Renew 9
Heater Hoses, Renew 10

1—RADIATOR, R&R OR RENEW
1971-73 ....0.5

2—RADIATOR HOSES, RENEW
1971-73, Each 0.3

3—WATER PUMP, OR RENEW
1971-73 ....0.6

4—THERMOSTAT OR HOUSING, RENEW
1971-73 ....0.3

5—HEATER ASSY, RENEW
1971-73 ....1.7

6—HEATER CORE, RENEW
1971-73 ....1.9

7—HEATER BLOWER MOTOR, RENEW
1971-73 ....2.0

8—HEATER TEMPERATURE CONTROL VALVE, RENEW
1971-73 ....2.0

9—HEATER CONTROL, RENEW
1971-73 ....0.6

10—HEATER HOSES, RENEW
1971-73—
One 0.3
All 0.5

Engine—TIME

OPERATION INDEX

Engine, R&R 1
Engine, R&R & Overhaul 2
Engine (Short), Renew & Grind Valves 3
Cylinder Head, R&R Or Gasket Renew 4
Valves, Grind 5
One Valve, Renew & Grind 6
Valve Springs, Renew 7
Rocker Arm Cover Gasket, Renew 8
Push Rods, Renew 9
Valve Rocker Arm Assy, Clean Or Overhaul 10
Oil Pan Or Gasket, R&R Or Renew 11
Valve Tappets, Renew 12
Valve Tappets, Adjust 13
Timing Cover Seal & Gasket, Renew 14
Timing Chain Or Gears, Renew 15
Timing Chain Tensioner, Renew 16
Camshaft, R&R Or Renew 17
Camshaft Bearings, Renew 18
Oil Pump, R&R Or Renew 19
Camshaft Rear Welch Plug, Renew 20
Piston Ring(S), Renew 21
Rings & Main Bearings, Renew & Grind Valves 22
Rod Bearing(S), Renew 23
Main Bearings, Renew 24
Main & Rod Bearings, Renew 25
Crankshaft, R&R Or Renew 26
Crankshaft Rear Main Oil Seal, Renew 27
Piston(S), Renew 28
Connecting Rod(S), Renew 29
Crankshaft Pulley, Renew 30

(Continued)

Engine—TIME Cont'd

1—ENGINE, R&R
Does not include transfer of any part of engine or replacement of special equipment.
1971-73—
Auto Trans 4.2
Std Trans 3.5

—NOTE—
To Renew Engine: For Transfer Of All Parts Not Included With New Engine And Not Including Special Equipment, Add 2.0

2—ENGINE, R&R & OVERHAUL
Includes rebore cylinders with boring bar, renew pistons, rings, pins & all bearings, grind valves, plastigage bearings & perform minor tune-up.
1971-73—
Auto Trans 14.9
Std Trans 14.2

3—ENGINE (SHORT), RENEW & GRIND VALVES
1971-73—
Auto Trans 9.2
Std Trans 8.5

—NOTE—
To Renew Cylinder Block, Add 1.5

4—CYLINDER HEAD, R&R OR GASKET, RENEW
Includes adjust tappets.
1971-73 ....2.7

5—VALVES, GRIND
Includes R&R head & adjust tappets
1971-73 ....4.5

6—ONE VALVE, RENEW & GRIND
Includes R&R head & adjust tappets.
1971-73 ....3.2

7—VALVE SPRINGS, RENEW
Includes replace valve stem oil seals & adjust tappets.
1971-73—
One 1.2
All 2.9

—NOTE—
Use Air To Hold Up Valves.

8—ROCKER COVER GASKET, RENEW
1971-73 ....0.4

9—PUSH RODS, RENEW
Includes adjust tappets.
1971-73—
One 1.0
All 1.3

10—VALVE ROCKER ARM ASSY, CLEAN OR OVERHAUL
1971-73 ....1.5

11—OIL PAN OR GASKET, R&R OR RENEW
1971-73 ....1.0

12—VALVE TAPPETS, RENEW
1971-73—
One 1.0
All 1.3

13—VALVE TAPPETS, ADJUST
1971-73 ....0.8

14—TIMING CASE COVER SEAL & GASKET, RENEW
1971-73—
Oil Seal 0.4
Cover Gasket 1.3

15—TIMING CHAIN OR GEARS, RENEW
1971-73 ....1.7

16—TIMING CHAIN TENSIONER, RENEW
1971-73 ....1.4

17—CAMSHAFT, R&R OR RENEW
1971-73 ....4.9

18—CAMSHAFT BEARINGS, RENEW
Includes R&R engine
1971-73—
Auto Trans 7.1
Std Trans 6.4

19—OIL PUMP, R&R OR RENEW
1971-73 ....1.3

—NOTE—
For Overhaul, Add 0.3

20—CAMSHAFT REAR WELCH PLUG, RENEW
1971-73—
Auto Trans 2.8
Std Trans 2.1

21—PISTON RING(S), RENEW
1971-73—
One 3.7
All 4.9

22—RINGS & MAIN BEARINGS, RENEW & GRIND VALVES
1971-73 ....8.4

23—ROD BEARING(S), RENEW
1971-73—
One 1.6
All 2.2

24—MAIN BEARINGS, RENEW
Includes plastigauge bearings.
1971-73 ....2.5

25—MAIN & ROD BEARINGS, RENEW
Includes plastigauge bearings.
1971-73 ....3.7

—NOTE—
To Renew Oil Pump, Add 0.3

26—CRANKSHAFT, R&R OR RENEW
1971-73—
Auto Trans 6.1
Std Trans 5.4

27—CRANKSHAFT REAR MAIN OIL SEAL, RENEW
1971-73—
Auto Trans 4.0
Std Trans 3.3

28—PISTONS(S), RENEW
Includes replace rings & rod bearings
1971-73—
One 4.3
All 5.5

29—CONNECTING ROD(S), RENEW
Includes replace rod bearings
1971-73—
One 4.2
All 5.3

30—CRANKSHAFT PULLEY, RENEW
1971-73 ....0.3

Clutch, Mounts & Transmissions—TIME

OPERATION INDEX
Flywheel, R&R Or Renew 1
Flywheel Ring Gear, Renew 2
Clutch Or Disc, Renew 3
Release Bearing, Renew 4
Pilot Bearing, Renew 5
Release Fork (Or Lever) Renew 6
Clutch Pedal, Adjust 7
Engine Mounts, Renew 8
Transmission Assy, R&R Or Renew 9
Manual Trans Case, Renew 10
Trans Case Cover Or Gasket, R&R Or Renew 11
Main Drive Pinion Retainer Or Seal, Renew 12
Extension Housing Or Bushing, Renew 13
Extension Housing Gasket, Renew 14
Extension Housing Oil Seal, Renew 15
Torque Converter Ring Gear, Renew 16
Oil Pan Gasket, Renew 17
Front & Rear Bands, Adjust 18
Manual Trans, R&R & Overhaul 19
Mainshaft Rear Bearing, Renew 20
Gear Selector Forks, Renew 21
Reverse Selector Lever, Renew 22
Shift Lever&Shaft, Renew 23
Speedometer Pinion Oil Seal, Renew 24
Gearshift Or Selector Lever, Renew 25
Throttle Valve Cable, Renew 26
Gear Selector Cable, Renew 27

1—FLYWHEEL, R&R OR RENEW
1971-73 ....2.8

2—FLYWHEEL RING GEAR, RENEW
1971-73 ....3.2

3—CLUTCH OR DISC, RENEW
Includes replace release bearing
1971-73 ....2.8

4—RELEASE BEARING, RENEW
1971-73 ....2.5

5—PILOT BEARING, RENEW
1971-73 ....3.0

6—RELEASE FORK (OR LEVER), RENEW
1971-73 ....2.1

7—CLUTCH PEDAL, ADJUST
1971-73 ....0.3

8—ENGINE MOUNTS, RENEW
1971-73—
Front—
One 0.4
Both 0.7
Rear 0.4

9—TRANSMISSION ASSY, R&R OR RENEW
1971-73—
Auto Trans 3.1
Std Trans 2.4

10—MANUAL TRANS CASE, RENEW
1971-73 ....3.7

11—TRANS CASE COVER OR GASKET, R&R OR RENEW
1971-73 ....2.1

12—MAIN DRIVE PINION RETAINER OR SEAL, RENEW
1971-73 ....2.1

13—EXTENSION HOUSING OR BUSHING, RENEW
Includes replace oil seal & gasket
1971-73—
Auto Trans 1.5
Std Trans 1.3

14—EXTENSION HOUSING GASKET, RENEW
1971-73—
Auto Trans ....(1)1.5
Std Trans 0.9

(1)*Includes Replace Extn Seal.*

15—EXTENSION HOUSING OIL SEAL, RENEW
1971-73—
Auto Trans 0.4
Std Trans 0.5

16—TORQUE CONVERTER RING GEAR, RENEW
1971-73 ....3.5

17—OIL PAN GASKET, RENEW
1971-73 ....0.6

(Continued)

Clutch, Mounts & Transmissions—TIME Cont'd

18—FRONT & REAR BANDS, ADJUST
1971-73 ....2.9

19—MANUAL TRANS, R&R & OVERHAUL
1971-73 ....6.7

20—MAINSHAFT REAR BEARING, RENEW
Includes replace extension oil seal & bushing.
1971-73 ....3.8

21—GEAR SELECTOR FORKS, RENEW
1971-73, One Or Both 2.6

22—REVERSE SELECTOR LEVER, RENEW
1971-73 ....2.8

23—SHIFT LEVER & SHAFT, RENEW
Includes remove extension housing
1971-73 ....1.6

24—SPEEDOMETER PINION OIL SEAL, RENEW
1971-73 ....0.3

25—GEARSHIFT OR SELECTOR LEVER, RENEW
1971-73—
Auto Trans Select Lever 0.7
Std Trans Gearshift 0.4

26—THROTTLE VALVE CABLE, RENEW
1971-73 ....0.7

27—GEAR SELECTOR CABLE, RENEW
1971-73 ....0.5

Brakes, Steering, Suspension, Universals & Rear Axle—TIME

OPERATION INDEX

Brake Shoes Or Friction Pads, Renew 1
Master Cylinder, Renew 2
Master Cylinder, R&R & Overhaul 3
Wheel Cylinders, Renew 4
Wheel Cylinders, R&R & Overhaul 5
Caliper Assy, Renew 6
Caliper Assy, R&R & Overhaul 7
Bleed System 8
Brake Hose, Renew 9
Hub, Disc Or Shield, Renew 10
Power Brake Unit, Renew 11
Power Brake Check Valve, Renew 12
Brake Drum, Renew 13
Brake Adjuster, Renew 14
Brake Proportioning Valve, Renew 15
Brake Pedal, Renew 16
Parking Brake Cable, Renew 17
Parking Brake Lever, Renew 18
Coupling Disc (Gear To Shaft), Renew 19
Rack & Pinion Assy, Renew 20
Spring(S), Renew 21
Strut Assy, Renew 22
Strut Assy, Overhaul 23
Track Control Arm, Renew 24
Steering Arm, Renew 25
Front Hub Bearings, Renew 26
Sway Bar Or Links, Renew 27
Drag Strut Or Bushing, Renew 28
Shock Absorbers, Renew 29
Rear Upper Link Assy, Renew 30
Rear Upper Link Front Bushing, Renew 31
Rear Lower Link Assy, Renew 32
Rear Lower Link Rear Bushing, Renew 33
Universal Joints, Renew 34
Propeller Shaft Sliding Yoke, Renew 35
Propeller Shaft Flange (On Rear Axle), Renew 36
Differential Axle Housing, Renew 37
Axle Shaft, Renew 38
Axle Shaft Bearings, Renew 39
Differential Assy, Overhaul 40
Pinion Shaft Front Bearing, Renew 41
Pinion Shaft Oil Seal, Renew 42
Differential Cover Or Gasket, Renew 43

1—BRAKE SHOES OR FRICTION PADS, RENEW
1971-73—
Front Disc 0.5
Rear Drum 1.2

2—MASTER CYLINDER, RENEW
Includes: Bleed system
1971-73 ....0.6

3—MASTER CYLINDER, R&R & OVERHAUL
Includes: Bleed system
1971-73 ....1.1

4—WHEEL CYLINDER, RENEW
Includes: Bleed system & adjust brakes.
1971-73—
One 0.7
Both 1.2

5—WHEEL CYLINDERS, R&R & OVERHAUL
Includes: Bleed system & adjust brakes.
1971-73—
One 0.8
Both 1.4

6—CALIPER ASSY, RENEW
Includes: Bleed system.
1971-73—
One 0.7
Both 1.2

7—CALIPER ASSY, R&R & OVERHAUL
Includes: Bleed system
1971-73—
One 1.2
Both 2.2

8—BLEED SYSTEM
1971-73 ....0.3

9—BRAKE HOSE, RENEW
Includes: Bleed system
1971-73, Each 0.6

10—HUB, DISC OR SHIELD, RENEW
1971-73, Each 0.8

11—POWER BRAKE UNIT, RENEW
1971-73 ....0.6

12—POWER BRAKE CHECK VALVE, RENEW
1971-73 ....0.2

13—BRAKE DRUM, RENEW
Includes: Adjust brakes.
1971-73 ....0.4

14—BRAKE ADJUSTER, RENEW
1971-73 ....0.8

15—BRAKE PROPORTIONING VALVE, RENEW
Includes: Bleed system
1971-73 ....0.5

16—BRAKE PEDAL, RENEW
1971-73 ....1.5

17—PARKING BRAKE CABLE, RENEW
1971-73 ....0.8

18—PARKING BRAKE LEVER, RENEW
1971-73 ....0.6

19—COUPLING DISC (GEAR TO SHAFT), RENEW
1971-73 ....0.5

20—RACK & PINION ASSY, RENEW
1971-73 ....0.8

21—SPRING(S), RENEW
1971-73—
Front (Each) 1.3
Rear (Each) 0.5

22—STRUT ASSY, RENEW
1971-73 ....0.9

23—STRUT ASSY, OVERHAUL
1971-73 ....1.5

24—TRACK CONTROL ARM, RENEW
1971-73 ....0.8

25—STEERING ARM, RENEW
1971-73 ....0.5

26—FRONT HUB BEARING, RENEW
1971-73—
One Side—
Inner & Outer 0.8
Both Sides—
Inner & Outer 1.4

27—SWAY BAR OR LINKS, RENEW
1971-73—
Sway Bar 0.5
Sway Bar Links 0.4

28—DRAG STRUT OR BUSHING, RENEW
1971-73—
Drag Strut 0.5
Strut Bushing 0.6

29—SHOCK ABSORBERS, RENEW
1971-73—
One (Rear) 0.4
Both (Rear) 0.7

30—REAR UPPER LINK ASSY, RENEW
1971-73 ....0.5

31—REAR UPPER LINK FRONT BUSHING, RENEW
1971-73 ....0.5

32—REAR LOWER LINK ASSY, RENEW
1971-73 ....0.8

33—REAR LOWER LINK REAR BUSHING, RENEW
1971-73 ....0.7

34—UNIVERSAL JOINTS, RENEW
1971-73—
One 0.6
Both 1.0

35—PROPELLER SHAFT SLIDING YOKE, RENEW
1971-73 ....0.6

36—PROPELLER SHAFT FLANGE (ON REAR AXLE), RENEW
1971-73 ....0.6

37—DIFFERENTIAL AXLE HOUSING, RENEW
1971-73 ....3.4

38—AXLE SHAFT, RENEW
Includes: Replace bearing & retainer gasket.
1971-73 ....0.5

39—AXLE SHAFT BEARINGS, RENEW
1971-73, Each 0.5

40—DIFFERENTIAL ASSY, OVERHAUL
1971-73 ....3.0

41—PINION SHAFT FRONT BEARING, RENEW
1971-73 ....2.3

(Continued)

Brakes, Steering, Suspension, Universals & Rear Axle—TIME Cont'd

42—PINION SHAFT OIL SEAL, RENEW
1971-73 ....0.6

43—DIFFERENTIAL COVER OR GASKET, RENEW
1971-73 ....0.4

Speedometer, Wipers & Instruments—TIME

OPERATION INDEX

Speedometer Cable & Housing, Renew 1
Speedometer Head, Renew 2
W/S Wiper Motor, Renew 3
W/S Wiper Link Set, Renew 4
W/S Wiper Arm, Renew 5
Fuel Gauge (Dash Unit), Renew 6
Fuel Tank Gauge, Renew 7
Oil Gauge (Dash Unit), Renew 8
Oil Gauge Sending Unit, Renew 9
Temperature Gauge (Dash Unit), Renew 10
Temperature Gauge Sending Unit, Renew 11
Ammeter, Renew 12
Instrument Cluster Voltage Limiter, Renew 13
Headlight Switch, Renew 14
Headlamp Foot Dimmer Switch, Renew 15
Stop Light Switch, Renew 16
Turn Signal & Horn Switch, Renew 17
Hazard Flasher Switch, Renew 18

1—SPEEDOMETER CABLE & HOUSING, RENEW
1971-73 ....0.9

2—SPEEDOMETER HEAD, RENEW
1971-73 ....0.9

3—W/S WIPER MOTOR, RENEW
1971-73 ....1.4

4—W/S WIPER LINK SET, RENEW
1971-73 ....1.4

5—W/S WIPER ARM, RENEW
1971-73 ....0.2

6—FUEL GAUGE (DASH UNIT), RENEW
1971-73 ....0.9

7—FUEL TANK GAUGE, RENEW
1971-73 ....0.3

8—OIL GAUGE (DASH UNIT), RENEW
1971-73 ....0.9

9—OIL GAUGE SENDING UNIT, RENEW
1971-73 ....0.3

10—TEMPERATURE GAUGE (DASH UNIT), RENEW
1971-73 ....0.9

11—TEMPERATURE GAUGE SENDING UNIT, RENEW
1971-73 ....0.3

12—AMMETER, RENEW
1971-73 ....0.9

13—INSTRUMENT CLUSTER VOLTAGE LIMITER, RENEW
1971-73 ....0.7

14—HEADLIGHT SWITCH, RENEW
1971-73 ....0.5

15—HEADLAMP FOOT SWITCH, RENEW
1971-73 ....0.3

16—STOP LIGHT SWITCH, RENEW
1971-73 ....0.2

17—TURN SIGNAL & HORN SWITCH, RENEW
1971-73 ....0.4

18—HAZARD FLASHER SWITCH, RENEW
1971-73 ....0.4

IDENTIFICATION

ALL MODELS.......................... 126

ILLUSTRATIONS

FIG 1 – ENGINE – 4 CYL – BLOCK & OIL PAN
FIG 2 – ENGINE – 4 CYL – CYLINDER HEAD
FIG 3 – ENGINE – 4 CYL – CRANKSHAFT & PISTONS
FIG 4 – ENGINE – 4 CYL – CAMSHAFT & VALVES
FIG 5 – ENGINE – 6 CYL – BLOCK & OIL PAN
FIG 6 – ENGINE – 6 CYL – CYLINDER HEAD
FIG 7 – ENGINE – 6 CYL – CRANKSHAFT & PISTONS
FIG 8 – ENGINE – 6 CYL – CAMSHAFT & VALVES
FIG 9 – TRANSMISSION GEARS – 4 SPEED
FIG 10 – FRONT SUSPENSION – 610
FIG 11 – FRONT SUSPENSION – 240 Z
FIG 12 – STEERING – 240 Z

OPERATION TIMES

A

Air Pump.. 134
Alternator.. 134
Automatic Transmission.................... 137
Axle Shaft.. 138

B

Brake Drums...................................... 137
Brakes.. 137

C

Cables (Ignition)................................ 134
Calipers.. 137
Camshaft... 135
Carburetor... 134
Clutch... 136
Coil, Ignition..................................... 134
Compression Test 134
Connecting Rods................................ 136
Cooling System.................................. 135
Crankshaft... 136
Cylinder Block................................... 135
Cylinder Head.................................... 135

D

Dash Gauges...................................... 138
Differential.. 138
Disc Brakes.. 137
Distributor... 134

E

Emission Controls.............................. 134
Engine Assembly................................ 135
Engine Mountings.............................. 136
Engine Oiling..................................... 135
Engine Tune-Up.................................. 134
Exhaust Gas Recirculation................. 134
Exhaust System.................................. 134

F

Flywheel.. 136
Front Suspension............................... 138
Fuel Gauges....................................... 138
Fuel Pump... 134
Fuel Tank.. 134

H

Hand Brake.. 138
Headlight Switch............................... 139
Heater... 135
Hose (Brake)...................................... 137
Hose (Radiator).................................. 135
Hydraulic Brakes............................... 137

I

Ignition... 134
Ignition Coil...................................... 134
Ignition Switch.................................. 134
Intake Manifold................................. 135

L

Light Switches................................... 139

M

Main Bearings.................................... 136
Master Cylinder................................. 137
Muffler.. 135

O

Oil Gauge.. 138
Oiling, Engine.................................... 135
Oil Pan.. 135
Oil Pump... 135

P

Parking Brake.................................... 138
Piston Rings....................................... 136
Pistons... 136
Power Brake....................................... 137

R

Radiator.. 135
Radiator Hose.................................... 135
Rear Axle.. 138
Regulator (Alternator)....................... 134
Rocker Arms...................................... 135
Rod Bearings..................................... 136

S

Shocks (Front)................................... 138
Shocks (Rear).................................... 138
Speedometer...................................... 138
Springs (Front).................................. 138
Springs (Rear)................................... 138
Stabilizer... 138
Starting Motor................................... 134
Steering Gear..................................... 138
Steering Linkage................................ 138
Switches (Light)................................. 139
Synchro-Mesh Trans.......................... 136

T

Tachometer....................................... 139
Temperature Gauge........................... 139
Thermostat.. 135
Timing Case Cover............................ 135
Timing Chain..................................... 135
Transverse Link................................. 138
Transmission, Manual........................ 136
Transmission, Automatic.................. 137
Tune-Up, Engine............................... 134

V

Vacuum Control Unit........................ 134
Valve Lifters...................................... 135
Valve System..................................... 135

W

Water Pump...................................... 135
Wheel Cylinders................................ 137
Windshield Wiper............................. 138

DATSUN TYPE
ENGINE CAPACITY
MAX HP at RPM
WHEEL BASE
ENGINE NO.
CAR NO.
NISSAN MOTOR CO., LTD.
YOKOHAMA JAPAN

IDENTIFICATION PLATE LOCATIONS

TYPE PLATE (CAR NUMBER PLATE) —
710-610-510-520-521-1600-2000
On Cowl Dash Panel
620-240Z-411
On Left Front Wheelhouse
1200-260Z
On Right Front Wheelhouse

CAR SERIAL NUMBER
620- On Right Frame Rail
All Others — On Cowl Dash Panel

ENGINE NUMBER
On Right Side of Cylinder Block

MODEL IDENTIFICATION

MODEL	YEAR	STARTING CHASSIS NO.
240Z	1970	HLS30-00013
240Z	1971	HLS30-21001
240Z	1972	HLS30-46001
240Z	1973	HLS30-120001
260Z (2seater)	1974	RLS30-000001
260Z (2+2)	1974	GRL30-000001
260Z (2-Seater)	1975	RLS30-060001
260Z 2+2	1975	GRLS30-015001
280Z (2-Seater)	1975	HLS 30 - 200001
280Z (2-Seater)	1976	HLS 30 - 270001
280Z 2+2	1975	GHLS30 - 000001
280Z 2+2	1976	GHLS30 - 030001
1200 Sedan	1971	LB110-000001
1200 Coupe	1971	KLB110-000001
510 2-Dr.	1968	L510-000011
510 4-Dr.		PL510-000011
510 Wgn		WPL510-800001
510 2-Dr.	1969	L510-010000
510 4-Dr.		PL510-040011
510 Wgn.		WPL510-820001
510 2-Dr.	1970	L510-040000
510 4-Dr.		PL510-095000
510 Wgn.		WPL510-853001
510 2-Dr.	1971	
510 4-Dr.		PL510-200011
510 Wgn.		WPL510-883501
510 2-Dr.	1972	
510 4-Dr.		PL510-295003
510 Wgn.		WPL510-927564
520	1965	000001
520	1966	004604
520	1967	019001
520	1968	160001
521	1968	000001
521	1969	038555
521	1970	180071
521	1970	255905
521	1970	350001
521	1971	587182
521	1972	910001
1600 (Early)	1967	SPL311-10001
1600 (Late)		SPL311-11001
2000		SRL311-00001
1600	1968	SPL311-17001
2000		SRL311-01001
1600	1969	SPL311-24001
2000		SRL311-07001
1600	1970	SPL311-27001
2000		SRL311-13001

MODEL	YEAR	STARTING CHASSIS NO.
PL620	1972	PL620-000001
PL620	1973	PL620-092942
620 Pick-Up	1974	PL620 - 324001
620 Pick-Up	1975	HL620 - 000001
620 Pick-Up	1976	HL620 - 090001
610 2-Dr.	1973	KPL610-000000
610 4-Dr.		PL610-000000
610 Wgn.		WPL610-000000
610 2-Dr	1974	KHL610-000001
610 4-Dr	1974	HL610-000001
610 Wagon	1974	WHL610-800001
610 4-Dr. Sedan	1975	HL610 - 040001
610 4-Dr. Sedan	1976	HL610 - 070014
610 2-Dr. Hard Top	1975	KHL610 - 040001
610 2-Dr. Hard Top	1976	KHL610 - 070014
610 Sta Wgn	1975	WHL610 - 840001
610 Sta Wgn	1976	WHL610 - 880007
B210 4-Dr. Sedan	1974	HLB210TU 400001
	1975	HLB210TU 510001
	1976*	HLB210TU 710001
	1976**	HLB210TU 900001
2-Dr. Sedan	1974	HLB210TRU 400001
	1975	HLB210TRU 510001
	1976*	HLB201TRU 710001
	1976**	HLB210TRU 900001
Coupe	1974#	HLB210U 000001
	1974*	HLB210U 400001
	1975 #	HLB210U 070001
	1975 *	HLB210U 510001
	1976 #	HLB210U 140001
	1976 *	HLB210U 710001
710 Sta Wgn	1974	WHL710 - 000001
710 Sta Wgn	1975	WHL710 - 840001
710 Sta Wgn	1976	WHL710 - 890009
710 2-Dr. Sedan	1974	HL710R - 000001
710 2-Dr. Sedan	1975	HL710R - 038001
710 2-Dr. Sedan	1976	HL710R - 070007
710 4-Dr. Sedan	1974	HL710 - 000001
710 4-Dr. Sedan	1975	HL710 - 038001
710 4-Dr. Sedan	1976	HL710 - 070007
710 2-Dr. Hard Top	1974	KHL710 - 000001
710 2-Dr. Hard Top	1975	KHL710 - 025001
710 2-Dr. Hard Top	1976	KHL710 - 040007

* Zama Plant ** Oppama Plant # Fuji Plant

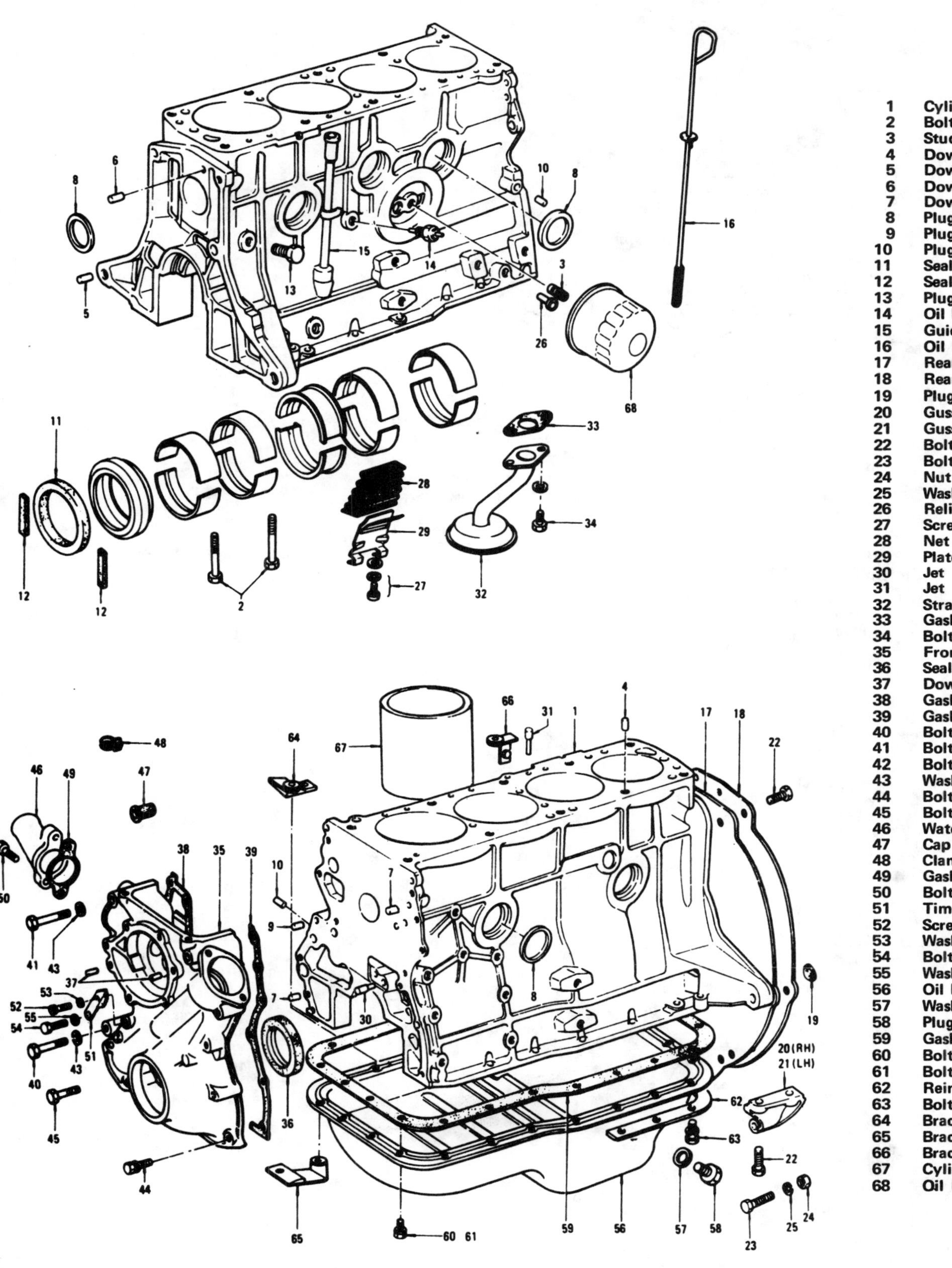

FIG 1 – ENGINE – 4 CYLINDER – BLOCK & OIL PAN

1	Cylinder Block
2	Bolt
3	Stud
4	Dowel
5	Dowel
6	Dowel
7	Dowel
8	Plug
9	Plug
10	Plug
11	Seal
12	Seal
13	Plug
14	Oil Pressure Switch
15	Guide
16	Oil Level Gauge
17	Rear Plate (Std Trans)
18	Rear Plate (Auto Trans)
19	Plug
20	Gusset
21	Gusset
22	Bolt
23	Bolt
24	Nut
25	Washer
26	Relief Valve
27	Screw
28	Net
29	Plate
30	Jet
31	Jet
32	Strainer
33	Gasket
34	Bolt
35	Front Cover
36	Seal
37	Dowel
38	Gasket
39	Gasket
40	Bolt
41	Bolt
42	Bolt
43	Washer
44	Bolt
45	Bolt
46	Water Inlet
47	Cap
48	Clamp
49	Gasket
50	Bolt
51	Timing Indicator
52	Screw
53	Washer
54	Bolt
55	Washer
56	Oil Pan
57	Washer
58	Plug
59	Gasket
60	Bolt
61	Bolt
62	Reinforcement
63	Bolt
64	Bracket
65	Bracket
66	Bracket
67	Cylinder Liner
68	Oil Filter Element

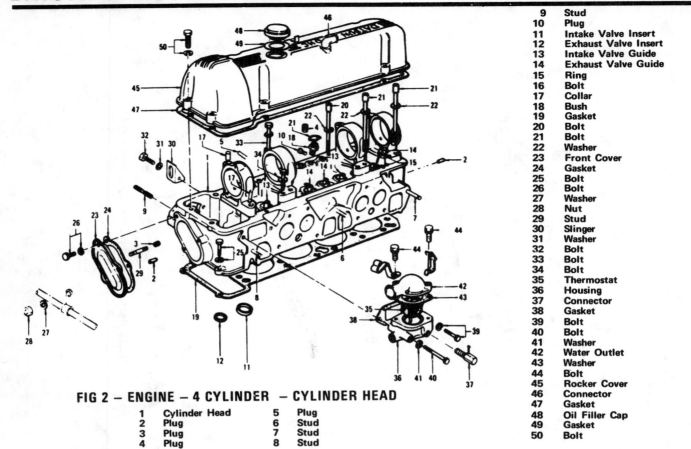

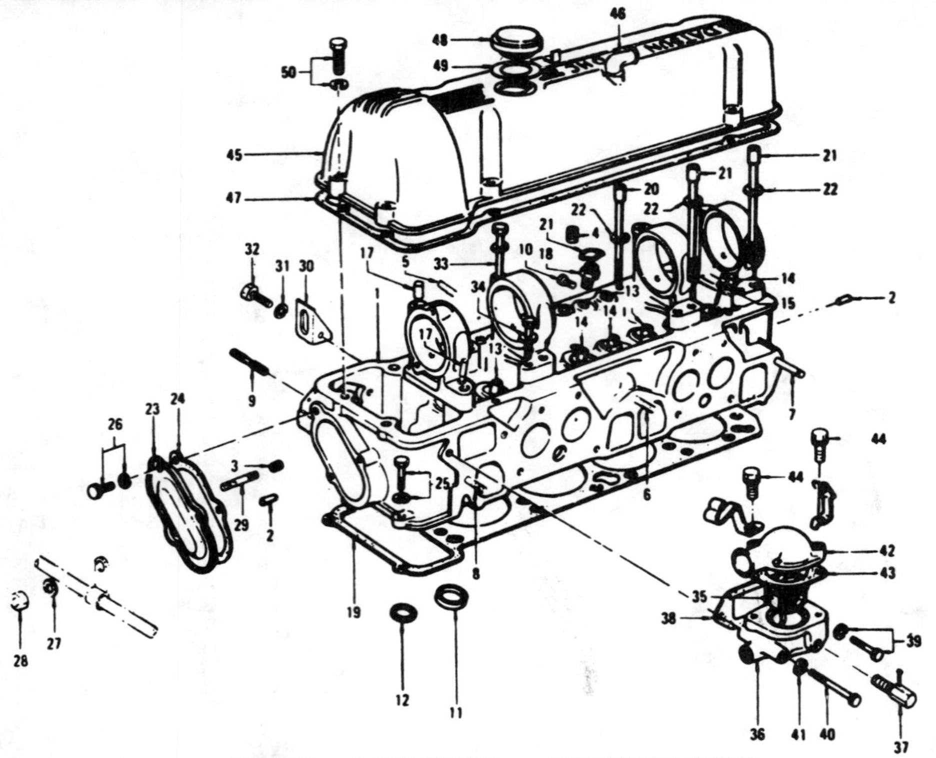

FIG 2 – ENGINE – 4 CYLINDER – CYLINDER HEAD

1 Cylinder Head
2 Plug
3 Plug
4 Plug
5 Plug
6 Stud
7 Stud
8 Stud
9 Stud
10 Plug
11 Intake Valve Insert
12 Exhaust Valve Insert
13 Intake Valve Guide
14 Exhaust Valve Guide
15 Ring
16 Bolt
17 Collar
18 Bush
19 Gasket
20 Bolt
21 Bolt
22 Washer
23 Front Cover
24 Gasket
25 Bolt
26 Bolt
27 Washer
28 Nut
29 Stud
30 Slinger
31 Washer
32 Bolt
33 Bolt
34 Bolt
35 Thermostat
36 Housing
37 Connector
38 Gasket
39 Bolt
40 Bolt
41 Washer
42 Water Outlet
43 Washer
44 Bolt
45 Rocker Cover
46 Connector
47 Gasket
48 Oil Filler Cap
49 Gasket
50 Bolt

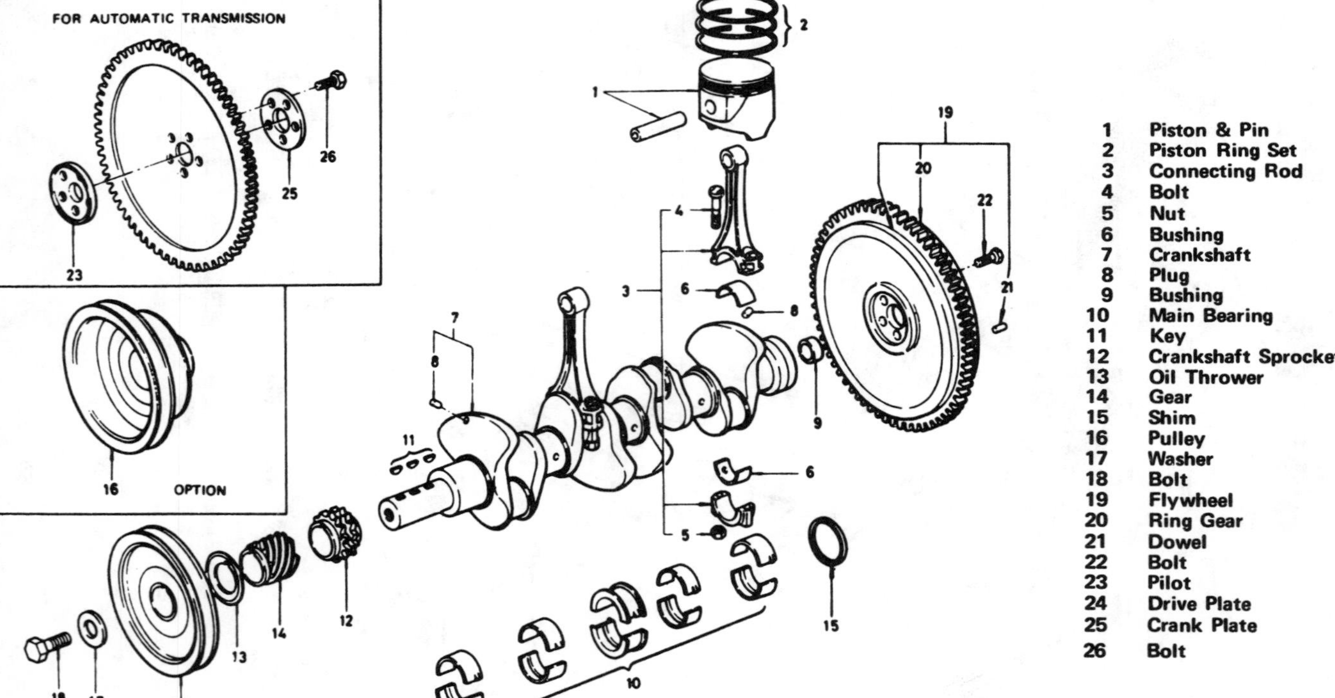

FIG 3 – ENGINE – 4 CYLINDER – CRANKSHAFT & PISTONS

1 Piston & Pin
2 Piston Ring Set
3 Connecting Rod
4 Bolt
5 Nut
6 Bushing
7 Crankshaft
8 Plug
9 Bushing
10 Main Bearing
11 Key
12 Crankshaft Sprocket
13 Oil Thrower
14 Gear
15 Shim
16 Pulley
17 Washer
18 Bolt
19 Flywheel
20 Ring Gear
21 Dowel
22 Bolt
23 Pilot
24 Drive Plate
25 Crank Plate
26 Bolt

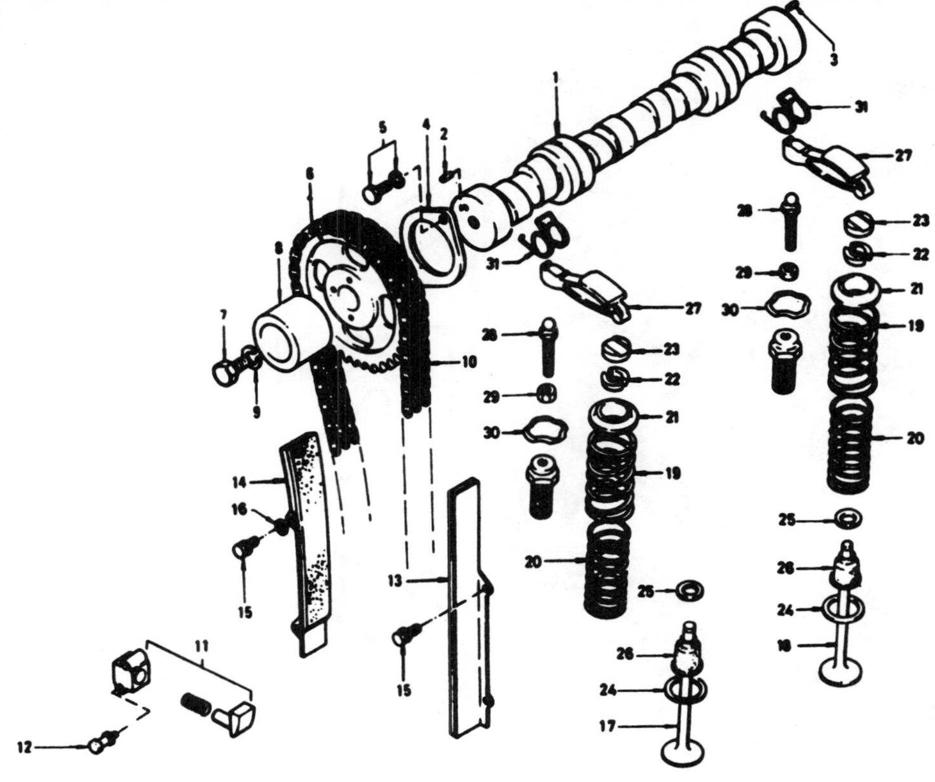

FIG 4 – ENGINE – 4 CYLINDER – CAMSHAFT & VALVES

1 Camshaft
2 Dowel
3 Plug
4 Plate
5 Bolt
6 Camshaft Sprocket
7 Bolt
8 Cam
9 Washer
10 Timing Chain
11 Tensioner
12 Bolt
13 Guide
14 Guide
15 Bolt
16 Washer
17 Intake Valve
18 Exhaust Valve
19 Spring
20 Spring
21 Retainer
22 Collar
23 Guide
24 Seat
25 Seat
26 Seal
27 Rocker
28 Pivot
29 Nut
30 Retainer
31 Spring

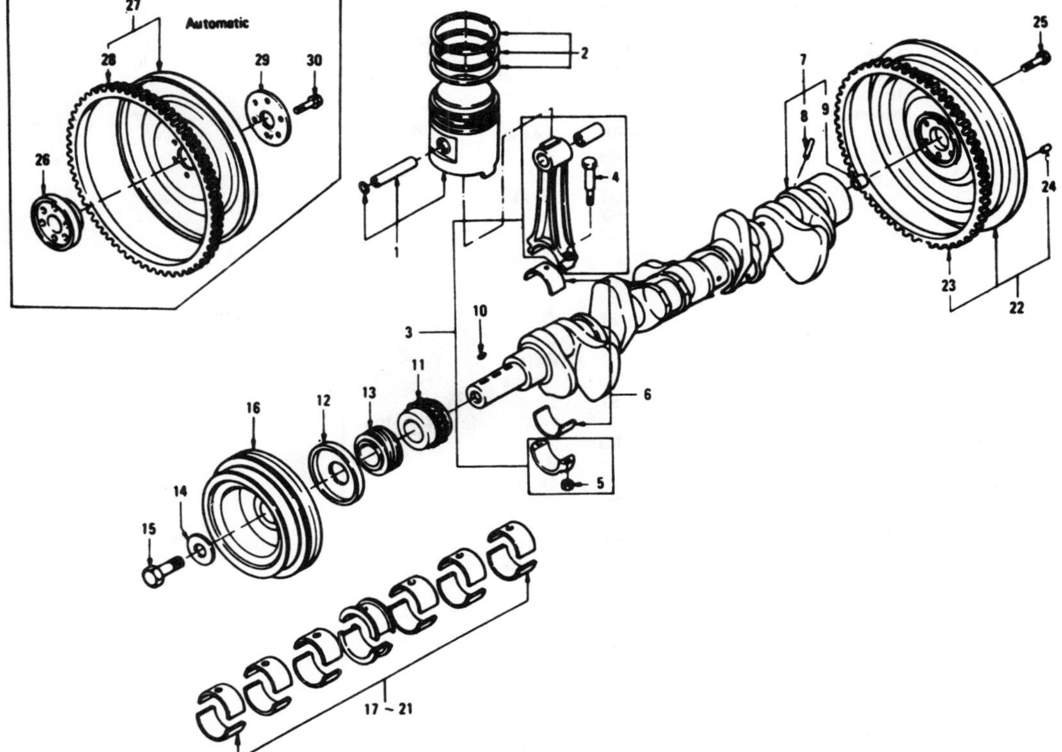

FIG 7 – ENGINE – 6 CYLINDER – CRANKSHAFT & PISTONS

1 Piston & Pin
2 Piston Ring Set
3 Connecting Rod
4 Bolt
5 Nut
6 Bushing
7 Crankshaft
8 Plug
9 Bush
10 Key
11 Crankshaft Gear
12 Oil Thrower
13 Gear
14 Washer
15 Bolt
16 Pulley
17 Main Bearing
18 Main Bearing
19 Main Bearing
20 Main Bearing
21 Main Bearing
22 Flywheel
23 Ring Gear
24 Dowel
25 Bolt
26 Pilot
27 Drive Plate
28 Ring Gear
29 Plate
30 Bolt

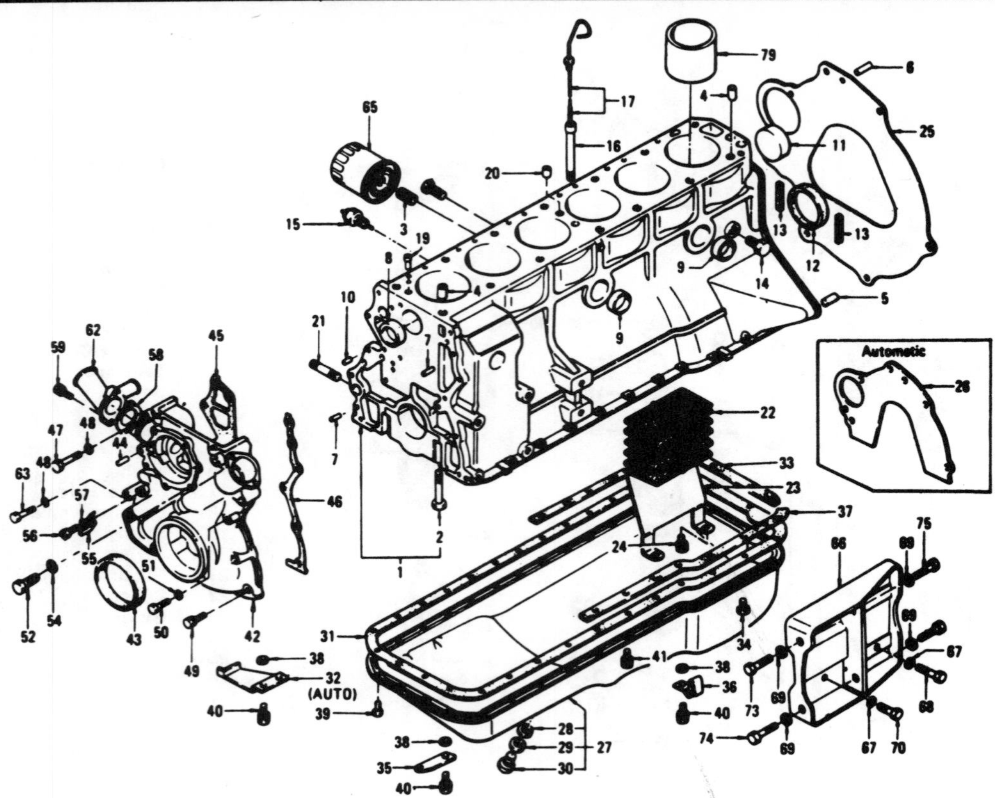

FIG 5 – ENGINE – 6 CYLINDER – BLOCK & OIL PAN

1 Cylinder Block
2 Bolt
3 Stud
4 Dowel
5 Dowel
6 Dowel
7 Dowel
8 Plug
9 Plug
10 Plug
11 Plug
12 Seal
13 Seal
14 Plug
15 Oil Pressure Switch
16 Guide
17 Oil Level Gauge
18 Relief Valve
19 Jet
20 Jet
21 Stud
22 Net
23 Plate
24 Screw
25 Rear Plate (Std Trans)
26 Rear Plate (Auto Trans)
27 Oil Pan
28 Seat
29 Washer
30 Plug
31 Gasket
32 Bracket
33 Reinforcement
34 Bolt
35 Bracket
36 Clamp
37 Reinforcement
38 Spacer
39 Bolt
40 Bolt
41 Bolt
42 Front Cover
43 Oil Seal
44 Dowel
45 Gasket
46 Gasket
47 Bolt
48 Washer
49 Bolt
50 Bolt
51 Washer
52 Bolt
53 Bolt
54 Washer
55 Timing Indicator
56 Screw
57 Washer
58 Gasket
59 Bolt
60 Washer
61 Bolt
62 Water Inlet
63 Bolt
64 Bolt
65 Oil Filter Element
66 Bracket
67 Washer
68 Bolt
69 Washer
70 Bolt
71 Bolt
72 Washer
73 Bolt
74 Bolt
75 Bolt
76 Washer
77 Shim
78 Shim
79 Cylinder Liner

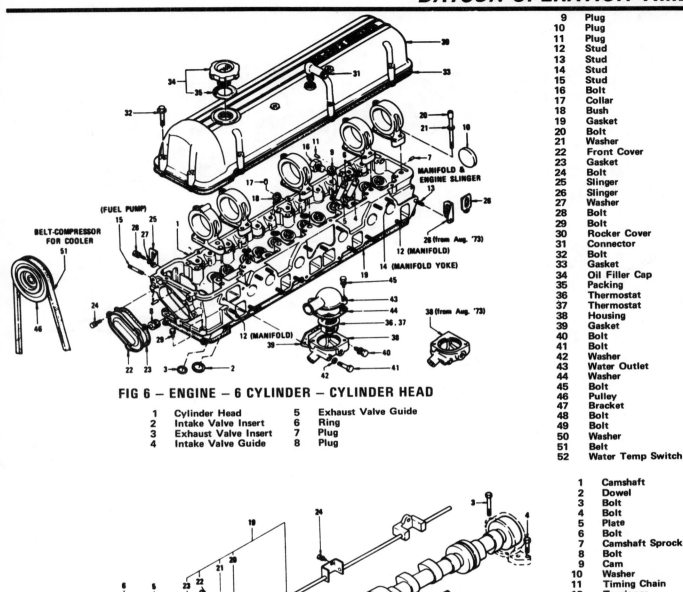

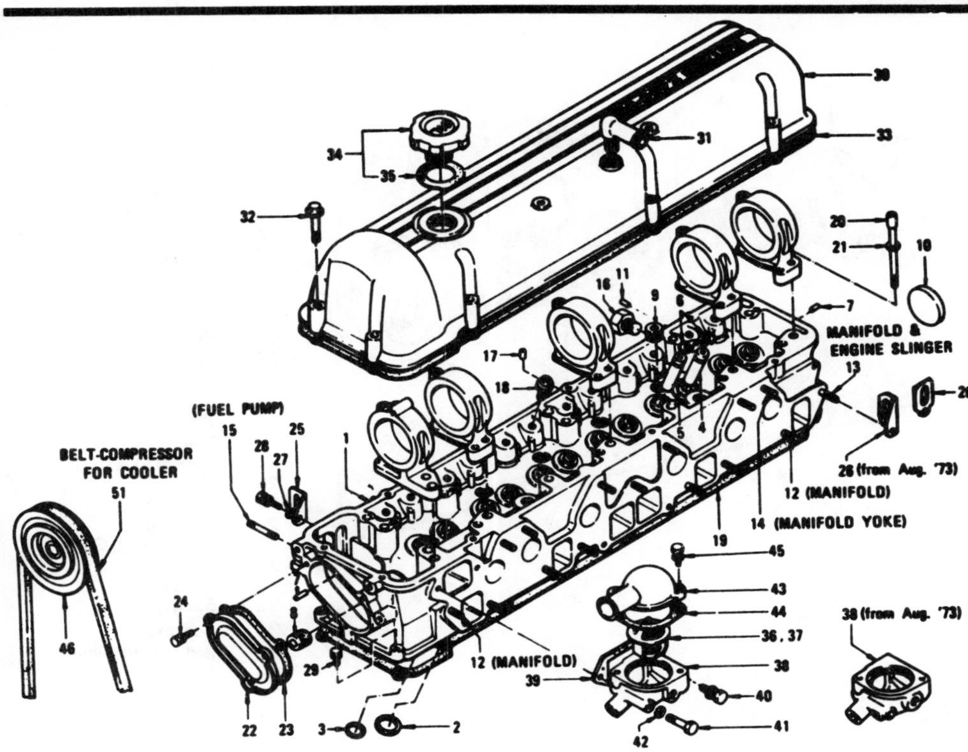

FIG 6 – ENGINE – 6 CYLINDER – CYLINDER HEAD

1	Cylinder Head
2	Intake Valve Insert
3	Exhaust Valve Insert
4	Intake Valve Guide
5	Exhaust Valve Guide
6	Ring
7	Plug
8	Plug
9	Plug
10	Plug
11	Plug
12	Stud
13	Stud
14	Stud
15	Stud
16	Bolt
17	Collar
18	Bush
19	Gasket
20	Bolt
21	Washer
22	Front Cover
23	Gasket
24	Bolt
25	Slinger
26	Slinger
27	Washer
28	Bolt
29	Bolt
30	Rocker Cover
31	Connector
32	Bolt
33	Gasket
34	Oil Filler Cap
35	Packing
36	Thermostat
37	Thermostat
38	Housing
39	Gasket
40	Bolt
41	Bolt
42	Washer
43	Water Outlet
44	Washer
45	Bolt
46	Pulley
47	Bracket
48	Bolt
49	Bolt
50	Washer
51	Belt
52	Water Temp Switch

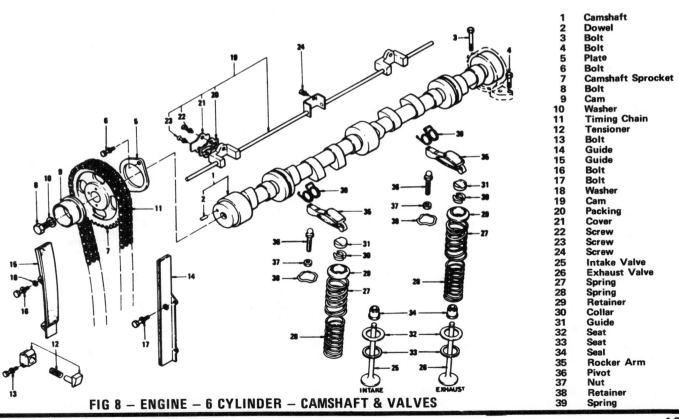

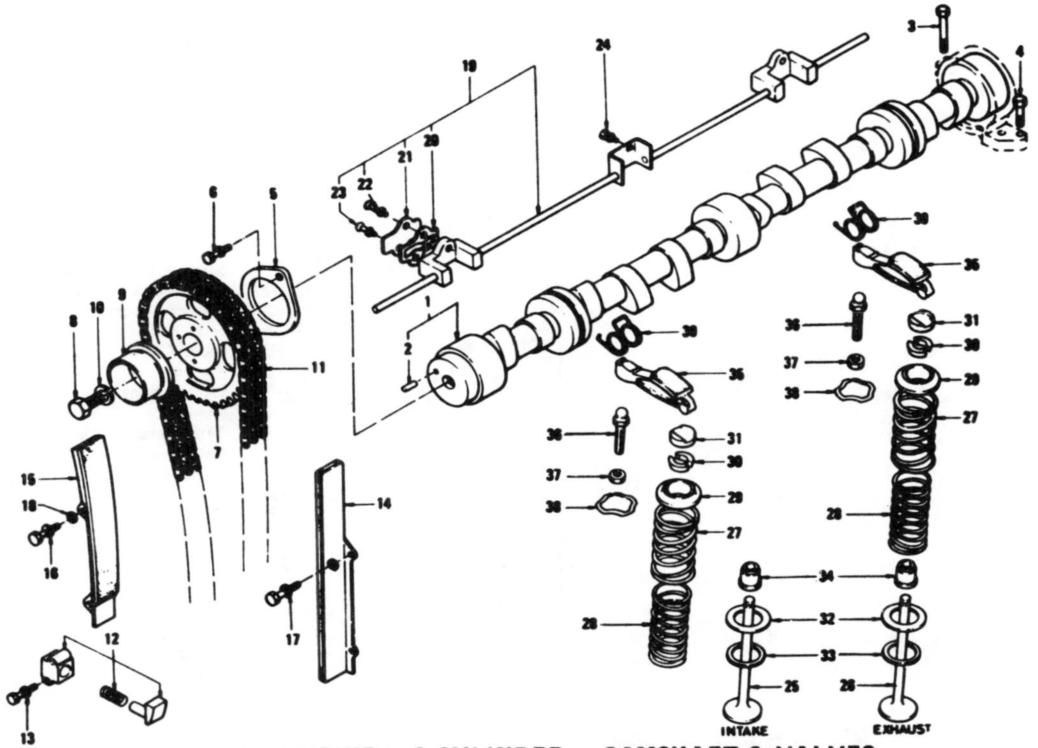

FIG 8 – ENGINE – 6 CYLINDER – CAMSHAFT & VALVES

1	Camshaft
2	Dowel
3	Bolt
4	Bolt
5	Plate
6	Bolt
7	Camshaft Sprocket
8	Bolt
9	Cam
10	Washer
11	Timing Chain
12	Tensioner
13	Bolt
14	Guide
15	Guide
16	Bolt
17	Bolt
18	Washer
19	Cam
20	Packing
21	Cover
22	Screw
23	Screw
24	Screw
25	Intake Valve
26	Exhaust Valve
27	Spring
28	Spring
29	Retainer
30	Collar
31	Guide
32	Seat
33	Seat
34	Seal
35	Rocker Arm
36	Pivot
37	Nut
38	Retainer
39	Spring

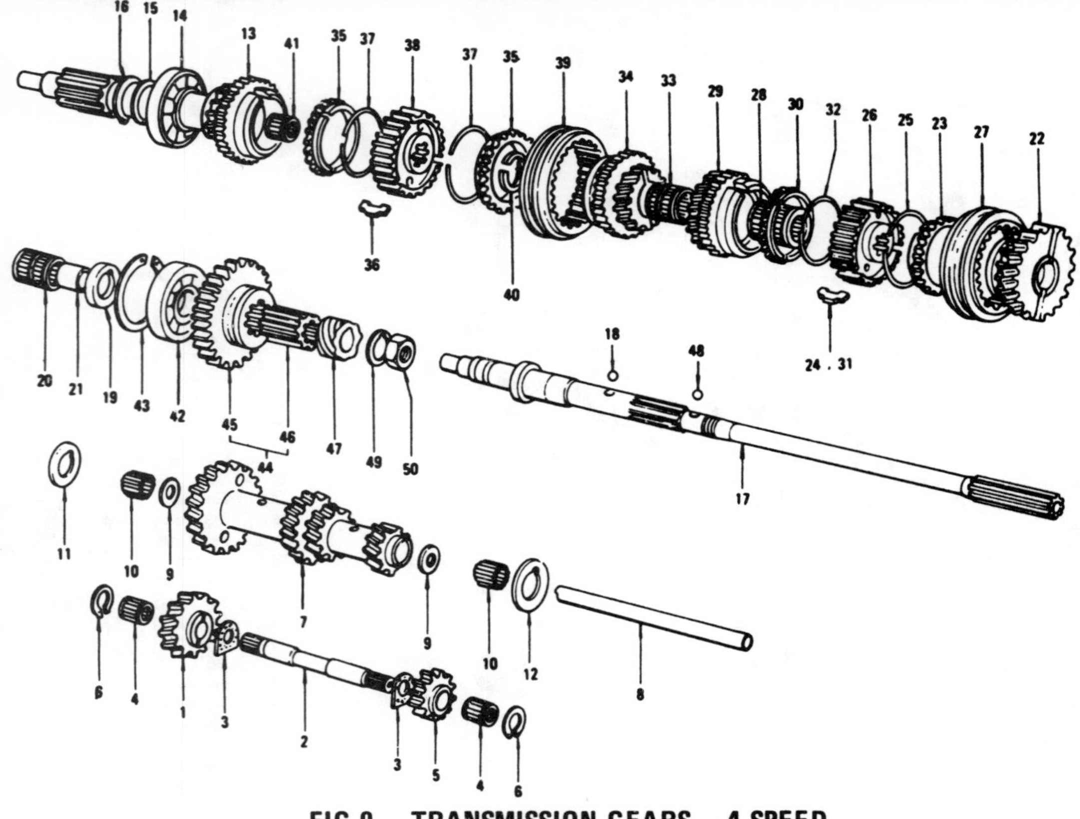

FIG 9 – TRANSMISSION GEARS – 4 SPEED

1 Reverse Idler Gear (Counter)
2 Reverse Idler Shaft
3 Washer
4 Bearing
5 Reverse Idler Gear (Main)
6 Ring
7 Counter Gear
8 Counter Gear Shaft
9 Spacer
10 Bearing
11 Washer
12 Washer
13 Mainshaft Gear
14 Bearing
15 Spacer
16 Ring
17 Main Shaft
18 Ball
19 Washer
20 Bearing
21 Bushing
22 1st Speed Gear
23 Ring
24 Insert
25 Spring
26 Hub
27 Sleeve
28 Bearing
29 2nd Speed Gear
30 Ring
31 Insert
32 Spring
33 Bearing
34 3rd Speed Gear
35 Ring
36 Insert
37 Spring
38 Hub
39 Sleeve
40 Ring
41 Bearing
42 Bearing
43 Ring
44 Reverse Gear & Hub
45 Reverse Gear Shaft
46 Hub
47 Speedometer Drive Gear
48 Ball
49 Washer
50 Nut

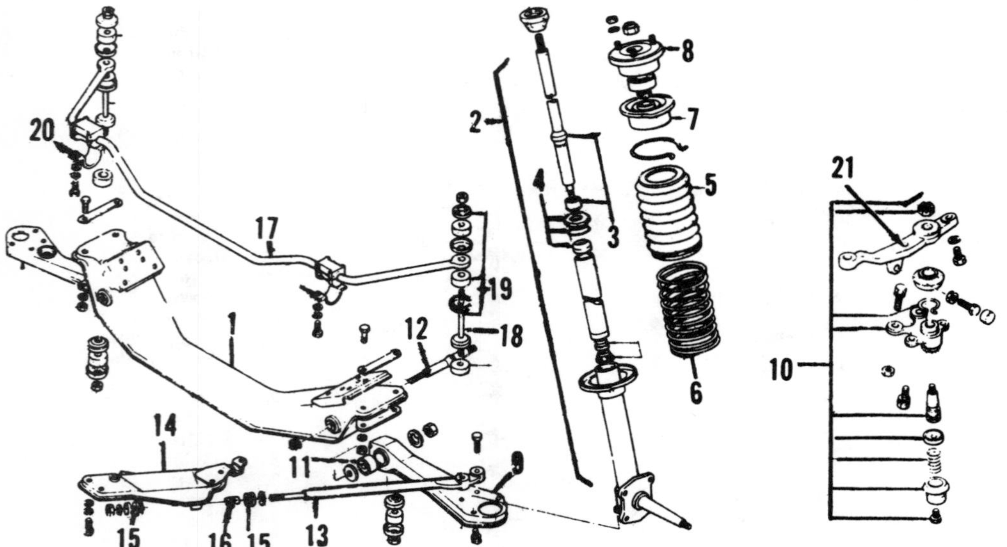

FIG 10 – FRONT SUSPENSION – 610

1 Susp Mount Crossmember
2 Knuckle & Shock
3 Shock Insert
4 Seal Kit
5 Dust Cover
6 Spring
7 Upper Seat
8 Insulator
9 Transverse Link
10 Ball Joint
11 Inner Bushing
12 Link Pin
13 Strut Rod
14 Bracket
15 Bushing
16 Collar
17 Stabilizer Bar
18 Link
19 Bushing
20 Bracket
21 Arm

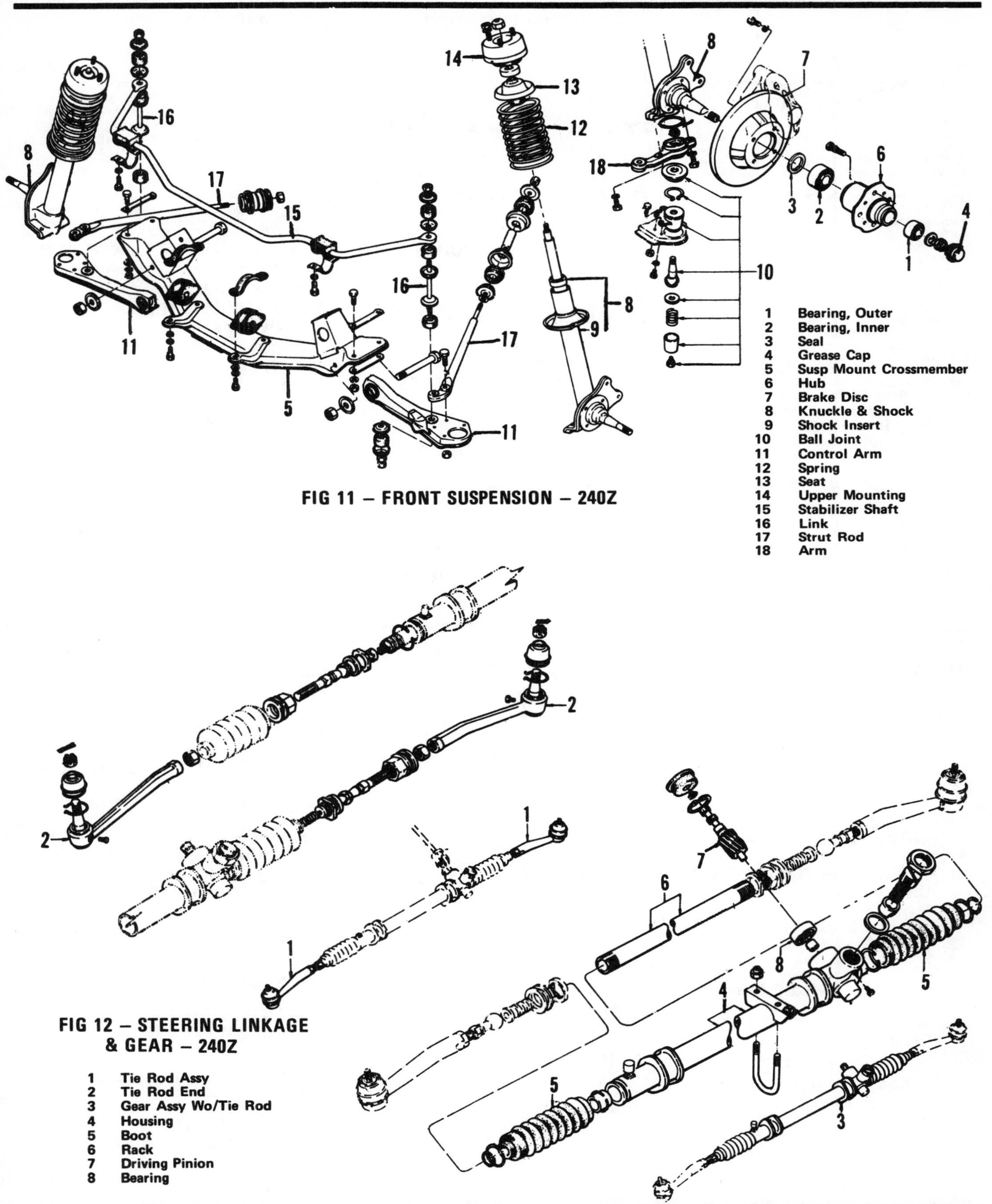

FIG 11 – FRONT SUSPENSION – 240Z

1 Bearing, Outer
2 Bearing, Inner
3 Seal
4 Grease Cap
5 Susp Mount Crossmember
6 Hub
7 Brake Disc
8 Knuckle & Shock
9 Shock Insert
10 Ball Joint
11 Control Arm
12 Spring
13 Seat
14 Upper Mounting
15 Stabilizer Shaft
16 Link
17 Strut Rod
18 Arm

FIG 12 – STEERING LINKAGE & GEAR – 240Z

1 Tie Rod Assy
2 Tie Rod End
3 Gear Assy Wo/Tie Rod
4 Housing
5 Boot
6 Rack
7 Driving Pinion
8 Bearing

Ignition, Starting & Charging—TIME

OPERATION INDEX

Tune-Up, Minor *1*
Tune-Up, Major *2*
Compression Test *3*
Distributor, R&R Or Renew *4*
Distributor Cap, Renew *5*
Ignition Cable Set, Renew *6*
Vacuum Control Unit, Renew *7*
Ignition Coil, Renew *8*
Transistorized Ignition Unit, Renew *8A*
Starter & Ignition Switch, Renew *9*
Starter, R&R Or Renew *10*
Magnetic Switch Assy, Renew *11*
Starter Clutch Pinion Assy, Renew *12*
Starter, R&R & Overhaul *13*
Starter Brushes, Renew *14*
Starter Armature, Renew *15*
Alternator Regulator, Renew *16*
Alternator, R&R Or Renew *17*
Alternator, R&R & Overhaul *18*
Alternator Diodes, Renew *19*
Alternator Bearings, Renew *20*
Alternator Brushes, Renew *21*
Alternator Pulley, Renew *22*

1—TUNE-UP, MINOR
Includes renew points, condenser & plugs, set spark timing & adjust carburetor idle.
Except Below 1.1
1300, 1600 .... 1.4
240z, 260z, 280z, F10 .... 1.8

2—TUNE-UP, MAJOR
Includes check compression, clean or renew & adjust spark plugs, R&R distributor, renew points & condenser. Adjust ignition timing, carburetor & fan belts. Clean battery terminals check coil & clean or renew fuel strainer.
Except Below 2.5
1200 .... 3.1
240z, 260z, 280z, F10 .... 3.0

3—COMPRESSION TEST
Except Below 0.3
1200 .... 0.4
240z, 260z, 280z, F10 .... 0.5

4—DISTRIBUTOR, R&R OR RENEW
All Models 0.5

5—DISTRIBUTOR CAP, RENEW
All Models 0.3

6—IGNITION CABLE SET, RENEW
All Models 0.3

7—VACUUM CONTROL UNIT, RENEW
All Models 0.3

8—IGNITION COIL, RENEW
All Models 0.2

8A—TRANSISTORIZED IGNITION UNIT, RENEW
All Models 0.3

9—STARTER & IGNITION SWITCH, RENEW
Except Below 0.3
240z, 260z, 280z 1.1

10—STARTER, R&R OR RENEW
All Models 0.5

11—MAGNETIC SWITCH ASSY, RENEW
Except Below 0.8
1200 .... 0.6

12—STARTER CLUTCH PINION ASSY, RENEW
Except Below 1.0
1200 .... 0.9

13—STARTER, R&R & OVERHAUL
All Models 1.3

14—STARTER BRUSHES, RENEW
All Models 0.8

15—STARTER ARMATURE, RENEW
All Models 1.0

16—ALTERNATOR REGULATOR, RENEW
All Models 0.3

17—ALTERNATOR, R&R OR RENEW
Except Below 0.5
1300, 1600 .... 0.4

18—ALTERNATOR, R&R & OVERHAUL
All Models 1.3

19—ALTERNATOR DIODES, RENEW
Exc Below 0.9
1200 .... 0.7

20—ALTERNATOR BEARINGS, RENEW
Except Below 1.0
1200 .... 0.6

21—ALTERNATOR BRUSHES, RENEW
Except Below 0.8
1200 .... 0.7

22—ALTERNATOR PULLEY, RENEW
All Models 0.4
& service air cleaner.

Fuel, Emission Controls, Intake & Exhaust Systems—TIME

OPERATION INDEX

Carburetor, R&R Or Renew *1*
Carburetor, R&R & Overhaul *2*
Fuel Pump, R&R Or Renew *3*
Fuel Pump, R&R & Overhaul *4*
Fuel Tank, R&R Or Renew *5*
Choke Cable Assy, Renew *6*
Emission Control Valve, Renew *7*
P C V Valve, R&R Or Renew *8*
Servo Diaphragm, Renew *9*
Thermo Switch, Renew *10*
Throttle Switch, Renew *11*
Water Temp Switch, Renew *12*
Vapor Canister, Renew *13*
Air Pump, R&R Or Renew *14*
Air Pump, R&R & Overhaul *15*
Relief Valve, Renew *16*
Anti-Backfire Valve, Renew *17*
Check Valve, Renew *18*
Exhaust Gas Recirculation Valve, Renew *19*
Solenoid Valve, Renew *20*
Intake Manifold Or Gasket, Renew *21*
Exhaust Manifold Or Gasket, Renew *22*
Exhaust Front Tube, Renew *23*
Pre-Muffler, Renew *24*
Muffler, Renew *25*

1—CARBURETOR, R&R OR RENEW
1967-73—
Exc Below 0.4
1300, 1600—
One 0.5
Both 0.9
240z—
One 0.6
Both 0.9
1974-78—
Exc Below 0.6
260z, 280z—
One 1.0
Both 1.8

2—CARBURETOR, R&R & OVERHAUL
1967-73—
Exc Below ①1.3
1300, 1600—
Single Carb 1.3
Twin Carb, One 1.0
Twin Carb, Both 1.9
240z—
One 1.1
Both 2.1
1974-78—
Exc Below 1.3
260z, 280z—
One 1.5
Both 2.5
①*With Emission Controls, Add* *0.2*

3—FUEL PUMP, R&R OR RENEW
Exc Below 0.4
1200 .... 0.5
240z, 260z, 280z, F10 .... 0.6

4—FUEL PUMP, R&R & OVERHAUL
Exc Below 0.7
1200 .... 0.8
240z, 260z, 280z, F10 .... 0.9

5—FUEL TANK, R&R OR RENEW
Exc Below 0.8
1200—
Sedan 0.6
Wagon & Van 0.5
Coupe 0.4
1300, 1600—
Sedan 1.0
Wagon 0.8
510, 610, 710 .... 1.1
240z, 260z, 280z, F10 .... 0.9

6—CHOKE CABLE ASSY, RENEW
Exc Below 0.3
1300, 1600 .... 0.2

7—EMISSION CONTROL VALVE, RENEW
All Models 0.3

8—PCV VALVE, R&R OR RENEW
Exc Below 0.2
F10 .... 0.4

9—SERVO DIAPHRAGM, RENEW
1200, 1300 .... 0.6
240z, 260z, 280z 0.5
F10 .... 0.8

10—THERMO SWITCH, RENEW
All Models 0.3

11—THROTTLE SWITCH, RENEW
All Models 0.4

12—WATER TEMPERATURE SWITCH, RENEW
240z, 260z, 280z 0.3

13—VAPOR CANISTER, RENEW
240z, 260z, 280z 0.2

14—AIR PUMP, R&R OR RENEW
Exc Below 0.5
F10 .... 0.9

15—AIR PUMP, R&R & OVERHAUL
Exc Below 1.1
F10 .... 1.7

16—RELIEF VALVE, RENEW
All Models 0.6

17—ANTI-BACKFIRE VALVE, RENEW
Exc Below 0.2
F10 .... 0.4

18—CHECK VALVE, RENEW
Exc Below 0.3
240z, 260z, 280z 0.2

19—EXHAUST GAS RECIRCULATION VALVE, RENEW
Exc Below 0.4
240z, 260z, 280z 0.3

(Continued)

Fuel, Emission Controls, Intake & Exhaust Systems—TIME Cont'd

20—SOLENOID VALVE, RENEW
Exc Below 0.4
240z, 260z, 280z 0.2

21—INTAKE, MANIFOLD OR GASKET, RENEW
Exc Below 1.3
1300, 1600—
One Carb ①1.1
Two Carbs ①1.5
240z ②1.3
260z, 280z 1.7
F10 ....4.0
①With Emission Controls, Add 0.2
②With Emmission Controls, Add 0.4

22—EXHAUST MANIFOLD OR GASKET, RENEW
Exc Below 1.5
1300, 1600—
One Carb ①1.1
Two Carbs ①1.5
240z ①1.8
260z, 280z 2.2
①With Emission Controls, Add 0.4

23—EXHAUST FRONT TUBE, RENEW
Exc Below 0.6
1200 ....0.4
240z, 260z, 280z 0.7

24—PRE-MUFFLER, RENEW
Exc Below 0.3
240z 0.5

25—MUFFLER, RENEW
All Models 0.5

Engine Cooling & Heater System—TIME

OPERATION INDEX

Radiator, R&R Or Renew 1
Radiator Hoses, Renew 2
Water Pump, R&R Or Renew 3
Thermostat Or Housing, Renew 4
Heater Assy, Renew 5
Heater Core, Renew 6
Heater Blower Motor, Renew 7
Heater Control, Renew 8
Heater Hoses, Renew 9

1—RADIATOR, R&R OR RENEW
Exc Below ①0.4
1300, 1600 ....0.6
240z, 260z, 280z 0.8
F10 ....1.0
①To Remove Shroud On 1200, Add 0.2

2— RADIATOR HOSES, RENEW
Upper 0.3
Lower 0.4

3—WATER PUMP, R&R OR RENEW
Exc Below 1.1
240z, 260z, 280z 1.2
F10 ....1.0

4—THERMOSTAT OR HOUSING, RENEW
Exc Below 0.3
1200 ....0.2
F10 ....0.4

5—HEATER ASSY, RENEW
240z, 260z, 280z 3.4

6—HEATER CORE, RENEW
Exc Below 1.1
1300 ....1.3
240z, 260z, 280z 3.6

7—HEATER BLOWER MOTOR, RENEW
Exc Below 1.0
240z, 260z, 280z 3.6

8—HEATER CONTROL, RENEW
Exc Below 1.0
1300, 1600 ....0.4

9—HEATER HOSES, RENEW
Each, Except 0.3
1200 ....0.4
240z, 26oz, 280z 0.7

Engine—TIME

OPERATION INDEX

Engine, R&R 1
Engine, R&R & Overhaul 2
Engine (Short), Renew & Grind Valves 3
Cylinder Head, R&R Or Gasket, Renew 4
Valves, Grind 5
One Valve, Renew & Grind 6
Valve Springs, Renew 7
Rocker Arm Cover Gasket, Renew 8
Push Rods, Renew 9
Valve Rocker Arm Assy Overhaul 10
Valve Rockers, Renew 11
Valve Lifters, Renew 12
Valve Lifters, Adjust 13
Timing Cover Seal & Gasket, Renew 14
Timing Chain, Renew 15
Oil Pan Or Gasket, R&R Or Renew 16
Oil Pump, R&R Or Renew 17
Oil Pump, Overhaul 18
Camshaft, R&R Or Renew 19
Camshaft Bearings, Renew 20
Piston Rings, Renew 21
Rings & Main Bearings Renew & Grind Valves 22
Rod Bearings, Renew 23
Main Bearings, Renew 24
Main & Rod Bearings, Renew 25
Crankshaft, R&R Or Renew 26
Crankshaft Rear Main Oil Seal, Renew 27
Pistons, Renew 28
Connecting Rods, Renew 29
Crankshaft Pulley, Renew 30

1—ENGINE, R&R
Does not include transfer of any part of engine or replacement of special equipment.
Exc Below 4.1
1200 ....3.8
240z, 260z, 280z 4.4
F10 ....4.0

—NOTE—
To Renew Engine, For Transfer Of Parts, Add 1.0

2—ENGINE, R&R & OVERHAUL
Includes rebore cylinders with boring bar, renew pistons, rings, pins, main & rod bearings, grind valves, plastigauge bearings & perform, minor tune-up.
Exc Below 18.9
240z, 260z, 280z 22.4
F10 ....18.5

3—ENGINE (SHORT) RENEW & GRIND VALVES
Exc Below 8.7
1200 ....8.3
240z, 260z, 280z 10.2
F10 ....7.5

4—CYLINDER HEAD, R&R OR GASKET, RENEW
Exc Below 2.3
1200 ....2.1
1300 ....2.4
240z 2.5
260z, 280z 3.8
F10 ....2.5

5—VALVES, GRIND
Exc Below 4.1
1200 ....3.6
240z 4.3
260z, 280z 5.0
F10 ....5.0

6—ONE VALVE, RENEW & GRIND
Exc Below ①2.7
1200 ....2.5
240z ②2.9
260z, 280z 3.8
F10 ....2.5
①With Emission Controls, Add 0.3
②With Emission Controls, Add 0.2

7—VALVE SPRINGS, RENEW
Includes R&R head.
One—
Exc Below ①2.4
1200 ....2.5
240z ①2.7
260z, 280z 3.0
Each Additional 0.1
①With Emission Controls, Add 0.3

8—ROCKER ARM COVER GASKET, RENEW
All Models 0.4

9—PUSH RODS, RENEW
1200 ....0.9
F10 ....1.0

10—VALVE ROCKER ARM ASSY, OVERHAUL
1200 ....1.1

11—VALVE ROCKERS, RENEW
1300, 1600 ....0.6
240z, 260z, 280z 0.8

12—VALVE LIFTERS, RENEW
1200, All 5.9
F10 ....6.0

13—VALVE LIFTERS, ADJUST
Exc Below 0.6
1300, 1600 ....0.5

14—TIMING COVER SEAL & GASKET, RENEW
Exc Below 3.0
1200 ....2.2
240z, 260z, 280z 4.0
F10 ....4.5

15—TIMING CHAIN, RENEW
Exc Below ①2.2
1300, 1600 ....②3.2
240z, 260z, 280z ②4.2
F10 ....5.0
①Includes R&R Sprockets.
②Includes R&R Chain Tensioner & Guides.

16—OIL PAN OR GASKET, R&R OR RENEW
1200 ....1.0
1300, 1600 ....①4.2
510, 610, 710 ....1.8
521, 620 ....1.0
240z, 260z, 280z ②1.5
F10 ....4.5
①Includes R&R Engine.
②Includes R&R Front Eng Mount.

17—OIL PUMP R&R OR RENEW
Exc Below 1.0
1200 ....①2.3
F10 ....1.5
①Includes Jack Engine For Clearance.

18—OIL PUMP, OVERHAUL
Pump removed
Exc Below 0.7
1200 ....0.5
240z, 260z, 280z 0.8
F10 ....2.0

19—CAMSHAFT, R&R OR RENEW
Exc Below 1.5
1200 ....5.8
240z, 260z, 280z 2.2
F10 ....6.0

20—CAMSHAFT BEARINGS, RENEW
1200 ....6.8

(Continued)

Engine—TIME Cont'd

21—PISTON RINGS, RENEW

One—
- Exc Below ①7.5
- 1200 ..... 6.8
- 240z, 260z, 280z ①9.5

F10 ..... 9.5

Each Additional—
- Exc Below 0.3
- 1200 ..... 0.2
- 240z, 260z, 280z 0.5

①With Emission Controls Add 0.3

22—RINGS & MAIN BEARINGS, RENEW & GRIND VALVES

Exc Below ①10.1
1200 ..... 9.5
240z, 260z, 280z ①12.6
F10 ..... 12.6
①With Emission Controls, Add 0.3

23—ROD BEARINGS, RENEW

One—
- Exc Below ①6.3
- 1200 ..... 4.5
- 240z, 260z, 280z ①5.0

Each Additional—
- Exc Below 0.3
- 1200 ..... 0.2

①With Emission Controls Add 0.3

24—MAIN BEARINGS RENEW

Exc Below ①8.9
1200 ..... 8.8
240z, 260z, 280z ①9.5
F10 ..... 10.0
①With Emission Controls, Add 0.3

25—MAIN & ROD BEARINGS, RENEW

Exc Below ①8.9
1200 ..... 8.8
240z, 260z, 280z ①9.5
F10 ..... 10.0
①With Emission Controls, Add 0.3

26—CRANKSHAFT, R&R OR RENEW

Exc Below ①8.9
1200 ..... 8.8
240z, 260z, 280z ①9.5
F10 ..... 10.0
①With Emission Controls, Add 0.3

27—CRANKSHAFT REAR MAIN OIL SEAL, RENEW

Exc Below 3.2
1200 ..... 4.9
240z, 260z, 280z 3.6
F10 ..... 5.0

28—PISTONS, RENEW

One—
- Exc Below 6.2
- 1200 ..... 6.9
- 240z, 260z, 280z ②8.5
- F10 ..... 9.5

Each Additional—
- Exc Below 0.5
- 1200 ..... 0.2

①Includes Minor Tune-Up.
②With Emission Controls, Add 0.3

29—CONNECTING RODS, RENEW

One—
- Exc Below ②6.2
- 1200 ..... ①6.9
- 240z, 260z, 280z ②8.5
- F10 ..... 9.5

Each Additional—
- Exc Below 0.5
- 1200 ..... 0.2

①Includes Minor Tune-Up.
②With Emission Controls, Add 0.3

30—CRANKSHAFT PULLEY, RENEW

Exc Below ①0.5
1200 ..... ②0.4
240z, 260z, 280z ①0.6
①With Emission Controls, Add 0.1
②With Shroud, Add 0.2

Clutch, Mounts & Manual Transmission—TIME

OPERATION INDEX

Flywheel, R&R Or Renew 1
Flywheel Ring Gear, Renew 2
Clutch Or Disc, Renew 3
Release Bearings, Renew 4
Pilot Bearing, Renew 5
Release Fork (Or Lever) Renew 6
Clutch Pedal, Adjust 7
Clutch Master Cylinder, R&R Or Renew 8
Clutch Master Cylinder, R&R & Overhaul 9
Clutch Operating Cylinder, R&R Or Renew 10
Clutch Operating Cylinder, R&R & Overhaul 11
Engine Mounts, Renew 12
Transmission, R&R Or Renew 13
Trans Case, Renew 14
Front Cover Or Oil Seal, Renew 15
Extension Housing Gasket, Renew 16
Extension Housing Oil Seal, Renew 17
Oil Pan Gasket, Renew 18
Trans, R&R & Overhaul 19
Rear Extn Bearing, Renew 20
Gear Selector Forks, Renew 21
Gearshift Or Selector Lever Renew 22

1—FLYWHEEL, R&R OR RENEW

Exc Below 3.1
1200 ..... 2.7
240z, 260z, 280z 3.4
521, 620 ..... 3.0
F10 ..... 4.0

2—FLYWHEEL RING GEAR, RENEW

Exc Below 3.5
1200 ..... 3.1
240z, 260z, 280z 3.9
521, 620 ..... 3.4
F10 ..... 4.4

3—CLUTCH (OR DISC), RENEW

Exc Below 3.0
1200 ..... 2.5
240z, 260z, 280z 3.2
521, 620 ..... 3.4
F10 ..... 2.0

4—RELEASE BEARING, RENEW

Exc Below 2.7
1200 ..... 2.3
240z, 260z, 280z 2.9
521, 620 ..... 3.2
F10 ..... 1.0

5—PILOT BEARING, RENEW

Exc Below 3.1
1200 ..... 2.6
240z, 260z, 280z 3.4
521, 620 ..... 3.0

6—RELEASE FORK (OR LEVER), RENEW

Exc Below 2.7
1200 ..... 2.2
240z, 260z, 280z 2.9
521, 620 ..... 2.8

7—CLUTCH PEDAL, ADJUST

All Models 0.2

8—CLUTCH MASTER CYLINDER, R&R OR RENEW

Exc Below 0.5
1200 ..... 0.4

9—CLUTCH MASTER CYLINDER, R&R & OVERHAUL

Exc Below 0.9
1200 ..... 0.8

10—CLUTCH OPERATING CYLINDER, R&R OR RENEW

All Models 0.4

11—CLUTCH OPERATING CYLINDER, R&R & OVERHAUL

All Models 0.6

12—ENGINE MOUNTS, RENEW

Front (One)—
- Exc Below 0.7
- 1200 ..... 0.5
- 240z, 260z, 280z 0.4

Rear—
- Exc Below 0.6
- 1200 ..... 0.4
- 240z, 260z, 280z 0.4

13—TRANSMISSION, R&R OR RENEW

Exc Below 2.6
1200 ..... 2.1
240z, 260z, 280z 2.8
521, 620 ..... 2.7

14—TRANSMISSION CASE, RENEW

Exc Below 4.1
1200—
- 3 Speed 2.5
- 4 Speed 2.6

240z, 260z, 280z 3.9

15—FRONT COVER OR OIL SEAL, RENEW

Exc Below 2.8
1200 ..... 2.3
240z, 260z, 280z 3.1
521, 620 ..... 2.9

16—EXTENSION HOUSING GASKET, RENEW

Exc Below 1.6
1200—
- 3 Speed 2.3
- 4 Speed 2.4

240z, 260z, 280z 3.4
521, 620 ..... 3.0

—NOTE—
To Renew Bushing, Add 0.2

17—EXTENSION HOUSING OIL SEAL, RENEW

Exc Below 0.5
240z, 260z, 280z 0.7

18—OIL PAN GASKET, RENEW

Exc Below 0.7
1200 ..... 0.5

19—TRANSMISSION, R&R & OVERHAUL

Exc Below 5.5
1200—
- 3 Speed 3.5
- 4 Speed 3.8

240z, 260z, 280z—
- 4 Speed 6.4
- 5 Speed 6.8

521, 620 ..... 5.6

20—REAR EXTENSION BEARINGS, RENEW

5 Speed Trans 3.7

21—GEAR SELECTOR FORKS, RENEW

Exc Below—
- 3 Speed 2.8
- 4 Speed 3.0

240z, 260z, 280z 4.2

22—GEARSHIFT OR SELECTOR LEVER, RENEW

Exc Below 0.2
240z, 260z, 280z 0.3

Automatic Transmission—TIME

OPERATION INDEX

Transmission, R&R Or Renew 1
Transmission, R&R & Overhaul 2
Oil Pan Or Gasket, R&R Or Renew 3
Torque Converter, R&R Or Renew 4
Vacuum Control Unit, Renew 5

(Continued)

Automatic Transmission—TIME Cont'd

Valve Body, Renew *6*
Valve Body, R&R & Overhaul *7*
Governor, R&R Or Renew *8*
Governor, R&R & Overhaul *9*
Front Servo, Renew *10*
Front Servo, R&R & Overhaul *11*
Rear Servo, Renew *12*
Rear Servo, R&R & Overhaul *13*
Front Pump, Renew *14*
Front Band, Adjust *15*
Rear Band, Adjust *16*
Front Oil Seal, Renew *17*
Rear Oil Seal, Renew *18*
Rear Extn Oil Seal, Renew *19*
Kickdown Switch, Renew *20*
Downshift Solenoid, Renew *21*
Inhibitor Switch, Renew *22*

1—TRANSMISSION, R&R OR RENEW
Exc Below 2.5
1200, 1300 .... 2.3
240z, 260z, 280z 3.2
620 .... 2.8
510, 610, 710 .... 2.5

2—TRANSMISSION, R&R & OVERHAUL
Exc Below 10.0
1200, 1300 .... 9.5
240z, 260z, 280z 10.7
620 .... 10.3
510, 610, 710 .... 10.0

3—OIL PAN OR GASKET, R&R OR RENEW
Exc Below 0.5
510, 610, 710 .... 0.7

4—TORQUE CONVERTER, R&R OR RENEW
Exc Below 2.5
1200, 1300 .... 2.3
240z, 260z, 280z 3.5
620 .... 3.0
510, 610, 710 .... 2.8

5—VACUUM CONTROL UNIT, RENEW
All Models 0.3

6—VALVE BODY RENEW
Exc Below 1.0
510, 610, 710 .... 1.5

7—VALVE BODY, R&R & OVERHAUL
Exc Below 1.8
510, 610, 710 .... 2.3

8—GOVERNOR, R&R OR RENEW
Exc Below 1.9
620 .... 3.4
240z, 260z, 280z 2.3
510, 610, 710 .... 1.6

9—GOVERNOR, R&R & OVERHAUL
Exc Below 2.1
620 .... 3.6
240z, 260z, 280z 2.5
510, 610, 710 .... 1.9

10—FRONT SERVO, RENEW
510 .... 1.6

11—FRONT SERVO, R&R & OVERHAUL
510 .... 1.8

12—REAR SERVO, RENEW
510 .... 2.4

13—REAR SERVO, R&R & OVERHAUL
510 .... 2.7

14—FRONT PUMP, RENEW
510 .... 3.4

15—FRONT BAND ADJUST
Exc Below 1.0
510 .... 1.2

16—REAR BAND, ADJUST
Exc Below 0.3
510 .... 1.9

17—FRONT OIL SEAL, RENEW
Exc Below 2.8
1200, 1300 .... 2.5
240z, 260z, 280z 3.6
620 .... 3.2
510 .... 2.8

18—REAR OIL SEAL, RENEW
Exc Below 2.3
620 .... 2.4
510 .... 1.8

19—REAR EXTENSION OIL SEAL, RENEW
Exc Below 0.5
620 .... 0.6
240z, 260z, 280z 0.7

20—KICKDOWN SWITCH, RENEW
All Models 0.2

21—DOWNSHIFT SOLENOID, RENEW
All Models 1.0

22—INHIBITOR SWITCH, RENEW
Exc Below 0.4
510 .... ①2.8
①*Includes R&R Trans.*

Brakes, Steering, Suspension, Universals & Rear Axle—TIME

OPERATION INDEX

Brake Shoes Or Friction Pads, Renew *1*
Master Cylinder, Renew *2*
Master Cylinder, R&R & Overhaul *3*
Tandem Type Master Cylinder, Renew *4*
Tandem Type Master Cylinder, Overhaul *5*
Brake Fluid Reservoir, R&R Or Renew *6*
Wheel Cylinders, Renew *7*
Wheel Cylinder, R&R & Overhaul *8*
Caliper Assy, Renew *9*
Caliper, R&R & Overhaul *10*
Bleed System *11*
Brake Hose, Renew *12*
Disc Or Shield, Renew *13*
Hub, R&R Or Renew *14*
Power Brake Unit, Renew *15*
Power Brake Unit, R&R & Overhaul *16*
Brake Drums, Renew *17*
Brake Adjuster, Renew *18*
Brake Pedal, Renew *19*
Parking Brake Cable Or Control Rod, Renew *20*
Parking Brake Lever, Renew *21*
Strg Gear Box, R&R Or Renew *22*
Strg Gear Box, R&R & Overhaul *23*
Strg Linkage Assy, R&R Or Renew *24*
Side Rod Assy, Renew *25*
Cross Rod Assy, Renew *26*
Idler Assy, Renew *27*
Idler Arm Or Bush, Renew *28*
Strg Gear Arm, Renew *29*
Strut, R&R Or Renew *30*
Springs, Renew *31*
Shocks Or Struts, Renew *32*
Ball Joints, Renew *33*
Stabilizer, R&R Or Renew *34*
Transverse Link, R&R Or Renew *35*
Transverse Link Bushing, Renew *36*
Compression Rod, Renew *37*
Front Suspension Member, Renew *38*
Rear Axle & Suspension Assy, R&R Or Renew *39*
Rear Axle Oil Seal, Renew *40*
Rear Susp Arm, Renew *41*
Rear Axle Shaft Or Bearing, Renew *42*
Rear Axle Drive Shaft Assy, Renew *43*
Rear Axle Drive Shaft Assy, R&R & Overhaul *44*
Rear Axle Housing, R&R Or Renew *45*
Rear Axle Assy, R&R Or Renew *46*
Differential Carrier, R&R Or Renew *47*
Differential Carrier, R&R & Overhaul *48*
Pinion Bearing, Renew *49*
Side Flange Or Oil Seal, Renew *50*

1—BRAKE SHOES OR FRICTION PADS, RENEW
One Wheel—
Drum Type 0.8
Disc Type 0.6

2—MASTER CYLINDER, RENEW
Exc Below 0.5
240z, 260z, 280z 0.6

3—MASTER CYLINDER, R&R & OVERHAUL
Exc Below 0.9
1200 .... 0.7

4—TANDEM TYPE MASTER CYLINDER, RENEW
1200 .... 0.6

5—TANDEM TYPE MASTER CYLINDER, OVERHAUL
1200 .... 0.9

6—BRAKE FLUID RESERVOIR, R&R OR RENEW
Exc Below, One 0.2
240z, 260z, 280z, All 0.5

7—WHEEL CYLINDER, RENEW
Exc Below 0.5
240z, 260z, 280z 0.6

8—WHEEL CYLINDER, R&R & OVERHAUL
Exc Below—
Front 0.6
Rear 0.7
240z, 260z, 280z 0.8

9—CALIPER ASSY, RENEW
Exc Below 0.5
1200 .... 0.8
240z, 260z, 280z 0.6

10—CALIPER ASSY, R&R OVERHAUL
Exc Below 0.7
1200 .... 1.1
240z, 260z, 280z 0.8

11—BLEED SYSTEM
All Models 0.3

12—BRAKE HOSE, RENEW
All Models, Each 0.3

13—DISC OR SHIELD, RENEW
Exc Below 0.8
1200 .... 1.0
240z, 260z, 280z 0.4

14—HUB, R&R OR RENEW
Front, Each Side—
Exc Below ①0.4
1200—
Drum Type ②0.5
Disc Type ②0.6
240z, 260z, 280z ③0.6
Rear, Each Side (Or Bearing)—
510, 1300, 1600 .... 1.0
①*To Renew Bearings, Add* *0.2*
②*To Renew Bearings, Add* *0.1*
③*To Renew Bearings, Add* *0.3*

15—POWER BRAKE UNIT, RENEW
Exc Below 1.0
240z, 260z, 280z 1.1

16—POWER BRAKE UNIT, R&R & OVERHAUL
All Models 2.0

17—BRAKE DRUMS, RENEW
All Models, Each 0.3

18—BRAKE ADJUSTER, RENEW
All Models, Each 0.3

19—BRAKE PEDAL, RENEW
Exc Below 0.3
1200 .... 0.2

(Continued)

Brakes, Steering, Suspension, Universals & Rear Axle—TIME Cont'd

20—PARKING BRAKE CABLE, OR CONTROL ROD, RENEW
Front—
Exc Below 0.5
1300, 1500 ....0.3
240z, 260z, 280z 0.8
610, 620 ....0.4
710 ....0.8
Rear—
Exc Below 0.3
1200 ....0.5
240z, 260z, 280z 0.4

21—PARKING BRAKE LEVER, RENEW
Exc Below 0.3
240z, 260z, 280z, 710 ....0.7

22—STEERING GEAR BOX, R&R OR RENEW
Collapsible Type—
Exc Below 0.6
240z, 260z, 280z ①1.0
Std Type—
Exc Below 1.8
1200 ....1.7
①*Includes R&R Linkage Assy.*

23—STEERING GEAR BOX, R&R & OVERHAUL
Collapsible Type—
Exc Below 3.1
240z, 260z, 280z ①1.8
Std Type—
Exc Below 1.9
1200 ....2.6
①*Includes Linkage Overhaul*

24—STEERING LINKAGE ASSY, R&R OR RENEW
All Models 0.9

25—SIDE ROD ASSY, RENEW
One—
Exc Below 0.4
240z, 260z, 280z 1.3

26—CROSS ROD ASSY, RENEW
Exc Below 0.4
1200 ....0.6

27—STEERING IDLER ASSY, RENEW
All Models 0.3

28—IDLER ARM OR BUSHING, RENEW
All Models 0.5

29—STEERING GEAR ARM, RENEW
All Models 0.6

30—STRUT ASSY, R&R OR RENEW
Front, One 1.2
Rear, One—
240z, 260z, 280z 1.5

31—SPRINGS, RENEW
Front, Each 1.4
Rear—
Exc Below 0.8
1300, 1600 Sedan 1.6
1300, 1600 Wagon 1.2
240z, 260z, 280z 1.7

32—SHOCK ABSORBERS OR STRUTS, RENEW
Front, Each—
Shock 1.6
Strut Exc 2.0
F10 ....1.5
Rear, Each—
Shock—
Exc Below 0.3
1200—
Sedan 0.6
Van & Wagon 0.4
Coupe 0.5
F10 ....0.5
Strut 3.9

33—BALL JOINTS, RENEW
Each Side—
Exc Below 0.8
1200 ....0.7
F10 ....0.5

34—STABILIZER, R&R OR RENEW
Exc Below 0.5
1200 ....0.4

35—TRANSVERSE LINK, R&R OR RENEW
Front, Each Side—
Exc Below 0.5
1200 ....0.7
Rear, Each Side—
240z, 260z, 280z 1.2

36—TRANSVERSE LINK BUSHING, RENEW
One Side—
Exc Below 0.5
1200 ....0.3
240z, 260z, 280z 0.3

37—COMPRESSION ROD, RENEW
All Models 0.4

38—FRONT SUSPENSION MEMBER, RENEW
1200 ....1.4

39—REAR AXLE & SUSPENSION. ASSY, R&R OR RENEW
Exc Below 1.9
1300, 1600—
Sedan 2.4
Wagon 2.0
240z, 260z, 280z, F10 ....2.6

40—REAR AXLE OIL SEAL, RENEW
One Side—
Exc Below 0.7
1200 ....0.8

41—REAR SUSPENSION ARM, RENEW
1300, 1600 ....2.0
F10 ....1.8

42—REAR AXLE SHAFT OR BEARING, RENEW
Each Side—
Exc Below 1.0
1200 ....0.9

43—REAR AXLE DRIVE SHAFT ASSY, RENEW
240z, 260z, 280z 0.7

44—REAR AXLE DRIVE SHAFT ASSY, R&R & OVERHAUL
240z, 260z, 280z 1.0

45—REAR AXLE HOUSING, R&R OR RENEW
1200 ....2.5
521, 620 ....3.0

46—REAR AXLE ASSY, R&R OR RENEW
1200 ....1.6

47—DIFFERENTIAL CARRIER, R&R OR RENEW
Exc Below 1.6
1300, 1600—
Sedan 1.8
Wagon 2.4
240z, 260z, 280z 2.0

48—DIFFERENTIAL CARRIER, R&R & OVERHAUL
Exc Below 4.5
1300, 1600—
Sedan 4.8
Wagon 4.5
240z, 260z, 280z 5.0

49—PINION BEARING, RENEW
Exc Below 3.2
1300, 1600—
Sedan 2.6
Wagon 2.6
240z, 260z, 280z 3.8

50—SIDE FLANGE OR OIL SEAL, RENEW
Exc Below 0.9
240z, 260z, 280z 1.0

Speedometer W/S Wipers, Switches & Instruments—TIME

OPERATION INDEX
Speedometer Cable & Housing Renew 1
Speedometer Head, Renew 2
W/S Wiper Motor, Renew 3
W/S Wiper Link Set, Renew 4
W/S Wiper Arm, Renew 5
Fuel Gauge (Dash Unit) Renew 6
Fuel Tank Gauge, Renew 7
Oil Gauge (Dash Unit) Renew 8
Oil Gauge Sending Unit, Renew 9
Temperature Gauge (Dash Unit) Renew 10
Temperature Gauge Sending Unit, Renew 11
Tachometer, Renew 12
Instrument Cluster Voltage Limiter, Renew 13
Headlight Switch, Renew 14
Turn Signal & Dimmer Switch, Renew 15
Stop Light Switch, Renew 16
Turn Signal Switch, Renew 17
Back-Up Lamp Switch, Renew 18

1—SPEEDOMETER CABLE & HOUSING, RENEW
Exc Below 0.9
1200 ....0.3
240z, 260z, 280z 0.5

2—SPEEDOMETER HEAD, RENEW
Exc Below 0.7
1300 ....0.9
510, 521, 620 ....0.5
610 ....0.5
710 ....0.8
240z, 260z, 280z 0.7

3—W/S WIPER MOTOR, RENEW
Exc Below 0.5
1200 ....0.4
240z, 260z, 280z 0.6

4—W/S WIPER LINK SET, RENEW
Exc Below 0.3
240z, 260z, 280z 0.8

5—W/S WIPER ARM, RENEW
All Models 0.2

6—FUEL GAUGE (DASH UNIT) RENEW
Exc Below 0.8
1200 ....0.2
240z, 260z, 280z 0.9

7—FUEL TANK GAUGE, RENEW
Exc Below 0.3
1200—
Sedan 0.3
Wagon & Van 0.5
Coupe 0.4
F10 ....0.6

8—OIL GAUGE (DASH UNIT) RENEW
Exc Below 0.8
1200 ....0.2
240z, 260z, 280z 0.9

(Continued)

Speedometer W/S Wipers, Switches & Instruments—TIME Cont'd

9—OIL GAUGE SENDING UNIT, RENEW

Exc Below 0.2
240z, 260z, 280z 0.3

10—TEMPERATURE GAUGE (DASH UNIT) RENEW

Exc Below 0.8
1200 ....0.2
240z, 260z, 280z 0.9

11—TEMPERATURE GAUGE SENDING UNIT, RENEW

Exc Below 0.3
1200 ....0.2

12—TACHOMETER, RENEW

Exc Below 0.8
1200, 710 ....0.6
260z, 260z, 280z 0.5
510, 521, 620 ....0.5
610 ....0.4

13—INSTRUMENT CLUSTER VOLTAGE LIMITER, RENEW

Exc Below 0.7
240z, 260z, 280z 0.9

14—HEADLIGHT SWITCH, RENEW

Exc Below 0.2
240z, 260z, 280z 0.4

15—TURN SIGNAL & DIMMER SWITCH, RENEW

All Models 0.4

16— STOP LIGHT SWITCH, RENEW

Exc Below 0.2
240z, 260z, 280z 0.3

17—TURN SIGNAL SWITCH, RENEW

Exc Below 0.2
240z, 260z, 280z 0.3

18—BACK-UP LAMP SWITCH, RENEW

All Models 0.3

IDENTIFICATION

ALL MODELS.................................... 141

ILLUSTRATIONS

FIG 1 – ENGINE BLOCK & COMPONENTS
FIG 2 – ENGINE OIL PAN & CRANKCASE COVERS
FIG 3 – ENGINE CRANKSHAFT & FLYWHEEL
FIG 4 – ENGINE PISTONS & RINGS
FIG 5 – ENGINE CAMSHAFT DRIVE
FIG 6 – ENGINE CAMSHAFT & VALVES
FIG 7 – TRANSMISSION CASE & RELATED PARTS
FIG 8 – TRANSMISSION GEARS
FIG 9 – FRONT SUSPENSION & STEERING – X1/9
FIG 10 – FRONT SUSPENSION & STEERING – 128 SL SPORT COUPE
FIG 11 – FRONT SUSPENSION & STEERING – 128 SEDAN & STATION WAGON
FIG 12 – FRONT SUSPENSION & STEERING – 124 4-DOOR SEDAN & STATION WAGON
FIG 13 – FRONT SUSPENSION & STEERING – 850

OPERATION TIMES

A

Air Pump.................................... 150
Alternator.................................... 150
Automatic Transmission.................... 153
Axle Shaft.................................... 154

B

Back-Up Lamp Switch.................... 155
Brake Drums.................................... 154
Brakes.................................... 153

C

Cables (Ignition).................................... 150
Calipers.................................... 154
Camshaft.................................... 152
Carburetor.................................... 150
Catalytic Converter.................................... 151
Clutch.................................... 153
Coil, Ignition.................................... 150
Compression Test.................................... 150
Connecting Rods.................................... 152
Cooling System.................................... 151
Crankshaft.................................... 152
Cylinder Block.................................... 151
Cylinder Head.................................... 152

D

Dash Gauges.................................... 155
Differential.................................... 154
Disc Brakes.................................... 153
Distributor.................................... 150

E

Emission Controls.................................... 150
Engine Assembly.................................... 151
Engine Mountings.................................... 153
Engine Oiling.................................... 152
Engine Tune-Up.................................... 150
Exhaust Gas Recirculation.................... 150
Exhaust System.................................... 151

F

Flywheel.................................... 153
Front Suspension.................................... 154
Fuel Gauges.................................... 155
Fuel Pump.................................... 150
Fuel Tank.................................... 150

H

Hand Brake.................................... 154
Headlight Switch.................................... 155
Heater.................................... 151
Hose (Brake).................................... 154
Hose (Radiator).................................... 151
Hydraulic Brakes.................................... 153

I

Ignition.................................... 150
Ignition Coil.................................... 150
Ignition Switch.................................... 150
Intake Manifold.................................... 151

L

Light Switches.................................... 155

M

Main Bearings.................................... 152
Master Cylinder.................................... 153
Muffler.................................... 151

O

Oil Gauge.................................... 155
Oiling, Engine.................................... 152
Oil Pan.................................... 152
Oil Pump.................................... 152

P

Parking Brake.................................... 154
Piston Rings.................................... 152
Pistons.................................... 152
Power Brake.................................... 154

R

Radiator.................................... 151
Radiator Hose.................................... 151
Rear Axle.................................... 154
Regulator (Alternator).................... 150
Rocker Arms.................................... 152
Rod Bearings.................................... 152

S

Shocks (Front).................................... 154
Shocks (Rear).................................... 154
Speedometer.................................... 155
Springs (Front).................................... 154
Springs (Rear).................................... 154
Stabilizer Bar.................................... 154
Starting Motor.................................... 150
Steering Gear.................................... 154
Steering Linkage.................................... 154
Switches (Light).................................... 155
Synchro-Mesh Trans.................................... 153

T

Temperature Gauge.................................... 155
Thermostat.................................... 151
Timing Case Cover.................................... 152
Timing Chain.................................... 152
Track Rod.................................... 154
Transmission, Manual.................................... 153
Transmission, Automatic.................... 153
Transverse Rod & Link.................................... 154
Tune-Up, Engine.................................... 150

U

Universals.................................... 154

V

Valve Lifters.................................... 152
Valve System.................................... 152

W

Water Pump.................................... 151
Wheel Alignment.................................... 154
Wheel Cylinders.................................... 153
Windshield Wiper.................................... 155

VEHICLE IDENTIFICATION PLATE

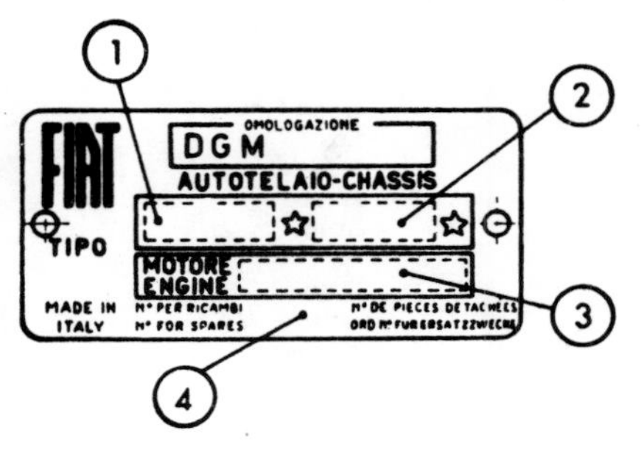

850

124 Sport Coupe & Spider – 1968-72

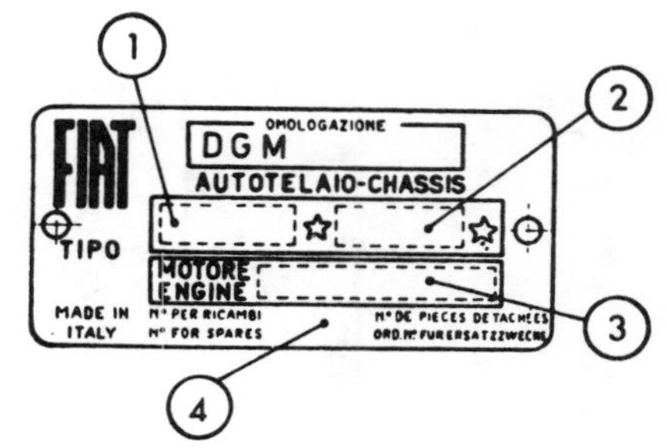

124 Sedan & Station Wagon

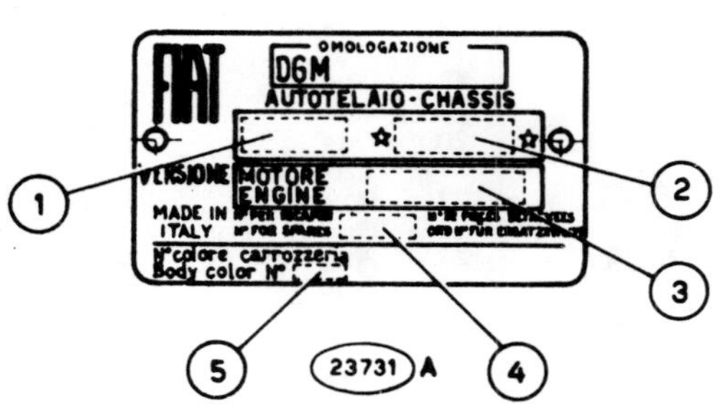

124 Sport Coupe & Spider – 1973

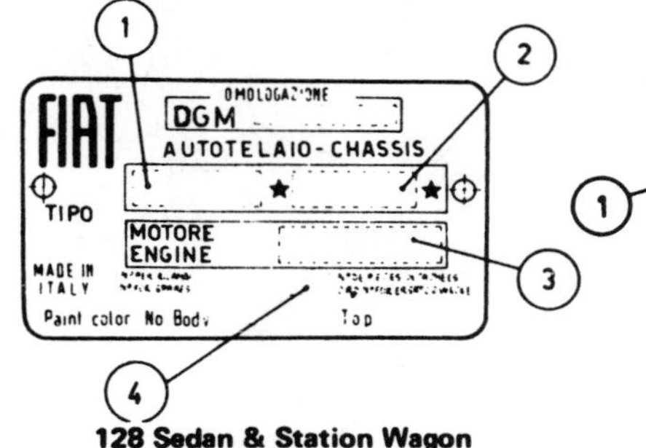

128 Sedan & Station Wagon
128 AS X1/9 Spider
131 Sedan & Station Wagon

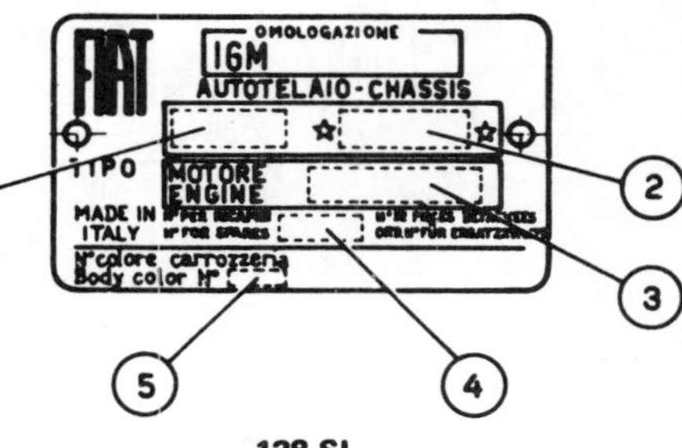

128 SL

(1) CHASSIS TYPE
(2) CHASSIS NUMBER
(3) ENGINE TYPE
(4) NUMBER FOR ORDERING PARTS
(5) EXTERIOR PAINT COLOR CODE

ENGINE NUMBER LOCATION

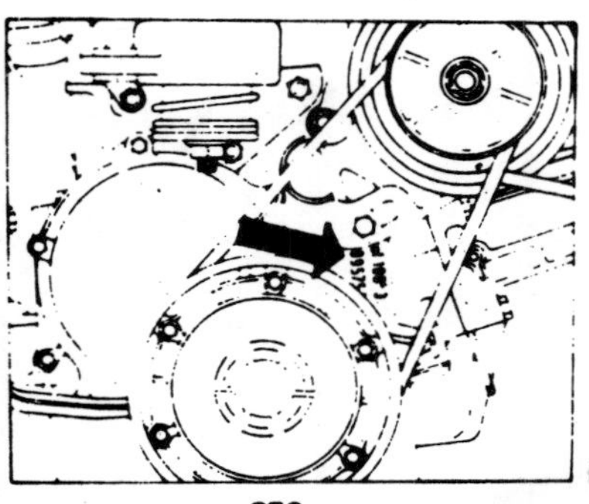

850

124 Sedan & Station Wagon

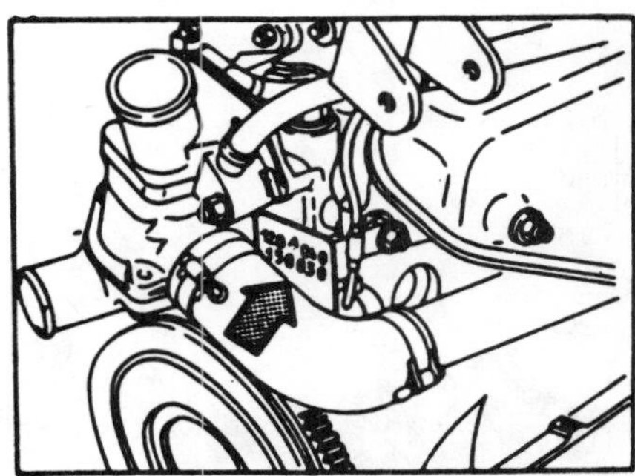

128 Sedan & Station Wagon
128 AS X1/9 Spider
131 Sedan & Station Wagon

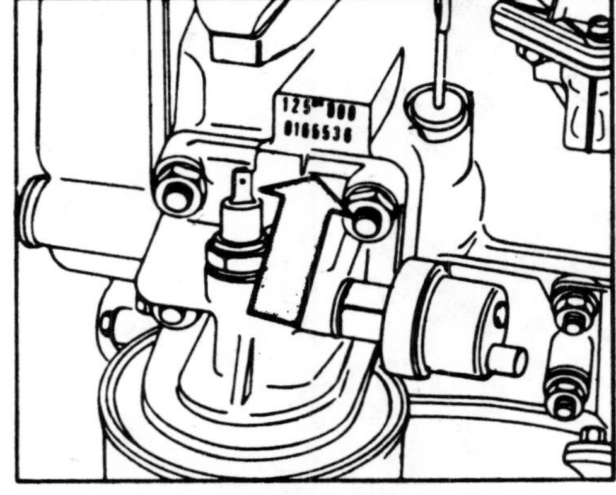

124 Sport Coupe & Spider

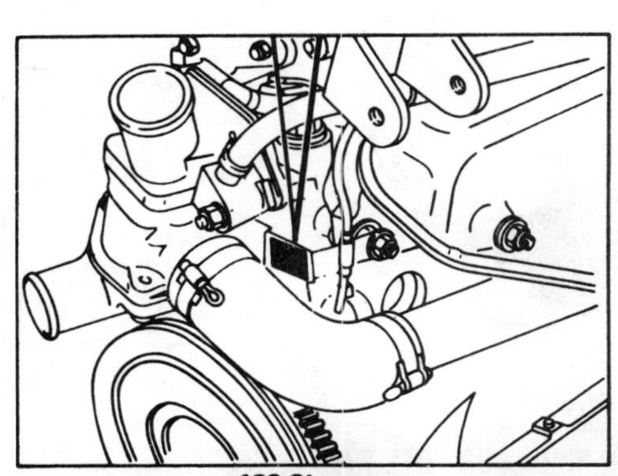

128 SL

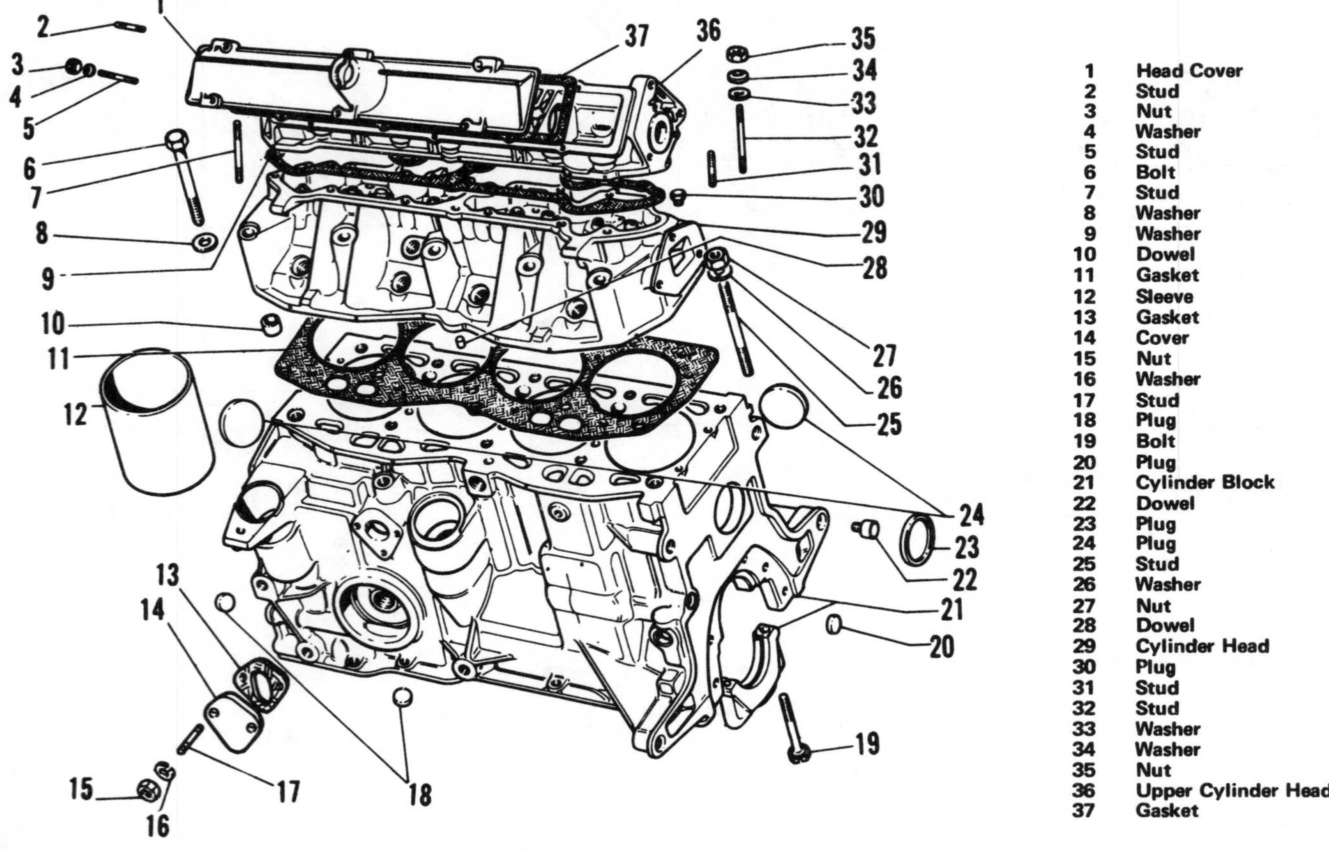

1 Head Cover
2 Stud
3 Nut
4 Washer
5 Stud
6 Bolt
7 Stud
8 Washer
9 Washer
10 Dowel
11 Gasket
12 Sleeve
13 Gasket
14 Cover
15 Nut
16 Washer
17 Stud
18 Plug
19 Bolt
20 Plug
21 Cylinder Block
22 Dowel
23 Plug
24 Plug
25 Stud
26 Washer
27 Nut
28 Dowel
29 Cylinder Head
30 Plug
31 Stud
32 Stud
33 Washer
34 Washer
35 Nut
36 Upper Cylinder Head
37 Gasket

FIG 1 – ENGINE – CYLINDER BLOCK & COMPONENTS

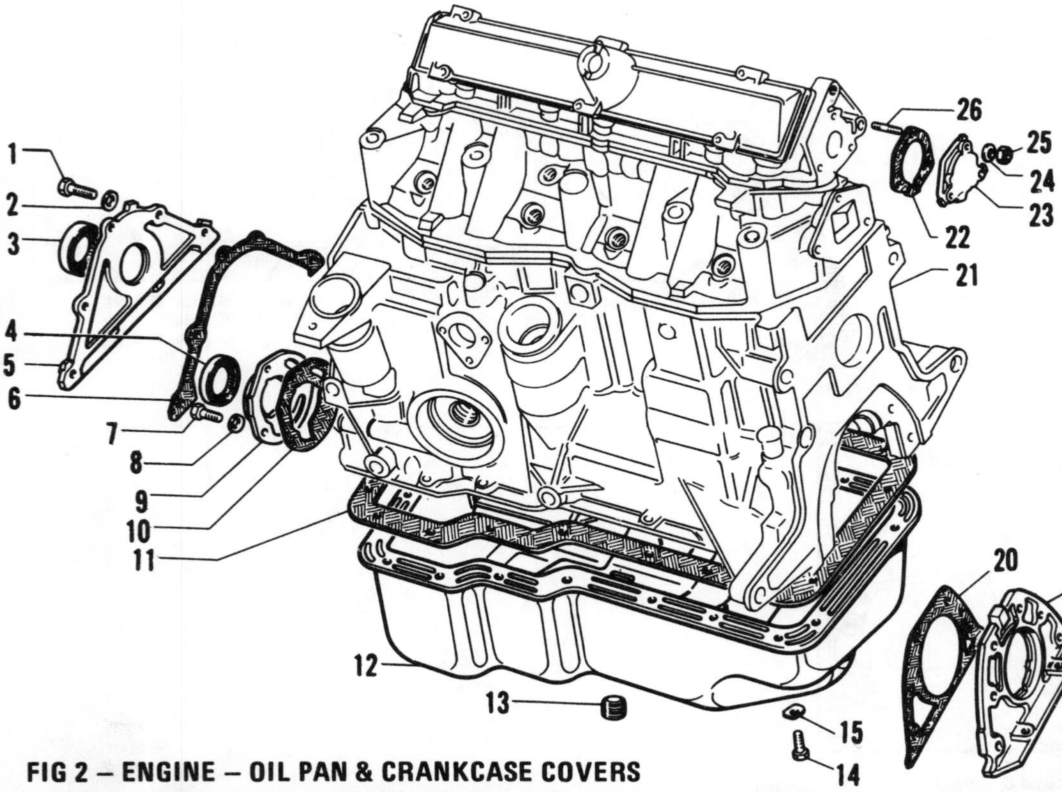

1 Bolt
2 Washer
3 Oil Seal
4 Oil Seal
5 Cover
6 Gasket
7 Bolt
8 Washer
9 Cover
10 Gasket
11 Gasket
12 Oil Pan
13 Drain Plug
14 Bolt
15 Washer
16 Bolt
17 Washer
18 Oil Seal
19 Cover
20 Gasket
21 Cylinder Block
22 Gasket
23 Cover
24 Washer
25 Nut
26 Stud

FIG 2 – ENGINE – OIL PAN & CRANKCASE COVERS

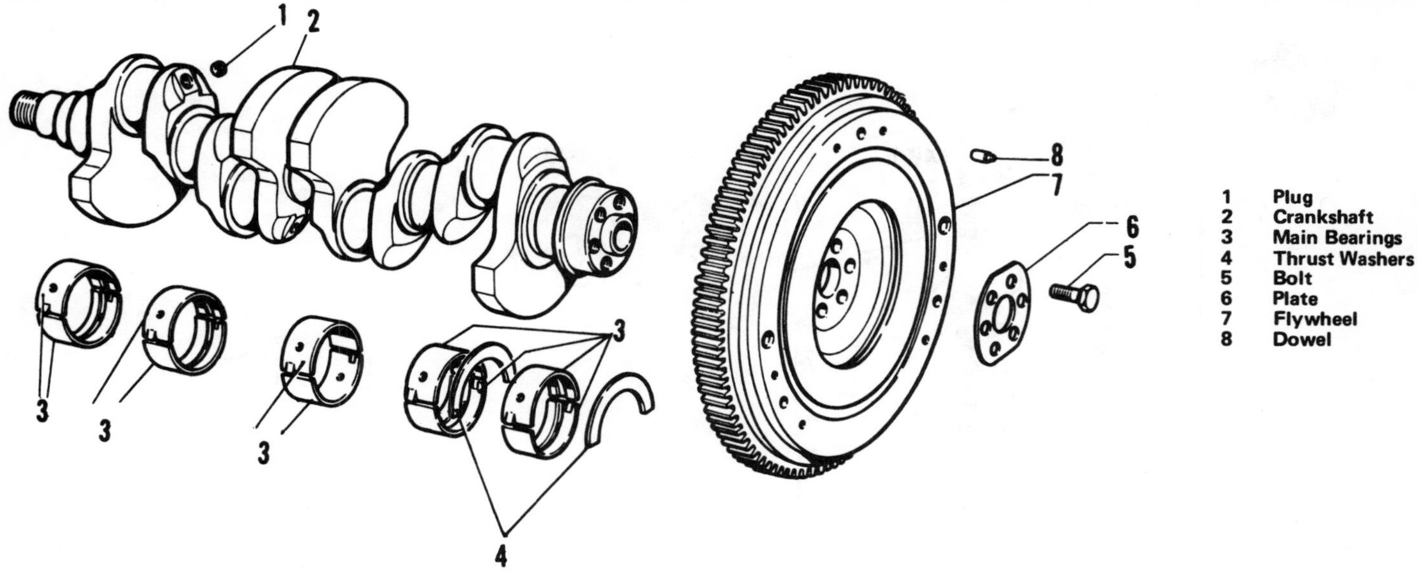

1	Plug
2	Crankshaft
3	Main Bearings
4	Thrust Washers
5	Bolt
6	Plate
7	Flywheel
8	Dowel

FIG 3 – ENGINE – CRANKSHAFT & FLYWHEEL

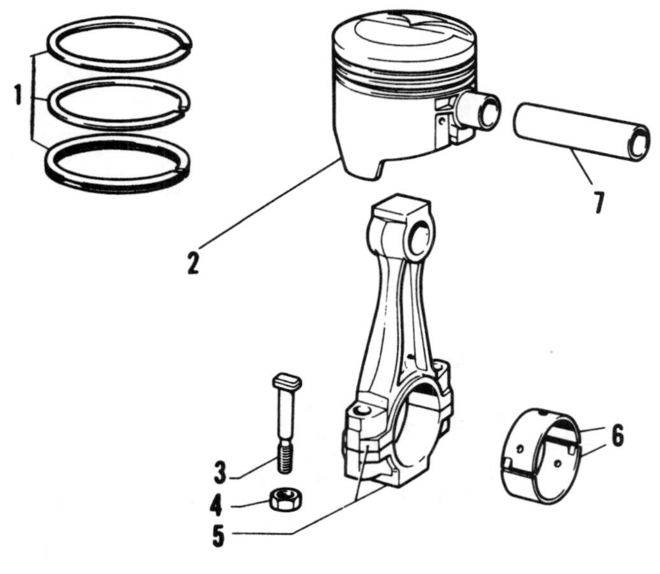

FIG 4 – ENGINE – PISTONS & RINGS

1	Piston Rings
2	Piston
3	Bolt
4	Nut
5	Conn Rod
6	Bearing
7	Piston Pin

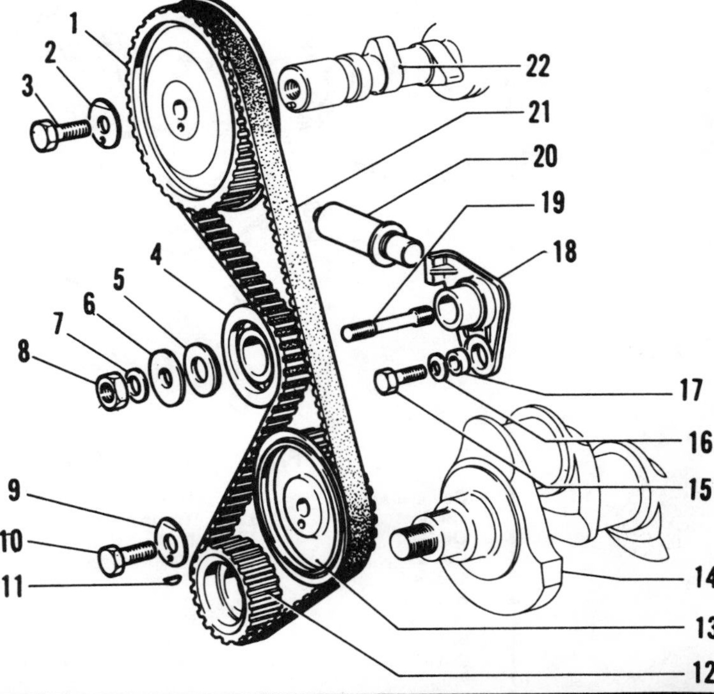

FIG 5 – ENGINE – CAMSHAFT DRIVE

1	Gear	12	Gear
2	Washer	13	Gear
3	Bolt	14	Crankshaft
4	Pulley	15	Bolt
5	Washer	16	Washer
6	Washer	17	Spacer
7	Washer	18	Support
8	Nut	19	Stud
9	Washer	20	Rod
10	Bolt	21	Drive Belt
11	Key	22	Cam Shaft

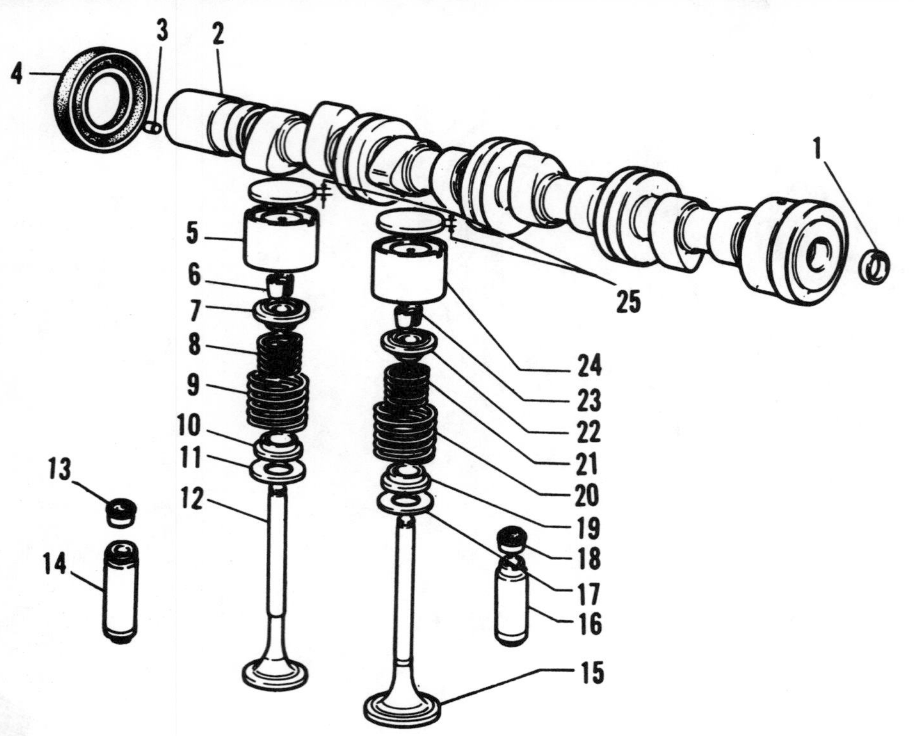

1	Plug
2	Cam Shaft
3	Dowel
4	Oil Seal
5	Tappet
6	Valve Keys
7	Cup
8	Spring
9	Spring
10	Cup
11	Washer
12	Exhaust Valve
13	Valve Boot
14	Valve Guide
15	Inlet Valve
16	Valve Guide
17	Washer
18	Valve Boot
19	Cup
20	Spring
21	Spring
22	Cup
23	Valve Keepers
24	Tappet
25	Valve Shims

FIG 6 – ENGINE – CAMSHAFT & VALVES

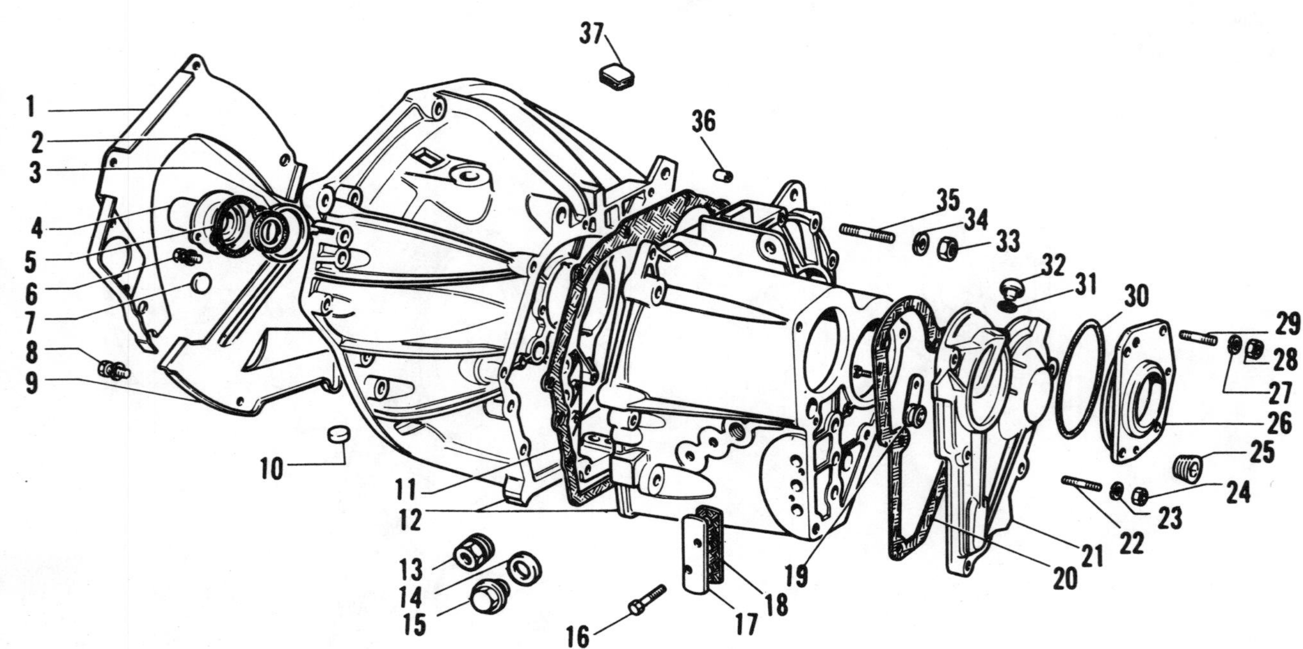

FIG 7 – TRANSMISSION CASE & RELATED PARTS

1	Cover Plate	11	Gasket	20	Gasket	29	Stud
2	Oil Seal	12	Transmission Case	21	Cover Plate	30	O-Ring
3	Oil Seal	13	Nut	22	Stud	31	Washer
4	Cover	14	Washer	23	Washer	32	Breather
5	Gasket	15	Bolt	24	Nut	33	Nut
6	Bolt	16	Bolt	25	Plug	34	Washer
7	Plug	17	Cover Plate	26	Cover	35	Stud
8	Bolt	18	Gasket	27	Washer	36	Spacer
9	Cover Plate	19	Magnetic Plate	28	Nut	37	Plug
10	Plug						

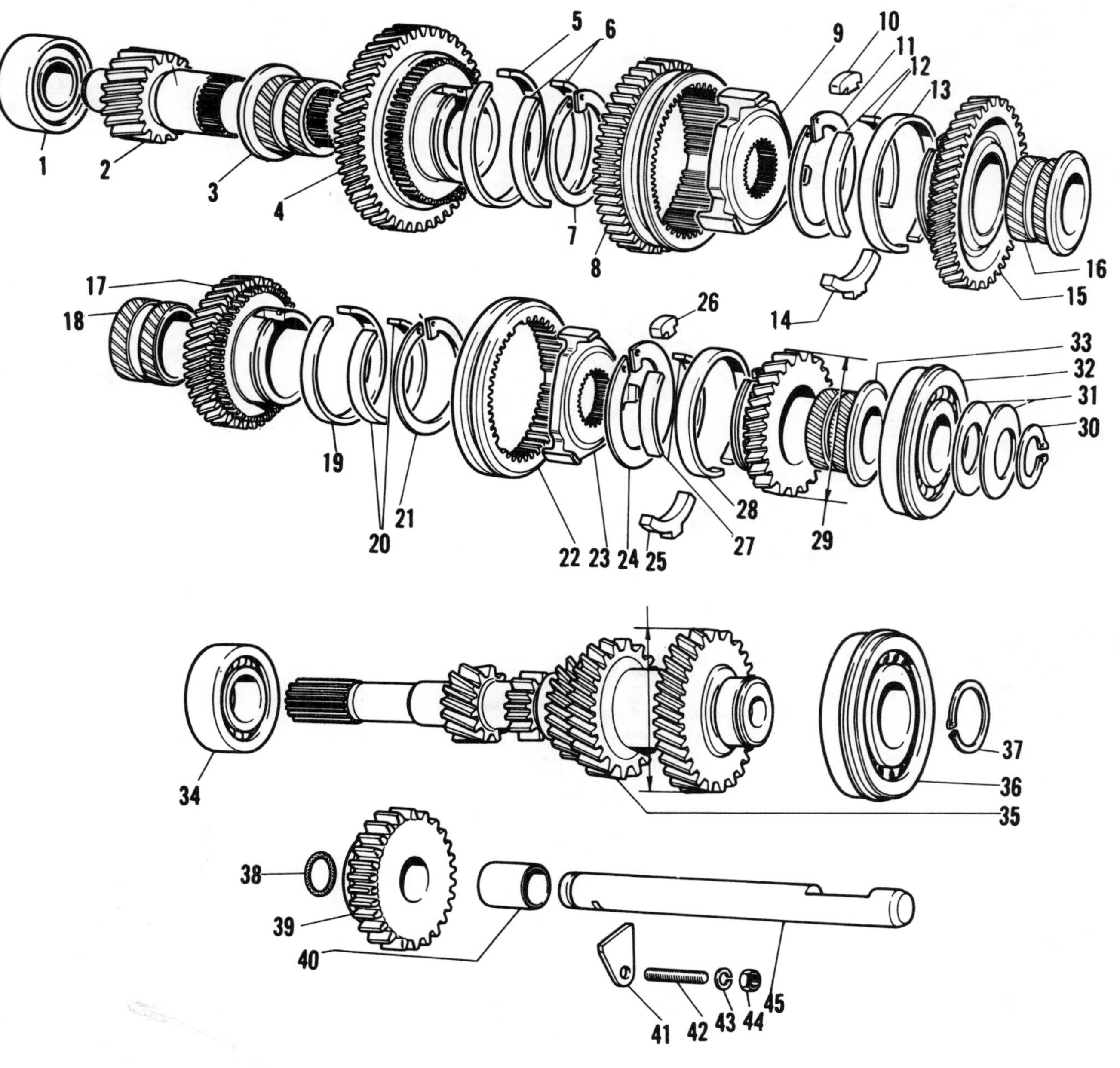

FIG 8 – TRANSMISSION GEARS

1	Bearing	16	2nd Speed Hub & Gear	31	Washers
2	Secondary Shaft	17	3rd Speed Gear	32	Bearing
3	1st Speed Bushing	18	3rd Speed Hub & Gear	33	4th Speed Bushing
4	1st Speed Gear	19	Synchronizer Ring	34	Bearing
5	Synchronizer Ring	20	Synchronizer Clip	35	Countershaft Cluster
6	Synchronizer Clip	21	Lock Ring	36	Bearing
7	Lock Ring	22	Synchronizer Sleeve	37	Lock Ring
8	2nd Speed Syncro Sleeve	23	Synchronizer Hub	38	Seal
9	2nd Speed Syncro Hub	24	Lock Ring	39	Reverse Gear
10	Synchronizer Pad	25	Synchronizer Pad	40	Bushing
11	Lock Ring	26	Synchronizer Pad	41	Lock Plate
12	Synchronizer Clip	27	Synchronizer Clip	42	Stud
13	Synchronizer Ring	28	Synchronizer Ring	43	Washer
14	Synchronizer Pad	29	4th Speed Gear	44	Nut
15	2nd Speed Gear	30	Lock Ring	45	Idler Shaft

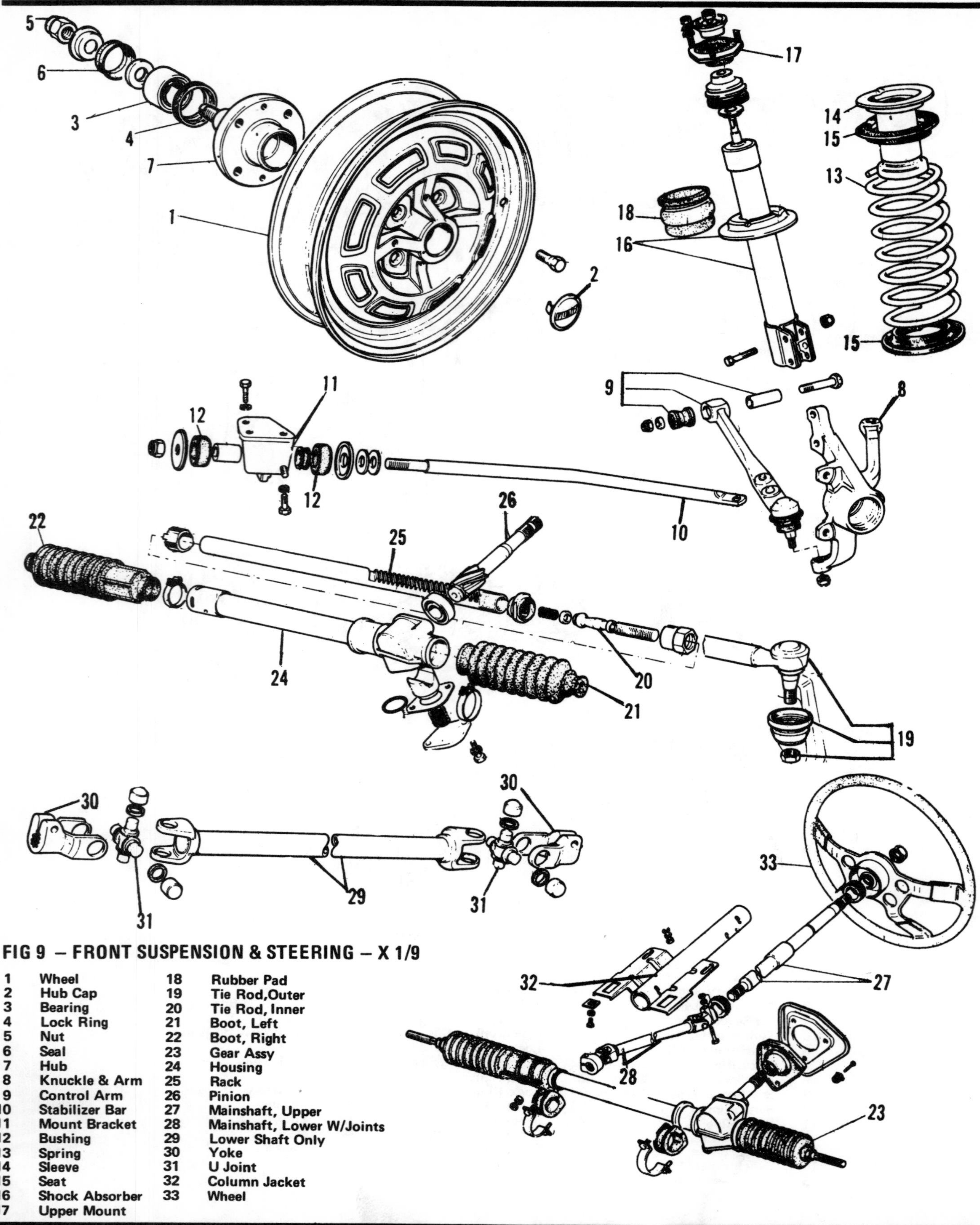

FIG 9 – FRONT SUSPENSION & STEERING – X 1/9

1	Wheel	18	Rubber Pad
2	Hub Cap	19	Tie Rod,Outer
3	Bearing	20	Tie Rod, Inner
4	Lock Ring	21	Boot, Left
5	Nut	22	Boot, Right
6	Seal	23	Gear Assy
7	Hub	24	Housing
8	Knuckle & Arm	25	Rack
9	Control Arm	26	Pinion
10	Stabilizer Bar	27	Mainshaft, Upper
11	Mount Bracket	28	Mainshaft, Lower W/Joints
12	Bushing	29	Lower Shaft Only
13	Spring	30	Yoke
14	Sleeve	31	U Joint
15	Seat	32	Column Jacket
16	Shock Absorber	33	Wheel
17	Upper Mount		

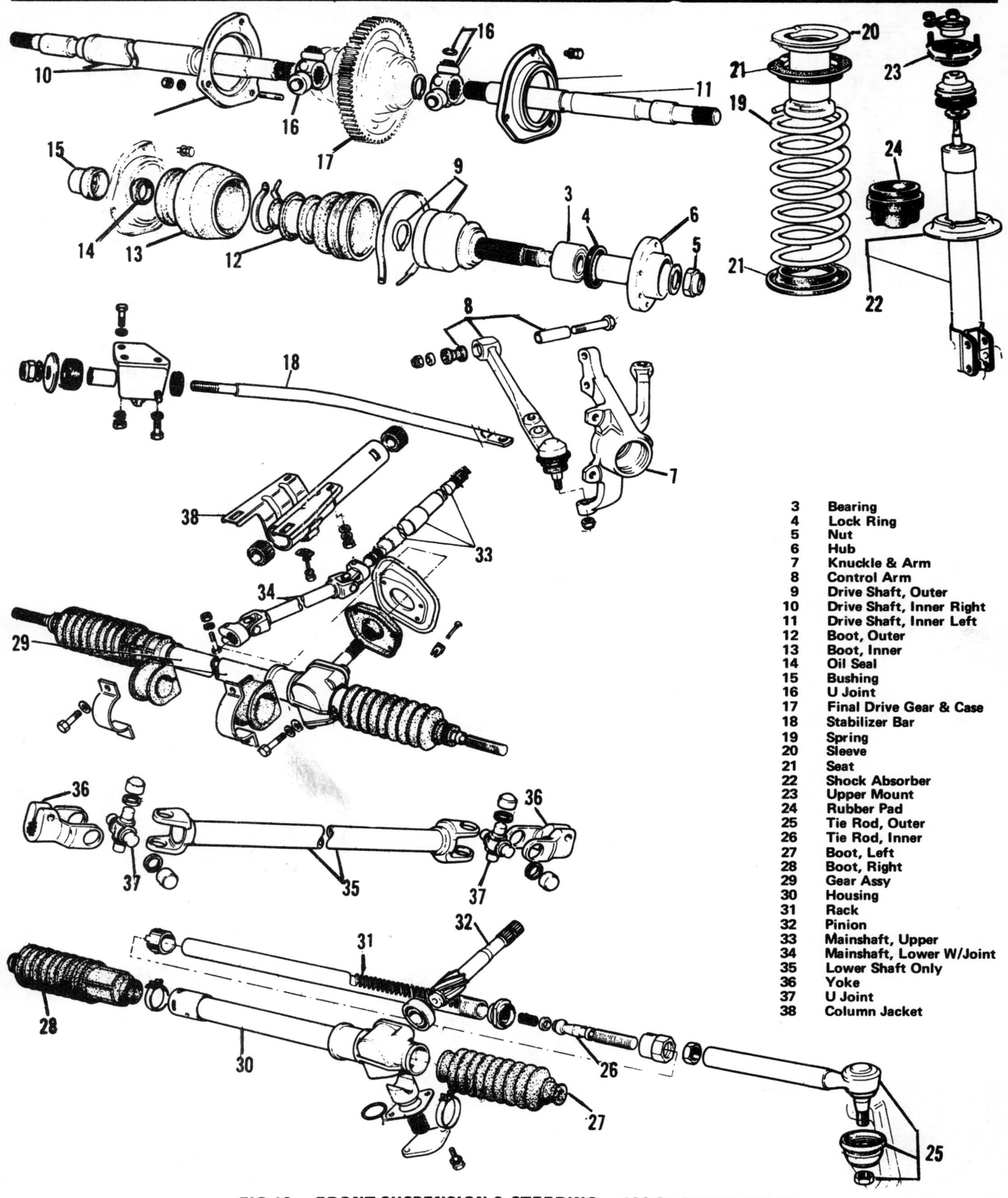
3 Bearing
4 Lock Ring
5 Nut
6 Hub
7 Knuckle & Arm
8 Control Arm
9 Drive Shaft, Outer
10 Drive Shaft, Inner Right
11 Drive Shaft, Inner Left
12 Boot, Outer
13 Boot, Inner
14 Oil Seal
15 Bushing
16 U Joint
17 Final Drive Gear & Case
18 Stabilizer Bar
19 Spring
20 Sleeve
21 Seat
22 Shock Absorber
23 Upper Mount
24 Rubber Pad
25 Tie Rod, Outer
26 Tie Rod, Inner
27 Boot, Left
28 Boot, Right
29 Gear Assy
30 Housing
31 Rack
32 Pinion
33 Mainshaft, Upper
34 Mainshaft, Lower W/Joint
35 Lower Shaft Only
36 Yoke
37 U Joint
38 Column Jacket

FIG 10 – FRONT SUSPENSION & STEERING – 128 SL SPORT COUPE

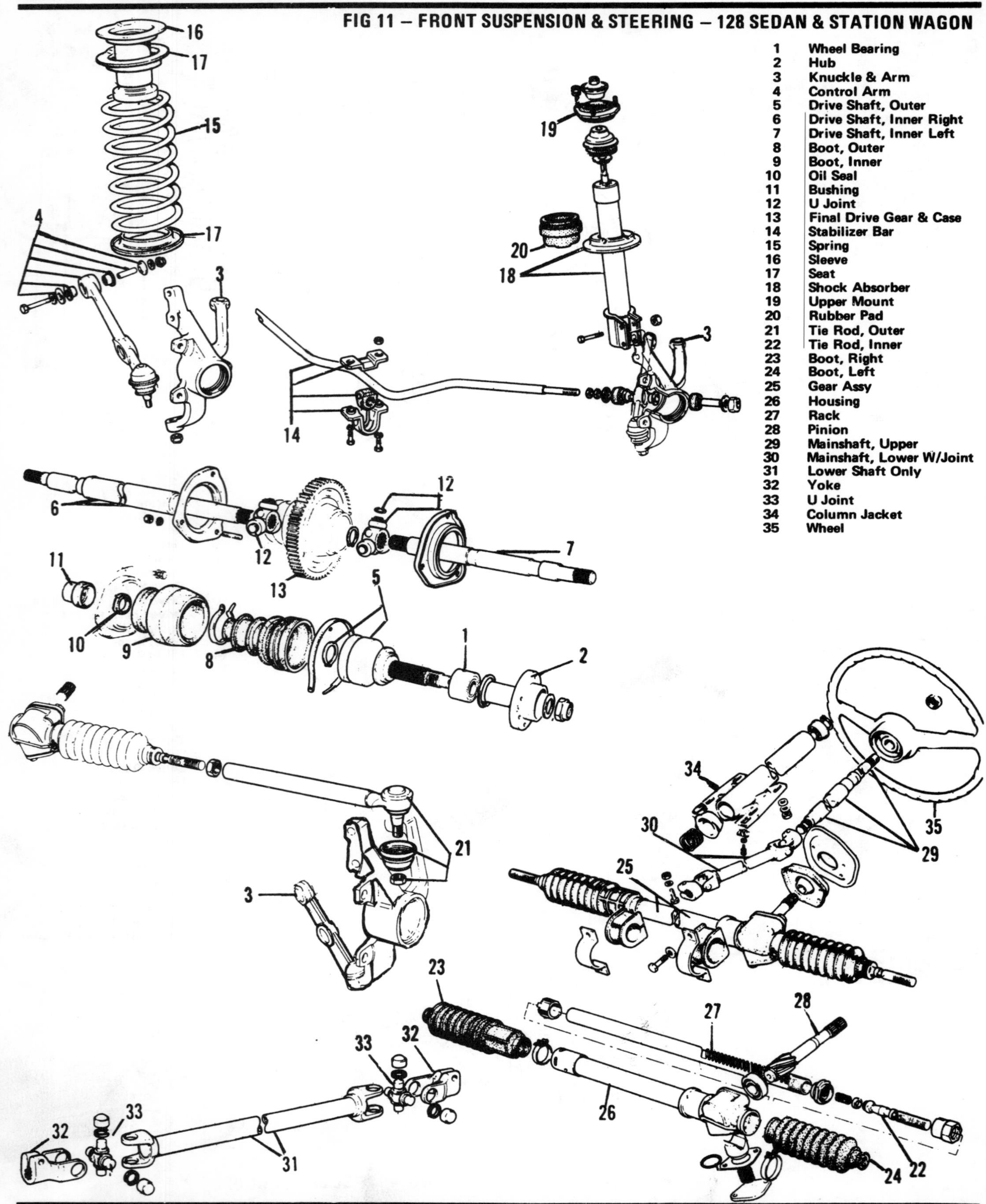
FIG 11 – FRONT SUSPENSION & STEERING – 128 SEDAN & STATION WAGON
1 Wheel Bearing
2 Hub
3 Knuckle & Arm
4 Control Arm
5 Drive Shaft, Outer
6 Drive Shaft, Inner Right
7 Drive Shaft, Inner Left
8 Boot, Outer
9 Boot, Inner
10 Oil Seal
11 Bushing
12 U Joint
13 Final Drive Gear & Case
14 Stabilizer Bar
15 Spring
16 Sleeve
17 Seat
18 Shock Absorber
19 Upper Mount
20 Rubber Pad
21 Tie Rod, Outer
22 Tie Rod, Inner
23 Boot, Right
24 Boot, Left
25 Gear Assy
26 Housing
27 Rack
28 Pinion
29 Mainshaft, Upper
30 Mainshaft, Lower W/Joint
31 Lower Shaft Only
32 Yoke
33 U Joint
34 Column Jacket
35 Wheel

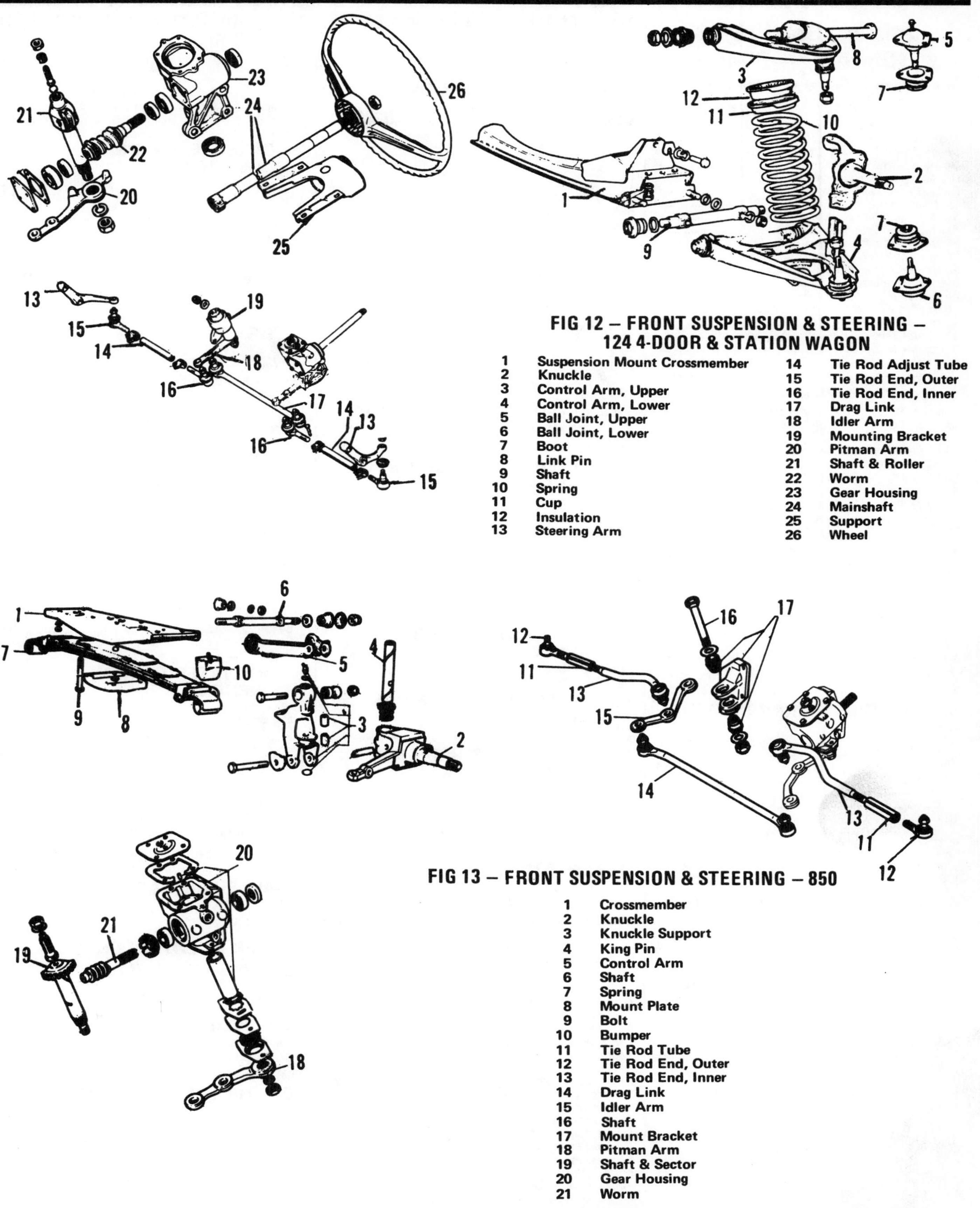

FIG 12 – FRONT SUSPENSION & STEERING – 124 4-DOOR & STATION WAGON

1 Suspension Mount Crossmember
2 Knuckle
3 Control Arm, Upper
4 Control Arm, Lower
5 Ball Joint, Upper
6 Ball Joint, Lower
7 Boot
8 Link Pin
9 Shaft
10 Spring
11 Cup
12 Insulation
13 Steering Arm
14 Tie Rod Adjust Tube
15 Tie Rod End, Outer
16 Tie Rod End, Inner
17 Drag Link
18 Idler Arm
19 Mounting Bracket
20 Pitman Arm
21 Shaft & Roller
22 Worm
23 Gear Housing
24 Mainshaft
25 Support
26 Wheel

FIG 13 – FRONT SUSPENSION & STEERING – 850

1 Crossmember
2 Knuckle
3 Knuckle Support
4 King Pin
5 Control Arm
6 Shaft
7 Spring
8 Mount Plate
9 Bolt
10 Bumper
11 Tie Rod Tube
12 Tie Rod End, Outer
13 Tie Rod End, Inner
14 Drag Link
15 Idler Arm
16 Shaft
17 Mount Bracket
18 Pitman Arm
19 Shaft & Sector
20 Gear Housing
21 Worm

Ignition, Starting & Charging—TIME

OPERATION INDEX

Tune-Up, Minor ... 1
Tune-Up, Major ... 2
Compression Test ... 3
Distributor, R&R Or Renew ... 4
Distributor Cap, Replace ... 5
Ignition Cable Set, Renew ... 6
Ignition Coil, Renew ... 7
Starter & Ignition Switch, Renew ... 8
Starter, R&R Or Renew ... 9
Starter Bendix Drive, Renew ... 10
Starter, R&R & Overhaul ... 11
Starter Brushes, Renew ... 12
Starter Armature, Renew ... 13
Alternator Regulator, Renew ... 14
Alternator, R&R Or Renew ... 15
Alternator, Overhaul ... 16
Alternator Diodes, Renew ... 17
Alternator Bearings ... 18
Alternator Brushes ... 19

1—TUNE-UP, MINOR

Includes: Renew points, condenser & plugs, set spark timing & adjust carburetor idle.

124—
Exc Below ... 2.8
Sedan & Wagon ... 2.5
128 ... 2.6
850 ... 2.5
X 1/9 & 131 ... 2.8

2—TUNE-UP, MAJOR

Includes: Check compression, clean or renew & adjust spark plugs. Renew points & condenser. Adjust ignition timing, carburetor & fan belts. Clean battery terminals & replace or clean fuel line filter & R&R distributor.

124—
Exc Below ... 4.0
Sedan & Wagon ... 3.7
128 & 850 ... 3.7
X 1/9 & 131 ... 4.0

3—COMPRESSION TEST

All Models ... 0.5

4—DISTRIBUTOR, R&R OR RENEW

124—
Exc Below ... 0.5
Sedan & Wagon ... 0.4
850 ... 0.4
128 ... 0.6
X 1/9 ... 0.7
131 ... 0.5
124 T.C. ... 0.5

5—DISTRIBUTOR CAP, RENEW

Exc Below ... 0.2
124 T.C. & 131 ... 0.3
124 Coupe & Spider ... 0.3

6—IGNITION CABLE SET, RENEW

All Models ... 0.7

7—IGNITION COIL, RENEW

Exc Below ... 0.3
124 Coupe & Spider ... 0.5

8—STARTER & IGNITION SWITCH, RENEW

850, 128 ... 0.5
X 1/9 ... 0.4
124 Exc ... 0.3
Sport Coupe & Spider ... 0.5
131 ... 0.3

9—STARTER, R&R OR RENEW

124—
Exc Below ... ①1.1
Sedan & Wagon ... ①0.9
128 ... 0.6
850 ... 0.9
X 1/9 ... 0.5
131 ... 0.7
①With Air Cond, 1974 & Prior, Add ... *0.9*

10—STARTER BENDIX DRIVE, RENEW

Does not include R&R starter.
All Models ... 0.8

11—STARTER, R&R & OVERHAUL

124—
Exc Below ... ①1.9
Sedan & Wagon ... ①1.6
128 ... 1.4
850 ... 1.8
X 1/9 ... 1.3
131 ... 1.5
①With Air Cond, 1974 & Prior, Add ... *0.9*

12—STARTER BRUSHES, RENEW

Does not include R&R starter.
All Models ... 0.8

13—STARTER ARMATURE, RENEW

127—
Exc Below ... 1.7
Sedan & Wagon ... 1.4
128 ... 1.2
850 ... 1.6
X 1/9 ... 1.1
131 ... 1.3

14—ALTERNATOR REGULATOR, RENEW

All Models ... 0.2

15—ALTERNATOR, R&R OR RENEW

850 ... 0.4
128 ... 0.7
X 1/9 ... 0.6
124 ... 0.7
124 T.C. ... 0.5
131 ... 0.5

16—ALTERNATOR, OVERHAUL

After alternator is removed.
All Models ... 1.0

17—ALTERNATOR DIODES, RENEW

All Models, Each ... 0.4
Each Additional ... 0.1

18—ALTERNATOR BEARINGS, RENEW

All Models ... 0.9

19—ALTERNATOR BRUSHES, RENEW

All Models ... 0.9

Fuel, Emission Controls, Intake Manifold & Exhaust System—TIME

OPERATION INDEX

Carburetor, R&R Or Renew ... 1
Carburetor, R&R & Overhaul ... 2
Fuel Pump, R&R Or Renew ... 3
Fuel Pump, Overhaul ... 4
Fuel Tank, R&R Or Renew ... 5
Activated Carbon Trap, Renew ... 6
Three Way Valve, Renew ... 7
Vapor Liquid Separator, Renew ... 8
Air Pump, R&R Or Renew ... 9
Air Inj Check Valve, Renew ... 10
Diverter Valve, Renew ... 11
Egr Valve, Renew ... 12
Egr Thermo Valve, Renew ... 13
Intake Manifold Or Gasket, Renew ... 14
Exhaust Manifold Or Gasket, Renew ... 15
Exhaust Pipe Muffler, Renew ... 16
Muffler, Renew ... 17
Intermediate Pipe, Renew ... 18
Catalytic Converter, Renew ... 19

1—CARBURETOR, R&R OR RENEW

124 ... 0.7
128 ... 1.0
850—
Exc Below ... 0.6
Coupe & Spider ... 1.0
X 1/9, 131 ... 1.0
124 T.C. ... 1.0

2—CARBURETOR, R&R & OVERHAUL

124 ... 2.0
128 ... 1.8
850—
Exc Below ... 1.4
Coupe & Spider ... 2.0
X 1/9, 131 ... 1.9
124 T.C. ... 1.9

3—FUEL PUMP, R&R OR RENEW

Mechanical Less Air Cond—
124—
Exc Below ... 0.4
Sport Coupe & Spider ... 0.5
128 ... 0.3
850 ... 0.4
X 1/9 ... 0.5
Mechanical With Air Cond ... 0.8
Electric—
All Models ... 0.5

4—FUEL PUMP, OVERHAUL (MECHANICAL)

Pump removed
All Models ... 0.5

5—FUEL TANK, R&R OR RENEW

131—
Sedan ... 1.2
Wagon ... 0.7
128 ... 1.3
850—
Exc Below ... 5.2
Sport Coupe ... 5.1
Spider ... 4.6
X 1/9 ... 1.6
124—
Sedan ... 0.9
Sport Coupe ... 1.2
Wagon ... 1.7

6—ACTIVATED CARBON TRAP, RENEW

124—
Exc Below ... 0.2
Coupe & Spider ... 0.3
128 & 850 ... 0.3
X 1/9 ... 0.6
124 T.C. ... 0.3
131 ... 0.5

7—THREE WAY VALVE, RENEW

All Models ... 0.2

8—VAPOR LIQUID SEPARATOR, RENEW

All Models ... 0.4

9—AIR PUMP, R&R OR RENEW

128 ... 2.2
X 1/9 ... 2.5
124 & 131 ... 0.8

10—AIR INJECTION CHECK VALVE, RENEW

128 & 124 ... 0.4
X 1/9 ... 0.8
131 ... 0.6

11—DIVERTER VALVE, RENEW

All Models ... 0.3

12—EGR VALVE, RENEW

All Models ... 0.5

13—EGR THERMO VALVE, RENEW

128 & X 1/9 ... 0.4
124 & 131 ... 0.5

14—INTAKE MANIFOLD OR GASKET, RENEW

124—
Exc Below ... 1.2
Coupe & Spider ... 3.4

(Continued)

Fuel, Emission Controls, Intake Manifold & Exhaust System—TIME Cont'd

128 .....1.2
124 T.C. 2.4
131 .....2.2

15—EXHAUST MANIFOLD OR GASKET, RENEW

124—
Exc Below 2.3
Coupe & Spider 3.6
128 .....2.0
850 .....0.6
X 1/9, Exc 2.2
W/Air Cond 2.7
131 Exc 3.4
W/Air Cond 3.8

16—EXHAUST PIPE & MUFFLER, RENEW

124 .....1.5
128 .....1.2
850—
Exc Below 0.7
Sport Coupe & Spider 1.3
X 1/9 .....1.2
131 .....1.5

17—MUFFLER, RENEW

124—
Exc Below 0.6
Rear Only 0.5
128 .....0.4
850 .....1.0
124 T.C. 0.5
131 .....0.5

18—INTERMEDIATE PIPE, RENEW

128 .....0.6
124 .....0.7
131 .....0.7

19—CATALYTIC CONVERTER, RENEW

128 .....0.5
X 1/9 .....0.7
124 .....0.5
131 .....0.5

Engine Cooling & Heater System—TIME

OPERATION INDEX

Radiator, R&R Or Renew 1
Radiator Hoses, Renew 2
Cololant Expansion Tank, Renew 3
Water Pump, R&R Or Renew 4
Water Pump, Overhaul 5
Thermostat Or Housing, Renew 6
Heater & Core, R&R Or Renew 7
Heater Temperature Control Valve, Renew 8
Heater Hoses, Renew 9
Heater Blower Motor, Renew 10

1—RADIATOR, R&R OR RENEW

124 Sed & Wgn Exc 0.6
W/Air Cond 1.0
W/Auto Trans 0.9
124 Coupe & Spider Exc 0.8
W/Air Cond 1.1
128 .....0.8
850 .....1.0
X 1/9 Exc 1.1
W/Air Cond 1.3
131 Exc 0.7
W/Air Cond 1.0
W/Auto Trans 0.9

2—RADIATOR HOSES, RENEW

Upper Hose—
124, 128, 131 .....0.4
850 .....0.5
X 1/9 .....0.6
Lower Hose—
124, X 1/9 .....0.6
128, 131 .....0.6
850 .....0.7

3—COOLANT EXPANSION TANK, RENEW

Exc Below 0.2
X 1/9 .....0.6

4—WATER PUMP, R&R OR RENEW

850 .....0.8
128 Exc 2.5
1974 & Later Exc 3.0
With Air Cond 4.3
X 1/9 Exc 4.0
W/Air Cond 5.6
124 Sed & Wgn Exc 1.5
W/Air Cond 1.7
124 Coupe & Spider Exc 1.8
W/Air Cond 2.1
124 T.C. Exc 1.8
With Air Cond 2.0
131 Exc 1.6
With Air Cond 1.8

5—WATER PUMP, OVERHAUL

After pump is removed
124 & 131 .....0.8
850 & 128 .....1.0
X 1/9 .....0.9

6—THERMOSTAT OR HOUSING, RENEW

124—
Exc Below 0.5
Sport Coupe & Spider 0.6
128 .....0.7
850—
Exc Below 0.8
Sport Coupe 0.9
X 1/9 .....1.0
131 .....0.6

7—HEATER & CORE, R&R OR RENEW

124—
Exc Below 2.3
Sport Coupe & Spider 2.5
128 .....0.8
850—
Exc Below 1.4
Coupe & Spider 1.0
X 1/9 .....2.2
131 .....2.0

8—HEATER TEMPERATURE CONTROL VALVE, RENEW

124—
Exc Below 1.1
Spec Sed & Wagon 0.7
128 .....00.6
850—
Exc Below 0.7
Sport Coupe 0.9
Spider 0.5

9—HEATER HOSES, RENEW

124 .....0.3
128 .....0.4
850—
Exc Below 0.4
Spider 0.6

10—HEATER BLOWER MOTOR, RENEW

124—
Exc Below 0.6
Sport Coupe & Spider 1.4
128 .....1.0
850—
Exc Below 0.7
Spider 0.4
Spec Sedan 0.5
X 1/9 .....1.1
124 T.C. 0.8
131 .....1.0

Engine—TIME

OPERATION INDEX

Engine, R&R 1
Engine, R&R & Overhaul 2
Engine Short Block, Renew & Grind Valves 3
Cylinder Head Or Gasket Renew 4
Valves, Grind (Head Off) 5
One Valve, Renew & Grind 6
Valve Spring, Renew 7
Rocker Arm Or Cam Housing Assy, Renew 8
Rocker Arm Or Cam Housing Gasket, Renew 9
Oil Pan Or Gasket, Renew 10
Valve Lifters, Adjust 11
Timing Cover Seal & Gasket, Renew 12
Timing Chain Or Sprockets, Renew 13
Timing Belt Tensioner, Renew 14
Camshaft, R&R Or Renew 15
Oil Pump, R&R Or Renew 16
Oil Pump, R&R & Overhaul 17
Piston Ring(S), Renew 18
Rings & Main Bearings, Renew 19
Rod Bearings, Renew 20
Main Bearings, Renew 21
Main & Rod Bearings, Renew 22
Crankshaft, R&R Or Renew 23
Piston & Connecting Rod (One), Renew 24
Piston & Connecting Rods (All), Renew 25
Crankshaft Pulley, Renew 26

1—ENGINE, R&R

Does not include transfer of any part of engine or replacement of special equipment. Includes R&R clutch from engine.
124—
Sed & Wgn Exc 5.6
W/Air Cond 6.3
Cpe & Spider Exc 6.2
1974 & Later Exc 7.2
W/Air Cond 7.6
124 T.C. Exc 6.9
W/Air Cond 7.5
850—
Exc Below 3.9
Sport Coupe 3.7
Spider 4.3
128 Exc 6.8
1974 & Later 7.8
X 1/9—
1974 .....7.3
1975-76 .....7.7
W/Air Cond 8.8
131 Exc 6.9
W/Air Cond 7.5

2—ENGINE, R&R & OVERHAUL

Includes rebore cylinders with boring bar, renew pistons, rings, bearings, grind valves, plastigauge bearings and perform minor tune-up
124—
Exc Below 21.6
Sport Coupe 23.4
Spider 23.1
128 .....20.7
124 T.C. 23.5
850—
Exc Below 18.2
Sport Coupe 18.6
Spider 19.2
X 1/9 .....25.0
131 .....23.5

3—ENGINE SHORT BLOCK, RENEW & GRIND VALVES

124—
Exc Below 13.3
Sport Coupe 16.5
Spider 16.2
124 T.C. Exc 13.6
W/Air Cond 14.2
850—
Exc Below 10.4
Sport Coupe 10.2
Spider 10.2
128 Exc 10.5
1974 & Later 11.5
X 1/9 Exc 11.0
W/Air Cond 11.5
131 Exc 13.6
W/Air Cond 14.2

4—CYLINDER HEAD OR GASKET, RENEW

124—
Exc Below 2.8
Sport Coupe 4.5
Spider 4.5
124 T.C. Exc 4.3
W/Air Cond 4.5
128 .....4.7

(Continued)

Engine—TIME Cont'd

850—
Exc Below 2.5
Sport Coupe 2.9
Spider 2.8
X 1/9 ..... 4.7
131 Exc 4.3
W/Air Cond 4.5

5—VALVES, GRIND (HEAD OFF)

124—
Exc Below 3.8
Sport Coupe 4.3
Spider 4.3
124 T.C. 4.3
128 ..... 3.1
850—
Exc Below 2.7
Sport Coupe 3.4
Spider 3.4
X 1/9 ..... 3.1
131 ..... 4.3

6—ONE VALVE, RENEW & GRIND

124—
Exc Below 4.2
Sport Coupe 5.2
Spider 5.2
124 T.C. 4.4
128 ..... 4.0
850—
Exc Below 3.9
Sport Coupe 3.7
Spider 3.7
X 1/9 ..... 4.5
131 ..... 4.4

7—VALVE SPRING, RENEW

All Models 0.8

8—ROCKER ARM OR CAM HOUSING ASSY, RENEW

124—
1200cc Eng 0.7
1400cc Eng 4.3
124 T.C. 3.6
128 ..... 3.4
850—
Exc Below 1.0
Spider 0.8
X 1/9 ..... 3.4

9—ROCKER ARM OR CAM HOUSING GASKET, RENEW

124—
1200cc Eng 0.2
1400cc Eng 3.5
128 ..... 3.1
850—
Exc Below 0.5
Spider 0.3
X 1/9 ..... 3.1
124 T.C. 3.3

10—OIL PAN OR GASKET, RENEW

128 ..... 1.4
850—
Exc Below 1.0
Sport Coupe 1.2
Spider 1.2
X 1/9 ..... 1.4
124 Exc 1.6
Coupe & Spider 2.3
124 T.C. 1.6
131 ..... 1.2

—NOTE—

To Renew Gasket, Add 0.3

11—VALVE LIFTERS, ADJUST

124—
Exc Below 0.6
Sport Coupe 0.9
Spider 0.9
128, X 1/9 ..... 0.9
850—
Exc Below 0.6
Sport Coupe 0.7
Spider 0.5
124 T.C. 0.9

12—TIMING COVER SEAL & GASKET, RENEW

124—
Exc Below 2.4
Sport Coupe 3.4
Spider 3.4
128 ..... 2.5
850—
Exc Below 1.9
Sport Coupe 2.0
Spider 2.7
X 1/9, 131 ..... 2.7
124 T.C. 2.7

13—TIMING CHAIN OR SPROCKETS, RENEW

124—
Exc Below 1.2
Sedan & Wagon ①2.9
128 ..... ②1.2
850—
Exc Below 2.9
Sport Coupe 3.0
Spider 3.8
X 1/9 ..... 2.7
131, 124 T.C. 2.3

①Includes R&R Radiator On Sedan & Wagon
②Includes R&R Timing Belt

14—TIMING BELT TENSIONER, RENEW

124 ..... 2.1
128 ..... 1.4

15—CAMSHAFT, R&R OR RENEW

124—
Exc Below 5.9
OHV Models 4.9
128, X 1/9 ..... 3.7
850—
Exc Below 5.5
Sport Coupe 5.9
Spider 6.5
124 T.C. 4.8

16—OIL PUMP, R&R OR RENEW

128, X 1/9 ..... 1.5
850—
Exc Below 1.2
Sport Coupe 1.4
Spider 1.4
124 Exc 1.6
Coupe & Spider 2.4
131 ..... 1.6

17—OIL PUMP, R&R & OVERHAUL

128, X 1/9 ..... 2.2
850—
Exc Below 2.0
Sport Coupe 2.2
Spider 2.2
124 Exc 2.1
Coupe & Spider 2.9
131 ..... 2.1

18—PISTON RING(S), RENEW

124—
Exc Below 7.3
Sport Coupe 8.0
Spider 8.0
128 ..... 7.3
850—
Exc Below 5.8
Sport Coupe 6.5
Spider 6.3
X 1/9 ..... 7.8
124 T.C. 7.6
131 ..... 7.7

19—RINGS & MAIN BEARINGS, RENEW & GRIND VALVES

124—
Exc Below 10.5
Sport Coupe 12.8
Spider 12.8
128 ..... 10.6
850—
Exc Below 9.1
Sport Coupe 9.6
Spider 9.4
X 1/9 ..... 12.8

20—ROD BEARINGS, RENEW

128 ..... 2.5
850—
Exc Below 2.1
Sport Coupe 2.2
Spider 2.2
X 1/9 ..... 2.5
124 Exc 2.7
Coupe & Spider 3.4
124 T.C. 2.7
131 ..... 2.3

21—MAIN BEARINGS, RENEW

128 ..... 1.9
850—
Exc Below 1.6
Sport Coupe 1.8
Spider 1.8
X 1/9 ..... 2.2
124 Exc 2.4
Coupe & Spider 3.1
124 T.C. 2.4
131 ..... 2.0

22—MAIN & ROD BEARINGS, RENEW

128 ..... 2.8
850—
Exc Below 2.5
Sport Coupe 2.7
Spider 2.7
X 1/9 ..... 3.1
124 Exc 3.3
Coupe & Spider 4.0
124 T.C. 3.3
131 ..... 2.9

23—CRANKSHAFT, R&R OR RENEW

124—
Exc Below 9.5
Sport Coupe 10.5
Spider 10.2
128 ..... 11.8
850—
Exc Below 6.7
Sport Coupe 6.9
Spider 7.5
X 1/9 ..... 12.2
131 ..... 11.4

24—PISTON & CONNECTING ROD (ONE), RENEW

124—
Exc Below 5.6
Sport Coupe 6.2
Spider 6.2
128 ..... 6.1
850—
Exc Below 4.7
Sport Coupe 5.3
Spider 5.2
X 1/9 ..... 6.1
124 T.C. 5.4
131 ..... 5.5

25—PISTONS & CONNECTING RODS (ALL), RENEW

124—
Exc Below 7.3
Sport Coupe 8.0
Spider 8.0
128 ..... 7.8
850—
Exc Below 5.8
Sport Coupe 6.5
Spider 6.3
X 1/9 ..... 7.8
124 T.C. 7.6
131 ..... 7.7

26—CRANKSHAFT PULLEY, RENEW

124—
Exc Below 1.1
Sport Coupe 2.5
128 ..... 0.5

Clutch, Mounts, Manual & Automatic Transmissions—TIME

OPERATION INDEX

Flywheel, R&R Or Renew ...1
Flywheel Ring Gear, Renew ...2
Clutch Assy, Renew ...3
Pilot Bearing, Renew ...4
Clutch Pedal, Adjust ...5
Clutch Master Cylinder, R&R Or Renew ...6
Clutch Operating Cylinder, R&R Or Renew ...7
Clutch Fluid Reservoir, R&R Or Renew ...8
Engine Mounts, Renew ...9
Transmission Assy, R&R Or Renew ...10
Oil Pan Gasket, Renew ...11
Manual Trans, R&R & Overhaul ...12
Automatic Transmission, R&R & Overhaul ...13
Extension Housing Oil Seal, Renew ...14
Rear Extension, R&R ...15
Trans Side Cover, Renew ...16
Rear Shaft Oil Seal, Renew ...17
Lower Case Cover, R&R ...18
Gearshift Or Selector Lever, Renew ...19

1—FLYWHEEL, R&R OR RENEW
124—
Exc Below ...4.0
Sport Coupe ...4.3
Spider ...4.3
128 ...3.9
850 ...3.7
X 1/9 ...4.9
131 ...3.4

2—FLYWHEEL RING GEAR, RENEW
124—
Exc Below ...4.3
Sport Coupe ...4.6
Spider ...4.3
128 ...4.2
850 ...4.0
X 1/9 ...5.2
131 ...3.7

3—CLUTCH ASSY, RENEW
Includes R&R release bearing.
124—
Exc Below ...3.6
Sport Coupe ...3.4
Spider ...3.4
128 ...3.9
850 ...3.3
X 1/9 ...4.5
124 T.C. ...3.6
131 ...3.4

4—PILOT BEARING, RENEW
124—
Exc Below ...3.8
Sport Coupe ...3.6
Spider ...3.6
128 ...4.1
850 ...3.5
X 1/9 ...4.7
124 T.C. ...3.8
131 ...3.6

5—CLUTCH PEDAL, ADJUST
All Models ...0.2

6—CLUTCH MASTER CYLINDER, R&R OR RENEW
X 1/9 ...2.6

7—CLUTCH OPERATING CYLINDER, R&R OR RENEW
X 1/9 ...1.5

8—CLUTCH FLUID RESERVOIR, R&R OR RENEW
X 1/9 ...0.8

9—ENGINE MOUNTS, RENEW
124—
Exc Below ...1.0
Sport Coupe & Spider ...1.2
124 T.C. Exc ...1.3
W/Air Cond ...1.5
128 ...1.0
850 ...0.5
X 1/9 ...1.2
131 ...1.2

10—TRANSMISSION ASSY, R&R OR RENEW
124—
Synchromesh—
Exc Below ...3.3
Sport Coupe ...3.6
Automatic ...3.8
128 ...3.6
850—
Exc Below ...3.1
Indroconvert ...3.8
X 1/9 ...4.2
124 T.C. & 131—
Synchro-Mesh ...3.1
Automatic ...3.8

11—OIL PAN GASKET, RENEW
All Models ...0.5

12—MANUAL TRANS, R&R & OVERHAUL
124—
Exc Below ...7.4
Sport Coupe ...7.7
Spider ...7.7
128 ...6.5
850 ...6.2
X 1/9 ...7.1
124 T.C. ...7.2
131 ...7.5

13—AUTOMATIC TRANS, R&R & OVERHAUL
124 & 131 ...10.5

14—EXTENSION HOUSING OIL SEAL, RENEW
124 ...0.7

15—REAR EXTENSION, R&R
128, X 1/9 ...0.7
124 ...2.5
131 ...1.8

16—TRANSMISSION SIDE COVER, RENEW
850 ...1.2

17—REAR SHAFT OIL SEAL, RENEW
124—
Exc Below ...1.6
Sport Coupe ...1.7
Spider ...1.7

18—LOWER CASE COVER, R&R
124 ...0.7

19—GEARSHIFT OR SELECTOR LEVER, RENEW
124—
Exc Below ...4.8
Sport Coupe ...5.0
Spider ...4.5
128 ...3.8
850 ...4.5

Brakes, Steering, Suspension, Universals & Rear Axle—TIME

OPERATION INDEX

Brake Shoes Or Friction Pads, Renew ...1
Master Cylinder , Renew ...2
Master Cylinder, R&R & Overhaul ...3
Wheel Cylinders, Renew ...4
Wheel Cylinders, R&R & Overhaul ...5
Caliper Assy, Renew ...6
Caliper Assy, R&R & Overhaul ...7
Bleed System ...8
Brake Hose, Renew ...9
Brake Hub, Renew ...10
Brake Discs, Renew ...11
Servo Brake, Renew ...12
Brake Drum, Renew ...13
Self Adjustment Device, R&R Or Overhaul ...14
Pressure Regulator Cylinder, Renew ...15
Brake Pedal, Overhaul ...16
Parking Brake Lever, Renew ...17
Steering Box, R&R Or Renew ...18
Steering Box, R&R & Overhaul ...19
Springs, Renew (Front) ...20
Springs, Renew (Rear) ...21
Fraont Suspension Assy, R&R Or Renew ...22
Upper Control Arms, R&R Or Renew ...23
Lower Control Arm, R&R Or Renew ...23A
Front Suspension Wishbone Upper (One), R&R Or Renew ...24
Caster, Camber & Toe-In, Adjust ...25
Track &(Link Rods, Renew ...26
Idler Arm, R&R Or Renew ...27
Front Hub Bearing, Renew ...28
Shock Absorbers, Renew ...29
Thrust Rod And Transverse Link, R&R Or Renew ...30
Longitudinal Thrust Rods, R&R Or Renew ...31
Longitudinal Links Or Push Rods, R&R Or Renew ...32
Stabilizer Bar, R&R Or Renew ...33
Universal Joints, Renew ...34
Axle Shift, Renew ...35
Axle Shaft Bearing, Renew ...36
Differential Assy, Overhaul ...37
Differential Assy, R&R Or Renew ...38

1—BRAKE SHOES OR FRICTION PADS, RENEW
124—
Front ...0.8
Rear ...1.1
All ...1.8
128, 131—
Front ...0.7
Rear ...1.3
All ...1.8
850—
Exc Sport Coupe & Spider—
Front ...1.1
Rear ...1.3
All ...2.3
Sport Coupe & Spider—
Front ...0.7
Rear ...1.3
All ...1.9
X 1/9—
Front ...0.7
Rear ...0.9

2—MASTER CYLINDER, RENEW
124—
Exc Below ...0.3
Sport Coupe ...0.6
Spider ...0.6
128 ...0.4
850 ...0.3
X 1/9 ...2.4
124 T.C. ...0.6
131 ...0.6

3—MASTER CYLINDER, R&R & OVERHAUL
124—
Exc Below ...0.8
Sport Coupe ...1.1
Spider ...1.1
128 ...0.9
850 ...0.8
X 1/9 ...2.9
124 T.C. ...1.1
131

4—WHEEL CYLINDERS, RENEW
850—
Exc Below—
Front ...1.5
Rear ...1.7
Sport Coupe & Spider—
Front ...1.1
Rear ...1.7

(Continued)

Brakes, Steering, Suspension, Universals & Rear Axle—TIME Cont'd

5—WHEEL CYLINDERS, R&R & OVERHAUL

850—
Exc Below—
Front 1.7
Rear 1.9
Sport Coupe & Spider—
Front 1.3
Rear 1.9

6—CALIPER ASSY, RENEW

All Models—
Front 1.0
Rear 1.5

7—CALIPER ASSY, R&R & OVERHAUL

All Models—
Front 1.7
Rear 2.7

8—BLEED SYSTEM

All Models 0.6

9—BRAKE HOSE, RENEW

Front 0.5
Rear—
850 ....0.6
128, X 1/9 ....0.5
124, 131 ....0.3

10—BRAKE HUB, RENEW

All Models 1.1

11—BRAKE DISC, RENEW

Front 1.2
Rear 1.6

12—SERVO BRAKE, RENEW

124—
Exc Below 1.0
Sport Coupe 1.2
Spider 1.2

13—BRAKE DRUM, RENEW

Front 0.6
Rear—
Exc Below 0.6
128 ....0.8

14—SELF ADJUSTMENT DEVICE, R&R OR OVERHAUL

128—
Front 0.8
Rear 1.4
850—
Exc Coupe & Spider—
Front 1.2
Rear 1.4
Coupe & Spider—
Front 0.8
Rear 1.4

15—PRESSURE REGULATOR CYLINDER, RENEW

124 ....0.6
128 ....0.9
131 ....0.6

16—BRAKE PEDAL, OVERHAUL

124—
Exc Below 1.9
Sport Coupe 1.0
Spider 1.0
128 ....1.0
850 ....0.9
X 1/9 ....0.6
124 T.C. 0.7
131 ....1.1

17—PARKING BRAKE LEVER, RENEW

124—
Exc Below 0.8
Sport Coupe 1.3
Spider 1.3
128 ....0.8
850—
Exc Below 1.2
Sport Coupe 1.3
Spider 1.3
X 1/9 ....1.3
131 ....0.7

18—STEERING BOX, R&R OR RENEW

124—
Exc Below 1.4
Sport Coupe 2.5
Spider 1.6
128 ....0.8
850—
Exc Below 1.3
Sport Coupe 0.8
Spider 0.8
X 1/9 ....1.2
131 ....0.6

19—STEERING BOX, R&R & OVERHAUL

124—
Exc Below 0.5
Sport Coupe 4.6
Spider 0.7
128 ....2.0
850—
Exc Below 3.2
Sport Coupe 2.7
Spider 2.7
X 1/9 ....2.4
131 ....2.0

20—SPRINGS, RENEW (FRONT)

124—
One 1.4
Both 2.5
128, 131, X 1/9—
One 0.7
Both 1.1
850 ....1.4

21—SPRINGS, RENEW (REAR)

128 ....1.2
850—
One 0.8
Both 1.2
X 1/9—
One 0.6
Both 1.0
124, 131—
One 0.9
Both 1.1

22—FRONT SUSPENSION ASSY, R&R OR RENEW

124—
Exc Below ....(1)5.1
Sport Coupe ....(1)5.0
Spider ....(1)5.0
128 ....3.9
850 ....2.6
(1)To R&R Crossmember, Add 1.0

23—UPPER CONTROL ARMS, R&R OR RENEW

124 ....2.3
850 ....1.2

23A—LOWER CONTRAOL ARM, R&R OR RENEW

850 ....1.0
128 ....1.2
131 ....1.5
X 1/9 ....0.7
124 ....1.4

24—FRONT SUSPENSION WISHBONE UPPER (ONE), R&R OR RENEW

Does not include wheel alignment,
124 ....1.5
850 ....0.7

25—CASTER, CAMBER & TOE-IN, CHECK & ADJUST

850 ....1.3
128, X 1/9 ....1.4
124 ....2.0
131 ....1.4

26—TRACK & LINK RODS, RENEW

Includes wheel alignment
124 ....1.4
128, X 1/9 ....1.3
850 ....1.4
131 ....0.9

27—IDLER ARM, R&R OR RENEW

124—
Exc Below 0.6
Sport Coupe & Spider 0.7
850 ....0.5

28—FRONT HUB BEARING, RENEW

All Models 0.9

29—SHOCK ABSORBERS, RENEW

124—
One Front 0.6
One Rear 0.9
Two Front 1.0
Two Rear 1.1
128, X 1/9—
One Front 0.7
One Rear 0.6
Two Front 1.1
Two Rear 1.0
850—
One Front 0.4
One Rear 0.5
Two Front 0.7
Two Rear 0.7
131—
One Front 0.6
One Rear 0.9
Two Front 0.9
Two Rear 1.1

30—THRUST ROD AND TRANSVERSE LINK, R&R OR RENEW

124 ....0.5

31—LONGITUDINAL THRUST RODS, R&R OR RENEW

124 ....1.1

32—LONGITUDINAL OR PUSH RODS, R&R OR RENEW

124 ....0.6

33—STABILIZER BAR, R&R OR RENEW

Front—
124—
Exc Below 0.7
Sport Coupe 0.9
128 ....1.1
850, 131 ....0.5
Rear 0.5

34—UNIVERSAL JOINTS, RENEW

124 ....2.9

35—AXLE SHAFT, RENEW

124 ....1.1
128, X 1/9 ....1.0
850 ....0.9
131 ....0.7

36—AXLE SHAFT BEARING, RENEW

124 ....1.3

37—DIFFERENTIAL ASSY, R&R & OVERHAUL

124 ....4.4
128 ....7.1
850 ....6.5
X 1/9 ....7.7

38—DIFFERENTIAL ASSY, R&R OR RENEW

124 ....2.2
128 ....3.6
850—
Exc Below 3.1
Sport Coupe 3.0
Spider 3.0
X 1/9 ....4.2

Speedometer, W/S Wipers & Instruments—TIME

OPERATION INDEX

Speedometer Head, Renew *1*
W/S Wiper Motor, Renew *2*
W/S Woper Assy, R&R Or Renew *3*
Fuel Gauge (Dash Unit), Renew *4*
Fuel Tank Gauge, Renew *5*
Oil Gauge (Dash Unit), Renew *6*
Oil Gauge Sending Unit, Renew *7*
Temperature Gauge (Dash Unit), Renew *8*
Temperature Gauge Sending Unit, Renew *9*
Headlight Switch, Renew *10*
High Beam Relay, Renew *11*
Stop Light Switch, Renew *12*
Turn Signal Switch, Renew *13*
Back-Up Lamp Switch, Renew *14*

1—SPEEDOMETER HEAD, RENEW

Includes: R&R instrument board

124—
- Exc Below 0.7
- Sport Coupe 0.5
- Spider 0.5

128 .... 0.7

850—
- Exc Below 0.4
- Sport Coupe 0.8
- Spider 0.8

X 1/9 .... 0.7

131 .... 0.7

2—W/S WIPER MOTOR, RENEW

124—
- Exc Below 0.5
- Spider 0.6

128 .... 0.5

850—
- Exc Below 0.6
- Sport Coupe 1.3
- Spider 0.8

X 1/9 .... 0.5

131 .... 0.8

3—W/S WIPER ASSY, R&R OR RENEW

124—
- Exc Below 1.0
- Spider 1.1

128 .... 0.6

850—
- Exc Below 1.4
- Sport Coupe 1.7
- Spider 1.2

X 1/9 .... 0.7

131 .... 1.0

4—FUEL GAUGE (DASH UNIT), RENEW

Includes R&R inst board.

124—
- Exc Below 0.7
- Sport Coupe 0.5
- Spider 0.5

128 .... 0.7

850—
- Exc Below 0.4
- Sport Coupe 1.0
- Spider 0.8

X 1/9 .... 0.7

124 T.C. 0.7

131 .... 0.7

5—FUEL TANK GAUGE, RENEW

124—
- Exc Below 0.4
- Sport Coupe 0.3
- Spider 0.3

128 .... 1.4

850—
- Exc Below 0.6
- Spider 0.4

X 1/9 .... 0.8

131—
- Sedan 0.7
- Wagon 1.0

6—OIL GAUGE (DASH UNIT), RENEW

Includes R&R inst board

124—
- Exc Below 0.4
- Sport Coupe 1.4

850 .... 0.8

128 .... 0.5

X 1/9 .... 0.7

7—OIL GAUGE SENDING UNIT, RENEW

124—
- Exc Below 0.2
- Sport Coupe 0.3
- Spider 0.3

128 .... 0.2

850 .... 0.3

X 1/9 .... 0.4

131 .... 0.3

8—TEMPERATURE GAUGE (DASH UNIT), RENEW

Includes R&R inst board.

124—
- Exc Below 0.7
- Sport Coupe 0.5
- Spider 0.5

128 .... 0.7

850—
- Exc Below 0.4
- Sport Coupe 0.8
- Spider 0.8

X 1/9 .... 0.7

124 T.C. 0.7

131 .... 0.7

9—TEMPERATURE GAUGE SENDING UNIT, RENEW

124 .... 0.3

128 .... 0.2

850—
- Exc Below 0.2
- Sport Coupe 0.3
- Spider 0.3

X 1/9 .... 0.3

131 .... 0.3

10—HEADLIGHT SWITCH, RENEW

All Models 0.2

11—HIGH BEAM RELAY, RENEW

All Models 0.2

12—STOP LIGHT SWITCH, RENEW

All Models 0.2

13—TURN SIGNAL SWITCH, RENEW

124—
- Exc Below 0.6
- Sport Coupe 0.4
- Spider 0.4

128 .... 0.6

850 .... 0.7

X 1/9 .... 0.6

14—BACK-UP LAMP SWITCH, RENEW

Exc Below 0.2

124 & 131 Auto Trans 0.4

IDENTIFICATION

ALL MODELS....................................157 & 158

ILLUSTRATIONS

FIG 1 – ENGINE CYLINDER HEAD & ROCKER ARM
FIG 2 – ENGINE BLOCK & PLUGS
FIG 3 – ENGINE TIMING GEAR & CHAIN COVER
FIG 4 – ENGINE OIL PAN & FILTER
FIG 5 – ENGINE CAMSHAFT & VALVES
FIG 6 – ENGINE CRANKSHAFT & PISTONS
FIG 7 – CLUTCH
FIG 8 – TRANSAXLE CASE
FIG 9 – TRANSAXLE GEAR TRAIN
FIG 10 – TRANSAXLE DIFFERENTIAL
FIG 11 – TRANSAXLE SHIFT FORKS & PIVOT SHAFT
FIG 12 – FRONT SUSPENSION ARMS, BRACKETS & BAR
FIG 13 – FRONT SUSPENSION SPRING & SHOCK ABSORBER
FIG 14 – STEERING GEAR & LINKAGE
FIG 15 – STEERING COLUMN
FIG 16 – REAR SUSPENSION

OPERATION TIMES

A

Air Pump.. 174
Alternator.. 174
Ammeter.. 177
Automatic Transmission.................... 175
Axle Shaft.. 176

B

Brake Drums.. 176
Brakes.. 176

C

Cables (Ignition).............................. 174
Calipers.. 176
Camshaft.. 175
Carburetor.. 174
Clutch.. 175
Coil, Ignition.. 174
Compression Test.............................. 174
Connecting Rods.............................. 175
Cooling System.............................. 174
Crankshaft.. 175
Cylinder Block.............................. 175
Cylinder Head.............................. 175

D

Dash Gauges.. 176
Differential.. 176
Disc Brakes.. 176
Distributor.. 174

E

Emission Controls.............................. 174
Engine Assembly.............................. 175
Engine Mountings.............................. 175
Engine Oiling.............................. 175
Engine Tune-Up.............................. 174
Exhaust System.............................. 174

F

Flywheel.. 175
Front Suspension.............................. 176
Fuel Gauges.. 176
Fuel Pump.. 174
Fuel Tank.. 174

H

Hand Brake.. 176
Headlight Switch.............................. 177
Heater.. 174
Hose (Brake).. 176
Hose (Radiator).............................. 174
Hydraulic Brakes.............................. 176

I

Ignition.. 174
Ignition Coil.. 174
Ignition Switch.............................. 174
Intake Manifold.............................. 174

L

Light Switches.............................. 177

M

Main Bearings.............................. 175
Master Cylinder.............................. 176
Muffler.. 174

O

Oil Gauge.. 176
Oiling, Engine.............................. 175
Oil Pan.. 175
Oil Pump.. 175

P

Parking Brake.............................. 176
Piston Rings.............................. 175
Pistons.. 175
Power Brake.............................. 176

R

Radiator.. 174
Radiator Hose.............................. 174
Rear Axle.. 176
Regulator (Alternator).................... 174
Rocker Arms.............................. 175
Rod Bearings.............................. 175

S

Shocks (Front).............................. 176
Shocks (Rear).............................. 176
Speedometer.............................. 176
Springs (Front).............................. 176
Springs (Rear).............................. 176
Starting Motor.............................. 174
Steering Gear.............................. 176
Steering Linkage.............................. 176
Switches (light).............................. 177
Synchro-Mesh Trans.................... 175

T

Tachometer.. 177
Temperature Gauge.................... 177
Thermostat.. 174
Timing Case Cover.................... 175
Timing Chain.............................. 175
Timing Gears.............................. 175
Transmission, Manual.................... 175
Transmission, Automatic.................... 175
Tune-Up, Engine.............................. 174

U

Universals.. 176

V

Vacuum Control Unit.................... 174
Valve Lifters.............................. 175
Valve System.............................. 175

W

Water Pump.. 174
Wheel Cylinders.............................. 176
Windshield Wiper.............................. 176

FIESTA WARRANTY PLATE - TYPICAL

Located on the right hand fender apron in the engine compartment

The Warranty Plate includes -

1. Type and Vehicle Number (first line) consists of codes which identify Body Type, Year of Model Introduction, Country of Origin, Assembly Plant, Body Type, Calendar Year, Month and Numerical Sequence of Assembly.
2. Miscellaneous Vehicle Date (second line) consists of codes which identify Drive, Engine, Transmission, Rear Axle Ratio, Color of Exterior Paint and Trim.

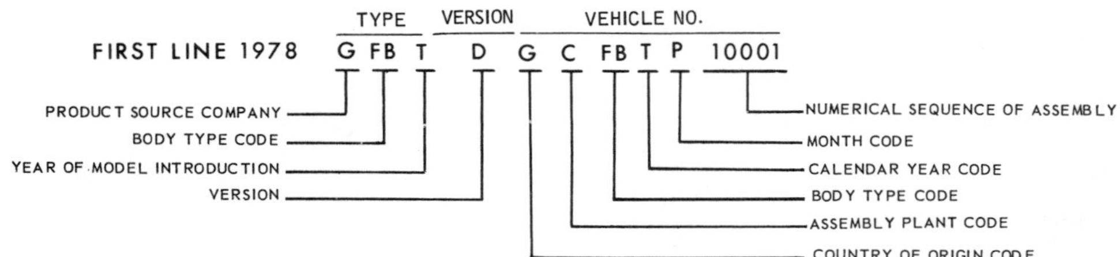

FB	---	3 Door Hatchback
G	---	Germany
C	---	Assembled at Saarlouis
T-U	---	T-1977 (Calendar Year) U-1978 (Calendar Year)
P	---	Month Code
10001	---	Numerical Sequence of Assembly

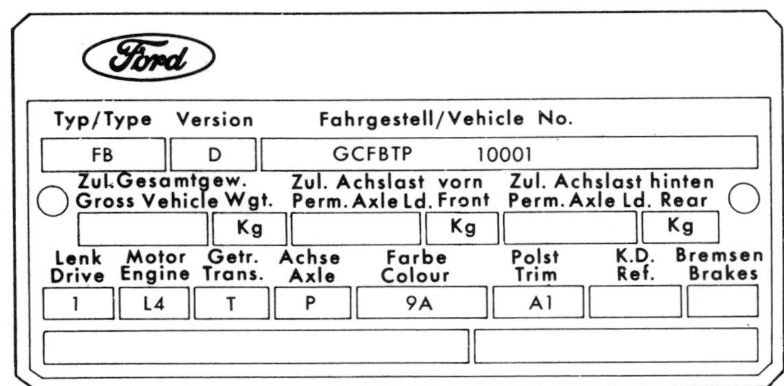

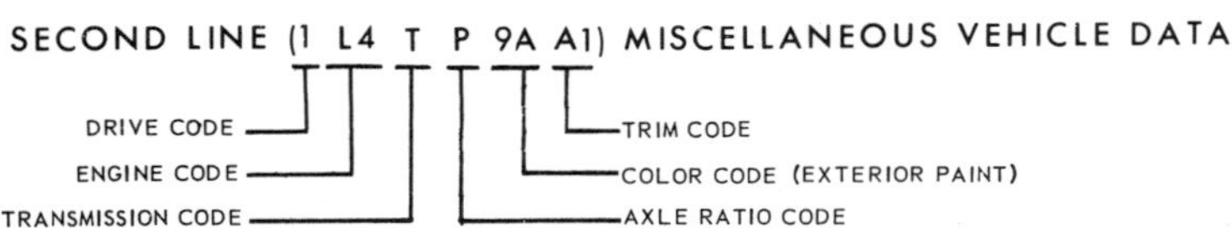

1	---	Left Hand Drive
L4	---	1.6 Litre
T	---	4 Speed Manual
P	---	Axle Ratio of 3.58 to 1
9A	---	Yellow (9) with Black Vinyl Roof (A)
A1	---	Black (A) with Cloth/Vinyl (1)

FIESTA WARRANTY PLATE - TYPICAL - continued

DRIVE CODES

1 - Left Hand Drive

YEAR of MODEL INTRODUCTION

U - 1978: For Model Year 1978

ENGINE CODES

L4 - (1.6 Litre)

TRANSMISSION CODES

T - 4 Speed Manual Transmission

AXLE RATIO CODES

P - 3.58 to 1

COUNTRY of ORIGIN CODES

G - Germany

ASSEMBLY PLANT CODES

C - Sarrlouis

VERSION

D - 64D (Decor 3 Door Sedan)
P - 64P (Ghia 3 Door Sedan)
R - 64R (Sport 3 Door Sedan)
S - 64S (3 Door Sedan)

BODY TYPE CODES

FB - 3 Door Hatchback

CALENDAR YEAR CODES

(First Digit of Date Code)
T - 1977
U - 1978

COLOR CODES (EXTERIOR PAINT)

Single digit code indicates solid color. Two digit code indicates solid color with vinyl roof cover. For a listing of these codes and the part number of the required paint refer to Paint Section.

TRIM CODES

First digit indicates color. . . . . Second digit indicates type of fabric

MONTH CODES

(Second Digit of Date Code)

MONTH CODE	1977 CALENDAR YEAR CODE T	1978 CALENDAR YEAR CODE U
A	July	November
B	May	September
C	September	
D	November	
E	December	
G	August	December
J	January	May
K	October	
L		January
M	March	July
P	April	August
R	June	October
S		March
T		April
U	February	June
Y		February

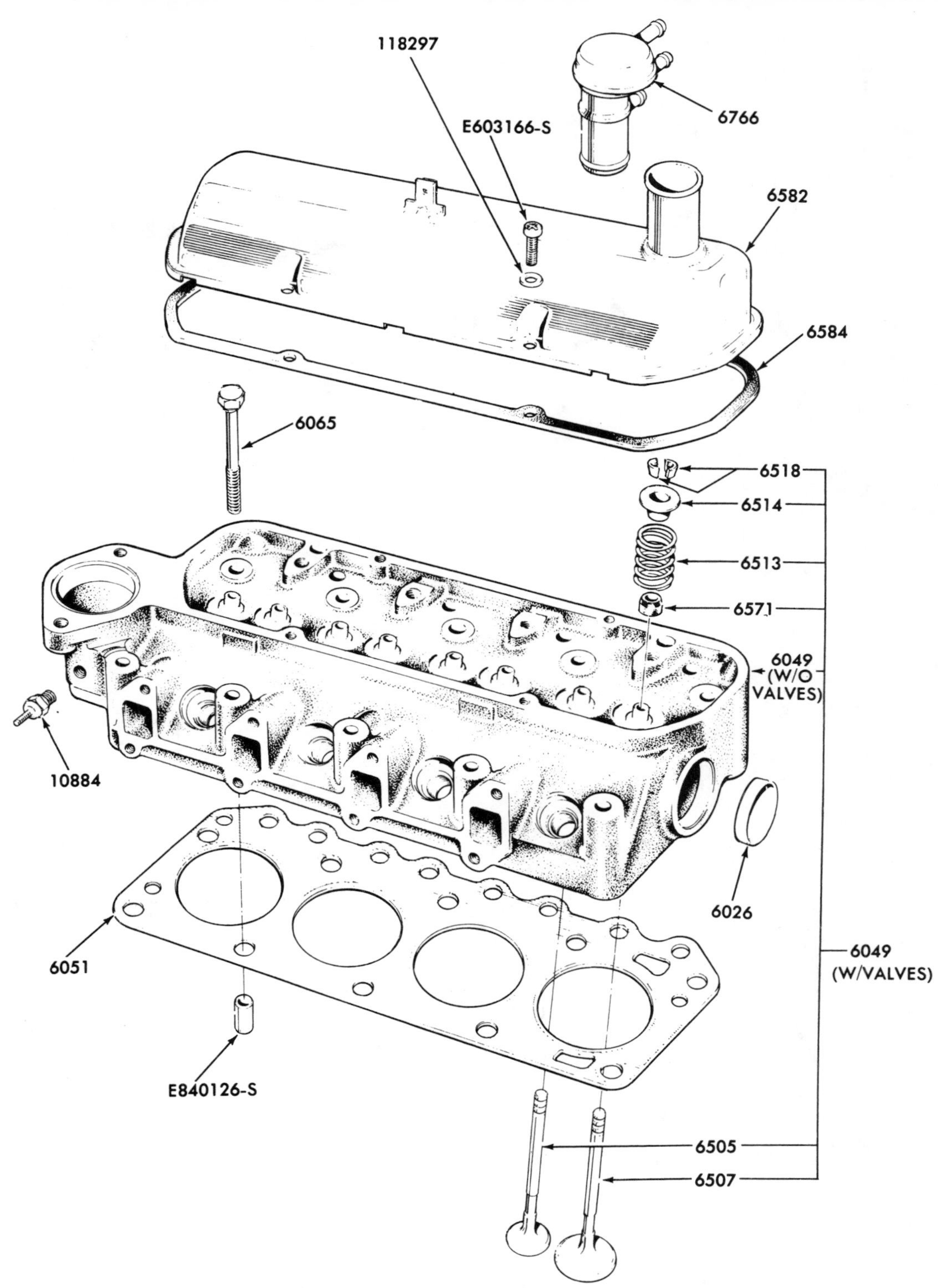

FIG 1 – ENGINE CYLINDER HEAD & ROCKER ARM

6026	Plug	6514	Retainer
6049	Head	6518	Key
6051	Gasket	6571	Seal
6065	Bolt	6582	Cover
6505	Valve-Exhaust	6584	Gasket
6507	Valve Intake	6766	Cap
6513	Spring		

6055
87837-S
(P-15)
9278
6767
87837-S
(P-15)
E830100-S
87837-S
(P-15)
6026
6026
6010
6345
6026

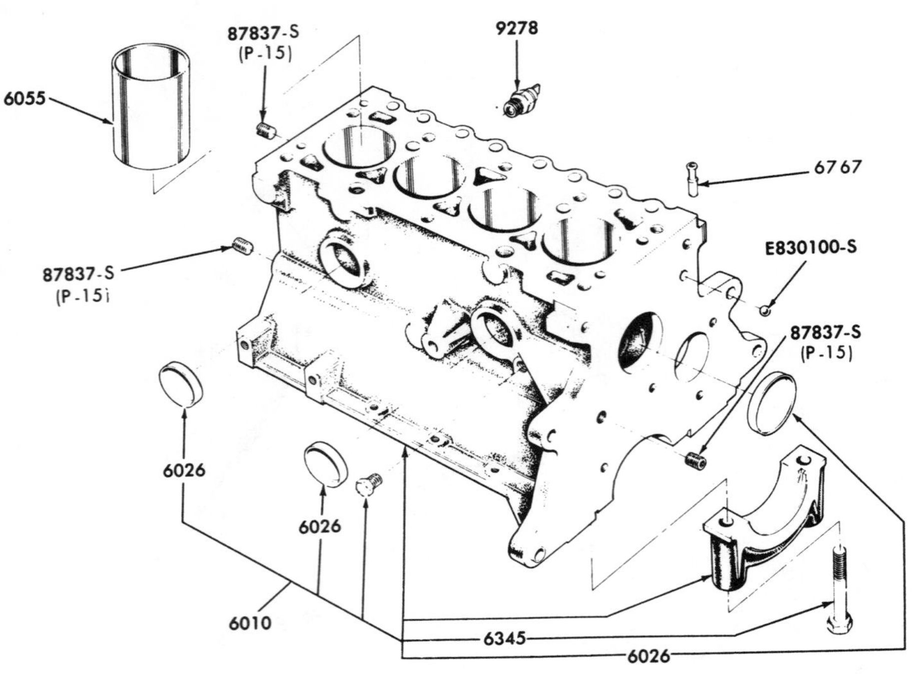

FIG 2 – ENGINE BLOCK & PLUGS

6010	Block
6026	Plug
6055	Liner
6345	Bolt
6767	Elbow
9278	Gauge

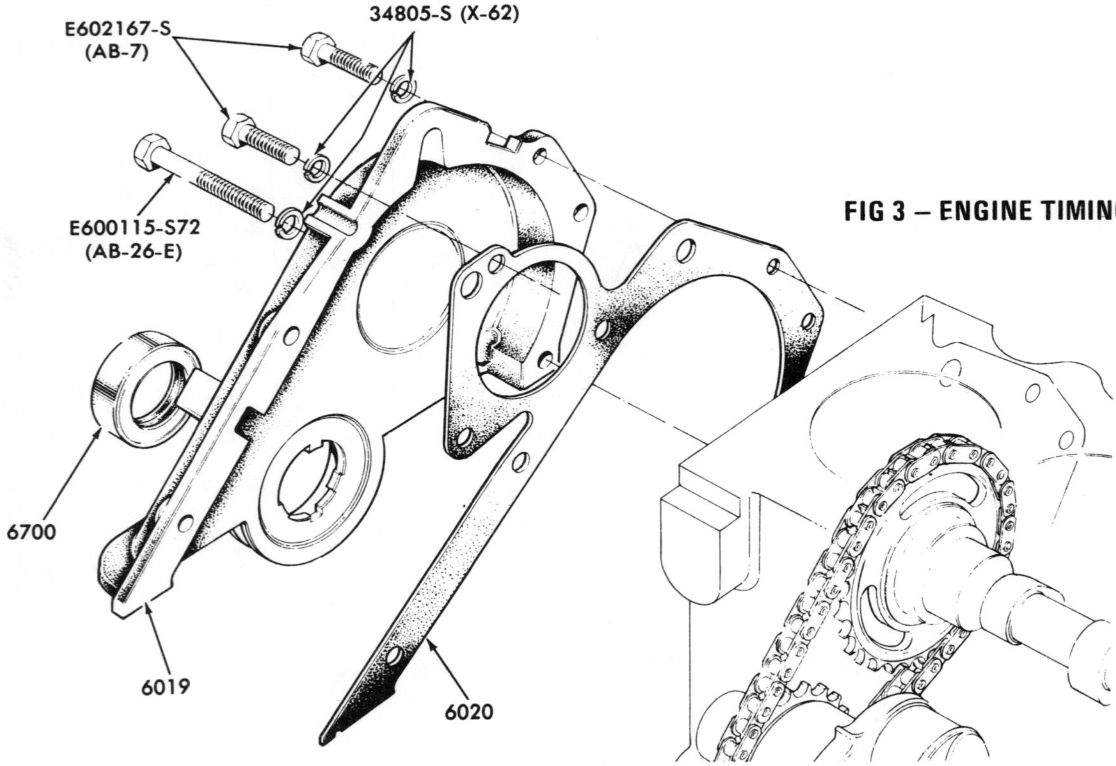

E602167-S
(AB-7)
34805-S (X-62)
E600115-S72
(AB-26-E)
6700
6019
6020

FIG 3 – ENGINE TIMING GEAR & CHAIN COVER

6019	Cover
6020	Gasket
6700	Seal

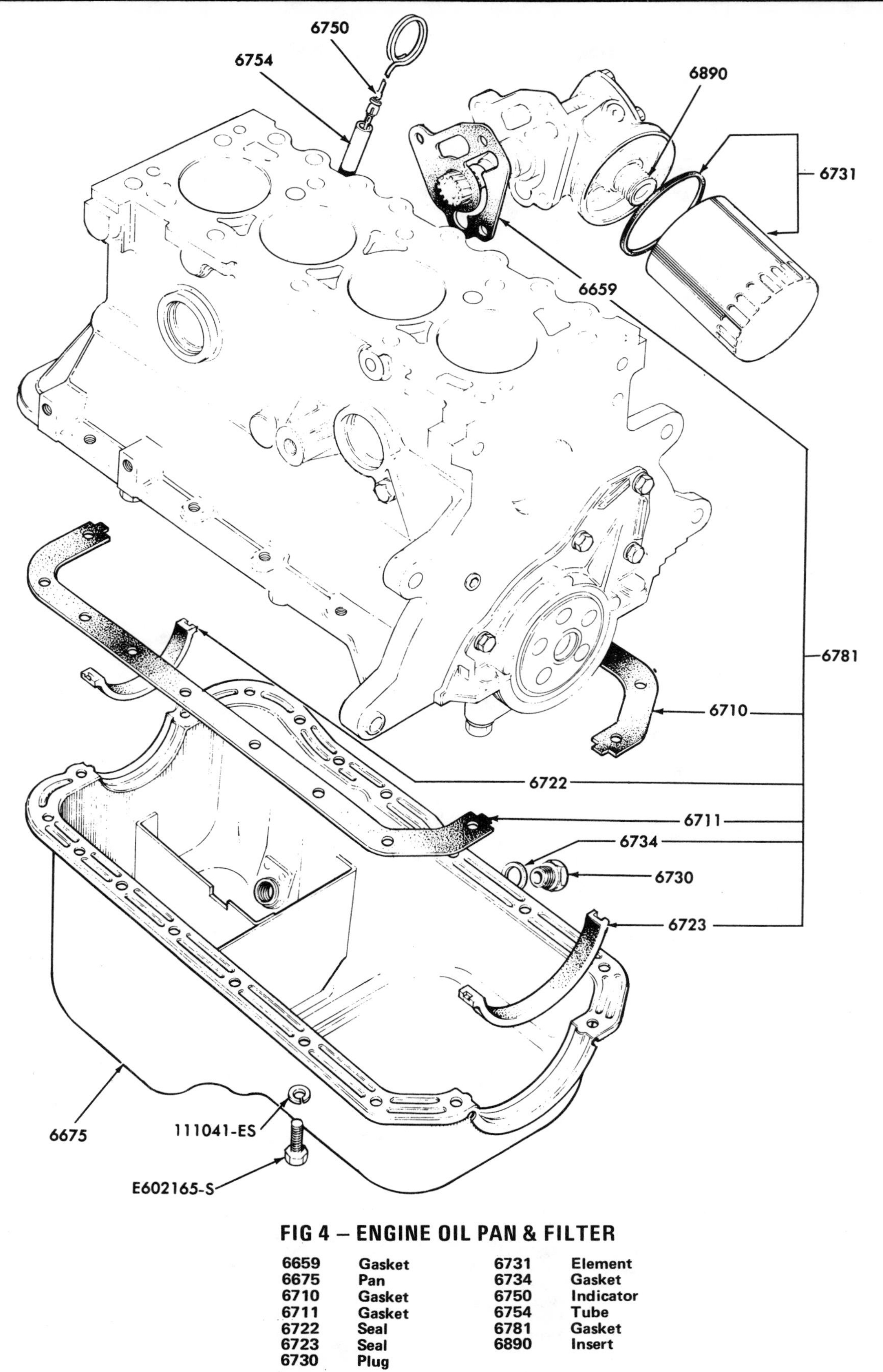

FIG 4 – ENGINE OIL PAN & FILTER

6659	Gasket	6731	Element
6675	Pan	6734	Gasket
6710	Gasket	6750	Indicator
6711	Gasket	6754	Tube
6722	Seal	6781	Gasket
6723	Seal	6890	Insert
6730	Plug		

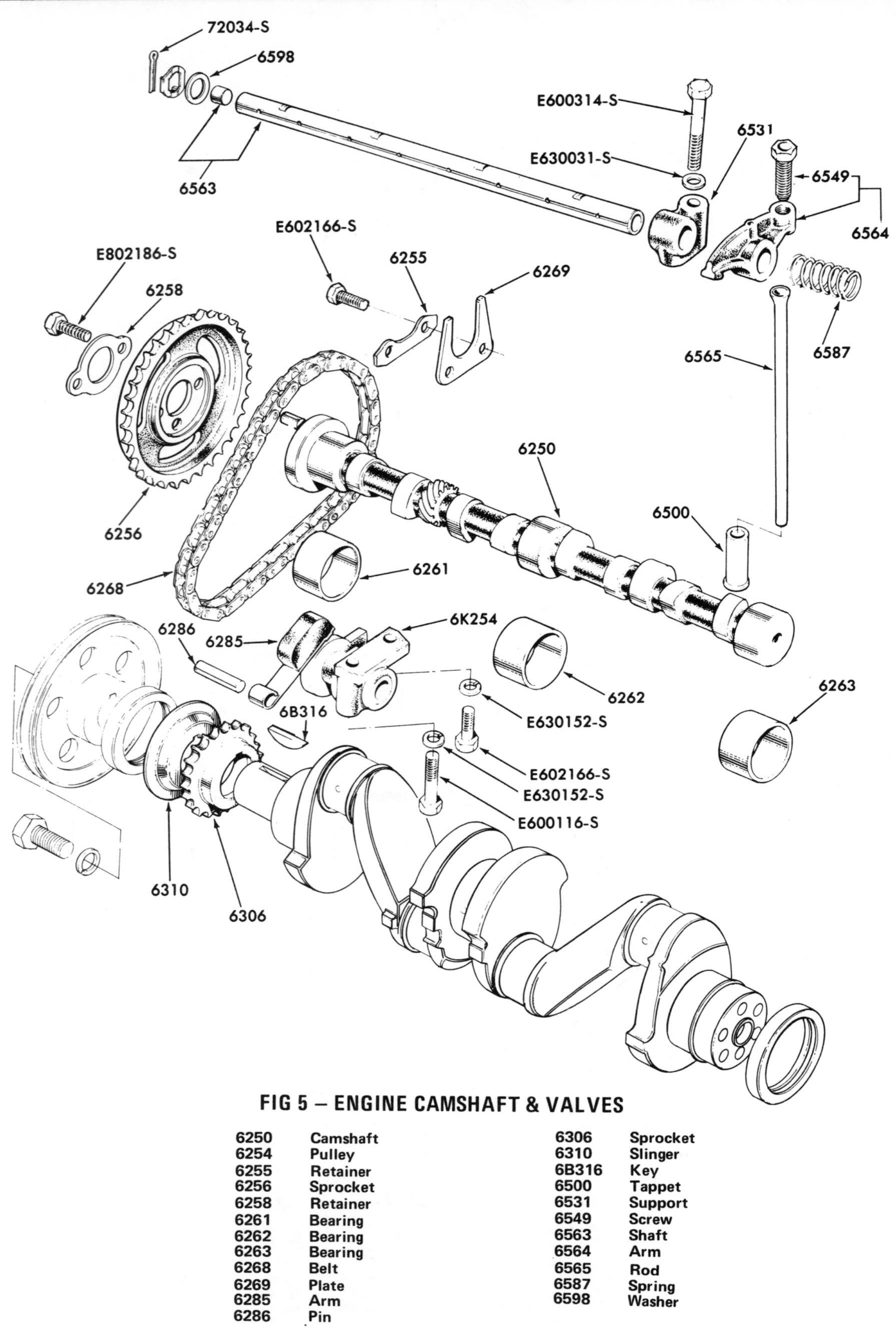

FIG 5 – ENGINE CAMSHAFT & VALVES

6250	Camshaft	6306	Sprocket
6254	Pulley	6310	Slinger
6255	Retainer	6B316	Key
6256	Sprocket	6500	Tappet
6258	Retainer	6531	Support
6261	Bearing	6549	Screw
6262	Bearing	6563	Shaft
6263	Bearing	6564	Arm
6268	Belt	6565	Rod
6269	Plate	6587	Spring
6285	Arm	6598	Washer
6286	Pin		

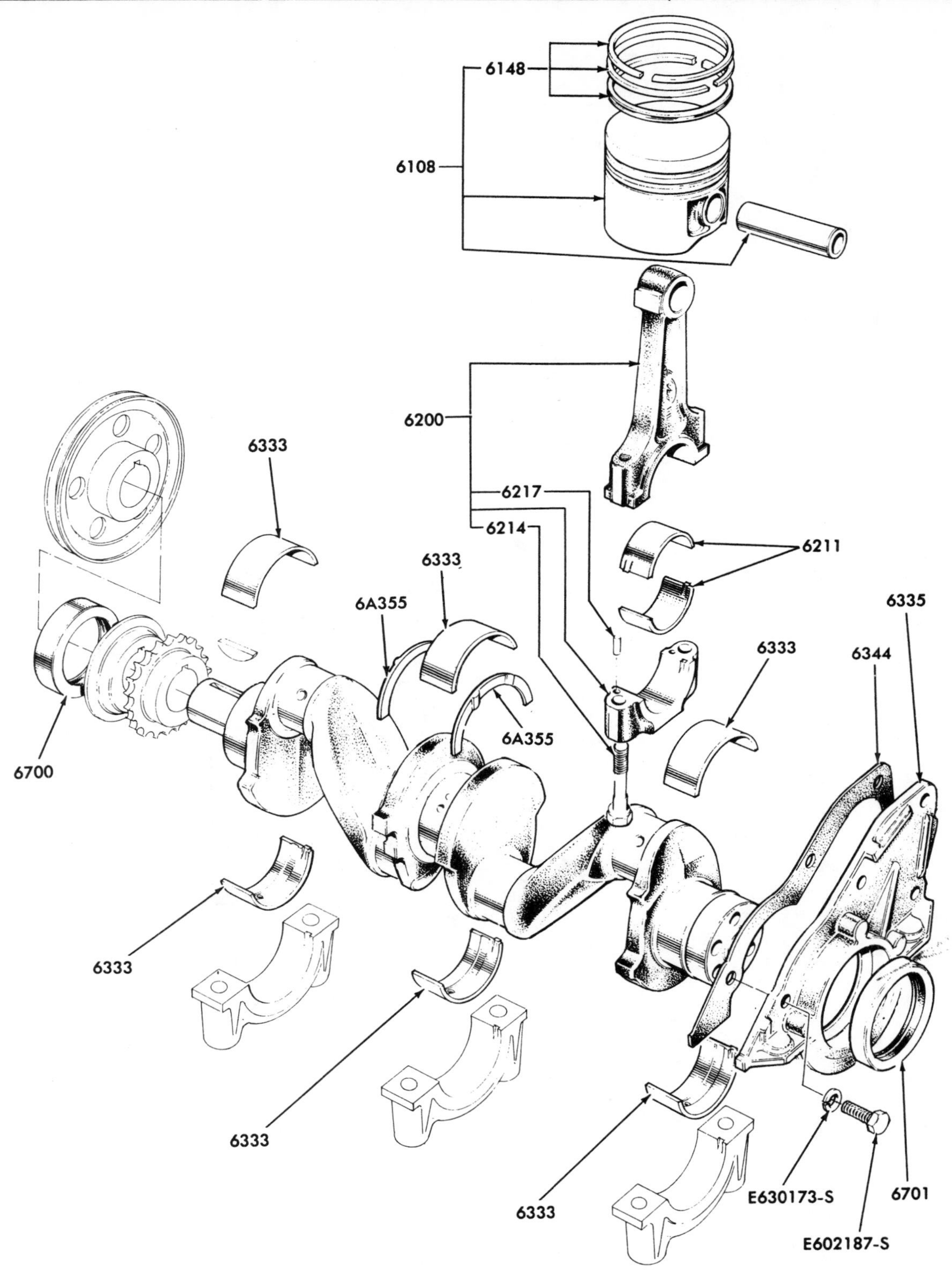

FIG 6 – ENGINE CRANKSHAFT & PISTONS

6108	Piston	6333	Bearing
6148	Ring Set	6335	Bearing
6200	Rod	6344	Gasket
6211	Bearing	6A355	Washer
6214	Bolt	6700	Seal
6217	Dowel		

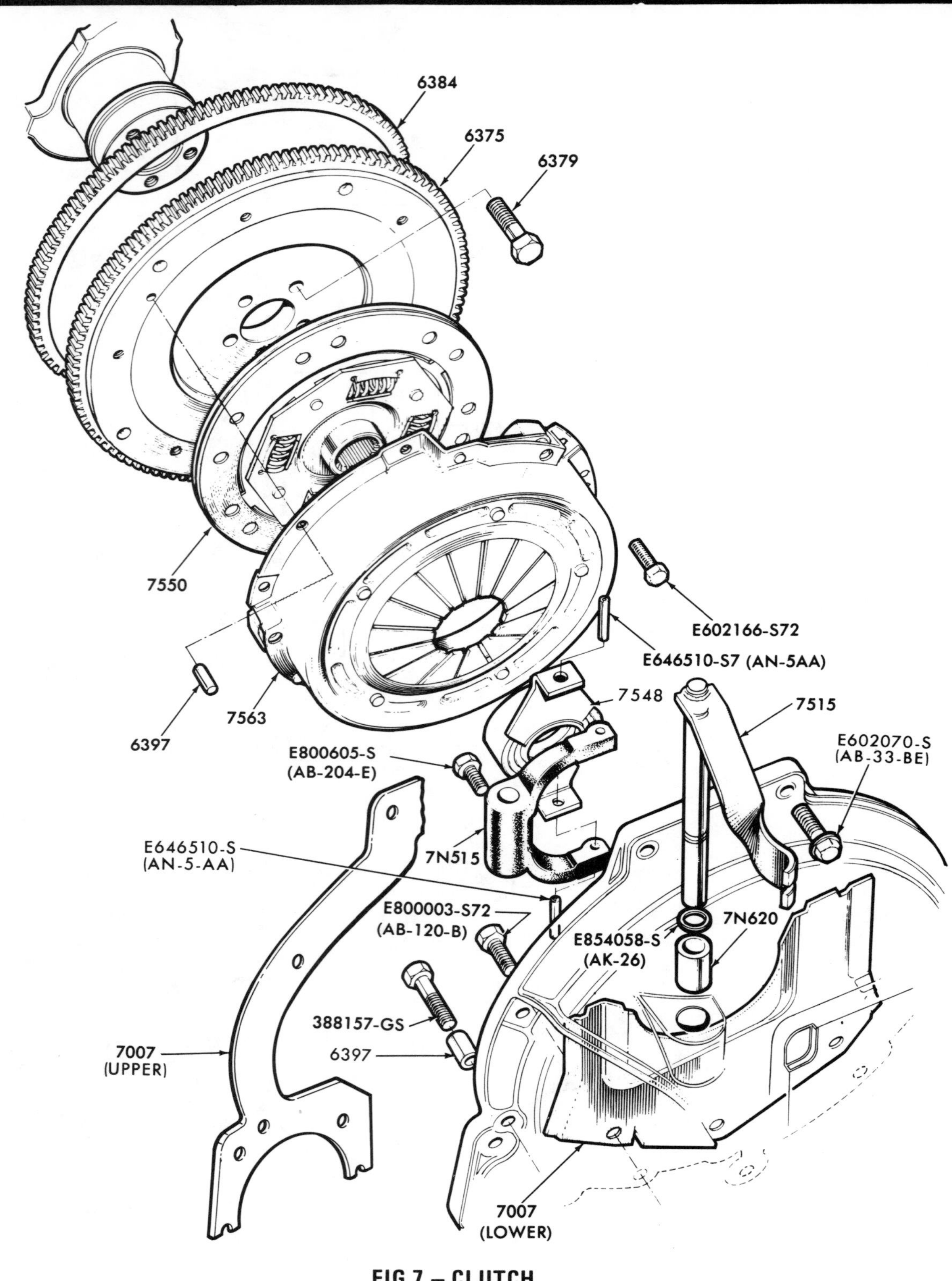

FIG 7 – CLUTCH

6375	Flywheel	7N515	Fork
6379	Bolt	7548	Hub
6384	Gear	7550	Disc
6397	Dowel	7563	Plate
7007	Plate	7N620	Bushing
7515	Lever		

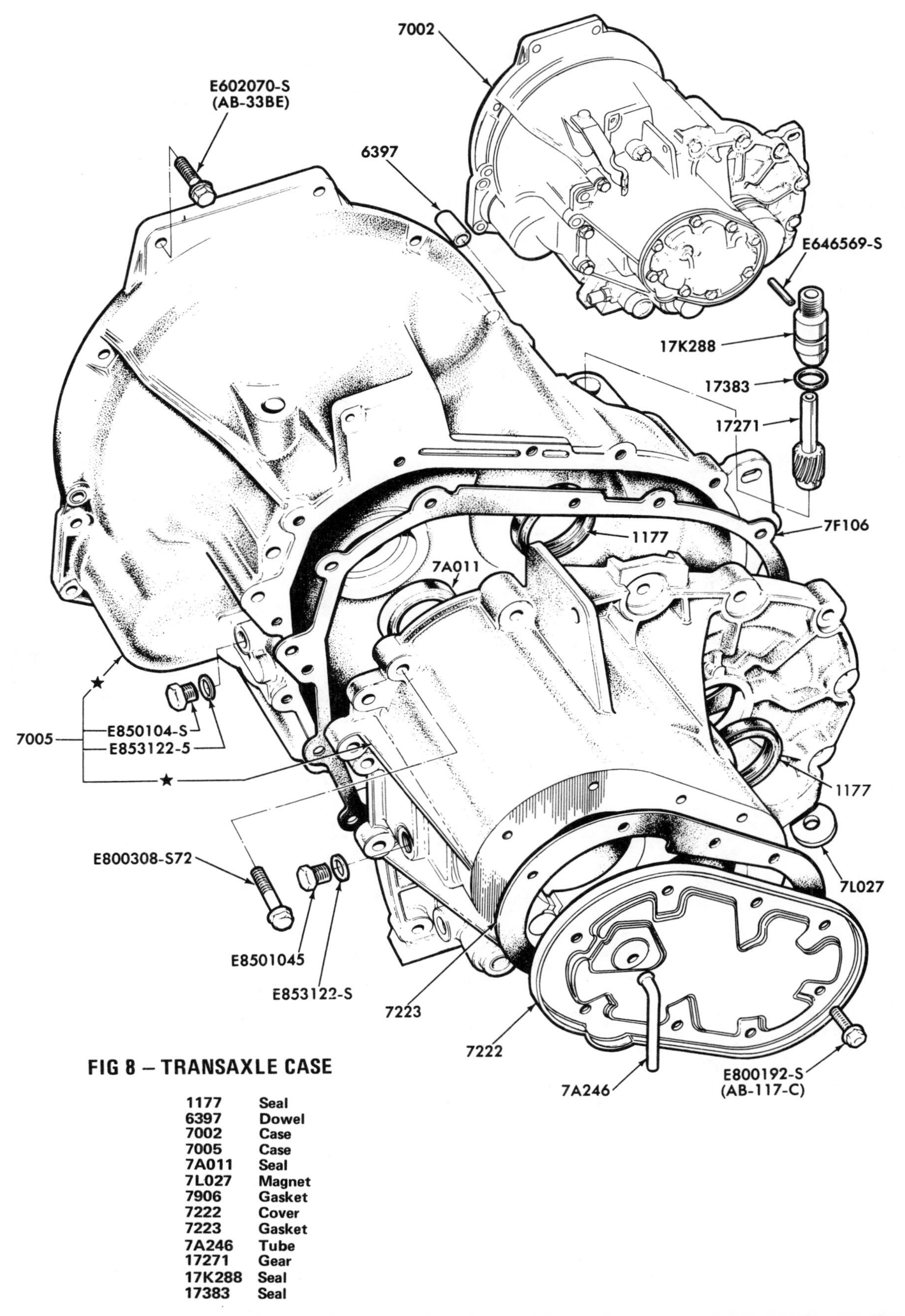

FIG 8 – TRANSAXLE CASE

1177	Seal
6397	Dowel
7002	Case
7005	Case
7A011	Seal
7L027	Magnet
7906	Gasket
7222	Cover
7223	Gasket
7A246	Tube
17271	Gear
17K288	Seal
17383	Seal

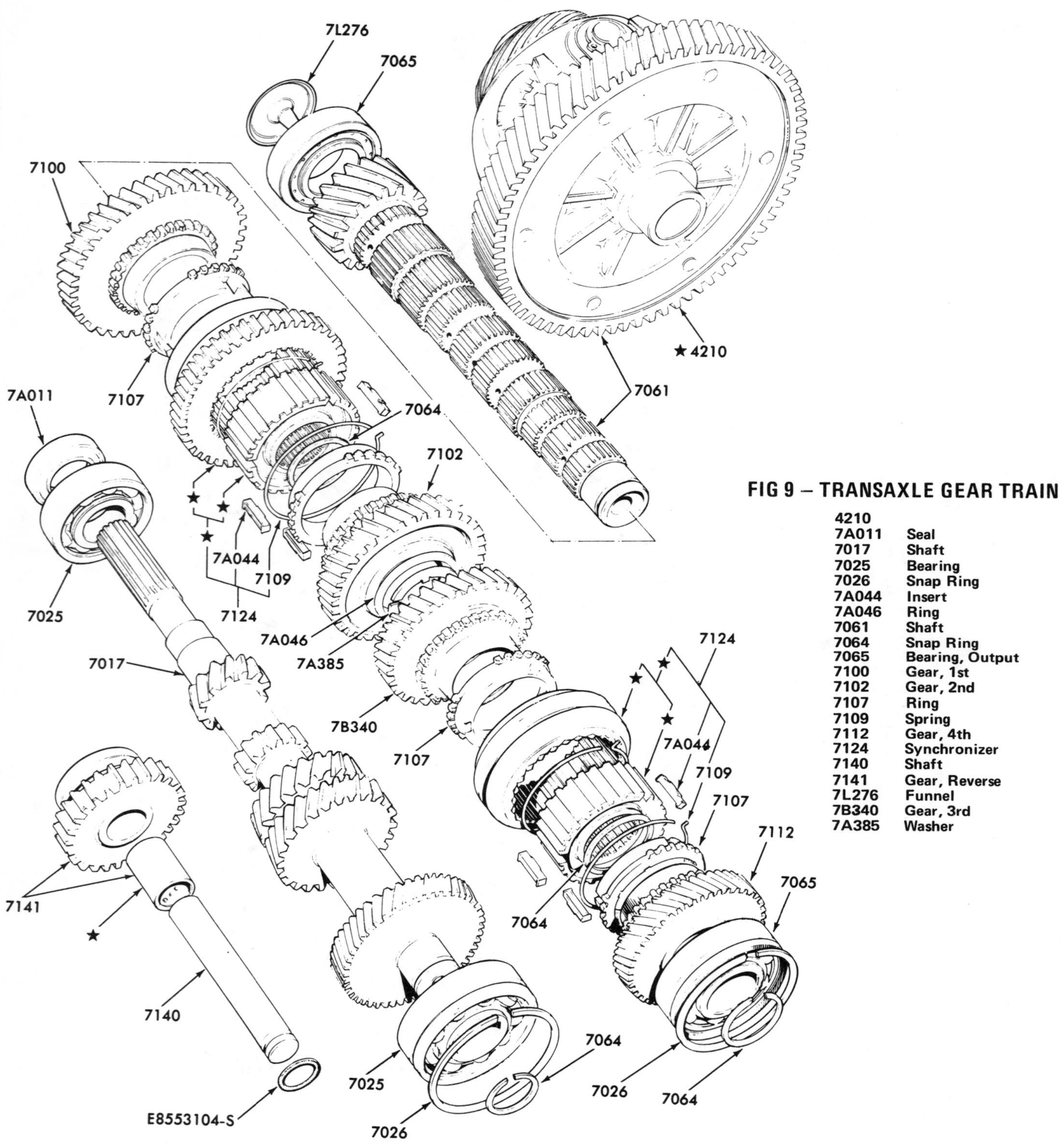

FIG 9 – TRANSAXLE GEAR TRAIN

4210	
7A011	Seal
7017	Shaft
7025	Bearing
7026	Snap Ring
7A044	Insert
7A046	Ring
7061	Shaft
7064	Snap Ring
7065	Bearing, Output
7100	Gear, 1st
7102	Gear, 2nd
7107	Ring
7109	Spring
7112	Gear, 4th
7124	Synchronizer
7140	Shaft
7141	Gear, Reverse
7L276	Funnel
7B340	Gear, 3rd
7A385	Washer

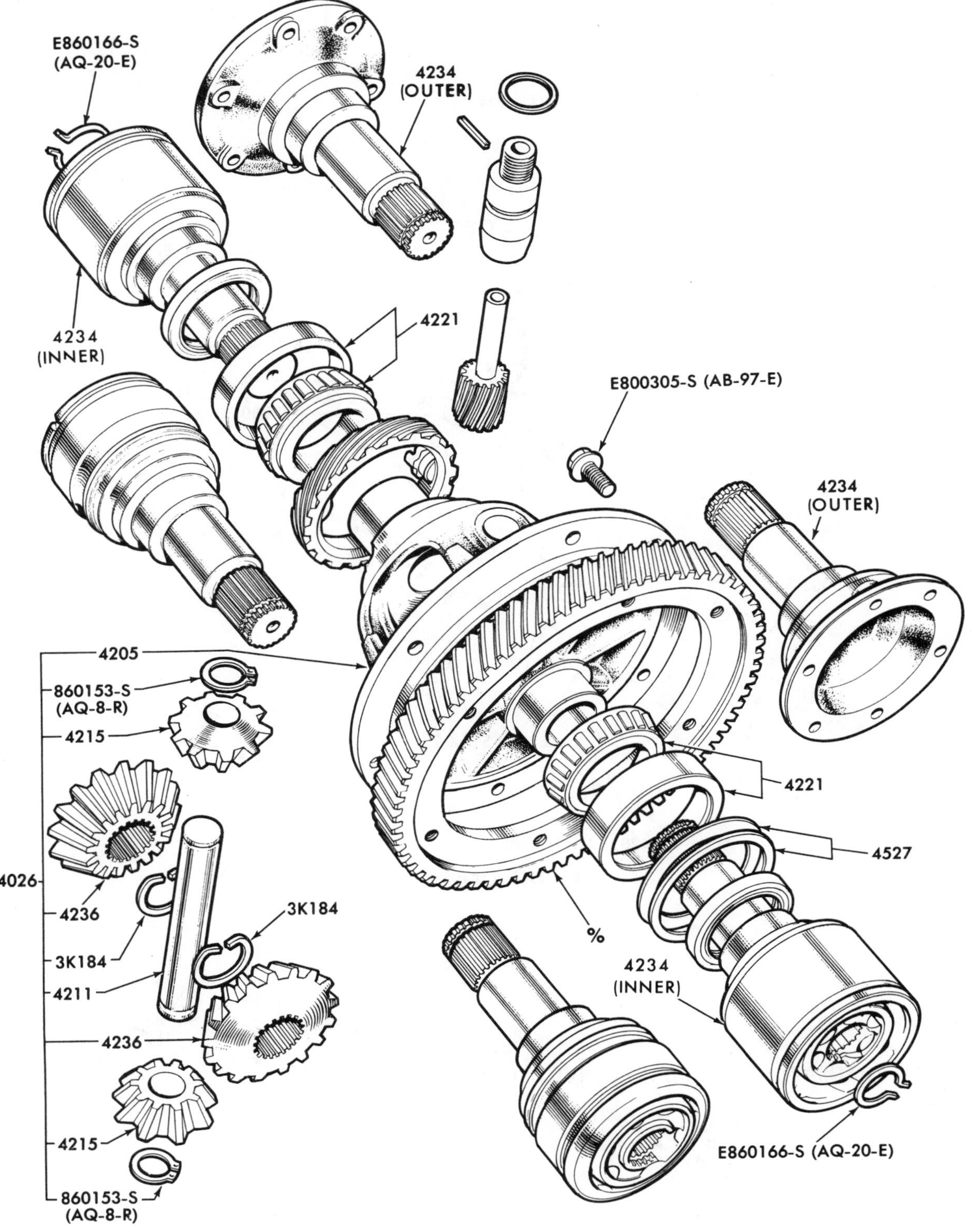

%SERVICED ONLY IN 7061 OUTPUT SHAFT GEAR SET

FIG 10 – TRANSAXLE DIFFERENTIAL

3K184	Ring
4026	Differential
4211	Shaft
4215	Pinion
4221	Cone & Roller
4234	Shaft
4236	Gear

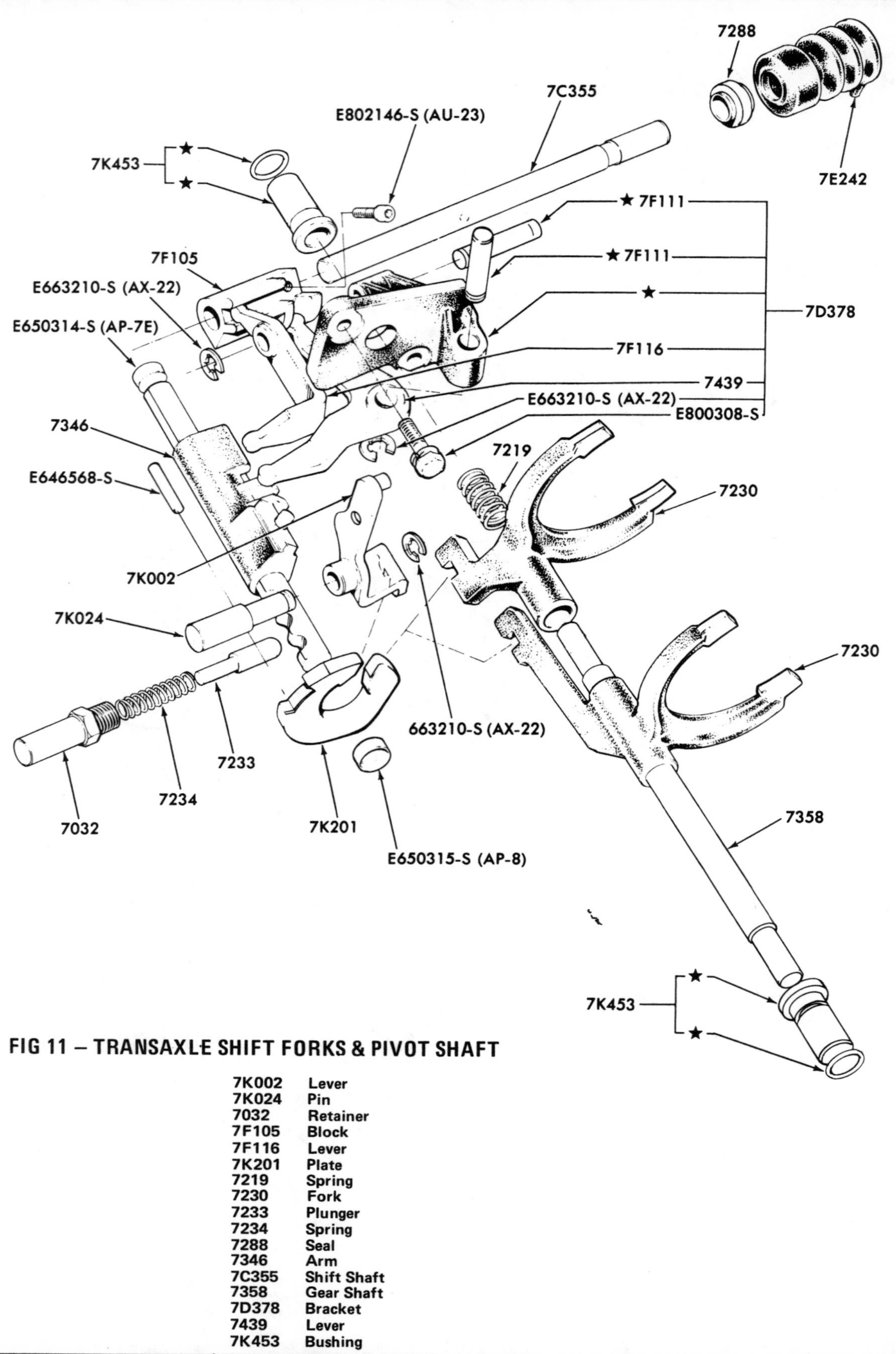

FIG 11 – TRANSAXLE SHIFT FORKS & PIVOT SHAFT

7K002	Lever
7K024	Pin
7032	Retainer
7F105	Block
7F116	Lever
7K201	Plate
7219	Spring
7230	Fork
7233	Plunger
7234	Spring
7288	Seal
7346	Arm
7C355	Shift Shaft
7358	Gear Shaft
7D378	Bracket
7439	Lever
7K453	Bushing

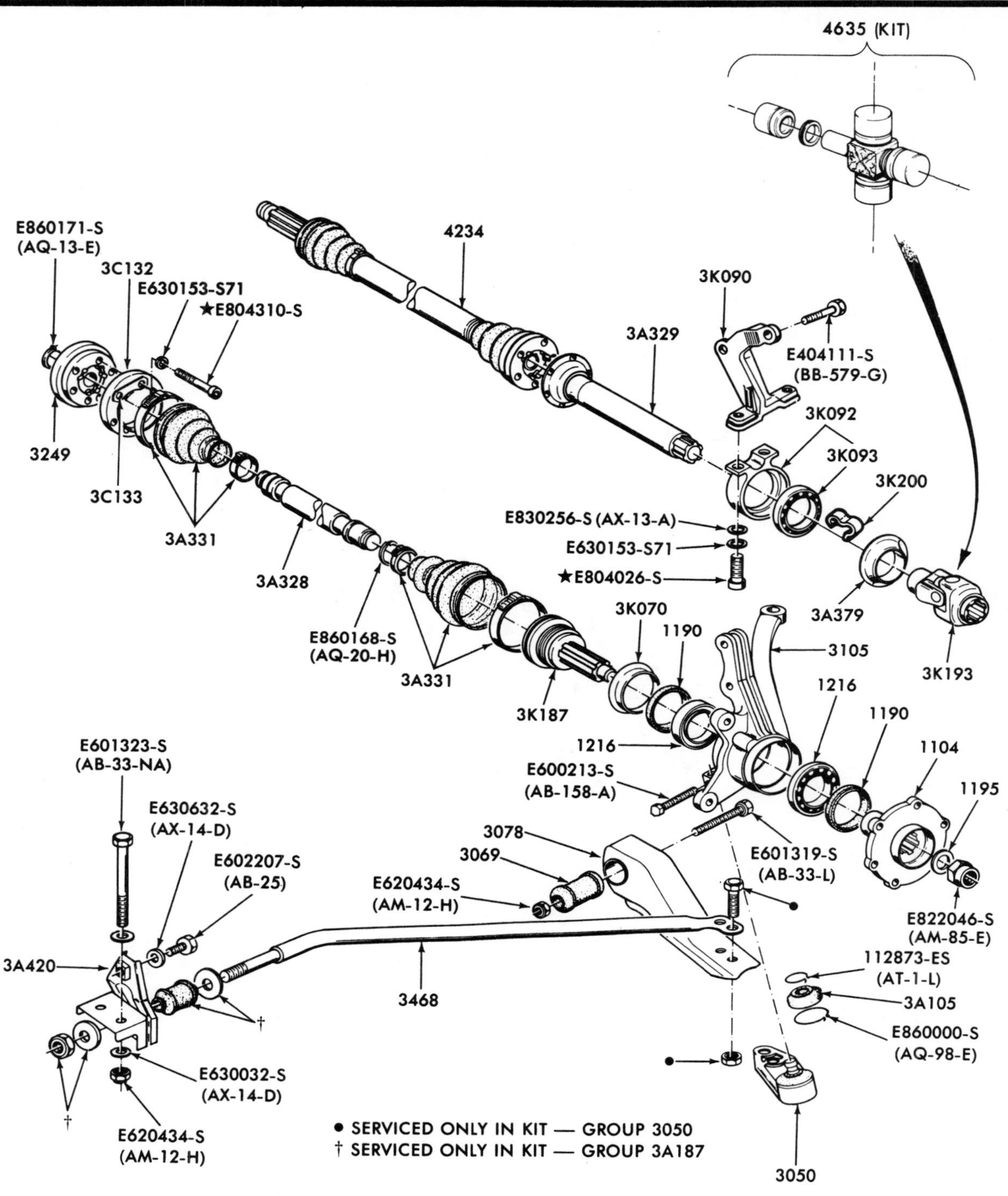

FIG 12 – FRONT SUSPENSION ARMS, BRACKETS & BAR

1104	Hub	3K092	Support	3249	Universal
1190	Retainer	3K093	Bearing	3A329	Shaft
1195	Washer	3105	Spindle	3A331	Boot
1216	Cone & Roller	3C132	Slinger	3A379	Deflector
3050	Joint	3C133	Plate	3A420	Bracket
3069	Bushing	3K187	Joint	3468	Strut
3K070	Shield	3K193	Yoke	4234	Shaft
3078	Arm	3K200	Clip	4635	Universal
3K090	Bracket				

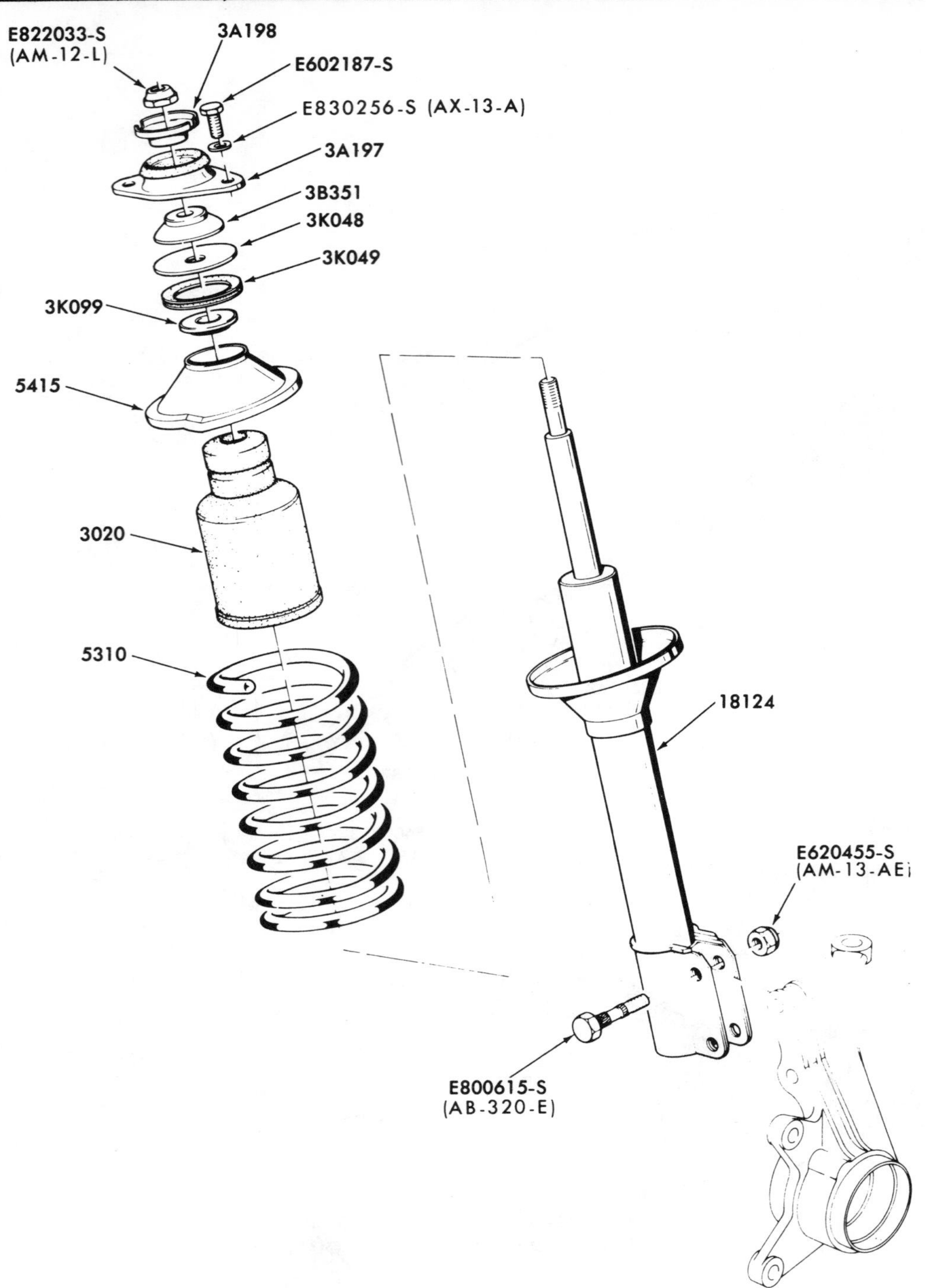

FIG 13 – FRONT SUSPENSION SPRING & SHOCK ABSORBER

3020	Bumper
3K048	Bushing
3K049	Seal
3K099	Bearing
3A197	Plate
3A198	Retainer
3B351	Spacer
5310	Spring
5415	Insulator
18124	Shock

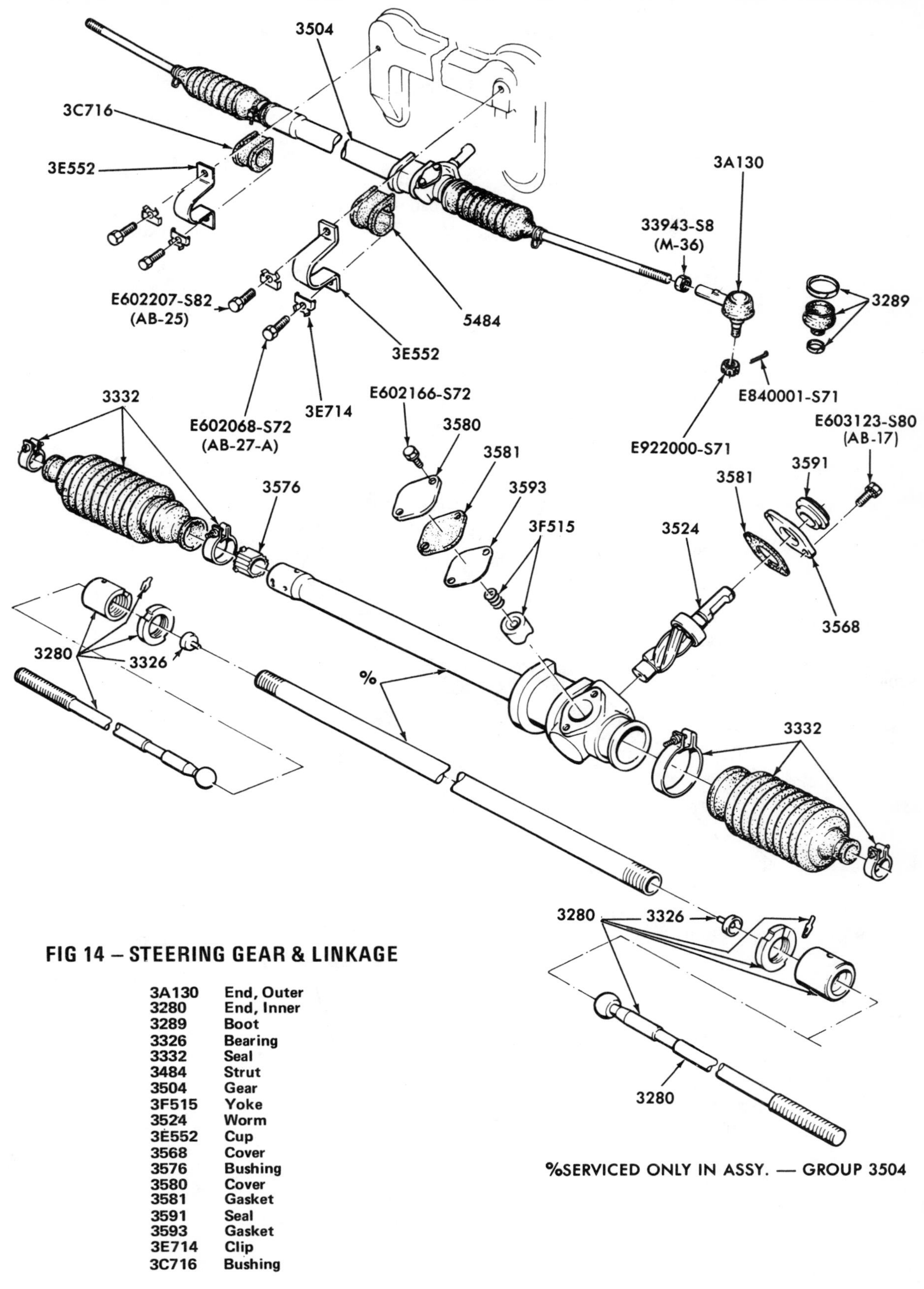

FIG 14 – STEERING GEAR & LINKAGE

3A130	End, Outer
3280	End, Inner
3289	Boot
3326	Bearing
3332	Seal
3484	Strut
3504	Gear
3F515	Yoke
3524	Worm
3E552	Cup
3568	Cover
3576	Bushing
3580	Cover
3581	Gasket
3591	Seal
3593	Gasket
3E714	Clip
3C716	Bushing

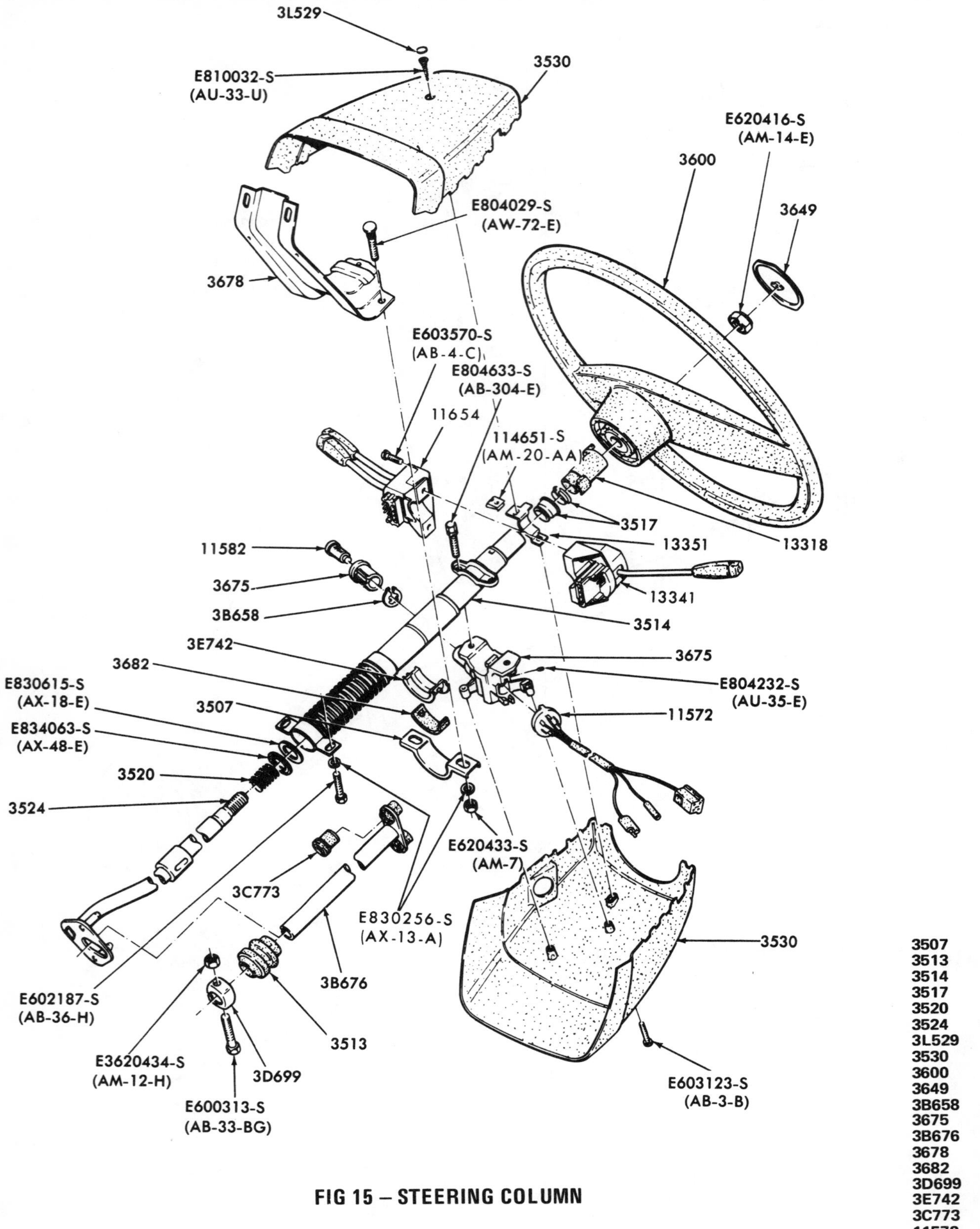

FIG 15 – STEERING COLUMN

3507	Clamp
3513	Seal
3514	Tube
3517	Bearing
3520	Spring
3524	Worm
3L529	Bumper
3530	Shroud
3600	Wheel
3649	Emblem
3B658	Plate
3675	Cylinder
3B676	Tube
3678	Bracket
3682	Insulator
3D699	Clamp
3E742	Spacer
3C773	Bushing
11572	Cylinder
11582	Switch
13318	Cam
13341	Switch

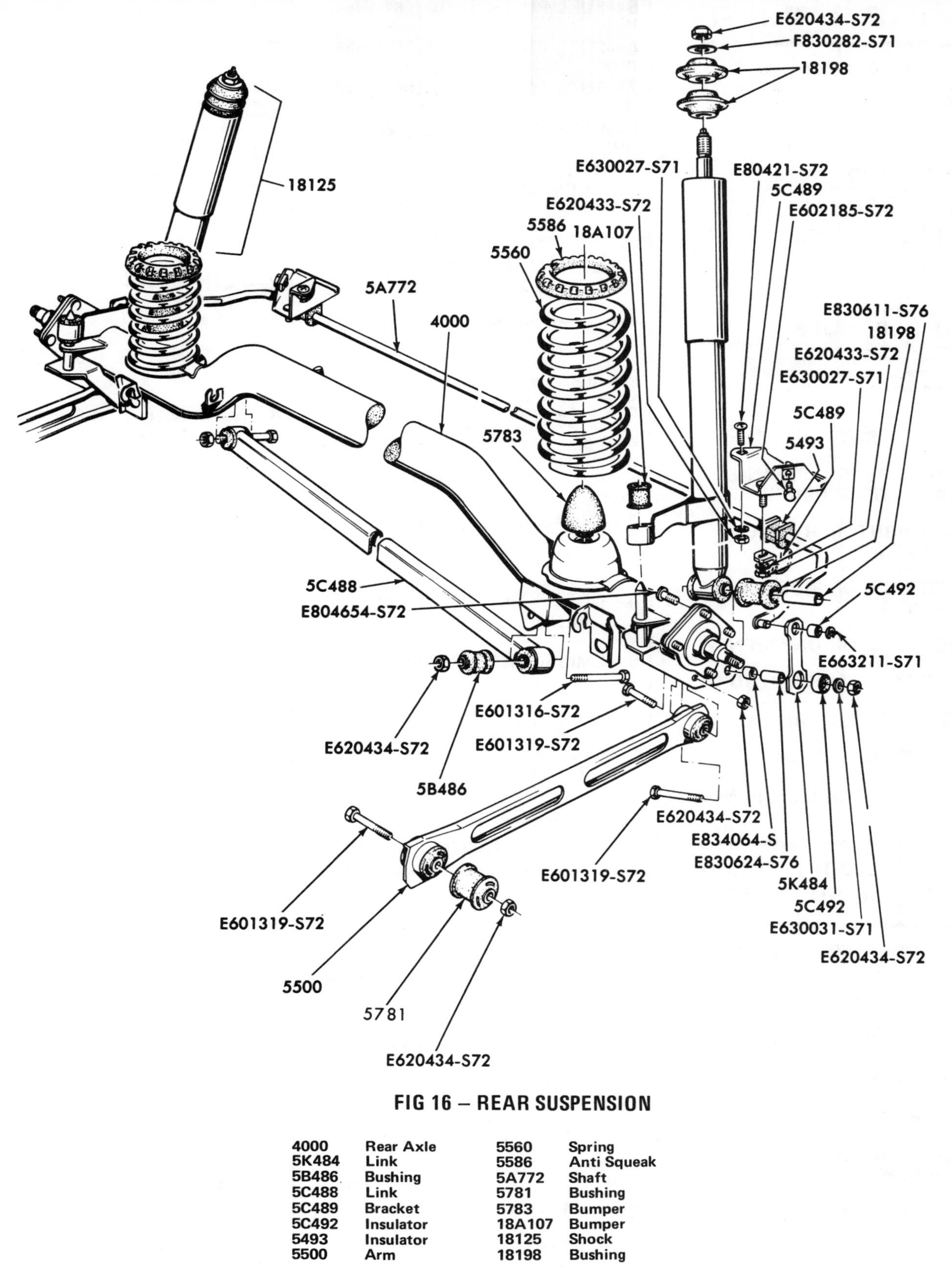

FIG 16 – REAR SUSPENSION

4000	Rear Axle	5560	Spring
5K484	Link	5586	Anti Squeak
5B486	Bushing	5A772	Shaft
5C488	Link	5781	Bushing
5C489	Bracket	5783	Bumper
5C492	Insulator	18A107	Bumper
5493	Insulator	18125	Shock
5500	Arm	18198	Bushing

Tune-Up & Ignition—TIME

OPERATION INDEX

Tune-Up, Minor *1*
Tune-Up, Major *2*
Compression, Test *3*
Spark Plugs, Clean & Adjust Or Renew *4*
Distributor, R & R Or Renew *5*
Distributor Modulator, Renew *6*
Distributor Cap, Renew *7*
Ignition Timing, Adjust *8*
Ignition Coil, Renew *9*
Ignition Switch, Renew *10*
Ignition Cables, Renew *11*

1—TUNE-UP, MINOR
Includes renew plugs, set spark timing & adjust carburetor idle.
1978 .... 0.9

2—TUNE-UP, MAJOR
Includes check compression, clean or renew & adjust spark plugs, R & R distributor, adjust ign timing, carburetor & fan belts. Clean battery terminals & service air cleaner. Check coil, replace fuel filter.
1978 .... 1.9

3—COMPRESSION, TEST
1978 .... 0.3

4—SPARK PLUGS, CLEAN & ADJUST OR RENEW
1978 .... 0.3

5—DISTRIBUTOR, R & R OR RENEW
1978 .... 0.5

6—DISTRIBUTOR MODULATOR, RENEW
1978 .... 0.4

7—DISTRIBUTOR CAP, RENEW
1978 .... 0.3

8—IGNITION TIMING, ADJUST
1978 .... 0.3

9—IGNITION COIL, RENEW
1978 .... 0.4

10—IGNITION SWITCH, RENEW
1978 .... 0.3

11—IGNITION CABLES, RENEW
1978 .... 0.4

Fuel System & Intake Manifold—TIME

OPERATION INDEX

Carburetor, Adjust *1*
Carburetor, R & R Or Renew *2*
Carburetor, R & R & Overhaul *3*
Float Needle & Seat, Renew *4*
Fuel Pump, Test *5*
Fuel Pump, R & R Or Renew *6*
Fuel Tank, R & R Or Renew *7*
Intake Manifold, Renew *8*
Intake Manifold Basket, Renew *9*

1—CARBURETOR, ADJUST
1978 .... 0.4

2—CARBURETOR, R & R OR RENEW
1978 .... 0.5

3—CARBURETOR, R & R & OVERHAUL
1978 .... 1.1

4—FLOAT NEEDLE & SEAT, RENEW
1978 .... 0.5

5—FUEL PUMP, TEST (ON CAR)
1978 .... 0.3

6—FUEL PUMP, R & R OR RENEW
1978 .... 0.3

7—FUEL TANK, R & R OR RENEW
1978 .... 0.9

8—INTAKE MANIFOLD, RENEW
1978 .... 1.4

9—INTAKE MANIFOLD GASKET, RENEW
1978 .... 1.1

Exhaust & Emission Systems—TIME

OPERATION INDEX

Exhaust Manifold, Renew *1*
Exhaust Pipe, Renew *2*
Muffler, Renew *3*
Catalytic Converter, Renew *4*
Emission Air Pump, Renew *5*
E.G.R. Valve, Renew *6*

1—EXHAUST MANIFOLD, RENEW
1978 .... 1.5

2—EXHAUST PIPE, RENEW
1978 .... 0.6

3—MUFFLER, RENEW
1978 .... 0.6

4—CATALYTIC CONVERTER, RENEW
1978 .... 0.4

5—EMISSION AIR PUMP, RENEW
1978—
Less Air Cond 1.0
With Air Cond 0.6

6—EXHAUST GAS RECIRCULATION VALVE, RENEW
1978 .... 0.3

Starting Motor—TIME

OPERATION INDEX

Starter, R & R Or Renew *1*
Starter R & R & Overhaul *2*
Starter Drive, Renew *3*
Brushes, Renew *4*
Armature, Renew *5*
Solenoid, Renew *6*
Starter Switch, Renew *7*

1—STARTER, R & R OR RENEW
1978 .... 0.4

2—STARTER, R & R & OVERHAUL
1978 .... 1.3

3—STARTER DRIVE, RENEW
1978 .... 0.7

4—BRUSHES, RENEW
1978 .... 0.6

5—ARMATURE, RENEW
1978 .... 0.8

6—SOLENOID, RENEW
1978 .... 0.5

7—STARTER SWITCH, RENEW
1978 .... 0.3

Alternator—TIME

OPERATION INDEX

Regulator, Check & Adjust *1*
Regulator, Renew *2*
Alternator, R & R Or Renew *3*
Alternator, R & R & Overhaul *4*
Alternator Rectifier, Renew *5*
Alternator Stator, Renew *6*
Alternator Bearings, Renew *7*
Alternator Brushes, Renew *8*

1—ALTERNATOR REGULATOR, CHECK & ADJUST
1978 .... 0.3

2—ALTERNATOR REGULATOR, RENEW
Includes check & adjust
1978 .... 0.5

3—ALTERNATOR, R & R OR RENEW
1978 .... 0.5

4—ALTERNATOR, R & R & OVERHAUL
1978 .... 0.9

5—ALTERNATOR RECTIFIER, RENEW
1978 .... 0.8

6—ALTERNATOR STATOR, RENEW
1978 .... 0.8

7—ALTERNATOR BEARINGS, RENEW
Front Or Rear 0.8

8—ALTERNATOR BRUSHES, RENEW
1978 .... 0.7

Dash Gauges, Speedometer, Windshield Wiper—TIME

OPERATION INDEX

Fuel Gauge, Dash, Renew *1*
Fuel Gauge, Tank, Renew *2*
Oil Gauge Sending Unit, Renew *3*
Temperature Gauge Sending Unit, Renew *4*
Temperature Gauge, Dash, Renew *5*
Speedometer Head, R & R Or Renew *6*
Speedometer Cable, Renew *7*
Speedometer Cable, Lubricate *8*
Windshield Wiper Motor, Renew *9*
Windshield Wiper Switch, Renew *10*

1—FUEL GAUGE, DASH UNIT, RENEW
1978 .... 0.6

2—FUEL GAUGE, TANK UNIT, RENEW
1978 .... 0.5

3—OIL GAUGE SENDING UNIT, RENEW
1978 .... 0.3

4—TEMPERATURE GAUGE SENDING UNIT, RENEW
1978 .... 0.3

5—TEMPERATURE GAUGE, DASH UNIT, RENEW
1978 .... 0.6

(Continued)

Dash Gauges, Speedometer, Windshield Wiper—TIME Cont'd

6—SPEEDOMETER HEAD, R & R OR RENEW
1978 .... 0.5

7—SPEEDOMETER CABLE, RENEW
1978 .... 0.3

8—SPEEDOMETER CABLE, LUBRICATE
1978 .... 0.2

9—WINDSHIELD WIPER MOTOR, RENEW
1978 .... 0.4

10—WINDSHIELD WIPER SWITCH, RENEW
1978 .... 0.4

Battery Cable & Horn—TIME

OPERATION INDEX
Battery Cables, Renew *1*
Horn, Renew *2*
Horn Relay, Renew *3*

1—BATTERY CABLES, RENEW
Starter To Relay 0.3
Battery To Relay 0.3
Ground 0.3

2—HORN, RENEW
1978 .... 0.3

3—HORN RELAY, RENEW
1978 .... 0.3

Lamps & Light Switches—TIME

OPERATION INDEX
Headlamps, Aim *1*
Lamp Lenses Or Bulbs, Renew *2*
Light Switch, Renew *3*
Stop Light Switch, Renew *4*
Back-Up Lamp Switch, Renew *5*
Direction Signal Flasher, Renew *6*
Headlamp Dimmer Switch, Renew *7*
Turn Signal Switch, Renew *8*

1—HEADLAMPS, AIM
1978 .... 0.4

2—LAMPS LENSES OR BULBS, RENEW
1978 Exc 0.2
Seal Beam 0.3
Tail Lamp 0.3

3—LIGHT SWITCH, RENEW
1978 .... 0.4

4—STOP LIGHT SWITCH, RENEW
1978 .... 0.3

5—BACK-UP LAMP SWITCH, RENEW
1978 .... 0.3

6—DIRECTION SIGNAL FLASHER, RENEW
1978 .... 0.3

7—HEADLAMP DIMMER SWITCH, RENEW
1978 .... 0.4

8—TURN SIGNAL SWITCH, RENEW
1978 .... 0.4

Cooling System—TIME

OPERATION INDEX
Radiator, R & R Or Renew *1*
Radiator Hoses, Renew *2*
Fan, Renew *3*
Fan Belts, Renew *4*
Water Pump, R & R Or Renew *5*
Thermostat, Renew *6*

1—RADIATOR, R & R OR RENEW
1978 .... 0.6

2—RADIATOR HOSES, RENEW
Upper 0.3
Lower 0.4
Both 0.5

3—FAN, RENEW
1978 .... 0.4

4—FAN BELTS, RENEW
1978, Each 0.4

5—WATER PUMP, R & R OR RENEW
1978 .... 1.2

6—THERMOSTAT, RENEW
1978 .... 0.4

Cylinder Head & Valves—TIME

OPERATION INDEX
Cylinder Head, R & R *1*
Cylinder Head, Renew *2*
Cylinder Head Gasket, Renew *3*
Cylinder Head, Tighten *4*
Valves, Grind *5*
Valves, Grind (Head Off) *6*
Rocker Arm Cover Gasket, Renew *7*
Valve Tappets, Adjust *8*
Valve Spring Or Seal, Renew *9*
Push Rod, Renew *10*
Rocker Arm, Renew *11*
Rocker Shaft, Overhaul *12*

1—CYLINDER HEAD, R & R
1978 .... 1.8

2—CYLINDER HEAD, RENEW
Includes transfer all parts & grind valves
1978 .... 4.0

3—CYLINDER HEAD GASKET, RENEW
Includes check head & block flatness, adjust carburetor, ignition timing (when distributor is removed) & valves.
1978 .... 1.8

4—CYLINDER HEAD, TIGHTEN
1978 .... 0.4

5—VALVES, GRIND & TUNE-UP, MINOR
1978 .... 4.8

6—VALVES, GRIND (HEAD OFF)
1978 .... 2.0

7—ROCKER ARM COVER GASKET, RENEW
1978 .... 0.5

8—VALVE TAPPETS, ADJUST
1978 .... 0.7

9—VALVE SPRING OR STEM SEAL, RENEW
1978—
One 1.0
All 1.7

10—PUSH ROD, RENEW
1978 .... 0.8

11—ROCKER ARM, RENEW
1978 .... 1.0

12—ROCKER ARM SHAFT ASSY, OVERHAUL
1978 .... 1.0

Timing Case & Camshaft—TIME

OPERATION INDEX
Timing Cover Or Gasket, Renew *1*
Timing Cover Oil Seal, Renew *2*
Timing Chain Or Sprockets, Renew *3*
Camshaft, Renew *4*

1—TIMING COVER OR GASKET, RENEW
1978 .... 1.1

2—TIMING COVER OIL SEAL, RENEW
1978 .... 0.5

3—TIMING CHAIN OR SPROCKETS, RENEW
Includes adjust timing
1978 .... 1.4

4—CAMSHAFT, RENEW
1978 .... 5.8

Engine/Pistons, Rings, Bearings & Crankshaft—TIME

OPERATION INDEX
Pistons Or Rings, Renew *1*
Rings, Renew & Grind Valves *2*
Rings & Main Bearings, Renew *3*
Rod Bearings, Renew *4*
Main Bearings, Renew *5*
Rod & Main Bearings, Renew *6*
Crankshaft, Renew *7*
Rear Main Oil Seal, Renew *8*
Engine, R & R *9*
Cylinder Assy, Renew *10*
Cylinder Block, Renew *11*

1—PISTONS OR RINGS, RENEW
Includes check rod bearing clearances, replace necessary bearings, adjust carburetor, ignition timing & valves, replace oil filter, clean carbon & hone cylinder walls.
1978, One 4.1
All 5.7

2—RINGS, RENEW & GRIND VALVES
1978 .... 7.7

3—RINGS & MAIN BEARINGS, RENEW & GRIND VALVES
1978 .... 8.9

4—ROD BEARINGS, ALL, RENEW
Includes plastigage.
1978 .... 2.9

5—MAIN BEARINGS, RENEW
Includes plastigage.
1978 .... 3.2

(Continued)

Engine/Pistons, Rings, Bearings & Crankshaft—TIME Cont'd

6—MAIN & ROD BEARINGS, RENEW
Includes plastigage.
1978 ....4.1

7—CRANKSHAFT, RENEW
Includes R & R engine, check bearing clearance & adjust ignition timing.
1978 Exc 7.2
With Air Cond 8.2

8—REAR MAIN BEARING OIL SEAL, RENEW
1978 ....2.8

9—ENGINE, R & R
1978 Exc 3.3
With Air Cond 4.3

10—CYLINDER ASSY, RENEW
Includes R & R engine, transfer & clean all component parts without disassembly, adjust valves & ignition timing.
1978 Exc 6.5
With Air Cond 7.5

11—CYLINDER BLOCK, RENEW
Includes R & R engine, transfer & clean all component parts without disassembly, replace rings & bearings, adjust clearance valves & ignition timing.
1978 Exc 10.7
With Air Cond 11.7

Vibration Damper, Flywheel & Engine Mounts—TIME

OPERATION INDEX
Vibration Damper, Renew 1
Flywheel, Renew 2
Engine Mounts, Renew 3

1—VIBRATION DAMPER, RENEW
1978 ....0.4

2—FLYWHEEL, RENEW (TRANSMISSION OUT)
1978 ....0.3

3—ENGINE MOUNTS, RENEW
1978—
Front Right 0.7
Front Left 0.3
Rear 0.5

Engine Oiling—TIME

OPERATION INDEX
Oil Pan, R & R Or Renew Gasket 1
Oil Pump, Renew 2
Oil Pump, Overhaul 3

1—OIL PAN R & R OR RENEW GASKET
1978 ....2.0

2—OIL PUMP, RENEW
1978 ....0.5

3—OIL PUMP, OVERHAUL (PUMP OFF)
1978 ....0.2

Clutch—TIME

OPERATION INDEX
Free Pedal Travel, Adjust 1
Clutch Or Disc, R & R Or Renew 2
Clutch Pilot Bearing, Renew 3
Clutch Operating Cable, Renew 4

1—CLUTCH PEDAL FREE TRAVEL, ADJUST
1978 ....0.4

2—CLUTCH OR DISC, R & R OR RENEW
1978 ....2.5

3—CLUTCH PILOT BEARING, RENEW (CLUTCH OUT)
1978 ....0.2

4—CLUTCH OPERATING CABLE, RENEW
1978 ....0.3

4-Speed Transmission—TIME

OPERATION INDEX
Transmission, R & R Or Renew 1
Transmission, R & R & Overhaul 2
Gear Selector Lever, Renew 3
Linkage Rods, Adjust 4

1—TRANSMISSION, R & R OR RENEW
1978 ....2.3

2—TRANSMISSION, R & R & OVERHAUL
1978 ....3.6

3—GEAR SELECTOR LEVER, RENEW
1978 ....0.7

4—LINKAGE RODS, ADJUST
1978 ....0.3

Rear Suspension—TIME

OPERATION INDEX
Rear Spring, Renew 1
Rear Shock Absorber, Renew 2
Rear Suspension Arm, Renew 3
Rear Stabilizer Bar, Renew 4
Rear Wheel Bearing, Renew 5

1—REAR SPRING, RENEW
1978—
One 0.4
Both 0.7

2—REAR SHOCK ABSORBER, RENEW
1978—
One 0.4
Both 0.5

3—REAR SUSPENSION ARM, RENEW
1978—
One 0.4
Both 0.5

4—REAR STABILIZER BAR, RENEW
1978 ....0.3

5—REAR WHEEL BEARINGS, RENEW
1978—
One 0.5
Both 0.8

Brakes—TIME

OPERATION INDEX
Brake Shoes Or Pads, Renew 1
Brake Shoes, Reline 2
Disc Rotor, Renew 3
Disc Rotor, Resurface 4
Caliper, Renew 5
Caliper, Overhaul 6
Parking Brake, Adjust 7
Parking Brake Cable, Renew 8
Parking Brake Control, Renew 9
Master Cylinder, R & R Or Renew 10
Wheel Cylinder, Renew 11
Wheel Cylinder, Overhaul 12
Flush & Refill System 13
Bleed System 14
Brake Hose, Renew 15
Brake Booster, Renew 16
Rear Brake Drum, Renew 17
Rear Brake Drum, Reface 18

1—BRAKE OR PADS, RENEW
1978—
Front 0.8
Rear 1.1
All 1.3

2—BRAKE SHOES, RELINE (RIVETED TYPE)
After shoes are removed
1978 ....0.4

3—FRONT DISC ROTOR, RENEW
1978 ....0.9

4—FRONT DISC ROTOR, REFACE
After rotor is removed
1978—
One 0.7
Both 1.2

5—FRONT BRAKE CALIPER, RENEW
1978—
One 0.6
Both 0.8

6—FRONT BRAKE CALIPER, R & R & OVERHAUL
1978—
One 1.1
Both 1.5

7—PARKING BRAKE, ADJUST
1978 ....0.2

8—PARKING BRAKE CABLE, RENEW
1978—
Rear, One 0.3
Rear, Both 0.4
Control To Adjuster 1.0

9—PARKING BRAKE CONTROL, RENEW
1978 ....0.6

10—MASTER CYLINDER, R & R OR RENEW
Includes bleed brakes.
1978 ....0.6

11—WHEEL CYLINDER, RENEW
Includes bleed brakes.
1978—
One 1.4
Both 1.5

(Continued)

Brakes—TIME Cont'd

12—WHEEL CYLINDER, R & R & OVERHAUL
Includes bleed brakes.
1978—
One 1.6
Both 1.8

13—FLUSH & REFILL SYSTEM
1978 ....1.0

14—BLEED SYSTEM
1978 ....0.3

15—BRAKE HOSP, RENEW
Includes bleed brakes.
1978—
Front, One 0.5
Front, Both 0.6
Rear 0.4

16—BRAKE BOOSTER, RENEW
1978 ....0.8

17—REAR BRAKE DRUM, RENEW
1978—
One 0.4
Both 0.5

18—REAR BRAKE DRUM, REFACE
After drum is removed.
1978, Both 0.8

Front Suspension—TIME

OPERATION INDEX

Toe-In, Adjust 1
Wheel Alignment 2
Steering Spindle, Renew 3
Control Arm, Renew 4
Ball-Joint, Renew 5
Control Arm Strut, Renew 6
Strut Bushings, Renew 7
Drive Shaft Assy, Renew 8
Universal Joints, Renew 9
Spring, Renew 10
Shock Absorber, Renew 11
Front Wheel Bearings, Renew 12

1—TOE-IN, ADJUST
1978 ....0.4

2—CASTER, CAMBER & TOE-IN, CHECK & ADJUST
1978 ....1.2

3—STEERING SPINDLE (KNUCKLE), RENEW
Does not include wheel alignment,
1978 ....1.2

4—CONTROL ARM, RENEW
Does not include wheel alignment.
1978—
One Side 0.4
Both Sides 0.6

5—BALL-JOINT, RENEW
Does not include wheel alignment.
1978—
One Side 0.4
Both Sides 0.7

6—CONTROL ARM STRUT, RENEW
Does not include wheel alignment.
1978—
One Side 0.4
Both Sides 0.7

7—CONTROL ARM STRUT BUSHINGS, RENEW
1978—
One Side 0.5
Both Sides 0.8

8—DRIVE SHIFT ASSY, RENEW
1978—
Right 0.9
Left 0.9
Both 1.7

9—UNIVERSAL JOINTS, RENEW OR OVERHAUL
After drive shaft is removed
1978—
Right 1.8
Left 0.9
Both 2.5

10—SPRING, RENEW
1978—
One Side 0.7
Both Sides 1.1

11—SHOCK ABSORBER, RENEW
1978—
One Side 0.6
Both Sides 1.0

12—FRONT WHEEL BEARINGS, RENEW
1978—
One Side 0.7
Both Sides 1.2

Steering Linkage—TIME

OPERATION INDEX

Tie Rod Ends, Renew 1
Steering Relay Rod, Renew 2
Idler Arm, Renew 3
Pitman Arm, Renew 4

1—TIE ROD ENDS, RENEW
1978—
One Side 0.7
Both Sides 0.8

2—STEERING RELAY ROD, RENEW
1978 ....0.8

3—IDLER ARM, RENEW
1978 ....0.9

4—PITMAN ARM, RENEW
1978 ....0.5

Steering Gear—TIME

OPERATION INDEX

Steering Gear, Adjust 1
Steering Gear, R&R Or Renew 2
Column Upper Bearing, Renew 3
Steering Wheel, Renew 4

1—STEERING GEAR, ADJUST (ON CAR)
1978 ....0.7

2—STEERING GEAR, R&R OR RENEW
1978 ....0.9

3—COLUMN UPPER BEARING, RENEW
1978 ....0.7

4—STEERING WHEEL, RENEW
1978 ....0.2

Heater—TIME

OPERATION INDEX

Heater Core, R&R Or Renew 1
Heater Hose, Renew 2
Blower Moter, Renew 3
Heater Switch, Renew 4
Heater Control, Renew 5
Heater Control Cable, Renew 6

1—HEATER CORE, R&R OR RENEW
1978 ....0.9

2—HEATER HOSE, RENEW
1978 ....0.4

3—BLOWER MOTER, RENEW
1978 ....1.2

4—HEATER SWITCH, RENEW
1978 ....0.3

5—HEATER CONTROL, RENEW
1978 ....0.7

6—HEATER CONTROL CABLE, RENEW
1978 ....0.6

Air Conditioner—TIME

OPERATION INDEX

Evacutate & Charge System 1
Compressor, Renew 2
Clutch Bearing, Renew 3
Condenser, Renew 4
Receiver-Dehydrator, Renew 5
Expansion Valve, Renew 6
Evaporator Core, Renew 7
Hoses, Renew 8
Blower Motor, Renew 9
Blower Switch, Renew 10

1—EVACUATE & CHARGE SYSTEM
1978 ....1.5

2—COMPRESSOR, RENEW
Does not include charge system.
1978 ....1.0

3—COMPRESSOR CLUTCH BEARING, RENEW
1978 ....0.9

4—CONDENSER, RENEW
Does not include charging system.
1978 ....1.1

5—RECEIVER-DEHYDRATOR, RENEW
Does not include charging system
1978 ....0.3

6—EXPANSION VALVE, RENEW
Does not include charging system.
1978 ....0.5

7—EVAPORATOR CORE, RENEW
Does not include charging system.
1978 ....1.8

8—AIR COND HOSES, RENEW
1978—
Dehydrator To Evaporator 0.4
Evaporator To Compressor 0.6
Evaporator To Compressor 0.6

9—BLOWER MOTOR, RENEW
1978 ....0.7

10—BLOWER SWITCH, RENEW
1978 ....0.6

IDENTIFICATION

ALL MODELS..179

ILLUSTRATIONS

FIG 1 – ENGINE – CYLINDER HEAD COVER – CIVIC
FIG 2 – ENGINE – VALVES & COVERS – CIVIC
FIG 3 – ENGINE – CAMSHAFT & TIMING BELT
FIG 4 – ENGINE – CYLINDER HEAD
FIG 5 – ENGINE – PISTON & CONNECTING ROD
FIG 6 – ENGINE – CRANKSHAFT
FIG 7 – ENGINE – CYLINDER BLOCK & OIL PAN
FIG 8 – TRANSMISSION HOUSING
FIG 9 – STANDARD TRANSMISSION GEARS
FIG 10 – DIFFERENTIAL
FIG 11 – HONDAMATIC TORQUE CONVERTER HOUSING
FIG 12 – HONDAMATIC TORQUE CONVERTER
FIG 13 – HONDAMATIC TRANSMISSION HOUSING
FIG 14 – HONDAMATIC MAINSHAFT
FIG 15 – HONDAMATIC COUNTERSHAFT
FIG 16 – HONDAMATIC CLUTCH
FIG 17 – FRONT SUSPENSION
FIG 18 – STEERING
FIG 19 – REAR SUSPENSION

OPERATION TIMES

A

Alternator.. 189
Automatic Transmission.................... 193

B

Back-Up Light Switch........................ 194
Brake Drums.. 194
Brakes... 193

C

Cables (Ignition)................................ 189
Calipers.. 193
Camshaft, 600.................................... 191
-Civic.. 191
Carburetor.. 189
Clutch.. 192
Coil, Ignition...................................... 189
Compression Test.............................. 189
Connecting Rods................................ 191
Cooling System, 600.......................... 190
-Civic.. 190
Crankshaft, 600.................................. 190
-Civic.. 191
Cylinder Block, Civic......................... 191
Cylinder Head, 600............................ 190
-Civic.. 191

D

Differential.. 194
Disc Brakes... 194
Distributor... 189

E

Emission Controls.............................. 189
Engine Assembly, 600........................ 190
Engine Cooling, 600........................... 190
-Civic.. 190
Engine Heating, 600........................... 190
-Civic.. 190
Engine Mountings, 600....................... 191
-Civic.. 191
Engine Oiling, 600.............................. 191
-Civic.. 191
Engine Tune-Up................................... 189
Exhaust System.................................. 189

F

Flywheel.. 191
Front Suspension............................... 194
Fuel Pump... 189
Fuel Tank.. 189

G

Generator.. 189

H

Hand Brake... 193
Headlight Switch................................. 194
Heater... 190
Hose (Brake)....................................... 193
Hose (Radiator)................................... 190
Hydraulic Brakes................................ 193

I

Ignition.. 189
Ignition Coil.. 189
Ignition Switch.................................... 189
Intake Manifold................................... 189

L

Light Switches.................................... 194

M

Master Cylinder.................................. 193
Muffler.. 189

O

Oiling, Engine, 600............................. 191
-Civic.. 191
Oil Pan... 191
Oil Pump, 600...................................... 191
-Civic.. 191

P

Parking Brake..................................... 193
Piston Rings, 600................................ 190
-Civic.. 191
Pistons, 600.. 190
-Civic.. 191
Power Brake....................................... 193

R

Radiator.. 190
Radiator Hose..................................... 190
Rear Axle.. 194
Regulator.. 189

S

Shocks (Front).................................... 194
Shocks (Rear)..................................... 194
Speedometer....................................... 194
Springs (Front).................................... 194
Springs (Rear)..................................... 194
Stabilizer Shaft................................... 194
Starting Motor..................................... 189
Steering Gear...................................... 194
Steering Linkage................................. 194
Switches (Light).................................. 194
Synchro-Mesh Trans, 600................... 192
-Civic.. 192

T

Thermostat.. 190
Timing Belt Cover............................... 192
Timing Belt.. 192
Transmission, Manual, 600................. 192
-Civic.. 192
Transmission, Automatic.................... 193
Tune-Up, Engine................................. 189

V

Valve System, 600.............................. 191
-Civic.. 191

W

Water Pump... 190
Wheel Cylinders.................................. 193
Windshield Wiper................................ 194

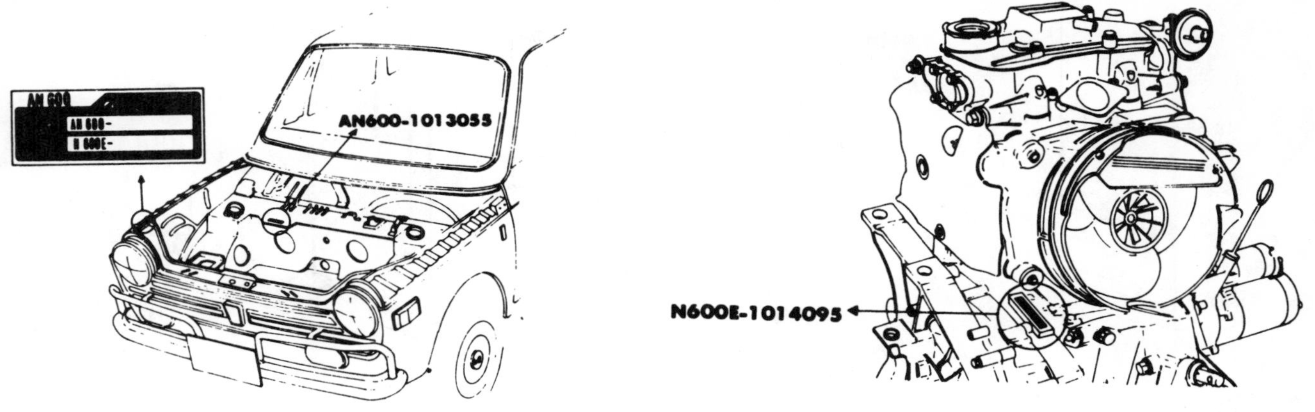

IDENTIFICATION PLATES — 600 SEDAN

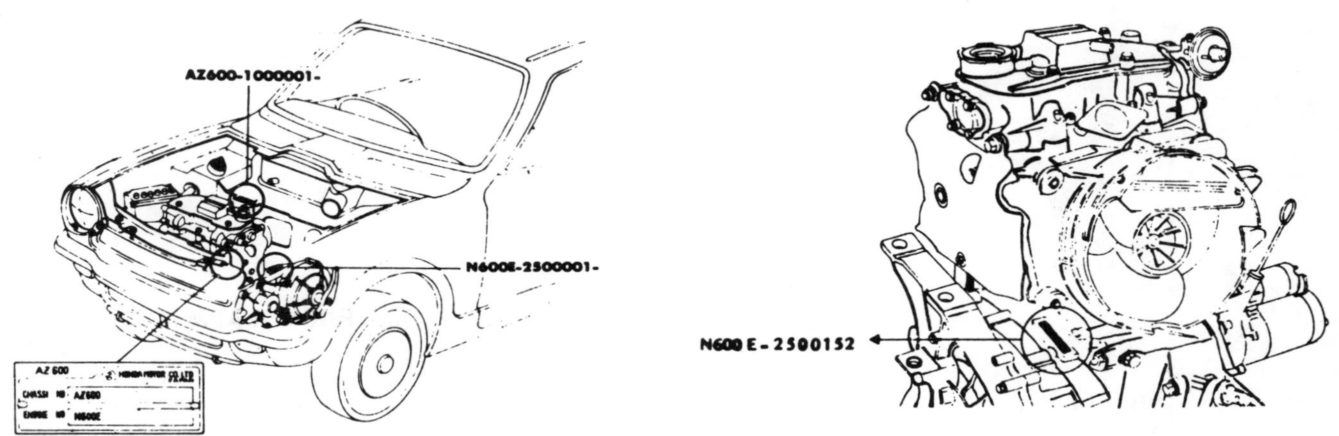

IDENTIFICATION PLATES — 600 COUPE

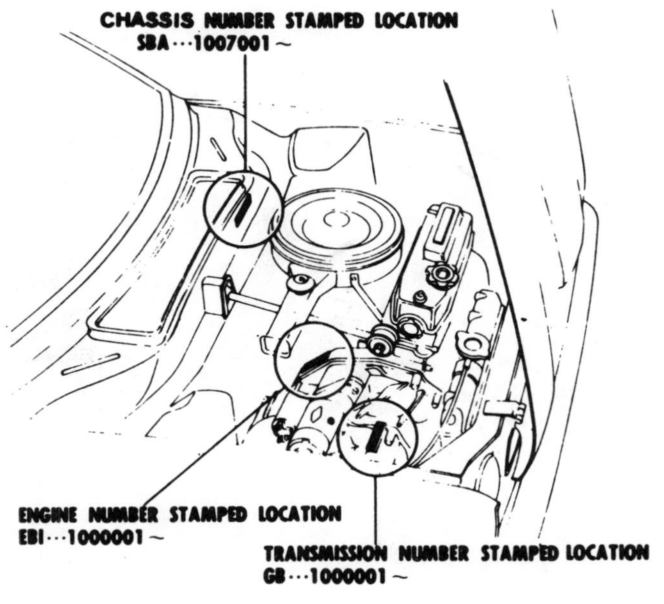

IDENTIFICATION PLATES — CIVIC — CVCC — ACCORD

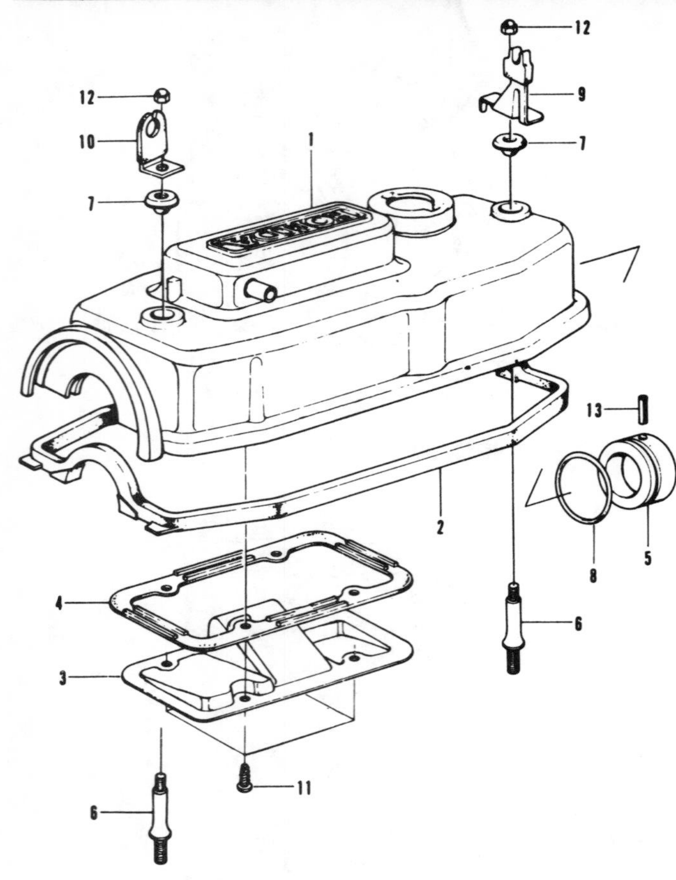

FIG 1 – CYLINDER HEAD COVER – CIVIC

1	Head Cover	8	O Ring
2	Gasket	9	Bracket
3	Breather Cover	10	Bracket
4	Gasket	11	Screw
5	Seal	12	Nut
6	Bolt	13	Roller
7	Washer		

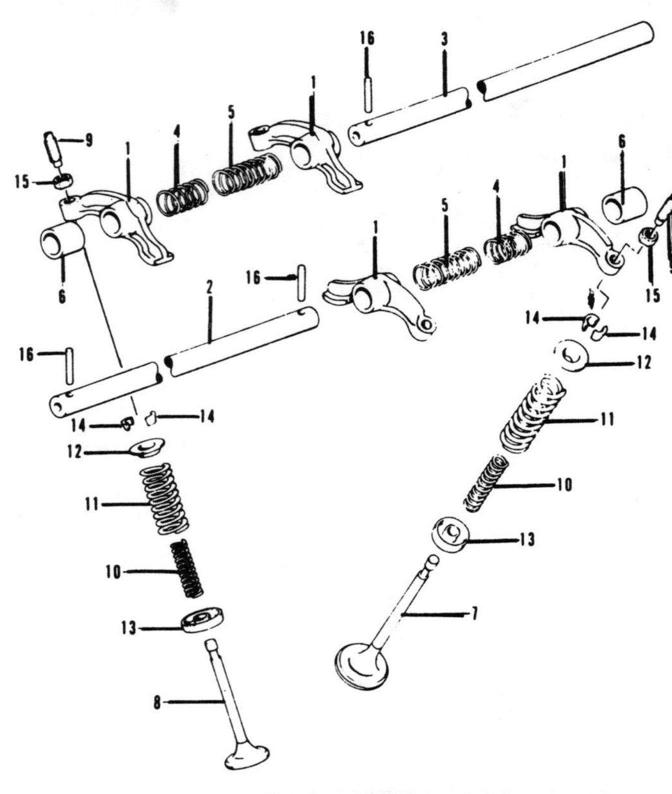

FIG 2 – VALVES & ROCKER ARMS – CIVIC

1	Rocker Arm	9	Screw
2	Intake Rocker Shaft	10	Spring
3	Exhaust Rocker Shaft	11	Spring
4	Spring	12	Retainer
5	Spring	13	Seat
6	Spacer	14	Keeper
7	Intake Valve	15	Nut
8	Exhaust Valve	16	Pin

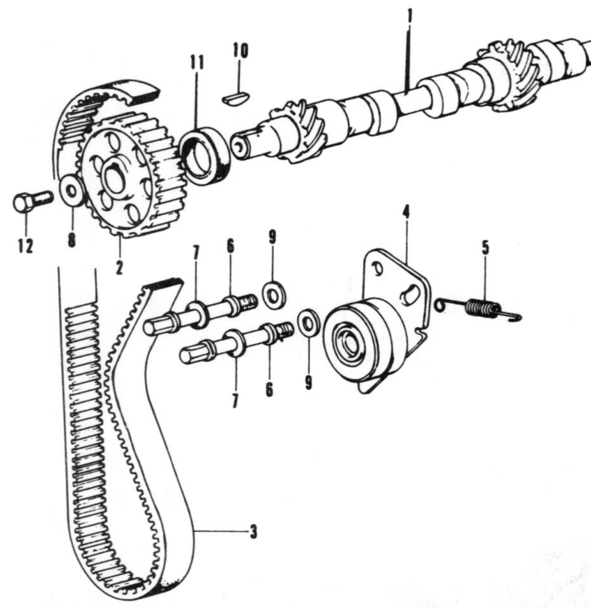

FIG 3 – CAMSHAFT & TIMING BELT

1	Camshaft
2	Pulley
3	Timing Belt
4	Adjuster
5	Spring
6	Bolt
7	Rubber
8	Washer
9	Washer
10	Key
11	Oil Seal
12	Bolt

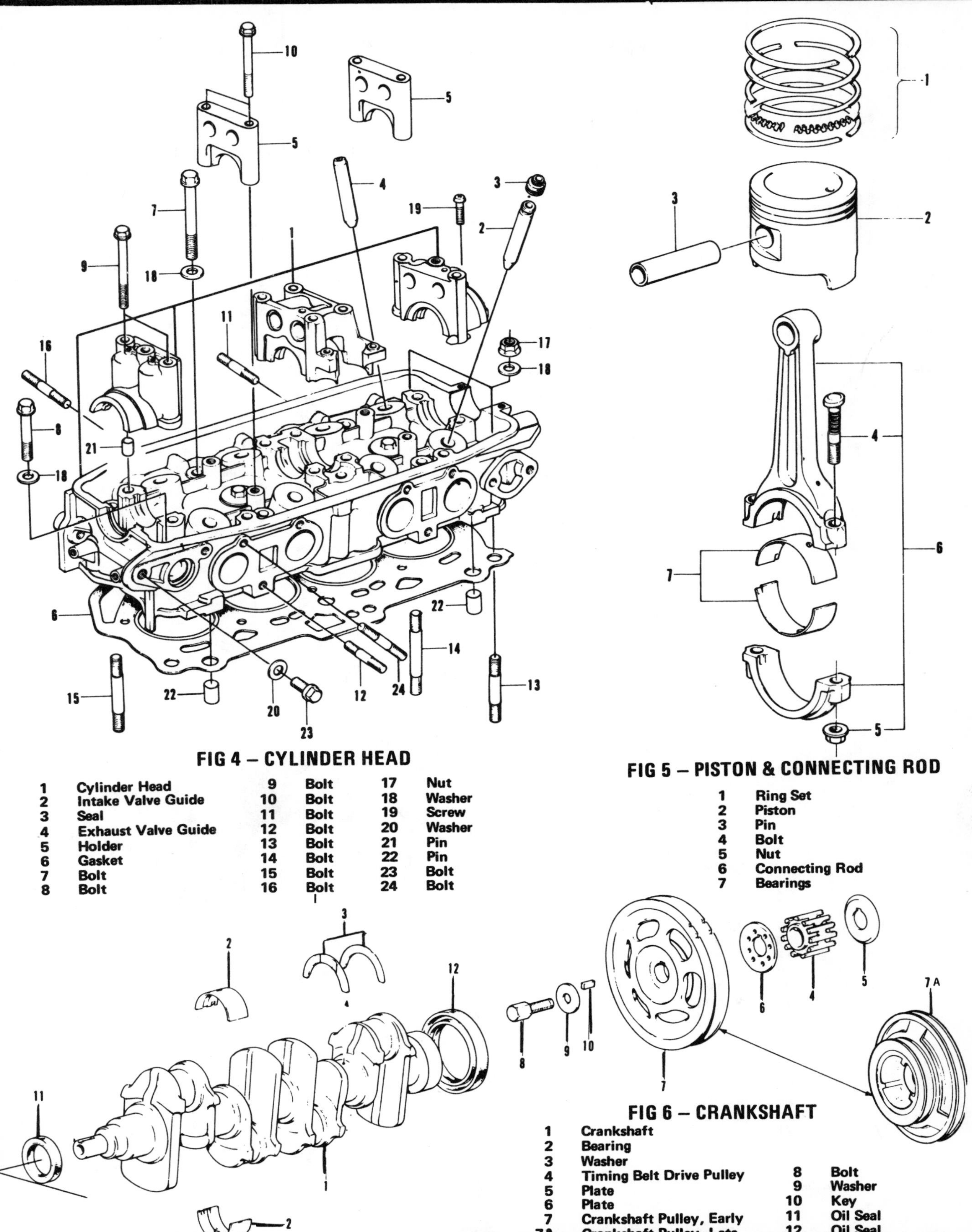

FIG 4 – CYLINDER HEAD

1	Cylinder Head	9	Bolt	17	Nut
2	Intake Valve Guide	10	Bolt	18	Washer
3	Seal	11	Bolt	19	Screw
4	Exhaust Valve Guide	12	Bolt	20	Washer
5	Holder	13	Bolt	21	Pin
6	Gasket	14	Bolt	22	Pin
7	Bolt	15	Bolt	23	Bolt
8	Bolt	16	Bolt	24	Bolt

FIG 5 – PISTON & CONNECTING ROD

1	Ring Set
2	Piston
3	Pin
4	Bolt
5	Nut
6	Connecting Rod
7	Bearings

FIG 6 – CRANKSHAFT

1	Crankshaft		
2	Bearing		
3	Washer		
4	Timing Belt Drive Pulley	8	Bolt
5	Plate	9	Washer
6	Plate	10	Key
7	Crankshaft Pulley, Early	11	Oil Seal
7A	Crankshaft Pulley, Late	12	Oil Seal

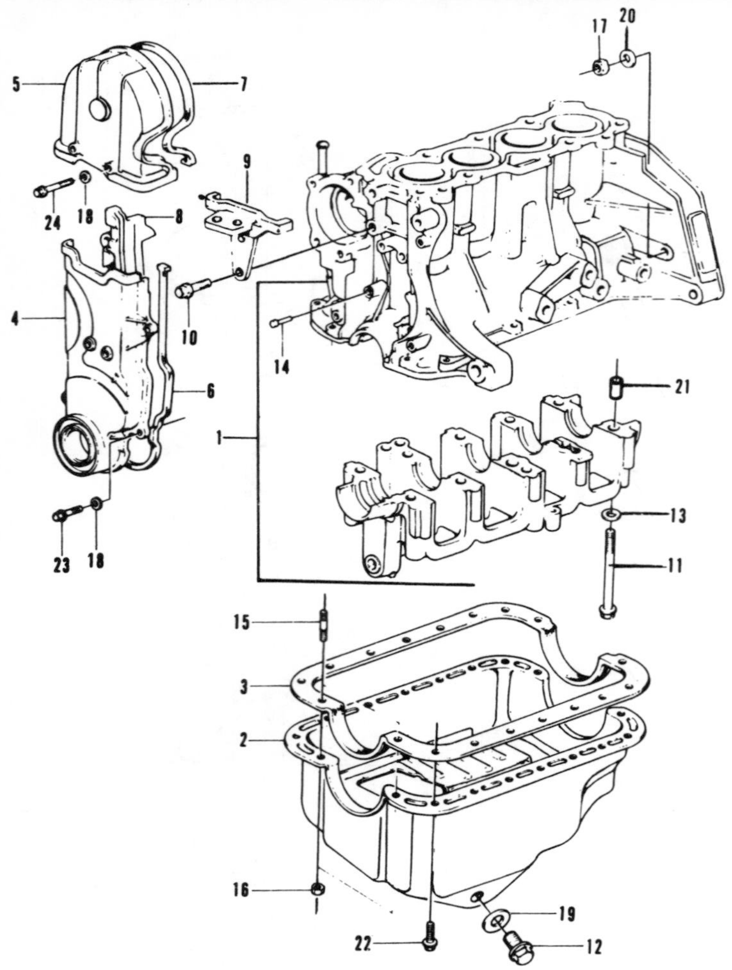

FIG 7 – CYLINDER BLOCK & OIL PAN

1 Block
2 Oil Pan
3 Gasket
4 Timing Belt Lower Cover
5 Timing Belt Upper Cover
6 Seal
7 Seal
8 Seal
9 Mount Bracket
10 Bolt
11 Bolt
12 Bolt
13 Washer
14 Pin
15 Bolt
16 Nut
17 Nut
18 Washer
19 Washer
20 Washer
21 Pin
22 Bolt
23 Bolt
24 Bolt

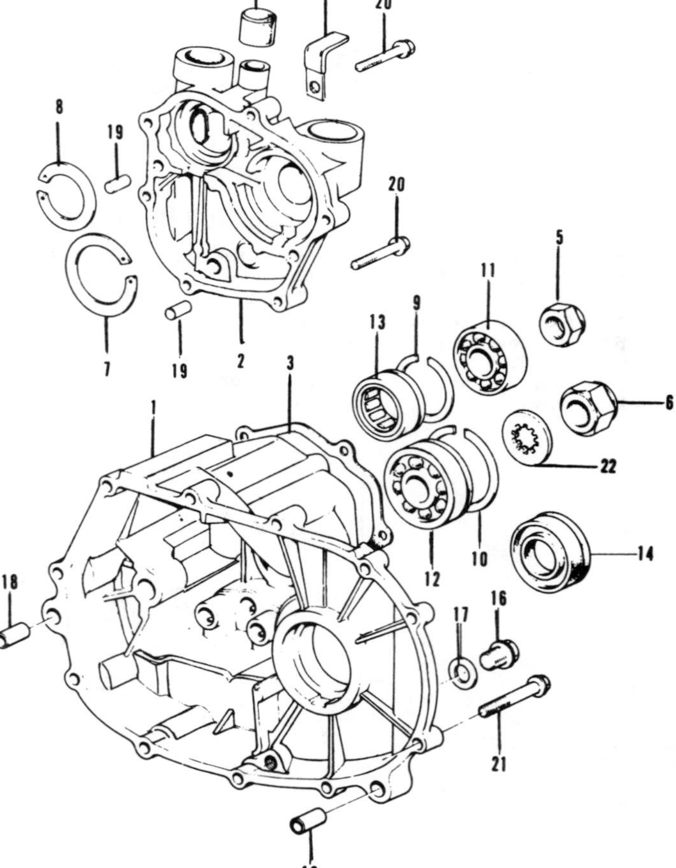

FIG 8 – TRANSMISSION HOUSING

1 Housing
2 Cover
3 Gasket
4 Cap
5 Nut
6 Nut
7 Ring
8 Ring
9 Ring
10 Ring
11 Bearing
12 Bearing
13 Bearing
14 Oil Seal
15 Bracket
16 Bolt
17 Washer
18 Pin
19 Pin
20 Bolt
21 Bolt
22 Plate

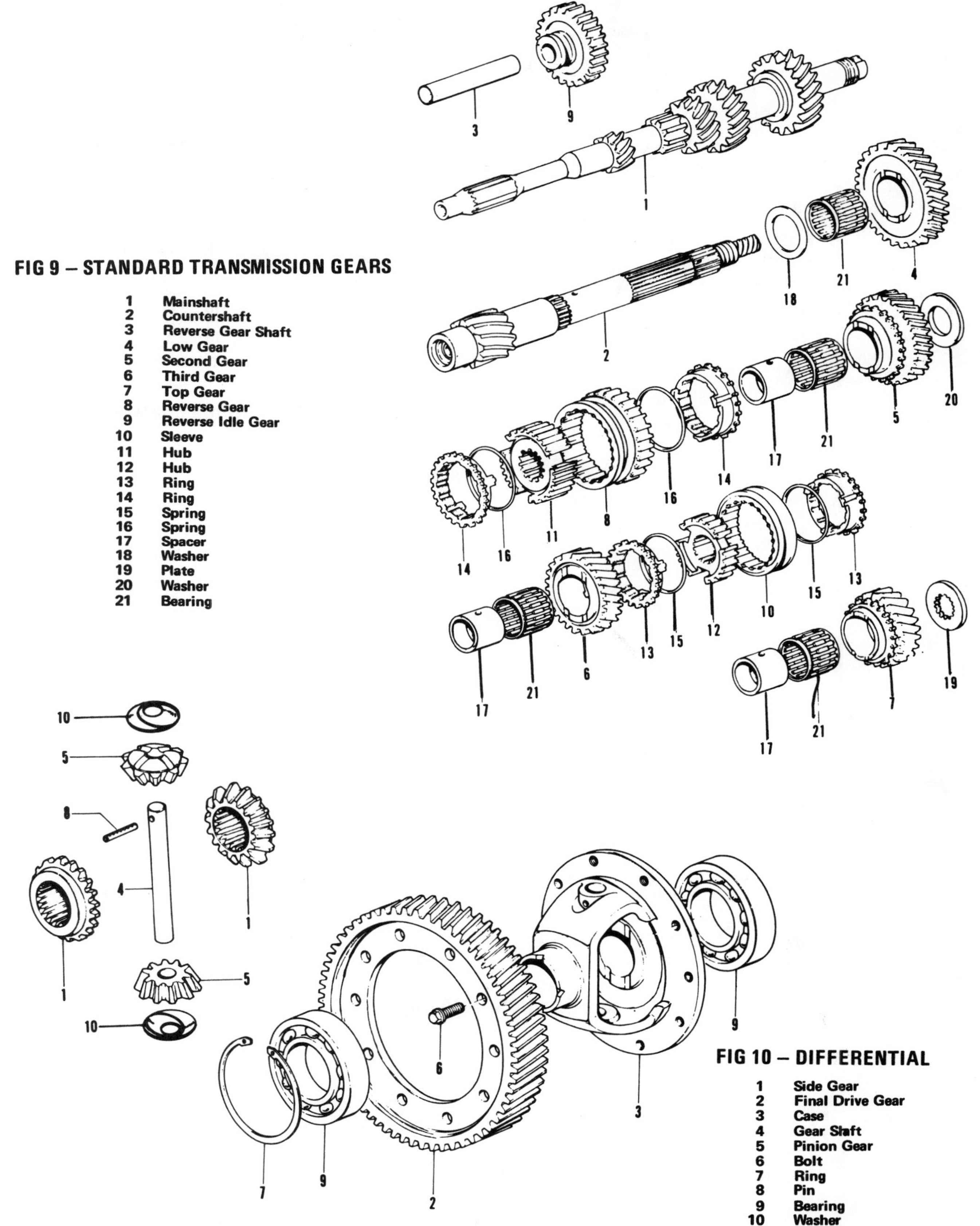

FIG 9 – STANDARD TRANSMISSION GEARS

1 Mainshaft
2 Countershaft
3 Reverse Gear Shaft
4 Low Gear
5 Second Gear
6 Third Gear
7 Top Gear
8 Reverse Gear
9 Reverse Idle Gear
10 Sleeve
11 Hub
12 Hub
13 Ring
14 Ring
15 Spring
16 Spring
17 Spacer
18 Washer
19 Plate
20 Washer
21 Bearing

FIG 10 – DIFFERENTIAL

1 Side Gear
2 Final Drive Gear
3 Case
4 Gear Shaft
5 Pinion Gear
6 Bolt
7 Ring
8 Pin
9 Bearing
10 Washer

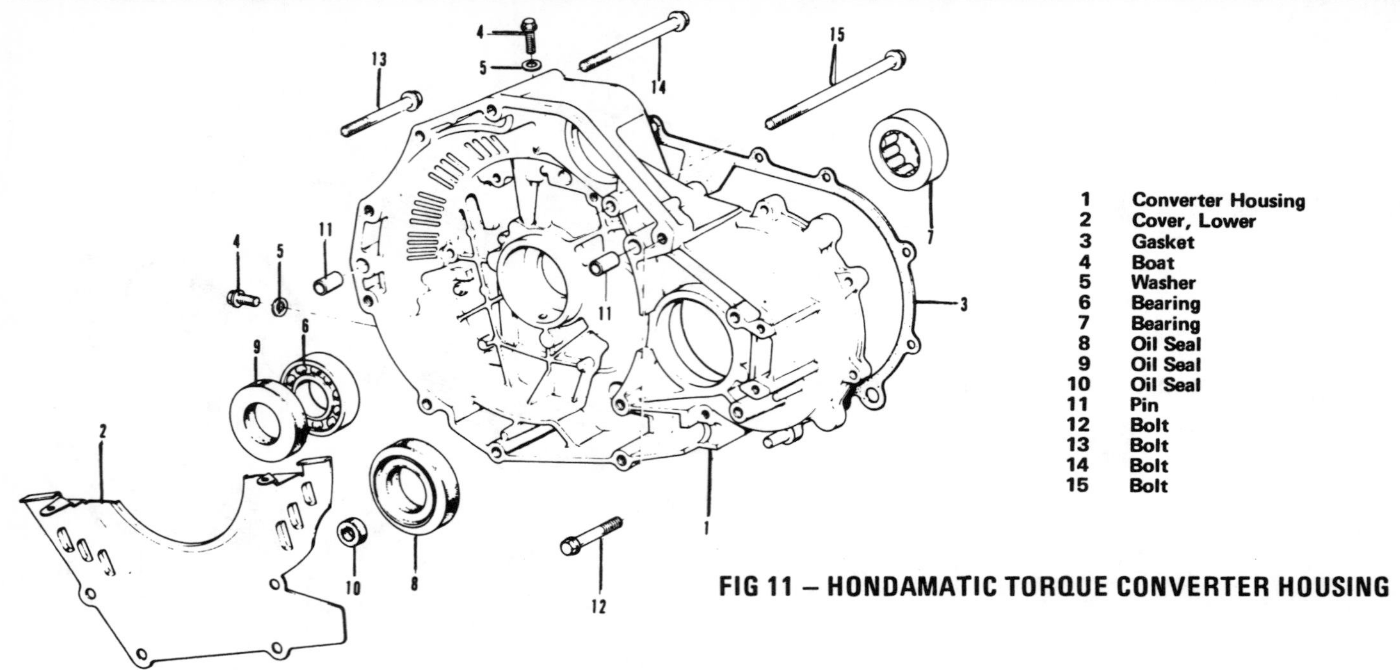

1 Converter Housing
2 Cover, Lower
3 Gasket
4 Boat
5 Washer
6 Bearing
7 Bearing
8 Oil Seal
9 Oil Seal
10 Oil Seal
11 Pin
12 Bolt
13 Bolt
14 Bolt
15 Bolt

FIG 11 – HONDAMATIC TORQUE CONVERTER HOUSING

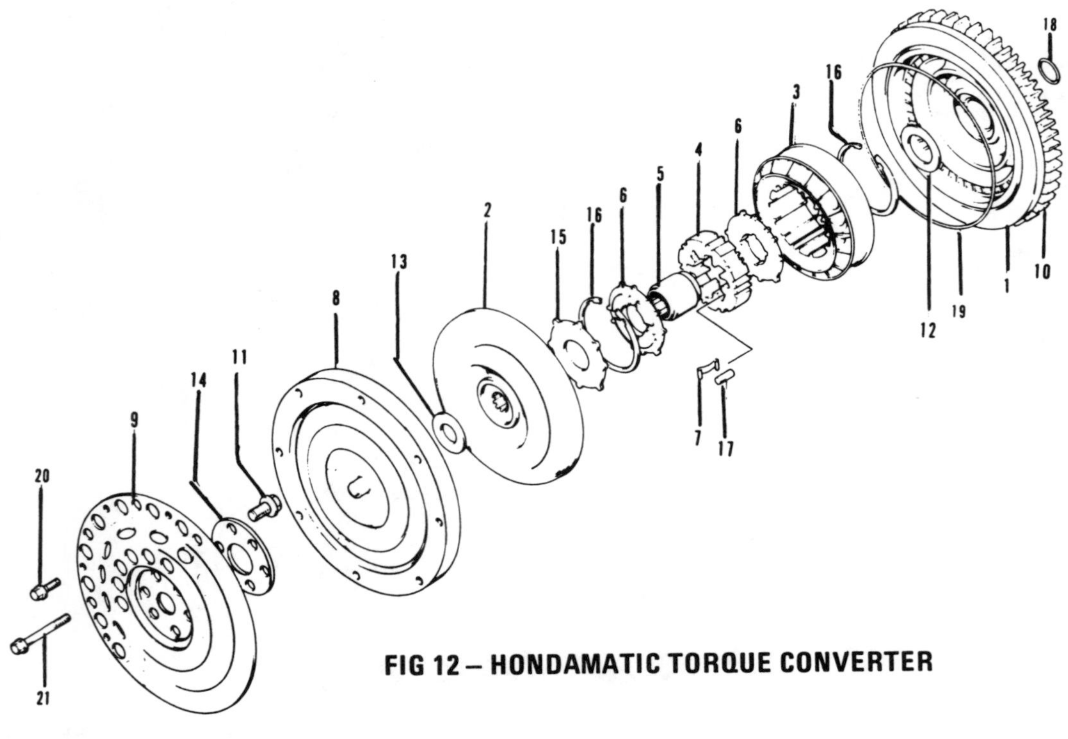

FIG 12 – HONDAMATIC TORQUE CONVERTER

1 Converter Pump
2 Turbine
3 Stator
4 Stator Cam
5 Stator Hub
6 Side Plate
7 Spring
8 Converter Cover
9 Drive Plate
10 Ring Gear
11 Bolt
12 Washer
13 Washer
14 Washer
15 Washer
16 Ring
17 Roller
18 O Ring
19 O Ring
20 Bolt
21 Bolt

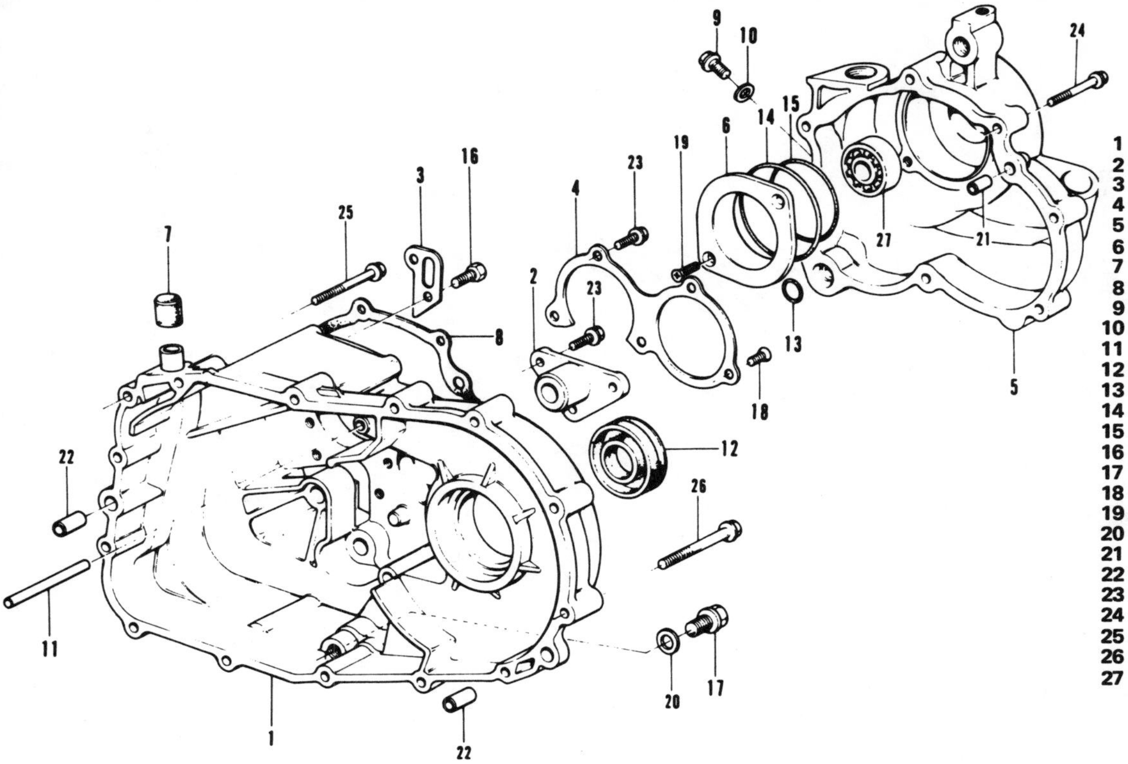

1	Transmission Housing
2	Reverse Idle Shaft Holder
3	Bracket
4	Plate
5	Cover
6	Retainer
7	Breather Cap
8	Gasket
9	Bolt
10	Washer
11	Pin
12	Oil Seal
13	O Ring
14	O Ring
15	O Ring
16	Bolt
17	Bolt
18	Screw
19	Screw
20	Washer
21	Pin
22	Pin
23	Bolt
24	Bolt
25	Bolt
26	Bolt
27	Bearing

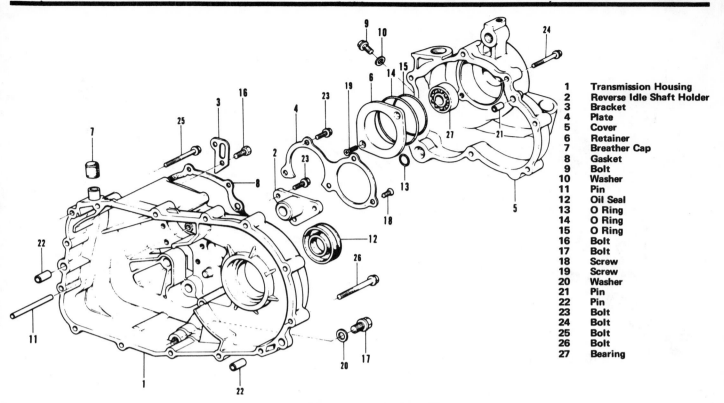

FIG 13 – HONDAMATIC TRANSMISSION HOUSING

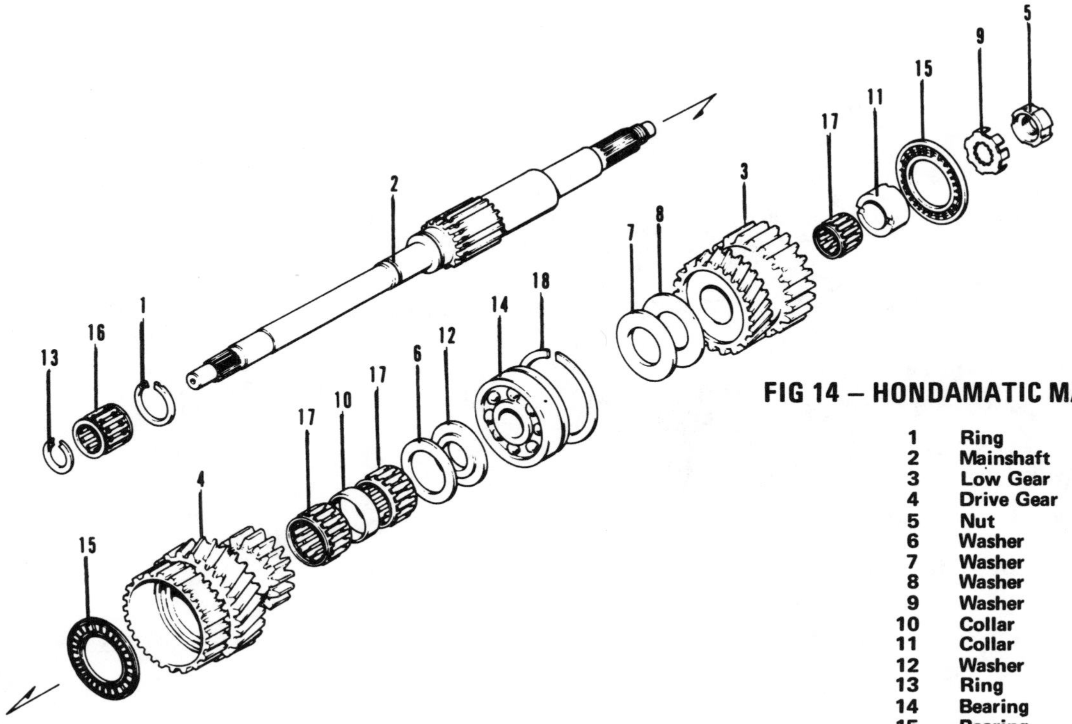

FIG 14 – HONDAMATIC MAINSHAFT

1	Ring
2	Mainshaft
3	Low Gear
4	Drive Gear
5	Nut
6	Washer
7	Washer
8	Washer
9	Washer
10	Collar
11	Collar
12	Washer
13	Ring
14	Bearing
15	Bearing
16	Bearing
17	Bearing
18	Ring

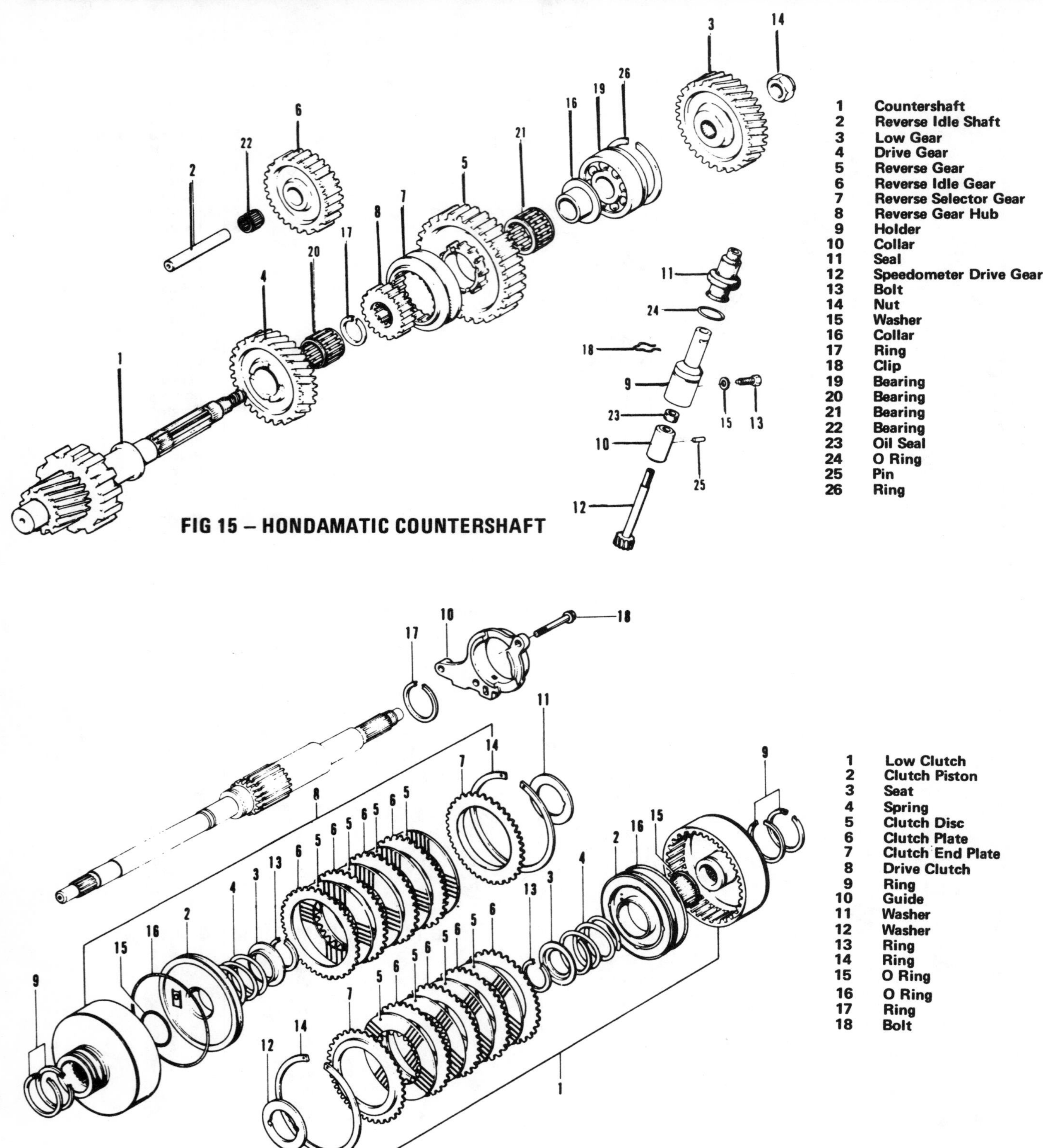

FIG 15 – HONDAMATIC COUNTERSHAFT

FIG 16 – HONDAMATIC CLUTCH

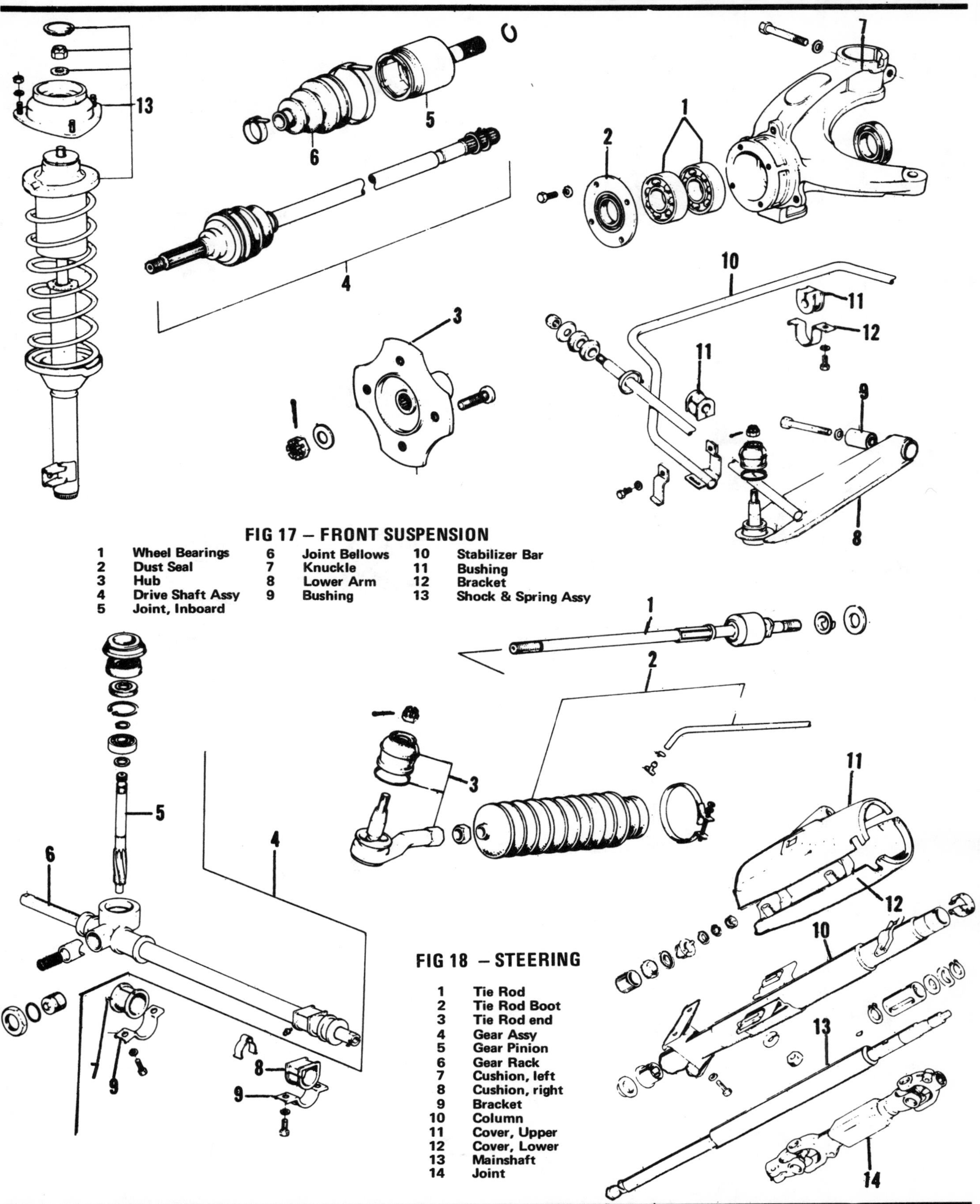

FIG 17 – FRONT SUSPENSION

1	Wheel Bearings	6	Joint Bellows	10	Stabilizer Bar
2	Dust Seal	7	Knuckle	11	Bushing
3	Hub	8	Lower Arm	12	Bracket
4	Drive Shaft Assy	9	Bushing	13	Shock & Spring Assy
5	Joint, Inboard				

FIG 18 – STEERING

1	Tie Rod
2	Tie Rod Boot
3	Tie Rod end
4	Gear Assy
5	Gear Pinion
6	Gear Rack
7	Cushion, left
8	Cushion, right
9	Bracket
10	Column
11	Cover, Upper
12	Cover, Lower
13	Mainshaft
14	Joint

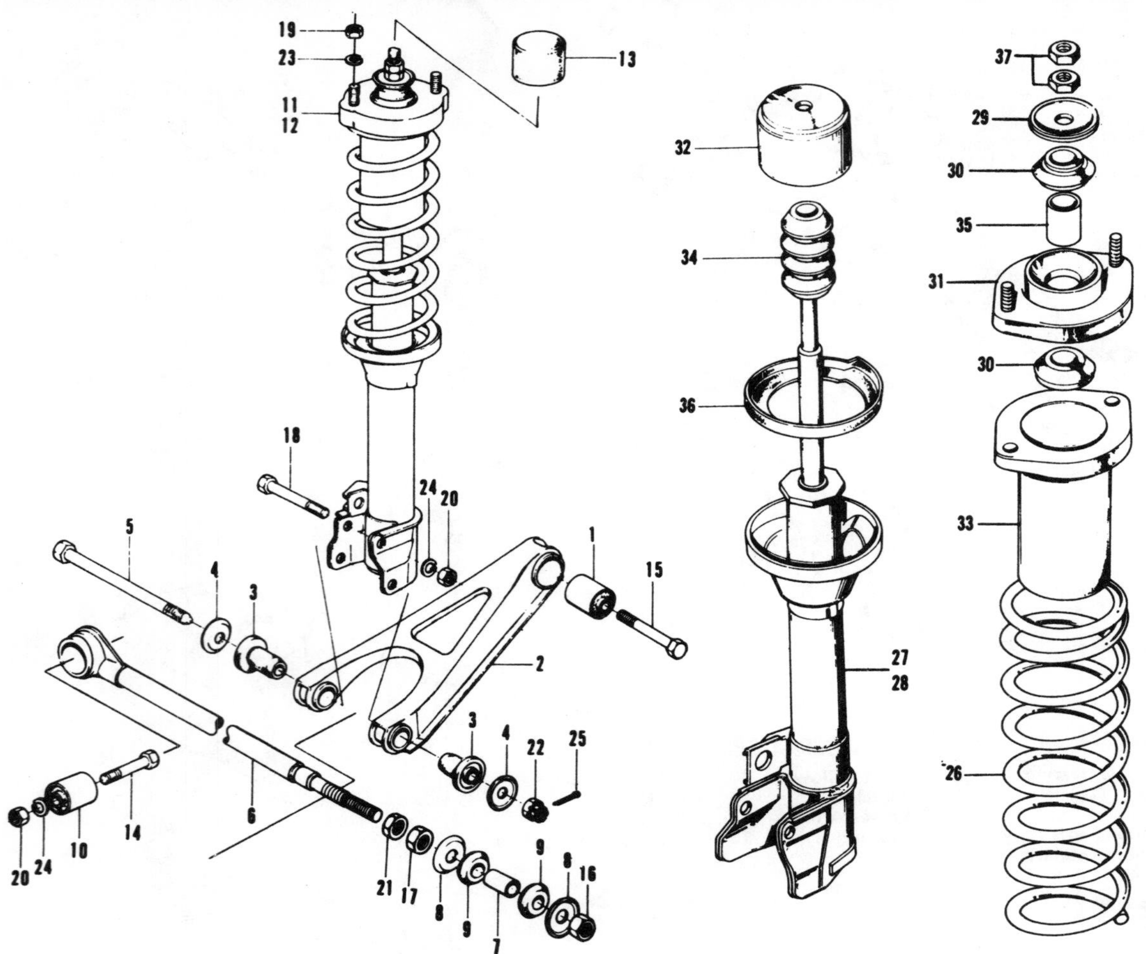

FIG 19 – REAR SUSPENSION

1	Bushing
2	Lower Arm
3	Bushing
4	Washer
5	Bolt
6	Radius Rod
7	Spacer
8	Washer
9	Bushing
10	Bushing
11	Shock Absorber Assy
12	Shock Absorber Assy
13	Cap
14	Bolt
15	Bolt
16	Nut
17	Nut
18	Bolt
19	Nut
20	Nut
21	Nut
22	Nut
23	Washer
24	Washer
25	Pin
26	Spring
27	Damper
28	Damper
29	Washer
30	Bushing
31	Seat
32	Guide
33	Cover
34	Bumper
35	Spacer
36	Rubber
37	Nut

Ignition, Starting & Charging—TIME

OPERATION INDEX

Tune-Up, Minor *1*
Tune-Up, Major *2*
Compression Test *3*
Distributor R&R Or Renew *3A*
Distributor, Overhaul *4*
Distributor Cap, Renew *5*
Ignition Cable Set, Renew *6*
Ignition Coil, Renew *7*
Starter And Ignition Switch, Renew *8*
Starter Assy, R & R Or Renew *9*
Starter, Overhaul *10*
Starter Brushes, Renew *11*
Starter Armature, Renew *12*
Voltage Regulator, Renew *13*
Rectifier, Renew *14*
Generator (Flywheel Housing), R&R *15*
Generator Cover, Renew *16*
Generator Rotor, Renew *17*
Generator Starter, Renew *18*
Generator Brush Assy, Renew *19*
Generator Pulley, Renew *20*
Generator Dust Seal Cover, Renew *21*
Alternator, R&R Or Renew *22*
Alternator, R&R & Overhaul *23*
Alternator Brushes, Renew *24*
Alternator Diodes, Renew *25*
Alternator Pulley, Renew *26*

1—TUNE-UP, MINOR
Includes: Renew points, condenser and plugs, set spark timing and adjust carburetor idle.
600 .... 0.9
Civic, CVCC, Accord 1.2

2—TUNE-UP, MAJOR
Includes: Check compression clean or renew and adjust spark plugs, renew points and condenser. Adjust ignition timing, carburetor and fan belts. Clean battery terminals and service air cleaner.
600 .... 1.5
Civic, CVCC, Accord 2.0

3—COMPRESSION TEST
All Models 0.3

3A—DISTRIBUTOR, R&R OR RENEW
600 .... 0.3
Civic, CVCC, Accord 0.5

4—DISTRIBUTOR, R&R & OVERHAUL
600 .... 0.5
Civic 0.9
CVCC 1.1
Accord 1.1

5—DISTRIBUTOR CAP, RENEW
All Models 0.2

6—IGNITION CABLE SET, RENEW
All Models 0.3

7—IGNITION COIL, RENEW
600 .... 0.3
Civic 0.2
Civic A.I.R. & CVCC 0.3
Accord 0.3

8—STARTER & IGNITION SWITCH, RENEW
600 .... 0.3
Civic & Accord 0.4

9—STARTER ASSY, R&R OR RENEW
600 .... 0.3
Civic & Accord 0.4

10—STARTER, OVERHAUL
Civic & Accord 0.9

11—STARTER BRUSHES, RENEW
600 .... 0.6
Civic & Accord 0.7

12—STARTER ARMATURE RENEW
600 .... 0.5
Civic & Accord 0.6

13—VOLTAGE REGULATOR, RENEW
600 .... 0.4
Civic & Accord 0.3

14—RECTIFIER, R&R OR RENEW
600 .... 0.4

15—GENERATOR (FLYWHEEL HOUSING), R&R
600 .... 1.1

16—GENERATOR COVER, RENEW
600 .... 0.8

17—GENERATOR ROTOR, RENEW
600 .... 1.0

18—GENERATOR STATOR, RENEW
600 .... 1.1

19—GENERATOR BRUSH ASSY, RENEW
600 .... 0.3

20—GENERATOR PULLEY, RENEW
600 .... 0.2

21—GENERATOR DUST SEAL COVER, RENEW
600 .... 0.2

22—ALTERNATOR, R&R OR RENEW
Civic & Accord Exc 0.3
With Air Cond 0.4

23—ALTERNATOR, R&R & OVERHAUL
Civic & Accord Exc 0.9
With Air Cond 1.0

24—ALTERNATOR BRUSHES, RENEW
Civic & Accord 0.6

25—ALTERNATOR DIODES, RENEW
Civic & Accord 0.4

26—ALTERNATOR PULLEY, RENEW
Civic & Accord 0.3

Fuel, Emission Control, Intake & Exhaust Systems—TIME

OPERATION INDEX

Carburetor, R&R Or Renew *1*
Carburetor, Overhaul *2*
Carburetor Float, Renew *3*
Carburetor Air Funnel , R&R *4*
Fuel Pump, R&R Or Renew *5*
Fuel Filter, Renew *6*
Fuel, Tank, R&R Or Renew *7*
Fuel Meter Assy, Renew *8*
Intake Manifold, R&R Or Renew *9*
Air Filter Element, Renew *10*
Air Cleaner Sealing Plug, Renew *11*
Air Cleaner Bellows, R&R *12*
Exhaust Manifold, Renew *13*
Heater Exhaust Pipe, Renew *14*
Mufflers, Renew *15*
Heat Exchanger, Renew *16*
Double Nutted Heat Exchanger, Renew *17*
Exhaust Pipe, Renew *18*
Emission Control Units, Renew (Civic) *19*

1—CARBURETOR, R&R OR RENEW
600 .... 0.4
Civic & Civic A.I.R. 0.7
CVCC, CVCC Wagon 1.0
Accord 1.6

2—CARBURETOR, R&R & OVERHAUL
600 .... 0.8
Civic & Civic A.I.R. 1.6
CVCC, CVCC Wagon 2.0
Accord 2.6

3—CARBURETOR FLOAT, RENEW
600 .... 0.5
Civic 1.1

4—CARBURETOR AIR FUNNEL, R&R
600 .... 0.3

5—FUEL PUMP, R&R OR RENEW
600 .... 0.2
Civic & Civic A.I.R. 0.2
CVCC Exc 0.4
Wagon 0.2
Accord 0.5

6—FUEL FILTER, RENEW
600 .... 0.3
Civic & CVCC 0.2
Accord 0.4

7—FUEL TANK, R&R OR RENEW
600 .... 0.8
Civic & Accord 0.7
CVCC 0.9

8—FUEL METER ASSY IN TANK, RENEW
600 .... 0.9

8A—FUEL-TEMPERATURE GAUGE, RENEW
Civic & Civic A.I.R. 0.6
CVCC, CVCC Wagon 0.5
Accord 0.7

9—INTAKE MANIFOLD, R&R OR RENEW
600 .... 0.2
Civic Exc A.I.R. ①0.8

9A—INTAKE & EXHAUST MANIFOLDS, RENEW
CVCC, 73-75 .... 2.0
CVCC, 76-78 .... 2.3
Accord 2.3

10—AIR FILTER ELEMENT, RENEW
All Models 0.1

11—AIR CLEANER SEALING PLUG, RENEW
600 .... 0.3

12—AIR CLEANER BELLOWS, R&R
600 .... 0.4

13—EXHAUST MANIFOLD, RENEW
600 & Civic Exc A.I.R. 0.5

14—HEATER EXHAUST PIPE, RENEW
600, Exc 0.5
From Eng 1500000 .... 0.1

15—MUFFLERS, RENEW
600—
To Eng 1500000—
Front 0.6
Rear 0.4
Both 1.0
From Eng 1500000—
Front 0.3
Rear 0.2
Both 0.4
Civic & Civic A.I.R. 0.4
Civic CVCC 0.5
CVCC Wagon 0.4
Accord 0.3

16—HEAT EXCHANGER, RENEW
600, Exc 0.8
From Eng 1500000 .... 1.3

17—DOUBLE NUTTED HEAT EXCHANGER, RENEW
600 .... 1.2

Fuel, Emission Control, Intake & Exhaust Systems—TIME Cont'd

18—EXHAUST PIPE, RENEW
All Models 0.5

Emission Control System—TIME

OPERATION INDEX

Intake Air Temperture & Crankcase Vent 1
Ignition Timing Controls 2
Air Injection System 3
Evaporative System 4

1—INTAKE AIR TEMPERATURE & CRANKCASE VENT
Breather Drain Tube 0.2
Check Valve Or Hose Exc 0.1
CVCC & Accord 0.2
Control Valve Diaphragm Exc 0.1
CVCC & Accord 0.2
Air Intake Sensor Exc 0.3
CVCC 0.2
Breather Tube Exc 0.3
CVCC & Accord 0.2
Breather Chamber Exc 0.3
CVCC & Accord 0.2
Hot Air Pipe Exc 0.1
CVCC & Accord 0.2
Hot Air Cover, Civic 0.2
Civic A.I.R. 0.7
CVCC & Accord 0.7

2—IGNITION TIMING CONTROLS
Throttle Control Valve 0.3
Throttle Positioner Solenoid ValVE 0.3
Dashpot Solenoid Valve 0.3
Dashpot Check Valve 0.3
Delay Valve 0.3
Ign Timing Control Check Valve 0.4
Start Control Valve 0.2
Ignition Solenoid Valve 0.4
Temperture Sensor 0.3
Thermoswitch 0.5

3—AIR INJECTION SYSTEM
Control Valve 0.3
Air Nozzles 0.5
Air Manifold 0.3
Air Pump 0.4
Check Valve Hose 0.2
Check Valve 0.2
Air By-Pass Valve 0.4
Air Delay Valve 0.3
Anti-Afterburn Valve 0.4

4—EVAPORATIVE SYSTEM
T-Joint Or Vent Hose 0.3
Cannister 0.2
2-Way Vent Valve Or Hose 0.4
Check Valve Or Hose 0.3
Vapor Separator Pipe 0.4
4- Way Joint 0.3

Engine Cooling & Heating System - 600—TIME

OPERATION INDEX

Fan, R&R 1
Fan Belt, Renew 2
Belt, Pulleys, R&R 3
Fan Housing, R&R Or Renew 4
Fan Housing Cushion, R&R Or Renew 5
Pulley, Cooling Fan, R&R 6
Shroud Assy (Eng) R&R 7
Heater Switch, Renew 8
Heater, Heat Exchanger, Renew 9
Heater Blower Unit, Renew 10
Heater Control Valve, Renew 11

1—FAN, R&R
600 ....0.7

2—FAN BELT, RENEW
600 ....0.2

3—BELT, PULLEYS, R&R
600, Each 0.1

4—FAN HOUSING, R&R OR RENEW
600 ....0.7

5—FAN HOUSING CUSHION, R&R
600 ....0.5

6—PULLEY, COOLING FAN, R&R
600 ....0.6

7—SHROUD ASSY (ENGINE), R&R OR RENEW
600, Right 0.2
Left 0.4

8—HEATER SWITCH, RENEW
600 ....0.2

9—HEATER, HEAT EXCHANGER, RENEW
600 ....0.8

10—HEATER BLOWER UNIT, RENEW
600 ....0.2

11—HEATER CONTROL VALVE, RENEW
600 ....0.7

Engine Cooling & Heating System - Civic—TIME

OPERATION INDEX

Radiator, R&R Or Renew 1
Coolant Recovery Tank, Renew 2
Water Pump, R&R Or Renew 3
Thermostat, R&R Or Renew 4
Radiator Hoses, R&R Or Renew 5
Coolant Tube, Renew 6
Fan, R&R Or Renew 7
Fan Belt, Renew 8
Fan Housing, Renew 9
Heater, R&R Or Renew 10
Heater Core, Renew 11
Heater Motor, Renew 12
Heater Control, Renew 13
Heater Water Valve, Renew 14
Heater Water Hose, Renew 15

1—RADIATOR, R&R OR RENEW
Civic & Civic A.I.R. Exc 1.1
Automatic Trans 1.2
CVCC, CVCC Wagon Exc 0.7
Automatic Trans 0.8
Accord Exc 0.8
Automatic Trans 0.9

2—COOLANT RECOVERY TANK, R&R OR RENEW
All Models 0.2

3—WATER PUMP, R&R OR RENEW
Civic & CVCC 0.5
Accord 0.7

4—THERMOSTAT, R&R OR RENEW
All Models 0.4

5—RADIATOR HOSES, R&R OR RENEW
Civic & Accord—
Upper 0.4
Lower 0.6
By-Pass 0.5
CVCC—
Upper 0.2
Lower 0.3
By-Pass 0.4

6—COOLANT TUBE, RENEW
Civic & Accord 0.6
CVCC 0.5

7—FAN, R&R OR RENEW
All Models 0.4

8—FAN BELT, RENEW
All Models 0.2

9—FAN HOUSING, RENEW
All Models 0.5

10—HEATER ASSY, R&R OR RENEW
Civic & CVCC 1.1
Accord 1.6

11—HEATER CORE, RENEW
Civic & CVCC 1.4
Accord 1.8

12—HEATER MOTOR, RENEW
Civic 1.1
CVCC 1.3
Accord 0.5

13—HEATER CONTROL, RENEW
Civic & CVCC 0.3
Accord 1.0

14—HEATER WATER VALVE, RENEW
Civic & CVCC 0.5
Accord 0.4

15—HEATER WATER HOSE, RENEW
Civic & CVCC 0.5
Accord 0.3

Engine - 600—TIME

OPERATION INDEX

Engine, R & R 1
Engine, R & R & Overhaul 2
Cylinder Barrel, R&R Or Renew 3
Cylinder Head, Renew 4
Piston & Or Rings, Renew 5
Crankshaft, R&R Or Renew 6
Crankshaft Main Bearing Holders, R&R Or Renew 7
Camshaft Drive Chain Slipper, Renew 8
Valve Guides, Renew 9
Camshaft, Renew 10
Cam Chain Tensioner Assy, Renew 11
Cam Chain Roller Guide, R&R 12
Valves, Renew 13
Rocker Arm, Renew 14
Crankcase, Renew 15
Crankcase Cover, Renew 16
Oil Guide, Renew 17
Nozzle, Chain Oiler, Renew 18
Oil Pump Rod, Renew 19
Oil Pump Plunger, Renew 20
Oil Pump Body, Renew 21
Oil Passage Pipe Seal, Renew 22
Oil Filter, Renew 23
Engine Mounting & Front Suspension Crossmember, R&R Or Renew 24
Engine Mounts, Renew 25
Crossmember Mounting Cushions, Renew 26

1—ENGINE, R&R
Note: Does not include transfer of any part of engine or replacement of special equipment.
600 ....2.0

2—ENGINE, R&R & OVERHAUL
600 ....12.8

3—CYLINDER BARREL, R&R OR RENEW
600 ....3.1

4—CYLINDER HEAD, RENEW
600 ....2.8

5—PISTON & OR RINGS, RENEW
600, One 3.1
Both 3.4

6—CRANKSHAFT, R&R OR RENEW
600 ....4.9

(Continued)

Engine - 600—TIME Cont'd

7—CRANKSHAFT MAIN BEARING HOLDERS, R&R OR RENEW
600, Center 3.5
Right Or Left 3.4

8—CAMSHAFT DRIVER CHAIN SLIPPER, RENEW
600 ....3.1

9—VALVE GUIDES, RENEW
600, One 2.6
Each Additional, Add 0.1

10—CAMSHAFT, RENEW
600 ....1.3

11—CAM CHAIN TENSIONER ASSY, RENEW
600 ....3.4

12—CAM CHAIN ROLLER GUIDE, R&R
600 ....2.4

13—VALVES, RENEW
600, One 2.6
Each Additional, Add 0.3

14—ROCKER AR, RENEW
600, Right 0.4
Left 0.3

15—CRANKCASE, RENEW
600, Upper 5.2
Lower 3.5

16—CRANKCASE COVER, RENEW
600, Right 0.7
Left 1.4

17—OIL GUIDE, RENEW
600 ....3.5

18—NOZZLE, CHAIN OILER, RENEW
600 ....1.6

19—OIL PUMP ROD, RENEW
600 ....1.8

20—OIL PUMP PLUNGER, RENEW
600 ....1.8

21—OIL PUMP BODY, RENEW
600 ....1.8

22—OIL PASSAGE PIPE SEAL, RENEW
600 ....3.4

23—OIL FILTER, RENEW
600 ....0.1

24—ENGINE MTG & FRONT SUSP CROSSMEMBER, R&R OR RENEW
600 ....2.0

25—ENGINE MOUNTS, RENEW
600—
Front 0.5
Rear 0.8

26—CROSSMEMBER MOUNTING CUSIONS, RENEW
600—
Front, One Side 0.3
Both Sides 0.4
Rear, One Side 0.5
Both Sides 0.6
All 0.8

Engine - Civic & Accord—TIME

OPERATION INDEX

Engine & Trans, R&R *1*
Cylinder Block, Renew *1A*
Cylinder Head, R&R Or Renew *2*
Cylinder Head Gasket, R&R Or Renew *3*
Prechambers, Overhaul *4*
Piston Rings, Renew *5*
Pistons Or Rods, Renew *6*
Rod Bearings, Renew *7*
Crankshaft Or Main Bearings, Renew *8*
Crankshaft Rear Oil Seal, Renew *9*
Crankshaft Pulley, R&R Or Renew *10*
Valves, Renew Or Grind *11*
Valve Spring Or Seal, Renew *11A*
Crankshaft, Renew *12*
Rocker Arms, Overhaul *13*
Valve Cover, R&R Or Renew *14*
Timing Belt Cover, Renew *15*
Timing Belt, Renew *16*
Timing Belt Adjuster, Renew *17*
Oil Pan Or Gasket, Renew *19*
Oil Pump, R&R & Overhaul *20*
Oil Filter, R&R Or Renew *21*
Engine Mounts, Renew *22*
Left Eng Supt Bracket, Renew *23*
Eng Support Frame, Renew *24*
Front Frame Beam, Renew *25*
Eng Torque Rod, Renew *26*

1—ENGINE & TRANSMISSION, REMOVE & REINSTALL
Civic & CVCC 3.5
Accord 3.6

1A—CYLINDER BLOCK, RENEW
Includes transfer and/or replace all components not furnished with new block.
Civic 9.0
Civic A.I.R. 9.4
CVCC, CVCC Wagon 9.3
Accord 9.6
Includes R&R cylinder head & manifolds as a unit & replace all rings.
Civic 8.8

2—CYLINDER HEAD, R&R OR RENEW
Includes replace or reface valves, check seats & guides, transfer prechambers, adjust valves, timing & dwell.
Civic Exc 4.9
With Air Cond 5.6
Civic A.I.R. Exc 5.3
With Air Cond 6.0
Civic CVCC, CVCC Wagon—
73-75 Exc 4.4
With Air Cond 4.7
76-78 Exc 4.6
With Air Cond 4.9
Accord Exc 5.3
With Air Cond 5.6

3—CYLINDER HEAD GASKET, R&R OR RENEW
Includes check head surface, valve ajdustment, dwell & timing adjustments
Civic Exc 1.8
With Air Cond 2.5
Civic A.I.R. Exc 2.2
With Air Cond 2.9
Civic CVCC, CVCC Wagon—
73-75 Exc 3.7
With Air Cond 4.0
76-78 Exc 3.9
With Air Cond 4.2
Accord Exc 4.3
With Air Cond 4.7

4—PRECHAMBERS, ALL, OVERHAUL
Includes replace valve, reface seat & replace all seals.
CVCC & Accord 1.7

5—PISTON RINGS, RENEW
Civic—
One Piston 4.6
All Pistons 5.5
Civic A.I.R.—
One Piston 5.0
All Pistons 5.9
Civic CVCC, CVCC Wagon—
One Piston 5.3
All Pistons 6.2
Accord—
One Piston 4.9
All Pistons 5.8

6—PISTONS OR RODS, RENEW
Civic—
One 4.8
All 6.1
Civic A.I.R.—
One 5.2
All 5.8
CVCC, CVCC Wagon—
One 5.5
All 6.1
Accord—
One 5.1
All 5.7

7—ROD BEARINGS, RENEW
One—
Civic & Civic A.I.R. 1.2
CVCC, CVCC Wagon 0.7
Accord 1.0
Each Additional 0.3

8—CRANKSHAFT OR MAIN BEARINGS, RENEW
Includes R&R engine, crankshaft pulley and gear. Does not includes R&R cylinder head or pistons.
Civic 4.7
Civic A.I.R. 5.1
CVCC, CVCC Wagon 5.7
Accord 5.2

9—CRANKSHAFT REAR OIL SEAL, RENEW
Includes R&R transmission, flywheel & clutch.
Civic & Civic A.I.R. Exc 2.5
With Hondamatic 3.5
CVCC Exc 2.2
With Hondamatic 3.2
Accord Exc 2.4
With Hondamatic 3.4

10—CRANKSHAFT PULLEY, R&R OR RENEW
Civic & CVCC 0.2
Accord 0.3

11—VALVES, RENEW OR GRIND
Includes grind all seats & valve adjustment
Civic Exc 4.4
With Air Cond 5.1
Civic A.I.R. Exc 4.8
With Air Cond 5.5
Civic CVCC, CVCC Wagon—
73-75 Exc 5.3
With Air Cond 5.6
76-78 Exc 5.5
With Air Cond 5.8
Accord Exc 6.1
With Air Cond 6.4

—NOTE—
For Each Valve Guide, Add *0.1*

11A—VALVE SPRINGS OR SEALS, RENEW
Includes valve adjustment
All Models—
One 0.9
Each Additional 0.1

12—CAMSHAFT, RENEW
Civic & Civic A.I.R. Exc 1.3
With Air Cond 2.0
Civic CVCC, CVCC Wagon—
Less Air Cond 1.7
With Air Cond 2.0
Accord Exc 1.6
With Air Cond 1.9

13—ROCKER ARMS, OVERHAUL
Includes disassemble, inspect
Accord 1.2
& measure, replace any or all components & adjust valves.
Civic & Civic A.I.R. 1.2
Civic CVCC, CVCC Wgn 1.3

14—VALVE COVER, R&R OR RENEW
Civic & CVCC 0.2
Accord 0.3

(Continued)

Engine - Civic & Accord—TIME Cont'd

15—TIMING BELT COVER, RENEW
Upper—
- Civic Exc 0.2
  - With Air Cond 0.9
- CVCC Exc 0.2
  - With Air Cond 0.5
- Accord Exc 0.3
  - With Air Cond 0.6

Lower—
- Civic Exc 0.8
  - With Air Cond 1.5
- CVCC Exc 0.5
  - With Air Cond 0.8
- Accord Exc 0.5
  - With Air Cond 0.8

16—TIMING BELT, RENEW
Civic Exc 1.0
- With Air Cond 1.7

CVCC Exc 1.6
- With Air Cond 1.9

Accord Exc 1.3
- With Air Cond 1.6

17—TIMING BELT ADJUSTER, RENEW
Civic Exc 1.1
- With Air Cond 1.8

CVCC Exc 1.6
- With Air Cond 1.9

Accord Exc 1.2
- With Air Cond 1.5

19—OIL PAN &/OR CASKET, RENEW
Civic & Civic A.I.R. 1.0
CVCC, CVCC Wagon 0.4
Accord 0.5

20—OIL PUMP, R&R & OVERHAUL
Civic & Civic A.I.R. 1.2
CVCC, CVCC Wagon 0.7
Accord 1.0

21—OIL FILTER, R&R OR RENEW
All Models 0.2

22—ENGINE MOUNTS, RENEW
Front—
- CVCC & Accord 0.5

Center—
- All Models 0.3

Rear—
- CVCC 1.4
- Accord 0.7

23—LEFT ENGINE SUPPORT BRACKET, RENEW
Civic & CVCC Exc 0.4
- With Air Cond 1.0

Accord Exc 0.6
- With Air Cond 1.2

24—ENGINE SUPPORT FRAME, RENEW
All Models 2.3

25—FRONT FRAME BEAM, RENEW
Civic & CVCC 1.6
Accord 1.2

26—ENGINE TORQUE ROD, RENEW
All Models 0.3

Clutch, Manual Trans & Primary Drives - 600—TIME

OPERATION INDEX

Clutch Housing, Renew 1
Clutch Housing Bushing, Renew 2
Clutch Drum, Renew 3
Clutch Friction Disc, Renew 4
Clutch Pressure Disc, Renew 5
Clutch Pressure Disc Retainer, Renew 6
Clutch Diaphragm Spring, Renew 7
Clutch Torque Spring Assy, Renew 8
Clutch Release Rod Assy, Renew 9
Clutch Release Bearing, Renew 10
Clutch Cable, Renew 11
Clutch Oil Seal, Renew 12
Primary Driver Chain Tensioner, Renew 13
Primary Drive Chain, Renew 14
Primary Driver Shaft, Renew 15
Primary Driver Sprockets, Renew 16
Primary Driven Sprockets Hub, Renew 17
Std Trans Mainshaft, Renew 18
Std Trans Countershaft, Renew 19
Std Trans Shift Forks, Renew 20
Std Trans Shift Fork Shafts, Renew 21
Std Trans Shift Plates Or Guides, Renew 22

1—CLUTCH HOUSING, RENEW
600 ....0.9

2—CLUTCH HOUSING BUSHING, RENEW
600 ....1.1

3—CLUTCH DRUM, RENEW
600 ....1.3

4—CLUTCH FRICTION DISC, RENEW
600 ....1.2

5—CLUTCH PRESSURE DISC, RENEW
600 ....1.4

6—CLUTCH PRESSURE DISC RETAINER, RENEW
600 ....1.4

7—CLUTCH DIAPHRAGM SPRING, RENEW
600 ....1.4

8—CLUTCH TORQUE SPRING ASSY, RENEW
600 ....1.4

9—CLUTCH RELEASE ROD ASSY,RENEW
600 ....1.0

10—CLUTCH RELEASE BEARING, RENEW
600 ....1.0

11—CLUTCH CABLE, RENEW
600 ....0.2

12—CLUTCH OIL SEAL, RENEW
600 ....1.3

13—PRIMARY DRIVE CHAIN TENSIONER, RENEW
600 ....1.5

14—PRIMARY DRIVE CHAIN, RENEW
600 ....1.5

15—PRIMARY DRIVE SHAFT, RENEW
600 ....1.5

16—PRIMARY DRIVE SPROCKETS, RENEW
600, Each 2.0

17—PRIMARY DRIVEN SPROCKET HUB, RENEW
600 ....1.7

18—STD. TRANS. MAINSHAFT, RENEW
600 ....3.7

19—STD. TRANS. COUNTERSHAFT, RENEW
600 ....3.7

20—STD. TRANS. SHIFT FORKS, RENEW
600—
- Forward Gears, Each 3.8
- Reverse Gear 1.2

21—STD. TRANS. SHIFT FORK SHAFTS, RENEW
600, Each 3.8

22—STD. TRANS. SHIFT PLATES OR GUIDES, RENEW
600 ....3.9

Clutch & Manual Transmission - Civic—TIME

OPERATION INDEX

Clutch Disc &/Or Pressure Plate, Renew 1
Clutch Throwout Bearing, Renew 2
Clutch Release Shaft, Renew 3
Flywheel & Pilot Bearing, Renew 4
Clutch Pedal, Renew 5
Clutch Master Cylinder, Renew 6
Clutch Slave Cylinder, Renew 7
Clutch Hydraulic Line, Renew 8
Transmission, R&R Or Renew 9
Transmission, R&R & Overhaul 10
Transmission, Reseal 11
Shifter Fork Or Shafts, Renew 12
Detent, Renew 13
Gearshift Lever, Overhaul 14
Extension Bushing, Renew 15

1—CLUTCH DISC &/OR PRESSURE PLATE, RENEW
Includes R & R transmission
Civic & CVCC 2.2
Accord 2.1

2—CLUTCH THROWOUT BEARING, RENEW
All Models 2.0

3—CLUTCH RELEASE SHAFT, RENEW
Includes R & R transmission
All Models 2.0

4—FLYWHEEL & PILOT BEARING, RENEW
Civic & Accord 2.3
CVCC 2.0

5—CLUTCH PEDAL, RENEW
Civic 0.2
Accord 1.0

6—CLUTCH MASTER CYLINDER, RENEW
Includes bleeding system.
Accord 0.7

7—CLUTCH SLAVE CYLINDER, RENEW
Includes bleeding system.
Accord 0.7

8—CLUTCH HYDRAULIC LINE, RENEW
Includes bleeding system.
Accord 0.5

9—TRANSMISSION R&R OR RENEW
Civic & CVCC 2.0
Accord 1.8

10—TRANSMISSION, R&R & OVERHAUL
All Models 3.9

—NOTE—

For 5 Speed, Add 0.3
To Overhaul Differential, Add 0.9

11—TRANSMISSION, RESEAL
Civic & Civic A.I.R. 3.0
CVCC Exc 2.8
- 5 Speed 3.0

Accord 3.3

(Continued)

Clutch & Manual Transmission - Civic—TIME Cont'd

12—SHIFTER FORK OR SHAFTS, RENEW

Civic & Civic A.I.R. 2.5
CVCC Exc 3.2
5 Speed 3.4
Accord 3.1

13—DETENT, RENEW

Civic & CVCC 0.2
Accord 0.4

14—GEAR SHIFT LEVER, OVERHAUL

Civic & Civic A.I.R. 0.5
CVCC 0.9
Accord 0.7

15—EXTENSION BUSHING, RENEW

Civic & Civic A.I.R. 0.5
CVCC 0.2
Accord 0.5

Automatic Transmission—TIME

OPERATION INDEX

Trans & Converter, R&R Or Renew 1
Trans & Converter, Overhaul 2
Transmission, Reseal 3
Torque Converter, Reseal 4
Converter Drive Plate, Renew 5
Valve Body, Renew 6
Parking Pawl, Renew 7
Reverse Fork Or Shaft, Renew 8
Main Shaft Oil Seal, Renew 9
Oil Cooler, Renew 10
Inhibitor & Back-Up Lamp Switch, Renew 11
Gearshfit Selector Lever, Renew 12
Gearshift Control Cable, Renew 13

1—TRANSMISSION & CONVERTER, R&R OR RENEW

Includes pressure test & road test.
Civic & CVCC 3.3
Accord 2.4

2—TRANSMISSION & CONVERTER, R&R & OVERHAUL

Civic & CVCC 6.0
Accord 5.1

—NOTE—
To Overhaul Differential, Add 0.9

3—TRANSMISSION, R&R & RESEAL

Includes replace all gaskets & seals. Does not include dissassembly of any components.
Civic & CVCC 4.0
Accord 3.3

—NOTE—
To Replace Converter Seals, Add 0.8

3—TORQUE CONVERTER, CLEAN & RESEAL

Includes R&R transmission & converter.
Civic & CVCC 4.1
Accord 2.7

5—CONVERTER DRIVE PLATE, RENEW

Includes R&R transmission.
Civic & CVCC 3.4
Accord 2.4

6—VALVE BODY, RENEW

Includes R&R transmission.
Civic & CVCC 4.0
Accord 3.3

7—PARKING PAWL, RENEW

Includes R&R transmission.
Civic & CVCC 4.0
Accord 3.1

8—REVERSE FORK &/OR SHAFT, RENEW

Includes R&R transmission.
Civic & CVCC 4.0
Accord 3.1

9—MAINSHAFT OIL SEAL, RENEW

Includes R&R transmission
Civic & CVCC 3.4
Accord 2.5

10—OIL COOLER, RENEW

Includes bleed cooling system
Civic & A.I.R. 1.1
CVCC 0.8
Accord 0.8

11—INHIBITOR SWITCH & BACK-UP LAMP SWITCH, RENEW

Civic & Civic A.I.R. 0.3
CVCC 0.2
Accord 0.4

12—GEARSHIFT SELECTOR LEVER, RENEW

Civic & Civic A.I.R. 0.4
CVCC 0.6
Accord 0.8

13—GEARSHIFT CONTROL CABLE, RENEW

Civic & CVCC 0.7
Accord 0.8

Brakes, Steering, Suspension & Differential—TIME

OPERATION INDEX

Brake Shoes Or Friction Pads, Renew 1
Master Cylinder, Renew 2
Master Cylinder, Overhaul 3
Fluid Reservoir, Renew 4
Master Cylinder Check Valve, Renew 5
Vacuum Booster, Overhaul 6
Vacuum Booster, R & R 7
Brakeline Protector Valve, Renew 8
Brake Hose, Front Or Rear, Renew 9
Caliper Assy, Renew 10
Caliper Assy, Overhaul 11
Disc Brake Rotors, Renew 11A
Wheel Cylinder, Renew 12
Bleed System 13
Proportioning Valve Assy, Renew 14
Mud Guard (Disc Brakes), Renew 15
Hub & Disc (Front), Renew 16
Brake Drum Rear, R & R Or Renew 17
Wheel Bearings, Renew 18
Parking Brake Arm, Renew 19
Parking Brake Cable, Renew 20
Parking Brake, Adjust 21
Parking Brake Pawl, Renew 22
Parking Brake Lever, Renew 23
Steering Gear Box, Renew 24
Steering Gear Rack, Adjust 25
Steering Pinion Dust Seal, Renew 26
Steering Rack End Assy, Renew 27
Tie Rod End Assy, Renew 28
Steering Rack Guide, Replace 29
Steering Shaft Joint Assy, Renew 30
Steering Column Main Shaft, Renew 31
Steering Col. Main Shaft Bushing, Renew 32
Steering Column Lock Assy, Renew 33
Front Suspension Driveshaft, Renew 34
Driveshaft Bellows, Renew 35
Driveshaft Joint, Inner, Renew 36
Front Suspension Knuckle, Renew 37
Front Suspension Ball Joint, Renew 38
Stabilizer Shaft, Renew 39
Lower Control Arm, Renew 40
Springs, Renew 41
Shock Absorbers, Renew 42
Front Suspension Main Shaft, Renew 43
Front Suspension Mounting Pad, Renew 44
Rear Axle Beam, R & R As Assy 45
Rear Axle Beam, Renew 46
Rear Lower Arm, Renew 47
Rear Hub Shaft, Renew 48
Rear Radius Rod, Renew 49
Differential Final Driven Gear Unit, Renew 50
Differential, Overhaul 51
Differential Ball Bearing, Renew 52
Differential Flange Joint, Renew 53
Differential Flange Joint Seal, Renew 54
Front Susp Mtg Sub Frame 55

1—BRAKE SHOES OR FRICTION PADS, RENEW

Drum Type—
600, One Wheel 0.3
Civic & Accord, One Wheel 0.6
Disc Type—
600, One Wheel 0.2
Civic & Accord, Two Wheels 0.6

2—MASTER CYLINDER, RENEW

600 .... 1.0
Civic & CVCC 0.6
Accord 1.0

3—MASTER CYLINDER, OVERHAUL

All Models 1.2

4—FLUID RESERVOIR, RENEW

All Models 0.4

5—MASTER CYLINDER CHECK VALVE, RENEW

600 .... 0.4
Civic 0.7

6—VACUUM BOOSTER, OVERHAUL

600 .... 1.0
Civic 0.8
Accord 1.6

7—VACUUM BOOSTER, R & R

All Models 0.5
Accord 1.1

8—BRAKELINE PROTECTOR VALVE, RENEW

600 .... 0.3

9—BRAKE HOSE, FRONT OR REAR, RENEW

600 .... 0.3
Civic & Accord 0.6

10—CALIPER ASSY, RENEW

600—
One 0.5
Both 0.7
Civic—
One 0.6
Both 1.0
Accord—
One 0.8
Both 1.0

11—CALIPER ASSY, OVERHAUL

600 .... 0.6

11A—DISC BRAKE ROTORS, BOTH, RENEW

Includes replace wheel bearings & bleed brakes.
Civic 2.0
Accord 2.2

12—BRAKE WHEEL CYLINDER, RENEW

600 .... 0.6
Civic & Accord 1.0

13—BLEED SYSTEM

All Models 0.3

14—PROPORTIONING VALVE ASSY, RENEW

CVCC 0.5
Civic & Civic A.I.R. 0.7
Accord 0.6

15—MUD GUARD (DISC BRAKES), RENEW

600 .... 0.3
Civic 1.2

(Continued)

Brakes, Steering, Suspension & Differential—TIME Cont'd

16—HUB & DISC (FRONT), RENEW
600 .... 0.4
Civic ①1.3
Accord ①1.6
①Includes Replace Wheel Bearings & Bleed Brakes.

17—BRAKE DRUM, REAR, R & R OR RENEW
600 .... 0.3
Civic & Accord 0.6

18—WHEEL BEARINGS, RENEW
600—
  Rear 0.3
  Front 1.0
Civic & Accord—
  Front 1.3
  Rear 0.6

19—PARKING BRAKE ARM, RENEW
600 .... 0.6
Civic & Accord 0.7

20—PARKING BRAKE CABLE, RENEW
600 .... 0.6
Civic & Accord 0.5

21—PARKING BRAKE, ADJUST
600 .... 0.1

22—PARKING BRAKE PAWL, RENEW
600 .... 0.2

23—PARKING BRAKE LEVER, RENEW
All Models 0.2

24—STEERING GEAR, RENEW
600 .... 1.9
Civic & Accord 1.4

24A—STEERING GEAR, R&R & OVERHAUL
Civic 1.6
CVCC & Accord 2.4

25—STEERING GEAR RACK, ADJUST
600 .... 0.3

26—STEERING PINION DUST SEAL, RENEW
All Models 0.5

27—STEERING RACK END ASSY, RENEW
600, Right 1.0
  Left 1.8

28—TIE ROD END ASSY, RENEW
All Models, Each 0.6

29—STEERING RACK GUIDE, REPLACE
All Models 0.5

30—STEERING SHAFT JOINT ASSY, RENEW
600 .... 0.2

31—STEERING COLUMN MAIN SHAFT, RENEW
600 .... 0.5
Civic 1.1
Accord 0.8

32—STEERING COLUMN MAIN SHAFT BUSHING, RENEW
600 .... 0.5

33—STEERING COLUMN LOCK ASSY, RENEW
600 .... 0.5
Civic & Accord 0.4

34—FRONT SUSPENSION DRIVESHAFT, RENEW
600 .... 1.0
Civic & Accord—
  One 0.7
  Both 1.2

35—DRIVESHAFT BELLOWS, RENEW
600, Inner Or Outer 1.0
Civic & Accord—
  One 0.8
  Both 1.4

36—DRIVESHAFT JOINT, INNER, RENEW
600 .... 1.0
Civic & Accord—
  One 0.8
  Both 1.5

37—FRONT SUSPENSION KNUCKLE, RENEW
600 .... 1.0
Civic 1.3
Accord 1.4

38—FRONT SUSPENSION BALL JOINT, RENEW
600, One 0.3

39—STABILIZER SHAFT, RENEW
600 .... 0.3
Civic & Accord 0.4

40—LOWER CONTROL ARM, RENEW
Civic 0.7
Civic A.I.R. 0.9
CVCC 1.1
Accord 0.9

41—SPRING(S), RENEW
Front—
  600 .... 0.8
  Civic 1.2
  Accord 1.3
Rear—
  600 .... 0.6
  Civic Exc 0.8
    Wagon 0.6
  Accord 1.0

42—SHOCK ABSORBERS, RENEW
Front—
  600 .... 0.6
  Civic 1.2
  Accord 1.3
Rear—
  600 .... 0.2
  Civic Exc 0.8
    Wagon 0.2
  Accord 1.0

43—FRONT SUSPENSION MAIN SHAFT, RENEW
600 .... 0.8

44—FRONT SUSPENSION MOUNTING PAD, RENEW
600 .... 0.6

45—REAR AXLE BEAM, R & R AS ASSY
600 .... 1.0

46—REAR AXLE BEAM, RENEW
600 .... 1.5

47—REAR LOWER ARM, RENEW
Civic 0.5
Accord 0.7

48—REAR HUB SHAFT, RENEW
Civic 1.1
Accord 1.0

49—REAR RADIUS ROD, RENEW
Civic 0.5
Accord 0.6

50—DIFFERENTIAL FINAL DRIVEN GEAR UNIT, RENEW
600 .... 3.8

51—DIFFERENTIAL, OVERHAUL
600 .... 3.8
Civic & Accord—
  4 Speed 2.9
  5 Speed 3.3
  Automatic 4.2

52—DIFFERENTIAL BALL BEARING, RENEW
600 .... 3.5
Civic 3.0

53—DIFFERENTIAL FLANGE JOINT, RENEW
600 .... 0.5

54—DIFFERENTIAL FLANGE JOINT SEAL, RENEW
All Models 0.6

55—FRONT SUSPENSION MOUNTING SUB FRAME
See engine mountings

Speedometer, W/S Wiper, Switches & Instruments—TIME

OPERATION INDEX
Speedometer Cable, Renew 1
Speedometer Head, Renew 2
W/S Wiper & Washer Switch, Renew 3
W/S Wiper Motor, Renew 4
W/S Wiper Drive Arm Assy, Renew 5
Lighting Switch Assy, Renew 6
Turn Signal Switch, Renew 7
Back-Up Light Switch, Renew 8
Stop Light Switch, Renew 9
Hazard Flasher Switch, Renew 10

1—SPEEDOMETER CABLE, RENEW
600 .... 0.2
Civic & Accord 0.6
CVCC 0.7

2—SPEEDOMETER HEAD, RENEW
600 .... 0.2
Civic & Accord 0.6
CVCC 0.5

3—W/S WIPER & WASHER SWITCH, RENEW
600 .... 0.3
Civic & Accord 0.4

4—W/S WIPER MOTOR, RENEW
600 .... 0.3
Civic 0.5
Accord 0.3

5—W/S WIPER DRIVE ARM ASSY, RENEW
600 .... 0.3
Civic 0.4
Accord 0.3

6—LIGHTING SWITCH ASSY, RENEW
1971-75 .... 0.2
1976-78 .... 0.4

7—TURN SIGNAL SWITCH, RENEW
All Models 0.4

8—BACK-UP LIGHT SWITCH, RENEW
600 .... 0.1
Civic & Accord Exc 0.2
  With Automatic Trans 0.3

9—STOP LIGHT SWITCH, RENEW
All Models 0.2

10—HAZARD FLASHER SWITCH, RENEW
All Models Exc 0.2
  Accord 0.3

IDENTIFICATION

ALL MODELS.................................. 196

ILLUSTRATIONS

FIG 1 – ENGINE – BLOCK, OIL PAN & CRANKSHAFT
FIG 2 – ENGINE – HEAD & VALVES
FIG 3 – TRANSMISSION CASE
FIG 4 – TRANSMISSION GEARS
FIG 5 – FRONT SUSPENSION
FIG 6 – STEERING

OPERATION TIMES

A

Air Conditioner.................................. 204
Alternator.................................. 203
Ammeter.................................. 203
Automatic Transmission.................................. 205

B

Brakes.................................. 206

C

Cables (Ignition).................................. 203
Calipers.................................. 206
Camshaft.................................. 204
Carburetor.................................. 203
Clutch.................................. 205
Coil, Ignition.................................. 203
Compression Test.................................. 203
Cooling System.................................. 204
Crankshaft.................................. 205
Cylinder Head.................................. 204

D

Dash Gauges.................................. 207
Differential.................................. 207
Disc Brakes.................................. 206
Distributor.................................. 203

E

Emission Controls.................................. 203
Engine Assembly.................................. 205
Engine Mountings.................................. 204
Engine Oiling.................................. 204
Engine Tune-Up.................................. 203
Exhaust System.................................. 203

F

Flywheel.................................. 205
Front Suspension.................................. 206
Fuel Gauges.................................. 207
Fuel Pump.................................. 203
Fuel Tank.................................. 203

H

Hand Brake.................................. 206
Headlight Switch.................................. 208
Heater.................................. 204
Hose (Brake).................................. 206
Hose (Radiator).................................. 204
Hydraulic Brakes.................................. 206

I

Ignition.................................. 203
Ignition Coil.................................. 203
Ignition Switch.................................. 203
Intake Manifold.................................. 203

L

Light Switches.................................. 208

M

Main Bearings.................................. 205
Master Cylinder.................................. 206
Muffler.................................. 203

O

Oil Gauge.................................. 207
Oiling, Engine.................................. 204
Oil Pan.................................. 204
Oil Pump.................................. 204
Overdrive.................................. 205

P

Parking Brake.................................. 206
Piston Rings.................................. 205
Pistons.................................. 205
Power Brake.................................. 206
Power Steering.................................. 206

R

Radiator.................................. 204
Radiator Hose.................................. 204
Rear Axle.................................. 207
Regulator (Alternator).................................. 203
Rod Bearings.................................. 205

S

Shocks (Front).................................. 207
Shocks (Rear).................................. 207
Speedometer.................................. 207
Springs (Front).................................. 207
Springs (Rear).................................. 207
Starting Motor.................................. 203
Steering Gear.................................. 206
Steering Linkage.................................. 206
Switches (Light).................................. 208
Synchro-Mesh Trans.................................. 205

T

Tachometer.................................. 207
Temperature Gauge.................................. 207
Thermostat.................................. 204
Timing Case Cover.................................. 204
Timing Chain.................................. 204
Timing Gears.................................. 204
Torsion Bar.................................. 207
Transmission, Manual.................................. 205
Transmission, Automatic.................................. 205
Tune-Up, Engine.................................. 203

U

Universals.................................. 207

V

Valve Lifters.................................. 204
Valve System.................................. 204

W

Water Pump.................................. 204
Windshield Wiper.................................. 207

VEHICLE IDENTIFICATION

STARTING CHASSIS NUMBERS

E TYPE SERIES 3

MODEL	YEAR	STARTING CHASSIS NO.
OPEN CAR	1971	1S 7001
	1972	1S 72335
	1973	UD1S 73856
2 + 2 COUPE	1971	1S 20001
	1972	1S 20103
	1973	UD1S 21029
	1974	UE1S 23240

XJ6

MODEL	YEAR	STARTING CHASSIS NO.
XJ6 SED SER 1	1969	1L 5001
	1970	1L 53203
	1971	1L 55686
	1972	1L 64129
	1973	UD1L 69908BW
XJ6 SED SER 2	1974	UE2N 50001BW
XJ6L SED SER 2	1975	UF2T 54779
	1976	UG2T 56746BW
XJ6C COUPE SER 2	1975	UF2J 50045BW
	1976	UG2J 51369BW

X J 12

MODEL	YEAR	STARTING CHASSIS NO.
XJ12 SED SER 1	1973	UD1P 50153
XJ12L SED SER 2	1974	UE2R 50001BW
	1975	UF2R 53930BW
	1976	UG2R 54264BW
XJ12 C COUPE SER 2	1975	UF2G 50060BW
	1976	UG2G 50426BW

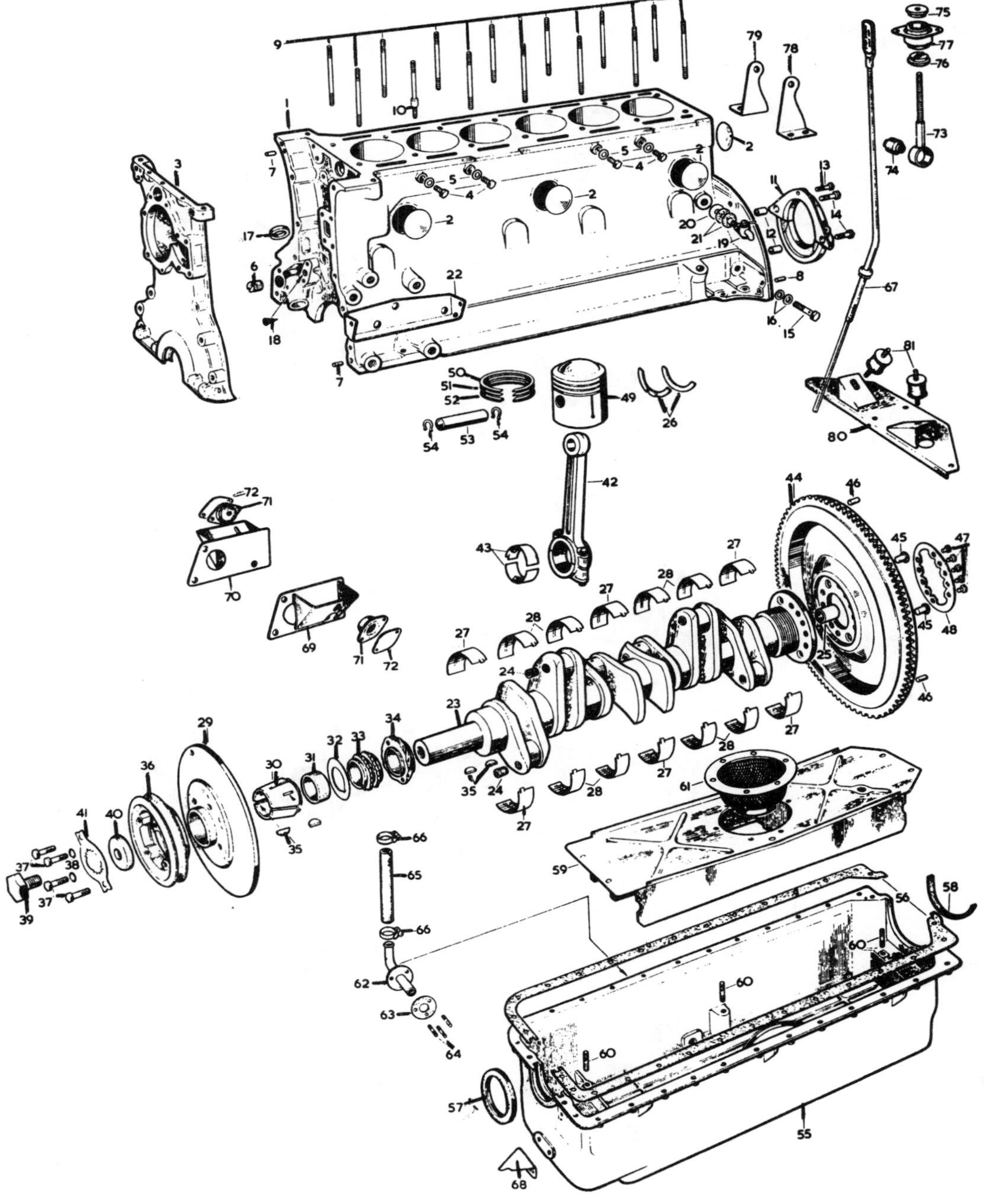

FIG 1 – ENGINE BLOCK, OIL PAN & CRANKSHAFT

1	Cylinder Block
2	Plug
3	Timing Cover
4	Screw
5	Washer
6	Plug
7	Dowel
8	Dowel
9	Stud
10	Stud
11	Rear Cover
12	Ring Dowel
13	Screw
14	Bolt
15	Union
16	Washer
17	Seal Ring
18	Filter Gauze
19	Drain Tap
20	Washer
21	Washer
22	Bracket
23	Crankshaft
24	Plug
25	Bush
26	Washer
27	Bearing
28	Bearing
29	Damper
30	Cone
31	Distance Piece
32	Oil Thrower
33	Gear
34	Gear
35	Key
36	Pulley
37	Bolt
38	Washer
39	Bolt
40	Washer
41	Tab Washer
42	Connecting Rod
43	Bearing
44	Flywheel
45	Dowel
46	Dowel
47	Screw
48	Plate
49	Piston
50	Ring
51	Ring
52	Ring
53	Pin
54	Circlip
55	Oil Pan
56	Gasket
57	Seal
58	Seal
59	Baffle
60	Stud
61	Filter Basket
62	Adapter
63	Gasket
64	Stud
65	Hose
66	Clip
67	Dipstick
68	Timing Pointer
69	Bracket
70	Bracket
71	Rubber Mount
72	Packing Plate
73	Stabilizing Link
74	Bush
75	Washer
76	Washer
77	Rubber Mount
78	Bearing Bracket
79	Bearing Bracket
80	Support Bracket
81	Rubber Mount

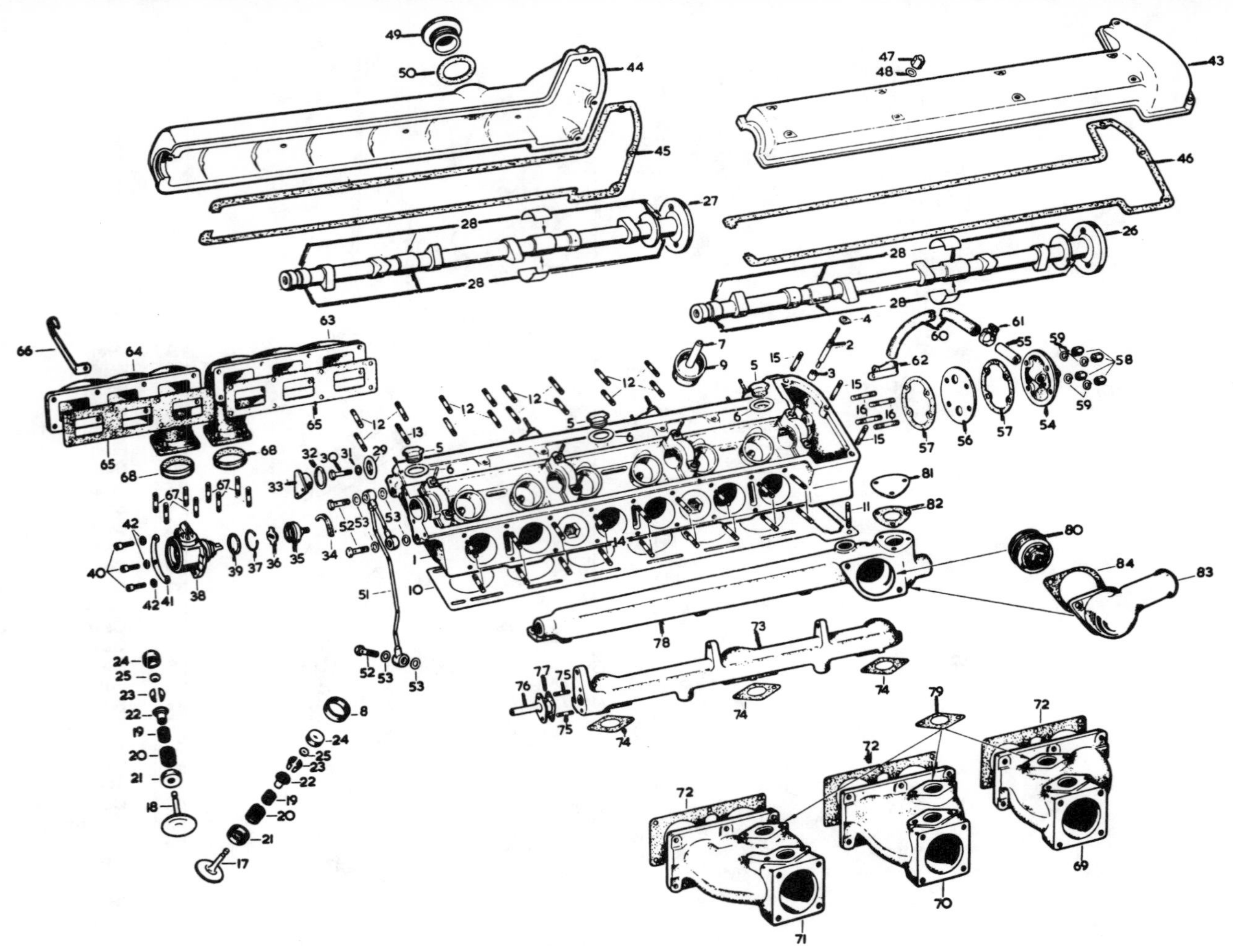

FIG 2 – ENGINE HEAD & VALVES

1 Cylinder Head
2 Stud
3 Ring Dowel
4 Washer
5 Plug
6 Washer
7 Guide
8 Insert
9 Guide
10 Gasket
11 Stud
12 Stud
13 Stud
14 Stud
15 Stud
16 Stud
17 Intake Valve
18 Exhaust Valve
19 Spring, Inner
20 Spring, Outer
21 Seat
22 Collar
23 Cotter
24 Tappet
25 Pad
26 Camshaft, Inlet
27 Camshaft, Exhaust
28 Bearing
29 Oil Thrower
30 Screw
31 Washer
32 Ring
33 Plug
34 Seal
35 Adapter
36 Driving Dog
37 Circlip
38 Inlet Camshaft Generator
39 O Ring
40 Screw
41 Washer
42 Washer
43 Cover
44 Cover
45 Gasket
46 Gasket
47 Nut
48 Washer
49 Filler Cap
50 Washer
51 Oil Pipe
52 Bolt
53 Washer
54 Front Cover
55 Pipe
56 Baffle
57 Gasket
58 Nut
59 Washer
60 Pipe
61 Clip
62 Clip
63 Exhaust Manifold, Front
64 Exhaust Manifold, Rear
65 Gasket
66 Clip
67 Stud
68 Ring
69 Intake Manifold, Front
70 Intake Manifold, Center
71 Intake Manifold, Rear
72 Gasket
73 Pipe
74 Gasket
75 Stud
76 Adapter
77 Gasket
78 Pipe
79 Gasket
80 Thermostat
81 Plate
82 Gasket
83 Elbow
84 Gasket

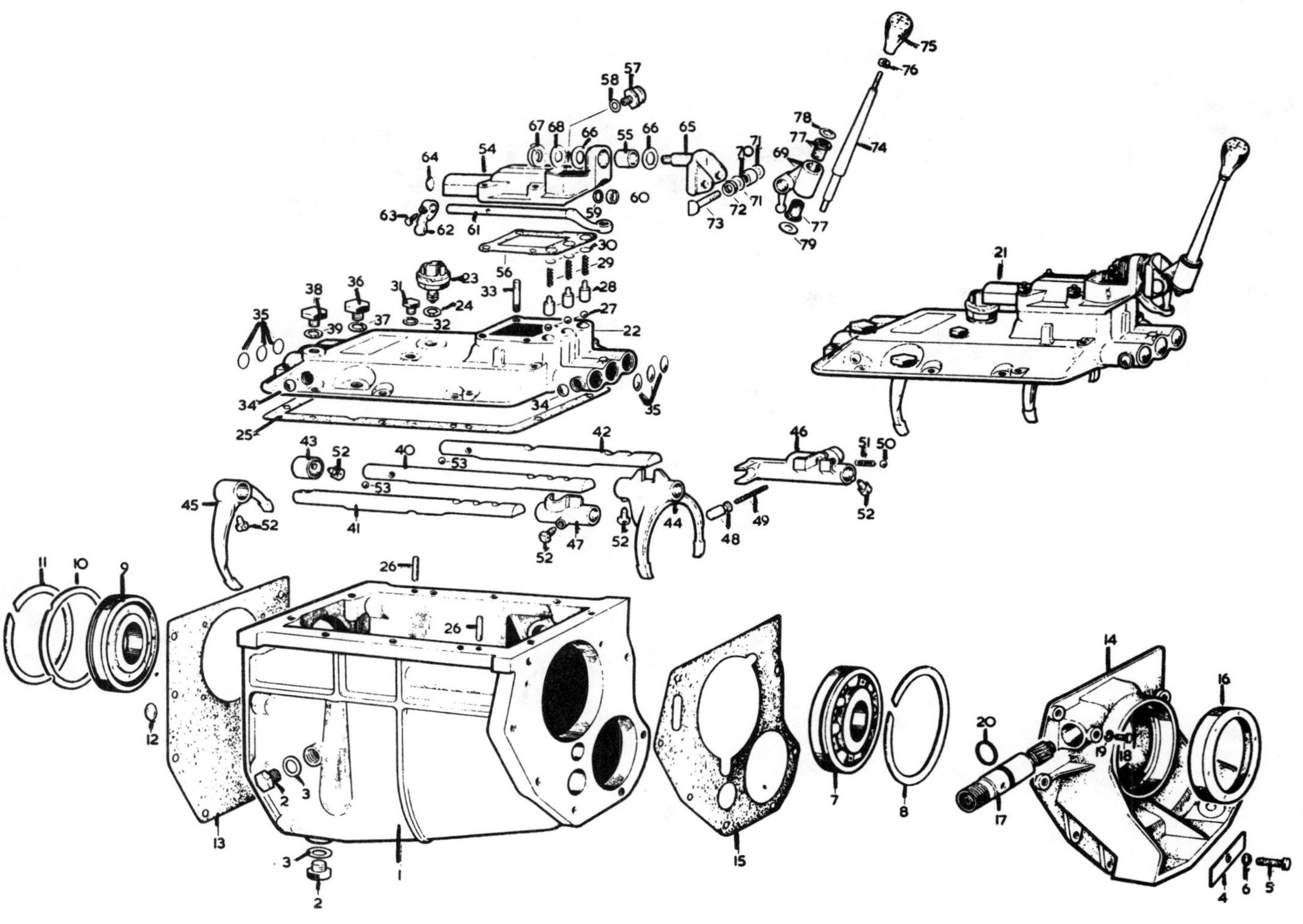

FIG 3 – TRANSMISSION CASE

1 Transmission Case
2 Plug
3 Washer
4 Plate
5 Screw
6 Washer
7 Bearing
8 Circlip
9 Bearing
10 Collar
11 Circlip
12 Washer
13 Gasket
14 Rear Cover
15 Gasket
16 Seal
17 Speedometer Driven Gear
18 Screw
19 Washer
20 Ring
21 Gearshift Remote Control
22 Top Cover
23 Back-Up Lamp Switch
24 Gasket
25 Gasket
26 Dowel
27 Ball
28 Plunger
29 Spring
30 Shim
31 Plug
32 Washer
33 Stud
34 Washer
35 Washer
36 Plug
37 Washer
38 Plug
39 Washer
40 Striking Rod
41 Striking Rod
42 Striking Rod
43 Stop
44 Fork
45 Fork
46 Fork
47 Selector
48 Plunger
49 Spring
50 Ball
51 Spring
52 Dowel
53 Ball
54 Housing
55 Bush
56 Gasket
57 Breather
58 Washer
59 O Ring
60 Retainer Cup
61 Remote Control Shaft
62 Selector Finger
63 Screw
64 Washer
65 Lever
66 Washer
67 Washer
68 Washer
69 Lever
70 Bush
71 Washer
72 Washer
73 Pin
74 Lever
75 Knob
76 Nut
77 Rubber Bush
78 Washer
79 Washer

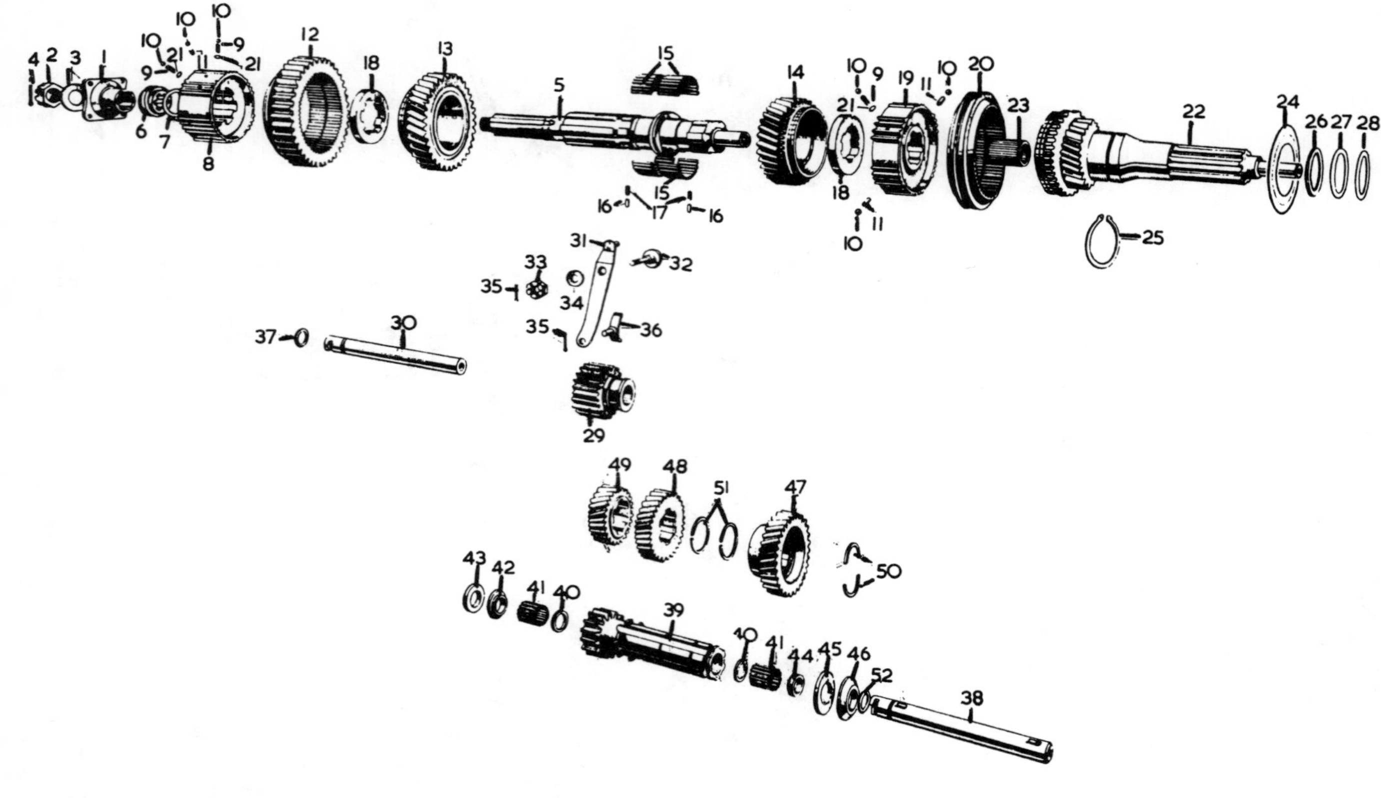

FIG 4 – TRANSMISSION GEARS

1	Flange
2	Nut
3	Washer
4	Pin
5	Mainshaft
6	Speedometer Driving Gear
7	Distance Piece
8	Sleeve
9	Spring
10	Ball
11	Plunger
12	1st Speed Gear
13	2nd Speed Gear
14	3rd Speed Gear
15	Roller
16	Plunger
17	Spring
18	Washer
19	Sleeve
20	Sleeve
21	Shim
22	Pinion Shaft
23	Bearing
24	Oil Thrower
25	Circlip
26	Washer
27	Shim
28	Shim
29	Reverse Gear
30	Spindle
31	Lever
32	Pin
33	Nut
34	Washer
35	Pin
36	Slipper
37	Ring
38	Countershaft
39	Countershaft 1st Gear
40	Ring
41	Roller
42	Washer
43	Washer
44	Ring
45	Washer
46	Washer
47	Constant Wheel
48	Countershaft 3rd Gear
49	Countershaft 2nd Gear
50	Ring
51	Circlip
52	Ring

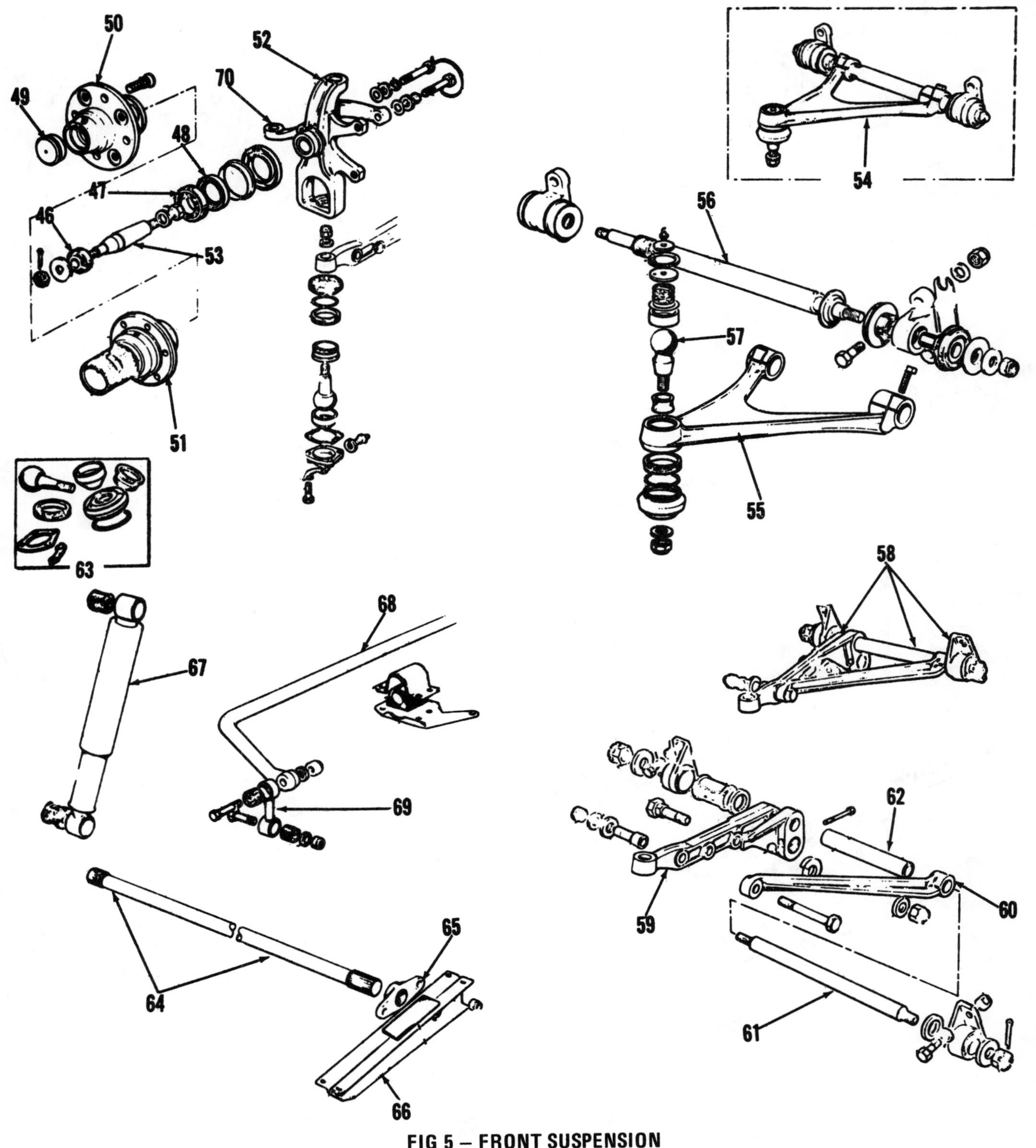

FIG 5 – FRONT SUSPENSION

46	Bearing, Outer	51	Hub, Wire Wheel	56	Shaft	61	Shaft	66	Mounting Bracket
47	Bearing, Inner	52	Vertical Link	57	Ball	62	Collar	67	Shock Absorber
48	Oil Seal	53	Stub Shaft	58	Lower Control Arm Assy	63	Ball Joint	68	Stabilizer Bar
49	Grease Cap	54	Upper Control Arm Assy	59	Lower Arm, Front	64	Torsion Bar	69	Link
50	Hub, Disc Wheel	55	Upper Control Arm	60	Lower Arm, Rear	65	End Bracket	70	Arm

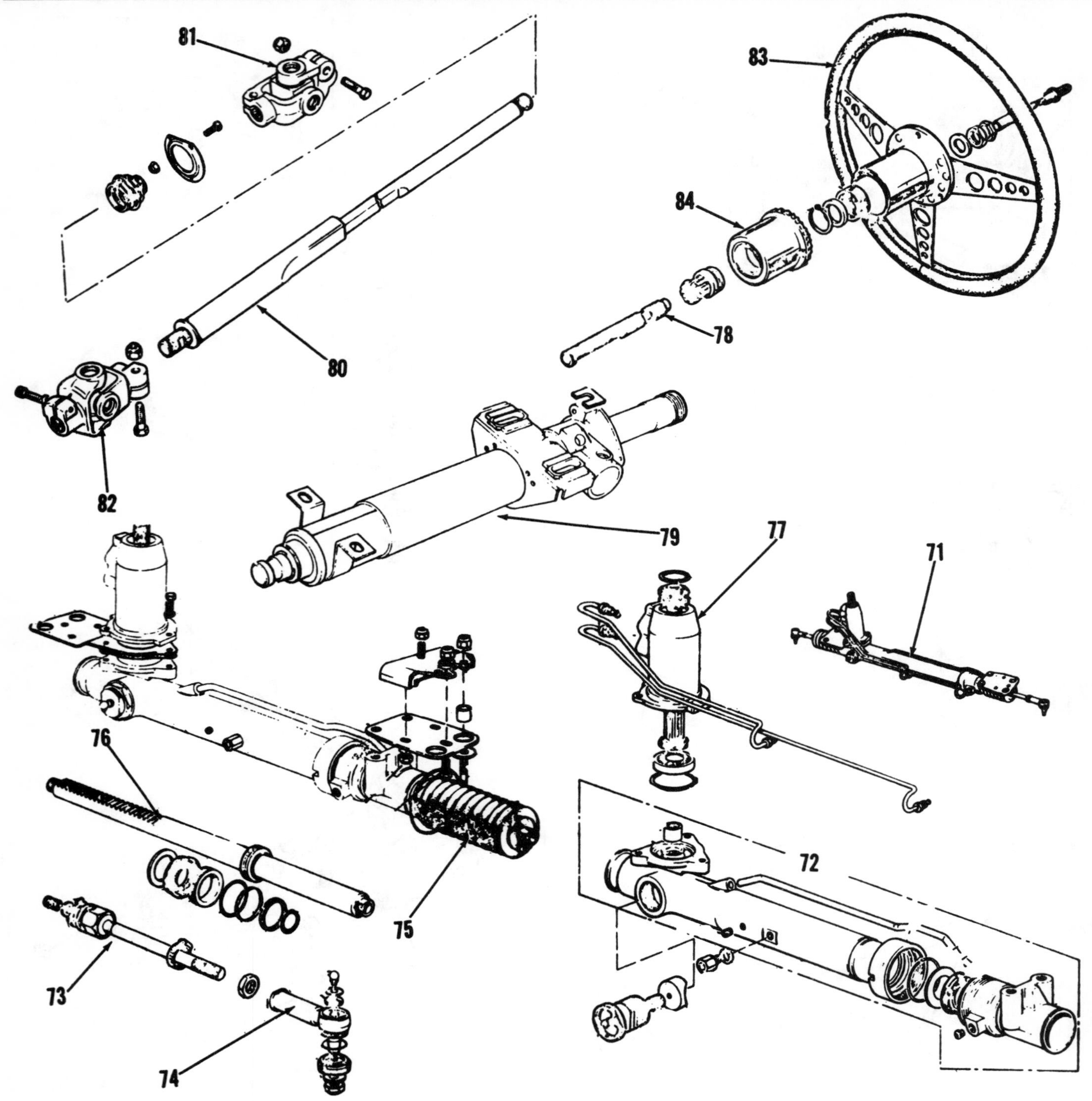

FIG 6 – STEERING

71	Gear Assy W/Tie Rods	78	Mainshaft, Upper
72	Housing	79	Mainshaft, Center
73	Tie Rod	80	Mainshaft, Lower
74	End	81	Joint, Upper
75	Boot	82	Joint, Lower
76	Rack	83	Wheel
77	Pinion	84	Sleeve

Ignition, Starting & Charging—TIME

OPERATION INDEX

Tune-Up, Minor 1
Tune-Up, Major 2
Compression Test 3
Distributor, R&R Or Renew 4
Distributor, Overhaul 4A
Distributor Cap, Renew 5
Ignition Cable Set, Renew 6
Ignition Coil, Renew 7
Starter & Ignition Switch, Renew 8
Starter, R&R Or Renew 9
Starter Solenoid, Renew 10
Starter Bendix Drive, Renew 11
Starter, R&R & Overhaul 12
Alternator Regulator, Renew 13
Alternator, R&R Or Renew 14
Alternator, R&R & Overhaul 15
Alternator Pulley, Renew 16
Alternator Belt, Renew 17

1—TUNE-UP, MINOR

Includes: Renew points, condenser and plugs, set spark timing and adjust carburetor idle.

6 Cyl 1.5
12 Cyl 2.4

2—TUNE-UP, MAJOR

Includes: Check compression, clean or renew and adjust spark plugs. R&R distributor, renew points and condenser. Adjust ignition timing, carburetor and fan belts. Clean battery terminals and service air cleaner. Check coil and clean or replace fuel filter.

6 Cyl 3.1
12 Cyl 5.4

3—COMPRESSION TEST

6 Cyl 0.5
12 Cyl Exc 0.6
W/Elec Fuel Injection 0.9
XJS 1.0

4—DISTRIBUTOR, R&R OR RENEW

6 Cyl 1.0
12 Cyl Exc 1.3
XJS 1.7

4A—DISTRIBUTOR, OVERHAUL

6 Cyl 1.7
12 Cyl Exc 2.0
XJS 2.4

5—DISTRIBUTOR CAP, RENEW

6 Cyl 0.3
12 Cyl Exc 0.7
XJS 0.8

6—IGNITION CABLE SET, RENEW

6 Cyl 1.5
12 Cyl 1.8

7—IGNITION COIL, RENEW

6 Cyl 0.2
12 Cyl 0.4

8—STARTER & IGNITION SWITCH, RENEW

6 Cyl Exc 1.1
XJ6 Sedan 1.3
12 Cyl 1.2

9—STARTER, R&R OR RENEW

6 Cyl Exc 3.5
XJ6 Sedan 2.0
12 Cyl Exc 1.2
XJ12, XJS 3.0

10—STARTER SOLENOID, RENEW

6 Cyl Exc 3.8
XJ6 Sedan 2.1
12 Cyl Exc 1.3
XJ12, XJS 3.5

11—STARTER BENDIX DRIVE, RENEW

6 Cyl Exc 3.9
XJ6 Sedan 2.1
12 Cyl Exc 1.5
XJ12, XJS 3.6

12—STARTER, R&R & OVERHAUL

6 Cyl Exc 4.5
XJ6 Sedan 2.6
12 Cyl Exc 2.3
XJ12, XJS 4.5

13—ALTERNATOR REGUALTOR, RENEW

E Series 0.3
XJ6 ......0.7
XJ12 ......1.1
XJS 0.9

14—ALTERNATOR, R&R OR RENEW

6 Cyl 0.5
12 Cyl Exc 1.0
XJ12 EXC 1.0
With Air Pump 2.0
XJS 1.0

15—ALTERNATOR, R&R & OVERHAUL

6 Cyl 1.5
12 Cyl 2.0

16—ALTERNATOR PULLEY, RENEW

6 Cyl 0.3
12 Cyl 0.7

17—ALTERNATOR BELT, RENEW

All Models 0.4

Fuel, Emission Control, Intake & Exhaust System—TIME

OPERATION INDEX

Carburetor, R&R Or Renew 1
Carburetor, R&R & Overhaul 2
Carb Emission Pack, R&R Or Renew 3
Fuel Pump, R&R Or Renew 4
Fuel Pump, Overhaul 5
Fuel Tank, R&R Or Renew 6
Vapor Emission Controls, R&R Or Renew 7
Choke Cable Assy, Renew 8
Intake Manifold Or Gasket, Renew 9
Induction Manifolds &/Or Housings, Renew 10
Exhaust Manifold Or Gasket, Renew 11
Exhaust Down Pipe, Renew 12
Exhaust Tailpipe &/Or Silencer, Renew 13
Muffler, Renew 14
Exhaust Port Air Inj Pump, R&R Or Renew 15
Exhaust Port Pump Belt, R&R Or Renew 16
Exhaust Port Pump Cleaner, R&R Or Renew 17
Exhaust Port Rails, R&R Or Renew 18
Exhaust Port Check Valve, R&R Or Renew 19
Exhaust Port Gulp Valve, R&R Or Renew 20

1—CARBURETOR, R&R OR RENEW

6 Cyl 1.0
12 Cyl—
Front 0.7
Rear 0.7
Both 1.8

2—CARBURETOR, R&R & OVERHAUL

6 Cyl (Pair) 2.5
12 Cyl—
Front 1.7
Rear 1.7
Both 3.4

3—CARB EMISSION PACK, R&R OR RENEW

12 Cyl 3.7

4—FUEL PUMP, R&R OR RENEW

6 Cyl 0.5
12 Cyl Exc 0.9
XJS 0.7

5—FUEL PUMP, OVERHAUL

6 Cyl 0.7
12 Cyl Exc 1.6
XJS 1.1

6—FUEL TANK, R&R OR RENEW

E Ser II 2.5
E Ser III 2.0
XJ6, XJ12 ......1.8
XJ12 FUEL INJ, EACH 2.2
XJS 2.8

7—VAPOR EMISSION CONTROLS, R&R OR RENEW

E-Type V-12—
Vapor Canister 0.4
Expansion Tank 2.1
Control Pipe—
Canister To Expansion Tank 0.9
Tank To Expansion Tank 2.0
Purge Pipe 0.3

8—CHOKE CABLE ASSY, RENEW

E-Type, Exc ......(1)2.0
V-12 ......1.8
XJ6 Sedan 0.5
XJ12 ......1.2
(1)With Air Conditioner, Add 0.5

9—INTAKE MANIFOLD OR GASKET, RENEW

6 Cyl Exc 2.2
XJ6 ......1.5
12 Cyl Exc 2.0
XJ12 ......3.0
Manifold Each 0.5
Housings, Each 1.7

11—EXHAUST MANIFOLD OR GASKET, RENEW

6 Cyl 1.0
12 Cyl Exc 1.7
XJ12, EACH 4.0
XJS, Right 3.5
XJS, Left 4.5

12—EXHAUST DOWNPIPE, RENEW

Front—
Exc Below 0.7
Type E 0.5
V-12, Each 0.7
Rear—
Exc Below ......(1)0.7
XJ6 Sedan ......(1)0.9
(1)Includes Front Pipe.

13—EXHAUST TAILPIPE &/OR SILENCER, RENEW

Exc Below 0.8
XJ6 ......1.1
XJ12 ......0.8
XJS 0.6

14—MUFFLER, RENEW

Exc Below 1.2
XJ6 Sedan 0.8
XJ12, XJS, One 1.0
Both 1.2

15—EXHAUST PORT AIR INJ. PUMP, R&R OR RENEW

E-Type V-12 ......0.9

16—EXHAUST PORT PUMP BELT, R&R OR RENEW

E-Type V-12 ......0.6

17—EXHAUST PORT PUMP CLEANER, R&R OR RENEW

E-Type V-12 ......0.4

18—EXHAUST PORT RAILS, R&R OR RENEW

E-Type V-12, Each 0.6
Both 0.9

19—EXHAUST PORT CHECK VALVE, R&R OR RENEW

E-Type V-12 ......0.3

20—EXHAUST PORT GULP VALVE, R&R OR RENEW

E-Type V-12 ......0.4

Engine Cooling & Heating System—TIME

OPERATION INDEX

Radiator, R&R Or Renew 1
Expansion Tank, Renew 2
Radiator Hoses, Renew 3
Water Pump, R&R Or Renew 4
Water Pump, Overhaul 5
Belts, R&R Or Renew 6
Thermostat Or Housing, Renew 7
Heater Core, Renew 8
Heater Blower Motor, Renew 9
Heater Temperature Control Valve, Renew 10
Modulator Heat Control, Renew 11
Heater Hoses, Renew 12
Recharge Air Conditioner 13
Condenser, R&R Or Renew 14
Compressor, R&R Or Renew 15
Receiver Dehydrator, R&R Or Renew 16
Evaporator, R&R Or Renew 17

1—RADIATOR, R&R OR RENEW
6 Cyl Exc 1.7
XJ6 ....1.4
12 Cyl Exc 1.2
XJ12 ....2.2
XJS 3.5

2—EXPANSION TANK, RENEW
6 Cyl 0.3
12 Cyl Exc 0.6
XJ12, XJS 1.0

3—RADIATOR HOSES, RENEW
6 Cyl—
Upper 0.3
Lower 0.5
12 Cyl, Upper 0.5
Lower 0.8

4—WATER PUMP, R&R OR RENEW
6 Cyl Exc 2.5
XJ Sedan 1.6
12 Cyl Exc 2.5
XJ12, XJS 4.5

5—WATER PUMP, OVERHAUL
6 Cyl Exc 3.5
XJ6 Sedan 2.6
12 Cyl Exc 3.5
XJ12, XJS 5.0

6—BELTS, R&R OR RENEW
Fan, Exc Below ①0.3
XJ6 ....0.5
Alternator 0.4
①*E-Type, Add*
With Power Steering *0.2*
With Air Conditioner *0.4*

7—THERMOSTAT OR HOUSING, RENEW
Exc Below 0.5
XJ12, One 1.0
Both 1.4
XJS, One 0.7
Both 1.0

8—HEATER CORE, RENEW
Exc Below 1.5
XJ6, XJ12 ....10.0
E-Type V-12 XJS 8.0

9—HEATER BLOWER MOTOR, RENEW
Exc Below 1.5
XJ6 Sedan 0.5
E-Type V-12 ....0.6

10—HEATER TEMPERATURE CONTROL VALVE, RENEW
Exc Below 1.5
XJ6 Sedan 0.3
E-Type V-12 ....1.1

11—MODULATOR HEAT CONTROL, RENEW
XJ6 Sedan 0.4

12—HEATER HOSES, RENEW
Exc Below, Pair 0.4
XJ6 Sedan 0.6
E-Type V-12 ....0.4

13—RECHARGE AIR CONDITIONER
All Models 1.5

14—CONDENSER, R&R OR RENEW
Does not include recharge
Exc Below 1.5
XJ6 ....1.0
XJS 1.2

15—COMPRESSOR, R&R OR RENEW
Does not include recharge
Exc Below 1.0
XJ6 ....1.2
XJ12 ....1.1
XJS 1.3

16—RECEIVER DEHYDRATOR, R&R OR RENEW
Does not include recharge
Exc Below 0.3
XJ12, XJS 0.6

17—EVAPORATOR, R&R OR RENEW
Does not include recharge
Exc Below 3.0
XJ6 Sedan 12.0
E-Type V-12 ....4.1
XJ12 ....10.5
XJS 9.5

Engine—TIME

OPERATION INDEX

Engine, R&R 1
Engine, R&R & Overhaul 2
Engine Short, Renew 3
Cylinder Head, R&R Or Gasket, Renew 4
Valves, Grind 5
One Valve, Renew & Grind 6
Valve Springs, Renew 7
Rocker Or Cam Cover Gasket, Renew 8
Valve Tappets, Renew 9
Valve Tappets, Adjust 10
Oil Sump Gasket, R&R Or Renew 11
Oil Pump, R&R Or Renew 12
Timing Cover Seal, Renew 13
Timing Chains, Replace 14
Timing Gears Or Vernier, Renew 15
Timing Chain Tensioner, Replace 16
Camshafts Or Bearings, Renew 17
Piston Ring (S), Renew 18
Rings & Main Bearings, Renew & Grind Valves 19
Rod Bearings, Renew 20
Main Bearings, Renew 21
Crankshaft Or Rear Seal Housing, Renew 22
Piston (S), Renew 23
Crankshaft Damper Or Pulley, Renew 24

1—ENGINE, R&R
Does not include transfer of any part of engine or replacement of special equipment. Includes R&R trans
6 Cyl Exc 11.0
XJ6 Sedan 10.0
12 Cyl Exc 9.5
XJ12 ....11.0
XJS 12.0

2—ENGINE, R&R & OVERHAUL
Includes rebore cylinders with boring bar, renew pistons, rings, bearings, grind valves, plastigauge bearings and perform minor tune-up.
6 Cyl Exc 26.7
XJ6 Sedan 24.2
12 Cyl Exc 37.4
XJ12 ....40.0
XJS 41.5

3—ENGINE SHORT, RENEW
Includes R&R engine & trans.
Exc Below 26.0
XJ6 Sedan 23.0
E-Type V-12 ....28.0

4—CYLINDER HEAD, RENEW
6 Cyl 9.3
V12 Exc 8.5
XJ12, Right 9.3
XJ12, Left 10.5
XJS, Right 10.0
XJS, Left 12.0

5—VALVES, GRIND
Includes: R&R head & minor tune-up
6 Cyl 11.0
12 Cyl Exc 17.5
E-Type V-12 XJ12 ....19.5
XJS 25.0

6—ONE VALVE, RENEW & GRIND
Exc Below 7.0
Type E 2 Plus 2 ....7.5
E-Type V-12 ....5.3

7—VALVE SPRING, RENEW ONE
Exc Below 1.5
E-Type V-12 ....2.7

8—ROCKER OR CAM COVER GASKET, RENEW
6 Cyl 0.8
12 Cyl Exc 0.9
XJS, Right 3.0
XJS, Left 2.0

9—VALVE TAPPETS, RENEW
Exc Below 4.0
E-Type V-12 ....5.1
XJ12 ....5.5

10—VALVE TAPPETS, ADJUST
All models each side
6 Cyl 1.4
12 Cyl Exc 5.1

11—OIL SUMP GASKET, R&R OR RENEW
6 Cyl Exc 2.6
XJ6 Sedan 3.8
12 Cyl Exc 2.2
XJS 1.7

12—OIL PUMP, R&R OR RENEW
6 Cyl Exc 3.0
XJ6 Sedan 6.0
E-Type—
Exc Below 2.0
2 Plus 2 ....3.0
V-12 ....14.6
XJ12 ....13.5
XJS 12.5

13—TIMING COVER SEAL, RENEW
XJ6 Sedan 4.0
E-Type—
Exc Below 1.7
2 Plus 2 ....2.7
V-12 ....14.3

14—TIMING CHAINS, REPLACE
Exc Below 14.0
E-Type V-12 ....14.5
XJ12 ....20.5
XJS 22.5

15—TIMING GEARS OR VERNIER, RENEW
6 Cyl 1.0

16—TIMING CHAIN TENSIONER, RENEW
Exc Below 11.0
E-Type V-12 ....11.4

17—CAMSHAFTS OR BEARINGS, RENEW
6 Cyl 4.0
E-Type V-12, Each Shaft 2.6
Both 5.1

18—PISTON RING (S), RENEW
Exc Below 11.5
E-Type V-12 ....13.9
XJ6 Sedan ①16.0
XJ12 ....20.0
XJS 22.0
①*Includes R&R Engine & Trans.*

(Continued)

Engine—TIME Cont'd

19—RINGS & MAIN BEARINGS, RENEW & GRIND VALVES

Includes: Minor tune-up
Exc Below 22.4
E-Type V-12 .... 25.3
XJ6 Sedan .... (1)27.8
(1)*Includes R&R Engine & Trans.*

20—ROD BEARINGS, RENEW

One Pair—
Exc Below 4.0
E-Type, Exc 1.9
2 Plus 2 .... 2.9
V-12 .... 2.6
Each Additional Pair 0.4

21—MAIN BEARINGS, RENEW

Exc Below 5.3
Type-E, Exc 3.0
2 Plus 2 .... 4.0
V-12 .... 3.0
XJ12 .... 8.0
XJS 7.5

22—CRANKSHAFT OR REAR SEAL HOUSING, RENEW

Sedan 21.0
E-Type, Exc 22.0
V-12 .... 17.2

23—PISTON (S), RENEW

Exc Below 11.5
E-Type V-12 .... 13.9
XJ6 Sedan .... (1)16.0
XJ12 .... 20.0
XJS 22.0
(1)*Includes R&R Engine & Trans.*

24—CRANKSHAFT DAMPER OR PULLEY, RENEW

Exc Below 1.0
E-Type V-12 .... 0.9
XJ12 .... 3.5
XJS 3.0

Clutch, Mounts, Transmissions & Overdrive—TIME

OPERATION INDEX

Flywheel Or Ring Gear, R&R Or Renew 1
Clutch Or Disc, Renew 2
Release Fork (Or Lever), Renew 3
Clutch Master Cylinder, R&R Or Renew 4
Clutch Master Cylinder, R&R & Overhaul 5
Slave Cylinder, R&R Or Renew 6
Slave Cylinder, R&R & Overhaul 7
Clutch System, Bleed & Adjust 8
Reservoir, Renew 9
Engine Mounts, Renew 10
Transmission Assy, R&R Or Renew 11
Manual Transmission, R&R & Overhaul 12
Extension Case Seal, Renew 13
Oil Pan Gasket, Renew 14
Front Band, Adjust 15
Mainshaft Rear Bearing, Renew 16
Shift Forks Or Rails, Renew 17
Gear Selector Lever Assy, Renew 18
Gear Selector Cable, Renew 19
Overdrive, Renew 20
Overdrive, Overhaul 21
Rear Oil Seal, Renew 22
Solenoid, Replace 23
Oil Filter, Renew 24
Overdrive Control Or Isolating Switch, Renew 25

1—FLYWHEEL OR RING GEAR, R&R OR RENEW

Exc Below 11.9
XJ6 Sedan 9.2
E-Type V-12 .... 9.1

2—CLUTCH OR DISC, RENEW

Exc Below 11.7
XJ6 Sedan 9.0
E-Type V-12 .... 8.9

3—RELEASE FORK (OR LEVER), RENEW

Exc Below 11.7
XJ6 Sedan 8.9
E-Type V-12 .... 9.3

4—CLUTCH MASTER CYLINDER, R&R OR RENEW

Exc Below 1.1
E-Type, Exc 0.9
V-12 .... 0.8

5—CLUTCH MASTER CYLINDER, R&R & OVERHAUL

Exc Below 1.4
E-Type, Exc 1.0
V-12 .... 1.0

6—SLAVE CYLINDER, R&R OR RENEW

Exc Below 0.3
E-Type V-12 .... 0.7

7—SLAVE CYLINDER, R&R & OVERHAUL

Exc Below 0.4
E-Type V-12 .... 0.8

8—CLUTCH SYSTEM, BLEED & ADJUST

Exc Below 0.2
E-Type V-12 .... 0.3

9—RESERVOIR, RENEW

Exc Below 0.2
E-Type V-12 .... 0.4

10—ENGINE MOUNTS, RENEW

Front Set—
Exc Below 1.0
XJ6 Sedan 0.8
E-Type V-12 .... 1.3
XJ12 .... 0.8
XJS 1.3
Rear Set—
Exc Below 1.0
XJ6 Sedan 0.7
E-Type V-12 .... 0.8
XJ12 .... 0.7
XJS 1.3

11—TRANSMISSION ASSY, R&R OR RENEW

Manual Trans—
Exc Below 11.3
XJ6 Sedan 8.5
E-Type V-12 .... 9.0

12—MANUAL TRANSMISSION, R&R & OVERHAUL

Exc Below 16.3
XJ6 Sedan 13.5
E-Type V-12 .... 13.6

13—EXTENSION CASE SEAL, RENEW

E-Type, Exc 1.1
2 Plus 2 .... 11.1
V-12 .... 8.7

14—OIL PAN GASKET, RENEW

Exc Below 1.1
Type E, 2 Plus 2 .... 0.8

15—FRONT BAND, ADJUST

All Models 1.2

16—MAINSHAFT REAR BEARING, RENEW

Trans removed
All Models 1.0

17—SHIFT FORK OR RAILS, RENEW

Exc Below 3.0
XJ6 Sedan 2.9

18—GEAR SELECTOR LEVER ASSY, RENEW

Auto Trans—
E-Type, Exc 2.0
V-12 .... 0.8
XJ6 Sedan 0.5

19—GEAR SELECTOR CABLE, RENEW

Exc Below 1.4
2 Plus 2 Auto Trans 1.5
Type E V-12 .... 0.8

20—OVERDRIVE, RENEW

XJ6 Sedan 2.0

21—OVERDRIVE, OVERHAUL

XJ6 Sedan 5.5

22—REAR OIL SEAL, RENEW

XJ6 Sedan 1.0

23—SOLENOID, REPLACE

XJ6 Sedan 1.4

24—OIL FILTER, RENEW

XJ6 Sedan 0.2

25—OVERDRIVE CONTROL OR ISOLATING SWITCH, RENEW

XJ6 Sedan—
Control Switch 0.2
Isolationg Switch 1.4

Automatic Transmission—TIME

OPERATION INDEX

Transmission, R&R Or Renew 1
Transmission, R&R & Overhaul 2
Converter, R&R Or Renew 3
Oil Pan, R&R Or Renew 4
Valve Body, Overhaul 5
Pump Assy, Renew 6
Band, Adjust 7

1—TRANSMISSION ASSY, R&R OR RENEW

2 Plus 2 .... 11.5
E Series 9.5
XJ6 .... 9.5
XJ12 .... 10.0
XJS 10.5

2—TRANSMISSION ASSY, R&R & OVERHAUL

2 Plus 2 .... 19.0
E Series 16.5
XJ6 .... 16.5
XJ12 .... 17.5
XJS 18.0

3—CONVERTER ASSY, R&R OR RENEW

2 Plus 2 .... 11.8
E Series 10.0
XJ6 .... 10.0
XJ12 .... 10.5
XJS 11.0

4—OIL PAN, R&R OR RENEW

Exc Below 1.5
2 Plus 2 .... 1.0

5—VALVE BODY, R&R & OVERHAUL

2 Plus 2 .... 3.5
E Series 3.0
XJ6 .... 3.0
XJS 3.5

6—PUMP ASSY, RENEW

2 Plus 2 .... 10.5
E Series 10.0
XJ6 .... 9.5

7—BAND, ADJUST

2 Plus 2 .... 1.5
XJ6 .... 1.0
XJ12, XJS 1.4

Brakes, Steering, Suspension, Universals & Rear Axle—TIME

OPERATION INDEX

Brake Shoes Or Friction Pads, Renew 1
Master Cylinder, Renew 2
Master Cylinder, R&R & Overhaul 3
Caliper Assy, Renew 4
Caliper Assy, R&R & Overhaul 5
Bleed System 6
Brake Hose, Renew 7
Disc, Renew 8
Vacuum Tank, Renew 9
Check Valve, Renew 10
Brake Booster Or Servo, Renew 11
Brake Booster Or Servo, Overhaul 12
Brake Fluid Reservoir, Renew 13
Brake Pedal, Renew 14
Hand Brake Pads, Renew 15
Hand Brake Caliper, Renew 16
Parking Brake Cable, Renew 17
Hand Brake Compensator Assy, Renew 18
Hand Brake Assy, Renew 19
Steering Column Universal Joint, Renew 20
Rack & Pinion Assy, Renew 21
Rack & Pinion Assy, R&R & Overhaul 22
Stub Axle Carrier, Renew 23
Tie-Rod Ball Ends, Renew 24
Cross Rod Or Ball Ends, Renew 25
Power Steering Pump, Renew 26
Power Steering Pump, Overhaul 27
Power Steering Reservoir, Renew 28
Power Steering Pump Pulley, Renew 29
Flow Control Valve, Renew 30
Spring (S) Or Torsion Bars, Renew 31
Fulcrum Shaft, Replace 32
Wishbone Pivot Or Bushings, Renew 33
Anti Roll Bar Link Or Bushings, Renew 34
Ball Joints, Adjust 35
Ball Joints, Overhaul 36
Rear Suspension Radius Arm Or Bushing, Renew 37
Wishbone Assy Or Inner Bearing, Renew 38
Inner Fulcrum Shaft Mounting, Renew 39
Shock Absorber, Renew 40
Hubs Or Bearings, Renew 41
Rear Suspension Assy, Renew 42
Universal Joints, Rnew 43
Center Bearing, Renew 44
Axle Assy Complete, Renew 45
Axle Assy, R&R & Overhaul 46
Pinion Bearings, Renew 47
Differential Cage Bearings, Renew 48
Output Shaft Bearings Or Seals, Renew 49
Axle Shaft Universal Joints, Renew 50
Pinion Oil Seal, Renew 51
Differential Cover Seal Or Gasket, Renew 52

1—BRAKE SHOES OR FRICTION PADS, RENEW

Front Exc 0.4
XJ Models 0.7
Rear, Exc 0.4
E-Type V-12 ....0.7
XJ6 ....0.7
XJ12, XJS 0.9

2—MASTER CYLINDER, RENEW

Exc Below 2.0
XJ6, XJS 0.7
E-Type V-12 ....1.2
XJ12 ....1.0

3—MASTER CYLINDER, R&R & OVERHAUL

Exc Below 2.3
XJ6 Sedan 1.2
E-Type V-12 ....1.4
XJ12 ....1.4

4—CALIPER ASSY, RENEW

Front Each—
Exc Below 0.6
XJ6 Sedan 1.0
E-Type V-12 ....1.1
XJ12, XJS 1.2
Rear—
One—
Exc Below 8.8
XJ6 Sedan 1.9
E-Type V-12 ....3.8
XJ12, XJS 2.5
Both—
Exc Below 9.0
XJ6 Sedan 3.5
E-Type V-12 ....4.5
XJ12, XJS 4.0

5—CALIPER ASSY, R&R & OVERHAUL

Front Each—
Exc Below 1.1
XJ Models 1.6
E-Type V-12 ....1.5
Rear—
One—
Exc Below 9.3
XJ6, XJ12 ....2.3
XJS 3.0
E-Type V-12 ....4.1
Both—
Exc Below 9.8
XJ6, XJ12 ....4.3
E-Type V-12 ....5.1
XJS 4.0

6—BLEED SYSTEM

All Models 0.6

7—BRAKE HOSE, RENEW

Exc Below 0.3
E-Type V-12 ....0.4
XJ6, XJ12 ....1.2
XJS 1.0

8—DISC, RENEW

Front Each—
Exc Below 0.7
XJ Models 1.0
E-Type V-12 ....0.9
Rear—
One—
Exc Below 8.8
XJ Models 4.0
E-Type V-12 ....4.9
Both—
Exc Below 9.0
XJ Models 7.0
E-Type V-12 ....5.3

9—VACUUM TANK, RENEW

Exc Below 0.5
XJ Models 1.0

10—CHECK VALVE, RENEW

Exc Below 0.2
XJ Models 0.3
E-Type V-12 ....0.4

11—BRAKE BOOSTER OR SERVO, RENEW

Exc Below 2.0
XJ6 Sedan 2.5
E-Type V-12 ....1.5
XJ12 ....2.0
XJS 1.0

12—BRAKE BOOSTER OR SERVO, OVERHAUL

All Models 3.0

13—BRAKE FLUID RESERVOIR, RENEW

Exc Below 0.2
XJ6 Sedan 1.3
E-Type V-12 Front 0.4
Rear 0.6

14—BRAKE PEDAL, RENEW

Exc Below 3.0
XJ6, XJ12 ....2.5
XJS 1.0
E-Type V-12 ....1.9

15—HAND BRAKE PADS, RENEW

Exc Below 3.2
XJ6 Sedan 2.6
E-Type V-12 ....3.4
XJ12 ....2.0
XJS 3.0

16—HAND BRAKE CALIPER, RENEW

One—
Exc Below 3.1
XJ Models 1.3
E-Type V-12 ....3.3
Both—
Exc Below 3.2
XJ Models 2.4
E-Type V-12 ....3.6

—NOTE—

To Overhaul Each, Add 0.2

17—PARKING BRAKE CABLE, RENEW

Exc Below 0.2
E-Type V-12 ....0.7
XJ6 ....1.0
XJ12 ....0.8
XJS 1.2

18—HAND BRAKE COMPENSATOR ASSY, RENEW

Exc Below 0.5
E-Type V-12 & XJ6 ....3.2

19—HAND BRAKE ASSY, RENEW

Exc Below 1.0
XJ6 Sedan 0.8
XJ Series II 1.5
XJ12 ....1.5
XJS 1.2

20—STEERING COLUMN UNIVERSAL JOINT, RENEW

Exc Below 1.5
E-Type V-12 ....1.0

21—RACK & PINION ASSY, RENEW

Manual—
All Models 1.7
Power—
Exc Below 2.7
XJ6, XJ12 ....2.5
XJS 3.0
E-Type V-12 ....3.6

22—RACK & PINION ASSY, R&R & OVERHAUL

Manual—
All Models 2.9
Power—
Exc Below 5.7
XJ6, XJ12 ....5.0
XJS 4.5
E-Type 5.0

23—STUB AXLE CARRIER, RENEW

Each, Exc 1.8
XJ6, XJ12 ....2.0
XJS 2.5

24—TIE ROD BALL ENDS, RENEW

All Models, Each 0.5

25—CROSS ROD OR BALL ENDS, RENEW

Exc Below 1.0
E-Type V-12 ....1.2

26—POWER STEERING PUMP, RENEW

Exc Below 1.8
XJ Models 1.5
E-Type V-12 ....0.5

27—POWER STEERING PUMP, OVERHAUL

Exc Below 2.6
XJ Models 2.0
E-Type V-12 ....1.3

28—POWER STEERING RESERVOIR, RENEW

Exc Below 0.4
XJ6 Sedan 0.7

29—POWER STEERING PUMP PULLEY, RENEW

Exc Below 2.2
XJ6 Sedan 0.8

(Continued)

Brakes, Steering, Suspension, Universals & Rear Axle—TIME Cont'd

30—FLOW CONTROL VALVE, RENEW
Exc Below 2.6
XJ6 Sedan 0.5
E-Type V-12 ....3.7

31—SPRING (S) OR TORSION BARS, RENEW
Front—
E-Type, Exc 1.4
2 Plus 2 ....1.8
V-12 ....1.5
XJ Models 1.3
Rear—
Each—
Exc Below 1.0
E-Type V-12 ....1.2
XJ Models 1.3
Both—
Exc Below 1.3
E-Type V-12 ....2.1
XJ Models 2.3

32—FULCRUM SHAFT, REPLACE
All Models, Each 2.0

33—WISHBONE PIVOT OR BUSHINGS, RENEW
Exc Below (Upper) Each 1.0
XJ6 Sedan (Upper) Each 2.0
E-Type V-12 ....2.3
XJ12 ....1.5
XJS 1.0

34—ANTI ROLL BAR LINK OR BUSHINGS, RENEW
Exc Below 0.2
E-Type V-12 ....0.5

35—BALL JOINTS, ADJUST
Upper—
All Models, Each 0.3
Lower—
All Models, Each 0.6

36—BALL JOINTS, OVERHAUL
Upper—
Exc Below 0.7
E-Type V-12 ....1.0
XJ6, XJ12 ....1.1
Lower—
Exc Below 1.5
E-Type V-12 ....1.7
XJ6, XJ12 ....1.5

37—REAR SUSPENSION RADIUS ARM OR BUSHING, RENEW
All Models Exc 0.6
XJS 0.9

—NOTE—

To Replace Bushings, Add 0.1

38—WISHBONE ASSY, OR INNER BEARING, RENEW
Exc Below 3.6
E-Type V-12 ....2.3
XJS 2.0
XJ12 ....2.5

—NOTE—

To Replace Inner Brgs, Add 0.1

39—INNER FULCRUM SHAFT MOUNTING, RENEW
Exc Below 9.0
XJ6 Sedan 3.0
E-Type V-12 ....3.3
XJS 2.0
XJ12 ....2.5

40—SHOCK ABSORBER, RENEW
Front, One—
Exc Below 0.6
E-Type V-12 ....0.4
Rear, One—
Exc Below 1.0
E-Type V-12 (Pair) 1.2
Rear, Both—
Exc Below 1.0
E-Type V-12 ....2.1

41—HUBS OR BEARINGS, RENEW
Front—
All Models Each 0.8
Rear—
All Models 1.3

42—REAR SUSPENSION ASSY, RENEW
Exc Below 3.0
E-Type V-12 ....2.9

43—UNIVERSAL JOINTS, RENEW
Front Or Rear, Each—
Exc Below 1.5
E-Type, Exc 3.4
2 Plus 2 ....4.3
V-12 ....3.7
Both—
Exc Below 1.8
E-Type, Exc 3.7
2 Plus 2 ....4.6
V-12 ....3.9

44—CENTER BEARING, RENEW
XJ6 Sedan 2.0

45—AXLE ASSY COMPLETE, RENEW
Exc Below 10.0
E-Type V-12 ....9.0
XJS 8.0

46—AXLE ASSY, R&R & OVERHAUL
Exc Below 16.0
E-Type V-12 ....13.8

47—PINION BEARINGS, RENEW
All Models 13.5

48—DIFFERENTIAL CAGE BEARINGS, RENEW
Exc Below 12.0
E Type V-12 ....11.0

49—OUTPUT SHAFT BEARINGS OR SEALS, RENEW
Exc Below 10.5
XJ6 Sedan 7.6
E-Type V-12 ....9.4

50—AXLE SHAFT UNIVERSAL JOINTS, RENEW
Each Side 1.8

51—PINION OIL SEAL, RENEW
Exc Below 3.2
XJ6 Sedan 0.7
E-Type V-12 ....0.7

52—DIFFERENTIAL COVER SEAL OR GASKET, RENEW
Exc Below 0.7
E-Type V-12 ....1.1

Speedometer, W/S Wipers & Instruments—TIME

OPERATION INDEX

Speedometer Cable, Renew 1
Speedometer Head, Renew 2
Speedometer Right Angle Drive, Renew 3
W/S Wiper Motor, Renew 4
W/S Wiper Wheel Box Assy, Replace 5
W/S Wiper Motor Cable & Box Assy, Renew 6
W/S Wiper Linkage, Renew 7
W/S Wiper Arm, Renew 8
Fuel Gauge (Dash Unit), Renew 9
Fuel Tank Gauge, Renew 10
Oil Gauge (Dash Unit), Renew 11
Oil Gauge Sending Unit, Renew 12
Temperature Gauge (Dash Unit), Renew 13
Temperature Gauge Sending Unit, Renew 14
Ammeter, Renew 15
Tachometer, Renew 16
Instrument Cluster Voltage Limiter, Renew 17
Headlight Switch, Renew 18
Headlamp Dimmer Switch, Renew 19
Stop Light Switch, Renew 20
Flasher Switch, Renew 21
Reverse Lamp Switch, Renew 22

1—SPEEDOMETER CABLE, RENEW
Exc Below 1.2
XJ6 Sedan 1.9
E-Type V-12 ....0.8
XJ12 ....2.3
XJS 1.2

2—SPEEDOMETER HEAD, RENEW
Exc Below 0.6
XJ6, XJ12 ....0.4
XJS 1.0
E-Type V-12 ....0.7
XJS 1.0

3—SPEEDOMETER RIGHT ANGLE DRIVE, RENEW
Exc Below 0.3
E-Type, Exc 2.0
W/Auto Trans 0.5
V-12 ....0.6
XJ6, XJ12 ....0.8

4—W/S WIPER MOTOR, RENEW
Exc Below 1.5
XJ Models 1.0
E-Type V-12 ....0.8

5—W/S WIPER WHEEL BOX ASSY'S, REPLACE
Exc Below 2.5
XJ Models 1.0

6—W/S WIPER MOTOR CABLE & BOX ASSY'S, RENEW
Exc Below 5.0
XJ6 Sedan 1.5

7—W/S WIPER LINKAGE, RENEW
E-Type V-12 ....1.4

8—W/S WIPER ARM, RENEW
Exc Below 0.1
E-Type V-12 ....0.3

9—FUEL GAUGE (DASH UNIT), RENEW
Exc Below 0.2
E-Type V-12 ....0.3
XJS 1.0
XJ6, XJ12 ....0.5

10—FUEL TANK GAUGE, RENEW
Exc Below 0.6
E-Type V-12 ....0.4
XJ6 ....0.7
XJ12 ....1.0
XJS 1.5

11—OIL GAUGE (DASH UNIT), RENEW
Exc Below 0.4
XJ12 ....0.7
XJS 1.2

12—OIL GAUGE SENDING UNIT, RENEW
Exc Below 0.2
E-Type V-12 ....0.5

13—TEMPERATURE GAUGE (DASH UNIT), RENEW
Exc Below 0.4
XJ12 ....0.6
XJS 1.2

14—TEMPERATURE GAUGE SENDING UNIT, RENEW
Exc Below 0.3
XJ6, XJ12 ....0.5

15—AMMETER, RENEW
Exc Below 0.4
XJ12 ....0.6
XJS 1.2

16—TACHOMETER, RENEW
Exc Below 0.6
XJ6 Sedan 0.7
E-Type V-12 ....0.5
XJS 1.2
XJ12 ....0.5

(Continued)

Speedometer, W/S Wipers & Instruments—TIME Cont'd

17—INSTRUMENT CLUSTER VOLTAGE LIMITER, RENEW

Exc Below 0.3
XJ6 Sedan 0.2

18—HEADLIGHT SWITCH, RENEW

Exc Below 0.3
XJ6, XJ12 ....0.8
XJS 1.2

19—HEADLAMP DIMMER SWITCH, RENEW

Exc Below 0.4
XJ Models 1.2

20—STOP LIGHT SWITCH, RENEW

Exc Below 0.3
XJ6, XJ12 ....0.5
E-Type V-12 ....0.3
XJS 0.4

21—FLASHER SWITCH, RENEW

Exc Below 0.8
XJ6 Sedan 0.4
E-Type V-12 ....0.3
XJS 0.3

22—REVERSE LAMP SWITCH, RENEW

Exc Below 1.1
XJ Models 0.7

A

Air Conditioner.................................. 215
Air Pump.................................. 210
Alternator.................................. 210
Axle Shaft.................................. 213

B

Ball Joints.................................. 214
Back-Up Lamp Switch.................................. 211
Brakes.................................. 214

C

Cables (Ignition).................................. 210
Calipers.................................. 214
Camshaft.................................. 212
Carburetor.................................. 210
Catalytic Converter.................................. 210
Clutch.................................. 212
Coil Ignition.................................. 210
Compression Test.................................. 210
Connecting Rods.................................. 212
Cooling System.................................. 211
Crankshaft.................................. 212
Cylinder Head.................................. 212

D

Dash Gauges.................................. 211
Differential.................................. 213
Disc Brakes.................................. 214
Distributor.................................. 210

E

Emission Controls.................................. 210
Engine Assembly.................................. 212
Engine Oiling.................................. 212
Engine Tune-Up.................................. 210
Exhaust System.................................. 210

F

Flywheel.................................. 212
Front Suspension.................................. 214
Fuel Gauges.................................. 211
Fuel Pump.................................. 210
Fuel Tank.................................. 210

H

Hand Brake.................................. 214
Hazard Light Switch.................................. 211
Heat Gauge.................................. 211
Heated Rear Window Switch.................................. 211
Heater Core.................................. 215
Hose (Brake).................................. 214
Hose (Radiator).................................. 211
Hydraulic Brakes.................................. 214

I

Ignition.................................. 210
Ignition Coil.................................. 210
Ignition Switch.................................. 210

L

Light Switches.................................. 211

M

Master Cylinder.................................. 214

O

Oil Gauge.................................. 211
Oiling, Engine.................................. 212
Oil Pan.................................. 212
Oil Pump.................................. 212

P

Parking Brake.................................. 214
Pistons.................................. 212
Power Brake.................................. 214

R

Radiator.................................. 211
Radiator Hose.................................. 211
Rear Axle.................................. 213
Regulator (Alternator).................................. 210
Rod Bearings.................................. 212

S

Shocks (Front).................................. 214
Shocks (Rear).................................. 213
Speedometer.................................. 211
Stabilizer.................................. 214
Starting Motor.................................. 210
Steering Gear (Manual).................................. 214
Steering Gear (Power).................................. 215
Steering Linkage.................................. 214
Stop Light Switch.................................. 211
Switches (Light).................................. 211

T

Tachometer.................................. 211
Temperature Gauge.................................. 211
Thermostat.................................. 211
Timing Case Cover.................................. 212
Timing Chain.................................. 212
Timing Gears.................................. 212
Transmission.................................. 213
Transverse Bar.................................. 213
Tune-Up, Engine.................................. 211

V

Valve System.................................. 212

W

Water Pump.................................. 211
Windshield Wiper.................................. 211

Emission Control Systems—TIME

OPERATION INDEX

Fuel Evaporative System *1*
Emission Control System *2*
Crankcase Emission Controls *3*

1—FUEL EVAPORATIVE SYSTEM UNITS, RENEW

3-Way Control Valve 0.3
Liquid Separator Exc 0.4
Scorpion 0.6
Charcoal Cannister Exc 0.4
Scorpion 0.6

2—EMISSION CONTROL SYSTEM UNITS, RENEW

Air Pump Exc 1.0
Scorpion 0.6
Air Pump Belt 0.3
Diverter Valve Exc 0.4
Scorpion 0.5
Check Valve 0.3
Injection Manifold 1.2
E.G.R. Control Valve 0.8
Vapor Separator 0.7
E.G.R. Thermo Valve 0.5
Relays, Each 0.2

3—CRANKCASE EMISSION CONTROL SYSTEM

Flame Trap 0.3
P.C.V. Valve 0.3
Vapor Separator Exc 0.8
With Air Cond 1.0
Hose, Air Cleaner To Separator—
Less Air Cond 0.3
With Air Cond 1.0
Hose, Separator To Crankcase 0.2
Hose, Air Cleaner To Carb 0.2

Tune-Up & Ignition—TIME

OPERATION INDEX

Tune-Up, Minor *1*
Tune-Up, Major *2*
Compression, Check *3*
Points & Condenser, Renew *4*
Distributor, R&R Or Renew *5*
Distributor, R&R & Overhaul *6*
Dist Cap, Renew *7*
Ignition Coil, Renew *8*
Spark Plugs, Renew *9*
Ignition Timing, Check *10*
Ignition Cables, Renew *11*
Ignition Switch, Renew *12*

1—TUNE-UP, MINOR

Includes renew points, condenser & plugs, set spark timing & adjust carburetor idle.
All Models 1.5

2—TUNE-UP, MAJOR

Includes check compression, clean or renew & adjust spark plugs. R&R distributor, renew points & condenser. Adjust ignition timing, carburetor & fan belts. Clean battery terminals & service air cleaner. Check coil, clean fuel pump sediment bowl & replace or clean fuel line filter.
All Models 3.5

3—COMPRESSION, CHECK

All Models 0.5

4—POINTS & CONDENSER, RENEW

Includes set spark timing.
All Models 0.7

5—DISTRIBUTOR, R&R OR RENEW

Sedan, Coupe, H.P.E. 0.5
Scorpion 0.7

6—DISTRIBUTOR, R&R & OVERHAUL

Sedan, Coupe, H.P.E. 1.0
Scorpion 1.2

7—DISTRIBUTOR CAP, RENEW

All Models 0.3

8—IGNITION COIL, RENEW

All Models 0.3

9—SPARK PLUGS, CLEAN & ADJUST OR RENEW

All Models 0.4

10—IGNITION TIMING, CHECK

Sedan, Coupe, H.P.E. 0.3
Scorpion 0.5

11—IGNITION CABLES, RENEW

All Models 0.4

12—IGNITION SWITCH, RENEW

All Models 0.5

Fuel System & Intake Manifold—TIME

OPERATION INDEX

Carburetor, R&R Or Renew *1*
Carburetor, R&R & Overhaul *2*
Carburetor, Adjust *3*
Automatic Choke, Renew *4*
Automatic Choke, Adjust *5*
Accelerator Cable, Renew *6*
Accelerator Pedal, Renew *7*
Fuel Pump, R&R Or Renew *8*
Fuel Filter, Renew *9*
Anti-Spill Valve, Renew *10*
Fuel Tank, Renew *11*
Intake Manifold, Renew *12*
Intake & Exhaust Manifolds, Renew *13*

1—CARBURETOR, R&R OR RENEW

All Models 0.9

2—CARBURETOR, R&R & OVERHAUL

All Models 2.3

3—CARBURETOR, ADJUST IDLE & C.O.

All Models 0.4

4—AUTOMATIC CHOKE, RENEW

All Models 0.9

5—AUTOMATIC CHOKE, ADJUST

All Models 0.2

6—ACCELERATOR CONTROL CABLE, RENEW

Sedan, Coupe, H.P.E. 0.4
Scorpion 0.9

7—ACCELERATOR CONTROL PEDAL, RENEW

Sedan, Coupe, H.P.E. 0.5
Scorpion 1.5

8—FUEL PUMP, R&R OR RENEW

All Models 0.6

9—FUEL FILTER, ENGINE COMPT, RENEW

Sedan, Coupe, H.P.E. 0.2
Scorpion 0.3

10—ANTI-SPILL VALVE, RENEW

All Models 0.2

11—FUEL TANK, RENEW

Sedan, Coupe, H.P.E. 1.0
Scorpion 1.3

12—INTAKE MANIFOLD OR GASKET, RENEW

Less Air Cond 2.2
With Air Cond 2.8

13—INTAKE & EXHAUST MANIFOLDS, RENEW

Less Air Cond 5.1
With Air Cond 5.7

Exhaust System—TIME

OPERATION INDEX

Exhaust Manifold, Renew *1*
Front Pipe, Renew *2*
Muffler, Renew *3*
Resonator, Renew *4*
Intermediate Pipe, Renew *5*
Catalytic Converter, Renew *6*
Exhaust System, Renew *7*

1—EXHAUST MANIFOLD OR GASKET, RENEW

All Models 3.2

2—EXHAUST FRONT PIPE, RENEW

All Models 0.7

3—MUFFLER, RENEW

Sedan, Coupe, H.P.E. 0.4
Scorpion 0.6

4—RESONATOR, RENEW

All Models 0.5

5—INTERMEDIATE PIPE, RENEW

All Models 0.5

6—CATALYTIC CONVERTER, RENEW

Sedan, Coupe, H.P.E. 0.5
Scorpion 0.7

7—EXHAUST SYSTEM (EXC MANIFOLDS) RENEW

Less Catalytic Converter 1.5
With Converter Exc 1.7
Scorpion 1.5

Starting Motor—TIME

OPERATION INDEX

Starter, R&R Or Renew *1*
Starter, R&R & Overhaul *2*
Starter Drive, Renew *3*
Starter Armature, Renew *4*
Starter Solenoid, Renew *5*

1—STARTER, R&R OR RENEW

Less Air Cond Exc 0.7
Scorpion 1.3
With Air Cond 1.3

2—STARTER, R&R & OVERHAUL

Includes R&R armature drive, brushes, bushings & test starter. Does not include R&R armature.
Less Air Cond Exc 1.9
Scorpion 2.5
With Air Cond 2.5

3—STARTER DRIVE, RENEW

After starter is removed.
All Models 0.5

4—STARTER ARMATURE, RENEW

After starter is removed.
All Models 0.5

5—STARTER SOLENOID, RENEW

After starter is removed.
All Models 0.3

Alternator—TIME

OPERATION INDEX

Regulator, Renew *1*
Alternator, R&R Or Renew *2*
(Continued)

Alternator—TIME Cont'd

Alternator, Overhaul *3*
Brushes, Renew *4*
Rectifier Diode, Renew *5*

1—ALTERNATOR REGULATOR, RENEW
All Models 0.3

2—ALTERNATOR, R&R OR RENEW
Less Air Cond Exc 0.6
Scorpion 0.9
With Air Cond Exc 0.7
Scorpion 0.9

3—ALTERNATOR, OVERHAUL
After alternator is removed.
Sedan, Coupe, H.P.E. 1.2
Scorpion 0.9

4—ALTERNATOR BRUSHES, RENEW
All Models 0.2

5—RECTIFIER DIODE, ONE, RENEW
After alternator is removed.
All Models 0.4

Dash Gauges, Speedometer & Windshield Wiper—TIME

OPERATION INDEX

Fuel Gauge, Dash Unit, Renew *1*
Fuel Gauge, Tank Unit, Renew *2*
Oil Gauge, Dash Unit, Renew *3*
Oil Gauge Sending Unit, Renew *4*
Temperature Gauge, Dash Unit, Renew *5*
Temperature Gauge Sending Unit, Renew *6*
Speedometer Head, Renew *7*
Speedometer Cable, Renew *8*
Windshield Wiper Motor, Renew *9*
Windshield Wiper Switch, Renew *10*
Tachometer, Renew *11*

1—FUEL GAUGE, DASH UNIT, RENEW
Sedan 0.6
Coupe & H.P.E. 0.8
Scorpion 0.8

2—FUEL GAUGE, TANK UNIT, RENEW
Sedan, Coupe, H.P.E. 0.4
Scorpion 0.7

3—OIL GAUGE, DASH UNIT, RENEW
Sedan 0.6
Coupe & H.P.E. 0.8
Scorpion 0.8

4—OIL GAUGE SENDING UNIT, RENEW
Sedan, Coupe, H.P.E. Exc 0.2
With Air Cond 0.7
Scorpion Exc 0.4
With Air Cond 0.9

5—TEMPERATURE GAUGE, DASH UNIT, RENEW
Sedan 0.6
Coupe & H.P.E. 0.8
Scorpion 0.8

6—TEMPERATURE GAUGE SENDING UNIT, RENEW
All Models 0.3

7—SPEEDOMETER HEAD, RENEW
Sedan 0.6
Coupe & H.P.E. 0.8
Scorpion 0.8

8—SPEEDOMETER CABLE, RENEW
Btwn Trans & Counter Switch—
Sedan, Coupe, H.P.E. 0.4
Scorpion 0.3
Btwn Counter Switch & SpeedometeR-
Sedan, Coupe, H.P.E. 0.4
Scorpion 1.2

9—WINDSHIELD WIPER MOTOR, RENEW
Sedan, Coupe, H.P.E. 0.7
Scorpion 0.3

10—WINDSHIELD WIPER SWITCH, RENEW
Intermittent Exc 0.3
Scorpion 0.5
High & Low Speed Exc 0.2
Scorpion 0.5

11—TACHOMETER, RENEW
Sedan 0.6
Coupe & H.P.E. 0.8
Scorpion 0.8

Battery Cables & Horns—TIME

OPERATION INDEX

Battery Cables, Renew *1*
Horn, Renew *2*
Electro-Compressor, Renew *3*

1—BATTERY CABLES, RENEW
Ground 0.2
Positive 0.3

2—HORN, RENEW
One 0.2
Two Exc 0.3
Scorpion 0.4

3—HORN ELECTRO-COMPRESSOR, RENEW
Sedan, Coupe, H.P.E. 0.2
Scorpion 0.4

Lamps & Light Switches—TIME

OPERATION INDEX

Headlamps, Aim *1*
Lamp Lenses Or Bulbs, Renew *2*
Headlamp Motor, Renew *3*
Signaling Switch, Renew *4*
Stop Light Switch, Renew *5*
Back-Up Lamp Switch, Renew *6*
Direction Signal Flasher, Renew *7*
Hazard Flasher Switch, Renew *8*
Electric Window Switch, Renew *9*
Rear Window Defogger Switch, Renew *10*
Fasten Belt Delay Switch, Renew *11*
Fasten Belt Seat Switch, Renew *12*

1—HEADLAMPS, AIM
All Models 0.2

2—LAMP LENSES OR BULBS, RENEW
Each Exc Seal Beam 0.2
Seal Beam—
One Exc 0.3
Scorpion 0.6
Two Exc 0.5
Scorpion 0.9

3—HEADLAMP MOTOR, RENEW
Scorpion 0.5

4—SIGNALING SWITCH, RENEW
Includes turn signal, windshield washer/wiper, high/low beams, & outer lighting.
All Models 0.7

5—STOP LIGHT SWITCH, RENEW
All Models 0.2

6—BACK-UP LIGHT SWITCH, RENEW
Sedan, Coupe, H.P.E. 1.2
Scorpion 0.7

7—DIRECTION SIGNAL FLASHER, RENEW
Sedan, Coupe, H.P.E. 0.2
Scorpion 0.4

8—HAZARD SIGNAL SWITCH, RENEW
Sedan 0.2
Coupe & H.P.E. 0.4
Scorpion 1.5

9—ELECTRIC WINDOW SWITCH, RENEW
All Models 0.3

10—REAR WINDOW DEFOGGER SWITCH, RENEW
All Models Exc 0.4
Sedan 0.2

11—FASTEN BELTS DELAY SWITCH, RENEW
All Models 0.3

12—FASTEN BELTS SEAT SWITCH, RENEW
All Models 0.8

Cooling System—TIME

OPERATION INDEX

Radiator, R&R Or Renew *1*
Expansion Tank, Renew *2*
Radiator Hoses, Renew *3*
Fan Motor, Renew *4*
Thermostatic Switch, Renew *5*
Relay, Renew *6*
Water Pump, Renew *7*
Fan Belt, Renew *8*
Thermostat, Renew *9*

1—RADIATOR, R&R OR RENEW
Less Air Cond 0.9
With Air Cond 1.1

2—EXPANSION TANK, R&R OR RENEW
Sedan, Coupe & H.P.E. 0.4
Scorpion 0.3

3—RADIATOR HOSES, RENEW
Upper 0.3
Lower Exc 0.4
Scorpion 0.3

4—FAN MOTOR, R&R OR RENEW
Sedan, Coupe & H.P.E.—
Less Air Cond 0.7
With Air Cond 0.9
Scorpion 0.5

5—FAN MOTOR THERMOSTATIC SWITCH, RENEW
All Models 0.3

6—RELAY, RENEW
Each 0.2

7—WATER PUMP, R&R OR RENEW
Less Air Cond 1.6
With Air Cond 1.8

8—FAN BELT, RENEW
Less Air Cond 0.3
With Air Cond 1.3

9—THERMOSTAT, RENEW
Sedan, Coupe, H.P.E. 0.5
Scorpion 0.3

Engine—TIME

OPERATION INDEX

Engine Assy, Exc Scorpion 1
Engine Assy, Scorpion 2
Short Block, Renew 3
Engine Block (Crankcase) Renew 4
Freeze Plug, Renew 5
Engine Mount, Renew 6
Engine Mount Buffer, Renew 7
Cylinder Head Or Gasket, Renew 8
Cylinder Head, Resurface 9
Valve Tappets, Renew 10
Valve Tappets, Adjust 11
Valve Timing, Check 12
Valves & Seats, Recondition 13
Valves, Renew 14
Pistons & Rods, Renew 15
Rod Bearings, Renew 16
Piston Rings, Renew 17
Camshaft, Renew 18
Camshaft Seal, Renew 19
Camshaft Housings, Renew 20
Camshaft Housing Cover, Renew 21
Timing Belt Cover, Renew 22
Timing Belt, Renew 23
Belt Tensioner, Renew 24
Timing Sprockets & Auxiliary Shaft, Renew 25
Timing Sprockets, Renew 26
Oil Pan Or Gasket, Renew 27
Oil Pump, Renew 28
Oil Pump, Overhaul 29
Crankshaft Driving Pulley, Renew 30
Crankshaft, Renew 31
Main Bearings, Renew 32
Flywheel, Renew 33
Flywheel Ring Gear, Renew 34

1—ENGING ASSY, R&R (EXC SCORPION)

Complete with transmission & sub-frame. Includes R & R engine from sub-frame. R & R trans & clutch from engine.

Sedan, Coupe & H.P.E.—
Less Air Cond 4.9
With Air Cond 6.4

2—ENGINE ASSY, R&R (SCORPION)

Complete with transmission. Includes R & R transmission & clutch from engine.

Scorpion—
Less Air Cond Or Pwr Strg 6.5
With Air Cond Or Pwr Strg 8.5

3—SHORT BLOCK, RENEW

Includes R & R engine & cylinder head, transfer component parts from replaced short block. Adjust carburetor, timing & tappet clearance. Road test.

Less Air Cond Exc 9.7
Scorpion 11.3
With Air Cond Exc 12.0
Scorpion 13.5

4—ENGINE BLOCK (CRANKCASE) RENEW

Includes R & R engine & transfer components from replaced block.

Less Air Cond Exc 15.7
Scorpion 17.2
With Air Cond Exc 18.0
Scorpion 19.5

5—FREEZE PLUG, RENEW

Includes R & R exhaust manifold.

Less Air Cond Exc 3.4
Scorpion 3.5
With Air Cond 3.6

6—ENGINE MOUNT, FRONT UPPER, RENEW

Engine To Body Exc 0.2
Scorpion 0.6

7—ENGINE MOUNT BUFFER, RENEW

All Models 0.5

8—CYLINDER HEAD &/OR GASNET, RENEW

Includes adjust tappets & carburetor idle after road test

Less Air Cond 4.3
With Air Cond 4.5

9—CYLINDER HEAD, RESURFACE

Head removed

All Models 0.7

10—VALVE TAPPETS, RENEW

With engine on car. Includes R & R camshaft housings, disassemble, clean & reassemble. Adjust tappet clearance.

Less Air Cond 5.3
With Air Cond 5.5

11—VALVE TAPPETS, ADJUST CLEARANCE

All Models 2.2

12—VALVE TIMING, CHECK

Less Air Cond 0.8
With Air Cond 1.0

13—VALVES & VALVE SEATS, RECONDITION

With engine on car. Includes R & R cylinder heads, intake & exhaust manifolds & camshaft housings. Replace valve seals.

All Models 7.5

14—VALVES, RENEW (HEAD OFF)

Includes hand lapping.

One 0.2
All 1.0

15—PISTONS & RODS, RENEW ALL

Less Air Cond 9.0
With Air Cond 9.2

16—CONNECTING ROD BEARINGS, RENEW

Includes R & R oil pan.

All Models Exc 4.1
Scorpion 2.1

17—PISTON RINGS, RENEW

Less Air Cond 9.8
With Air Cond 10.0

18—CAMSHAFTS, RENEW

Includes R & R camshaft housings. Replace parts as required. Adjust tappet clearance.

Both—
Less Air Cond 5.8
With Air Cond 6.0
Intake Only—
Less Air Cond 3.1
With Air Cond 3.3
Exhaust Only—
Less Air Cond 3.6
With Air Cond 3.9

19—CAMSHAFT FRONT SEALS, RENEW

All Models 2.2

20—CAMSHAFT HOUSINGS, RENEW

Includes replace gaskets. R & R air cleaner, emission control items, lines, hoses, gaskets & timing belt. Disconnect & reconnect air pump. Adjust tappet clearance.

Both—
Less Air Cond 5.4
With Air Cond 5.6
Intake Only—
Less Air Cond 2.7
With Air Cond 2.9
Exhaust Only—
Less Air Cond 3.0
With Air Cond 3.3

21—CAMSHAFT HOUSING COVER, RENEW

All Models—
Intake 0.7
Exhaust 0.5

22—TIMING BELT COVER, RENEW

Less Air Cond 1.3
With Air Cond 1.8

23—TIMING BELT, RENEW

Includes set valve & ignition timing.

Less Air Cond 2.0
With Air Cond 2.5

24—BELT TENSIONER &/OR BEARING, RENEW

Includes R & R timing belt

Less Air Cond 2.4
With Air Cond 2.9

25—TIMING SPROCKETS & AUXILIARY SHAFT, RENEW

Includes R & R timing belt.

Less Air Cond 2.8
With Air Cond 3.3

26—TIMING SPROCKETS, RENEW

includes R & R timing belt.

Less Air Cond—
Driven 2.2
Driving 2.3
With Air Cond—
Driven 2.7
Driving 2.8

27—OIL PAN OR GASKET, RENEW

Sedan, Coupe & H.P.E.—
Less Air Cond 3.0
With Air Cond 3.7
Scorpion 1.0

28—OIL PUMP, RENEW

Sedan, Coupe & H.P.E.—
Less Air Cond 3.2
With Air Cond 3.9
Scorpion 1.2

29—OIL PUMP, OVERHAUL (PUMP REMOVED)

All Models 0.5

30—CRANKSHAFT DRIVING PULLEY, RENEW

Sedan, Coupe & H.P.E.—
Less Air Cond 0.8
With Air Cond 1.1
Scorpion—
Less Air Cond 1.7
With Air Cond 2.0

31—CRANKSHAFT, RENEW (ENGINE ON BENCH)

All Models Exc 4.0
Scorpion 4.5

32—MAIN BEARINGS, RENEW (ENGINE ON BENCH)

All Models 2.5

33—FLYWHEEL, RENEW (CLUTCH REMOVED)

All Models 0.3

34—FLYWHEEL RING GEAR, RENEW (FLYWHEEL REMOVED)

All Models 0.4

Clutch—TIME

OPERATION INDEX

Pedal Free Travel, Adjust 1
Cable, Renew 2
Clutch Or Disc, Renew 3
Release Bearing, Renew 4
Release Lever, Renew 5
Master Cylinder, R&R Or Renew 6
Master Cylinder, R&R & Overhaul 7
Operating Cylinder, R&R Or Renew 8
Operating Cylinder, Overhaul 9
Hydraulic System, Bleed 10
Hydraulic Reservoir, Renew 11
Hose, Res To Cyl, Renew 12
Hose, Cyl To Tube, Renew 13

(Continued)

Clutch—TIME Cont'd

1—CLUTCH PEDAL FREE TRAVEL, ADJUST
All Models 0.4

2—CLUTCH CABLE, RENEW
All Models 0.8

3—CLUTCH OR DISC, R&R OR RENEW
Sedan 4.9
Coupe, H.P.E. 5.1
Scorpion 4.1

4—CLUTCH RELEASE BEARING, RENEW
After transmission is removed.
All Models 0.2

5—CLUTCH RELEASE LEVER, RENEW
All Models 0.2

6—MASTER CYLINDER, R&R OR RENEW
Includes bleeding.
Scorpion 2.2

7—MASTER CYLINDER, R&R & OVERHAUL
Includes bleeding.
Scorpion 2.7

8—OPERATING CYLINDER, R&R OR RENEW
Includes bleeding.
Scorpion 0.8

9—OPERATING CYLINDER, R&R & OVERHAUL
Includes bleeding.
Scorpion 1.3

10—HYDRAULIC SYSTEM, BLEED
Scorpion 0.5

11—CLUTCH HYDRAULIC RESERVOIR, RENEW
Does not include bleeding.
Scorpion 0.4

12—HOSE, RESERVOIR TO CYLINDER, RENEW
Includes bleeding
Scorpion 0.8

13—HOSE, CYLINDER TO REAR TUBE, RENEW
Includes bleeding
Scorpion 0.7

Transmission—TIME

OPERATION INDEX

Trans, R&R (Exc Scorpion) 1
Trans, R&R (Scorpion) 2
Minor Overhaul 3
Major Overhaul 4
Case, Renew 5
Gear Shift Lever, Renew 6
Support & Shift Lever, Renew 7
Rear Control Shaft, Renew 8
Differential, Overhaul 9
Diff Side Gear Seal, Renew 10

1—TRANSMISSION, R&R (EXCEPT SCORPION)
Includes R&R engine assy with sub-frame & R&R transmission from engine.
Sedan, Coupe, H.P.E. Exc 4.9
With A.C. &/Or Pwr Strg 6.4

2—TRANSMISSION, R&R (SCORPION)
Scorpion 3.8

3—TRANSMISSION, MINOR OVERHAUL
Includes replace all gaskets, seals & packings with transmission on bench.
All Models 1.2

4—TRANSMISSION, MAJOR OVERHAUL
Includes repair or replace defective parts as necessary with transmission on bench.
All Models 2.5

5—TRANSMISSION CASE, RENEW
After transmission is removed. Includes overhaul transmission.
All Models 3.0

6—GEAR SHIFT LEVER, RENEW
Scorpion 0.4

7—SUPPORT & GEAR SHIFT LEVER, RENEW
Sedan 1.2
Coupe & H.P.E. 1.4

8—REAR GEAR CONTROL SHAFT, RENEW
Sedan 1.7
Coupe & H.P.E. 1.9

9—DIFFERENTIAL, OVERHAUL ON BENCH
Includes repair or replace parts as necessary & overhaul transmission.
All Models 3.5

10—DIFF SIDE GEAR SEAL, RENEW
Includes R&R drive shaft.
Engine End Exc 1.2
Scorpion 1.0
Transmission End 1.0

Rear Suspension—TIME

OPERATION INDEX

Camber & Toe-In, Check 1
Strut, Renew 2
Strut, Disassemble & Assemble 3
Transverse Link, Renew 4
Lower Arms, Renew 5
Lower Arm Bushings, Renew 6
Stabilizer Bar, Renew 7
Shock Absorber, Renew 8
Crossmember, Renew 9
Rear Wheel Shaft, Renew 10
Hub Carrier, Renew 11
Hub Or Bearing, Renew 12

1—REAR WHEEL CAMBER & TOE-IN, CHECK
Includes correct toe-in on both sides.
All Models 1.0

2—REAR STRUT, RENEW
One Exc 0.6
Scorpion 0.5
Both Exc 0.9
Scorpion 0.8

3—REAR STRUT, DISASSEMBLE & ASSEMBLE
After strut is removed
One Exc 0.5
Scorpion 0.6
Both Exc 0.9
Scorpion 1.0

4—TRANSVERSE LINK, RENEW
Does not include alignment.
Scorpion 0.6
Sedan, Coupe, H.P.E.—
Front 0.8
Rear 0.9

5—LOWER ARMS, RENEW
Scorpion, One 0.8
Both 1.2

6—LOWER ARM BUSHINGS, RENEW
Scorpion, One Arm 0.9
Both Arms 1.4

7—STABILIZER BAR, RENEW
Sedan, Coupe, H.P.E. 1.0
Scorpion 0.9

8—SHOCK ABSORBER, RENEW
After spring is removed.
One 0.2
Both 0.3

9—CROSSMEMBER, RENEW
Sedan, Coupe, H.P.E. 1.0
Scorpion 2.0

10—REAR WHEEL SHAFT, RENEW
Sedan, Coupe, H.P.E.—
One Shaft 1.2
Both Shafts 2.2

11—REAR WHEEL HUB CARRIER, RENEW
Scorpion—
One Carrier 1.0
Both Carriers 1.7

12—REAR HUB OR BEARING, RENEW ON BENCH
One Exc 0.3
Scorpion 0.7
Both Exc 0.5
Scorpion 1.2

Driving Axle Shaft—TIME

OPERATION INDEX

Driving Axle Shafts, Renew 1
Shaft, Overhaul 2
Constant Speed Joint, Renew 3
Joints, Check Tightness 4
Extension Shaft, Renew 5
Extn Shaft Support, Renew 6
Extn Shaft Bearing, Renew 7

1—DRIVING AXLE SHAFTS, RENEW
One Exc 0.9
Scorpion 0.8
Both 1.4

2—DRIVING AXLE SHAFT, OVERHAUL ON BENCH
Includes repair or replace parts as necessary
All Models 0.6

3—CONSTANT SPEED JOINT, RENEW
With shaft removed
All Models 0.3

4—CONSTANT SPEED JOINT, OUTBOARD, CHECK TIGHTNESS
All Models 0.5

5—EXTENSION SHAFT, RIGHT HAND, RENEW
Sedan, Coupe, H.P.E. 1.0

6—EXTENSION SHAFT SUPPORT, RENEW
Sedan, Coupe, H.P.E. 1.3

7—EXTENSION SHAFT BEARING, RENEW
Shaft removed
Sedan, Coupe, H.P.E. 0.3

Brakes—TIME

OPERTAION INDEX

Brake Pads, Renew 1
Brake Discs, Renew 2
Front Caliper, Renew 3
Rear Caliper, Renew 4
Caliper, Overhaul 5
Caliper Cylinders, Renew 6
Master Cylinder, Renew 7
Master Cylinder, Overhaul 8
Servo Unit, Renew 9
Servo Unit, Overhaul 10
Fluid Reservoir, Renew 11
Brakes, Complete Bleed 12
Brakes, Bleed Partial 13
Brake Hose, Renew 14
Pressure Warning Switch, Renew 15
Action Compensator, Adjust 16
Action Compensator, Renew 17
Compensator Lever, Renew 18
Pedal Assy, Renew 19
Hand Brake Lever, Renew 20
Hand Brake Lever, Adjust 21
Hand Brake Tie Rod, Renew 22
Hand Brake Cable, Renew 23

1—BRAKE PADS, RENEW
Front 0.9
Rear 0.8

2—BRAKE DISCS, RENEW
Includes partially R&R caliper &/or replace pads.
Front, One Side 0.7
Both Sides Exc 1.1
Scorpion 1.3
Rear, One Side 0.7
Both Sides Exc 1.1
Scorpion 1.3

3—FRONT BRAKE CALIPERS, RENEW
Includes R&R cylinders & pads. Does not include bleeding.
One Side 0.6
Both Sides Exc 1.0
Scorpion 0.8

4—REAR BRAKE CALIPERS, RENEW
Includes R&R cylinders & pads & connect & disconnect hand brake cables. Does not include bleeding.
One Side 0.7
Both Sides 1.2

5—CALIPER, OVERHAUL
After caliper is removed
Front Exc 0.6
Scorpion 0.3
Rear 0.7

6—CALIPER CYLINDERS, RENEW
After caliper is removed
One Side 0.3
Both Sides 0.4

7—MASTER CYLINDER, RENEW
Does not include bleeding.
Sedan, Coupe, H.P.E. 0.8
Scorpion 2.0

8—MASTER CYLINDER, OVERHAUL
After cylinder is removed
All Models 0.6

9—SERVO UNIT, RENEW
Includes R&R master cylinder (exc scorpion). Does not include bleeding.
Sedan, Coupe, H.P.E. 1.5
Scorpion 1.0

10—SERVO UNIT, OVERHAUL
After servo is removed
All Models 0.8

11—BRAKE FLUID RESERVOIR, RENEW
Does not include bleeding.
All Models 0.2

12—BRAKES, BLEED COMPLETE
Sedan, Coupe, H.P.E. 1.0
Scorpion 0.8

13—BRAKES, BLEED PARTIAL
Use this opertaion to cure spongy pedal.
Sedan, Coupe, H.P.E. 0.6
Scorpion 0.5

14—BRAKE HOSE, RENEW
Does not include bleeding.
Front, One 0.5
Both 0.9
Rear, One 0.4
Both 0.7
Vacuum, To Servo Unit 0.3

15—BRAKE PRESSURE WARNING SWITCH, RENEW
Does not include bleeding
Sedan, Coupe, H.P.E. 0.9
Scorpion 0.6

16—BRAKE ACTION COMPENSATOR, ADJUST
Sedan, Coupe, H.P.E. 0.3

17—BRAKE ACTION COMPENSATOR, RENEW
Does not include bleeding.
Sedan, Coupe, H.P.E. 0.6

18—COMPENSATOR CONTROL LEVER, RENEW & ADJUST
Sedan, Coupe, H.P.E. 0.7

19—PEDAL ASSY, RENEW &/OR ADJUST FREE PLAY
Includes R&R support & bleed clutch & brakes on scorpion.
Sedan, Coupe, H.P.E. 0.6
Scorpion 2.2

20—HAND BRAKE CONTROL LEVER, R&R & OVERHAUL
Sedan, Coupe, H.P.E. 1.3
Scorpion 0.8

21—HAND BRAKE LEVER, ADJUST FREE PLAY
Sedan, Coupe, H.P.E. 0.2
Scorpion 0.4

22—HAND BRAKE TIE ROD, RENEW
All Models 1.0

23—HAND BRAKE CABLE, RENEW & ADJUST
Sedan, Coupe, H.P.E. 0.6
Scorpion 0.8

Front Suspension—TIME

OPERATION INDEX

Toe-In Or Toe-Out 1
Wheel Alignment 2
Strut, Renew 3
Strut, Disassemble & Reassemble 4
Lower Arm, R&R Or Renew 5
Lower Ball-Joint, Renew 6
Lower Arm Bushings, Renew 7
Anchorage Rod, Renew 8
Stabilizer Bar, Renew 9
Shock Absorber, Renew 10
Front Swivel Assy, Renew 11
Hub Or Bearing, Renew 12

1—TOE-IN OR TOE-OUT, CHECK & ADJUST
Check 0.4
Check & Adjust 0.8

2—WHEEL ALIGNMENT
All Models 1.5

3—STRUT ASSY, RENEW
One Side 0.6
Both Sides 0.9

4—STRUT ASSY, DISASSEMBLE & REASSEMBLE
After strut is removed.
One 0.5
Both Exc 0.9
Scorpion 1.0

5—LOWER ARM, R&R OR RENEW
Does not include alignment.
One Exc 0.8
Scorpion 0.9
Both Exc 1.4
Scorpion 1.5

6—LOWER BALL-JOINT, RENEW
Sedan, Coupe & H.P.E.—
One 0.4
Both 0.7

7—LOWER ARM BUSHINGS, RENEW
Sedan, Coupe, H.P.E.—
One 1.3
Both 2.4
Scorpion—
One 0.8
Both 1.4

8—ANCHORAGE ROD, RENEW
Scorpion 0.3

9—STABILIZER BAR, RENEW
Includes replace bushings. Does not include alignment.
Sedan, Coupe, H.P.E. 1.2
Scorpion 0.8

10—SHOCK ABSORBER, RENEW
With springs removed
One 0.2
Both 0.3

11—FRONT SWIVEL ASSY, RENEW
One Exc 1.0
Scorpion 0.8
Both Exc 1.9
Scorpion 1.4

12—FRONT HUB OR BEARING, RENEW ON BENCH
One Exc 0.3
Scorpion 0.8
Both Exc 0.5
Scorpion 1.4

Manual Steering Gear—TIME

OPERATION INDEX

Gear Assy, Renew 1
Gear, Overhaul 2
Boot Or Bushing, Renew 3
Damper, Renew 4
Tie Rods, Renew 5
Column Jacket, Renew 6

1—STEERING GEAR ASSY & RODS, RENEW
Does not include check & adjust toe-out
Sedan, Coupe, H.P.E. 1.1
Scorpion 1.6

2—STEERING GEAR, OVERHAUL
After gear is removed.
All Models 1.5

3—BOOT &/OR BUSHING, RIGHT SIDE, RENEW
All Models 1.5

4—STEERING DAMPER, RENEW
All Models 0.6

5—TIE RODS, RENEW
One Side Exc 0.8
Scorpion 0.9
Both Sides Exc 1.4
Scorpion 1.5

(Continued)

Manual Steering Gear—TIME Cont'd

6—COLUMN JACKET, RENEW
Sedan, Coupe, H.P.E. 0.5
Scorpion 0.6

Power Steering Gear—TIME

OPERATION INDEX

Gear Assy, Renew 1
Gear, Overhaul 2
Reservoir, Renew 3
Pump, Renew 4
Pump Belt, Renew 5
Pump Pulley Renew 6
Pump Arm, Renew 7

1—STEERING GEAR ASSY & RODS, RENEW
Includes bleeding. Does not include check & adjust toe-out
Less Air Cond 3.6
With Air Cond 4.0

2—STEERING GEAR, OVERHAUL
After gear is removed
All Models 2.0

3—RESERVOIR, RENEW
All Models 0.3

4—PUMP, RENEW
Includes adjust drive belt & bleeding
Less Air Cond 1.5
With Air Cond 1.7

5—PUMP BELT, RENEW
Less Air Cond 1.2

6—PUMP PULLEY, RENEW
All Models 1.4

7—PUMP ARM, FRONT OR RENEW, RENEW
Less Air Cond 0.3

Heater—TIME

OPERATION INDEX

Heater Assy, Renew 1
Heater Assy, Overhaul 2
Heater Valve, Renew 3
Heater Core, Renew 4
Heater Core, Overhaul 5
Heater Motor, Renew 6
Heater Control Lever, Renew 7
Fan Motor Switch, Renew 8

1—HEATER ASSY, RENEW
Sedan 1.1
Coupe & H.P.E. 2.7
Scorpion 2.0

2—HEATER ASSY, OVERHAUL
Heater removed
All Models 0.7

3—HEATER VALVE, RENEW
Sedan 0.6
Coupe & H.P.E. 1.8
Scorpion 0.6

4—HEATER CORE, RENEW
Sedan 1.3
Coupe & H.P.E. 2.7
Scorpion 2.2

5—HEATER CORE, OVERHAUL
After core is removed. Includes test, repair or replace parts as necessary.
All Models 0.7

6—HEATER MOTOR, RENEW
Sedan 1.3
Coupe & H.P.E. 2.9
Scorpion 1.4

7—HEATER CONTROL LEVER, RENEW
Sedan, Coupe, H.P.E 1.1

8—FAN MOTOR SWITCH RENEW
Sedan, Coupe, H.P.E. 0.6

Air Conditioner—TIME

OPERATION INDEX

Evacuate & Recharge System 1
Check Operation Of System 2
Compressor, Renew 3
Compressor Belts, Renew 4
Compressor Clutch, Renew 5
Compressor Front Seal, Renew 6
Receiver-Dryer, Renew 7
Expansion Valve, Renew 8
Condenser, Renew 9
Condenser Fan, Renew 10
Condenser Fan Switch, Renew 11
Blower Control Switch, Renew 12
Blower Motor, Renew 13
Vacuum Motor, Renew 14
Vacuum Reserve Tank, Renew 15
Hoses, Renew 16
Evaporator Renew 17

1—EVACUATE & RECHARGE SYSTEM
All Models 0.6

2—CHECK OPERATION OF SYSTEM
Includes hook up gauges, check operation & refrigeration.
Sedan, Coupe, H.P.E. 0.5
Scorpion 0.7

3—COMPRESSOR, RENEW
Does not include evacuate & recharge.
Sedan, Coupe, H.P.E. 2.0
Scorpion 1.7

4—COMPRESSOR BELTS, RENEW
All Models 1.2

5—COMPRESSOR CLUTCH, RENEW
Sedan, Coupe, H.P.E. 1.8
Scorpion 1.5

6—COMPRESSOR FRONT SEAL, RENEW
All Models 1.6

7—RECEIVER-DRYER, RENEW
Sedan, Coupe, H.P.E. 0.5
Scorpion 0.7

8—EXPANSION VALVE, RENEW
Sedan, Coupe, H.P.E. 0.5
Scorpion 0.8

9—CONDENSER RENEW
All Models 1.0

10—CONDENSER FAN, RENEW
All Models 0.5

11—CONDENSER FAN SWITCH, RENEW
Sedan, Coupe, H.P.E. 0.4
Scorpion 0.5

12—BLOWER CONTROL SWITCH, RENEW
Sedan, Coupe, H.P.E. 0.4
Scorpion 1.6

13—BLOWER MOTOR, RENEW
Scorpion 1.0

14—VACUUM MOTOR, RENEW
Scorpion 2.5

15—VACUUM RESERVE TANK, RENEW
Scorpion 1.2

16—AIR COND HOSES, RENEW
Evap To Comp Exc 1.2
Scorpion 1.5
Comp To Cond Exc 1.5
Scorpion 2.0

17—EVAPORATOR ASSY, RENEW
Sedan, Coupe, H.P.E. 3.5
Scorpion 8.0

IDENTIFICATION

ALL MODELS....217

ILLUSTRATIONS

FIG 1 – ENGINE CAMSHAFT CARRIER & COVER – SERIES 1
FIG 2 – ENGINE CAMSHAFT CARRIER & COVER – SERIES 2, 3, 4
FIG 3 – ENGINE CYLINDER HEAD & COVER – SERIES 5, 6
FIG 4 – ENGINE CYLINDER HEAD – SERIES 1
FIG 5 – ENGINE CYLINDER HEAD – SERIES 2, 3, 4
FIG 6 – ENGINE CYLINDER HEAD – SERIES 5, 6
FIG 7 – ENGINE CYLINDER BLOCK & OIL PAN – SERIES 1
FIG 8 – ENGINE CYLINDER BLOCK & OIL PAN – SERIES 2, 3, 4
FIG 9 – ENGINE CYLINDER BLOCK & OIL PAN – SERIES 5, 6
FIG 10 – ENGINE TIMING GEAR CASE & WATER PUMP – 1
FIG 11 – ENGINE TIMING GEAR CASE & WATER PUMP – 2,3,4
FIG 12 – ENGINE REAR COVER, WATER & OIL PUMPS – 5,6
FIG 13 – ENGINE CRANKSHAFT & PISTONS – SERIES 1
FIG 14 – ENGINE CRANKSHAFT & PISTONS – SERIES 2, 3, 4
FIG 15 – ENGINE CRANKSHAFT & PISTONS – SERIES 5, 6
FIG 16 – ENGINE CAMSHAFT & VALVES – SERIES 1
FIG 17 – ENGINE CAMSHAFT & VALVES – SERIES 2, 3, 4
FIG 18 – ENGINE CAMSNAFT & VALVES – SERIES 5, 6
FIG 19 – MANUAL TRANSMISSION
FIG 20 – AUTOMATIC TRANSMISSION – INTERNAL COMPONENTS
FIG 21 – AUTOMATIC TRANSMISSION – CASE & RELATED PARTS
FIG 22 – FRONT SUSPENSION UPPER & LOWER ARMS – SERIES 1
FIG 23 – FRONT SUSPENSION UPPER & LOWER ARMS – 2 thru 6
FIG 24 – FRONT SUSPENSION SPRING & SHOCK ABSORBER
FIG 25 – STEERING GEAR – SERIES 1 THRU 5
FIG 26 – STEERING GEAR – SERIES 6
FIG 27 – STEERING LINKAGE – SERIES 1
FIG 28 – STEERING LINKAGE – SERIES 2 THRU 6
FIG 29 – REAR AXLE

OPERATION TIMES

A

Air Pump.... 234
Alternator.... 235
Alternator Regulator.... 235
Axle Shaft.... 237
Automatic Transmission.... 237

B

Back-Up Lamp Switch.... 235
Ball Joints, Front.... 238
Battery Cables.... 235
Brakes.... 237
Brake Drum.... 237
Brake Hose.... 238

C

Cables, Battery.... 235
Cables, Ignition.... 234
Camshaft.... 236
Carburetor.... 234
Clutch.... 236
Coil, Ignition.... 234
Compression, Test.... 234
Condenser, Distributor.... 234
Control Arms, Front.... 238
Controlled Combustion System.... 234
Cooling System.... 235
Crankcase Vent Valve.... 236
Crankshaft.... 236
Cylinder Head.... 235

D

Dash Gauges.... 235
Differential.... 237
Directional Flasher.... 235
Directional Switch.... 235
Distributor.... 234

E

Emission Control System.... 234
Engine Assembly.... 236
Engine Mounting.... 236
Engine Oiling.... 236
Engine Tune-Up.... 234
Evaporative Emission.... 234
Exhaust System.... 234

F

Fan.... 235
Flywheel.... 236
Front End Adjustments.... 238
Front Suspension.... 238
Front Wheel Bearings.... 238
Fuel Gauge.... 235
Fuel Pump.... 234
Fuel Tank.... 234

H

Handbrake.... 238
Headlamp.... 235
Heater Core.... 235
Horn.... 235
Hose, Brake.... 238
Hose, Radiator.... 235
Hydraulic Brake System.... 238

I

Idler Arm.... 238
Ignition System.... 234
Intake Manifold Gasket.... 234

L

Lamps.... 235
Layshaft.... 236
Lens, Lamp.... 235
Light Switch.... 235

M

Manual Transmission.... 237
Main Bearings.... 236
Master Cylinder.... 238
Muffler.... 234

O

Oiling, Engine.... 236
Oil Gauge.... 235
Oil Pan.... 236
Oil Pump.... 236

P

Parking Brake.... 238
Piston.... 236
Piston Rings.... 236
Pitman Arm.... 238
Power Brake.... 237
Propeller Shaft.... 237

R

Radiator.... 235
Radiator Hose.... 235
Regulator (Alternator).... 235
Rings (Piston).... 236
Rocker Arm.... 235
Rod Bearings.... 236

S

Shocks, Front.... 238
Shocks, Rear.... 238
Spark Plugs.... 234
Speedometer.... 235
Spring, Rear.... 238
Stabilizer Shaft.... 238
Starting Motor.... 234
Steering Gear.... 238
Steering Knuckle.... 238
Steering Linkage.... 238
Stop Light Switch.... 235
Strut Rod.... 238
Switches –
- Back-Up Lamp.... 235
- Ignition.... 234
- Light.... 235
- Stop Light.... 235
- Turn Signal.... 235

T

Tail Pipe.... 234
Temperature Gauge.... 235
Thermostat.... 235
Tie Rod.... 238
Timing Case.... 236
Timing Chain.... 236
Torsion Bar.... 238
Transmission.... 237
Tune-Up , Engine.... 234
Turn Signal Switch.... 235

U

Universal Joint.... 237

V

Vacuum Control Unit.... 234
Valve System.... 235

W

Water Pump.... 235
Wheel Alignment.... 238
Wheel Bearing, Front.... 238
Wheel Bearing, Rear.... 238
Windshield Wiper.... 235

VEHICLE IDENTIFICATION NUMBER PLATE

LOCATION – On left side lock pillar within the cab.

SERIES I – Begins with LUV 82
SERIES II – Begins with CLN 14282
SERIES III – Begins with CLN 14382
SERIES IV – Begins with CLN14482
SERIES V – Begins with CLN14582
SERIES VI – Begins with CLN14682

ENGINE NUMBER

LOCATION – Stamped on right upper center section of block.

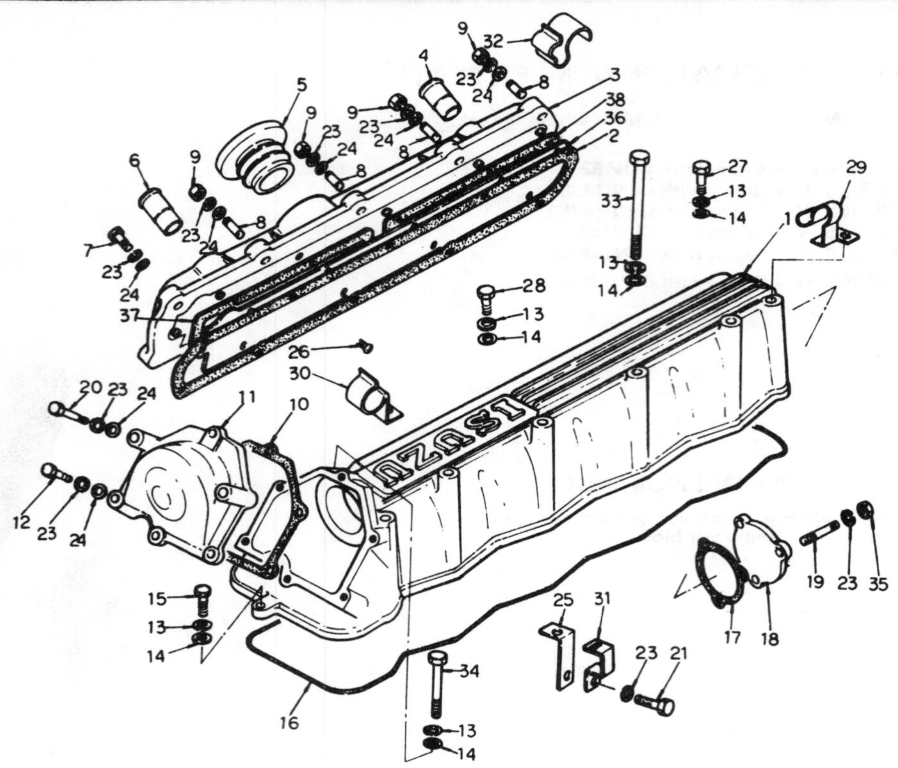

1	Camshaft Carrier
2	Gasket
3	Cover
4	Pipe
5	Cap
6	Pipe
7	Bolt
8	Stud
9	Nut
10	Gasket
11	Cover
12	Bolt
13	Washer
14	Washer
15	Bolt
16	Seal
17	Gasket
18	Cover
19	Stud
20	Bolt
21	Bolt
22	Washer
23	Washer
24	Washer
25	Bracket
26	Screw
27	Bolt
28	Bolt
29	Clip
30	Clip
31	Clip
32	Clip
33	Bolt
34	Bolt
35	Nut
36	Plate
37	Gasket
38	Gasket

FIG 1 – ENGINE CAMSHAFT CARRIER & COVER – SERIES 1

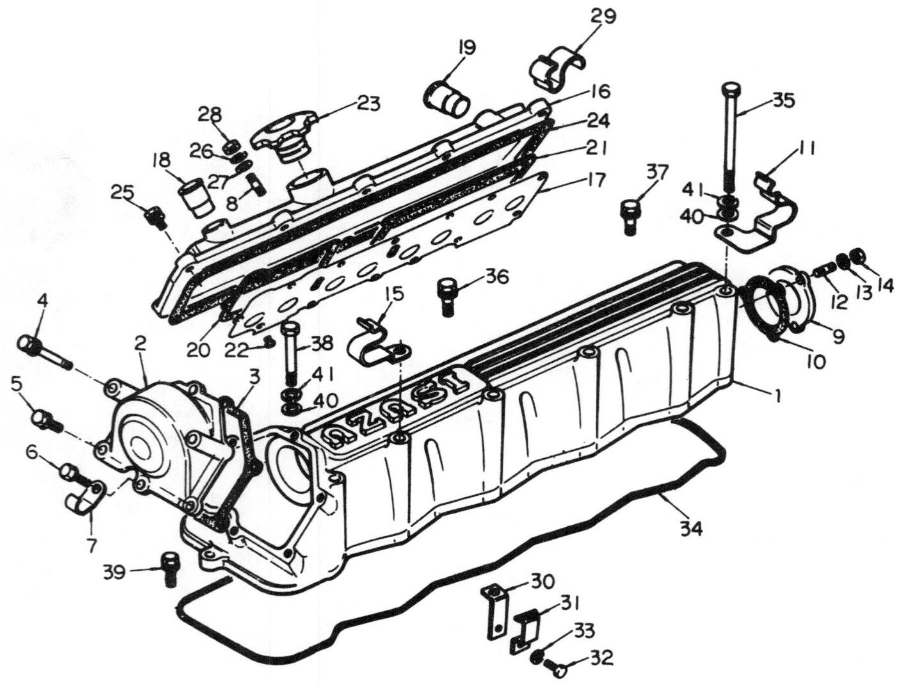

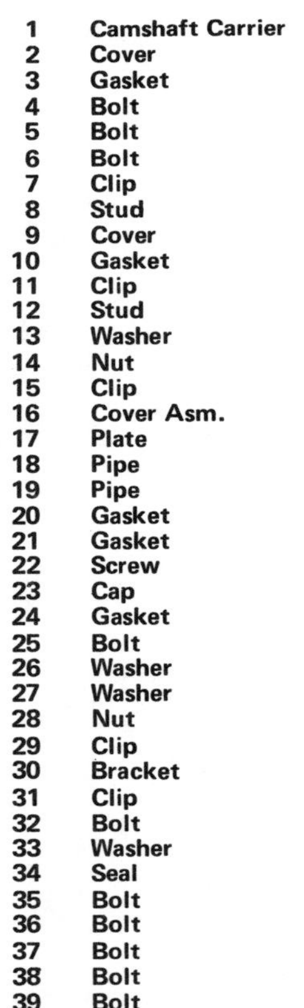

1	Camshaft Carrier
2	Cover
3	Gasket
4	Bolt
5	Bolt
6	Bolt
7	Clip
8	Stud
9	Cover
10	Gasket
11	Clip
12	Stud
13	Washer
14	Nut
15	Clip
16	Cover Asm.
17	Plate
18	Pipe
19	Pipe
20	Gasket
21	Gasket
22	Screw
23	Cap
24	Gasket
25	Bolt
26	Washer
27	Washer
28	Nut
29	Clip
30	Bracket
31	Clip
32	Bolt
33	Washer
34	Seal
35	Bolt
36	Bolt
37	Bolt
38	Bolt
39	Bolt
40	Washer
41	Washer

FIG 2 – ENGINE CAMSHAFT CARRIER & COVER – SERIES 2, 3, 4

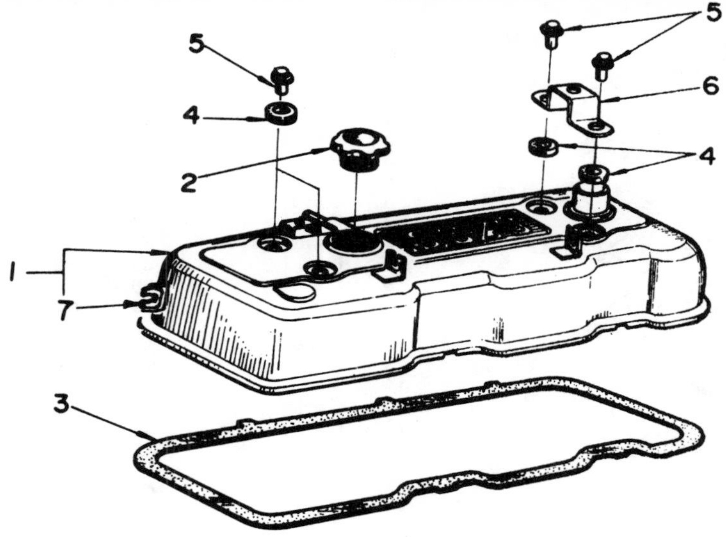

1	Cover
2	Cap
3	Gasket
4	Gasket
5	Nut
6	Bracket
7	Clip

FIG 3 – ENGINE CYLINDER HEAD & COVER – SERIES 5, 6

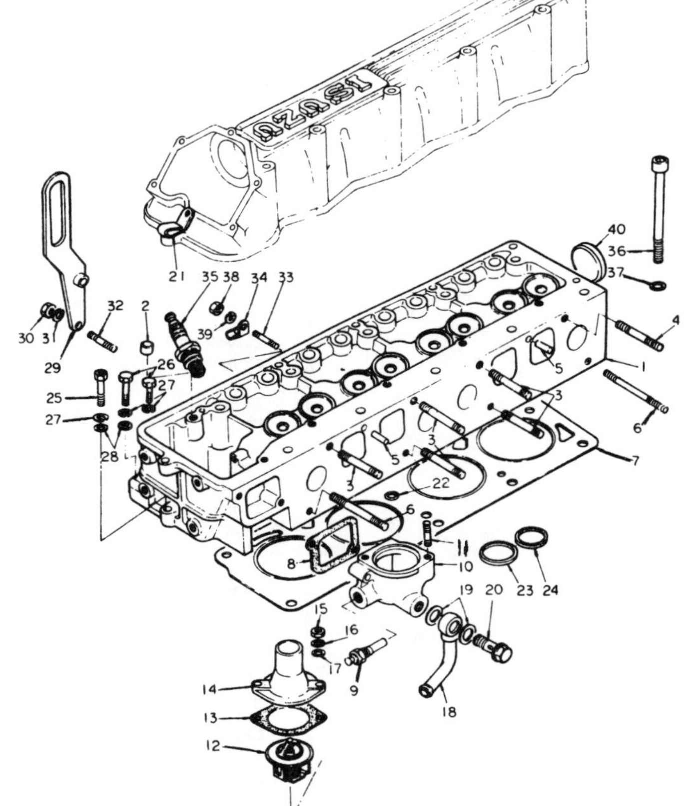

1	Cylinder Head
2	Dowel
3	Stud
4	Stud
5	Pin
6	Stud
7	Gasket
8	Gasket
9	Thermometer Unit
10	Housing
11	Stud
12	Thermostat
13	Gasket
14	Pipe (Outlet)
15	Nut
16	Washer
17	Washer
18	Pipe
19	Seal
20	Connector (Joint Bolt)
21	Clip
22	Seal
23	Insert
24	Insert
25	Bolt
26	Bolt
27	Washer
28	Washer
29	Hanger
30	Nut
31	Washer
32	Stud
33	Stud
34	Clip
35	Spark Plug
36	Bolt
37	Washer
38	Nut
39	Washer
40	Cup

FIG 4 – ENGINE CYLINDER HEAD – SERIES 1

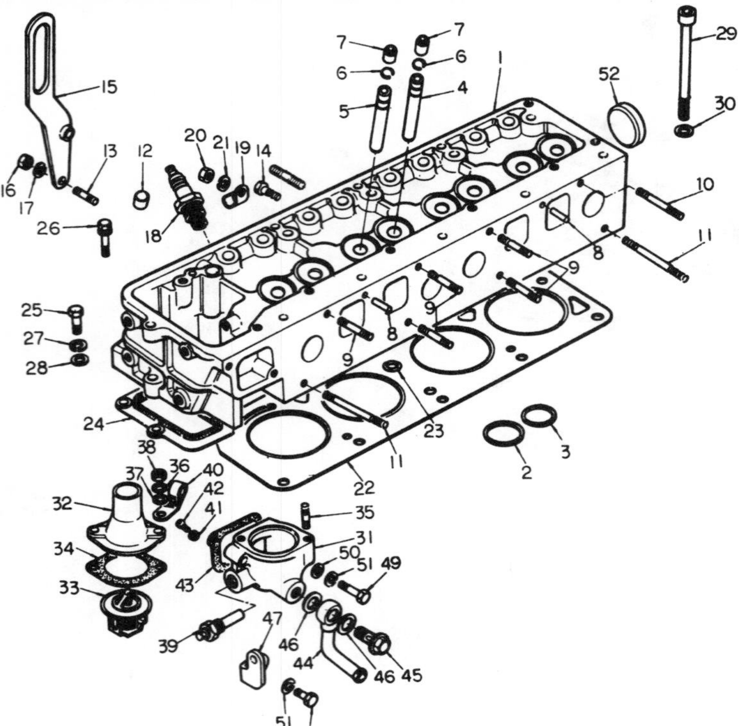

No.	Part	No.	Part
1	Cylinder Head	27	Washer
2	Insert	28	Washer
3	Insert	29	Bolt
4	Valve Guide	30	Washer
5	Valve Guide	31	Housing
6	Ring	32	Pipe (Outlet)
7	Controller	33	Thermostat
8	Pin	34	Gasket
9	Stud	35	Stud
10	Stud	36	Washer
11	Stud	37	Washer
12	Dowel	38	Nut
13	Stud	39	Thermometer Unit
14	Stud	40	Clip
15	Hanger	41	Washer
16	Nut	42	Screw
17	Washer	43	Gasket
18	Spark Plug	44	Pipe
19	Clip	45	Connector (Joint Bolt)
20	Nut	46	Seal
21	Washer	47	Bracket
22	Gasket	48	Bolt
23	Seal	49	Bolt
24	Gasket	50	Washer
25	Bolt	51	Washer
26	Bolt	52	Cup

FIG 5 – ENGINE CYLINDER HEAD – SERIES 2,3,4

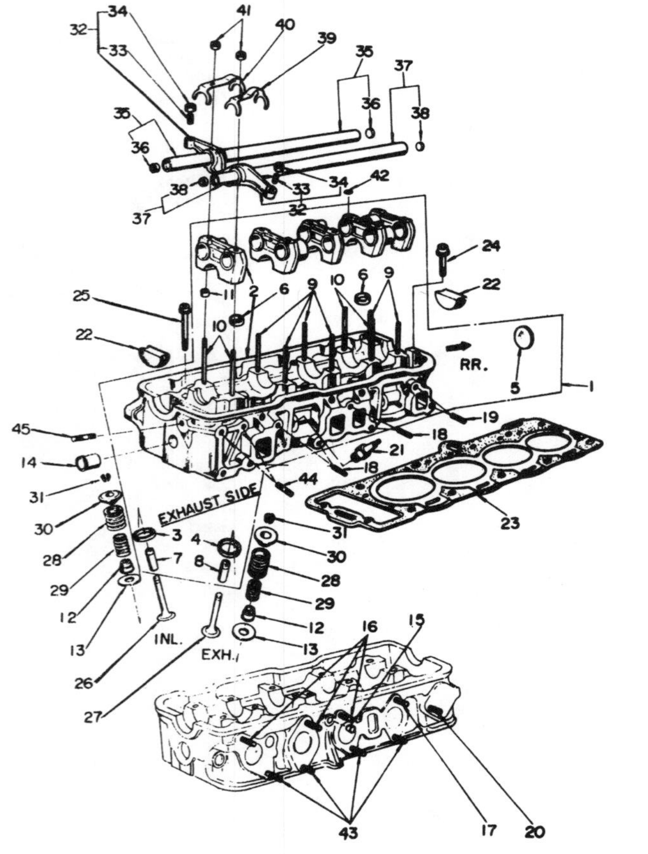

No.	Part
1	Cylinder Head Assy
2	Head, part of head asm.
3	Insert
4	Insert
5	Cup, rear
6	Cup, upper
7	Valve Guide
8	Valve Guide
9	Stud
10	Stud
11	Dowel
12	Controller
13	Cap
14	Pipe
15	Plug
16	Stud
17	Stud
18	Stud
19	Stud
20	Stud
21	Spark Plug
22	Plug
23	Gasket
24	Bolt
25	Bolt
26	Valve, inlet
27	Valve, exhaust
28	Spring
29	Spring
30	Cap
31	Key
32	Arm
33	Screw
34	Nut
35	Shaft
36	Plug
37	Shaft
38	Plug
39	Spring
40	Spring
41	Nut
42	Washer
43	Stud
44	Stud
45	Stud

FIG 6 – ENGINE CYLINDER HEAD – SERIES 5, 6

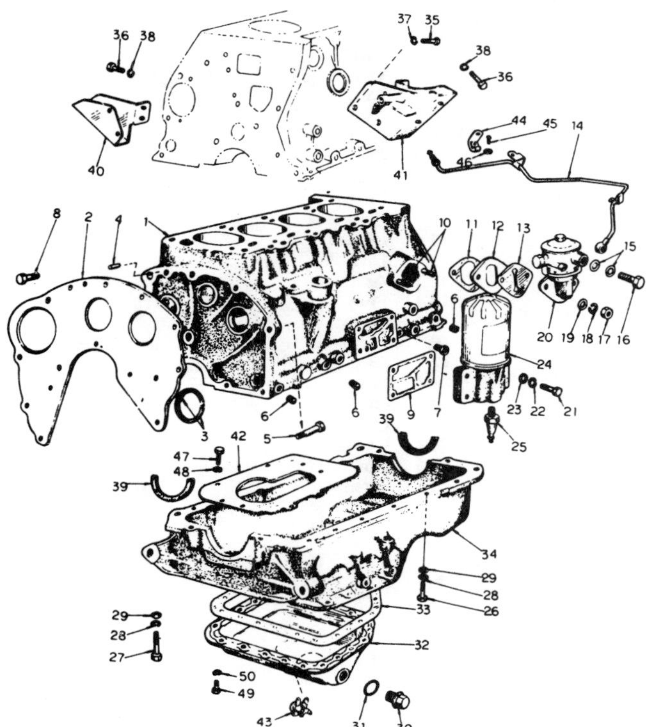

FIG 7 – ENGINE CYLINDER BLOCK & OIL PAN – SERIES 1

1	Cylinder Block	26	Bolt
2	Plate	27	Bolt
3	Seal	28	Washer
4	Pin	29	Washer
5	Bolt	30	Plug
6	Plug	31	Seal
7	Nipple	32	Pan
8	Bolt	33	Gasket
9	Gasket	34	Crankcase
10	Stud	35	Bolt
11	Gasket	36	Bolt
12	Pad	37	Washer
13	Gasket	38	Washer
14	Pipe	39	Packing
15	Seal	40	Bracket, R.H.
16	Connector (Joint Bolt)	41	Bracket, L.H.
17	Nut	42	Plate
18	Washer	43	Seat
19	Washer	44	Clip
20	Pump	45	Screw
21	Bolt	46	Washer
22	Washer	47	Bolt
23	Washer	48	Washer
24	Filter	49	Bolt
25	Unit	50	Washer

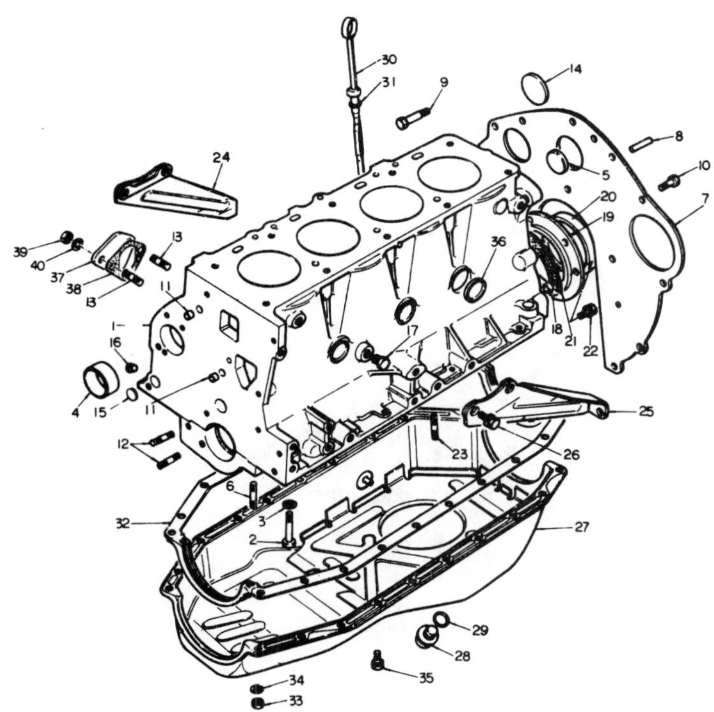

FIG 8 – ENGINE CYLINDER BLOCK & OIL PAN – SERIES 2, 3, 4

1	Cylinder Block
2	Bolt
3	Washer
4	Bearing
5	Cup
6	Stud
7	Plate
8	Pin
9	Bolt
10	Bolt
11	Dowel
12	Stud
13	Stud
14	Plug
15	Plug
16	Plug
17	Plug
18	Dowel
19	Retainer
20	Seal
21	Gasket
22	Bolt
23	Stud
24	Support, R.H.
25	Support, L.H.
26	Bolt
27	Pan
28	Plug
29	Seal
30	Gauge
31	Seal
32	Gasket
33	Nut
34	Washer
35	Bolt
36	Cup
37	Cover
38	Gasket
39	Nut
40	Washer

FIG 9 – ENGINE CYLINDER BLOCK & OIL PAN – SERIES 5, 6

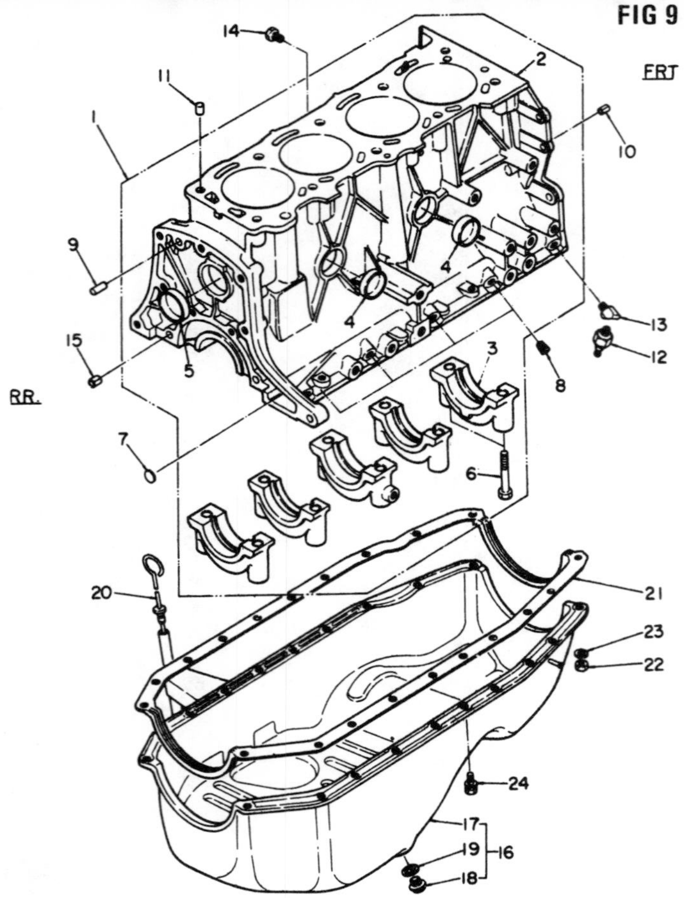

1	Block
2	Body Assy
3	Cap, brg.,part of block assy.
4	Cup
5	Cup
6	Bolt
7	Plug
8	Plug
9	Pin
10	Dowel
11	Dowel
12	Unit
13	Adapter
14	Plug
15	Dowel
16	Pan Assy
17	Pan, part of oil pan assy
18	Plug
19	Gasket
20	Gauge
21	Gasket
22	Nut
23	Washer
24	Bolt

FIG 10 – ENGINE TIMING GEAR CASE & WATER PUMP – SERIES 1

1	Fan	36	Cup
2	Bolt	37	Connector (Joint Bolt)
3	Washer	38	Seal
4	Spacer	39	Bolt
5	Pulley	40	Washer
6	Pulley	41	Washer
7	Belt	42	Pump
8	Plug	43	Gasket
9	Seal	44	Bolt
10	Case	45	Bolt
11	Cover	46	Bolt
12	Gasket	47	Washer
13	Pointer	48	Washer
14	Bolt	49	Clip
15	Nut	50	Hose
16	Washer	51	Stud
17	Washer	52	Oil Pipe
18	Bolt	53	Nipple
19	Plug	54	Gasket
20	Seal	55	Clip
21	Gasket	56	Clip
22	Gasket	57	Plug
23	Plate	58	Plug
24	Gauge Asm	59	Bolt
25	Gasket	60	Bolt
26	Bearing	61	Seal
27	Dowel	62	Washer
28	Brace	63	Washer
29	Bolt	64	Bolt
30	Bolt	65	Washer
31	Washer	66	Washer
32	Bolt	67	Washer
33	Washer	68	Washer
34	Clip	69	Bolt
35	Bolt		

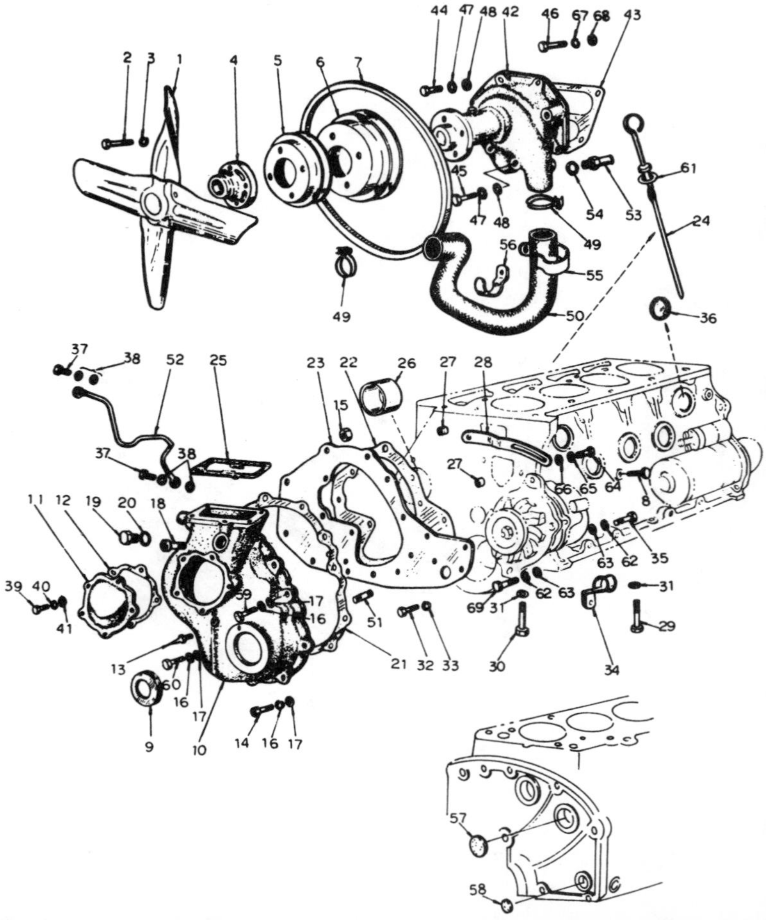

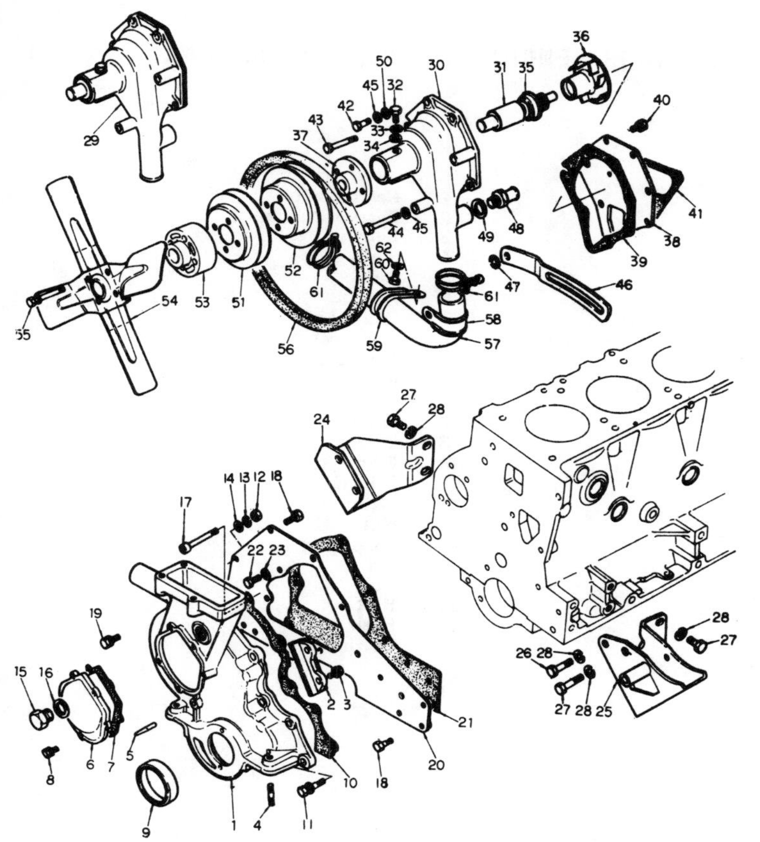

1	Case	32	Screw
2	Damper Assy	33	Washer
3	Bolt	34	Washer
4	Stud	35	Seal Unit
5	Pointer	36	Impeller
6	Cover	37	Center
7	Gasket	38	Cover
8	Bolt	39	Gasket
9	Seal	40	Bolt
10	Gasket	41	Gasket
11	Bolt	42	Bolt
12	Nut	43	Bolt
13	Washer	44	Bolt
14	Washer	45	Washer
15	Plug	46	Brace
16	Seal	47	Washer
17	Bolt	48	Nipple
18	Bolt	49	Gasket
19	Bolt	50	Washer
20	Plate	51	Pulley
21	Gasket	52	Pulley
22	Bolt	53	Spacer
23	Washer	54	Fan
24	Bracket, R.H.	55	Bolt
25	Bracket, L. H.	56	Belt
26	Bolt	57	Hose
27	Bolt	58	Clip
28	Washer	59	Clip
29	Pump	60	Bolt
30	Bpdy	61	Clip
31	Bearing Unit	62	Washer

FIG 11 – ENGINE TIMING GEAR CASE & WATER PUMP – SERIES 2, 3, 4

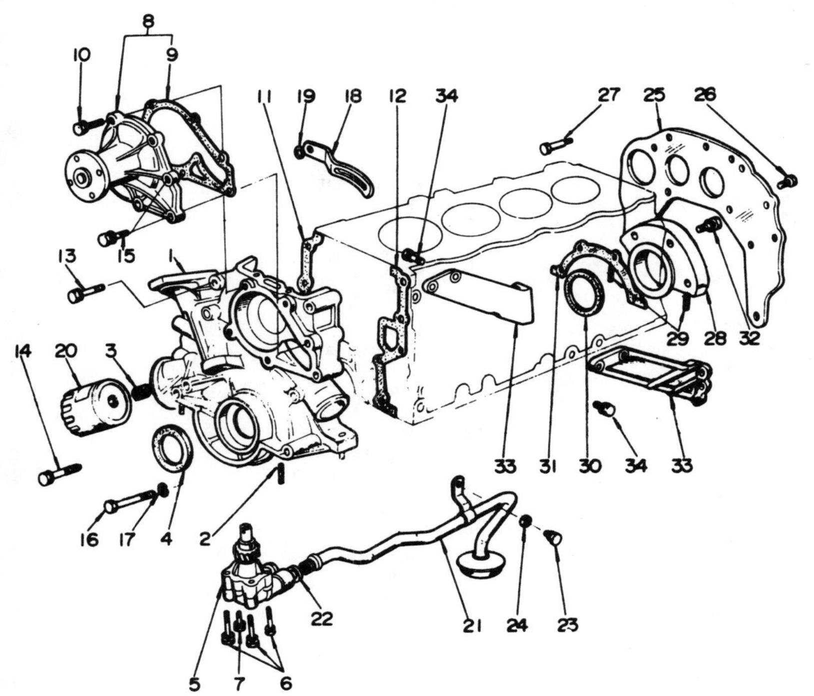

1	Cover
2	Stud
3	Fitting
4	Seal
5	Pump
6	Bolt
7	Bolt
8	Pump
9	Gasket
10	Bolt
11	Gasket R.H.
12	Gasket, L.H.
13	Bolt
14	Bolt
15	Bolt
16	Bolt
17	Washer
18	Brace
19	Washer
20	Element
21	Pipe Asm.
22	Seal
23	Bolt
24	Washer
25	Plate
26	Bolt
27	Bolt
28	Retainer
29	Stud
30	Seal
31	Gasket
32	Bolt
33	Support
34	Bolt

FIG 12 – ENGINE & REAR COVER, WATER & OIL PUMPS – SERIES 5, 6

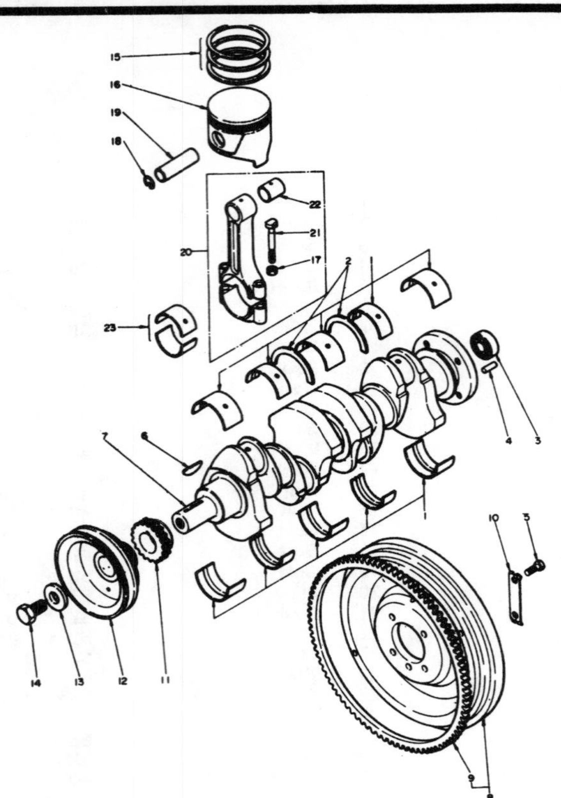

FIG 13 – ENGINE CRANKSHAFT & PISTONS – SERIES 1

1	Bearing Kit
2	Bearing Washer
3	Bearing
4	Pin
5	Bolt
6	Key
7	Crankshaft
8	Flywheel
9	Ring Gear
10	Plate
11	Sprocket
12	Pulley
13	Washer
14	Bolt
15	Ring Kit
16	Piston
17	Nut
18	Snap Ring
19	Pin
20	Rod
21	Bolt
22	Bush
23	Bearing Set

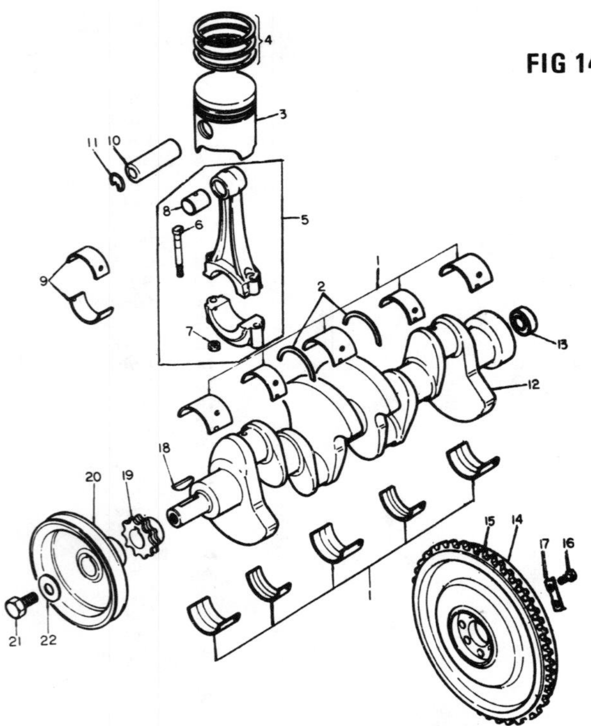

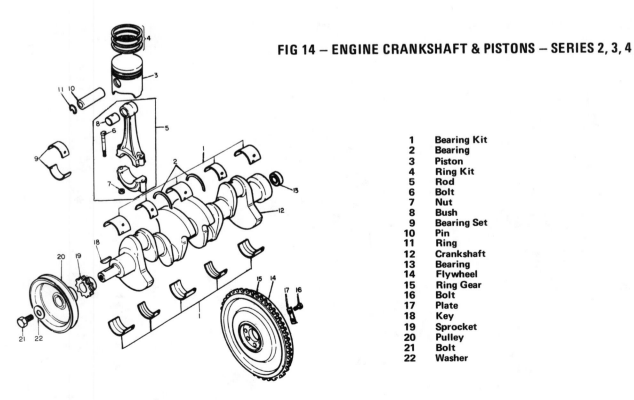

FIG 14 – ENGINE CRANKSHAFT & PISTONS – SERIES 2, 3, 4

1	Bearing Kit
2	Bearing
3	Piston
4	Ring Kit
5	Rod
6	Bolt
7	Nut
8	Bush
9	Bearing Set
10	Pin
11	Ring
12	Crankshaft
13	Bearing
14	Flywheel
15	Ring Gear
16	Bolt
17	Plate
18	Key
19	Sprocket
20	Pulley
21	Bolt
22	Washer

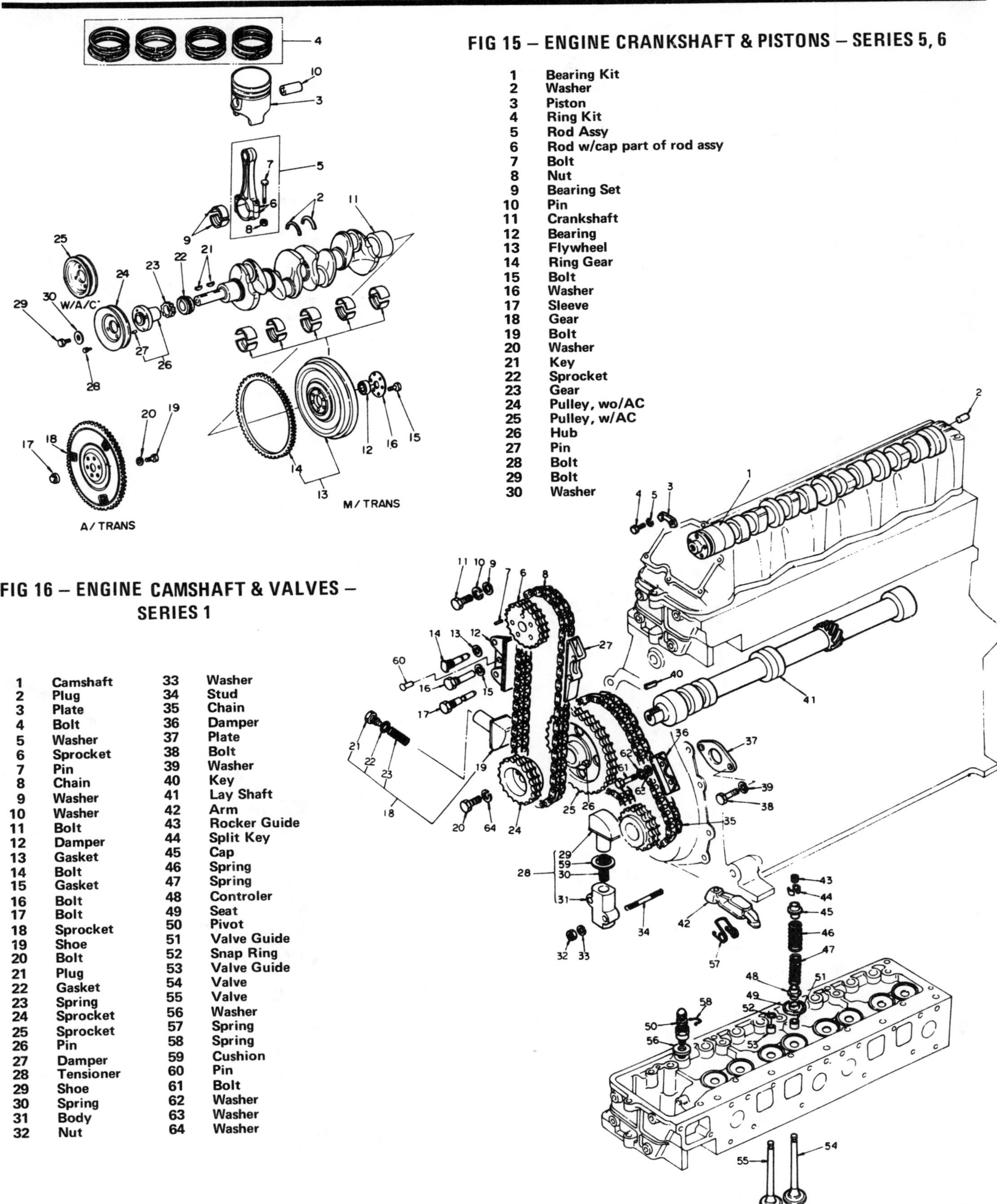

FIG 15 – ENGINE CRANKSHAFT & PISTONS – SERIES 5, 6

1 Bearing Kit
2 Washer
3 Piston
4 Ring Kit
5 Rod Assy
6 Rod w/cap part of rod assy
7 Bolt
8 Nut
9 Bearing Set
10 Pin
11 Crankshaft
12 Bearing
13 Flywheel
14 Ring Gear
15 Bolt
16 Washer
17 Sleeve
18 Gear
19 Bolt
20 Washer
21 Key
22 Sprocket
23 Gear
24 Pulley, wo/AC
25 Pulley, w/AC
26 Hub
27 Pin
28 Bolt
29 Bolt
30 Washer

FIG 16 – ENGINE CAMSHAFT & VALVES – SERIES 1

1 Camshaft
2 Plug
3 Plate
4 Bolt
5 Washer
6 Sprocket
7 Pin
8 Chain
9 Washer
10 Washer
11 Bolt
12 Damper
13 Gasket
14 Bolt
15 Gasket
16 Bolt
17 Bolt
18 Sprocket
19 Shoe
20 Bolt
21 Plug
22 Gasket
23 Spring
24 Sprocket
25 Sprocket
26 Pin
27 Damper
28 Tensioner
29 Shoe
30 Spring
31 Body
32 Nut
33 Washer
34 Stud
35 Chain
36 Damper
37 Plate
38 Bolt
39 Washer
40 Key
41 Lay Shaft
42 Arm
43 Rocker Guide
44 Split Key
45 Cap
46 Spring
47 Spring
48 Controler
49 Seat
50 Pivot
51 Valve Guide
52 Snap Ring
53 Valve Guide
54 Valve
55 Valve
56 Washer
57 Spring
58 Spring
59 Cushion
60 Pin
61 Bolt
62 Washer
63 Washer
64 Washer

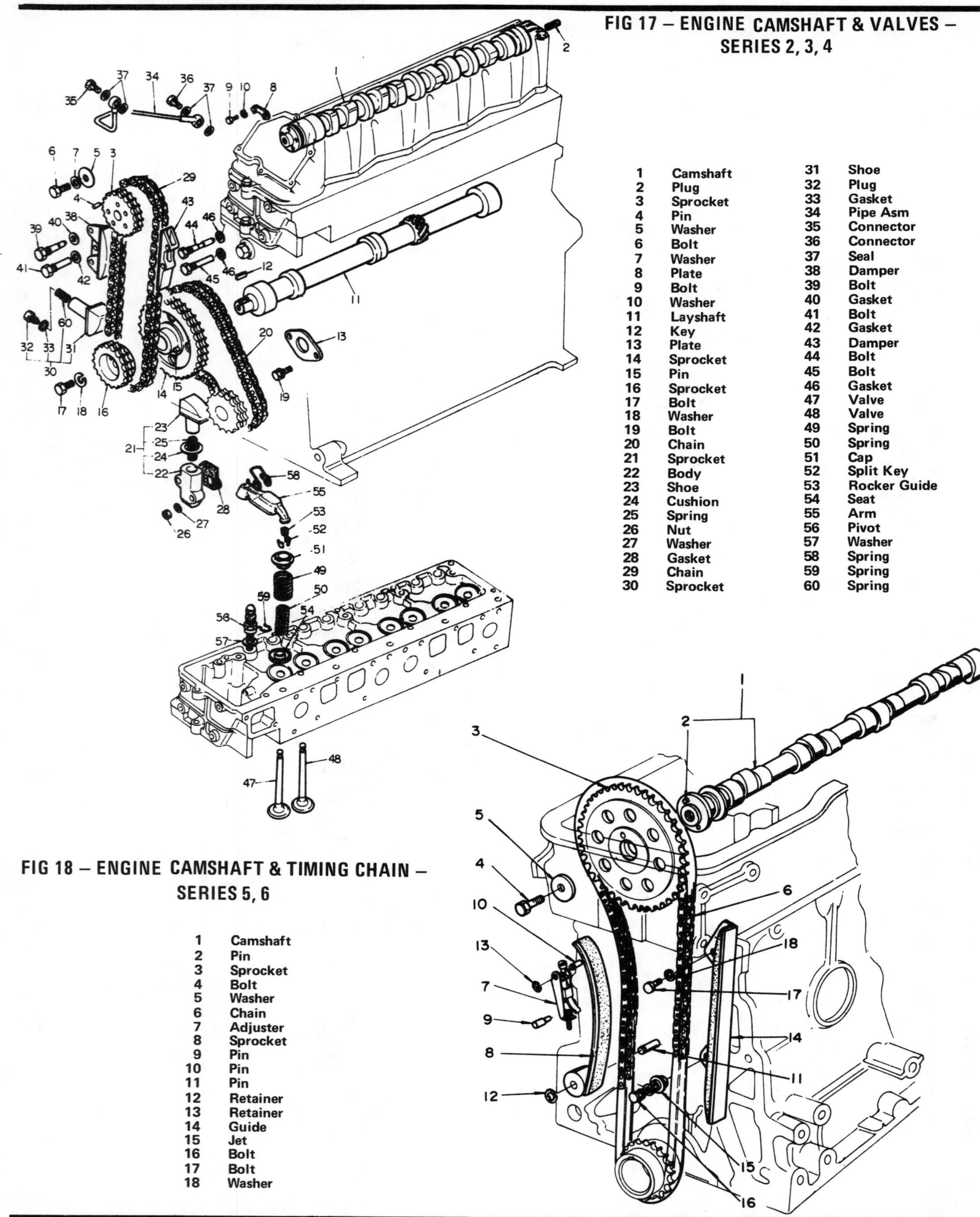

FIG 17 – ENGINE CAMSHAFT & VALVES – SERIES 2, 3, 4

1	Camshaft	31	Shoe
2	Plug	32	Plug
3	Sprocket	33	Gasket
4	Pin	34	Pipe Asm
5	Washer	35	Connector
6	Bolt	36	Connector
7	Washer	37	Seal
8	Plate	38	Damper
9	Bolt	39	Bolt
10	Washer	40	Gasket
11	Layshaft	41	Bolt
12	Key	42	Gasket
13	Plate	43	Damper
14	Sprocket	44	Bolt
15	Pin	45	Bolt
16	Sprocket	46	Gasket
17	Bolt	47	Valve
18	Washer	48	Valve
19	Bolt	49	Spring
20	Chain	50	Spring
21	Sprocket	51	Cap
22	Body	52	Split Key
23	Shoe	53	Rocker Guide
24	Cushion	54	Seat
25	Spring	55	Arm
26	Nut	56	Pivot
27	Washer	57	Washer
28	Gasket	58	Spring
29	Chain	59	Spring
30	Sprocket	60	Spring

FIG 18 – ENGINE CAMSHAFT & TIMING CHAIN – SERIES 5, 6

1	Camshaft
2	Pin
3	Sprocket
4	Bolt
5	Washer
6	Chain
7	Adjuster
8	Sprocket
9	Pin
10	Pin
11	Pin
12	Retainer
13	Retainer
14	Guide
15	Jet
16	Bolt
17	Bolt
18	Washer

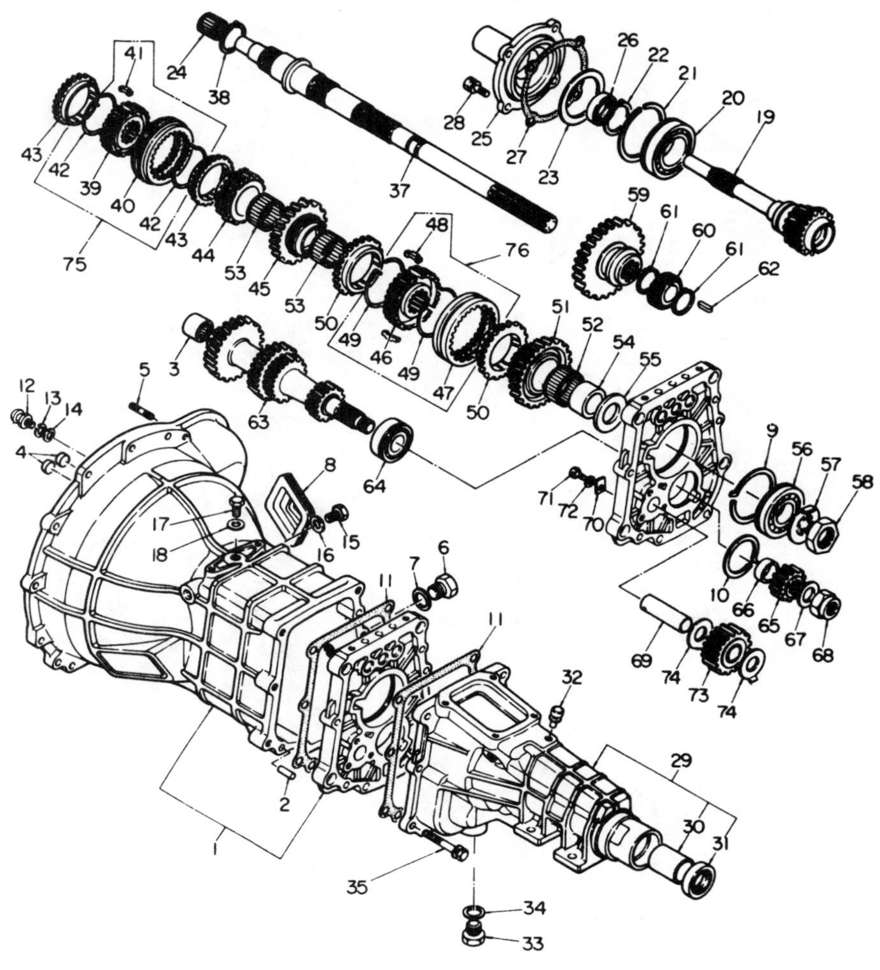

FIG 19 – MANUAL TRANSMISSION

1	Case
2	Pin
3	Bearing
4	Plug
5	Stud
6	Plug
7	Gasket (O-Ring)
8	Cover
9	Ring
10	Ring
11	Gasket
12	Ball Stud (Support)
13	Washer
14	Washer
15	Plug
16	Gasket (Packing)
17	Plug
18	Gasket
19	Gear (Shaft)
20	Bearing
21	Ring
22	Ring
23	Spring
24	Bearing
25	Cover
26	Seal
27	Gasket
28	Bolt
29	Extension (Cover)
30	Bushing
31	Seal
32	Ventilator (Breather)
33	Plug
34	Gasket (O-Ring)
35	Bolt
37	Shaft
38	Ring
39	Hub
40	Sleeve
41	Key
42	Spring
43	Ring
44	Gear
45	Gear
46	Hub
47	Sleeve
48	Key
49	Spring
50	Ring
51	Gear
52	Bearing
53	Bearing
54	Collar
55	Washer
56	Bearing
57	Washer
58	Nut
59	Gear
60	Gear
61	Ring
62	Key
63	Gear
64	Bearing
65	Gear
66	Washer
68	Nut
69	Shaft
70	Plate
71	Bolt
72	Washer
73	Gear
74	Washer
75	Synchronizer Assy
76	Synchronizer Assy

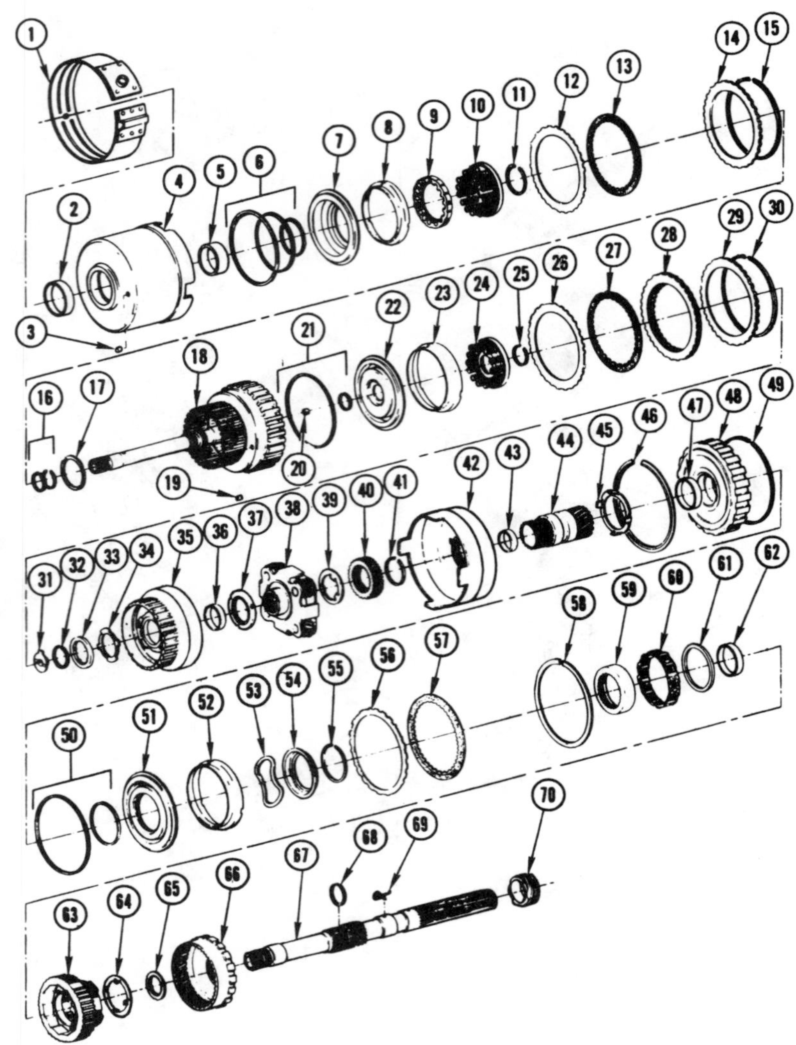

FIG 20 – AUTOMATIC TRANSMISSION – INTERNAL COMPONENTS

1	Band	24	Retainer	47	Bushing
2	Bushing	25	Ring	48	Housing
3	Retainer	26	Plate	49	Spacer
4	Housing w/Drum	27	Plate	50	Seal
5	Bushing	28	Plate	51	Piston
6	Seal Unit	29	Plate	52	Ring
7	Piston	30	Ring	53	Spring
8	Ring	31	Washer	54	Retainer
9	Guide	32	Ring	55	Ring
10	Retainer	33	Washer	56	Plate
11	Ring	34	Washer	57	Plate
12	Plate	35	Gear	58	Washer
13	Plate	36	Bushing	59	Race
14	Plate	37	Bearing	60	Roller
15	Ring	38	Carrier	61	Washer
16	Seal	39	Bearing	62	Bushing
17	Washer	40	Gear	63	Carrier
18	Housing	41	Ring	64	Washer
19	Retainer	42	Drum	65	Bearing
20	Plug	43	Bushing	66	Gear
21	Seal	44	Gear	67	Shaft
22	Piston	45	Washer	68	Ring
23	Ring	46	Ring	69	Clip
				70	Gear

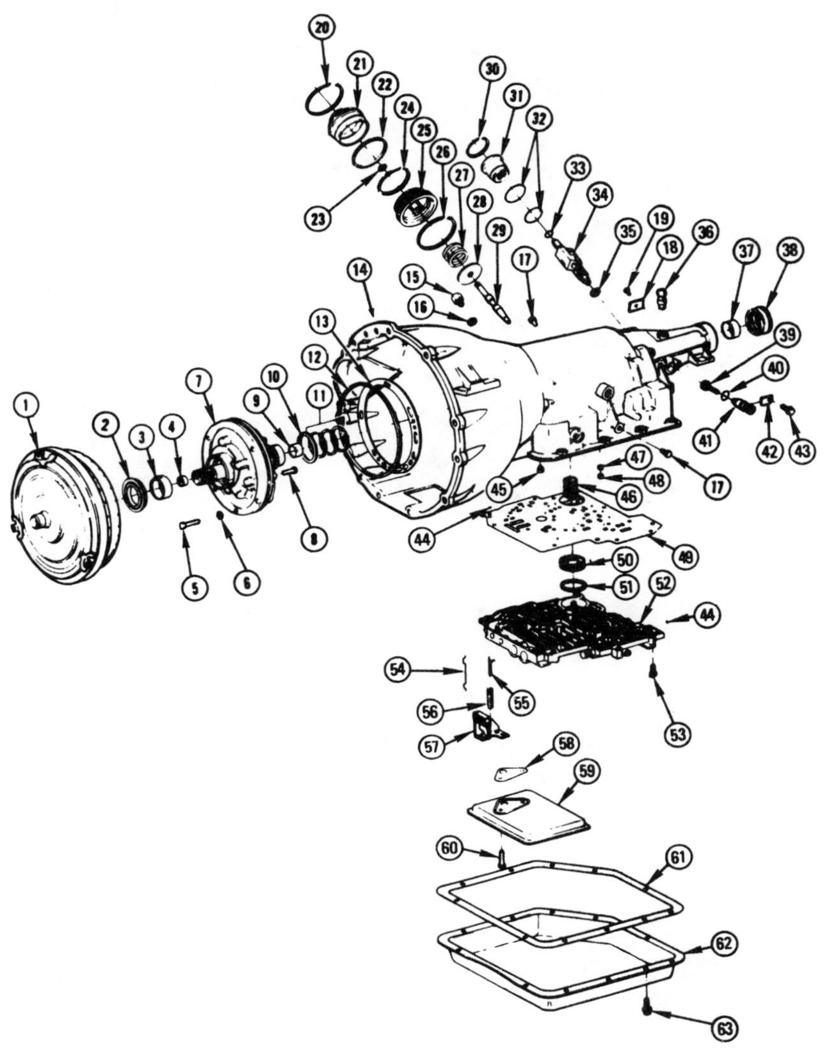

FIG 21 – AUTOMATIC TRANSMISSION – CASE & RELATED PARTS

1	Converter	22	Seal	43	Bolt
2	Seal	23	Ring	44	Ball
3	Bushing	24	Ring	45	Pin
4	Bushing	25	Piston	46	Spring
5	Bolt	26	Ring	47	Seal
6	Washer	27	Spring	48	Plug
7	Pump	28	Washer	49	Plate
8	Bolt	29	Pin	50	Piston Asm
9	Bushing	30	Ring	51	Seal
10	Washer	31	Cover	52	Valve Asm
11	Ring	32	Seal	53	Bolt
12	Ring	33	Ring	54	Link
13	Gasket	34	Governor	55	Lifter
14	Case	35	Washer	56	Spring
15	Connector	36	Vent	57	Lever
16	Gasket	37	Bushing	58	Gasket
17	Plug	38	Seal	59	Screen
18	Name Plate	39	Gear	60	Bolt
19	Screw	40	Seal "O" Ring	61	Gasket
20	Ring	41	Fitting	62	Pan
21	Cover	42	Retainer	63	Bolt

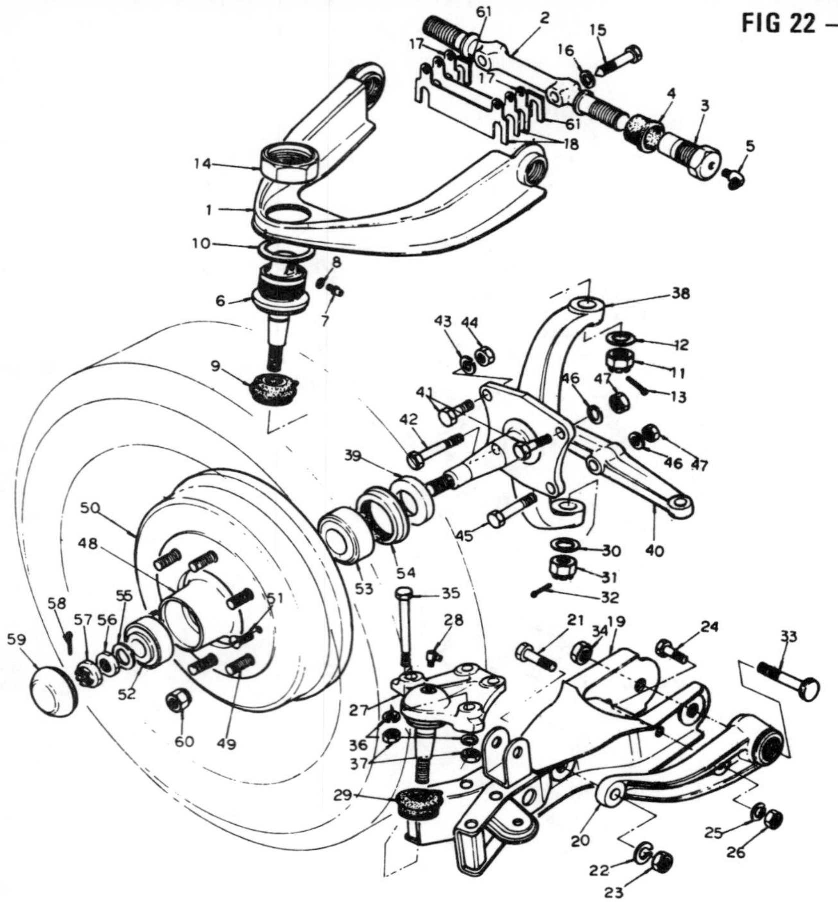

FIG 22 – FRONT SUSPENSION UPPER & LOWER ARMS – SERIES 1

1	Arm	31	Nut
2	Shaft	32	Cotter Pin
3	Bushing	33	Bolt
4	Seal	34	Nut
5	Fitting	35	Bolt
6	End	36	Washer
7	Nipple	37	Nut
8	Packing	38	Knuckle
9	Boot	39	Spacer
10	Shim	40	Arm
11	Nut	41	Bolt
12	Washer	42	Bolt
13	Cotter Pin	43	Washer
14	Nut	44	Nut
15	Bolt	45	Bolt
16	Washer	46	Washer
17	Shim	47	Nut
18	Shim	48	Hub
19	Link	49	Bolt (Pin)
20	Arm	50	Drum
21	Bolt	51	Screw
22	Washer	52	Bearing
23	Nut	53	Bearing
24	Bolt	54	Seal
25	Washer	55	Washer
26	Nut	56	Nut
27	End	57	Nut
28	Nipple	58	Cotter Pin
29	Boot	59	Cap
30	Washer	60	Nut
		61	Shim

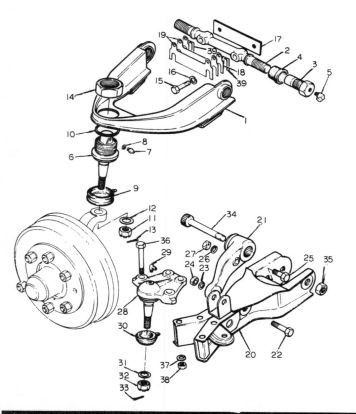

FIG 23 – FRONT SUSPENSION UPPER & LOWER ARMS – SERIES 2 THRU 6

1	Arm	21	Arm
2	Shaft	22	Bolt
3	Bushing	23	Washer
4	Seal	24	Nut
5	Fitting	25	Bolt
6	End	26	Washer
7	Nipple	27	Nut
8	Packing	28	End
9	Boot	29	Nipple
10	Shim	30	Boot
11	Nut	31	Washer
12	Washer	32	Nut
13	Cotter Pin	33	Cotter Pin
14	Nut	34	Bolt
15	Bolt	35	Nut
16	Washer	36	Bolt
17	Nut	37	Washer
18	Shim	38	Nut
19	Shim	39	Shim
20	Link		

FIG 24 – FRONT SUSPENSION SPRING & SHOCK ABSORBER

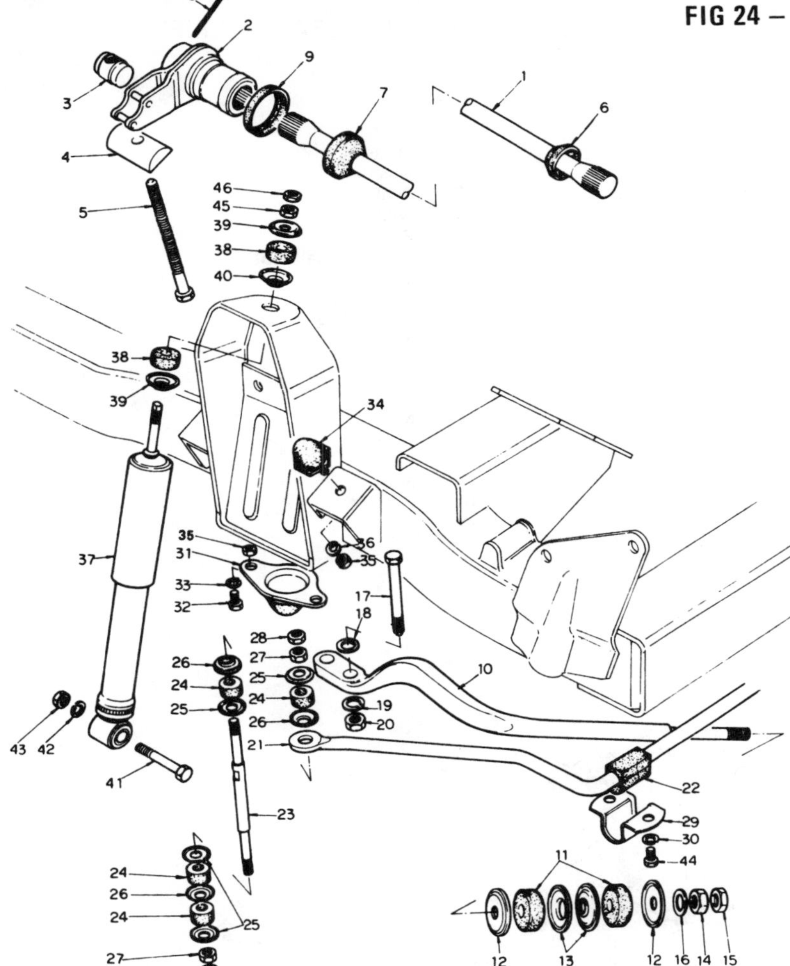

1	Bar	24	Grommet
2	Arm	25	Washer
3	Anchor	26	Washer
4	Seat	27	Nut
5	Bolt	28	Nut
6	Boot	29	Bracket
7	Boot	30	Washer
8	Cotter Pin	31	Rubber
9	Seal	32	Bolt
10	Bar Asm	33	Washer
11	Bushing	34	Rubber
12	Retainer	35	Nut
13	Retainer	36	Washer
14	Nut	37	Absorber
15	Nut	38	Bushing
16	Washer	39	Washer
17	Bolt	40	Washer
18	Washer	41	Bolt
19	Washer	42	Washer
20	Nut	43	Nut
21	Shaft	44	Bolt
22	Bushing	45	Nut
23	Link	46	Nut

FIG 25 – STEERING GEAR – SERIES 1 THRU 5

1	Housing
2	Bushing
3	Seal
4	Seal
5	Plug
6	Worm & Ball Nut
7	Bearing
8	Cover
9	Cover
10	Shim
11	Gasket
12	Bolt
13	Washer
14	Screw
15	Nut
16	Shaft
17	Shim
18	Nut
19	Washer

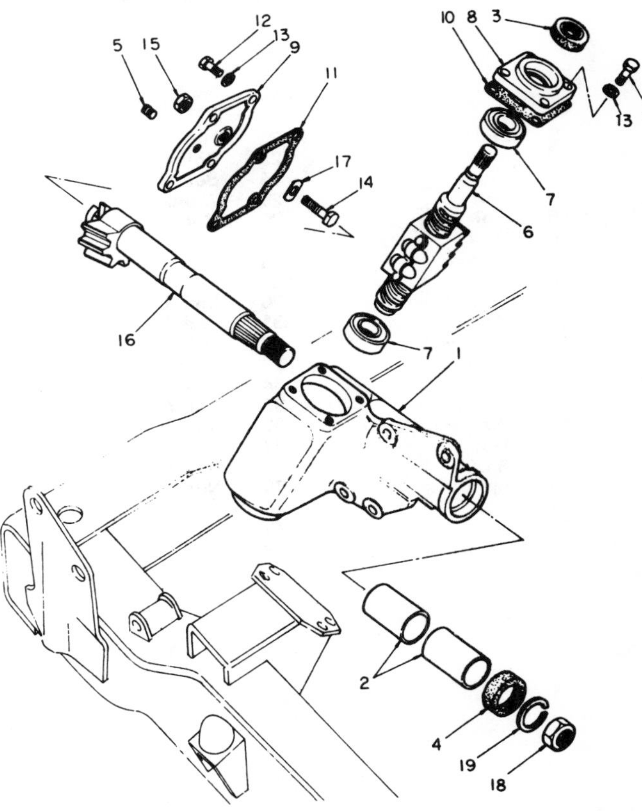

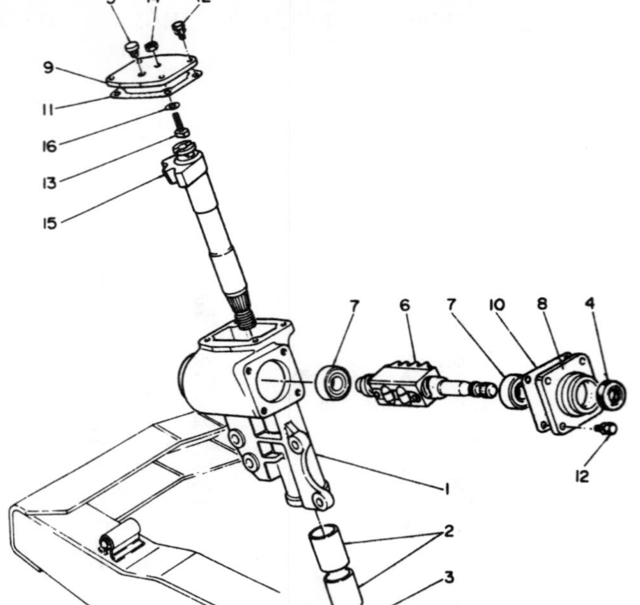

FIG 26 – STEERING GEAR – SERIES 6

1	Housing
2	Bushing
3	Seal
4	Seal
5	Plug
6	Worm & Ball Nut
7	Bearing
8	Cover, rear
9	Cover, top
10	Shim
11	Gasket
12	Bolt
13	Screw
14	Nut
15	Shaft
16	Shim
17	Nut
18	Washer

FIG 27 – STEERING LINKAGE – SERIES 1

1	Bolt	22	Nut
2	Washer	23	Bolt
3	Washer	24	Bolt
4	Nut	25	Washer
5	Bolt	26	Rod
6	Bolt	27	Nut
7	Washer	28	Nut
8	Arm	29	Nut
9	Arm (Lever)	30	End, R.H.
10	Bracket	31	End, L.H.
11	Bushing	32	Nipple
12	Fitting	33	Boot
13	Seal	34	Retainer
14	Bushing	35	Rod Asm
15	Washer	36	Nipple
16	Nut	37	Boot
17	Shaft	38	Retainer
18	Spring	39	Nut
19	Bolt	40	Cotter Pin
20	Washer	41	Bolt
21	Washer	42	Nut

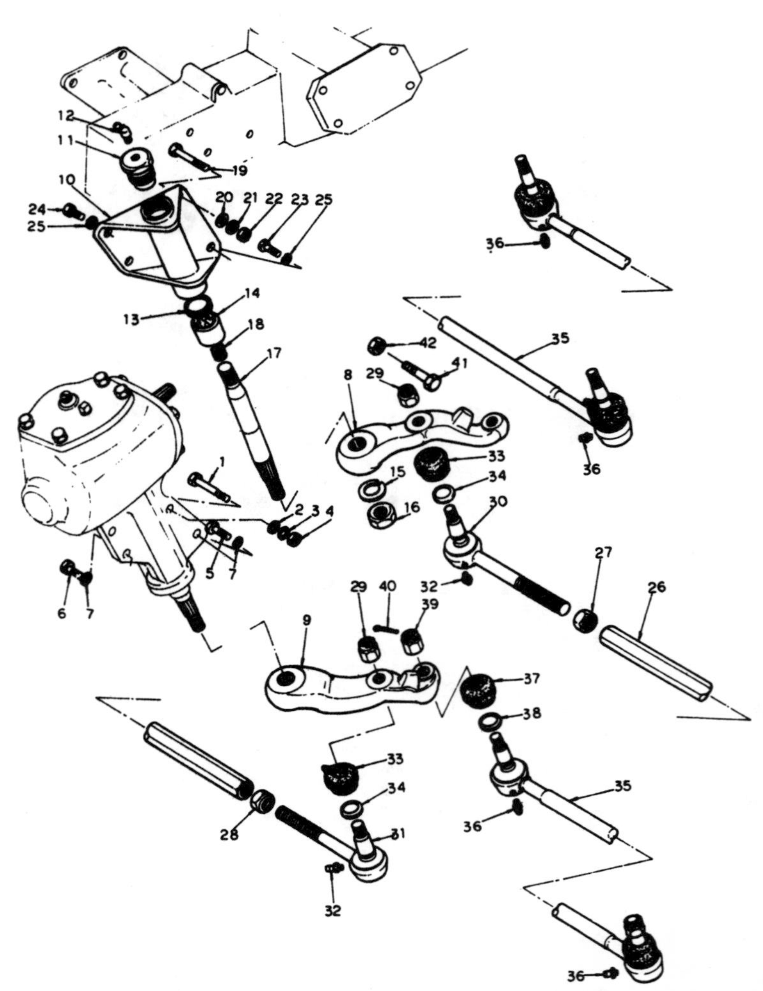

FIG 28 – STEERING LINKAGE – SERIES 2 THRU 6

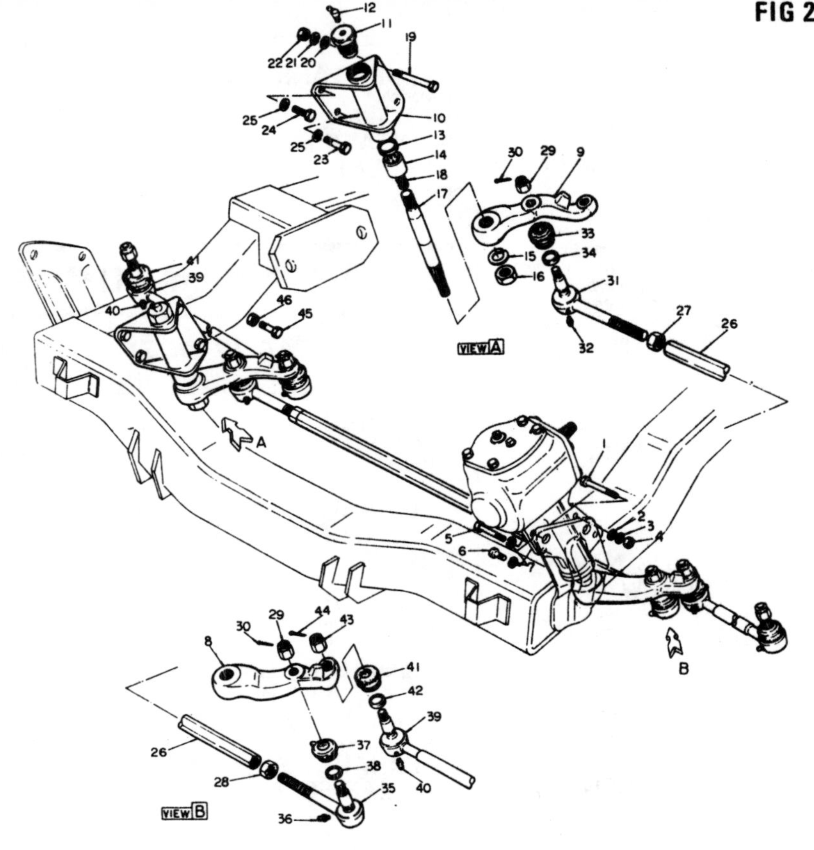

1	Bolt	24	Bolt
2	Washer	25	Washer
3	Washer	26	Rod
4	Nut	27	Nut
5	Bolt	28	Nut
6	Bolt	29	Nut
7	Washer	30	Cotter Pin
8	Arm	31	End, R.H.
9	Arm (Lever)	32	Nipple
10	Bracket	33	Boot
11	Bushing	34	Retainer
12	Fitting	35	End, L.H.
13	Seal	36	Nipple
14	Bushing	37	Boot
15	Washer	38	Retainer
16	Nut	39	Rod Asm
17	Shaft	40	Nipple
18	Spring	41	Boot
19	Bolt	42	Retainer
20	Washer	43	Nut
21	Washer	44	Cotter Pin
22	Nut	45	Bolt
23	Bolt	46	Nut

FIG 29 – REAR AXLE

1	Housing	27	Washer
2	Stud	28	Carrier Asm.
3	Stud	29	Carrier
4	Ventilation	30	Stud
5	Plug	31	Nut
6	Gasket	32	Washer
7	Plug	33	Gear Set
8	Gasket	34	Bearing
9	Seal	35	Shim
10	Shaft	36	Bearing
11	Bolt	37	Shim
12	Bearing	38	Spacer
13	Retainer	39	Seal
14	Washer	40	Bolt
15	Nut	41	Case
16	Seal	42	Bearing
17	Shim	43	Shim
18	Bolt	44	Pinion
19	Bolt	45	Gear
20	Washer	46	Pin
21	Nut	47	Washer
22	Drum	48	Pin
23	Screw	49	Spacer
24	Nut	50	Flange
25	Gasket	51	Washer
26	Nut	52	Nut

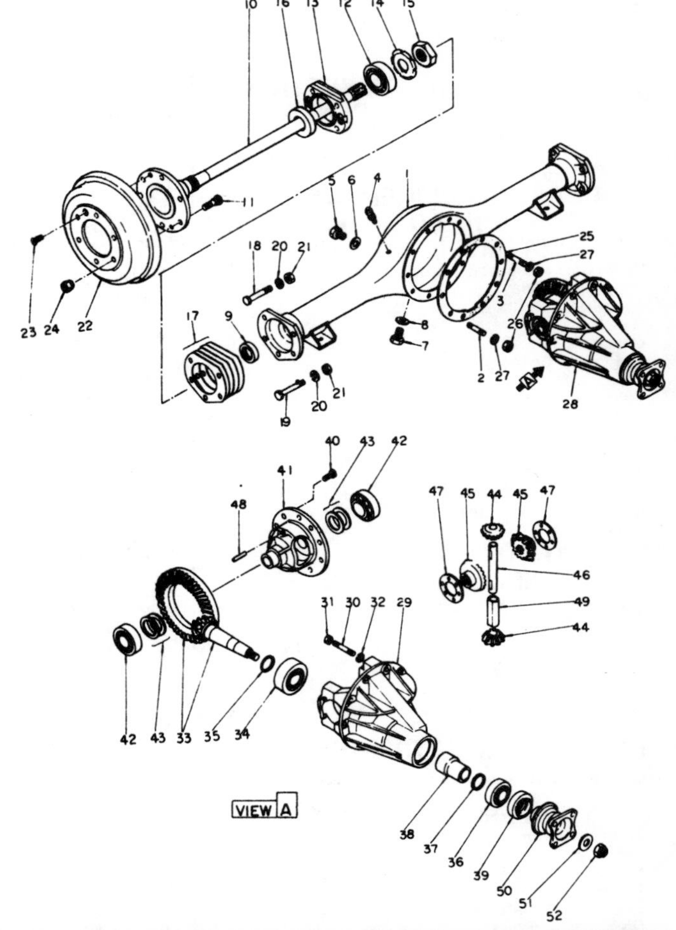

Emission Control Systems—TIME

OPERATION INDEX

Emission Control Check 1
Air Pump, R & R Or Renew 2
Air Pump Hose, Renew 3
Air Pump Check Valve, Renew 4
Air Pump Manifold, Renew 5
Crankcase Vent Valve, Renew 6
Controlled Combustion System 7
Coasting Richer Or Controlled Spark Systems 8
Evaporative Emission Controls 9
Exhaust Gas Recirculation System 10

1—EMISSION CONTROL CHECK
Includes check & adjust engine idle speed, ignition timing & PCV Valve
All Models 0.5

2—AIR PUMP, R & R OR RENEW
Ser 1, 2, 3, 4—
R & R 0.4
Renew 0.6
Ser 5, 6, 8—
R & R 0.3
Renew 0.5

3—AIR PUMP HOSE, RENEW
All Models 0.2

4—AIR PUMP CHECK VALVE, RENEW
Ser 1, 2, 3, 4 .... 0.3
Ser 5, 6, 8 .... 0.2

5—AIR PUMP MANIFOLD, RENEW
Ser 1, 2, 3, 4 .... 0.4
Ser 5, 6, 8 .... 0.6

6—CRANKCASE VENT VALVE, RENEW
All Models 0.2

7—CONTROLLED COMBUSTION SYSTEM PARTS, RENEW
Air Cleaner Vacuum Motor 0.2
Temperature Sensor 0.3
Hot Idle Compensator 0.3

8—COASTING RICHER OR CONTROLLED SPARK SYSTEM, RENEW
Distributor Relay 0.2
Accelerator Relay 0.2
Accelerator Switch 0.2
Clutch Switch 0.2
Clutch Relay 0.2
3rd & 4th Gear Switch, Exc 0.6
Ser 5, 6, 8 .... 0.3
Transmission Relay 0.2
Coasting Valve Solenoid 0.3
Throttle Switch 0.3

9—EVAPORATIVE EMISSION CONTROL PARTS, RENEW
Separator, Stand Pipe 0.3
Check & Relief Valve 0.2

10—EXHAUST GAS RECIRCULATION SYSTEM
E G R Valve, Renew—
Ser 3, 4 .... 0.2
Ser 5, 6, 8 .... 0.2
E G R Adapter, Renew 0.6
E G R Pipe, Renew 0.5

Tune-Up & Ignition—TIME

OPERATION INDEX

Tune-Up Minor 1
Tune-Up Major 2
Compression Test 3
Points & Condenser, Renew 4
Spark Plugs, Clean Or Renew 5
Distributor, Renew 6
Distributor, Overhaul 7
Distributor Cap, Renew 8
Vacuum Control Unit, Renew 9
Ignition Coil, Renew 10
Ignition Switch, Renew 11
Ignition Cable Set, Renew 12

1—TUNE UP, MINOR
Includes renew points, condenser & plugs, set spark timing & adjust carburetor idle.
All Models 1.2

2—TUNE-UP, MAJOR
Includes check compression, clean or renew & adjust spark plugs. R & R distributor, renew points & condenser. Adjust ignition timing, carburetor & fan belts. Clean battery terminals & service air cleaner. Check coil & service manifold heat control valve. Clean fuel pump sediment bowl & replace or clean fuel line filter.
All Models 2.8

3—COMPRESSION, TEST
All Models 0.4

4—POINTS & CONDENSER, RENEW
Includes set spark timing.
Ser 1, 2, 3, 4 .... 0.7
Ser 5, 6, 8 .... 0.5

5—SPARK PLUGS, CLEAN & ADJUST OR RENEW
All Models 0.3

6—DISTRIBUTOR, R & R OR RENEW
All Models 0.4

7—DISTRIBUTOR, R & R & OVERHAUL
All Models 1.0

8—DISTRIBUTOR CAP, RENEW
All Models 0.2

9—VACUUM CONTROL UNIT, RENEW
Ser 1, 2, 3, 4 .... 0.5
Ser 5, 6, 8 .... 0.3

10—IGNITION COIL, RENEW
All Models 0.3

11—IGNITION SWITCH, RENEW
All Models 0.2

12—IGNITION CABLE SET, RENEW
Time allowance covers installation of factory supplied sets.
All Models 0.3

Fuel System & Intake Manifold—TIME

OPERATION INDEX

Carburetor, R & R Or Renew 1
Carburetor, R & R & Overhaul 2
Manual Choke Cable, Renew 3
Anti-Dieseling Solenoid, Renew 4
Fuel Pump, R & R Or Renew 5
Fuel Tank, R & R Or Renew 6
Intake Manifold Gasket, Renew 7

1—CARBURETOR, R & R OR RENEW
All Models 0.7

2—CARBURETOR, R & R & OVERHAUL
All Models 1.8

3—MANUAL CHOKE CABLE, RENEW
All Models 0.3

4—ANTI-DIESELING SOLENOID, RENEW
All Models 0.4

5—FUEL PUMP, R & R OR RENEW
Ser 1, 2, 3, 4 .... 0.2
Ser 5, 6, 8 .... 0.4

6—FUEL TANK, R & R OR RENEW
All Models Exc 0.9
Series 1 .... 1.1

7—INTAKE MANIFOLD GASKET, RENEW
Ser 1, 2, 3, 4 .... 1.0
Ser 5, 6, 8 .... 1.4

Exhaust System—TIME

OPERATION INDEX

Exhaust Manifold, Renew 1
Exhaust Pipe, Renew 2
Muffler, Renew 3
Tail Pipe, Renew 4
Exhaust System (Exc Manifold) Renew 5
Converter, Renew 6

1—EXHAUST MANIFOLD (OR GASKETS), RENEW
Ser 1, 2, 3, 4 .... 1.3
Ser 5, 6, 8 .... 1.0

2—EXHAUST PIPE, RENEW
Models Less Converter 0.9
Models With Converter 0.5

3—MUFFLER, RENEW
All Models 0.4

4—TAIL PIPE, RENEW
All Models 0.4

5—EXHAUST SYSTEM (EXC MANIFOLDS), RENEW
All Models 1.0

6—CONVERTER, RENEW
Ser 5, 6, 8 .... 0.9

Starting Motor—TIME

OPERATION INDEX

Starter, R & R Or Renew 1
Starter, R & R & Overhaul 2
Starter Drive, Renew 3
Brushes, Renew 4
Armature & Brushes, Renew 5
Starter Switch, Renew 6
Starter Solenoid, Renew 7

1—STARTER, R & R OR RENEW
Ser 1, 2, 3, 4 .... 0.4
Ser 5, 6, 8 .... 0.5

2—STARTER, R & R & OVERHAUL
Includes turn down armature and replace all necessary parts.
All Models 1.5

3—STARTER DRIVE, RENEW
Ser 1, 2, 3, 4 .... 0.9
Ser 5, 6, 8 .... 1.0

4—BRUSHES, RENEW & TURN DOWN COMMUTATOR
Includes R & R starter.
All Models 1.2

5—ARMATURE & BRUSHES, RENEW
Includes R & R starter.
All Models 1.0

6—STARTER SWITCH (ON DASH), RENEW
All Models 0.2

7—STARTER SOLENOID, RENEW
Includes R & R starter.
Ser 1, 2, 3, 4 .... 0.6
Ser 5, 6, 8 .... 0.7

Alternator—TIME

OPERATION INDEX

Regulator, Check & Adjust *1*
Regulator, Renew *2*
Alternator, R & R Or Renew *3*
Alternator, R & R & Overhaul *4*
Fan Or Pulley, Renew *5*
Bearings, Renew *6*

1—ALTERNATOR REGULATOR, CHECK & ADJUST
All Models 0.2

2—ALTERNATOR REGULATOR, RENEW
Includes check & adjust.
All Models 0.5

3—ALTERNATOR, R & R OR RENEW
All Models 0.5

4—ALTERNATOR, R & R & OVERHAUL
All Models 1.0

5—FAN OR PULLEY, RENEW
All Models 0.2

6—BEARINGS, RENEW
One 0.7
Both 0.8

Dash Gauges, Speedometer & W/S Wiper—TIME

OPERATION INDEX

Fuel Dash Gauge, Renew *1*
Fuel Tank Gauge, Renew *2*
Oil Gauge Sending Unit, Renew *3*
Temp Gauge Sending Unit, Renew *4*
Temp Gauge Dash Unit, Renew *5*
Speedometer Head, R & R Or Renew *6*
Speed Cable, Lubricate *7*
Speed Cable & Housing, Renew *8*
Windshield Wiper Motor, Renew *9*
W/S Wiper Transmission, Renew *10*
W/S Wiper Switch, Renew *11*

1—FUEL DASH GAUGE, RENEW
All Models 0.4

2—FUEL TANK GAUGE, RENEW
All Models Exc 0.6
Series 1 .... 1.1

3—OIL GAUGE SENDING UNIT, RENEW
Ser 1, 2, 3, 4 .... 0.2
Ser 5, 6, 8 .... 0.3

4—TEMPERATURE GAUGE SENDING UNIT, RENEW
Ser 1, 2, 3, 4 .... 0.2
Ser 5, 6, 8 .... 0.3

5—TEMPERATURE GAUGE DASH UNIT, RENEW
All Models 0.4

6—SPEEDOMETER HEAD, R & R OR RENEW
All Models 0.4

7—SPEEDOMETER CABLE, LUBRICATE
All Models 0.2

8—SPEEDOMETER CABLE & HOUSING, RENEW
All Models 0.3

9—W/S WIPER MOTOR, RENEW
Ser 1, 2, 3, 4 .... 0.4
Ser 5, 6, 8 .... 0.5

10—W/S WIPER TRANSMISSION, RENEW
Ser 1, 2, 3, 4 .... 0.5
Ser 5, 6, 8 .... 0.6

11—W/S WIPER SWITCH, RENEW
All Models 0.2

Battery Cables & Horns—TIME

OPERATION INDEX

Battery Cables, Renew *1*
Horn, Renew *2*
Horn Relay, Renew *3*

1—BATTERY CABLES, RENEW, EACH
Ser 1, 2, 3, 4 .... 0.2
Ser 5, 6, 8 .... 0.3

2—HORN, RENEW
All Models 0.2

3—HORN RELAY, RENEW
All Models 0.2

Lamps & Light Switches—TIME

OPERATION INDEX

Headlamps, Aim *1*
Lamp Lens Or Bulbs, Renew *2*
Light Switch, Renew *3*
Stop Light Switch, Renew *4*
Back-Up Lamp Switch, Renew *5*
Turn Signal Switch, Renew *6*
Direction Signal Flasher, Renew *7*

1—HEADLAMPS, AIM
All Models 0.3

2—LAMP LENS OR BULBS, RENEW
Each Exc 0.2
Seal Beam 0.3

3—LIGHT SWITCH, RENEW
All Models 0.2

4—STOP LIGHT SWITCH, RENEW
All Models 0.2

5—BACK-UP LAMP SWITCH, RENEW
All Models 0.2

6—TURN SIGNAL SWITCH, RENEW
All Models 0.3

7—DIRECTION SIGNAL FLASHER, RENEW
All Models 0.2

Cooling System—TIME

OPERATION INDEX

Radiator, R & R Or Renew *1*
Radiator Hoses, Renew *2*
Fan, Renew *3*
Fan Belt, Renew *4*
Water Pump, R & R Or Renew *5*
Thermostat, Renew *6*
Heater Core, R & R Or Renew *7*

1—RADIATOR, R & R OR RENEW
Ser 1, 2, 3, 4 .... 0.4
Ser 5, 6, 8 .... 0.7

2—RADIATOR HOSES, RENEW
Upper 0.3
Lower, Ser 2, 3, 4 .... 0.5
Ser 1 .... 0.4
Ser 5, 6, 8 .... 0.3
Both, Ser 2, 3, 4 .... 0.6
Ser 1 .... 0.5
Ser 5, 6, 8 .... 0.4

3—FAN, RENEW
All Models 0.3

4—FAN BELT, RENEW
One 0.2
Each Additional 0.2

5—WATER PUMP, R & R OR RENEW
Ser 2, 3, 4 .... 1.5
Ser 1 .... 2.1
Ser 5, 6, 8 .... 0.8

6—THERMOSTAT, RENEW
All Models 0.3

7—HEATER CORE, R & R OR RENEW
All Models 0.9

Cylinder Head & Valves—TIME

OPERATION INDEX

Cylinder Head, R & R *1*
Cylinder Head, Renew *2*
Cylinder Head Gasket, Renew *3*
Cylinder Head, Tighten *4*
Valves, Grind *5*
Valves, Grind (Head Off) *6*
One Valve, Renew & Grind *7*
One Valve Spring, Renew *8*
Rocker Arm, Renew *9*
Rocker Pivot Assy, Renew *10*
Rocker Arm Cover Gasket, Renew *11*

1—CYLINDER HEAD, R & R
Use Cylinder Head Gasket, Renew.

2—CYLINDER HEAD, RENEW
Includes drain radiator & block, R & R intake & exhaust manifolds, transfer all component parts, grind valves, clean & adjust spark plugs, adjust valves & carburetor.
Ser 1, 2, 3, 4 .... 3.6
Ser 5, 6, 8 .... 4.3

3—CYLINDER HEAD GASKET, RENEW
Includes drain radiator & block, R & R cylinder head, clean & adjust spark plugs & adjust valves.
Ser 1, 2, 3, 4 .... 2.2
Ser 5, 6, 8 .... 2.3

4—CYLINDER HEAD, TIGHTEN
All Models 0.5

5—VALVES, GRIND & TUNE-UP MINOR
All Models 4.1

6—VALVES, GRIND (HEAD OFF)
All Models 1.9

7—ONE VALVE, RENEW & GRIND
All Models 2.0

8—ONE VALVE SPRING, RENEW
Ser 1, 2, 3, 4 .... 1.1
Ser 5, 6, 8 .... 0.7

9—ROCKER ARM, RENEW
Ser 1, 2, 3, 4—
One Or Two 0.3
Three Or More 0.6

(Continued)

Cylinder Head & Valves—TIME Cont'd

Ser 5, 6, 8—
 One Or Two 0.6
 Three Or More 0.7

10—ROCKER PIVOT ASSY, RENEW
All Models 0.3

11—ROCKER ARM COVER GASKET, RENEW
Ser 1, 2, 3, 4 ....0.2
Ser 5, 6, 8 ....0.4

Timing Case & Camshaft—TIME

OPERATION INDEX
Timing Cover, Gasket Or Seal 1
Timing Chain, R & R Or Renew 2
Camshaft, R & R Or Renew 3
Layshaft, R & R Or Renew 4

1—TIMING CASE COVER, GASKET OR SEAL, RENEW
Ser 2, 3, 4 ....2.6
 Ser 1 ....1.1
Ser 5, 6, 8 ....5.0

2—TIMING CHAIN, RENEW
Camshaft, Ser 2, 3, 4 ....0.6
 Ser 1 ....0.5
 Ser 5, 6, 8 ....4.9
Layshaft, Ser 2, 3, 4 ....2.7
 Ser 1 ....1.3

3—CAMSHAFT, R & R OR RENEW
Includes adjust valves.
Ser 1, 2, 3, 4 ....1.0
Ser 5, 6, 8 ....0.8

4—LAYSHAFT, R & R OR RENEW
Ser 2, 3, 4 ....3.9

Engine/Pistons, Rings, Bearings & Crankshaft—TIME

OPERATION INDEX
Rings (One Piston), Renew 1
Rings, Renew 2
Rings, Renew & Grind Valves 3
Rings & Main Bearings, Renew & Grind Valves 4
Piston (One), Renew 5
Rod Bearing (One), Renew 6
Rod Bearings (All), Renew 7
Main Bearings, Renew 8
Main & Rod Bearings, Renew 9
Crankshaft, Renew 10
Rear Main Bearing Oil Seal, Renew 11
Engine, R & R 12
Engine, Partial, Renew 13
Engine, R & R & Overhaul 14

1—RINGS (ONE PISTON), RENEW
Ser 1, 2, 3, 4 ....3.2
Ser 5, 6, 8 ....3.7

2—RINGS, RENEW
Includes minor tune-up.
Ser 1, 2, 3, 4 ....5.2
Ser 5, 6, 8 ....5.7

3—RINGS, RENEW & GRIND VALVES
Includes minor tune-up.
Ser 1, 2, 3, 4 ....6.6
Ser 5, 6, 8 ....7.0

4—RINGS & MAIN BEARINGS, RENEW & GRIND VALVES
Includes minor tune-up.
Ser 1, 2, 3, 4 ....9.3
Ser 5, 6, 8 ....9.7

5—PISTON (ONE), RENEW, WITH RINGS & PIN
Includes adjust valves & clean & adjust spark plugs.
Ser 1, 2, 3, 4 ....3.1
Ser 5, 6, 8 ....3.7

6—ROD BEARING (ONE), RENEW
Includes plastigage.
Ser 1, 2, 3, 4 ....1.0
Ser 5, 6, 8 ....1.5

7—ROD BEARINGS (ALL), RENEW
Includes plastigage.
Ser 1, 2, 3, 4 ....1.9
Ser 5, 6, 8 ....2.5

8—MAIN BEARINGS, RENEW
Includes plastigage.
Ser 1, 2, 3, 4 ....2.2
Ser 5, 6, 8 ....3.1

9—MAIN & ROD BEARINGS, RENEW
Includes plastigage.
Ser 1, 2, 3, 4 ....3.5
Ser 5, 6, 8 ....4.0

10—CRANKSHAFT, RENEW
Includes R & R engine and plastigage all bearings & clean & adjust spark plugs.
Ser 1, 2, 3, 4 ....6.6
Ser 5, 6, 8 ....7.0

11—REAR MAIN BEARING OIL SEAL, RENEW
Ser 1 ....1.1
Ser 2, 3, 4 ....2.6
Ser 5, 6, 8—
 Std Trans 3.0
 Auto Trans 3.5

12—ENGINE, R & R
Does not include transfer of any parts.
All Models 3.1

13—ENGINE (PARTIAL), RENEW & GRIND VALVES
Includes R & R engine & trans assy, transfer cylinder head, intake manifold, cam cover, oil pump & oil pan. Adjust valves, dwell angle, timing & carburetor, clean & adjust spark plugs.
Ser 1, 2, 3, 4 ....9.2
Ser 5, 6, 8 ....7.6

14—ENGINE, R & R & OVERHAUL
Includes rebore cylinders with boring bar, renew timing chains, pistons, rings, pins, main & rod bearings, grind valves & tune-up minor.
Ser 1, 2, 3, 4 ....13.0
Ser 5, 6, 8 ....13.5

Flywheel & Engine Mounts—TIME

OPERATION INDEX
Flywheel, Renew 1
Engine Mount, Front, Renew 2
Engine Mount, Rear, Renew 3

1—FLYWHEEL, RENEW
All Models Exc 1.8
 Series 1 ....2.1

2—ENGINE MOUNT, FRONT, RENEW
Series 1, Right 0.3
 Left 0.5
 Both 0.6
All Others, Right 0.5
 Left 0.5
 Both 0.7

3—ENGINE MOUNT, REAR, RENEW
All Models 0.4

Engine Oiling—TIME

OPERATION INDEX
Oil Pan, R & R Or Renew Gasket 1
Oil Pump, Renew 2
Crankcase Vent Valve 3

1—OIL PAN, R & R OR RENEW GASKET
Ser 1 ....0.6
Ser 2, 3, 4 ....0.8
Ser 5, 6, 8 ....1.2

2—OIL PUMP, R & R OR RENEW
Ser 1, 2, 3, 4 ....0.9
Ser 5, 6, 8 ....1.3

3—POSITIVE CRANKCASE VENT VALVE, RENEW OR CLEAN
Renew 0.2
Clean 0.4

Clutch—TIME

OPERATION INDEX
Pedal Free Travel, Adjust 1
System, Bleed 2
Master Cylinder, Renew 3
Master Cylinder, R & R & Overhaul 4
Slave Cylinder, Renew 5
Slave Cylinder, Overhaul 6
Clutch (Or Disc), R & R Or Renew 7
Clutch Release Bearing, Renew 8
Pilot Bearing, Renew (Clutch Out) 9

1—CLUTCH PEDAL FREE TRAVEL, ADJUST
All Models 0.3

2—CLUTCH SYSTEM, BLEED
All Models 0.3

3—CLUTCH MASTER CYLINDER, RENEW
All Models 0.3

4—CLUTCH MASTER CYLINDER, R & R & OVERHAUL
All Models 0.5

5—CLUTCH SLAVE CYLINDER, RENEW
All Models 0.4

6—CLUTCH SLAVE CYLINDER, OVERHAUL
All Models 0.6

7—CLUTCH (OR DISC), R & R OR RENEW
All Models Exc 1.7
 Series 1 ....2.0

8—CLUTCH RELEASE BEARING, RENEW
Includes R & R transmission.
All Models 1.5

9—CLUTCH PILOT BEARING, RENEW (CLUTCH OUT)
All Models 0.2

Manual Transmission—TIME

OPERATION INDEX

Trans, R & R Or Renew 1
Trans, R & R & Overhaul 2
Trans Case, Renew 3
Case Extn Rear Oil Seal, Renew 4

1—TRANSMISSION, R & R OR RENEW
All Models Exc 1.6
Series 1 ....2.1

2—TRANSMISSION, R & R & OVERHAUL
All Models Exc 3.2
Series 1 ....3.7

3—TRANSMISSION CASE, RENEW
All Models Exc 3.2
Series 1 ....2.7

4—CASE EXTENSION REAR OIL SEAL, RENEW
All Models 0.4

Automatic Transmission—TIME

OPERATION INDEX

Trans, R & R Or Renew 1
Converter Assy, Renew 2
Flex Plate, Renew 3
Oil Pump, R & R Or Renew 4
Oil Pump, R & R & Overhaul 5
Governor Assy, Renew 6
Oil Pan, Renew 7
Intermediate Servo, Renew 8
Intermediate Accumulator, Renew 9
Pressure Regulator, Renew 10
Valve Body, R & R Or Renew 11
Valve Body, R & R & Overhaul 12
Parking Pawl, Renew 13
Direct & Forward Clutches, Renew 14
Output Carrier & Sungear, Renew 15
Low & Reverse Clutch Hsng, Renew 16
Transmission Case, Renew 17
Oil Cooler Pipe, Renew 18
Oil Cooler Hose, Renew 19

1—TRANSMISSION, R & R OR RENEW
All Models 2.1

2—CONVERTER ASSY, RENEW
Includes remove & replace transmission, pressure check converter & check converter end play
All Models 2.4

3—FLEX PLATE, RENEW
Includes remove transmission.
All Models 2.1

4—OIL PUMP, R & R
Includes remove transmission.
All Models 2.6

5—OIL PUMP, R & R & OVERHAUL
Includes remove transmission.
All Models 3.1

6—GOVERNOR ASSY, RENEW
All Models 0.6

7—OIL PAN, RENEW
All Models 0.6

8—INTERMEDIATE SERVO, RENEW
All Models 0.5

9—INTERMEDIATE ACCUMULATOR, RENEW
All Models 0.9

10—PRESSURE REGULATOR, RENEW
All Models 0.7

11—VALVE BODY, R & R & RENEW
All Models 0.9

12—VALVE BODY, R & R & OVERHAUL
All Models 1.6

13—PARKING PAWL, RENEW
All Models 1.3

14—DIRECT & FORWARD CLUTCH & INTERMEDIATE BAND, RENEW
All Models 3.4

15—OUTPUT CARRIER, SUNGEAR & DRIVE SHELL, RENEW
All Models 3.7

16—LOW & REVERSE CLUTCH HOUSING, RENEW
All Models 4.0

17—TRANSMISSION CASE, RENEW
Includes remove & reinstall trans & replace all parts.
All Models 4.5

18—OIL COOLER PIPE, RENEW
One 0.6
Both 0.8

19—OIL COOLER HOSE, RENEW
One 0.3
Both 0.4

Universals, Propeller Shaft & Rear Axle—TIME

OPERATION INDEX

Universal Joint, Renew 1
Propeller Shaft, R & R Or Renew 2
Differential, R & R Or Renew 3
Differential, R & R & Overhaul 4
Pinion Shaft Oil Seal, Renew 5
Axle Shaft, Renew 6
Axle Shaft Bearing, Renew 7
Axle Shaft Oil Seal, Renew 8

1—UNIVERSAL JOINT, RENEW OR OVERHAUL
One 0.6
Both 1.0

2—PROPELLER SHAFT, R & R OR RENEW
All Models 0.3

3—DIFFERENTIAL CASE & CARRIER ASSY, R & R OR RENEW
Ser 1, 2, 3, 4 ....1.4
Ser 5, 6, 8 ....1.8

4—DIFFERENTIAL CASE & CARRIER, R & R & OVERHAUL
Ser 1, 2, 3, 4 ....3.8
Ser 5, 6, 8 ....4.0

5—PINION SHAFT FLANGE OR OIL SEAL, RENEW
All Models 0.5

6—AXLE SHAFT, RENEW
One Side 1.0
Both Sides 1.8

7—AXLE SHAFT BEARINGS, RENEW
One Side 1.2
Both Sides 2.2

8—AXLE SHAFT OIL SEAL, RENEW
One Side 1.2
Both Sides 2.2

Rear Suspension—TIME

OPERATION INDEX

Rear Spring, Renew 1
Shackle & Bushings, Renew 2
Rear Shock Absorber, Renew 3

1—REAR SPRING, RENEW
One Side 0.9
Both Sides 1.4

2—REAR SPRING SHACKLE & BUSHINGS, RENEW
One Side 0.4
Both Sides 0.6

3—REAR SHOCK ABSORBER, RENEW
One Side 0.4
Both Sides 0.5

Brakes—TIME

OPERATION INDEX

Self Adj Mechanism 1
Brake Shoes, All, Renew 2
Brake Shoes, Front, Renew 3
Brake Shoes, Rear, Renew 4
Disc Brake Lined Pads, Renew 4A
Disc Brake Rotor, Renew 4B
Disc Brake Caliper, Renew 4C
Parking Brake Cable, Renew 5
Parking Brake Control & Ratchet, Renew 6
Master Cylinder, R & R Or Renew 7
Master Cylinder, R & R & Overhaul 8
Wheel Cylinder, Renew 9
Wheel Cylinder, Overhaul 10
Flush & Refill System 11
Bleed System 12
Front Wheel Hub, Renew 13
Front Drum, R & R Or Renew 14
Rear Drum, R & R Or Renew 15
Front Brake Hose, Renew 16
Rear Brake Hose, Renew 17
Power Cylinder, R & R Or Renew 18
Power Cylinder, Overhaul 19

1—SELF ADJUSTING MECHANISM, RENEW OR CLEAN
All Models 0.4

2—BRAKE SHOES (ALL WHEELS), RENEW & BLEED SYSTEM
Ser 1, 2, 3, 4 ....2.4

3—BRAKE SHOES (FRONT WHEELS), RENEW & BLEED SYSTEM
Ser 1, 2, 3, 4 ....1.2

4—BRAKE SHOES (REAR WHEELS), RENEW & BLEED SYSTEM
All Models 1.6

4A—DISC BRAKE LINED PADS, BOTH WHEELS, RENEW
Ser 5, 6, 8 ....①1.1
①To Reface Each Disc, Add 0.6

4B—DISC BRAKE ROTOR, RENEW
Ser 5, 6, 8—
One Side ①0.6
Both Sides ①1.0
①To Reface Rotors Add-
One 0.4
Both 0.7

(Continued)

Brakes—TIME Cont'd

4C—DISC BRAKE CALIPER, RENEW
Ser 5, 6, 8—
One Side ①0.6
Both Sides ①0.9
① *To Overhaul, Add-*
One 0.5
Both 0.8

5—PARKING BRAKE CABLE, RENEW
Front, Ser 1, 2, 3, 4 .... 1.4
Front, Ser 5, 6, 8 .... 0.8
Intermediate 0.5
Rear 1.4

6—PARKING BRAKE CONTROL & RATCHET, RENEW
Ser 1, 2, 3, 4 .... 1.4
Ser 5, 6, 8 .... 0.8

7—MASTER CYLINDER, R & R OR RENEW
Includes bleed at main cylinder only.
All Models 0.4

8—MASTER CYLINDER, R & R & OVERHAUL
Includes bleed at main cylinder only.
All Models 1.0

9—WHEEL CYLINDER, RENEW
Includes bleed brakes.
One Side 0.6
Both Sides 1.2

10—WHEEL CYLINDER, OVERHAUL (CYLINDER OFF)
All Models 0.2

11—FLUSH & REFILL SYSTEM
All Models 0.7

12—BLEED SYSTEM
All Models 0.4

13—FRONT WHEEL HUB, RENEW
Ser 1, 2, 3, 4—
One Side 0.5
Both Sides 0.9
Ser 5, 6, 8—
One Side 0.6
Both Sides 1.1

14—FRONT BRAKE DRUM, R & R OR RENEW
Ser 1, 2, 3, 4 .... ①0.5
① *To Reface Drum, Add 0.3*

15—REAR BRAKE DRUM, R & R OR RENEW
All Models ①0.3
① *To Reface Drum, Add 0.3*

16—FRONT BRAKE HOSE, RENEW
Includes bleed system.
One Side 0.4
Both Sides 0.7

17—REAR BRAKE HOSE, RENEW
All Models 0.5

18—POWER BRAKE CYLINDER, R & R OR RENEW
All Models Exc 0.6
Series 1 .... 0.4

19—POWER BRAKE CYLINDER, R & R & OVERHAUL
All Models Exc 1.2
Series 1 .... 0.8

Front Suspension—TIME

OPERATION INDEX

Toe-In, Adjust 1
Caster, Camber & Toe-In 2
Steering Knuckle, Renew 3
Upper Control Arm, Renew 4
Lower Control Arm, Renew 5
Upper Ball Joint, Renew 6
Lower Ball Joint, Renew 7
Torsion Bar, Renew 8
Shock Absorber, Renew 9
Wheel Bearing, Renew 10
Wheel Oil Seal, Renew 11
Stabilizer Shaft, Renew 12
Stabilizer Shaft, Rebush 13
Strut Rod, Renew 14

1—TOE-IN, ADJUST
All Models 0.5

2—CASTER, CAMBER & TOE-IN, ADJUST
All Models 1.5

3—STEERING KNUCKLES, RENEW
Does not include wheel alignment.
Ser 1, 2, 3, 4—
One Side 0.7
Both Sides 1.3
Ser 5, 6, 8—
One Side 0.8
Both Sides 1.3

4—UPPER CONTROL ARM, RENEW
Does not include wheel alignment.
One Side 0.7
Both Sides 1.3

5—LOWER CONTROL ARM, RENEW
Does not include wheel alignment.
Ser 1, 2, 3, 4—
One Side 1.1
Both Sides 2.1
Ser 5, 6, 8—
One Side 0.9
Both Sides 1.6

6—UPPER BALL JOINT, RENEW
Does not include wheel alignment.
One Side 0.7
Both Sides 1.3

7—LOWER BALL JOINT, RENEW
Does not include wheel alignment.
One Side 0.8
Both Sides 1.4

8—TORSION BAR, RENEW
One Side 0.5
Both Sides 0.8

9—SHOCK ABSORBER, RENEW
One Side 0.3
Both Sides 0.4

10—FRONT WHEEL BEARING, RENEW
Ser 1, 2, 3, 4—
One Side 0.4
Both Sides 0.6
Ser 5, 6, 8—
One Side 0.6
Both Sides 1.1

11—FRONT WHEEL OIL SEAL, RENEW
Ser 1, 2, 3, 4—
One Side 0.4
Both Sides 0.5
Ser 5, 6, 8—
One Side 0.6
Both Sides 0.8

12—FRONT STABILIZER SHAFT, RENEW
All Models 0.6

13—FRONT STABILIZER SHAFT, REBUSH
All Models 0.4

14—STRUT ROD, RENEW
One Side 0.4
Both Sides 0.5

Steering Linkage—TIME

OPERATION INDEX

Tie Rod Or Ends, Renew 1
Relay Rod, Renew 2
Idler Arm, Renew 3
Pitman Arm, Renew 4

1—TIE ROD OR ENDS, RENEW
One Side 0.7
Both Sides 0.9

2—STEERING RELAY ROD, RENEW
Includes adjust toe-in.
All Models 0.8

3—IDLER ARM, RENEW
All Models 0.3

4—PITMAN ARM, RENEW
All Models 0.5

Steering Gear—TIME

OPERATION INDEX

Steering Gear, Renew 1
Steering Gear, R & R & Overhaul 2
Pitman Shaft Seal, Renew 3
Flexible Coupling, Renew 4
Mast Jacket, R & R Or Renew 5

1—STEERING GEAR, RENEW
All Models 0.6

2—STEERING GEAR, R & R & OVERHAUL
All Models 1.7

3—PITMAN SHAFT SEAL, RENEW
All Models 0.5

4—FLEXIBLE COUPLING, RENEW
All Models 0.5

5—MAST JACKET, R & R OR RENEW
All Models 0.7

Air Conditioning—TIME

OPERATION INDEX

Compressor, R & R & Renew 1
Compressor, R & R & Overhaul 2
Comp Pulley & Bearings, Renew 3
Comp Coil & Housing, Renew 4
Hoses, Renew 5
Condenser, Renew 6
Receiver Dehydrator, Renew 7
Evaporator Core, Renew 8
Expansion Valve, Renew 9
Partial Charge 10

1—COMPRESSOR, R & R & RENEW
Includes purge, evacuate, add oil, charge, leak & performance test systems.
Ser 1, 2, 3, 4 .... 1.2
Ser 5, 6, 8 .... 2.4

2—COMPRESSOR, R & R & OVERHAUL
Includes purge, evacuate, add oil, charge, leak & performance test systems.
Ser 1, 2, 3, 4 .... 2.9
Ser 5, 6, 8 .... 4.2

3—COMPRESSOR PULLEY &/OR BEARINGS, RENEW
Ser 1, 2, 3, 4 .... 0.6
Ser 5, 6, 8 .... 2.3

(Continued)

Air Conditioning—TIME Cont'd

4—COMPRESSOR COIL & HOUSING, RENEW

Ser 1, 2, 3, 4 .... 0.4
Ser 5, 6, 8 .... 2.3

5—HOSES, RENEW

Includes purge, evacuate, add oil, charge, leak & performance test systems.

Comp To Evap 0.8
Comp Discharge 1.0

6—CONDENSER, RENEW

Includes purge, evacuate, add oil, charge, leak & performance test systems.

All Models 1.4

7—RECEIVER-DEHYDRATOR, RENEW

Includes purge, evacuate, add oil, charge, leak & performance test systems.

All Models 0.9

8—EVAPORATOR CORE, RENEW

Includes purge, evacuate, add oil, charge, leak & performance test systems

All Models 2.4

9—EXPANSION VALVE, RENEW

Includes purge, evacuate, add oil, charge, leak & performance test systems.

All Models 2.1

10—PARTIAL CHARGE

Includes leak test system & tighten connections

All Models 0.5

IDENTIFICATION

ALL MODELS.................................. 241-242

ILLUSTRATIONS

FIG 1 – 4 CYLINDER ENGINE – CYLINDER HEAD
FIG 2 – 4 CYLINDER ENGINE – CYLINDER BLOCK & OIL PAN
FIG 3 – 4 CYLINDER ENGINE – CRANKSHAFT & PISTONS
FIG 4 – 4 CYLINDER ENGINE – CAMSHAFT & VALVES
FIG 5 – ROTARY ENGINE – ROTOR HOUSING
FIG 6 – ROTARY ENGINE – ROTOR
FIG 7 – TRANSMISSION GEARS
FIG 8 – FRONT SUSPENSION & STEERING – R X4
FIG 9 – FRONT SUSPENSION & STEERING – B1600 PICK-UP
FIG 10 – FRONT SUSPENSION & STEERING – 618

OPERATION TIMES

A

Air Pump.......... 253
Alternator.......... 253
Ammeter.......... 260
Automatic Transmission.......... 258
Axle Shaft.......... 259

B

Brake Drums.......... 259
Brakes.......... 259

C

Cables (Ignition).......... 253
Calipers.......... 259
Camshaft.......... 255
Carburetor.......... 253
Catalytic Converter.......... 253
Clutch.......... 257
Coil, Ignition.......... 253
Compression Test.......... 253
Connecting Rods.......... 255
Cooling System.......... 254
Crankshaft.......... 255
Cylinder Block.......... 255
Cylinder Head.......... 255

D

Dash Gauges.......... 260
Differential.......... 260
Disc Brakes.......... 259
Distributor.......... 253

E

Emission Controls.......... 253
Engine Assembly, Conv Eng.......... 255
-Rotary.......... 256
Engine Mountings.......... 257
Engine Oiling, Conv. Eng.......... 255
-Rotary.......... 257
Engine Tune-Up.......... 253
Exhaust Gas Recirculation.......... 253
Exhaust System.......... 253

F

Flywheel.......... 257
Front Suspension.......... 259
Fuel Gauges.......... 260
Fuel Pump.......... 253
Fuel Tank.......... 253

H

Hand Brake.......... 259
Heater.......... 254
Hose (Brake).......... 259
Hose (Radiator).......... 254
Hydraulic Brakes.......... 259

I

Ignition.......... 253
Ignition Coil.......... 253
Ignition Switch.......... 253
Intake Manifold.......... 254

L

Light Switches.......... 261

M

Main Bearings, Conv. Eng.......... 255
-Rotary.......... 256
Master Cylinder.......... 259
Muffler.......... 254

O

Oil Gauge.......... 261
Oiling, Engine Conv Eng.......... 255
-Rotary.......... 256
Oil Pan, Conv Eng.......... 255
-Rotary.......... 256
Oil Pump.......... 255

P

Parking Brake.......... 259
Piston Rings, Conv.......... 255
Pistons, Conv.......... 255
Power Brake.......... 259
Power Steering.......... 259

R

Radiator.......... 254
Radiator Hose.......... 254
Rear Axle.......... 260
Regulator (Alternator).......... 253
Rocker Arms.......... 255
Rod Bearings.......... 255
Rotary Engine.......... 256

S

Shocks (Front).......... 259
Shocks (Rear).......... 259
Speedometer.......... 261
Springs (Front).......... 259
Springs (Rear).......... 259
Stabilizer Bar.......... 259
Starting Motor.......... 253
Steering Gear.......... 259
Steering Linkage.......... 259
Switches (Light).......... 261
Synchro-Mesh Trans.......... 258

T

Tachometer.......... 261
Temperature Gauge.......... 261
Thermostat.......... 254
Timing Case Cover.......... 255
Timing Chain.......... 255
Timing Gears.......... 255
Transmission, Manual.......... 257
Transmission, Automatic.......... 258
Tune-Up, Engine.......... 253

U

Universals.......... 259

V

Vacuum Control Unit.......... 253
Valve Clearance.......... 255
Valve System.......... 255

W

Water Pump.......... 254
Wheel Alignment.......... 260
Wheel Cylinders.......... 259
Windshield Wiper.......... 261

IDENTIFICATION PLATE

LOCATION: On the dash panel, below rear edge of hood.

FIRST LINE indicates Model/Type
See Model Identification below.
SECOND LINE indicates Engine.
THIRD LINE indicates Bore & Stroke.
FOURTH LINE indicates displacement.
FIFTH LINE indicates serial number.

MODEL IDENTIFICATION

RX 4 — 1973-74

(From Sept. 1973 to Sept. 1974)

Sedan & Hard Top -From Chassis 100070 to 136402
Station Wagon - From chassis 100011 to 125520

MODEL NUMBER	MODEL TYPE	BODY TYPE
1755	LA23S	Sedan
1757	LA23S-CA	Hard Top
1767 (1)	LA23S	Sedan
1769 (1)	LA23S-CA	Hard Top
1775 (1)	LA23W	Sta Wgn
1791	LA23W	Sta Wgn
3521 (2)	LA23S	Sedan
3523 (2)	LA23S-CA	Hard Top
3525 (3)	LA23S	Sedan
3527 (3)	LA23S-CA	Hard Top
3537 (2)	LA23W	Sta Wgn
3539 (3)	LA23W	Sta Wgn

RX 4 — 1974

(From Feb. 1974 to Sept. 1974)

Sedan & Hard Top from Chassis 115925
Station Wagon From Chassis 111857

MODEL NUMBER	MODEL TYPE	BODY TYPE
1756	LA23S-T	Sedan
1758	LA23S-CAT	Hard Top
1768 (1)	LA23S-T	Sedan
1770 (1)	LA23S-CAT	Hard Top
1776 (1)	LA23W-T	Sta Wgn
1792	LA23W-T	Sta Wgn
3522 (2)	LA23S-T	Sedan
3524 (2)	LA23S-CAT	Hard Top
3526 (3)	LA23S-T	Sedan
3528 (3)	LA23S-CAT	Hard Top
3538 (2)	LA23W-T	Sta Wgn
3540 (3)	LA23W-T	Sta Wgn

RX 4 — 1975

Sedan & Hard Top from Chassis SLA23S-127229
Station Wagon from Chassis SLA23W-115564

MODEL NUMBER	MODEL TYPE	BODY TYPE
3558	SLA23S	Sedan
3559 (1)	SLA23S	Sedan
3560 (2)	SLA23S	Sedan
3561 (3)	SLA23S	Sedan
3562 (2)	SLA23S-T	Sedan
3563 (3)	SLA23S-T	Sedan
3564 (2)	SLA23S-CA	Hard Top
3565 (3)	SLA23S-CA	Hard Top
3566 (2)	SLA23S-CAT	Hard Top
3567 (3)	SLA23S-CAT	Hard Top
3568	SLA23W	Sta Wgn
3569 (1)	SLA23W	Sta Wgn
3570 (2)	SLA23W	Sta Wgn
3571 (3)	SLA23W	Sta Wgn
3572 (2)	SLA23W-T	Sta Wgn
3573 (3)	SLA23W-T	Sta Wgn
3574	SLA23S-T	Sedan
3575 (1)	SLA23S-T	Sedan
3576	SLA23S-CA	Hard Top
3577 (1)	SLA23S-CA	Hard Top
3578	SLA23S-CAT	Hard Top
3579 (1)	SLA23S-CAT	Hard Top
3580	SLA23W-T	Sta Wgn
3581 (1)	SLA23W-T	Sta Wgn

RX 4 — 1976-77

MODEL NUMBER	MODEL TYPE	BODY TYPE
3646 (5)	LA23S-P	Sedan
3647 (5)	LA23S-T	Sedan
3648 (5)	LA23S-CAP	Hard Top
3649 (5)	LA23S-CAT	Hard Top
3650 (5)	LA23W-P	Sta Wgn
3651 (5)	LA23W-T	Sta Wgn
3652 (5) (2)	LA23W-T	Sta Wgn
3653 (4)	LA 23S	Sedan
3654 (4) (1)	LA 23S	Sedan
3655 (4) (2)	LA23S	Sedan
3656 (4) (3)	LA23S	Sedan
3657 (4)	LA23S-P	Sedan
3658 (4) (2)	LA23S-P	Sedan
3659 (4)	LA23S-T	Sedan
3660 (4) (1)	LA23S-T	Sedan
3661 (4) (2)	LA23S-T	Sedan
3662 (4) (2)	LA23S-T	Sedan
3663 (4)	LA23S-CA	Hard Top
3664 (4) (1)	LA23S-CA	Hard Top
3665 (4) (2)	LA23S-CA	Hard Top
3666 (4) (3)	LA23 S-CA	Hard Top
3667 (4)	LA23S-CAP	Hard Top
3668 (4) (2)	LA23S-CAP	Hard Top
3669 (4)	LA23S-CAT	Hard Top
3670 (4) (1)	LA23S-CAT	Hard Top
3671 (4) (2)	LA23S-CAT	Hard Top
3672 (4) (3)	LA23S-CAT	Hard Top
3673 (4)	LA23W	Sta Wgn
3674 (4) (1)	LA23W	Sta Wgn
3675 (4) (2)	LA23W	Sta Wgn
3676 (4) (3)	LA23W	Sta Wgn
3677 (4)	LA23W-P	Sta Wgn
3678 (4) (2)	LA23W-P	Sta Wgn
3679 (4)	LA23W-T	Sta Wgn
3680 (4) (2)	LA23W-T	Sta Wgn
3681 (5)	LA23S	Sedan
3682 (5) (2)	LA23S	Sedan
3683 (5) (2)	LA23S-P	Sedan
3684 (5) (2)	LA23S-T	Sedan
3685 (5)	LA23S-CA	Hard Top
3686 (5) (2)	LA23S-CA	Hard Top
3687 (5)	LA23S-CAP	Hard Top
3688 (5)	LA23S-CAT	Hard Top
3689 (5)	LA23W	Sta Wgn
3690 (5) (2)	LA23W	Sta Wgn
3691 (5)	LA23W-P	Sta Wgn

RX 3 — 1972

MODEL NUMBER	MODEL TYPE	BODY TYPE
1570	S124A	Sedan
1571	S124W	Wagon
1572	S124A-CA	Coupe

(1) With Air Cond
(2) With Pwr Strg
(3) With Air Cond & Pwr Strg
(4) Federal
(5) California

RX 3 — 1973

MODEL NUMBER	MODEL TYPE	BODY TYPE
1608	S124A-CAP	Coupe
1620	S124A	Sedan
1621	S124A-T	Sedan
1622	S124A-CA	Coupe
1623	S124A-CAT	Coupe
1624	S124W	Wagon
1625	S124W-T	Wagon
1693	S124A	Sedan
1694	S124A-CA	Coupe
1695	S124A-CAP	Coupe
1696	S124W	Wagon
1697	S124A-T	Sedan
1698	S124A-CAT	Coupe
1699	S124W-T	Wagon

RX 3 — 1974

MODEL NUMBER	MODEL TYPE	BODY TYPE
1881	S124A	Sedan
1882	S124A-CA	Coupe
1883	S124A-T	Sedan
1884	S124A-CAT	Coupe
1889	S124W	Sta Wgn
1890	S124W-T	Sta Wgn

RX 3 — 1975

MODEL NUMBER	MODEL TYPE	BODY TYPE
3625	S124A	Sedan
3626	S124A-T	Sedan
3627	S124A-CA	Coupe
3628	S124A-CAT	Coupe
3629	S124W	Sta Wgn
3630	S124W-T	Sta Wgn

RX 3 — 1976

MODEL NUMBER	MODEL TYPE	BODY TYPE
3704 (4)	124A-CAP	Coupe
3705 (4)	S124W-P	Sta Wgn
3706 (5)	S124A-CAP	Coupe
3707 (5)	S124W-P	Sta Wgn
3737 (4)	S124A	Sedan
3738 (4)	S124A-T	Sedan
3739 (4)	S124A-CA	Coupe
3740 (4)	S124A-CAT	Coupe
3741 (4)	S124W	Sta Wgn
3742 (4)	S124 W-T	Sta Wgn
3743 (5)	S124A	Sedan
3744 (5)	S124 A-T	Sedan
3745 (5)	S124A-CA	Coupe
3746 (5)	S124A-CAT	Coupe
3747 (5)	S124W	Sta Wgn
3748 (5)	S124W-T	Sta Wgn

RX 3 — 1977

MODEL NUMBER	MODEL TYPE	BODY TYPE
8648 (5)	S124A-CA	Coupe
8649 (5)	S124A-CAP	Coupe
8650 (5)	S124A-CAT	Coupe
8651 (4)	S124A-CA	Coupe
8652 (4)	S124A-CAP	Coupe
8653 (4)	S124A-CAT	Coupe

MODEL IDENTIFICATION CONTINUED

GLC – 1977

MODEL NUMBER	MODEL TYPE	BODY TYPE
3958 (4)	FA4TS	4-Speed
3960 (5)	FA4TS	4-Speed
3959 (4)	FA4TS-T	Auto
3961 (5)	FA4TS-T	Auto
8601 (4)	FA4TS-P	5-Speed
8602 (5)	FA4TS-P	5-Speed

COSMO – 1976

(From September 1975)

MODEL NUMBER	MODEL TYPE	BODY TYPE
3597	CD23C	Coupe
3598	CD23C-T	Coupe
3599	CD23C	Coupe
3600	CD23C-T	Coupe

RX 2 – 1971

From March 1971 to Aug. 1971
From Chassis Number 61649 to 96266

MODEL NUMBER	MODEL TYPE	BODY TYPE
2081	S122A-S	Sedan
2090	S122A-SCA	Coupe

RX 2 – 1972

From Sept. 1971 to July 1972
From Chassis Number 96267 to 139694

MODEL NUMBER	MODEL TYPE	BODY TYPE
1662	S122A-S	Sedan
1663	S122A-SCA	Coupe
1664	S122A-S	Sedan
1665	S122A-SCA	Coupe

RX 2 – 1973

From Aug. 1972 to Aug. 1973
From Chassis Number 139695

MODEL NUMBER	MODEL TYPE	BODY TYPE
1666	S122A-S	Sedan
1667	S122A-ST	Sedan
1668	S122A-SCA	Coupe
1669	S122A-SCAT	Coupe
1686	S122A-S	Sedan
1687	S122A-SCA	Coupe
1688	S122A-ST	Sedan
1689	S122A-SCAT	Coupe

618 – 1972

From Sept. 1971 to July 1972

MODEL NUMBER	MODEL TYPE	BODY TYPE
1650	SV2A	Sedan
1651	SV2A-T	Sedan
1652	SV2A-SCA	Coupe
1653	SV2A-SCAT	Coupe
1654	SV2A	Sedan
1655	SV2A-T	Sedan
1656	SV2A-SCA	Coupe
1657	SV2A-SCAT	Coupe

618 – 1973

From August 1972

MODEL NUMBER	MODEL TYPE	BODY TYPE
1674	SV2A	Sedan
1675	SV2A-T	Sedan
1676	SV2A-SCA	Coupe
1677	SV2A-SCAT	Coupe
1682	SV2A	Sedan
1683	SV2A-T	Sedan
1684	SV2A-SCA	Coupe
1685	SV2A-SCAT	Coupe

808 – 1972

From Nov. 1971 to July 1972
From Chassis 100011 to 114957 Sedan & Coupe
From Chassis 100006 to 103365 Station Wagon

MODEL NUMBER	MODEL TYPE	BODY TYPE
1540	SN3A	Sedan
1541	SN3A-T	Sedan
1542	SN3A-CA	Coupe
1543	SN3A-CAT	Coupe
1544	SN3AV	Wagon
1545	SN3AV-T	Wagon
1546	SN3A-T	Sedan
1547	SN3A-CAT	Coupe
1548	SN3AV-T	Wagon

808 – 1973-75

From August 1972
From Chassis 114958 Sedan & Coupe
From Chassis 103366 Station Wagon

MODEL NUMBER	MODEL TYPE	BODY TYPE
1632	SN3A	Sedan
1633	SN3A-T	Sedan
1634	SN3A-CA	Coupe
1635	SN3A-CAT	Coupe
1636	SN3AV	Wagon
1637	SN3AV-T	Wagon
1644	SN3A	Sedan
1645	SN3A-T	Sedan
1646	SN3A-CA	Coupe
1647	SN3A-CAT	Coupe
1648	SN3AV	Wagon
1649	SN3AV-T	Wagon

808 – 1976

From November 1975 1300 Eng (Mizer)
From August 1975 1600 Eng.

MODEL NUMBER	MODEL TYPE	BODY TYPE
3710	STC	Sedan
3711	STC-CA	Coupe
3712	STCV	Sta Wgn
3713	STC	Sedan
3714	STC-CA	Coupe
3715	STCV	Sta Wgn
3719	SN3A	Sedan
3720	SN3A-T	Sedan
3721	SN3A-CA	Coupe
3722	SN3A-CAT	Coupe
3723	SN3AV	Sta Wgn
3724	SN3AV-T	Sta Wgn
3725	SN3A	Sedan
3726	SN3A-T	Sedan
3727	SN3A-CA	Coupe
3728	SN3A-CAT	Coupe
3729	SN3AV	Sta Wgn
3730	SN3AV-T	Sta Wgn

B1600 – 1972-76

1972 From Chassis 21289
1973 From Chassis 33621
1974 From Chassis 62109
1975 From Chassis 67534
1976 From Chassis 106444

MODEL NUMBER	MODEL TYPE	BODY TYPE
1819	BNA61	Pick-Up
2628	BNA61	Pick-Up
1836	BNA61	Pick-Up
1838	BNA61	Pick-Up
3916	SBNA61-F	Pick-Up
3768	BNA61-F	Pick-Up

ROTARY PICK-UP – 1974-77

1974 From Chassis 100173
1975 From Chassis 112286
1976 From Chassis 150001
1977 From Chassis

MODEL NUMBER	MODEL TYPE	BODY TYPE
1854	PA136	Pick-Up, Std
1856	PA136-T	Pick-Up, Auto
3900	SPA136	Pick-Up, Std
3902	SPA136-T	Pick-Up, Auto
3775	PA136-C	Pick-Up, 4-Speed
3776	PA136-TC	Pick-Up, Auto
3777	PA136-PC	Pick-Up, 5-Speed
3778 (5)	PA136-PC	Pick-Up, 5-Speed
3787 (4)	PA136-P	Pick-Up, Std
3789 (4)	PA136-TC	Pick-Up, Auto
3790 (5)	PA136-PC	Pick-Up, Std
3791 (5)	PA136-TC	Pick-Up, Auto

(4) Federal
(5) California

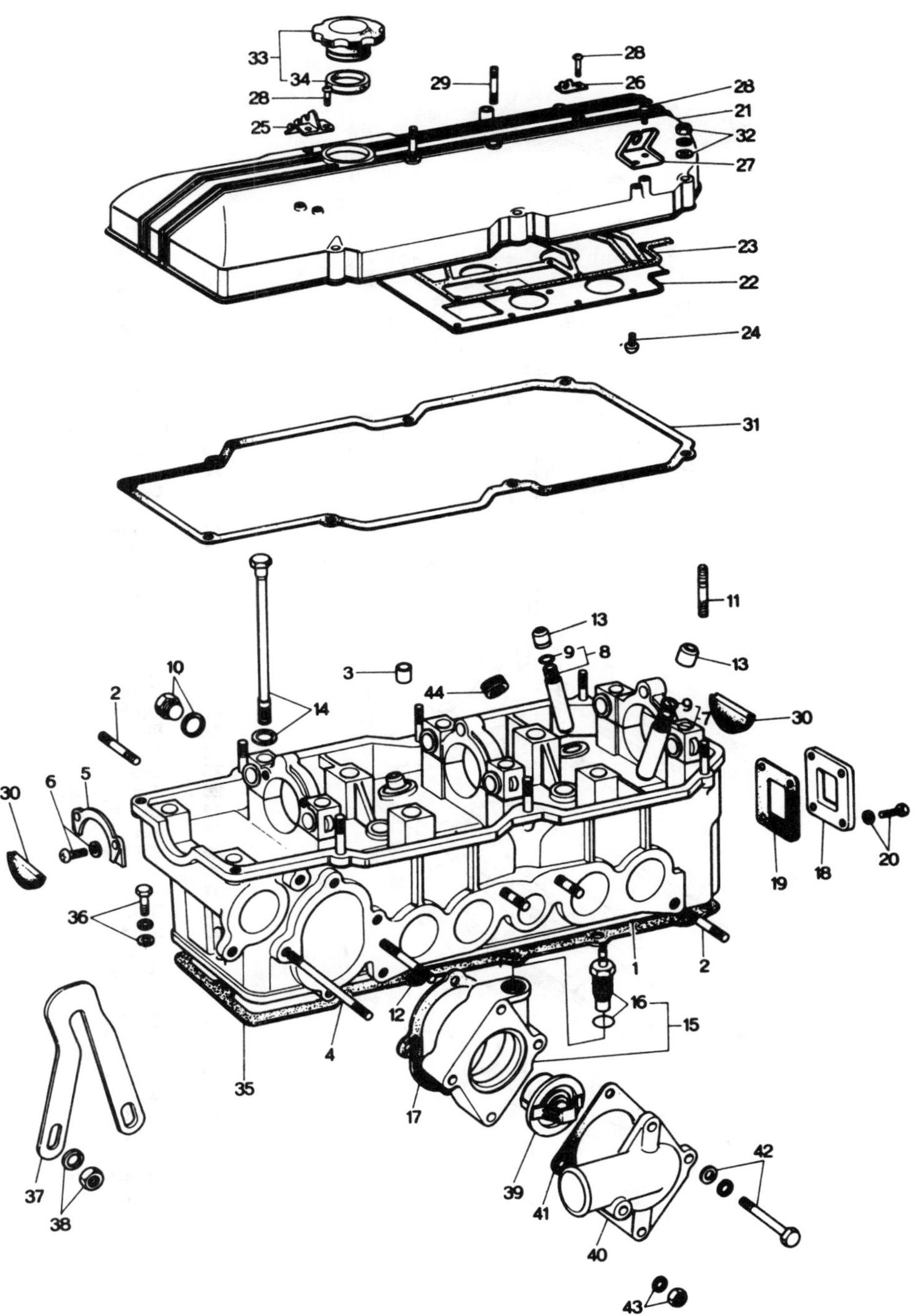

1	Cylinder Head
2	Stud
3	Pin
4	Stud
5	Plate
6	Screw
7	Intake Valve Guide
8	Exhaust Valve Guide
9	Clip
10	Plug
11	Stud
12	Stud
13	Seal
14	Bolt
15	Thermostat Housing
16	Water Heat Gauge
17	Gasket
18	Cover
19	Gasket
20	Bolt
21	Cylinder Head Cover
22	Baffle Plate
23	Gasket
24	Screw
25	Protector
26	Protector
27	Support
28	Screw
29	Stud
30	Oil Seal
31	Gasket
32	Nut
33	Oil Filler Cap
34	Gasket
35	Gasket
36	Bolt
37	Hanger
38	Nut
39	Thermostat
40	Water Outlet
41	Gasket
42	Bolt
43	Nut
44	Insert

FIG 1 – 4 CYLINDER ENGINE – CYLINDER HEAD

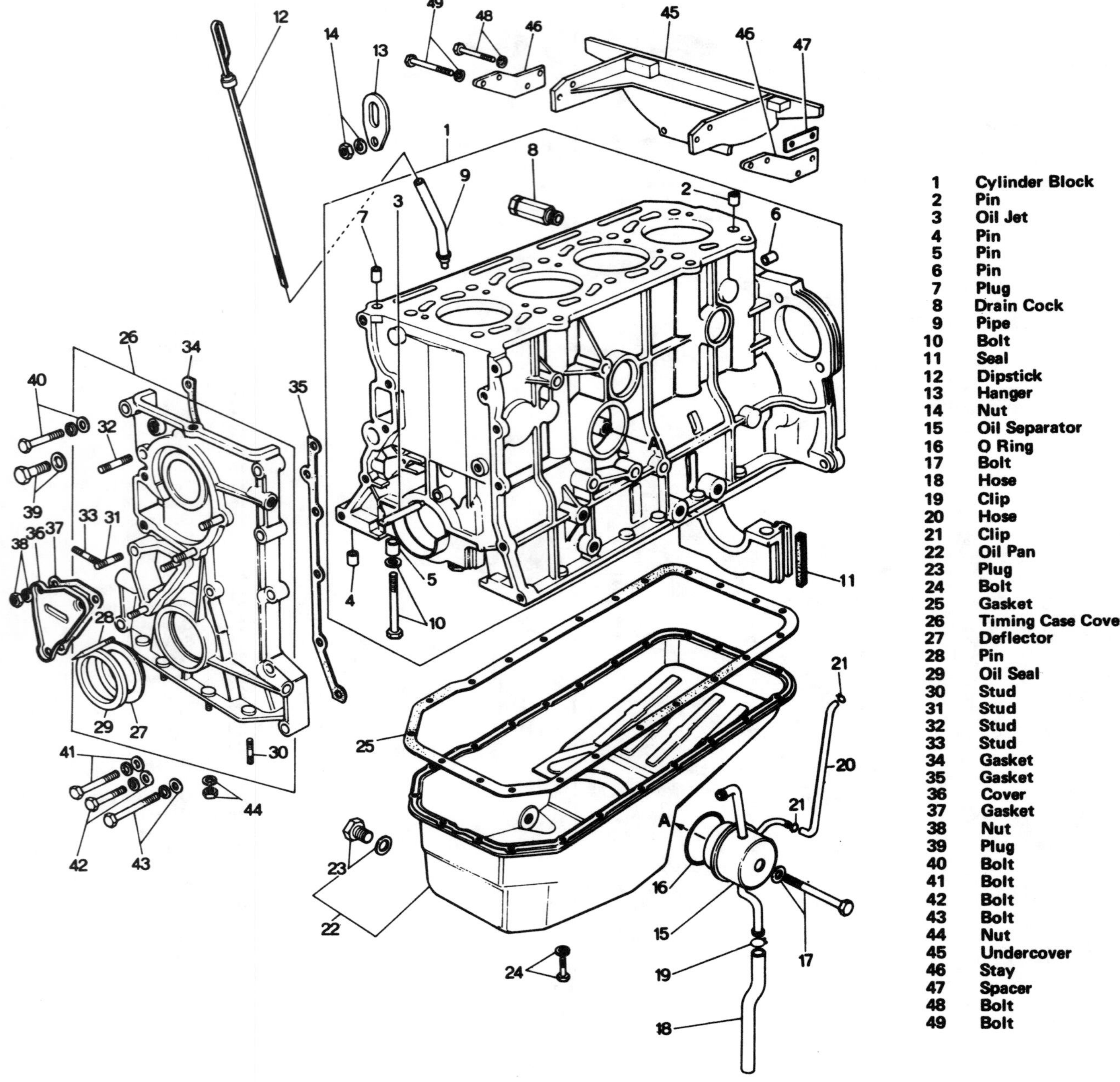
1 Cylinder Block
2 Pin
3 Oil Jet
4 Pin
5 Pin
6 Pin
7 Plug
8 Drain Cock
9 Pipe
10 Bolt
11 Seal
12 Dipstick
13 Hanger
14 Nut
15 Oil Separator
16 O Ring
17 Bolt
18 Hose
19 Clip
20 Hose
21 Clip
22 Oil Pan
23 Plug
24 Bolt
25 Gasket
26 Timing Case Cover
27 Deflector
28 Pin
29 Oil Seal
30 Stud
31 Stud
32 Stud
33 Stud
34 Gasket
35 Gasket
36 Cover
37 Gasket
38 Nut
39 Plug
40 Bolt
41 Bolt
42 Bolt
43 Bolt
44 Nut
45 Undercover
46 Stay
47 Spacer
48 Bolt
49 Bolt

FIG 2 – 4 CYLINDER ENGINE – CYLINDER BLOCK & OIL PAN

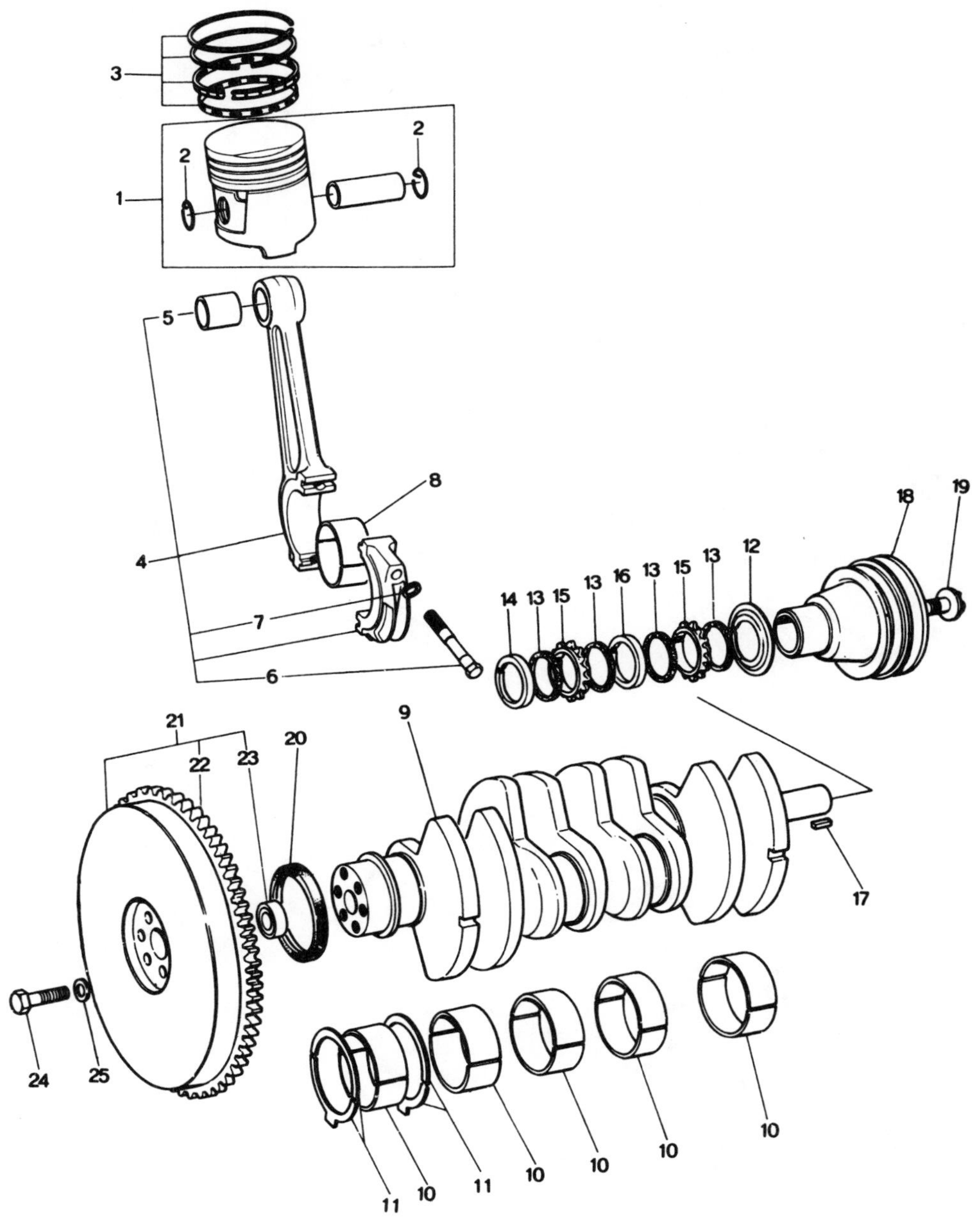

FIG 3 – 4 CYLINDER ENGINE – CRANKSHAFT & PISTONS

1	Piston	14	Spacer
2	Clip	15	Timing Sprocket
3	Ring Set	16	Spacer
4	Connecting Rod	17	Key
5	Bushing	18	Pulley
6	Bolt	19	Bolt
7	Washer	20	Oil Seal
8	Bearing	21	Flywheel
9	Crankshaft	22	Ring Gear
10	Bearing	23	Bearing
11	Washer	24	Bolt
12	Baffle Plate	25	Washer
13	Ring		

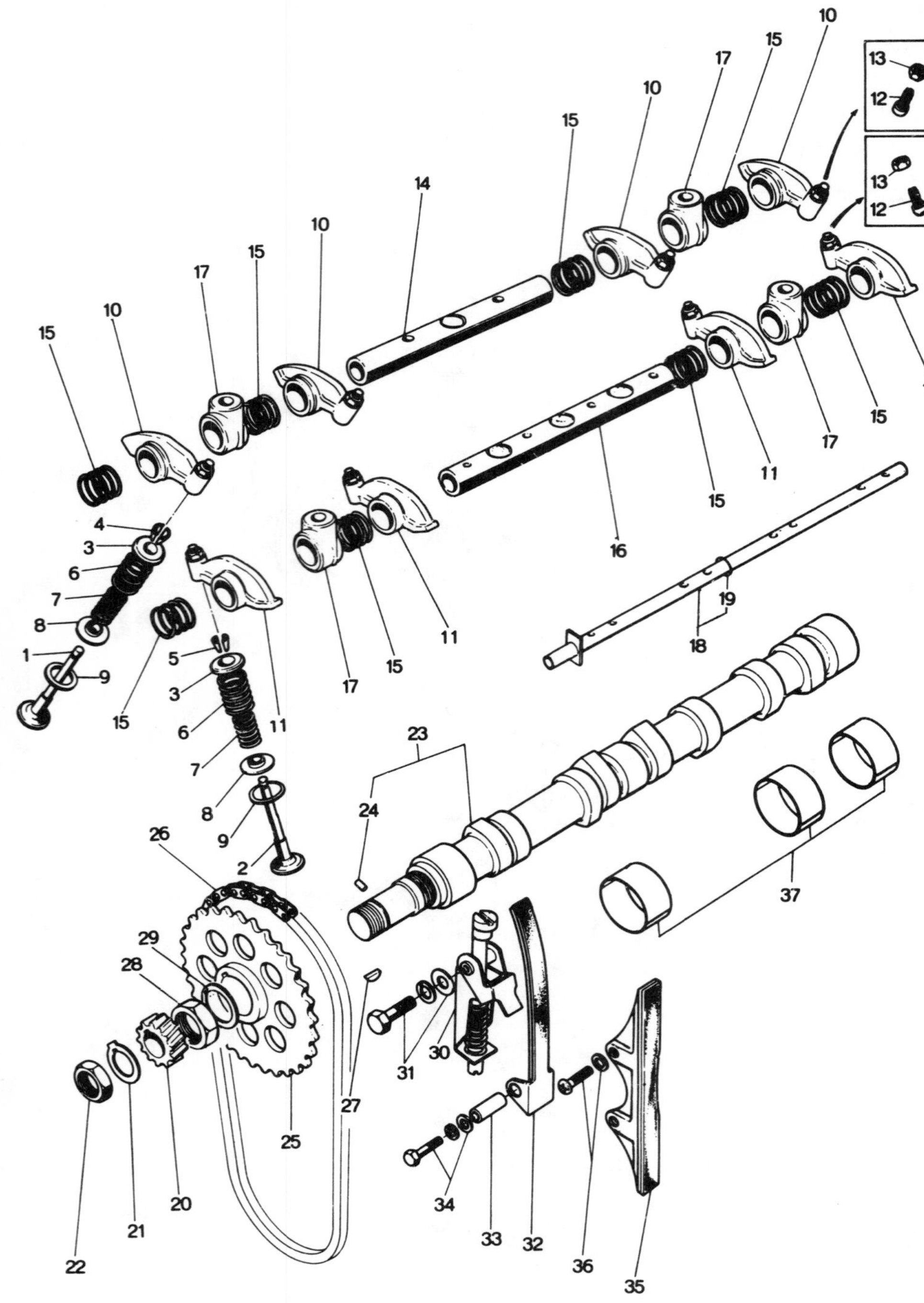

1	Intake Valve
2	Exhaust Valve
3	Seat
4	Sleeve
5	Sleeve
6	Spring
7	Spring
8	Seat
9	Spacer
10	Rocker Arm
11	Rocker Arm
12	Screw
13	Nut
14	Shaft
15	Spring
16	Shaft
17	Support
18	Pipe
19	O Ring
20	Dist. Drive Gear
21	Washer
22	Nut
23	Camshaft
24	Pin
25	Camshaft Sprocket
26	Timing Chain
27	Key
28	Nut
29	Washer
30	Chain Adjuster
31	Bolt
32	Adjuster Blade
33	Spacer
34	Bolt
35	Vibration Damper
36	Bolt
37	Bearings

FIG 4 – 4 CYLINDER ENGINE – CAMSHAFT & VALVES

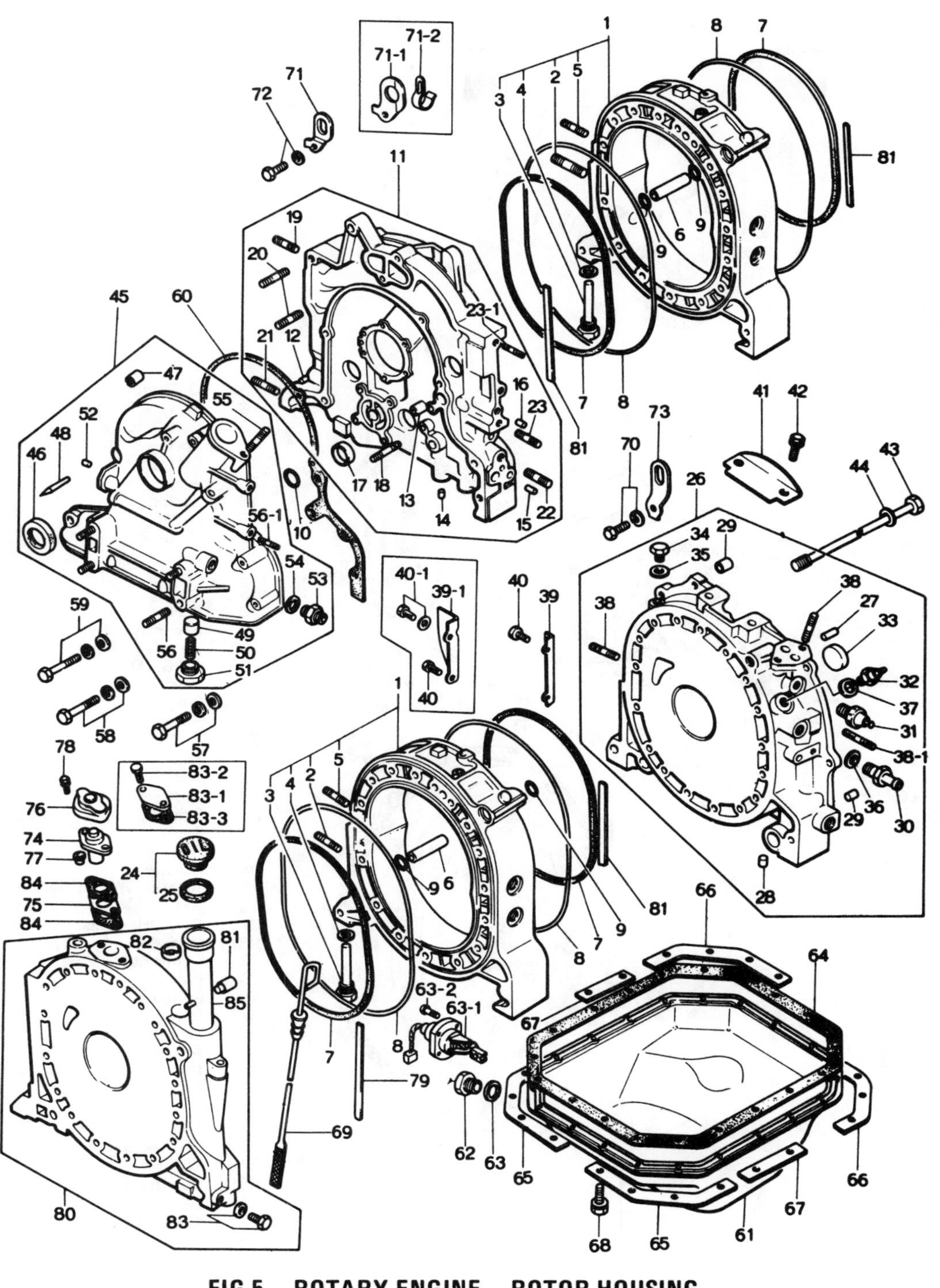

FIG 5 – ROTARY ENGINE – ROTOR HOUSING

1	Rotor Housing
2	Stud
3	Air Nozzle
4	Gasket
5	Stud
6	Dowel
7	Ring
8	O Ring
9	O Ring
10	O Ring
11	Housing, front
12	Pin
13	Dowel
14	Plug
15	Plug
16	Plug
17	Plug
18	Stud
19	Stud
20	Stud
21	Stud
22	Stud
23	Stud
23-1	Stud
24	Oil Filler Cap
25	Gasket
26	Housing, Rear
27	Pin
28	Plug
29	Pin
30	Hose Joint
31	Oil Pressure Switch
32	Heat Gauge
33	Plug
34	Plug
35	Gasket
36	Gasket
37	Gasket
38	Stud
38-1	Plug
39	Cover
39-1	Cover
40	Bolt
40-1	Bolt
41	Cover
42	Bolt
43	Bolt
44	Washer
45	Front Cover
46	Oil Seal
47	Pin
48	Pin
49	Plunger
50	Spring
51	Plug
52	Plug
53	Joint
54	Gasket
55	Stud
56	Stud
56-1	Stud
57	Bolt
58	Bolt
59	Bolt
60	Gasket
61	Oil Pan
62	Plug
63	Gasket
63-1	Oil Level Sensor
63-2	Screw
64	Gasket
65	Plate
66	Plate
67	Plate
68	Bolt
69	Oil Level Gauge
70	Bolt
71	Hanger
71-1	Hanger
71-2	Clip
72	Bolt
73	Hanger
74	Sensor
75	Insulator
76	Cover
77	Washer
78	Bolt
79	Protector
80	Intermediate Housing
81	Pipe Joint
82	Plug
83	Plug
83-1	Plate
83-2	Bolt
83-3	Gasket
84	Gasket
85	Pipe

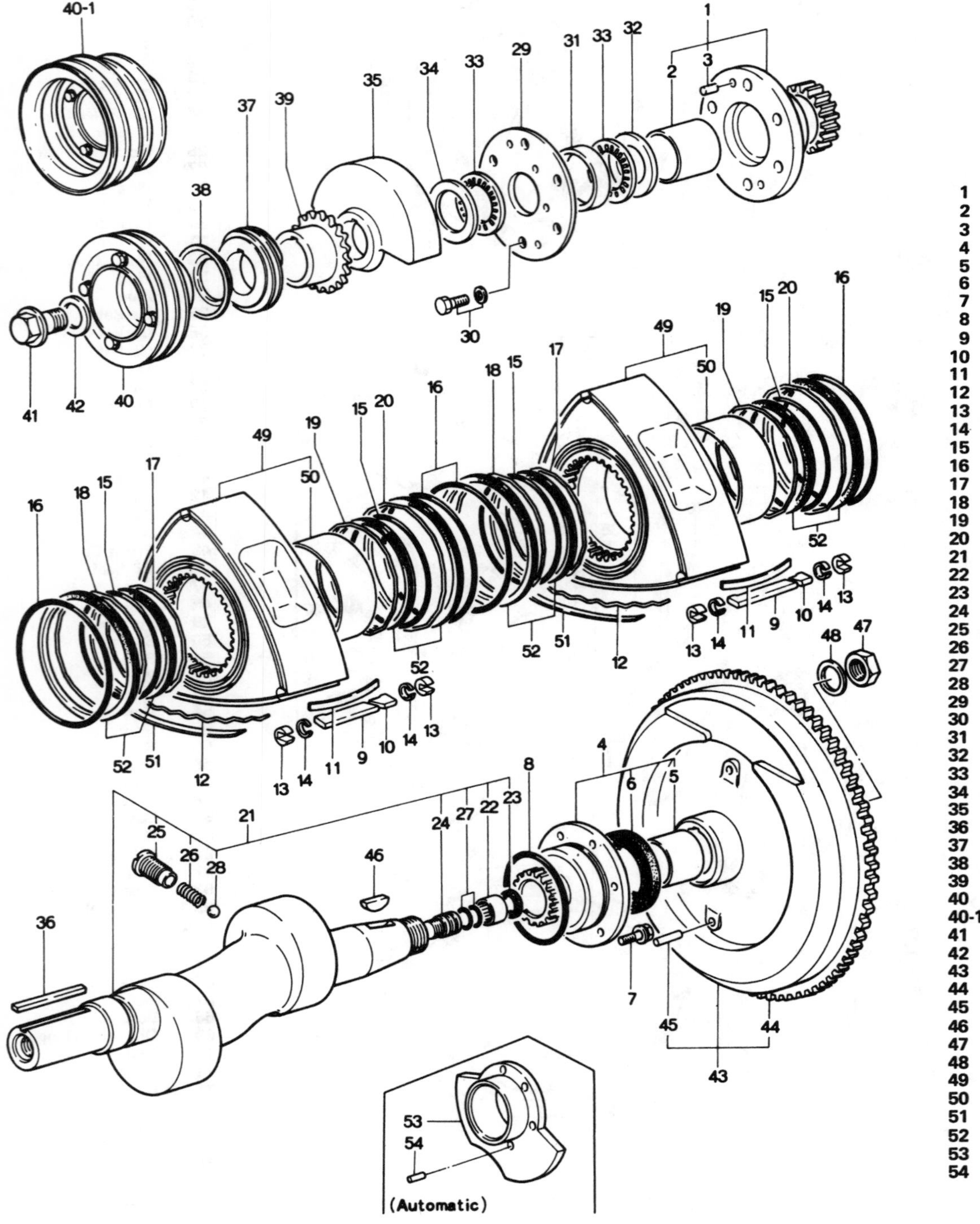

1	Front Stationary Gear
2	Main Bearing
3	Pin
4	Rear Staionary Gear
5	Main Bearing
6	Oil Seal
7	Bolt
8	O Ring
9	Seal
10	Side Piece
11	Spring
12	Spring
13	Seal
14	Spring
15	O Ring
16	O Ring
17	Spring
18	Spring
19	Spring
20	Spring
21	Eccentric Shaft
22	Needle Bearing
23	Oil Seal
24	Plug
25	Plug
26	Spring
27	O Ring
28	Ball
29	Plate
30	Bolt
31	Spacer
32	Plate
33	Needle Bearing
34	Washer
35	Balance Weight
36	Key
37	Dist Drive Gear
38	Plate
39	Pump Drive Gear
40	Pulley
40-1	Pulley
41	Bolt
42	Gasket
43	Flywheel
44	Ring Gear
45	Pin
46	Key
47	Nut
48	Washer
49	"C" Rotor
50	Bearing
51	Seal
52	Oil Seal Pkg
53	Counterweight
54	Pin

FIG 6 – ROTARY ENGINE – ROTOR

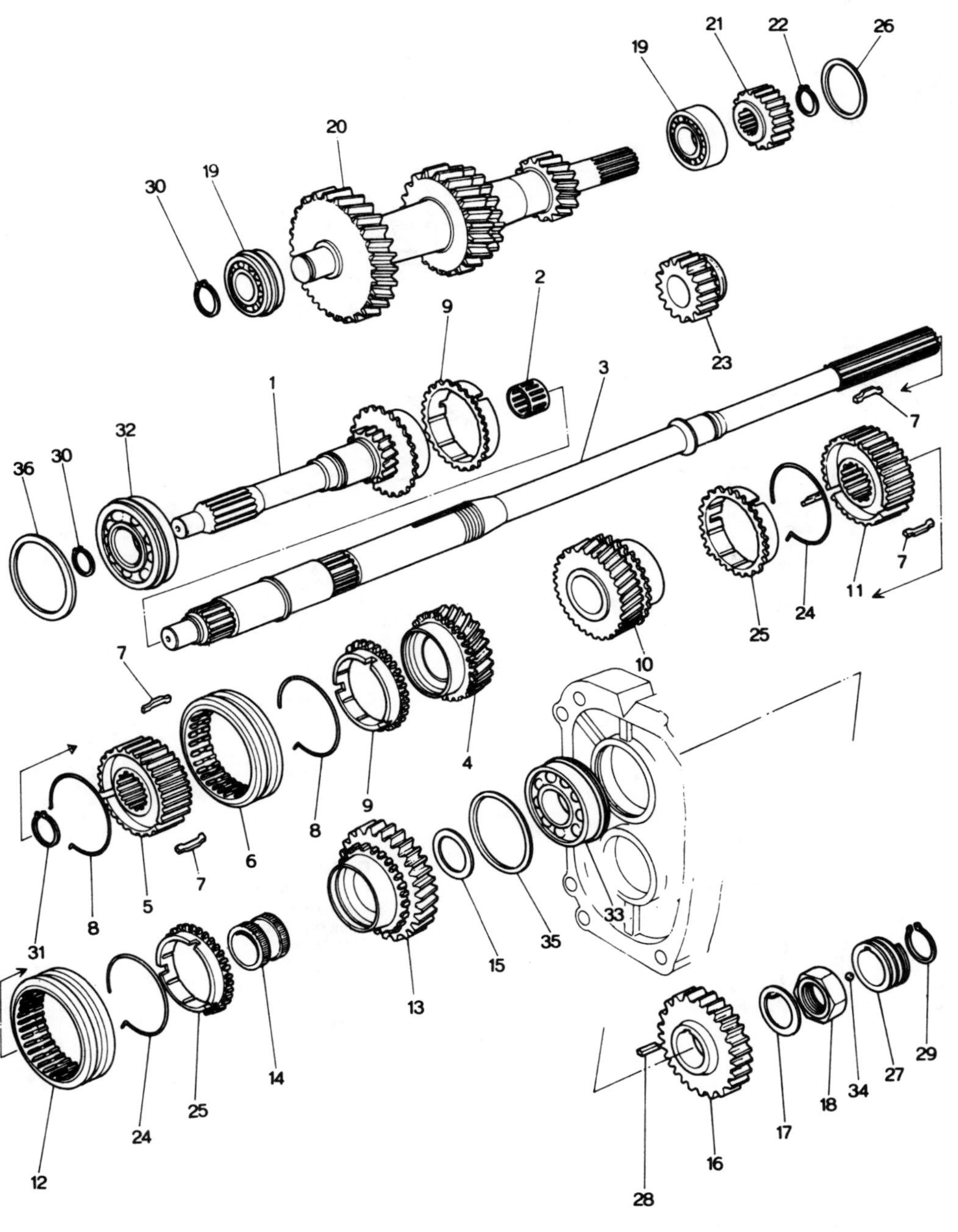

1	Main Drive Gear
2	Needle Bearing
3	Main Shaft
4	3rd Gear
5	Clutch Hub
6	Sleeve
7	Key
8	Spring
9	Ring
10	2nd Gear
11	Clutch Hub
12	Sleeve
13	1st Gear
14	Sleeve
15	Washer
16	Reverse Gear
17	Washer
18	Nut
19	Bearing
20	Countershaft Gear
21	Counter Reverse Gear
22	Ring
23	Reverse Idler Gear
24	Spring
25	Ring
26	Shim
27	Speedometer Drive Gear
28	Key
39	Ring
30	Ring
31	Ring
32	Bearing
33	Bearing
34	Ball
35	Shim
36	Shim

FIG 7 – TRANSMISSION GEARS

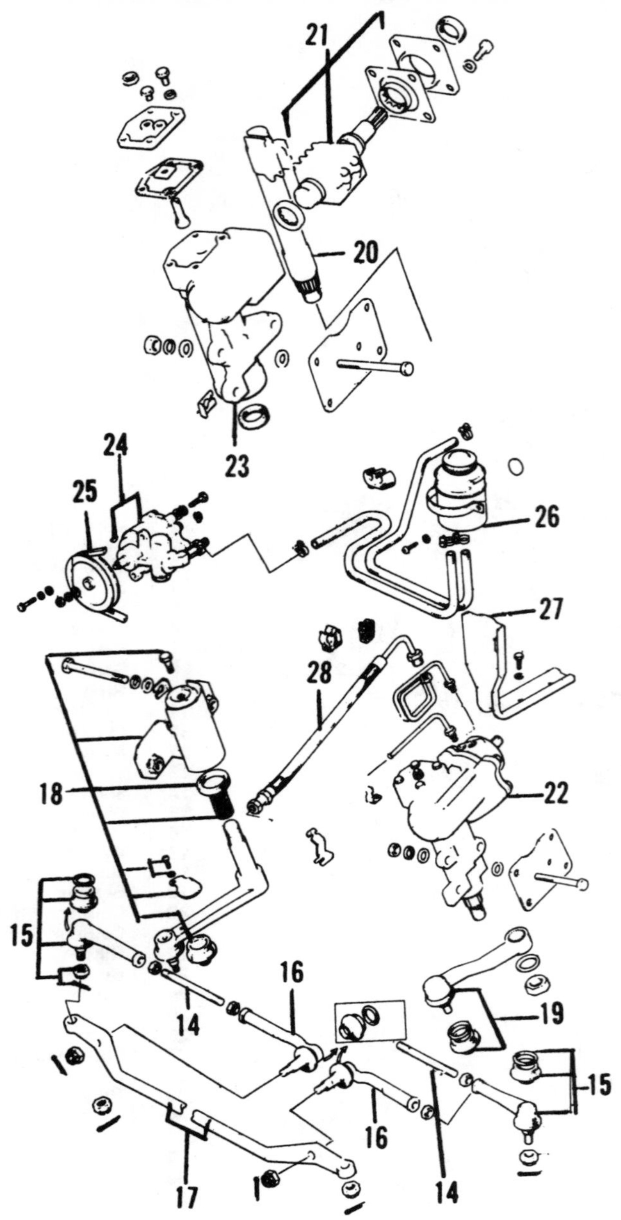

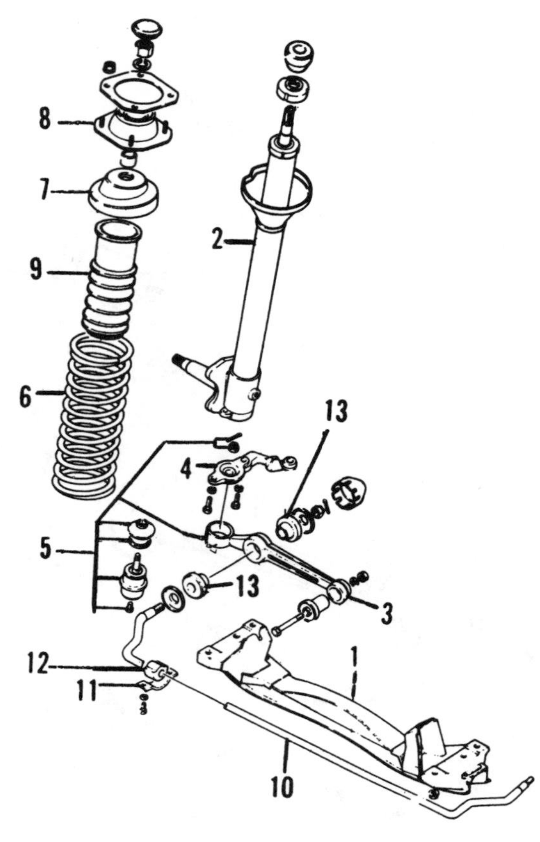

FIG 8 – FRONT SUSPENSION & STEERING – RX4

1 Crossmember
2 Knuckle & Shock
3 Control Arm
4 Steering Arm
5 Ball Joint
6 Spring
7 Upper Seat
8 Mount Plate
9 Boot
10 Stabilizer Bar
11 Support Bracket
12 Bushing, Inner
13 Bushing Outer
14 Tie Rod Adjust Tube
15 Tie Rod End, Outer
16 Tie Rod End, Inner
17 Drag Link
18 Idler Arm & Bracket
19 Pitman Arm
20 Sector Shaft
21 Worm & Ball-Nut
22 Gear Assy, Power Strg
23 Housing, Std Strg
24 Pump
25 Pulley
26 Reservoir
27 Mounting Bracket
28 Pressure Hose

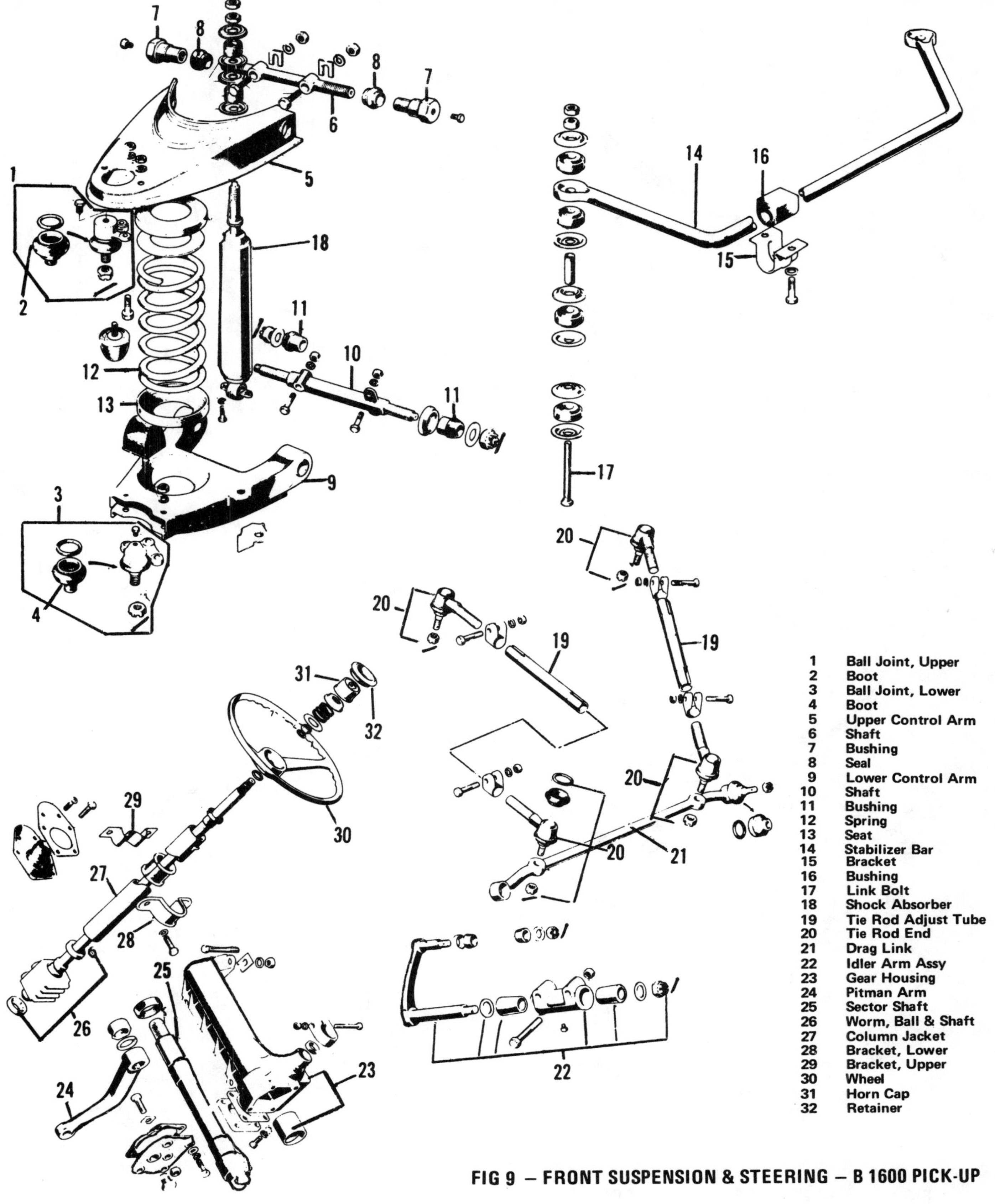
1 Ball Joint, Upper
2 Boot
3 Ball Joint, Lower
4 Boot
5 Upper Control Arm
6 Shaft
7 Bushing
8 Seal
9 Lower Control Arm
10 Shaft
11 Bushing
12 Spring
13 Seat
14 Stabilizer Bar
15 Bracket
16 Bushing
17 Link Bolt
18 Shock Absorber
19 Tie Rod Adjust Tube
20 Tie Rod End
21 Drag Link
22 Idler Arm Assy
23 Gear Housing
24 Pitman Arm
25 Sector Shaft
26 Worm, Ball & Shaft
27 Column Jacket
28 Bracket, Lower
29 Bracket, Upper
30 Wheel
31 Horn Cap
32 Retainer

FIG 9 – FRONT SUSPENSION & STEERING – B 1600 PICK-UP

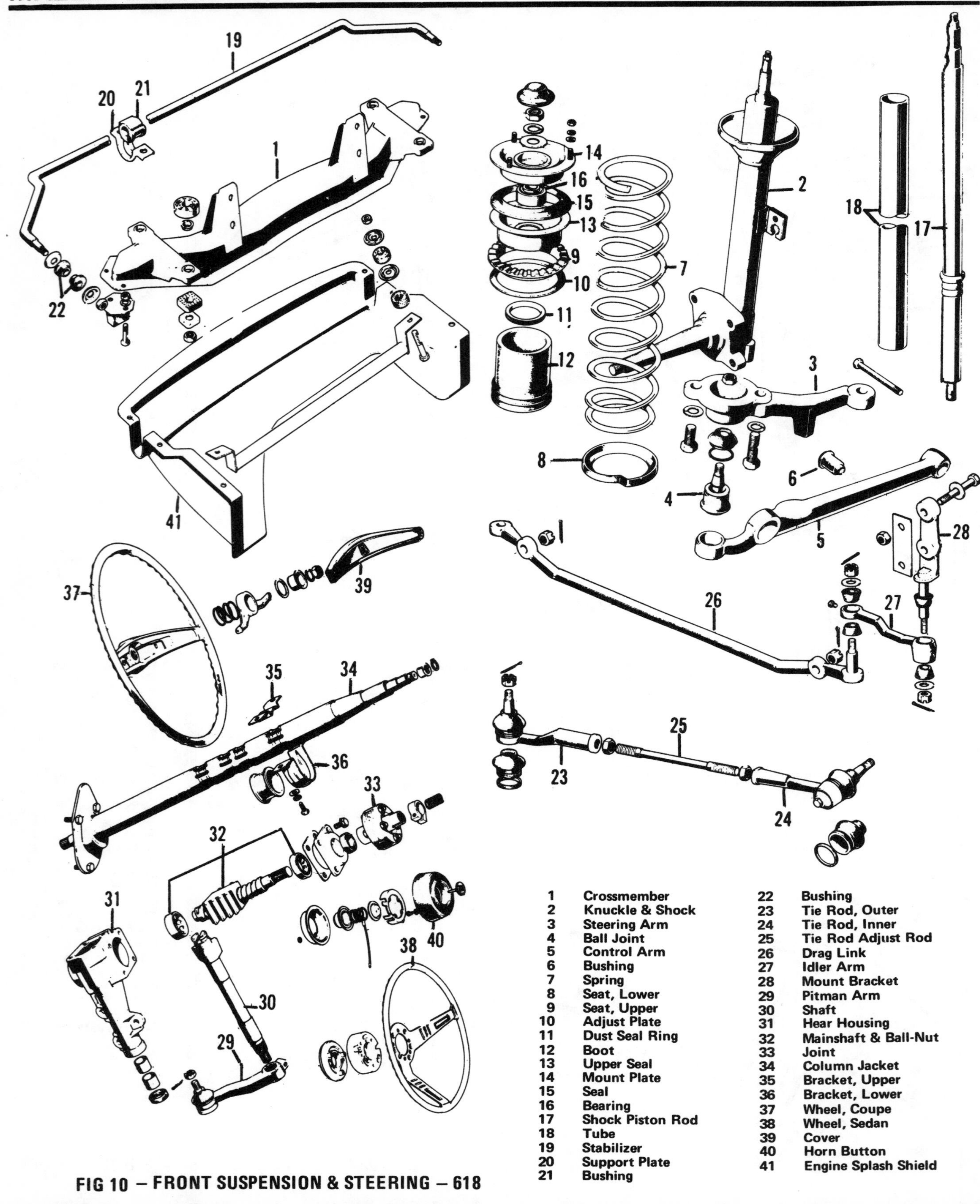

FIG 10 – FRONT SUSPENSION & STEERING – 618

Ignition, Starting & Charging—TIME

OPERATION INDEX

Tune-Up, Minor 1
Tune-Up, Major 2
Compression Test 3
Distributor, R&R Or Renew 4
Distributor, R&R & Overhaul 4A
Distributor Cap, Renew 5
Ignition Cable Set, Renew 6
Vacuum Control Unit, Renew 7
Ignition Coil, Renew 8
Starter & Ignition Switch, Renew 9
Starter, R&R Or Renew 10
Starter Solenoid, Renew 11
Starter Bendix Drive, Renew 12
Starter, R&R & Overhaul 13
Starter Brushes, Renew 14
Regulator, Renew 15
Regulator, Adjust 16
Alternator, R&R Or Renew 17
Alternator, R&R & Overhaul 18
Alternator Brushes, Renew 19
Alternator Pulley, Renew 20

1—TUNE-UP, MINOR
Includes: Renew points, condenser and plugs, set spark timing and adjust carburetor idle.

All Models 1.8

2—TUNE-UP, MAJOR
Includes: Check compression, clean or renew and adjust spark plugs, R&R distributor, renew points and condenser. Adjust ignition timing, carburetor and fan belts. Clean battery terminals and service air cleaner. Check coil and renew fuel filter.

All Models 3.5

3—COMPRESSION TEST
All Models 0.4

4—DISTRIBUTOR, R&R OR RENEW
616 .... 0.4
RX2 .... 0.6
RX3-4, Cosmo 0.5
Rotary Pick-Up 0.5
808 (1300 Eng) Exc 0.7
California 0.4
808 (1600 Eng) 0.4
GLC 0.4
B1800 .... 0.4

4A—DISTRIBUTOR, R&R & OVERHAUL
Exc Below 1.4
GLC 1.2
808 (1300 Eng) Exc 1.5
California 1.2
808 (1600 Eng) 1.2
B1800 .... 1.2

5—DISTRIBUTOR CAP, RENEW
All Models 0.2

6—IGNITION CABLE SET, RENEW
All Models 0.3

7—VACUUM CONTROL UNIT, RENEW
One 0.3
Two 0.4

8—IGNITION COIL, RENEW
Each 0.2

9—STARTER & IGNITION SWITCH, RENEW
All Models 0.3

—NOTE—
To Renew Steering Lock, Add
Exc Below *0.7*
Cosmo *1.1*

10—STARTER, R&R OR RENEW
616, 808, B1600 .... 0.5
RX2-3-4, Cosmo 0.4
Rotary Pick-Up 0.4
GLC 0.5
B1800 .... 0.7

11—STARTER SOLENOID, RENEW
616, 808, B1600 .... 0.7
RX2-3-4, Cosmo 0.6
Rotary Pick-Up 0.6
GLC 0.7
B1800 .... 0.8

12—STARTER BENDIX DRIVE, RENEW
616, 808, B1600 .... 1.2
RX2-3-4, Cosmo 1.1
Rotary Pick-Up 1.1
GLC 1.2
B1800 .... 1.4

13—STARTER, R&R & OVERHAUL
616 .... 1.8
RX2 .... 1.7
RX3-4, Cosmo 1.4
Rotary Pick-Up 1.4
808, B1600 .... 1.5
GLC 1.5
B1800 .... 1.7

14—STARTER BRUSHES, RENEW
616, 808, B1600 .... 1.0
RX2-3-4, Cosmo 0.9
Rotary Pick-Up 0.9
GLC 1.0
B1800 .... 1.2

15—REGULATOR, RENEW
All Models 0.2

16—REGULATOR, ADJUST
All Models 0.6

17—ALTERNATOR, R&R OR RENEW
Exc Below 0.3
808, B1600 .... 0.4
GLC 0.4
B1800 .... 0.4

18—ALTERNATOR, R&R & OVERHAUL
Exc Below 1.3
808, B1600, B1800 .... 1.4
GLC 1.4

19—ALTERNATOR BRUSHES, RENEW
Exc Below 0.6
808, B1600, B1800 .... 0.7
GLC 0.7

20—ALTERNATOR PULLEY, RENEW
Exc Below 0.4
808, B1600, B1800 .... 0.5
GLC 0.5

Fuel, Emission Controls, Intake & Exhaust Systems—TIME

OPERATION INDEX

Carburetor Or Insulator, R & R Or Renew 1
Carburetor, R & R & Overhaul 2
Fuel Pump, R & R Or Renew 3
Fuel Pump, R & R & Overhaul 4
Fuel Tank, R & R Or Renew 5
Choke Cable Assy, Renew 6
Air Pump, R & R Or Renew 7
Air Control Valve Or Check Valve, Renew 8
Anti-After Burn Valve, Renew 9
Positive Crankcase Ventilation Valve, Renew 10
Air Control Valve, Renew 11
Deceleration Control Valve, Renew 12
Air Injector Nozzle, Renew 13
Condense Tank, Renew 14
Charcoal Canister, Renew 15
Thermal Reactor, Renew 16
Deceleration Control Solenoid Valve, Renew 17
Power Solenoid Valve, Renew 18
Vacuum Control Valve, Renew 19
Egr Control Valve, Renew 20
Emission Control Unit, Renew 21
Heat Exchanger, Renew 22
Intake Manifold, Renew 23
Intake Manifold Gasket, Renew 24
Exhaust Manifold, Renew 25
Exhaust Manifold Gasket, Renew 26
Front Exhaust Pipe, Renew 27
Center Exhaust Pipe, Renew 28
Silencer, Renew 29
Catalytic Converter, Renew 30

1—CARBURETOR OR INSULATOR, R & R OR RENEW
616 .... 0.7
RX2 .... 1.0
RX3 .... 1.1
RX4, Cosmo 0.9
Rotary Pick-Up 0.9
808 (1300 Eng) 0.6
808 (1600 Eng) 0.8
B1600, B1800 .... 0.8
GLC 0.6

2—CARBURETOR, R & R & OVERHAUL
616 .... 1.5
RX2 .... 2.0
RX3 .... 2.1
RX4, Cosmo 1.9
Rotary Pick-Up 1.9
808 (1300 Eng) 1.3
808 (1600 Eng) 1.6
B1600, B1800 .... 1.6
GLC 1.3

3—FUEL PUMP, R & R OR RENEW
Exc Below 0.3
616 .... 0.4
RX2 .... 0.5
B1800 .... 0.6

4—FUEL PUMP, R & R & OVERHAUL
616, 808 .... 0.8
GLC 0.8

5—FUEL TANK, R & R OR RENEW
616 .... 1.2
RX2 .... 1.0
Cosmo, RX3-4, Exc Wgn 0.9
RX3 Wagon 1.1
RX4 Wagon 1.4
Rotary Pick-Up 0.9
808, Exc 0.9
Wagon 1.1
B1600, B1800 .... 0.8
GLC 0.8

6—CHOKE CABLE ASSY, RENEW
Exc Below 0.6
RX3-4, Cosmo 0.4
Rotary Pick-Up 0.3
808, B1600, B1800 .... 0.4
GLC 0.4

7—AIR PUMP, R & R OR RENEW
616 .... 0.2
RX2-3 .... 0.5
RX4, Cosmo 0.4
Rotary Pick-Up 0.4
808, B1600, B1800 .... 0.4
GLC 0.3

8—AIR CONTROL VALVE OR CHECK VALVE, RENEW
616 .... 0.1
RX2 .... 0.5
RX3-4, Cosmo 0.4
Rotary Pick-Up 0.4
808, B1600, B1800 .... 0.2
GLC 0.2

9—ANTI-AFTERBURN VALVE, RENEW
All Models Exc 0.3
B1800 .... 0.2

10—POSITIVE CRANKCASE VENTILATION VALVE, RENEW
Exc Below 0.2
616, B1600, B1800 .... 0.1

11—AIR CONTROL VALVE, RENEW
RX3-4, Cosmo 0.4
Rotary Pick-Up 0.4
808, B1600 .... 0.3
GLC 0.3
B1800 .... 0.2

(Continued)

Fuel, Emission Controls, Intake & Exhaust Systems—TIME Cont'd

12—DECELERATION CONTROL VALVE, RENEW

RX3-4, Cosmo	0.3
Rotary Pick-Up	0.3

13—AIR INJECTOR NOZZLE, RENEW

616	0.9
RX2—	
One Or Two	1.4
Three Or Four	1.5
Rotary Pick-Up	1.0
808, B1600, B1800	0.3
GLC	0.4

14—CONDENSE TANK, RENEW

616, B1600	0.3
RX2	0.4
RX3-4	0.5
Cosmo	0.3
Rotary Pick-Up	0.4
808	0.5

15—CHARCOAL CANISTER, RENEW

All Models	0.2

16—THERMAL REACTOR OR GASKET, RENEW

RX2	1.9
RX3	2.6
RX4, Cosmo	2.9
Rotary Pick-Up	2.8

17—DECELERATION CONTROL SOLENOID VALVE, RENEW

RX3-4, Cosmo	0.3
Rotary Pick-Up	0.2

18—POWER SOLENOID VALVE, RENEW

RX3-4, Cosmo	0.2
Rotary Pick-Up	0.2

19—VACUUM CONTROL VALVE, RENEW

RX3-4, Cosmo	0.3
808, B1600	0.2
B1800	0.1
GLC	0.2

20—EGR CONTROL VALVE, RENEW

808	0.3
RX3-4, Cosmo	0.2
GLC	0.2
808 (1300 Eng)	0.2
808 (1600 Eng)	0.3
B1800	0.3

21—EMISSION CONTROL UNIT, RENEW

RX3, 808	0.3
RX4, Cosmo	0.5
Rotary Pick-Up	0.3
B1600	0.2

22—HEAT EXCHANGER, RENEW

RX3-4, Cosmo	0.6

23—INTAKE MANIFOLD, RENEW

Exc Below	1.8
RX3	1.7
RX4, Cosmo	1.8
Rotary Pick-Up	1.7
808 (1300)	1.3
808 (1600 Eng)	1.5
B1600	1.5
GLC	1.3
B1800	1.4

24—INTAKE MANIFOLD GASKET, RENEW

Exc Below	1.5
RX3	1.4
RX4, Cosmo	1.5
Rotary Pick-Up	1.4
808	1.0
B1600	0.9
GLC	1.0
B1800	1.1

25—EXHAUST MANIFOLD, RENEW

Exc Below	1.0
808 (1300 Eng)	0.7
808 (1600 Eng)	0.8
B1600	0.6
GLC	0.7
B1800	1.0

26—EXHAUST MANIFOLD GASKET, RENEW

Exc Below	0.7
808 (1300 Eng)	0.5
808 (1600 Eng)	0.6
B1600	0.4
GLC	0.5
B1800	0.8

27—FRONT EXHAUST PIPE, RENEW

RX 2	0.5
RX3-4, Cosmo	0.7
808	0.6
B1600	0.5
GLC	0.6
B1800	0.6

28—CENTER EXHAUST PIPE, RENEW

808	0.4
B1800	0.5

29—SILENCER, RENEW

Pre-Silencer, Exc	0.4
RX4, Cosmo	0.5
Rotary Pick-Up	0.6
808	0.7
B1800	0.9
Main Silencer, Exc	0.5
Cosmo	0.6
Rotary Pick-Up	0.4
808 (1300 Eng)	0.4
808 (1600 Eng)	0.6
B1600	0.4
GLC	0.4
B1800	0.5

30—CATALYTIC CONVERTER, RENEW

All Models	0.6

Engine Cooling & Heater System—TIME

OPERATION INDEX

Radiator, R & R Or Renew 1
Expansion Tank, R & R Or Renew 2
Fan Belt, Renew 3
Radiator Hoses, Renew 4
Water Pump, R & R Or Renew 5
Water Pump, R & R & Overhaul 6
Thermostat Or Housing, Renew 7
Heater Assy, Renew 8
Heater Blower Motor, Renew 9
Heater Control Cable, Renew 10
Heater Hoses, Renew 11

1—RADIATOR, R & R OR RENEW

616, B1600	0.5
808	0.6
RX2	0.8
RX3-4, Cosmo—	
Manual Trans	①0.7
Auto Trans	①0.8
Rotary Pick-Up—	
Manual Trans	0.7
Auto Trans	0.8
GLC—	
Manual Trans	①0.5
Auto Trans	①0.6
B1800	0.5
①With Air Cond, Add.	*0.1*

2—EXPANSION TANK, R & R OR RENEW

All Models	0.2

3—FAN BELT, RENEW

All Models, Exc	0.3
W/Air Cond	0.4

4—RADIATOR HOSES, RENEW

Rad To Thermostat	0.2
Rad To Pump, Exc	0.3
Rotary Pick-Up	0.2
GLC	0.2
RX3	0.4
Rad To Expansion Tank	0.2

5—WATER PUMP, R & R OR RENEW

Exc Below	1.0
808 (1300 Eng)	0.7
808 (1600 Eng)	0.8
B1600	0.9
GLC	0.7
B1800	0.9

6—WATER PUMP, R & R & OVERHAUL

Exc Below	1.6
808 (1300 Eng)	1.3
808 (1600 Eng)	1.4
B1600	1.5
GLC	1.3
B1800	1.5

7—THERMOSTAT HOUSING, RENEW

All Models Exc	0.3
B1800	0.2

8—HEATER ASSY, RENEW

Exc Below	2.0
RX3, Exc	1.2
W/Air Cond	2.0
RX4, Exc	1.3
W/Air Cond	3.0
Cosmo, Exc	1.5
W/Air Cond	3.2
Rotary Pick-Up	0.7
808, Exc	1.1
W/Air Cond	1.9
B1600	0.8
GLC Exc	0.6
W/Air Cond	2.2
B1800	0.8

9—HEATER BLOWER MOTOR, RENEW

Exc Below—	
W/Console	2.0
L/Console	1.8
RX3	0.7
RX4 Exc	0.5
W/Air Cond	0.7
Cosmo Exc	0.9
W/Air Cond	1.1
Rotary Pick-Up	1.0
808	0.7
B1600	1.0
GLC	0.5
B1800	1.0

10—HEATER CONTROL CABLE, RENEW

Exc Below	0.8
RX3, Exc	0.8
W/Air Cond	0.9
RX4, Exc	1.0
W/Air Cond	1.1
Cosmo, Exc	1.3
W/Air Cond	1.4
Rotary Pick-Up	0.7
808, Exc	0.6
W/Air Cond	0.7
B1600	0.6
GLC Exc	1.2
W/Air Cond	2.8
B1800	0.6

11—HEATER HOSES, RENEW

Exc Below	0.7
RX3, Exc	0.7
W/Air Cond	1.2
RX4, Exc	0.7
W/Air Cond	0.8
Cosmo, Exc	0.8
W/Air Cond	0.9
Rotary Pick-Up	0.6
808, Exc	0.6
W/Air Cond	1.1
B1600	0.5
GLC Exc	0.6
W/Air Cond	0.9
B1800	0.6

Engine (CONVENTIONAL)—TIME

OPERATION INDEX

Engine, R & R ... *1*
Cylinder Block, Renew ... *2*
Engine (Short), Renew & Grind Valves ... *3*
Cylinder Head Gasket, Renew ... *4*
Cylinder Head, Renew ... *4A*
Valves, Grind ... *5*
One Valve, Renew & Grind ... *6*
Valve Springs Or Seals, Renew ... *7*
Rocker Arm Cover Gasket, Renew ... *8*
Valve Rocker Arms, Shafts Or Supporters, R & R Or Renew ... *9*
Valve Clearances, Adjust ... *10*
Timing Chain Cover Oil Seal, Renew ... *11*
Timing Chain Cover, Renew ... *12*
Blind Cover (Timing Chain) Or Gasket, Renew ... *13*
Timing Chain Or Gears, Renew ... *14*
Chain Adjuster Assy, Renew ... *15*
Oil Pan Or Gasket, R & R Or Renew ... *16*
Oil Pump, R & R Or Renew ... *17*
Oil Pump, R & R & Overhaul ... *18*
Oil Pump Chain Or Sprocket, Renew ... *19*
Camshaft, R & R Or Renew ... *20*
Camshaft Bearings, Renew ... *21*
Piston Ring(S), Renew ... *22*
Rings & Main Bearings, Renew & Grind Valves ... *23*
Rod Bearing(S), Renew ... *24*
Main Bearings, Renew ... *25*
Main & Rod Bearings, Renew ... *26*
Crankshaft, R & R Or Renew ... *27*
Crankshaft Rear Main Oil Seal, Renew ... *28*
Main Bearing Cap Seals, Renew ... *29*
Piston(S), Renew ... *30*
Connecting Rod(S), Renew ... *31*
Vibration Damper, Renew ... *32*
Crankshaft Pulley, Renew ... *33*

1—ENGINE, R & R

Does not include transfer of any part of engine or replacement of special equipment.

616 ... 3.8
808 (1300 Eng) ... ①3.7
808 (1600 Eng)—
  Std Trans ... ①3.9
  Auto Trans ... ①4.4
B1600 ... 3.5
GLC—
  Std Trans Exc ... 3.7
    W/Air Cond ... 4.3
  Auto Trans Exc ... 4.2
    W/Air Cond ... 4.9
B1800 ... 3.9
① *With Air Cond, Add.* ... *0.7*

2—CYLINDER BLOCK, RENEW

616 ... 13.1
808 (1300 Eng), Exc ... 12.2
  W/Air Cond ... 12.8
808 (1600 Eng)—
  Std Trans, Exc ... 12.7
    Air Cond ... 13.3
  Auto Trans, Exc ... 13.2
    Air Cond ... 13.8
B1600 ... 12.2
GLC—
  Std Trans Exc ... 12.0
    W/Air Cond ... 12.6
  Auto Trans Exc ... 12.5
    W/Air Cond ... 13.1
B1800 ... 12.4

3—ENGINE (SHORT), RENEW & GRIND VALVES

Includes: R & R all necessary bearings, bushings, rings, gaskets & perform minor tune-up

616 ... 21.8

4—CYLINDER HEAD GASKET, RENEW

616 ... 5.1
808 (1300 Eng), Exc ... 3.6
  California ... 3.8
808 (1600 Eng), Exc ... 4.3
  California ... 4.5
B1600 ... 4.3
GLC ... 3.8
B1800 ... 4.0

4A—CYLINDER HEAD, R & R OR RENEW

616 ... 5.1
808 (1300 Eng), Exc ... 6.1
  California ... 6.3
808 (1600 Eng), Exc ... 6.8
  California ... 7.0
B1600 ... 6.8
GLC Exc ... 6.1
  California ... 6.3
B1800 Exc ... 6.5
  California ... 6.7

5—VALVES, GRIND

616 ... 8.4
808, GLC ... 7.5
B1600, B1800 ... 7.5

6—ONE VALVE, RENEW & GRIND

616 ... 5.7
808 (1300 Eng) ... 4.3
808 (1600 Eng) ... 4.9
B1600, B1800 ... 4.9
GLC ... 4.3

7—VALVE SPRINGS OR SEALS, RENEW

616—
  One ... 5.5
  All ... 6.2
808 (1300 Eng)—
  One ... 4.3
  All ... 5.0
808 (1600 Eng)—
  One ... 4.9
  All ... 5.5
B1600, B1800—
  One ... 4.7
  All ... 5.3
GLC—
  One ... 4.3
  All ... 5.0

8—ROCKER ARM COVER GASKET, RENEW

616 ... 0.2
808, B1600, B1800 ... 0.3
GLC ... 0.3

9—VALVE ROCKER ARMS, SHAFTS OR SUPPORTERS, RENEW

All Models ... 1.2

10—VALVE CLEARANCES, ADJUST

616 ... 0.7
808, B1600, B1800 ... 0.6
GLC ... 0.6

11—TIMING CHAIN COVER OIL SEAL, RENEW

All Models ... 1.3

12—TIMING CHAIN COVER, RENEW

616 ... 4.6
808 (1300 Eng) ... ①4.9
808 (1600 Eng) ... ①5.1
1600 ... 5.1
GLC Exc ... ①4.8
  California ... ①5.0
B1800 Exc ... 5.4
  California ... 5.6
① *With Air Cond, Add* ... *0.6*

13—BLIND COVER (TIMING CHAIN) OR GASKET, RENEW

616 ... 1.2
808 (1300 Eng) ... 0.7
808 (1600 Eng) ... 1.0
B1600 ... 1.1
GLC ... 0.2
B1800 ... 0.9

14—TIMING CHAIN OR GEARS, RENEW

616 ... 5.9
808 (1300 Eng) ... ①5.3
808 (1600 Eng) ... ①5.6
B1600 ... 5.6
GLC Exc ... ①5.1
  California ... ①5.3
B1800 Exc ... 5.8
  California ... 6.0
① *With Air Cond, Add.* ... *0.6*

15—CHAIN ADJUSTER ASSY, RENEW

616 ... 5.0
808 (1300 Eng), Exc ... 0.5
  W/Air Cond ... 1.1
808 (1600 Eng), Exc ... 1.2
  W/Air Cond ... 1.8
B1600, B1800 ... 1.2
GLC Exc ... 0.5
  W/Air Cond ... 1.1

16—OIL PAN OR GASKET, R & R OR RENEW

616 ... 1.6
808 (1300 Eng) ... 1.2
808 (1600 Eng) ... 1.4
B1600, B1800 ... 1.2
GLC ... 1.1

17—OIL PUMP, R & R OR RENEW

616 ... 2.0
808 (1300 Eng), Exc ... 5.4
  W/Air Cond ... 6.0
808 (1600 Eng) Exc ... 1.7
  W/Air Cond ... 2.3
B1600 ... 1.6
GLC—
  Wo/Air Cond Exc ... 5.2
    California ... 5.4
  W/Air Cond Exc ... 5.8
    California ... 6.0
B1800 ... 1.6

18—OIL PUMP, R & R & OVERHAUL

616 ... 2.2
808 (1300 Eng), Exc ... 5.5
  W/Air Cond ... 6.1
808 (1600 Eng) Exc ... 1.9
  W/Air Cond ... 2.5
B1600 ... 1.8
GLC—
  Wo/Air Cond Exc ... 5.3
    California ... 5.5
  W/Air Cond Exc ... 5.9
    California ... 6.1
B1800 ... 1.8

19—OIL PUMP CHAIN OR SPROCKET, RENEW

616 ... 4.0
808 (1300 Eng), Exc ... 5.1
  W/Air Cond ... 5.7
808 (1600 Eng), Exc ... 5.4
  W/Air Cond ... 6.1
B1600 ... 5.4
GLC—
  Wo/Air Cond Exc ... 4.9
    California ... 5.1
  W/Air Cond Exc ... 5.5
    California ... 5.7
B1800 ... 5.6

20—CAMSHAFT, R & R OR RENEW

616 ... 2.5
808 (1300 Eng), Exc ... 2.0
  California ... 2.2
808 (1600 Eng), Exc ... 2.5
  California ... 2.7
B1600 ... 2.5
GLC Exc ... 2.0
  California ... 2.2
B1800 Exc ... 2.2
  California ... 2.4

21—CAMSHAFT BEARINGS, RENEW

616 ... 2.5
808 (1300 Eng), Exc ... 2.0
  California ... 2.2
808 (1600 Eng), Exc ... 2.5
  California ... 2.7
B1600 ... 2.5
GLC EXC ... 2.0
  California ... 2.2
B1800 Exc ... 2.2
  California ... 2.4

(Continued)

Engine (CONVENTIONAL)—TIME Cont'd

22—PISTON RING(S), RENEW

616, B1600—
One 6.7
All 7.4
808 (1300 Eng)—
One 6.5
All 7.3
808 (1600 Eng)—
One 7.0
All 7.8
GLC—
One 6.5
All 7.3
B1800—
One 7.0
All 7.8

23—RINGS & MAIN BEARINGS, RENEW & GRIND VALVES

Includes: R & R engine
616 .... 18.5
808 (1300 Eng) 21.0
808 (1600 Eng) 22.0
B1600 .... 21.5
GLC 21.0
B1800 .... 21.5

24—ROD BEARING(S), RENEW

616—
One 2.5
All 2.9
808, B1800—
One 2.0
All 2.4
B1600, GLC—
One 1.9
All 2.3

25—MAIN BEARINGS, RENEW

Includes: R & R engine
616 .... 9.3
808 (1300 Eng) ①11.7
808 (1600 Eng) ②12.3
B1600 .... 11.9
GLC ①11.7
B1800 .... 12.3
①With Air Cond, Add. 0.6
②With Air Cond, Add. 0.7

26—MAIN & ROD BEARINGS, RENEW

Includes: R & R engine
616 .... 10.1
808 (1300 Eng) ①12.0
808 (1600 Eng) ②12.5
B1600 .... 12.3
GLC ①12.0
B1800 .... 12.5
①With Air Cond, Add. 0.6
②With Air Cond, Add. 0.7

27—CRANKSHAFT, R & R OR RENEW

Includes: R & R engine
616 .... 9.3
808 (1300 Eng) ①11.7
808 (1600 Eng) ②12.3
B1600 .... 11.9
①With Air Cond, Add. 0.6
②With Air Cond, Add. 0.7
GLC ①11.7
B1800 .... 12.3

28—CRANKSHAFT REAR MAIN OIL SEAL, RENEW

Includes: R & R trans & flywheel
616—
L/Console 2.9
W/Console 3.1
808 (1300 Eng) 2.7
808 (1600 Eng)—
Std Trans 2.8
Auto Trans 3.5
B1600 .... 2.7
GLC Exc 2.7
Auto Trans 3.4
B1800 Exc 2.8
Auto Trans 3.5

29—MAIN BEARING CAP SEALS, RENEW

616 .... 2.0
808, B1800 .... 1.6
B1600, GLC 1.5

30—PISTON(S), RENEW

616—
One 6.9
All 7.5
808 (1300 Eng) & GLC—
One 6.8
All 7.9
808 (1600 Eng) & B1800—
One 7.3
All 8.4
B1600—
One 6.9
All 8.0

—NOTE—
To Renew Small End Bushings-
One, Add. 0.5
All, Add. 1.0

31—CONNECTING ROD(S), RENEW

616—
One 6.6
All 7.2
808 (1300 Eng) & GLC—
One 6.6
All 7.5
808 (1600 Eng) & B1800—
One 7.1
All 8.0
B1600—
One 6.7
All 7.6

—NOTE—
To Renew Small End Bushings,-
One, Add. 0.5
All, Add. 1.0

32—VIBRATION DAMPER, RENEW

616 .... 5.0
808 (1300 Eng) ①5.0
808 (1600 Eng) ①5.4
B1600 .... 5.4
GLC Exc ①4.8
California ①5.0
B1800 Exc 5.2
California 5.4
With Air Cond, Add. 0.6

33—CRANKSHAFT PULLEY, RENEW

808 (1300 Eng), Exc 0.5
W/Air Cond 0.6
808 (1600 Eng), Exc 0.6
W/Air Cond 0.7
B1600 .... 1.0
GLC EXC 0.5
W/Air Cond 0.6
B1800 .... 0.6

Engine (ROTARY)—TIME

OPERATION INDEX

Engine, R & R 1
Engine, R & R & Overhaul 2
Front Cover, R & R Or Renew 3
Front Cover Oil Seal, Renew 4
Distributor Or Oil Pump Drive Gear, Renew 5
Eccentric Shaft Rear Oil Seal, Renew 6
Eccentric Shaft Rear Roller Bearing Or Plug, Renew 7
Oil Pan Or Gasket, Renew 8
Front Housing Or Sealing Rubbers, Renew 9
Tubulat Dowel, Renew 10
Rotor Assy Or Housing, Front Or Rear, R & R Or Renew 11
Apex Seal, Corner Seal, Side Seal Or Spring, Renew 12
Oil Seals, Rings Or Sprint, Renew 13
Rotor Bearings, Renew 14
Intermediate Or Rear Housing, Renew 15
Stationary Gear, Renew 16
Main Bearings, Renew 17
Stationary Gear Oil Seal Or "O" Ring, Renew 18
Eccentric Shaft, R & R Or Renew 19

1—ENGINE, R & R

Does not include transfer of any part of engine or replacement of special equipment.
RX2 .... 4.7
RX3—
Std Trans ①4.1
Auto Trans ①4.6
RX4, Rotary Pick-Up, Cosmo—
Std Trans ①3.8
Auto Trans ①4.3
①With Air Cond, Add. 0.6

2—ENGINE, R & R & OVERHAUL

Includes: R & R all worn bearings, bushings, gaskets & perform minor tune-up
RX2 .... 14.8
RX3—
Std Trans ①14.8
Auto Trans ①15.3
RX4, Cosmo, Rotary Pick-Up—
Std Trans ①14.5
Auto Trans ①15.0
①With Air Cond, Add. 0.6

3—FRONT COVER, R & R OR RENEW

RX2 .... 3.7
RX3, Exc 3.7
W/Air Cond 4.3
RX4, Cosmo, Exc 3.5
W/Air Cond 4.1
Rotary Pick-Up 3.5

4—FRONT COVER OIL SEAL, RENEW

RX2 .... 1.2
RX3-4, Cosmo, Exc 0.8
W/Air Cond 1.1
Rotary Pick-Up 0.8

5—DISTRIBUTOR OR OIL PUMP DRIVE GEAR, RENEW

RX2 .... 3.4
RX3, Exc 3.8
W/Air Cond 4.4
RX4, Cosmo, Exc 3.6
W/Air Cond 4.2
Rotary Pick-Up 3.6

6—ECCENTRIC SHAFT REAR OIL SEAL, RENEW

Includes: R & R trans & clutch
RX2—
L/Console 2.4
W/Console 2.6
RX3 .... 2.9
RX4, Cosmo 2.7
Rotary Pick-Up 2.7

7—ECCENTRIC SHAFT REAR ROLLER BEARING OR PLUG, RENEW

Includes: R & R trans & clutch
RX2—
L/Console 2.9
W/Console 3.1
RX3, Exc 3.4
W/Auto Trans 4.1
RX4, Cosmo, Exc 3.3
W/Auto Trans 4.0
Rotary Pick-Up, Exc 3.3
W/Auto Trans 4.0

8—OIL PAN OR GASKET, RENEW

All Models 0.8

9—FRONT HOUSING OR SEALING RUBBERS, RENEW

Includes: R & R engine, alternator, manifolds, oil pan & flywheel
RX2 .... 13.6
RX3, Exc ①13.0
Auto Trans ①13.5
RX4, Exc ①12.7
Auto Trans ①13.2
Rotary Pick-Up, Exc 12.7
Auto Trans 13.2
①With Air Cond, Add. 0.6

10—TUBULAR DOWEL, RENEW

Includes: R & R engine, alternator, manifolds, oil pan & flywheel
RX2 .... 13.6
RX3, Exc ①13.0
Auto Trans ①13.5
RX4 & Cosmo, Exc ①12.7
Auto Trans ①13.2

(Continued)

Engine (ROTARY)—TIME Cont'd

Rotary Pick-Up, Exc … 12.7
Auto Trans … 13.2
①*With Air Cond, Add.* … *0.6*

11—ROTOR ASSY OR HOUSING, FRONT OR REAR, R & R OR RENEW

RX2 … 14.0
RX3—
Std Trans … ①13.0
Auto Trans … ①13.5
RX4, Cosmo—
Std Trans … ①12.7
Auto Trans … ①13.2
Rotary Pick-Up—
Std Trans … 12.7
Auto Trans … 13.2
①*With Air Cond, Add.* … *0.6*

12—APEX SEAL, CORNER SEAL, SIDE SEAL OR SPRING, RENEW

Includes: R & R engine, alternator, manifolds, oil pan & flywheel

RX2 … 14.0
RX3—
Std Trans … ①13.0
Auto Trans … ①13.5
RX4, Cosmo—
Std Trans … ①12.7
Auto Trans … ①13.2
Rotary Pick-Up—
Std Trans … 12.7
Auto Trans … 13.2
①*With Air Cond, Add.* … *0.6*

13—OIL SEALS, RINGS OR SPRING, RENEW

Includes: R & R engine, alternator, manifolds, oil pan & flywheel

RX2—
Inner And/Or Outer … 14.0
RX3—
Std Trans … ①13.0
Auto Trans … ①13.5
RX4, Cosmo—
Std Trans … ①12.7
Auto Trans … ①13.2
Rotary Pick-Up—
Std Trans … 12.7
Auto Trans … 13.2
①*With Air Cond, Add.* … *0.6*

14—ROTOR BEARINGS, RENEW

Includes: R & R engine, alternator, manifolds, oil pan & flywheel

RX2—
One Rotor … 14.5
Two Rotors … 15.0
RX3—
Std Trans, One Rotor … ①13.3
Two Rotors … ①13.5
Auto Trans, One Rotor … ①13.8
Two Rotors … ①14.0
RX4, Cosmo, Rotary Pick-Up—
Std Trans, One Rotor … ①13.0
Two Rotors … ①13.2
Auto Trans, One Rotor … ①13.5
Two Rotors … ①13.7
①*With Air Cond, Add.* … *0.6*

15—INTERMEDIATE OR REAR HOUSING, RENEW

Includes: R & R engine, alternator, manifolds, oil pan & flywheel

RX2 … 14.0
RX3—
Std Trans … ①13.0
Auto Trans … ①13.5
RX4, Cosmo—
Std Trans … ①12.7
Auto Trans … ①13.2
Rotary Pick-Up—
Std Trans … 12.7
Auto Trans … 13.2
①*With Air Cond, Add.* … *0.6*

16—STATIONARY GEAR, RENEW

Includes: R & R engine, alternator, manifolds, oil pan, flywheel & stationary gear

RX2 … 14.0
RX3—
Std Trans … ①13.0
Auto Trans … ①13.5
RX4, Cosmo—
Std Trans … ①12.7
Auto Trans … ①13.2
Rotary Pick-Up—
Std Trans … 12.7
Auto Trans … 13.2
①*With Air Cond, Add.* … *0.6*

17—MAIN BEARINGS, RENEW

Includes: R & R engine, alternator, manifolds, oil pan, flywheel & stationary gear

RX2—
One … 14.3
Two … 14.5
RX3—
Std Trans, One … ①13.3
Two … ①13.5
Auto Trans, One … ①13.8
Two … ①14.0
RX4, Cosmo, Rotary Pick-Up—
Std Trans, One … ①13.0
Two … ①13.2
Auto Trans, One … ①13.5
Two … ①13.7
①*With Air Cond, Add.* … *0.6*

18—STATIONARY GEAR OIL SEAL OR "O" RING, RENEW

Includes: R & R engine, alternator, manifolds, oil pan, flywheel & stationary gear.

RX2 … 14.0
RX3—
Std Trans … ①13.0
Auto Trans … ①13.5
RX4, Cosmo—
Std Trans … ①12.7
Auto Trans … ①13.2
Rotary Pick-Up—
Std Trans … 12.7
Auto Trans … 13.2
①*With Air Cond, Add.* … *0.6*

19—ECCENTRIC SHAFT, R & R OR RENEW

Includes: R & R engine, manifolds, oil pan, flywheel, front, rear & intermediate housings & rotor

RX2 … 14.0
RX3—
Std Trans … ①13.0
Auto Trans … ①13.5
RX4, Cosmo—
Std Trans … ①12.7
Auto Trans … ①13.2
Rotary Pick-Up—
Std Trans … 12.7
Auto Trans … 13.2
①*With Air Cond, Add.* … *0.6*

Clutch, Mounts & Manual Transmission—TIME

OPERATION INDEX

Flywheel, R & R Or Renew … *1*
Flywheel Ring Gear, Renew … *2*
Clutch Or Disc, Renew … *3*
Release Bearing, Renew … *4*
Release Fork (Or Lever), Renew … *5*
Engine Mounts, Renew … *6*
Clutch Housing, Renew … *7*
Clutch Housing Oil Seal, Renew … *8*
Clutch Master Cylinder, Renew … *9*
Clutch Master Cylinder, R & R & Overhaul … *10*
Reservoir, Renew … *11*
Clutch Release Cylinder, Renew … *12*
Clutch Release Cylinder, R & R & Overhaul … *13*
Clutch System, Bleed … *14*
Transmission Assy, R & R Or Renew … *15*
Trans Case, Renew … *16*
Bearing Cover, Renew … *17*
Under Cover Or Gasket, Renew … *18*
Extension Housing, R & R Or Renew … *19*
Extension Housing Oil Seal, Renew … *20*
Trans Drive Shaft Shift Fork Or Shift Rod, Renew … *21*
Trans, R & R & Overhaul … *22*
Control Or Select (Inner Or Outer) Lever, Renew … *23*
Gear Shift Or Selector Lever, Renew … *24*
Gear Shift Control Case, Renew … *25*
Select Lock Spindle, Renew … *26*

1—FLYWHEEL, R & R OR RENEW

Exc Below—
L/Console … 2.7
W/Console … 2.9
RX3 … 3.2
RX4, Cosmo … 3.1
Rotary Pick-Up … 3.1
808 … 2.7
B1600, B1800 … 2.6
GLC … 2.6

2—FLYWHEEL RING GEAR, RENEW

Exc Below—
L/Console … 2.9
W/Console … 3.1
RX3 … 3.4
RX4, Cosmo … 3.3
Rotary Pick-Up … 3.3
808 … 2.9
B1600, B1800 … 2.8
GLC … 2.8

3—CLUTCH OR DISC, RENEW

Exc Below—
L/Console … 2.4
W/Console … 2.6
RX3 … 2.9
RX4, Cosmo … 2.8
Rotary Pick-Up … 2.8
808 … 2.4
B1600, B1800 … 2.3
GLC … 2.3

4—RELEASE BEARING, RENEW

Exc Below—
L/Console … 2.2
W/Console … 2.4
RX3 … 2.7
RX4, Cosmo … 2.6
Rotary Pick-Up … 2.6
808 … 2.2
B1600, B1800 … 2.1
GLC … 2.1

5—RELEASE FORK (OR LEVER), RENEW

Exc Below—
L/Console … 2.2
W/Console … 2.4
RX3 … 2.7
RX4, Cosmo … 2.6
Rotary Pick-Up … 2.6
808 … 2.2
B1600, B1800 … 2.1
GLC … 2.1

6—ENGINE MOUNTS, RENEW

616—
Each Side … 0.5
Rear … 0.2
B1600—
Right Side … 0.5
Left Side … 0.4
Both … 0.7
RX2—
Right Side … 0.8
Left Side … 0.5
Rear … 0.3
RX3—
Right Side … 0.6
Left Side … 0.5
Both … 1.0
RX4, Cosmo, Rotary Pick-Up—
Right Side … 0.4
Left Side … 0.3
Both … 0.5
808—
Right Side, Exc … 0.3
1300 Eng W/Air Cond … 0.9
Left Side, Exc … 0.3
1600 Eng W/Air Cond … 1.0
Both Sides, Exc … 0.5
With Air Cond … 1.2
GLC—
Right Exc … 0.3
W/Air Cond … 0.9
Left … 0.3
Both Exc … 0.5
W/Air Cond … 1.0

(Continued)

Clutch, Mounts & Manual Transmission—TIME Cont'd

B1800, One 0.3
Both 0.5

7—CLUTCH HOUSING, RENEW

RX2—
L/Console 2.2
W/Console 2.6
RX3 ....3.1
RX4, Cosmo 3.0
Rotary Pick-Up 3.0
808 ....2.5
B1600, B1800 ....2.4
GLC 2.4

8—CLUTCH HOUSING OIL SEAL, RENEW

RX2—
L/Console 2.4
W/Console 2.6
RX3 ....3.1
RX4, Cosmo 3.0
Rotary Pick-Up 3.0
808 ....2.5
B1600, B1800 ....2.4
GLC 2.4

9—CLUTCH MASTER CYLINDER, RENEW

All Models 0.4

10—CLUTCH MASTER CYLINDER, R & R & OVERHAUL

All Models 0.6

11—RESERVOIR, RENEW

All Models 0.2

12—CLUTCH RELEASE CYLINDER, RENEW

All Models 0.3

13—CLUTCH RELEASE CYLINDER, R & R & OVERHAUL

All Models 0.4

14—CLUTCH SYSTEM, BLEED

All Models 0.2

15—TRANSMISSION ASSY, R & R OR RENEW

616—
L/Console 2.1
W/Console 2.4
RX2—
L/Console 2.2
W/Console 2.5
RX3 ....2.6
RX4, Cosmo 2.5
Rotary Pick-Up 2.5
808 ....2.1
B1600, B1800 ....2.0
GLC 2.0

16—TRANSMISSION CASE, RENEW

Exc Below—
L/Console 4.6
W/Console 4.9
RX3—
4 Speed 5.0
5 Speed 5.9
RX4, Cosmo, Rotary Pick-Up—
4 Speed 4.9
5 Speed 5.8
808 (1300 Eng) 4.5
B1600 ....4.4
GLC—
4 Speed 4.4
5 Speed 4.9
808 (1600 Eng)—
4 Speed 4.5
5 Speed 5.4
B1800—
4 Speed 4.2
5 Speed 5.3

17—BEARING COVER, RENEW

616—
L/Console 2.5
W/Console 2.8

18—UNDER COVER OR GASKET, RENEW

All Models 0.4

19—EXTENSION HOUSING, R & R OR RENEW

Exc Below—
L/Console 1.4
W/Console 1.7
RX3 ....2.4
RX4, Cosmo 2.3
Rotary Pick-Up 3.2
808 ....2.1
B1600, B1800 ....1.9
GLC 2.1

20—EXTENSION HOUSING OIL SEAL, RENEW

Exc Below 0.4
RX3 ....0.7
RX4, Cosmo 0.8
Rotary Pick-Up 0.5

21—TRANS DRIVE SHAFT, SHIFT FORK OR SHIFT ROD, RENEW

616—
L/Console 4.3
W/Console 4.6
RX2—
L/Console 4.4
W/Console 4.7
808 ....3.6
B1600 ....3.5
RX3-4, Cosmo, Rotary Pick-Up—
4 Speed (Rod) 3.5
4 Speed (Fork) 4.8
5 Speed (Rod) 3.6
5 Speed (Fork) 5.7

22—TRANSMISSION, R & R & OVERHAUL

Exc Below—
L/Console 6.2
W/Console 6.5
RX3—
4 Speed 5.8
5 Speed 6.7
RX4, Cosmo, Rotary Pick-Up—
4 Speed 5.7
5 Speed 6.6
B1600 ....5.3
GLC—
4 Speed 5.3
5 Speed 5.9
808—
4 Speed 5.4
5 Speed 6.2
B1800—
4 Speed 4.9
5 Speed 6.1

23—CONTROL OR SELECT (INNER OR OUTER) LEVER, RENEW

616—
L/Console 1.5
W/Console 1.8
RX2—
L/Console 1.6
W/Console 1.9
RX3 ....2.1
RX4, Cosmo 2.0
Rotary Pick-Up 2.9
808 ....1.8
B1600, B1800 ....1.6
GLC 1.8

24—GEAR SHIFT OR SELECTOR LEVER, RENEW

Exc Below—
L/Console 0.2
W/Console 0.5
RX3-4, Cosmo, 808 ....0.5
Rotary Pick-Up 0.3
B1600, B1800, GLC 0.3

25—GEAR SHIFT CONTROL CASE, RENEW

Exc Below—
L/Console 0.4
W/Console 0.7
RX3-4, Cosmo 0.6
Rotary Pick-Up 0.5
808, GLC 0.6
B1600, B1800 ....0.5

26—SELECT LOCK SPINDLE, RENEW

Exc Below—
L/Console 0.5
W/Console 0.8
RX3-4, Cosmo 0.6
Rotary Pick-Up 0.5
808, GLC 0.6
B1600, B1800 ....0.5

Automatic Transmission—TIME

OPERATION INDEX

Trans, R & R Or Renew 1
Trans, R & R & Overhaul 2
Torque Converter, R & R Or Renew 3
Driveplate, R & R Or Renew 4
Oil Pan Or Gasket, R & R Or Renew 5
Valve Body, Renew 6
Extension Housing Or Gasket, R & R Or Renew 7
Governor, R & R Or Renew 8
Governor, R & R & Overhaul 9
Line Pressure, Check 10
Vacuum Control Unit, Renew 11
Kickdown Switch, Renew 12
Downshift Solenoid, Renew 13
Inhibitor Switch, Renew 14
Oil Cooler, R & R Or Renew 15
Gearshift Select Lever, Renew 16
Gearshift Lower Select Rod, Renew 17

1—TRANSMISSION, R & R OR RENEW

616, 808, GLC 2.6
RX3-4, Cosmo 3.0
Rotary Pick-Up 3.0

2—TRANSMISSION, R & R & OVERHAUL

616, 808, GLC 10.1
RX3-4, Cosmo 10.5
Rotary Pick-Up 10.5

3—TORQUE CONVERTER, R & R OR RENEW

616, 808, GLC 2.9
RX3-4, Cosmo 3.3
Rotary Pick-Up 3.3

4—DRIVE PLATE, R & R OR RENEW

616, 808 ....3.4
RX3-4, Cosmo 3.8
Rotary Pick-Up 3.8
GLC 3.1

5—OIL PAN OR GASKET, R & R OR RENEW

616 ....0.8
808, Rotary Pick-Up 0.6
RX3-4, Cosmo 0.7
GLC 0.5

6—VALVE BODY ASSY, RENEW

Exc Below 1.1
RX3-4, Cosmo 1.2
GLC 1.0

7—EXTENSION HOUSING OR GASKET, R & R OR RENEW

616, 808, GLC 1.4
RX3 ....1.5
RX4, Cosmo 1.6
Rotary Pick-Up 3.3

8—GOVERNOR, R & R OR RENEW

616, 808, GLC 1.6
RX3 ....1.7
RX4, Cosmo 1.8
Rotary Pick-Up 3.4

9—GOVERNOR, R & R & OVERHAUL

616, 808, GLC 1.8

(Continued)

Automatic Transmission—TIME Cont'd

RX3 ... 1.9
RX4, Cosmo ... 2.0
Rotary Pick-Up ... 3.6

10—LINE PRESSURE, CHECK

Exc Below ... 0.5
616, 808, GLC ... 0.4

11—VACUUM CONTROL UNIT, RENEW

All Models ... 0.3

12—KICKDOWN SWITCH, RENEW

All Models ... 0.2

13—DOWNSHIFT SOLENOID, RENEW

Exc Below ... 0.5
616, 808, GLC ... 0.4

14—INHIBITOR SWITCH, RENEW

808, GLC ... 0.4
RX3 ... 0.5
RX4, Cosmo ... 0.3
Rotary Pick-Up ... 0.3

15—OIL COOLER, R & R OR RENEW

808 ... 0.6
Rotary Pick-Up ... 0.8
RX3-4, Cosmo, Exc ... 0.8
  W/Air Cond ... 0.9

16—GEARSHIFT SELECT LEVER, RENEW

616 ... 0.5
808, GLC ... 0.6
RX3 ... 0.7
RX4, Cosmo ... 0.6
Rotary Pick-Up ... 0.6

17—GEARSHIFT LOWER SELECT ROD, RENEW

808, GLC ... 0.6
RX3-4, Cosmo ... 0.7
Rotary Pick-Up ... 0.6

Brakes, Steering, Suspension, Universals & Rear Axle—TIME

OPERATION INDEX

Brake Shoes Or Friction Pads, Renew ... 1
Master Cylinder, Renew ... 2
Master Cylinder, R & R & Overhaul ... 3
Reservoir, Renew ... 4
Wheel Cylinders, Renew ... 5
Wheel Cylinders, R & R & Overhaul ... 6
Caliper Assy, Renew ... 7
Caliper Assy, R & R & Overhaul ... 8
Bleed System ... 9
Brake Hose, Renew ... 10
Disc Or Hub, R & R Or Renew ... 11
Power Brake Unit, Renew ... 12
Power Brake Unit, R & R & Overhaul ... 13
Power Brake Check Valve, Renew ... 14
Brake Drum(S), Renew ... 15
Brake Pedal, Renew ... 16
Parking Brake Cable, Renew ... 17
Parking Brake Lever, Renew ... 18
Release Rod Or Button, Renew ... 19
Sector Assy, Renew ... 20
Brake Fail Indicator, Renew ... 21
Steering Joint, Renew ... 22
Steering Gear, R & R Or Renew ... 23
Steering Gear, R & R & Overhaul ... 24
Side Ocver Or Gasket, Renew ... 25
Sector Shaft Or Oil Seal, Renew ... 26
Pitman Arm, Renew ... 27
Worm Ball Nut Shaft Oil Seal, Renew ... 28
Front Wheel Alignment ... 29
Tie Rod, Renew ... 30
Ball Joints (Tie Rod), Renew ... 31
Center Link, Renew ... 32
Knuckle Arm, Renew ... 33
Idler Arm Or Bushings, Renew ... 34
Idler Arm Spindle, Renew ... 35
Suspension Arm Or Ball Joint, Renew ... 36
Upper Control Arm, Renew ... 37
Lower Control Arm, Renew ... 38
Steering Knuckle, Renew ... 39
Ball Joints, Upper Or Lower, Renew ... 40
Power Steering Pump, Renew ... 41
Power Steering Pump, R & R & Overhaul ... 42
Power Steering Hoses, Renew ... 43
Coil Springs, Renew ... 44
Shock Absorbers, Renew ... 45
Shock Absorbers, R & R & Overhaul ... 46
Knuckle Arm Ball Joint, Renew ... 47
Arm Bushing, Renew ... 48
Stabilizer Bar Or Rubber Bushings, Renew ... 49
Crossmember, Renew ... 50
Rear Lateral Rod, Renew ... 51
Rear Link Assy, Renew ... 52
Universal Joints, Renew ... 53
Rear Axle Shaft, R & R Or Renew ... 54
Wheel Bearings, Renew ... 55
Wheel Bearings Oil Seal(S), Renew ... 56
Rear Axle Casing, R & R Or Renew ... 57
Differential Assy, R & R Or Renew ... 58
Differential Assy, R & R & Overhaul ... 59
Companion Flange, Renew ... 60
Drive Pinion Oil Seal, Renew ... 61

1—BRAKE SHOES OR FRICTION PADS, RENEW

Drum Type—
  Each Wheel ... 0.5
Disc Type—
  Each Wheel ... 0.4

2—MASTER CYLINDER, RENEW

Exc Below ... 0.7
808 ... 0.8
B1600, B1800 ... 0.8

3—MASTER CYLINDER, R & R & OVERHAUL

Exc Below ... 1.0
RX3-4, Cosmo ... 0.9
Rotary Pick-Up ... 0.9

4—RESERVOIR, RENEW

All Models ... 0.2

5—WHEEL CYLINDERS, RENEW

Each, Exc ... 0.8
  B1600 ... 0.9

6—WHEEL CYLINDERS, R & R & OVERHAUL

Each, Exc ... 0.9
  B1600 ... 1.1

7—CALIPER ASSY, RENEW

Each, Exc ... 0.7
  RX4, Cosmo ... 0.6
  Rotary Pick-Up ... 0.6

8—CALIPER ASSY, R & R & OVERHAUL

Each, Exc ... 1.1
  RX4, Cosmo ... 0.9
  Rotary Pick-Up ... 0.9

9—BLEED SYSTEM

All Models ... 0.4

10—BRAKE HOSE, RENEW

Each ... 0.6

11—DISC OR HUB, R & R OR RENEW

Exc Below ... 0.9
B1600 ... 0.7

12—POWER BRAKE UNIT, RENEW

Exc Below ... 0.8
RX3-4 ... 0.9
Rotary Pick-Up ... 0.9
Cosmo, 808, B1800 ... 1.0

13—POWER BRAKE UNIT, R & R & OVERHAUL

Exc Below ... 1.2
Cosmo ... 1.3
808, B1800 ... 1.3

14—POWER BRAKE CHECK VALVE, RENEW

All Models ... 0.1

15—BRAKE DRUMS, RENEW

All Models, Each ... 0.4

16—BRAKE PEDAL, RENEW

Exc Below ... 0.4
RX3-4, GLC ... 0.3
Rotary Pick-Up, B1800 ... 0.5
808, B1600 ... 0.3

17—PARKING BRAKE CABLE, RENEW

Exc Below—
  Front—
    L/Console ... 0.6
    W/Console ... 0.8
  Rear—
    One ... 0.8
    Both ... 1.5
RX3-4, 808—
  Front ... 0.6
  Rear ... 0.7
Cosmo—
  Front ... 0.6
  Center ... 0.8
  Rear ... 0.3
Pick-Ups—
  Front ... 0.6
  Rear ... 0.7
GLC—
  Front ... 0.5
  Rear ... 0.7

18—PARKING BRAKE LEVER, RENEW

Exc Below—
  L/Console ... 0.3
  W/Console ... 0.5
RX3, 808 ... 0.3
RX4 ... 0.4
Pick-Ups ... 0.3
Cosmo ... 1.4

19—RELEASE ROD OR BUTTON, RENEW

Exc Below—
  L/Console ... 0.3
  W/Console ... 0.5
RX3, 808, GLC ... 0.3
RX4, Cosmo ... 0.5

20—SECTOR ASSY, RENEW

Exc Below—
  L/Console ... 0.4
  W/Console ... 0.6
RX3, 808, GLC ... 0.3
RX4, Cosmo ... 0.5

21—BRAKE FAIL INDICATOR, RENEW

All Models ... 0.3

22—STEERING JOINT, RENEW

Exc Below ... 0.5
RX4, Cosmo ... 0.8

23—STERING GEAR, R & R OR RENEW

616—
  L/Steering Lock—
    Column Shift ... 2.3
    Floor Shift ... 2.2
  W/Steering Lock ... 1.2
RX2—
  L/Steering Lock ... 2.2
  W/Steering Lock ... 1.2
RX3 ... 2.2
RX4, Cosmo ... 1.1
Rotary Pick-Up ... 0.8
808 ... 2.5
B1600 ... 2.3
GLC ... 1.6
B1800 ... 2.6

24—STEERING GEAR, R & R & OVERHAUL

616—
  L/Steering Lock—
    Column Shift ... 3.4
    Floor Shift ... 3.3
  W/Steering Lock ... 2.1
RX2—
  L/Steering Lock ... 3.3
  W/Steering Lock ... 2.1
RX3 ... 3.2

(Continued)

Brakes, Steering, Suspension, Universals & Rear Axle—TIME Cont'd

RX4, Cosmo 2.2
Rotary Pick-Up 1.5
808 ..... 3.5
B1600 ..... 3.4
GLC 2.3
B1800 ..... 3.6

25—SIDE COVER OR GASKET, RENEW

Exc Below 0.5
RX4, Cosmo 0.6
GLC 0.4

26—SECTOR SHAFT OR OIL SEAL, RENEW

Exc Below 0.9
RX4, Cosmo 1.2
GLC 0.8
B1800 ..... 1.1

27—PITMAN ARM, RENEW

All Models 0.4

28—WORM BALL NUT SHAFT OIL SEAL, RENEW

All Models 1.8

29—FRONT WHEEL ALIGNMENT

Exc Below 1.3
RX3, 808 ..... 1.1
Rotary Pick-Up 1.6
B1600, B1800 ..... 1.6

30—TIE ROD, RENEW

All Models—
Each 0.5
All 0.7

31—BALL JOINTS (TIE ROD), RENEW

All Models—
One Or Two 0.6
Three Or Four 0.9

32—CENTER LINK, RENEW

All Models 0.8

33—KNUCKLE ARM, RENEW

Includes: Toe-in adjust
Exc Below 0.8
RX3-4, Cosmo, B1600 ..... 0.6

34—IDLER ARM OR BUSHINGS, RENEW

All Models 0.4

35—IDLER ARM SPINDLE, RENEW

All Models 0.5

36—SUSPENSION ARM OR BALL JOINT, RENEW

RX3 ..... 0.8
808 (1300 Eng) 0.7
808 (1600 Eng) 0.8

37—UPPER CONTROL ARM, RENEW

Rotary Pick-Up 1.6
B1600 ..... 1.6

38—LOWER CONTROL ARM, RENEW

RX4, Cosmo 2.1
Rotary Pick-Up 2.3
B1600, B1800 ..... 2.3

39—STEERING KNUCKLE, RENEW

Rotary Pick-Up 1.6
GLC 1.3
B1600, B1800 ..... 1.6

40—BALL JOINTS, UPPER OR LOWER, RENEW

RX4, Cosmo 1.4
Rotary Pick-Up 0.5
B1600, B1800 ..... 0.5

41—POWER STEERING PUMP, RENEW

All Models, Exc 0.7
W/Air Cond 0.8

42—POWER STEERING PUMP, R & R & OVERHAUL

All Models, Exc 1.1
W/Air Cond 1.2

43—POWER STEERING HOSES, RENEW

Each 0.2
All 0.4

44—COIL SPRING(S), RENEW

Includes: R & R shock absorbers
Front, Each—
Exc Below 1.3
Rotary Pick-Up 0.9
B1600, B1800 ..... 0.9
RX3, 808, GLC 0.8
RX4, Cosmo 1.4
Rear, Each—
Exc Below 0.7
RX3-4, 808, B1600 ..... 0.9
Rotary Pick-Up 0.9
Pick-Ups 1.0
Cosmo 0.6
GLC, B1800 ..... 0.9

45—SHOCK ABSORBERS, RENEW

Front, Each—
Exc Below 1.3
Rotary Pick-Up 0.4
B1600 ..... 0.4
RX3, 808, GLC 1.1
RX4, Cosmo 1.8
Rear, Each—
Exc Below 0.7
RX3, Cosmo 0.4
RX4, Exc 0.5
Wagon 0.4
Rotary Pick-Up 0.4
808, B1600, B1800 ..... 0.4
GLC 0.3

46—SHOCK ABSORBERS, R & R & OVERHAUL

Front, Each—
Exc Below 2.0
RX3, 808, GLC 1.8
RX4, Cosmo 2.5

47—KNUCKLE ARM BALL JOINT, RENEW

All Models 1.1

48—ARM BUSHING, RENEW

All Models 0.6

49—STABILIZER BAR OR RUBBER BUSHINGS, RENEW

Exc Below 0.5
RX3, 808 ..... 0.6
RX4, Cosmo 0.7

50—CROSSMEMBER, RENEW

Includes: R & R stabilizer, arm, engine mounting & wheel alignment adjust.
Exc Below 3.0
RX3-4, Cosmo 2.0
808 (1300 Eng) 2.7
808 (1600 Eng) 2.8
GLC 2.3

51—REAR LATERAL ROD ASSY, RENEW

All Models 0.3

52—REAR LINK ASSY, RENEW

All Models—
Lower Or Upper 0.3

583—UNIVERSAL JOINTS, RENEW

616—
One 0.7
Two 1.2
RX2—
One 0.8
Two 1.3
Three 1.8
RX3, 808, GLC—
One 0.7
Two 1.0
RX4, Cosmo—
One 1.2
Two 1.5
Three 1.8
Rotary Pick-Up, B1600, B1800—
One 0.8
Two 1.1
Three 1.4

54—REAR AXLE SHAFT, R & R OR RENEW

Exc Below 1.4
RX3-4, 808 ..... 1.0
Cosmo 1.4
Rotary Pick-Up 1.3
B1600, B1800 ..... 1.3
GLC 1.3

55—WHEEL BEARINGS, RENEW

Front, Each, Exc 0.7
B1600 ..... 0.6
Rear, Each, Exc 1.4
RX3-4 ..... 1.0
808 ..... 1.0

56—WHEEL BEARING OIL SEAL(S), RENEW

Front, Each, Exc 0.5
B1600 ..... 0.3
Rear, Each, Exc 0.8
Cosmo 1.2
Rotary Pick-Up 1.0
B1600, B1800 ..... 1.0
GLC 1.1

57—REAR AXLE CASING, R & R OR RENEW

Exc Below 3.3
RX3-4, 808 ..... 3.4
Cosmo 4.2
Rotary Pick-Up 3.5
B1600, B1800 ..... 3.5
GLC 3.6

58—DIFFERENTIAL ASSY, R & R OR RENEW

Exc Below 1.6
RX3, 808 ..... 1.5
RX4 ..... 1.6
Cosmo 2.4
Rotary Pick-Up 1.8
B1600, B1800 ..... 1.8
GLC 1.9

59—DIFFERENTIAL ASSY, R & R & OVERHAUL

Exc Below 4.0
RX3, 808 ..... 3.2
RX4 ..... 3.3
Cosmo 4.1
Rotary Pick-Up 3.5
B1600, B1800 ..... 3.5
GLC 3.6

60—COMPANION FLANGE, RENEW

All Models 0.5

61—DRIVE PINION OIL SEAL, RENEW

All Models 0.6

Speedometer, W/S Wipers, Switches & Instruments—TIME

OPERATION INDEX

Speedometer Cable, Renew 1
Speedometer Head, Renew 2
W/S Wiper Motor, Renew 3
W/S Wiper Link Set, Renew 4
W/S Wiper Arm, Renew 5
Fuel Gauge (Dash Unit), Renew 6
Fuel Tank Gauge, Renew 7
Oil Pressure Switch, Renew 8
Temperature Gauge (Dash Unit), Renew 9
Temperature Gauge Sending Unit, Renew 10
Ammeter, Renew 11
Tachometer, Renew 12
Combination Meter Assy, R & R Or Renew 13
Combination Switch, Renew 14

(Continued)

Speedometer, W/S Wipers, Switches & Instruments—TIME Cont'd

Stop Light Switch, Renew *15*
Hazard Flasher Unit, Renew *16*
Back-Up Lamp Switch, Renew *17*
Oil Level Warn Switch, Renew *18*
Water Temp Switch, Renew *19*
Thermo Switch, Renew *20*
Oil Thermo Switch, Renew *21*

1—SPEEDOMETER CABLE, RENEW
Exc Below 0.3
RX3-4, Cosmo 0.4
Rotary Pick-Up 0.4
B1600, B1800, GLC 0.4

2—SPEEDOMETER HEAD, RENEW
Exc Below 0.5
RX3, 808 .... 0.7
RX4 .... 0.9
Cosmo 1.2

3—W/S WIPER MOTOR, RENEW
Exc Below 0.5
RX4, Cosmo 0.4
Rotary Pick-Up 0.3
B1600 .... 0.3

4—W/S WIPER LINK SET, RENEW
Exc Below 0.5
RX4, Cosmo 0.4
Rotary Pick-Up 0.3
B1600 .... 0.3
B1800 .... 0.6

5—W/S WIPER ARM, RENEW
All Models, Each 0.1

6—FUEL GAUGE (DASH UNIT), RENEW
Exc Below 0.5
RX3 .... 0.6
RX4 .... 0.8
Cosmo 1.1
808 .... 0.7
B1800 .... 0.6

7—FUEL TANK GAUGE, RENEW
Exc Below 0.2
RX3, 808 .... 0.3
Rotary Pick-Up 0.7
GLC 0.6
B1800 .... 0.7

8—OIL PRESSURE SWITCH, RENEW
616 .... 0.1
RX2, 808, B1600 .... 0.2
GLC 0.4

9—TEMPERATURE GAUGE (DASH UNIT), RENEW
Exc Below 0.5
RX3, B1800 .... 0.6
RX4 .... 0.8
Cosmo 1.1
808 .... 0.7

10—TEMPERATURE GAUGE SENDING UNIT, RENEW
Exc Below 0.2
RX3-4, Cosmo 0.3
Rotary Pick-Up 0.3
808 .... 0.3

11—AMMETER, RENEW
Exc Below 0.5
RX3 .... 0.6
RX4 .... 0.8
Cosmo 1.1
808 .... 0.7

12—TACHOMETER, RENEW
Exc Below 0.5
RX3, 808 .... 0.7
RX4 .... 0.8
Cosmo 1.1

13—COMBINATION METER ASSY, R & R OR RENEW
Exc Below 0.3
RX3 .... 0.4

14—COMBINATION SWITCH, RENEW
All Models 0.4

15—STOP LIGHT SWITCH, RENEW
Exc Below 0.3
RX3-4, 808, B1600 .... 0.2
Rotary Pick-Up 0.2

16—HAZARD FLASHER UNIT, RENEW
Exc Below 0.1
Rotary Pick-Up 0.2

17—BACK-UP LAMP SWITCH, RENEW
All Models 0.2

18—OIL LEVEL WARNING SWITCH, RENEW
RX3-4, Cosmo 0.4
Rotary Pick-Up 0.4

19—WATER TEMPERATURE SWITCH, RENEW
In engine rear housing
RX3-4, Cosmo 0.2
Rotary Pick-Up 0.2

20—THERMO SWITCH, RENEW
Heat hazard warning system
All Models 0.2

21—OIL THERMO SWITCH, RENEW
RX3-4, Cosmo 0.3
Rotary Pick-Up 0.3

IDENTIFICATION

ALL MODELS.. 263

ILLUSTRATIONS

FIG 1 – ENGINE – CYLINDER BLOCK
FIG 2 – ENGINE – OIL PAN
FIG 3 – ENGINE – CYLINDER HEAD
FIG 4 – ENGINE – CRANKSHAFT & FLYWHEEL
FIG 5 – ENGINE – CAMSHAFT & TIMING MECHANISM
FIG 6 – TRANSMISSION CASE
FIG 7 – TRANSMISSION GEARS & SHAFTS
FIG 8 – FRONT SUSPENSION & STEERING – 250 SL, 280 SL
FIG 9 – FRONT SUSPENSION & STEERING – 250 SE/c, 280 SE/c/8, 280 SE/c/3.5
FIG 10 – FRONT SUSPENSION & STEERING – 250 C, 280 C, 350 SL/SLC, 450 SL/SLC

OPERATION TIMES

A

Alternator.. 272
Automatic Transmission.................... 277

B

Brakes.. 277

C

Cables (Ignition).............................. 272
Calipers.. 277
Camshaft.. 275
Carburetor.. 272
Catalytic Converter.......................... 273
Clutch.. 276
Coil, Ignition.................................. 272
Compression Test.............................. 272
Cooling System.............................. 273
Crankshaft.. 275
Cylinder Block.................................. 274
Cylinder Head.................................. 274

D

Dash Gauges.................................. 278
Differential.................................. 278
Disc Brakes.................................. 277
Distributor.................................. 272

E

Emission Controls.............................. 272
Engine Assembly.............................. 274
Engine Mountings.............................. 276
Engine Oiling.................................. 275
Engine Tune-Up.............................. 272
Exhaust System.............................. 273

F

Flywheel.. 276
Front Suspension.............................. 278
Fuel Gauges.................................. 278
Fuel Pump.. 272
Fuel Tank.. 272

G

Generator.. 272

H

Hand Brake.................................. 278
Headlight Switch.............................. 277
Heater.. 273
Hose (Brake).................................. 277
Hose (Radiator).............................. 273
Hydraulic Brakes.............................. 277

I

Ignition.. 272
Ignition Coil.................................. 272
Ignition Switch.............................. 272
Intake Manifold.............................. 273

L

Light Switches.................................. 279

M

Main Bearings.................................. 275
Master Cylinder.............................. 277

O

Oil Gauge.. 279
Oiling, Engine.................................. 275
Oil Pan.. 275
Oil Pump.. 275

P

Parking Brake.................................. 278
Piston Rings.................................. 275
Pistons.. 275
Power Brake.................................. 277
Power Steering.................................. 278

R

Radiator.. 273
Radiator Hose.................................. 273
Rear Axle.. 278
Regulator.. 272
Rocker Arms.................................. 275
Rod Bearings.................................. 275

S

Shocks (Front).................................. 278
Shocks (Rear).................................. 278
Speedometer.................................. 278
Springs (Front).................................. 278
Springs (Rear).................................. 278
Starting Motor.................................. 272
Steering.. 278
Switches (Light).............................. 279
Synchro-Mesh Trans.......................... 276

T

Temperature Gauge.......................... 279
Thermostat.................................. 273
Timing Chain.................................. 275
Torsion Bar.................................. 278
Transmission, Manual...................... 276
Transmission, Automatic.................. 277
Tune-Up, Engine.............................. 272

V

Valve System.................................. 274

W

Water Pump.................................. 273
Wheel Cylinders.............................. 277
Windshield Wiper.............................. 278

IDENTIFICATION PLATE LOCATIONS

TYPE PLATE (CHASSIS TYPE):

On left front door rear pillar face or on top of radiator header.

BODY & PAINT NUMBER PLATE:

250 SL, 280SL, on left front wheelhouse.

ALL OTHERS, on top of radiator header.

CHASSIS NUMBER:

350 SL/SLC, 450 SL/SLC, on top of radiator header.

450 SE, 450 SEL, on center portion of firewall.

ALL OTHERS, on right frame sidemember.

ENGINE NUMBER:

On left side of cylinder block.

To properly identify a Mercedes model, refer to the type plate on the vehicle:

MODEL	CHASSIS TYPE NUMBER	ENGINE TYPE NUMBER
450 SL/SLC	107.024	117.982
350 SL/SLC	107.044	117.982
250 S	108.012	108.920
250 SE	108.014	129.980
280 S/8	108.016	130.920
280 SE/8	108.018	130.980
280 SEL	108.019	130.980
280 SE 4.5	108.067	117.984
280 SEL 4.5	108.068	117.984
300 SEL	109.015	189.988
300 SEL/8	109.016	130.981
300 SEL 6.3	109.018	100.981
300 SEL 3.5	109.056	116.981
300 SEL 4.5	109.057	117.981
250 SE/C Coupe	111.021	129.981
250 SE/C Convertible	111.023	129.981
280 SE/C/8 Coupe	111.024	130.980
280 SE/C/8 Convertible	111.025	130.980
280 SE/C 3.5 Coupe	111.026	116.980
280 SE/C 3.5 Convertible	111.027	116.980
250 SL	113.043	129.982
280 SL	113.044	130.983
250/8 (1968-69) to 049262	114.010	114.920
250/8 (1970-72) to 016278	114.011	130.923
230/8 to 037477	114.015	180.954
250C from 009737	114.023	130.923
280	114.060	110.928
280C from 000333	114.073	110.921
220/8	115.010	115.920
220D/8	115.110	615.912
240D	115.117	616.916
450 SE	116.032	117.983
450 SEL	116.033	117.983
230/4	115.017	115.951
300 D	115.114	617.910
280 S	116.020	110.922

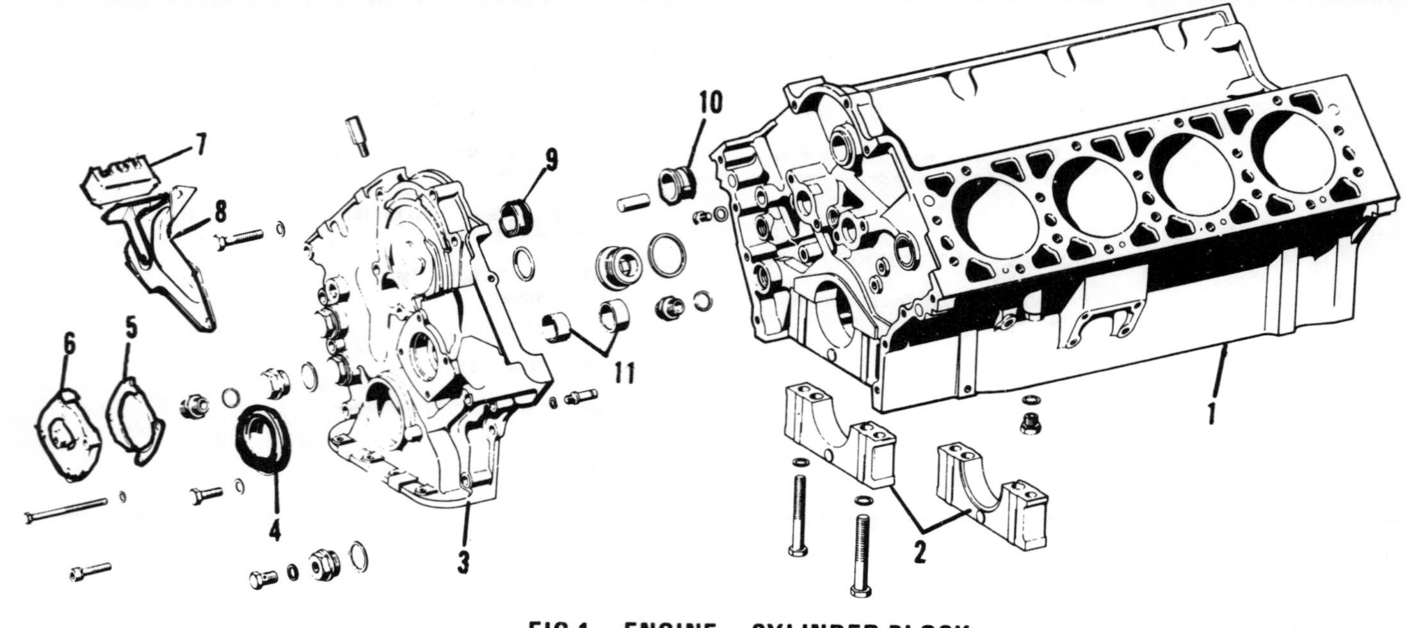

FIG 1 – ENGINE – CYLINDER BLOCK

1	Cylinder Block	7	Rubber Mount
2	Crankshaft Bearing Cap	8	Bracket
3	Timing Case Cover	9	Bushing
4	Seal Ring	10	Bushing
5	Gasket	11	Bushing
6	End Cover		

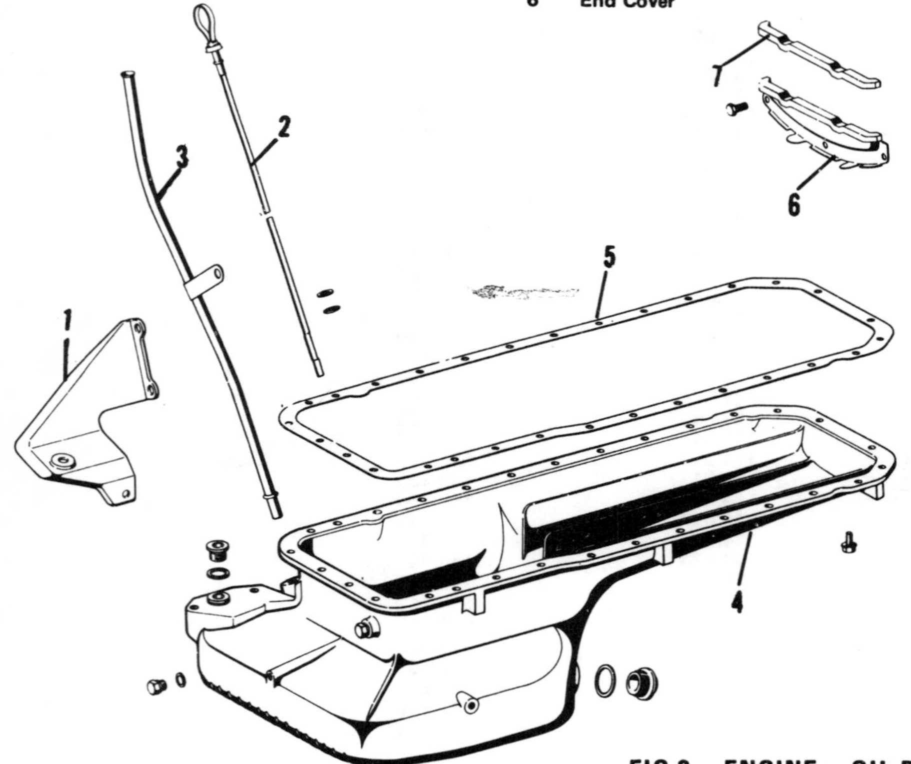

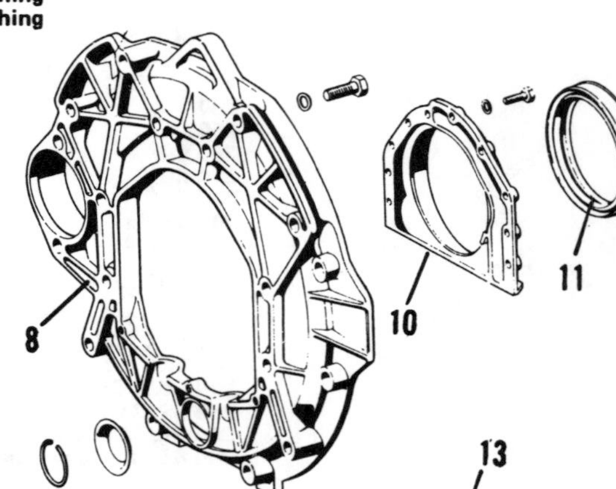

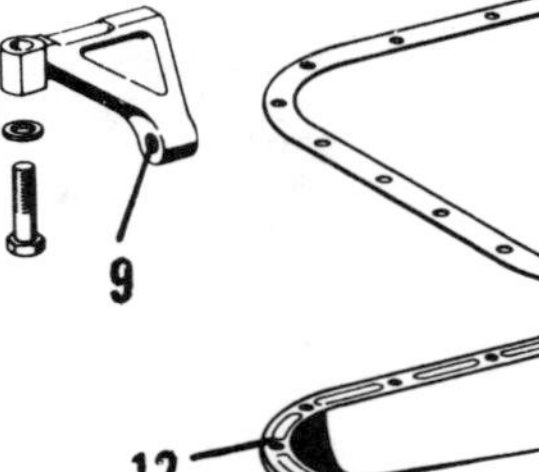

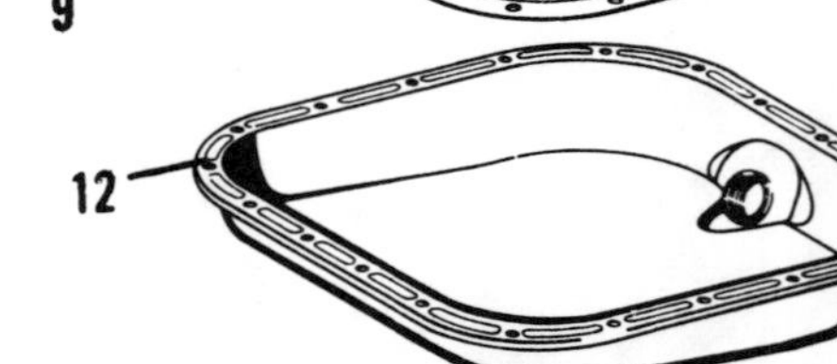

FIG 2 – ENGINE -- OIL PAN

1	Mount Bracket	8	Intermediate Flange
2	Oil Dipstick	9	Support Angle
3	Dipstick Tube	10	Rear Seal Cover
4	Oil Pan	11	Seal
5	Gasket	12	Oil Pan Sump
6	Cover Plate	13	Gasket
7	Sealing Strip		

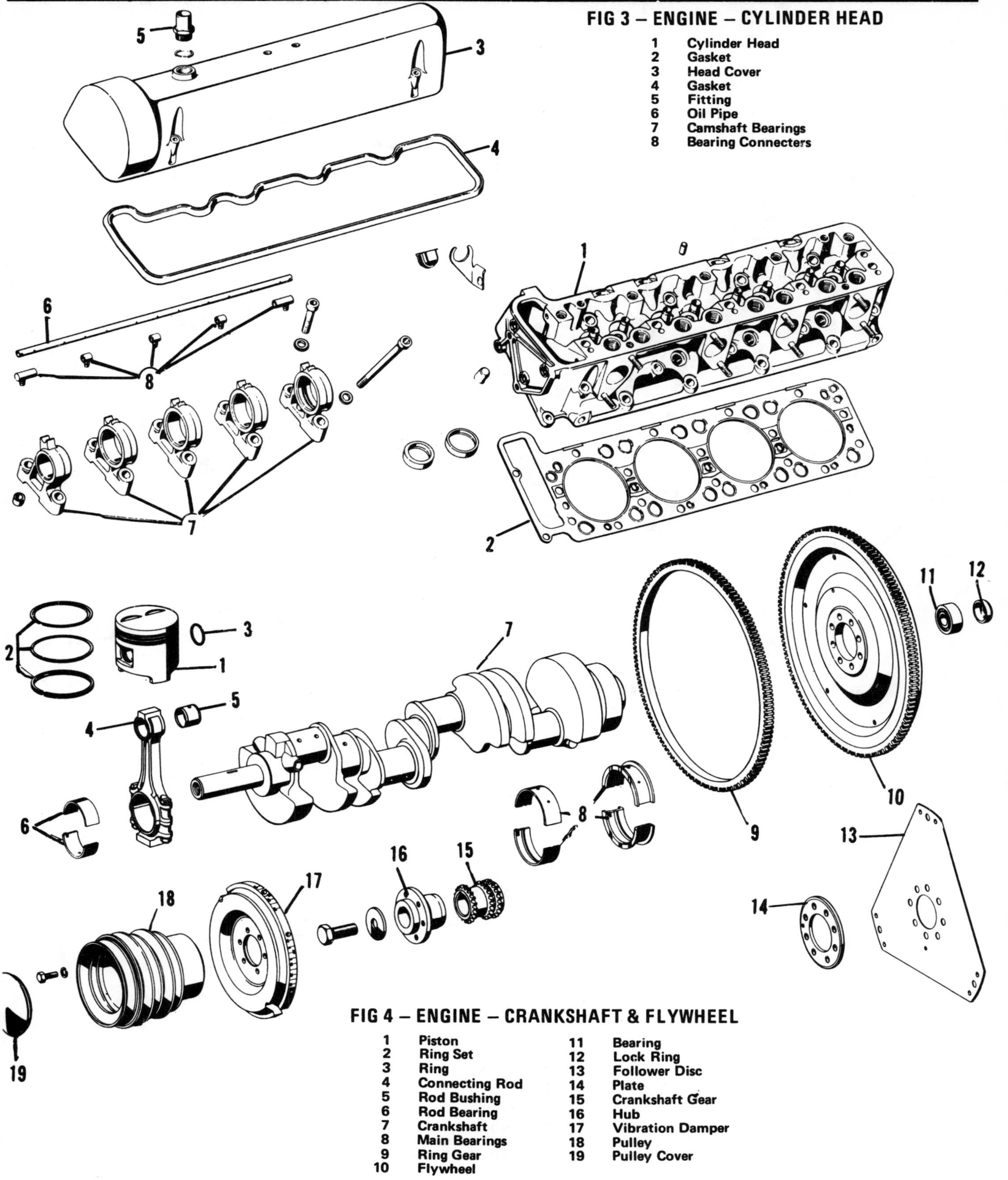

FIG 3 – ENGINE – CYLINDER HEAD

1 Cylinder Head
2 Gasket
3 Head Cover
4 Gasket
5 Fitting
6 Oil Pipe
7 Camshaft Bearings
8 Bearing Connecters

FIG 4 – ENGINE – CRANKSHAFT & FLYWHEEL

1 Piston
2 Ring Set
3 Ring
4 Connecting Rod
5 Rod Bushing
6 Rod Bearing
7 Crankshaft
8 Main Bearings
9 Ring Gear
10 Flywheel
11 Bearing
12 Lock Ring
13 Follower Disc
14 Plate
15 Crankshaft Gear
16 Hub
17 Vibration Damper
18 Pulley
19 Pulley Cover

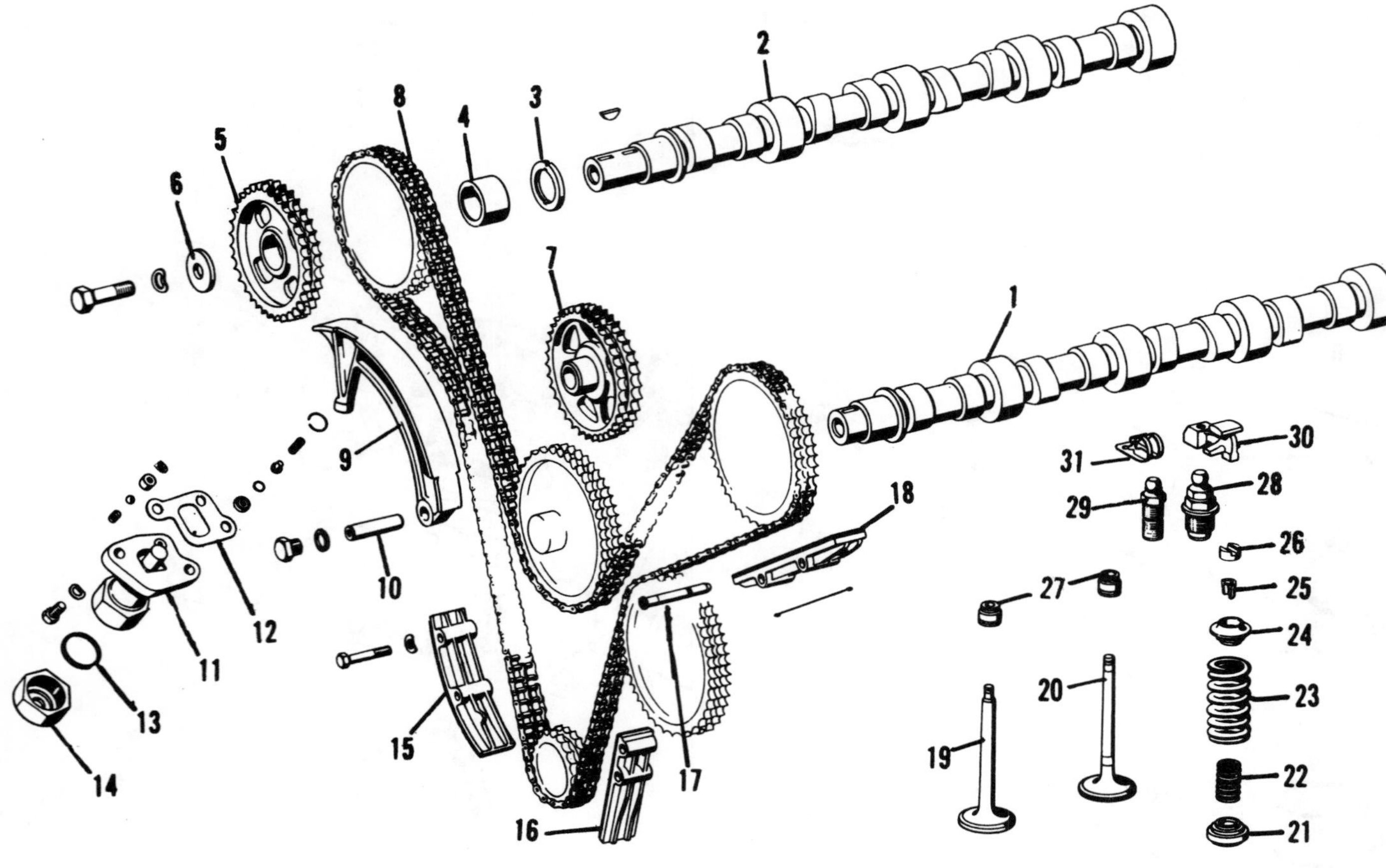

FIG 5 – ENGINE – CAMSHAFT & TIMING MECHANISM

1 Camshaft, Left
2 Camshaft, Right
3 Washer
4 Spacer Ring
5 Camshaft Gear
6 Washer
7 Guide Gear
8 Chain
9 Clamping Rail
10 Pivot Pin
11 Chain Tightener
12 Gasket
13 Seal Ring
14 Locknut
15 Sliding Rail
16 Sliding Rail
17 Pivot Pin
18 Sliding Rail
19 Exhaust Valve
20 Intake Valve
21 Rotocap
22 Spring
23 Spring
24 Retainer
25 Valve Keeper
26 Thrust Piece
27 Sealing Kit
28 Set Screw
29 Ball Head Bolt
30 Rocker Arm
31 Clamping Spring

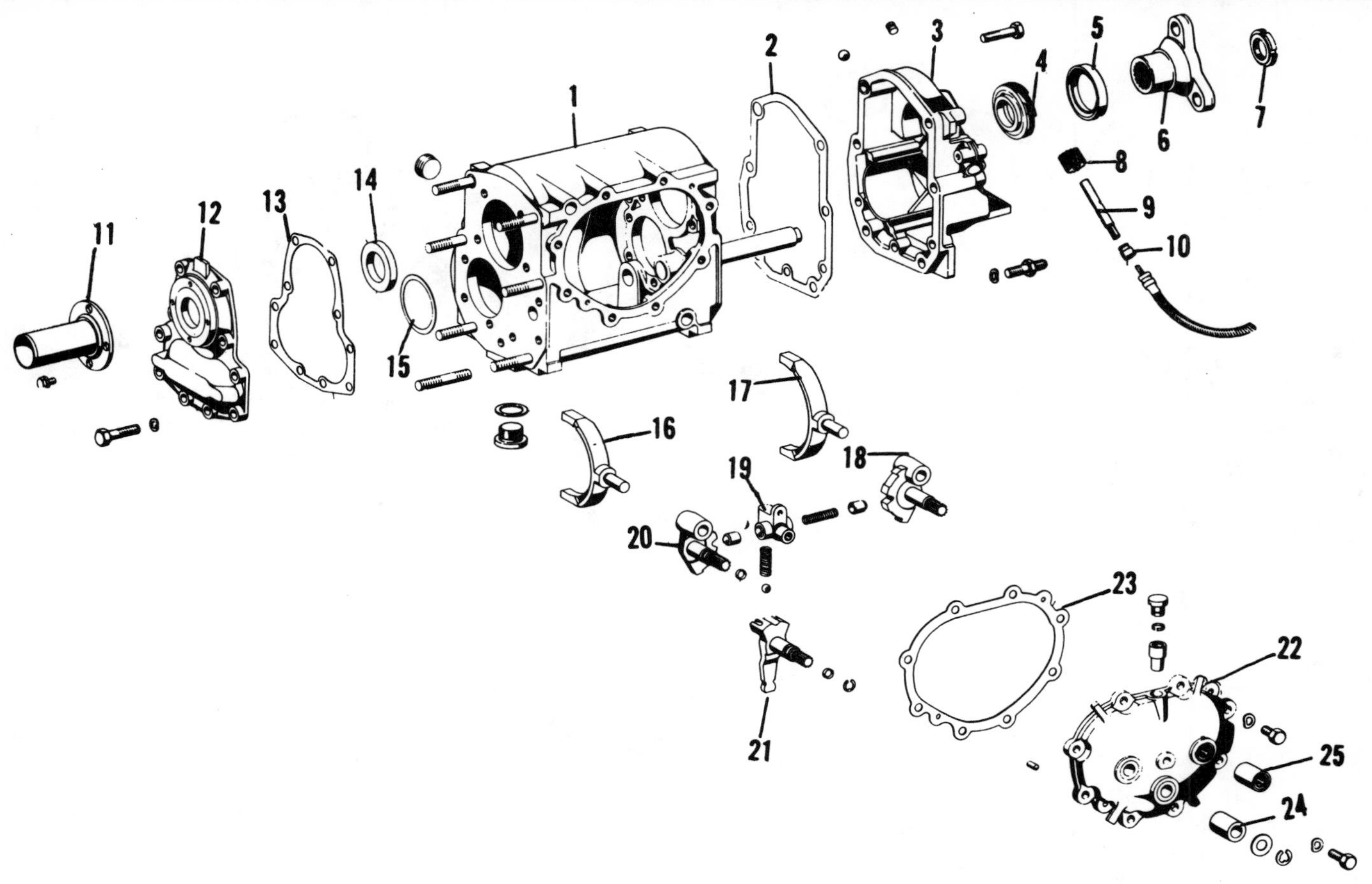

FIG 6 – TRANSMISSION CASE & RELATED PARTS

1	Transmission Case
2	Gasket
3	Rear Cover
4	Speedometer Drive Gear
5	Seal Ring
6	Joint Flange
7	Locknut
8	Speedometer Drive Pinion
9	Speedometer Drive Shaft
10	Seal Ring
11	Bearing Retainer
12	Case Front Cover
13	Gasket
14	Seal Ring
15	Washer
16	Shift Yoke
17	Shift Yoke
18	Shift Detent
19	Interlock Cage
20	Shift Detent
21	Shifting Shaft
22	Gearshift Cover
23	Gasket
24	Bushing
25	Needle Sleeve

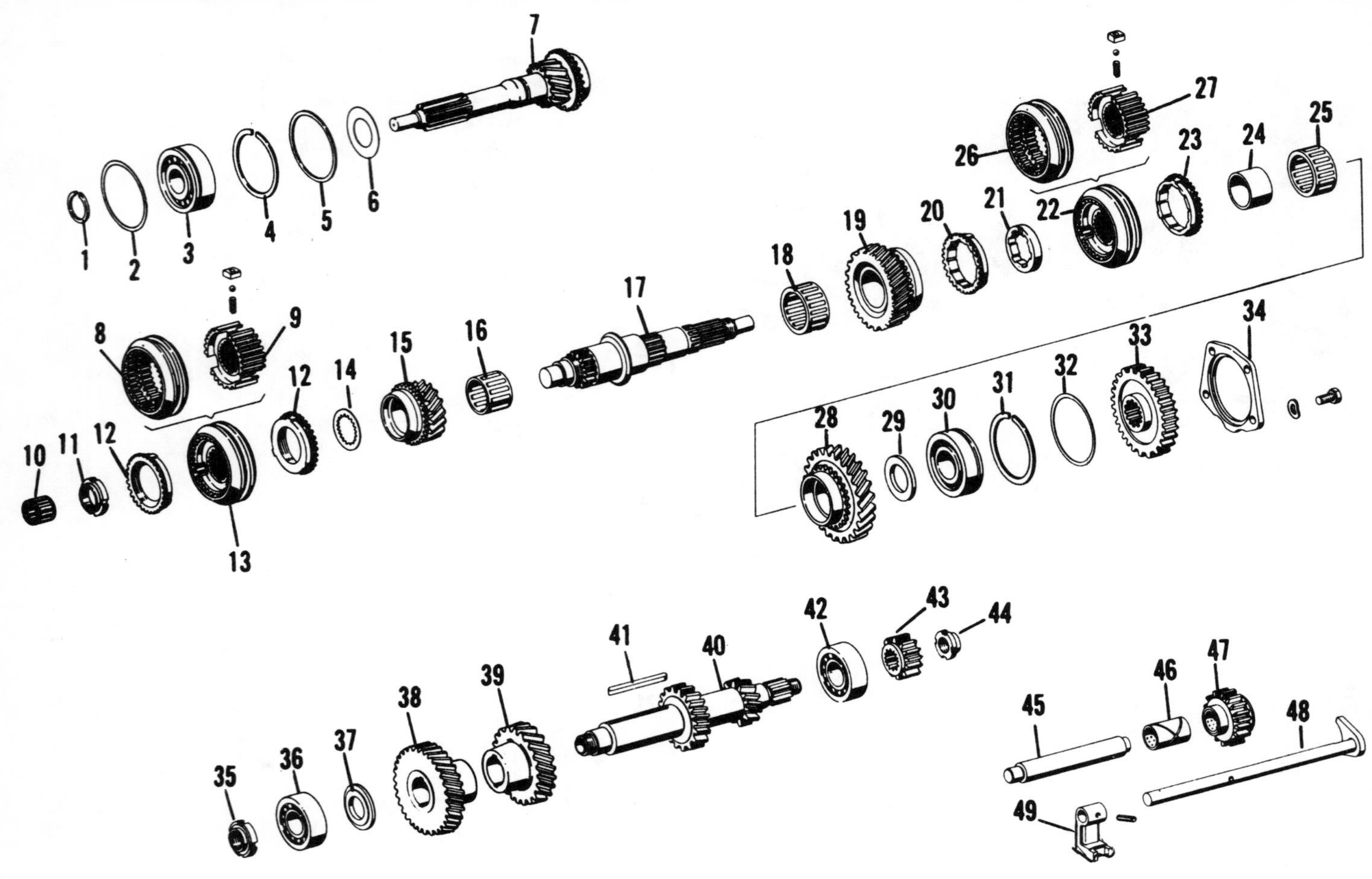

FIG 7 – TRANSMISSION GEARS & SHAFTS

1	Ring	26	Synchronizer Body
2	Washer	27	Sliding Collar
3	Bearing	28	1st Speed Gear
4	Ring	29	Guard Plate
5	Ring	30	Bearing
6	Oil Slinger	31	Ring
7	Clutch Shaft	32	Washer
8	Sliding Collar	33	Reverse Idler Gear (Mainshaft)
9	Synchronizer Body	34	Retaining Ring
10	Needle Cage	35	Nut
11	Nut	36	Bearing
12	Synchronizer Ring	37	Washer
13	Synchronizer Body Assy	38	Countershaft Gear
14	Guard Plate	39	Countershaft 3rd Speed Gear
15	3rd Speed Gear	40	Countershaft
16	Needle Cage	41	Key
17	Mainshaft	42	Bearing
18	Needle Cage	43	Reverse Idler Gear (Countershaft)
19	2nd Speed Gear	44	Nut
20	Synchronizer Ring	45	Reverse Idler Shaft
21	Guard Plate	46	Bushing
22	Synchronizer Body Assy	47	Reverse Idler Gear
23	Synchronizer Ring	48	Shifting Rod
24	Race	49	Follower
25	Needle Cage		

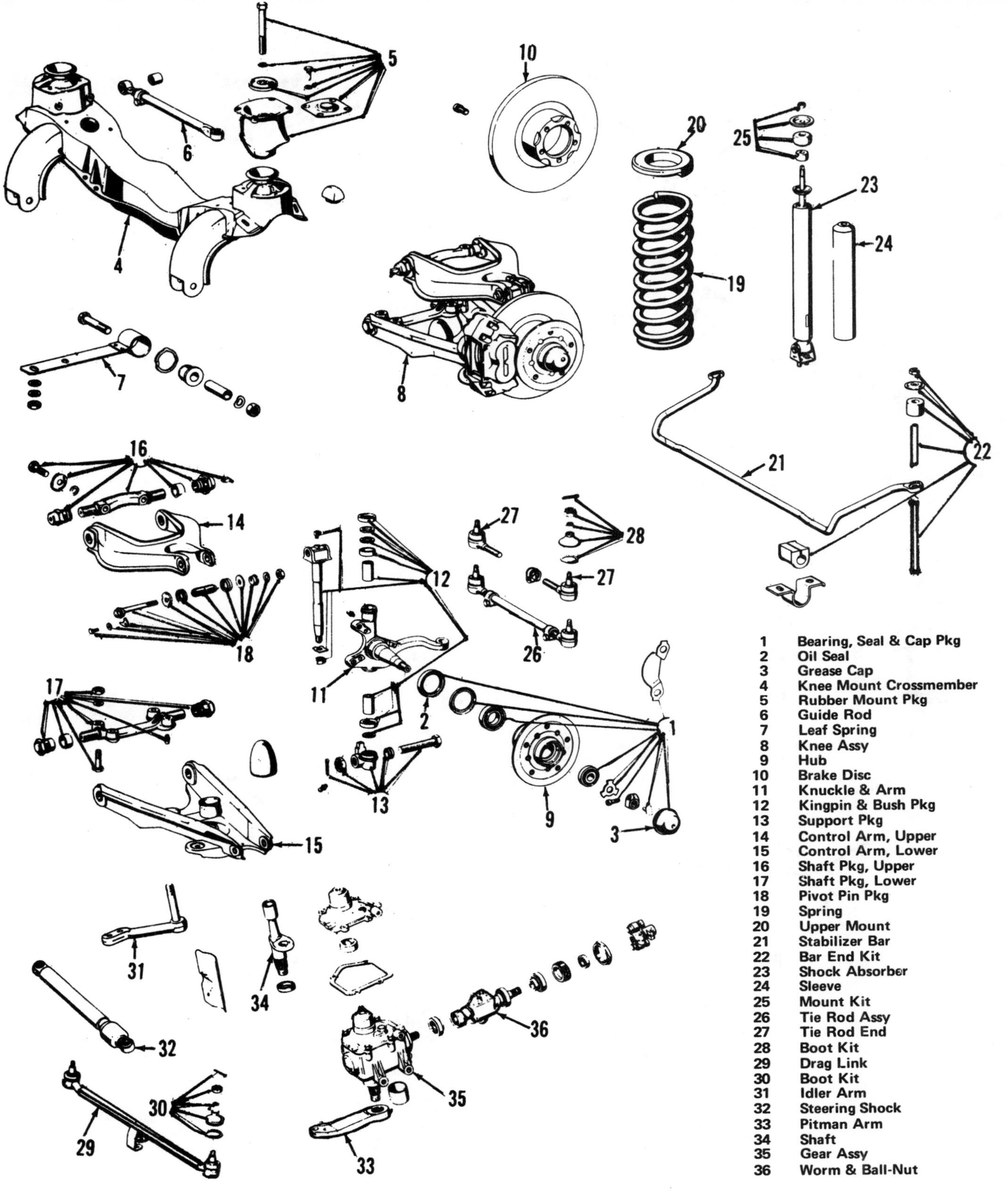
1 Bearing, Seal & Cap Pkg
2 Oil Seal
3 Grease Cap
4 Knee Mount Crossmember
5 Rubber Mount Pkg
6 Guide Rod
7 Leaf Spring
8 Knee Assy
9 Hub
10 Brake Disc
11 Knuckle & Arm
12 Kingpin & Bush Pkg
13 Support Pkg
14 Control Arm, Upper
15 Control Arm, Lower
16 Shaft Pkg, Upper
17 Shaft Pkg, Lower
18 Pivot Pin Pkg
19 Spring
20 Upper Mount
21 Stabilizer Bar
22 Bar End Kit
23 Shock Absorber
24 Sleeve
25 Mount Kit
26 Tie Rod Assy
27 Tie Rod End
28 Boot Kit
29 Drag Link
30 Boot Kit
31 Idler Arm
32 Steering Shock
33 Pitman Arm
34 Shaft
35 Gear Assy
36 Worm & Ball-Nut

FIG 8 – FRONT SUSPENSION & STEERING – 250 SL, 280 SL

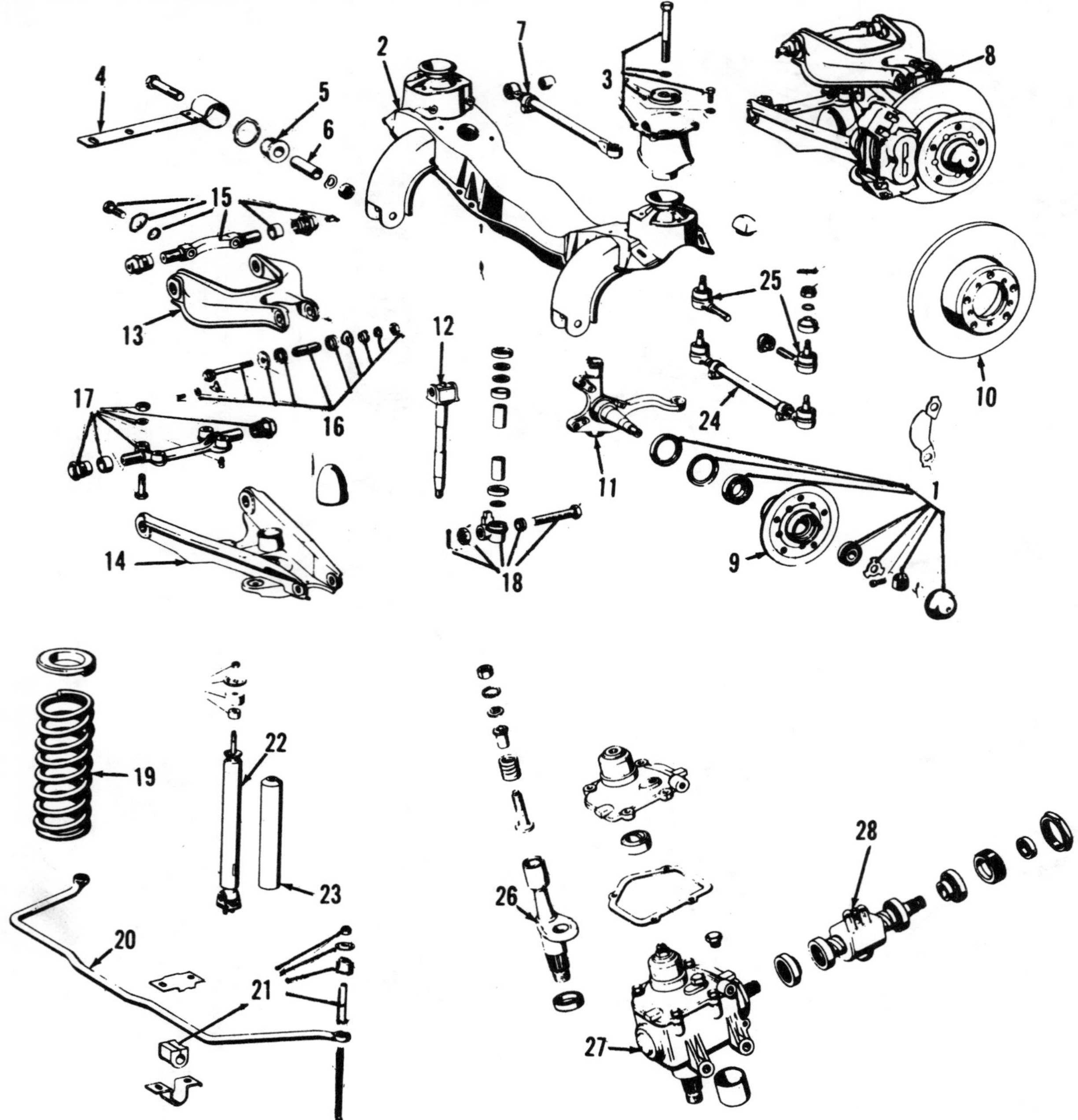

FIG 9 – FRONT SUSPENSION & STEERING – 250 SE/C, 280SE/C/8, 280SE/C 3.5

1	Bearing & Retainer Kit	16	Shaft Kit, Upper Outer
2	Knee Mount Crossmember	17	Shaft Kit, Lower Inner
3	Crossmember Mount Kit	18	Shaft Kit, Lower Outer
4	Bracing Spring	19	Spring
5	Bushing	20	Stabilizer Bar
6	Tube	21	Link & Bush Kit
7	Bracing Rod	22	Shock Absorber
8	Knee Assy	23	Protective Sleeve
9	Hub	24	Tie Rod Assy
10	Brake Disc	25	Tie Rod End
11	Knuckle & Arm	26	Pitman Shaft
12	King Pin	27	Gear Assy
13	Control Arm, Upper	28	Worm & Ball-Nut
14	Control Arm, Lower		
15	Shaft Kit, Upper Inner		

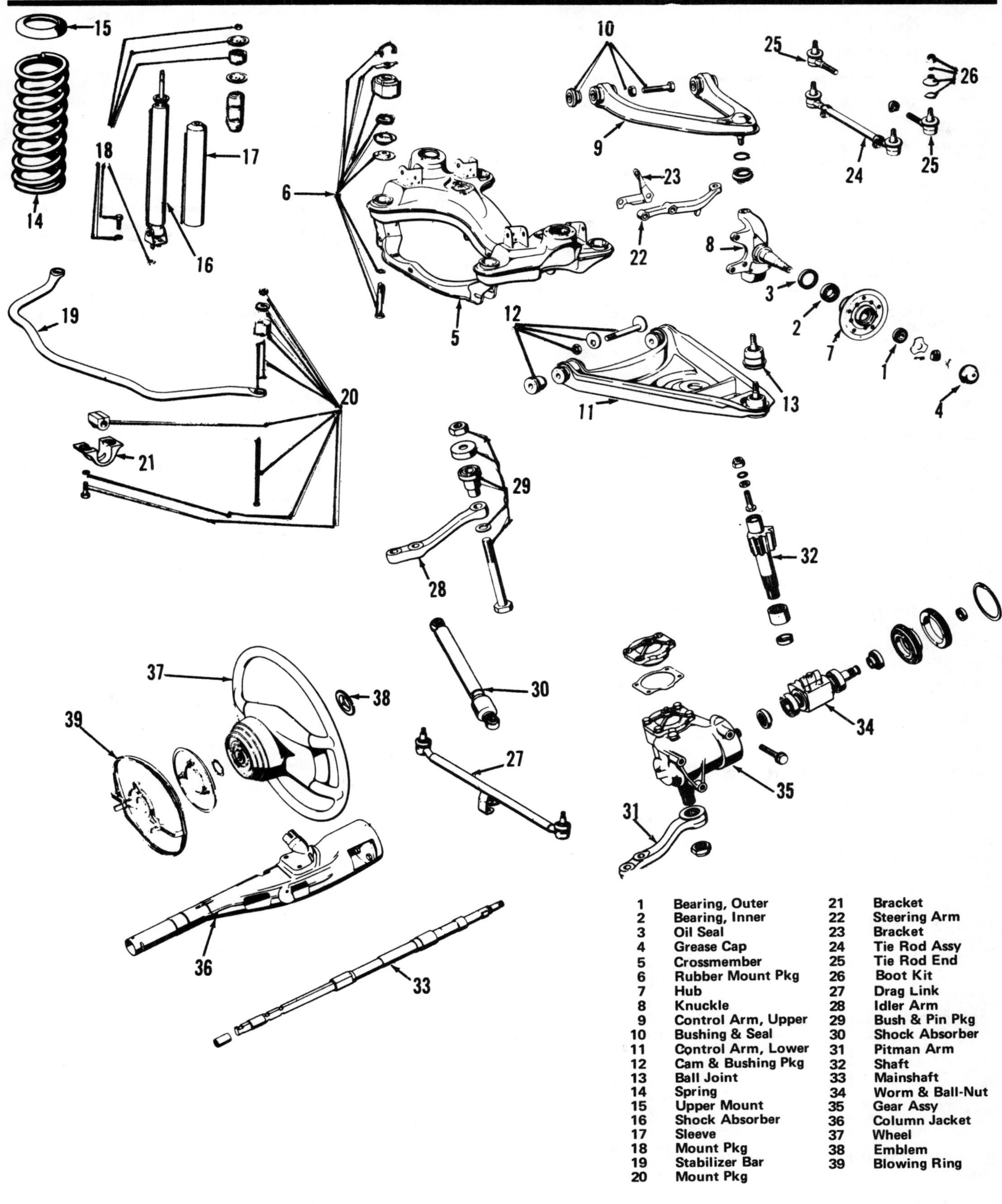

FIG 10 – FRONT SUSPENSION & STEERING – 250 C, 280C, 350 SL/SLC, 450 SL/SLC

Ignition, Starting & Charging—TIME

OPERATION INDEX

Tune-Up, Minor ... *1*
Compression Test ... *2*
Distributor, R & R Or Renew ... *3*
Distributor Cap, Renew ... *4*
Ignition Cable Set, Renew ... *5*
Ignition Coil, Renew ... *6*
Starter & Ignition Switch, Renew ... *7*
Starter, R & R Or Renew ... *8*
Starter, R & R & Overhaul ... *9*
Generator, R & R Or Renew ... *10*
Alternator, R & R Or Renew ... *11*
Generator, R & R & Overhaul ... *12*
Voltage Regulator, Renew ... *13*

1—TUNE-UP, MINOR

Includes: Renew points, plugs, set spark timing and adjust carburetor idle

- 1966-72—
  - Exc Below ... 3.5
  - 300 SE ... 3.9
- 1973-78—
  - 230, 280 ... 3.5
- 450 ... 4.5

2—COMPRESSION TEST

- 1966-72—
  - Exc Below ... 1.0
  - 200, 200/8 ... 0.9
  - 200, 200D8 ... 1.3
  - 200D ... 1.3
- 1973-78—
  - 280, 280C ... 0.6
  - 450 Models ... 1.3
  - 230 ... 0.4
  - 240D ... 1.0
  - 300D ... 1.3
  - 280S ... 0.6

3—DISTRIBUTOR, R & R OR RENEW

- 1966-72—
  - Exc Below ... 0.8
  - 300SEB ... 1.0
  - 300SEL ... 1.0
  - 300SE CP/CA ... 1.0
- 1973-78—
  - 280, 280C, 280S ... 0.7
  - 450 Models ... 1.0
  - 230 ... 0.8

4—DISTRIBUTOR CAP, RENEW

- All Models ... 0.3

5—IGNITION CABLE SET, RENEW

- 1966-72 ... 0.6
- 1973-78 ... 0.8

6—IGNITION COIL, RENEW

- All Models ... 0.3

7—STARTER & IGNITION SWITCH, RENEW

1966-72

- Exc Below ... 1.5
- 200, 220D/8 ... 1.1
- 200, 220/8 ... 0.9
- 230, 250/8 ... 0.9
- 200D ... 1.8
- 250SE CP/CA ... 2.3
- 300SE CP/CA ... 2.3
- 250SE, 230SL ... 3.2

1973-78

- 280, 280C ... 1.2
- 450SE, SEL ... 1.0
- 450SL, SLC ... 0.9
- 230 ... 1.2
- 240D ... 1.3
  - 300D ... 1.5
  - 280S ... 1.0

8—STARTER, R & R OR RENEW

1966-72

- 200, 200D, 230, 230/S, 250/S—
  - Exc Below ... 0.8
  - Auto Trans ... 0.9
- 200/D8, 220/D8—
  - Exc Below ... 1.1
  - Auto Trans ... 1.5
- 200/8, 220/8—
  - Exc Below ... 1.5
  - Auto Trans ... 1.7
- 230SL—
  - Exc Below ... 1.0
  - Auto Trans ... 1.2
- 230/8, 250/8—
  - Exc Below ... 0.8
  - Auto Trans ... 1.1
- 250/SE—
  - Exc Below ... 0.9
  - Auto Trans ... 1.2
- 250SL—
  - Exc Below ... 0.9
  - Auto Trans ... 1.1
- 280/S8—
  - Exc Below ... 0.7
  - Auto Trans ... 1.1
- 280/SE8, 280/SL8—
  - Exc Below ... 0.9
  - Auto Trans ... 1.1
- 300/SEL8 ... 1.1

1973-78

- 280, 280C, 280S ... 1.3
- 450SE, SEL ... 1.3
- 450SL, SLC ... 2.8
- 230 ... 1.9
- 240D ... 1.3
- 300D ... 1.4

9—STARTER, R & R & OVERHAUL

1966-72

- 200, 200D, 230, 230/S, 250/S—
  - Exc Below ... 1.6
  - Auto Trans ... 1.7
- 200D/8, 220D/8—
  - Exc Below ... 2.1
  - Auto Trans ... 2.5
- 200/8, 220/8—
  - Exc Below ... 2.5
  - Auto Trans ... 2.7
- 230SL—
  - Exc Below ... 1.8
  - Auto Trans ... 2.0
- 230/8, 250/8—
  - Exc Below ... 1.8
  - Auto Trans ... 2.1
- 250SE—
  - Exc Below ... 1.7
  - Auto Trans ... 2.0
- 250SL—
  - Exc Below ... 1.7
  - Auto Trans ... 1.9
- 280S/8—
  - Exc Below ... 1.7
  - Auto Trans ... 2.1
- 280SE/8, 280SL/8—
  - Exc Below ... 1.9
  - Auto Trans ... 2.1
- 300SEL/8 ... 2.1

1973-78

- 280, 280C, 280S ... 2.1
- 450SE, SEL ... 2.1
- 450SL, SLC ... 3.6
- 230 ... 2.7
- 240D ... 2.1
- 300D ... 2.2

10—GENERATOR, R & R OR RENEW

- 1966-72—
  - Exc Below ... 0.8
  - 280SL/8 ... 1.0
  - 230 & 250SL ... 1.0
  - 300SE, SEB, SEL ... 1.3

11—ALTERNATOR, R & R OR RENEW

- 1973-78—
  - 280, 280C ... 1.6
  - 450 Models ... 0.7
  - 230, 240D ... ①0.7
  - 300D ... 1.6
  - 280S ... 1.5

①*With Air Cond, Add.* ... *0.9*

12—GENERATOR, R & R & OVERHAUL

- 1966-72—
  - 300SE ... 3.4

13—VOLTAGE REGULATOR, RENEW

- 1966-72—
  - Exc Below ... 0.3
  - 300SEB, SEL ... 0.5
  - 300SE CP/CA ... 0.5
- 1973-78—
  - 280, 280C, 280S ... 0.9
  - 450 Models ... 0.5
  - 230 ... 0.9
  - 240D ... 0.3
  - 300D ... 0.7

Fuel, Emission Controls, Intake & Exhaust Systems—TIME

OPERATION INDEX

Carburetor (Front Or Rear), Renew ... *1*
Carburetors (Front & Rear), Renew ... *2*
Fuel Pump, R & R Or Renew ... *3*
Fuel Tank, R & R Or Renew ... *4*
Injection Pump, R & R Or Renew ... *5*
Injection Pump Pressure Valve, Renew ... *6*
Injection Nozzle (One), Renew ... *7*
Injection Valve (One), Renew ... *8*
Intake Manifold Or Gasket, Renew ... *9*
Exhaust Manifold Or Gasket, Renew ... *10*
Catalytic Converter, Renew ... *11*

1—CARBURETOR (FRONT OR REAR), RENEW

- 1966-72—
  - 200 ... 1.2
  - 230—
    - Exc Below ... 1.7
    - Downdraft Carb ... 1.2
  - 230/S, 250/S ... 1.7
  - 230/8, 280S/8 ... 1.6
  - 280S/8 ... 1.6
- 1973-78 ... 0.9

2—CARBURETORS (FRONT & REAR), RENEW

- 1966-72—
  - 200 ... 1.4
  - 230—
    - Exc Below ... 2.2
    - Downdraft Carb ... 1.4
  - 230/S, 250/S ... 2.2
  - 230/8, 250/8 ... 2.2
  - 280S/8 ... 2.2

3—FUEL PUMP, R & R OR RENEW

- 1966-72 ... 0.5
- 1973-78—
  - 280, 280C, 280S ... 0.8
  - 230 ... 0.3
  - 240D, 300D ... 0.4

4—FUEL TANK, R & R OR RENEW

- 1966-72—
  - Exc Below ... ①1.0
  - 250SE ... ①1.1
  - 300SE ... ①1.1
  - 230SL, 250SL ... ②1.3
  - 280SE/8, 300SEL/8 ... ①1.1
  - 280SL/8 ... ②1.5
- 1973-78—
  - 280, 280C ... ②0.9
  - 450SE, SEL ... ③1.5
  - 450SL ... ④2.5
  - 450SLC ... ④1.8
  - 230, 240D, 300D ... ②0.9
  - 280S ... ③1.5

①*To Renew, Add.* ... *0.2*
②*To Renew, Add.* ... *0.3*
③*To Renew, Add.* ... *0.5*
④*To Renew, Add.* ... *0.4*

(Continued)

Fuel, Emission Controls, Intake & Exhaust Systems—TIME Cont'd

5—INJECTION PUMP, R & R OR RENEW

1966-72—
- Exc Below ... 2.9
- 250SE, SL ... 3.3
- 230SL ... 2.8
- 300SE, SEB, SEL—
  - Exc Below ... 2.8
  - 2 Plunger Pump ... 2.5

1973-78—
- 240D ... 3.7
- 300D ... 3.5

6—INJECTION PUMP PRESSURE VALVE, RENEW

Includes: R & R pump

1966-72—
- Exc Below ... 3.3
- 250SE, SL ... 3.7
- 230SL ... 3.2
- 300SE, SEB, SEL—
  - Exc Below ... 3.2
  - 2 Plunger Pump ... 2.9

7—INJECTION NOZZLE (ONE), RENEW

1966-72 ... ①0.3
1973-78 ... 0.7
①*Does Not Include R & R Pump.*

8—INJECTION VALVE (ONE), RENEW

Does not include R & R pump.

1966-72 ... 0.2

9—INTAKE MANIFOLD OR GASKET, RENEW

1966-72—
- Exc Below ... 2.7
- 230 W/Downdraft Carb ... 2.3
- 200 ... 2.3
- 200D ... 1.0
- 220D/8 ... 1.0
- 300SEB, SEL ... 5.6
- 300SE CP/CA ... 5.6
- 300SEL/8 ... 2.9

1973-78—
- 280, 280C, 280S ... 2.5
- 450 Models ... 3.6
- 230 ... ①2.9
- 240D ... ①1.1
- 300D ... 3.4

①*With Air Cond, Add ... 2.3*

10—EXHAUST MANIFOLD OR GASKET, RENEW

1966-72
- Exc Below ... 2.7
- 200D ... 1.0
- 230S, 250S ... 3.0
- 220D/8 ... 1.0
- 220/8 ... 2.9
- 230/8, 250/8 ... 3.0
- 280S/8 ... 3.0
- 300SEL/8 ... 2.9
- 300SEB, SEL ... 5.6
- 300SE CP/CA ... 6.0

1973-78
- 280, 280C, Front ... 1.6
  - Rear ... 1.4
  - All ... 2.0
- 450SE, SEL, Right ... ①1.5
  - Left ... ①1.4
  - All ... ①2.5
- 450SL, SLC, Right ... ②2.9
  - Left ... ②2.5
  - All ... ②4.4
- 230 ... ③3.2
- 240D ... ③1.1
- 300D ... 3.4
- 280S ... 1.8

①*With Catalytic Converter, Add. ... 1.3*
②*With Catalytic Converter, Add. ... 0.6*
③*With Air Cond, Add. ... 2.3*

11—CATALYTIC CONVERTER, RENEW

Left Side—
- 450SE, SEL ... 3.1
- 450SL, SLC ... 3.5

Right Side—
- 280, 280C, 280S ... 1.7
- 450SE, SEL ... 2.6
- 450SL, SLC ... 3.1
- 230 ... 1.7

Both—
- 450SE, SEL ... 5.5
- 450SL, SLC ... 6.3

Engine Cooling & Heater System—TIME

OPERATION INDEX

Radiator, R & R Or Renew ... 1
Radiator Hoses, Renew ... 2
Water Pump, R & R Or Renew ... 3
Thermostat Or Housing, Renew ... 4
Heater, R&R Or Renew ... 4A
Heater Box, R & R & Overhaul ... 5
Heater Blower Motor, Renew ... 6
Heater Hoses, Renew ... 7

1—RADIATOR, R & R OR RENEW

1966-72

220/8, 220D/8, 230/8—
- Exc Below ... 0.7
- Auto Trans ... 0.9

250/8—
- Exc Below ... 0.9
- Auto Trans ... 1.1

280S/8, 280SE/8, 300SEL/8—
- Exc Below ... 0.9
- Auto Trans ... 1.1

200, 200D ... 1.0
230 ... 1.2

230S—
- Exc Below ... 1.0
- Auto Trans ... 1.2

250S, SE, SE CP/CA—
- Exc Below ... 1.1
- Auto Trans ... 1.3

300SEB ... 1.7
300SEL ... 2.1
300SE CP/CA ... 2.1

230 & 250SL—
- Exc Below ... 1.4
- Auto Trans ... 1.6

1973-78
- 280, 280C, 280S ... 1.1
- 450SE, SEL ... 1.1
- 450SL, SLC ... 1.2
- 230 ... 1.0
- 240D, 300D ... 1.1

2—RADIATOR HOSES, RENEW

1966-72

Upper—
- Exc Below ... 0.3
- 300SEB, SEL ... 0.6
- 300SE CP/CA ... 0.6

Lower—
Exc Below ... 0.3
- 280SL/8 ... 0.6
- 230 ... 0.4
- 230SL, 250SL ... 0.6
- 300SEB, SEL ... 0.8
- 300CP/CA ... 0.8

1973-78

Upper—
- 280, 280C, 280S ... 0.4
- 450 Models ... 0.5
- 230, 240D, 300D ... 0.4

Lower—
- 280, 280C, 280S ... 0.8
- 450 Models ... 0.6
- 230, 240D ... 0.4
- 300D ... 1.0

3—WATER PUMP, R & R OR RENEW

1966-72

200, 200D ... 1.5
230 ... 1.6

230S—
- Exc Below ... 1.5
- Auto Trans ... 1.7

250, 250SE ... 1.4
250SL ... 1.5

230SL—
- Exc Below ... 2.5
- Auto Trans ... 2.6

300SE, SEB, SEL ... 2.5
220/8, 220D/8 ... 1.0
230/8 ... 1.1
250/8 ... 1.2
280S/8, 230SE ... 1.3
280SE/8 CP/CA ... 1.3
300SEL/8 ... 1.3
280SL/8 ... 1.4

1973-78
- 280, 280C ... 3.3
- 450 Models ... 3.3
- 230, 240D ... 1.5
- 300D ... 3.5
- 280S ... 3.1

4—THERMOSTAT OR HOUSING, RENEW

1966-72—
- Exc Below ... 0.3
- 230SL, 250SL ... 0.6
- 300SE, SEB, SEL ... 0.5
- 280SE, SEL, SL/8 ... 0.5

1973-78 (Thermostat)—
- 280, 280C, 280S ... 0.9
- 450 Models ... 1.3
- 230, 240D, 300D ... 0.5

1973-78 (Housing)—
- 280, 280C, 280S ... 2.2
- 230, 240D ... ①0.9
- 300D ... 3.0

①*With Air Cond, Add. ... 2.2*

4A—HEATER, R&R OR RENEW

1973-78—
- 230-240D Exc ... 6.0
  - With Air Cond ... 9.0
- 280 Exc ... 9.0
  - 280E ... 6.0
- 450 Se, Sel ... 13.5
- 450 SL, SLC ... 15.5

5—HEATER BOX, R & R & OVERHAUL

1966-72
- 200, 200D, 230, 230S ... 4.1
- 250S, 250SE ... 7.1
- 250SE CP/CA ... 4.3
- 300SEB, SEL ... 7.3
- 300SE CP/CA ... 4.3
- 220/8, 220D/8 ... 5.0
- 230/8, 250/8 ... 5.0
- 280S/8, 280SE/8 ... 7.0
- 280SE/8 CP/CA ... 4.3
- 300SEL/8 ... 4.7

6—HEATER BLOWER MOTOR, RENEW

1966-72
- 200, 200D, 230, 230S ... 4.2
- 250S, 250SE ... 6.4
- 250SE CP/CA ... 4.3
- 300SEB, SEL ... 6.6
- 300SE CP/CA ... 4.3
- 230SL, 250SL ... 3.3
- 220/8, 220D/8 ... 5.6
- 230/8, 250/8 ... 5.6
- 280S/8, 280SE/8 ... 6.4
- 280SE/8 CP/CA ... 4.3
- 300SEL/8 ... 6.5
- 280SL/8 ... 3.3

1973-78
- 280, 280C ... 8.7
- 450SE, SEL ... 2.5
- 450SL, SLC ... 0.9
- 230, 240D ... ①5.6
- 300D ... 8.7
- 280S ... 2.5

①*With Air Cond, Add. ... 3.2*

7—HEATER HOSES, RENEW

1966-72
- Exc Below ... 0.7
- 250SE ... 0.8
- 230 ... 3.4
- 200, 200D ... 3.5
- 230S ... 3.5
- 300SE CP/CA ... 3.7
- 250SE CP/CA ... 3.8
  - 280S/8, 280SE/8 ... 0.8
- 280SL/8 ... 0.9
- 220/8, 220D/8 ... 1.6

(Continued)

Engine Cooling & Heater System—TIME Cont'd

230/8, 250/8 .... 1.8
280SE/8 CP/CA 3.9
1973-78
230-240D-300D 2.0
280 .... 2.5
450 .... 2.5

Engine—TIME

OPERATION INDEX

Engine, R & R *1*
Engine, Renew *2*
Engine (Short Block), Renew *3*
Engine Block (Fitted), Renew *4*
Engine, R & R & Overhaul *5*
Cylinder Head, R & R Or Gasket, Renew *6*
Valves, Grind (Head Off) *7*
Valve Guide(S), Renew *8*
Rocker Arm Cover Gasket, Renew *9*
Valve Rocker Arm Assy, R & R Or Renew *10*
Oil Pan Or Gasket, R & R Or Renew *11*
Oil Pan, Lower, R & R Or Renew *12*
Timing Chain Tensioner, R & R Or Renew *13*
Roller Chain, Renew *14*
Camshaft, R & R Or Renew *15*
Camshaft Bearings, Renew *16*
Oil Pump, R & R Or Renew *17*
Piston Rings, Renew *18*
Pistons, Renew *19*
Crankshaft, R & R Or Renew *20*
Main & Rod Bearings, Renew And Grind Valves *21*
Crankshaft Pulley, Renew *22*

1—ENGINE, R & R

Does not include transfer of any part of engine or replacement of special equipment includes: R & R trans & eng

1966-72
200—
Synchro-Mesh ①6.3
Auto Trans ②7.4
200D—
Synchro-Mesh ①6.8
Auto Trans ③7.8
220D/8—
Synchro-Mesh ⑤5.8
Auto Trans ⑥6.8
220/8—
Synchro-Mesh ①6.2
Auto Trans ⑦7.2
230—
Synchro-Mesh ①8.0
Auto Trans ①9.9
230S, 250S—
Synchro-Mesh ①6.5
Auto Trans ③7.8
230/8, 250/8—
Synchro-Mesh ①6.8
Auto Trans ①8.2
230SL, 250SL—
Synchro-Mesh ①8.7
Auto Trans ①10.2
250SE Coupe & Cabriolet—
Synchro-Mesh—
L/Power Steer ④8.4
W/Power Steer ④8.9
Auto Trans—
L/Power Steer ⑤9.8
W/Power Steer ⑥10.4
280S/8—
Synchro-Mesh ①6.5
Auto Trans ①7.8
280SE/8—
Synchro-Mesh ①8.3
Auto Trans ①9.8
280SE/8 Coupe & Cabriolet—
Synchro-Mesh—
L/Power Steer ④8.3
W/Power Steer ④8.8
Auto Trans—
L/Power Steer ④9.8
W/Power Steer ④10.3
280SL/8—
Synchro-Mesh ①8.7
Auto Trans ①10.2
300SEB—
Synchro-Mesh 9.3
Auto Trans 11.1
300SEL—
Synchro-Mesh 9.6
Auto Trans 11.4
300SEL/8—
Synchro-Mesh 9.6
Auto Trans 11.4
300SE Coupe & Cabriolet—
Synchro-Mesh ⑤9.4
Auto Trans ④11.3
1973-78
280, 280C ⑧10.3
450SE, SEL ⑧12.5
450SL, SLC ⑧13.9
230 .... ⑦8.0
240D, Manual ⑦6.9
240D, Automatic ⑦7.9
300D 8.9
280S 10.3
①For Pwr Strg, Add. *0.5*
②For Pwr Strg, Add. *0.4*
③For Pwr Strg, Add. *0.6*
④Conv Models, Add. *0.5*
⑤Conv Models, Add. *0.6*
⑥Conv Models, Add. *0.4*
⑦With Air Cond, Add. *0.9*
⑧With Air Injection, Add. *0.3*

2—ENGINE ASSY, RENEW

1973-78—
280, 280C ②14.6
450SE, SEL ③16.2
450SL, SLC ③17.5
230 .... ①12.1
240D, Manual ①9.8
240D, Automatic ①11.4
300D 13.4
280S 15.9
①With Air Cond, Add. *2.3*
②With Air Injection, Add. *0.5*
③With Air Injection, Add. *0.3*

3—ENGINE (SHORT BLOCK), RENEW

1973-78—
280, 280C 27.2
450SE, SEL 30.5
450SL, SLC 31.9
230 .... 22.0
240D 20.8
300D 24.3
280S 27.7

4—ENG BLOCK (FITTED WITH PISTONS-RINGS-PINS), RENEW

1973-78—
280, 280C ③33.2
450SE, SEL ④40.5
450SL, SLC ④42.4
230 .... ①③26.0
240D ①②24.8
300D 29.2
280S 33.7
①With Air Cond, Add. *2.3*
②With Auto Trans, Add *1.1*
③With Air Injection, Add. *0.5*
④With Air Injection, Add. *0.3*

5—ENGINE, R & R & OVERHAUL

Includes: Rebore cylinders with boring bar, renew pistons, rings, pins, main & rod bearings, grind valves, plastigauge bearings and perform minor tune-up. Includes: R & R trans w/eng

1966-72
200—
Synchro-Mesh ①23.6
Auto Trans ②24.7
200D—
Synchro-Mesh ①24.4
Auto Trans ③25.4
220D/8—
Synchro-Mesh ①23.4
Auto Trans ①24.4
220/8—
Synchro-Mesh ①24.0
Auto Trans ①25.0
230—
Synchro-Mesh ①27.5
Auto Trans ①29.4
230S—
Synchro-Mesh ①26.2
Auto Trans ③27.5
250S—
Synchro-Mesh ①26.9
Auto Trans ③28.2
230/8—
Synchro-Mesh ①26.4
Auto Trans ①27.8
250/8—
Synchro-Mesh ①27.4
Auto Trans ①28.8
230SL, 250SL—
Synchro-Mesh ①29.6
Auto Trans ①31.1
250SE Coupe & Cabriolet—
Synchro-Mesh—
L/Power Steer ④30.2
W/Power Steer ④30.7
Auto Trans—
L/Power Steer ⑤31.6
W/Power Steer ⑥32.2
280S/8—
Synchro-Mesh ①27.1
Auto Trans ①28.4
280SE/8—
Synchro-Mesh ①30.4
Auto Trans ①31.9
280SE/8 Coupe & Cabriolet—
Synchro-Mesh—
L/Power Steer ④30.4
W/Power Steer ④30.9
Auto Trans—
L/Power Steer ④31.9
W/Power Steer ④32.4
280SL/8—
Synchro-Mesh ①30.8
Auto Trans ①32.3
300SEB—
Synchro-Mesh 33.2
Auto Trans 35.0
300SEL—
Synchro-Mesh 34.0
Auto Trans 35.8
300SEL/8—
Synchro-Mesh 32.2
Auto Trans 34.0
300SE Coupe & Cabriolet—
Synchro-Mesh ⑤33.8
Auto Trans ④35.7
①For Pwr Strg, Add. *0.5*
②For Pwr Strg, Add. *0.4*
③For Pwr Strg, Add. *0.6*
④Conv Models, Add. *0.5*
⑤Conv Models, Add. *0.6*
⑥Conv Models, Add. *0.4*

6—CYLINDER HEAD, R & R OR GASKET, RENEW

1966-72
200 .... 1.8
200D 1.7
220/8 .... 1.9
220D/8 .... 2.0
230, 230S 1.9
230/8, 250/8 .... 1.9
250S 1.9
250SE 2.7
230SL, 250SL 2.8
280SE/8 .... 2.7
280SL/8 .... 2.8
300SEL/8 .... 2.7
300SEB 3.1
300SE, SEL 3.3
1973-78
280, 280C 3.8
450SE, SEL—
One 3.4
Both 5.2
450SL, SLC—
One 3.7
Both 5.7
230 .... 2.3
240D 2.1
300D 2.1
280S 3.8

7—VALVES, GRIND (HEAD OFF)

1966-72—
Exc Below 3.7
200, 220/8, 220D/8 .... 2.9
230, 230S 3.8
230SL, 250SL 3.8
250S, SE CP/CA 3.8
300SEB, SEL 4.0
300SE CP/CA 4.0

(Continued)

Engine—TIME Cont'd

1973-78—
280, 280C, 280S 3.0
450 Models 3.5
230, 240D 3.0
300D 4.0

8—VALVE GUIDE(S), RENEW

Valves removed

1966-72—
Exc Below—
One 0.3
All 1.0
200, 200D—
One 0.3
All 0.7
220/8, 220D/8—
One 0.2
All 0.6
230/8, 250/8—
One 0.2
All 1.0
280S, SE, SL/8, 300SEL/8—
One 0.2
All 1.0
1973-78—
One 0.3
All—
280, 280C, 280S 1.2
450 Models 1.5
230, 240D 0.8
300D 1.0

9—ROCKER ARM COVER GASKET, RENEW

1966-72—
Exc Below 0.4
220/8, D/8 .... 0.3
200, 200D 0.3
230S, 250S 0.3
1973-78—
280, 280C, 280S 0.9
450 Models 1.0
230, 240D, 300D 0.4

10—VALVE ROCKER ARM ASSY, R & R OR RENEW

Includes: Adjust valve clearance

1966-72—
Exc Below 2.0
220/8, D/8 .... 1.8
200, 200D 0.8
230, 230S 1.0
230S, 250S, SE 1.0
230SL, 250SL 1.0
300SE, SEB, SEL 1.0
1973-78—
230 .... 1.5
240D 1.8
280 .... 2.5
300D 2.0
450 .... 3.0

11—OIL PAN OR GASKET, R & R OR RENEW

1966-72
200, 200D—
L/Power Steer 3.5
W/Power Steer 4.2
220/8, 220D/8 .... 4.8
230/8, 250/8 .... 5.0
230 .... 5.0
230S 4.7
250S 5.2
250SE CP/CA 5.4
280S/8 .... 5.1
280SE/8 .... 5.4
230SL, 250SL 7.1
280SL/8 .... 7.0
300SEB 7.5
300SE, SEL 7.9
1973-78
280, 280C 5.8
450SE, SEL, SL, SLC 10.4
230, 240D Exc 5.3
1977-78 .... 2.0
300D Exc 5.5
1977-78 .... 2.0
280S 5.9

12—OIL PAN (LOWER), R & R OR RENEW

1973-78—
280, 280C 1.6
450SE, SEL 1.3
230, 240D, 300D 1.1
280S 1.3

13—TIMING CHAIN TENSIONER, R & R OR RENEW

1966-72—
Exc Below 1.1
220/8, D/8 .... 1.0
200, 200D 1.0
300SE, SEB, SEL 1.0
1973-78—
280, 280C 1.8
450 Models 1.3
230, 240D 1.1
300D 2.5
280S 1.8

14—ROLLER CHAIN, RENEW

1966-72—
Exc Below 1.9
220/8 .... 1.7
280SL/8 .... 2.1
200, 200D 2.1
250S, SE 2.1
300SEB 2.1
230SL, 250 SL 2.3
300SE, SEL 2.3
1973-78—
280, 280C 4.3
450 Models 4.3
230 .... 2.2
240D 3.1
300D 3.6
280S 4.3

15—CAMSHAFT, R & R OR RENEW

1966-72—
Exc Below 3.5
200D 3.0
200 .... 2.9
230, 230S, 250S 3.3
300SEB, SEL 4.0
300SE CP/CA 4.0
1973-78—
280, 280C, 280S—
One 7.5
Both 8.3
450 Models—
One 5.3
Both 9.3
230 .... 3.2
240D 3.5
300D 4.2

16—CAMSHAFT BEARINGS, RENEW

—NOTE—

Use Camshaft R & R Or Renew

17—OIL PUMP, R & R OR RENEW

1966-72—
Exc Below 1.4
220/8, 230/8, 250/8 .... 1.5
280S/8 .... 1.5
200, 200D 1.3
230, 230S 1.3
250S 1.5
300SE, SEL ①8.4
300SEB ①8.0
1973-78—
280, 280C, 280S 2.0
450SE, SEL 1.5
450SL, SLC 7.9
230 .... 1.5
240D 1.6
300D 1.5

①*Includes R & R Complete Pan.*

18—PISTON RINGS, RENEW

Engine removed

1966-72
200 .... 9.3
200D 10.2
220/8, D/8 .... 12.7
230/8 .... 12.8
250/8 .... 13.9
230 .... 9.5
230S 10.4
250S 10.7
250SE 11.5
230SL 11.4
250SL 11.8
280S/8 .... 13.9
280SE/8 .... 15.2
280SL/8 .... 15.2
300SEL/8 .... 16.0
300SEB, SEL 15.4

19—PISTONS, RENEW

Engine, clutch & cylinder head removed

1966-72
200 .... 12.0
200D 12.4
220/8, D/8 .... 12.7
230/8 .... 12.8
250/8 .... 13.9
230 .... 12.7
230S 12.9
250S 13.5
250SE 14.8
250SE CP/CA 14.8
230SL, 250SL 13.9
280S/8 .... 13.9
280SE/8 .... 15.2
280SL/8 .... 15.2
300SE, SE/L 16.8
300SEB 16.2
300SEL/8 .... 16.0

20—CRANKSHAFT, R & R OR RENEW

1966-72
220/8 .... ①5.0
220D/8 .... ①5.8
230/8 .... ①5.3
250/8 .... ①5.6
200 .... ①4.9
200D ①5.7
230, 230S ①5.3
250S ①5.7
250SE ①5.8
280S/8 .... ①5.6
280SE/8 .... ①5.8
280SL/8 .... ①5.8
230SL, 250SL ①5.5
300SE, SEB, SEL ①7.5
1973-78
280, 280C ②20.6
450 Models ②22.0
230 .... ②15.2
240D ②15.5
300D ②18.6
280S ②20.6

①*Engine & Clutch Removed*
②*Includes: R & R Engine*

21—MAIN & ROD BEARINGS, RENEW & GRIND VALVES

Engine & clutch removed

1966-72
200 .... 9.4
220D/8 .... 10.4
220/8 .... 9.5
230, 230S 11.0
230/8 .... 10.8
230SL, 250SL 11.1
250S 11.5
250SE 11.6
250/8, 280S/8 .... 11.4
280SE/8 .... 11.5
300SEB, SEL 13.5
300SE CP/CA 13.5

22—CRANKSHAFT PULLEY, RENEW

1966-72
220/8, D/8 .... 0.5
230/8 .... 0.9
250/8 .... 1.0
280S/8, SE/8, SE/8 CP/CA—
Exc Below 0.8
Pwr Strg Or Auto Trans 1.3
300SEL/8 .... 1.3
280SL/8—
Exc Below 1.0
Pwr Strg Or Auto Trans 1.5
200,200,D—
Exc Below 0.5
Pwr Strg 0.7
230—
Exc Below 1.3
Pwr Strg Or Auto Trans 1.5

(Continued)

Engine—TIME Cont'd

230S—
- Exc Below 0.7
- Pwr Strg Or Auto Trans 0.9

250S, SE, CP/CA—
- Exc Below 0.8
- Pwr Strg Or Auto Trans 1.3

230SL—
- Exc Below 0.8
- Pwr Strg Or Auto Trans 1.1

250SL—
- Exc Below 1.0
- Pwr Strg Or Auto Trans 1.5

300SE, SEL, SEB 1.1

1973-78

280, 280C 1.5
450 Models 2.4
230, 240D 0.7
300D 0.9
280S 1.5

Clutch, Mounts, Manual & Automatic Transmissions—TIME

OPERATION INDEX

Flywheel (Synchro-Mesh Trans), R & R Or Renew 1
Flywheel (Auto Trans), R & R Or Renew 2
Clutch & Driven Plate, Renew 3
Clutch Master Cylinder, R & R Or Renew 4
Clutch Slave Cylinder, R & R Or Renew 5
Front Engine Mounts, Renew 6
Rear Engine Mounts, Renew 7
Front & Rear Engine Mounts, Renew 8
Trans Assy (Manual) R & R Or Renew 9
Trans Assy (Automatic), R & R Or Renew 10
Trans Assy (Manual), Overhaul 11
Trans Assy (Automatic), Overhaul 12
Trans Kickdown Switch, Renew 13
Gearshift Or Selector Lever, Renew 14
Trans Shift Cover, R & R Or Renew 15
Extension Housing Oil Seal, Renew 16
Oil Pan Gasket, Renew 17
Governor, R & R Or Renew 18
Modulating Valve, Renew 19

1—FLYWHEEL (SYNCHRO-MESH TRANS), R & R OR RENEW

1966-72

200&D, 230&S, 250s&Se—
- L/Floor Shift 3.6
- W/Floor Shift 3.8

250SE Coupe & Cabriolet—
- L/Floor Shift 3.8
- W/Floor Shift 4.3

230SL, 250SL 4.3

300SEB, SEL—
- L/Floor Shift 3.8
- W/Floor Shift 3.9

300SE Coupe & Cabriolet—
- Exc Below 3.9
- Floor Shift Or Conv 4.4

220/8, 220D/8 .... 3.4
230/8, 250/8 .... 3.4

280S/8, 280SE/8—
- Exc Below 3.5
- Conv 3.7

280SE/8 Coupe & Cabriolet—
- Exc Below 3.5
- Conv 4.2

280SL/8 .... 4.2

300SEL/8—
- L/Floor Shift 3.5
- W/Floor Shift 3.8

1973-78

230, 240D 3.7

2—FLYWHEEL (AUTO TRANS), R & R OR RENEW

1966-72

200, 200D 4.6
230 .... 5.0
230S, 250S 5.3
230SL, 250SL 6.3
250SE 5.5

250SE Coupe & Cabriolet—
- Exc Below 5.5
- Conv 6.0

300SEB, SEL 6.2

300SE Coupe & Cabriolet—
- Exc Below 6.2
- Conv 6.7

220/8, 220D/8 .... 5.0
230/8, 250/8 .... 5.1
280S/8 .... 5.3
280SE/8 .... 5.5

280SE/8 Coupe & Cabriolet—
- Exc Below 5.5
- Conv 6.0

280SL/8 .... 6.3
300SEL/8 .... 5.5

1973-78

280, 280C 5.6
450SE, SEL 5.8
450SL, SLC 6.3
230, 240D, 300D 5.4
280S 5.6

3—CLUTCH & DRIVEN PLATE, RENEW

1966-72

200&D, 230&S, 250S&Se—
- Exc Below 3.3
- Floor Shift 3.4

250SE Coupe & Cabriolet—
- Exc Below 3.4
- Conv 3.9

230SL, 250SL 3.9

300SEB, SEL—
- Exc Below 3.4
- Floor Shift 3.6

300SE Coupe & Cabriolet—
- Exc Below 3.6
- Conv 4.1

220/8, 220D/8 .... 2.9
230/8, 250/8 .... 3.1

280S/8, 280SE/8—
- Exc Below 3.2
- Floor Shift 3.4

280SL/8 .... 3.9

280SE/8 Coupe & Cabriolet—
- Exc Below 3.4
- Conv 3.9

300SEL/8—
- Exc Below 3.2
- Floor Shift 3.4

1973-78

240D 3.2

4—CLUTCH MASTER CYLINDER, R & R OR RENEW

1966-72

220/8, 220D/8 .... 1.1
230/8, 250/8 .... 1.1
280S/8, SE/8 .... 1.5
280SL/8, 300SEL/8 .... 1.5
280SE/8, CP/CA 1.5
200, 200D, 230, 230S 1.0
230SL, 250SL 1.0
250S, SE, CP/CA 1.5
300SEB, SEL 1.5

300SE Coupe & Cabriolet—
- Exc Below 1.0
- On Firewall 1.3

1973-78

240D 1.3

5—CLUTCH SLAVE CYLINDER, R & R OR RENEW

1966-72—
- Exc Below 0.6
- 220/8, D/8 .... 1.1
- 230/8, 250/8 .... 1.1
- 280S/8, SE/8 .... 1.5
- 280SL/8 .... 1.5
- 300SEL/8 .... 1.5

1973-78—
- 240D 0.7

6—FRONT ENGINE MOUNTS, RENEW

1966-72

220/8 .... 0.7
220D/8 .... 0.9
230/8, 250/8 .... 0.9
280S/8 .... 0.9
280SE/8 .... 1.2
280SL/8 .... 1.2
200, 200D, 230 .... 0.9
230s, 250S 1.1
250SE, 300SEB 1.3
230SL, 250SL 1.3
300SEL, 300SE CP/CA 1.7

1973-78

280, 280C 1.4
450SE, SEL 1.7
450SL, SLC 2.3
230, 240D 1.0
300D 1.1
280S 1.6

7—REAR ENGINE MOUNTS, RENEW

1966-72—
- Exc Below 0.8
- 220/8, D/8 .... 0.6
- 280SL/8 .... 0.6
- 250SE, 280SE/8, 300SE Conv 1.3
- 200, 200D 0.7
- 230SL, 250SL 0.7

1973-78—
- All Models 0.6

8—FRONT & REAR ENGINE MOUNTS, RENEW

1966-72

220/8 .... 1.1
220D/8 .... 1.2
230/8, 250/8 .... 1.2
280S/8 .... 1.5
280SE/8 .... 1.8

280SE/8 Coupe & Cabriolet—
- Exc Below 1.8
- Conv 1.9

280SL/8 .... 1.6
200, 200D 1.4
230 .... 1.5
230S, 250S, SE 0.8

250SE Coupe & Cabriolet—
- Exc Below 1.8
- Conv 2.3

300SEB, SEL 0.8

300SE Coupe & Cabriolet—
- Exc Below 0.8
- Conv 1.3

230SL, 250SL 0.7

1973-78

280, 280C 1.8
450SE, SEL 1.8
450SL, SLC 2.6
230 .... 1.2
240D 1.4
300D 1.5
280S 1.7

9—TRANS ASSY (MANUAL), R & R OR RENEW

1966-72

220/8, 220D/8 .... ①2.5
230/8, 250/8 .... ①2.7

280S/8, SE/8—
- Exc Below ②2.8
- Floor Shift ②3.0

280SE/8 Coupe & Cabriolet—
- Floor Shift ③3.0
- Conv ①3.4

280SL/8 .... ①3.4

300SEL/8—
- Exc Below ②2.8
- Floor Shift ③3.0

200, 200D, 230, 230S—
- Exc Below ②2.8
- Floor Shift ②3.0

250s, 250SE—
- Exc Below ②2.8
- Floor Shift ②3.0

250SE Coupe & Cabriolet—
- Floor Shift ①3.0
- Conv ①3.5

230SL, 250SL ③3.5

300SEB, SEL—
- Exc Below ④3.0
- Floor Shift ④3.2

300SE Coupe & Cabriolet—
- Exc Below ④3.2
- Conv ④3.7

1973-78

240D ⑤2.7

①To Renew Trans, Add. 0.4
②To Renew Trans, Add. 0.2
③To Renew Trans, Add. 0.3
④To Renew Trans, Add. 1.3
⑤To Renew Trans, Add. 1.4

(Continued)

Clutch, Mounts, Manual & Automatic Transmissions—TIME Cont'd

10—TRANS ASSY (AUTOMATIC), R & R OR RENEW

1966-72
200, 200D ①4.3
230 .... ②4.7
230S, 250S ③5.0
250SE ③5.2
250SE Coupe & Cabriolet—
Exc Below ③5.2
Conv ③5.7
230SL, 250SL ③6.0
300SEB, SEL ③5.8
300SE Coupe & Cabriolet—
Exc Below ③5.8
Conv ③6.3
220/8, 220D/8 .... ②4.5
230/8, 250/8 .... ②4.8
280S/8 .... ③5.0
280SE/8 .... ④5.1
280SE/8 Coupe & Cabriolet—
Exc Below ④5.1
Conv ③5.7
280SL/8 .... ③6.0
300SEL/8 .... ④5.0
1973-78
280, 280C ⑤5.1
450SE, SEL ②5.4
450SL, SLC ①5.9
230, 240D, 300D ②4.9
280S ②5.2
①*To Renew Trans, Add.* *0.6*
②*To Renew Trans, Add.* *0.5*
③*To Renew Trans, Add.* *1.0*
④*To Renew Trans, Add.* *1.1*
⑤*To Renew Trans, Add.* *0.7*

11—TRANS ASSY (MANUAL), OVERHAUL

Shift cover removed
1966-72—
Exc Below 5.9
220/8, D/8 .... 4.5
230/8, 250/8 .... 4.5
280S/8, SE/8 .... 5.8
280SL/8 .... 5.8
300SEL/8 .... 5.8
1973-78—
240D 7.6

12—TRANS ASSY (AUTOMATIC), OVERHAUL

Transmission removed
1966-72 .... 12.1
1973-78 .... 12.6

13—TRANS KICKDOWN SWITCH, RENEW

1966-72 .... 0.6
1973-78 .... 0.4

14—GEARSHIFT OR SELECTOR LEVER, RENEW

1966-72—
Column Shift 0.3
Floor Shift—
Exc Below 2.1
220/8, D/8 .... 2.3
230/8, 250/8 .... 2.3
1973-78, Exc Floor Shift 0.4
Floor Shift 0.7

15—TRANS SHIFT COVER, R & R OR RENEW

1966-72—
Exc Below 0.4
220/8, D/8 .... 0.8
230/8, 250/8 .... 0.8

16—EXTENSION HOUSING OIL SEAL, RENEW

1966-72—
Exc Below 0.4
280S/8, SE/8 .... 0.6
280SL/8, 300SEL/8 .... 0.6
1973-78—
Exc Below 1.8
450SL 2.7
450SLC 2.2

17—OIL PAN GASKET, RENEW

1966-72—
Exc Below 1.1
250SE, 300SE CP/CA—
Exc Conv 1.1
Conv 1.6
220/8, D/8 .... 0.6
1973-78 .... 0.6

18—GOVERNOR, R & R OR RENEW

1966-72 .... 0.3

19—MODULATING VALVE, RENEW

1966-72—
Exc Below 1.2
230SL, 250SL 1.5
250SE CP/CA 1.3
300SEB, SEL, SE CP/CA 1.3
220/8, D/8, 230/8, 250/8 .... 2.9
280S/8, SE/8 .... 1.1
280SE/8 CP/CA 1.3
300SEL/8 .... 1.1
280SL/8 .... 1.5

Brakes, Steering, Suspension, Universals & Rear Axle—TIME

OPERATION INDEX

Brake Disc Pads, Renew *1*
Master Cylinder, Renew *2*
Master Cylinder, R & R & Overhaul *3*
Wheel Cylinder (One), Overhaul *4*
Brake Caliper, R & R Or Renew *5*
Brake Caliper, R & R & Overhaul *6*
Bleed System *7*
Brake Hose, Renew *8*
Brake Disc, R & R Or Renew *9*
Power Brake Unit, Renew *10*
Power Brake Regulator, Renew *11*
Parking Brake Cable, Renew *12*
Parking Brake Lever, Renew *13*
Steering Coupling, Renew *14*
Steering Gear Assy, R & R Or Renew *15*
Spring(S), Renew *16*
Torsion Bar, Renew *16A*
Cross Strut (Axle Support), Renew *17*
Steering Knuckle, R & R Or Renew *18*
Front Hub Bearongs, Renew *19*
Shock Absorbers, Renew *20*
Drive Shaft Intermediate Bearing, Renew *21*
Differential Axle Housing, Renew *22*
Front Axle Subframe With Half Axle, R & R Or Renew *23*

1—BRAKE DISC PADS, RENEW

1966-72, Front Or Rear 0.3
1973-78, Front Or Rear 0.8

2—MASTER CYLINDER, RENEW

1966-72—
Exc Below 0.7
220/8, D/8 .... 0.6
300SEL/8 .... 0.8
300SEB, SEL 0.8
300SE CP/CA 0.8
1973-78—
Exc Below 0.8
280, 280C 1.1

3—MASTER CYLINDER, R & R & OVERHAUL

1966-72—
Exc Below 1.4
220/8, D/8 .... 1.2
300SEL/8 .... 1.4
300SEB, SEL 1.5
300SE CP/CA 1.5
1973-78 .... 1.3

4—WHEEL CYLINDER (ONE), OVERHAUL

1966-72 .... 0.3

5—BRAKE CALIPER, R & R OR RENEW

1966-72—
Exc Below 0.7
220/8, D/8 .... 0.5
230/8, 250/8 .... 0.5
280S/8, SE/8, SL/8 .... 0.5
300SEL/8 .... 0.5
1973-78 .... 0.8

6—BRAKE CALIPER, R & R & OVERHAUL

1966-72—
Exc Below 1.5
220/8, D/8 .... 1.3
230/8, 250/8 .... 1.3
280S/8, SE/8, SL/8 .... 1.3
300SEL/8 .... 1.3
1973-78 .... 1.6

7—BLEED SYSTEM

All Models 0.5

8—BRAKE HOSE, RENEW

1966-72—
Both, Front 0.6
Both Rear 0.6
1973-78—
One, Front Or Rear 0.7
Both, Front Or Rear 0.9
All 1.2

9—BRAKE DISC, R & R OR RENEW

1966-72
Front (One)—
Exc Below 1.3
220/8, D/8 .... 1.1
230/8, 250/8 .... 1.1
280S/8, SE/8 .... 1.1
280SL/8 .... 1.1
300SEL/8 .... 1.1
Rear (One)—
Exc Below 0.8
220/8, D/8 .... 0.6
230/8, 250/8 .... 0.6
280S/8, SE/8 .... 0.6
280SL/8 .... 0.6
300SEL/8 .... 0.6
1973-78
Front, One 1.6
Both 2.7
Rear, One 1.0
Both 1.8

10—POWER BRAKE UNIT, RENEW

1966-72—
Exc Below 1.3
230SL, 250SL 1.0
300SEB 1.4
300SEL, CP/CA 1.5
280SL/8 .... 1.0
220/8, D/8 .... 1.2
230/8, 250/8 .... 1.2
1973-78—
280, 280C 1.6
450SE, SEL 1.7
450SL, SLC 1.5
230, 240D, 300D 1.4
280S 1.7

11—POWER BRAKE REGULATOR, RENEW

1966-72 .... 0.5

12—PARKING BRAKE CABLE, RENEW

1966-72—
Front—
Exc Below 1.1
280SL/8 .... 0.4
Center 0.4
Rear—
Exc Below 0.6
250SL 0.3
250S, SE, 300SEB 0.3
300SE, SEL 0.3

(Continued)

Brakes, Steering, Suspension, Universals & Rear Axle—TIME Cont'd

1973-78—
Front—
280, 280C 1.3
450SE, SEL 1.9
450SL, SLC 2.6
230, 240D, 300D 1.3
280S 1.9
Rear—
Exc Below 0.6
450 Models & 280S 1.4

13—PARKING BRAKE LEVER, RENEW

1966-72 ....0.4

14—STEERING COUPLING, RENEW

1966-72—
220/8, 230/8, 250/8 ....1.0
280S/8, SE/8—
Exc Below 1.0
Pwr Strg 1.2
300SEL/8 ....1.2
200, 200D, 230, 230S—
Exc Below 1.0
Pwr Strg 1.1
250SE, 300SEB, SEL—
Exc Below 1.0
Pwr Strg 1.2
1973-78—
280, 280C, 280S 1.1
450SE, SEL 1.1
450SL, SLC 1.3
230 ....1.1
240D, 300D 1.2

15—STEERING GEAR ASSY, R & R OR RENEW

1966-72—
Exc Below 1.3
220D/8 ....1.5
200/8, D/8 ....1.4
230/8, 250/8 ....1.4
280S/8, SE/8, SL/8 ....1.2
1973-78 (Power)—
280, 280C 2.9
450SE, SEL 1.9
450SL, SLC 2.6
230 ....2.1
240D, 300D 2.4
280S 1.7

16—SPRING(S), RENEW

1966-72-
220/8, 220D/8, 230/8, 250/8—
One Front 1.0
Both Front 2.0
One Rear 0.8
280S/8, SE/8, SL/8, 300SEL/8—
One Front 1.2
Both Front 2.3
One Rear 0.8
200, 200D, 230, 230S, 250S, SE, 230SL, 250SL, 300SEB—
One Front 1.3
Both Front 2.5
One Rear 0.8
1973-78
Both Front—
Exc Below 1.9
450SE, SEL 2.8
280S 2.2
Both Rear—
450SE, SEL 2.2
450SL 3.1
450SLC 2.8
280S 2.2

16A—TORSION BAR, RENEW

1973-76 (Front)—
Exc Below 1.0
450SE, SEL 5.2
280S 4.8
1973-78 (Rear)—
Exc Below 1.4
450SE, SEL 0.9
450SL 1.3
450SLC 1.6
280S 0.9

17—CROSS STRUT (AXLE SUPPORT), RENEW

1966-72—
Exc Below 1.0
230SL, 250SL 1.6
280SL/8 ....1.6

18—STEERING KNUCKLE, R & R OR RENEW

1966-72—
Exc Below—
One 1.8
Both 3.1
220/8, D/8, 230/8, 250/8—
One 1.5
Both 2.5
1973-78—
One—
280, 280C 1.6
450SE, SEL 1.4
450SL, SLC 2.0
230, 240D, 300D 1.6
280S 1.4
Both—
280, 280C 2.7
450SE, SEL 2.3
450SL, SLC 3.3
230, 240D, 300D 2.7
280S 2.3

19—FRONT HUB BEARINGS, RENEW

1966-72—
One Side 1.8
Both Sides 3.1

20—SHOCK ABSORBERS, RENEW

1966-72
Exc Below—
One Front 0.6
Both Front 0.8
One Rear 0.5
Both Rear 0.7
200, 200D, 230, 230S, 250S, SE—
One Front 0.6
Both Front 0.8
One Rear 0.5
Both Rear 0.8
230SL, 250SL—
One Front 0.7
Both Front 1.0
One Rear 0.6
Both Rear 0.8
1973-78
Front, One 0.6
Front, Both—
280, 280C, 280S 0.9
450SE, SEL 0.9
450SL, SLC 1.0
230, 240D, 300D 0.8
Rear, One—
280, 280C 0.5
450SE, SEL, SLC 1.0
450SL 1.1
230, 240D, 300D 0.5
280S 1.0
Rear, Both—
280, 280C 0.8
450SE, SEL 1.3
450SL 1.6
450SLC 1.5
230, 240D, 300D 0.8
280S 1.3

21—DRIVE SHAFT INTERMEDIATE BEARING, RENEW

Drive shaft removed
1966-72—
Exc Below 0.7
300SEL 1.0
230SL 0.8
220/8, D/8, 230/8, 250/8—
One Bearing 0.5
Both Bearings 0.8
280S/8, SE/8, SL/8 ....0.5
300SEL/8 ....0.5

22—DIFFERENTIAL AXLE HOUSING, RENEW

1966-72—
Exc Below 5.6
300SEL, SE CP/CA 6.3
220/8, D/8, 230/8, 250/8 ....5.3
280SL/8 ....5.6
300SEL/8 ....6.2

23—FRONT AXLE SUBFRAME WITH HALF AXLE, R & R OR RENEW

1966-72—
Exc Below 4.6
300SEL, SE CP/CA 5.0
300SEL/8 ....5.0
220/8, D/8, 230/8, 250/8 ....3.3
1973-78—
280, 280C 3.5
450SL, SLC 4.3
230, 240D, 300D 3.5

Speedometer, W/S Wipers, Switches & Instruments—TIME

OPERATION INDEX

Speedometer Head, Renew 1
Speedometer Cable, Renew 2
W/S Wiper Motor, Renew 3
W/S Washer Pump, Renew 4
Fuel Gauge (Dash Unit), Renew 5
Fuel Tank Gauge, Renew 6
Oil Gauge (Dash Unit), Renew 7
Temperature Gauge (Dash Unit), Renew 8
Headlight Switch, Renew 9
Stop Light Switch, Renew 10
Turn Signal Switch, Renew 11
Turn Signal & Hazard Warning Switch, Renew 12

1—SPEEDOMETER HEAD, RENEW

Includes: R & R cluster
1966-72—
200, 200D, 230, 230S 1.1
250S, SE, SE CP/CA 1.2
300SEB, SEL, SE CP/CA 1.2
230SL, 250SL 1.5
1973-78 ....0.8

2—SPEEDOMETER CABLE, RENEW

1966-72—
Exc Below 1.2
200, 200D, 230, 230S 0.8
1973-78 ....0.9

3—W/S WIPER MOTOR, RENEW

1966-72 ....0.8
1973-78—
280, 280C 0.7
450SE, SEL 2.3
450SL, SLC 1.0
230, 240D, 300D 0.7
280S 2.3

4—W/S WASHER PUMP, RENEW

1966-72—
Exc Below 0.3
230SL, 250SL 0.5
1973-78 ....0.4

5—FUEL GAUGE (DASH UNIT), RENEW

1966-72—
Exc Below 0.2
250S, SE, 300SEB, SEL 0.7
220/8, D/8, 230/8, 250/8 ....0.5
280S/8, SE/8, 300SEL/8 ....0.6
1973-78 ....1.0

6—FUEL TANK GAUGE, RENEW

1966-72—
Exc Below 0.7
220/8, D/8, 230/8, 250/8 ....0.5
280S/8, SE/8, SL/8 ....0.5
300SEL/8 ....0.5

(Continued)

Speedometer, W/S Wipers, Switches & Instruments—TIME Cont'd

1973-78—
- 280, 280C 0.5
- 450 Models 0.6
- 230, 240D, 300D 0.4
- 280S 0.6

7—OIL GAUGE (DASH UNIT), RENEW

Includes: R & R cluster

1966-72—
- 220/8, D/8 .....1.1
- 230/8, 250/8 .....1.1
- 280S/8, SE/8 .....1.5
- 280SE/8 CP/CA 1.2
- 280SL/8 .....1.3
- 300SEL/8 .....1.5
- 200, 200D, 230, 230S 1.1
- 250S, SE, CP/CA 1.4
- 230SL, 250SL 1.4
- 300SEB, SEL 1.4
- 300SE CP/CA 1.2

1973-78 .....1.0

8—TEMPERATURE GAUGE (DASH UNIT), RENEW

Includes: R & R cluster

1966-72—
- 220/8, D/8 .....1.1
- 230/8, 250/8 .....1.1
- 280S/8, SE/8 .....1.5
- 280SE/8 CP/CA 1.2
- 280SL/8 .....1.3
- 300SEL/8 .....1.5
- 200, 200D, 230, 230S 1.2
- 250S, SE 1.5
- 250SE CP/CA 1.3
- 230SL, 250SL 1.4
- 300SE CP/CA 1.3
- 300SEB, SEL 1.5

1973-78 .....1.0

9—HEADLIGHT SWITCH, RENEW

1966-72—
- Exc Below 0.5
- 250S, SE, 300SEB 0.8
- 300SEL 0.8
- 220/8, D/8 .....0.7
- 230/8, 250/8 .....0.7
- 280S/8, SE/8 .....0.7
- 300SEL/8 .....0.7

1973-78—
- 280, 280C 1.0
- 280S 1.1
- 450SE, SEL 1.1
- 450SL, SLC 0.8
- 230, 240D 0.8
- 300D 0.8

10—STOP LIGHT SWITCH, RENEW

1966-72—
- Exc Below 0.3
- 220/8, D/8 .....0.8
- 230/8, 250/8 .....0.8

1973-78—
- Exc Below 0.5
- 280S 0.8
- 450 Models 0.8

11—TURN SIGNAL SWITCH, RENEW

1966-72 .....0.3

1973-78—
- 280, 280C 0.6
- 450SE, SEL 0.9
- 450SL, SLC 0.7
- 230, 240D, 300D 0.6
- 280S 0.9

12—TURN SIGNAL & HAZARD WARNING SWITCH, RENEW

1966-72—
- Exc Below 0.7
- 230SL, 250SL 0.8
- 220/8, D/8, 230/8, 250/8 .....0.6
- 280S/8, SE/8 .....0.6
- 280SL/8, 300SEL/8 .....0.6

1973-78 .....0.3

IDENTIFICATION

ALL MODELS.............................. 281

ILLUSTRATIONS

FIG 1 – ENGINE – BLOCK
FIG 2 – ENGINE – CRANKSHAFT, CAMSHAFT & FLYWHEEL
FIG 3 – TRANSMISSION
FIG 4 – FRONT SUSPENSION
FIG 5 – STEERING
FIG 6 – REAR AXLE

OPERATION TIMES

A

Air Pump.......... 287
Alternator.......... 287
Automatic Transmission.......... 289

B

Brake Drums.......... 290
Brakes.......... 289

C

Cables (Ignition).......... 287
Calipers.......... 290
Camshaft.......... 288
Carburetor.......... 287
Clutch.......... 289
Coil, Ignition.......... 287
Compression Test.......... 287
Cooling System.......... 287
Crankshaft.......... 288
Cylinder Head.......... 288

D

Dash Gauges.......... 291
Differential.......... 290
Disc Brakes.......... 290
Distributor.......... 287

E

Emission Controls.......... 287
Engine Assembly.......... 288
Engine Mountings.......... 289
Engine Oiling.......... 288
Engine Tune-Up.......... 287
Exhaust System.......... 287

F

Flywheel.......... 289
Front Suspension.......... 290
Fuel Gauges.......... 291
Fuel Pump.......... 287
Fuel Tank.......... 287

G

Generator.......... 287

H

Hand Brake.......... 290
Headlight Switch.......... 291
Heater.......... 288
Hose (Brake).......... 296
Hose (Radiator).......... 287
Hydraulic Brakes.......... 289

I

Ignition.......... 287
Ignition Coil.......... 287
Ignition Switch.......... 287
Intake Manifold.......... 287

L

Light Switches.......... 291

M

Main Bearings.......... 288
Master Cylinder.......... 289
Muffler.......... 287

O

Oil Gauge.......... 291
Oiling, Engine.......... 288
Oil Pan.......... 288
Oil Pump.......... 288
Overdrive.......... 289

P

Parking Brake.......... 290
Piston Rings.......... 288
Pistons.......... 288
Power Brake.......... 290

R

Radiator.......... 287
Radiator Hose.......... 287
Regulator.......... 287
Resonator.......... 287
Rocker Arms.......... 288
Rod Bearings.......... 288

S

Shocks (Front).......... 290
Shocks (Rear).......... 290
Speedometer.......... 291
Springs.......... 290
Starting Motor.......... 287
Steering Gear.......... 290
Steering Linkage.......... 290
Switches (Light).......... 291
Synchro-Mesh Trans.......... 289

T

Tachometer.......... 291
Temperature Gauge.......... 291
Thermostat.......... 288
Timing Case Cover.......... 288
Timing Chain.......... 288
Timing Gears.......... 288
Torsion Bar.......... 290
Transmission, Manual.......... 289
Transmission, Automatic.......... 289
Tune-Up Engine.......... 287

U

Universals.......... 290

V

Vacuum Control Unit.......... 287
Valve Lifters.......... 288
Valve System.......... 288

W

Water Pump.......... 288
Wheel Cylinders.......... 290
Windshield Wiper.......... 291

MGB VEHICLE IDENTIFICATION PLATES

The **Car Number** is stamped on a plate secured to the left-hand wing valance forward of the radiator

The **Body Number** is stamped on a plate secured to the left-hand front valance behind the radiator diaphragm

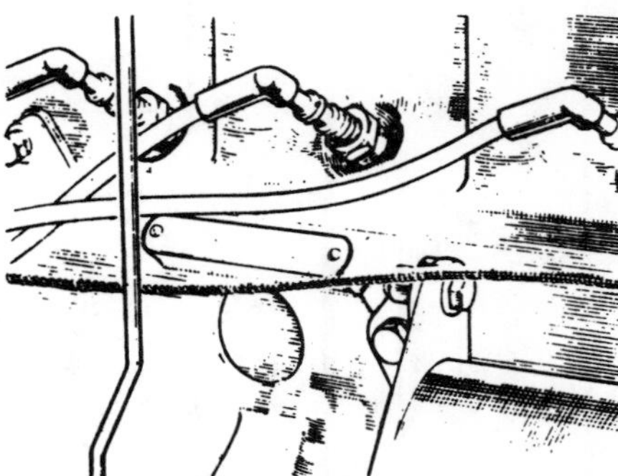

The **Engine Number** is stamped on a plate secured to the right-hand side of the cylinder block

The **Gearbox Number** is stamped on the top of the gearbox casing adjacent to the dipstick

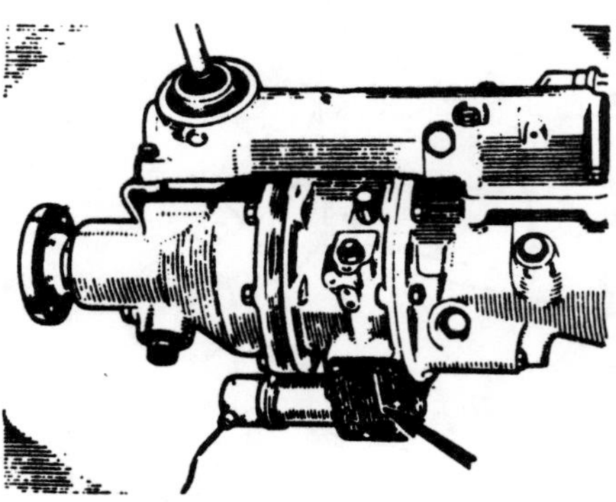

The **Overdrive Unit Number** is stamped on the solenoid side cover on the right-hand side of the unit

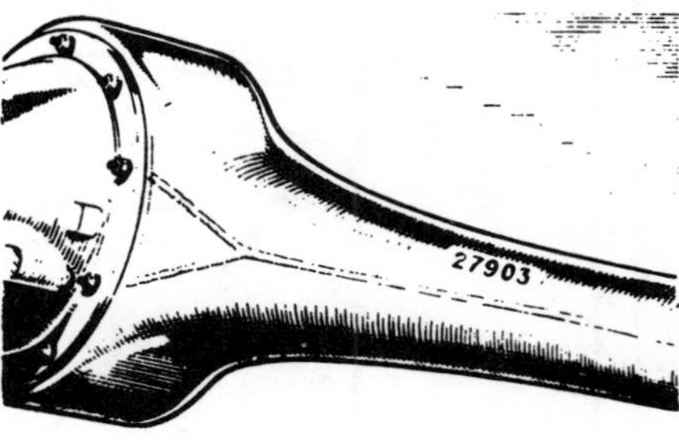

The **Rear Axle Number** is stamped on the front of the axle tube on the left-hand side adjacent to the spring seat

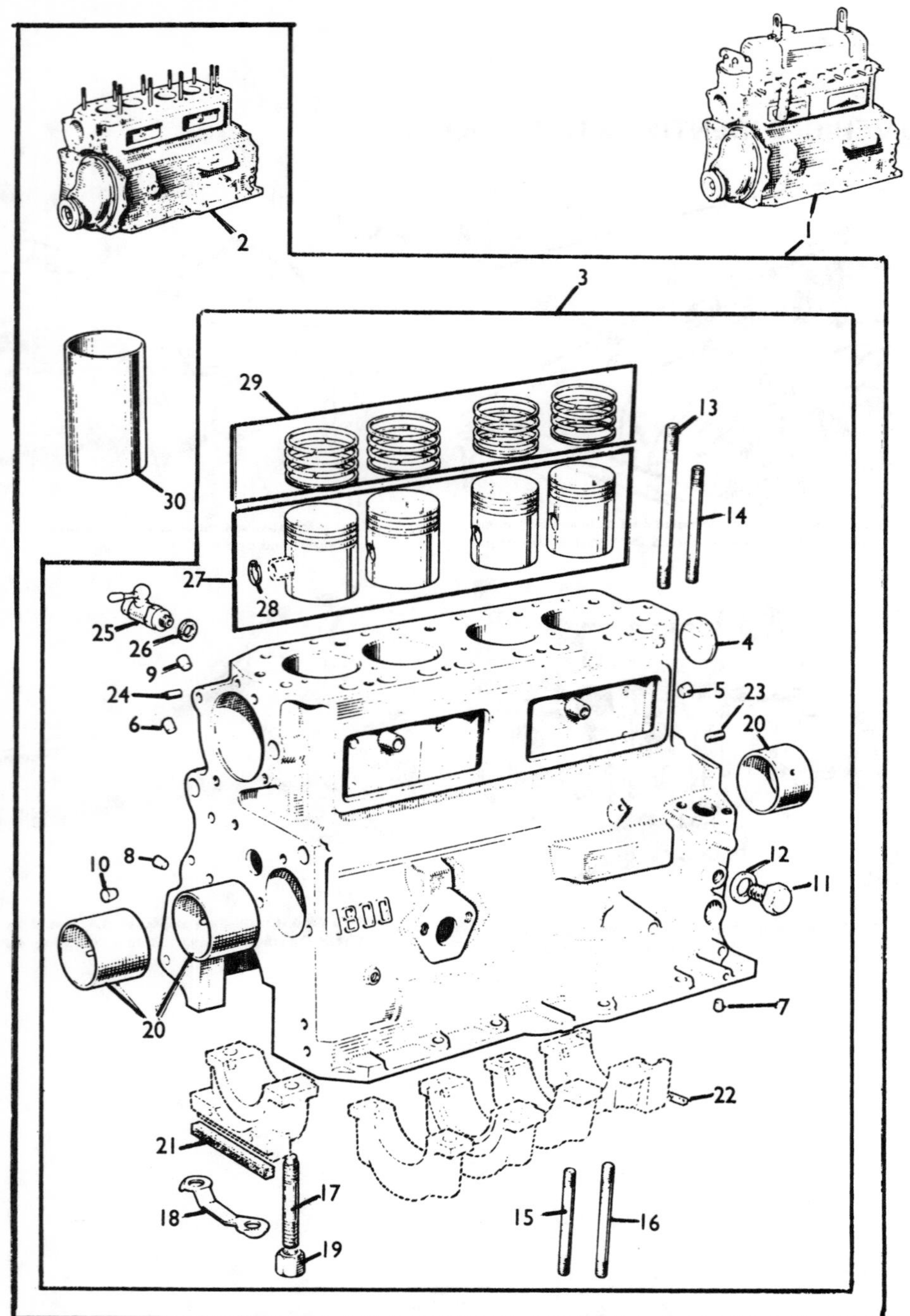

1	Engine Strippped
2	Engine Partial
3	Cylinder Block
4	Plug
5	Plug
6	Plug
7	Plug
8	Plug
9	Plug
10	Plug
11	Plug
12	Washer
13	Stud
14	Stud
15	Stud
16	Stud
17	Stud
18	Washer
19	Nut
20	Bearing
21	Joint
22	Joint
23	Dowel
24	Dowel
25	Drain Tap
26	Washer
27	Piston & Rings
28	Circlip
29	Ring Set
30	Cylinder Liner

FIG 1 – ENGINE BLOCK

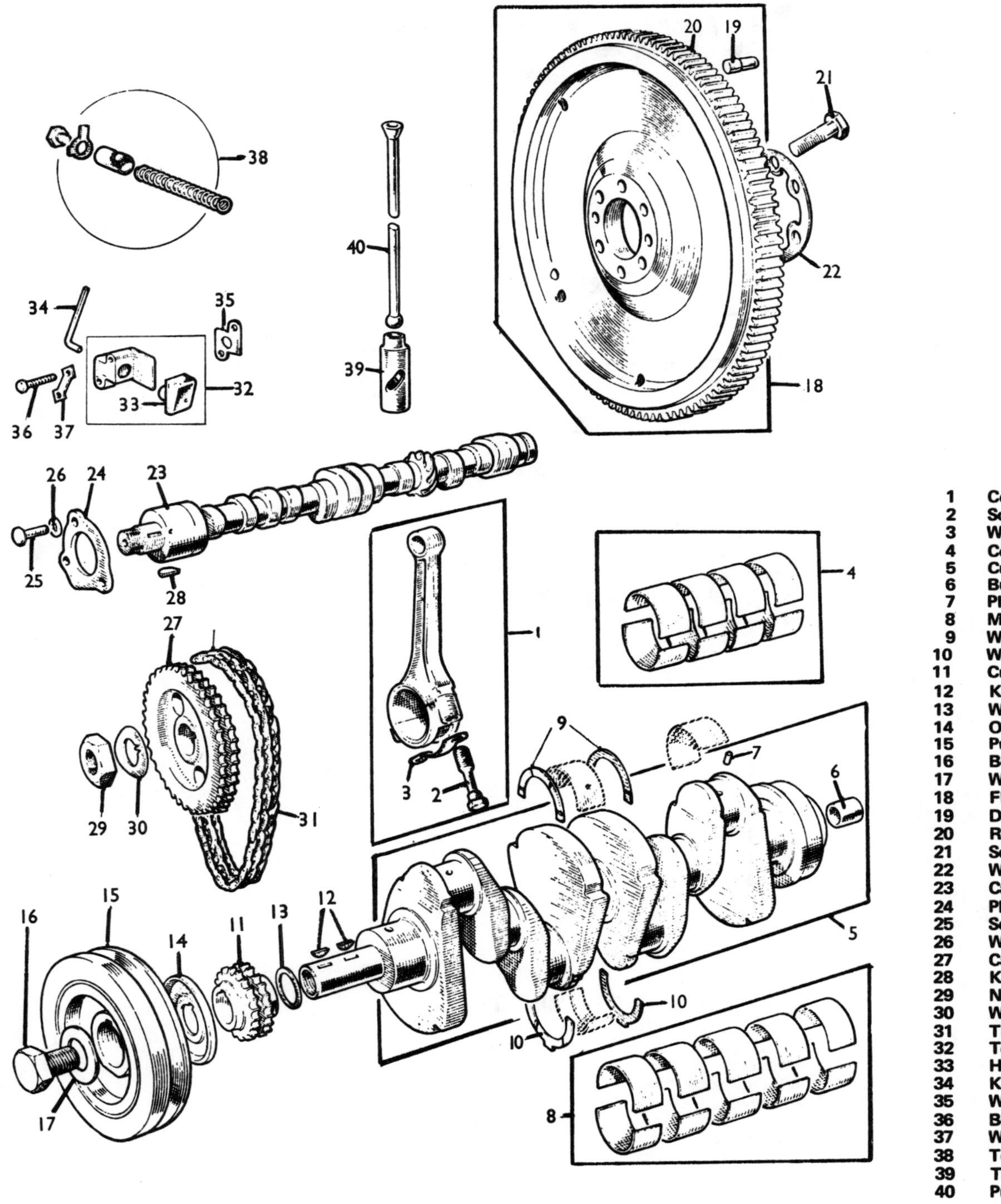

1 Connecting Rod
2 Screw
3 Washer
4 Connecting Rod Bearings
5 Crankshaft
6 Bush
7 Plug
8 Main Bearings
9 Washer
10 Washer
11 Crankshaft Gear
12 Key
13 Washer
14 Oil Thrower
15 Pulley
16 Boot
17 Washer
18 Flywheel
19 Dowel
20 Ring Gear
21 Screw
22 Washer
23 Camshaft
24 Plate
25 Screw
26 Washer
27 Camshaft Gear
28 Key
29 Nut
30 Washer
31 Timing Chain
32 Tensioner
33 Head
34 Key
35 Washer
36 Bolt
37 Washer
38 Tensioner Repair Kit
39 Tappet
40 Push Rod

FIG 2 – ENGINE CRANKSHAFT, CAMSHAFT & FLYWHEEL

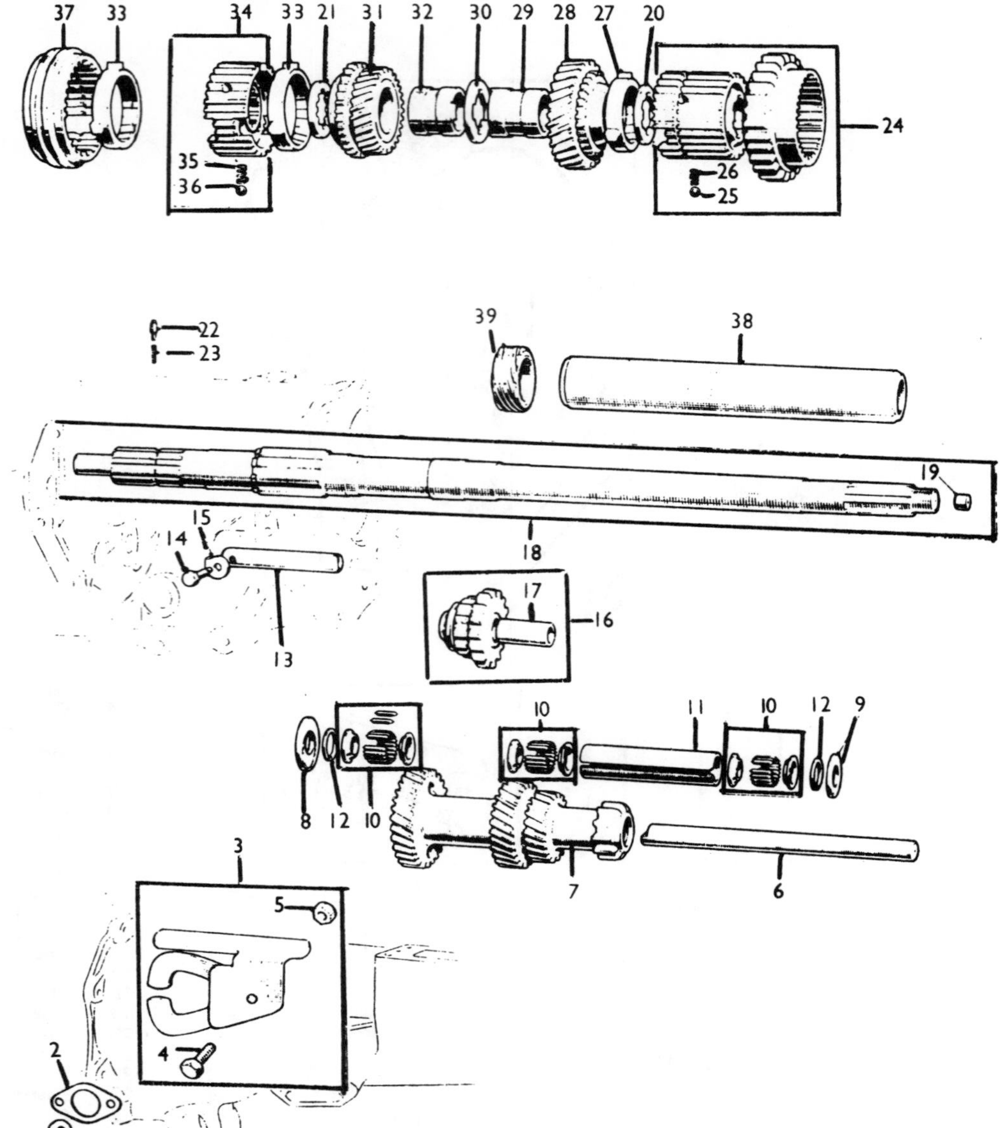

FIG 3 – TRANSMISSION

1	Seal	20	Washer
2	Washer	21	Washer
3	Interlocking Arm	22	Peg
4	Screw	23	Spring
5	Nut	24	1st Speed Gear & Synchronizer
6	Layshaft	25	Ball
7	Layshaft Gear Unit	26	Spring
8	Washer	27	Ring
9	Washer	28	2nd Speed Gear
10	Roller Bearing	29	Bushing
11	Tube	30	Ring
12	Ring	31	3rd Speed Gear
13	Reverse Shaft	32	Bushing
14	Screw	33	Ring
15	Washer	34	Synchronizer Assy
16	Reverse Gear	35	Spring
17	Bushing	36	Ball
18	3rd Speed Shaft	37	Coupling
19	Oil Restrictor	38	Distance Piece
		39	Speedometer Gear

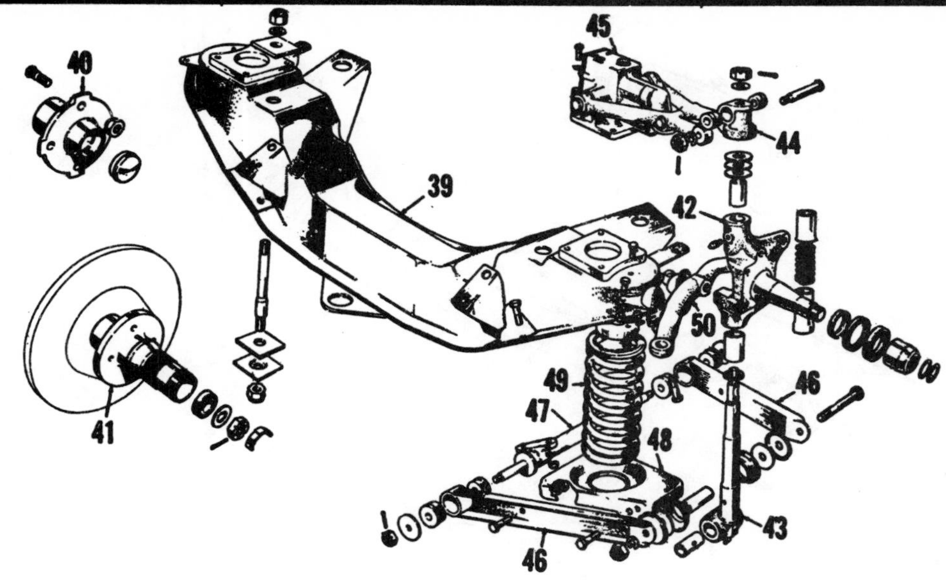

FIG 4 – FRONT SUSPENSION

39 Crossmember
40 Hub, Disc Wheel
41 Hub, Wire Wheel
42 Steering Knuckle
43 Swivel Pin Support
44 Support Link, Upper
45 Upper Arm & Shock
46 Control Arm
47 Shaft
48 Spring Seat
49 Spring
50 Arm

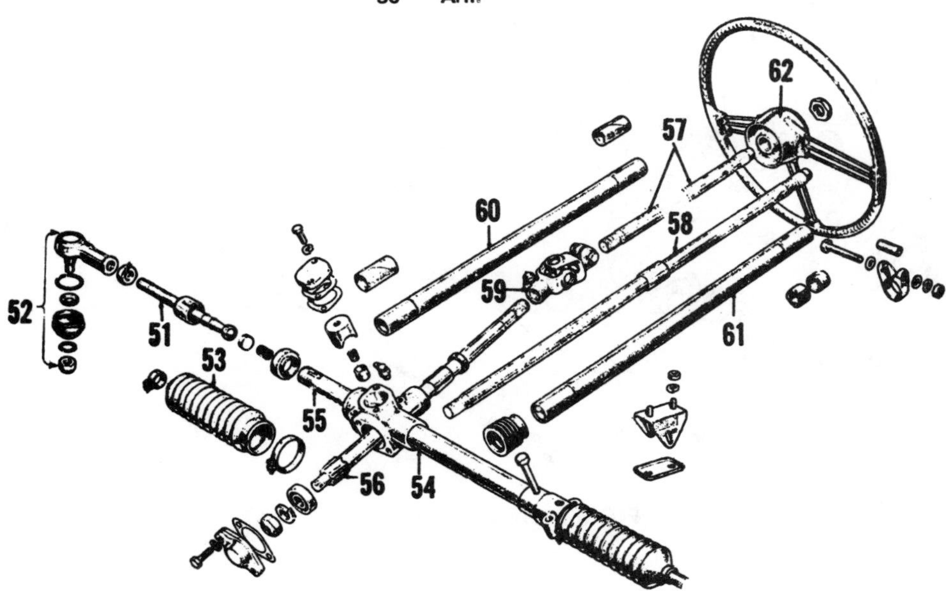

FIG 5 – STEERING

51 Tie Rod
52 End
53 Boot
54 Gear Housing
55 Rack
56 Pinion
57 Main Shaft
58 Main Shaft (W/Strg Lock)
59 Universal Joint
60 Column Jacket
61 Column Jacket (W/Strg Lock)
62 Wheel

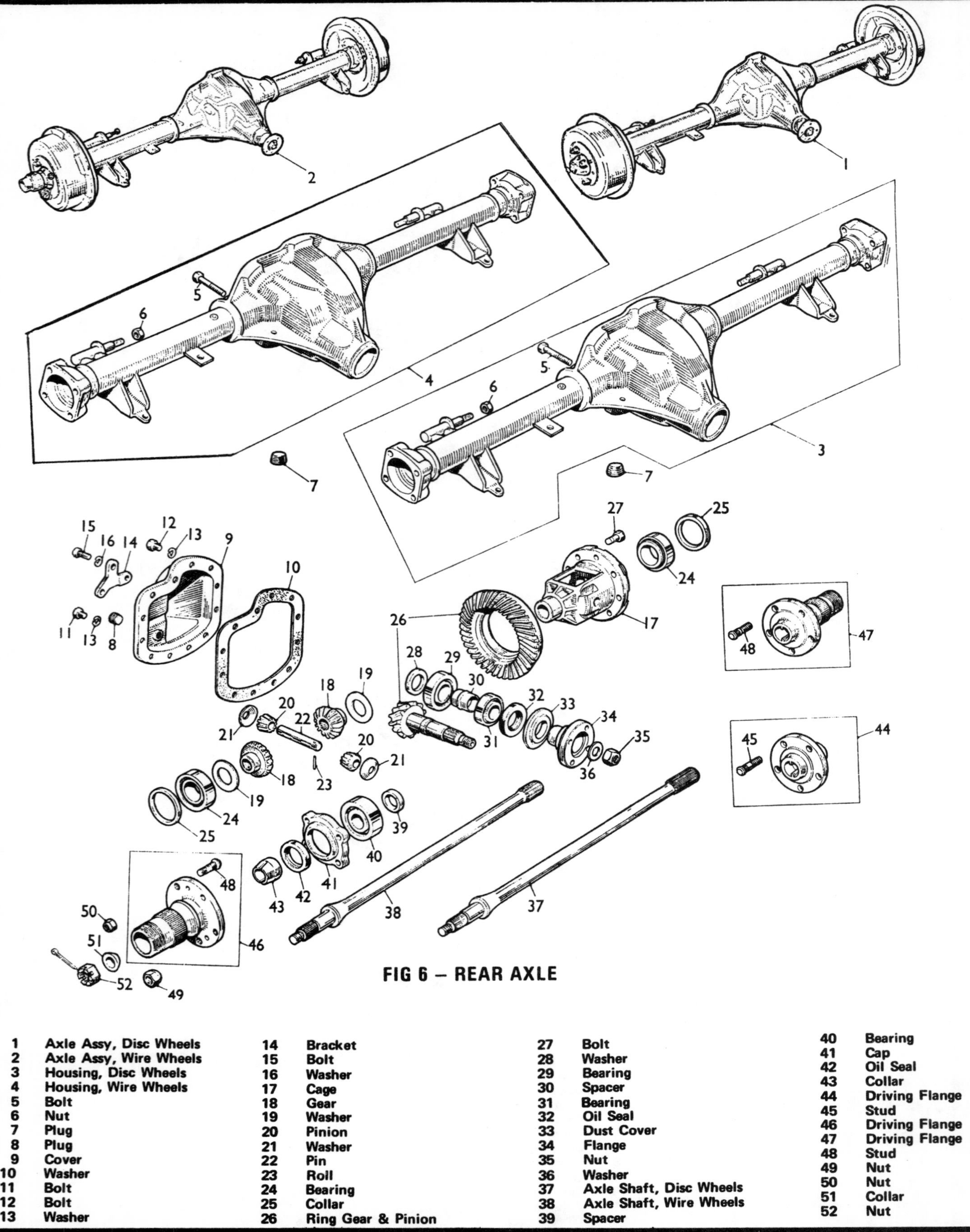

FIG 6 – REAR AXLE

1	Axle Assy, Disc Wheels	14	Bracket	27	Bolt	40	Bearing
2	Axle Assy, Wire Wheels	15	Bolt	28	Washer	41	Cap
3	Housing, Disc Wheels	16	Washer	29	Bearing	42	Oil Seal
4	Housing, Wire Wheels	17	Cage	30	Spacer	43	Collar
5	Bolt	18	Gear	31	Bearing	44	Driving Flange
6	Nut	19	Washer	32	Oil Seal	45	Stud
7	Plug	20	Pinion	33	Dust Cover	46	Driving Flange
8	Plug	21	Washer	34	Flange	47	Driving Flange
9	Cover	22	Pin	35	Nut	48	Stud
10	Washer	23	Roll	36	Washer	49	Nut
11	Bolt	24	Bearing	37	Axle Shaft, Disc Wheels	50	Nut
12	Bolt	25	Collar	38	Axle Shaft, Wire Wheels	51	Collar
13	Washer	26	Ring Gear & Pinion	39	Spacer	52	Nut

Ignition, Starting & Charging—TIME

OPERATION INDEX

Tune-Up, Minor *1*
Tune-Up, Major *2*
Compression Test *3*
Distrubutor, R & R Or Renew *4*
Distributor Cap, Renew *5*
Ignition Cable Set, Renew *6*
Vacuum Control Unit, Renew *7*
Ignition Coil, Renew *8*
Starter & Ignition Switch, Renew *9*
Starter, R & R Or Renew *10*
Starter Solenoid, Renew *11*
Starter, R & R & Overhaul *12*
Regulator, Renew *13*
Alternator Or Generator, R & R Or Renew *14*
Alternator Or Generator, R & R & Overhaul *15*

1—TUNE-UP, MINOR
Includes: Renew points, condenser & plugs, set spark plugs & adjust carburetor idle, check exhaust emissions.
Exc Below 2.8
MGC & Gt 2.6
MGC & Gt Auto Trans 3.3

2—TUNE-UP, MAJOR
Includes: Check compression, clean or renew and adjust spark plugs. R & R distributor, renew points and condenser. Adjust ignition timing, carburetor and fan belts. Clean battery terminals and service air cleaner. Check coil, exhaust emissions & clean or replace fuel filter.
Exc Below 4.3
MCG & Gt 4.1
MGC & Gt—
  Auto Trans 5.2
  Std Trans 4.7

3—COMPRESSION TEST
Exc Below 0.5
MGC & Gt 0.9

4—DISTRIBUTOR, R & R OR RENEW
Exc Below 0.6
MGC & Gt 0.4

5—DISTRIBUTOR CAP, RENEW
Exc Below 0.8
MGC & Gt 0.9

6—IGNITION CABLE SET, RENEW
Exc Below 0.8
MGC & Gt 0.9

7—VACUUM CONTROL UNIT, RENEW
All Models 0.2

58—IGNITION COIL, RENEW
All Models 0.2

9—STARTER & IGNITION SWITCH, RENEW
Exc Below 0.9
MGB & Gt 0.4

10—STARTER, R & R OR RENEW
Exc Below 1.0
MGB & Gt Mk II 0.5
MGB & Gt 1.6

11—STARTER SOLENOID, RENEW
Exc Below 0.6
MGB & Gt 0.4

12—STARTER, R & R & OVERHAUL
Exc Below 1.0
MGB & Gt 2.1
MGC & Gt 2.0

13—REGULATOR, RENEW
Exc Below 0.2
MGB & Gt 0.3

14—ALTERNATOR OR GENERATOR, R & R OR RENEW
Exc Below 0.5
MGB & Gt Mk II 0.6

15—ALTERNATOR OR GENERATOR, R & R & OVERHAUL
All Models 1.4

Fuel, Emission Controls, Intake & Exhaust Systems—TIME

OPERATION INDEX

Carburetor, R & R Or Renew *1*
Carburetor, R & R & Overhaul *2*
Fuel Pump, R & R Or Renew *3*
Fuel Pump, R & R & Overhaul *4*
Fuel Tank, R & R Or Renew *5*
Choke Control Cable(S), Renew *6*
Air Pump, Renew *7*
Air Pump, R & R & Overhaul *8*
Pressure Relief Valve, Renew *9*
Pump Cleaner Element, Renew *10*
Air Pump Pulley, Renew *11*
Air Manifold, Renew *12*
Manifold Check Valve, Renew *13*
Emission Gulp Valve, Renew *14*
Intake Manifold Or Gasket, Renew *15*
Exhaust Manifold Or Gasket, Renew *16*
Exhaust System Assy, Renew *17*
Exhaust Pipe Front, Renew *18*
Muffler Front, Renew *19*
Resonator Or Rear, Renew *20*
Exhaust Pipe Intermediate, Renew *21*
Exhaust Tailpipe Or Silencer, Renew *22*

1—CARBURETOR, R & R OR RENEW
Exc Below, Both 1.2
MGC & Gt, Both—
  Auto Trans 1.9
  Std Trans 1.4

2—CARBURETOR, R & R & OVERHAUL
Exc Below, Both 2.9
MGC & Gt, Both—
  Auto Trans 3.8
  Std Trans 3.4

3—FUEL PUMP, R & R OR RENEW
All Models 0.5

4—FUEL PUMP, R & R & OVERHAUL
All Models 1.7

5—FUEL TANK, R & R OR RENEW
All Models 1.0

6—CHOKE CONTROL CABLE(S), RENEW
Exc Below 1.1
MGC & Gt 0.5

7—AIR PUMP, RENEW
Exc Below 0.9
MGB & Gt Mk II 0.4

8—AIR PUMP, R & R & OVERHAUL
Exc Below 1.4
MGB & Gt Mk II 0.9

9—PRESSURE RELIEF VALVE, RENEW
Exc Below 1.0
MGB & Gt Mk II 0.5

10—PUMP CLEANER ELEMENT, RENEW
Exc Below 0.2
MGB & Gt Mk II 0.1

11—AIR PUMP PULLEY, RENEW
Exc Below 1.0
MGB & Gt Mk II 0.3

12—AIR MANIFOLD, RENEW
Exc Below 0.8
MGB & Gt Mk II 0.3

13—MANIFOLD CHECK VALVE, RENEW
All Models 0.2

14—EMISSION GULG VALVE, RENEW
Exc Below 0.5
MGB & Gt 0.2

15—INTAKE MANIFOLD OR GASKET, RENEW
Exc Below 1.5
MGC & Gt—
  Auto Trans 2.8
  Std Trans 2.2

16—EXHAUST MANIFOLD OR GASKET, RENEW
Exc Below 2.2
MGC & Gt 2.9

17—EXHAUST SYSTEM ASSY, RENEW
Exc Below 0.7
MGC & Gt 0.8

18—EXHAUST PIPE FRONT, RENEW
All Models 0.9

19—MUFFLER, FRONT, RENEW
Exc Below 1.5
MGC & Gt 0.9

20—RESONATOR OR REAR, RENEW
MGB, All Models 1.2

21—EXHAUST PIPE INTERMEDIATE, RENEW
MGB, All Models 1.5

22—EXHAUST TAIL PIPE OR SILENCER, RENEW
MGC, All Models 0.9

Engine Cooling & Heater System—TIME

OPERATION INDEX

Radiator, R & R Or Renew *1*
Radiator Hoses, Renew *2*
By-Pass Hose, Renew *3*
Water Pump, R & R Or Renew *4*
Water Pump, R & R & Overhaul *5*
Thermostat Or Housing, Renew *6*

Expansion Tank, Renew

Heater Assy, Renew *8*
Heater Matrix, Renew *9*
Heater Blower Motor, Renew *10*
Heater Temperature Control Valve, Renew *11*
Heater Control, Renew *12*
Demister Duct, Renew *13*
Heater Hoses, Renew *14*

1—RADIATOR, R & R OR RENEW
Exc Below 1.1
MGC & Gt 0.9

2—RADIATOR HOSES, RENEW
Upper—
  Exc Below 0.3
  MGB & Gt Mk II 0.4
Lower—
  Exc Below 0.4
  MGC & Gt 1.2

(Continued)

Engine Cooling & Heater System—TIME Cont'd

Both—
- Exc Below 0.7
- MGB & Gt 0.6
- MGC & Gt 1.4

3—BY-PASS HOSE, RENEW
All Models 0.5

4—WATER PUMP, R & R OR RENEW
Exc Below 1.4
MGB & Gt 1.3
MGC & Gt 2.0

5—WATER PUMP, R & R & OVERHAUL
Exc Below 2.2
MGC & Gt 2.9

6—THERMOSTAT OR HOUSING, RENEW
Exc Below 0.4
MGB & Gt Mk II 0.7

7—EXPANSION TANK, RENEW
All Models 0.2

8—HEATER ASSY, RENEW
All Models 1.3

9—HEATER MATRIX, RENEW
All Models 1.3

10—HEATER BLOWER MOTOR, RENEW
All Models 0.3

11—HEATER TEMPERATURE CONTROL VALVE, RENEW
All Models 0.4

12—HEATER CONTROL, RENEW
Exc Below 0.4
MGB & Gt 0.2

13—DEMISTER DUCT, RENEW
Exc Below 3.2
MGB & Gt, Both 0.7

14—HEATER HOSES, RENEW
All Models—
- One 0.2
- Both 0.3

Engine—TIME

OPERATION INDEX

Engine, R & R 1
Engine, Renew 2
Engine, R & R & Overhaul 3
Engine (Short), Renew & Grind Valves 4
Cylinder Head, R & R Or Gasket, Renew 5
Valves, Grind 6
One Valve, Renew & Grind 7
Rocker Arm Cover Gasket, Renew 8
Valve Rocker Arm Assy, Clean Or Overhaul 9
Valve Tappets, Renew 10
Valve Tappets, Adjust 11
Timing Cover Seal & Gasket, Renew 12
Timing Chain Or Gears, Renew 13
Timing Chain Tensioner, Renew 14
Oil Sump Or Gasket, Renew 15
Camshaft, R & R Or Renew 16
Camshaft Bearings, Renew 17
Oil Pump, R & R Or Renew 18
Piston Ring(S), Renew 19
Rings & Main Bearings, Renew & Grind Valves 20
Rod Bearing(S), Renew 21
Main Bearings, Renew 22
Main & Rod Bearings, Renew 23
Crankshaft, R & R Or Renew 24
Crankshaft Thrust Washer, Renew 25
Crankshaft Rear Main Oil Seal, Renew 26
Piston(S), Renew 27
Crankshaft Damper, Renew 28
Crankshaft Pulley, Renew 29

1—ENGINE, R & R
Does not include transfer of any part of engine or replacement of special equipment.
Exc Below 6.3
MGC & Gt 6.8

2—ENGINE, RENEW
Includes: Fit replacement over ancillary equipment, clean & adjust carburetors.
Exc Below 9.5
MGB & Gt 8.8
MGC & Gt—
- Auto Trans 11.9
- Std Trans 10.8

3—ENGINE, R & R & OVERHAUL
Includes: Rebore cylinders with boring bar, renew pistons, rings, bearings, grind valves, plastigauge bearings and perform minor tune-up.
Exc Below 26.5
MGC & Gt—
- Auto Trans 31.9
- Std Trans 31.4

—NOTE—
Include On Transverse Engines; Clutch Overhaul & Adjustment Of Idler Gear.

4—ENGINE (SHORT), RENEW & GRIND VALVES
Includes: Minor tune-up
Exc Below 19.9
MGB & Gt 18.6
MGC & Gt—
- Auto Trans 25.5
- Std Trans 24.7

5—CYLINDER HEAD, R & R OR GASKET, RENEW
Exc Below 3.4
MGC & Gt—
- Auto Trans 6.1
- Std Trans 5.6

6—VALVES, GRIND
Includes: Minor tune-up
Exc Below 3.4
MGC & Gt—
- Auto Trans 6.1
- Std Trans 5.6

7—ONE VALVE, RENEW & GRIND
Exc Below 3.5
MGC & Gt—
- Auto Trans 6.3
- Std Trans 5.8

8—ROCKER ARM COVER GASKET, RENEW
Exc Below 0.4
MGC & Gt 0.5

9—VALVE ROCKER ARM ASSY, CLEAN OR OVERHAUL
Exc Below 1.0
MGC & Gt 2.0

10—VALVE TAPPETS, RENEW
Exc Below 2.7
MGC & Gt 2.6

11—VALVE TAPPETS, ADJUST
Exc Below 0.7
MGC & Gt 1.3

12—TIMING COVER SEAL & GASKET, RENEW
Exc Below 2.0
MGC & Gt 2.8

13—TIMING CHAIN OR GEARS, RENEW
Exc Below 2.3
MGC & Gt 3.8

14—TIMING CHAIN TENSIONER, RENEW
Exc Below 2.3
MGC & Gt 3.8

15—OIL SUMP OR GASKET, RENEW
Exc Below 1.4
MGC & Gt—
- Auto Trans 7.5
- Std Trans 4.3

16—CAMSHAFT, R & R OR RENEW
Exc Below 7.0
MGC & Gt 7.4

17—CAMSHAFT BEARINGS, RENEW
All Models (MGB) 17.8

18—OIL PUMP, R & R OR RENEW
Exc Below 1.6
MGC & Gt—
- Auto Trans 7.6
- Std Trans 4.5

19—PISTON RING(S), RENEW
Exc Below 7.0
MGC & Gt—
- Auto Trans 11.2
- Std Trans 10.8

20—RINGS & MAIN BEARINGS, RENEW & GRIND VALVES
Exc Below 13.5
MGC & Gt—
- Auto Trans 16.6
- Std Trans 15.4

21—ROD BEARING(S), RENEW
Exc Below (One Pair) 1.8
MGC & Gt—
- Auto Trans 7.9
- Std Trans 4.7

Each Additional 0.4

22—MAIN BEARINGS, RENEW
Exc Below 9.3
MGC & Gt—
- Auto Trans 10.4
- Std Trans 9.8

23—MAIN & ROD BEARINGS, RENEW
Exc Below 10.9
MGC & Gt—
- Auto Trans 12.0
- Std Trans 11.4

24—CRANKSHAFT, R & R OR RENEW
Exc Below 9.5
MGC & Gt—
- Auto Trans 10.7
- Std Trans 10.1

25—CRANKSHAFT THRUST WASHER, RENEW
Exc Below 1.9
MGC & Gt—
- Auto Trans 7.8
- Std Trans 4.6

26—CRANKSHAFT REAR MAIN OIL SEAL, RENEW
Exc Below 7.6
MGC & Gt—
- Auto Trans 9.0
- Std Trans 8.5

27—PISTON(S), RENEW
Exc Below 7.0
MGC & Gt—
- Auto Trans 11.2
- Std Trans 10.8

28—CRANKSHAFT DAMPER, RENEW
Transverse Engine—
- All Models 1.5

29—CRANKSHAFT PULLEY, RENEW
Exc Below 0.4
MGC & Gt 1.5

Clutch, Mounts, Transmissions & Overdrive—TIME

OPERATION INDEX

Flywheel, R & R Or Renew 1
Flywheel Ring Gear, Renew 2
Clutch Or Disc, Renew 3
Release Bearing, Renew 4
Clutch Master Cylinder, Renew 5
Clutch Master Cylinder, R & R & Overhaul 6
Slave Cylinder, Renew 7
Slave Cylinder, R & R & Overhaul 8
Bleed System 9
Engine Mounts, Renew 10
Transmission Assy, R & R Or Renew 11
Gearbox Front Plate Or Gasket & Seal, Renew 12
Gearbox Rear Extension Gasket, Renew 13
Extension Housing Oil Seal, Renew 14
Gearbox Side Plate Gasket, Renew 15
Gearbox Top Cover Gasket, Renew 16
Shift Forks Or Rail, Renew 17
Gearbox, R & R & Overhaul 18
Oil Pan Gasket, Renew 19
Front & Rear Band, Adjust 20
Gearshift Or Selector Lever, Renew 21
Throttle Valve Cable, Renew 22
Gear Selector Cable, Renew 23
Overdrive, R & R Or Renew 24
Overdrive, R & R & Overhaul 25
Overdrive Operating Valve, Renew 26
Overdrive Relief Valve, Renew 27
Overdrive Oil Pump, Renew 28

1—FLYWHEEL, R & R OR RENEW
Exc Below 7.1
MGC & Gt—
Auto Trans 8.1
Std Trans 7.5

2—FLYWHEEL RING GEAR, RENEW
Exc Below 8.3
MGC & Gt 8.7

3—CLUTCH OR DISC, RENEW
Exc Below 6.8
MGC & Gt 7.0

4—RELEASE BEARING, RENEW
Exc Below 6.7
MGC & Gt 6.9

5—CLUTCH MASTER CYLINDER, RENEW
Includes: Bleed system
Exc Below 0.8
MGB & Gt Mk II 1.2

6—CLUTCH MASTER CYLINDER, R & R & OVERHAUL
Includes: Bleed system
Exc Below 2.0
MGB & Gt Mk II 2.5

7—SLAVE CYLINDER, RENEW
Includes: Bleed system
All Models 0.6

8—SLAVE CYLINDER, R & R & OVERHAUL
Includes: Bleed system
All Models 1.4

9—BLEED SYSTEM
All Models 0.3

10—ENGINE MOUNTS, RENEW
Front—
Left—
Exc Below 0.8
MGC & Gt 1.9
Right—
Exc Below 1.2
MGC & Gt 1.0
Both—
Exc Below 2.0
MGC & Gt 2.7
Rear Set—
Exc Below 0.7
MGC & Gt 0.8

11—TRANSMISSION ASSY, R & R OR RENEW
Exc Below 6.6
MGC & Gt—
Auto Trans 7.3
Std Trans 6.9

12—GEARBOX FRONT PLATE OR GASKET & SEAL, RENEW
Exc Below 6.9
MGC & Gt 7.1

13—GEARBOX REAR EXTENSION GASKET, RENEW
Exc Below 7.1
MGC & Gt 7.4

14—EXTENSION HOUSING OIL SEAL, RENEW
Std Trans 0.7
Auto Trans 0.8

15—GEARBOX SIDE PLATE GASKET, RENEW
Exc Below 6.8
MGC & Gt 7.1

16—GEARBOX TOP COVER GASKET, RENEW
Exc Below 6.2
MGC & Gt 6.7

17—SHIFT FORKS OR RAILS, RENEW
Exc Below 8.4
MGC & Gt 8.8

18—GEARBOX, R & R & OVERHAUL
Exc Below 11.5
MGC & Gt 11.9

19—OIL PAN GASKET, RENEW
MGC & Gt, Auto Trans 0.7

20—FRONT & REAR BAND, ADJUST
Front 0.8
Rear 0.5
Both 1.3

21—GEARSHIFT OR SELECTOR LEVER, RENEW
Exc Below 0.3
MGC & Gt, Auto Trans 0.9

22—THROTTLE VALVE CABLE, RENEW
MGC & Gt, Auto Trans 1.3

23—GEAR SELECTOR CABLE, RENEW
MGC & Gt, Auto Trans 0.3

24—OVERDRIVE, R & R OR RENEW
Exc Below 6.6
MGC & Gt 7.0

25—OVERDRIVE, R & R & OVERHAUL
Exc Below 9.3
MGC & Gt 9.2

26—OVERDRIVE OPERATING VALVE, RENEW
All Models 0.3

27—OVERDRIVE RELIEF VALVE, RENEW
All Models 0.2

28—OVERDRIVE OIL PUMP, RENEW
Exc Below 7.8
MGC & Gt 8.0

Brakes, Steering, Suspension, Universals & Rear Axle—TIME

OPERATION INDEX

Brake Shoes Or Friction Pads, Renew 1
Master Cylinder, Renew 2
Master Cylinder, R & R & Overhaul 3
Brake Fluid Reservoir, Renew 4
Wheel Cylinders, Renew 5
Wheel Cylinder, R & R & Overhaul 6
Caliper Assy, Renew 7
Caliper Assy, R & R & Overhaul 8
Bleed System 9
Brake Hose, Renew 10
Hub Or Bearing, Renew 11
Disc Or Shield, Renew 12
Brake Drum, Renew 13
Brake Booster Or Servo, Renew 14
Brake Booster Or Servo, R & R & Overhaul 15
Pedal Assy, Renew 16
Pedal Assy, R & R & Overhaul 17
Handbrake Assy, Renew 18
Handbrake Lever Ratchet, Renew 19
Rack & Pinion Assy, Renew 20
Rack & Pinion Assy, R & R & Overhaul 21
Column Universal Joint, Renew 22
Swivel Axle Or Hub Pins & Bushings, Renew 23
Swivel Pin Trunnion Link, Renew 24
Swivel Pin Trunnion Bushing, Renew 25
Steering Lever, Renew 26
Tie Rod Ball Ends, Renew 27
Front Suspension Assy, Renew 28
Front Suspension Assy, Overhaul 29
Upper Arm Or Bushings, Renew 30
Lower Arm Or Bushings, Renew 31
Wishbone Pivot Or Bushings, Renew 32
Tie Rod Front Assy, Renew 33
Spring(S), Renew 34
Leaf Spring, Renew 35
Leaf Spring, Overhaul 36
Anti-Roll Bar (Front) Link Or Bushings, Renew 37
Shock Absorber, Renew 38
Torsion Bar (Front), Renew 39
Universal Joints, Renew 40
Half Shaft Or Gasket, Renew 41
Final Drive Or Axle Assy, Renew 42
Differential Cage Bearings, Renew 43
Differential Drive Gear & Pinion, Overhaul 44
Pinion Oil Seal, Renew 45
Half Shaft Oil Seal, Renew 46

1—BRAKE SHOES OR FRICTION PADS, RENEW
Exc Below 0.5
MGC & Gt 0.9

2—MASTER CYLINDER, RENEW
Exc Below 2.2
MGC & Gt 0.8
MGC & Gt 1.9

3—MASTER CYLINDER, R & R & OVERHAUL
Exc Below 1.9
MGB & Gt 1.2
MGC & Gt 2.5

4—BRAKE FLUID RESERVOIR, RENEW
Exc Below 1.9
MGB & Gt Mk II 2.3

(Continued)

Brakes, Steering, Suspension, Universals & Rear Axle—TIME Cont'd

5—WHEEL CYLINDERS, RENEW
Rear—
One—
Exc Below 1.2
MGC & Gt 1.3
Both—
Exc Below 2.2
MGC & Gt 2.3

6—WHEEL CYLINDERS, R & R & OVERHAUL
Rear—
One—
Exc Below 1.5
MGC & Gt 1.7
Both—
Exc Below 2.9
MGC & Gt 3.0

7—CALIPER ASSY, RENEW
Each—
Exc Below 0.8
MGC & Gt 0.9
Both—
Exc Below 1.2
MGC & Gt 1.3

8—CALIPER ASSY, R & R & OVERHAUL
Each—
Exc Below 1.2
MGC & Gt 1.3
Both—
Exc Below 2.0
MGC & Gt 2.2

9—BLEED SYSTEM
All Models 0.4

10—BRAKE HOSE, RENVE
All Models 0.5

11—HUB OR BEARING, RENEW
Front—
Exc Below 1.2
MGC & Gt 2.0
Rear—
All Models 0.6

12—DISC OR SHIELD, RENEW
Disc—
Each—
Exc Below 1.0
MGC & Gt 1.6
Both—
Exc Below 1.9
MGC & Gt 2.8
Shield—
Each—
Exc Below 0.8
MGC & Gt 1.4
Both—
Exc Below 1.5
MGC & Gt 2.3

13—BRAKE DRUM, RENEW
All Models—
Each 0.6
Both 1.0

14—BRAKE BOOSTER OR SERVO, RENEW
Front System—
All Models 0.9
Rear System—
All Models 0.7

15—BRAKE BOOSTER OR SERVO, R & R & OVERHAUL
Front System—
All Models 1.7
Rear System—
All Models 1.5

16—PEDAL ASSY, RENEW
All Models 0.4

17—PEDAL ASSY, R & R & OVERHAUL
All Models 0.6

18—HANDBRAKE ASSY, RENEW
All Models 0.8

19—HANDBRAKE LEVER RATCHET, RENEW
All Models 1.0

20—RACK & PINION ASSY, RENEW
Exc Below 0.7
Mgc & Gt 1.0

21—RACK & PINION, R & R & OVERHAUL
Exc Below 1.7
Mgc & Gt 1.9

22—COLUMN UNIVERSAL JOINT, RENEW
Exc Below ①1.6
Mgb & Gt ①0.6
Mgc & Gt ②1.9
①To Overhaul, Add. 0.4
②To Overhaul, Add. 0.6

23—SWIVEL AXLE OR HUB PINS & BUSHINGS, RENEW
One Side—
All Models 3.3
Both Sides—
All Models 6.5

24—SWIVEL PIN TRUNNION LINK, RENEW
Each Side—
Exc Below 1.1
MGC & Gt 0.5

25—SWIVEL PIN TRUNNION BUSHING, RENEW
Each Side—
Exc Below 0.4
MGC & Gt 0.3

26—STEERING LEVER, RENEW
All Models, Each 0.8

27—TIE ROD BALL ENDS, RENEW
MGC & Gt—
Each 0.3
Both 0.4

28—FRONT SUSPENSION ASSY, RENEW
One Side—
Exc Below 2.3
MGC & Gt 1.5
Both Sides—
Exc Below 4.4
MGC & Gt 2.6

29—FRONT SUSPENSION ASSY, OVERHAUL
One Side—
Exc Below 2.6
MGC & Gt 1.9
Both Sides—
Exc Below 4.9
MGC & Gt 3.3

30—UPPER ARM OR BUSHINGS, RENEW
MGC & Gt 1.0

31—LOWER ARM OR BUSHINGS, RENEW
Exc Below 0.9
MGC & Gt 1.4

32—WISHBONE PIVOT OR BUSHINGS, RENEW
MGB & Gt 1.2

33—TIE ROD FRONT ASSY, RENEW
MGC & Gt 0.7

34—SPRING(S), RENEW
MGC & Gt—
Each 0.6
Both 1.2

35—LEAF SPRING, RENEW
Each 1.1
Both 2.1

36—LEAF SPRING, OVERHAUL
Each 1.7
Both 3.3

37—ANTI-ROLL BAR (FRONT) LINK OR BUSHING, RENEW
Exc Below 0.2
MGC & Gt 0.4

—NOTE—
To Renew Anti-Roll Bar, Add. 0.1

38—SHOCK ABSORBER, RENEW
Front—
Each—
Exc Below 0.6
MGC & Gt 0.7
Both, All Models 1.2
Rear Each—
All Models 0.5

39—TORSION BAR (FRONT), RENEW
MGC & Gt 1.2

40—UNIVERSAL JOINTS, RENEW
Front Or Rear—
Exc Below 0.9
MGC & Gt 1.3
Both—
Exc Below 1.3
MGC & Gt 1.7

41—HALF SHAFT OR GASKET, RENEW
All Models 2.1

42—FINAL DRIVE OR AXLE ASSY, RENEW
Exc Below 2.6
MGC & Gt 2.5

43—DIFFERENTIAL CAGE BEARINGS, RENEW
Exc Below 4.9
MGC & Gt 4.8

44—DIFFERENTIAL DRIVE GEAR & PINION, OVERHAUL
Exc Below 6.7
MGC & Gt 6.6

45—PINION OIL SEAL, RENEW
All Models 0.6

46—HALF SHAFT OIL SEAL, RENEW
All Models 1.9

Speedometer, W/S Wipers, Switches & Instruments—TIME

OPERATION INDEX

Speedometer Cable, Renew 1
Speedometer Head, Renew 2
W/S Wiper Motor, Renew 3
W/S Wiper Wheel Box Assy, Renew 4
W/S Wiper Arm, Renew 5
Fuel Gauge (Dash Unit), Renew 6
Fuel Tank Gauge, Renew 7
Oil Gauge (Dash Unit), Renew 8
Oil Gauge Sending Unit, Renew 9
Temperature Gauge (Dash Unit), Renew 10
Temperature Gauge Sending Unit, Renew 11
Tachometer Head, Renew 12
Instrument Cluster Voltage Limiter, Renew 13
Headlight Switch, Renew 14
Dimmer Switch, Renew 15
Headlamp Flasher Switch, Renew 16
Turn Signal Flasher Switch, Renew 17
Stop Light Switch, Renew 18
Hazard Flasher Switch, Renew 19
Overdrive Operating Solenoid, Renew 20
Overdrive, Manual Or Vacuum Switch, Renew 21
Overdrive Throttle Switch, Renew 22

(Continued)

Speedometer, W/S Wipers, Switches & Instruments—TIME Cont'd

1—SPEEDOMETER CABLE, RENEW
Exc Below 1.3
MGC & Gt 0.6

2—SPEEDOMETER HEAD, RENEW
Exc Below 0.6
MGB & Gt 0.3

3—W/S WIPER MOTOR, RENEW
Exc Below 0.7
MGB & Gt 0.6

4—W/S WIPER WHEEL BOX ASSY, RENEW
Exc Below 0.9
MGB & Gt 0.8

5—W/S WIPER ARM, RENEW
All Models, Each 0.3

6—FUEL GAUGE (DASH UNIT), RENEW
Exc Below 0.4
MGB & Gt 0.2

7—FUEL TANK GAUGE, RENEW
All Models 0.4

8—OIL GAUGE (DASH UNIT), RENEW
All Models 0.8

9—OIL GAUGE SENDING UNIT, RENEW
All Models 0.2

10—TEMPERATURE GAUGE (DASH UNIT), RENEW
Exc Below 0.6
MGB & Gt 0.8

11—TEMPERATURE GAUGE SENDING UNIT, RENEW
All Models 0.4

12—TACHOMETER HEAD, RENEW
Exc Below 0.5
MGB & Gt 0.3
Exc Below 0.4
MGC & Gt 0.3

14—HEADLIGHT SWITCH, RENEW
Exc Below 0.5
MGB & Gt 0.2

15—DIMMER SWITCH, RENEW
Exc Below 0.8
MGB & Gt 0.3

16—HEADLAMP FLASHER SWITCH, RENEW
Exc Below 0.8
MGB 0.5

17—TURN SIGNAL FLASHER SWITCH, RENEW
Exc Below 0.8
MGB & Gt 0.4

18—STOP LIGHT SWITCH, RENEW
Exc Below 0.2
MGB & Gt 0.5

19—HAZARD FLASHER SWITCH, RENEW
All Models 0.4

20—OVERDRIVE OPERATING SOLENOID, RENEW
All Models 1.2

21—OVERDRIVE, MANUAL OR VACUUM SWITCH, RENEW
Exc Below 0.7
MGB & Gt 0.2

22—OVERDRIVE THROTTLE SWITCH, RENEW
All Models 1.5

13—INSTRUMENT CLUSTER VOLTAGE LIMITER, RENEW

IDENTIFICATION

ALL MODELS....... 293

ILLUSTRATIONS

FIG 1 – ENGINE
FIG 2 – TRANSMISSION
FIG 3 – FRONT SUSPENSION
FIG 4 – STEERING GEAR
FIG 5 – STEERING COLUMN
FIG 6 – REAR AXLE

OPERATION TIMES

A

Air Pump....... 299
Alternator....... 299
Ammeter....... 303
Automatic Transmission....... 301
Axle Shaft....... 302

B

Brake Drums....... 302
Brakes....... 302

C

Cables (Ignition)....... 299
Calipers....... 302
Camshaft....... 301
Carburetor....... 299
Clutch....... 301
Coil, Ignition....... 299
Compression Test....... 299
Connecting Rods....... 299
Cooling System....... 300
Crankshaft....... 301
Cylinder Head....... 300

D

Dash Gauges....... 303
Differential....... 302
Disc Brakes....... 302
Distributor....... 299

E

Electronic Fuel Injection....... 300
Emission Controls....... 299
Engine Assembly....... 300
Engine Mountings....... 301
Engine Oiling....... 301
Engine Tune-Up....... 299
Exhaust System....... 299

F

Flywheel....... 301
Front Suspension....... 302
Fuel Gauges....... 303
Fuel Pump....... 299
Fuel Tank....... 299

G

Generator....... 299

H

Hand Brake....... 302
Headlight Switch....... 303
Heater....... 300
Hose (Brake)....... 302
Hose (Radiator)....... 300
Hydraulic Brakes....... 302

I

Ignition....... 299
Ignition Coil....... 299
Ignition Switch....... 299
Intake Manifold....... 299

L

Light Switches....... 303

M

Main Bearings....... 301
Master Cylinder....... 302
Muffler....... 289

O

Oil Gauge....... 303
Oiling, Engine....... 301
Oil Pan....... 301
Oil Pump....... 301

P

Parking Brake....... 302
Piston Rings....... 301
Pistons....... 301
Power Brake....... 302

R

Radiator....... 300
Radiator Hose....... 300
Rear Axle....... 302
Regulator....... 299
Rocker Arms....... 300
Rod Bearings....... 301

S

Shocks (Front)....... 302
Shocks (Rear)....... 302
Speedometer....... 303
Springs (Front)....... 302
Springs (Rear)....... 302
Stabilizer....... 302
Starting Motor....... 299
Steering Gear....... 302
Steering Linkage....... 302
Switches (Light)....... 303
Synchro-Mesh Trans....... 301

T

Tachometer....... 303
Temperature Gauge....... 303
Thermostat....... 300
Timing Case Cover....... 300
Timing Chain....... 300
Timing Gears....... 300
Track Rod....... 302
Transmission, Manual....... 301
Transmission, Automatic....... 301
Tune-Up, Engine....... 299

U

Universals....... 302

V

Vacuum Control Unit....... 299
Valve Lifters....... 300
Valve System....... 300

W

Water Pump....... 300
Wheel Cylinders....... 302
Windshield Wiper....... 303

MODEL IDENTIFICATION PLATE

LOCATION –

Kadett & 30 Series – On dash panel inboard of battery.
1900 & Manta – On right front fender skirt.
GT Models – On top right side of cowl.

The first 2 digits of the Serial Number represents the Body Style. The ramaining digits are the actual serial number.

SERIAL NUMBER PLATE – 1968-72

LOCATION –

On top left side of instrument panel or left hinge pillar post visible through windshield.

VEHICLE IDENTIFICATION PLATE – 1973-75
OL15ND9123456 (TYPICAL)

LOCATION –

On top left side of instrument panel or left hinge pillar post, visible through windshield.

First 4 digits indicate Models –
- OL 11 – Opel 1900 2-Door Sedan
- OL 15 – Opel 1900 Wagon
- OL 60 – Opel 1900 4-Door Sedan
- OL 77 – Manta
- OY 07 – GT 2-Door Coupe

Fifth Digit (Letter) indicates engine
- N – 1.9 engine

Sixth Digit (Letter) indicates year
- C – 1973
- D – 1974
- 5 – 1975

Seventh Digit indicates assembly plant
- 2 – Bochum
- 9 – Antwerp
- 5 - Antwerp

Last 6 digits indicate sequence numbers

ENGINE NUMBER

LOCATION – Stamped on a flat boss on the left side of block.

TRANSMISSION NUMBER

LOCATION – Manual – On Cover Plate
Automatic – On left side of case

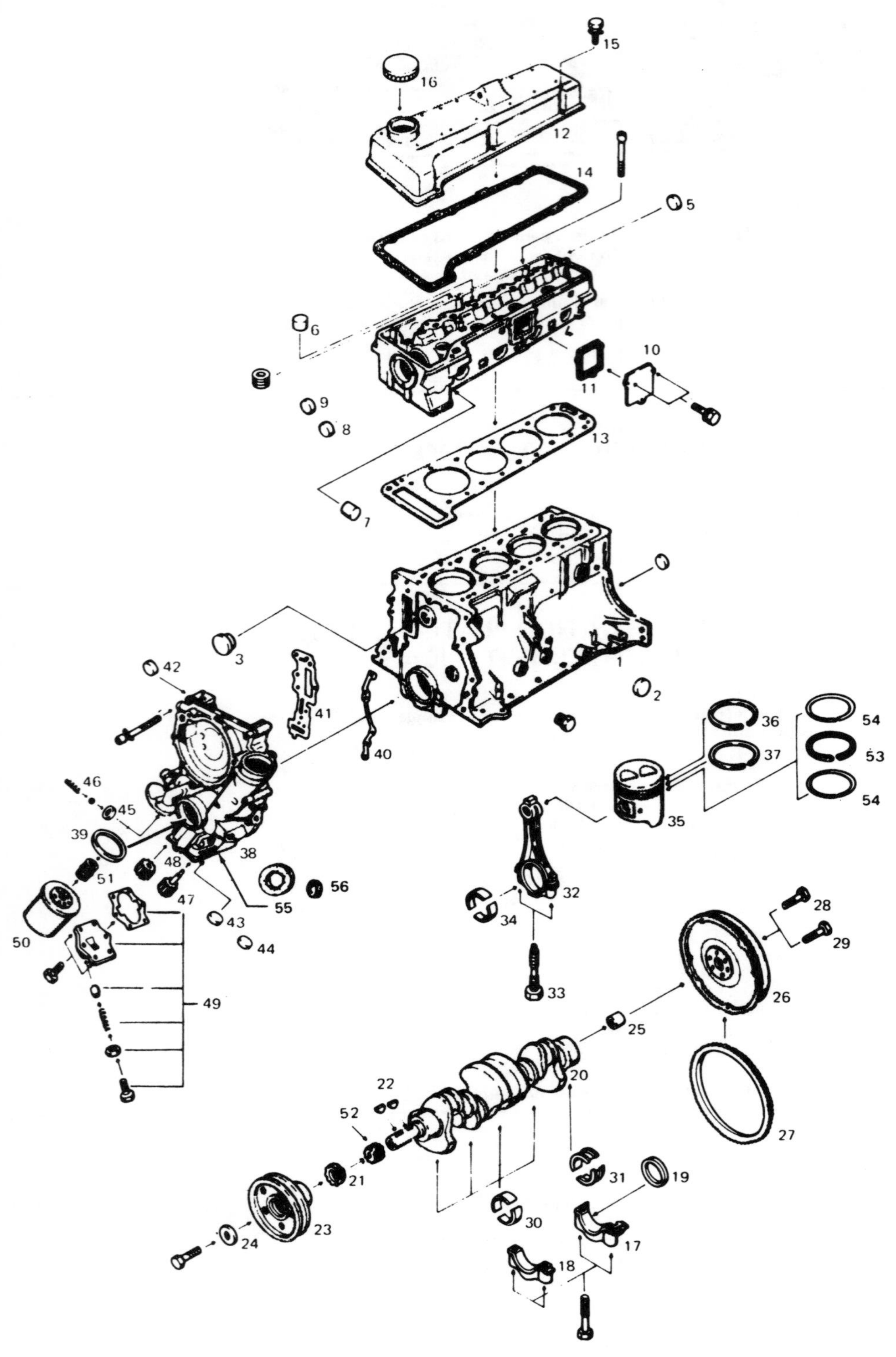

1	Cylinder Block
2	Plug
3	Plug Screw
4	Cylinder Head
5	Plug
6	Plug
7	Plug
8	Plug
9	Plug
10	Cover
11	Gasket
12	Cover
13	Head Gasket
14	Gasket
15	Screw
16	Oil Filler Cap
17	Cap
18	Cap
19	Seal Ring
20	Crankshaft
21	Worm Gear
22	Key
23	Pulley
24	Washer
25	Bushing
26	Flywheel
27	Ring Gear
28	Screw
29	Screw
30	Bearings
31	Bearings
32	Rod
33	Bolt
34	Bearing
35	Piston
36	Ring
37	Ring
38	Housing
39	Seal
40	Gasket
41	Gasket
42	Plug
43	Plug
44	Plug
45	Sleeve
46	Spring
47	Shaft
48	Gear
49	Cover Kit
50	Element
51	Connector
52	Gear
53	Ring
54	Ring
55	Seal
56	Seal

FIG 1 – ENGINE – 1971-75 MODEL 50 – 1.9 LITER

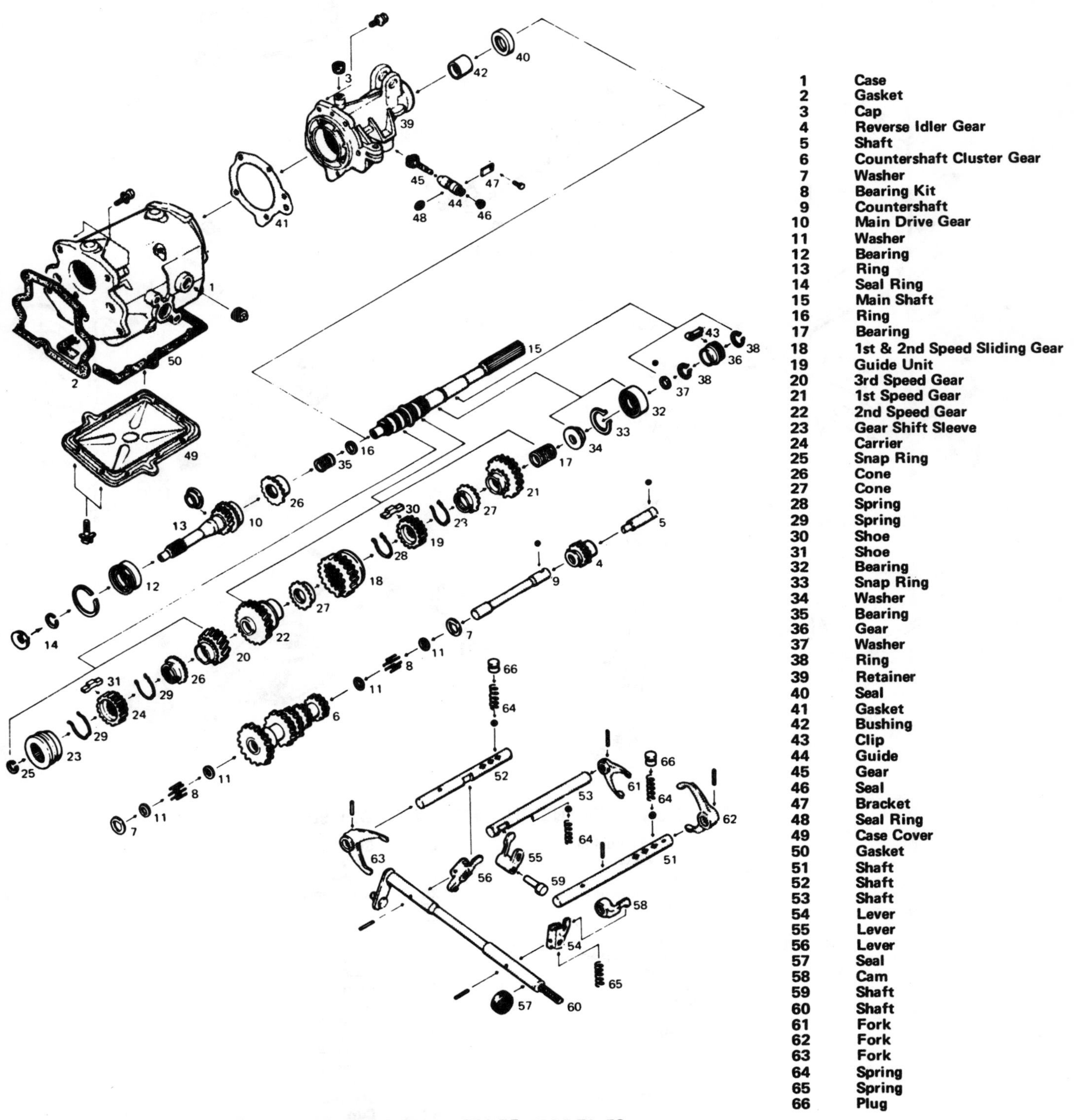
1 Case
2 Gasket
3 Cap
4 Reverse Idler Gear
5 Shaft
6 Countershaft Cluster Gear
7 Washer
8 Bearing Kit
9 Countershaft
10 Main Drive Gear
11 Washer
12 Bearing
13 Ring
14 Seal Ring
15 Main Shaft
16 Ring
17 Bearing
18 1st & 2nd Speed Sliding Gear
19 Guide Unit
20 3rd Speed Gear
21 1st Speed Gear
22 2nd Speed Gear
23 Gear Shift Sleeve
24 Carrier
25 Snap Ring
26 Cone
27 Cone
28 Spring
29 Spring
30 Shoe
31 Shoe
32 Bearing
33 Snap Ring
34 Washer
35 Bearing
36 Gear
37 Washer
38 Ring
39 Retainer
40 Seal
41 Gasket
42 Bushing
43 Clip
44 Guide
45 Gear
46 Seal
47 Bracket
48 Seal Ring
49 Case Cover
50 Gasket
51 Shaft
52 Shaft
53 Shaft
54 Lever
55 Lever
56 Lever
57 Seal
58 Cam
59 Shaft
60 Shaft
61 Fork
62 Fork
63 Fork
64 Spring
65 Spring
66 Plug

FIG 2 – MANUAL TRANSMISSION – 1971-75 MODEL 50

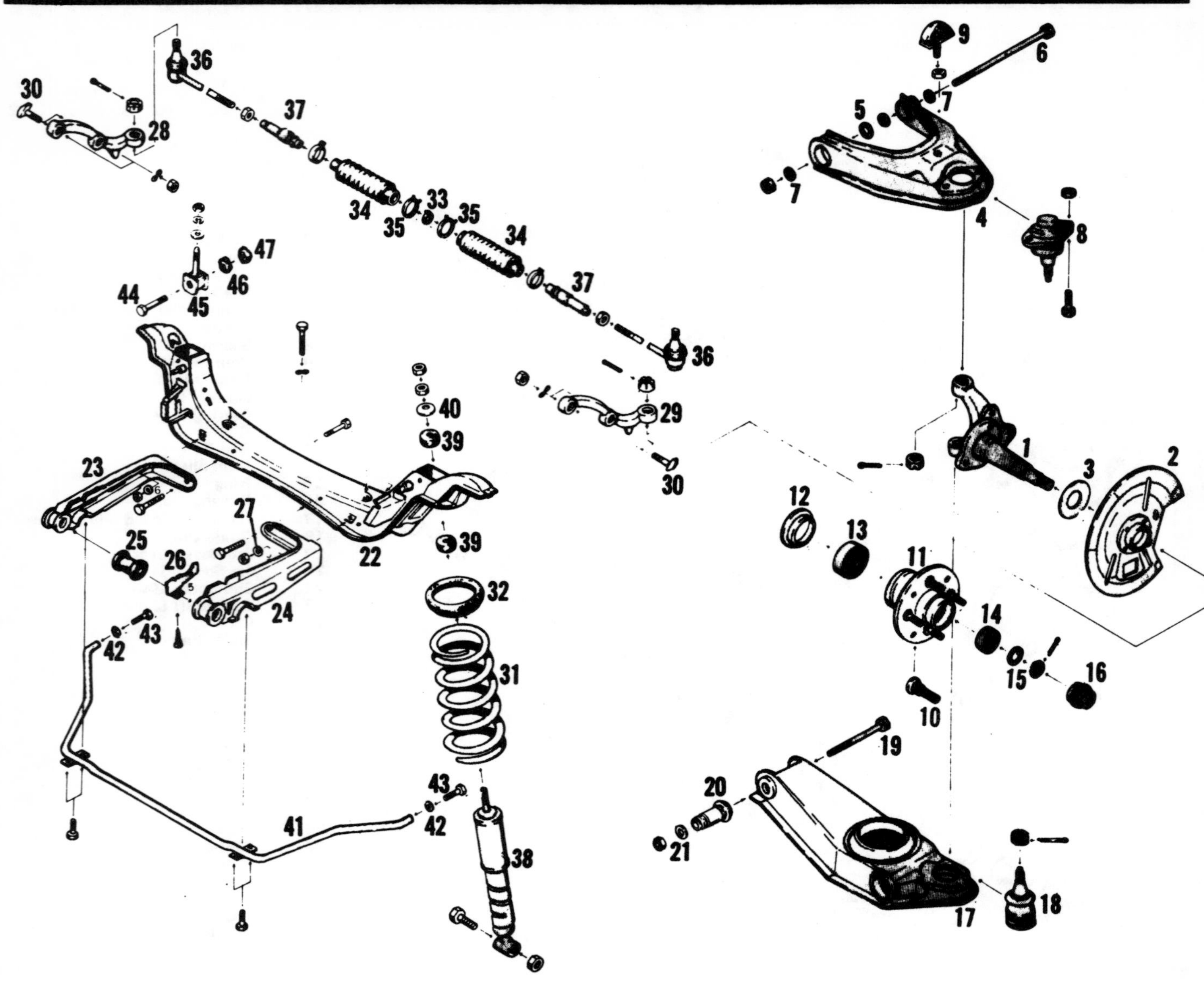

FIG 3 – FRONT SUSPENSION – 1971-75 MODEL 50

1	Steering Knuckle	25	Bushing
2	Cover Plate	26	Plate
3	Gasket	27	Washer
4	Upper Control Arm	28	Lever, left
5	Washer	29	Lever, right
6	Bolt	30	Screw
7	Washer	31	Spring
8	Ball Joint, Upper	32	Ring
9	Bumper	33	Plate
10	Bolt	34	Boot
11	Hub	35	Clamp
12	Seal Ring	36	Tie Rod End
13	Bearing, Inner	37	Joint
14	Bearing, Outer	38	Shock Absorber
15	Washer	39	Bumper
16	Cap	40	Cup
17	Lower Control Arm	41	Stabilizer Shaft
18	Ball Joint, Lower	42	Cup
19	Bolt	43	Screw
20	Bushing	44	Screw
21	Washer	45	Bushing
22	Front Suspension Crossmember	46	Washer
23	Support	47	Nut
24	Support		

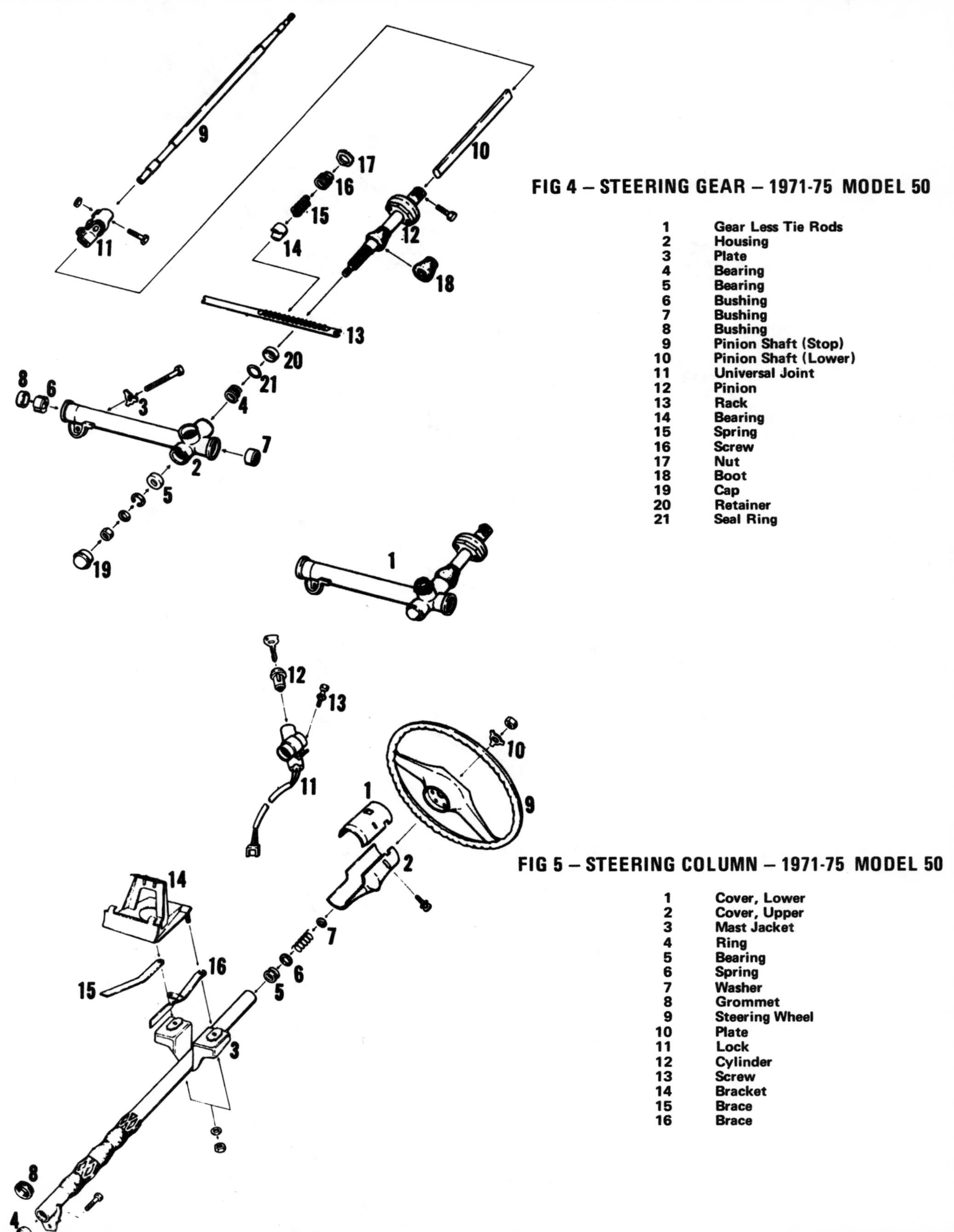

FIG 4 – STEERING GEAR – 1971-75 MODEL 50

1 Gear Less Tie Rods
2 Housing
3 Plate
4 Bearing
5 Bearing
6 Bushing
7 Bushing
8 Bushing
9 Pinion Shaft (Stop)
10 Pinion Shaft (Lower)
11 Universal Joint
12 Pinion
13 Rack
14 Bearing
15 Spring
16 Screw
17 Nut
18 Boot
19 Cap
20 Retainer
21 Seal Ring

FIG 5 – STEERING COLUMN – 1971-75 MODEL 50

1 Cover, Lower
2 Cover, Upper
3 Mast Jacket
4 Ring
5 Bearing
6 Spring
7 Washer
8 Grommet
9 Steering Wheel
10 Plate
11 Lock
12 Cylinder
13 Screw
14 Bracket
15 Brace
16 Brace

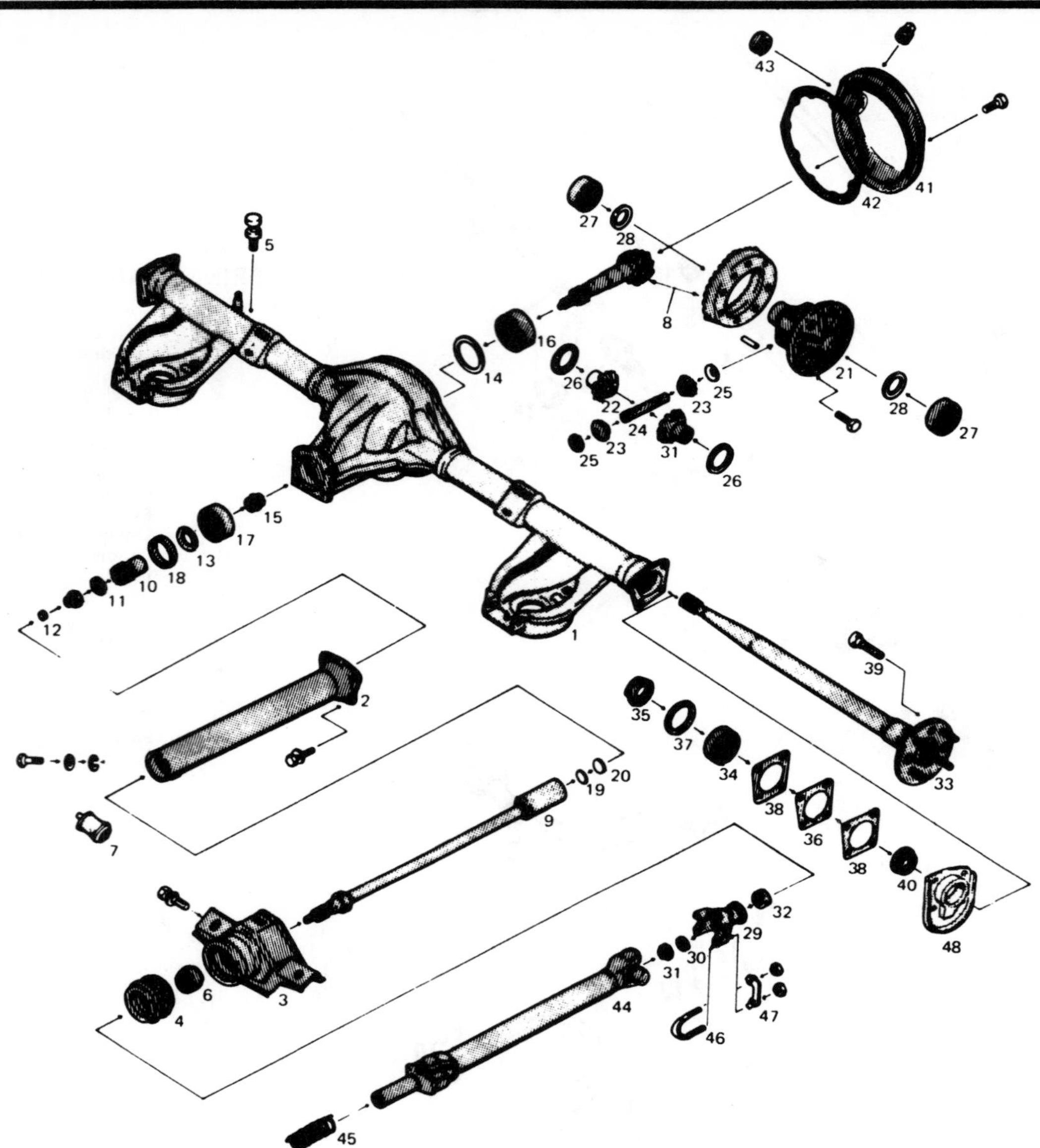

FIG 6 – REAR AXLE – 1971-75 MODEL 50

1	Axle Housing	25	Washer
2	Extension	26	Washer
3	Support	27	Bearing
4	Ring	28	Shim
5	Ventilator	29	Flange
6	Bearing	30	Washer
7	Bumper	31	Nut
8	Overhauling Parts	32	Ring
9	Extension	33	Axle Shaft
10	Cam Sleeve	34	Axle Shaft Bearing
11	Washer	35	Retainer
12	Cap	36	Ring
13	Shim	37	Ring
14	Shim	38	Gasket
15	Ring	39	Bolt
16	Bearing, Inner	40	Deflector
17	Bearing, Outer	41	Housing Cover
18	Oil Seal	42	Gasket
19	Washer	43	Plug
20	Bumper	44	Propeller Shaft
21	Differential Case	45	Spring
22	Differential Side Gear	46	Bracket
23	Differential Pinion Gear	47	Plate
24	Pinion Gear Shaft	48	Baffle

Ignition, Starting & Charging—TIME

OPERATION INDEX

Tune-Up, Minor 1
Tune-Up, Major 2
Compression Test 3
Distributor, R&R Or Renew 4
Distributor Cap, Renew 5
Ignition Cables, Renew 6
Vacuum Control Unit, Renew 7
Ignition Coil, Renew 8
Starter & Ignition Switch Renew 9
Starter, R&R Or Renew 10
Starter Solenoid, Renew 11
Starter Bendix Drive, Renew 12
Starter, R&R & Overhaul 13
Starter Brushes, Renew 14
Starter Armature, Renew 15
Voltage Regulator, Renew 16
Generator Or Alternator, R&R Or Renew 17
Generator Or Alternator, R&R & Overhaul 18
Alternator Diodes , Renew 19
Alternator Or Generator Brushes Or Bearings, Renew 20

1—TUNE-UP, MINOR

Inlcudes renew points condenser & plugs, set spark timing & adjust carburetor idle.

1966-75 ..... 1.8

2—TUNE-UP, MAJOR

Inlcudes check compression, clean or renew & adjust spark plugs, R & R distributor. Renew points & condenser. Adjust ignition timing carburetor & fan belts. Clean batterty terminals & service air cleaner. Check coil and clean or renew

1966-75 ..... 3.0

3—COMPRESSION TEST

1966-75 ..... 0.5

4—DISTRIBUTOR, R&R OR RENEW

1966-73—
 1.9 Liter Opel & G.T.—
  L/Air Cond 0.5
  W/Air Cond 1.5
 1.1 Liter 1.4
 1900 (1.9 Liter) 0.5
1974-75 ..... 0.8

—NOTE—

Includes R & R Fuel Pump On 1.5 & 1.9 Litre Engines.

5—DISTRIBUTOR CAP, RENEW

1966-75 ..... 0.2

6—IGNITION CABLE SET, RENEW

1966-75—
 One 0.1
 All 0.3

7—VACUUM CONTROL UNIT, RENEW

1966-75 ..... 0.5

8—IGNITION COIL, RENEW

1966-75 ..... 0.2

9—STARTER & IGNITION SWITCH, RENEW

1966-73 ..... 0.4
1974-75 ..... 0.8

10—STARTER, R&R OR RENEW

1966-73—
 Exc Below 0.5
 1.1 Liter 1.0
1974-75 ..... 0.7

11—STARTER SOLENOID, RENEW

1966-73—
 Exc Below 0.7
 1.1 Liter 1.2
1974-75 ..... 0.8

12—STARTER BENDIX DRIVE, RENEW

1966-75
 Exc Below 0.7
 1.1 Liter 1.2

13—STARTER, R&R & OVERHAUL

1966-73—
 Exc Below 0.9
 1.1 Liter 1.4
1974-75 ..... 0.9

14—STARTER BRUSHES, RENEW

1966-73—
 Exc Below 0.9
 1.1 Liter 1.4
1974-75 ..... 0.9

15—STARTER ARMATURE, RENEW

1966-73—
 Exc Below 0.9
 1.1 Liter 1.4
1974-75 ..... 0.9

16—VOLTAGE REGULATOR, RENEW

1966-75 ..... 0.5

17—GENERATOR OR ALTERNATOR, R&R OR RENEW

Generator—
 Less Air Cond 0.3
 With Air Cond 0.8
Alternator—
 Model 1900 (1.9 Liter)—
  Less Air Cond 0.4
  With Air Cond 0.6
 All Others, 1966-73—
  Less Air Cond 0.4
  With Air Cond 0.9
 All Others, 1974-75—
  Less Air Cond 0.4
  With Air Cond 0.6

18—GENERATOR OR ALTERNATOR R&R & OVERHAUL

Generator—
 Less Air Cond 1.3
 With Air Cond 1.8
Alternator
 Model 1900 (1.9 Liter)—
  Less Air Cond 1.5
  With Air Cond 1.7
 All Others, 1966-73—
  Less Air Cond 1.5
  With Air Cond 2.0
 All Others, 1974-75—
  Less Air Cond 1.5
  With Air Cond 1.8

19—ALTERNATOR DIODES, RENEW

Model 1900 (1.9 Liter)—
 Less Air Cond 0.7
 With Air Cond 0.9
All Others—
 Less Air Cond 0.7
 With Air Cond 1.2

20—ALTERNATOR OR GENERATOR BRUSHES OR BEARINGS, RENEW

Generator—
 Less Air Cond 0.4
 With Air Cond 0.9
Alternator—
 Model 1900 (1.9 Liter)—
  Less Air Cond 0.5
  With Air Cond 0.7
 All Others—
  Less Air Cond 0.5
  With Air Cond 1.0

Fuel, Emission Controls, Intake & Exhaust Systems—TIME

OPERATION INDEX

Carburetur Or Flange Gasket, R&R Or Renew 1
Fuel Pump, R&R Or Renew 2
Fuel Tank, R&R Or Renew 3
Choke Cable Assy, Renew 4
Automatic Choke Diaphragm, Renew 5
Emission Control Vacuum Motor, Renew 6
Air Injector Reactor Pump, Renew 7
Air Injector Reactor Check Valve, Renew 8
Air Injector Reactor Air Distributor, Renew 9
Evaporative Emission Vapor Separator, Renew 10
Evaporative Emission Relief Valve, Renew 11
Intake Manifold Or Gasket, Renew 12
Exhaust Manifold Or Gasket, Renew 13
Exhaust Pipe, Renew 14
Muffler, Renew 15
Tail Pipe, Renew 16
Electronic Fuel Injection 17

1—CARBURETOR OR FLANGE GASKET, R&R OR RENEW

1966-75—
 One 0.3
 Both 0.6

2—FUEL PUMP, R&R OR RENEW

1966-75 ..... 0.2

—NOTE—

To Overhaul, Add 0.1
With Air Cond. 1.9 Liter, Add 1.0

3—FUEL TANK, R&R OR RENEW

1966-75 Except 0.6
 Model 1900 ..... 0.4
 G.T. 1.7

4—CHOKE CONTROL CABLE, RENEW

1.1 Liter 0.2

5—AUTOMATIC CHOKE DIAPHRAM, RENEW

1966-75 ..... 0.4

6—EMISSION CONTROL VACUUM MOTOR, RENEW

All Models 0.3

7—AIR INJECTOR REACTOR PUMP, RENEW

All Models 0.4

8—AIR INJECTOR REACTOR CHECK VALVE, RENEW

All Models 0.3

9—AIR INJECTOR REACTOR AIR DISTRIBUTOR, RENEW

Except Below 1.0
1.1 Liter 0.3

10—EVAPORATIVE EMISSION VAPOR SEPARATOR, RENEW

All Models 0.3

11—EVAPORATIVE EMISSION RELIEF VALVE, RENEW

All Models 0.3

12—INTAKE MANIFOLD OR GASKET, RENEW

1966-73—
 Except Below 1.1
 1.1 Liter 0.4
1974-75 ..... 0.8

13—EXHAUST MANIFOLD OR GASKET RENEW

1966-73—
 Except Below 1.1
 1.1 Liter 0.3
1974-75 ..... 1.5

14—EXHAUST PIPE, RENEW

1966-75 ..... 0.6

15—MUFFLER, RENEW

Includes R&R tail pipe.

1966-75—
 Each 0.6
 Both 1.0

(Continued)

Fuel, Emission Controls, Intake & Exhaust Systems—TIME Cont'd

16—TAIL PIPE, RENEW
1966-75—
Each 0.6
Both 1.0

17—ELECTRONIC FUEL INJECTION ITEMS, RENEW
Temperature Sensor 0.2
Dual Relay 0.2
Thermostatic Time Switch 0.2
Cold Start Injector 0.2
Auxiliary Air Valve 0.2
Deceleration Valve 0.2
Pressure Regulator Valve 0.3
Throttle Valve Switch 0.2
Pre-Resistors 0.2
Injectors Or Plates
One Pair 0.4
Both Pairs 0.8
Fuel Distributor Pipe 0.6
Throttle Plate Housing 0.8
Air Flow Meter 0.5
Flow Meter Outlet Hose 0.2
Wiring Harness 0.5
Control Unit 0.2
Idle Drop Test 0.3
Fuel Pump 0.3
Fuel Filter 0.2
Accelerator Cable 0.3

Engine Cooling & Heater Systems—TIME

OPERATION INDEX
Radiator, R&R Or Renew *1*
Radiator Hoses, Renew *2*
Water Pump, R&R Or Renew *3*
Thermostat Or Housing, Renew *4*
Heater Blower Motor Or Housing, Renew *5*
Heater Core, Renew *6*
Heater Control Switch, Renew *7*
Heater Regulator Valve Renew *8*
Heater Hoses, Renew *9*

1—RADIATOR, R&R OR RENEW
1966-73—
Std Trans 0.3
Auto Trans 0.6
1974-75—
Std Strans 0.5
Auto Trans 0.8
Noted
For Air Cond, Add
1900 ....*0.2*
1974-75 ....*0.5*

2—RADIATOR HOSES, RENEW
1966-75—
Upper 0.2
Lower 0.3
Both 0.4

—NOTE—

With Air Cond, Add *0.5*

3—WATER PUMP, R&R OR RENEW
1966-73—
Model 1900 & 1.1 Liter—
L/Air Cond 0.6
W/Air Cond 1.4
Opel 1.9 & G.T.—
L/Air Cond Exc 0.8
W/Auto Trans 1.4
W/Air Cond Exc 1.8
W/Auto Trans 2.4
1974-75 Exc 0.9
W/Air Cond 1.4
W/Auto Trans 1.2

4—THERMOSTAT OR HOUSING, RENEW
1966-73 ....0.3
1974-75—
Thermostat 0.6
Housing 1.1

5—HEATER BLOWER MOTOR OR HOUSING, RENEW
1966-73 Except 0.5
Model 1900 ....0.8
G.T. 2.1
1974-75 ....0.3

6—HEATER CORE, RENEW
1966-73 Except ①0.6
Model 1900 ....①0.8
G.T. ①2.1
1974-75 ....0.9
①With Air Cond, Add *0.3*

7—HEATER CONTROL SWITCH, RENEW
1966-73 Except ①0.2
Model 1900 ....①0.3
G.T. ①2.0
1974-75 ....0.3
①With Air Cond, Add *0.3*

8—HEATER REGULATOR VALVE, RENEW
1966-75—
Except Below 0.3
G.T. 2.0

9—HEATER HOSES, RENEW
1966-75—
Upper 0.2
Lower 0.2

Engine—TIME

OPERATION INDEX
Engine, R&R *1*
Engine, R&R Or Overhaul *2*
Engine (Short) Renew & Grine Valves *3*
Cylinder Head, Renew *4*
Cylinder Head, R&R Or Gasket, Renew *5*
Valves, Grind *6*
Rocker Arm Cover Gasket, Renew *7*
Push Rods, Renew *8*
Rocker Arms, R&R Or Renew *9*
Valve Lifters (All) Renew *10*
Timing Cover Seal & Gasket, Renew *11*
Timing Chain Or Gears, Renew *12*
Oil Pan Or Gasket, R&R Or Renew *13*
Camshaft, R&R Or Renew *14*
Oil Pump, R&R & Overhaul *15*
Piston Ring(S), Renew *16*
Rings & Main Bearings, Renew & Grind Valves *17*
Rod Bearing(S), Renew *18*
Main Bearings, Renew *19*
Main & Rod Bearings, Renew *20*
Crankshaft, R&R Or Renew *21*
Crankshaft Rear Main Oil Seal, Renew *22*
Piston(S), Renew *23*
Connecting Rod(S), Renew *24*
Crankshaft Pulley, Renew *25*

1—ENGINE, R&R
Does not include transfer of any part of engine or replacement of special equipment.
1966-75—
Exc Below 3.2
Opel 1.9 Liter—
L/Air Cond 4.4
W/Air Cond 4.9
Model 1900—
L/Air Cond 3.1
W/Air Cond 3.9
G.T.—
L/Air Cond 3.8
W/Air Cond 4.8

2—ENGINE, R&R & OVERHAUL
Includes rebore cylinders with boring bar, renew pistone, rings, pins, main & rod bearings, grind valves, plastigauge bearings and perform minor tune-up
1966-75—
Except Below 16.7
Opel 1.9 Liter 19.1
Model 1900 ....17.8
G.T. 18.5

3—ENGINE (SHORT), RENEW & GRIND VALVES
1966-75—
Except Below 7.5
Opel 1.9 Liter 9.9
Model 1900 ....8.6
G.T. 9.3

4—CYLINDER HEAD, RENEW
1966-73—
Except Below 3.4
Opel 1.9 Liter—
L/Air Cond 3.9
W/Air Cond 4.9
Model 1900 ....3.9
G.T.—
L/Air Cond 4.2
W/Air Cond 4.7
1974-75 ....4.7

5—CYLINDER HEAD, R&R OR GASKET, RENEW
1966-73—
Except Below 1.8
Opel 1.9 Liter—
L/Air Cond 2.3
W/Air Cond 3.3
Model 1900 ....2.3
G.T.—
L/Air Cond 2.6
W/Air Cond 3.1
1974-75 ....3.1

6—VALVES, GRIND
1966-75—
Except Below 3.5
1.1 Liter 3.1
G.T. 3.9

7—ROCKER ARM COVER GASKET, RENEW
1966-75—
Except Below 0.2
G.T. 0.5

8—PUSH RODS, RENEW
1.1 Liter 0.8

9—ROCKER ARMS, R&R OR RENEW
1966-75 All—
Except Below 1.1
G.T. 1.4

10—VALVE LIFTERS (ALL) RENEW
1966-75—
Except Below 0.8
1.1 Liter 6.2
Model 1900 ....0.6
G.T. 1.1

11—TIMING COVER SEAL & GASKET, RENEW
1966-73—
1.1 Liter 0.6
1.9 Liter (Opel)—
L/Air Cond 6.5
W/Air Cond 7.5
Model 1900—
L/Air Cond 6.0
W/Air Cond 6.8
G.T.—
L/Air Cond 4.5
W/Air Cond 5.5
1974-75 ....6.8

12—TIMING CHAIN OR GEARS, RENEW
1966-73—
1.1 Liter 0.9
1.9 Liter (Opel)—
L/Air Cond 6.8
W/Air Cond 7.8
Model 1900—
L/Air Cond 6.3
W/Air Cond 7.1
G.T.—
L/Air Cond 4.8
W/Air Cond 5.8
1974-75 ....7.1

(Continued)

Engine—TIME Cont'd

13—OIL PAN OR GASKET, R&R OR RENEW
1966-73—
Except Below 2.8
Model 1900—
L/Air Cond 3.6
W/Air Cond 4.4
G.T. 0.8
1974-75—
L/Air Cond 3.6
W/Air Cond 4.4

14—CAMSHAFT, R&R OR RENEW
1966-73—
1.1 Liter 5.7
1.9 Liter (Opel)—
L/Air Cond 2.8
W/Air Cond 3.3
Model 1900—
L/Air Cond 2.8
W/Air Cond 3.6
G.T.—
L/Air Cond 3.1
W/Air Cond 4.1
1974-75 ..... 3.6

15—OIL PUMP, R&R & OVERHAUL
1966-73—
Except Below 0.7
1.1 Liter 3.2

16—PISTON RING(S), RENEW
1966-75—
One Except Below 5.6
1.1 Liter 5.1
Model 1900 ..... 6.0
G.T. 3.9
Each Additional 0.5
With Air Cond, Add 0.5

17—RINGS & MAIN BEARINGS, RENEW & GRIND VALVES
1966-75—
1.1 Liter 9.3
1.9 Liter Opel 10.8
Model 1900 ..... 11.2
G.T. 9.1

18—ROD BEARING(S), RENEW
1966-75—
One Except Below 3.0
Model 1900 ..... (1)3.8
G.T. 1.4
Each Additional 0.2
(1)*With Air Cond, Add 0.2*

19—MAIN BEARINGS, RENEW
1966-75—
One Except Below 3.3
Model 1900 ..... (1)4.1
G.T. 1.3
Each Additional 0.5
(1)*With Air Cond, Add 0.8*

20—MAIN & ROD BEARINGS, RENEW
1966-75—
Except Below 4.1
Model 1900 ..... 4.9
G.T. 2.1

21—CRANKSHAFT, R&R OR RENEW
1966-73—
Except Below 8.9
1.1 Liter 6.0
Model 1900 ..... 7.6
G.T. 8.3
1974-75 Exc 7.6
W/Air Cond 8.0

22—CRANKSHAFT REAR MAIN OIL SEAL, RENEW
1966-73—
Except Below 2.4
G.T. W/Air Cond 3.5
1974-75 Except 2.7
W/Auto Trans 3.7

23—PISTON(S), RENEW
1966-75—
One Except Below 5.4
1.1 Liter 4.9
Model 1900 ..... 5.8
G.T. 3.7
Each Additional 0.3
With Air Cond, Add 0.5

24—CONNECTING ROD(S), RENEW
1966-75—
One Except Below 5.4
1.1 Liter 4.9
Model 1900 ..... 5.8
G.T. 3.7
Each Additional 0.3
With Air Cond, Add 0.5

25—CRANKSHAFT PULLEY, RENEW
1966-73—
Except Below 0.6
1.1 Liter 0.2
1974-75 ..... 0.7

—NOTE—

With Air Cond, Add 0.2
With Auto Trans, Add 0.3
Fuel filter.
1966-75 ..... 0.5

Clutch, Mounts & Transmission—TIME

OPERATION INDEX
Flywheel, R&R Or Renew 1
Clutch Or Disc, Renew 2
Release Bearing, Renew 3
Release Fork (Or Lever) Renew 4
Clutch Pedal, Adjust 5
Engine Mounts, Renew 6
Trans Assy, R&R Or Renew 7
Manual Trans Case, Renew 8
Trans Side Cover Or Gasket, R&R Or Renew 9
Main Drive Pinion Retainer Or Seal, Renew 10
Extension Housing, Gasket Or Bushing, Renew 11
Extension Housing Oil Seal, Renew 12
Converter Housing Seal, Renew 13
Oil Pan Gasket, Renew 14
Detent Cable, Adjust 15
Manual Trans, R&R & Overhaul 16
Shift Lever Reverse Cable, Renew 17
Gear Shift Lever, Renew 18
Clutch Cable, Renew 19

1—FLYWHEEL, R&R OR RENEW
1966-75—
Except Below 2.2
1.9 Liter Opel & 1900—
L/Air Cond 2.3
W/Air Cond 2.4
G.T.—
L/Air Cond 2.3
W/Air Cond 4.4

2—CLUTCH OR DISC, RENEW
1966-75—
Except Below 2.0
1.1 Liter 2.1

3—RELEASE BEARING, RENEW
1966-75—
Except Below 2.0
1.1 Liter 1.9

4—RELEASE FORK (OR LEVER), RENEW
1966-75—
Except Below 2.0
1.1 Liter 1.9

5—CLUTCH PEDAL, ADJUST
1966-75 ..... 0.2

6—ENGINE MOUNTS, RENEW
1966-75—
Left Except 0.6
1.1 Liter 0.8
Right Except 0.6
1.1 Liter 0.9
Both Except 1.1
1.1 Liter 1.6
Rear, All Models 0.3

7—TRANSMISSION ASSY, R&R OR RENEW
1966-75—
Std Trans Exc 0.9
1.1 Liter 1.8
Auto Trans Exc 2.3
G.T. 3.3

8—MANUAL TRANS CASE, RENEW
1966-75 Except 3.9
1.1 Liter & G.T. 4.1

9—TRANS SIDE COVER OR GASKET, R&R OR RENEW
1966-75 Except 0.3
1.1 Liter 1.9

10—MAIN DRIVE PINION RETAINER OR SEAL, RENEW
1966-75 Except 1.1
1.1 Liter 2.0

11—EXTENSION HOUSING, GASKET OR BUSHING, RENEW
1966-75—
Std Trans, Exc 2.8
1.1 Liter 2.3
Auto Trans 0.9

12—EXTENSION HOUSING OIL SEAL, RENEW
1966-75—
Std Trans, Exc 0.4
1.1 Liter 0.5
Auto Trans 0.4

13—CONVERTER HOUSING SEAL, RENEW
1966-75 Except 2.4
G.T. 3.4

14—OIL PAN GASKET, RENEW
1966-75 ..... 0.5

15—DETENT CABLE, ADJUST
1966-75 ..... 0.8

16—MANUAL TRANS, R & R & OVERHAUL
1966-75 Except 4.1
1.1 Liter 4.3
G.T. 4.5

17—SHIFT LEVER REVERSE CABLE, RENEW
1.1 Liter Eng 0.5

18—GEAR SHIFT LIVER, RENEW
1966-75 Except 0.2
G.T. 0.3

19—CLUTCH CABLE, RENEW
1966-75 ..... 0.3

Brakes, Steering, Suspension, Universals & Rear Axle—TIME

OPERATION INDEX
Brake Shoes Or Friction Pads, Renew 1
Master Cylinder, Renew 2
Master Cylinder, R & R & Overhaul 3
Brake Master Cylinder Reservoir, Renew 4
Wheel Cylinders, Renew 5
Wheel Cylinders, Overhaul 6
Caliper Assy, Renew 7
Caliper Assy, R & R & Overhaul 8
(Continued)

Brakes, Steering, Suspension, Universals & Rear Axle—TIME Cont'd

Bleed System 9
Brake Hose, Renew 10
Hub Or Disc, R & R Or Renew 11
Power Brake Vacuum Cylinder, Renew 12
Power Brake Vacuum Check Valve, Renew 13
Brake Drum, Renew 14
Brake Pedal, Renew 15
Parking Brake Cable, Renew 16
Parking Brake Lever, Renew 17
Steering Gear Assy, R & R Or Renew 18
Steering Gear Assy, R & R & Overhaul 19
Tie Rod Or Ends, Renew 20
Steering Arm(S), Renew 21
Steering Knuckle(S), Renew 22
Control Arm(S), Renew 23
Ball Joint(S), Renew 24
Spring(S), Renew 25
Front Hub Bearings, Renew 26
Shock Absorbers, Renew 27
Stabilizer, R & R Or Renew 28
Rear Lower Control Arm(S), R & R Or Renew 29
Track Rod, Renew 30
Universal Joints, R & R & Overhaul 31
Rear Axle Assy, R & R Or Renew 32
Differential Case, R & R Or Renew 33
Differential Side Bearings, Renew 34
Pinion Bearings & Races, Renew 35
Pinion Oil Seal, Renew 36
Companion Flange, Renew 37
Rear Axle Housing, R & R Or Renew 38
Rear Axle Shafts, Renew 39
Rear Axle Shaft Bearings, Renew 40

1—BRAKE SHOES OR FRICTION PADS, RENEW

1966-75—
Drum Type—
Front, Each 0.6
Front, Both 1.0
Rear, Each 0.6
Rear, Both 1.0
Disc Type—
Each 0.7
Both 1.0

2—MASTER CYLINDER, RENEW

1966-75 .... 0.6

3—MASTER CYLINDER, R & R & OVERHAUL

1966-75 .... 1.0

4—BRAKE MASTER CYLINDER RESERVOIR, RENEW

1966-75 .... 0.6

5—WHEEL CYLINDERS, RENEW

1966-75—
Each Side 0.9
Both, Front Or Rear 1.4

6—WHEEL CYLINDERS, OVERHAUL

1966-75—
Each Side 0.9
Both, Front Or Rear 1.4

7—CALIPER ASSY, RENEW

1966-75—
Each Side 0.6
Both Sides 1.1

8—CALIPER ASSY, R & R & OVERHAUL

1966-75—
Each Side 0.9
Both Sides 1.7

9—BLEED SYSTEM

1966-75 .... 0.3

10—BRAKE HOSE, RENEW

1966-75—
Front, Each 0.6
Front, Both 0.8
Rear 0.7

11—HUB OR DISC, R & R OR RENEW

1966-75—
Hub—
Each Side 0.2
Both Sides 0.3
Disc—
Each Side 0.8
Both Sides 1.5

12—POWER BRAKE VACUUM CYLINDER, RENEW

1966-75 .... 0.8

13—POWER BRAKE VACUUM CHECK VALVE, RENEW

1966-75 .... 0.2

14—BRAKE DRUM, RENEW

1966-75—
Each Side 0.2
Both Sides 0.3

15—BRAKE PEDAL, RENEW

1966-75 .... 0.2

16—PARKING BRAKE CABLE, RENEW

1966-75 .... 0.6

17—PARKING BRAKE LEVER, RENEW

1966-75 .... 0.2

18—STEERING GEAR ASSY, R & R OR RENEW

1966-75 .... 1.1

19—STEERING GEAR ASSY, R & R & OVERHAUL

1966-75 .... 1.4

22—TIE ROD OR ENDS, RENEW

1966-75—
Each Side 0.3
Both Sides 0.5

21—STEERING ARM(S), RENEW

1966-75—
Each Side 0.6
Both Sides 1.1

22—STEERING KNUCKLE(S), RENEW

1966-75—
One, Exc 0.7
Model 1900 .... 1.1
Both, Exc 1.3
Model 1900 .... 2.1

23—CONTROL ARM(S), RENEW

1966-75—
Upper, Each, Exc 0.7
Model 1900 .... 0.9
Upper, Both, Exc 1.0
Model 1900 .... 1.4
Lower, Each, Exc 0.6
Model 1900 .... 1.3
Lower, Both, Exc 1.1
Model 1900 .... 2.2

24—BALL JOINT(S), RENEW

1966-75—
Upper, Each, Exc 0.3
Model 1900 .... 0.4
Upper, Both, Exc 0.5
Model 1900 .... 0.7
Lower, Each, Exc 0.7
Model 1900 .... 0.4
Lower, Both, Exc 1.3
Model 1900 .... 0.7

25—SPRING(S), RENEW

1966-75—
One Front—
Coil Type 1.1
Leaf Type 0.9
Both Front—
Coil Type 2.1
One Rear—
Exc Below 0.5
Model 1900 .... 0.3
Both Rear—
Exc Below 0.7
Opel (1966-67) 0.9
Model 1900 .... 0.5

26—FRONT HUB BEARINGS, RENEW

1966-75—
Each Side 0.6
Both Sides 1.1

27—SHOCK ABSORBER, RENEW

1966-75—
One Front, Exc 0.4
Model 1900 .... 0.3
Both Front, Exc 0.7
Model 1900 .... 0.5
One Rear 0.3
Both Rear 0.5

28—STABILIZER, R & R OR RENEW

1966-75—
Front, Model 1900 .... 0.4
Rear, Exc 0.5
Model 1900 .... 0.4

29—REAR LOWER CONTROL ARM, R & R OR RENEW

1966-75—
One, Exc 0.4
Model 1900 .... 0.3
Both, Exc 0.7
Model 1900 .... 0.5

30—TRACK ROD, RENEW

1966-75 .... 0.3

31—UNIVERSAL JOINTS, R & R OR RENEW

1966-75, Each 0.7

32—REAR AXLE ASSY, R & R OR RENEW

1966-75 .... 1.7

33—DIFFERENTIAL CASE, R & R OR RENEW

1966-75 .... 3.3

34—DIFFERENTIAL SIDE BEARINGS, RENEW

1966-75 .... 1.7

35—PINION BEARINGS & RACES, RENEW

1966-75, Front Or Rear 4.1

36—PINION OIL SEAL, RENEW

1966-75 .... 0.7

37—COMPANION FLANGE, RENEW

1966-75 .... 0.7

38—REAR AXLE HOUSING, R & R OR RENEW

1966-75 .... 4.0

39—REAR AXLE SHAFTS, RENEW

1966-70—
One Side—
1.1 Liter 0.6
1.9 Liter 0.9
Both Sides—
1.1 Liter 1.1
1.9 Liter 1.5
1971-73—
One Side—
1.1 Liter 0.6
1.9 Liter 0.7
Both Sides—
1.1 Liter 1.1
1.9 Liter 1.3
1974-75
One Side 0.7
Both Sides 1.3

40—REAR AXLE SHAFT BEARINGS, RENEW

1966-70—
One Side—
1.1 Liter ①0.7
1.9 Liter 1.1
Both Sides—
1.1 Liter ①1.3
1.9 Liter 1.7

(Continued)

Brakes, Steering, Suspension, Universals & Rear Axle—TIME Cont'd

1971-73—
One Side—
1.1 Liter ....① 0.7
1.9 Liter 0.9
Both Sides—
1.1 Liter ....① 1.3
1.9 Liter 1.7
1974-75—
One Side ....① 0.9
Both Sides 1.7
① To Renew Seal, Add 0.3

Speedometer, Wipers, Switches & Instruments—TIME

OPERATION INDEX

Speedometer Cable, Renew 1
Speedometer Head, Renew 2
W/S Wiper Motor, Renew 3
W/S Wiper Motor, R & R & Overhaul 4
W/S Wiper Transmission Links, Renew 5
W/S Wiper Control Switch, Renew 6
Fuel Gauge (Dash Unit), Renew 7
Fuel Tank Gauge, Renew 8
Oil Gauge (Dash Unit), Renew 9
Oil Gauge Sending Unit, Renew 10
Temperature Gauge (Dash Unit), Renew 11
Temperature Gauge Sending Unit, Renew 12
Ammeter, Renew 13
Tachometer, Renew 14
Headlight Switch, Renew 15
Headlamp Dimmer Switch, Renew 16
Stop Light Switch, Renew 17
Directional Signal Switch, Renew 18
Hazard Flasher Switch, Renew 19

1—SPEEDOMETER CABLE, RENEW
1966-73—
Except Below 0.3
G.T. Less Air Cond 0.8
G.T. With Air Cond 1.1
1974-75 ....0.4

2—SPEEDOMETER HEAD, RENEW
1966-73—
Except Below 0.3
Model 1900 ....0.5
G.T. 0.8
1974-75 ....0.5

3—W/S WIPER MOTOR, RENEW
1966-73—
Except Below 0.2
G.T. 0.6
1974-75 ....0.4

4—W/S WIPER MOTOR, R & R & OVERHAUL
1966-73—
Except Below 0.7
G.T. 1.2
1974-75 ....0.9

5—W/S WIPER TRANSMISSION LINKS, RENEW
1966-73—
Left, Exc 0.4
Model 1900 ....0.5
Right, Exc 0.3
Model 1900 ....1.2
Both, Exc 0.5
Model 1900 ....1.4
G.T. 0.6
1974-75—
Left 0.5
Right 1.2
Both 1.4

6—W/S WIPER CONTROL SWITCH, RENEW
1966-73—
Exc Below 0.3
Model 1900 ....0.2
G.T. 0.8
1974-75 ....0.3

7—FUEL GAUGE (DASH UNIT), RENEW
1966-73—
Exc Below 0.3
Model 1900 ....0.5
G.T. 1.1
1974-75 ....0.5

8—FUEL TANK GAUGE, RENEW
1966-73—
Exc Below 0.6
Model 1900 ....0.3
G.T. 1.1
1974-75 ....0.4

9—OIL GAUGE (DASH UNIT), RENEW
1966-73—
Exc Below 0.3
G.T., L/Air Cond 0.8
G.T., W/Air Cond 1.1
1974-75 ....0.3

10— OIL GAUGE SENDING UNIT, RENEW
1966-75 ....0.3

11—TEMPERATURE GAUGE (DASH UNIT), RENEW
1966-73—
Exc Below 0.6
G.T., L/Air Cond 0.8
G.T., W/Air Cond 1.1
1974-75 ....0.6

12—TEMPERATURE GAUGE SENDING UNIT, RENEW
1966-73 ....0.3
1974-75 ....0.2

13—AMMETER, RENEW
1966-73—
Exc Below 0.3
G.T., L/Air Cond 0.8
G.T., W/Air Cond 1.1
1974-75 ....0.3

14—TACHOMETER, RENEW
1966-73—
Exc Below 0.3
Model 1900 ....0.5
G.T. 0.8
1974-75 ....0.5

15—HEADLIGHT SWITCH, RENEW
1966-73—
Exc Below 0.3
G.T., L/Air Cond 0.8
G.T., W/Air Cond 1.1
1974-75 ....0.4

16—HEADLAMP DIMMER SWITCH, RENEW
1966-73 ....0.3
1974-75 ....0.7

17—STOP LIGHT SWITCH, RENEW
1966-75 ....0.2

18—DIRECTIONAL SIGNAL SWITCH, RENEW
1966-75 ....0.7

19—HAZARD FLASHER SWITCH, RENEW
1966-73—
Exc Below 0.2
Model 1900 ....0.7
G.T. 0.8
1974-75 ....0.2

ILLUSTRATIONS

FIG 1 — ENGINE — CYLINDER HEAD
FIG 2 — ENGINE — CYLINDER BLOCK & OIL PAN
FIG 3 — ENGINE — CRANKSHAFT PISTONS
FIG 4 — ENGINE — CAMSHAFT & TIMING CHAIN
FIG 5 — ENGINE — CYLINDER HEAD COVER
FIG 6 — ENGINE — OILING & COOLING
FIG 7 — STARTING MOTOR
FIG 8 — ALTERNATOR
FIG 9 — DISTRIBUTOR
FIG 10 — FOUR SPEED MANUAL TRANSMISSION
FIG 11 — FIVE SPEED MANUAL TRANSMISSION
FIG 12 — AUTOMATIC TRANSMISSION — CASE & RELATED PARTS
FIG 13 — AUTOMATIC TRANSMISSION — INTERNAL PARTS
FIG 14 — AUTOMATIC TRANSMISSION — PUMP
FIG 15 — AUTOMATIC TRANSMISSION — CONTROL VALVE
FIG 16 — FRONT SUSPENSION
FIG 17 — STEERING GEAR
FIG 18 — STEERING COLUMN
FIG 19 — REAR AXLE

OPERATION TIMES

A

Air Conditioning.... 326
Air Pump.... 321
Alternator.... 322
Ammeter.... 322
Automatic Transmission.... 324
Axle Shaft.... 325

B

Battery.... 322
Brake Drums & Discs.... 325
Brakes.... 325

C

Cables (Ignition).... 321
Calipers.... 325
Camshaft.... 323
Carburetor.... 321
Clock.... 322
Clutch.... 323
Coil, Ignition.... 321
Compression Test.... 321
Connecting Rods.... 323
Cooling System.... 322
Crankshaft.... 323
Cylinder Head.... 323

D

Dash Gauges.... 322
Differential.... 325
Disc Brakes.... 325
Distributor.... 321

E

Emission Controls.... 321
Engine Assembly.... 323
Engine Mountings.... 323
Engine Oiling.... 323
Engine Tune-Up.... 321
Exhaust System.... 321

F

Front Suspension.... 325
Fuel Gauges.... 322
Fuel Pump.... 321
Fuel Tank.... 321

G

Generator.... 322

H

Hand Brake.... 325
Headlight Switch.... 322
Heater.... 326
Horn.... 322
Hose (Brake).... 325
Hose (Radiator).... 323
Hydraulic Brakes.... 325

I

Ignition.... 321
Ignition Coil.... 321
Ignition Switch.... 321
Intake Manifold.... 321

L

Lamps & Switches.... 322

M

Main Bearings.... 323
Master Cylinder.... 325
Muffler.... 321

O

Oil Gauge.... 322
Oiling, Engine.... 323
Oil Pan.... 323
Oil Pump.... 323

P

Parking Brake.... 325
Piston Rings.... 323
Pistons.... 323
Power Brake.... 325

R

Radiator.... 323
Radiator Hose.... 323
Radio.... 322
Rear Axle.... 324
Regulator.... 322
Rocker Arms.... 323
Rod Bearings.... 323

S

Shocks (Front).... 326
Shocks (Rear.... 324
Speedometer.... 322
Springs (Front).... 326
Springs (Rear).... 324
Stabilizer.... 326
Starting Motor.... 321
Steering Gear.... 326
Steering Linkage.... 326
Switches (Light).... 322
Synchro-Mesh Trans.... 323

T

Tachometer.... 322
Temperature Gauge.... 322
Thermostat.... 323
Timing Case Cover.... 323
Timing Chain.... 323
Timing Gears.... 323
Track Rod.... 324
Transmission, Manual.... 323
Transmission, Automatic.... 324
Tune-Up, Engine.... 321

U

Universals.... 325

V

Vacuum Control Unit.... 321
Valve Lifters.... 323
Valve System.... 323

W

Water Pump.... 323
Wheel Cylinders.... 325
Windshield Wiper.... 322

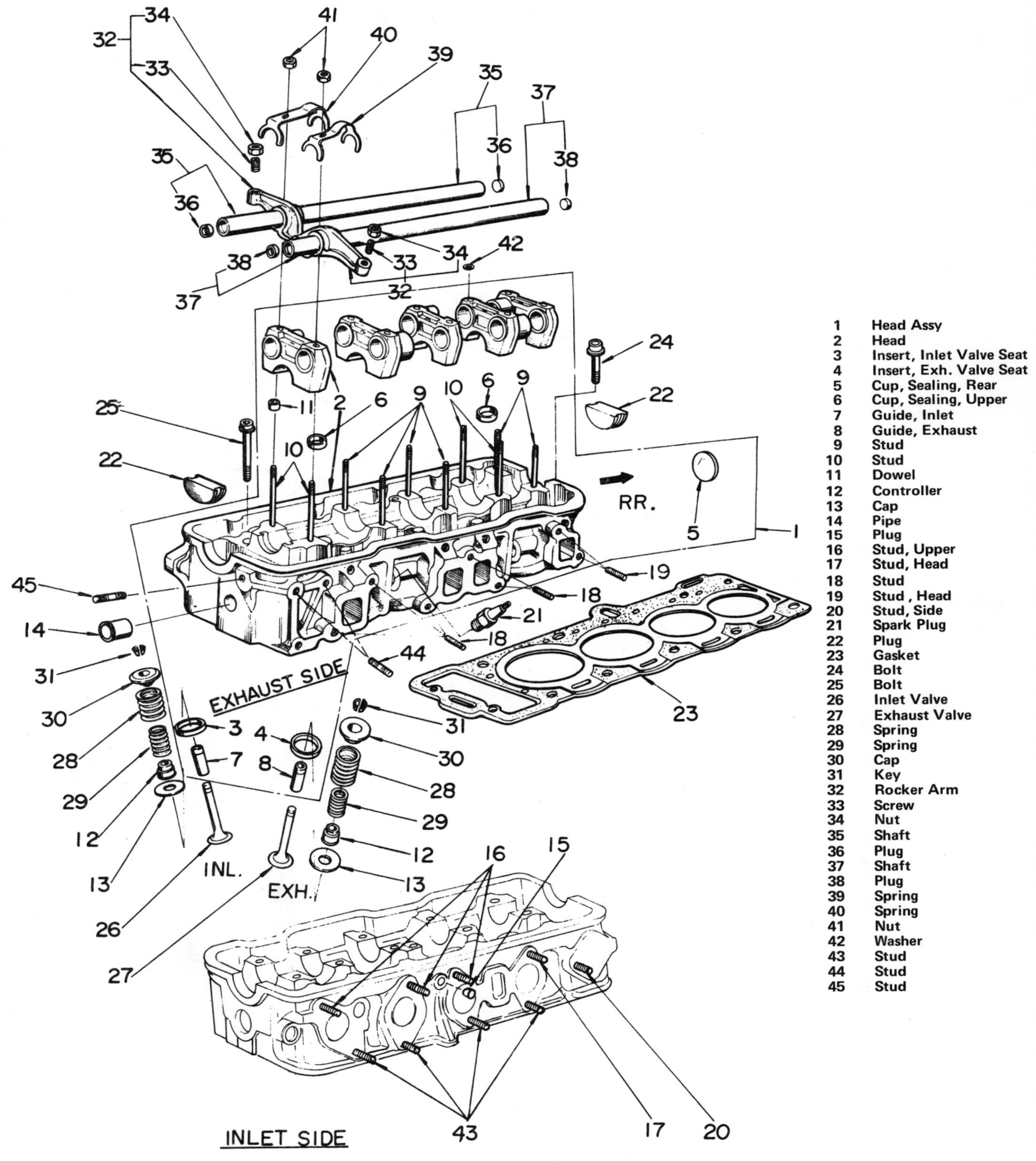
EXHAUST SIDE
INLET SIDE
RR.
INL.
EXH.
1 Head Assy
2 Head
3 Insert, Inlet Valve Seat
4 Insert, Exh. Valve Seat
5 Cup, Sealing, Rear
6 Cup, Sealing, Upper
7 Guide, Inlet
8 Guide, Exhaust
9 Stud
10 Stud
11 Dowel
12 Controller
13 Cap
14 Pipe
15 Plug
16 Stud, Upper
17 Stud, Head
18 Stud
19 Stud , Head
20 Stud, Side
21 Spark Plug
22 Plug
23 Gasket
24 Bolt
25 Bolt
26 Inlet Valve
27 Exhaust Valve
28 Spring
29 Spring
30 Cap
31 Key
32 Rocker Arm
33 Screw
34 Nut
35 Shaft
36 Plug
37 Shaft
38 Plug
39 Spring
40 Spring
41 Nut
42 Washer
43 Stud
44 Stud
45 Stud

FIG 1 – ENGINE – CYLINDER HEAD

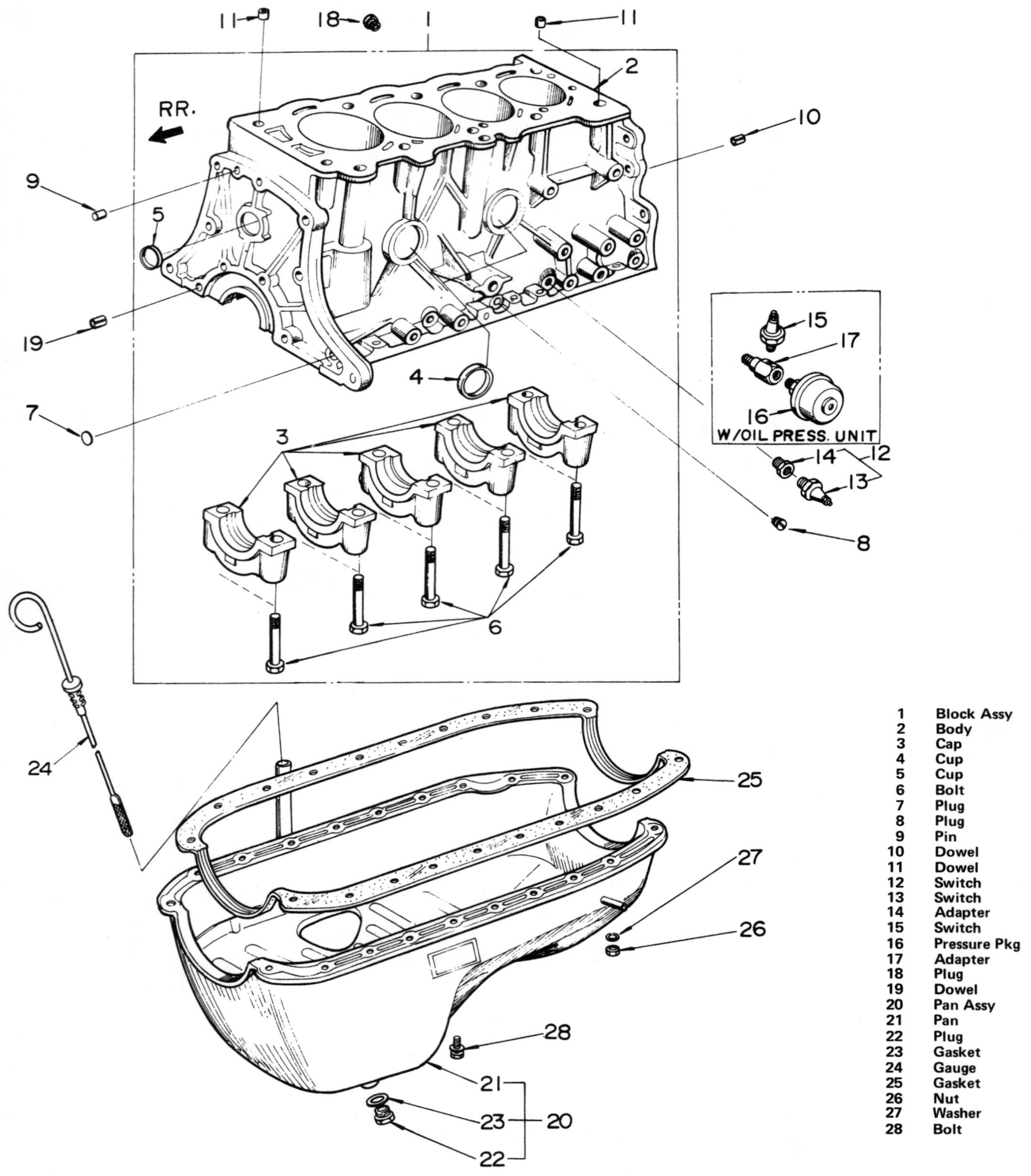

FIG 2 – ENGINE – CYLINDER BLOCK & OIL PAN

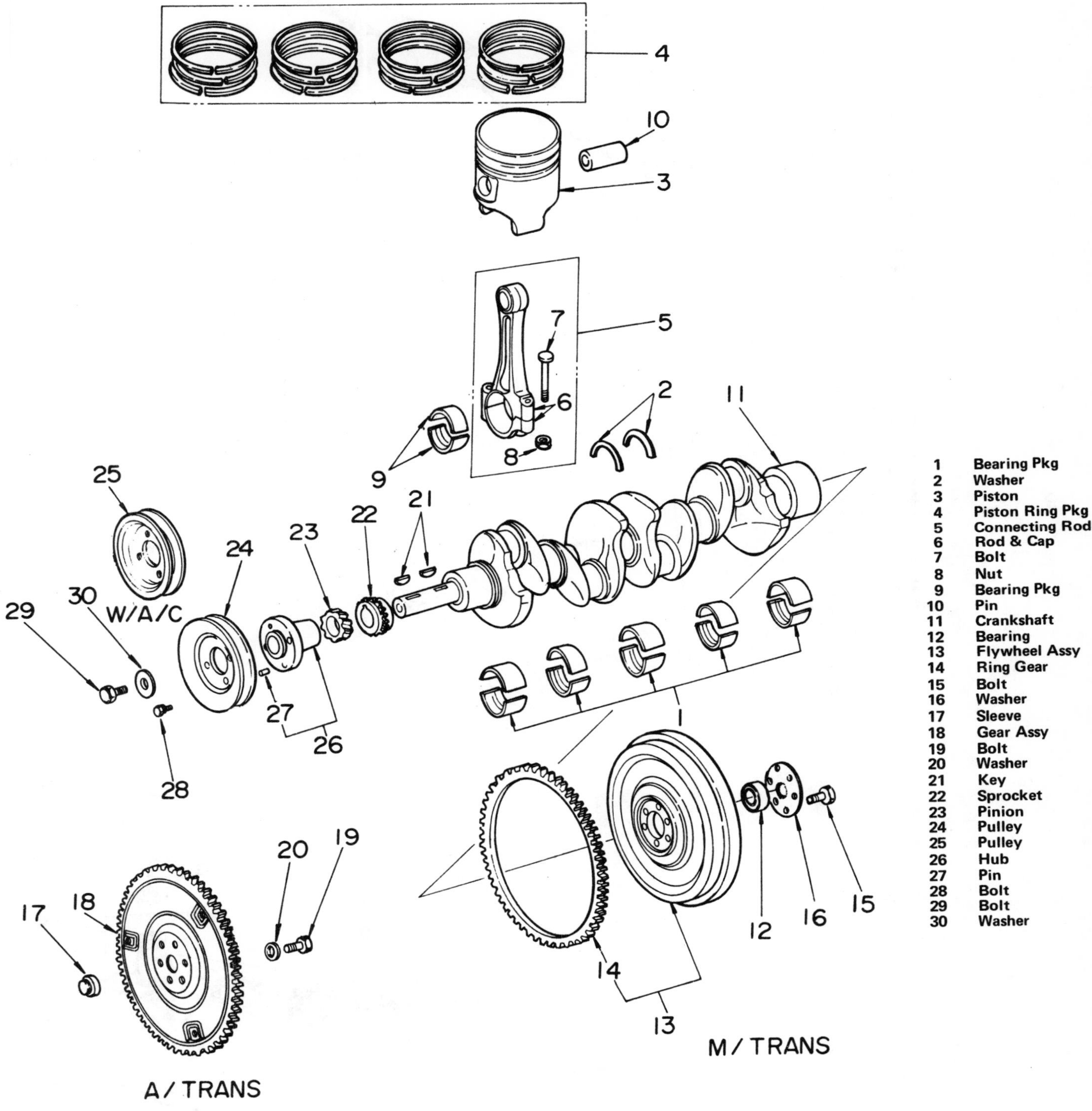
W/A/C
M/TRANS
A/TRANS
1 Bearing Pkg
2 Washer
3 Piston
4 Piston Ring Pkg
5 Connecting Rod
6 Rod & Cap
7 Bolt
8 Nut
9 Bearing Pkg
10 Pin
11 Crankshaft
12 Bearing
13 Flywheel Assy
14 Ring Gear
15 Bolt
16 Washer
17 Sleeve
18 Gear Assy
19 Bolt
20 Washer
21 Key
22 Sprocket
23 Pinion
24 Pulley
25 Pulley
26 Hub
27 Pin
28 Bolt
29 Bolt
30 Washer

FIG 3 – ENGINE – CRANKSHAFT & PISTONS

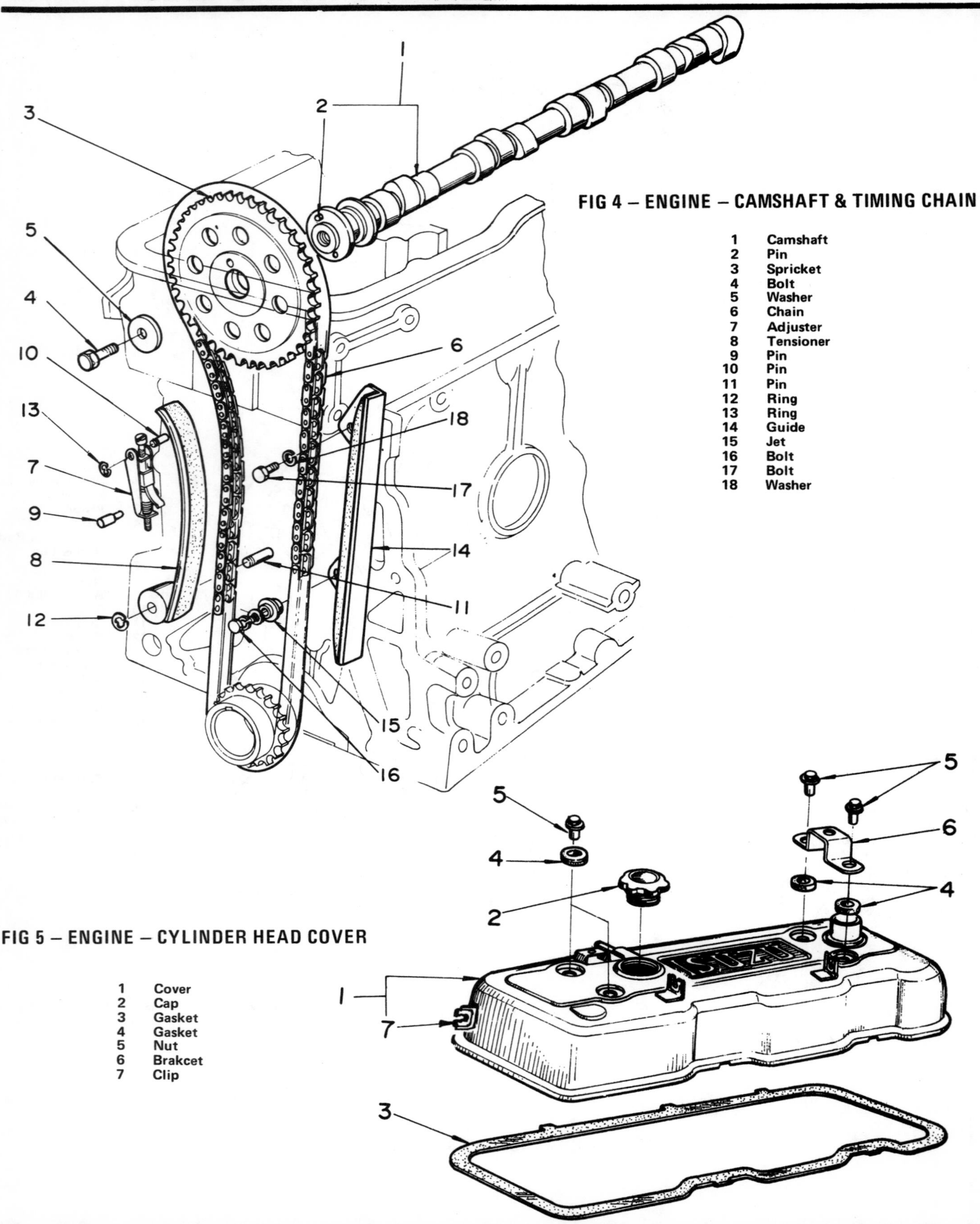

FIG 4 – ENGINE – CAMSHAFT & TIMING CHAIN

1 Camshaft
2 Pin
3 Spricket
4 Bolt
5 Washer
6 Chain
7 Adjuster
8 Tensioner
9 Pin
10 Pin
11 Pin
12 Ring
13 Ring
14 Guide
15 Jet
16 Bolt
17 Bolt
18 Washer

FIG 5 – ENGINE – CYLINDER HEAD COVER

1 Cover
2 Cap
3 Gasket
4 Gasket
5 Nut
6 Brakcet
7 Clip

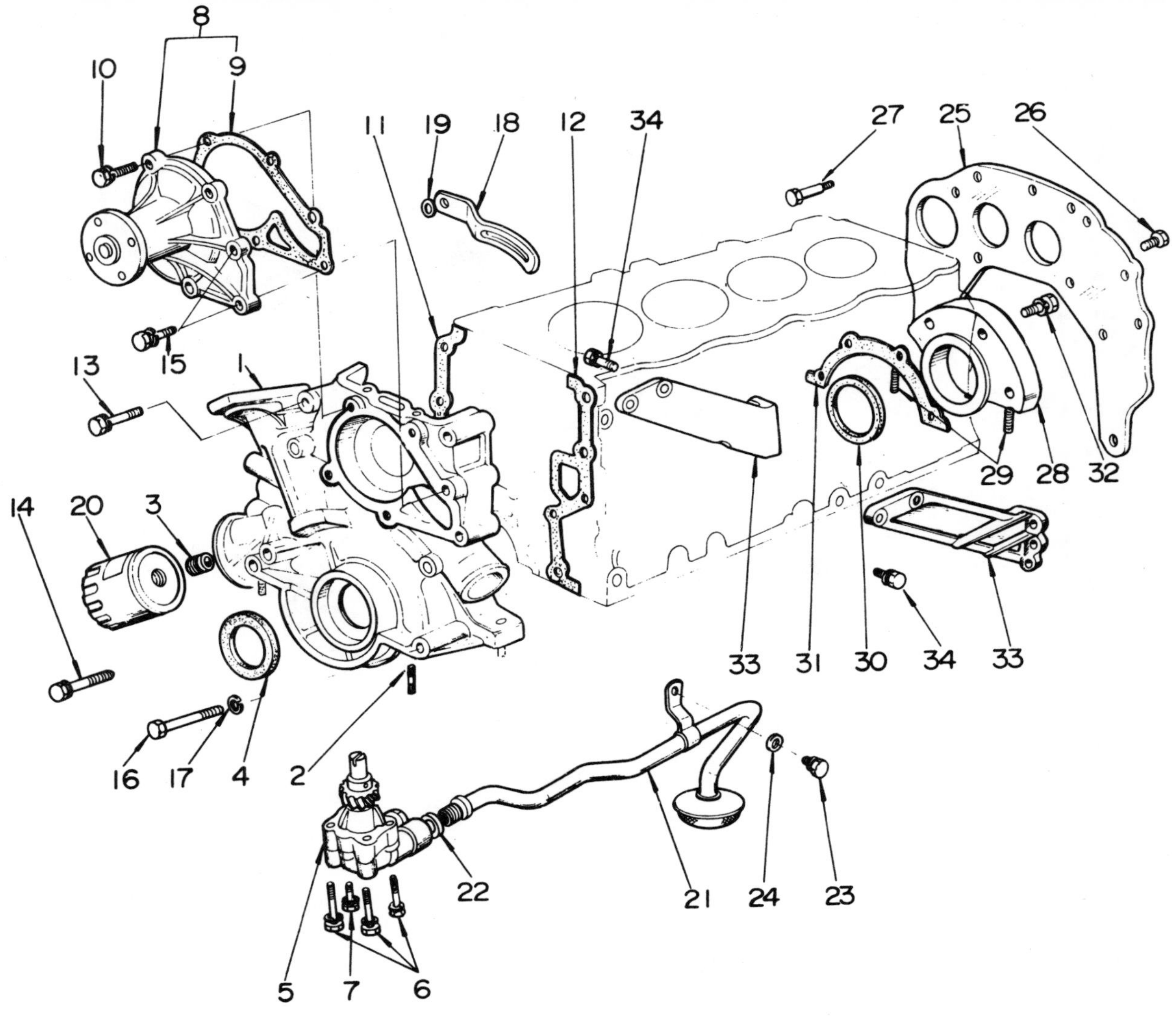

FIG 6 – ENGINE – OILING & COOLING

1 Timing Cover
2 Stud
3 Fitting
4 Seal
5 Oil Pump
6 Bolt
7 Bolt
8 Water Pump
9 Gasket
10 Bolt
11 Gasket
12 Gasket
13 Bolt
14 Bolt
15 Bolt
16 Bolt
17 Washer
18 Brace
19 Washer
20 Oil Filter Element
21 Pipe
22 Seal
23 Bolt
24 Washer
25 Plate
26 Bolt
27 Bolt
28 Retainer
29 Stud
30 Seal
31 Gasket
32 Bolt
33 Support
34 Bolt

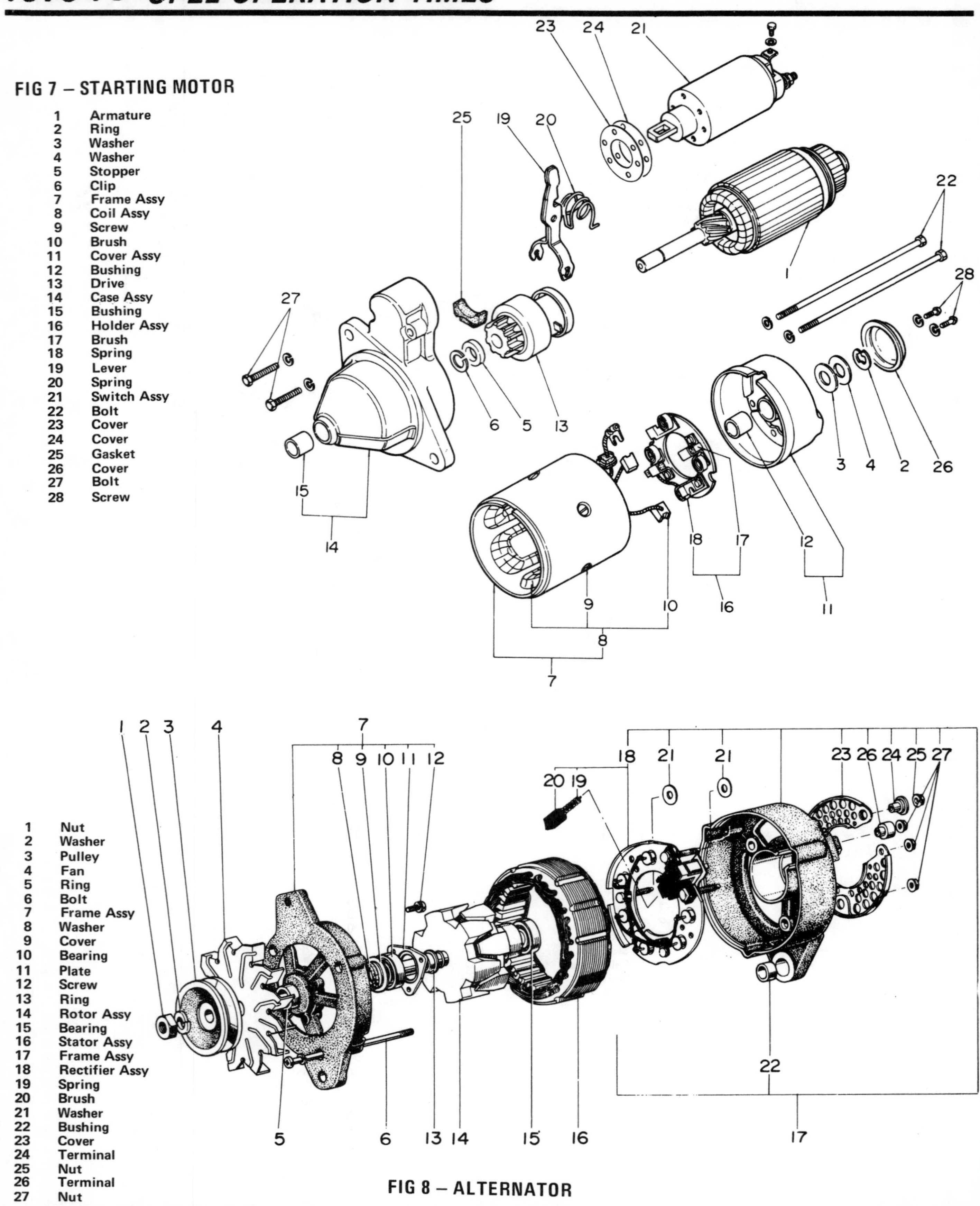
1 Armature
2 Ring
3 Washer
4 Washer
5 Stopper
6 Clip
7 Frame Assy
8 Coil Assy
9 Screw
10 Brush
11 Cover Assy
12 Bushing
13 Drive
14 Case Assy
15 Bushing
16 Holder Assy
17 Brush
18 Spring
19 Lever
20 Spring
21 Switch Assy
22 Bolt
23 Cover
24 Cover
25 Gasket
26 Cover
27 Bolt
28 Screw
1 Nut
2 Washer
3 Pulley
4 Fan
5 Ring
6 Bolt
7 Frame Assy
8 Washer
9 Cover
10 Bearing
11 Plate
12 Screw
13 Ring
14 Rotor Assy
15 Bearing
16 Stator Assy
17 Frame Assy
18 Rectifier Assy
19 Spring
20 Brush
21 Washer
22 Bushing
23 Cover
24 Terminal
25 Nut
26 Terminal
27 Nut

FIG 7 – STARTING MOTOR

FIG 8 – ALTERNATOR

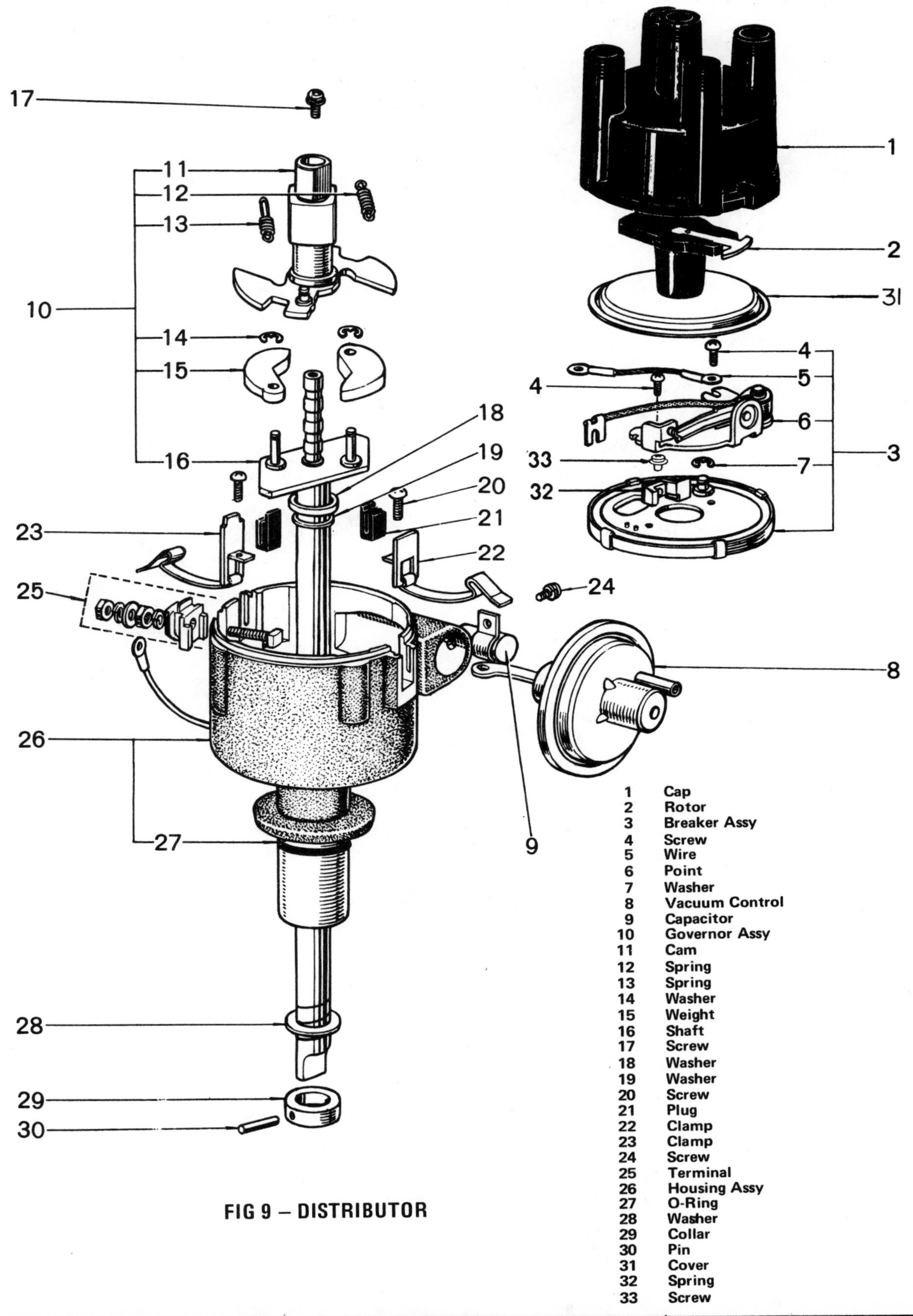
1 Cap
2 Rotor
3 Breaker Assy
4 Screw
5 Wire
6 Point
7 Washer
8 Vacuum Control
9 Capacitor
10 Governor Assy
11 Cam
12 Spring
13 Spring
14 Washer
15 Weight
16 Shaft
17 Screw
18 Washer
19 Washer
20 Screw
21 Plug
22 Clamp
23 Clamp
24 Screw
25 Terminal
26 Housing Assy
27 O-Ring
28 Washer
29 Collar
30 Pin
31 Cover
32 Spring
33 Screw

FIG 9 – DISTRIBUTOR

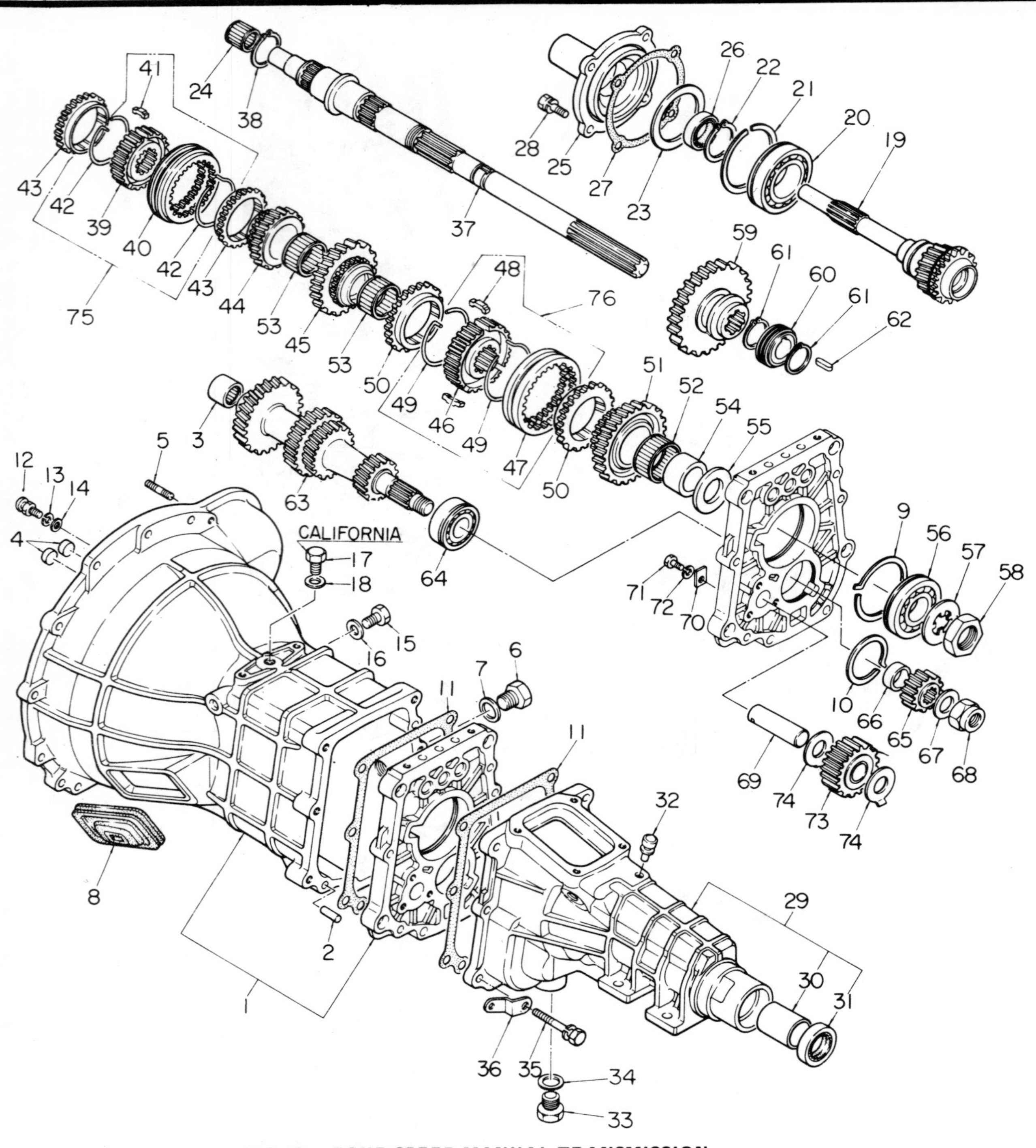

FIG 10 – FOUR SPEED MANUAL TRANSMISSION

1	Case Assy	15	Plug	29	Cover	43	Ring	57	Washer	71	Bolt
2	Pin	16	Gasket	30	Bush	44	Gear Assy	58	Nut	72	Washer
3	Bearing	17	Plug	31	Seal	45	Gear	59	Gear	73	Gear, Reverse Idler
4	Plug	18	Gasket	32	Ventilator	46	Hub	60	Gear	74	Washer
5	Stud	19	Shaft	33	Plug	47	Sleeve	61	Ring	75	Synchronizer Assy
6	Plug	20	Bearing	34	Ring	48	Insert	62	Key	76	Synchronizer Assy
7	Seal	21	Ring	35	Bolt	49	Spring	63	Gear		
8	Cover	22	Ring	36	Bracket	50	Ring	64	Bearing		
9	Ring	23	Spring	37	Main Shaft	51	Gear Assy	65	Gear, Center Reverse		
10	Ring	24	Bearing	38	Ring	52	Bearing	66	Spacer		
11	Gasket	25	Cover	39	Hub	53	Bearing	67	Washer		
12	Support	26	Seal	40	Sleeve	54	Collar	68	Nut		
13	Washer	27	Gasket	41	Insert	55	Washer	69	Shaft, Reverse Idler		
14	Washer	28	Bolt	42	Spring	56	Bearing	70	Plate		

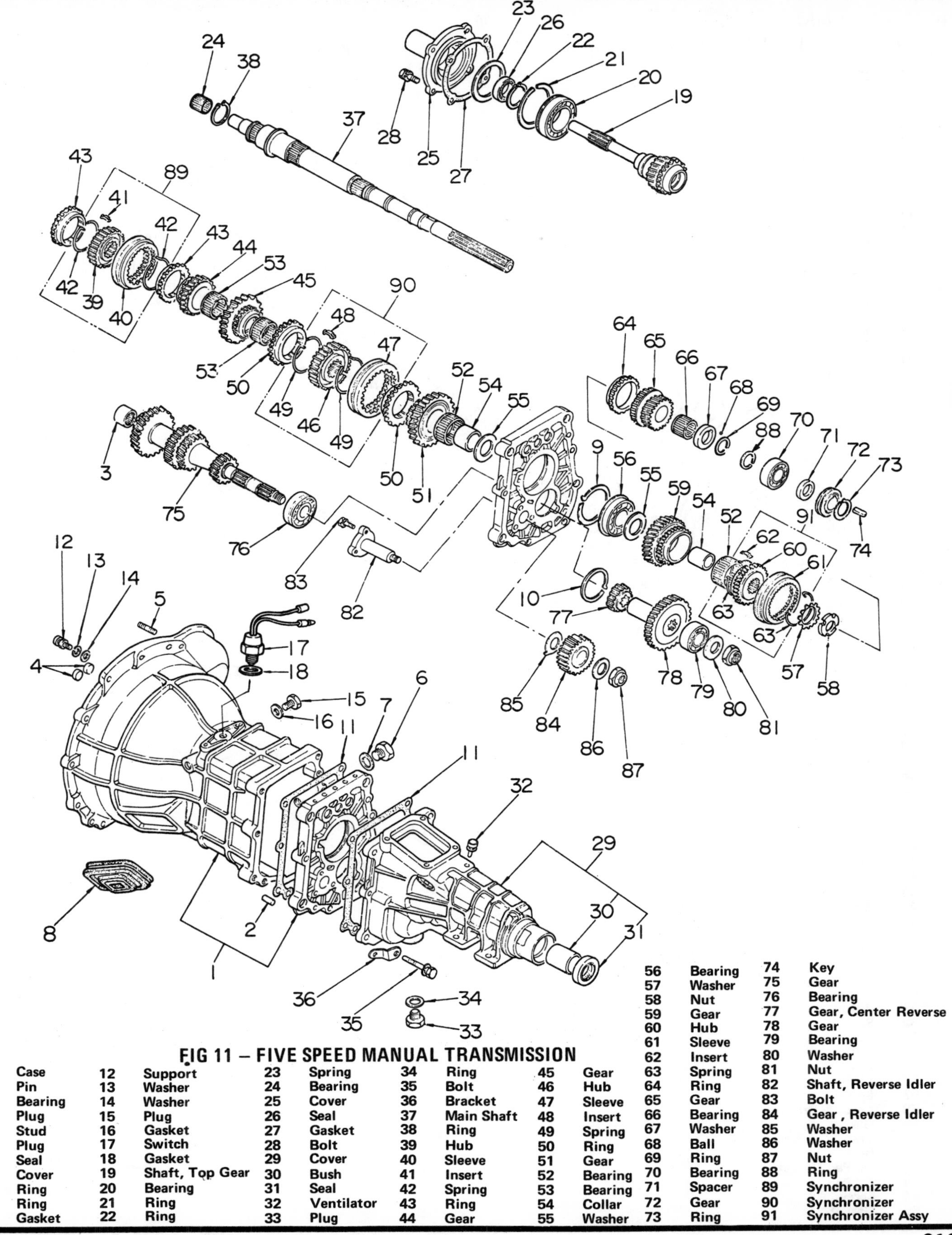

FIG 11 – FIVE SPEED MANUAL TRANSMISSION

										56	Bearing	74	Key
										57	Washer	75	Gear
										58	Nut	76	Bearing
										59	Gear	77	Gear, Center Reverse
										60	Hub	78	Gear
										61	Sleeve	79	Bearing
										62	Insert	80	Washer
1	Case	12	Support	23	Spring	34	Ring	45	Gear	63	Spring	81	Nut
2	Pin	13	Washer	24	Bearing	35	Bolt	46	Hub	64	Ring	82	Shaft, Reverse Idler
3	Bearing	14	Washer	25	Cover	36	Bracket	47	Sleeve	65	Gear	83	Bolt
4	Plug	15	Plug	26	Seal	37	Main Shaft	48	Insert	66	Bearing	84	Gear, Reverse Idler
5	Stud	16	Gasket	27	Gasket	38	Ring	49	Spring	67	Washer	85	Washer
6	Plug	17	Switch	28	Bolt	39	Hub	50	Ring	68	Ball	86	Washer
7	Seal	18	Gasket	29	Cover	40	Sleeve	51	Gear	69	Ring	87	Nut
8	Cover	19	Shaft, Top Gear	30	Bush	41	Insert	52	Bearing	70	Bearing	88	Ring
9	Ring	20	Bearing	31	Seal	42	Spring	53	Bearing	71	Spacer	89	Synchronizer
10	Ring	21	Ring	32	Ventilator	43	Ring	54	Collar	72	Gear	90	Synchronizer
11	Gasket	22	Ring	33	Plug	44	Gear	55	Washer	73	Ring	91	Synchronizer Assy

FIG 12 – AUTOMATIC TRANSMISSION – CASE & RELATED PARTS

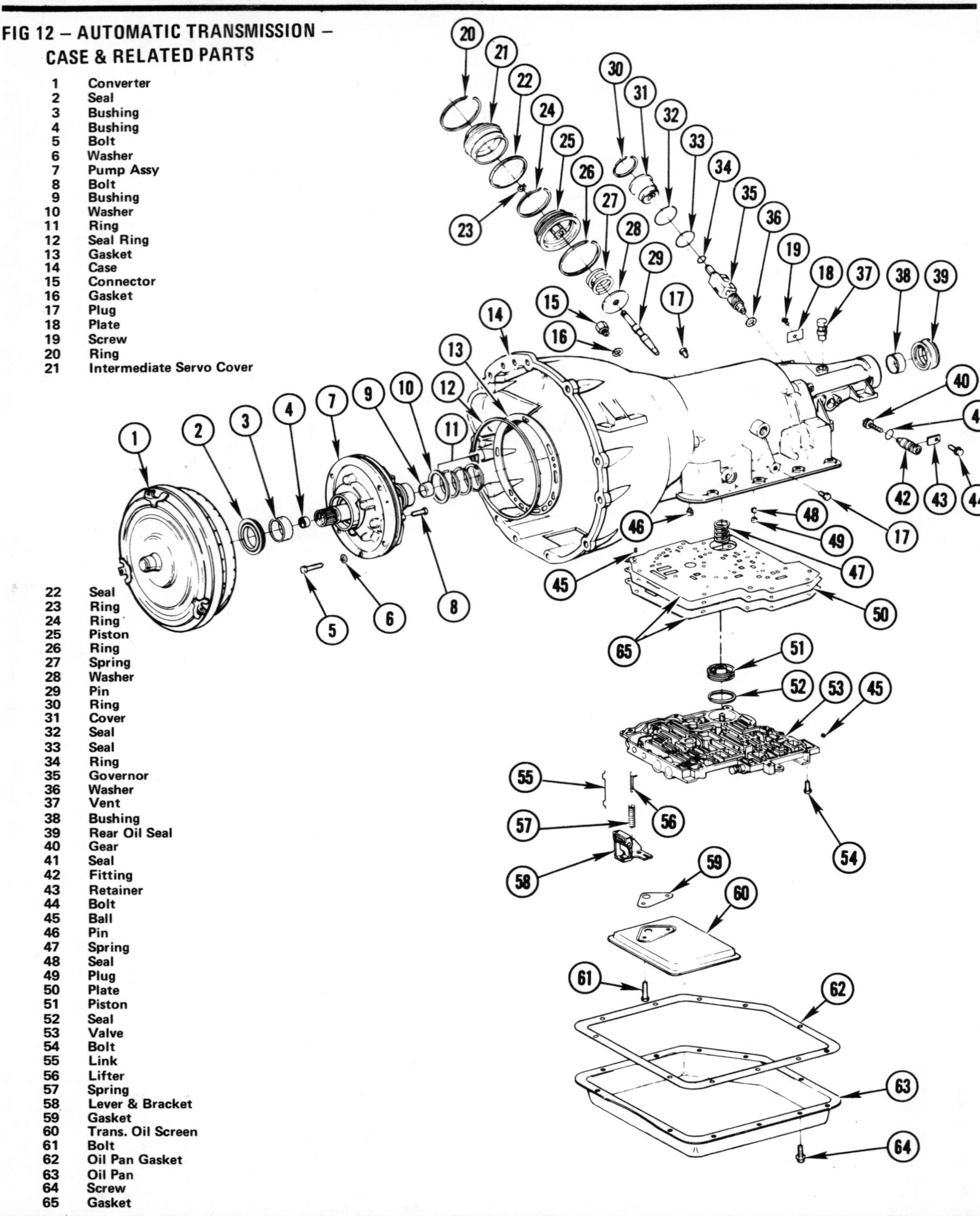

1 Converter
2 Seal
3 Bushing
4 Bushing
5 Bolt
6 Washer
7 Pump Assy
8 Bolt
9 Bushing
10 Washer
11 Ring
12 Seal Ring
13 Gasket
14 Case
15 Connector
16 Gasket
17 Plug
18 Plate
19 Screw
20 Ring
21 Intermediate Servo Cover
22 Seal
23 Ring
24 Ring
25 Piston
26 Ring
27 Spring
28 Washer
29 Pin
30 Ring
31 Cover
32 Seal
33 Seal
34 Ring
35 Governor
36 Washer
37 Vent
38 Bushing
39 Rear Oil Seal
40 Gear
41 Seal
42 Fitting
43 Retainer
44 Bolt
45 Ball
46 Pin
47 Spring
48 Seal
49 Plug
50 Plate
51 Piston
52 Seal
53 Valve
54 Bolt
55 Link
56 Lifter
57 Spring
58 Lever & Bracket
59 Gasket
60 Trans. Oil Screen
61 Bolt
62 Oil Pan Gasket
63 Oil Pan
64 Screw
65 Gasket

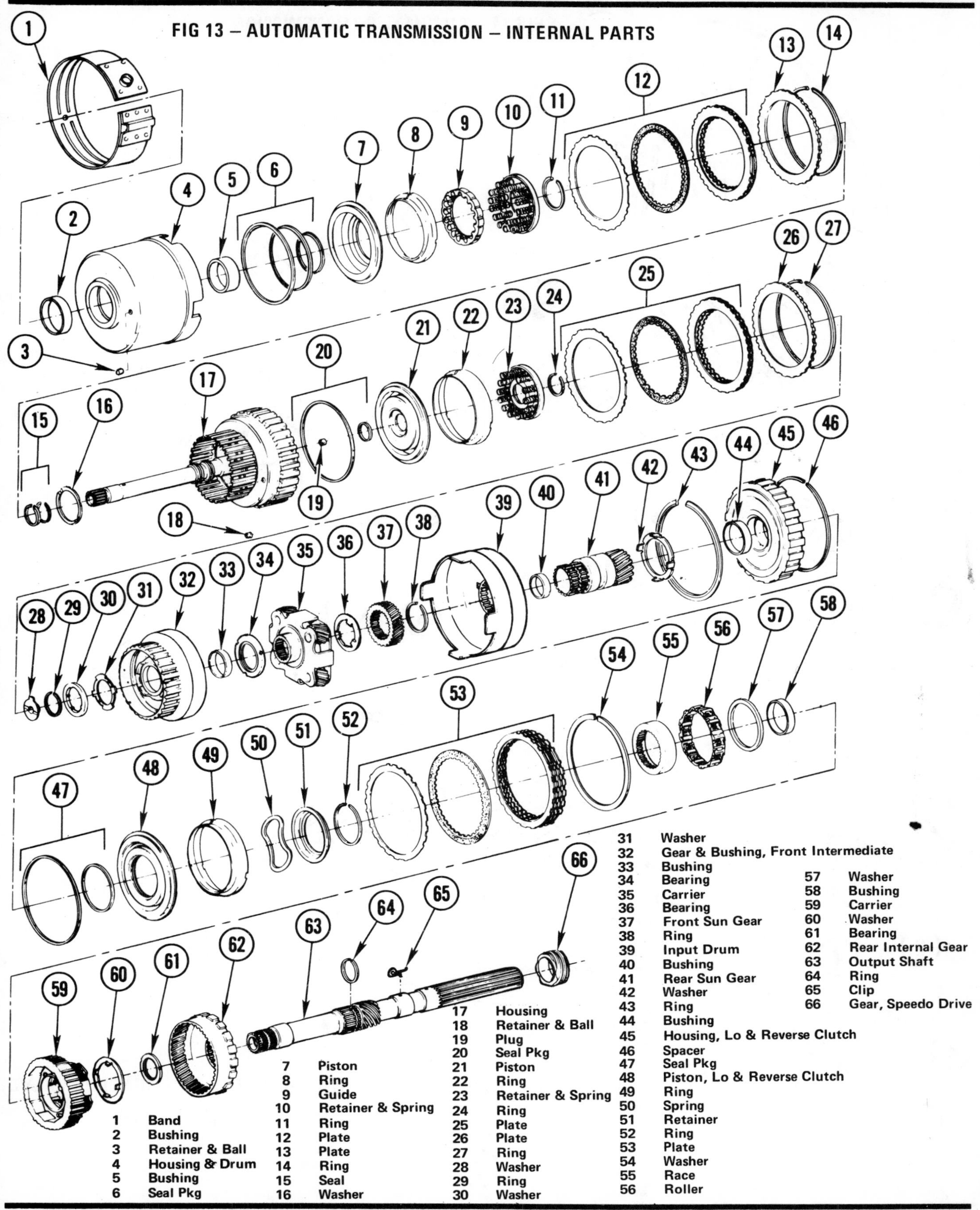
1 Band
2 Bushing
3 Retainer & Ball
4 Housing & Drum
5 Bushing
6 Seal Pkg
7 Piston
8 Ring
9 Guide
10 Retainer & Spring
11 Ring
12 Plate
13 Plate
14 Ring
15 Seal
16 Washer
17 Housing
18 Retainer & Ball
19 Plug
20 Seal Pkg
21 Piston
22 Ring
23 Retainer & Spring
24 Ring
25 Plate
26 Plate
27 Ring
28 Washer
29 Ring
30 Washer
31 Washer
32 Gear & Bushing, Front Intermediate
33 Bushing
34 Bearing
35 Carrier
36 Bearing
37 Front Sun Gear
38 Ring
39 Input Drum
40 Bushing
41 Rear Sun Gear
42 Washer
43 Ring
44 Bushing
45 Housing, Lo & Reverse Clutch
46 Spacer
47 Seal Pkg
48 Piston, Lo & Reverse Clutch
49 Ring
50 Spring
51 Retainer
52 Ring
53 Plate
54 Washer
55 Race
56 Roller
57 Washer
58 Bushing
59 Carrier
60 Washer
61 Bearing
62 Rear Internal Gear
63 Output Shaft
64 Ring
65 Clip
66 Gear, Speedo Drive

FIG 13 – AUTOMATIC TRANSMISSION – INTERNAL PARTS

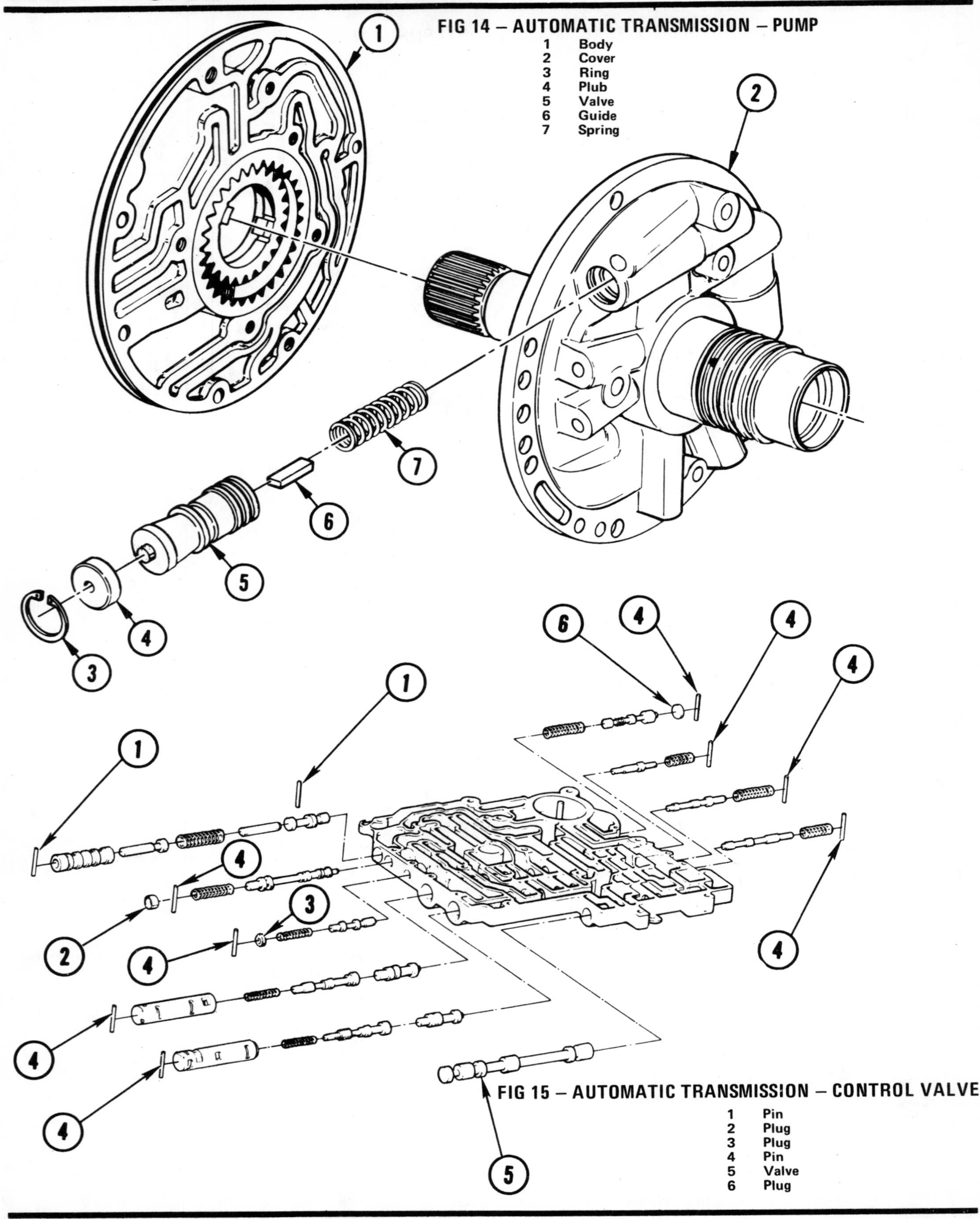

FIG 14 – AUTOMATIC TRANSMISSION – PUMP

1 Body
2 Cover
3 Ring
4 Plub
5 Valve
6 Guide
7 Spring

FIG 15 – AUTOMATIC TRANSMISSION – CONTROL VALVE

1 Pin
2 Plug
3 Plug
4 Pin
5 Valve
6 Plug

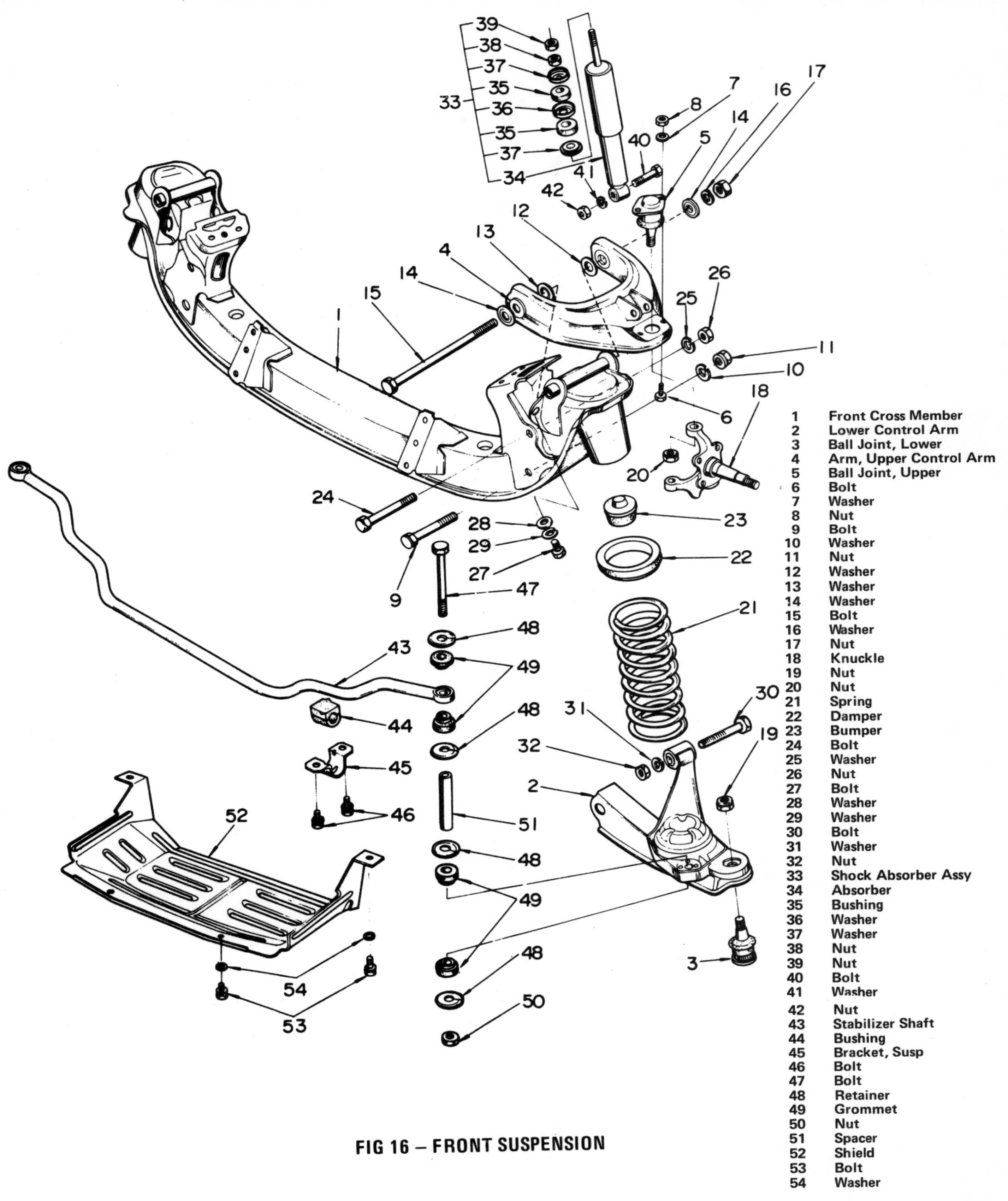
1 Front Cross Member
2 Lower Control Arm
3 Ball Joint, Lower
4 Arm, Upper Control Arm
5 Ball Joint, Upper
6 Bolt
7 Washer
8 Nut
9 Bolt
10 Washer
11 Nut
12 Washer
13 Washer
14 Washer
15 Bolt
16 Washer
17 Nut
18 Knuckle
19 Nut
20 Nut
21 Spring
22 Damper
23 Bumper
24 Bolt
25 Washer
26 Nut
27 Bolt
28 Washer
29 Washer
30 Bolt
31 Washer
32 Nut
33 Shock Absorber Assy
34 Absorber
35 Bushing
36 Washer
37 Washer
38 Nut
39 Nut
40 Bolt
41 Washer
42 Nut
43 Stabilizer Shaft
44 Bushing
45 Bracket, Susp
46 Bolt
47 Bolt
48 Retainer
49 Grommet
50 Nut
51 Spacer
52 Shield
53 Bolt
54 Washer

FIG 16 – FRONT SUSPENSION

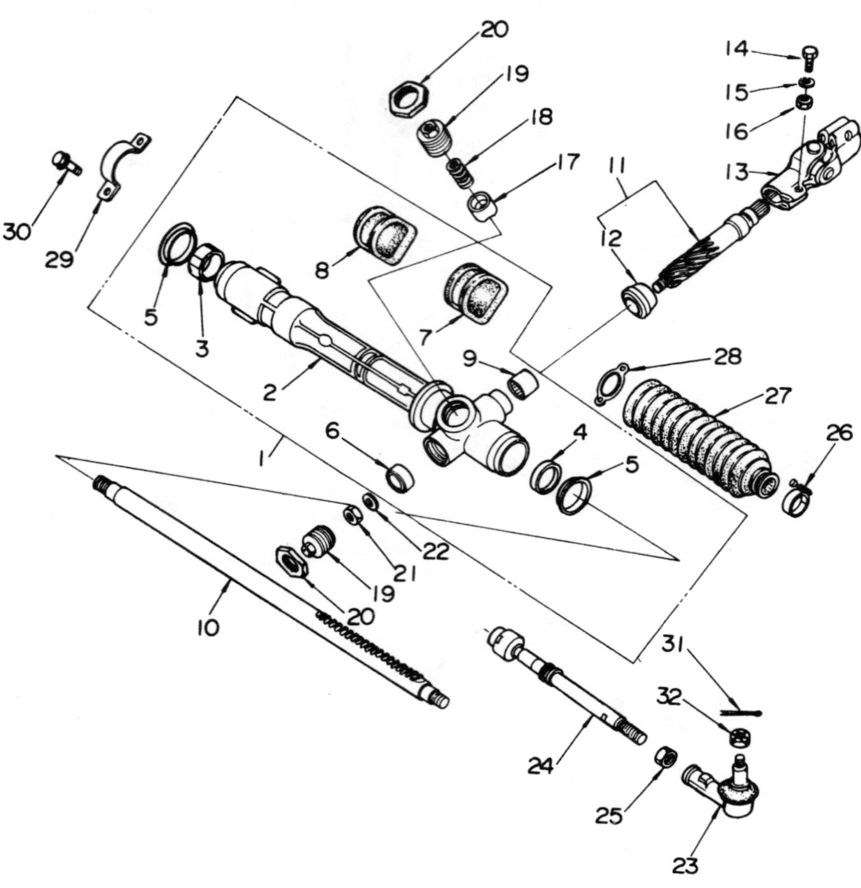

FIG 17 – STEERING GEAR

1	Housing Assy
2	Housing
3	Bushing
4	Bushing
5	Retainer
6	Bearing
7	Grommet
8	Grommet
9	Bearing
10	Rack
11	Pinion Assy
12	Seal
13	Joint
14	Bolt
15	Washer
16	Nut
17	Bearing
18	Spring
19	Plug
20	Nut
21	Nut
22	Washer
23	End Assy
24	Rod
25	Nut
26	Clip
27	Boot
28	Clamp
29	Bracket
30	Bolt
31	Pin
32	Nut

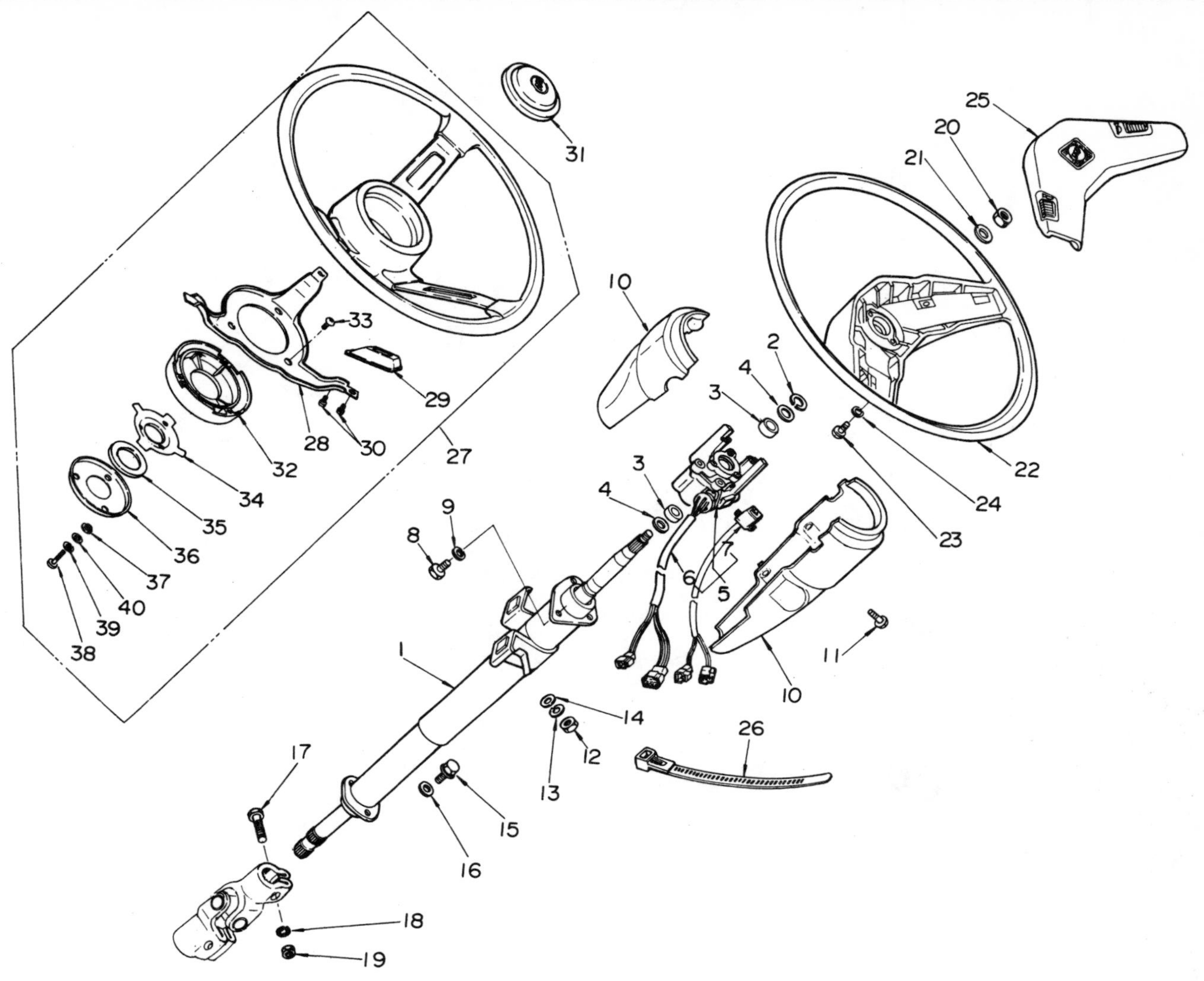

FIG 18 – STEERING COLUMN

1	Column Assy	21	Washer
2	Ring	22	Wheel
3	Grommet	23	Screw
4	Washer	24	Washer
5	Lock Pkg	25	Shroud & Horn Button
6	Switch	26	Clip
7	Switch	27	Wheel (Sport)
8	Bolt	28	Lever
9	Washer	29	Button
10	Cover Set	30	Screw
11	Screw	31	Shroud
12	Nut	32	Cover
13	Washer	33	Screw
14	Washer	34	Spring
15	Bolt	35	Packing
16	Washer	36	Ring
17	Bolt	37	Insulator
18	Washer	38	Screw
19	Nut	39	Washer
20	Nut	40	Washer

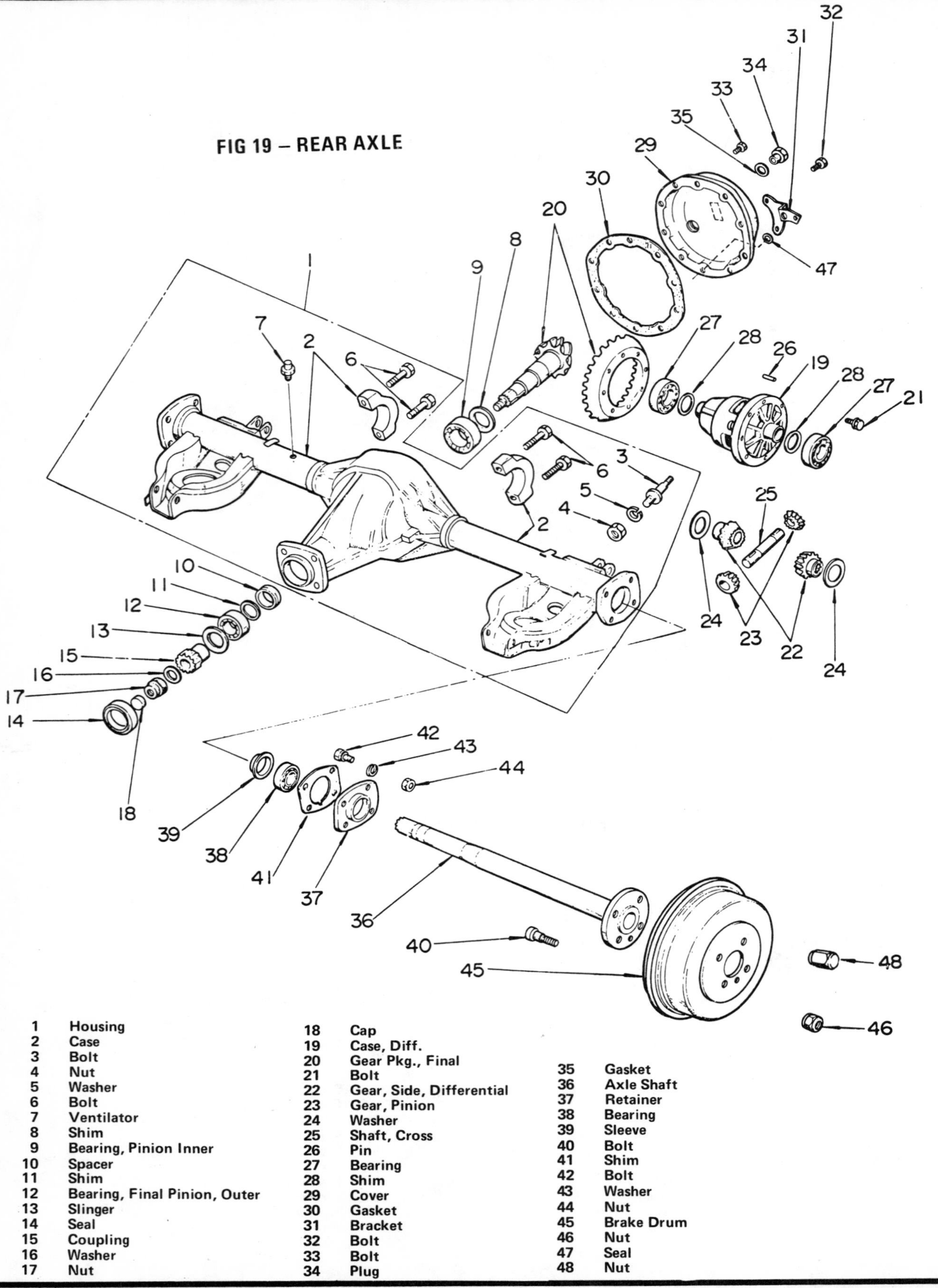

FIG 19 – REAR AXLE

1	Housing	18	Cap	35	Gasket
2	Case	19	Case, Diff.	36	Axle Shaft
3	Bolt	20	Gear Pkg., Final	37	Retainer
4	Nut	21	Bolt	38	Bearing
5	Washer	22	Gear, Side, Differential	39	Sleeve
6	Bolt	23	Gear, Pinion	40	Bolt
7	Ventilator	24	Washer	41	Shim
8	Shim	25	Shaft, Cross	42	Bolt
9	Bearing, Pinion Inner	26	Pin	43	Washer
10	Spacer	27	Bearing	44	Nut
11	Shim	28	Shim	45	Brake Drum
12	Bearing, Final Pinion, Outer	29	Cover	46	Nut
13	Slinger	30	Gasket	47	Seal
14	Seal	31	Bracket	48	Nut
15	Coupling	32	Bolt		
16	Washer	33	Bolt		
17	Nut	34	Plug		

Emission Controls—TIME

OPERATION INDEX

Air Injection Reactor System 1
Exhaust Gas Recirculation System 2
Controlled Combustion System 3
Coasting Richer System 4
Over Temperature Control System 5
Evap Emission Control System 6
Positive Crankcase Vent System 7

1—AIR INJECTOR REACTOR SYSTEM

Pump, Renew 0.4
By-Pass Valve, Renew 0.3
Hose, Renew 0.2
Drive Belt, Renew 0.2
Manifold, Renew 0.4
Mixture Control Valve, Renew 0.3
Check Valve, Renew 0.2

2—EXHAUST GAS RECIRCULATION SYSTEM

Thermal Vacuum Valve, Renew 0.2
E G R Valve, Renew 0.6
E G R Pipe, Renew 0.7

3—CONTROLLED COMBUSTION SYSTEM

Thermo Sensor, Renew 0.3
Hot Idle Compensator, Renew 0.3
Vacuum Motor, Renew 0.2
Hot Air Hose, Renew 0.2

4—COASTING RICHER SYSTEM

Accelerator Switch, Renew 0.3
Clutch Switch, Renew 0.3
Inhibitor Switch, Renew 0.3
Engine Speed Sensor, Renew 0.2
Solenoid, Renew 0.7
Transmission Switch, Renew 0.5
Closing Dash Pot, Renew 0.3

5—OVER TEMPERATURE CONTROL SYSTEM

Vacuum Switching Valve, Renew 0.3
Air Switching Valve, Renew 0.3
Thermo Sensor, Renew 0.3
Thermo Controller, Renew 0.2

6—EVAPORATIVE EMISSION CONTROL SYSTEM

Check & Relief Valve, Renew 0.2
Vapor Tank, Renew 0.2
Hoses, Renew—
  Engine Area 0.2
  Rear Compartment 0.3

7—POSITIVE CRANKCASE VENT SYSTEM

P. C. V. Hoses, Renew 0.3
P. C. V. Valve, Renew 0.2

Tune-Up & Ignition—TIME

OPERATION INDEX

Tune-Up, Minor 1
Tune-Up, Major 2
Compression, Test 3
Distributor, R&R Or Renew 4
Distributor, Overhaul 5
Distributor Cap, Renew 6
Distributor Rotor, Renew 7
Points & Condenser, Renew 8
Vacuum Advance, Renew 9
Ignition Coil, Renew 10
Ignition Cable Set, Renew 11
Spark Plugs, Renew 12
Ignition Switch, Renew 13
Ignition Lock Cylinder, Renew 14
Ign Lock Cyl Housing, Renew 15

1—TUNE-UP, MINOR

Includes renew points, condenser & spark plugs, set spark timing & adjust carburetor idle.

1976-78 .... 1.8

2—TUNE-UP, MAJOR

Includes check compression, clean or renew & adjust spark plugs. R&R distributor, renew points & condenser. Adjust ignition timing, carburetor & fan belts. Clean battery terminals & service air cleaner. Check coil & clean or renew fuel filter.

1976-78 .... 3.0

3—COMPRESSION, TEST

1976-78 .... 0.5

4—DISTRIBUTOR, R&R OR RENEW

1976-78 .... 0.3

5—DISTRIBUTOR, OVERHAUL

Distributor removed

1976-78 .... 0.4

6—DISTRIBUTOR CAP, RENEW

1976-78 .... 0.2

7—DISTRIBUTOR ROTOR, RENEW

1976-78 .... 0.2

8—POINTS & CONDENSER, RENEW

1976-78 .... 0.3

9—VACUUM ADVANCE UNIT, RENEW

1976-78 .... 0.3

10—IGNITION COIL, RENEW

1976-78 .... 0.3

11—IGNITION CABLE SET, RENEW

1976-78 .... 0.3

12—SPARK PLUGS, RENEW

1976-78 .... 0.3

13—IGNITION SWITCH, RENEW

1976-78 .... 0.3

14—IGNITION LOCK CYLINDER, RENEW

1976-78 .... 0.3

15—IGNITION LOCK CYLINDER HOUSING, RENEW

1976-78 .... 0.7

Fuel System & Intake Manifold—TIME

OPERATION INDEX

Intake Manifold Gasket, Renew 1
Intake Manifold, Renew 2
Carburetor, Renew 3
Carburetor Float, Renew 4
Carburetor Jets, Renew 5
Carb Accelerator Pump, Renew 6
Carb Throttle Body, Renew 7
Fuel Pump, Renew 8
Fuel Filter, Renew 9
Accelerator Cable, Renew 10
Accelerator Pedal, Renew 11
Fuel Tank, Renew 12
Fuel Gauge, Tank Unit, Renew 13
Fuel System, Clean & Flush 14

1—INTAKE MANIFOLD GASKET, RENEW

1976-78 .... 2.3

2—INTAKE MANIFOLD, RENEW

1976-78 .... 2.7

3—CARBURETOR, RENEW

1976-78 .... 0.6

4—CARBURETOR FLOAT, RENEW

1976-78 .... 0.5

5—CARBURETOR JETS, RENEW

1976-78 .... 1.1

6—CARB ACCELERATOR PUMP, RENEW

1976-78 .... 1.0

7—CARB THROTTLE BODY, RENEW

1976-78 .... 1.4

8—FUEL PUMP, RENEW

1976-78 .... 0.4

9—FUEL FILTER, RENEW

1976-78 .... 0.2

10—ACCELERATOR CABLE, RENEW

1976-78 .... 0.3

11—ACCELERATOR PEDAL, RENEW

1976-78 .... 0.3

12—FUEL TANK, RENEW

1976-78 .... 0.6

13—FUEL GAUGE, TANK UNIT, RENEW

1976-78 .... 0.3

14—FUEL SYSTEM, CLEAN & FLUSH

1976-78 .... 1.3

Exhaust System—TIME

OPERATION INDEX

Exhaust Manifold, Renew 1
Exhaust Pipe, Renew 2
Catalytic Converter, Renew 3
Converter Catalyst, Renew 4
Muffler, Renew 5
Resonator, Renew 6
Exhaust System Complete, Renew 7

1—EXHAUST MANIFOLD &/OR GASKET, RENEW

1976-78 .... 1.6

2—EXHAUST PIPE, FRONT, RENEW

1976-78 .... 0.6

3—CATALYTIC CONVERTER, RENEW

1976-78 .... 0.6

4—CONVERTER CATALYST, RENEW

1976-78 .... 0.5

5—MUFFLER, RENEW

1976-78 .... 0.8

6—RESONATOR, RENEW

1976-78 .... 0.6

7—EXHAUST SYSTEM, COMPLETE, RENEW

1976-78 .... 1.2

Starting Motor—TIME

OPERATION INDEX

Starter, Renew 1
Starter, R&R & Overhaul 2
Starter Solenoid, Renew 3
Starter Clutch, Renew 4
Starter Armature, Recondition 5
Starter Safety Switch, Renew 6

1—STARTER, RENEW

1976-78—
  Less Air Cond 0.4
  With Air Cond 0.6

(Continued)

Starting Motor—TIME Cont'd

2—STARTER, R&R & OVERHAUL
1976-78—
Less Air Cond 1.2
With Air Cond 1.4

3—STARTER SOLENOID, RENEW
1976-78—
Less Air Cond 0.5
With Air Cond 0.7

4—STARTER CLUTCH, RENEW
1976-78—
Less Air Cond 0.8
With Air Cond 1.0

5—STARTER ARMATURE, RECONDITION
Armature removed
1976-78 ....0.4

6—STARTER SAFETY SWITCH, RENEW
1976-78—
Manual Trans 0.2
Automatic Trans 0.3

Alternator—TIME

OPERATION INDEX
Alternator, Renew 1
Alternator, R&R & Overhaul 2
Voltage Regulator, Renew 3

1—ALTERNATOR ASSY, RENEW
1976-78 ....0.6

2—ALTERNATOR, R&R & OVERHAUL
1976-78 ....1.4

3—VOLTAGE REGULATOR, RENEW
1976-78 ....0.3

Dash Gauges, Speedometer & Windshield Wiper—TIME

OPERATION INDEX
Fuel Gauge, Dash Unit, Renew 1
Oil Gauge, Dash Unit, Renew 2
Oil Pressure Sending Switch, Renew 3
Temperature Gauge, Dash Unit 4
Temperature Sending Unit, Renew 5
Ammeter, Renew 6
Tachometer, Renew 7
Clock, Renew 8
Radio Receiver, Renew 9
Instrument Cluster, Renew 10
Printed Circuit, Renew 11
Speedometer Head, Renew 12
Speedometer Cable, Renew 13
Windshield Wiper Motor, Renew 14
Wiper Motor, Overhaul 15
Wiper Transmission, Renew 16
Wiper Arm Or Blade, Renew 17
Wiper Switch, Renew 18
Windshield Washer Pump, Renew 19
Wiper Nozzle, Renew 20

1—FUEL GAUGE (DASH UNIT) RENEW
1976-78 ....0.4

2—OIL PRESSURE GAUGE (DASH UNIT) RENEW
1976-78 ....0.3

3—OIL PRESSURE SENDING SWITCH, RENEW
1976-78 ....0.3

4—TEMPERATURE GAUGE (DASH UNIT) RENEW
1976-78 ....0.4

5—TEMPERATURE SENDING UNIT, RENEW
1976-78 ....0.3

6—AMMETER, RENEW
1976-78 ....0.3

7—TACHOMETER, RENEW
1976-78 ....0.4

8—CLOCK, RENEW
1976-78, Console Mounted 0.3
Instrument Cluster 0.4

9—RADIO RECEIVER, RENEW
1976-78 ....0.5

10—INSTRUMENT CLUSTER, RENEW
1976-78 ....0.6

11—PRINTED CIRCUIT, RENEW
1976-78 ....0.4

12—SPEEDOMETER HEAD, RENEW
1976-78 ....0.4

13—SPEEDOMETER CABLE, RENEW
1976-78 ....0.4

14—WINDSHIELD WIPER MOTOR, RENEW
1976-78 ....0.5

15—WIPER MOTOR, R & R & OVERHAUL
1976-78 ....1.0

16—WIPER TRANSMISSION, RENEW
1976-78—
Right 0.4
Left 0.5
Both 0.8

17—WIPER ARM OR BLADE, RENEW
1976-78 ....0.2

18—WIPER SWITCH, RENEW
1976-78 ....0.6

19—WINDSHIELD WASHER PUMP, RENEW
1976-78 ....0.2

20—WIPER NOZZLE, RENEW
1976-78—
Less Air Cond 0.3
With Air Cond 0.4

Battery Cables & Horns—TIME

OPERATION INDEX
Battery Cables, Renew 1
Horn, Renew 2
Horn Relay, Renew 3

1—BATTERY CABLES, RENEW
1976-78, Each—
Less Air Cond 0.2
With Air Cond 0.3

2—HORN, RENEW
1976-78 ....0.2

3—HORN RELAY, RENEW
1976-78 ....0.2

Lamps & Light Switches—TIME

OPERATION INDEX
Headlamps, Aim 1
Headlamp Switch, Renew 2
Stop Lamp Switch, Renew 3
Back-Up Lamp Switch, Renew 4
Park Brake Lamp Switch, Renew 5
Turn Signal, Dimmer, Hazard Warning Switch, Renew 6
Direction Signal Flasher, Renew 7
Hazard Warning Flasher, Renew 8
Turn, Signal & Dimmer Switch, Renew 9
Key Warning Buzzer Switch, Renew 10
Key Warning Buzzer, Renew 11
Converter Warning Buzzer, Renew 12
Seat Belt Warning Buzzer, Renew 13
Heated Back Glass Switch, Renew 14
Heated Back Glass Relay, Renew 15

1—HEADLAMPS, AIM
1976-78 ....0.5

2—HEADLAMP SWITCH, RENEW
1976-78 ....0.2

3—STOP LAMP SWITCH, RENEW
1976-78 ....0.2

4—BACK-UP LAMP SWITCH, RENEW
1976-78 ....0.3

5—PARKING BRAKE LAMP SWITCH, RENEW
1976-78 ....0.6

6—TURN SIGNAL, DIMMER, HAZARD WARNING SWITCH, RENEW
1976-78 ....0.6

7—DIRECTION SIGNAL FLASHER, RENEW
1976-78 ....0.2

8—HAZARD WARNING FLASHER, RENEW
1976-78 ....0.3

9—TURN, SIGNAL & DIMMER SWITCH, RENEW
1976-78 ....0.6

10—KEY WARNING BUZZER SWITCH, RENEW
1976-78 ....0.3

11—KEY WARNING BUZZER, RENEW
1976-78 ....0.3

12—CONVERTER WARNING BUZZER, RENEW
1976-78 ....0.3

13—SEAT BELT WARING BUZZER, RENEW
1976-78 ....0.5

14—HEATED BACK GLASS SWITCH, RENEW
1976-78 ....0.3

15—HEATED BACK GLASS RELAY, RENEW
1976-78 ....0.2

Cooling—TIME

OPERATION INDEX
Radiator, Renew 1
Radiator Hoses, Renew 2

(Continued)

Cooling—TIME Cont'd

Water Pump, Renew *3*
Thermostat Or Housing, Renew *4*
Fan Belts, Renew *5*
Fan Blade Or Clutch, Renew *6*
Fan Pulley, Renew *7*
Cooling System, Flush *8*

1—RADIATOR, RENEW
1976-78—
- Standard Trans 0.6
- Automatic Trans 0.9
- Air Cond 1.4

2—RADIATOR HOSES, RENEW
1976-78—
- Upper 0.3
- Lower 0.4
- Both 0.5

3—WATER PUMP, RENEW
1976-78—
- Standard Trans 1.0
- Automatic Trans 1.3
- Air Cond 1.8

4—THERMOSTAT OR HOUSING, RENEW
1976-78 .... 0.5

5—FAN BELTS, RENEW
1976-78—
- Less Air Cond 0.3
- With Air Cond 0.5

6—FAN BLADE OR CLUTCH, RENEW
1976-78 .... 0.5

7—FAN PULLEY, RENEW
1976-78 .... 0.6

8—COOLING SYSTEM, FLUSH
1976-78 .... 0.5

Engine—TIME

OPERATION INDEX

Engine (Basic) Renew *1*
Cylinder Head Gasket, Renew *2*
Cylinder Head, Renew *3*
Valves, Grind *4*
Valve Lash Adjustment *5*
Valves, Renew *6*
Valve Spring Or Seal, Renew *7*
Valve Guides, Renew *8*
Rocker Arm Cover &/Or Gasket, Renew *9*
Rocker Arms, Renew *10*
Camshaft, Renew *11*
Timing Case Cover &/Or Gasket, Renew *12*
Timing Chain Or Gears, Renew *13*
Crankshaft, Renew *14*
Main Bearings, Renew *15*
Rod Bearings, Renew *16*
Crankshaft Pulley Or Balancer, Renew *17*
Rear Main Bearing Seal, Renew *18*
Piston & Rod, Renew *19*
Piston Rings, Renew *20*
Oil Pan &/Or Gasket, Renew *21*
Oil Pump, R & R & Overhaul *22*
Engine Mounts, Renew *23*

1—ENGINE (BASIC) RENEW
Includes R&R engine assy, transfer parts not furnished with basic engine & make necessary adjustments.
1976-78—
- Less Air Cond 6.0
- With Air Cond 7.0

2—CYLINDER HEAD GASKET, RENEW
Includes adjust valve lash.
1976-78 .... 2.3

3—CYLINDER HEAD, RENEW
Includes transfer all attaching parts, reface valves & seats & adjust valve lash.
1976-78 .... 4.3

4—VALVES, GRIND
Head removed
1976-78 .... 2.5

5—VALVE LASH ADJUSTMENT
1976-78 .... 0.6

6—VALVES, RENEW
Includes grind & adjust lash.
1976-78—
- One Cylinder 3.4
- All Cylinders 4.0

7—VALVE SPRING OR SEAL, RENEW
Includes adjust valve lash.
1976-78—
- One Cylinder 1.3
- All Cylinders 2.2

8—VALVE GUIDES, RENEW
Includes adjust valve lash
1976-78—
- One Cylinder 3.4
- All Cylinders 4.0

—NOTE—
To Grind Valves & Seats, Add-
Each Cylinder *0.2*

9—ROCKER ARM COVER &/OR GASKET, RENEW
1976-78 .... 0.4

10—ROCKER ARMS, ONE OR ALL, RENEW
Includes adjust valve lash.
1976-78 .... 1.1

11—CAMSHAFT, RENEW
Includes adjust valve lash
1976-78 .... 1.2

12—TIMING CASE COVER &/OR GASKET, RENEW
Includes R & R engine assy, balancer, oil pan & cylinder head.
1976-78—
- Less Air Cond 6.1
- With Air Cond 7.1

13—TIMING CHAIN OR GEARS, RENEW
After cover is removed.
1976-78 .... 0.2

14—CRANKSHAFT, RENEW
Includes R & R engine, oil pan, front cover, chain & sprockets. Plastigauge all main & rod bearings, clean carbon from pistons, head & block
1976-78—
- Less Air Cond 7.6
- With Air Cond 8.5

15—MAIN BEARINGS, RENEW
Includes R & R engine assy.
1976-78—
- One, Less Air Cond 4.9
- One, With Air Cond 5.8
- All, Less Air Cond 5.8
- All, With Air Cond 6.7

16—ROD BEARINGS, RENEW
Includes R & R engine assy.
1976-78—
- One, Less Air Cond 4.8
- One, With Air Cond 5.7
- All, Less Air Cond 5.4
- All, With Air Cond 6.3

17—CRANKSHAFT PULLEY OR BALANCER, RENEW
Includes R & R radiator
1976-78 .... 1.0

—NOTE—
With Automatic Trans, Add *0.3*
With Air Cond Add *0.8*
To Replace Oil Seal, Add *0.2*

18—REAR MAIN BEARING SEAL, RENEW
Includes R & R transmission, clutch or converter and flywheel or flex-plate.
1976-78—
- Standard Trans 2.6
- Automatic Trans 2.9

19—PISTON & ROD ASSY, RENEW
Includes R & R engine assy
1976-78—
- One, Less Air Cond 5.8
- One, With Air Cond 6.7
- All, Less Air Cond 7.0
- All, With Air Cond 7.9

20—PISTON RINGS, RENEW
Includes R & R engine assy.
1976-78—
- Less Air Cond 7.8
- With Air Cond 8.7

21—OIL PAN &/OR GASKET, RENEW
Includes R & R engine assy.
1976-78—
- Less Air Cond 4.6
- With Air Cond 5.5

22—OIL PUMP, R & R & OVERHAUL
Includes R & R engine assy.
1976-78—
- Less Air Cond 5.0
- With Air Cond 5.9

23—ENGINE MOUNTS, RENEW
1976-78—
- Front, One 1.4
- Front, Both 1.7
- Rear 0.3

Clutch—TIME

OPERATION INDEX

Clutch Or Disc, Renew *1*
Clutch Pedal, Renew *2*
Clutch Pedal, Adjust *3*
Clutch Cable, Renew *4*
Release Fork &/Or Bearing, Renew *5*

1—CLUTCH OR DISC, RENEW
Includes R & R transmission
1976-78 .... 2.3

2—CLUTCH PEDAL &/OR BUSHING, RENEW
1976-78 .... 0.6

3—CLUTCH PEDAL, ADJUST
1976-78 .... 0.3

4—CLUTCH CABLE, RENEW
1976-78 .... 0.5

5—CLUTCH RELEASE FORK &/OR BEARING, RENEW
Includes R & R transmission
1976-78 .... 2.1

Manual Transmission-4 Speed—TIME

OPERATION INDEX

Transmission, Renew *1*
Transmission, Overhaul *2*
Case, Renew *3*
Front Cover &/Or Oil Seal, Renew *4*
Extension Housing &/Or Gasket, Renew *5*
Case Extension Seal, Renew *66*
Shift Lever, Renew *7*

1—TRANSMISSION ASSY, RENEW
1976-78 .... 2.1

2—TRANSMISSION, R & R & OVERHAUL
1976-78 .... 4.0

3—TRANSMISSION CASE, RENEW
1976-78 .... 2.6

(Continued)

Manual Transmission-4 Speed—TIME Cont'd

4—FRONT COVER &/OR OIL SEAL, RENEW
Includes R & R transmission
1976-78 .... 2.2

5—EXTENSION HOUSING &/OR GASKET, RENEW
1976-78 .... 1.3

6—CASE EXTENSION SEAL, RENEW
Includes R & R propeller shaft
1976-78 .... 0.4

7—SHIFT LEVER, RENEW
1976-78 .... 0.3

Manual Transmission-5 Speed—TIME

OPERATION INDEX

Transmission, Renew 1
Transmission, Overhaul 2
Case, Renew 3
Front Cover &/Or Gasket, Renew 4
Extension Housing, Renew 5
Case Extension Seal, Renew 6
Shift Lever, Renew 7

1—TRANSMISSION ASSY, RENEW
1977-78 .... 2.1

2—TRANSMISSION, R & R & OVERHAUL
1977-78 .... 4.3

3—TRANSMISSION CASE, RENEW
1977-78 .... 2.6

4—FRONT COVER &/OR GASKET, RENEW
Includes R & R transmission
1977-78 .... 2.2

5—EXTENSION HOUSING, RENEW
1977-78 .... 1.0

6—CASE EXTENSION SEAL, RENEW
Includes R & R propeller shaft.
1977-78 .... 0.4

7—SHIFT LEVER, RENEW
1977-78 .... 0.3

Automatic Transmission—TIME

OPERATION INDEX

Transmission, Renew 1
Converter, Renew 2
Case, Renew 3
Front Pump, Renew 4
Front Pump, Overhaul 5
Front Pump Seal, Renew 6
Direct & Forward Clutches & Inter Band, Overhaul 7
Output Carrier, Sun Gear & Drive Shell, Overhaul 8
Input Drum & Rear Sun Gear, Overhaul 9
Low & Reverse Clutch & Output Shaft, Overhaul 10
Oil Pan &/Or Gasket, Renew 11
Valve Body, Renew 12
Valve Body, Overhaul 13
Detent Valve, Renew 14
Parking Pawl, Renew 15
Rear Seal, Renew 16
Governor Assy, Renew 17
Governor Assy, Overhaul 18
Intermediate Servo, Renew 19
Intermediate Servo, Overhaul 20
Oil Cooler Pipes, Renew 21
Shift Lever, Renew 22
Shift Link Lever, Renew 23
Shift Control Linkage, Renew 24
Shift Linkage, Adjust 25
Detent Valve Cable, Renew 26

1—TRANSMISSION ASSY, RENEW
1976-78 .... 2.4

2—CONVERTER ASSY, RENEW
1976-78 .... 2.6

3—TRANSMISSION CASE, RENEW
1976-78 .... 4.8

—NOTE—
Add To:
Overhaul Roller Clutch 0.2
Overhaul Direct Clutch 0.3
Overhaul Forward Clutch 0.4
Overhaul Valve Body 0.7
Overhaul Oil Pump 0.5
Overhaul Low & Reverse Clutch 0.3
Overhaul Servo 0.2
Overhaul Sun Gear & Drum 0.2

4—TRANS FRONT PUMP, RENEW
Includes R & R transmission
1976-78 .... 2.8

5—TRANS FRONT PUMP, R & R & OVERHAUL
Includes R & R transmission
1976-78 .... 3.3

6—FRONT PUMP SEAL, RENEW
Includes R & R transmission
1976-78 .... 2.5

7—DIRECT & FORWARD CLUTCHES & INTER BAND, R & R OH
Includes R & R transmission
1976-78 .... 3.6

8—OUTPUT CARRIER, SUN GEAR & DRIVE SHELL, R & R & OH
Includes R & R transmission
1976-78 .... 3.9

9—INPUT DRUM & REAR SUN GEAR, R & R & OH
Includes R & R transmission
1976-78 .... 4.0

10—LOW & REVERSE CLUTCH & OUTPUT SHAFT, R & R & OH
Includes R & R transmission
1976-78 .... 4.3

11—OIL PAN &/OR GASKET, RENEW
1976-78 .... 0.5

12—VALVE BODY, RENEW
Includes R & R oil pan
1976-78 .... 0.6

13—VALVE BODY, R & R & OVERHAUL
Includes R & R oil pan
1976-78 .... 1.3

14—DETENT VALVE ASSY, RENEW
Includes R & R oil pan
1976-78 .... 0.6

15—PARKING PAWL, RENEW
Includes R & R oil pan
1976-78 .... 0.9

16—REAR SEAL, RENEW
Includes R & R propeller shaft.
1976-78 .... 0.4

17—GOVERNOR ASSY, RENEW
Includes R & R propeller shaft
1976-78 .... 0.6

18—GOVERNOR ASSY, R & R & OVERHAUL
Includes R & R propeller shaft
1976-78 .... 0.9

19—INTERMEDIATE SERVO ASSY, RENEW
Includes R & R propeller shaft
1976-78 .... 0.6

20—INTERMEDIATE SERVO ASSY, R & R & OVERHAUL
Includes R & R propeller shaft
1976-78 .... 0.8

21—OIL COOLER PIPES, RENEW
Includes R & R propeller shaft & lower trans at rear mount
Each 0.7
Both 0.9

22—SHIFT LEVER, RENEW
1976-78 .... 0.5

23—SHIFT LINK LEVER, RENEW
1976-78 .... 0.7

24—SHIFT CONTROL LINKAGE, RENEW
1976-78 .... 0.4

25—SHIFT LINKAGE, ADJUST
1976-78 .... 0.2

26—DETENT VALVE CONTROL CABLE, RENEW
1976-78 .... 0.6

Rear Suspension—TIME

OPERATION INDEX

Shock Absorber, Renew 1
Spring, Renew 2
Lower Control Arm, Renew 3
Track Rod, Renew 4

1—SHOCK ABSORBER, RENEW
1976-78—
One 0.4
Both 0.6

2—SPRING, RENEW
Includes R & R wheel & tire assys, disconnect shocks at axle end & track rod at frame, R & R propeller shaft and lower axle assy.
1976-78, One Or Both 0.8

3—LOWER CONTROL ARM, RENEW
1976-78—
One 0.4
Both 0.6

4—TRACK ROD, RENEW
1976-78 .... 0.4

Universals, Propeller Shaft & Rear Axle—TIME

OPERATION INDEX

Universal Joint, Renew 1
Propeller Shaft, Renew 2
Companion Flange, Renew 3
Axle Assy, Renew 4
Axle Housing, Renew 5
Axle Housing Cover &/Or Gasket, Renew 6
Ring Gear & Pinion, Renew 7
Differential Case, Renew 8
Diff Side Bearings, Renew 9
Pinion Bearings & Outer Race, Renew 10
Diff Side &/Or Pinion Gears, Renew 11
Pinion Oil Seal, Renew 12
Axle Shaft, Renew 13
Axle Shaft Bearing, Renew 14
Axle Shaft Oil Seal, Renew 15

(Continued)

Universals, Propeller Shaft & Rear Axle—TIME Cont'd

1—UNIVERSAL JOINT, RENEW
1976-78—
Front 0.6
Rear 0.7

2—PROPELLER SHAFT, RENEW
1976-78 ....0.3

3—COMPANION FLANGE, RENEW
1976-78 ....0.5

4—AXLE ASSY, RENEW
1976-78 ....2.0

5—AXLE HOUSING ASSY, RENEW
Includes R&R axle assy, transfer differential & brake parts to new housing, check & adjust ring gear backlash, side bearing preload, pinion depth & bleed brake system
1976-78 ....3.3

6—AXLE HOUSING COVER &/OR GASKET, RENEW
Includes R & R right rear brake line & bleed rear brakes.
1976-78 ....0.6

7—RING GEAR & PINION, RENEW
1976-78 ....3.1

8—DIFFERENTIAL CASE, RENEW
1976-78 ....2.3

9—DIFFERENTIAL SIDE BEARINGS, RENEW
1976-78 ....1.7

10—PINION BEARING & OUTER RACE, RENEW
1976-78—
Front 2.6
Rear 2.9

11—DIFFERENTIAL SIDE &/OR PINION GEARS, RENEW
1976-78 ....2.1

12—PINION SEAL, RENEW
1976-78 ....1.0

13—AXLE SHAFT, RENEW
1976-78—
One 0.6
Both 1.0

14—AXLE SHAFT BEARING, RENEW
1976-78—
One 0.6
Both 1.0

15—AXLE SHAFT OIL SEAL, RENEW
1976-78—
One 0.5
Both 0.7

Brakes—TIME

OPERATION INDEX

Front Disc Brake Pads, Renew 1
Front Brake Rotor, Renew 2
Front Brake Rotor, Reface 3
Front Brake Caliper, Overhaul 4
Rear Brake Shoe & Lining, Renew 5
Rear Brake Drum, Renew 6
Rear Wheel Cylinder, Renew 7
Rear Brake Backing Plate, Renew 8
Rear Brake Adjuster Mechanism, Renew 9
Master Cylinder, Renew 10
Master Cylinder, Overhaul 11
Master Cylinder Reservoir, Renew 12
Combination Valve, Renew 13
Brake System, Bleed 14
Brake Pedal, Renew 15
Parking Brake Cable, Adjust 16
Parking Brake Cable, Renew 17
Parking Brake Lever, Renew 18
Power Vacuum Cylinder, Renew 19
Power Cylinder, Overhaul 20
Vacuum Check Valve, Renew 21
Vacuum Hose, Renew 22
Brake Hoses, Renew 23

1—FRONT DISC BRAKE PADS, RENEW
1976-78—
One Side 0.3
Both Sides 0.5

2—FRONT BRAKE ROTOR, RENEW
1976-78—
One Side 0.5
Both Sides 0.9

—NOTE—
To Replace Brake Pads, Add-
One Side 0.2
Both Sides 0.3

3—FRONT BRAKE ROTOR, REFACE
After rotor is removed
1976-78—
One 0.6
Both 1.1

4—FRONT BRAKE CALIPER, R & R & OVERHAUL
1976-78—
One Side 0.8
Both Sides 1.5

5—REAR BRAKE SHOE & LINING, RENEW
1976-78—
One Side 0.6
Both Sides 1.2

—NOTE—
To Resurface Drums, Add-
One 0.4
Both 0.7

6—REAR BRAKE DRUM, RENEW
1976-78—
One 0.3
Both 0.5

—NOTE—
To Resurface Drums, Add-
One 0.4
Both 0.7

7—REAR WHEEL CYLINDER, RENEW
Includes bleed at affected wheel.
1976-78—
One 0.5
Both 0.8

8—REAR BRAKE BACKING PLATE, RENEW
Includes bleed at affected wheel.
1976-78—
One 0.9
Both 1.6

9—REAR BRAKE ADJUSTER MECHANISM, RENEW
1976-78—
One Side 0.6
Both Sides 0.9

10—MASTER CYLINDER, RENEW
Includes bleed brakes
1976-78 ....0.5

11—MASTER CYLINDER, R & R & OVERHAUL
Includes bleed brakes.
1976-78 ....1.3

12—MASTER CYLINDER RESERVOIR, RENEW
Includes bleed brakes.
1976-78 ....0.4

13—BRAKE COMBINATION VALVE, RENEW
Includes bleed brakes
1976-78 ....0.5

14—BRAKE SYSTEM, BLEED
1976-78 ....0.3

15—BRAKE PEDAL, RENEW
1976-78 ....0.6

16—PARKING BRAKE CABLE, ADJUST
1976-78 ....0.3

17—PARKING BRAKE CABLE, RENEW
1976-78 ....0.8

18—PARKING BRAKE LEVER, RENEW
1976-78 ....0.6

19—POWER VACUUM CYLINDER, RENEW
Includes R & R master cylinder & bleed brakes
1976-78 ....0.8

20—POWER BRAKE CYLINDER, OVERHAUL
Cylinder removed
1976-78 ....0.5

21—VACUUM CHECK VALVE, RENEW
1976-78 ....0.2

22—VACUUM HOSE, RENEW
1976-78 ....0.2

23—BRAKE HOSES, RENEW
Includes bleed at affected wheel.
Front, One 0.6
Front, Both 0.8
Rear 0.4

Front Suspension—TIME

OPERATION INDEX

Toe-In, Adjust 1
Caster, Camber & Toe-In, Adjust 2
Steering Knuckle, Renew 3
Upper Control Arm, Renew 4
Lower Control Arm, Renew 5
Upper Ball Joints, Renew 6
Lower Ball Joints, Renew 7
Front Spring, Renew 8
Stabilizer Shaft, Renew 9
Shock Absorber, Renew 10
Front Wheel Bearings, Renew 11
Front Wheel Oil Seal, Renew 12

1—TOE-IN, ADJUST
1976-78 ....0.4

2—CASTER, CAMBER & TOE-IN, ADJUST
1976-78 ....0.7

3—STEERING KNUCKLE, RENEW
Does not include wheel alignment
1976-78—
One 1.0
Both 1.8

4—UPPER CONTORL ARM, RENEW
Includes check & adjust caster & camber.
1976-78—
One 1.0
Both 1.4

5—LOWER CONTROL ARM, RENEW
Includes check & adjust caster & camber
1976-78—
One 1.3
Both 2.1

6—UPPER BALL JOINTS, RENEW
Includes check & adjust caster & camber
1976-78—
One 0.9
Both 1.3

(Continued)

Front Suspension—TIME Cont'd

7—LOWER BALL JOINTS, RENEW
Includes check caster & camber
1976-78—
One 1.1
Both 1.8

8—FRONT SPRING, RENEW
1976-78—
One 1.3
Both 2.2

9—STABILIZER SHAFT &/OR BUSHINGS, RENEW
1976-78 ....0.6

10—SHOCK ABSORBERS, RENEW
1976-78—
One 0.3
Both 0.5

11—FRONT WHEEL BEARINGS, RENEW
1976-78 Outer—
One Wheel 0.5
Both Wheels 0.8
1976-78 Inner—
One Wheel 0.6
Both Wheels 1.0
1976-78 Outer & Inner—
One Wheel 0.7
Both Wheels 1.2

12—FRONT WHEEL OIL SEAL, RENEW
1976-78—
One 0.5
Both 0.8

Steering Linkage & Gear—TIME

OPERATION INDEX

Tie Rod, Renew 1
Tie Rod End Or Boots, Renew 2
Gear Assy, Renew 3
Gear Assy, Overhaul 4
Mast Jacket, Renew 5
Steering Shaft, Renew 6
Shaft Upper Bearing, Renew 7
Steering Wheel, Renew 8

1—TIE ROD, RENEW
Includes check & adjust toe-in
1976-78—
One 1.1
Both 1.3

2—TIE ROD ENDS OR BOOTS, RENEW
Includes check & adjust toe-in
1976-78—
One 0.7
Both 0.9

3—GEAR ASSY, RENEW
Includes check & adjust toe-in
1976-78 ....1.1

4—GEAR ASSY, R & R & OVERHAUL
Includes check & adjust toe-in.
1976-78 ....1.4

5—MAST JACKET, RENEW
1976-78 ....1.0

6—STEERING SHAFT, RENEW
1976-78 ....0.8

7—STEERING SHAFT UPPER BEARING, RENEW
1976-78 ....0.8

8—STEERING WHEEL, RENEW
1976-78 ....0.3

Heater—TIME

OPERATION INDEX

Blower Motor Or Impeller, Renew 1
Case Or Core, Renew 2
Blower Motor Switch, Renew 3
Blower Motor Resistor, Renew 4
High Blower Relay, Renew 5
Water Control Valve, Renew 6
Control Assy, Renew 7
Control Cables, Renew 8
Control Cables, Adjust 9
Heater Hoses, Renew 10

1—HEATER BLOWER MOTOR &/OR IMPELLER, RENEW
1976-78 ....0.4

2—HEATER CASE &/OR CORE, RENEW
Includes drain & refill cooling system, R & R blower unit cover, steering wheel, instrument cluster, console, radio, heater control & instrument panel pad.
1976-78 ....2.6

3—BLOWER MOTOR SWITCH, RENEW
1976 ....1.1
1977-78 ....1.0

4—BLOWER MOTOR RESISTOR, RENEW
1976-78 ....0.5

5—HIGH BLOWER RELAY, RENEW
1976-78 ....0.2

6—WATER CONTROL VALVE, RENEW
1976-78 ....0.3

7—CONTROL ASSEMBLY, RENEW
1976-78 ....1.1

8—CONTROL CABLES, RENEW
1976-78 ....1.1

9—CONTROL CABLES, ADJUST
1976-78 ....0.2

10—HEATER HOSES, RENEW
Each Exc 0.3
Oil Head To Tee Block 0.5
All 0.8

Air Conditioning—TIME

OPERATION INDEX

Compressor Assy, Renew 1
Compressor Clutch Plate & Hub Assy, Renew 2
Compressor Pulley &/Or Bearings, Renew 3
Clutch Coil, Renew 4
Compressor, Overhaul 5
Compressor Belt, Renew 6
Hoses, Renew 7
Liquid Line, Renew 8
Condenser, Renew 9
Receiver-Dehydrator, Renew 10
Evaporator Core, Renew 11
Expansion Valve, Renew 12

1—COMPRESSOR ASSY, RENEW
Includes R & R belly pan & distributor assy, transfer clutch assy & compressor manifolds, check & adjust timing, add oil as necessary, evacuate & recharge system.
1976-78 ....1.8

2—COMPRESSOR PLATE & HUB ASSY, RENEW
Includes R & R compressor, adjust clutch clearance, evacuate & recharge system
1976-78 ....1.5

3—COMPRESSOR PULLEY &/OR BEARINGS, RENEW
Includes evacuate & recharge.
1976-78 ....1.6

4—COMPRESSOR CLUTCH COIL, RENEW
Includes evacuate & recharge.
1976-78 ....1.6

5—COMPRESSOR ASSY, R & R & OVERHAUL
Includes evacuate & recharge.
1976-78 ....3.5

6—COMPRESSOR BELT, RENEW
1976-78 ....0.2

7—HOSES, SUCTION OR DISCHARGE, RENEW
Includes evacuate & recharge
One 0.9
Both 1.0

8—LIQUID LINE, RENEW
Includes evacuate & recharge.
One 0.9
Both 1.1

9—CONDENSER, RENEW
Includes evacuate & recharge.
1976-78 ....1.4

10—RECEIVER-DEHYDRATOR, RENEW
Includes evacuate & recharge.
1976-78 ....1.0

11—EVAPORATOR CORE, RENEW
Includes evacuate & recharge.
1976-78 ....1.6

12—EXPANSION VALVE, RENEW
Includes evacuate & recharge.
1976-78 ....1.6

IDENTIFICATION

ALL MODELS 328

ILLUSTRATIONS

FIG 1 – ENGINE – OIL PAN & TIMING GEAR HOUSING
FIG 2 – ENGINE – CAMSHAFT & TIMING CHAIN
FIG 3 – ENGINE – CRANKSHAFT & FLYWHEEL
FIG 4 – TRANSMISSION
FIG 5 – FRONT SUSPENSION
FIG 6 – STEERING

OPERATION TIMES

A

Alternator 333
Ammeter 336
Axle Shaft 335

B

Brake Drums 335
Brakes 335

C

Cables (Ignition) 333
Calipers 335
Camshaft 334
Carburetor 333
Clutch 334
Coil, Ignition 333
Compression Test 333
Cooling System 333
Crankshaft 334
Cylinder Head 334

D

Dash Gauges 336
Differential 335
Disc Brakes 335
Distributor 333

E

Emission Controls 333
Engine Assembly 334
Engine Mountings 334
Engine Oiling 334
Engine Tune-Up 333
Exhaust System 333

F

Flywheel 334
Front Suspension 335
Fuel Gauges 336
Fuel Pump 333
Fuel Tank 333

G

Generator 333

H

Hand Brake 335
Headlight Switch 336
Heater 333
Hose (Brake) 335
Hose (Radiator) 333
Hydraulic Brakes 335

I

Ignition 333
Ignition Coil 333
Ignition Switch 333
Intake Manifold 333

L

Light Switches 336

M

Master Cylinder 335
Muffler 333

O

Oil Gauge 336
Oiling, Engine 334
Oil Pan 334
Oil Pump 334

P

Parking Brake 335
Piston Rings 334
Pistons 334
Power Brake 335

R

Radiator 333
Radiator Hose 333
Rear Axle 336
Regulator 333
Resonator 333
Rocker Arms 334
Rod Bearings 334

S

Shocks (Front) 335
Shocks (Rear) 335
Speedometer 336
Springs (Front) 335
Springs (Rear) 335
Starting Motor 333
Steering Gear 335
Steering Linkage 335
Switches (Light) 336

T

Temperature Gauge 336
Thermostat 333
Timing Case Cover 334
Timing Chain 334
Transmission 334
Tune-Up, Engine 333

U

Universals 335

V

Valve Lifters 334
Valve System 334

W

Water Pump 333
Wheel Cylinders 335
Windshield Wiper 336

VEHICLE IDENTIFICATION

YEAR		STARTING CHASSIS NUMBER
	504	
1968	Std Trans	1.000.001
	Auto Trans.	1.009.801
1969		1.065.501
1970		1.178.001
1971		1.322.001
1972		1.489.001
1973		1.697.001
1974		1.897.001
1975		2.142.001

91=Standard Transmission, w/Gas Eng
90=Standard Transmission,w/Diesel Eng
93=Automatic Transmission

YEAR		STARTING CHASSIS NUMBER
	304	
1970	Sedan	3.067.001
1971	Sedan	3.213.301
1970	Sta Wgn	3.124.401
1971	Sta Wgn	3.213.301

304A = Sedan
304C = Station Wagon

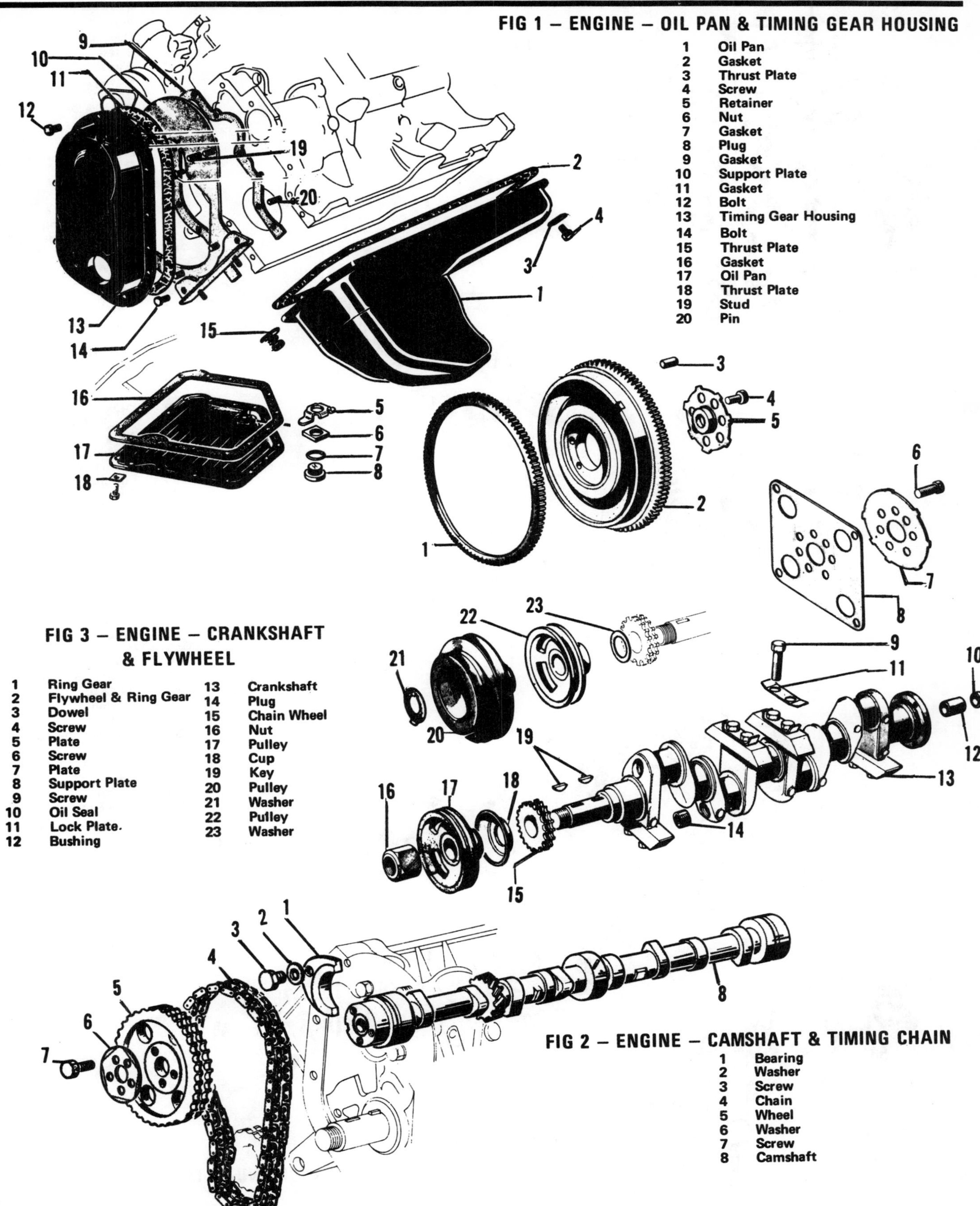

FIG 1 – ENGINE – OIL PAN & TIMING GEAR HOUSING

1 Oil Pan
2 Gasket
3 Thrust Plate
4 Screw
5 Retainer
6 Nut
7 Gasket
8 Plug
9 Gasket
10 Support Plate
11 Gasket
12 Bolt
13 Timing Gear Housing
14 Bolt
15 Thrust Plate
16 Gasket
17 Oil Pan
18 Thrust Plate
19 Stud
20 Pin

FIG 3 – ENGINE – CRANKSHAFT & FLYWHEEL

1 Ring Gear
2 Flywheel & Ring Gear
3 Dowel
4 Screw
5 Plate
6 Screw
7 Plate
8 Support Plate
9 Screw
10 Oil Seal
11 Lock Plate.
12 Bushing
13 Crankshaft
14 Plug
15 Chain Wheel
16 Nut
17 Pulley
18 Cup
19 Key
20 Pulley
21 Washer
22 Pulley
23 Washer

FIG 2 – ENGINE – CAMSHAFT & TIMING CHAIN

1 Bearing
2 Washer
3 Screw
4 Chain
5 Wheel
6 Washer
7 Screw
8 Camshaft

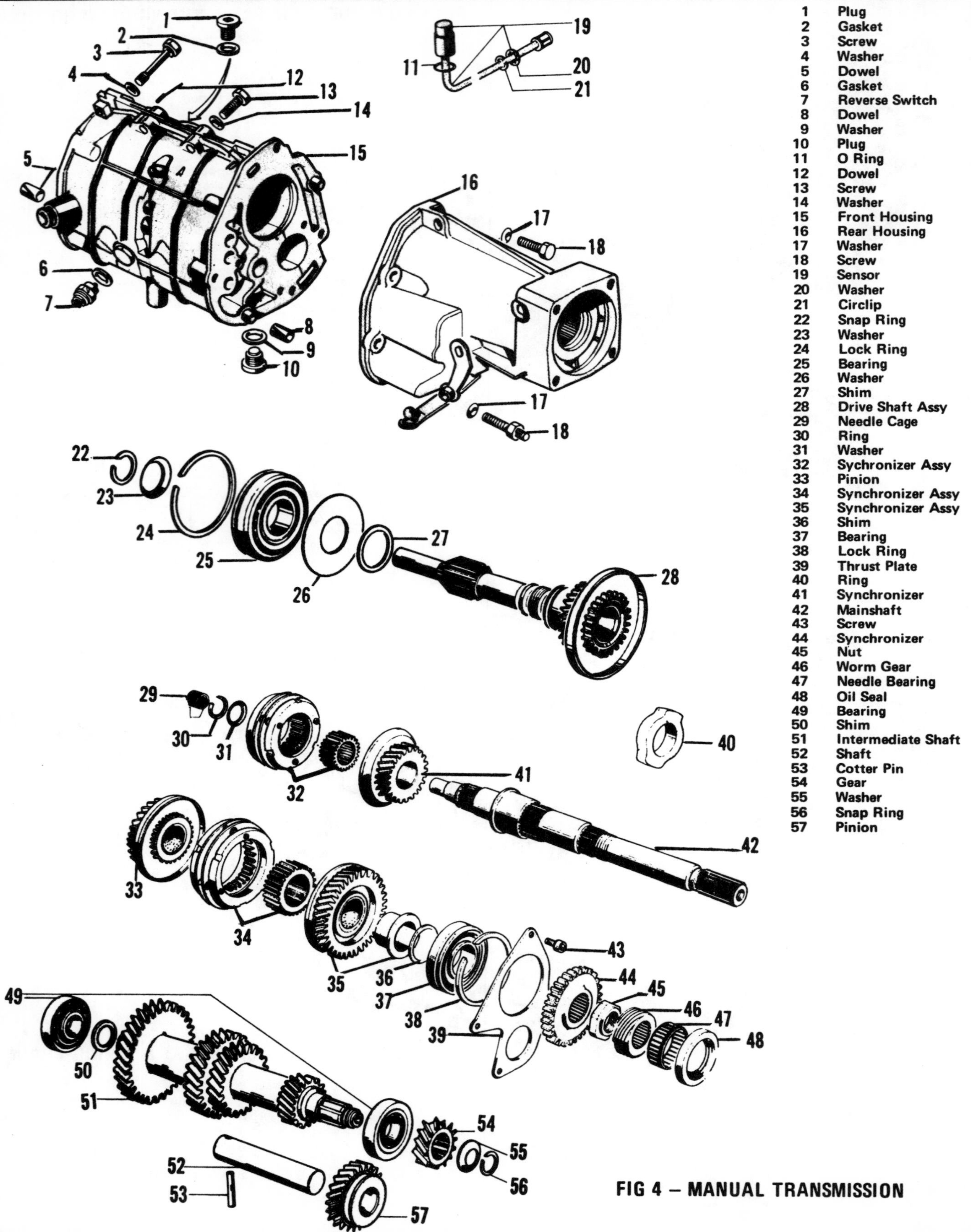
1 Plug
2 Gasket
3 Screw
4 Washer
5 Dowel
6 Gasket
7 Reverse Switch
8 Dowel
9 Washer
10 Plug
11 O Ring
12 Dowel
13 Screw
14 Washer
15 Front Housing
16 Rear Housing
17 Washer
18 Screw
19 Sensor
20 Washer
21 Circlip
22 Snap Ring
23 Washer
24 Lock Ring
25 Bearing
26 Washer
27 Shim
28 Drive Shaft Assy
29 Needle Cage
30 Ring
31 Washer
32 Sychronizer Assy
33 Pinion
34 Synchronizer Assy
35 Synchronizer Assy
36 Shim
37 Bearing
38 Lock Ring
39 Thrust Plate
40 Ring
41 Synchronizer
42 Mainshaft
43 Screw
44 Synchronizer
45 Nut
46 Worm Gear
47 Needle Bearing
48 Oil Seal
49 Bearing
50 Shim
51 Intermediate Shaft
52 Shaft
53 Cotter Pin
54 Gear
55 Washer
56 Snap Ring
57 Pinion

FIG 4 – MANUAL TRANSMISSION

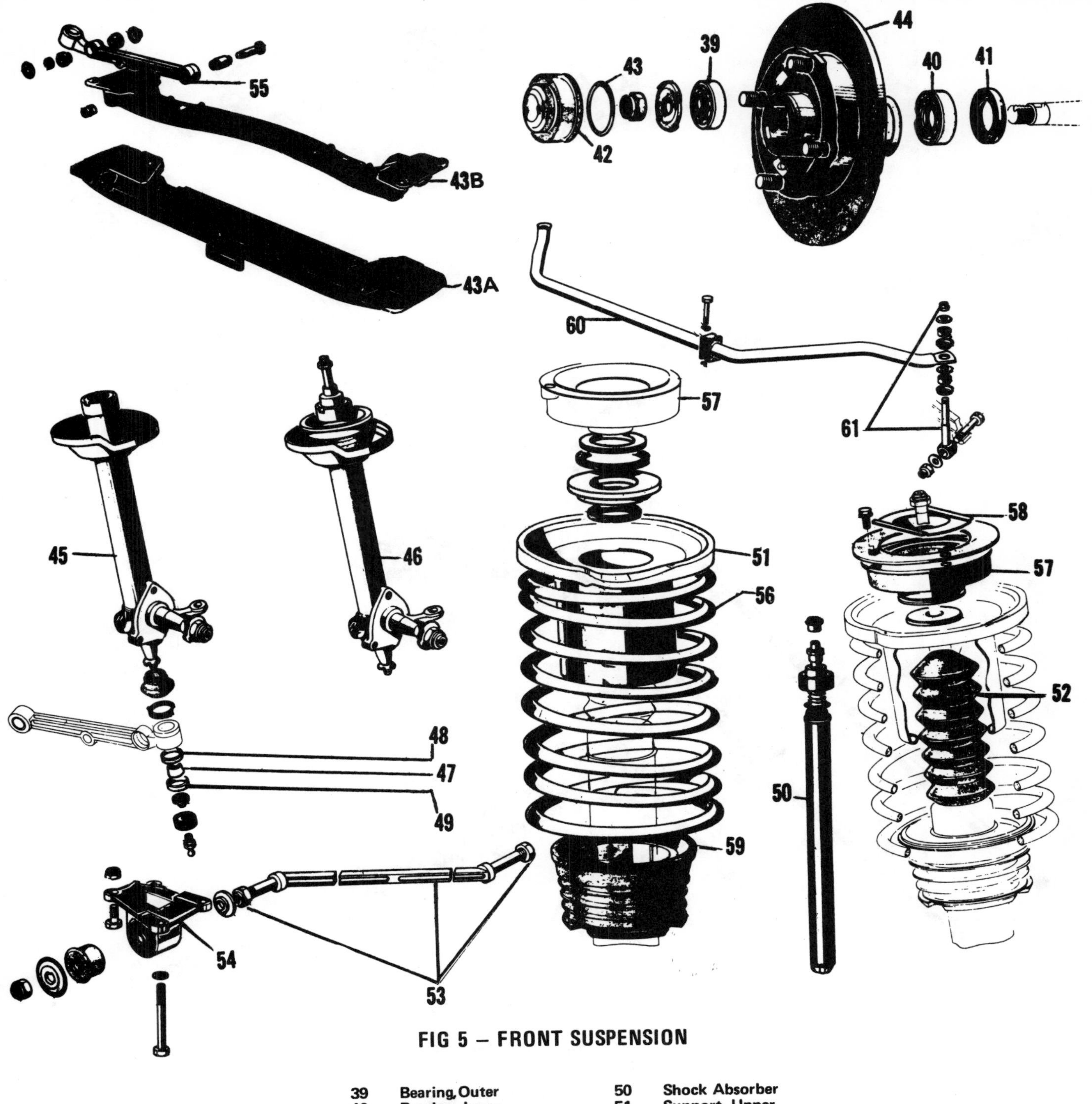

FIG 5 – FRONT SUSPENSION

39	Bearing, Outer
40	Bearing, Inner
41	Oil Seal
42	Grease Cap
43	Seal
43A	Crossmember, Front
43B	Crossmember, Rear
44	Hub & Disc
45	Swivel Wo/Shock
46	Swivel W/Shock
47	Ball Joint Head
48	Half Bearing, Upper
49	Half Bearing, Lower
50	Shock Absorber
51	Support, Upper
52	Rubber Boot
53	Control Arm, Front
54	Support
55	Control Arm, Rear
56	Spring
57	Support, Upper
58	Cup Plate
59	Rebound Stop
60	Stabilizer Bar
61	Link Pin

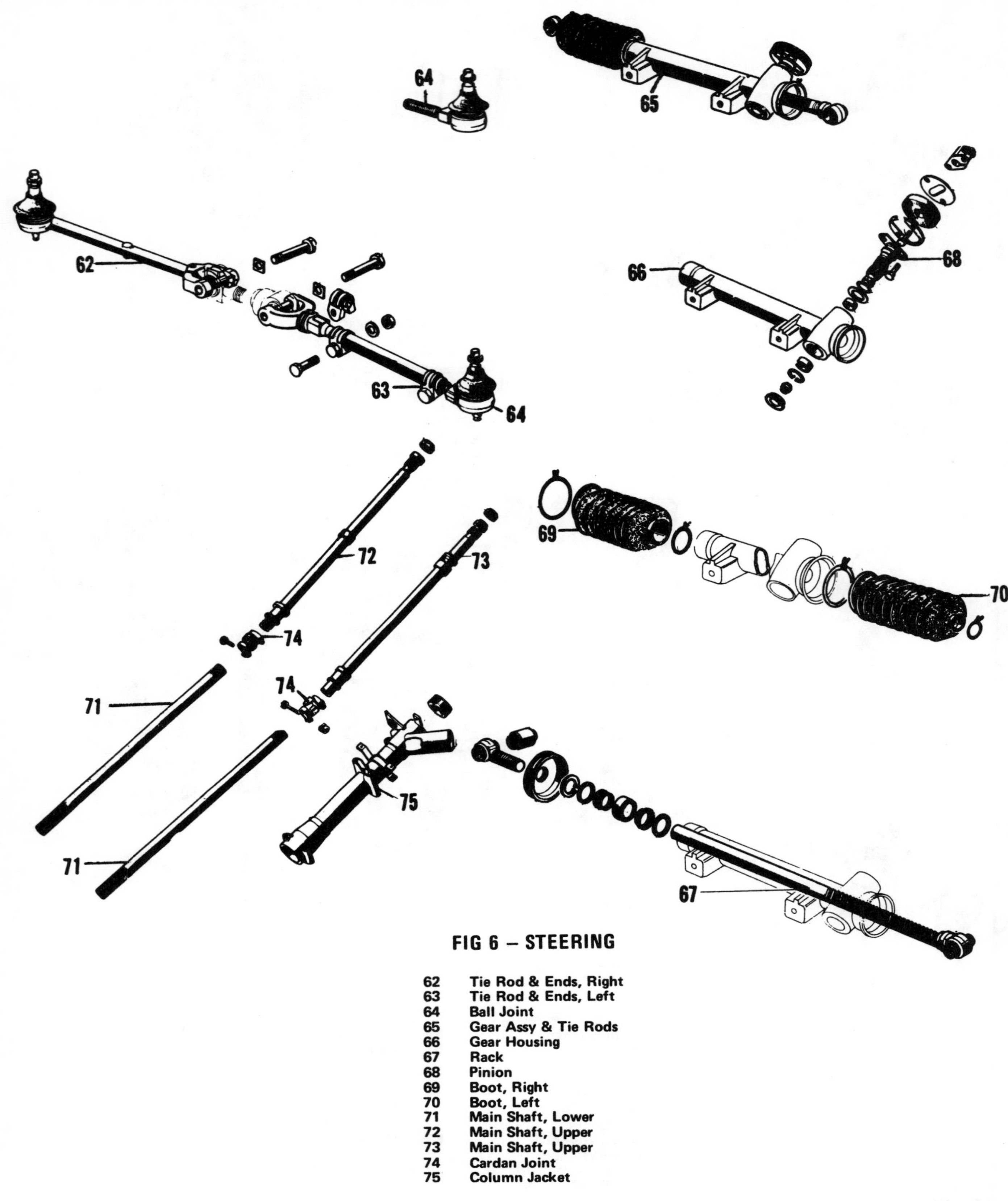

FIG 6 – STEERING

62 Tie Rod & Ends, Right
63 Tie Rod & Ends, Left
64 Ball Joint
65 Gear Assy & Tie Rods
66 Gear Housing
67 Rack
68 Pinion
69 Boot, Right
70 Boot, Left
71 Main Shaft, Lower
72 Main Shaft, Upper
73 Main Shaft, Upper
74 Cardan Joint
75 Column Jacket

Ignition, Starting & Charging—TIME

OPERATION INDEX

Tune-Up, Minor 1
Tune-Up, Major 2
Compression Test 3
Distributor, R&R Or Renew 4
Distributor, R&R & Overhaul 5
Distributor Cap, Renew 6
Ignition Cable Set, Renew 7
Ignition Coil, Renew 8
Starter & Ignition Switch Renew 9
Starter, R&R Or Renew 10
Starter Solenoid, Renew 11
Starter Bendix Drive, Renew 12
Starter, R&R & Overhaul 13
Starter Armature, Renew 14
Voltage Regulator, Renew 15
Alternator, R&R Or Renew 16
Alternator, R&R & Overhaul 17
Alternator Pulley, Renew 18
Generator, R&R Or Renew 19
Generator, R&R & Overhaul 20
Generator Pulley, Renew 21

1—TUNE-UP, MINOR
Includes: Renew points, condenser & plugs. Set spark timing and adjust carburetor idle.
All Models 1.3

2—TUNE-UP, MAJOR
Includes: Check compression, clean or renew & adjust spark plugs, R&R distributor, renew points & condenser. Adjust valves, ignition timing, carburetor & fan belts, clean battery terminals and service air cleaner, chek coil & clean or replace fuel filter.
All Models 3.3

3—COMPRESSION TEST
All Models 0.5

4—DISTRIBUTOR, R&R OR RENEW
All Models 0.8

—NOTE—
For Stroboscope Adjustment, Add *0.3*

5—DISTRIBUTOR, R&R & OVERHAUL
All Models 2.0

6—DISTRIBUTOR CAP, RENEW
All Models 0.3

7—IGNITION CABLE SET, RENEW
All Models—
One 0.1
All 0.4

8—IGNITION COIL, RENEW
All Models 0.3

9—STARTER & IGNITION SWITCH, RENEW
All Models 0.5

10—STARTER, R&R OR RENEW
Exc Below 0.5
304 ....1.0

11—STARTER SOLENOID, RENEW
Includes: Starter R&R
Exc Below 1.3
304 ....1.5

12—STARTER BENDIX DRIVER, RENEW
Includes: Starter R&R
All Models 1.5

13—STARTER, R&R & OVERHAUL
Includes: Turn down commutator and replace all parts necessary.
All Models 2.0

14—STARTER ARMATURE, RENEW
All Models 1.7

15—VOLTAGE REGULATOR, RENEW
All Models 0.3

16—ALTERNATOR, R&R OR RENEW
Exc Below 0.5
304 ....0.8

17—ALTERNATOR, R&R & OVERHAUL
All Models 2.0

18—ALTERNATOR PULLEY, RENEW
Includes: Alternator R&R.
Exc Below 0.8
304 ....1.0

19—GENERATOR, R&R OR RENEW
All Models 0.5

20—GENERATOR, R&R & OVERHAUL
All Models 2.0

—NOTE—
To Renew Field Coils, Add *0.5*

21—GENERATOR PULLEY, RENEW
Includes: Generator R&R.
All Models 0.8

Fuel, Emission Controls, Intake & Exhaust Systems—TIME

OPERATION INDEX

Carburetor, R&R Or Renew 1
Carburetor, R&R & Overhaul 2
Choke Control, Renew 3
Fuel Pump, Renew 4
Fuel Pump, R&R & Overhaul 5
Fuel Tank, Renew 6
Coppolair Fast Idle Control Rod, Renew 7
Coppolair Dash Pot Or Electro Valve, Renew 8
Governor Or Transducer, Renew 9
Coppolair System, Adjust 10
Intake Manifold Or Gasket, Renew 11
Exhaust Manifold, Renew 12
Front Resonator, Renew 13
Front Exhaust Pipe, Renew 14
Intermediate Muffler, Renew 15
Rear Muffler & Pipe, Renew 16
Exhaust System Complete, Renew 17
Fuel Injection 18

1—CARBURETOR, R&R OR RENEW
Includes: Coppolair adjustment
Exc Below 1.3
304 & 403 ....0.8

2—CARBURETOR, R&R & OVERHAUL
Exc Below 1.8
403 ....1.1

3—CHOKE CONTROL, RENEW
All Models 0.5

4— FUEL PUMP, R&R OR RENEW
All Models 0.5

5—FUEL PUMP, R&R & OVERHAUL
All Models 1.0

6—FUEL TANK, R&R OR RENEW
Exc Below 1.0
304 ....1.5
403 Sta Wagon 1.3
404 Sta Wagon 1.3

7—COPPOLAIR FAST IDLE CONTROL ROD, RENEW
All Models 0.3

8—COPPOLAIR DASH POT OR ELECTRO VALVE, RENEW
All Models 0.3

9—GOVERNOR OR TRANSDUCER, RENEW
All Models 0.5

10—COPPOLAIR SYSTEM, ADJUST
All Models 0.5

11—INTAKE MANIFOLD OR GASKET, RENEW
Exc Below 1.5
304 & 403 ....1.8

12—EXHAUST MANIFOLD, RENEW
All Models 1.0

13—FRONT RESONATOR, RENEW
All Models 0.5

14—FRONT EXHAUST PIPE, RENEW
All Models 1.0

15—INTERMEDIATE MUFFLER, RENEW
Includes: R&R heat shield & strap.
Exc Below 1.0
504 ....0.8

16—REAR MUFFLER & PIPE, RENEW
Includes: R&R exhaust pipes & muffler.
Exc Below 1.5
304 ....0.8
504 ....1.3

17—EXHAUST SYSTEM COMPLETE, RENEW
Exc Below 2.3
304 ....1.3
Pipes 1.0
Nozzle 0.3
Fuel Filter 1.0
Fuel Filter Element 1.2
Fuel Filter Cartridge 1.2
Priming Pump Overhaul 1.2

Engine Cooling & Heater System—TIME

OPERATION INDEX

Radiator, R&R Or Renew 1
Radiator Hoses, Renew 2
Water Pump, R&R Or Renew 3
Water Pump, R&R & Overhaul 4
Thermostat, Renew 5
Heater Blower Motor & Fan, Renew 6
Heater Control Switch, Renew 7

1—RADIATOR, R&R OR RENEW
All Models 0.8
Diesel 1.2

2—RADIATOR HOSES, RENEW
Upper—
All Models 0.3
Lower—
All Models 0.5

3—WATER PEMP, R&R OR RENEW
Exc Below 1.5
304 ....1.3

4—WATER PUMP, R&R OR OVERHAUL
All Models 2.0

—NOTE—
To R&R Self-Disengaging Fan, Add *0.3*

5—THERMOSTAT, RENEW
All Models 0.5

6—HEATER BLOWER MOTOR & FAN, RENEW
Includes: R&R heater front housing.
Exc Below 0.8
304 ....1.0

(Continued)

Engine Cooling & Heater System—TIME Cont'd

504 .... 1.3

7—HEATER CONTROL SWITCH, RENEW

Exc Below 0.8
304 .... 1.3
504 .... 1.0

Engine—TIME

OPERATION INDEX

Engine, R&R 1
Engine, R&R & Overhaul 2
Cylinder Head, R&R Or Gasket, Renew 3
Valves, Grind 4
One Valve, Renew & Grind 5
Valve Spring, Renew 6
Rocker Cover Gasket, Renew 7
Spark Plug Protecting Tube, Renew 8
Push Rods, Renew 9
Valve Rocker Arm Assy, R&R & Overhaul 10
Valve Tappets, Renew 11
Valve Tappets, Adjust 12
Oil Pan Or Gasket, R&R Or Renew 13
Timing Gear Cover Or Gasket, R&R Or Renew 14
Chain Tensioner, Renew 15
Camshaft, R&R Or Renew 16
Oil Pump, R&R Or Renew 17
Oil Pump, R&R & Overhaul 18
Piston Rings, Renew 19
Water Jackets & Piston, R&R Or Renew 20
Rod Bearing, Renew 21
Crankshaft Rear Main Seal, Renew 22
Crankshaft Pulley, Renew 23

1—ENGINE, R&R

Does not include transfer of any part of engine or replacement of special equipment.

Exc Below 4.5
403 .... 5.0
Diesel 7.5

—NOTE—

To Renew Engine, For Transfer Or Parts Not Included With New Engine, Excluding Special Equipment, Add 2.0 .

2—ENGINE, R&R OR OVERHAUL

Includes rebore cylinders with boring bar, renew pistons, rings, bearings, grind valves, plastigauge bearings and perform minor tune-up.

Exc Below 15.5
304 .... 16.5
Diesel 30.0

3—CYLINDER HEAD, R&R OR GASKET, RENEW

Exc Below 4.0
304 .... 5.0
Diesel 6.5

4—VALVES, GRIND

Excludes: R&R cylinder head & minor tune-up

Exc Below 6.5
304 .... 7.0
Diesel 13.0

5—ONE VALVE, RENEW & GRIND

Includes, minor tune-up

Ecx Below 5.0
304 .... 5.5

6—VALVE SPRING, RENEW

All Models 1.0
Diesel 1.5

7—ROCKER COVER GASKET, RENEW

All Models 0.5

8—SPARK PLUG PROTECTING TUBE, RENEW

Includes; R&R valve cover

All Models 0.8

—NOTE—

To Renew Spark Plug Tubes, Add 0.3

9—PUSH RODS, RENEW

Includes: Adjustment of vlave clearances.

Exc Below 1.3
403 .... 0.8

10—VLAVE ROCKER ARM ASSY, R&R 3 OVERHAUL

Includes: R&R cylinder head when necessary.

Exc Below 5.0
304 .... 6.0
403 .... 1.5
Diesel 2.5

11—VALVE TAPPETS, RENEW

Includes: R&R of cylinder head.

All Models 4.0

12—VALVE TAPPETS, ADJUST

All Models 0.5
Diesel 1.0

13—OIL PAN OR GASKET, R&R OR RENEW

Exc Below 1.0
304 .... 0.5
403 .... 0.5
Diesel 2.0

14—TIMING GEAR COVER OR GASKET, R&R OR RENEW

Exc Below 0.5
304 .... (1)2.0
403 .... (2)1.5

(1)Includes: R&R Distributor, Dynåmo & Set Timing.
(2)Includes: R&R Radiator & Crankshaft Pulley.

15—CHAIN TENSIONER, RENEW

Exc Below 1.0
304 .... 1.0
504 .... 1.5

16—CAMSHAFT, R&R OR RENEW

403 .... 6.5
304 .... 4.5
404 (3 Main Bearings) 9.5
404 (5 Main Bearings) 8.5
504 .... 8.5
Diesel 16.5

17—OIL PUMP, R&R OR RENEW

Exc Below 1.8
304 .... 2.5
Diesel 2.5

18—OIL PUMP, R&R & OVERHAUL

Exc Below 2.5
304 .... 3.0

19—PISTON RINGS, RENEW

Exc Below 8.0
304 .... (1)12.0
403 .... (1)10.0

(1)Includes: Engine R&R.

Diesel 17.0

20—WATER JACKETS & PISTON, R&R OR RENEW

Includes: Minor tune-up

Exc Below 10.5
304 .... (1)15.0
403 .... (1)12.5

(1)Includes: Engine R&R

21—ROD BEARINGS, RENEW

Exc Below 3.0
304 .... (1)10.0
403 .... (1)7.5
Diesel 16.0

(1)Includes: Engine R&R.

22—CRANKSHAFT REAR MAIN OIL SEAL, RENEW

All Models 2.0
Diesel 9.0

23—CRANKSHAFT PULLEY, RENEW

All Models 0.5

Clutch, Mounts & Transmission—TIME

OPERATION INDEX

Flywheel Or Release Shaft & Fork, Renew 1
Flywheel Ring Gear, Renew 2
Clutch Or Disc, Renew 3
Pilot Bearing, Renew 4
Clutch Pedal, Adjust 5
Engine Mounts, Renew 6
Front Engine Support Brakets, Renew 7
Transmission Assy, R&R Or Renew 8
Transmission, R&R & Overhaul 9
Speedometer Drive Gear, Renew 10
Oil Pan Gasket Or Screen, Renew 11
Pump Assy, Renew 12
Valve Body, R & R & Overhaul 13

1—FLYWHEEL OR RELEASE SHAFT & FORK, RENEW

Exc Below 5.8
304 .... 6.8

2—FLYWHEEL RING GEAR, EWNEW

Exc Below 6.3
304 .... 7.3

3—CLUTCH OR DISC, RENEW

Exc Below 5.2
304 .... 6.2
Diesel 6.0

4—PILOT BEARING, RENEW

Exc Below 6.0
304 .... 5.0

5—CLUTCH PEDAL, ADJUST

All Models 0.3

6—ENGINE MOUNTS, RENEW

Front—
Exc Below 1.0
403 .... 0.8
Rear—
All Models 3.0
Station Wagon 3.5

7—FRONT ENGINE SUPPORT BRACKETS, RENEW

All Models 0.8

8—TRANSMISSION ASSY, R&R OR RENEW

Exc Below 5.0
304 .... 8.5
Automatic 5.0

9—TRANSMISSION, R&R & OVERHAUL

Exc Below 8.0
304 .... 14.5
Automatic 12.0

10—TORQUE CONVERTER, R & R OR RENEW

Automatic Trans 5.0
304 .... (1)10.0

(1)Includes: Engine R&R

11—OIL PAN GASKET OR SCREEN, RENEW

All Models 0.8

—NOTE—

To Replace Screen, Add 0.2

12—PUMP ASSY, RENEW

Automatic Trans 5.2

13—VALVE BODY, R & R & OVERHAUL

Automatic Trans 3.5

Brakes, Steering, Suspension, Universals & Rear Axle—TIME

OPERATION INDEX

Brake Shoes Or Friction Pads, Renew *1*
Master Cylinder, Renew *2*
Master Cylinder, R&R & Overhaul *3*
Wheel Cylinders, Renew *4*
Brake Drums, Renew *5*
Caliper Assy, Renew *6*
Caliper Assy, R&R & Overhaul *7*
Bleed System *8*
Brake Hose, Renew *9*
Hub Or Disc, Renew *10*
Vacuum Reservoir Or Non-Return Valve, Renew *11*
Hydrovac Or Mastervac Unit, Renew *12*
Brake Compensator, Renew *13*
Brake Compensator, R&R & Overhaul *14*
Pressure Limiter, Renew *15*
Pedal Support, R&R Or Renew *16*
Parking Brake Cable, Renew *17*
Parking Brake Control Cable, Renew *18*
Parking Brake Control Lever, Renew *19*
Rack To Column Flex Coupling, Renew *20*
Steering Gear Rack Plungers, Renew *21*
Steering Gear Rack Eyes, Renew *22*
Steering Rack Assy, Renew *23*
Steering Rack Assy, R&R & Overhaul *24*
Steering Rack Ball Joint, Renew *25*
Tie Rod, Renew *26*
Tie Rods Ends, Renew *27*
Spring(S), Renew *28*
Anti-Roll Bar, R&R Or Renew *29*
Anti-Roll Bar Rubber Bushings, Renew *30*
Front Or Rear Arm Rubber Bushings, Renew *31*
Front Triangle Rubber Bushings, Renew *32*
"A" Frame Rubber Bushings, Renew *33*
Front Spring Rubber Bushings, Renew *34*
Shock Absorbers, Renew *35*
Front And Rear Hub Bearings, Renew *36*
Universal Joint, Renew *37*
Differential Pinion Shaft Oil Seal, Renew *38*
Torque Tube Center Bearing, Renew *39*
Differential Assy, R&R Or Renew *40*
Differential Assy, R&R & Overhaul *41*
Rear Axle & Shaft Assy, Housing, R&R Or Renew *42*
Rear Axle Assy, R&R Or Renew *43*
Rear Axle Suspension Arms, R&R Or Renew *44*

1—BRAKE SHOES OR FRICTION PADS, RENEW
Front Or Rear (Two)—
- Drum Type 1.5
- Disc Type 0.5

2—MASTER CYLINDER, RENEW
Exc Below 1.3
404 .... 1.5

3—MASTER CYLINDER, R&R & OVERHAUL
Exc Below 1.8
403 .... 1.5

4—WHEEL CYLINDERS, RENEW
Front—
- One—
  - Exc Below 1.0
  - 404 .... 1.5
- All On One Wheel—
  - Exc Below 1.3
  - 404 .... 1.8
- All Both Wheels—
  - Exc Below 2.0
  - 404 .... 3.0

Rear—
- One—
  - Exc Below 1.0
  - 404 .... 1.3
- Both All Models 1.5

5—BRAKE DRUMS, RENEW
All Models, Each 0.3

6—CALIPER ASSY, RENEW
All Models—
- Each 0.8
- Two 1.3

7—CLIPER ASSY, R&R & OVERHAUL
Exc Below, Two 1.3
304, Two 1.5

8—BLEED SYSTEM
All Models 0.5

9—BRAKE HOSE, RENEW
All Models, Each 0.8

10—HUB OR DISC, RENEW
Exc Below, Each 0.8
304, Each 1.8

11—VACUUM RESERVOIR OR NON-RETURN VALVE, RENEW
All Models 0.3

12—HYDROVAC OR MASTERVAC UNIT, RENEW
All Models 1.5

13—BRAKE COMPENSATOR, RENEW
All Models 1.0

14—BRAKE COMPENSATOR, R&R & OVERHAUL
All Models 1.5

15—PRESSURE LIMITER, RENEW
All Models 0.8

16—PEDAL SUPPORT, R&R OR RENEW
Exc Below 1.5
403 .... 1.0
404 .... 1.0

—NOTE—

For Overhaul, Add 0.7

17—PARKING BRAKE CABLE, RENEW
Exc Below 1.0
504 .... 0.8

18—PARKING BRAKE CONTROL CABLE, RENEW
Exc Below 1.0
304 .... 0.8

19—PARKING BRAKE CONTROL LEVER, RENEW
All Models 0.5

—NOTE—

To Replace Handle Sector & Trigger, Add
- *Exc Below 0.3*
- *304 .... 0.5*

20—RACK TO COLUMN FLEX COUPLING, RENEW
All Models 0.8

21—STEERING GEAR RACK PLUNGERS, RENEW
All Models 0.5

22—STEERING GEAR RACK EYES, RENEW
All Models 1.3

23—STEERING RACK ASSY, RENEW
Includes: Set toe-in.
All Models 1.5

24—STEERING RACK ASSY, R&R & OVERHAUL
Includes: Set toe-in
Exc Below 2.8
403 .... 2.5

25—STEERING RACK BALL JOINT, RENEW
All Models 1.0

26—TIE ROD, RENEW
Includes: Set toe-in
All Models 0.5

27—TIE ROD ENDS, RENEW
Includes: Set toe-in
All Models—
- Each 0.8
- Both 1.3

28—SPRING(S), RENEW
Front—
- One—
  - Exc Below 2.0
  - 304 .... 2.3
- Both—
  - Exc Below 3.5
  - 304 .... 4.0

Rear Both—
- 304 .... 1.5
- 504 .... 1.5
- 403—
  - Exc Below 0.8
  - Sta Wagon 2.3
- 404—
  - Exc Below 0.8
  - Sta Wagon 1.3

29—ANTI-ROLL BAR, R&R OR RENEW
All Models—
- Front Or Rear 0.8

30—ANTI-ROLL BAR RUBBER BUSHINGS, RENEW
Front 0.3
Rear 1.0

31—FRONT OR REAR ARM RUBBER BUSHINGS, RENEW
All Models, Each 1.0

32—FRONT TRIANGLE RUBBER BUSHINGS, RENEW
Exc Below 1.8
304 .... 1.0

33—A-FRAME RUBBER BUSHINGS, RENEW
Exc Below 3.3
304 .... 2.5

34—FRONT SPRING RUBBER BUSHINGS, RENEW
403—
- Each 1.0
- Both 1.3

35—SHOCK ABSORBER, RENEW
Front—
- Each—
  - Exc Below 3.0
  - 403 .... 1.0
  - 404 .... 2.8
- Both—
  - Exc Below 4.5
  - 403 .... 1.8
  - 504 .... 4.8

Rear—
- Each—
  - Exc Below 0.5
  - 304 .... 1.5
  - 403 Sta Wagon 1.0
- Both—
  - Exc Below 1.0
  - 304 .... 2.3
  - 403 Sta Wagon 2.0

36—FRONT & REAR HUB BEARINGS, RENEW
Front—
- One Hub—
  - Exc Below 1.3
  - 304 .... 1.8
- Both Hubs—
  - Exc Below 2.0
  - 304 .... 2.3

Rear—
- 304 .... 1.3
- 504 .... 2.0

37—UNIVERSAL JOINT, RENEW
All Models 3.0

(Continued)

Brakes, Steering, Suspension, Universals & Rear Axle—TIME Cont'd

38—DIFFERENTIAL PINION SHAFT OIL SEAL, RENEW
Exc Below 3.8
504 .... 1.8

39—TORQUE TUBE CENTER BEARING, RENEW
Exc Below 4.0
504 .... 2.0

40—DIFFERENTIAL ASSY, R&R OR RENEW
Exc Below 4.0
304 .... 3.0
504 .... 2.5

41—DIFFERENTIAL ASSY, R&R & OVERHAUL
Worm Type 6.0
Hypoid Type ①4.0
①Does Not Include R&R On Sta Wagon

42—REAR AXLE & SHAFT ASSY HOUSING, R&R OR RENEW
Exc Below 2.0
404 Sta Wagon 3.0

43—REAR AXLE ASSY, R&R OR RENEW
Exc Below 3.5
304 .... 3.0
504 .... 3.0

44—REAR AXLE SUSPENSION ARMS, R&R OR RENEW
304—
One 1.3
Both 2.0
To Renew Each Arm, Add 1.0

—NOTE—

Sppedometerm W/S Wipers & Instruments—TIME

OPERATION INDEX

Speedometer Cable, Renew 1
Speedometer Head, Renew 2
W/S Wiper Motor, Renew 3
W/S Wiper Connecting Link, Renew 4
W/S Wiper Spindle, Renew 5
W/S Wiper Motor Activating Set, Renew 6
Fuel Gauge (Dash Unit), Renew 7
Fuel Tank Gauge, Renew 8
Oil Gauge (Dash Unit), Renew 9
Temperature Gauge (Dash Unit), Renew 10
Ammeter, Renew 11
Headlight Switch, Renew 12
Stop Light Switch, Renew 13
Turn Signal Switch, Renew 14
Hazard Flasher Switch, Renew 15

1—SPEEDOMETER CABLE, RENEW
All Models 0.5

2—SPEEDOMETER HEAD, RENEW
All Models 0.8

3—W/S WIPER MOTOR, RENEW
All Models 0.5

4—W/S WIPER CONNECTING LINK, RENEW
Includes: R&R glove box.
All Models 0.5

5—W/S WIPER SPINDLE, RENEW
All Models 1.0

6—W/S WIPER MOTOR ACTIVATING SET, RENEW
Exc, Below 1.3
304 .... 1.0

7—FUEL GAUGE (DASH UNIT), RENEW
Exc Below 0.5
304 .... 0.3
404 Sta Wagon ①0.8
①Includes R&R Of Rear Floor.

8—FUEL TANK GAUGE, RENEW
Includes R&R of instrument panel.
All Models 0.5

9—OIL GAUGE (DASH UNIT), RENEW
Includes R&R of instrument panel.
All Models 0.8

10—TEMPERATURE GAUGE (DASH UNIT), RENEW
Includes R&R of instrument panel.
All Models 0.8

11—AMMETER, RENEW
Includes R&R of instrument panel.
All Models 0.8

12—HEADLIGHT SWITCH, RENEW
Exc Below 0.5
504 .... 1.5

13—STOP LIGHT SWITCH, RENEW
All Models 0.3

14—TURN SIGNAL SWITCH, RENEW
Exc Below 0.8
304 .... 0.5
403 .... 0.5

15—HAZARD FLASHER SWITCH, RENEW
Exc Below 0.3
404 .... 0.5

IDENTIFICATION

ALL MODELS.................................... 338

ILLUSTRATIONS

FIG 1 – ENGINE – 914/6 CRANKSHAFT
FIG 2 – ENGINE – 914/6 CYLINDER HEAD
FIG 3 – ENGINE – 914 CRANKCASE, CYLINDER & HEAD
FIG 4 – ENGINE – 914 CRANKSHAFT, PISTON & FLYWHEEL
FIG 5 – FIVE SPEED TRANSMISSION HOUSING
FIG 6 – SPORTOMATIC TORQUE CONVERTER
FIG 7 – FRONT SUSPENSION
FIG 8 – STEERING – 914/6
FIG 9 – STEERING - 914

OPERATION TIMES

A

Alternator.. 347

B

Brakes.. 350

C

Cables (Ignition).. 347
Calipers.. 351
Camshaft.. 349
Carburetor.. 347
Clutch.. 350
Coil, Ignition.. 347
Compression Test.. 347
Connecting Rods.. 350
Cooling System.. 348
Crankcase.. 349
Crankshaft.. 349
Cylinder Head.. 348

D

Dash Gauges.. 352
Differential.. 350
Disc Brakes.. 351
Distributor.. 347

E

Electronic Control Unit.. 348
Emission Controls.. 347
Engine Assembly.. 348
Engine Mountings.. 350
Engine Oiling.. 349
Engine Tune-Up.. 347
Exhaust System.. 348

F

Flywheel.. 350
Front Suspension.. 351
Fuel Gauges.. 352
Fuel Pump.. 348
Fuel Tank.. 348

G

Generator.. 347

H

Hand Brake.. 351
Headlight Switch.. 352
Heater.. 348
Hose (Brake).. 351
Hydraulic Brakes.. 350

I

Ignition.. 347
Ignition Coil.. 347
Ignition Switch.. 347
Injection Pump.. 347
Intake Manifold.. 348

L

Light Switches.. 352

M

Main Bearings.. 349
Master Cylinder.. 350
Muffler.. 348

O

Oil Gauge.. 352
Oiling, Engine.. 349
Oil Pump.. 349

P

Parking Brake.. 351
Piston Rings.. 349
Pistons.. 349
Power Brake.. 351

R

Rear Axle.. 351
Regulator.. 347
Rocker Arms.. 349
Rod Bearings.. 349

S

Shocks (Front).. 351
Shocks (Rear).. 351
Speedometer.. 351
Springs.. 351
Starting Motor.. 347
Steering Gear.. 347
Steering Linkage.. 347
Switches (Light).. 352
Synchro-Mesh Trans.. 350

T

Tachometer.. 352
Thermostat.. 348
Torsion Bars.. 351
Transmission.. 350
Tune-Up, Engine.. 347

V

Vacuum Control Unit.. 347
Valve System.. 348

W

Windshield Wiper.. 352

CHASSIS NUMBER LOCATION

In luggage compartment at wheelhouse or on left windshield pillar.

STARTING CHASSIS NUMBERS

Year	Model	Chassis Number
1968	911	11800001
	912	12800001
1969	911T	119100001
	911E	119200001
	911S	119300001
	912	129000001
1970	911T	9110100001
	911E	9110200001
	911S	9110300001
	914-6	9140430001
	914	4702900001
1971	911T	9111100001
	911E	9111200001
	911S	9111300001
	914-6	9141430001
	914	4712900001
1972	911T Coupe	9112100001
	Targa	9112110001
	911E Coupe	9112200001
	Targa	9112210001
	911S Coupe	9112300001
	Targa	9112310001
	914	4722900001
	914-6	9142430001
1973	914	4732900001
	911 Coupe	9113300001
	911 Targa	9113310001
1974	914	4742900001
	911 Coupe	9114300001
	911 Targa	9114310001
1975	914	4752900001
	911 Coupe	9115200001
	911 Targa	9115210001
1976	914	4762900001
	911S Coupe	9116200001
	911S Targa	9116210001
	912 Coupe	9126000001

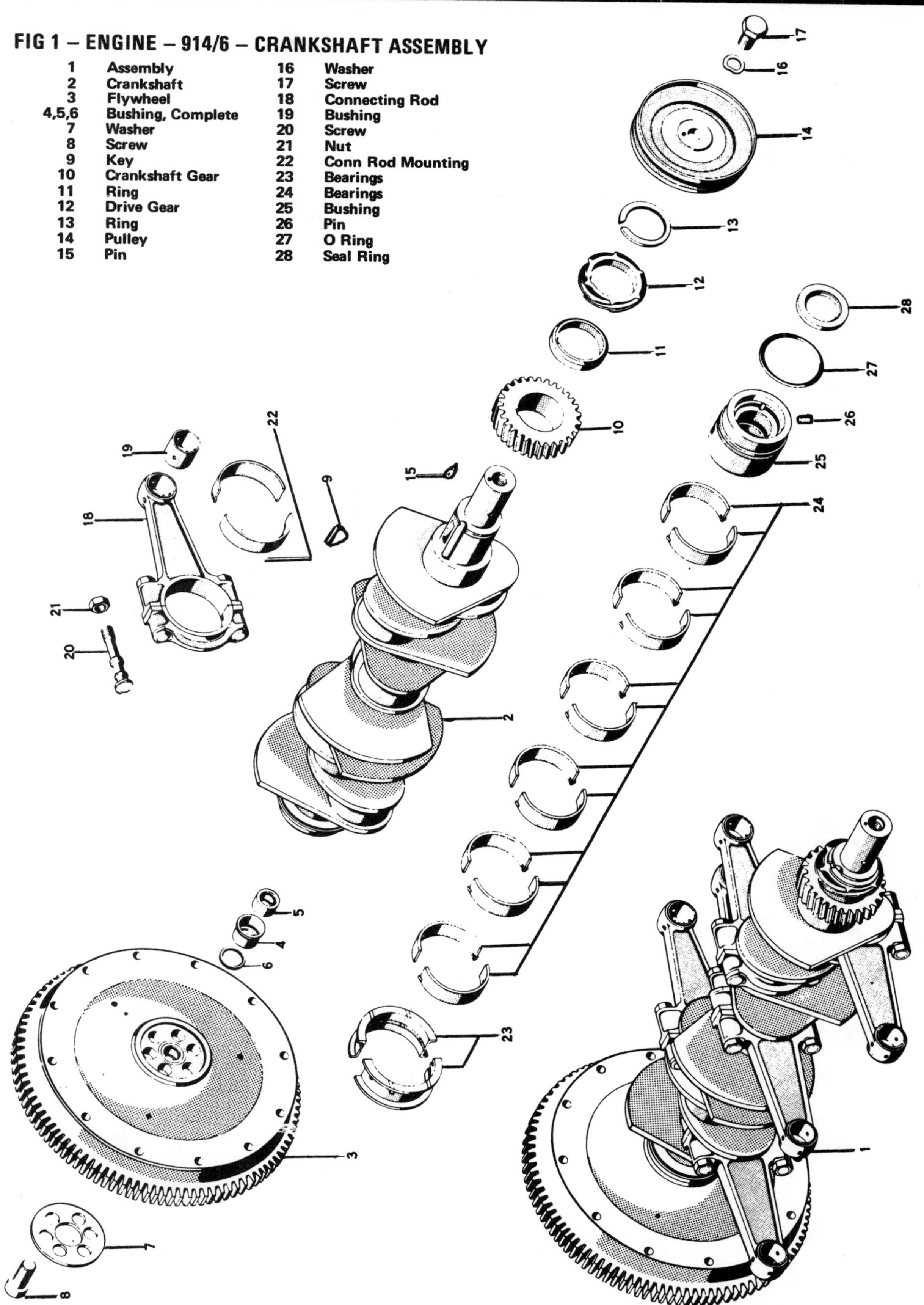

FIG 1 – ENGINE – 914/6 – CRANKSHAFT ASSEMBLY

1	Assembly	16	Washer
2	Crankshaft	17	Screw
3	Flywheel	18	Connecting Rod
4,5,6	Bushing, Complete	19	Bushing
7	Washer	20	Screw
8	Screw	21	Nut
9	Key	22	Conn Rod Mounting
10	Crankshaft Gear	23	Bearings
11	Ring	24	Bearings
12	Drive Gear	25	Bushing
13	Ring	26	Pin
14	Pulley	27	O Ring
15	Pin	28	Seal Ring

FIG 2 — ENGINE — 914/6 — CYLINDER HEAD

1	– Head, Complete
2	– Valve Guide
3	– Valve Seat, Intake
4	– Valve Seat, Exhaust
6	Stud
6/1	Stud
7	Stud
8	Pin
9	Intake Valve
10	Exhaust Valve
11	Washer
12	Ring
13	Spring
14	Spring
15	Seat
16	Valve Keeper
17	Washer
18	Nut
19	Seal
20 to 26	Cylinder & Piston Complete
21 to 26	Piston Complete
22 to 24	Ring Set
25	Pin
26	Ring
27	Gasket, Base
28	Gasket, Head

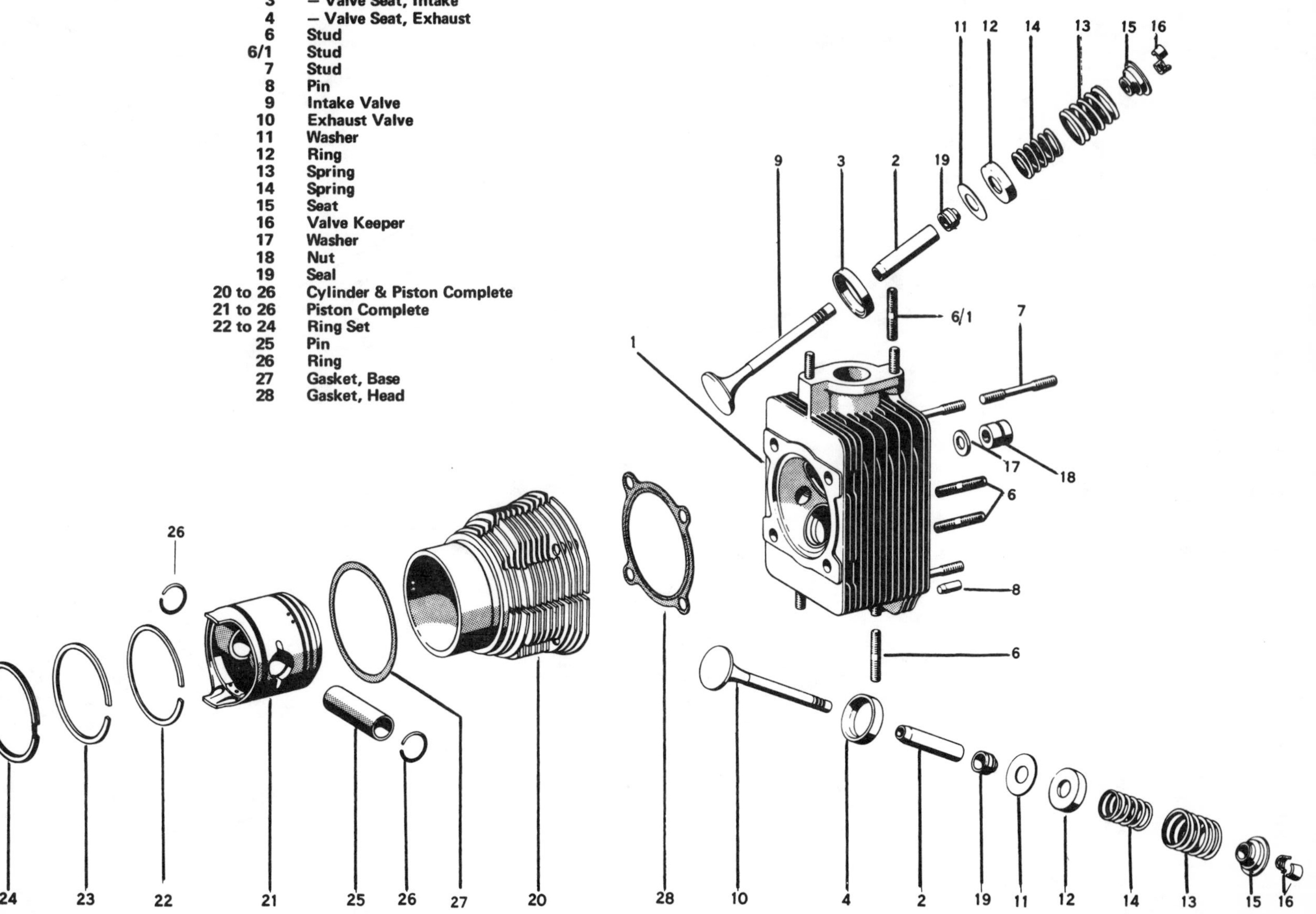

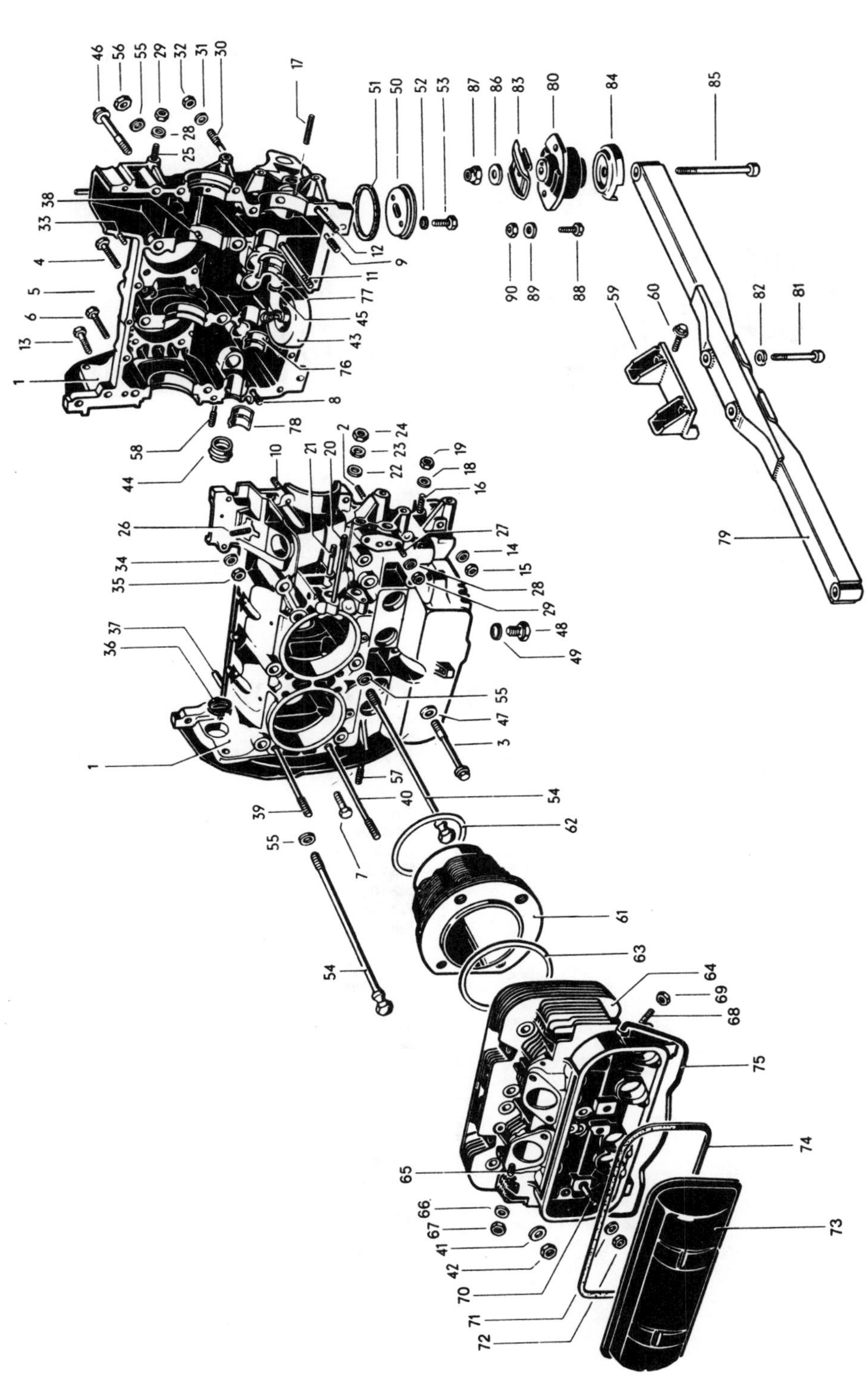

FIG 3 – ENGINE – 914 – CRANKCASE, CYLINDER & HEAD

1	Crankcase
2	Stud
3	Bolt
4	Bolt
5	Bolt
6	Bolt
7	Bolt
8	Stud
9	Stud
10	Stud
11	Stud
12	Stud
13	Bolt
14	Washer
15	Nut
16	Stud
17	Stud
18	Washer
19	Nut
20	Stud
21	Stud
22	Washer
23	Washer
24	Nut
25	Stud
26	Stud
27	Stud
28	Washer
29	Nut
30	Stud
31	Washer
32	Nut
33	Stud
34	Washer
35	Nut
36	Cover
37	Dowel Pin
38	Dowel Pin
39	Stud
40	Stud
41	Washer
42	Nut
43	Oil Pipe
44	Plug
45	Seal
46	Bolt
47	Seal
48	Plug
49	Ring
50	Cover
51	Seal
52	Ring
53	Bolt
54	Bolt
55	Washer
56	Nut
57	Stud
58	Stud
59	Support
60	Bolt
61	Cylinder
62	Gasket
63	Gasket
64	Head
65	Stud
66	Washer
67	Nut
68	Stud
69	Nut
70	Stud
71	Washer
72	Nut
73	Head Cover
74	Gasket
75	Clamp
76	Bearing
77	Bearing
78	Bearing
79	Engine Carrier
80	Engine Mount
81	Screw
82	Ring
83	Plate
84	Plate
85	Screw
86	Washer
87	Nut
88	Bolt
89	Washer
90	Nut

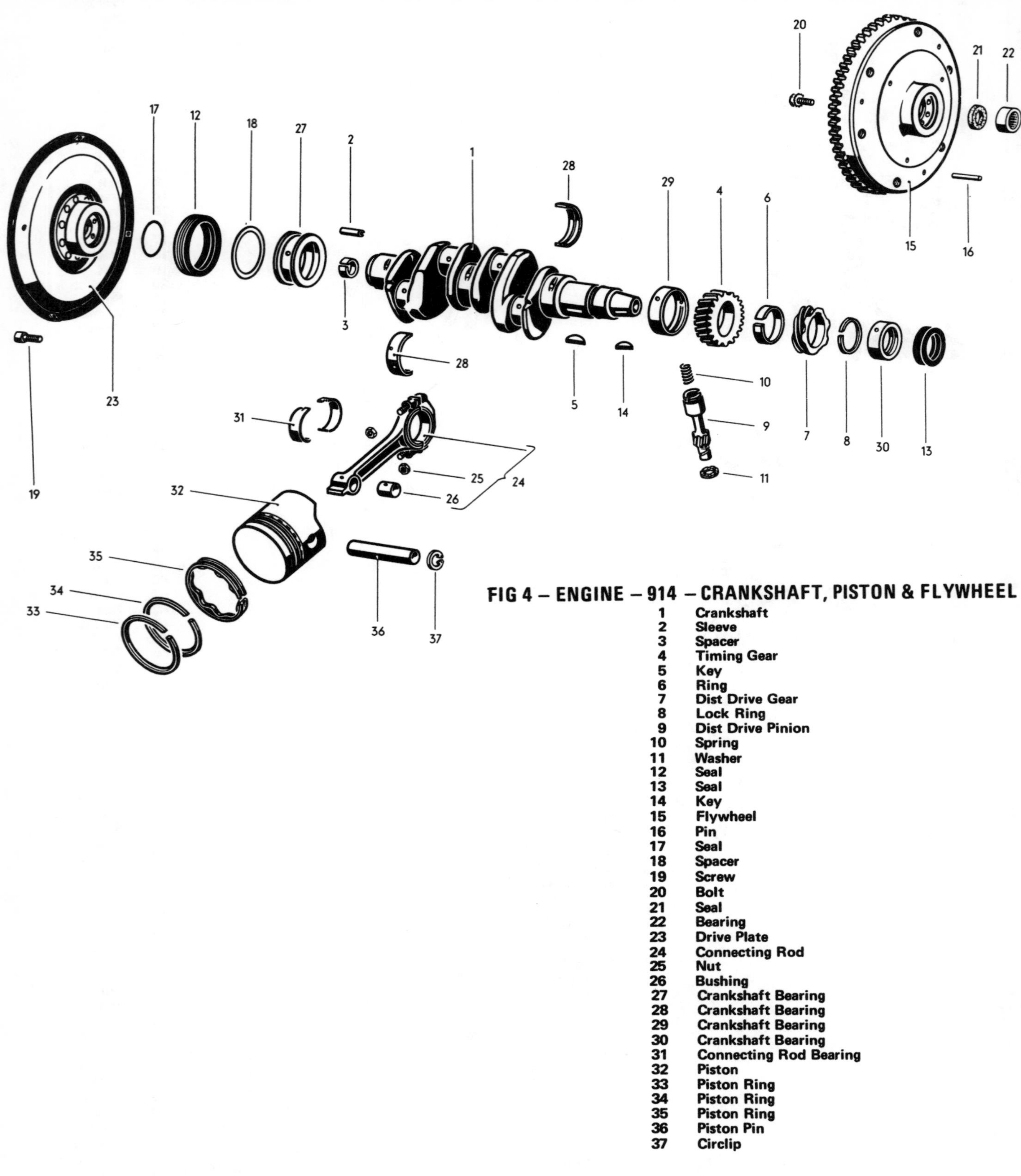

FIG 4 – ENGINE – 914 – CRANKSHAFT, PISTON & FLYWHEEL

1 Crankshaft
2 Sleeve
3 Spacer
4 Timing Gear
5 Key
6 Ring
7 Dist Drive Gear
8 Lock Ring
9 Dist Drive Pinion
10 Spring
11 Washer
12 Seal
13 Seal
14 Key
15 Flywheel
16 Pin
17 Seal
18 Spacer
19 Screw
20 Bolt
21 Seal
22 Bearing
23 Drive Plate
24 Connecting Rod
25 Nut
26 Bushing
27 Crankshaft Bearing
28 Crankshaft Bearing
29 Crankshaft Bearing
30 Crankshaft Bearing
31 Connecting Rod Bearing
32 Piston
33 Piston Ring
34 Piston Ring
35 Piston Ring
36 Piston Pin
37 Circlip

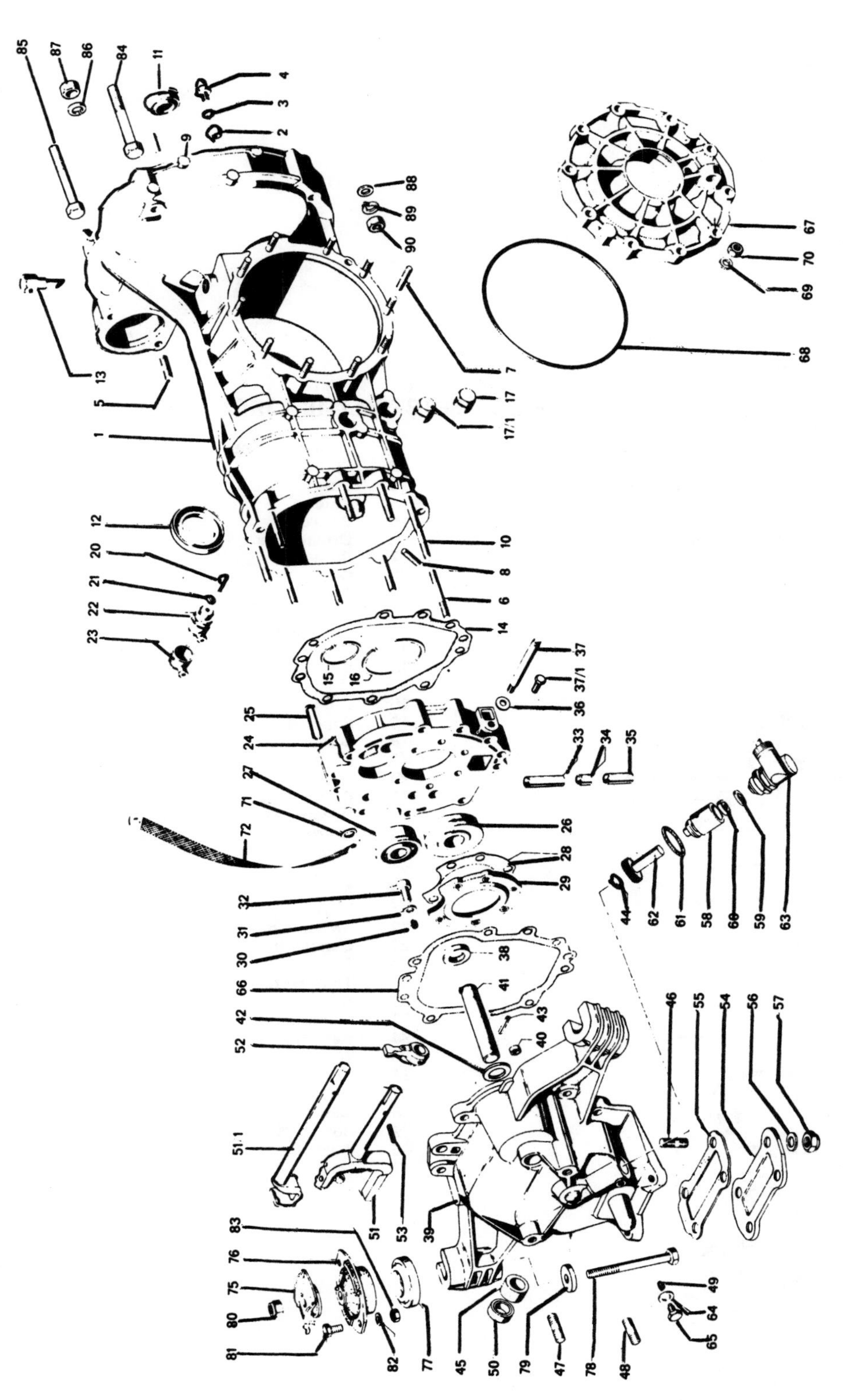

FIG 5 – 5 SPEED TRANSMISSION HOUSING

1	Housing
2	Bushing
3	Washer
4	Pin
5	Stud
6	Stud
7	Stud
8	Stud
9	Stud
10	Stud
11	Ring
12	Ring
13	Ventilator
14	Gasket
15	Ring
16	Ring
17	Screw
17/1	Screw
20	Tappet
21	Washer
22	Reverse Light Switch
23	Cap
24	Plate
25	Pin
26	Bearing
27	Bearing
28	Plate
29	Plate
30	Insert
31	Washer
32	Screw
33	Bushing
34	Bushing
35	Bushing
36	Washer
37	Pin
37/1	Bolt
38	Disc
39	Cover
40	Bearing Bush
41	Pin
42	Washer
43	Sleeve
44	Pin
45	Bush
46	Stud
47	Stud
48	Stud
49	Insert
50	Ring
51	Pin
52	Lever
53	Pin
54	Cover
55	Gasket
56	Washer
57	Nut
58	Guide Bush
59	Washer
60	Ring
61	O Ring
62	Shaft
63	Gear
64	Washer
65	Screw
66	Gasket
67	Cover
68	Gasket
69	Washer
70	Nut
71	Washer
72	Strap
75	Plate
76	Mount
77	Washer
78	Bolt
79	Washer
80	Nut
81	Bolt
82	Washer
83	Nut
84	Screw
85	Screw
86	Washer
87	Nut
88	Washer
89	Washer
90	Nut

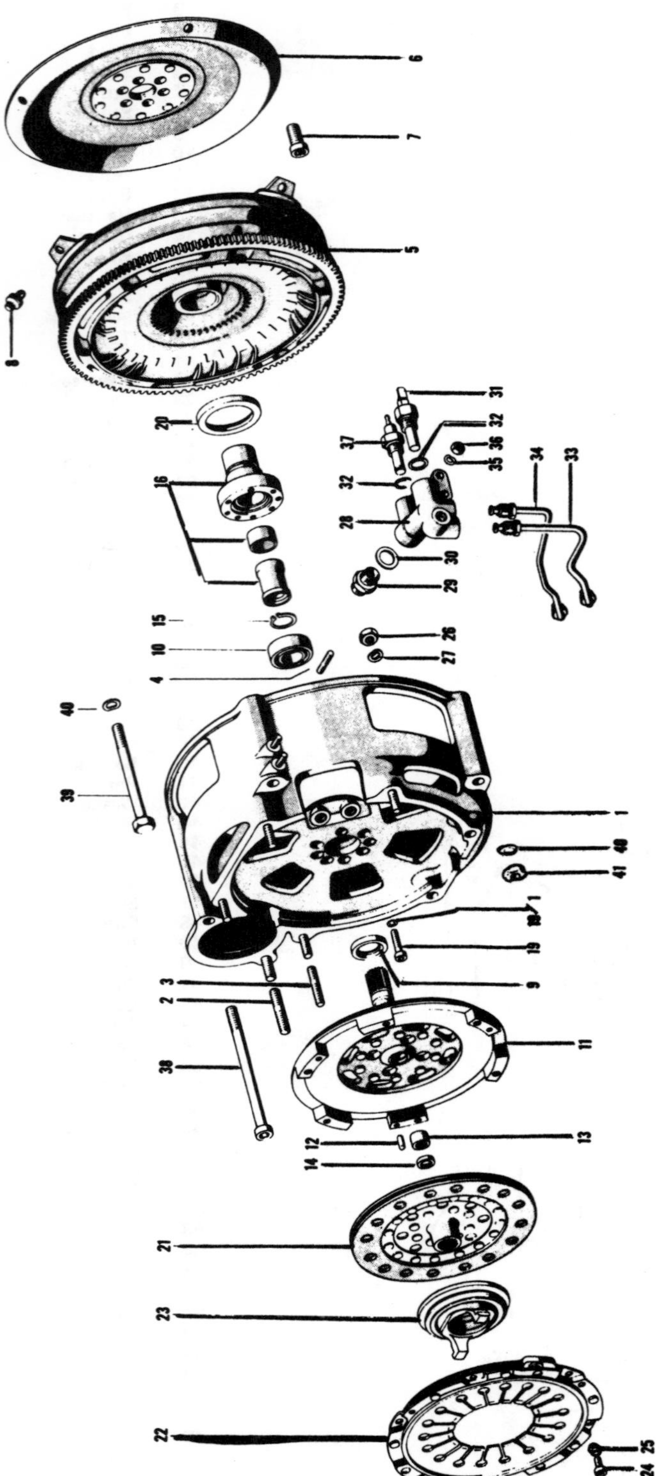

FIG 6 – SPORTOMATIC TORQUE CONVERTER

1	Converter Housing
2	Stud
3	Stud
4	Stud
5	Converter
6	Driving Disc
7	Screw
8	Screw
9	Ring
10	Bearing
11	Turbine Shaft
12	Pin
13	Bush
14	Ring
15	Ring
16	Support
19	Screw
19/1	Ring
20	Ring
21	Clutch Disc
22	Pressure Plate
23	Bearing
24	Screw
25	Ring
26	Nut
27	Washer
28	Switch Housing
29	Connecting Piece
30	Ring
31	Temperature Switch
32	Ring
33	Pressure Pipe
34	Return Pipe
35	Washer
36	Nut
37	Thermometer Element
38	Screw
39	Bolt
40	Washer
41	Nut

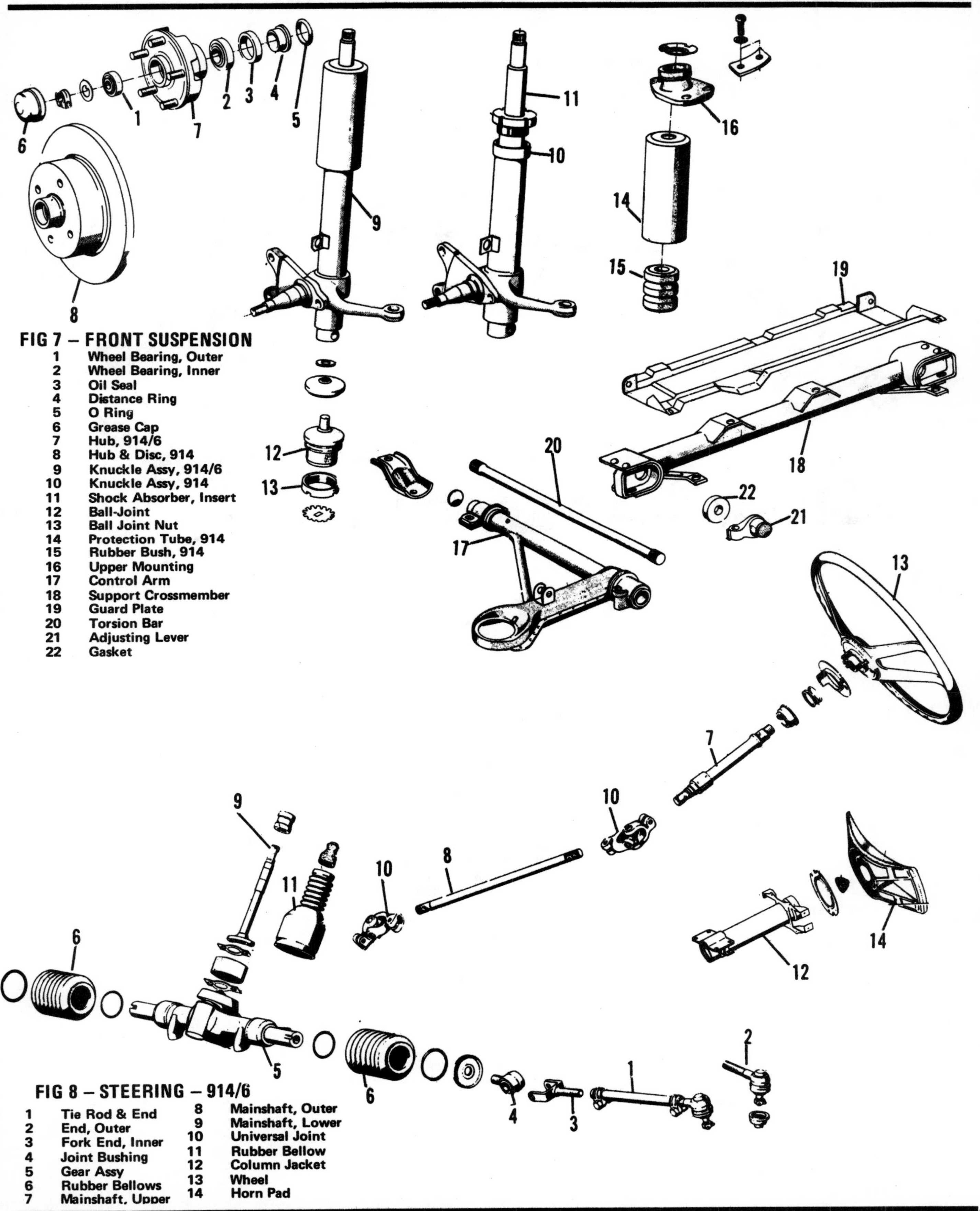

FIG 7 – FRONT SUSPENSION

1 Wheel Bearing, Outer
2 Wheel Bearing, Inner
3 Oil Seal
4 Distance Ring
5 O Ring
6 Grease Cap
7 Hub, 914/6
8 Hub & Disc, 914
9 Knuckle Assy, 914/6
10 Knuckle Assy, 914
11 Shock Absorber, Insert
12 Ball-Joint
13 Ball Joint Nut
14 Protection Tube, 914
15 Rubber Bush, 914
16 Upper Mounting
17 Control Arm
18 Support Crossmember
19 Guard Plate
20 Torsion Bar
21 Adjusting Lever
22 Gasket

FIG 8 – STEERING – 914/6

1 Tie Rod & End
2 End, Outer
3 Fork End, Inner
4 Joint Bushing
5 Gear Assy
6 Rubber Bellows
7 Mainshaft, Upper
8 Mainshaft, Outer
9 Mainshaft, Lower
10 Universal Joint
11 Rubber Bellow
12 Column Jacket
13 Wheel
14 Horn Pad

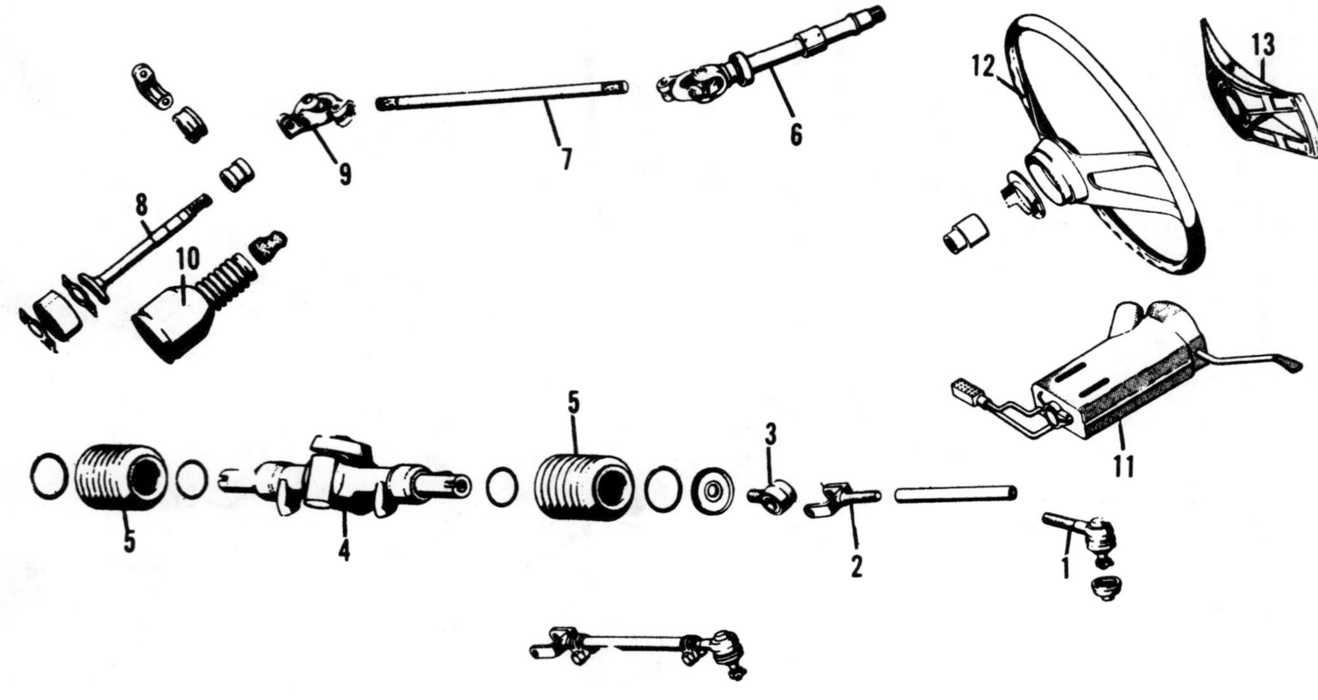

FIG 9 – STEERING – 914

1	Tie Rod End, Outer
2	Fork End, Inner
3	Joint Bushing
4	Gear Assembly
5	Rubber Bellows
6	Mainshaft, Upper
7	Mainshaft, Center
8	Mainshaft, Lower
9	Universal Joint
10	Rubber Bellow
11	Column Jacket
12	Wheel
13	Horn Pad

Ignition, Starting & Charging—TIME

OPERATION INDEX

Tune-Up, Minor *1*
Tune-Up, Major *2*
Compression Test *3*
Distributor, R & R Or Renew *4*
Distributor Cap, Renew *5*
Ignition Cable Set, Renew *6*
Vacuum Control Unit, Renew *7*
Ignition Coil, Renew *8*
Starter & Ignition Switch, Renew *9*
Starter, R & R Or Renew *10*
Starter Solenoid, Renew *11*
Starter Bendix Drive, Renew *12*
Starter, R & R & Overhaul *13*
Voltage Regulator, Renew *14*
Generator Or Alternator, R & R Or Renew *15*
Generator Or Alternator, R & R & Overhaul *16*
Alternator Diodes, Renew *17*
Generator Carbon Brushes, Renew *18*
Generator Ball Bearings, Renew *19*
Generator Or Alternator Pulley, Renew *20*

1—TUNE-UP, MINOR
Includes: Renew points, condenser and plugs, set spark timing and adjust carburetor idle or fuel injection system
Type 911 .... 1.6
Type 912 .... 1.3
Type 914 .... 2.5
Type 914/6 .... 2.1

2—TUNE-UP, MAJOR
Includes: Check compression, clean or renew and adjust spark plugs. R & R distributor, renew points and condenser. Adjust ignition and timing, carburetor and fan belts. Clean battery terminals and service air cleaner. Check oil and adjust valve clearance.
Type 911 .... 3.7
Type 912 .... 2.3
Type 914 .... 1.9
Type 914/6 .... 4.2

3—COMPRESSION TEST
Exc Below 0.5
Type 911 .... 0.8
Type 914/6 .... 0.7

4—DISTRIBUTOR, R & R OR RENEW
Exc Below 0.5
Type 912 .... 0.4
Type 914 .... 0.7

5—DISTRIBUTOR CAP, RENEW
Exc Below 0.3
Type 914 .... 0.2

6—IGNITION CABLE SET, RENEW
Exc Below 0.5
Type 912 & 914 .... 0.4

7—VACUUM CONTROL UNIT RENEW
All Models 0.9

8—IGNITION COIL, RENEW
Exc Below 0.3
Type 914 & 914/6 .... 0.2

9—STARTER & IGNITION SWITCH, RENEW
Exc Below 0.4
Type 914 .... 1.8

10—STARTER, R & R OR RENEW
Exc Below 0.7
Type 914 .... 0.6

11—STARTER SOLENOID, RENEW
Exc Below 0.8
Type 914/6 .... 0.9

12—STARTER BENDEX DRIVE, RENEW
Exc Below 1.4
Type 914/6 .... 1.5

13—STARTER, R & R & OVERHAUL
Exc Below 2.2
Type 914/6 .... 2.3

14—VOLTAGE REGULATOR, RENEW
Exc Below 0.2
Type 911 & 912 .... 0.3

15—GENERATOR OR ALTERNATOR, R & R OR RENEW
Type 911 .... 0.6
Type 912 .... 1.1
Type 914 .... 2.0
Type 914/6 .... 4.2

16—GENERATOR OR ALTERNATOR, R & R & OVERHAUL
Type 911 .... 1.6
Type 912 .... 2.6
Type 914/6 .... 5.2

17—ALTERNATOR DIODES, RENEW
Type 914—
Positive 2.6
Exciter 2.7
Negative 2.8
All 3.2
Type 914/6—
Positive 4.8
Exciter 4.9
Negative 5.0
All 5.4

18—GENERATOR CARBON BRUSHES, RENEW
Generator removed
All Models 0.5

19—GENERATOR BALL BEARINGS, RENEW
Generator removed
Exc Below 0.6
Type 912 .... 0.2

20—GENERATOR OR ALTERNATOR PULLEY, RENEW
All Models 0.2

Fuel, Emission Controls, Intake & Exhaust Systems—TIME

OPERATION INDEX

Carburetor(S), R & R Or Renew *1*
Carburetor(S), R & R & Overhaul *2*
Mechanical Fuel Injection Pump, R & R Or Renew *3*
Injection Pipe(S), Renew *4*
Fuel Delivery Pump, Renew *5*
Intake Pipe(S), Renew *6*
Intake Venturis, Renew *7*
Throttle Butterfly Housing, Renew *8*
Injection Valves Renew *9*
Changeover Shaft, Renew *10*
Torsion Springs Or Lever, Renew *11*
Injection Pump Belt, Renew *12*
Cold Start Magnet, Renew *13*
Engine Speed Relay Or Delay Switch, Renew *14*
Series Switch, Renew *15*
Single Element Regulator, Renew *16*
Electronic Control Unit Cables, Renew *17*
Electronic Control Unit, Renew *18*
Power Supply Or Fuel Pump Relay, Renew *19*
Electric Fuel Pump, Renew *20*
Intake Air Distributor, R & R Or Renew *21*
Temperature Sensor(S), Renew *22*
Additional Air Regulator Renew *23*
Pressure Regulator Or Sensor, Renew *24*
Throttle Butterfly Stud Pipes, Renew *25*
Temperature Switch, Renew *26*
Cold Start Switch, Renew *27*
Throttle Butterfly Switch, R & R & Adjust *28*
Injection Valve(S), Renew *29*
Fuel Pump, R & R Or Renew *30*
Fuel Tank, R & R Or Renew *31*
Intake Manifold, Renew *32*
Muffler, Renew *33*
Tail Pipe With Muffler, Renew *34*
Tail Pipe Extension Renew *35*

1—CARBURETOR(S),R & R OR RENEW
Solex 40 PI Or 40 PII4 —
One 0.9
Two—
Type 911 .... 1.1
Type 912 .... 1.3
Three 1.3
Six 2.1
Weber 40 IDA Or 40 IDS—
Left Or Right—
Type 911 .... 0.9
Type 914/6 .... 1.2
Both—
Type 911 .... 1.2
Type 914/6 .... 1.6

2—CARBURETOR(S), R & R & OVERHAUL
Solex 40 PI Or 40 PII4—
One—
Type 911 .... 1.6
Type 912 .... 1.9
Two—
Type 911 .... 2.0
Type 912 .... 3.2
Three 2.4
Six 4.1
Weber 40 IDA Or 40 IDS—
Left Or Right—
Type 911 .... 2.7
Type 914/6 .... 2.8
Both—
All Models 4.6

3—MECHANICAL FUEL INJECTION PUMP, R & R OR RENEW
Type 911 .... 1.5

4—INJECTION PIPE(S), RENEW
Type 911—
Left Each 0.5
Right Each 0.4
Each Additional 0.1
All 1.2

5—FUEL DELIVERY PUMP, RENEW
Type 911 .... 0.7

6—INTAKE PIPE(S), RENEW
Type 911—
Left 1.0
Right 0.6
Both 1.2

7—INTAKE VENTURIS, RENEW
Type 911—
One 0.3
All 0.6

8—THROTTLE BUTTERFLY HOUSING, RENEW
Type 911—
Left 1.2
Right 0.8
Both 1.6

9—INJECTION VALVES, RENEW
Type 911—
One Side 0.5
All 0.7

10—CHANGEOVER SHAFT, RENEW
Type 911—
Exc Below 1.1
Sportomatic 1.2

11—TORSION SPRINGS OR LEVER, RENEW
Type 911 .... 0.3

(Continued)

Fuel, Emission Controls, Intake & Exhaust Systems—TIME Cont'd

12—INJECTION PUMP BELT, RENEW
Type 911—
Exc Below 1.4
Sportomatic 1.6

13—COLD START MAGNET, RENEW
Type 911 ....0.4

14—ENGINE SPEED RELAY OR DELAY SWITCH, RENEW
Type 911 ....0.2

15—SERIES SWITCH, RENEW
Type 911 ....0.3

16—SINGLE ELEMENT REGULATOR, RENEW
Type 911 ....0.2

17—ELECTRONIC CONTROL UNIT CABLES, RENEW
Type 914 ....1.1

18—ELECTRONIC CONTROL UNIT, RENEW
Type 914 ....0.4

19—POWER SUPPLY OR FUEL PUMP RELAY, RENEW
Type 914 ....0.2

20—ELECTRIC FUEL PUMP, RENEW
Type 914 ....0.6

21—INTAKE AIR DISTRIBUTOR, R & R OR RENEW
Type 914 ....1.3

22—TEMPERATURE SENSOR(S), RENEW
Type 914—
Cylinder Head 0.3
Intake Air Distributor 0.2

23—ADDITIONAL AIR REGULATOR, RENEW
Type 914 ....0.2

24—PRESSURE REGULATOR OR SENSOR, RENEW
Type 914 ....0.3

25—THROTTLE BUTTERFLY STUB PIPES, RENEW
Includes: Adjust throttle butterfly switch & engine idle
Type 914 ....0.7

26—TEMPERATURE SWITCH, RENEW
Type 914 ....0.3

27—COLD START SWITCH, RENEW
Type 914 ....0.5

28—THROTTLE BUTTERFLY SWITCH, R & R & ADJUST
Type 914 ....0.6

29—INJECTION VALVE(S), RENEW
Type 914—
One 0.4
Two On Same Side 0.7
All 1.0

30—FUEL PUMP, R & R OR RENEW
Mechanical—
All Models 0.4
Electrical—
Exc Below 0.6
Type 911 ....0.3

31—FUEL TANK, R & R OR RENEW
Type 911 & 912 ....1.4
Type 914 & 914/6 ....0.8

32—INTAKE MANIFOLD, RENEW
Left Or Right—
Type 911 ....1.5
Type 912 ....1.1
Type 914/6 ....①5.1
①Includes R & R Engine

33—MUFFLER, RENEW
Exc Below 0.4
Type 912 ....①1.2
①Includes R & R Tail Pipe

34—TAIL PIPE WITH MUFFLER, RENEW
Type 912 & 914 ....0.3

35—TAIL PIPE EXTENSIN, RENEW
All Models 0.3

Engine Cooling & Heater System—TIME

OPERATION INDEX

Blower, R & R Or Renew 1
Impeller, Renew 2
Blower Or Air Guide Housing, Renew 3
Thermostat, Renew 4
Heating System, Repair 5
Control Valve, Renew 6
Heat Exchanger, R & R Or Renew 7
Heat Control Box, R & R Or Renew 8
Distributor Pipe, Renew 9
Heat Control Cable, Renew 10

1—BLOWER, R & R OR RENEW
Exc Below 0.8
Type 912 ....0.7
—NOTE—
To Renew, Add 0.1

2—IMPELLER, RENEW
Type 911 ....0.2
Type 912 ....0.1
Type 914 ....①4.2
Type 914/6 ....①3.6
①Includes: R & R Engine

3—BLOWER OR AIR GUIDE HOUSING, RENEW
Type 911 ....0.5
Type 912 ....①2.4
Type 914 ....①5.1
①Includes: R & R Engine

4—THERMOSTAT, RENEW
Exc Below 0.4
Type 914 ....0.5

5—HEATING SYSTEM, REPAIR
Includes: Free & adjust flaps, joints & control cables.
All Models 1.0

6—CONTROL VALVE, RENEW
All Models 0.8

7—HEAT EXCHANGER, R & R OR RENEW
Left Or Right—
Exc Below 0.6
Type 914 ....0.7
Type 914/6 ....0.9
Both—
Exc Below 1.0
Type 914 ....1.2
Type 914/6 ....1.3

8—HEAT CONTROL BOX, R & R OR RENEW
Left Or Right—
Exc Below 0.5
Type 914 & 914/6 ....0.3
Both—
Exc Below 0.9
Type 914 & 914/6 ....0.5

9—DISTRIBUTOR PIPE, RENEW
All Models 1.3

10—HEAT CONTROL CABLE, RENEW
Exc Below 0.6
Type 914 ....0.5

Engine—TIME

OPERATION INDEX

Engine, R & R 1
Engine, R & R & Overhaul 2
Cylinder Head(S), Renew 3
Valves, Grind 4
Valve Spring, Renew 5
Valve Cover Or Gasket, Renew 6
Rocker Arm Carrier, Renew 7
Rocker Arm Shaft, Renew 8
Rocker Arm, Renew 9
Valves, Adjust 10
Push Rods, Renew 11
Push Rod Tubes Or Oil Return Tubes, Seal 12
Chain Housing, R & R Or Renew 13
Chain Housing Covers, R & R Or Renew 14
Chain Sprocket, Renew 15
Chain Tensioner, Renew 16
Chain Guide Ramps, Renew 17
Camshaft Housings, Renew 18
Camshaft, Renew 19
Intermediate Shaft, Renew 20
Camshaft Sprocket, Renew 21
Oil Pump, Renew 22
Oil Cooler, R & R Or Renew 23
Piston Ring(S), Renew 24
Cylinder Banks With Camshaft Housings, Renew 25
Crankcase, Renew 26
Connecting Rod Bearings, Renew 27
Main Bearings, Renew 28
Main Bearings & Connecting Rod Bearings, Renew 29
Crankshaft Oil Seal, Renew 30
Crankcase, R & R Or Renew 31
Piston(S), Renew 32
Connecting Rods, R & R Or Renew 33
Crankshaft Pulley, Renew 34

1—ENGINE, R & R
Does not include transfer of any part of engine or replacement of special equipment
Type 911 ....①2.7
Type 912 ....1.5
Type 914 ....①3.8
Type 914/6 ....①3.5
①Includes R & R Transmission

2—ENGINE, R & R & OVERHAUL
Includes: Rebore cylinders with boring bar, renew pistons, rings, pins, bearings, grind valves, plastigauge bearings and perform minor tune-up.
Type 911 ....42.7
Type 912 ....40.7
Type 914 ....23.3
Type 914/6 ....45.7

3—CYLINDER HEAD(S), RENEW
Includes: R & R engine
One—
Type 912 ....3.9
Type 914 ....6.7
Two—
Type 912 ....5.0
Type 914 ....8.1
All One Side—
Type 911 ....7.2
Type 914/6 ....10.0
All Both Sides—
Type 911 ....14.7
Type 914/6 ....15.5

4—VALVES, GRIND
Includes: R & R engine
One Cylinder Head—
Type 911 ....①8.1
Type 912 ....5.2
Type 914 ....7.7
Type 914/6 ....①10.9
Two Cylinder Heads—
Type 912 ....7.4
Type 914 ....9.8

(Continued)

Engine—TIME Cont'd

- All One Bank—
  - Type 911 ... 9.7
  - Type 914/6 ... 12.5
- All Both Banks—
  - Type 911 ... 19.7
  - Type 914/6 ... 20.5

①Includes: R & R All Cylinders On One Bank.

5—VALVE SPRING, RENEW

- Each—
  - Type 911—
    - Intake ... 1.0
    - Exhaust ... ①3.2
  - Type 912 ... 0.6
  - Type 914 ... ①4.3
  - Type 914/6 ... ①4.1

①Includes: R & R Engine.

6—VALVE COVER OR GASKET, RENEW

- Upper Each—
  - Exc Below ... 0.4
  - Type 912 & 914 ... 0.3
- Upper Both—
  - Exc Below ... 0.7
  - Type 912 & 914 ... 0.4
- Lower Each—
  - Type 911 ... 0.4
  - Type 914/6 ... 1.2
- Lower Both—
  - Type 911 ... 0.7
  - Type 914/6 ... 2.0
- All Four—
  - Type 911 ... 1.0
  - Type 914/6 ... 2.8

7—ROCKER ARM CARRIER, RENEW

- One Side—
  - Type 912 ... 0.8
- Both Sides—
  - Type 912 ... 1.4

8—ROCKER ARM SHAFT, RENEW

- Type 911 ... 1.0
- Type 914/6 ... ①4.1

①Includes: R & R Engine.

9—ROCKER ARMS RENEW

- Upper—
  - Left Or Right (One)—
    - Type 911 ... 1.0
    - Type 912 ... 0.5
    - Type 914 ... 0.9
    - Type 914/6 ... 0.8
  - Each Additional ... 0.4
- Lower—
  - Left Or Right Each—
    - Type 911 ... 1.0
    - Type 914/6 ... 1.5
  - Each Additional ... 0.5

10—VALVES, ADJUST

- Type 911 ... 1.3
- Type 912 ... 0.4
- Type 914 ... 02.7
- Type 914/6 ... 1.1

11—PUSH RODS, RENEW

- One Side—
  - Type 912 ... 0.6
  - Type 914 ... ①4.4
- Both Sides—
  - Type 912 ... 1.2
  - Type 914 ... ①4.8

①Includes: R & R Engine

12—PUSH ROD TUBES OR OIL RETURN TUBES, SEAL

Includes: R & R engine

- One Side—
  - Type 911 ... 6.9
  - Type 912 ... 3.9
  - Type 914 ... 4.7
  - Type 914/6 ... 7.7
- Both Sides—
  - Type 911 ... 11.0
  - Type 912 ... 5.0
  - Type 914 ... 5.4
  - Type 914/6 ... 11.8

13—CHAIN HOUSING, R & R OR RENEW

Includes: R & R engine

- Left Or Right—
  - Type 911 ... 7.7
  - Type 914/6 ... 8.5
- Both—
  - Type 911 ... 11.7
  - Type 914/6 ... 12.5

14—CHAIN HOUSING COVERS, R & R OR RENEW

- Left Or Right—
  - Type 911 ... 1.1
  - Type 914/6 ... ①4.1
- Both—
  - Type 911 ... 1.4
  - Type 914/6 ... ①4.5

①Includes: R & R Engine

15—CHAIN SPROCKET, RENEW

- Left Or Right—
  - Type 911 ... 2.0
  - Type 914/6 ... ①4.5

①Includes: R & R Engine

16—CHAIN TENSIONER, RENEW

- Mechanical—
  - Both—
    - Type 911 ... 3.5
    - Type 914/6 ... ①5.4
- Oil Type—
  - One—
    - Type 911 ... 1.6
    - Type 914/6 ... ①4.5
  - Both—
    - Type 911 ... 2.3
    - Type 914/6 ... ①5.4

①Includes: R & R Engine

17—CHAIN GUIDE RAMPS, RENEW

- Left Or Right—
  - Type 911 ... 2.0
  - Type 914/6 ... ①6.8

①Includes: R & R Engine

18—CAMSHAFT HOUSINGS, RENEW

Includes: R & R engine

- Left Or Right—
  - Type 911 ... 9.2
  - Type 914/6 ... 10.0
- Both—
  - Type 911 ... 14.7
  - Type 914/6 ... 15.5

19—CAMSHAFT, RENEW

Includes: R & R engine

- One—
  - Type 911 ... 6.5
  - Type 912 ... 11.5
  - Type 914 ... 11.1
  - Type 914/6 ... 7.3
- Both—
  - Type 911 ... 9.5
  - Type 914/6 ... 10.3

20—INTERMEDIATE SHAFT, RENEW

- Type 911 ... 20.0
- Type 914/6 ... 20.8

21—CAMSHAFT SPROCKET, RENEW

- Left Or Right—
  - Type 911 ... 4.7
  - Type 914/6 ... 5.5
- Both—
  - Type 911 ... 5.5
  - Type 914/6 ... 6.3

22—OIL PUMP, RENEW

- Exc Below ... 17.3
- Type 912 ... 1.1
- Type 914 ... ②5.4

①Includes: R & R Engine, Disassemble & Assemble.
②Includes R & R Engine.

23—OIL COOLER, R & R OR RENEW

Includes: R & R engine

- Exc Below ... 4.2
- Type 911 ... 3.4
- Type 912 ... 2.6

24—PISTON RING(S), RENEW

Pistons removed.

- One Piston—
  - Exc Below ... 0.3
  - Type 914 ... 0.2
- All One Side—
  - Exc Below ... 0.6
  - Type 912 ... 0.4
  - Type 914 ... 0.3
- All Both Sides—
  - Exc Below ... 1.0
  - Type 912 ... 0.8
  - Type 914 ... 0.6

25—CYLINDER BANKS WITH CAMSHAFT HOUSINGS, RENEW

Includes: R&R engine

- One—
  - Type 911 ... 6.7
  - 914/6 ... 7.5
- Both—
  - Type 911 ... 10.3
  - Type 914/6 ... 11.1

26—CRANKCASE, RENEW

Includes: R&R engine, disassemble, inspect, clean, reassemble & tune.

- Type 911 ... 25.5
- Type 912 ... 13.5
- Type 914 ... 14.2
- Type 914/6 ... 26.3

27—CONNECTING ROD BEARINGS, RENEW

Includes: R&R engine, disassemble, clean, inspect, reassemble & tune.

- Type 911 ... 25.0
- Type 912 ... 13.3
- Type 914 ... 13.4
- Type 914/6 ... 25.8

28—MAIN BEARINGS, RENEW

Includes: R&R engine. Disassemble, inspect, clean, reassemble & tune.

- Type 911 ... 26.2
- Type 912 ... 14.4
- Type 914 ... 14.6
- Type 914/6 ... 27.0

29—MAIN BEARINGS & CONNECTING ROD BEARINGS, RENEW

Includes: R&R engine, disassemble, inspect, clean, reassemble & tune.

- Exc Below ... 15.2
- Type 911 ... 27.5
- Type 914/6 ... 28.3

30—CRANKSHAFT OIL SEAL, RENEW

- Front—
  - Type 911 ... 0.7
  - Type 912 ... 1.0
  - Type 914 ... ①4.2
  - Type 914/6 ... ①4.1
- Rear—
  - Exc Below ... ①4.5
  - Type 911 ... ①3.7
  - Type 912 ... ①2.5

①Includes: R&R Engine

31—CRANKSHAFT, R&R OR RENEW

Includes: R&R engine, desassemble, inspect, clean, reassemble & tune.

- Type 911 ... 25.7
- Type 912 ... 14.0
- Type 914 ... 14.2
- Type 914/6 ... 26.5

—NOTE—

To Renew Distributor Drive Gear, Add ... 0.5

32—PISTON(S), RENEW

Includes: R&R engine, disassemble, inspect, clean, reassemble & tune.

- One—
  - Type 911 ... 26.0
  - Type 912 ... 14.3
  - Type 914 ... 14.5
  - Type 914/6 ... 26.7

(Continued)

Engine—TIME Cont'd

Each Additional (03) 0.3

—NOTE—

To Ream & Renew Connecting Rod Bushings, Each, Add 0.5

33—CONNECTING RODS, R&R OR RENEW

Includes: R&R engine, disassemble, inspect, clean, reassemble & tune.

One—
- Type 911 .... 26.0
- Type 912 .... 14.3
- Type 914 .... 14.5
- Type 914/6 .... 26.7

Each Additional 0.3

—NOTE—

To Ream & Renew Connecting Rod Bushings, Each, Add 0.5

34—CRANKSHAFT PULLEY, RENEW

Type 911 .... 0.3
Type 912 .... 0.9
Type 914/6 .... ①3.7
①*Includes: R&R Engine,*

Clutch, Mounts, Transmissions & Differentials—TIME

OPERATION INDEX

Flywheel, R&R Or Renew 1
Flywheel Starter Gear, Renew 2
Clutch Or Disc, Renew 3
Release Bearings, Renew 4
Input Shaft Needle Roller Bearing, Renew 5
Release Fork (Or Lever), Renew 6
Clutch Pedal, Adjust 7
Throwout Or Clutch Lever, Renew 8
Servo Motor, Renew 9
Clutch Cable, Renew 10
Vacuum Reservoir, Renew 11
Engine Mounts, Renew 12
Gear Box, R&R Or Renew 13
Manual Trans., R&R & Overhaul 14
Transmission Housing, Renew 15
Differential Side Cover Seal, Renew 16
Axle Flange Oil Seals, Renew 17
Clutch Lever Shaft Bushing, Renew 18
Differential Housing, R&R Or Renew 19
Gearbox Cover, Renew 20
Selector Forks, Sleeves Or Shafts, Renew 21
Input Shaft Oil Seal, Renew 22
Converter & Starter Ring, Renew 23
Driving Disc, Renew 24
Turbine Shaft, R&R Or Renew 25
Turbine Shaft Oil Seal Or Sealing Ring, Renew 26
Thermostat, Renew 27

1—FLYWHEEL, R&R OR RENEW

Type 911 .... ①3.5
Type 912 .... ①2.1
Type 914 .... ②4.6
Type 914/6 .... ①4.3
①*Includes: R&R Engine*
②*Includes: R&R Engine & Clutch.*

2—FLYWHEEL STARTER GEAR, RENEW

Type 911 .... ①4.3
Type 912 .... ①2.9
Type 914 .... ②5.4
Type 914/6 .... ①5.4
①*Includes: R&R Engine*
②*Includes: R&R Engine & Clutch*

3—CLUTCH OR DISC, RENEW

Type 911 .... ①3.0
Type 912 .... ①1.8
Type 914 .... ②2.5
Type 914/6 .... ②2.6
①*Includes: R&R Engine*
②*Includes: R&R Gearbox*

4—RELEASE BEARING, RENEW

Gearbox removed
All Models 0.3

5—INPUT SHAFT NEEDLE ROLLER BEARING, RENEW

Includes: R&R engine
Type 911 .... 3.8
Type 912 .... 1.9
Type 914 .... 4.4
Type 914/6 .... 4.6

6—RELEASE FORK (OR LEVER), RENEW

Gearbox removed
Exc Below 0.2
Type 912 .... 0.3

7—CLUTCH PEDAL, ADJUST

All Models 0.2

8—THROWOUT OR CLUTCH LEVER, RENEW

Gearbox removed
All Models 0.5

9—SERVO MOTOR, RENEW

Gearbox removed
All Models 0.3

10—CLUTCH CABLE, RENEW

Exc Below 0.8
Type 911 .... 0.7

11—VACUUM RESERVOIR, RENEW

Exc Below 0.2
Type 911 .... 0.4

12—ENGINE MOUNTS, RENEW

Engine, One—
- Exc Below, ... 0.4
- Type 914/6 .... ①04.2

Engine, Two—
- Type 914 .... 0.8

Trans—
- Exc Below 0.7
- Type 911 & 912 .... 0.4

①*Includes: R&R Engine*

13—GEARBOX, R&R OR RENEW

Exc Below 2.7
Type 914 .... 2.2
Type 914/6 .... 2.3

14—MANUAL TRANS., R&R & OVERHAUL

Exc Below 8.7
Type 914 .... 8.2
Type 914/6 .... 8.3

—NOTE—

For Sportomatic, Add 0.4

15—TRANSMISSION HOUSING, RENEW

Exc Below 6.3
Type 914 .... 5.8
Type 914/6 .... 5.9

16—DIFFERENTIAL SIDE COVER SEAL, RENEW

All Models 1.0

17—AXLE FLANGE OIL SEALS, RENEW

Left Or Right—
- Exc Below 0.9
- Type 914 & 914/6 .... 0.5

18—CLUTCH LEVER SHAFT BUSHING, RENEW

Trans. Removed
All Models 0.4

19—DIFFERENTIAL HOUSING, R&R OR RENEW

Trans removed
All Models 2.4

20—GEARBOX COVER, RENEW

All Models—
- Front Or Rear 0.5

21—SELECTOR FORKS, SLEEVES OR SHAFTS, RENEW

Trans removed
All Models 2.7

22—INPUT SHAFT OIL SEAL, RENEW

Exc Below 0.4
Type 911 .... 0.3

23—CONVERTER & STARTER, RING GEAR, RENEW

Trans removed
All Models 0.2

24—DRIVING DISC, RENEW

Trans removed
All Models 0.6

25—TURBINE SHAFT, R&R OR RENEW

Trans removed
All Models 0.7

26—TURBINE SHAFT OIL SEAL OR SEALING RING, RENEW

Trans removed
All Models 0.9

27—THERMOSTAT, RENEW

All Models 0.6

Brakes, Steering, Suspension & Rear Axle—TIME

OPERATION INDEX

Brake Shoes Or Friction Pads, Renew 1
Master Cylinder, Renew 2
Master Cylinder, R&R & Overhaul 3
Hydraulic Brake Fluid Reservoir, Renew 4
Calipers, R&R Or Renew 5
Calipers, R&R & Overhaul 6
Disc(S), Renew 7
Disc Shroud, Renew 8
Power Brake Control, Renew 9
Bleed Brake System 10
Brake Hose, Renew 11
Handbrake Shoes, Renew 12
Handbrake Lever, Renew 13
Handbrake Cable(S), Renew 14
Pedal Cluster, R&R & Overhaul 15
Steering Gear, R&R Or Renew 16
Steering Gear, Overhaul 17
Tie Rods, Renew 18
Front Axle Assy, R&R Or Renew 19
Ball Joints, Renew 20
Torsion Bars, Renew 21
Struts Shock Abosrbers, Renew 22
Steering Lever, Renew 23
Wishbone, Renew 24
Hub(S), Renew 25
Hub Bearings, Renew 26
Hub Bearing Seals, Renew 27
Stabilizer Or Bushings, Renew 28
Rear Axle Complete, Overhaul 29
Radius Arm Bushing, Renew 30
Rear Coil Springs, Renew 31
Rear Control Arms, Renew 32
Rear Wheel Bearings, Renew 33
Half Shafts, Renew 34

1—BRAKE SHOES OR FRICTION PADS, RENEW

All Models—
- Front—
  - Left & Right 0.5
- Rear—
  - Left & Right—
    - Exc Below 0.8
    - Type 911 & 912 .... 0.5

2—MASTER CYLINDER, RENEW

Exc Below 1.3
Type 914 .... 1.6
Type 914/6 .... 1.7

3—MASTER CYLINDER, R&R & OVERHAUL

Exc Below 1.6
Type 914 .... 1.9

(Continued)

Brakes, Steering, Suspension & Rear Axle—TIME Cont'd

Type 914/6 .....2.0

4—HYDRAULIC BRAKE FLUID RESERVOIR, RENEW
Does not include bleed system.
Exc Below 0.3
Type 911 & 912 .....0.6

5—CALIPERS, R&R OR RENEW
Front—
Left Or Right—
Exc Below 0.6
Type 911 & 912 .....0.4
Both—
Exc Below 0.9
Type 911 & 912 .....0.8
Rear—
Left Or Right—
Exc Below 0.9
Type 911 & 912 .....0.4
Both—
Exc Below 1.3
Type 911 & 912 .....0.8

6—CALIPER, R&R & OVERHAUL
Front—
Each—
Exc Below 1.1
Type 911 & 912 .....0.9
Both—
Exc Below 1.8
Type 911 & 912 .....1.7
Rear—
Left Or Right—
Exc Below 1.4
Type 911 & 912 .....0.9
Both—
Exc Below 2.3
Type 911 & 912 .....1.7

7—DISC(S), RENEW
Front—
Each—
Exc Below 0.7
Type 914 .....0.9
Both—
Exc Below 1.2
Type 914 .....1.3
Rear—
Each—
Exc Below 1.0
Type 911 & 912 .....0.5
Both—
Exc Below 1.0
Type 911 & 912 .....0.5

8—DISC SHROUD, RENEW
Front—
Left Or Right—
Exc Below 0.7
Type 911 & 912 .....0.4
Both—
Exc Below 1.0
Type 911 & 912 .....0.6
Rear—
Left Or Right—
Exc Below 0.2
Type 911 & 912 .....0.4
Both—
Exc Below 0.3
Type 911 & 912 .....0.6

9—POWER BRAKE CONTROL, RENEW
Exc Below 1.6
Type 914 .....1.4

10—BLEED BERAKE SYSTEM
Single Circuit 0.5
Dual Circuit—
Exc Below 0.9
Type 911 & 912 .....0.7

11—BRAKE HOSE, RENEW
Front—
One—
Exc Below 0.7
Type 911 & 912 .....0.6
Both 0.8
Rear—
One—
Exc Below 0.8
Type 911 & 912 .....0.6
Both—
Exc Below 0.8
Type 914 .....1.0
Type 914/6 .....0.9

12—HANDBRAKE SHOES, RENEW
Each—
All Models 1.8
Both—
All Models 1.4

13—HANDBRAKE LEVER, RENEW
Exc Below 1.1
Type 914 .....0.8
Type 914/6 .....0.9

14—HANDBRAKE CABLE(S), RENEW
Left Or Right—
All Models 0.8
Both—
Exc Below 1.2
Type 914 .....1.0
Type 914/6 .....1.1

15—PEDAL CLUSTER, R&R & OVERHAUL
All Models 1.1

16—STEERING GEAR, R&R OR RENEW
L/Aux Heater 1.6
W/Aux Heater—
Exc Below 1.5
Type 914 .....1.6
Type 914/6 .....1.7

17—STEERING GEAR, OVERHAUL
Exc Below 1.0
Type 911 & 912 .....0.9

18—TIE RODS, RENEW
All Models—
Left Or Right 1.0
Both 1.2

19—FRONT AXLE ASSY, R&R OR RENEW
Exc Below 2.1
Type 914 .....2.0
Type 914/6 .....1.9

20—BALL JOINTS, RENEW
Left Or Right—
All Models 0.5
Both—
All Models 0.7

21—TORSION BARS, RENEW
All Models—
Front—
Each 0.5
Both 1.0
Rear—
Each 1.8
Both 3.3

22—STRUTS SHOCK ABSORBERS, RENEW
Front—
Each 1.2
Both 2.3
Rear—
Each—
Exc Below 0.9
Type 911 & 912 .....0.3
Both—
Exc Below 1.4
Type 911 & 912 .....0.4

—NOTE—
To Renew Thrust Bearings, Each, Add 0.2

23—STEERING LEVER, RENEW
All Models—
Left Or Right 0.8

24—WISHBONE, RENEW
Left Or Right—
All Models 0.9
Both—
All Models 1.4

25—HUB(S), RENEW
All Models—
Front—
One 0.9
Both 1.8

26—HUB BEARINGS, RENEW
All Models, Each 0.7

27—HUB BEARING SEALS, RENEW
All Models 0.5

28—STABILIZER OR BUSHING, RENEW
All Models 1.3

29—REAR AXLE COMPLETE, OVERHAUL
Trans removed
Exc Below 4.9
Type 911 & 912 .....7.0

30—RADIUS ARM BUSHINGS, RENEW
All Models 1.8

31—REAR COIL SPRINGS, RENEW
Type 914 & 914/6—
One 0.9
Both 1.4

32—REAR CONTROL ARMS, RENEW
Each—
Exc Below 2.5
Type 914 .....2.6
Type 914/6 .....2.7
Both—
Exc Below 4.6
Type 911 & 912 .....5.0

33—REAR WHEEL BEARINGS, RENEW
Left Or Right—
All Models 1.1
Both—
All Models 2.0

34—HALF SHAFTS, RENEW
Nadella—
Each 0.5
Both 0.9
Lobro—
Each—
Exc Below 1.2
Type 911 & 912 .....0.6
Both—
Exc Below 2.0
Type 911 & 912 .....1.1

Speedometer, W/S Wipers, Switches & Instruments—TIME

OPERATION INDEX
Speedometer Drive Cable, Renew 1
Speedometer, Renew 2
W/S Wiper Motor, Renew 3
W/S Wiper Mechanism, Renew 4
W/S Wiper Arm, Renew 5
W/S Wiper Control Switch, Renew 6
Combines Instrument, Renew 7
Fuel Gauge Sending Unit, Renew 8
Oil Pressure Sending Unit, Renew 9
Thermometer Element, Renew 10
Tachometer, Renew 11
Headlight Switch, Renew 12
Turn Flasher/Dimmer Switch, Renew 13
Dimmer Or Turn Flasher Switch, Renew 14
Stop Light Switch, Renew 15
Hazard Flasher Switch, Renew 16

1—SPEEDOMETER DRIVE CABLE, RENEW
Exc Below 0.7

(Continued)

Speedometer, W/S Wipers, Switches & Instruments—TIME Cont'd

Type 911 & 912 ....0.9

2—SPEEDOMETER, RENEW
Exc Below 0.2
Type 911 & 912 ....0.3

3—W/S WIPER MOTOR, RENEW
Type 911 ....1.3
Type 912 ....1.1
Type 914 ....0.3
Type 914/6 ....(1)2.4
(1)*Includes R&R Tank & Blower.*

4—W/S WIPER MECHANISM, RENEW
Exc Below 1.9
Type 911 ....1.2
Type 912 ....1.0

5—W/S WIPER ARM, RENEW
All Models, Each 0.2

6—W/S WIPER CONTROL SWITCH, RENEW
Exc Below 0.4
Type 914 ....0.5
Type 914/6 ....0.7

7—COMBINED INSTRUMENT, RENEW
Exc Below 0.2
Type 911 & 912 ....0.3

8—FUEL GAUGE SENDING UNIT, RENEW
All Models 0.2

9—OIL PRESSURE SENDING UNIT, RENEW
All Models 0.3

10—THERMOMETER ELEMENT, RENEW
All Models 0.3

11—TACHOMETER, RENEW
All Models 0.2

12—HEADLIGHT SWITCH, RENEW
All Models 0.3

13—TURN FLASHER/DIMMER SWITCH, RENEW
Type 914 ....1.8
Type 914/6 ....0.5

14—DIMMER OR TURN FLASHER SWITCH, RENEW
Type 911 &.912 ....0.4

15—STOP LIGHT SWITCH, RENEW
All Models—
Hydraulic 1.0
Mechanical 0.3

16—HAZARD FLASHER SWITCH, RENEW
Exc Below 0.2
Type 911 & 912 ....0.3

IDENTIFICATION

VEHICLE IDENTIFICATION........................354
ENGINE IDENTIFICATION..........................355

ILLUSTRATIONS

FIG 1 – ENGINE – BLOCK, OIL PAN & CRANKSHAFT
FIG 2 – ENGINE – HEAD, VALVES & MANIFOLD
FIG 3 – TRANSAXLE
FIG 4 – FRONT SUSPENSION & STEERING – R12, R15, R17
FIG 5 – FRONT SUSPENSION & STEERING – R8, R10
FIG 6 – FRONT SUSPENSION – R5
FIG 7 – STEERING – R5

OPERATION TIMES

A

Air Conditioner.................................. 364
Alternator.. 363
Automatic Transmission.................... 365
Axle Shaft.. 366

B

Brake Drums....................................... 366
Brakes... 365

C

Cables (Ignition)................................ 363
Calipers.. 366
Camshaft.. 365
Carburetor.. 363
Catalytic Converter........................... 364
Clutch... 365
Coil, Ignition....................................... 363
Compression Test.............................. 363
Cooling System.................................. 364
Crankshaft.. 365
Cylinder Block.................................... 364
Cylinder Head.................................... 364

D

Dash Gauges...................................... 367
Differential... 366
Disc Brakes.. 366
Distributor.. 363

E

Emission Controls.............................. 363
Engine Assembly............................... 364
Engine Mountings.............................. 365
Engine Oiling...................................... 364
Engine Tune-Up.................................. 363
Exhaust Gas Recirculation................ 364
Exhaust System.................................. 363

F

Flywheel.. 365
Front Suspension............................... 366
Fuel Gauges.. 367
Fuel Pump... 363
Fuel Tank.. 363

G

Generator.. 363

H

Hand Brake... 366
Headlight Switch................................ 367
Heater.. 364
Hose (Brake)....................................... 366
Hose (Radiator).................................. 364
Hydraulic Brakes................................ 365

I

Ignition.. 363
Ignition Coil.. 363
Ignition Switch................................... 363
Intake Manifold.................................. 363

L

Light Switches.................................... 367

M

Master Cylinder.................................. 365
Muffler.. 363

O

Oil Gauge.. 367
Oiling, Engine..................................... 364
Oil Pan.. 364
Oil Pump... 365

P

Parking Brake...................................... 366
Pistons... 365

R

Radiator... 364
Radiator Hose..................................... 364
Rear Axle... 367
Regulator... 363
Resonator.. 363
Rocker Arms....................................... 364

S

Shocks (Front).................................... 366
Shocks (Rear)...................................... 366
Speedometer....................................... 367
Springs (Front).................................... 366
Springs (Rear)..................................... 366
Starting Motor..................................... 363
Steering Gear...................................... 366
Steering Linkage................................. 366
Switches (Light).................................. 367

T

Temperature Gauge............................ 367
Thermostat.. 364
Timing Case Cover............................. 364
Timing Chain...................................... 364
Timing Gears...................................... 364
Torsion Bars.. 366
TransAxle.. 365
Transmission, Automatic.................... 365
Tune-Up, Engine................................. 363

U

Universals... 366

V

Valve Lifters.. 364
Valve System....................................... 364

W

Water Pump.. 364
Wheel Cylinders................................. 366
Windshield Wiper............................... 367

VEHICLE IDENTIFICATION

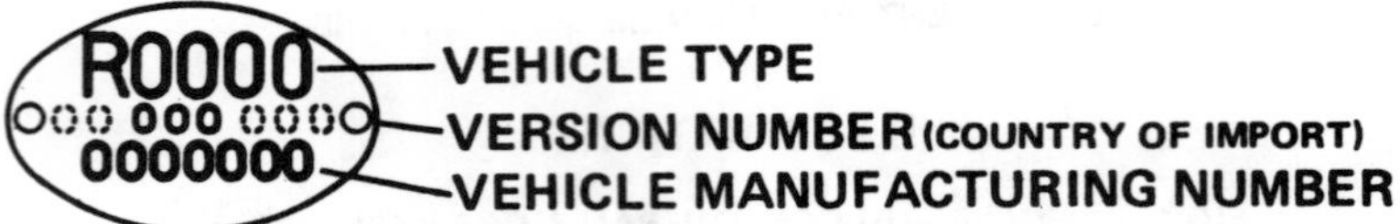

VEHICLE TYPES

R1130	R8	R1301	R15
R1132	R8	R1304	R15
R1152	R16	R1313	R17
R1153	R16	R1314	R17TL
R1172	R12 Sedan	R1323	R17
R1178	R12 Sedan	R1324	R17TL
R1190	R10	R1331	R12 Sta Wgn
R1192	R10	R1332	R12 Sta Wgn
R1228	R5		

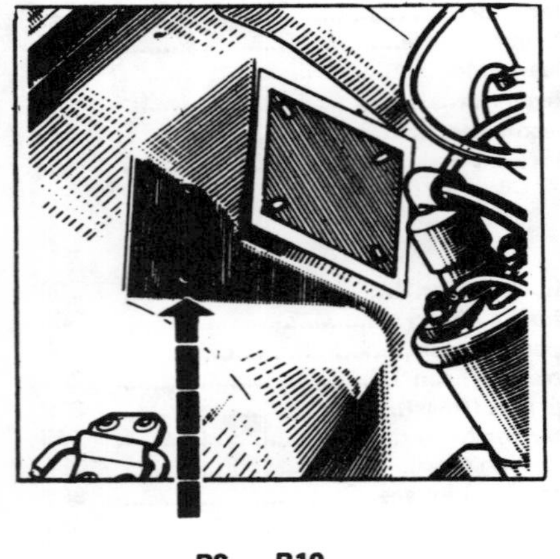

R8 R10

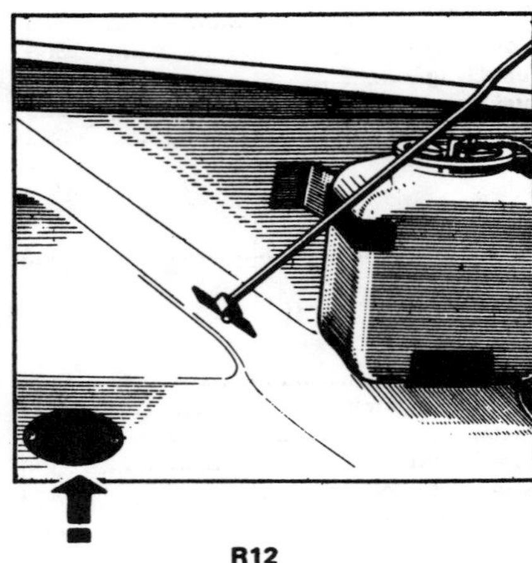

R12

R15

R16

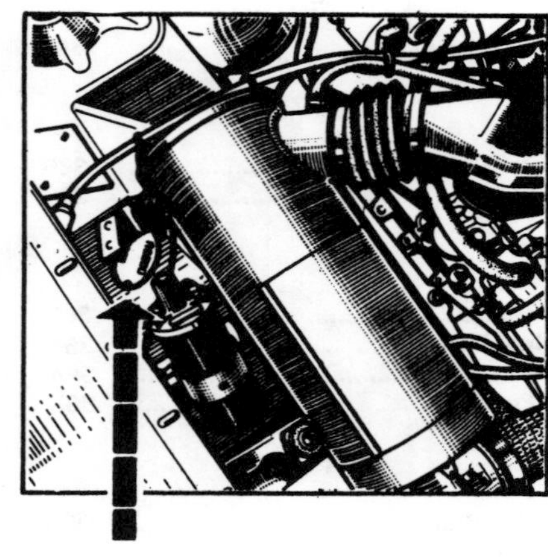

R17

R5

ENGINE IDENTIFICATION

R8 R10

R12

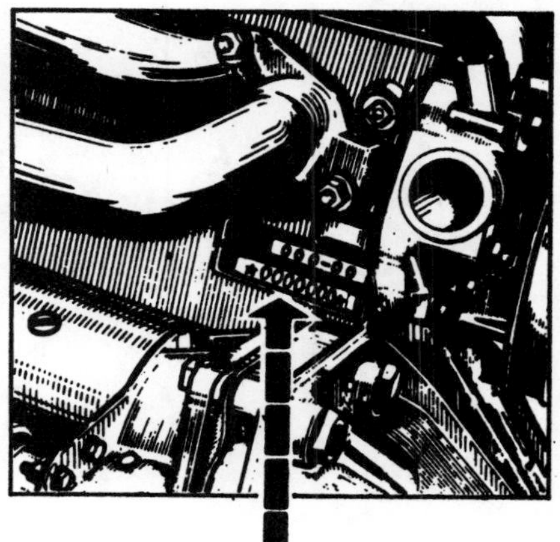

R15

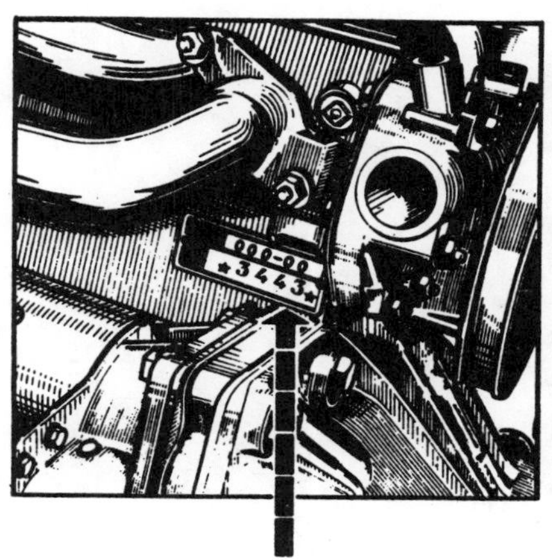

R16

R17

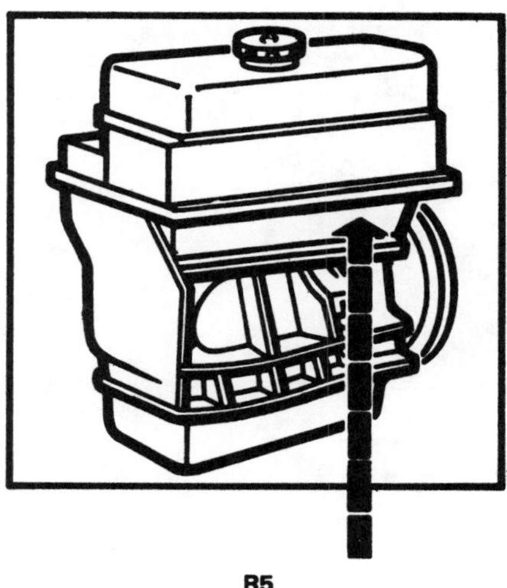

R5

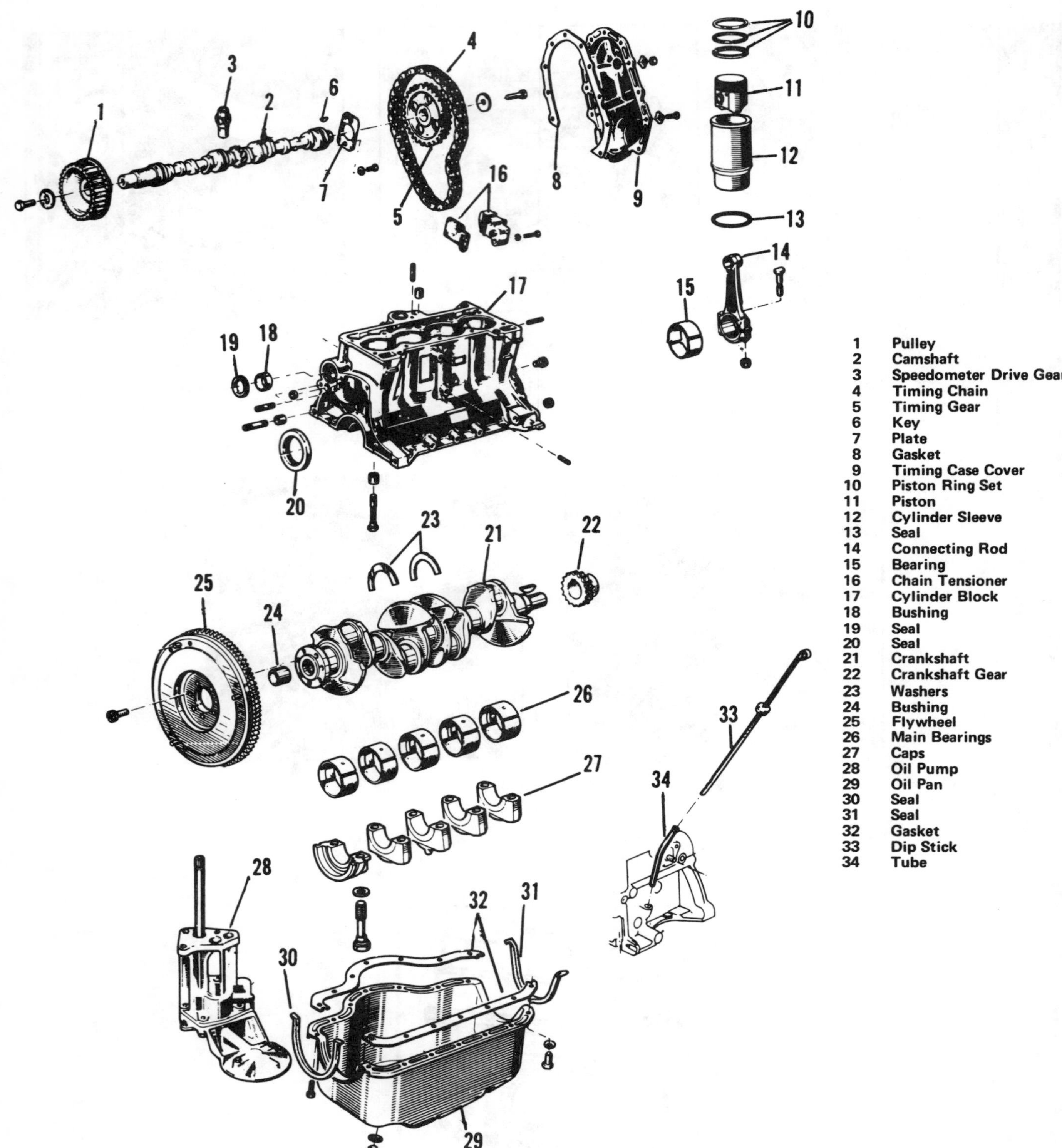
1
2
3
4
5
6
7
8
9
10
11
12
13
14
15
16
17
18
19
20
21
22
23
24
25
26
27
28
29
30
31
32
33
34
1 Pulley
2 Camshaft
3 Speedometer Drive Gear
4 Timing Chain
5 Timing Gear
6 Key
7 Plate
8 Gasket
9 Timing Case Cover
10 Piston Ring Set
11 Piston
12 Cylinder Sleeve
13 Seal
14 Connecting Rod
15 Bearing
16 Chain Tensioner
17 Cylinder Block
18 Bushing
19 Seal
20 Seal
21 Crankshaft
22 Crankshaft Gear
23 Washers
24 Bushing
25 Flywheel
26 Main Bearings
27 Caps
28 Oil Pump
29 Oil Pan
30 Seal
31 Seal
32 Gasket
33 Dip Stick
34 Tube

FIG 1 – ENGINE BLOCK, OIL PAN & CRANKSHAFT

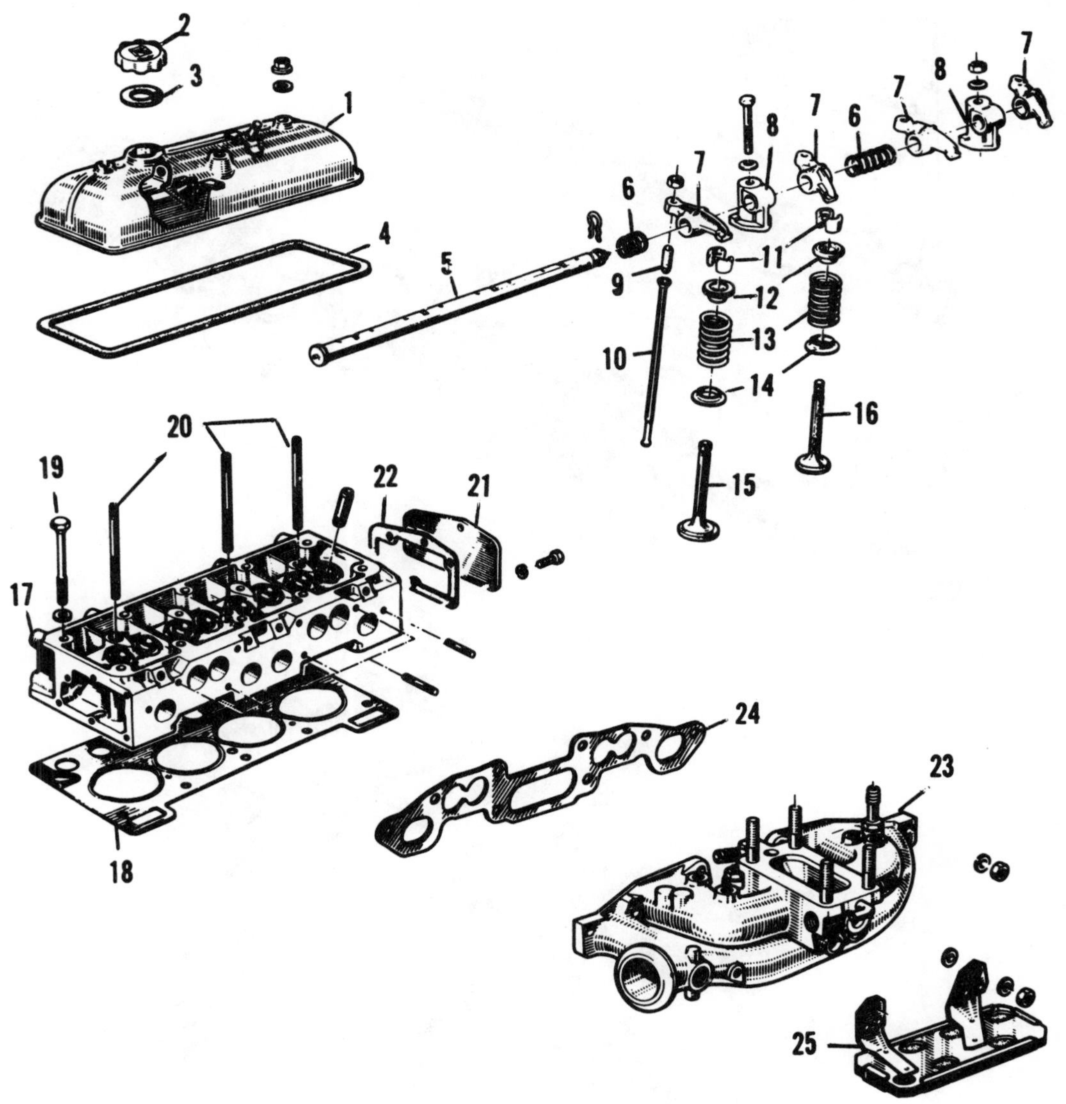

FIG 2 – ENGINE HEAD, VALVES & MANIFOLD

1	Rocker Cover	14	Washer
2	Oil Cap	15	Intake Valve
3	Gasket	16	Exhaust Valve
4	Gasket	17	Cylinder Head
5	Shaft	18	Gasket
6	Spring	19	Bolt
7	Rocker Arm	20	Studs
8	Support	21	Cover Plate
9	Adjuster Screw	22	Gasket
10	Push Rod	23	Manifold Assy
11	Valve Keepers	24	Gasket
12	Cap	25	Heat Shield
13	Spring		

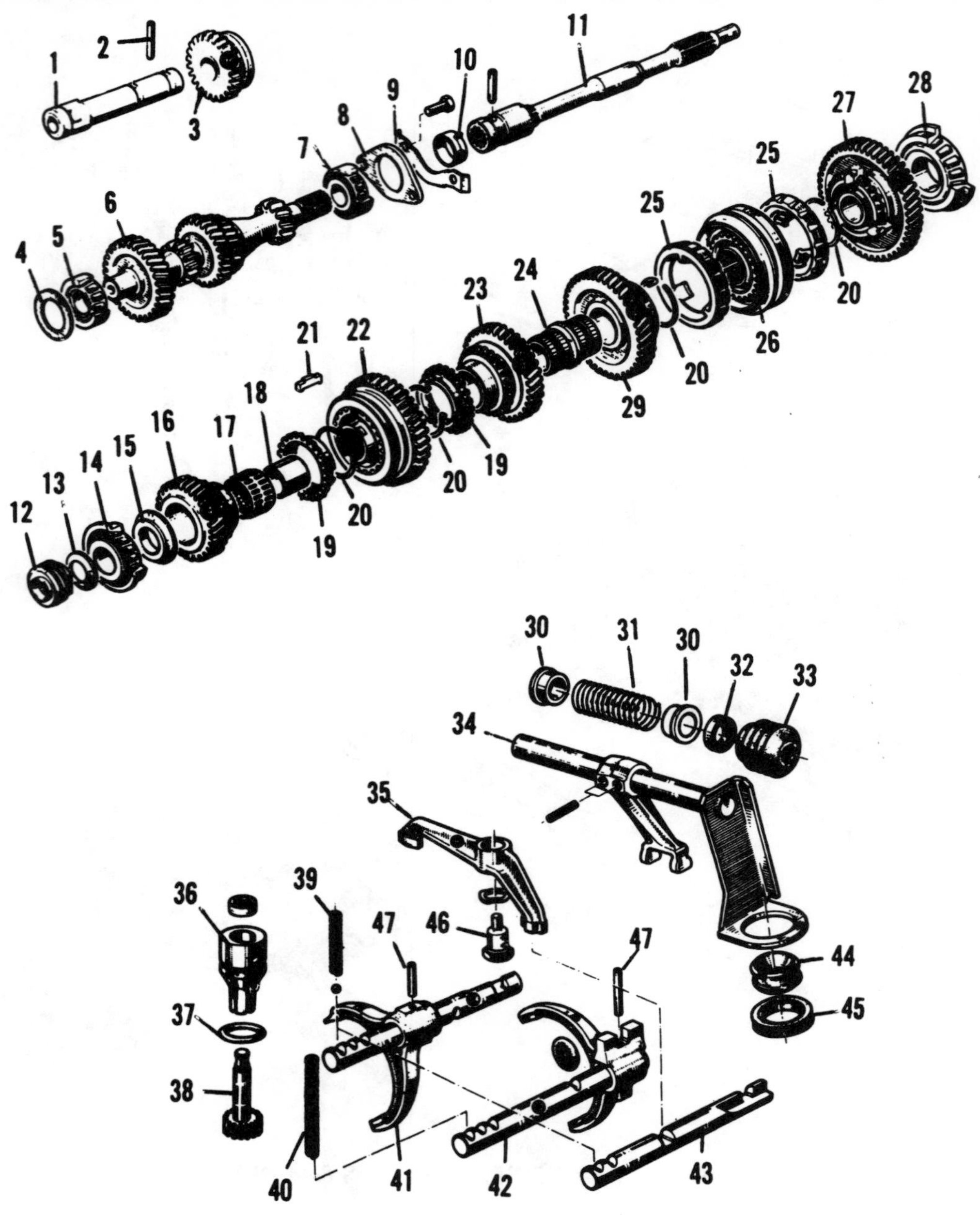

FIG 3 – TRANSAXLE

1	Reverse Shaft	17	Needle Bearing	33	Boot
2	Pin	18	Bushing	34	Fork & Shaft
3	Reverse Gear	19	Synchro Ring	35	Reverse Fork
4	Washer	20	Spring	36	Guide
5	Bearing	21	Key	37	Seal
6	Cluster Gear	22	Synchro Gear	38	Tachometer Gear
7	Bearing	23	3rd Speed Gear	39	Spring
8	Plate	24	Spacer	40	Spring
9	Lock Plate	25	Synchro Ring	41	Fork
10	Spring	26	Synchro Hub	42	Fork
11	Clutch Shaft	27	1st Speed Gear	43	Fork
12	Tachometer Drive Gear	28	Bearing	44	Plug
13	Washer	29	2nd Speed Gear	45	Washer
14	Bearing	30	Bushing	46	Rod
15	Washer	31	Spring	47	Pin
16	4th Speed Gear	32	Seal		

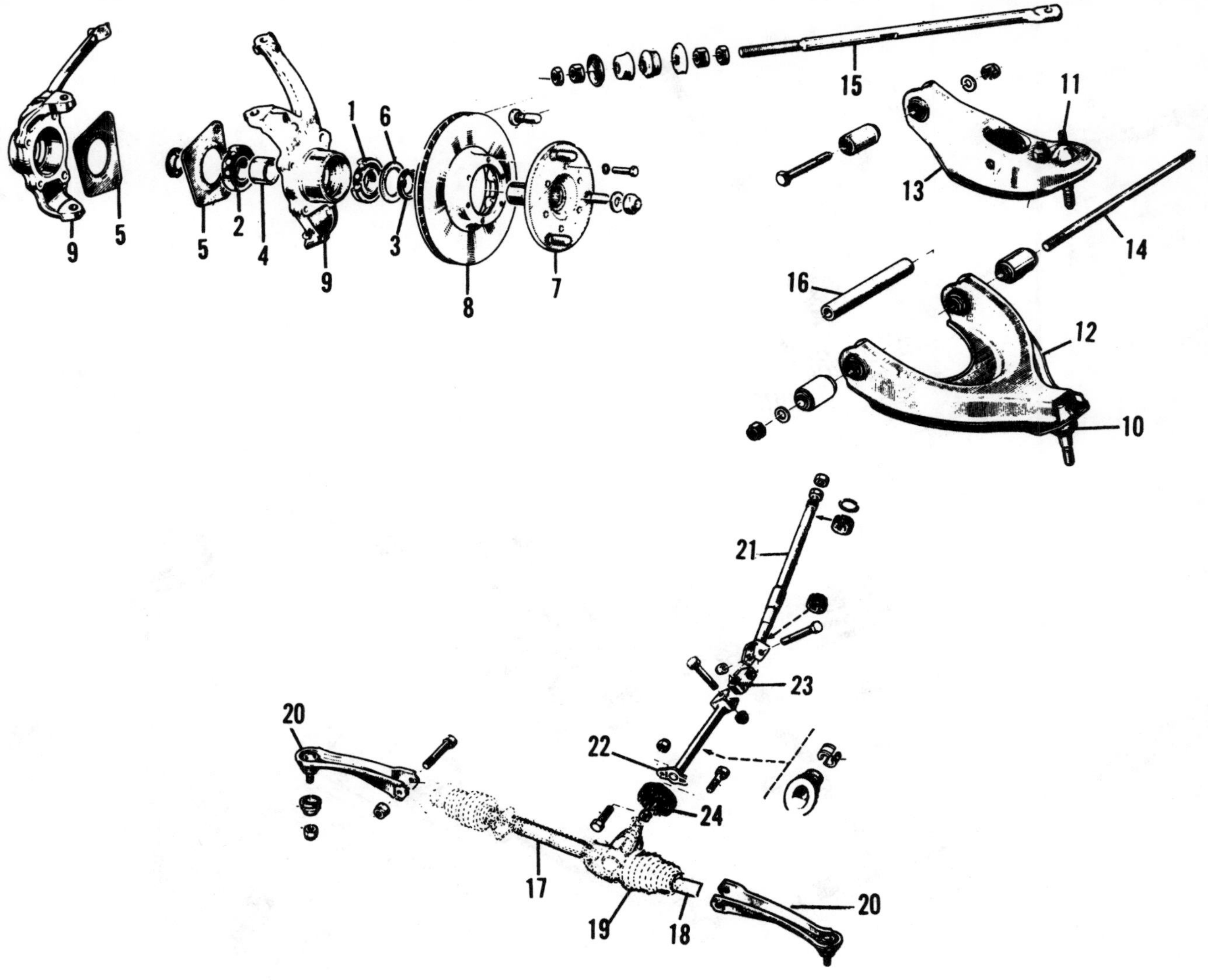

FIG 4 – FRONT SUSPENSION & STEERING – R12, R15, R17

1	Bearing, Outer
2	Bearing, Inner
3	Spacer, Outer
4	Spacer, Inner
5	Plate
6	Seal
7	Hub
8	Brake Disc
9	Steering Knucle & Arm
10	Ball Joint, Upper
11	Ball Joint, Lower
12	Control Arm, Upper
13	Control Arm, Lower
14	Shaft
15	Strut
16	Spacer
17	Gear & Tie Rod Assy
18	End
19	Boot
20	Link
21	Mainshaft, Upper
22	Mainshaft, Lower
23	Joint
24	Disc

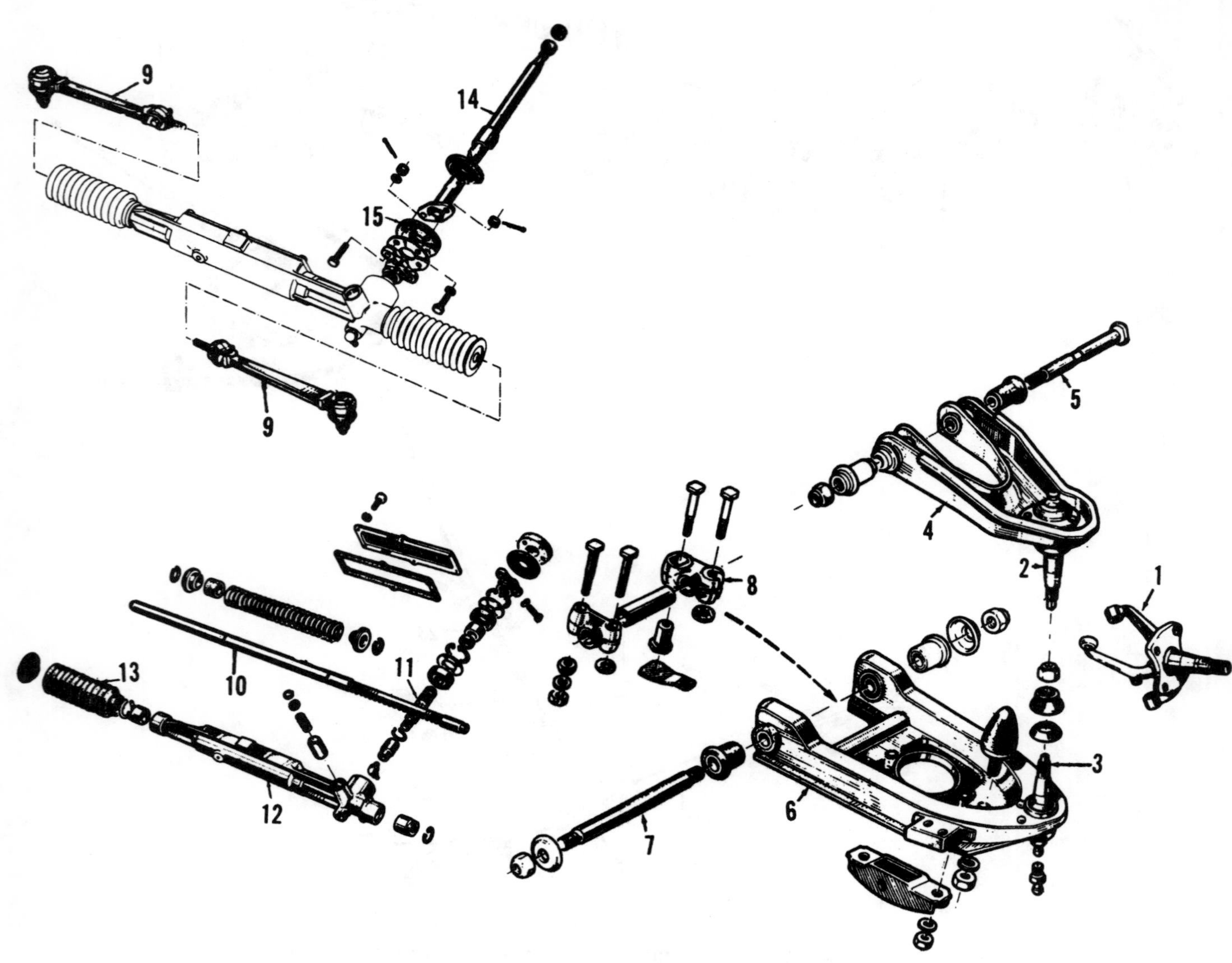

FIG 5 – FRONT SUSPENSION & STEERING – R8, R10

1 Steering Knuckle & Arm
2 Ball Joint, Upper
3 Ball Joint, Lower
4 Control Arm, Upper
5 Upper Shaft
6 Control Arm, Lower
7 Lower Shaft
8 Yoke
9 Tie Rod & Ends
10 Rack
11 Pinion
12 Gear Housing
13 Boot
14 Mainshaft
15 Flexible Disc

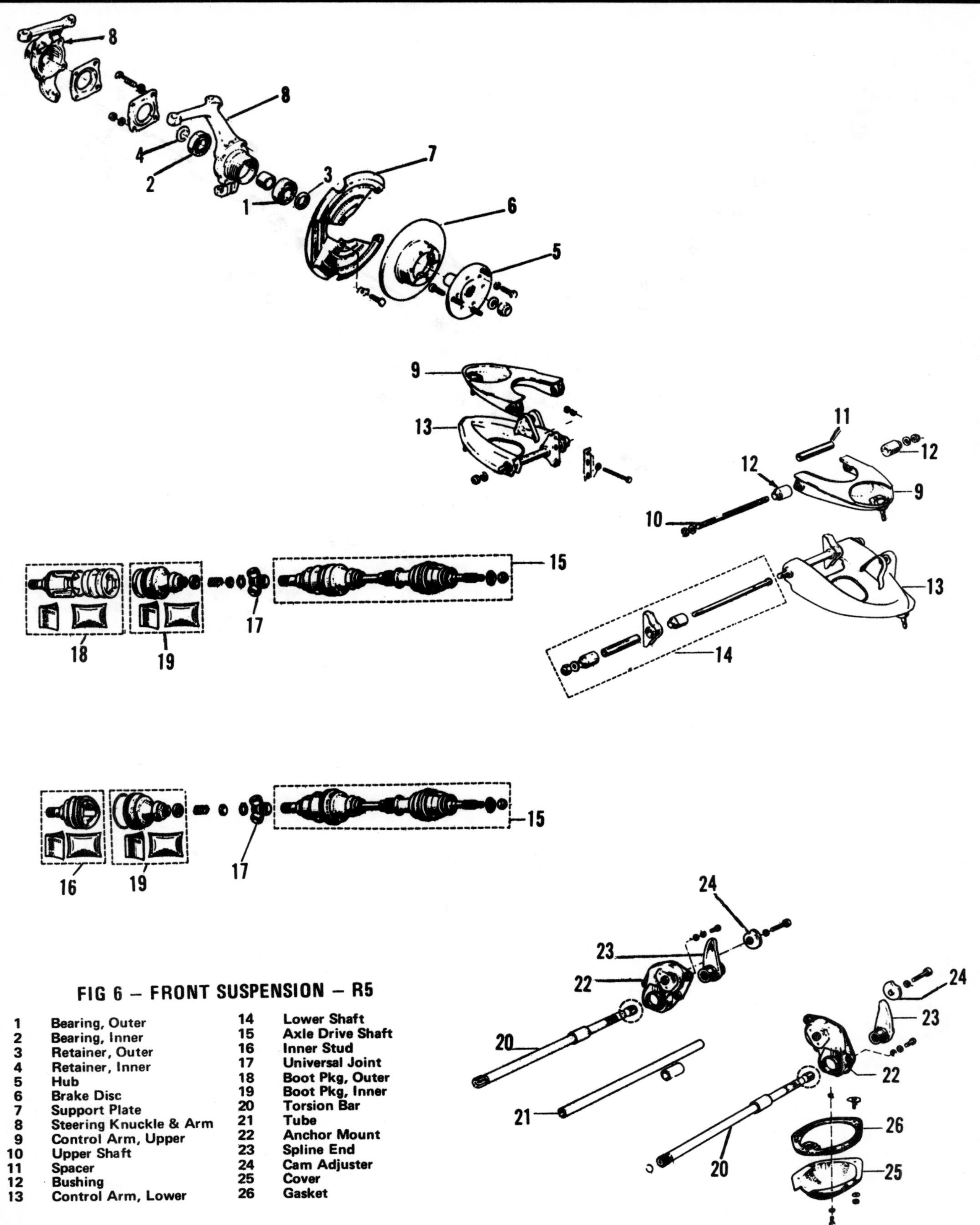

FIG 6 – FRONT SUSPENSION – R5

1	Bearing, Outer	14	Lower Shaft
2	Bearing, Inner	15	Axle Drive Shaft
3	Retainer, Outer	16	Inner Stud
4	Retainer, Inner	17	Universal Joint
5	Hub	18	Boot Pkg, Outer
6	Brake Disc	19	Boot Pkg, Inner
7	Support Plate	20	Torsion Bar
8	Steering Knuckle & Arm	21	Tube
9	Control Arm, Upper	22	Anchor Mount
10	Upper Shaft	23	Spline End
11	Spacer	24	Cam Adjuster
12	Bushing	25	Cover
13	Control Arm, Lower	26	Gasket

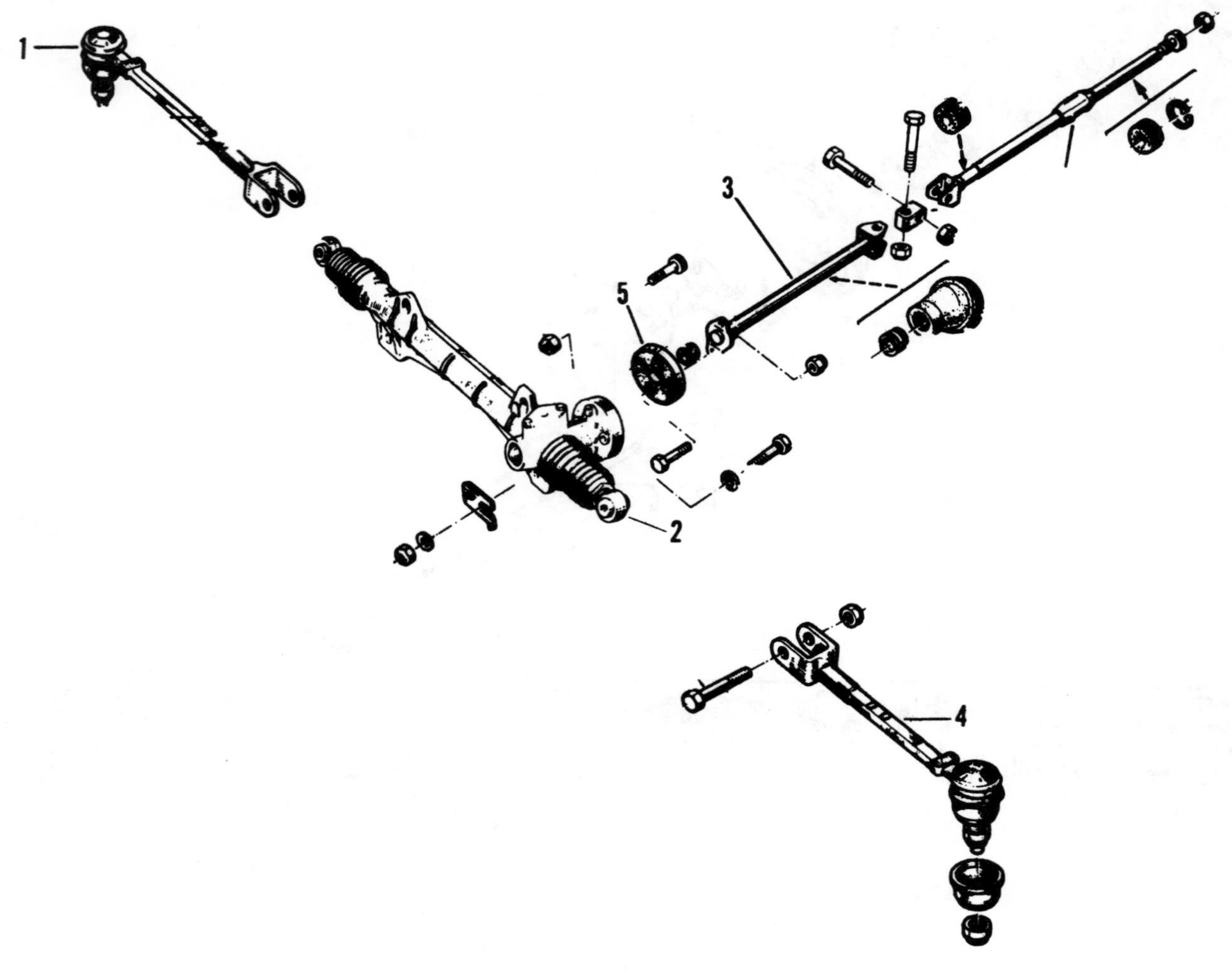

FIG 7 – STEERING - R5

1 Tie Rod End
2 Gear Assy
3 Mainshaft, Lower
4 Mainshaft, Upper
5 Coupling

Ignition, Starting & Charging—TIME

OPERATION INDEX

Tune-Up, Minor ... *1*
Tune-Up, Major ... *2*
Compression Test ... *3*
Distributor, R & R Or Renew ... *4*
Distributor Cap, Renew ... *5*
Ignition Cable Set, Renew ... *6*
Ignition Coil, Renew ... *7*
Starter, R & R Or Renew ... *8*
Starter, R & R & Overhaul ... *9*
Starter Solenoid, Renew ... *10*
Starter Bendix Drive, Renew ... *11*
Starter Brushes, Renew ... *12*
Alternator Or Generator, R & R Or Renew ... *13*
Alternator Or Generator, R & R & Overhaul ... *14*
Voltage Regulator, Renew ... *15*
Alternator Or Generator Brushes, Renew ... *16*
Ignition Switch, Renew ... *17*

1—TUNE-UP, MINOR

Includes: Renew points, condenser & plugs. Set spark timing and adjust carburetor idle.

R10 ... 1.0
R16 ... 1.7
R12, 15 ... 1.3
R17, Exc ... 1.3
Gordini ... 1.4
R5 ... 0.9

2—TUNE-UP, MAJOR

Includes: Check compression, clean or renew and adjust spark plugs. R & R distributor, renew points and condenser. Adjust ignition timing, carburetor and fan belts. Clean battery terminals and service air cleaner. Check coil & clean or replace fuel filter.

R10 ... 2.3
R16 ... 2.6
R12 ... 2.0
R15, 17, Exc ... 2.5
Gordini ... 2.7
R5 ... 1.7

3—COMPRESSION TEST

R10 ... 0.3
R16 ... 0.6
R12 ... 0.3
R15, 17 ... 0.5
R5 ... 0.4

4—DISTRIBUTOR, R & R OR RENEW

R10 ... 0.5
R16 ... 0.9
R12, 15, 17, Exc ... 0.4
R17 Gordini ... 0.5
R5 ... 0.5

5—DISTRIBUTOR CAP, RENEW

All Models ... 0.3

6—IGNITION CABLE SET, RENEW

All Models ... 0.2

7—IGNITION COIL, RENEW

R10 ... 0.5
R16 ... 0.7
R12, 15, 17 ... 0.2
R5 ... 0.3

8—STARTER, R & R OR RENEW

R10 ... 0.8
R16 ... 2.2
R12 ... 0.8
R15, 17, Exc ... 1.2
R17 Gordini ... 1.0
R5 ... 2.5

9—STARTER, R & R & OVERHAUL

R10 ... 2.0
R16 ... 4.2
R12, 15, 17, Exc ... 1.9
1974 Gordini ... 1.7
1975 All ... 1.5
R5 ... 3.2

10—STARTER SOLENOID, RENEW

R10 ... 1.0
R16 ... 2.0
R12, 15, 17, Exc ... 1.5
1974 Gordini ... 1.3
1975 All ... 1.0
R5 ... 0.5

11—STARTER BENDIX DRIVE, RENEW

R10 ... 1.2
R16 ... 2.0
R12, 15, 17, Exc ... 1.7
1974 Gordini ... 1.5
1975 All ... 1.2
R5 ... 3.0

12—STARTER BRUSHES, RENEW

R10 ... 1.2
R16 ... 2.0
R12, 15, 17, Exc ... 1.5
1974 Gordini ... 1.3
1975 All ... 1.0
R5 ... 3.2

13—ALTERNATOR OR GENERATOR, R & R OR RENEW

Exc Below ... 0.5
R10 ... 0.4

14—ALTERNATOR OR GENERATOR, R & R & OVERHAUL

R10 ... 1.7
R16 ... 1.5
R12, 15, 17 ... 1.9
R5 ... 2.0

15—VOLTAGE REGULATOR, RENEW

R10 ... 0.3
R16 ... 0.5
R12, 15, 17 ... 0.3
R5 ... 0.5

16—ALTERNATOR BRUSHES, RENEW

R10 ... 0.6
R16 ... 0.8
R12, 15, 17 ... 0.3
R5 ... 1.2

17—IGNITION SWITCH, RENEW

R10 ... 0.5
R16 ... 1.5
R12, 15, 17 ... 0.5
R5 ... 1.0

Fuel, Emission Controls, Intake & Exhaust Systems—TIME

OPERATION INDEX

Carburetor, R & R Or Renew ... *1*
Fuel Pump, R & R Or Renew ... *2*
Fuel Pump, R & R & Overhaul ... *3*
Fuel Tank, R & R Or Renew ... *4*
Choke Cable, Renew ... *5*
Intake Manifold Or Gasket, Renew ... *6*
Exhaust Manifold Or Gasket, Renew ... *7*
Exhaust Pipe, Renew ... *8*
Muffler, Renew ... *9*
Resonator, Renew ... *10*
Exhaust Expansion Chamber, Renew ... *11*
Charcoal Canister, Renew ... *12*
Air Injection Pump, Renew ... *13*
Air Pump Fulter, Renew ... *14*
Relief Diverter Valve, Renew ... *15*
Air Control Valve, Renew ... *16*
Check Valve, Renew ... *17*
Governor, Air Pump, Renew ... *18*
Solenoid Valve, Renew ... *19*
Fuel Expansion Tank, Renew ... *20*
Throttle Switch, Renew ... *21*
Auxiliary Air Control Valve, Renew ... *22*
Thermical Switch, Renew ... *23*
Fuel Pressure Regulator, Renew ... *24*
Injector(S), Renew ... *25*
Egr Valve, Renew ... *26*
Catalytic Converter, Renew ... *27*

1—CARBURETOR, R & R OR RENEW

R10—
Exc Below ... 0.4
T-124 Transaxle ... 0.6
R16 ... 0.8
R12, 15, 17 ... 1.0
R5 ... 1.2

2—FUEL PUMP, R & R OR RENEW

R10 ... 0.6
R16 ... 0.7
R12, 15, 17 ... 0.3
R5 ... 0.6

3—FUEL PUMP, R & R & OVERHAUL

R10 ... 0.8
R16 ... 1.2
R12, 15, 17 ... 0.6
R5 ... 1.0

4—FUEL TANK, R & R OR RENEW

Exc Below ... 1.0
R10 ... 6.0
R5 ... 1.2

5—CHOKE CABLE, RENEW

R10 ... 1.5
R16 ... 0.5
R12, 15, 17—
Single ... 0.5
Twin, Primary ... 0.3
Twin, Secondary ... 0.2
R5 ... 0.5

6—INTAKE MANIFOLD OR GASKET, RENEW

Exc Below ... 1.5
R17 Gordini ... ①2.0
R5 ... 2.6
①*Includes Exhaust Manifold.*

7—EXHAUST MANIFOLD OR GASKET, RENEW

R10 ... 1.5
R16 ... 1.5
R12, 15, 17, Exc ... ①1.8
R17 Gordini ... 0.8
R5 ... 2.3
①*Includes Exhaust Manifold.*

8—EXHAUST PIPE, RENEW

R10 ... 0.5
R16 ... 0.7
R12, 15, 17 ... 1.0
R5 ... 0.8

9—MUFFLER, RENEW

R10 ... 1.0
R16 ... 1.2
R12, 15, 17 ... 1.0
R5 ... 1.0

10—RESONATOR, RENEW

All Models ... 1.0

11—EXHAUST EXPANSION CHAMBER, RENEW

R12 ... 1.0

12—CHARCOAL CANISTER, RENEW

R5 ... 0.3

13—AIR INJECTION PUMP, RENEW

All Models ... 0.8

14—AIR PUMP FILTER, RENEW

All Models ... 0.4

15—RELIEF DIVERTER VALVE, RENEW

Exc Below ... 0.3
R5 ... 0.5

16—AIR CONTROL VALVE, RENEW

Exc Below ... 0.5
R5 ... 0.3

(Continued)

Fuel, Emission Controls, Intake & Exhaust Systems—TIME Cont'd

17—CHECK VALVE, RENEW
Exc Below 0.2
R5 ....0.5

18—GOVERNOR, AIR PUMP, RENEW
All Models 0.4

19—SOLENOID VALVE, RENEW
R12 ....0.3
R5, 17 ....0.5

20—FUEL EXPANSION TANK, RENEW
All Models 0.5

21—THROTTLE SWITCH, RENEW
R17 Gordini 0.3

22—AUXILIARY AIR CONTROL VLAVE, RENEW
R17 Gordini 0.5

23—THERMICAL SWITCH, RENEW
R17 Gordini 0.3

24—FUEL PRESSURE REGULATOR, RENEW
R17 Gordini 0.3

25—INJECTOR(S), RENEW
One, Exc 0.2
1975-76 ....0.5
All, Exc 0.8
1975-76 ....1.5

26—EGR VALVE, RENEW
Exc Below 0.3
1975, R15, 17 ....0.5

27—CATALYTIC CONVERTER, RENEW
All Models 0.5

Engine Cooling & Heater System—TIME

OPERATION INDEX

Radiator, R & R Or Renew 1
Radiator Hoses, Renew 2
Water Pump, R & R Or Renew 3
Thermostat Or Housing, Renew 4
Heater Blower Motor, Renew 5
Heater Blower Motor, R & R & Overhaul 6
Heater Hoses, Renew 7
Cooling Fan, Renew 8
Heater Core, R & R Or Renew 9
Cooling Fan Temperature Switch, Renew 10
Air Conditioner Compressor, Renew 11
Clutch Rotor Or Bearing, Renew 12
Air Conditioner Condenser, Renew 13
Receiver Drier, Renew 14
Blower Motor (Air Conditioner), Renew 15

1—RADIATOR, R & R OR RENEW
R10 ....2.0
R16 ....1.5
R12, 15, 17, Exc 1.2
R17 Gordini 1.4
R5 ....1.7

2—RADIATOR HOSES, RENEW
Upper—
Exc Below 0.5
R10 ....0.7
Lower—
R10 ....0.8
R16 ....0.5
R12, 15, 17, Exc 0.7
R17 Gordini 0.5
R5 ....0.8

3—WATER PUMP, R & R OR RENEW
R10 ....①2.0
R16 ....2.2
R12, 15, 17, Exc 2.0
1974 R17 Gordini 2.3
1975 All 2.3
R5 ....3.0
①*With Air Cond, Add.* *0.2*

4—THERMOSTAT OR HOUSING, RENEW
Exc Below 0.5
R10 ....0.3

5—HEATER BLOWER MOTOR, RENEW
R10, R16 ....2.0
R12 ....1.3
R15, 17 ....4.3
R5 ....0.5

6—HEATER BLOWER MOTOR, R & R & OVERHAUL
R10 ....2.5
R16 ....3.0
R12 ....2.0
R15, 17 ....5.0
R5 ....1.4

7—HEATER HOSES, RENEW
R10—
One Hose 1.5
Two Hoses 2.0
R16 ....0.5
R12 ....0.8
R15, 17 ....1.0
R5 ....1.2

8—COOLING FAN, RENEW
R5 ....0.5

9—HEATER CORE, R & R OR RENEW
R10 ....2.5
R16 ....2.0
R12 ....1.5
R15, 17 ....4.8
R5 ....1.2

10—COOLING FAN TEMPERATURE SWITCH, RENEW
R5 ....0.6

11—AIR CONDITIONER COMPRESSOR, RENEW
Exc Below 1.4
R17 Gordini 2.2

12—CLUTCH ROTOR OR BEARING, RENEW
All Models 0.6

13—CONDENSER (AIR COND), RENEW
All Models 1.1

14—RECEIVER DRIER, RENEW
All Models 0.5

15—BLOWER MOTOR (AIR COND), RENEW
All Models 1.0

Engine—TIME

OPERATION INDEX

Engine, R & R 1
Engine, R & R & Overhaul 2
Engine (Short Block), Renew & Grind Valves 3
Cylinder Head, R & R Or Gasket Renew 4
Valves, Grind 5
Valve Spring (One), Renew 6
Rocker Arm Cover Gasket, Renew 7
Rocker Arm Shaft, Renew 8
Oil Pan Or Gasket, R & R Or Renew 9
Valve Tappets, Renew 10
Timing Cover Seal & Gasket, Renew 11
Timing Chain Or Gears, Renew 12
Timing Chain Tensioner, Renew 13
Camshaft, R & R Or Renew 14
Oil Pump, R & R Or Renew 15
Crankshaft, R & R Or Renew 16
Pistons & Liners, Renew 17
Crankshaft Pulley, Renew 18

1—ENGINE, R & R
Does not include transfer of any part of engine or replacement or special equipment.
R10 ....5.0
R16 ....8.5
R12, 15, 17, Exc 5.7
R17 Gordini 6.7
R5 ....6.0

2—ENGINE, R & R & OVERHAUL
R10 ....①12.5
R16 ....18.0
R12, 15, 17 ....①14.5
R5 ....18.0
①*With Air Cond, Add.* *1.0*

3—ENGINE (SHORT BLOCK), RENEW & GRIND VALVES
R10 ....21.0
R16 ....19.1
R12, 15, 17, Exc 17.2
R17 Gordini 18.2
R5 ....17.1

4—CYLINDER HEAD, R & R OR GASKET, RENEW
R10 ....2.5
R16 ....4.5
R12, 15, 17, Exc 3.9
R17 Gordini 4.8
R5 ....6.0

5—VALVES, GRIND
R10 ....6.0
R16 ....5.7
R12, 15, 17, Exc 4.9
R17 Gordini 5.8
R5 ....7.2

6—VALVE SPRING (ONE), RENEW
R10 ....①0.8
R16 ....①1.0
R12, 15, 17 ....①1.3
R5 ....①1.4
①*For Each Additional, Add.* *0.1*

7—ROCKER ARM COVER GASKET, RENEW
Exc Below 0.5
R10 ....0.3
R16 ....0.6

8—ROCKER ARM SHAFT, RENEW
R10 ....①0.6
R16 ....①1.2
R12, 15, 17 ....①2.0
R5 ....①1.2
①*Does Not Include R & R Head.*

9—OIL PAN OR GASKET, R & R OR RENEW
R10 ....1.5
R16 ....1.2
R12, 15, 17 ....1.0
R5 ....2.0

10—VALVE TAPPETS, RENEW
After head is removed.
Exc Below 0.5
R12, 15, 17 ....0.3

11—TIMING COVER SEAL & GASKET, RENEW
R10 ....①0.6
R16 ....①7.7
R12, 15, 17 ....①6.7
R5 ....7.0
①*With Air Cond, Add.* *0.2*

12—TIMING CHAIN OR GEARS, RENEW
R10 ....①2.5
R16 ....8.0
R12, 15, 17, Exc ①8.0
1974 R17 Gordini ①9.5
1975 ....①9.5
R5 ....9.2
①*With Air Cond, Add.* *0.2*

(Continued)

Engine—TIME Cont'd

13—TIMING CHAIN TENSIONER, RENEW

R10 .... ①2.1
R16 .... 7.2
R12, 15, 17, Exc 7.2
1974 R17 Gordini 8.7
1975 .... 8.7
R5 .... 8.2
①With Air Cond, Add. 0.2

14—CAMSHAFT, R & R OR RENEW

R10 .... ①8.5
R16 .... ①14.7
R12, 15, 17, Exc 8.2
1974 R17 Gordini 9.7
1975 .... 9.7
R5 .... ①12.0
①Includes R & R Engine.

15—OIL PUMP, R & R OR RENEW

Exc Below 1.7
R10 .... 2.0
R5 .... 2.3

16—CRANKSHAFT, R & R OR RENEW

R10 .... 9.5
R16 .... 18.0
R12, 15, 17, Exc 12.9
1974 R17 Gordini 13.9
1975 .... 13.9
R5 .... 10.0

17—PISTONS & LINERS, RENEW

R10 .... ①9.5
R16 .... ①17.5
R12, 15, 17 .... ①9.8
R5 .... 11.0
①Includes R & R Engine.

18—CRANKSHAFT PULLEY, RENEW

Exc Below 0.8
R10, 16 .... 0.4

Clutch, Mounts, Manual & Automatic Transmissions—TIME

OPERATION INDEX

Flywheel, R & R Or Renew 1
Flywheel Ring Gear, Renew 2
Clutch Assy, Renew 3
Release Bearing, Renew 4
Pilot Bearing, Renew 5
Clutch Release Fork, Renew 6
Clutch Pedal, Adjust 7
Engine Mounts, Renew 8
Transaxle Assy, R & R Or Renew 9
Transaxle Assy, R & R & Overhaul 10
Automatic Trans Relay Case, Renew 11
Automatic Trans Coupling, Renew 12
Automatic Trans Governor, Renew 13
Automatic Trans Actuator, Renew 14
Automatic Trans Decelerator, Renew 15
Gearshift Lever, Renew 16
Electric Comp Unit, Renew 17
Converter, Renew 18
Oil Pan Or Gasket, Renew 19
Automatic Trans R & R & Overhaul 20
Trans Axle Mounts, Renew 21

1—FLYWHEEL, R & R OR RENEW

R10 .... ①0.3
R16 .... ①0.5
R12, 15, 17 .... ①0.5
R5 .... ①1.5
①After Engine Is Removed.

2—FLYWHEEL RING GEAR, RENEW

R10 .... ①0.5
R16 .... ①1.0
R12, 15, 17 .... ①0.9
R5 .... ①0.5
①After Flywheel Is Removed.

3—CLUTCH ASSY, RENEW

R10 .... 5.2
R16 .... 5.5
R12, 15, 17 .... 6.4
R5 .... 7.5

4—RELEASE BEARING, RENEW

R10 .... ①0.3
R16 .... ①0.5
R12, 15, 17 .... ①0.2
R5 .... ①0.3
①After Transmission Or Trans Axle Is Removed.

5—PILOT BEARING, RENEW

Exc Below ①0.3
R16 .... ①0.7
①After Clutch Is Removed.

6—CLUTCH RELEASE FORK, RENEW

R10 .... ①0.3
R16 .... ①0.5
R12, 15, 17 .... ①0.3
R5 .... ①0.4
①After Engine, Trans Axle Or Transmission Is Removed.

7—CLUTCH PEDAL, ADJUST

R10 .... 0.4
R16 .... 0.5
R12, 15, 17 .... 0.2
R5 .... 0.3

8—ENGINE MOUNTS, RENEW

R10 .... 1.2
R16 .... 0.7
R12, 15, 17 .... 0.8
R5 .... 1.5

9—TRANSAXLE ASSY, R & R OR RENEW

R10 .... 4.5
R16 .... 5.2
R12, 15, 17 .... 6.0
R5 .... 7.0

10—TRANSAXLE ASSY, R & R & OVERHAUL

R10 .... 10.0
R16 .... 12.7
R12, 15, 17, Exc 11.6
395, 5 Speed 12.6
R5 .... 12.0

11—AUTOMATIC TRANS RELAY CASE, RENEW

Includes: Check and adjust.
R10 .... 1.3

12—AUTOMATIC TRANS COUPLING, RENEW

Includes: R & R engine.
R10 .... 5.7

13—AUTOMATIC TRANS GOVERNOR, RENEW

R10 .... 0.5
R12, 15, 17 .... 0.9

14—AUTOMATIC TRANS ACTUATOR, RENEW

R10 .... 1.3

15—AUTOMATIC TRANS DECELERATOR, RENEW

R10 .... 0.8

16—GEARSHIFT LEVER, RENEW

R10 .... 1.0
R5 .... 1.2

17—ELECTRIC COMP UNIT, RENEW

R12 .... 0.7

18—CONVERTER, RENEW

Includes: Replacing converter seal
R12, 15, 17 .... 7.5

19—OIL PAN OR GASKET, RENEW

R12, 15, 17 .... 0.5

20—AUTOMATIC TRANS, R & R & OVERHAUL

R12, 15, 17 .... 11.5

21—TRANS AXLE MOUNTS, R & R OR RENEW

R5 .... 0.8
R12, 15, 17 .... 0.7

Brakes, Steering, Suspension, Universals & Rear Axle—TIME

OPERATION INDEX

Brake Shoes Or Friction Pads, Renew 1
Master Cylinder, Renew 2
Master Cylinder, R & R & Overhaul 3
Wheel Cylinder(S), Renew 4
Caliper(S) Assy, Renew 5
Caliper(S) Assy, R & R & Overhaul 6
Bleed System 7
Brake Hose, Renew 8
Hub Or Disc, Renew 9
Brake Drum, Renew 10
Brake Pressure Control Valve, Renew 11
Brake Pedal, Renew 12
Parking Brake Cable, Renew 13
Parking Brake Lever, Renew 14
Steering Coupling, Renew 15
Steering Link, R & R Or Renew 16
Tie Rod, Renew 17
Spring(S), Renew 18
Torsion Bar(S), Renew 19
Stabilizer Shaft Bushing, Renew 20
Front Hub Bearings, Renew 21
Shock Absorbers, Renew 22

3—MASTER CYLINDER, R & R & OVERHAUL

Upper Control Arm Assy, Renew 23
Lower Control Arm Assy, Renew 24
Universal Joints, Renew 25
Axle Shaft (One), Renew 26
Differential Carrier Seal & Gasket (One Side), Renew 27
Differential Carrier Seal & Gasket (Both Sides), Renew 28
Brake Servo, Renew 29
Ball Joints, Renew 30
Steering Knuckle, Renew 31
Front Axle Carrier(S), Renew 32
Rear Suspension Control Arm(S) Rod(S), Renew 33
Differential, Renew 34
Rear Hub (Wheel) Bearing, Renew 35
Steering Gear (Rack), R & R Or Renew 36

1—BRAKE SHOES OR FRICTION PADS, RENEW

Includes: Bleed system
R10 Drum Brakes—
Front 1.7
Rear 2.0
R10 Disc Brakes—
Front 1.0
Rear 1.2
All 1.7
R16—
Front (Disc) 1.5
Rear (Drum) 2.5
All 3.0
R12, 15, 17—
Front 1.0
Rear 1.5
All 2.3
R5—
Front 0.7
Rear 1.4
All 2.0

2—MASTER CYLINDER, RENEW

Includes: Bleed system
R10 .... 1.5
R16 .... 1.2

(Continued)

Brakes, Steering, Suspension, Universals & Rear Axle—TIME Cont'd

R12, 15, 17 .....1.0
R5 .....1.3
Includes: Bleed system
R10 .....2.2
R16 .....2.0
R12, 15, 17 .....1.5
R5 .....2.0

4—WHEEL CYLINDER(S), RENEW

Includes: Bleed system
R10—
Front & Rear 1.5
R16—
One 1.2
Both 2.0
R12, 15, 17—
One 1.2
Both 1.7
R5—
One 1.3
Both 2.1

5—CALIPER(S), RENEW

Includes: Bleed system
R10—
Front, One 0.7
Both 1.0
Rear, One 0.9
Both 1.5
R16—
Front, One 1.0
Both 1.2
R12, 15, 17—
Front, One 0.6
Both 1.0
Rear, One 0.6
Both 1.0
All Four 1.7
R5—
Front, One 0.8
Both 1.2

6—CALIPER(S) ASSY, R & R & OVERHAUL

Includes: Bleed system
R10—
Front, One 1.1
Both 1.8
Rear, One 1.3
Both 2.1
All Four 3.5
R16—
Front, One 1.7
Both 2.7
R12, 15, 17—
Front, One 0.9
Both 1.6
Rear, One 1.0
Both 1.7
All Four 3.0
R5—
Front, One 1.1
Both 2.1

7—BLEED SYSTEM

Includes: Adjust handbrake
R10 .....1.0
R16 .....1.7
R12, 15, 17 .....0.8
R5 .....0.5

8—BRAKE HOSE, RENEW

Includes: Bleed system
R10—
One 0.7
Two 1.1
All Four 2.0
R16—
One 1.0
Two 1.5
All Four 2.2
R12, 15, 17—
One 1.0
Two 1.5
All Four 1.8
R5—
One 0.8
Two 1.2

9—HUB OR DISC, RENEW

R10—
One 1.0
Two 1.9
R16—
One 1.5
Both 2.7
R12, 15, 17—
One 2.0
Both 3.8
R5—
One 1.5
Both 2.7

10—BRAKE DRUM(S), RENEW

R10—
Front, Both 1.2
Rear, Both 2.3
All Four 3.5
R16—
Front, One 1.5
Both 2.7
Rear, One 0.5
Both 1.0
R12, 15, 17—
One 0.4
Both 0.7
R5—
One 0.5
Both 1.0

11—BRAKE PRESSURE CONTROL VALVE, RENEW

Includes: Bleed system
Exc Below 1.2
R12, 15, 17 .....1.0

12—BRAKE PEDAL, RENEW

Exc Below 1.0
R10 .....1.2
R5 .....1.6

13—PARKING BRAKE CABLE, RENEW

R10 .....1.5
R16 .....2.0
R12, 15, 17—
Primary 1.5
Secondary, Exc 1.4
R17 Gordini 0.7
R5 .....1.0

14—PARKING BRAKE LEVER, RENEW

R10 .....1.0
R1l 1.2
R12, 15, 17 .....0.8
R5 .....1.0

15—STEERING COUPLING, RENEW

R10 .....0.9
R16 .....0.5
R12, 15, 17 .....0.5
R5 .....1.8

16—STEERING LINK, R & R OR RENEW

R16 .....1.5

17—TIE ROD, RENEW

R10 .....1.2
R16 .....0.5
R12, 15, 17 .....0.4
R5 .....1.7

18—SPRING(S), RENEW

R10—
Front, One 1.2
Both 2.2
Rear, One 1.5
Both 2.5
R12, 15, 17—
Front 1.3
Rear 0.8

19—TORSION BAR(S), RENEW

R16—
Front, One 1.0
Both 1.5
Rear, One 2.0
Both 3.5
R5—
Front, One 1.4
Both 2.4
Rear, One 1.3
Both 2.0

20—STABILIZER SHAFT BUSHING, RENEW

Exc Below 0.7
R10 .....0.8
R5 .....0.5

21—FRONT HUB BEARINGS, RENEW

R10—
One Side 1.3
Both Sides 2.3
R16—
One Side 2.0
Both Sides 3.1
R12, 15, 17—
One Side 2.0
Both Sides 3.0
R5—
One Side 2.2
Both Sides 3.0

22—SHOCK ABSORBERS, RENEW

R10—
Front, One 0.6
Both 1.0
Rear, One 1.5
Both 2.5
All Four 3.5
R16—
Front, One 0.7
Both 1.2
Rear, One 1.0
Both 1.7
All Four 2.5
R12, 15, 17—
Front, One 1.0
Both 1.8
Rear, One 0.8
Both 1.3
All Four 2.9
R5—
Front, One 1.0
Both 1.7
Rear, One 0.8
Both 1.2
All Four 2.7

23—UPPER CONTROL ARM ASSY, RENEW

Includes: Front end align
R10—
One Side 1.5
Both Sides 2.5
R16—
One Side 2.5
Both Sides 4.0
R12, 15, 17—
One Side 1.5
Both Sides 2.8
R5—
One Side 2.0
Both Sides 3.5

24—LOWER CONTROL ARM ASSY, RENEW

R10—
One .....(1)2.0
Both .....(1)3.5
R16—
One .....(1)3.0
Both .....(1)5.0
R12, 15, 17—
One 1.0
Both 1.7
R5—
One .....(1)3.0
Both .....(1)4.9
(1)*Includes: Front End Align*

25—UNIVERSAL JOINTS, RENEW

R10—
One 1.7
Both 3.0

26—AXLE SHAFT (ONE), RENEW

R10 .....1.0
R16 .....1.5

27—DIFFERENTIAL CARRIER SEAL & GASKET (ONE SIDE), RENEW

R10 .....2.0
R16 .....1.5
R12, 15, 17 .....1.4

(Continued)

Brakes, Steering, Suspension, Universals & Rear Axle—TIME Cont'd

R5 .... 1.8

28—DIFFERENTIAL CARRIER SEAL & GASKET (BOTH SIDES), RENEW

R10 .... 3.0
R16 .... 2.7
R12, 15, 17 .... 2.7
R5 .... 2.8

29—BRAKE SERVO, RENEW

R5 .... 1.8
R12, 15, 17 .... 1.2

30—BALL JOINTS, RENEW

R10—
Upper Or Lower 1.2
Both One Side 2.0
R16—
Upper 1.2
Lower 1.5
Both One Side 2.5
R12, 15, 17—
Upper 1.0
Lower 1.0
Both One Side 1.8
R5—
Upper 1.4
Lower 1.7
Both One Side 2.5

31—STEERING KNUCKLE, RENEW

R10 .... 2.5
R16 .... ①2.7
①Includes Wheel Alignment.

32—AXLE CARRIER(S), RENEW

Includes: Wheel alignment
R12—
One 1.8
Both 3.5
R5—
One 2.7
Both 4.5

33—REAR SUSPENSION CONTROL ARM(S) ROD(S), RENEW

R10—
Rods, All 0.5
R16—
Arm, One ①4.0
Both ①7.0
R12, 15, 17—
Side, One 0.5
Center 0.7
R5—
Arm, One ①3.7
Both ①4.4
①Includes Adjust Body Height & Bleed Brakes.

34—DIFFERENTIAL, RENEW

R10—
325 .... 6.5
330 .... 7.0
R16, See Transaxle Overhaul—
R12, 15, 17, Exc 10.4
5 Speed 10.9
R5 .... 12.0

35—REAR HUB (WHEEL) BEARING, RENEW

R10—
One 1.0
Both 1.9
R16—
One 1.0
Both 1.8
R12, 15, 17—
One 1.0
Both 1.8
R5—
One 1.0
Both 1.7

36—STEERING GEAR (RACK), R & R OR RENEW

Includes: Wheel alignment
R10 .... 1.7
R16 .... 2.7
R12, 15, 17 .... 1.8
R5 .... 3.0

Speedometer, W/S Wipers, Switches & Instruments—TIME

OPERATION INDEX

Speedometer Cable & Housing, Renew 1
Speedometer Head, Renew 2
W/S Wiper Motor, Renew 3
W/S Wiper Link Set, Renew 4
W/S Wiper Arm, Renew 5
Fuel Gauge (Dash Unit), Renew 6
Fuel Tank Gauge, Renew 7
Oil Gauge Sending Unit, Renew 8
Temperature Gauge Sending Unit, Renew 9
Headlight Switch, Renew 10
Headlight Foot Dimmer Switch, Renew 11
Turn Signal Switch, Renew 12
Hazard Flasher Switch, Renew 13

1—SPEEDOMETER CABLE & HOUSING, RENEW

Exc Below 1.5
R5 .... 0.7

2—SPEEDOMETER HEAD, RENEW

R10 .... 2.0
R16, 12 .... 1.5
R15, 17 .... 1.9
R5 .... 0.8

3—W/S WIPER MOTOR, RENEW

R10 .... 0.5
R16 .... 1.5
R12, 15, 17 .... 0.8
R5 .... 0.7

4—W/S WIPER LINK SET, RENEW

R10 .... 1.5
R16 .... 1.2
R12, 15, 17 .... 1.4
R5 .... 1.0

5—W/S WIPER ARM, RENEW

Exc Below 0.2
R16 .... 0.4

6—FUEL GAUGE (DASH UNIT), RENEW

R10 .... 1.3
R16 .... 2.5
R12 .... 1.4
R15, 17 .... 1.8
R5 .... 0.6

7—FUEL TANK GAUGE, RENEW

R10 .... 0.8
R16 .... 0.5
R12, 15, 17, Exc 0.5
1974-76 .... 1.5
R5 .... 1.5

8—OIL GAUGE SENDING UNIT, RENEW

R10 .... 0.2
R16 .... 0.7
R12, 15, 17 .... 0.3
R5 .... 0.3

9—TEMPERATURE GAUGE SENDING UNIT, RENEW

Exc Below 0.5
R10 .... 0.2

10—HEADLIGHT SWITCH, RENEW

Exc Below 1.2
R5 .... 0.5

11—HEADLAMP FOOT DIMMER SWITCH, RENEW

R10 .... 0.3
R16 .... 0.5
R12 .... 0.4
R5 .... 0.3

12—TURN SIGNAL SWITCH, RENEW

R10 .... 0.8
R16 .... 0.7
R12, 15, 17 .... ①0.8
R5 .... 0.5
①Includes Headlamp Dimmer On Some Models.

13—HAZARD FLASHER SWITCH, RENEW

Exc Below 0.4
R10, 12 .... 0.2
R15, 17 .... 0.3

IDENTIFICATION

ALL MODELS.................................. 369

ILLUSTRATIONS

FIG 1 – CYLINDER HEAD & CAMSHAFT – 4 CYL IN-LINE
FIG 2 – CYLINDER BLOCK – 4 CYL IN-LINE
FIG 3 – CRANKSHAFT & PISTONS – 4 CYL IN-LINE
FIG 4 – CAMSHAFT & ROCKER ARMS – V4
FIG 5 – CRANKSHAFT & PISTONS – V4
FIG 6 – TRANSMISSION SHAFTS, GEARS, SHIFT BARS
FIG 7 – TRANSMISSION DIFFERENTIAL, INNER UNIVERSAL
FIG 8 – FRONT SUSPENSION
FIG 9 – STEERING

OPERATION TIMES

A

Alternator.................................. 377

B

Brake Drums.................................. 379
Brakes.................................. 379

C

Cables (Ignition).................................. 377
Calipers.................................. 379
Camshaft.................................. 378
Carburetor.................................. 377
Clutch.................................. 378
Coil, Ignition.................................. 377
Compression Test.................................. 377
Cooling System.................................. 377
Crankshaft.................................. 378
Cylinder Block.................................. 378
Cylinder Head.................................. 378

D

Dash Gauges.................................. 380
Disc Brakes.................................. 379
Distributor.................................. 377

E

Engine Assembly.................................. 378
Engine Mountings.................................. 378
Engine Oiling.................................. 378
Engine Tune-Up.................................. 377
Exhaust System.................................. 377

F

Flywheel.................................. 378
Front Suspension.................................. 378
Fuel Gauges.................................. 380
Fuel Pump.................................. 377
Fuel Tank.................................. 377

G

Generator.................................. 377

H

Hand Brake.................................. 379
Headlight Switch.................................. 380
Heater.................................. 377
Hose (Brake).................................. 379
Hose (Radiator).................................. 377
Hydraulic Brakes.................................. 379

I

Ignition.................................. 377
Ignition Coil.................................. 377
Ignition Switch.................................. 377
Intake Manifold.................................. 377

L

Light Switches.................................. 380

M

Main Bearings.................................. 378
Master Cylinder.................................. 379
Muffler.................................. 377

O

Oil Gauge.................................. 380
Oiling, Engine.................................. 378
Oil Pan.................................. 378
Oil Pump.................................. 378

P

Parking Brake.................................. 379
Piston Rings.................................. 378
Pistons.................................. 378
Power Brake.................................. 379

R

Radiator.................................. 377
Radiator Hose.................................. 377
Rear Axle.................................. 379
Regulator.................................. 377
Rocker Arms.................................. 378
Rod Bearings.................................. 378

S

Shocks (Front).................................. 379
Shocks (Rear).................................. 379
Speedometer.................................. 380
Springs (Front).................................. 379
Springs (Rear).................................. 379
Stabilizer Bar.................................. 379
Starting Motor.................................. 377
Steering Gear.................................. 379
Steering Linkage.................................. 379
Switches (Light).................................. 380
Synchro-Mesh Trans.................................. 378

T

Tachometer.................................. 380
Temperature Gauge.................................. 380
Themostat.................................. 377
Timing Case Cover.................................. 378
Timing Chain.................................. 378
Timing Gears.................................. 378
Transmission.................................. 378
Tune-Up, Engine.................................. 377

U

Universals.................................. 379

V

Valve System.................................. 378

W

Water Pump.................................. 377
Wheel Cylinders.................................. 379
Windshield Wiper.................................. 380

MODEL IDENTIFICATION

The chart below shows the first and last chassis numbers for a given model and year. Before making an estimate or using any prices listed, it is recommended that the vehicle first be identified by the chassis number.

SAAB SONETT III

Model	Year	Chassis Numbers
Saab Sonett III	1970	70500001 - 70500303
	1971	71500001 - 71501265
	1972	97725000001 - 97725002000
	1973	97735000001-97735002300
	1974	97745000001

SAAB 99

Model	Year	Chassis Numbers
Saab 99	1969	99.001.001 - 99.014.259
	1970	99.020.001 - 99.043.053
	1971	99.050.001 - 99.075.331
	1972	99722000001 - 99722031968
Saab 99 EMS	1972	99722012833-99722031968
Saab 99 Land EMS	1973	99732000001
Saab 99L, EMS and X7	1974	99742000001- 99742038672
Saab 99 Cc	1974	99742012200 - 99742038672
Saab 99, 99L, EMS and Cc	1975	99752000001

SAAB 96

Model	Year	Chassis Numbers
Saab 95 V4	1968	52001 - 62059
	1969	95.065.001 - 074.986
	1970	95.080.001 - 088.371
	1971	95.095.001 - 102.180
	1972	95722000001 - 95722008323
	1973	95732000001 - 95732007767
	1974	95742000001 -
Saab 96V4	1968	47001 - 507018
	1969	96.520.001 - 552.859
	1970	96.560.001 - 592.844
	1971	96.600.001 - 627.413
	1972	96722000001 - 96722021567
	1973	96732000001 - 96732023028
	1974	96742000001 -

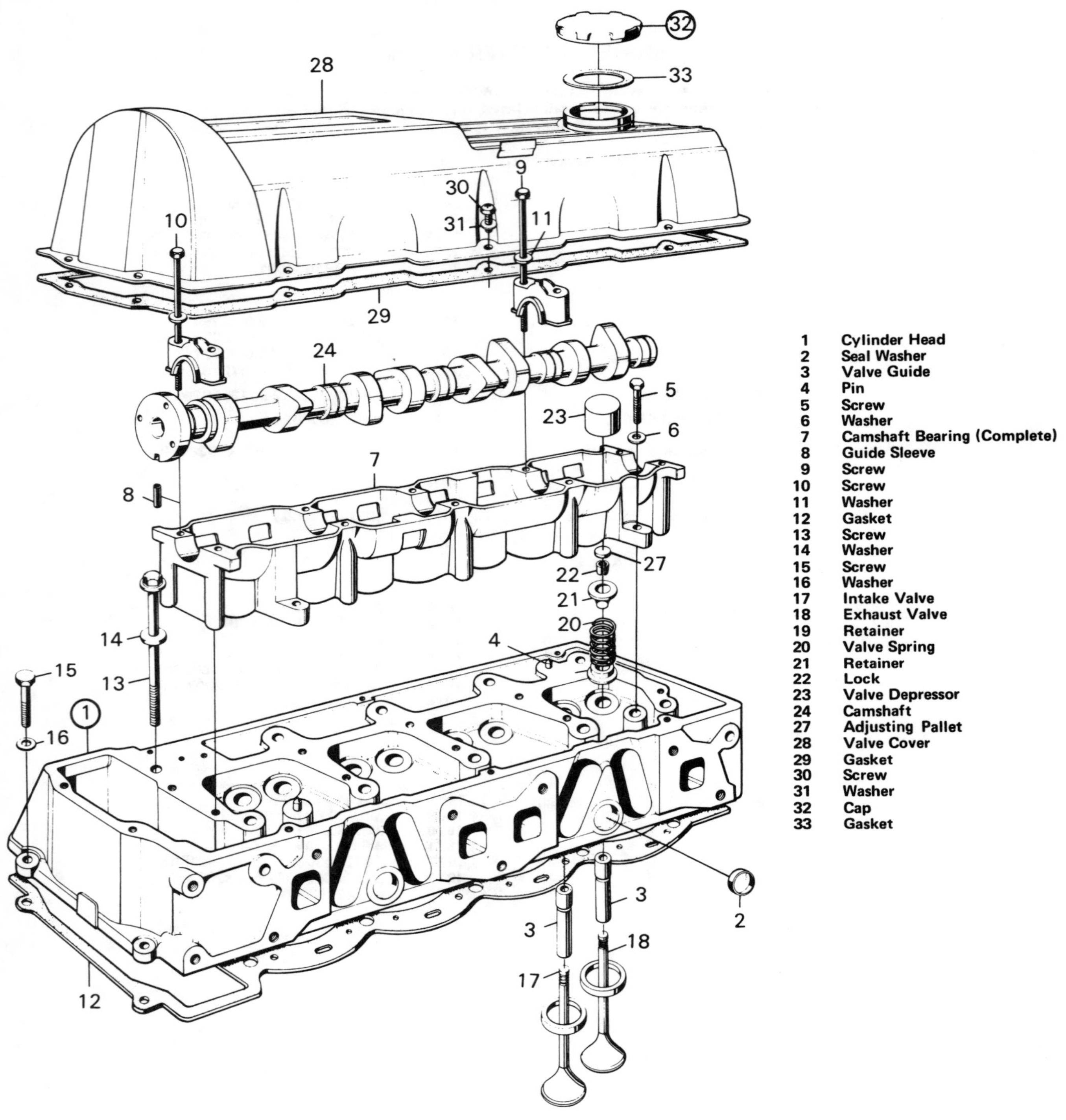

FIG 1 – CYLINDER HEAD & CAMSHAFT – 4 CYL IN LINE

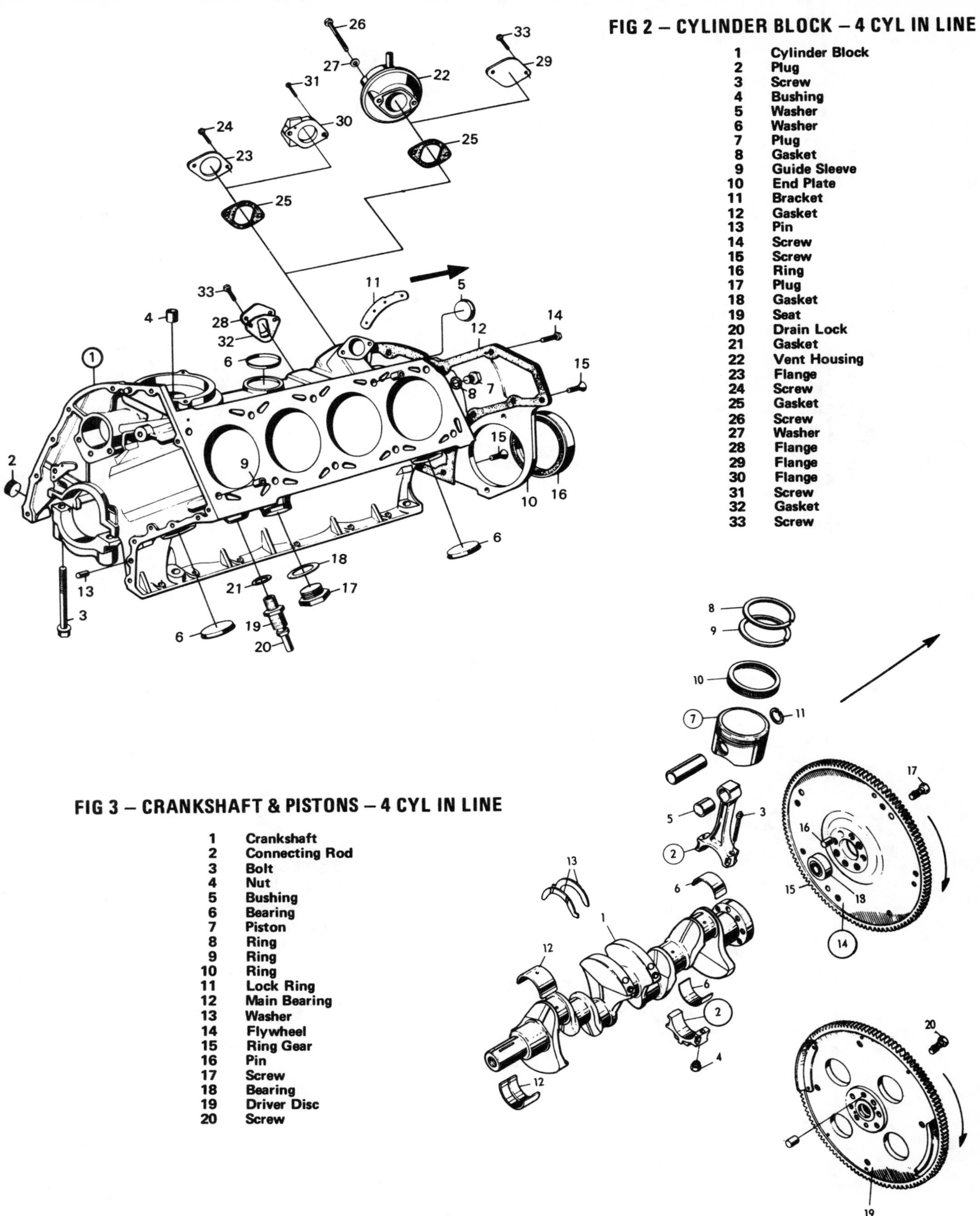

FIG 2 – CYLINDER BLOCK – 4 CYL IN LINE

1 Cylinder Block
2 Plug
3 Screw
4 Bushing
5 Washer
6 Washer
7 Plug
8 Gasket
9 Guide Sleeve
10 End Plate
11 Bracket
12 Gasket
13 Pin
14 Screw
15 Screw
16 Ring
17 Plug
18 Gasket
19 Seat
20 Drain Lock
21 Gasket
22 Vent Housing
23 Flange
24 Screw
25 Gasket
26 Screw
27 Washer
28 Flange
29 Flange
30 Flange
31 Screw
32 Gasket
33 Screw

FIG 3 – CRANKSHAFT & PISTONS – 4 CYL IN LINE

1 Crankshaft
2 Connecting Rod
3 Bolt
4 Nut
5 Bushing
6 Bearing
7 Piston
8 Ring
9 Ring
10 Ring
11 Lock Ring
12 Main Bearing
13 Washer
14 Flywheel
15 Ring Gear
16 Pin
17 Screw
18 Bearing
19 Driver Disc
20 Screw

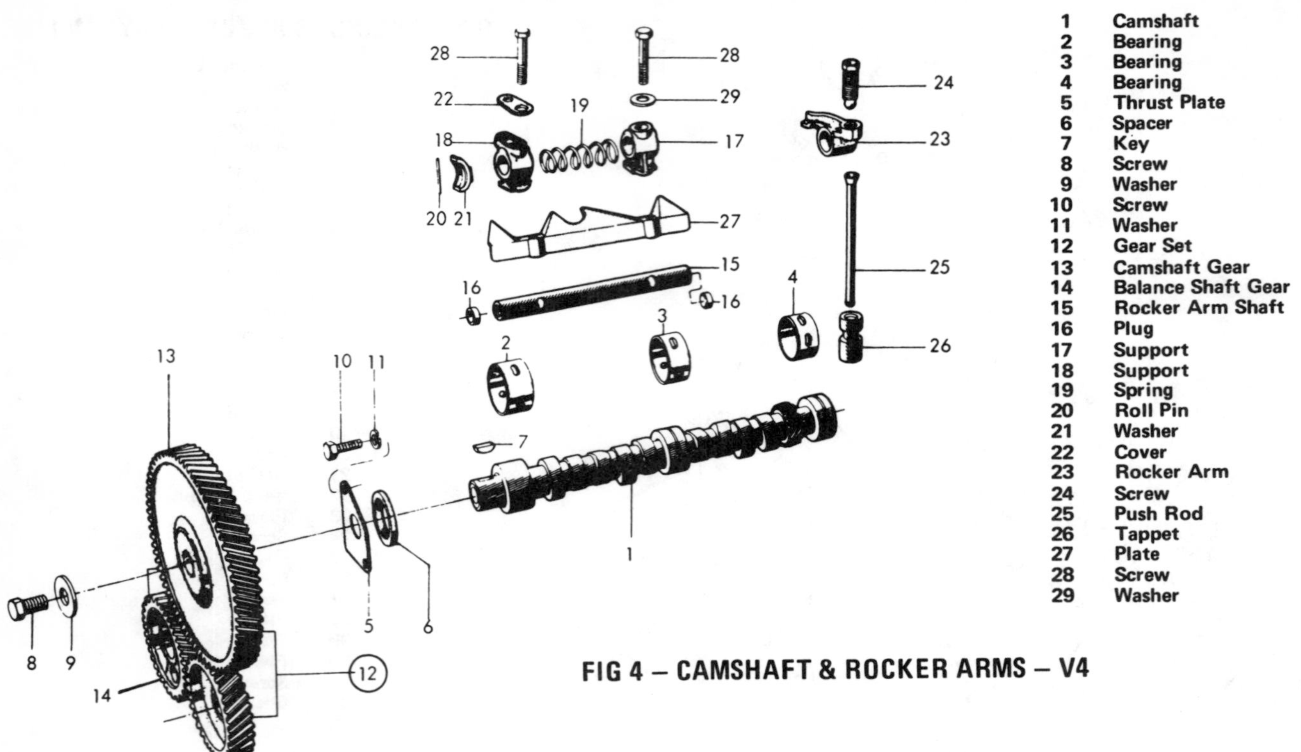
1 Camshaft
2 Bearing
3 Bearing
4 Bearing
5 Thrust Plate
6 Spacer
7 Key
8 Screw
9 Washer
10 Screw
11 Washer
12 Gear Set
13 Camshaft Gear
14 Balance Shaft Gear
15 Rocker Arm Shaft
16 Plug
17 Support
18 Support
19 Spring
20 Roll Pin
21 Washer
22 Cover
23 Rocker Arm
24 Screw
25 Push Rod
26 Tappet
27 Plate
28 Screw
29 Washer

FIG 4 – CAMSHAFT & ROCKER ARMS – V4

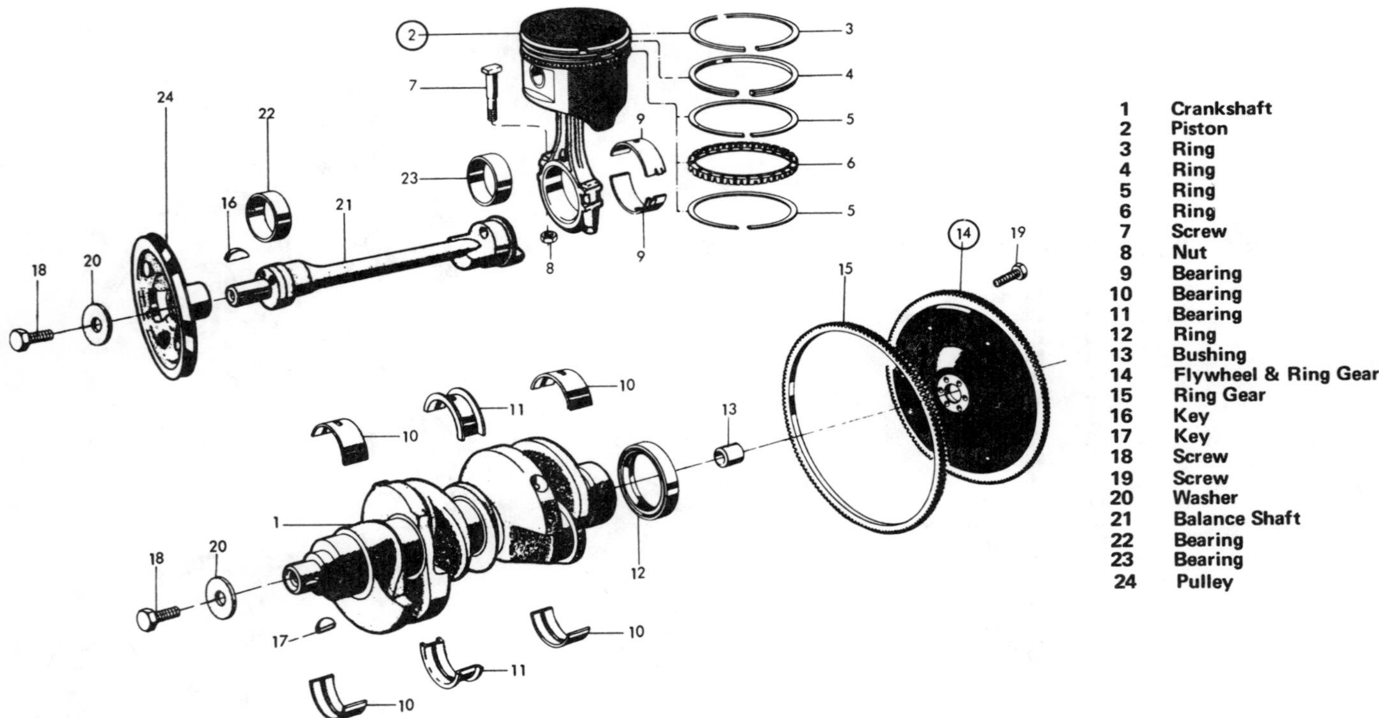
1 Crankshaft
2 Piston
3 Ring
4 Ring
5 Ring
6 Ring
7 Screw
8 Nut
9 Bearing
10 Bearing
11 Bearing
12 Ring
13 Bushing
14 Flywheel & Ring Gear
15 Ring Gear
16 Key
17 Key
18 Screw
19 Screw
20 Washer
21 Balance Shaft
22 Bearing
23 Bearing
24 Pulley

FIG 5 – CRANKSHAFT & PISTONS – V4

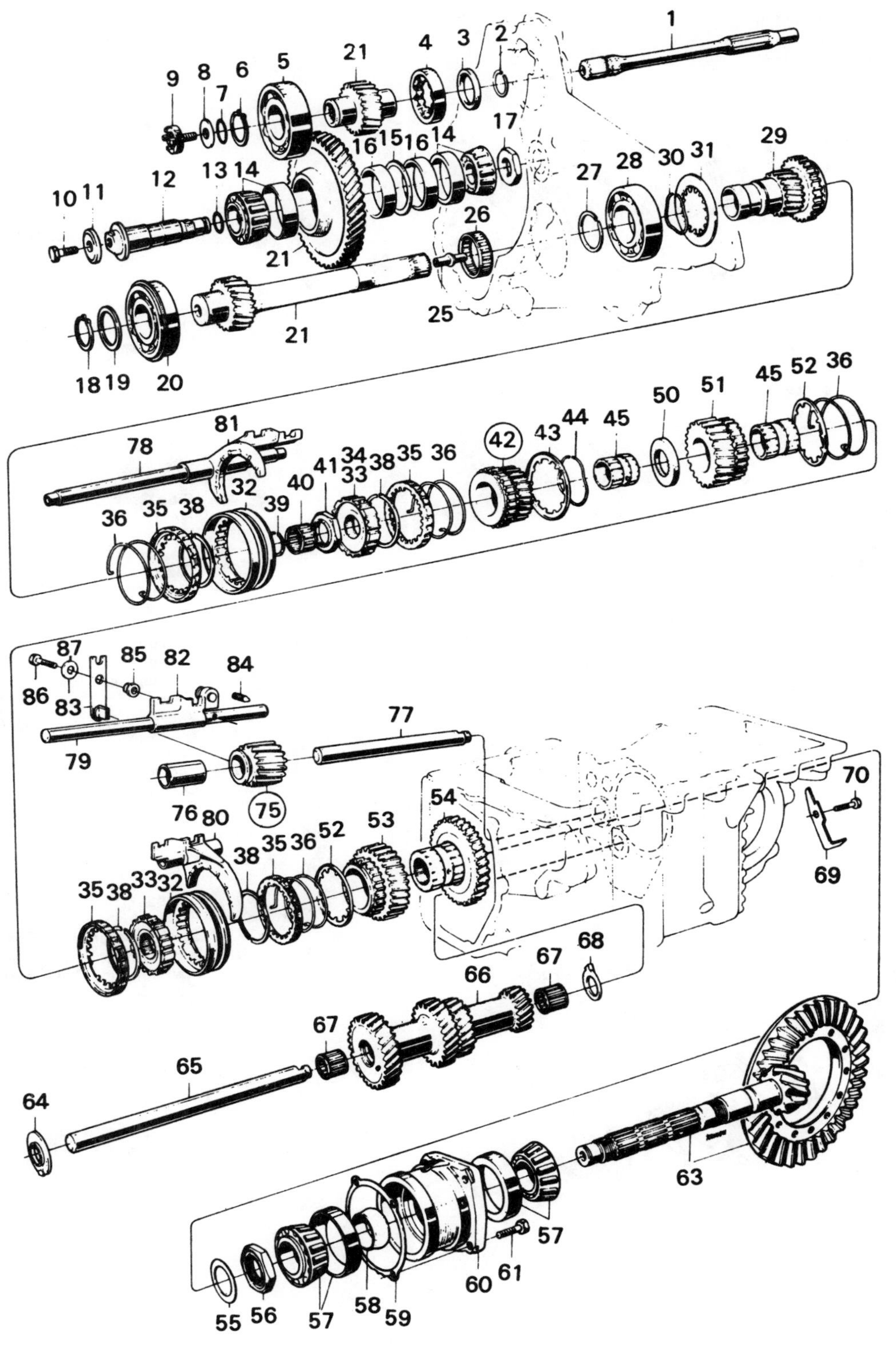

1	Shaft
2	Ring
3	Ring
4	Bearing
5	Bearing
6	Ring
7	O Ring
8	Washer
9	Screw
10	Screw
11	Washer
12	Shaft
13	O Ring
14	Bearing
15	Ring
16	Ring
17	Nut
18	Ring
19	Washer
20	Bearing
21	Primary Gear Set
25	Connecting Pipe
26	Bearing
27	Ring
28	Bearing
29	4th Gear
30	Ring
31	Ring
32	Sychronizer Muff
33	Synchronizer Hub
34	Synchronizer Hub
35	Synchronizer Ring
36	Spring
38	Ring
39	Ring
40	Bearing
41	Nut
42	3rd Gear
43	Ring
44	Ring
45	Bushing
50	Washer
51	2nd Gear
52	Ring
53	1st Gear
54	Reverse Gear
55	Shim
56	Nut
57	Bearing
58	Spacer
59	Shim
60	Retainer
61	Screw
63	Pinion & Gear
64	Washer
65	Shaft
66	Intermediate Gear
67	Bearing
68	Washer
69	Plate
70	Screw
75	Sliding Reverse Gear
76	Bushing
77	Shaft
78	Shaft
79	Shaft
80	Fork
81	Fork
82	Fork
83	Lever
84	Screw
85	Sleeve
86	Screw
87	Washer

FIG 6 – TRANSMISSION – SHAFTS, GEARS, SHIFT BARS

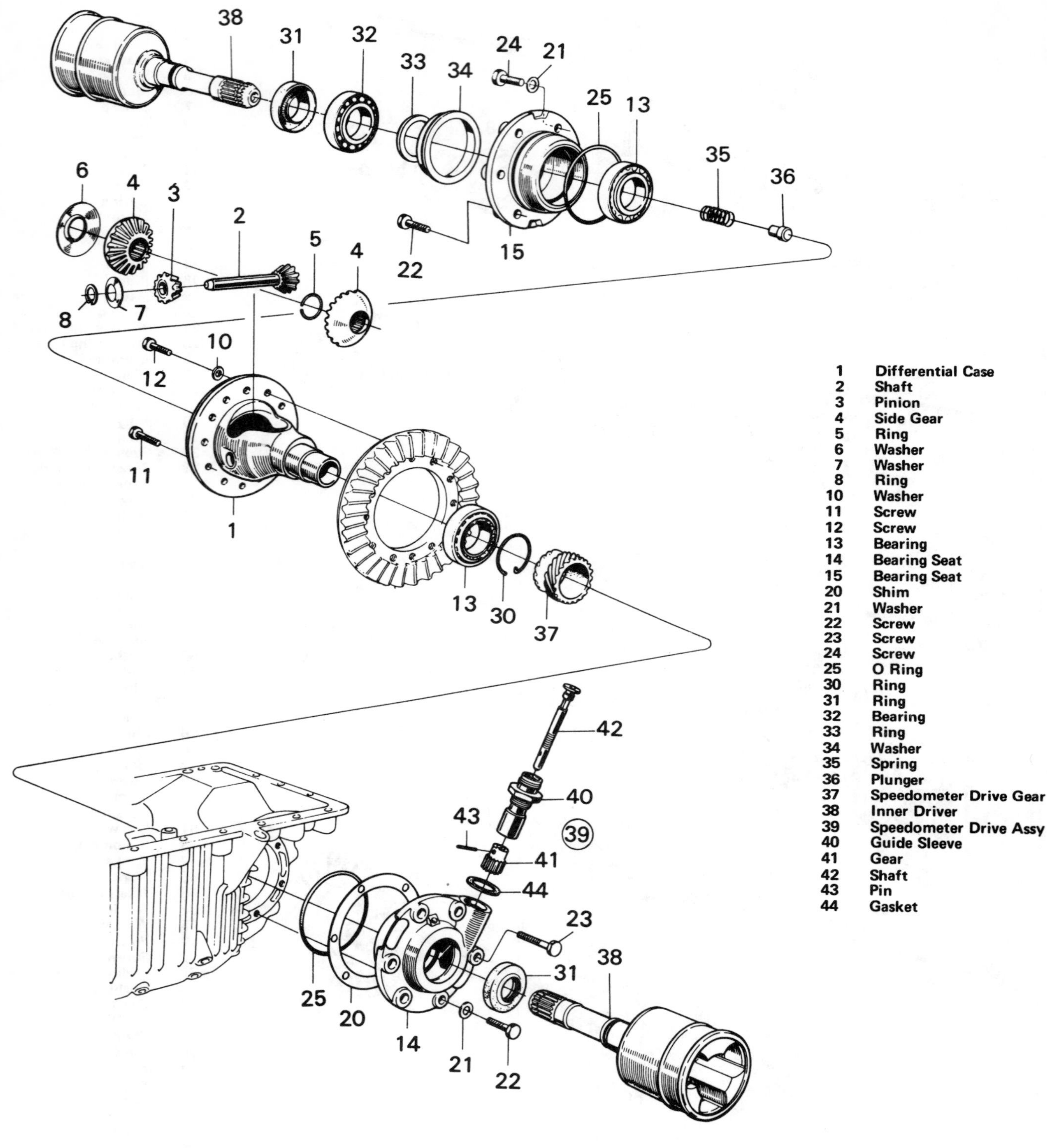
38
31
32
33
34
24
21
25
13
35
36
6
4
3
2
5
4
22
15
8
7
10
12
11
1
13
30
37
42
40
43
39
41
44
23
31
38
25
20
14
21
22
1 Differential Case
2 Shaft
3 Pinion
4 Side Gear
5 Ring
6 Washer
7 Washer
8 Ring
10 Washer
11 Screw
12 Screw
13 Bearing
14 Bearing Seat
15 Bearing Seat
20 Shim
21 Washer
22 Screw
23 Screw
24 Screw
25 O Ring
30 Ring
31 Ring
32 Bearing
33 Ring
34 Washer
35 Spring
36 Plunger
37 Speedometer Drive Gear
38 Inner Driver
39 Speedometer Drive Assy
40 Guide Sleeve
41 Gear
42 Shaft
43 Pin
44 Gasket

FIG 7 – TRANSMISSION – DIFFERENTIAL, INNER UNIVERSAL

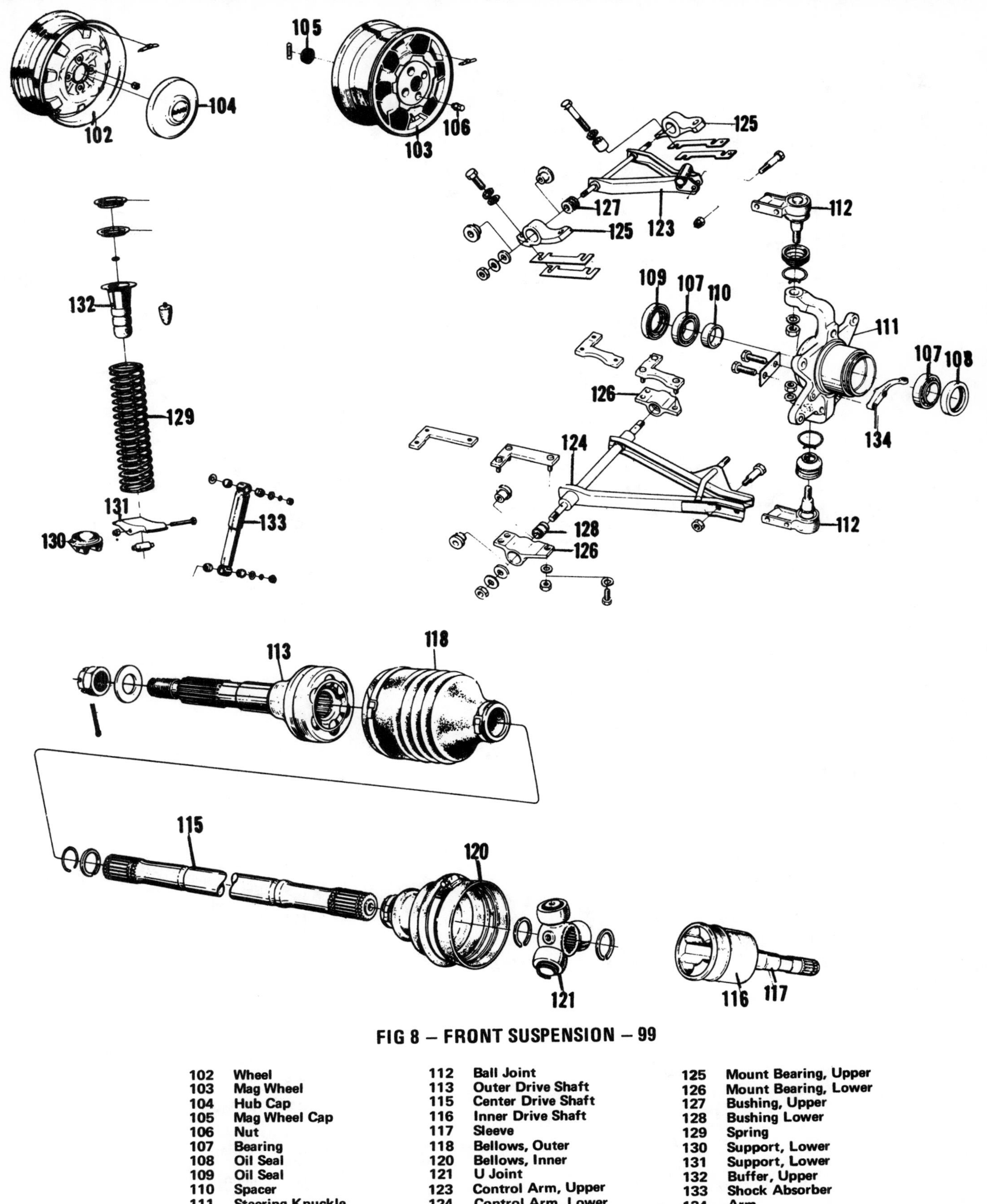

FIG 8 – FRONT SUSPENSION – 99

102 Wheel
103 Mag Wheel
104 Hub Cap
105 Mag Wheel Cap
106 Nut
107 Bearing
108 Oil Seal
109 Oil Seal
110 Spacer
111 Steering Knuckle
112 Ball Joint
113 Outer Drive Shaft
115 Center Drive Shaft
116 Inner Drive Shaft
117 Sleeve
118 Bellows, Outer
120 Bellows, Inner
121 U Joint
123 Control Arm, Upper
124 Control Arm, Lower
125 Mount Bearing, Upper
126 Mount Bearing, Lower
127 Bushing, Upper
128 Bushing Lower
129 Spring
130 Support, Lower
131 Support, Lower
132 Buffer, Upper
133 Shock Absorber
134 Arm

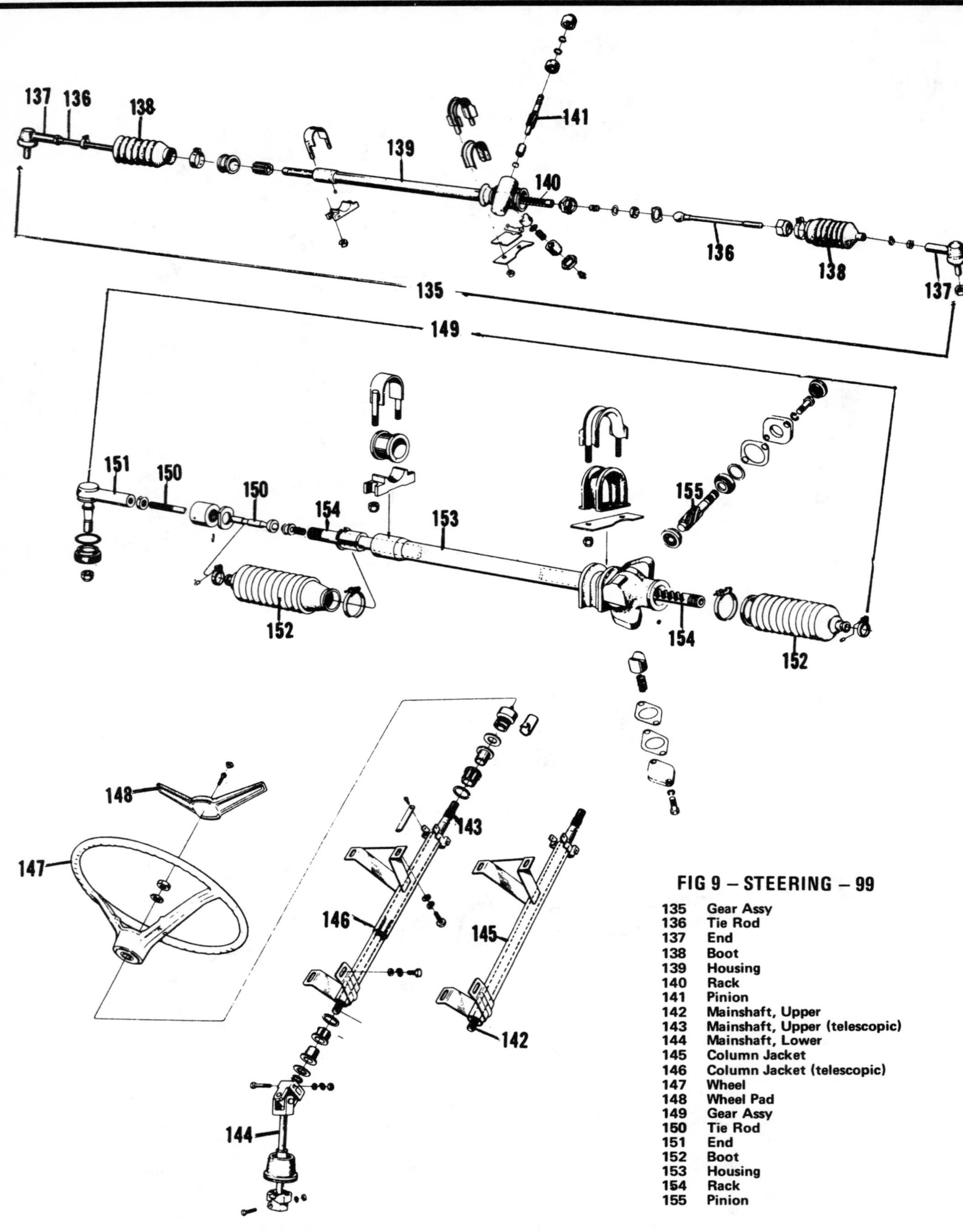

FIG 9 – STEERING – 99

135 Gear Assy
136 Tie Rod
137 End
138 Boot
139 Housing
140 Rack
141 Pinion
142 Mainshaft, Upper
143 Mainshaft, Upper (telescopic)
144 Mainshaft, Lower
145 Column Jacket
146 Column Jacket (telescopic)
147 Wheel
148 Wheel Pad
149 Gear Assy
150 Tie Rod
151 End
152 Boot
153 Housing
154 Rack
155 Pinion

Ignition, Starting & Charging—TIME

OPERATION INDEX

Tune-Up, Minor *1*
Tune-Up, Major *2*
Compression Test *3*
Distributor, R & R Or Renew *4*
Distributor, R & R & Overhaul *5*
Distributor Cap, Renew *6*
Ignition Cable Set, Renew *7*
Ignition Coil, Renew *8*
Starter & Ignition Switch, Renew *9*
Starter, R & R Or Renew *10*
Starter Solenoid, Renew *11*
Starter, R & R & Overhaul *12*
Starter Brushes, Renew *13*
Voltage Regulator, Renew *14*
Alternator Or Generator, R & R Or Renew *15*
Alternator Or Generator, R & R & Overhaul *16*
Alternator Or Generator Brushes, Renew *17*

1—TUNE-UP, MINOR
Includes: Renew points, condenser & plugs. Set spark timing and adjust carburetor idle.
Exc Below 1.3
Series 99 .... 1.4
V-4 Eng. 1.7

2—TUNE-UP, MAJOR
Includes: Check compression, clean or renew and adjust spark plugs. R & R distributor, renew points and condenser. Adjust ignition timing, carburetor and fan belts. Clean battery terminals and service air cleaner. Check coil & clean or replace fuel filter.

Exc Below 2.0
Series 99 .... 2.4
V-4 Eng. 2.6

3—COMPRESSION TEST
Exc Below 0.4
Series 99 & V-4 .... 0.6

4—DISTRIBUTOR, R & R OR RENEW
Exc Below 0.4
Series 99 .... 0.7
V-4 Eng 0.6

5—DISTRIBUTOR, R & R & OVERHAUL
Exc Below 1.7
Series 99 & V-4 .... 1.5

6—DISTRIBUTOR CAP, RENEW
Exc Below 0.3
Series 99 .... 0.2

7—IGNITION CABLE SET, RENEW
Exc Below 0.5
Series 99 .... 0.2

8—IGNITION COIL, RENEW
Exc Below 0.3
Series 99 .... 0.2

9—STARTER & IGNITION SWITCH, RENEW
Exc Below 0.5
Series 99 .... 0.3

10—STARTER, R & R OR RENEW
Exc Below 0.7
Series 99 .... 0.8
V-4 Eng 1.0

11—STARTER SOLENOID, RENEW
Exc Below 1.0
Series 99 .... 1.1
V-4 Eng 1.3

12—STARTER, R & R & OVERHAUL
Includes: Turn down commutator and replace all parts necessary.
Exc Below 1.7
Series 99 .... 2.3
V-4 Eng 2.2

13—STARTER BRUSHES, RENEW
Exc Below 1.3
Series 99 .... 1.7
V-4 Eng 1.8

14—VOLTAGE REGULATOR, RENEW
Exc Below 0.5
Series 99 & V-4 .... 0.2

15—ALTERNATOR OR GENERATOR, R & R OR RENEW
All Models 0.4

16—ALTERNATOR OR GENERATOR, R & R & OVERHAUL
Exc Below 1.3
Series 99 .... 1.9

17—ALTERNATOR RO GENERATOR BRUSHES, RENEW
All Models 1.1

Fuel, Intake & Exhaust Systems—TIME

OPERATION INDEX

Carburetor, R & R Or Renew *1*
Carburetor, R & R & Overhaul *2*
Fuel Pump, R & R Or Renew *3*
Fuel Pump, R & R & Overhaul *4*
Fuel Tank, R & R Or Renew *5*
Choke Cable Assy, Renew *6*
Intake Manifold Or Gasket, Renew *7*
Exhaust Manifold Or Gasket, Renew *8*
Exhaust System, Renew *9*
Exhaust Pipe, Renew *10*
Muffler, Renew *11*
Tail Pipe, Renew *12*

1—CARBURETOR, R & R OR RENEW
Exc Below 0.5
V-4 Eng 0.6

2—CARBURETOR, R & R & OVERHAUL
Exc Below 1.5
Series 99 .... 1.3
V-4 Eng 1.6

3—FUEL PUMP, R & R OR RENEW
Exc Below 0.5
Series 99 .... 0.3
V-4 Eng 0.4

4—FUEL PUMP, R & R & OVERHAUL
Exc Below 1.0
Series 99 .... 0.7

5—FUEL TANK, R & R OR RENEW
Exc Below 1.2
Series 99 .... 1.5
V-4 Eng—
  Exc Below 2.0
  Sonett 2.5

6—CHOKE CABLE ASSY, RENEW
All Models 0.4

7—INTAKE MANIFOLD OR GASKET, RENEW
Exc Below ①0.5
Series 99 .... ②1.0
V-4 Eng 1.5
①*To Renew Manifold, Add* *0.2*
②*To Renew Manifold, Add* *0.7*

8—EXHAUST MANIFOLD OR GASKET, RENEW
Exc Below 1.0
Series 99 .... 1.2
V-4 Eng 0.7

9—EXHAUST SYSTEM, RENEW
Exc Below 1.3
Series 99 .... 2.0
V-4 Eng 2.4

10—EXHAUST PIPE, RENEW
Exc Below 0.7
Series 99 .... 0.8

11—MUFFLER, RENEW
Front—
  Exc Below 0.7
  Series 99 .... ①1.0
  V-4 Eng 1.8
Rear—
  All Models 0.5
①*Includes R & R Exhaust Pipe*

12—TAIL PIPE, RENEW
Exc Below ①1.0
Series 99 .... 0.5
①*Includes R & R Rear Muffler*

Engine Cooling & Heater System—TIME

OPERATION INDEX

Radiator, R & R Or Renew *1*
Overflow Tank, Renew *2*
Radiator Hoses, Renew *3*
Water Pump, R & R Or Renew *4*
Water Pump, R & R & Overhaul *5*
Thermostat, Renew *6*
Heat Exchanger, Renew *7*
Heater Motor, Renew *8*
Heater Control Cables, Renew *9*
Heater Hoses, Renew *10*

1—RADIATOR, R & R OR RENEW
All Models 0.8

2—OVERFLOW TANK, RENEW
Exc Below 0.2
Series 99 .... 0.3

3—RADIATOR HOSES, RENEW
Exc Below 0.3
V-4 Eng—
  Radiator To Pump 0.8

4—WATER PUMP, R & R OR RENEW
Exc Below 1.0
Series 99 .... 1.2
V-4 Eng 2.0

5—WATER PUMP, R & R & OVERHAUL
Exc Below 4.5
Series 99 .... 1.5
V-4 Eng 2.5

6—THERMOSTAT, RENEW
Exc Below 0.4
V-4 Eng 0.5

7—HEAT EXCHANGER, RENEW
Exc Below 0.9
Series 97 .... 0.7
Series 99 .... 1.0

8—HEATER MOTOR, RENEW
Exc Below 0.5
Series 99 .... 0.4

9—HEATER CONTROL CABLES, RENEW
All Models 0.4

10—HEATER HOSES, RENEW
All Models 0.2

Engine—TIME

OPERATION INDEX

Engine, R & R *1*
Engine, R & R & Overhaul *2*
Engine (Short) Renew & Grind Valves *3*
Engine Block, Renew *4*
(Continued)

Engine—TIME Cont'd

Cylinder Head, R & R Or Gasket, Renew 5
Valves Grind 6
One Valve, Renew & Grind 7
Valve Springs, Renew 8
Rocker Arm Cover Gasket, Renew 9
Valve Rocker Arm Assy, Renew 10
Valves, Adjust 11
Oil Pan Or Gasket, R & R Or Renew 12
Front Engine Cover Or Gasket, R & R Or Renew 13
Timing Chain Or Drive Gears, Renew 14
Distributor Drive Cover Assy, Renew 15
Camshaft, R & R Or Renew 16
Balance Shaft, Renew 17
Idler Shaft, Renew 18
Oil Pump, R & R Or Renew 19
Piston(S) Or Ring(S), Renew 20
Rings & Main Bearings, Renew & Grind Valves 21
Rod Bearings(S), Renew 22
Main Bearings, Renew 23
Main & Rod Bearings, Renew 24
Crankshaft, R & R Or Renew 25
Crankshaft Pulley & Vibration Damper, Renew 26

1—ENGINE, R & R

Does not include transfer of any park of engine or replacement or special equipment.

Exc Below ①3.0
Series 99 ....②3.5
V-4 Eng ③4.5
Sonett ③5.0
①To Renew Engine, Add 0.8
②To Renew Engine, Add 3.0
③To Renew Engine, Add 1.5

2—ENGINE, R & R & OVERHAUL

Includes rebore cylinders with boring bar, renew pistons, rings, pins & bearings, plastigauge bearings and perform minor tune-up

Exc Below 8.8
Series 99 ....13.6
V-4 Eng 13.8
Sonett 14.3

3—ENGINE (SHORT), RENEW & GRIND VALVES

V-4 Eng 15.5

4—ENGINE BLOCK, RENEW

Exc Below 5.0
Series 99 ....10.9
V-4 Eng 13.5

5—CYLINDER HEAD, R & R OR GASKET, RENEW

Exc Below 1.2
Series 99 ....3.5
V-4 Eng ①1.7
①For 2nd Head, Add 1.0

6—VALVES, GRIND

Includes: R & R head(s) & adjust tappets

Exc Below 5.4
Series 99 ....8.0

7—ONE VALVE, RENEW & GRIND

Includes: R & R head & adjust tappets

Exc Below 2.8
Series 99 ....4.0

8—VALVE SPRINGS (ONE), RENEW

Includes replace valve stem oil seals & adjust tappets.

Exc Below ①1.0
Series 99 ....②1.5
①For Each Additional, Add 0.1
②For Each Additional, Add 0.4

9—ROCKER ARM COVER GASKET, RENEW

All Models 0.4

10—VALVE ROCKER ARM ASSY, RENEW

V-4 Eng, Each 0.8

11—VALVES, ADJUST

Exc Below 0.7
Series 99 ....1.0

12—OIL PAN OR GASKET, R & R OR RENEW

All Models 4.0

13—FRONT ENGINE COVER OR GASKET, R & R OR RENEW

Exc Below ①1.5
Series 99 ....②4.8
①To Renew Balance Shaft Seal, Add 0.2
②Includes R & R Engine.

14—TIMING CHAIN OR DRIVE GEARS, RENEW

Includes: R & R engine

Series 99 ....①5.7
①To Renew Drive Gear, Add 0.3

15—DISTRIBUTOR DRIVE COVER ASSY, RENEW

All Models 1.9

16—CAMSHAFT, R & R OR RENEW

Series 99 ....1.1
V-4 Eng ①5.1
①To Remove Balance Shaft Bearing, Add 0.5

17—BALANCE SHAFT, RENEW

V-4 Eng ①6.7
①To Renew Bearing, Add 0.5

18—IDLER SHAFT, RENEW

Series 99 ....①9.4
Includes R & R Engine & Head.

19—OIL PUMP, R & R OR RENEW

Exc Below 0.5
Series 99 ....0.3
V-4 Eng 5.2

—NOTE—

For Overhaul, Add 0.4

20—PISTON(S) OR RING(S), RENEW

Exc Below, All 6.0
Series 99 ....①6.5
V-4 Eng ②7.0
①For Each Additional, Add 0.5
②For Each Additional, Add 0.4

21—RINGS & MAIN BEARINGS, RENEW & GRIND VALVES

All Models 8.4

22—ROD BEARING(S), RENEW

Exc Below 7.5
Series 99 ....10.5

23—MAIN BEARINGS, RENEW

Includes plastigauge bearings.

Exc Below 8.0
Series 99 ....11.0

24—MAIN & ROD BEARINGS, RENEW

Includes plastigauge bearings

Exc Below 8.5
Series 99 ....11.5

25—CRANKSHAFT, R&R OR RENEW

Exc Below 6.0
Series 99 ....①12.8
V-4 Eng 7.0

—NOTE—

①To Renew Front Seal, Add 0.3

26—CRANKSHAFT PULLEY & VIBRATION DAMPER, RENEW

Exc Below 1.0
Series 99 ....3.5
V-4 Eng 0.5

Clutch, Mounts & Transmission—TIME

OPERATION INDEX

Flywheel, R&R & Renew 1
Flywheel Ring Gear, Renew 2
Clutch Or Disc, Renew 3
Clutch Master Cylinder Renew 4
Clutch Slave Cylinder, Renew 5
Bleed Hydraulic System 6
Release Bearing, Renew 7
Release Fork (Or Lever), Renew 8
Clutch Pedal, Adjust 9
Engine Mounts, Renew 10
Transmission Assy, R&R Or Renew 11
Transmission Assy, R&R & Overhaul 12
Flywheel Hub, Renew 13
Clutch Shaft Oil Seal, Renew 14
End Cover Gasket, R&R Or Renew 15
Gear Lever Housing (Top Cover), R&R Or Renew 16
Gear Shaft Joint, Renew 17
Adjust Shift Pattern 18
Gearshift Lever Stop, Renew 19

1—FLYWHEEL, R&R OR RENEW

Exc Below 3.3
Series 99 ....1.5
Sonett 5.3
V-4 Eng 4.8

2—FLYWHEEL RING GEAR, RENEW

Exc Below 3.6
Series 99 ....1.8
V-4 Eng 5.1
Sonett 5.6

3—CLUTCH OR DISC, RENEW

Exc Below 3.3
Series 99 ....1.5
V-4 Eng 4.8
Sonett 5.3

4—CLUTCH MASTER CYLINDER, RENEW

All Models 0.7

—NOTE—

To Overhaul, Add 0.5

5—CLUTCH SLAVE CYLINDER, RENEW

Exc Below 0.4
Series 99 ....0.5

—NOTE—

To Overhaul, Add 0.8

6—BLEED HYDRAULIC SYSTEM

All Models 0.2

7—RELEASE BEARING, RENEW

Exc Below 3.2
Series 99 ....1.5
V-4 Eng 4.7
Sonett 5.2

8—RELEASE FORK (OR LEVER), RENEW

Exc Below 4.9
Series 99 ....5.3

9—CLUTCH PEDAL ADJUST

All Models 0.2

10—ENGINE MOUNTS, RENEW

Engine—
Exc Below, One ①1.3
Series 99, One ①0.9
V-4 Eng, One ①1.0
Rear—
Exc Below 4.5
V-4 Eng 5.0
Sonett 5.5
①For Each Additional, Add 0.3

11—TRANSMISSION ASSY, R&R OR RENEW

Includes power unit

Exc Below 4.0
Series 99 ....4.4

(Continued)

Clutch, Mounts & Transmission—TIME Cont'd

V-4 Eng 5.0
Sonett 5.0

12—TRANSMISSION ASSY, R&R & OVERHAUL

4-Speed—
- Exc Below 11.0
- Series 99 ....8.4
- V-4 Eng 11.5
- Sonett 12.0

3-Speed—
- Exc Below 10.0
- Series 99 ....10.9
- V-4 Eng 10.5
- Sonett 11.0

13—FLYWHEEL HUB, RENEW

Includes: R&R trans

Exc Below 5.0
Series 99 ....5.9
V-4 Eng 5.5
Sonett 6.0

14—CLUTCH SHAFT OIL SEAL, RENEW

Exc Below 4.3
Series 99 ....6.7
V-4 Eng 4.8
Sonett 5.3

15—END COVER GASKET, R&R OR RENEW

Exc Below 4.4
V-4 Eng 4.9
Sonett 5.4

16—GEAR LEVER HOUSING (TOP COVER), R&R OR RENEW

Exc Below 4.4
V-4 Eng 4.9
Sonett 5.4

17—GEAR SHAFT JOINT, RENEW

Exc Below 0.5
Series 99 ....0.8

18—ADJUST SHIFT PATTERN

Exc Below 0.2
Series 99 ....0.4

19—GEARSHIFT LEVER STOP, RENEW

All Models 0.5

Brakes, Steering, Suspension, Universals & Rear Axle—TIME

OPERATION INDEX

Brake Shoes Or Friction Pads, Renew 1
Master Cylinder, Renew 2
Master Cylinder, R&R & Overhaul 3
Wheel Cylinder, Renew 4
Caliper Assy, Renew 5
Caliper Assy, R&R & Overhaul 6
Bleed System 7
Brake Hose, Renew 8
Disc, Renew 9
Vacuum Power Unit, Renew 10
Non Return Valve, Renew 11
Brake Drum, Renew 12
Parking Brake Cable, Renew 13
Rack & Pinion Assy, Renew 14
Rack & Pinion Assy, Overhaul 15
Rack & Pinion Boot, Renew 16
Tie Rod End, Renew 17
Front End, Alignment 18
Toe-In, Adjust 19
Spring(S), Renew 20
Ball Joints, Renew 21
Steering Knuckle Housing, Renew 22
Control Arm(S), Renew 23
Control Arm Brackets Or Bushings, Renew 24
Stabilizer Bar Or Bushings, Renew 25
Shock Absorbers, Renew 26
Rear Axle, R&R Or Renew 27
Rear Axle Center Bearing Bracket, Renew 28
Wheel Bearings, Renew 29
Wheel Bearing Seals, Renew 30
Universal Joints, Renew 31

1—BRAKE SHOES OR FRICTION PADS, RENEW

Drum Type—
- Each 0.8
- Front, Both 1.3
- Rear, Both 1.5
- All Four 2.5

Disc Pads—
- Each 0.3
- Front, Both 0.5
- Series 99, All Four 0.8

2—MASTER CYLINDER, RENEW

Exc Below 0.9
Series 97 ....1.5
Series 99 ....0.8

3—MASTER CYLINDER, R&R & OVERHAUL

Exc Below 0.9
Series 99 ....0.7

4—WHEEL CYLINDER, RENEW

Each 0.8

5—CALIPER ASSY, RENEW

Exc Below 0.7
Series 99 ....0.5

6—CALIPER ASSY, R&R & OVERHAUL

Exc Below 1.5
Series 99 ....1.3

2—BLEED SYSTEMS

All Models 0.5

8—BRAKE HOSE, RENEW

Exc Below, Each 0.5
Series 99, Each 0.4

9—DISC, RENEW

Exc Below, Each 0.7
Series 99, Each 0.4

10—VACUUM POWER UNIT, RENEW

Exc Below 0.5
Series 99 ....0.8

11—NON RETURN VALVE, RENEW

All Models 0.2

12—BRAKE DRUM, RENEW

Each 0.3

13—PARKING BRAKE CABLE, RENEW

Exc Below 1.2
Series 99 ....1.6

14—RACK & PINION ASSY, RENEW

Exc Below 2.5
Series 97 ....3.0
Series 99 ....1.5

15—RACK & PINION ASSY, OVERHAUL

Exc Below 3.5
Series 97 ....4.0
Series 99 ....2.5

16—RACK & PINION BOOT, RENEW

Exc Below 1.2
Series 99 ....1.4

17—TIE ROD END, RENEW

Includes: Adjust toe-in

Exc Below 1.6
Series 99 ....1.9

18—FRONT END ALIGNMENT

All Models 1.0

19—TOE-IN, ADJUST

Exc Below 0.5
Series 99 ....0.4

20—SPRING(S), RENEW

Front (Each)—
- Exc Below 1.0
- Series 99 ....0.9

Rear (Each) 0.6

21—BALL JOINTS, RENEW

Lower—
- Exc Below 0.5
- Series 99 ....0.6

Upper—
- Exc Below 0.9
- Series 99 ....1.0

22—STEERING KNUCKLE HOUSING, RENEW

Includes: Set toe-in

All Models 1.7

23—CONTROL ARM(S), RENEW

Lower (Each)—
- Exc Below 2.0
- Series 99 ....2.1

Upper (Each)—
- Exc Below 1.4
- Series 99 ....1.5

24—CONTROL ARM BRACKETS OR BUSHINGS, RENEW

Lower (Each)—
- Exc Below 1.7
- Series 99 ....1.9

Upper (Each)—
- Exc Below 2.0
- Series 99 ....2.1

25—STABILIZER BAR OR BUSHINGS, RENEW

All Models—
- Front Or Rear 0.8

26—SHOCK ABSORBERS, RENEW

Front (Each)—
- All Models 0.3

Rear (Each)—
- Exc Below 0.5
- Series 95 ....0.8

27—REAR AXLE, R&R OR RENEW

Exc Below 5.0
Series 99 ....4.0

28—REAR AXLE CENTER BEARING BRACKET, RENEW

All Models 2.5

29—WHEEL BEARINGS, RENEW

Front (Each)—
- All Models 1.7

Rear (Each)—
- All Models ①1.1

①*Includes Renew Grease Seals.*

30—WHEEL BEARING SEALS, RENEW

Front, All Models (Each)—
- Outer 0.5
- Inner 1.2

Rear (Each)—
- All Models 1.1

31—UNIVERSAL JOINTS, RENEW

Inner—
- Exc Below 0.8
- Series 99 ....0.9

Outer—
- Exc Below 1.5
- Series 99 ....1.6

Speedometer, W/S Wipers & Instruments—TIME

OPERATION INDEX

Speedometer Head, Renew 1
W/S Wiper Motor, Renew 2
W/S Wiper Motor, R&R & Overhaul 3
W/S Wiper Linkage, Renew 4
W/S Wiper Spindle, Renew 5
Fuel Gauge (Dash Unit), Renew 6
Fuel Gauge Transmitter Renew 7

(Continued)

Speedometer, W/S Wipers & Instruments—TIME Cont'd

Oil Pressure Switch, Renew *8*
Temperature Gauge (Dash Unit), Renew *9*
Temperature Transmitter Renew *10*
Tachometer, Renew *11*
Headlight Switch, Renew *12*
Headlamp Dimmer Switch, Renew *13*
Stop Light Switch, Renew *14*
Brake Warning Contact, Renew *15*
Directional Signal Switch, Renew *16*
Hazard Flasher Switch, Renew *17*

1—SPEEDOMETER HEAD, RENEW
Exc Below 0.5
Series 97 .... 0.7

2—W/S WIPER MOTOR, RENEW
Exc Below 0.5
Series 99 .... 0.6

3—W/S WIPER MOTOR, R&R & OVERHAUL
Exc Below 1.5
Series 99 .... 1.9

4—W/S WIPER LINKAGE, RENEW
Exc Below 0.4
Series 99 .... 1.4

5—W/S WIPER SPINDLE, RENEW
Exc Below 1.1
Series 97 .... 1.3

6—FUEL GAUGE (DASH UNIT), RENEW
Exc Below 0.5
Series 97 .... 0.7

7—FUEL GAUGE TRANSMITTER, RENEW
All Models 0.5

8—OIL PRESSURE SWITCH, RENEW
All Models 0.3

9—TEMPERATURE GAUGE (DASH UNIT), RENEW
Exc Below 0.5
Series 97 .... 0.8

10—TEMPERATURE TRANSMITTER, RENEW
All Models 0.4

11—TACHOMETER, RENEW
All Models 0.5

12—HEADLIGHT SWITCH, RENEW
Exc Below 0.4
Series 97 .... 0.6
Series 99 .... 0.3

13—HEADLAMP DIMMER SWITCH, RENEW
All Models 0.4

14—STOP LIGHT SWITCH, RENEW
Exc Below 0.3
Series 97 .... 0.4
Series 99 .... 0.4

15—BRAKE WARNING CONTACT, RENEW
All Models 0.3

16—DIRECTIONAL SIGNAL SWITCH, RENEW
Exc Below 0.5
Series 99 .... 0.4

17—HAZARD FLASHER SWITCH, RENEW
Exc Below 0.2
Series 97 .... 0.4

IDENTIFICATION

ALL MODELS............................. 382

ILLUSTRATIONS

FIG 1 – ENGINE – CYLINDER HEAD
FIG 2 – ENGINE – CRANKSHAFT
FIG 3 – ENGINE – CAMSHAFT & TIMING GEARS
FIG 4 – ENGINE – VALVES & ROCKERS
FIG 5 – TRANSMISSION ASSEMBLY
FIG 6 – TRANSMISSION MAINSHAFT & LOW GEARS
FIG 7 – TRANSMISSION COUNTERSHAFT
FIG 8 – FRONT SUSPENSION ARM & SPINDLES
FIG 9 – FRONT SUSPENSION LOWER ARMS
FIG 10 – FRONT TORSION BARS
FIG 11 – FRONT STABILIZER BAR
FIG 12 – STEERING WHEEL & HOUSING
FIG 13 – STEERING RACK & PINION
FIG 14 – REAR TORSION ARMS
FIG 15 – REAR LOWER ARMS
FIG 16 – DIFFERENTIAL

OPERATION TIMES

A

Alternator.. 390
Automatic Transmission..................... 392

B

Brake Drums...................................... 393
Brakes.. 392

C

Cables (Ignition)................................ 390
Calipers.. 392
Camshaft.. 391
Carburetor.. 390
Clutch... 392
Coil, Ignition...................................... 390
Compression Test............................... 390
Connecting Rods................................ 391
Cooling System................................... 390
Crankshaft.. 391
Cylinder Head..................................... 391

D

Dash Gauges....................................... 393
Differential... 393
Disc Brakes... 392
Distributor.. 390

E

Emission Controls............................... 390
Engine Assembly................................. 391
Engine Mountings................................ 392
Engine Oiling....................................... 391
Engine Tune-Up.................................. 390
Exhaust System.................................... 390

F

Flywheel.. 391
Front Suspension................................ 393
Fuel Gauges.. 393
Fuel Pump... 390
Fuel Tank.. 390

G

Generator.. 390

H

Hand Brake.. 393
Headlight Switch................................. 393
Heater.. 390
Hose (Brake).. 392
Hose (Radiator).................................... 390
Hydraulic Brakes.................................. 392

I

Ignition.. 390
Ignition Coil... 390
Ignition Switch..................................... 390
Intake Manifold.................................... 390

L

Light Switches...................................... 393

M

Main Bearings....................................... 391
Master Cylinder.................................... 392
Muffler.. 390

O

Oil Gauge... 393
Oiling, Engine....................................... 391
Oil Pan.. 391

P

Parking Brake....................................... 393
Piston Rings.. 391
Pistons.. 391

R

Radiator.. 390
Radiator Hose....................................... 390
Rear Axle.. 393
Regulator.. 390
Rocker Arms... 391
Rod Bearings... 391

S

Shocks (Front)....................................... 393
Shocks (Rear).. 393
Speedometer... 393
Springs (Front)...................................... 393
Springs (Rear)....................................... 393
Stabilizer Bar... 393
Starting Motor....................................... 390
Steering Gear.. 393
Steering Linkage.................................... 393
Switches (Light).................................... 393
Synchro-Mesh Trans.............................. 392

T

Temperature Gauge................................ 393
Thermostat.. 390
Timing Case Cover................................. 391
Timing Chain... 391
Timing Gears... 391
Torsion Bar... 393
Transaxle... 392
Transmission, Manual............................ 392
Transmission, Automatic....................... 392
Tune-Up, Engine.................................... 390

V

Vacuum Control Unit............................. 390
Valve Lifters.. 391
Valve System... 391

W

Water Pump... 390
Wheel Cylinders.................................... 392
Windshield Wiper.................................. 393

MODEL 1118

CAR SERIAL NUMBER – Stamped on the left side of the rear panel upper crossmember.

BODY NUMBER – Stamped on the right side of the rear panel upper crossmember.

ENGINE NUMBER – Stamped on a metal strip riveted to the cylinder block above timing gear cover.

TRANSMISSION NUMBER – Stamped on the side of the trans-axle.

MODEL 1204

ENGINE AND CAR SERIAL NUMBERS

A: SERIAL NUMBER
B: BODY SERIAL NUMBER
C: PAINT Ref. NUMBER

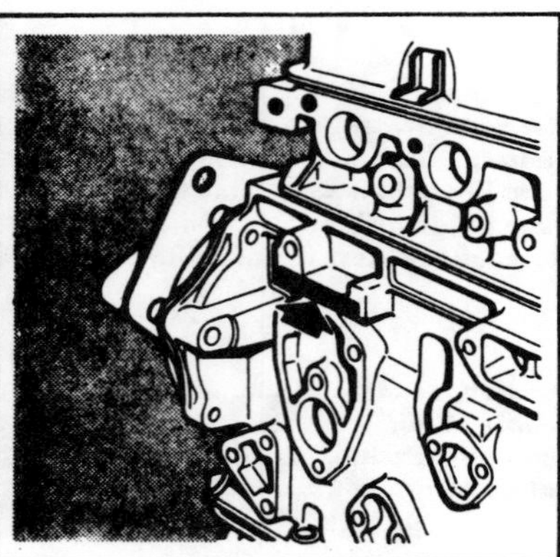

ENGINE SERIAL NUMBER

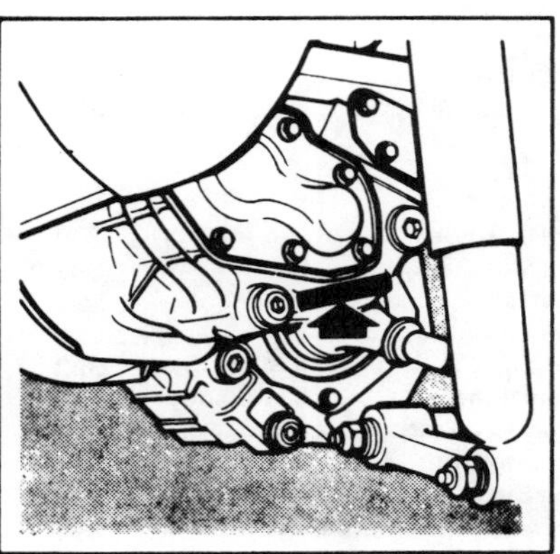

TRANS-AXLE SERIAL NUMBER

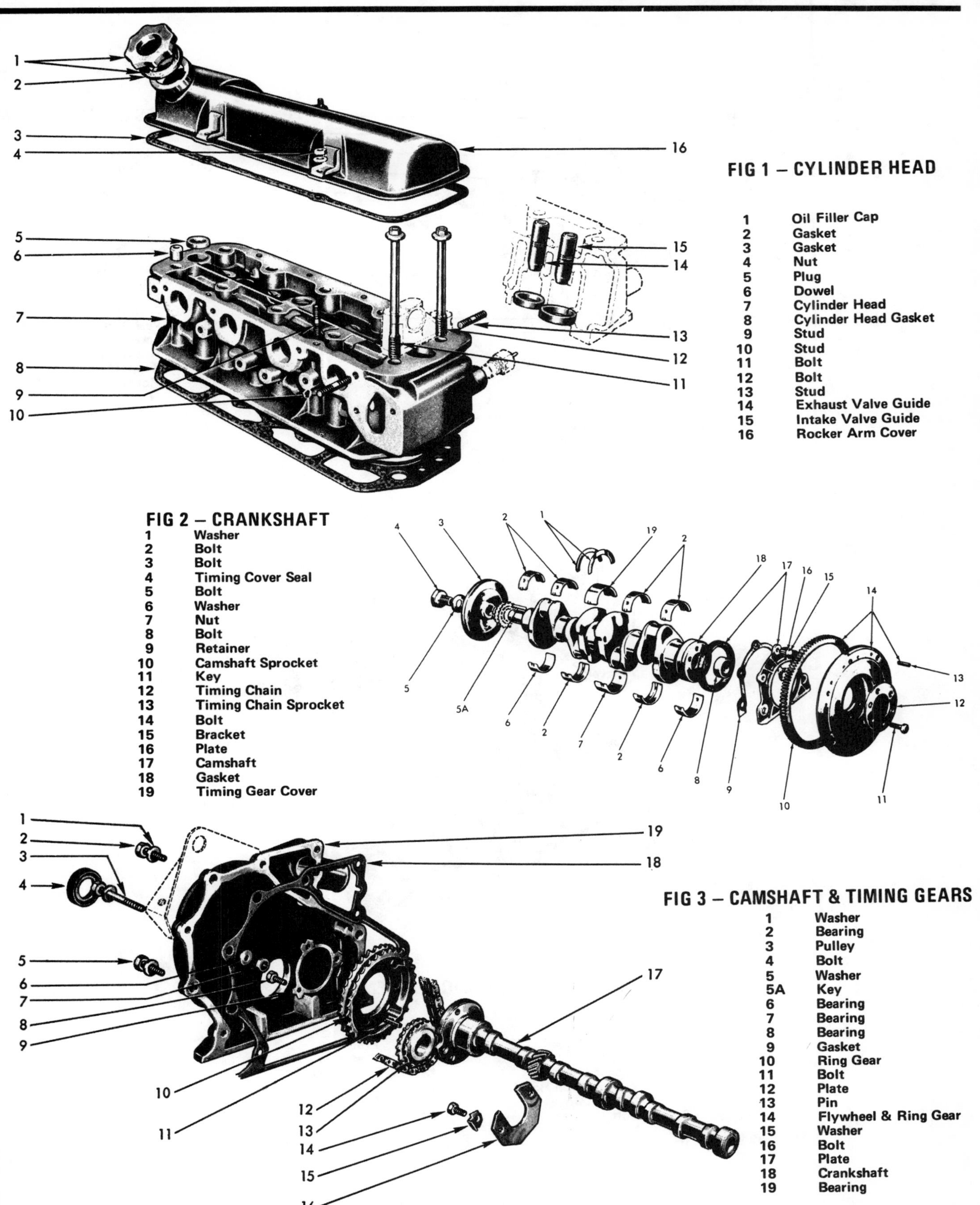

FIG 1 – CYLINDER HEAD

1 Oil Filler Cap
2 Gasket
3 Gasket
4 Nut
5 Plug
6 Dowel
7 Cylinder Head
8 Cylinder Head Gasket
9 Stud
10 Stud
11 Bolt
12 Bolt
13 Stud
14 Exhaust Valve Guide
15 Intake Valve Guide
16 Rocker Arm Cover

FIG 2 – CRANKSHAFT

1 Washer
2 Bolt
3 Bolt
4 Timing Cover Seal
5 Bolt
6 Washer
7 Nut
8 Bolt
9 Retainer
10 Camshaft Sprocket
11 Key
12 Timing Chain
13 Timing Chain Sprocket
14 Bolt
15 Bracket
16 Plate
17 Camshaft
18 Gasket
19 Timing Gear Cover

FIG 3 – CAMSHAFT & TIMING GEARS

1 Washer
2 Bearing
3 Pulley
4 Bolt
5 Washer
5A Key
6 Bearing
7 Bearing
8 Bearing
9 Gasket
10 Ring Gear
11 Bolt
12 Plate
13 Pin
14 Flywheel & Ring Gear
15 Washer
16 Bolt
17 Plate
18 Crankshaft
19 Bearing

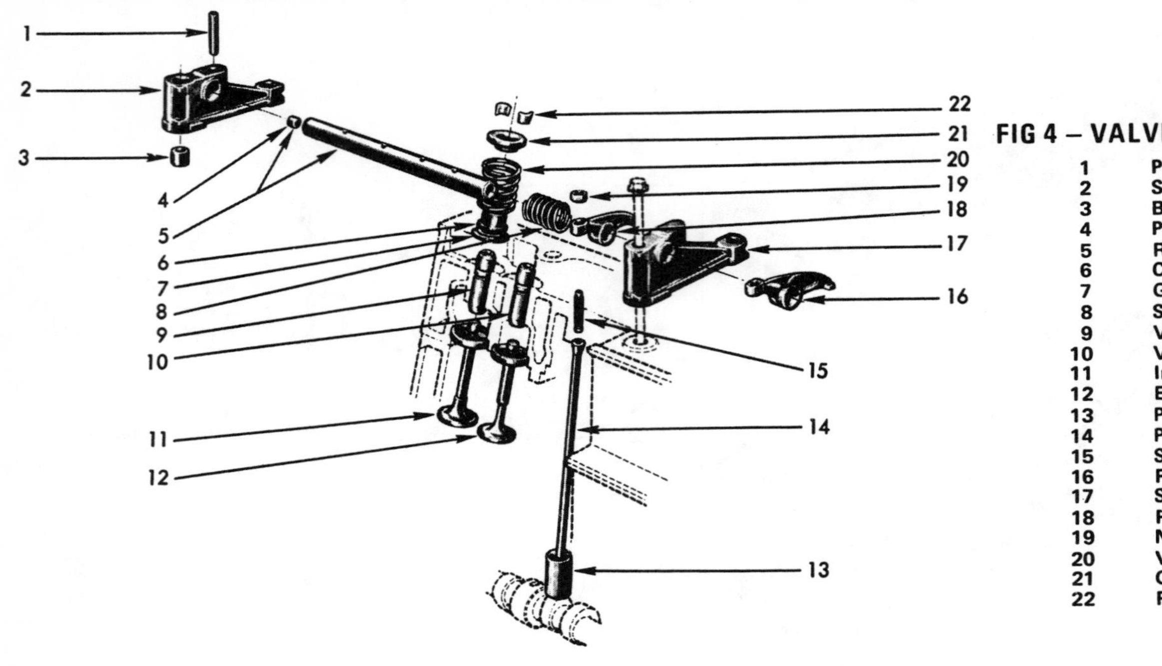

FIG 4 – VALVES & ROCKER ARMS

1	Pin
2	Support
3	Bushing
4	Plug
5	Rocker Arm Shaft
6	Cup
7	Guide
8	Spring
9	Valve Exhaust Guide
10	Valve Intake Guide
11	Intake Valve
12	Exhaust Valve
13	Push Rod Lever
14	Push Rod
15	Screw
16	Rocker
17	Support
18	Rocker
19	Nut
20	Valve Spring
21	Guide
22	Retainer

FIG 5 – TRANSMISSION ASSEMBLY

1	Bolt	10	Valve
2	Cover	11	Bolt
3	Bolt	12	Washer
4	Gasket	13	Rear Cover
5	Transmission Housing	14	Gasket
6	Dowel	15	Screw
7	Bolt	16	Seal
8	Washer	17	Transmission Assembly
9	Seal		

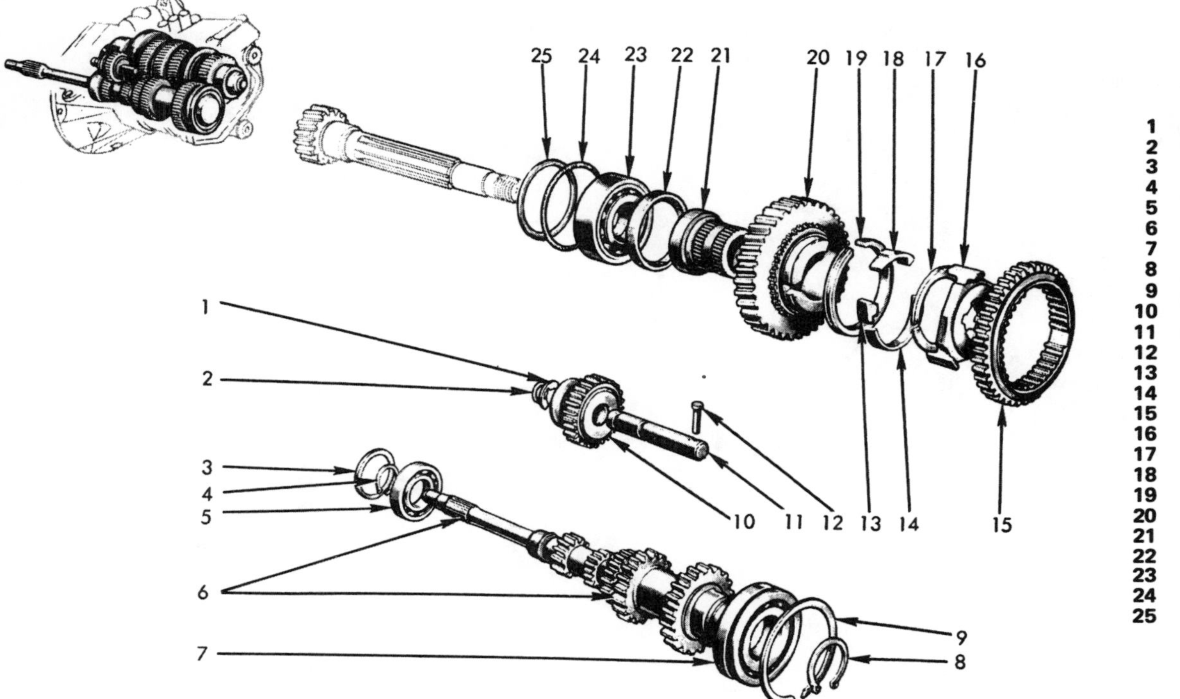

1	Washer
2	Snap Ring
3	Shim
4	Snap Ring
5	Bearing
6	Countershaft
7	Bearing
8	Snap Ring
9	Ring
10	Drive Gear
11	Shaft
12	Pin
13	Snap Ring
14	Spring
15	Gear
16	Hub
17	Ring
18	Strut
19	Ring
20	Countershaft Gear
21	Gear
22	Retainer
23	Bearing
24	Seal
25	Shim

FIG 6 – TRANSMISSION MAINSHAFT & LOW GEARS

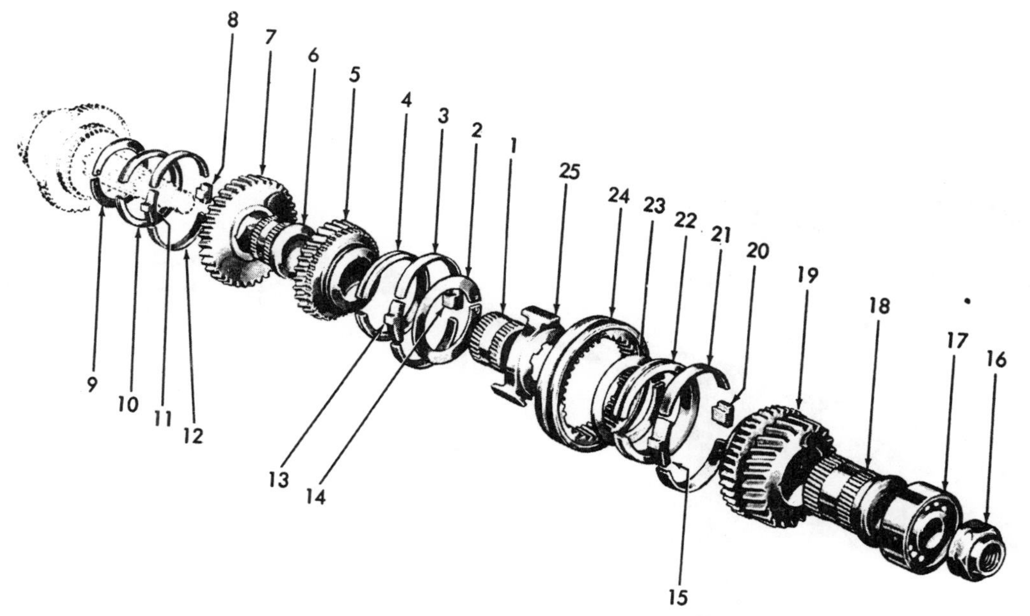

1	Gear
2	Ring
3	Spring
4	Ring
5	Gear
6	Gear
7	Gear
8	Snap Ring
9	Ring
10	Ring
11	Strut
12	Spring
13	Strut
14	Snap Ring
15	Strut
16	Nut
17	Bearing
18	Gear
19	Gear
20	Snap Ring
21	Spring
22	Ring
23	Ring
24	Synchronizer
25	Hub

FIG 7 – TRANSMISSION COUNTERSHAFT

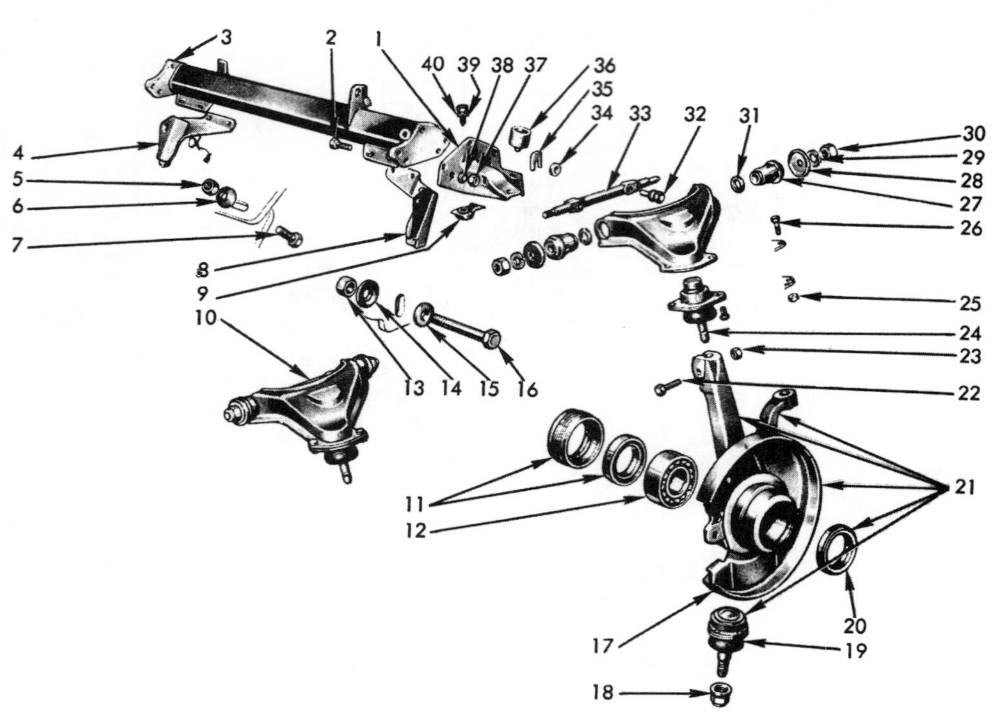

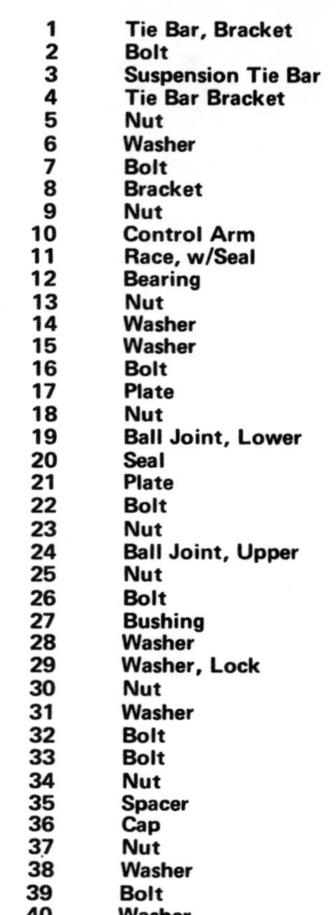

1	Tie Bar, Bracket
2	Bolt
3	Suspension Tie Bar
4	Tie Bar Bracket
5	Nut
6	Washer
7	Bolt
8	Bracket
9	Nut
10	Control Arm
11	Race, w/Seal
12	Bearing
13	Nut
14	Washer
15	Washer
16	Bolt
17	Plate
18	Nut
19	Ball Joint, Lower
20	Seal
21	Plate
22	Bolt
23	Nut
24	Ball Joint, Upper
25	Nut
26	Bolt
27	Bushing
28	Washer
29	Washer, Lock
30	Nut
31	Washer
32	Bolt
33	Bolt
34	Nut
35	Spacer
36	Cap
37	Nut
38	Washer
39	Bolt
40	Washer

FIG 8 – FRONT SUSPENSION ARM & SPINDLES

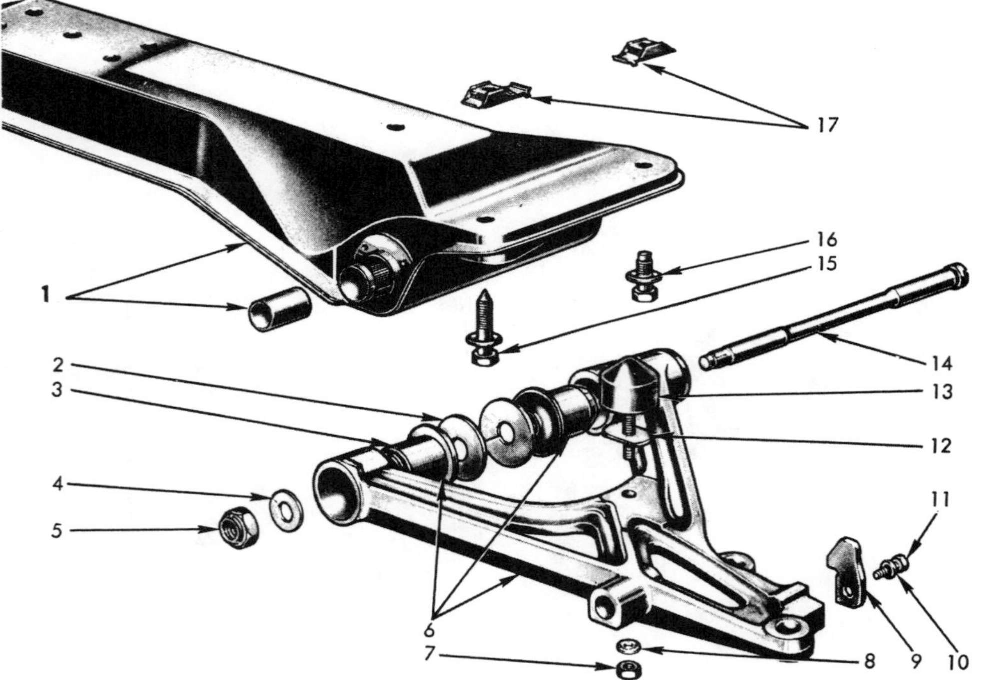

1	Crossmember
2	Washer
3	Bushing
4	Washer
5	Nut
6	Lower Control Arm
7	Nut
8	Washer
9	Bracket
10	Washer
11	Bolt
12	Plate
13	Bumper
14	Bolt
15	Bolt
16	Bolt
17	Nut

FIG 9 – FRONT SUSPENSION LOWER ARMS

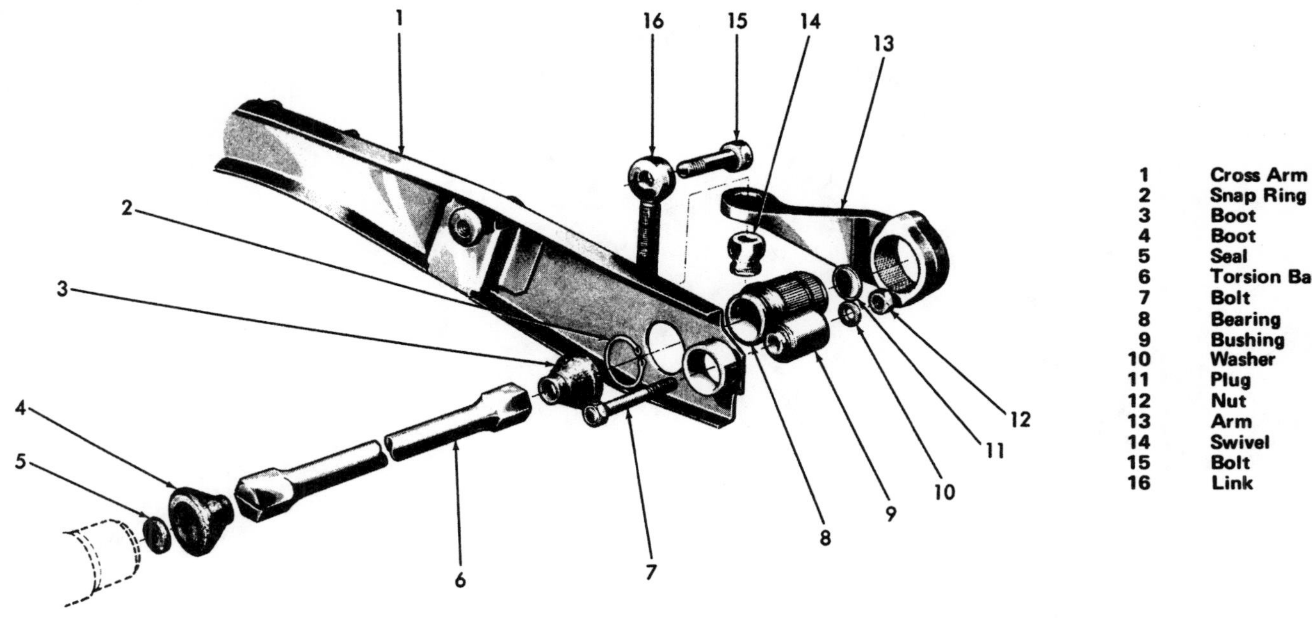

1	Cross Arm
2	Snap Ring
3	Boot
4	Boot
5	Seal
6	Torsion Bar
7	Bolt
8	Bearing
9	Bushing
10	Washer
11	Plug
12	Nut
13	Arm
14	Swivel
15	Bolt
16	Link

FIG 10 – FRONT TORSION BARS

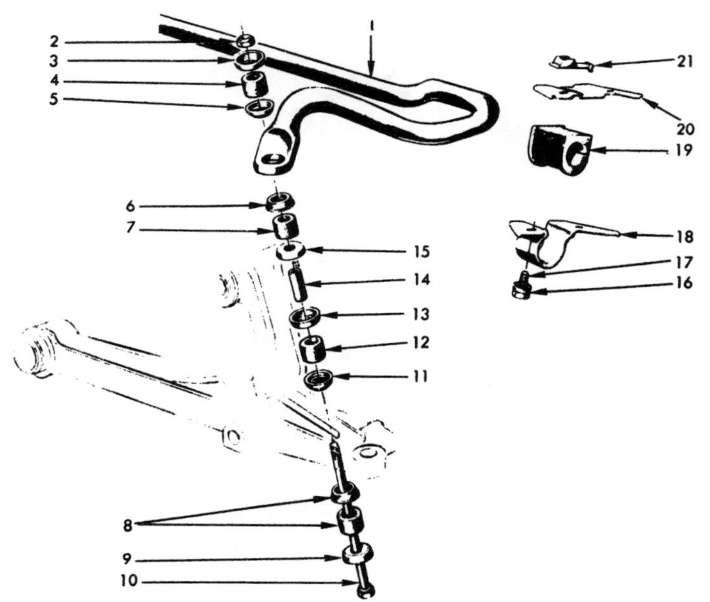

1	Stabilizer Bar
2	Nut
3	Retainer
4	Grommet
5	Retainer
6	Retainer
7	Grommet
8	Grommet
9	Retainer
10	Bolt
11	Retainer
12	Grommet
13	Retainer
14	Bushing
15	Retainer
16	Washer
17	Bolt
18	Bracket
19	Insulator
20	Plate
21	Nut

FIG 11 – FRONT STABILIZER BAR

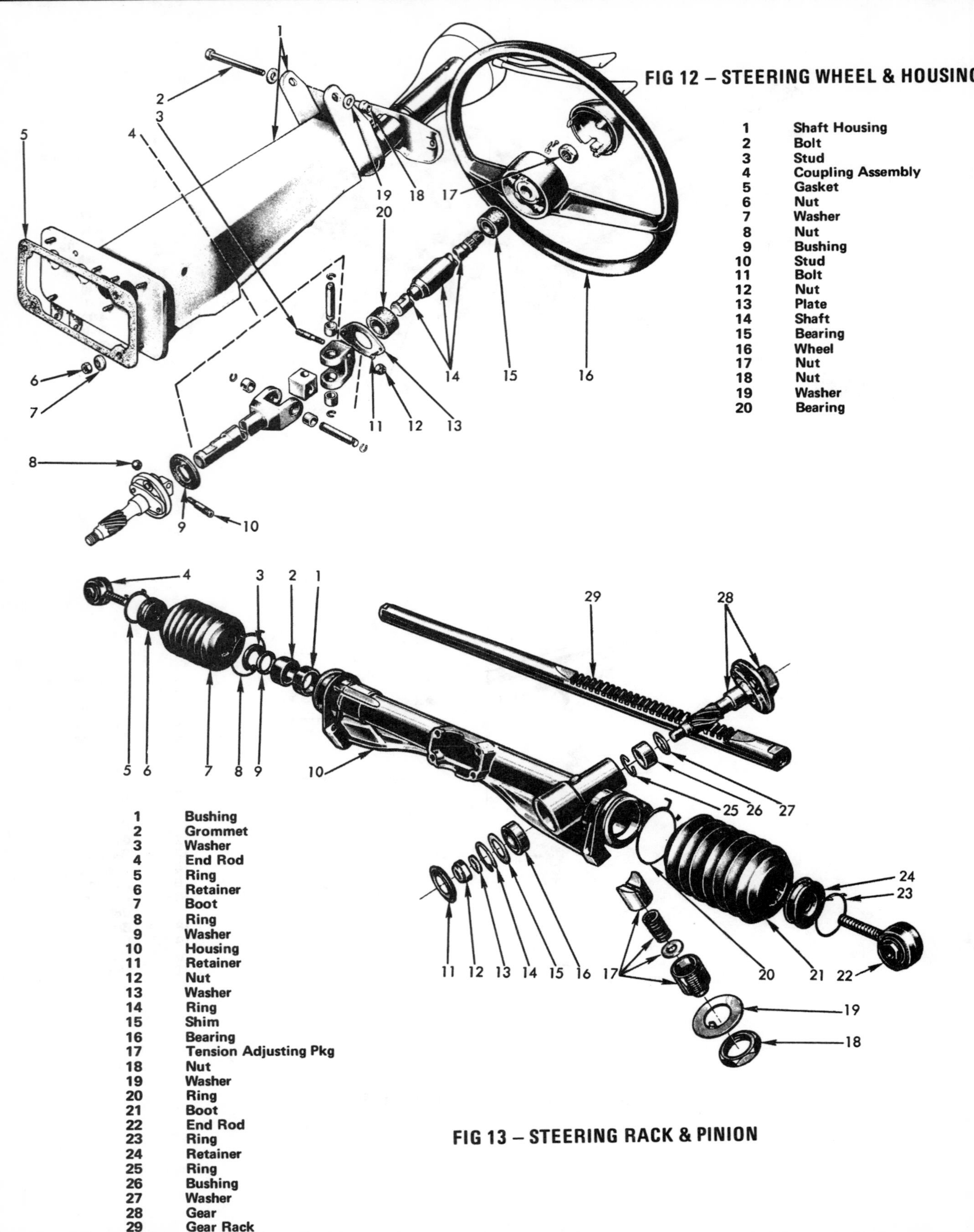

FIG 12 – STEERING WHEEL & HOUSING
1 Shaft Housing
2 Bolt
3 Stud
4 Coupling Assembly
5 Gasket
6 Nut
7 Washer
8 Nut
9 Bushing
10 Stud
11 Bolt
12 Nut
13 Plate
14 Shaft
15 Bearing
16 Wheel
17 Nut
18 Nut
19 Washer
20 Bearing
1 Bushing
2 Grommet
3 Washer
4 End Rod
5 Ring
6 Retainer
7 Boot
8 Ring
9 Washer
10 Housing
11 Retainer
12 Nut
13 Washer
14 Ring
15 Shim
16 Bearing
17 Tension Adjusting Pkg
18 Nut
19 Washer
20 Ring
21 Boot
22 End Rod
23 Ring
24 Retainer
25 Ring
26 Bushing
27 Washer
28 Gear
29 Gear Rack
FIG 13 – STEERING RACK & PINION

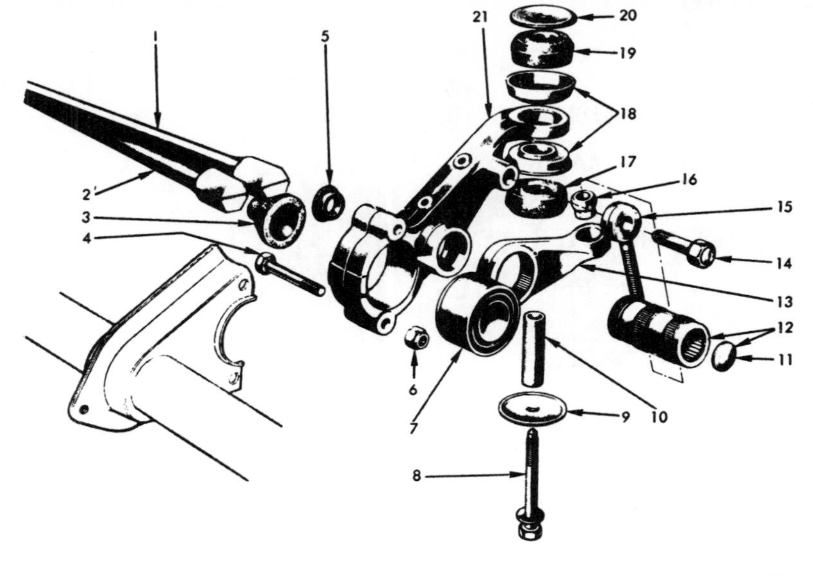

FIG 14 – REAR TORSION ARMS

1 Torsion Bar
2 Torsion Bar
3 Boot
4 Bolt
5 Grommet
6 Nut
7 Bushing
8 Bolt
9 Washer
10 Spacer
11 Plug
12 Bearing
13 Arm
14 Bolt
15 Link
16 Fitting
17 Bushing
18 Retainer
19 Bushing
20 Washer
21 Arm

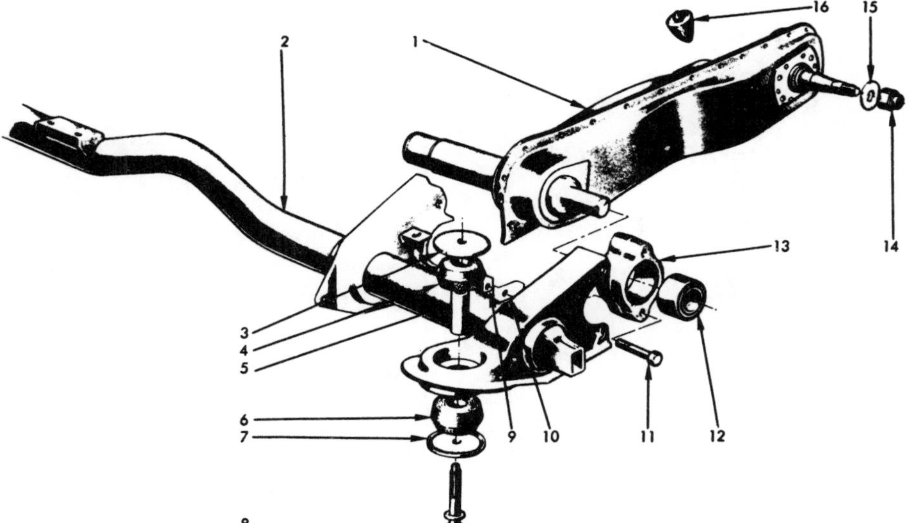

FIG 15 – REAR LOWER ARMS

1 Arm
2 Shaft
3 Washer
4 Bushing
5 Spacer
6 Bushing
7 Washer
8 Bolt
9 Nut
10 Clip
11 Bolt
12 Bearing
13 Housing
14 Nut
15 Washer
16 Bumper

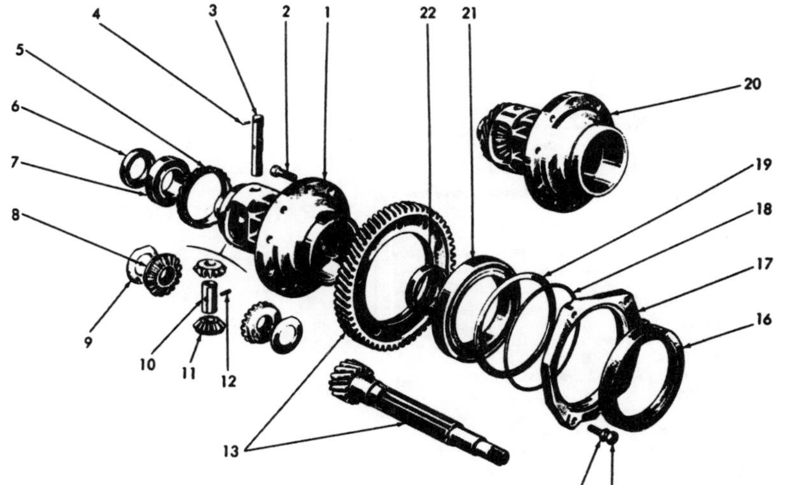

FIG 16 – DIFFERENTIAL

1 Differential Case
2 Bolt
3 Pinion Shaft
4 Pin
5 Pinion Gear
6 Seal
7 Bearing
8 Side Gear
9 Shim
10 Spacer
11 Gear
12 Pin
13 Gear, w/Pinion
14 Washer
15 Bolt
16 Seal
17 Platè
18 "O" Ring
19 Shim
20 Differential Assembly

Ignition, Starting & Charging—TIME

OPERATION INDEX

Tune-Up, Minor 1
Tune-Up, Major 2
Compression Test 3
Distributor, R & R Or Renew 4
Distributor, R & R & Overhaul 5
Distributor Cap, Renew 6
Ignition Cable Set, Renew 7
Vacuum Control Unit, Renew 8
Ignition Coil, Renew 9
Starter & Ignition Switch, Renew 10
Starter, R & R Or Renew 11
Starter Solenoid, Renew 12
Starter Bendix Drive, Renew 13
Starter, R & R & Overhaul 14
Starter Brushes, Renew 15
Starter Armature, Renew 16
Starter Relay, Renew 17
Alternator Regulator, Renew 18
Alternator, R & R Or Renew 19
Alternator, R & R & Overhaul 20
Alternator Diodes, Renew 21
Alternator Bearings, Renew 22
Alternator Brushes, Renew 23
Alternator Pulley, Renew 24
Generator, Renew 25
Generator, R & R & Overhaul 26
Voltage Regulator, Renew 27
Generator Armature, Renew 28
Generator Brushes, Renew 29
Generator Pulley, Renew 30

1—TUNE-UP, MINOR
Includes: Renew points, condenser & plugs. Set spark timing and adjust carburetor idle.
1969-72 ....1.4

2—TUNE-UP, MAJOR
Includes: Check compression, clean or renew and adjust plugs. R & R distributor, renew points and condenser. Adjust ignition timing, carburetor and fan belts. Clean battery terminals and service air cleaner. Check coil & clean or replace fuel filter.
1969-72 ....2.6

3—COMPRESSION TEST
1969-72 ....0.7

4—DISTRIBUTOR, R & R OR RENEW
1969-72 ....0.4

—NOTE—
For Stroboscope Adjustment, Add 0.3

5—DISTRIBUTOR, OVERHAUL
1969-72 ....1.2

6—DISTRIBUTOR CAP, RENEW
1969-72 ....0.2

7—IGNITION CABLE SET, RENEW
1969-72—
One 0.2
All 0.3

8—VACUUM CONTROL UNIT, RENEW
1969-72 ....0.4

9—IGNITION COIL, RENEW
1969-72 ....0.2

10—STARTER & IGNITION SWITCH, RENEW
1969-72 ....0.8

11—STARTER, R & R OR RENEW
1969-72 ....0.7

12—STARTER SOLENOID, RENEW
1969-72 ....0.3

13—STARTER BENDIX DRIVE, RENEW
1969-72 ....1.4

14—STARTER, R & R & OVERHAUL
Includes: Turn down commutator and replace all parts necessary.
1969-72 ....2.3

15—STARTER BRUSHES, RENEW
1969-72 ....1.3

16—STARTER ARMATURE, RENEW
1969-72 ....1.5

17—STARTER RELAY, RENEW
1969-72 ....0.3

18—ALTERNATOR REGULATOR, RENEW
1969-72 ....0.2

19—ALTERNATOR, R & R OR RENEW
1969-72 ....0.3

20—ALTERNATOR, R & R & OVERHAUL
1969-72 ....2.0

21—ALTERNATOR DIODES, RENEW
1969-72 ....1.0

22—ALTERNATOR BEARINGS, RENEW
1969-72 ....1.0

23—ALTERNATOR BRUSHES, RENEW
1969-72 ....0.8

24—ALTERNATOR PULLEY, RENEW
1969-72 ....0.3

25—GENERATOR, RENEW
1969 ....0.4

26—GENERATOR, R & R & OVERHAUL
1969 ....1.7

27—VOLTAGE REGULATOR, RENEW
Model 1118 ....0.3
Model 1204 ....0.2

28—GENERATOR ARMATURE, RENEW
1969 ....0.8

29—GENERATOR BRUSHES, RENEW
1969 ....0.6

30—GENERATOR PULLEY, RENEW
1969 ....0.2

Fuel, Emission Controls, Intake & Exhaust Systems—TIME

OPERATION INDEX

Carburetor Or Flange Gasket, Renew 1
Carburetor, R & R & Overhaul 2
Fuel Pump, R & R Or Renew 3
Fuel Tank, R & R Or Renew 4
Choke Cable Assy, Renew 5
Vacuum Control Valve, Renew 6
Intake Manifold Or Gasket, Renew 7
Exhaust Manifold Or Gasket, Renew 8
Exhaust Pipe, Renew 9
Exhaust Pipe Intermediate, Renew 10
Muffler & Pipe Assy, Renew 11

1—CARBURETOR OR FLANGE GASKET, RENEW
1969-72 ....0.4

2—CARBURETOR, R & R & OVERHAUL
1969-72 ....1.4

3—FUEL PUMP, R & R OR RENEW
1969-72—
1204 Models 0.5
1118 Models 0.3

4—FUEL TANK, R & R OR RENEW
1969-72—
1204 Models 0.8
1118 Models 6.0

5—CHOKE CABLE ASSY, RENEW
1969-72—
1204 Models 0.4
1118 Models 0.5

6—VACUUM CONTROL VALVE, RENEW
1969-72 ....0.2

7—INTAKE MANIFOLD OR GASKET, RENEW
1969-72—
Manifold 1.0
Gasket 0.9

8—EXHAUST MANIFOLD OR GASKET, RENEW
1969-72 ....0.5

9—EXHAUST PIPE, RENEW
1969-72—
1204 Models 0.9
1118 Models 0.5

10—EXHAUST PIPE INTERMEDIATE, RENEW
1969-72 ....0.8

11—MUFFLER & PIPE ASSY, RENEW
1969-72 ....0.5

Engine Cooling & Heater System—TIME

OPERATION INDEX

Radiator, R & R Or Renew 1
Radiator Reservoir, Renew 2
Radiator Hoses, Renew 3
Water Pump, R & R Or Renew 4
Thermostat Or Housing, Renew 5
Heater Assy, Renew 6
Heater Core, Renew 7
Heater Blower Motor, Renew 8
Heater Temperature Control Valve, Renew 9
Heater Control, Renew 10
Heater Hoses, Renew 11

1—RADIATOR, R & R OR RENEW
1969-72—
1204 Models 0.9
1118 Models 1.6

2—RADIATOR RESERVOIR, RENEW
1969-72 ....0.2

3—RADIATOR HOSES, RENEW
1969-72—
Lower 0.5
Upper 0.3

4—WATER PUMP, R & R OR RENEW
1969-72 ....0.8

5—THERMOSTAT, OR HOUSING, RENEW
1969-72 ....0.4

6—HEATER ASSY, RENEW
1969-72—
1204 Models 0.8
1118 Models 0.7

(Continued)

Engine Cooling & Heater System—TIME Cont'd

7—HEATER CORE, RENEW
1969-72—
1204 Models 1.0
1118 Models 0.8

8—HEATER BLOWER MOTOR, RENEW
1969-72 ....1.4

9—HEATER TEMPERATURE CONTROL VALVE, RENEW
1969-72—
1204 Models 1.0
1118 Models 0.3

10—HEATER CONTROL, RENEW
1969-72 ....1.0

11—HEATER HOSE, RENEW
1969 (1118 Models)—
One 0.4
Both 0.6
1969-72 (1204 Models)—
Manifold To Thermostat 0.2
Inlet Hsg To Mfld 0.3

Engine—TIME

OPERATION INDEX

Engine, R & R *1*
Engine, R & R & Overhaul *2*
.. ine (Short), Renew & Grind Valves *3*
CYLINDER HEAD, R & R OR

GASKET, RENEW

Valves, Grind *5*
One Valve, Renew & Grind *6*
Valve Springs, Renew *7*
Rocker Arm Cover Gasket, Renew *8*
Push Rods, Renew *9*
Valve Rocker Arm Assy, Clean Or Overhaul *10*
Oil Pan Or Gasket, R & R Or Overhaul *11*
Valve Tappets, Renew *12*
Valve Tappets, Adjust *13*
Timing Cover Seal & Gasket, Renew *14*
Timing Chain Or Gears, Renew *15*
Camshaft, R & R Or Renew *16*
Camshaft Bearings, Renew *17*
Oil Pump, R & R Or Renew *18*
Camshaft Rear Welch Plug, Renew *19*
Piston Ring(S), Renew *20*
Rings & Main Bearings, Renew & Grind Valves *21*
Rod Bearing(S), Renew *22*
Main Bearings, Renew *23*
Main & Rod Bearings, Renew *24*
Crankshaft, R & R Or Renew *25*
Crankshaft Rear Main Oil Seal, Renew *26*
Piston(S), Renew *27*
Connecting Rod(S), Renew *28*
Crankshaft Pulley, Renew *29*

1—ENGINE, R & R
Does not include transfer of any part of engine or replacement of special equipment
1969-72—
Model 1204 ....7.0
Model 1118 ....6.5

—NOTE—

To Renew Engine, For Transfer Of All Parts Not Included With New Engine And Not Including Special Equipment, Add *2.0*

2—ENGINE, R & R & OVERHAUL
Includes rebore cylinders with boring bar, renew pistons, rings, pins & all bearings, grind valves, plastigauge bearings and perform minor tune-up
1969-72 ....17.8

3—ENGINE (SHORT), RENEW & GRIND VALVES
1969-72—
Model 1204 ....9.6
Model 1118 ....10.1

4—CYLINDER HEAD, R & R OR GASKET, RENEW
Includes: Adjust tappets
1969-72 ....2.0

—NOTE—

To Renew Head, Add *1.1*

5—VALVES, GRIND
Includes R & R head and adjust tappets
1969-72 ....3.1

6—ONE VALVE, RENEW & GRIND
Includes: R & R head & adjust tappets
1969-72 ....2.4

7—VALVE SPRINGS, RENEW
Includes: Replace valve stem oil seals & adjust tappets.
1969-72—
One 0.9
All 2.9

—NOTE—

Use Air To Hold Up Valves.

8—ROCKER ARM COVER GASKET, RENEW
1969-72 ....0.3

9—PUSH RODS, RENEW
Includes: Adjust tappets.
1969-72—
One 0.9
All 1.0

10—VALVE ROCKER ARM ASSY, CLEAN OR OVERHAUL
1969-72 ....1.0

11—OIL PAN OR GASKET, R & R OR RENEW
1969-72—
Upper Pan 2.0
Upper Pan Gasket 1.3
Lower Pan Or Gasket—
Model 1204 ....0.5
Model 1118 ....1.0

12—VALVE TAPPETS, RENEW
1969-72—
Model 1204 ....1.7
Model 1118 ....3.5

13—VALVE TAPPETS, ADJUST
1971-72 ....0.4

14—TIMING CASE COVER SEAL & GASKET, RENEW
1969-72—
Oil Seal 1.2
Cover Gasket 1.2

15—TIMING CHAIN OR GEARS, RENEW
1969-72 ....1.8

16—CAMSHAFT, R & R OR RENEW
1969-72 ....5.8

17—CAMSHAFT BEARINGS, RENEW
1969-72—
Model 1204 ....7.5
Model 1118 ....7.0

18—OIL PUMP DRIVE SHAFT OR GEAR, RENEW
1969-72 ....1.0

19—CAMSHAFT REAR BEARING PLUG, RENEW
1969-72 ....2.6

20—PISTON RING(S), RENEW
1969-72—
One Piston 3.7
All Pistons 5.4

21—RINGS & MAIN BEARINGS, RENEW & GRIND VALVES
1969-72—
Model 1204 ....8.9
Model 1118 ....7.8

22—ROD BEARING(S), RENEW
1969-72—
One 1.7
All 2.6

23—MAIN BEARINGS, RENEW
Includes: Plastigauge bearings
1969-72—
Model 1204 ....3.5
Model 1118 ....2.4

24—MAIN & ROD BEARINGS, RENEW
Includes: Plastigauge bearings
1969-72—
Model 1204 ....4.8
Model 1118 ....3.7

25—CRANKSHAFT, R & R OR RENEW
1969-72 ....9.0

26—CRANKSHAFT REAR MAIN OIL SEAL, RENEW
1969-72—
Model 1204 ....3.0
Model 1118 ....2.6

27—PISTON(S), RENEW
Includes: Replace rings & rod bearings
1969-72—
One 3.7
All 6.5

28—CONNECTING ROD(S), RENEW
Includes: Replace rod bearings
1969-72—
One 3.7
All 6.5

29—CRANKSHAFT PULLEY, RENEW
1969-72 ....0.9

Clutch, Mounts & Transmissions—TIME

OPERATION INDEX

Flywheel, R & R Or Renew *1*
Flywheel Ring Gear, Renew *2*
Clutch Or Disc, Renew *3*
Release Bearing, Renew *4*

1969-72 ....0.3

Pilot Bearing, Renew *5*
Release Fork (Or Lever), Renew *6*
Clutch Pedal, Adjust *7*
Clutch Master Cylinder, Renew *8*
Clutch Master Cylinder, Overhaul *9*
Master Cyl To Slave Cyl Line, Renew *10*
Clutch Slave Cyl, Renew *11*
Clutch Slave Cyl, Overhaul *12*
Engine Mounts, Renew *13*
Transmission Assy, R & R Or Renew *14*
Manual Transmission Case, Renew *15*
Trans Shift Cover Or Gasket, Renew *16*
Trans Shift Cover, Overhaul *17*
Rear Cover Or Gasket, Renew *18*
Torque Converter, Renew *19*
Oil Pan Gasket, Renew *20*
Manual Trans, R & R & Overhaul *21*
Gearshift Lever, Renew *22*
Gearshift Control Rod, Renew *23*
Auto Trans Oil Cooler, Renew *24*
Transaxle Assy, Renew *25*
Transaxle Assy, Overhaul *26*
Transaxle Housing, Renew *27*
Transaxle Side Cover Or Gasket, Renew *28*
Transaxle Side Cover, Overhaul *29*

1—FLYWHEEL, R & R OR RENEW
1969-72 ....2.3

2—FLYWHEEL RING GEAR, RENEW
1969-72 ....2.6

(Continued)

Clutch, Mounts & Transmissions—TIME Cont'd

3—CLUTCH OR DISC, RENEW
Includes: Replace release bearing
1969-72—
Model 1204 .... 2.6
Model 1118 .... 2.8

4—RELEASE BEARING, RENEW
1969-72—
Model 1204 .... 2.3
Model 1118 .... 2.5

5—PILOT BEARING, RENEW
1969-72—
Model 1204 .... 2.9
Model 1118 .... 3.1

6—RELEASE FORK (OR LEVER), RENEW
Model 1204 .... 1.6
Model 1118 .... 1.8

7—CLUTCH PEDAL, ADJUST

8—CLUTCH MASTER CYLINDER, RENEW
Includes: Bleed system
1969-72 .... 0.8

9—CLUTCH MASTER CYLINDER, OVERHAUL
Includes: Bleed system
1969-72 .... 1.3

10—MASTER CYL TO SLAVE CYL LINE, RENEW
Includes: Bleed system
1969-72 .... 0.6

11—CLUTCH SLAVE CYLINDER, RENEW
Includes: Bleed system
1969-72 .... 1.0

12—CLUTCH SLAVE CYLINDER, OVERHAUL
Includes: Bleed system
1969-72 .... 1.5

13—ENGINE MOUNTS, RENEW
1969-72—
Front, Model 1204—
One 0.7
Both 1.1
Rear—
Model 1204 .... 0.8
Model 1118—
One 0.6
Both 1.1

14—TRANSMISSION ASSY, R & R OR RENEW
1969-72 Model 1204—
Auto Trans 1.4
Std Trans 1.5

15—MANUAL TRANS CASE, RENEW
1969-72 .... 4.0

16—TRANS SHIFT COVER OR GASKET, R & R OR RENEW
1969-72—
Auto Trans 2.1
Std Trans 1.6

17—TRANS SHIFT COVER, OVERHAUL
1969-72 Model 1204—
Std Trans 2.2

18—REAR COVER OR GASKET, RENEW
1969-72 Model 1024 .... 0.6

19—TORQUE CONVERTER, RENEW
1969-72 Model 1204 .... 6.2

—NOTE—
To Renew Oil Pump Seal, Add 0.2

20—OIL PAN GASKET, RENEW
1969-72 .... 6.0
1969-72 Model 1204 .... 0.4

21—MANUAL TRANS, R & R & OVERHAUL
Notes: To Renew Clutch Disc Add 0.5
To Overhaul Differential Assy, Add 3.4

22—GEARSHIFT LEVER RENEW
1969-72—
Model 1204 .... 0.4
Model 1118 .... 0.5

23—GEARSHIFT CONTROL ROD, RENEW
1969-72—
Model 1204 .... 0.4
Model 1118 .... 0.6

24—AUTO TRANS COOLER, RENEW
1969-72 Model 1204 .... 1.2

25—TRANSAXLE ASSY, RENEW
1969 Model 1118 .... 1.5

26—TRANSAXLE ASSY, OVERHAUL
1969 Model 1118 .... 6.0
Notes:
To Renew Clutch Disc Or Pressure Plate, Add 0.3
To Renew Clutch Release Bearing, Add 0.2
To Renew Flywheel Assy, Add 0.5
To Renew Mainshaft Oil Seal, Add 1.0

27—TRANSAXLE HOUSING, RENEW
1969 Model 1118 .... 5.5

28—TRANSAXLE SIDE COVER OR GASKET, RENEW
1969 Model 1118 .... 0.7

29—TRANSAXLE SIDE COVER, OVERHAUL
1969 Model 1118 .... 1.5

Brakes, Steering, Suspension & Differential—TIME

OPERATION INDEX

Brake Shoes Or Friction Pads, Renew 1
Master Cylinder, Renew 2
Master Cylinder, R & R & Overhaul 3
Wheel Cylinders, Renew 4
Wheel Cylinders, R & R & Overhaul 5
Caliper Assy, Renew 6
Caliper Assy, R & R & Overhaul 7
Bleed System 8
Brake Hose, Renew 9
Hub Or Disc, Renew 10
Brake Drum, Renew 11
Brake Pedal, Renew 12
Parking Brake Cable, Renew 13
Parking Brake Lever, Renew 14
Rack & Pinion Assy, Renew 15
Steering Tension Adjuster, Renew 16
Link, Rear To Adjuster, Renew 17
Tie Rod End Assy, Renew 18
Spring(S), Renew 19
Torsion Bar, Renew 20
Torsion Bar Adjusting Arm, Renew 21
Front Hub Bearings, Renew 22
Stabilizer Bar Or Link, Renew 23
Shock Absorbers, Renew 24
Steering Knuckle Assy, Renew 25
Upper Control Arm, Renew 26
Lower Control Arm, Renew 27
Ball Joints, Renew 28
Crossmember, Renew 29
Rear Suspension Lower Arm Or Bushings, Renew 30
Differential Assy, Renew 31
Differential Assy, Overhaul 32
Drive Pinion Oil Seal, Renew 33
Differential Side Gears & Pinions, Renew 34
Wheel Shafts, Renew 35

1—BRAKE SHOES OR FRICTION PADS, RENEW
1969-72—
Front Disc 0.5
Conventional Type—
Front—
One 0.6
Both 0.9
Rear—
One 0.8
Both 1.2
Model 1118, All 1.8

2—MASTER CYLINDER, RENEW
Includes: Bleed system
1969-72 .... 0.6

3—MASTER CYLINDER, R & R & OVERHAUL
Includes: Bleed system
1969-72 .... 1.3

4—WHEEL CYLINDER, RENEW
Includes: Bleed system & adjust brakes
1969-72—
Front—
One 0.7
Both 1.2
Rear—
One 0.5
Both 0.9

5—WHEEL CYLINDERS, R & R & OVERHAUL
Includes: Bleed system & adjust brakes
1969-72—
Front—
One 0.9
Both 1.6
Rear—
One 1.1
Both 1.9

6—CALIPER ASSY, RENEW
Includes: Bleed system
1969-72—
One 0.6
Both 0.9

7—CALIPER ASSY, R & R & OVERHAUL
Includes: Bleed system
1969-72—
One 1.0
Both 1.7

8—BLEED SYSTEM
1969-72 .... 0.4

9—BRAKE HOSE, RENEW
Includes: Bleed system
1969-72—
One 0.5
Both 0.8

10—HUB OR DISC, RENEW
1969-72—
Front Disc Type—
One 1.1
Both 1.8
Conventional Type—
Front—
One 0.5
Both 0.9
Rear—
Model 1204—
One 0.4
Both 0.7
Model 1118—
One 0.5
Both 0.9

(Continued)

Brakes, Steering, Suspension & Differential—TIME Cont'd

11—BRAKE DRUM, RENEW
Includes: Adjust brakes
1969-72—
One 0.3
Two 0.5
All 0.9

12—BRAKE PEDAL, RENEW
1969-72—
Model 1204 ....0.7
Model 1118 ....0.5

12—BRAKE PEDAL, RENEW
Includes: Adjust brakes
1969-72—
Model 1204 ....0.7
Model 1118 ....0.5

13—PARKING BRAKE CABLE, RENEW
1969-72 ....0.9

14—PARKING BRAKE LEVER, RENEW
1969-72 ....0.8

15—RACK & PINION ASSY, RENEW
1969-72—
Model 1204 ....3.0
Model 1118 ....1.5

16—STEERING TENSION ADJUSTER, RENEW
1969-72 ....0.4

17—LINK, REAR TO ADJUSTER, RENEW
1969-72 ....0.3

18—TIE ROD END ASSY, RENEW
1969-72—
One 0.4
Both 0.7

19—SPRING(S), RENEW
1969-72—
Front 1.5
Rear—
One 1.0
Both 1.9

20—TORSION BAR, RENEW
1969-72—
Front—
One 0.4
Both 0.7
Rear, One Or Both 2.8

21—TORSION BAR ADJUSTING ARM, RENEW
1969-72—
One 0.7
Both 0.8

22—FRONT HUB BEARING, RENEW
1969-72—
Model 1204—
One Side 1.2
Both Sides 2.2
Model 1118—
One Side 0.5
Both Sides 0.9

23—STABILIZER BAR OR LINK, RENEW
1969-72—
Front 0.7
Rear 0.4

24—SHOCK ABSORBERS, RENEW
1969-72—
One 0.4
Two 0.7
All 1.4

25—STEERING KNUCKLE ASSY, RENEW
1969-72—
Model 1204—
One ①1.0
Both ①1.9
Model 1118—
One ②0.7
Both ②1.3

①Includes Bearing & Cups
②To Renew Bearings, Add
One Side 0.5
Both Sides 0.7

26—UPPER CONTROL ARM, RENEW
1969-72—
One 1.0
Both 1.9

27—LOWER CONTROL ARM, RENEW
1969-72—
One 1.7
Both 3.0

28—BALL JOINTS, RENEW
Lower—
One 0.5
Both 0.9
Upper—
One 6
Both 1.1

29—CROSSMEMBER, RENEW
1969-72—
Front, Model 1204—
Upper 2.0
Lower 1.7
Rear—
Model 1204 ....2.4
Model 1118 ....8.0

30—REAR SUSPENSION LOWER ARM OR BUSHING, RENEW
1969-72 Model 1118—
One Side 1.5
Both Sides 2.9

21—DIFFERENTIAL ASSY, RENEW
1969-72—
Auto Trans 6.5
Std Trans 4.5

32—DIFFERENTIAL ASSY, OVERHAUL
1969-72—
Auto Trans 7.1
Std Trans 5.1

33—DRIVE PINION OIL SEAL, RENEW
1969-72—
Auto Trans 1.5
Std Trans 1.6

34—DIFFERENTIAL SIDE GEAR & PINIONS, RENEW
1969 Model 1118 ....2.3

35—WHEEL SHAFT, RENEW
1969-72—
One 0.5
Both 1.1

Speedometer, Wiper & Instruments—TIME

OPERATION INDEX

Speedometer Cable, Renew 1
Speedometer Head, Renew 2
W/S Wiper Motor, Renew 3
W/S Wiper Link Set, Renew 4
W/S Wiper Pivot, Renew 5
Fuel Gauge (Dash Unit), Renew 6
Fuel Tank Gauge, Renew 7
Oil Gauge Sending Unit, Renew 8
Temperature Gauge (Dash Unit), Renew 9
Temperature Gauge Sending Unit, Renew 10
Headlight Switch, Renew 11
Stop Light Switch, Renew 12
Turn Signal Relay, Renew 13
Sealed Beam Unit, Aim 14

1—SPEEDOMETER CABLE, RENEW
1969-72 ....0.3

2—SPEEDOMETER HEAD, RENEW
1969-72 ....0.8

3—W/S WIPER MOTOR, RENEW
1969-72 ....0.4

4—W/S WIPER LINK SET, RENEW
1969-72 ....0.6

5—W/S WIPER PIVOT, RENEW
1969-72 ....0.4

6—FUEL GAUGE (DASH UNIT), RENEW
1969-72—
Model 1204 ....0.6
Model 1118 ....0.2

7—FUEL TANK GAUGE, RENEW
1969-72 ....0.3

8—OIL GAUGE SENDING UNIT, RENEW
1969-72 ....0.3

9—TEMPERATURE GAUGE (DASH UNIT), RENEW
1969-72, Model 1204 ....0.6

10—TEMPERATURE GAUGE SENDING UNIT, RENEW
1969-72 ....0.4

11—HEADLIGHT SWITCH, RENEW
1969-72 ....0.3

12—STOP LIGHT SWITCH, RENEW
1969-72 ....0.3

13—TURN SIGNAL RELAY, RENEW
1969-72 ....0.2

14—SEALED BEAM UNIT, AIM
1969-72 (Both) 0.3

IDENTIFICATION

ALL MODELS.......................395

ILLUSTRATIONS

FIG 1 – ENGINE – CRANKCASE
FIG 2 – ENGINE – CYLINDER HEAD & HOUSING
FIG 3 – ENGINE – CRANKSHAFT & PISTONS
FIG 4 – ENGINE – CAMSHAFT & VALVE ROCKER
FIG 5 – TRANSMISSION CASE
FIG 6 – TRANSMISSION GEARS
FIG 7 – DIFFERENTIAL GEAR
FIG 8 – FRONT SUSPENSION
FIG 9 – STEERING
FIG 10 – REAR SUSPENSION

OPERATION TIMES

A

Alternator.......... 405
Automatic Transmission.......... 407
Axle Shaft.......... 408

B

Brake Drums.......... 407
Brakes.......... 407

C

Cables (Ignition).......... 405
Calipers.......... 407
Camshaft.......... 406
Carburetor.......... 405
Clutch.......... 406
Coil, Ignition.......... 405
Compression Test.......... 405
Connecting Rods.......... 406
Cooling System.......... 405
Crankshaft.......... 406
Cylinder Head.......... 406

D

Dash Gauges.......... 408
Differential.......... 406
Disc Brakes.......... 407
Distributor.......... 405

E

Emission Controls.......... 405
Engine Assembly.......... 406
Engine Mountings.......... 406
Engine Oiling.......... 406
Engine Tune-Up.......... 405
Exhaust System.......... 405

F

Flywheel.......... 406
Front Suspension.......... 407
Fuel Gauges.......... 408
Fuel Pump.......... 405
Fuel Tank.......... 405

H

Hand Brake.......... 407
Headlight Switch.......... 408
Heater.......... 406
Hose (Brake).......... 407
Hose (Radiator).......... 405
Hydraulic Brakes.......... 407

I

Ignition.......... 405
Ignition Coil.......... 405
Intake Manifold.......... 405

L

Light Switches.......... 408

M

Main Bearings.......... 406
Master Cylinder.......... 407
Muffler.......... 405

O

Oiling,Engine.......... 406
Oil Pan.......... 406
Oil Pressure Switch.......... 408
Oil Pump.......... 406

P

Parking Brake.......... 407
Piston Rings.......... 406
Pistons.......... 406
Power Brake.......... 407

R

Radiator.......... 405
Radiator Hose.......... 405
Rear Suspension.......... 408
Regulator (Alternator).......... 405
Rocker Arms.......... 406
Rod Bearings.......... 406

S

Shocks (Front).......... 408
Shocks (Rear).......... 408
Speedometer.......... 408
Stabilizer Bar.......... 408
Starting Motor.......... 405
Steering Gear.......... 408
Steering Linkage.......... 408
Switches (Light).......... 408
Synchro-Mesh Trans.......... 406

T

Tachometer.......... 408
Temperature Gauge.......... 408
Thermostat.......... 406
Torsion Bar.......... 408
Trans Axle.......... 406
Transmission, Manual.......... 406
Transmission, Automatic.......... 407
Tune-Up, Engine.......... 405

V

Vacuum Control Unit.......... 405
Valve System.......... 406

W

Water Pump.......... 405
Wheel Cylinders.......... 407
Windshield Wiper.......... 408

CHASSIS NUMBER

LOCATION – On top left side of instrument panel, visible through windshield or on firewall in engine compartment.

Year	Model	Chassis Number
1970 (1100 Phase 1)	2-Door Sedan	A14L – 700001 to 703999
	4-Door Sedan	A14L – 200001 to 203999
	Station Wagon	A43L – 200001 to 203999
1970 (1100 Phase 2)	2-Door Sedan	A14L – 704000 & Later
	4-Door Sedan	A14L – 204000 & Later
	Station Wagon	A43L – 204000 & Later
1971 (1300 G)	2-Door Sedan	A15L – 700001 to 702121
	4-Door Sedan	A15L – 200001 to 200986
	Station Wagon	A44L – 200001 to 202201
1972 (1300G)	2-Door Sedan	A15L – 702122 & Later
	4-Door Sedan	A15L – 200987 & Later
	Station Wagon	A44L – 202202 & Later
1972 (1300DL&GL)	Coupe	A23L – 700001 & Later
	2-Door Sedan	A23L – 900001 & Later
	4-Door Sedan	A23L – 800001 & Later
	Station Wagon	A63L – 700001 & Later
1973 Stage 1	Coupe	A22L – 700001 to 701102
	2-Door Sedan	A22L – 900001 to 900700
	4-Door Sedan	A22L – 800001 to 801000
	Station Wagon	A62L – 700001 to 701200
1973 Stage 2	Coupe	A22L – 701103 to 704200
	2-Door Sedan	A22L – 900701 to 902700
	4-Door Sedan	A22L – 801001 to 804108
	Station Wagon	A62L – 701201 to 703505
1973 State 3	Coupe	A22L – 704201 to 711000
	2-Door Sedan	A22L – 902701 to 908000
	4-Door Sedan	A22L – 804109 to 807000
	Station Wagon	A62L – 703506 to 708000
1974	Coupe	A22L – 711001 & Later
	2-Door Sedan	A22L – 908001 & Later
	4-Door Sedan	A22L – 807001 & Later
	Station Wagon	A62L – 708001 & Later
1975	Hardtop 4 Speed	A22L-020001 & Later
	Hardtop 5 Speed	A22L-002001 to 005060
	Hardtop A.T.	A22L-302001 to 305000
	Coupe 4 Speed	A22L-726001 & Later
	Coupe 5 Speed	A22L-402001 to 404000
	Coupe A. T.	A22L-202001 & Later
	2 Door Sedan	A22L-923001 to 924000
	2 Door Sedan A.T.	A22L-102001 to 106000
	4 Door Sedan	A22L-819001 to 819500
	4 Door Sedan,A.T.	A22L-602001 to 605000
	Station Wagon	A62L-725001 to 725500
	Station Wagon A.T.	A62L-602001 to 725500
	Station Wagon 4WD	A64L-802001 to 806000
1976	Hardtop 5 Speed	A22L-005001 & Later
	Hardtop A.T.	A26L-305001 & Later
	Coupe 5 Speed	A22L-404001 & Later
	2 Door Sedan:STD	A22L-924001 & Later
	2 Door Sedan:DL	A22L-726501 & Later
	2 Door Sedan A.T.	A26L-106001 & Later
	4 Door Sedan	A22L-819501 & Later
	4 Door Sedan A.T.	A26L-605001 & Later
	Station Wagon	A62L-725501 & Later
	Station Wagon A.T.	A66L-604001 & Later
	Station Wagon 4WD	A64L-[illegible] & Later

ENGINE NUMBERS

LOCATION – On front right side of cylinder block.

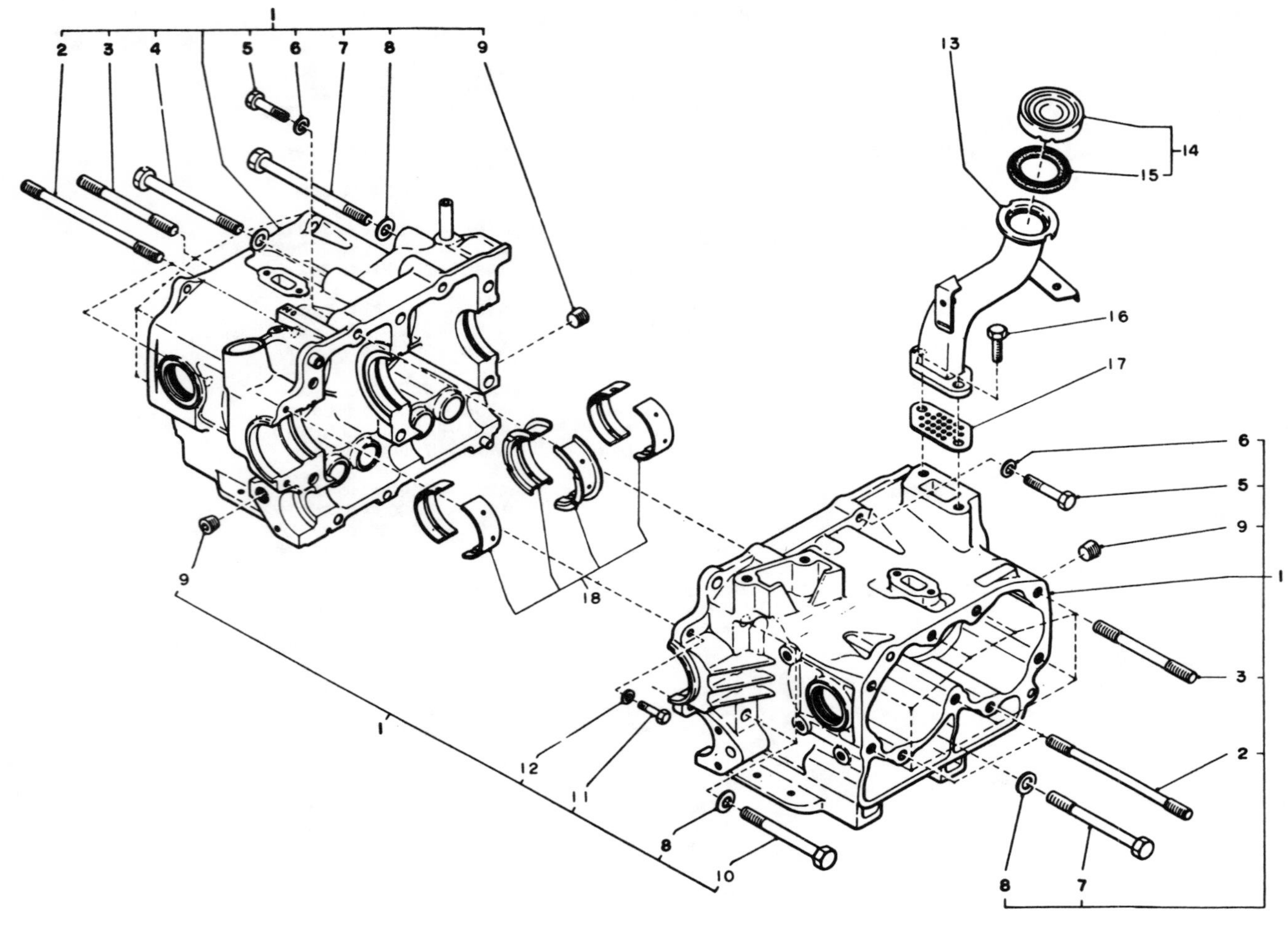

FIG 1 – ENGINE CRANKCASE

1	Crankcase Assy
2	Bolt
3	Bolt
4	Bolt
5	Bolt
6	Washer
7	Bolt
8	Washer
9	Plug
10	Bolt
11	Bolt
12	Washer
13	Oil Filler Duct
14	Oil Cap
15	Gasket
16	Bolt
17	Gasket
18	Crankshaft Bearing

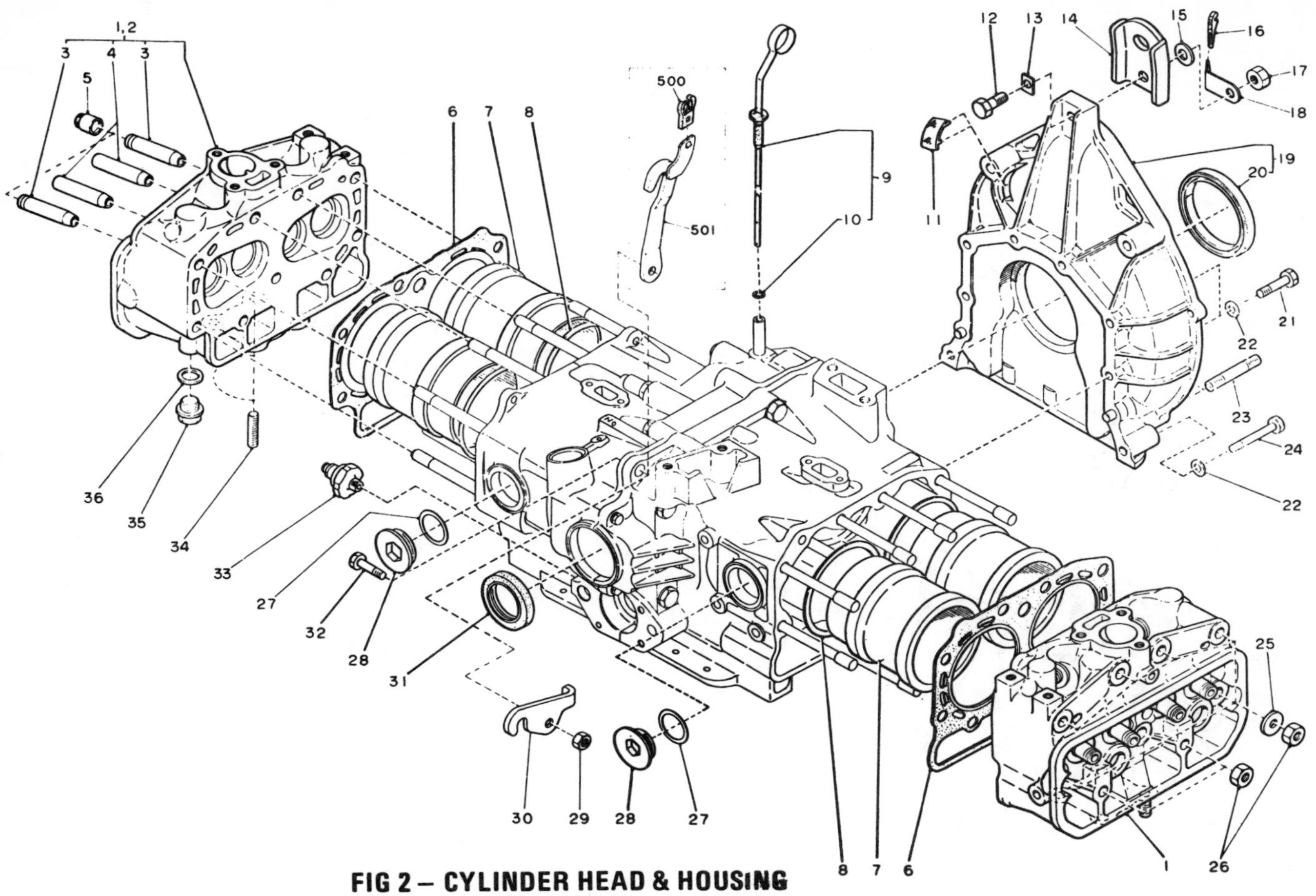

FIG 2 – CYLINDER HEAD & HOUSING

1 Head (Complete)
2 Head (Complete)
3 Valve Guide
4 Valve Guide
5 Oil Seal
6 Gasket
7 Cylinder Liner
8 Liner Gasket
9 Oil Level Gauge
10 O Ring
11 Plug
12 Bolt
13 Washer
14 Hanger
15 Washer
16 Support (Dist Cord)
17 Nut
18 Support (Battery Cable)
19 Flywheel Housing
20 Oil Seal
21 Bolt
22 Washer
23 Bolt
24 Bolt
25 Washer
26 Nut
27 Gasket
28 Plug
29 Nut
30 Hanger
31 Oil Seal
32 Bolt
33 Oil Pressure Switch
34 Bolt
35 Plug
36 Gasket
500 Supporter (Spark Plug Cord)
501 Hanger

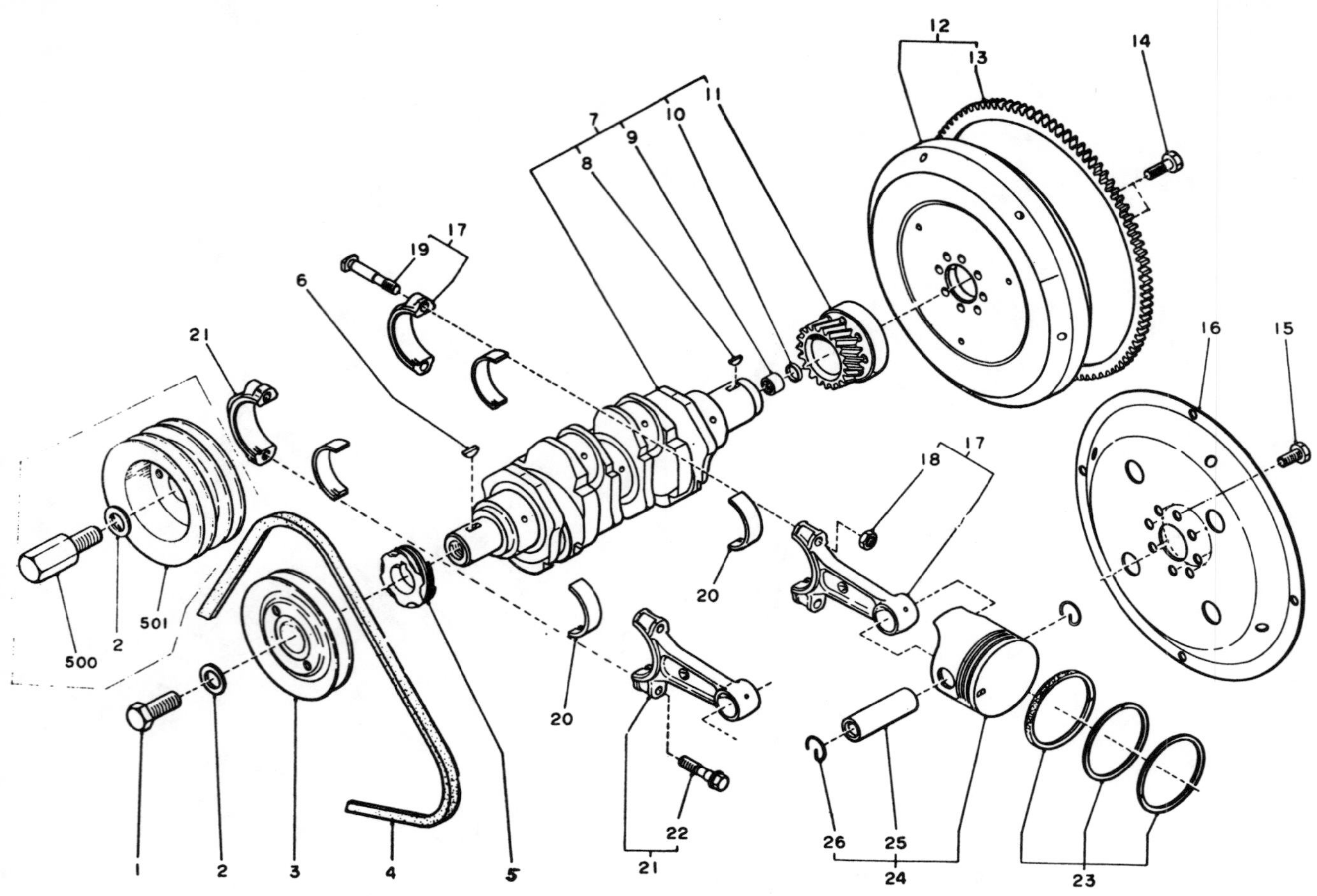

FIG 3 – CRANKSHAFT & PISTONS

1	Bolt
2	Washer
3	Crankshaft Pulley
4	Belt
5	Gear
6	Key
7	Crankshaft
8	Key
9	Needle Bearing
10	Oil Seal
11	Crankshaft Gear
12	Flywheel
13	Ring Gear
14	Bolt
15	Bolt
16	Converter Drive Plate
17	Connecting Rod
18	Nut
19	Bolt
20	Connecting Rod Bearing
21	Connecting Rod
22	Bolt
23	Piston Ring Set
24	Piston
25	Piston Pin
26	Circlip
500	Bolt
501	Crankshaft Pulley

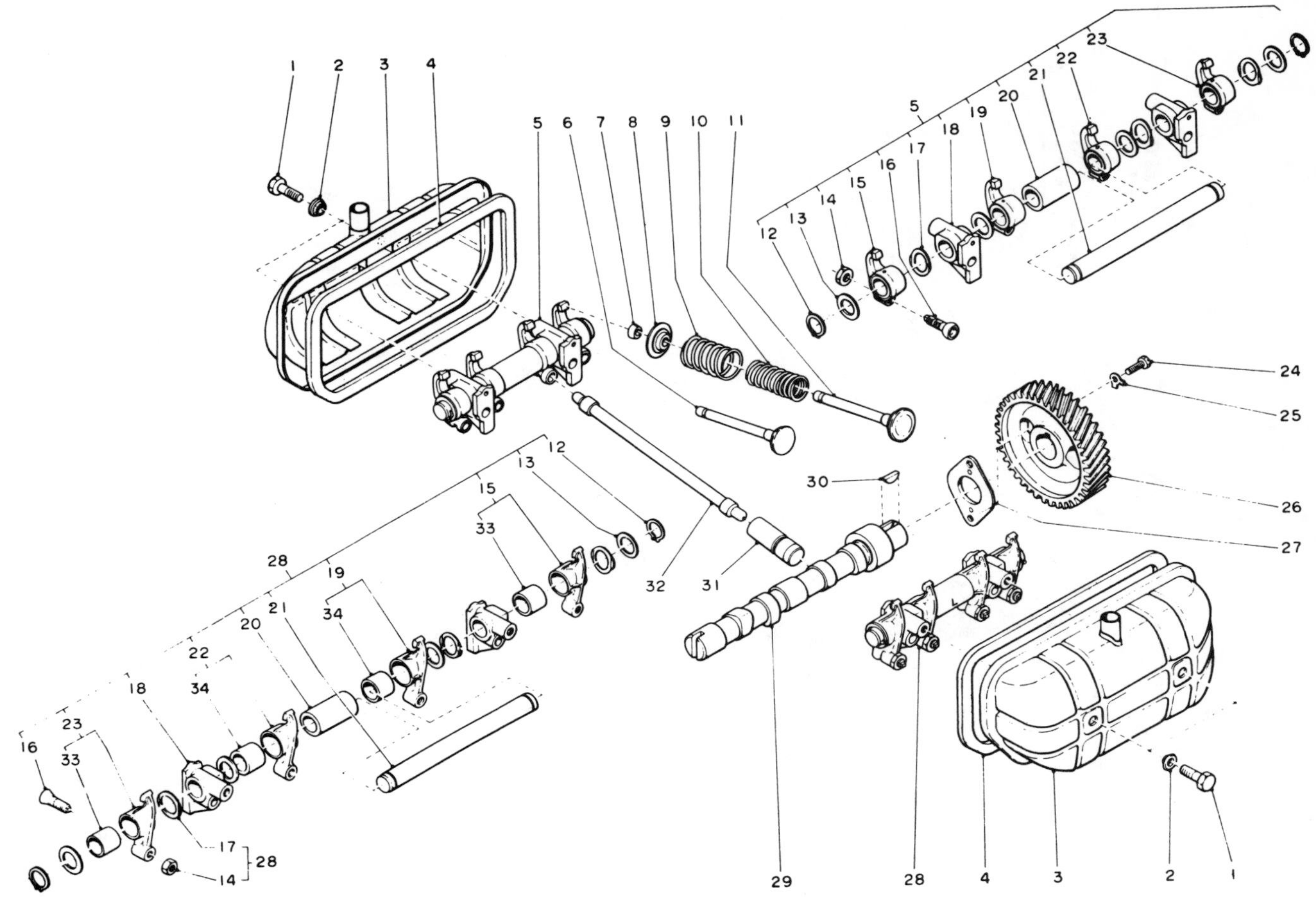

FIG 4 – CAMSHAFT & VALVE ROCKER

1	Bolt
2	Washer
3	Rocker Cover
4	Gasket
5	Rocker Assy
6	Exhaust Valve
7	Key
8	Retainer
9	Valve Spring
10	Valve Spring
11	Intake Valve
12	Snap Ring
13	Washer
14	Nut
15	Rocker Arm
16	Screw
17	Washer
18	Shaft Support
19	Rocker Arm
20	Spacer
21	Rocker Shaft
22	Rocker Arm
23	Rocker Arm
24	Bolt
25	Washer
26	Camshaft Gear
27	Plate
28	Rocker Assy
29	Camshaft
30	Key
31	Valve Lifter
32	Push Rod
33	Bushing
34	Bushing

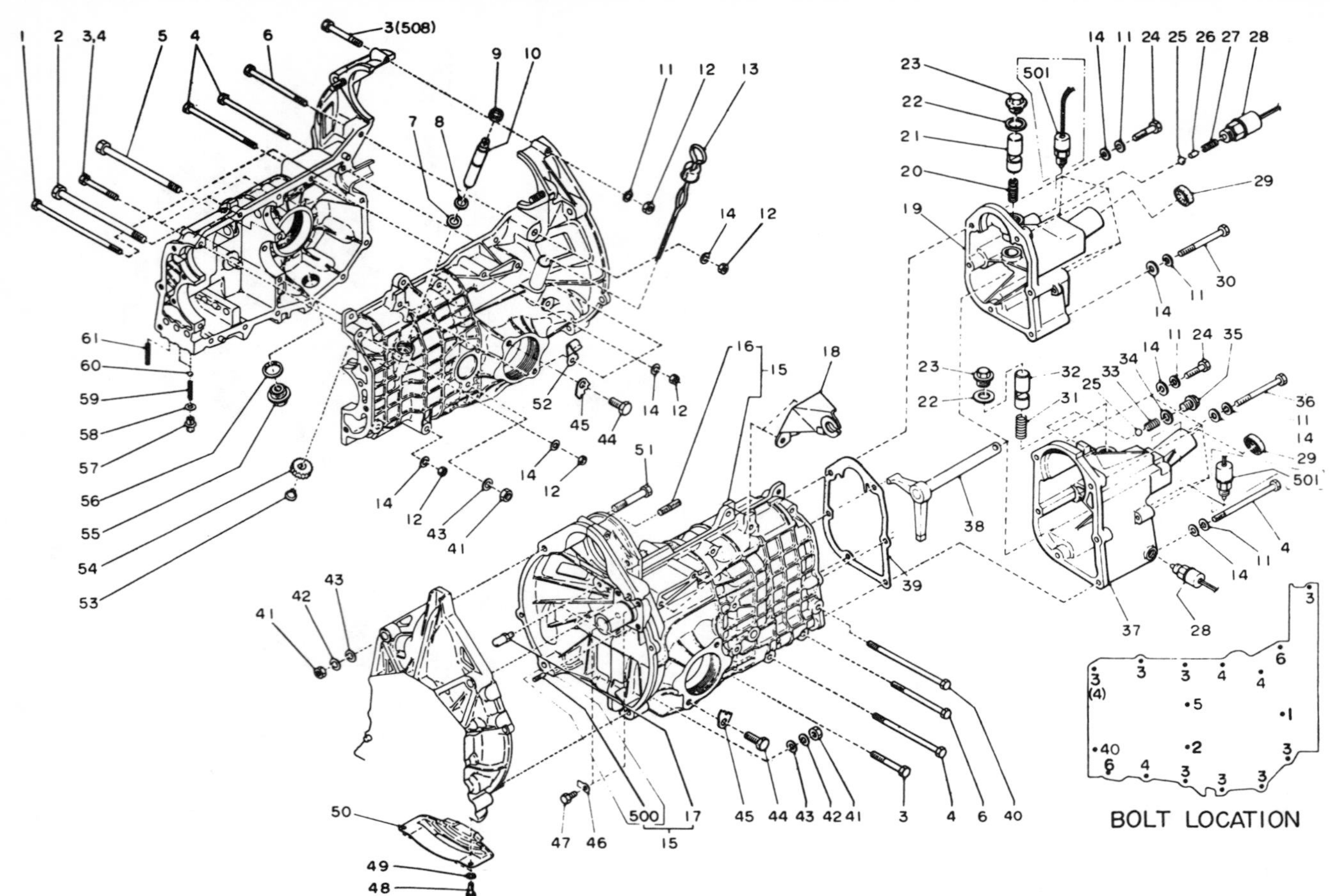

FIG 5 – TRANSMISSION CASE

1	Bolt
2	Bolt
3	Bolt
4	Bolt
5	Bolt
6	Bolt
7	Washer
8	Ring
9	Oil Seal
10	Speedometer Shaft
11	Washer
12	Nut
13	Oil Gauge
14	Washer
15	Trans Case
16	Bolt
17	Pivot
18	Bracket
19	Trans Cover
20	Spring
21	Shaft
22	Gasket (Aluminum)
23	Plug
24	Bolt
25	Bolt
26	Pin
27	Spring
28	Back-Up Lamp Switch
29	Oil Seal
30	Bolt
31	Spring
32	Shaft
33	Spring
34	Gasket (Aluminum)
35	Plug
36	Bolt
37	Trans Cover
38	Shifter Arm
39	Gasket
40	Bolt
41	Nut
42	Washer
43	Washer
44	Bolt
45	Plate
46	Bracket
47	Bolt
48	Bolt
49	Washer
50	Cover
51	Bolt
52	Clup
53	Ring
54	Gear
55	Plug
56	Gasket
57	Plug
58	Gasket (Aluminum)
59	Spring
60	Ball
61	Spring
500	Bolt
501	Neutral Switch
502	Bracket

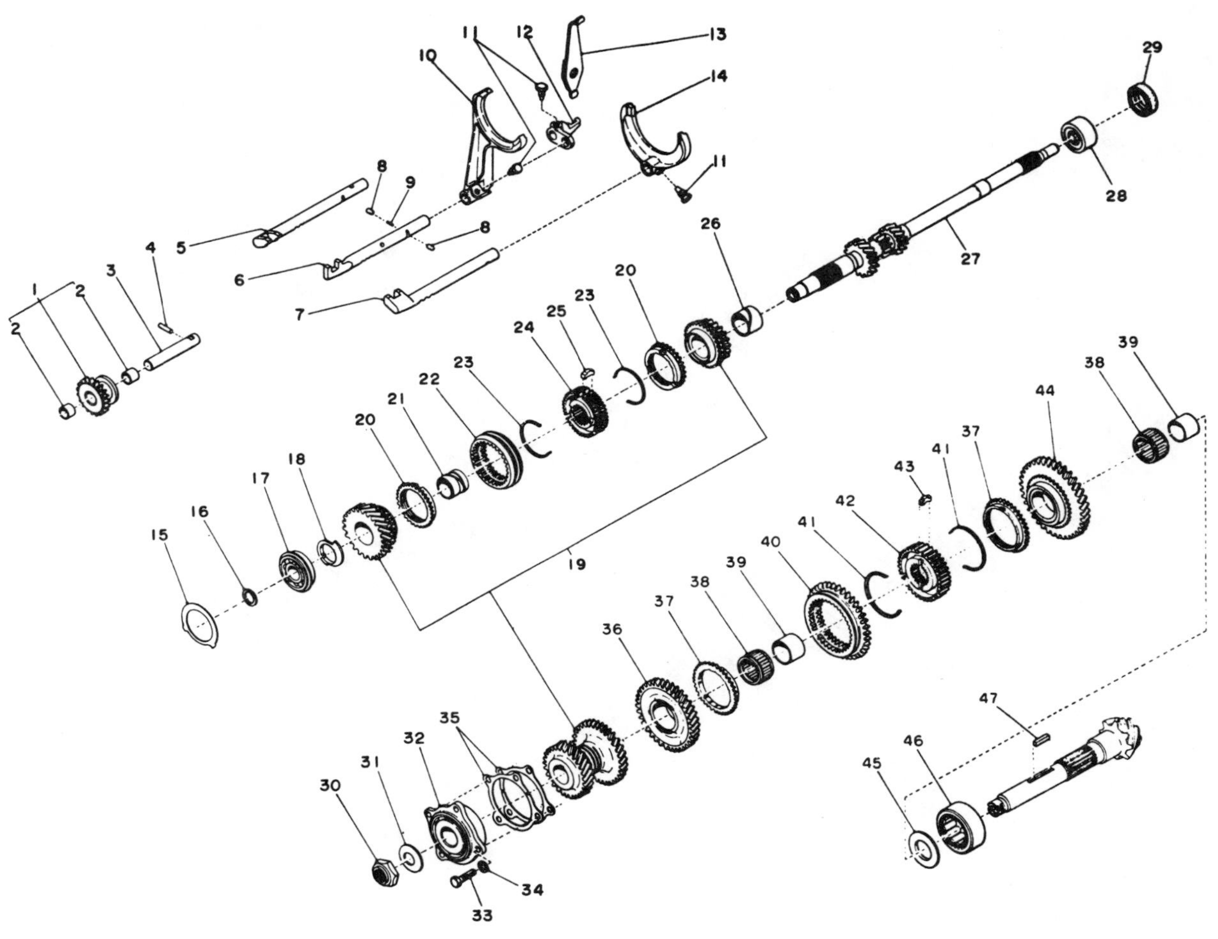

FIG 6 – TRANSMISSION GEARS

1 Reverse Idler Gear
2 Bushing
3 Shaft
4 Pin
5 Rail
6 Rail
7 Rail
8 Plunger
9 Plunger
10 Fork
11 Screw
12 Arm
13 Lever
14 Fork
15 Collar
16 Ring
17 Ball Bearing
18 Collar
19 Gear Set
20 Synchronizer Ring
21 Bushing
22 Sleeve
23 Spring
24 Hub
25 Insert
26 Bushing
27 Mainshaft
28 Needle Bearing
29 Oil Seal
30 Nut
31 Washer
32 Ball Bearing
33 Bolt
34 Washer
35 Shim
36 Second Driven Gear
37 Ring
38 Needle Bearing
39 Race
40 Reverse Driven Gear
41 Spring
42 Hub
43 Insert
44 Low Driven Gear
45 Spacer
46 Roller Bearing
47 Key

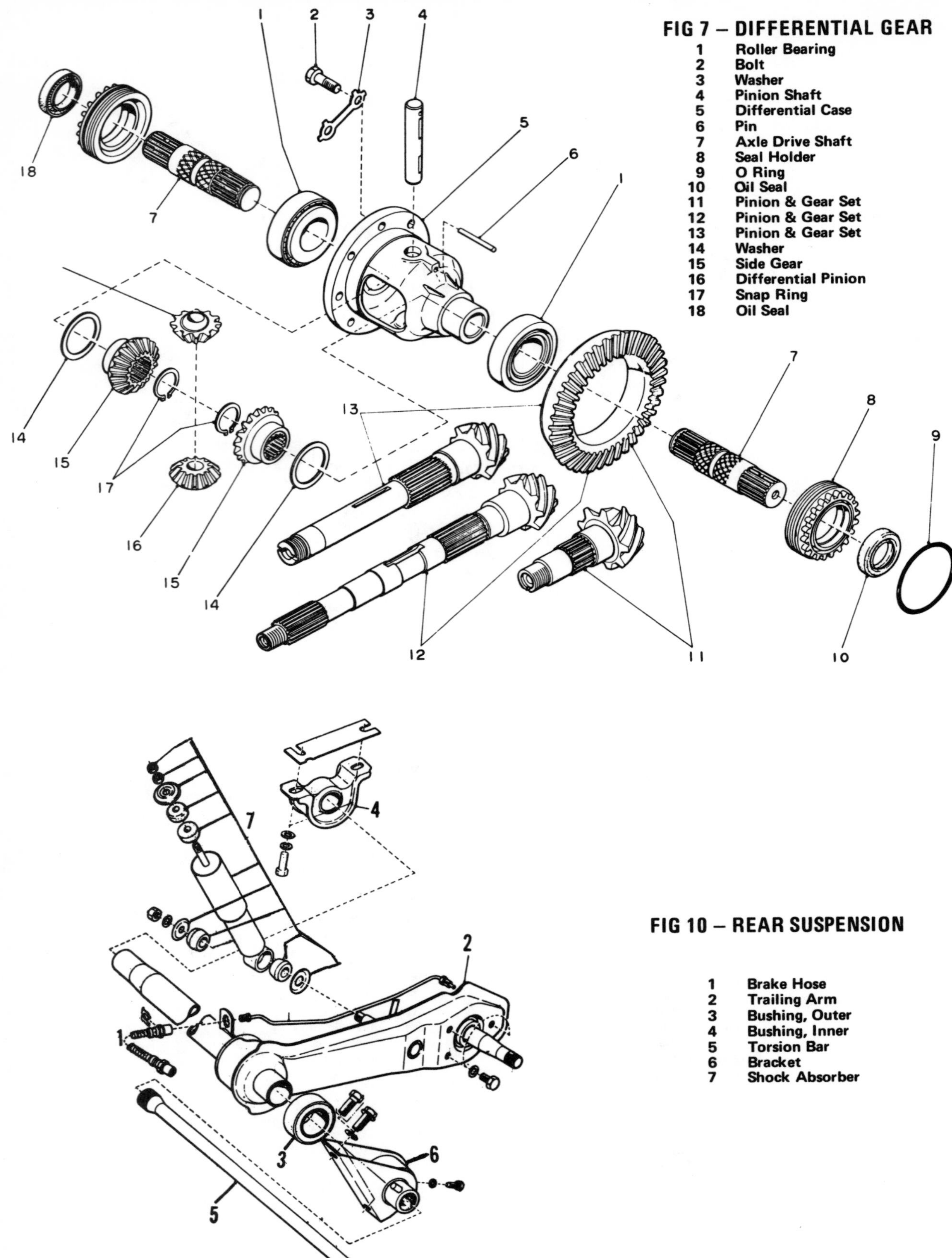

FIG 7 – DIFFERENTIAL GEAR

1 Roller Bearing
2 Bolt
3 Washer
4 Pinion Shaft
5 Differential Case
6 Pin
7 Axle Drive Shaft
8 Seal Holder
9 O Ring
10 Oil Seal
11 Pinion & Gear Set
12 Pinion & Gear Set
13 Pinion & Gear Set
14 Washer
15 Side Gear
16 Differential Pinion
17 Snap Ring
18 Oil Seal

FIG 10 – REAR SUSPENSION

1 Brake Hose
2 Trailing Arm
3 Bushing, Outer
4 Bushing, Inner
5 Torsion Bar
6 Bracket
7 Shock Absorber

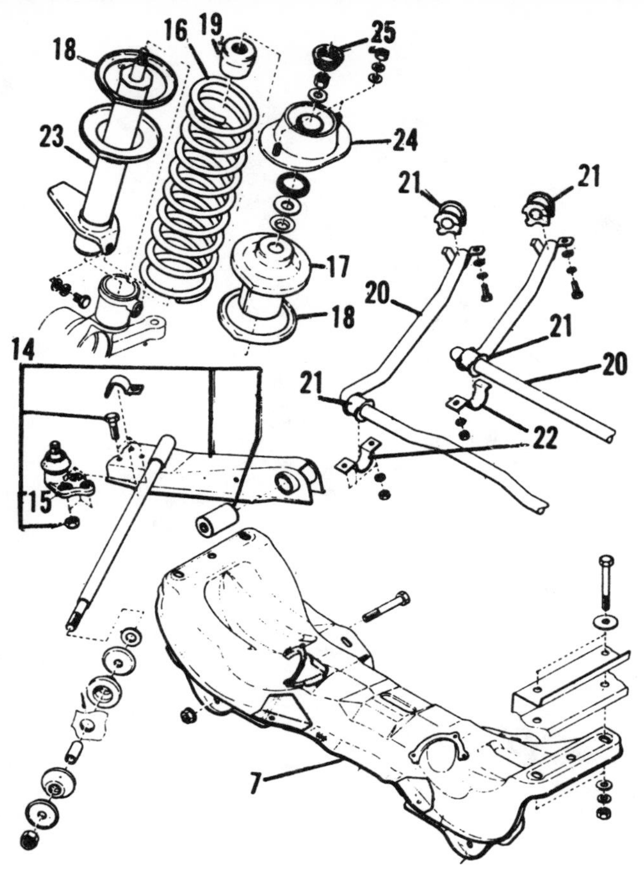

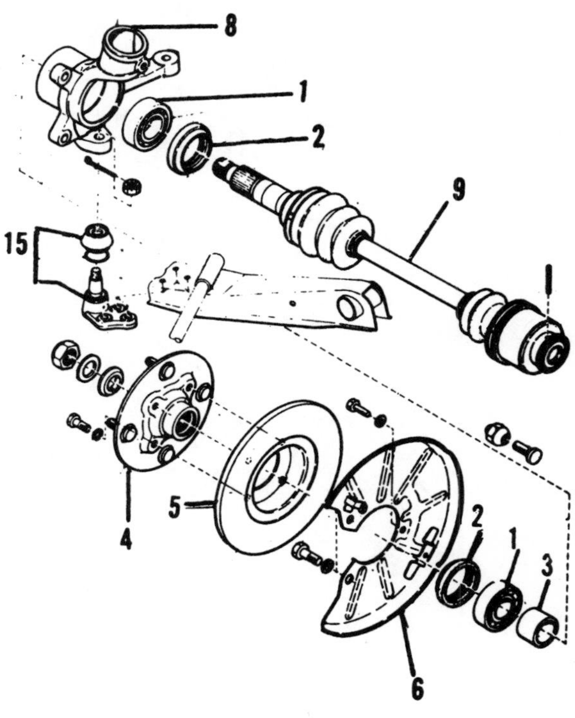

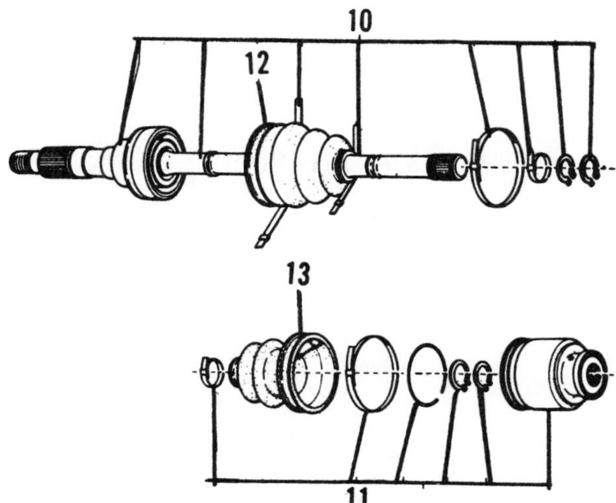

FIG 8 – FRONT SUSPENSION

1 Wheel Bearing
2 Seal
3 Spacer
4 Hub
5 Rotor
6 Shield
7 Crossmember
8 Steering Knuckle & Arm
9 Axle Shaft Assy & Inner Joint
10 Axle Shaft Wo/Inner Joint
11 Inner Joint
12 Boot, Outer
13 Boot, Inner
14 Control Arm & Transverse Link
15 Ball Joint
16 Spring
17 Seat, Upper
18 Rubber Seal
19 Bumper
20 Stabilizer Bar
21 Bushing
22 Bracket
23 Shock Absorber
24 Mount, Upper
25 Mount Cap

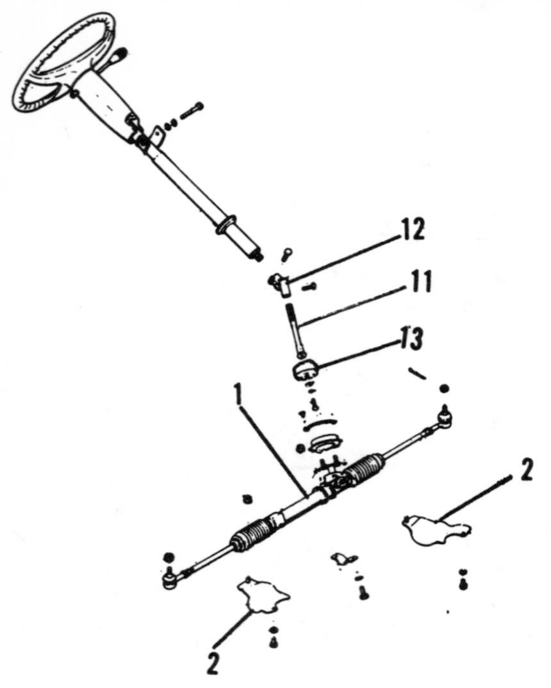

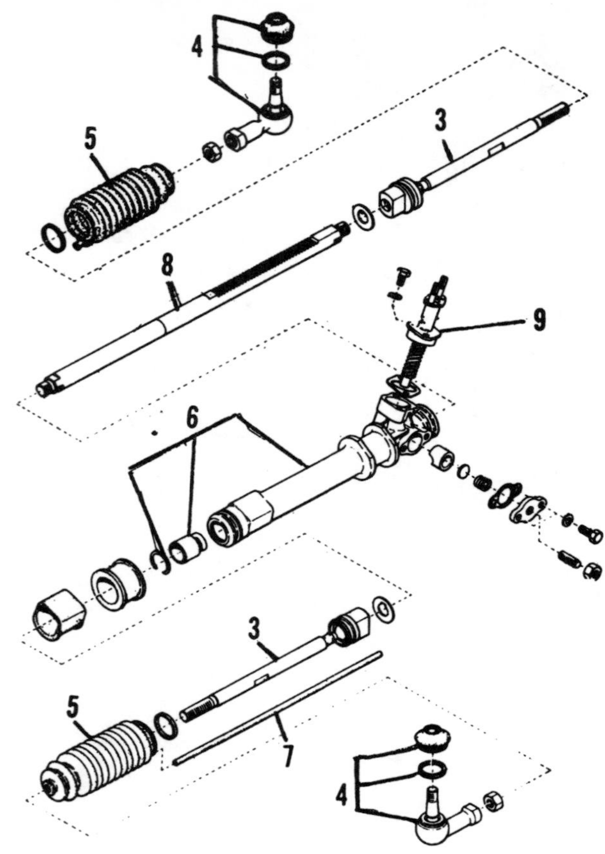

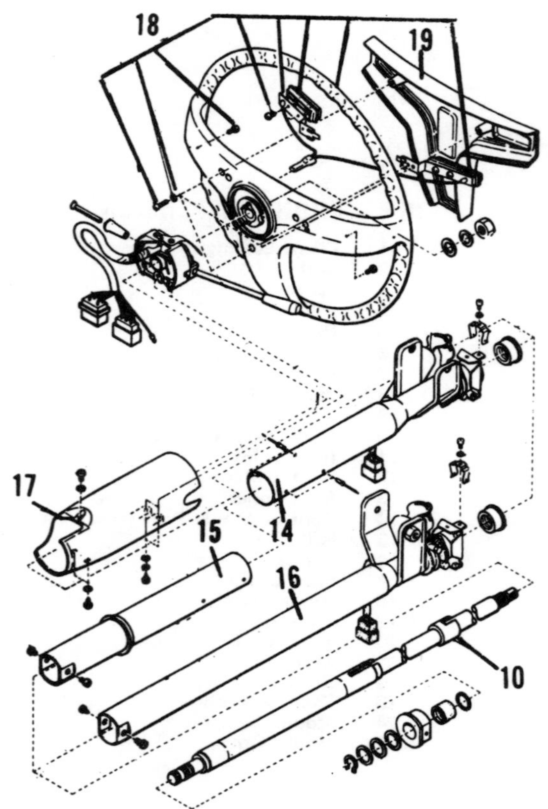

FIG 9 – STEERING

1	Gear Assy
2	Mounting Bracket
3	Tie Rod
4	Tie Rod End
5	Boot
6	Housing
7	Air Vent Pipe
8	Rack
9	Pinion
10	Upper Shaft
11	Lower Shaft
12	Universal Joint
13	Coupling
14	Column, Upper
15	Column, Lower
16	Column, 4-WD
17	Cover
18	Wheel
19	Horn Cover

Ignition, Starting & Charging—TIME

OPERATION INDEX

Tune-Up, Minor 1
Tune-Up, Major 2
Compression Test 3
Distributor, R&R Or Renew 4
Distributor, R&R & Overhaul 5
Distributor Cap Renew 6
Ignition Cable Set, Renew 7
Vacuum Control Unit, Renew 8
Points & Condenser, Renew 9
Ignition Timing 10
Ignition Coil, Renew 11
Starter, R&R Or Renew 12
Starter, R&R & Overhaul 13
Starter Solenoid, Renew 14
Starter Drive Unit, Renew 15
Starter Brushes, Renew 16
Voltage Regulator, Renew 17
Alternator, R&R Or Renew 18
Alternator, R&R & Overhaul 19
Alternator Diodes, Renew 20
Alternator Bearings, Renew 21
Alternator Pulley, Renew 22

1—TUNE-UP, MINOR
Includes renew points, condenser & plugs, set spark timing & adjust carburetor idle.
All Models 1.4

2—TUNE-UP, MAJOR
Includes check compression clean or renew & adjust spark plugs, R&R dist, renew points & condenser. Adjust ignition timing, carburetor & fan belts. Clean battery terminals & service air cleaner. Check coil & clean or renew fuel strainer.
All Models 2.5

3—COMPRESSION TEST
All Models 0.3

4—DISTRIBUTOR, R&R OR RENEW
All Models 0.4

5—DISTRIBUTOR, R&R & OVERHAUL
All Models 1.0

6—DISTRIBUTOR CAP, RENEW
All Models 0.2

7—IGNITION CABLE SET, RENEW
All Models 0.3

8—VACUUM CONTROL UNIT, RENEW
All Models 0.5

9—POINTS & CONDENSER, RENEW
Includes set dwell & adjust ignition timing.
All Models 0.4

10—IGNITION TIMING, CHECK OR ADJUST
All Models 0.3

11—IGNITION COIL, RENEW
All Models 0.2

12—STARTER, R&R OR RENEW
All Models 0.5

13—STARTER, R&R & OVERHAUL
All Models 1.5

14—STARTER SOLENOID, RENEW
All Models 0.7

15—STARTER DRIVE UNIT, RENEW
All Models 0.8

16—STARTER BRUSHES, RENEW
All Models 0.9

17—VOLTAGE REGULATOR RENEW
All Models 0.3

18—ALTERNATOR ASSY, R&R OR RENEW
All Models 0.5

19—ALTERNATOR, R&R & OVERHAUL
All Models 1.2

20—ALTERNATOR DIODES, RENEW
All Models 1.0

21—ALTERNATOR BEARINGS, RENEW
All Models 0.8

22—ALTERNATOR PULLEY, RENEW
All Models 0.3

Fuel, Emission Controls, Intake & Exhaust Systems—TIME

OPERATION INDEX

Carburetor, R&R Or Renew 1
Carburetor R&R & Overhaul 2
Choke Cable, Renew 3
Fuel Pump, R&R Or Renew 4
Fuel Filter, Renew 5
Fuel Tank, R&R Or Renew 6
Crankcase Emission Controls 7
Exhaust Emission Controls 8
Evaporative Emission Controls 9
Emission System, Check & Adjust 10
Intake Manifold, R&R Or Renew 11
Exhaust Manifold, R&R Or Renew 12
Exhuast System, Complete R&R 13
Exhaust Pipe, R&R Or Renew 14
Muffler, R&R Or Renew 15
Prechamber (Resonator) R&R Or Renew 16
Exhaust Heat Shield, R&R Or Renew 17

1—CARBURETOR R&R OR RENEW
All Models 0.6

2—CARBURETOR, R&R & OVERHAUL
All Models 1.5

3—CHOKE CABLE ASSY, RENEW
All Models 0.3

4—FUEL PUMP, R&R OR RENEW
All Models 0.3

5—FUEL FILTER, RENEW
All Models 0.2

6—FUEL TANK, R&R OR RENEW
Station Wagon 0.7
Seoans Exc 1.4
GL-DL 0.6

7—CRANKCASE EMISSION CONTROLS, RENEW
Oil Separator 0.3
Separator Drain Hose 0.2

8—EXHAUST EMISSION CONTROLS, RENEW
Vacuum Control Valve 0.4
Carb Servo Diaphragm 0.3
Anti-Dieseling Valve 0.2
Vacuum Dist Hose 0.2
Air Injection Pump—
Renew 0.5
Overhaul 1.0
Air Pump Pulley 0.3
Anti-After Burn Valve 0.3
Air Distribute Manifold 0.3
Manifold Check Valve 0.2
Air Distribute Valve 0.3

9—EVAPORATIVE EMISSION CONTROLS, RENEW
Air Breather Valve—
Except 0.3
GL-DL 0.6
Reservoir Separator—
Sedans 0.2
Wagons, One Side 0.2
Air Breather Tube—
Res To Valve 0.2
Res To Res 0.8
Valve To Pipe Exc 0.5
Sta Wagon 0.8
Pipe To Air Cleaner 0.2
Air Breather Pipe 0.8

10—EMISSION SYSTEM CHECK & ADJUST
All Models 0.5

11—INTAKE MANIFOLD, COMPLETE, R&R OR RENEW
Includes replace coolant-
All Models—
R&R 0.8
Renew 1.1

12—EXHAUST MANIFOLD, R&R OR RENEW
Each 0.5

13—EXHAUST SYSTEM COMPLETE, R&R
Does not include manifolds-
All Models 0.5

14—EXHAUST PIPE, R&R OR RENEW
All Models 0.4

15—MUFFLER, R&R OR RENEW
All Models 0.4

16—PRECHAMBER (RESONATOR), R&R OR RENEW
All Models 0.5

17—EXHAUST HEAT SHIELD, R&R OR RENEW
All Models 0.6

Engine Cooling & Heater System—TIME

OPERATION INDEX

Radiator, R & R Or Renew 1
Radiator Hoses, Renew 2
Water Pump, R&R Or Renew 3
Water Pump, R&R O Overhaul 4
Reserve Tank, R&R Or Renew 5
Thermoswitch, Renew 6
Eng Cooling Blower Or Fan Shroud, Renew 7
Fan Assy, Renew 8
Shutter Assy, Renew 9
Thermostat, Renew 10
Thermostat Housing, Renew 11
Heater Duct Assy, R&R 12
Heater Core, Renew 13
Hot Water Valve, Renew 14
Heater Hose, Renew 15
Heater Fan, Renew 16
Heater Fan Switch, Renew 17

1—RADIATOR, R&R OR RENEW
All Models—
W/1 Radiator 0.8
W/2 Radiators—
Main 0.6
Sub 0.6
Both 0.9

2—RADIATOR HOSES, RENEW
All Models, Each 0.4

3—WATER PUMP, R&R OR RENEW
All Models 0.5

(Continued)

Engine Cooling & Heater System—TIME Cont'd

4—WATER PUMP, R&R & OVERHAUL
All Models 1.0

5—RESERVE TANK, R&R OR RENEW
All Models 0.3

6—THERMOSWITCH, RENEW
All Models 0.2

7—ENG COOLING BLOWER OR FAN SHROUD, RENEW
All Models 0.4

8—FAN ASSY, RENEW
All Models 0.5

9—SHUTTER ASSY, RENEW
All Models 0.5

10—THERMOSTAT, RENEW
All Models 0.5

11—THERMOSTAT HOUSING, RENEW
All Models 0.6

12—HEATER DUCT ASSY, R&R
Except Below 2.5
GL-DL 1.2

13—HEATER CORE, RENEW
GL-DL 1.5

14—HOT WATER VALVE, RENEW
GL-DL 0.4

15—HEATER HOSE, RENEW
GL-DL, EACH 0.4

16—HEATER FAN ASSY, RENEW
GL-DL 0.8

17—HEATER FAN SWITCH, RENEW
Except Below 0.7
GL-DL 0.5

Engine—TIME

OPERATION INDEX

Engine, R&R 1
Engine, Renew 2
Engine (Short) Renew & Grind Valves 3
Engine, R&R & Overhaul 4
Cylinder Head, Renew 5
Cylinder Head, R&R Or Gasket, Renew 6
Valves, Adjust 7
Valves, Grind 8
One Valve, Renew & Grind 9
Valve Springs, Renew 10
Valve Cover Gaskets, Renew 11
Rocker Arm Assys, Renew 12
Rocker Arm Assys, Overhaul 13
Camshaft, R&R Or Renew 14
Camshaft Timing Gear, Renew 15
Oil Pan Or Gasket, Renew 16
Oil Pick-Up Tube, Renew 17
Oil Pump, R&R Or Renew 18
Oil Pump, R&R & Overhaul 19
Pistons Or Rings, Renew 20
Connecting Rod Or Bearing, Renew 21
Crankshaft, R&R Or Renew 22
Main Bearings, Renew 23
Main & Rod Bearings, Renew 24

1—ENGINE, R&R
Does not include transfer any part of engine or replacement of special equipment.
All Models 3.5

2—ENGINE, RENEW
Includes transfer all units. Does not include special equipment.
All Models 6.0

3—ENGINE (SHORT) RENEW & GRIND VALVES
All Models 9.0

4—ENGINE, R&R OVERHAUL
Includes rebore cylinders with boring bar, renew pistons, rings, pins, main & rod bearings, grind valves plastigauge bearings & perform minor tune-up.
All Models 18.5

5—CYLINDER HEAD, RENEW
All Models—
One 3.7
Both 6.6

6—CYLINDER HEAD, R&R OR GASKET, RENEW
All Models—
One 2.7
Both 4.6

7—VALVES, ADJUST
Includes torque cyl heads
All Models 0.6

8—VALVES, GRIND
All Models—
One Side 3.5
Both Sides 7.2

9—ONE VALVE, RENEW & GRIND
With head removed
All Models 0.5

10—VALVE SPRINGS. ALL RENEW
With head removed
All Models 1.0

11—VALVE COVER GASKETS, RENEW
Each Side 0.2

12—ROCKER ARM ASSEMBLES, RENEW
Each Side 0.5

13—ROCKER ARM ASSEMBLIES, OVERHAUL
With assemblies removed
Each Side 0.2

14—CAMSHAFT, R&R OR RENEW
All Models 7.0

15—CAMSHAFT TIMING GEAR, RENEW
After camshaft is removed
All Models 0.4

16—OIL PAN OR GASKET, RENEW
All Models 0.5

17—OIL PICK-UP TUBE, RENEW
After pan is removed
All Models 0.3

18—OIL PUMP, R&R OR RENEW
All Models 0.5

19—OIL PUMP, R&R & OVERHAUL
All Models 1.1

20—PISTONS OR RINGS, RENEW
Includes R&R engine.
All Models—
One 5.5
All 9.0

21—CONNECTING ROD OR BEARING, RENEW
After piston is removed.
All Models 0.4

22—CRANKSHAFT, R&R OR RENEW
After engine is removed.
All Models 6.2

23—MAIN BEARINGS, RENEW
After engine is removed
All Models 6.2

24—MAIN & ROD BEARINGS, RENEW
After engine is removed
All Models 7.0

Clutch, Engine Mounts, Manual Trans & Transaxle—TIME

OPERATION TIMES

Flywheel, R&R Or Renew 1
Flywheel Housing Or Oil Seal, Renew 2
Clutch Pedal, Adjust 3
Clutch, R&R Or Renew 4
Clutch Throw Out Bearing, Renew 5
Clutch Pilot Shaft Bearing, Renew 6
Engine Mounts, Renew 7
Transaxle Assy, R&R Or Renew 8
Transmission, Overhaul 9
Transaxle, Overhaul 10
Differentail Carrier, Overhaul 11
Trans End Cover Or Seal, Renew 12
Stub Axle Oil Seal, Renew 13
Input Shaft Seal, Renew 14
Shift Fork Or Rail, Renew 15

1—FLYWHEEL, R&R OR RENEW
After transaxle & clutch are removed.
All Models 0.5

2—FLYWHEEL HOUSING OR OIL SEAL, RENEW
After transaxle & clutch are removed.
All Models 0.9

3—CLUTCH PEDAL ADJUST
All Models 0.2

4—CLUTCH, R&R OR RENEW
After transaxle is removed
All Models 0.5

5—CLUTCH THROWOUT BEARING, RENEW
After clutch is removed.
All Models 0.2

6—CLUTCH PILOT SHAFT BEARINGS, RENEW
After clutch is removed
All Models 0.5

7—ENGINE MOUNTS RENEW
All Models—
Front—
One 0.3
Both 0.5
Rear Exc 0.5
GL-DL 0.3

8—TRANSAXLE ASSY, R&R OR RENEW
4 Speed Exc 3.5
GL-DL 3.0
5 Speed 3.0

9—TRANSMISSION, OVERHAUL
Transaxle removed
All Models 3.0

10—TRANSAXLE, OVERHAUL
Transaxle removed.
All Models 3.7

11—DIFFERENTIAL CARRIER, OVERHAUL
Transaxle Removed. 0.8

12—TRANS END COVER OR SEAL, RENEW
4 Speed 1.0
5 Speed 0.6

13—STUB AXLE OIL SEAL, ENTER, RENEW
4 Speed Exc 1.3
GL-DL 5

14—INPUT SHAFT SEAL, RENEW
Transaxle removed
All Models 0.5

15—SHIFT FORK OR RAIL, RENEW
Transaxle removed
All Models 1.1

Automatic Transmission & Transaxle—TIME

OPERATION INDEX

Transaxle Assy, R&R 1
Transmission, Overhaul 2
Converter Or Oil Seal, R&R Or Renew 3
Oil Pan, R&R Or Renew 4
Valve Body, R&R Or Renew 5
Valve Body, R&R & Overhaul 6
Governor, R&R & Clean 7
Oil Pump, R&R Or Renew 8
Oil Pump, R&R & Overhaul 9
Oil Coolant Line, R&R Or Renew 10
Band, Adjust 11
Manual Linkage, Adjust 12
Parking Pawl, R&R Or Renew 13
Vacuum Throttle Valve, Renew 14
Kickdown Solenoid, Renew 15
Inhibitor Switch, Renew 16
Differential Assy, R&R Or Renew 17
Pressure Test 18
Stall Test 19

1—TRANSAXLE ASSY, R&R
Includes engine R&R.
All Models 2.8

2—TRANSMISSION, OVERHAUL
Transaxle removed.
All Models 4.0

3—CONVERTER OR OIL SEAL, R&R OR RENEW
Includes engine R&R.
All Models 3.0

4—OIL PAN, R&R OR RENEW
All Models 0.4

5—VALVE BODY, R&R OR RENEW
All Models 0.7

6—VALVE BODY, R&R OVERHAUL
All Models 1.0

7—GOVERNOR ASSY, R&R OR & CLEAN
All Models 0.7

8—OIL PUMP, R&R OR RENEW
Transaxle removed
All Models 0.4

9—OIL PUMP, R&R & OVERHAUL
Transaxle removed.
All Models 0.8

10—OIL COOLANT LINE, R&R OR RENEW
One 0.4
Both 0.5

11—BAND, ADJUST
All Models 0.2

12—MANUAL LINKAGE, ADJUST
All Models 0.2

13—PARKING PAWL, R&R OR RENEW
Transaxle removed
All Models 0.8

14—VACUUM THROTTLE VALVE, RENEW
All Models 0.4

15—KICKDOWN SOLENOID, RENEW
All Models 0.4

16— INHIBITOR SWITCH, RENEW
All Models 0.4

17—DIFFERENTIAL ASSY, R&R OR RENEW
All Models 3.0

18—PRESSURE TEST
All Models 0.5

19—STALL TEST
All Models 0.2

Brakes—TIME

OPERATION INDEX

Brake Shoes Or Friction Pads, Renew 1
Caliper, R&R Or Renew 2
Caliper, R&R & Overhaul 3
Disc Brake Rotor, R&R Or Renew 4
Disc Brake Rotor, Resurface 5
Disc Brake Dust Shield, R&R Or Renew 6
Brake Drum, R&R Or Renew 7
Brake Drum, Resurface 8
Master Cylinder, R&R Or Renew 9
Master Cylinder, R&R & Overhaul 10
Wheel Cylinder, R&R Or Renew 11
Wheel Cyl, R&R & Overhaul 12
Bleed System 13
Brake Hose, Renew 14
Marking Brake Lever, Renew 15
Parking Brake Rod, Renew 16
Parking Brake Cables, Renew 17
Power Brake Unit, R&R Or Renew 18

1—BRAKE SHOES OR FRICTION PADS, RENEW
Drum Type—
One Wheel Exc 0.9
DL 0.8
Disc Type—
One Wheel 0.4

2—CALIPER ASSY, R&R OR RENEW
One Side 0.9
Both Sides 1.5

3—CALIPER ASSY, R&R & OVERHAUL
One Side 1.4
Both Sides 1.9

4—DISC BRAKE ROTOR, R&R OR RENEW
Each 1.1

5—DISC BRAKE ROTOR, RESURFACE
Rotor removed
Each 0.7

6—DISC BRAKE DUST SHIELD, R&R OR RENEW
GL 1.3

7—BRAKE DRUM, R&R OR RENEW
Front Exc 0.5
DL 0.3
Rear 0.6

8—BRAKE DRUM, RESURFACE
Drum removed
Each 0.2

9—MASTER CYLINDER, R&R OR RENEW
Includes bleed.
Except Below 0.7
GL-DL 0.4

10—MASTER CYLINDER, R&R OVERHAUL
Includes bleed.
Except Below 1.3
GL-DL 1.0

11—WHEEL CYLINDER, R&R OR RENEW
Includes bleed.
Front Exc 1.0
DL 0.8
Rear 0.9

12—WHEEL CYLINDER, R&R & OVERHAUL
Includes bleed.
Front Exc 1.3
DL 1.1
Rear 1.2

13—BLEED SYSTEM
All Models 0.3

14—BRAKE HOSE, RENEW
Includes bleed.
All Models 0.4

15—PARKING BRAKE LEVER, RENEW
All Models 0.5

16—PARKING BRAKE ROD ASSY, RENEW
All Models 0.3

17—PARKING BRAKE CABLES, RENEW
One Side Exc 1.2
GL-DL 0.6
Both Sides Exc 2.2
GL-DL 1.0

18—POWER BRAKE UNIT, R&R OR RENEW
Includes R&R master cylinder & bleed.
All Models 0.8

Front Suspension & Steering—TIME

OPERATION INDEX

Steering Knuckle, R&R Or Renew 1
Steering Knuckle, Overhaul 2
Ball-Joint, R&R Or Renew 3
Upper Control Arm, R&R Or Renew 4
Upper Arm Needle Bearing, Renew 5
Lower Control Arm, R&R Or Renew 6
Lower Arm & Strut, R&R Or Renew 7
Lower Arm Bushings Or Shaft, Renew 8
Lower Arm Bracket, Renew 9
Torsion Bar, R&R Or Renew 10
Strut Assy, R&R Or Renew 11
Stabilizer Bar, R&R Or Renew 12
Shock Absorber, R&R Or Renew 13
Axle Shaft, R&R Or Renew 14
Hub Assy, R&R Or Renew 15
Steering Rack Assy, R&R Or Renew 16
Steering Rack Assy, R&R & Overhaul 17
Tie Rod End, R&R Or Renew 18
Tie Rod Ball Joint, R&R Or Renew 19

1—STEERING KNUCKLE R&R OR RENEW
Includes R&R wheel, axle, align front end & adjust toe-in.
All Models 1.6

2—STEERING KNUCKLE, OVERHAUL
After knuckle is removed.
All Models 0.6

3—BALL JOINT, R&R OR RENEW
Upper 1.0
Lower Exc 1.0
1975 & Later 0.5

4—UPPER CONTROL ARM, R&R OR RENEW
Includes R&R torsion bar, shock absorber, & upper ball joint-
All Models 2.0

5—UPPER ARM NEEDLE BEARING, RENEW
After arm is removed.
All Models 0.8

6—LOWER CONTROL ARM, R&R OR RENEW
Except Below ①1.5
GL-DL ②1.2
①*Includes R&R Ball-Joint.*
②*Includes Arm & Knuckles*

(Continued)

Front Suspension & Steering—TIME Cont'd

7—LOWER ARM & STRUT, R&R OR RENEW
1975-76 .... 1.0

8—LOWER ARM BUSHINGS OR SHAFT, RENEW
After arm is removed.
All Models 0.3

9—LOWER ARM BRACKET, RENEW
After arm is removed
All Models 0.2

10—TORSION BAR, R&R OR RENEW
All Models 0.4

11—STRUT ASSY, R&R OR RENEW
GL-DL 0.6

12—STABILIZER BAR, R&R OR RENEW
GL-DL 0.3

13—SHOCK ABSORBER, R&R OR RENEW
All Models 0.3

14—AXLE SHAFT, R&R OR RENEW
Except Below 0.5
GL-DL 0.4

15—HUB ASSY, R&R OR RENEW
All Models 0.7

16—STEERING RACK ASSY, R&R OR RENEW
Except Below 1.2
GL-DL 1.0

17—STEERING RUCK ASSY, R&R& OVERHAUL
Except Below 2.1
GL-DL 1.7

18—TIE ROD END, R&R OR RENEW
Includes adjust toe-in.
All Models 0.7

19—TIE ROD BALL JOINT, R&R OR RENEW
All Models 0.8

Rear Suspension—TIME

OPERATION INDEX

Suspension Assy, R&R *1*
Trailing Arm, R&R Or Renew *2*
Trailing Arm Bushing Or Bearing, Renew *3*
Torsion Bar, R&R Or Renew *4*
Torsion Bar Center Arm, R&R Or Renew *5*
Shock Absorber, R&R Or Renew *6*

1—SUSPENSION ASSY, R&R
Except GL-DL 1.3

2—TRAILING ARM, R&R OR RENEW
All Models 1.6

3—TRAILING ARM BUSHING OR BEARING, RENEW
After arm is removed.
All Models—
Outer 0.4
Inner 0.7

4—TORSION BAR, R&R OR RENEW
All Models, Each 1.3

5—TORSION BAR CENTER ARM, R&R OR RENEW
Includes R&R torsion bar.
All Models 1.0

6—SHOCK ABSORBER, R&R OR RENEW
Each 0.3

Speedometer, W/S Wipers, Switches & Instruments—TIME

OPERATION INDEX

Speedometer Cable, R&R Or Renew *1*
Speedometer Head, Renew *2*
W/S Wiper Motor Or Link System, Renew *3*
W/S Wiper Arm Or Blade, Renew *4*
W/S Wiper Switch, Renew *5*
W/S Washer Pump, Renew *6*
Fule Gauge (Dash Unit), Renew *7*
Fuel Tank Gauge, Renew *8*
Oil Pressure Switch, Renew *9*
Temperature Gauge (Dash Unit), Renew *10*
Tempterature Gauge Sending Unit, Renew *11*
Headlight Switch, Renew *12*
Stop Light Switch, Renew *13*
Back-Up Light Switch, Renew *14*
Tachometer, Renew *15*
Turn Signal Or Hazard Flasher Unit, Renew *16*

1—SPEEDOMETER CABLE, R&R OR RENEW
All Models 0.3

2—SPEEDOMETER HEAD, RENEW
Except Below 0.3
GL-DL 0.6

3—W/S WIPER MOTOR OR LINK SYSTEM, RENEW
Except Below 0.9
GL-DL 0.3

4—W/S WIPER ARM OR BLADE, RENEW
All Models 0.2

5—W/S WIPER SWITCH, RENEW
Except Below 0.2
1974-76 GL-DL 0.5

6—W/S WASHER PUMP, RENEW
All Models 0.2

7—FUEL GAUGE (DASH UNIT), RENEW
Except Below 0.6
GL-DL 0.7

8—FUEL TANK GAUGE, RENEW
All Models 0.3

9—OIL PRESSURE SWITCH, RENEW
All Models 0.2

10—TEMPERATURE GAUGE (DASH UNIT), RENEW
Except Below 0.6
GL-DL 0.7

11—TEMPERATURE GAUGE SENDING UNIT, RENEW
All Models 0.2

12—HEADLIGHT SWITCH, RENEW
Except Below 0.4
GL-DL 0.2

13—STOP LIGHT SWITCH, RENEW
All Models 0.2

14—BACK-UP LIGHT SWITCH, RENEW
Except Below 1.0
GL-DL 0.3

15—TACHOMETER, RENEW
GL 0.2

16—TURN SIGNAL OR HAZARD FLASHER UNIT, RENEW
All Models 0.2

IDENTIFICATION

ALL MODELS........................... 410

ILLUSTRATIONS

FIG 1 – ENGINE – CYLINDER HEAD & COVER
FIG 2 – ENGINE – CYLINDER BLOCK & OIL PAN
FIG 3 – TIMING COVER & REAR END PLATE
FIG 4 – ENGINE – CAMSHAFT & VALVES
FIG 5 – ENGINE – TIMING CHAIN & DAMPER
FIG 6 – ENGINE – CRANKSHAFT & PISTONS
FIG 7 – TRANSMISSION CASE & EXTENSION HOUSING
FIG 8 – TRANSMISSION GEARS
FIG 9 – FRONT SUSPENSION – CARINA & CELICA
FIG 10 – FRONT SUSPENSION – CORONA
FIG 11 – FRONT SUSPENSION – CORONA MARK II
FIG 12 – STEERING – CARINA & CELICA
FIG 13 – STEERING – CORONA
FIG 14 – STEERING – CORONA MARK II
FIG 15 – REAR AXLE

OPERATION TIMES

A

Air Pump.......... 420
Alternator.......... 420
Ammeter.......... 425
Automatic Transmission.......... 423
Axle Shaft.......... 424

B

Brake Drums.......... 424
Brakes.......... 423

C

Cables (Ignition).......... 420
Calipers.......... 424
Camshaft.......... 422
Carburetor.......... 420
Clutch.......... 422
Coil, Ignition.......... 420
Compression Test.......... 420
Connecting Rods.......... 422
Cooling System.......... 421
Crankshaft.......... 422
Cylinder Head.......... 421

D

Dash Gauges.......... 425
Differential.......... 423
Disc Brakes.......... 423
Distributor.......... 420

E

Emission Controls.......... 420
Engine Assembly.......... 421
Engine Mountings.......... 423
Engine Oiling.......... 422
Engine Tune-Up.......... 420
Exhaust System.......... 420

F

Flywheel.......... 423
Front Suspension.......... 423
Fuel Gauges.......... 425
Fuel Pump.......... 420
Fuel Tank.......... 420

H

Hand Brake.......... 424
Headlight Switch.......... 425
Heater.......... 421
Hose (Brake).......... 424
Hose (Radiator).......... 421
Hydraulic Brakes.......... 423

I

Ignition.......... 420
Ignition Coil.......... 420
Ignition Switch.......... 420
Intake Manifold.......... 420

L

Light Switches.......... 425

M

Main Bearings.......... 422
Master Cylinder.......... 424
Muffler.......... 420

O

Oiling, Engine.......... 422
Oil Pan.......... 422
Oil Pump.......... 422

P

Parking Brake.......... 424
Piston Rings.......... 422
Pistons.......... 422

R

Radiator.......... 421
Radiator Hose.......... 421
Rear Axle.......... 423
Regulator (Alternator).......... 420
Rocker Arms.......... 422
Rod Bearings.......... 422

S

Shocks (Front).......... 424
Shocks (Rear).......... 424
Speedometer.......... 425
Springs (Front).......... 424
Springs (Rear).......... 424
Starting Motor.......... 420
Steering Gear.......... 424
Steering Linkage.......... 424
Switches (Light).......... 425
Synchro-Mesh Trans.......... 423

T

Tachometer.......... 425
Temperature Gauge.......... 425
Thermostat.......... 421
Timing Case Cover.......... 422
Timing Chain.......... 422
Timing Gears.......... 422
Transmission, Manual.......... 423
Transmission, Automatic.......... 423
Tune-Up Engine.......... 420

U

Universals.......... 424

V

Valve Lifters.......... 422
Valve System.......... 422

W

Water Pump.......... 421
Wheel Cylinders.......... 424
Windshield Wiper.......... 425

VEHICLE IDENTIFICATION PLATE

LOCATION: In the engine compartment on the firewall or the fender skirt.

This plate lists the model number, engine type, piston displacement, frame number, color code, trans-axle number and assembly plant code.

CHASSIS NUMBERS

LOCATION:
1 – On vehicle identification plate on the firewall or front fender skirt.
2 – Stamped on the firewall in the engine compartment.
3 – On the VIN plate located on top left side of instrument panel, visible thru windshield or on the front door hinge pillar.
4 – On vehicle production plate located on left front door lock pillar face.

PRODUCTION YEAR IDENTIFICATION

A vehicle production plate listing the month and year of production is located on the left front door lock pillar face. Model years can be determined by checking the following chart indicating the months produced.

MODEL YEAR	PRODUCTION MONTHS
1967	September 1966 thru August 1967
1968	September 1967 thru August 1968
1969	September 1968 thru August 1969
1970	September 1969 thru August 1970
1971	September 1970 thru August 1971
1972	September 1971 thru August 1972
1973	September 1972 thru August 1973
1974	September 1973 thru August 1974
1975	September 1974 thru August 1975
1976	September 1975 thru August 1976
1977	September 1976 thru August 1977

MODEL IDENTIFICATION

The model type is on the first line of the vehicle identification plate which is located on the firewall or the front fender skirt. To determine the model, use the chart below.

MODEL NUMBER	MODEL NAME
FJ 40-55	Land Cruiser
KE 10-11-15-16-17-18	Corolla
KE 20-25-26-30	Corolla
MS 53-55-63-65-75	Crown
MX 12-13-22-23-28-29	Corona Mark II
RA 20-21-22-24-29	Celica
RN 11-12-14-22-23-27-28	Hi-Lux
RT 62-63-72-73-78-79	Corona Mark II
RT 83-85-89-93-95	Corona
RT 104-105-114-115-118-119	Corona
TA 12	Carina
TE 21-27-28-31-37-38-51	Corolla

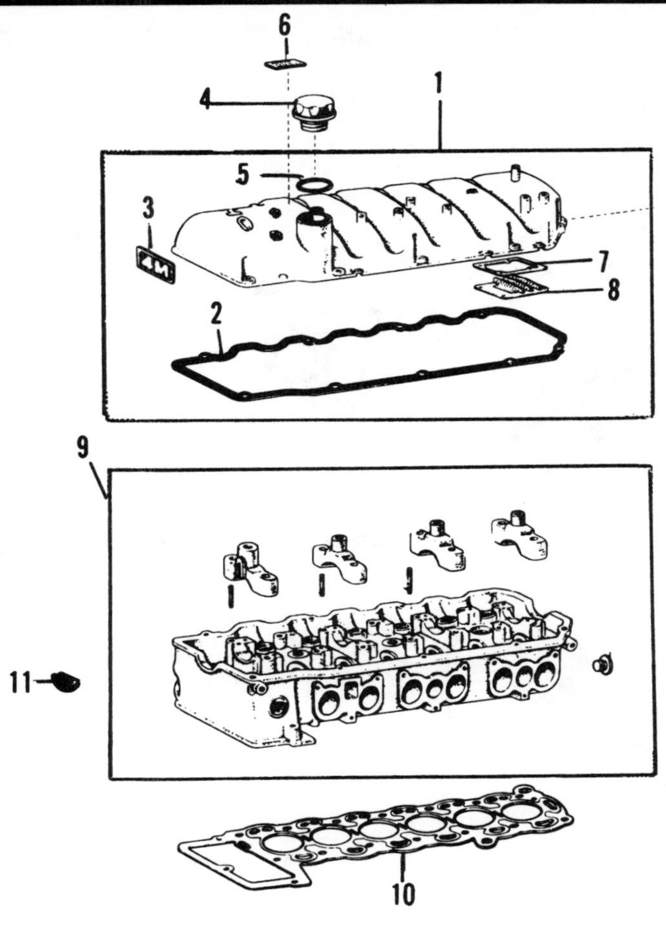

FIG 1 – ENGINE – CYLINDER HEAD & COVER

1	Cover Assy
2	Gasket
3	Plate
4	Cap
5	Ring
6	Plate
7	Gasket
8	Plate
9	Cylinder Head Assy
10	Gasket
11	Plug

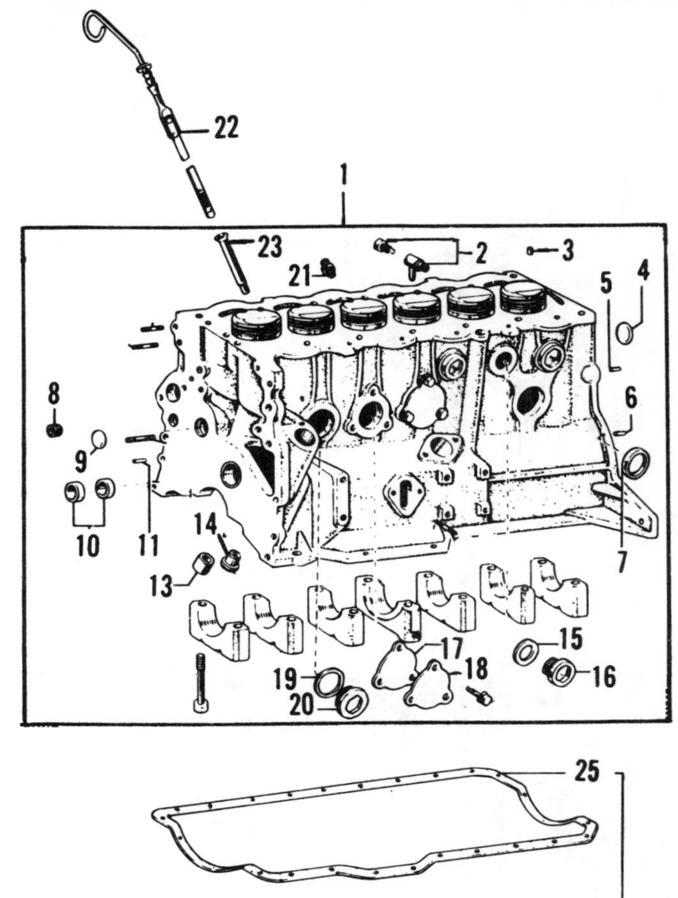

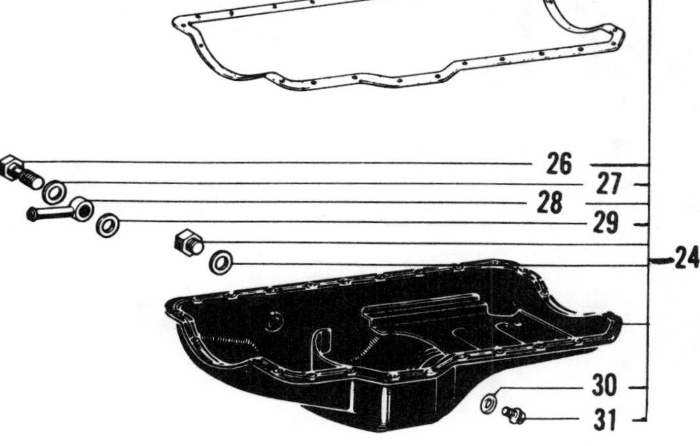

FIG 2 – ENGINE – CYLINDER BLOCK & OIL PAN

1	Cylinder Block Assy	17	Gasket
2	Drain Cock	18	Plate
3	Pin	19	Gasket
4	Plug	20	Plug
5	Pin	21	Union
6	Pin	22	Dip Stick
7	Plug	23	Guide
8	Plug	24	Oil Pan
9	Plug	25	Gasket
10	Bearing	26	Bolt
11	Pin	27	Gasket
12	Plug	28	Union
13	Bush	29	Gasket
14	Bush	30	Gasket
15	Gasket	31	Plug
16	Plug		

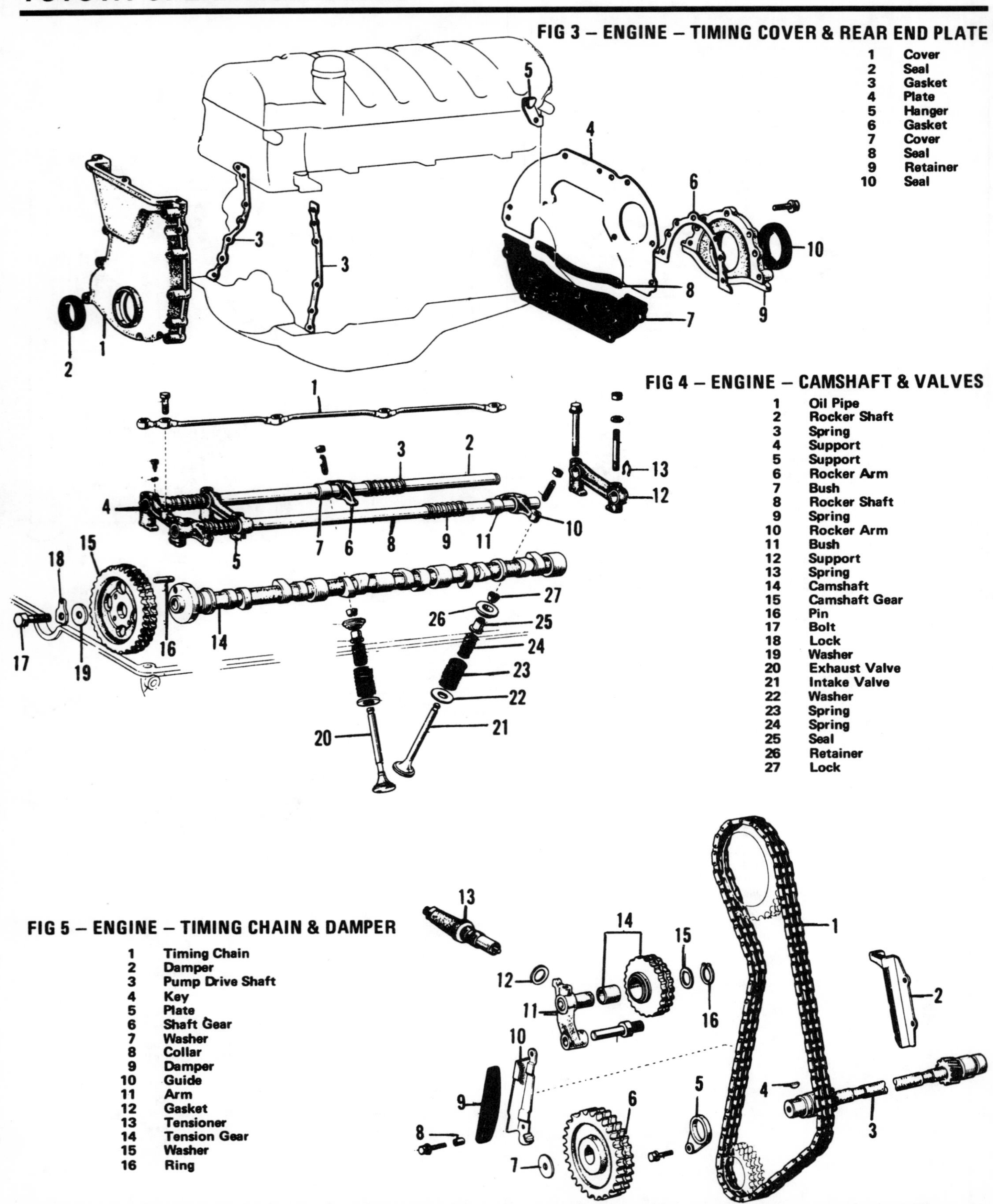

FIG 3 – ENGINE – TIMING COVER & REAR END PLATE

1 Cover
2 Seal
3 Gasket
4 Plate
5 Hanger
6 Gasket
7 Cover
8 Seal
9 Retainer
10 Seal

FIG 4 – ENGINE – CAMSHAFT & VALVES

1 Oil Pipe
2 Rocker Shaft
3 Spring
4 Support
5 Support
6 Rocker Arm
7 Bush
8 Rocker Shaft
9 Spring
10 Rocker Arm
11 Bush
12 Support
13 Spring
14 Camshaft
15 Camshaft Gear
16 Pin
17 Bolt
18 Lock
19 Washer
20 Exhaust Valve
21 Intake Valve
22 Washer
23 Spring
24 Spring
25 Seal
26 Retainer
27 Lock

FIG 5 – ENGINE – TIMING CHAIN & DAMPER

1 Timing Chain
2 Damper
3 Pump Drive Shaft
4 Key
5 Plate
6 Shaft Gear
7 Washer
8 Collar
9 Damper
10 Guide
11 Arm
12 Gasket
13 Tensioner
14 Tension Gear
15 Washer
16 Ring

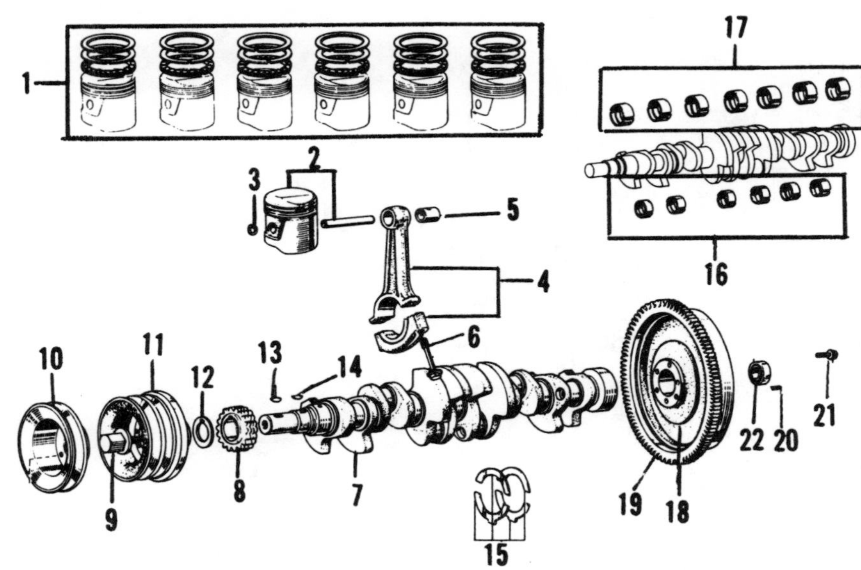

1 Piston Ring Set
2 Piston
3 Ring
4 Connecting Rod
5 Bushing
6 Bolt
7 Crankshaft
8 Crankshaft Gear
9 Boot
10 Pulley
11 Pulley
12 Washer
13 Key
14 Key
15 Washer
16 Connecting Rod Bearings
17 Main Bearings
18 Flywheel
19 Ring Gear
20 Pin
21 Bolt
22 Bearing

FIG 6 – ENGINE – CRANKSHAFT & PISTONS

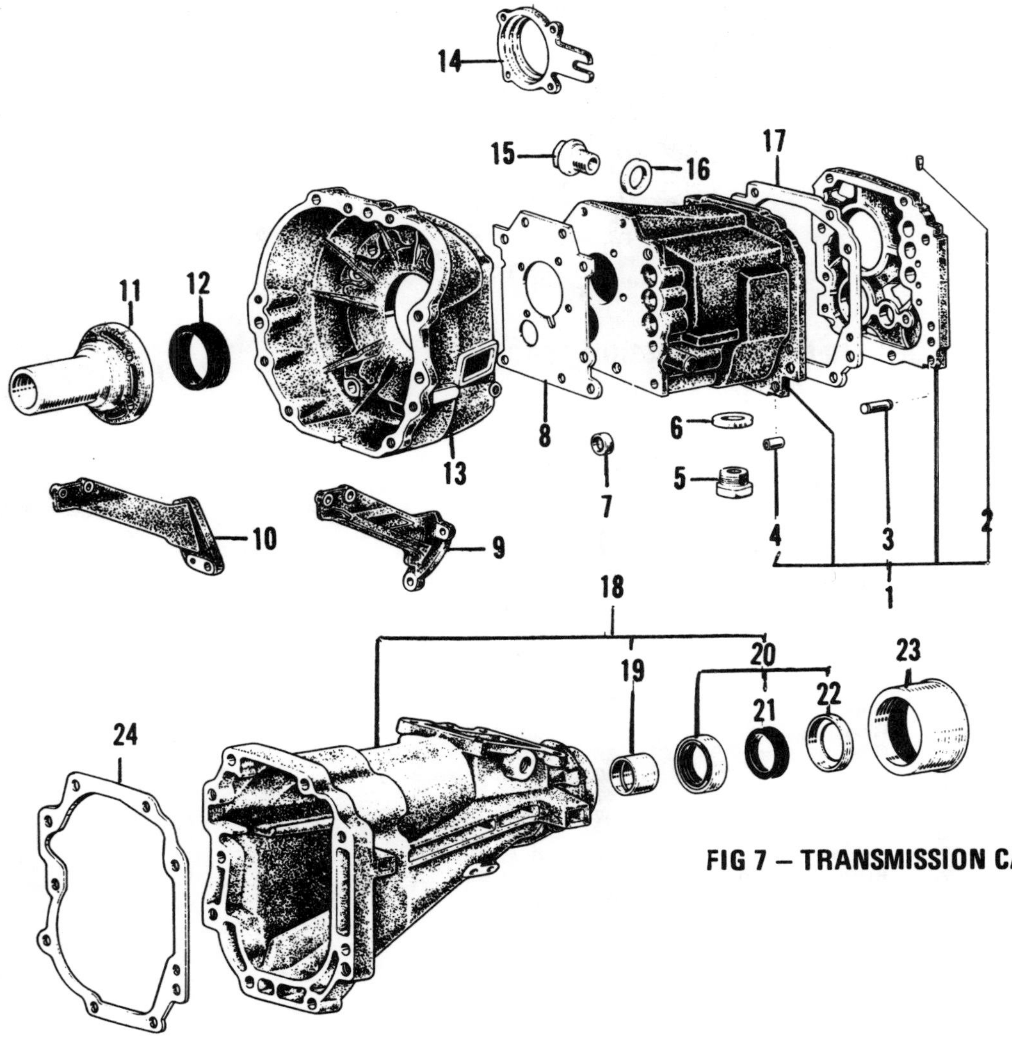

1 Transmission Case
2 Plug
3 Plug
4 Pin
5 Gasket
6 Gasket
7 Plug
8 Gasket
9 Plate
10 Plate
11 Bearing Retainer
12 Seal
13 Clutch Housing
14 Bearing Retainer
15 Plug
16 Gasket
17 Gasket
18 Extension Housing
19 Bushing
20 Seal Kit
21 Seal
22 Retainer
23 Deflector
24 Gasket

FIG 7 – TRANSMISSION CASE & EXTENSION HOUSING

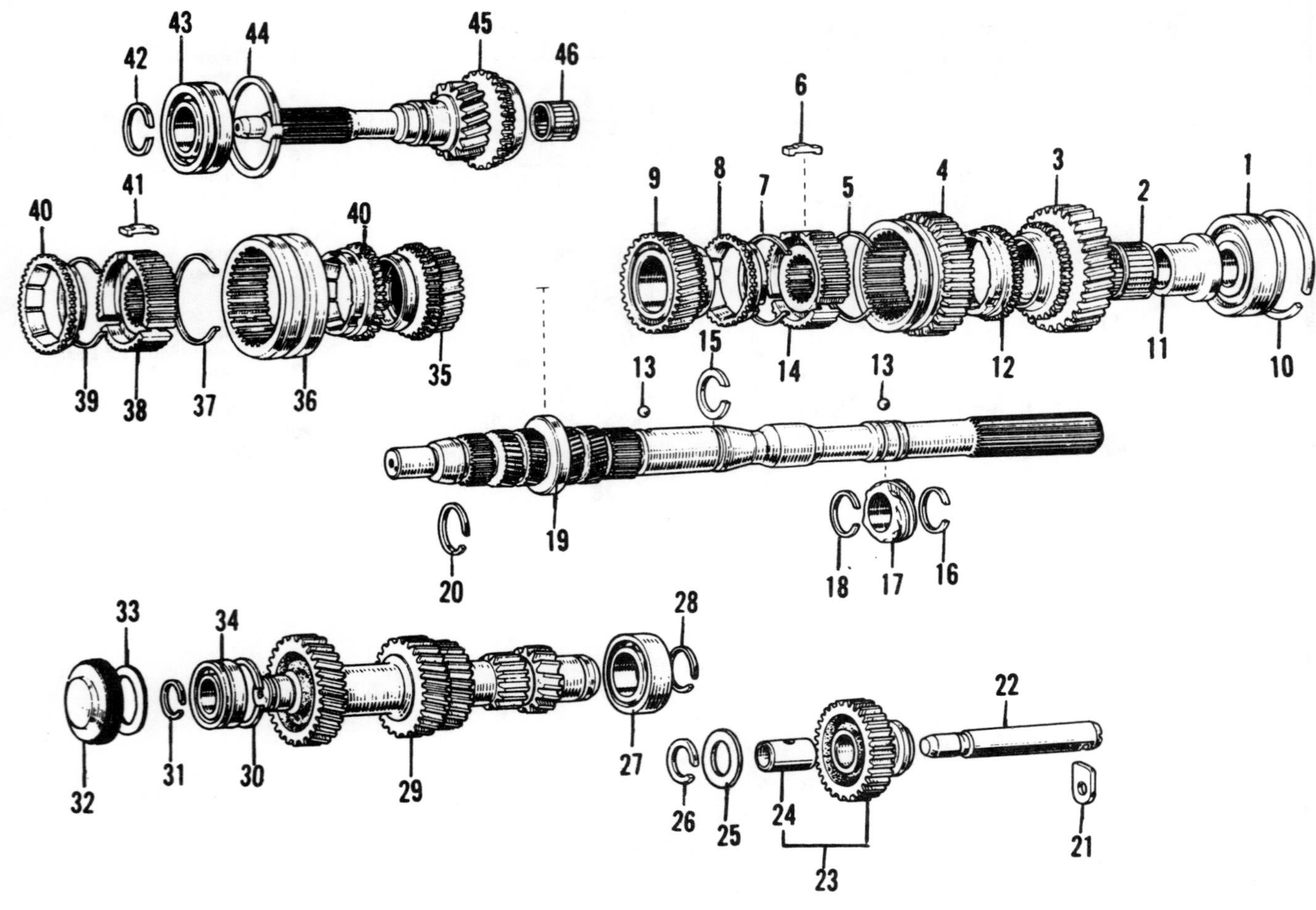

FIG 8 – TRANSMISSION GEARS

1	Bearing	24	Bushing
2	Bearing	25	Ring
3	1st Gear	26	Ring
4	Reverse Gear	27	Bearing
5	Spring	28	Ring
6	Key	29	Counter Gear
7	Spring	30	Ring
8	Ring	31	Ring
9	2nd Gear	32	Cover
10	Ring	33	Washer
11	Race	34	Bearing
12	Ring	35	3rd Gear
13	Ball	36	Sleeve
14	Hub	37	Spring
15	Ring	38	Hub
16	Ring	39	Spring
17	Gear	40	Synchronizer Ring
18	Ring	41	Key
19	Output Shaft	42	Ring
20	Ring	43	Bearing
21	Stopper	44	Ring
22	Reverse Idler Shaft	45	Input Shaft
23	Reverse Idler Gear	46	Bearing

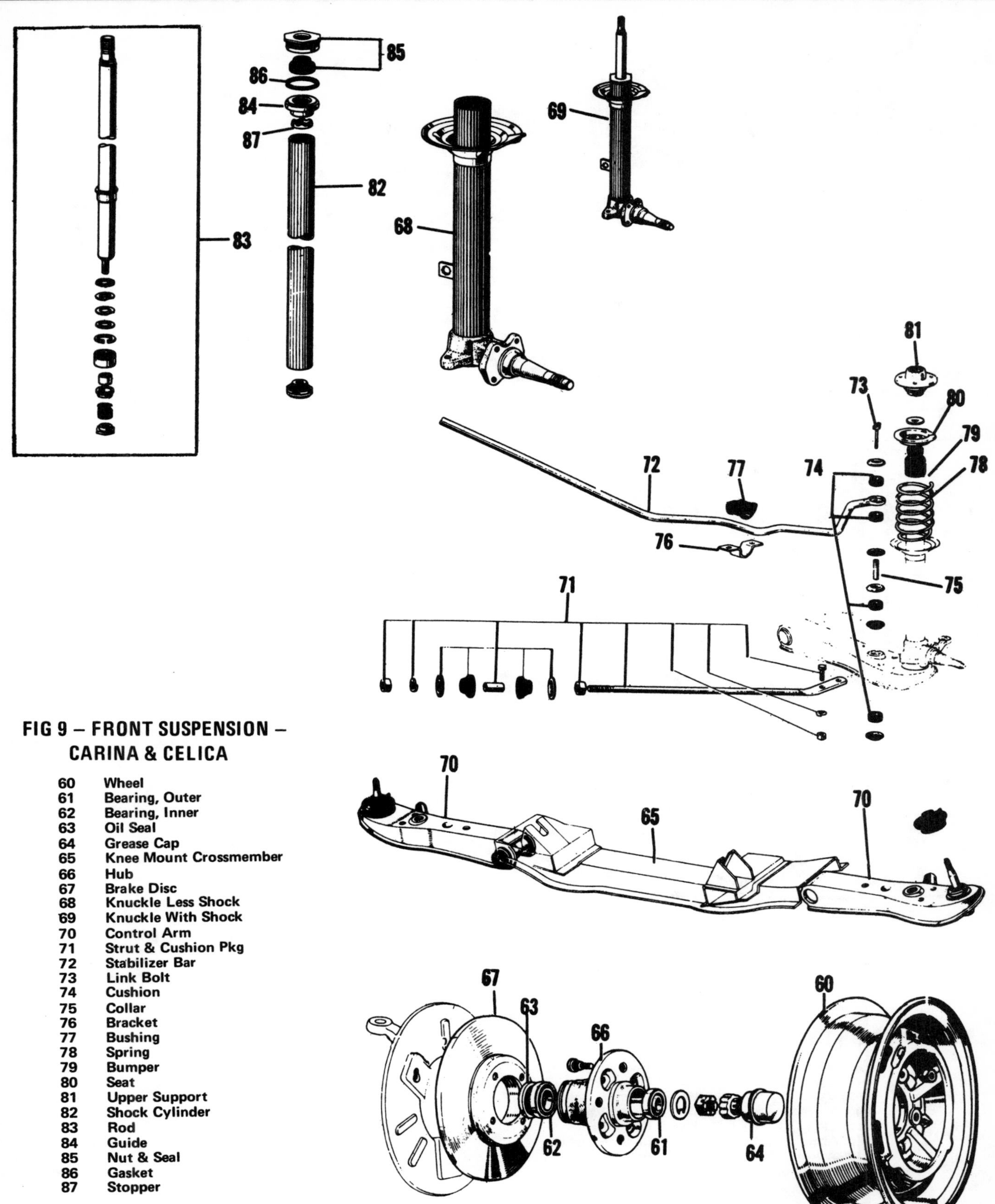

FIG 9 – FRONT SUSPENSION – CARINA & CELICA

60	Wheel
61	Bearing, Outer
62	Bearing, Inner
63	Oil Seal
64	Grease Cap
65	Knee Mount Crossmember
66	Hub
67	Brake Disc
68	Knuckle Less Shock
69	Knuckle With Shock
70	Control Arm
71	Strut & Cushion Pkg
72	Stabilizer Bar
73	Link Bolt
74	Cushion
75	Collar
76	Bracket
77	Bushing
78	Spring
79	Bumper
80	Seat
81	Upper Support
82	Shock Cylinder
83	Rod
84	Guide
85	Nut & Seal
86	Gasket
87	Stopper

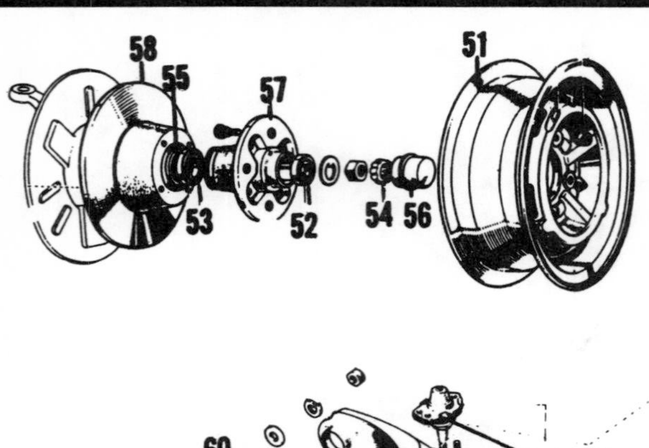

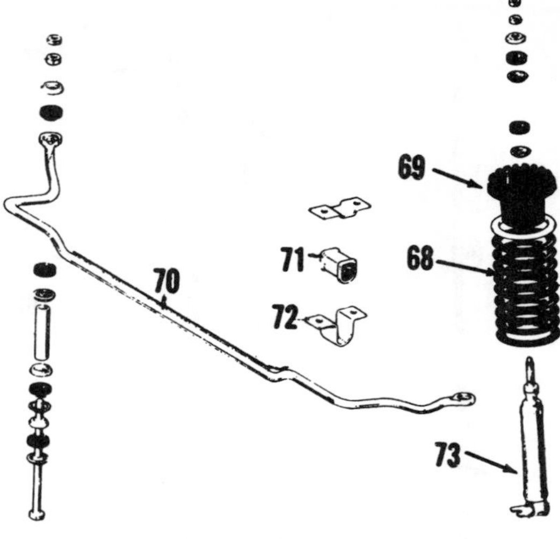

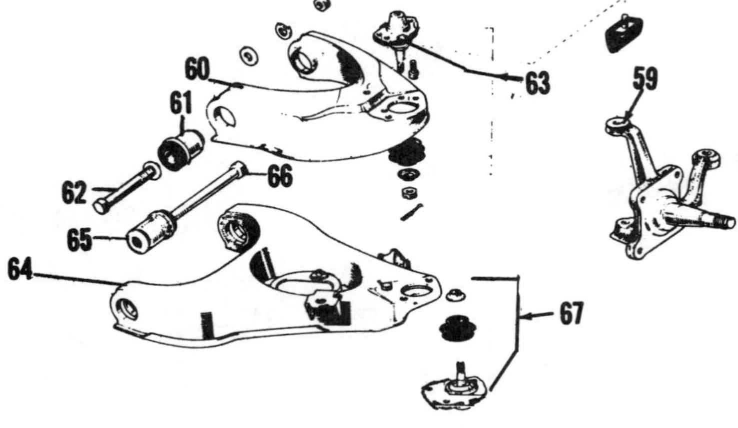

FIG 10 – FRONT SUSPENSION – CORONA

51	Wheel	63	Ball Joint
52	Bearing Outer	64	Lower Arm
53	Bearing, Inner	65	Bushing
54	Adjuster Cap	66	Cam
55	Oil Seal	67	Ball Joint
56	Grease Cap	68	Spring
57	Hub	69	Insulator
58	Brake Disc	70	Stabilizer Bar
59	Knuckle & Arm	71	Bushing
60	Upper Arm	72	Bracket
61	Bushing	73	Shock Absorber
62	Pin		

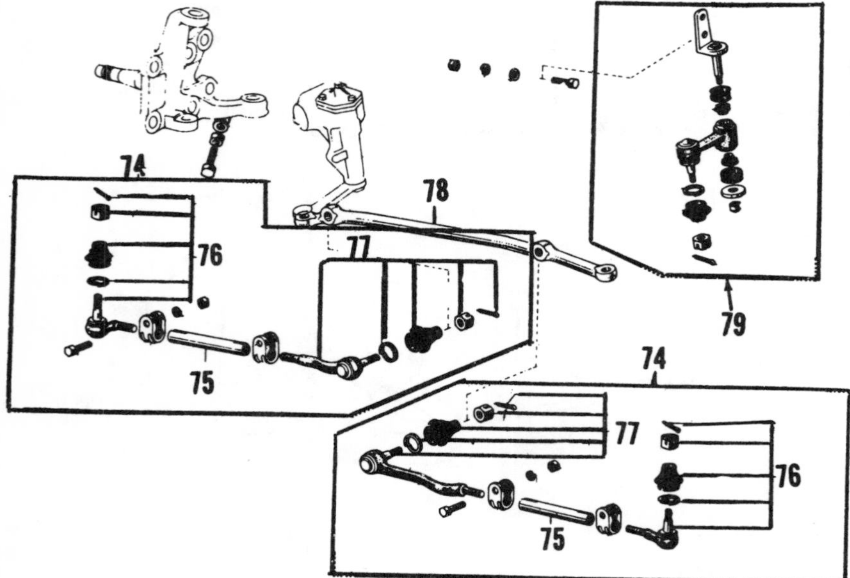

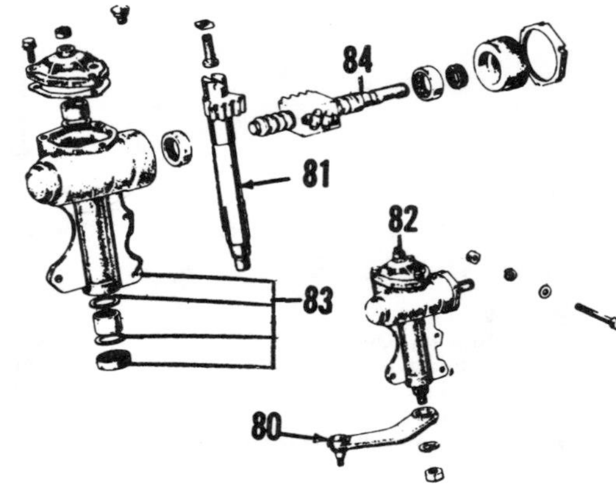

FIG 13 – STEERING – CORONA

74	Tie Rod Assy	82	Gear Assy
75	Adjusting Tube	83	Housing
76	End, Outer	84	Worm & Ball-Nut
77	End, Inner	85	Main Shaft
78	Drag Link	86	Coupling
79	Idler Arm & Bracket	87	Column Jacket
80	Pitman Arm	88	Bracket
81	Shaft & Sector	89	Bracket

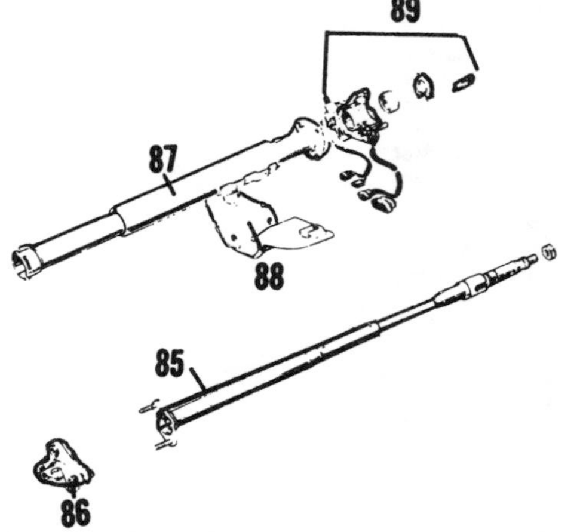

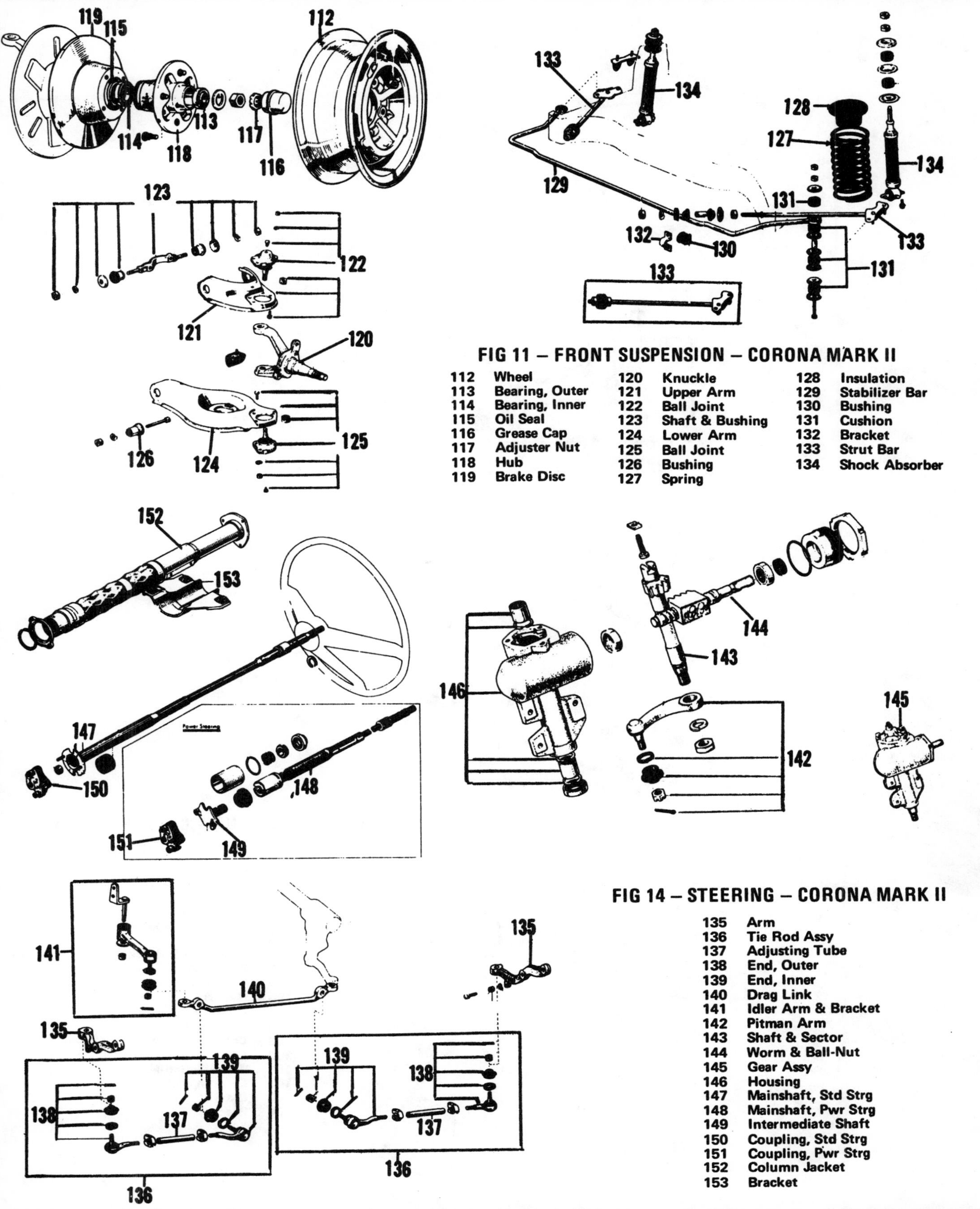

FIG 11 – FRONT SUSPENSION – CORONA MARK II

112	Wheel	120	Knuckle	128	Insulation
113	Bearing, Outer	121	Upper Arm	129	Stabilizer Bar
114	Bearing, Inner	122	Ball Joint	130	Bushing
115	Oil Seal	123	Shaft & Bushing	131	Cushion
116	Grease Cap	124	Lower Arm	132	Bracket
117	Adjuster Nut	125	Ball Joint	133	Strut Bar
118	Hub	126	Bushing	134	Shock Absorber
119	Brake Disc	127	Spring		

FIG 14 – STEERING – CORONA MARK II

135	Arm
136	Tie Rod Assy
137	Adjusting Tube
138	End, Outer
139	End, Inner
140	Drag Link
141	Idler Arm & Bracket
142	Pitman Arm
143	Shaft & Sector
144	Worm & Ball-Nut
145	Gear Assy
146	Housing
147	Mainshaft, Std Strg
148	Mainshaft, Pwr Strg
149	Intermediate Shaft
150	Coupling, Std Strg
151	Coupling, Pwr Strg
152	Column Jacket
153	Bracket

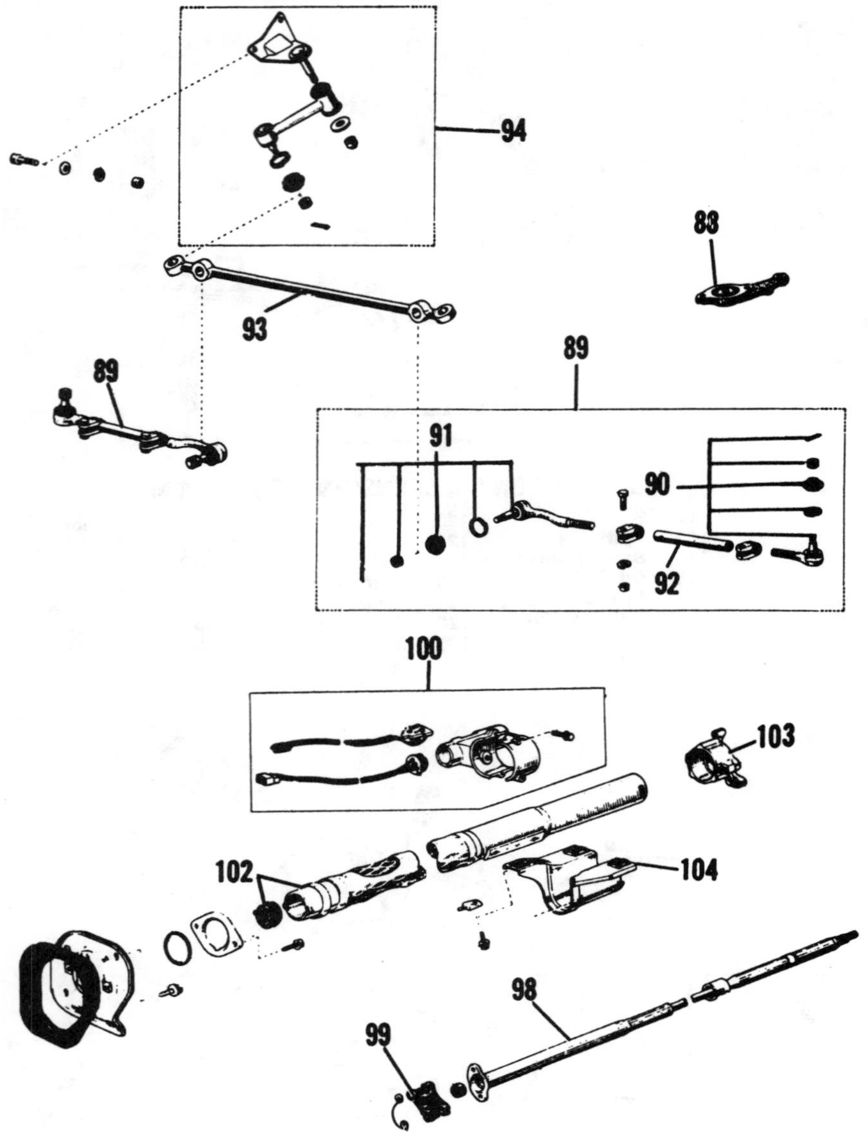

FIG 12 – STEERING – CARINA & CELICA

88 Arm
89 Tie Rod & Ends
90 End, Outer
91 End, Inner
92 Adjusting Tube
93 Drag Link
94 Idler Arm & Bracket
95 Pitman Arm
96 Shaft & Sector
96A Gear Assy
97 Housing
98 Mainshaft
99 Coupling & Yoke
100 Lock Assy
101 Worm & Ball-Nut
102 Column Jacket
103 Bracket
104 Bracket

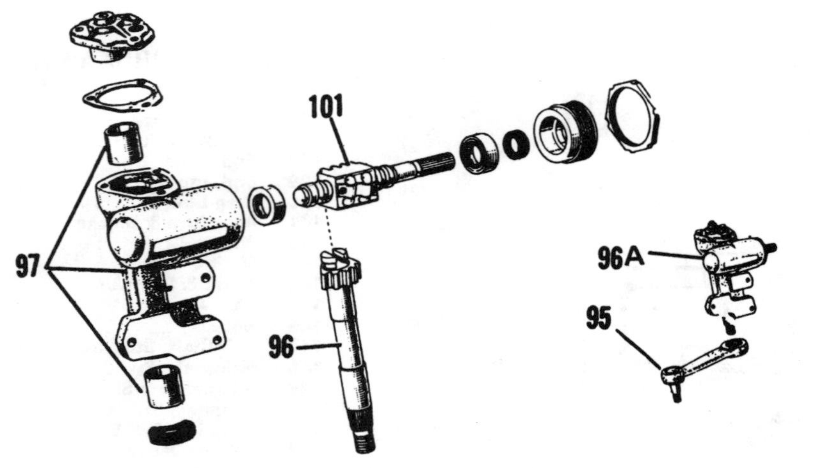

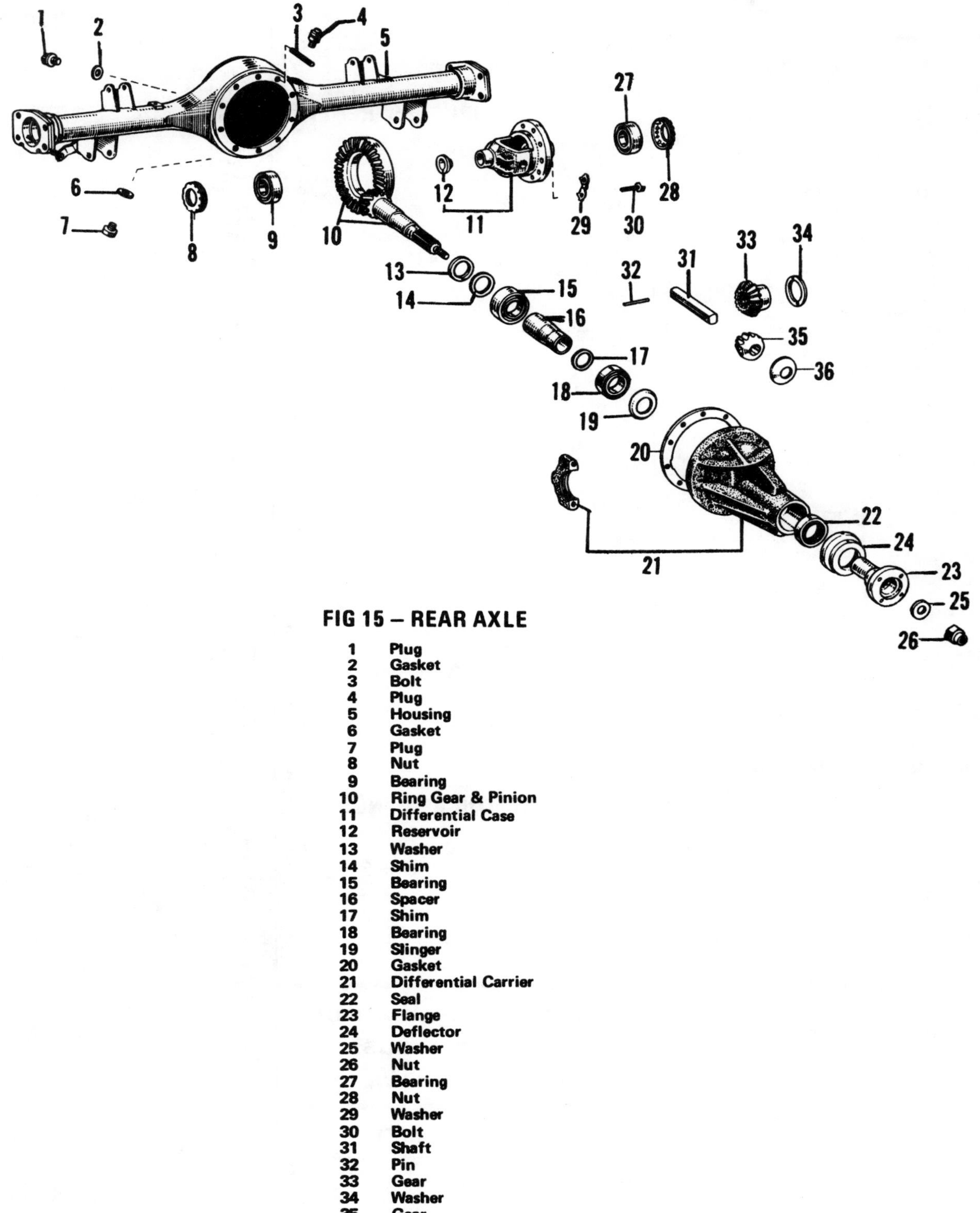

FIG 15 – REAR AXLE

1	Plug
2	Gasket
3	Bolt
4	Plug
5	Housing
6	Gasket
7	Plug
8	Nut
9	Bearing
10	Ring Gear & Pinion
11	Differential Case
12	Reservoir
13	Washer
14	Shim
15	Bearing
16	Spacer
17	Shim
18	Bearing
19	Slinger
20	Gasket
21	Differential Carrier
22	Seal
23	Flange
24	Deflector
25	Washer
26	Nut
27	Bearing
28	Nut
29	Washer
30	Bolt
31	Shaft
32	Pin
33	Gear
34	Washer
35	Gear
36	Washer

Ignition, Starting & Charging—TIME

OPERATION INDEX

Tune-Up, Minor *1*
Tune-Up, Major *2*
Compression Test *3*
Distributor, R&R Or Renew *4*
Distributor Cap, Renew *5*
Ignition Cable Set, Renew *6*
Ignition Coil, Renew *7*
Starter And Ignition Switch, Renew *8*
Starter Assy, R&R Or Renew *9*
Starter, R&R & Overhaul *10*
Starter Brushes, Renew *11*
Starter Armature, Renew *12*
Voltage Regulator, Renew *13*
Alternator, R&R Or Renew *14*
Alternator, R&R & Overhaul *15*
Alternator Bearings, Renew *16*
Alternator Brushes, Renew *17*

1—TUNE-UP, MINOR

Includes:rEnew points, condenser & plugs, set spark timing & adjust carburetor idle

Corolla, Celica, Carina 2.0
Corona 1.6
Crown—
 1966-67 .... 1.5
 1968-72 .... 1.8
Land Cruiser, Hi Lux, Stout 1.5

2—TUNE-UP, MAJOR

Includes:cHeck compression, clear or renew and adjust spark plugs. R&R distributor, renew points and condenser. Adjust ignition timing, carburetor and fan belts. Clean battery terminals and service air cleaner.

Corolla, Celica, Carina 2.9
Corona 2.4
Crown—
 1966-67 .... 2.2
 1968-72 .... 2.4
Land Cruiser, Hi Lux, Stout 2.2

3—COMPRESSION TEST

4 Cyl 0.6
6 Cyl 0.8

4—DISTRIBUTOR, R&R OR RENEW

Corolla, Celica, Carina 0.4
Corona 0.3
Crown—
 1966-67 .... 0.3
 1968-72 Four 0.5
 1968-72 Six 0.6
Land Cruiser, Hi Lux, Stout 0.5

5—DISTRIBUTOR CAP, RENEW

All Models 0.3

6—IGNITION CABLE SET, RENEW

All Models 0.5

7—IGNITION COIL, RENEW

All Models 0.3

8—STARTER & IGNITION SWITCH, RENEW

Corolla—
 K Eng 1.4
 KB Eng 2.2
 KC Eng 1.5
Corona 0.3
Crown 0.3
Celica, Carina 0.8
Land Cruiser, Hi Lux, Stout 0.6

9—STARTER ASSY, R&R OR RENEW

Corolla—
 K Eng 1.3
 KB Eng 2.1
 KC Eng 1.4
Corona 0.5
Crown 0.6
Celica, Carina 1.4
Land Cruiser, Hi Lux, Stout 0.5

10—STARTER, R&R & OVERHAUL

Corolla—
 K Eng 1.9
 KB Eng 2.7
 KC Eng 2.0
Corona 2.0
Crown 2.0
Celica, Carina 2.0
Land Cruiser, Hi Lux, Stout 1.8

11—STARTER BRUSHES, RENEW

Corolla—
 K Eng 1.6
 KB Eng 2.4
 KC Eng 1.7
Corona 0.8
Crown 0.9
Celica, Carina 1.7
Land Cruiser, Hi Lux, Stout 0.9

12—STARTER ARMATURE, RENEW

Corolla—
 K Eng 1.8
 KB Eng 2.6
 KC Eng 1.9
Corona 1.3
Crown 1.2
Celica, Carina 1.9
Land Cruiser, Hi Lux, Stout 1.1

13—VOLTAGE REGULATOR, RENEW

Corolla, Celica, Carina 0.4
Corona 0.3
Crown—
 1966-67 .... 0.3
 1968-72 .... 0.5
Land Cruiser, Hi Lux, Stout 0.4

14—ALTERNATOR, R&R OR RENEW

Corolla, Celica, Carina 0.6
Corona 0.4
Crown 0.5
Land Cruiser, Hi Lux, Stout 0.6

15—ALTERNATOR, R&R & OVERHAUL

Corolla, Celica, Carina 1.3
Corona 1.1
Crown—
 1966-67 .... 0.9
 1968-72 .... 1.3
Land Cruiser, Hi Lux, Stout 1.3

16—ALTERNATOR BEARINGS, RENEW

All Models 1.0

17—ALTERNATOR BRUSHES, RENEW

Corolla, Celica, Carina 1.0
Corona 0.8
Crown 0.7
Land Cruiser, Hi Lux, Stout 1.0

Fuel, Emission Control, Intake & Exhaust Systems—TIME

OPERATION INDEX

Carburetor, R&R Or Renew *1*
Carburetor, R&R & Overhaul *2*
Fuel Pump, R&R Or Renew *3*
Fuel Pump, Overhaul *4*
Fuel Tank, R&R Or Renew *5*
Air Injection Pump, Renew *6*
Anti-Afterburn Valve, Renew *7*
Check Valve, Renew *8*
Relief Valve, Renew *9*
Exhaust Gas Recirculation Valve, Renew *10*
Intake Manifold Or Gasket, Renew *11*
Exhaust Manifold Or Gasket, Renew *12*
Exhaust Pipe, Renew *13*
Muffler, Renew *14*
Tail Pipe, Renew *15*
Catalytic Converter, Renew *16*

1—CARBURETOR, R&R OR RENEW

Corolla—
 One Carb 0.8
 Two Carbs 0.9
Corona 0.6
Crown (1966-67)—
 4 Cyl 0.5
 6 Cyl 0.6
Crown (1968-72) 0.6
Celica 0.8
Carina 1.0
Land Cruiser 0.8
Hi Lux 0.9
Stout 1.1

2—CARBURETOR, R&R & OVERHAUL

Corolla—
 One Carb 1.4
 Two Carbs 2.2
Corona 1.5
Crown (1966-67) 1.8
Crown (1968-72)—
 4 Cyl 1.5
 6 Cyl 1.7
Celica 1.8
Carina 2.0
Land Cruiser 2.0
Hi Lux 2.3
Stout 2.2

3—FUEL PUMP, R&R OR RENEW

Corolla, Corona 0.3
Crown—
 1966-67 .... 0.3
 1968-72—
  4 Cyl 0.3
  6 Cyl 0.4
Celica, Carina 0.5
Land Cruiser 0.5
Hi Lux, Stout 0.4

4—FUEL PUMP, OVERHAUL

Corolla, Corona 0.7
Crown—
 1966-67 .... 0.7
 1968-72—
  4 Cyl 0.8
  6 Cyl 0.8
Celica, Carina 0.9
Land Cruiser 0.9
Hi Lux, Stout 0.8

5—FUEL TANK, R&R OR RENEW

Corolla—
 Exc Below 0.9
 KE 16V Ser 1.4
Corona 0.7
Crown (1966-67)—
 Sedan 0.6
 Wagon 0.8
Crown (1968-72)—
 Sedan 1.3
 Wagon 1.7
Celica, Carina 1.1
Land Cruiser 2.0
Hi Lux, Stout 1.5

6—AIR INJECTION PUMP, RENEW

Corolla 0.5
Crown 0.4
Corona, Celica 0.8
Land Cruiser 0.5
Hi Lux 0.6

7—ANTI-AFTERBURN VALVE, RENEW

All Models 0.2

8—CHECK VALVE, RENEW

All Models 0.3

9—RELIEF VALVE, RENEW

All Models 0.3

10—EXHAUST GAS RECIRCULATION VALVE, RENEW

All Models 0.4

(Continued)

Fuel, Emission Control, Intake & Exhaust Systems—TIME Cont'd

11—INTAKE MANIFOLD OR GASKET, RENEW

Corolla—
- Exc Below 0.9
- KC Model 1.0
- KB Model 1.6

Corona 0.6
Crown (1966-67) 0.8
Crown (1968-72)—
- 4 Cyl 0.8
- 6 Cyl 1.8

Celica 1.4
Carina 1.2
Land Cruiser, Hi Lux 1.2

12—EXHAUST MANIFOLD OR GASKET, RENEW

Corolla—
- Exc Below 0.9
- KC Model 1.0
- KB Model 1.6

Corona 1.0
Crown (1966-67) 0.6
Crown (1968-72)—
- 4 Cyl 0.8
- 6 Cyl 1.0

Carina 0.8

13—EXHAUST PIPE, RENEW

Corolla—
- Exc Below 0.7
- KC Model 0.8

Corona 0.8
Crown (1966-67)
Crown (1968-72)—
- Front 1.2
- Center 1.0

Celica, Carina 0.8
Land Cruiser, Hi Lux 0.7

14—MUFFLER, RENEW

Corolla 0.8
Corona, Carina 0.6
Crown (1966-67)—
- Front—
  - 4 Cyl 0.6
  - 6 Cyl 1.6
- Rear 0.6

Crown (1968-72)—
- 4 Cyl 1.0
- 6 Cyl 0.9

Celica 0.9
Land Cruiser, Hi Lux, Stout 0.7

15—TAIL PIPE, RENEW

Exc Below 0.4
Crown 0.6

16—CATALYTIC CONVERTER, RENEW

Exc Below 1.0
Corona Mark II 1.5

Engine Cooling & Heater System—TIME

OPERATION INDEX

Radiator, R&R Or Renew 1
Radiator Hoses, Renew 2
Water Pump, R&R Or Renew 3
Water Pump, R&R & Overhaul 4
Thermostat Or Housing, Renew 5
Heater Assy, R&R Or Renew 6
Heater Control Valve, Renew 7
Heater Hose(S), Renew 8

1—RADIATOR, R&R OR RENEW

Corolla—
- Manual Trans 0.5
- Auto Trans 0.7

Corona 0.6
Crown (1966-67)—
- Manual Trans 0.3
- Auto Trans 0.4

Crown (1968-72)—
- Manual Trans 0.6
- Auto Trans 0.8

Celica, Carina—
- Manual Trans 0.8
- Auto Trans 1.0

Land Cruiser 0.8
Hi Lux, Stout 0.8

2—RADIATOR HOSES, RENEW

Corolla, Celica, Carina—
- Upper 0.3
- Lower 0.4

Corona 0.3
Crown (1966-67) 0.3
Crown (1968-72)—
- Upper 0.3
- Lower 0.5

Land Cruiser 0.4
Hi Lux, Stout—
- Upper 0.3
- Lower 0.4

3—WATER PUMP, R&R OR RENEW

Corolla, Celica, Carina—
- Manual Trans 0.9
- Auto Trans 1.0

Corona 0.7
Crown (1966-67)—
- 4 Cyl—
  - Exc Deluxe 0.6
  - Deluxe 0.9
- 6 Cyl 0.6

Crown (1968-72) 0.8
Land Cruiser, Hi Lux, Stout 0.9

4—WATER PUMP, R&R & OVERHAUL

Corolla, Celica, Carina—
- Manual Trans 1.3
- Auto Trans 1.4

Corona 1.6
Crown (1966-67)—
- Exc Deluxe 0.8
- Deluxe 1.0

Crown (1968-72)—
- 4 Cyl 1.2
- 6 Cyl 1.5

Land Cruiser, Hi Lux, Stout 1.3

5—THERMOSTAT OR HOUSING, RENEW

Corolla, Celica, Carina 0.4
Corona 0.2
Crown—
- 1966-67 ....0.2
- 1968-72—
  - Exc Below 0.4
  - W/Emission Control 0.5

Land Cruiser, Hi Lux, Stout 0.4

6—HEATER ASSY, R&R OR RENEW

Corolla, Celica 1.2
Carina 0.9
Corona 1.2
Crown (1966-67) 1.8
Crown (1968-72) 1.7
Land Cruiser 0.9
Hi-Lux, Stout 1.1

7—HEATER CONTROL VALVE, RENEW

Corolla, Celica, Carina 0.5
Corona 0.5
Crown (1966-67) 0.6
Crown (1968-72) 1.0

8—HEATER HOSE(S), RENEW

Corolla—
- Defroster 0.2
- Inlet Or Outlet 0.4

Corona 0.3
Crown 0.4
Celica, Carina 0.5

Engine—TIME

OPERATION INDEX

Engine, R&R 1
Engine, R&R & Overhaul 2
Cylinder Head Gasket, Renew 3
Valves, Grind & Tune-Up, Minor 4
Valves Springs, Renew 5
Rocker Arm Cover Gasket, Renew 6
Push Rods, Renew 7
Oil Pan Or Gasket, R&R 8
Valve Tappets, Renew 9
Valve Tappets, Adjust 10
Timing Cover Seal & Gasket, Renew 11
Timing Chain Or Gears, Renew 12
Camshaft, R&R Or Renew 13
Camshaft Bearings, Renew 14
Oil Pump, R&R Or Renew 15
Piston Ring(S), Renew 16
Rod Bearing(S), Renew 17
Main Bearings, Renew 18
Crankshaft, R&R Or Renew 19
Crankshaft Rear Oil Seal, Renew 20
Pistons, Renew 21
Connecting Rods, Renew 22
Crankshaft Pulley, Renew 23

1—ENGINE, R&R

Does not include R&R clutch or transfer of parts or special equipment. Includes R&R trans with engine

Corolla—
- Manual Trans 4.1
- Auto Trans 4.3

Corona—
- Manual Trans 4.5
- Auto Trans 4.6

Crown (1966-67)—
- 4 Cyl W/Manual Trans—
  - Exc Deluxe 4.8
  - Deluxe 5.1
- 4 Cyl W/Auto Trans—
  - Exc Deluxe 5.1
  - Deluxe 5.2
- 6 Cyl W/Manual Trans—
  - Exc Deluxe 5.6
  - Deluxe 5.9
- 6 Cyl W/Auto Trans—
  - Exc Deluxe 6.1
  - Deluxe 6.2

Crown (1968-72)—
- 4 Cyl 6.0
- 6 Cyl—
  - Exc Below 6.9
  - Auto Trans 7.1
  - W/Emission Control 8.4

Celica 6.0
Carina 6.0
Land Cruiser 8.4
Hi Lux, Stout 6.0

2—ENGINE, R&R & OVERHAUL

Includes rebore cylinders with boring bar, renew pistons, rings, pins, main & rod bearings, grind valves, plastigauge bearings and perform minor tune-up

Corona 22.3
Crown (1966-67)—
- 4 Cyl W/Manual Trans—
  - Exc Deluxe 22.0
  - Deluxe 22.3
- 4 Cyl W/Auto Trans—
  - Exc Deluxe 22.3
  - Deluxe 22.4
- 6 Cyl W/Manual Trans—
  - Exc Deluxe 27.5
  - Deluxe 27.8
- 6 Cyl W/Auto Trans—
  - Exc Deluxe 27.9
  - Deluxe 28.0

Crown (1968-72)—
- 4 Cyl 17.4
- 6 Cyl 22.7

Celica 22.7
Carina 20.0
Land Cruiser 24.0
Hi Lux, Stout 22.7

3—CYLINDER HEAD GASKET, RENEW

Includes minor tune-up

Corolla—
- Exc Below 3.0
- 2 Carbs 3.2

Corona 2.4
Crown 3.5
Celica 3.2
Carina 3.0
Land Cruiser 3.5
Hi Lux, Stout 3.0

(Continued)

Engine—TIME Cont'd

4—VALVES, GRIND & TUNE-UP, MINOR

Corolla—
Exc Below 7.0
K & KC Ser 7.3
Corona 7.0
Crown (1966-67) 5.6
Crown (1968-72) 9.6
Celica 7.5
Carina 8.0
Land Cruiser 7.0
Hi Lux, Stout 7.5

5—VALVE SPRINGS, RENEW

Includes minor tune-up & adjust carburetor.
Corolla—
Exc Below 4.2
KB Series 4.6
Corona 4.3
Crown 4.2
Celica, Carina 4.6

6—ROCKER ARM COVER GASKET, RENEW

All Models 0.5

7—PUSH RODS, RENEW

Corolla—
Exc Below 1.1
KB & Kc Series 1.2
Corona 0.6
Crown 0.7

8—OIL PAN OR GASKET, R&R

Corolla 3.7
Corona 1.0
Crown (1966-67)—
4 Cyl ①1.0
6 Cyl ①1.9
Crown (1968-72)—
4 Cyl 1.6
6 Cyl 2.2
Celica 1.8
Carina 2.2
Land Cruiser 2.5
Hi Lux, Stout 1.8
①*Includes R&R Idler Arm Support.*

9—VALVE TAPPETS, RENEW

Includes adjust carb
Corolla, Carina 1.7
Corona 1.1
Crown 1.3
Land Cruiser 2.5
Hi Lux, Stout 1.5

10—VALVE TAPPETS, ADJUST

Corona 0.4
Crown—
Exc Below 0.4
6 Cyl 0.6
Corolla, Carina 0.6
Celica 0.7
Land Cruiser, Hi Lux, Stout 0.7

11—TIMING COVER SEAL & GASKET, RENEW

Corolla—
Exc Below 2.1
2 Carbs 2.0
Corona 3.0
Crown (1966-67)—
Manual Trans 1.2
Auto Trans 1.3
Crown (1968-72)—
4 Cyl 1.1
6 Cyl 5.8
Celica 4.2
Carina 1.9
Land Cruiser 2.3
Hi Lux, Stout 4.2

12—TIMING CHAIN OR GEARS, RENEW

Corolla 3.2
Corona 4.9
Crown 4 Cyl—
Manual Trans 5.6
Auto Trans 5.7
Crown 6 Cyl—
Chain 6.5
Gear 1.4
Celica 4.2
Carina 3.3
Hi Lux, Stout 4.2

13—CAMSHAFT, R&R OR RENEW

Corolla—
Manual Trans 4.9
Auto Trans 4.8
Corona 4.5
Crown (1966-67)—
4 Cyl 4.3
6 Cyl 2.3
Crown (1968-72)—
4 Cyl 3.7
6 Cyl 2.4
Celica 2.5
Carina 5.0
Land Cruiser 4.5
Hi Lux, Stout 2.5

14—CAMSHAFT BEARINGS, RENEW

Corolla 4.5
Crown 2.5
Corona 2.5
Celica 2.5
Hi Lux 2.5

15—OIL PUMP, R&R OR RENEW

Corolla—
Manual Trans ①4.7
Auto Trans ①4.8
Corona 1.3
Crown (1966-67)—
4 Cyl 1.3
6 Cyl 2.0
Crown (1968-72)—
4 Cyl 1.7
6 Cyl 2.2
Celica, Carina 2.1
Land Cruiser 2.8
Hi Lux, Stout 2.1
①*Includes R&R Engine*

16—PISTON RING(S), RENEW

Corolla—
Manual Trans 8.2
Auto Trans 8.4
Corona 5.2
Crown (1966-67)—
4 Cyl 5.2
6 Cyl 8.1
Crown (1968-72)—
4 Cyl 6.1
6 Cyl 8.3
Celica 7.2
Carina 8.5
Land Cruiser 8.5
Hi Lux, Stout 6.5

17—ROD BEARING(S), RENEW

Corolla 5.8
Corona—
One Set 1.5
All 2.6
Crown (1966-67)—
One (4 Cyl) 1.5
All (4 Cyl) 2.6
One (6 Cyl) 2.3
All (6 Cyl) 3.4
Crown (1968-72)—
4 Cyl 3.3
6 Cyl 4.5
Celica, Carina 3.5
Land Cruiser 4.5
Hi Lux, Stout 3.5

18—MAIN BEARINGS, RENEW

Corolla 7.4
Corona 9.4
Crown—
4 Cyl Manual Trans—
Exc Deluxe 9.0
Deluxe 9.3
4 Cyl Auto Trans—
Exc Deluxe 9.3
Deluxe 9.4
6 Cyl Manual Trans—
Exc Deluxe 9.9
Deluxe 10.2
6 Cyl Auto Trans—
Exc Deluxe 10.4
Deluxe 10.5
Celica 9.5
Carina 8.0
Land Cruiser 10.5
Hi Lux, Stout 9.5

19—CRANKSHAFT, R&R OR RENEW

Corolla 7.4
Corona 9.4
Crown—
4 Cyl Manual Trans—
Exc Deluxe 9.0
Deluxe 9.3
4 Cyl Auto Trans—
Exc Deluxe 9.3
Deluxe 9.4
6 Cyl Manual Trans—
Exc Deluxe 9.9
Deluxe 10.2
6 Cyl Auto Trans—
Exc Deluxe 10.4
Deluxe 10.5
Celica 9.5
Land Cruiser 10.5
Hi Lux, Stout 9.5
Carina 8.0

20—CRANKSHAFT REAR OIL SEAL, RENEW

Corona 8.4
Crown—
4 Cyl Manual Trans—
Exc Deluxe 8.0
Deluxe 8.3
4 Cyl Auto Trans—
Exc Deluxe 8.3
Deluxe 8.4
6 Cyl—
Manual Trans 4.2
Auto Trans 4.5
Corolla 5.0
Celica, Carina 3.5
Land Cruiser 4.5
Hi Lux, Stout 3.5

21—PISTONS, RENEW

Corolla—
Manual Trans 8.1
Auto Trans 8.3
Corona—
One 4.0
All 6.2
Crown—
4 Cyl (One) 4.0
4 Cyl (All) 6.2
6 Cyl (One) 5.8
6 Cyl (All) 9.9
Celica 6.5
Carina 7.0
Land Cruiser 8.5
Hi Lux, Stout 6.5

22—CONNECTING RODS, RENEW

Corolla—
Manual Trans 8.4
Auto Trans 8.7
Corona ①3.8
Crown—
4 Cyl ①3.8
6 Cyl ①5.4
①*One Rod*

23—CRANKSHAFT PULLEY, RENEW

Corolla 1.0
Corona 0.9
Crown 0.8
Celica, Carina 1.0
Land Cruiser 1.0
Hi Lux, Stout 0.9

Clutch, Mounts & Transmissions—TIME

OPERATION INDEX

Flywheel, R&R Or Renew 1
Flywheel Ring Gear, Renew 2
Clutch Or Disc, Renew 3
Release Bearing, Renew 4
Clutch Pedal, Adjust 5
Engine Mount(S), Renew 6
Trans Assy, R&R Or Renew 7
Manual Trans Case, Renew 8
Trans Case Cover Or Gasket, R&R Or Renew 9
(Continued)

Clutch, Mounts & Transmissions—TIME Cont'd

Extension Housing Or Bushing, Renew 10
Oil Pan Gasket, Renew 11
Front & Rear Bands, Renew 12
Manual Trans, R&R & Overhaul 13
Automatic Trans, R&R & Overhaul 14
Mainshaft Rear Bearing, Renew 15
Gear Selector Forks, Renew 16
Gearshift Or Selector Lever, Renew 17

1—FLYWHEEL, R&R OR RENEW

Corolla—
- Std Trans 2.1
- Auto Trans 3.2

Corona 3.0
Crown (1966-67)—
- 4 Cyl—
  - Std Trans 2.5
  - Auto Trans 2.7
- 6 Cyl—
  - Std Trans 3.0
  - Auto Trans 3.2

Crown (1968-72)—
- 4 Cyl 3.2
- 6 Cyl—
  - Std Trans 3.2
  - Auto Trans 4.0

Celica, Carina 3.5
Land Cruiser, Stout 3.8
Hi Lux—
- Std Trans 2.5
- Auto Trans 3.2

2—FLYWHEEL RING GEAR, RENEW

Corolla—
- Auto Trans 2.6
- Auto Trans 3.7

Corona 3.5
Crown (1966-67)—
- 4 Cyl—
  - Std Trans 3.0
  - Auto Trans 3.2
- 6 Cyl—
  - Std Trans 3.5
  - Auto Trans 3.7

Crown (1968-72)—
- 4 Cyl 3.7
- 6 Cyl—
  - Std Trans 3.7
  - Auto Trans 4.5

Celica, Carina 4.0
Land Cruiser, Stout 4.3
Hi Lux—
- Std Trans 3.0
- Auto Trans 3.7

3—CLUTCH OR DISC, RENEW

Corolla 2.4
Corona 2.5
Crown (1966-67)—
- 4 Cyl—
  - Std Trans 2.3
  - Auto Trans 2.5
- 6 Cyl—
  - Std Trans 2.8
  - Auto Trans 3.0

Crown (1968-72) 2.9
Celica, Carina 2.5
Land Cruiser 3.5
Hi Lux, Stout 2.5

4—RELEASE BEARING, RENEW

Corolla 2.5
Corona 2.5
Crown (1966-67)—
- 4 Cyl—
  - Std Trans 2.3
  - Auto Trans 2.5
- 6 Cyl—
  - Std Trans 2.8
  - Auto Trans 3.0

Crown (1968-72) 2.8
Celica, Carina 2.5
Land Cruiser 3.5
Hi Lux, Stout 2.5

5—CLUTCH PEDAL, ADJUST

All Models 0.3

6—ENGINE MOUNT(S), RENEW

Corolla 1.2
Corona—
- Right Side 1.3
- Left Side 1.5
- Both Sides 1.7

Crown (1966-67)—
- 4 Cyl Std Trans—
  - Exc Deluxe 0.8
  - Deluxe 0.9
- 4 Cyl Auto Trans—
  - Exc Deluxe 1.1
  - Deluxe 1.3
- 6 Cyl Std Trans—
  - Exc Deluxe 0.6
  - Deluxe 0.7
- 6 Cyl Auto Trans—
  - Exc Deluxe 0.8
  - Deluxe 1.0

Crown (1968-72)—
- 4 Cyl 0.4
- 6 Cyl 0.6

Celica, Carina 0.8
Land Cruiser 1.0
Hi Lux, Stout 0.8

7—TRANSMISSION ASSY, R&R OR RENEW

Manual—
- Corolla 2.0
- Corona 2.6
- Crown (1966-67)—
  - 4 Cyl—
    - Exc Deluxe 2.2
    - Deluxe 2.4
  - 6 Cyl—
    - Exc Deluxe 2.9
    - Deluxe 3.1
- Crown (1968-72)—
  - 3 Speed 3.0
  - 4 Speed 3.1
- Land Cruiser 3.7
- Celica, Hi Lux 3.5

Carina 3.0
Stout 3.0
5 Speed, All 3.0
Automatic—
- Crown 3.9
- Corolla 3.8
- Corona 3.5
- Celica, Hi Lux, Carina 3.5

8—MANUAL TRANS CASE, RENEW

Corolla 3.3
Corona 2.2
Crown (1966-67)—
- 4 Cyl 3.5
- 6 Cyl 4.4

Crown (1968-72)—
- 3 Speed 4.5
- 4 Speed 3.9

9—TRANS CASE COVER OR GASKET, R&R OR RENEW

Corona 1.8
Crown (1966-67)—
- 4 Cyl 2.2
- 6 Cyl 3.0

Crown (1968-72) 2.8

10—EXTENSION HOUSING OR BUSHING, RENEW

Corolla 2.5
Corona 2.2
Crown (1966-67)—
- 4 Cyl 3.0
- 6 Cyl 4.3

Crown (1968-72)—
- 3 Speed 3.8
- 4 Speed 4.0

Celica, Carina 3.5

11—OIL PAN GASKET, RENEW

All Models 1.0

12—FRONT & REAR BANDS, ADJUST

Corona 2.3
Crown 1.0

13—MANUAL TRANS, R&R & OVERHAUL

Corolla 7.5
Corona 4.5
Crown (1966-67)—
- 3 Speed, 4 Cyl 4.1
- 3 Speed, 6 Cyl 5.1
- 4 Speed, 4 Cyl—
  - Column 3.4
  - Floor 3.7
- 4 Speed, 6 Cyl—
  - Column 4.8
  - Floor 5.1

Crown (1968-72)—
- 3 Speed 5.6
- 4 Speed 4.9

Celica 5.0
Carina 4.5
Land Cruiser 5.5
Hi Lux, Stout 5.0

14—AUTOMATIC TRANS, R&R & OVERHAUL

Crown 8.9
Corolla 8.7
Corona 8.5
Celica, Hi Lux 8.5
Carina 8.5

15—MAINSHAFT REAR BEARING, RENEW

Corona 2.9
Crown—
- 3 Speed—
  - 4 Cyl 3.0
  - 6 Cyl 4.0
- 4 Speed 4 Cyl—
  - Column 2.9
  - Floor 3.2
- 4 Speed 6 Cyl—
  - Column 3.9
  - Floor 4.2

16—GEAR SELECTOR FORKS, RENEW

Corolla 2.8
Corona 3.0
Crown—
- 4 Cyl 2.9
- 6 Cyl 3.8

17—GEARSHIFT OR SELECTOR LEVER, RENEW

Corolla 0.4
Corona 0.3
Crown 0.4

Brakes, Steering, Suspension, Universals & Rear Axle—TIME

OPERATION INDEX

Brake Shoes Or Friction Pads, Renew 1
Master Cylinder, Renew 2
Master Cylinder, R&R & Overhaul 3
Wheel Cylinders, Renew 4
Wheel Cylinders, R&R & Overhaul 5
Caliper Assy, Renew 6
Caliper Assy, R&R & Overhaul 7
Bleed System 8
Brake Hose, Renew 9
Front Hub & Brake Drum Assy, Renew 10
Brake Shoe Adjusting Screw Set, Renew 11
Brake Pedal, Renew 12
Parking Brake Cable, Renew 13
Parking Brake Lever, Renew 14
Steering Post Assy, Renew 15
Spring(S), Renew 16
Strut Bar, Renew 17
Steering Relay Rod, Renew 18
Front Wheel Bearings, Renew 19
Shock Absorbers, Renew 20
Front Suspension Upper Control Arm Assy, Renew 21
Front Suspension Lower Control Arm Assy, Renew 22
Universal Joints, Renew 23
Axle Shaft, Renew 24
Axle Shaft Bearings, Renew 25

(Continued)

Brakes, Steering, Suspension, Universals & Rear Axle—TIME Cont'd

Differential Assy, Overhaul *26*
Differential Cover Or Gasket, Renew *27*

1—BRAKE SHOES OR FRICTION PADS, RENEW

Corolla—
Front Or Rear 1.4
All 2.4
Corona—
2 Front Wheels 1.0
2 Rear Wheels 1.1
All 2.1
Crown (1966-67)—
2 Front Wheels 0.9
2 Rear Wheels 1.1
All 1.4
Crown (1968-72)—
Exc Disc Brake—
Front 1.4
Rear 1.9
Disc Brake 0.6
Celica, Carina—
Front 0.9
Rear 1.5
All 2.2
Land Cruiser—
Front Or Rear 1.1
All 2.0
Hi Lux, Stout—
Front 1.2
Rear 1.4
All 2.2

2—MASTER CYLINDER, RENEW

Corolla 1.0
Corona 1.2
Crown—
1966-67 .... 0.9
1968-72 .... 1.6
Celica, Carina 0.8
Land Cruiser 1.0
Hi Lux, Stout 1.3

3—MASTER CYLINDER, R&R & OVERHAUL

Corolla 1.4
Corona 1.6
Crown (1966-67) 1.2
Crown (1968-72) 1.9
Celica, Carina 1.2
Land Cruiser 1.3
Hi Lux, Stout 1.6

4—WHEEL CYLINDERS, RENEW

Corolla—
Front—
One Side 1.0
Both Sides 1.5
Rear—
One Side 0.8
Both Sides 1.2
Corona—
Front 0.8
Rear 0.9
Crown (1966-67)—
Front One 1.5
Rear One 1.6
Crown (1968-72)—
Front One 1.1
Rear One 1.2
Celica, Carina—
One 1.0
Both 1.5
Land Cruiser, Hi Lux, Stout—
One 1.1
Both 1.7

5—WHEEL CYLINDERS, R&R & OVERHAUL

Corolla—
Front—
One Side 1.2
Both Sides 1.7
Rear—
One Side 1.0
Both Sides 1.5
Corona—
Front One 1.0
Rear One 1.2
Crown (1966-67)—
Front One 1.7
Rear One 1.8
Crown (1968-72)—
Front One 1.3
Rear One 1.4
Celica, Carina—
One 1.2
Both 1.6
Land Cruiser, Hi Lux, Stout—
One 1.3
Both 1.8

6—CALIPER ASSY, RENEW

One Side 0.9

7—CALIPER ASSY, R&R & OVERHAUL

One Side 1.1

8—BLEED SYSTEM

Corolla 0.6
Corona 0.5
Crown, Celica, Carina 0.6
Land Cruiser 0.9
Hi Lux, Stout 0.9

9—BRAKE HOSE, RENEW

Each 0.6

10—FRONT HUB & BRAKE DRUM ASSY, RENEW

Corolla—
L/Disc Brake—
One Side 1.2
Both Sides 1.7
W/Disc Brake—
One Side 1.1
Both Sides 1.8
Corona 0.9
Crown (1966-67) 0.9
Crown (1968-72)—
Drum 1.9
Disc 1.1
Hi Lux 1.1

11—BRAKE SHOE ADJUSTING SCREW SET, RENEW

Corolla 0.4
Corona 0.4

12—BRAKE PEDAL, RENEW

Corolla—
Std Trans 0.6
Auto Trans 0.4
Corona 0.3
Crown 0.2

13—PARKING BRAKE CABLE, RENEW

Corolla—
No. 1 Cable 0.7
No. 2 Cable 0.9
Corona—
No. 1 Cable 0.7
No. 2 & No. 3 Cable 1.1
Crown 1.2
Celica, Carina—
Front 0.6
Rear 1.0
Land Cruiser 1.5
Hi Lux 0.9
Stout 0.4

14—PARKING BRAKE LEVER, RENEW

Corolla 0.4
Corona 0.4
Crown 0.5

15—STEERING GEAR ASSY, RENEW

Corolla 2.2
Corona 1.4
Crown (1966-67)—
Exc Deluxe 1.4
Deluxe 1.6
Crown (1968-72) 1.5
Land Cruiser, Hi Lux, Stout 1.2
Celica, Carina 1.0

16—SPRING(S), RENEW

Corolla—
Front 2.0
Rear—
One Side 0.8
Both Sides 1.3
Corona—
Front—
One Side 1.0
Both Sides 1.6
Rear—
One Side 0.8
Both Sides 1.4
Crown (1966-67)—
Front—
One Side 0.6
Both Sides 1.2
Crown (1968-72)—
Front 2.4
Rear 0.9
Celica, Carina—
Front 0.9
Rear 0.5
Hi Lux, Stout—
Front 1.2
Rear 1.0
Land Cruiser—
Front 1.0
Rear 1.2

17—STRUT BAR, RENEW

One Side 2.4

18—STEERING RELAY ROD, RENEW

Corolla 2.0
Corona 0.9
Crown 1.0
Celica, Carina 1.2
Land Cruiser 0.7
Hi Lux, Stout 1.1

19—FRONT WHEEL BEARINGS, RENEW

Corolla—
L/Disc Brake—
One Side 0.6
Both Sides 0.9
W/Disc Brakes—
One Side 0.7
Both Sides 1.0
Corona—
One Side 1.0
Both Sides 1.2
Crown (1966-67)—
One Side 0.9
Both Sides 1.3
Crown (1968-72)—
One Side 1.4
Both Sides 1.7
Celica, Hi Lux, Carina, Stout—
One Side 0.8
Both Sides 1.2
Land Cruiser—
One Side 1.0
Both Sides 1.3

20—SHOCK ABSORBERS, RENEW

Corolla—
Front—
One Side 1.8
Both Sides 2.6
Rear—
One Side 0.5
Both Sides 0.7
Corona (Front Or Rear)—
One Side 0.3
Both Sides 0.4
Crown (Front)—
One Side 0.4
Both Sides 0.6
Crown (Rear)—
One Side 0.5
Both Sides 0.8

21—FRONT SUSPENSION UPPER CONTROL ARM, REAR

Corolla—
One Side 1.0
Both Sides 2.2
Corona—
One Side 1.2
Both Sides 2.0

(Continued)

Brakes, Steering, Suspension, Universals & Rear Axle—TIME Cont'd

Crown (1966-67)—
One Side 1.3
Both Sides 2.1
Crown (1968-72)—
One Side 1.8
Both Sides 2.6
Hi Lux—
One Side 2.2
Both Sides 3.0

22—FRONT SUSPENSION LOWER CONTROL ARM, RENEW

Corolla—
One Side 1.5
Both Sides 2.3
Corona—
One Side 1.8
Both Sides 2.5
Crown (1966-67)—
One Side 1.5
Both Sides 2.6
Crown (1968-72)—
One Side 2.4
Both Sides 3.0
Celica, Carina—
One Side 1.1
Both Sides 2.0
Hi Lux—
One Side 2.0
Both Sides 3.0

23—UNIVERSAL JOINTS, RENEW

Corolla—
One 0.9
Two 1.3
Corona—
One 0.9
Two 1.5
Crown 0.8
Celica, Carina 0.9
Land Cruiser 1.0
Hi Lux, Stout—
Front 0.8
Rear, Each 1.1

24—AXLE SHAFT, RENEW

Corolla—
One Side 1.3
Both Sides 2.1
Corona (One) 1.4
Crown (1966-67) 1.1
Crown (1968-72) 1.8
Celica, Hi Lux 1.2
Carina 1.2
Land Cruiser, Stout 1.2

25—AXLE SHAFT BEARINGS, RENEW

Corolla—
One Side 1.2
Both Sides 2.0
Corona—
One Side 1.3
Both Sides 2.6
Crown (1966-67)—
One Side 1.1
Both Sides 1.9
Crown (1968-72) 1.8
Celica, Hi Lux 1.2
Carina 1.2
Land Cruiser, Stout 1.5

26—DIFFERENTIAL ASSY, OVERHAUL

Corolla 4.5
Corona 5.2
Crown (1966-67) 4.5
Crown (1968-72)—
Exc Below 7.0
MS53, 57; RS56 ....6.0
Limited Diff 7.5
Celica, Carina 5.2
Hi Lux 5.5
Land Cruiser 4.5

27—DIFFERENTIAL COVER OR GASKET, RENEW

Corolla 1.9
Corona 1.7
Crown (1966-67) 1.9
Crown (1968-72)—
Exc Below 3.3
MS53, 57; RS56 ....2.2

Speedometer, W/S Wipers & Instruments—TIME

OPERATION INDEX

Speedometer Head, Renew 1
W/S Wiper Motor, Renew 2
W/S Wiper Link Assy, Renew 3
W/S Wiper Arm, Renew 4
Fuel Gauge (Dash Unit), Renew 5
Fuel Tank Gauge, Renew 6
Temperature Gauge (Dash Unit), Renew 7
Temperature Gauge Sending Unit, Renew 8
Ammeter, Renew 9
Tachometer, Renew 10
Headlight Switch, Renew 11
Headlamp Dimmer Switch, Renew 12
Stop Light Switch, Renew 13
Turn Signal Switch, Renew 14

1—SPEEDOMETER HEAD, RENEW

Corolla 0.6
Corona 0.8
Crown (1966-67) 0.4
Crown (1968-72) 1.6
Celica, Hi Lux 0.6
Land Cruiser 0.7
Carina 0.8

2—W/S WIPER MOTOR, RENEW

Corolla 0.8
Corona 1.1
Crown (1966-67)—
Exc Below 0.6
Deluxe 0.8
Crown (1968-72) 0.6
Celica, Carina 0.5
Land Cruiser 0.6

3—W/S WIPER LINK ASSY, RENEW

Corolla 0.8
Corona 1.1
Crown (1966-67)—
Exc Below 0.7
Deluxe 0.9
Crown (1968-72) 0.6
Celica, Carina 0.6
Land Cruiser 1.0

4—W/S WIPER ARM, RENEW

All Models 0.2

5—FUEL GAUGE (DASH UNIT), RENEW

Corolla 0.8
Corona 0.9
Crown 1.4
Celica 0.6
Land Cruiser 0.7
Carina 0.7

6—FUEL TANK GAUGE, RENEW

Corolla—
Exc Below 0.8
KE 16V Ser 1.4
Corona 0.3
Crown—
Exc Below 0.3
MS53 ....0.8
MS57, RS56 ....0.9
Land Cruiser 0.6
Hi-Lux 1.5
Celica 0.8
Carina 0.6

7—TEMPERATURE GAUGE (DASH UNIT), RENEW

Corolla 0.8
Corona 0.6
Crown 1.5
Celica 0.6
Land Cruiser 0.8
Carina 0.7

8—TEMPERATURE GAUGE SENDING UNIT, RENEW

Exc Below 0.4
Corona 0.5
Celica 0.5

9—AMMETER, RENEW

Crown—
Exc Below 1.1
MS55-D 1.4
Land Cruiser 0.8
Celica 0.6
Corona 0.7

10—TACHOMETER, RENEW

Crown 0.4

11—HEADLIGHT SWITCH, RENEW

Corolla 0.3
Corona 0.2
Crown, Celica 0.4
Hi Lux, Land Cruiser 0.4

12—HEADLAMP DIMMER SWITCH, RENEW

Corolla, Corona 0.2
Celica, Carina 0.3
Crown 1.2

13—STOP LIGHT SWITCH, RENEW

Corolla 0.3
Corona 0.2
Crown 0.3
Celica, Hi Lux, Carina 0.4
Land Cruiser 0.4

14—TURN SIGNAL SWITCH, RENEW

Corolla 0.4
Corona 0.3
Crown, Hi Lux 0.4
Celica, Land Cruiser, Carina 0.5

IDENTIFICATION

ALL MODELS.................................. 427

ILLUSTRATIONS

FIG 1 – ENGINE – BLOCK & OIL PAN
FIG 2 – ENGINE – CYLINDER HEAD & VALVES
FIG 3 – ENGINE – CAMSHAFT & CRANKSHAFT
FIG 4 – TRANSMISSION
FIG 5 – FRONT SUSPENSION & STEERING

OPERATION TIMES

A

Alternator.......... 433
Ammeter.......... 437
Axle Shaft.......... 435

B

Brake Drums & Rotors.......... 436
Brakes.......... 436

C

Cables (Ignition).......... 433
Calipers.......... 436
Camshaft.......... 434
Carburetor.......... 433
Clutch.......... 435
Coil, Ignition.......... 433
Compression Test.......... 433
Connecting Rods.......... 434
Cooling System.......... 434
Crankshaft.......... 434
Cylinder Block.......... 434
Cylinder Head.......... 434

D

Dash Gauges.......... 437
Differential.......... 435
Disc Brakes.......... 436
Distributor.......... 433

E

Emission Controls.......... 433
Engine Assembly.......... 434
Engine Mountings.......... 435
Engine Oiling.......... 434
Engine Tune-Up.......... 433
Exhaust System.......... 433

F

Flywheel.......... 435
Front Suspension.......... 436
Fuel Gauges.......... 437
Fuel Pump.......... 433
Fuel Tank.......... 433

G

Generator.......... 433

H

Hand Brake.......... 436
Headlight Switch.......... 437
Heater.......... 434
Hose (Brake).......... 436
Hose (Radiator).......... 434
Hydraulic Brakes.......... 436

I

Ignition.......... 433
Ignition Coil.......... 433
Ignition Switch.......... 433
Intake Manifold.......... 433

L

Light Switches.......... 437

M

Master Cylinder.......... 436
Muffler.......... 433

O

Oil Gauge.......... 437
Oiling Engine.......... 434
Oil Pan.......... 434
Oil Pump.......... 434
Overdrive.......... 435

P

Parking Brake.......... 436
Piston Rings.......... 434
Pistons.......... 434

R

Radiator.......... 434
Radiator Hose.......... 434
Rear Axle.......... 435
Regulator.......... 433
Rocker Arms.......... 434
Rod Bearings.......... 434

S

Shocks (Front).......... 436
Shocks (Rear).......... 436
Speedometer.......... 437
Springs (Front).......... 436
Springs (Rear).......... 436
Starting Motor.......... 433
Steering Gear.......... 436
Steering Linkage.......... 436
Switches (Light).......... 437

T

Tachometer.......... 437
Temperature Gauge.......... 437
Thermostat.......... 434
Timing Case Cover.......... 434
Timing Chain.......... 434
Timing Gears.......... 434
Transmission.......... 435
Tune-Up, Engine.......... 433

U

Universals.......... 436

V

Vacuum Control Unit.......... 433
Valve Lifters.......... 434
Valve System.......... 434

W

Water Pump.......... 434
Wheel Cylinders.......... 436
Windshield Wiper.......... 437

CHASSIS NUMBER LOCATION

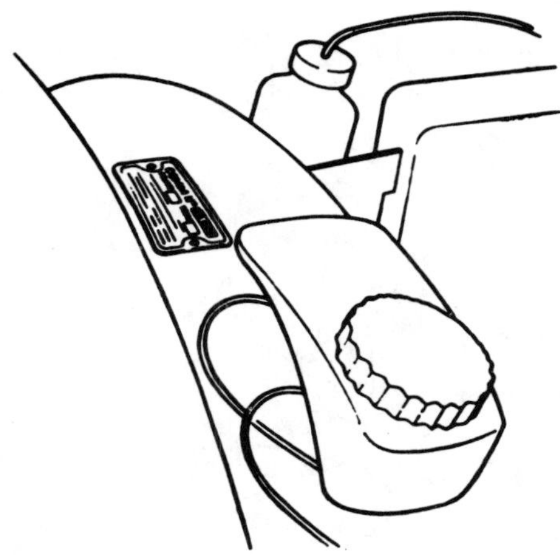

TR6 & TR250
On a plate riveted to the left front wheelhouse.

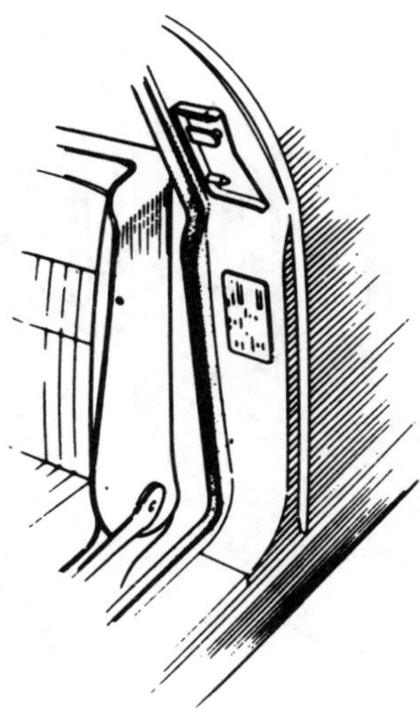

STAG
On a plate riveted to the left door lock pillar face below lock striker.

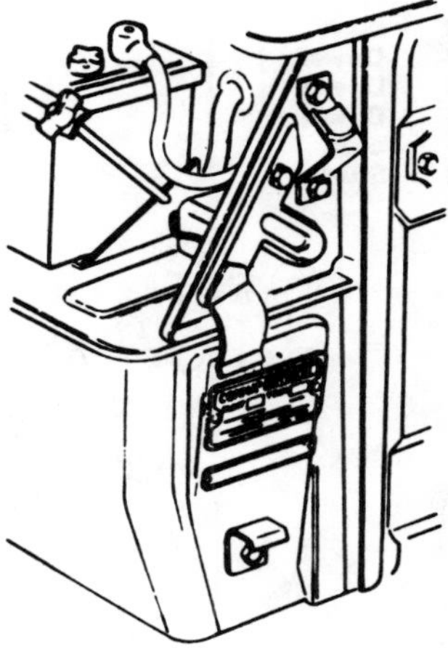

GT6 & SPITFIRE
On a plate riveted to the left hand bulkhead panel.

ENGINE NUMBER LOCATION

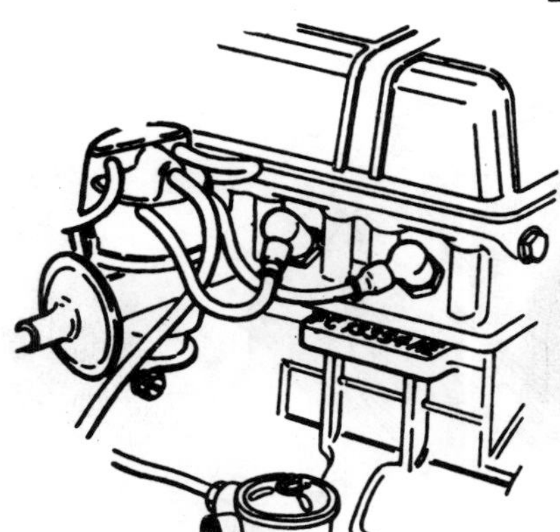

TR6–TR250–GT6–SPITFIRE
On a boss on the left hand side of the cylinder block.

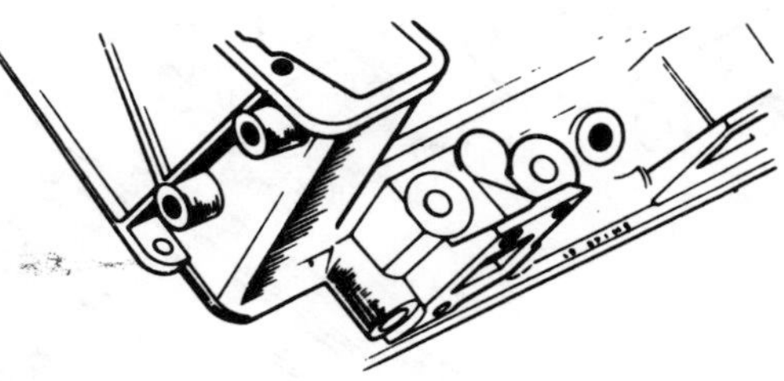

STAG
On a flange between No. 2&4 spark plugs on left hand side of engine.

FIG 1 – ENGINE BLOCK & OIL PAN

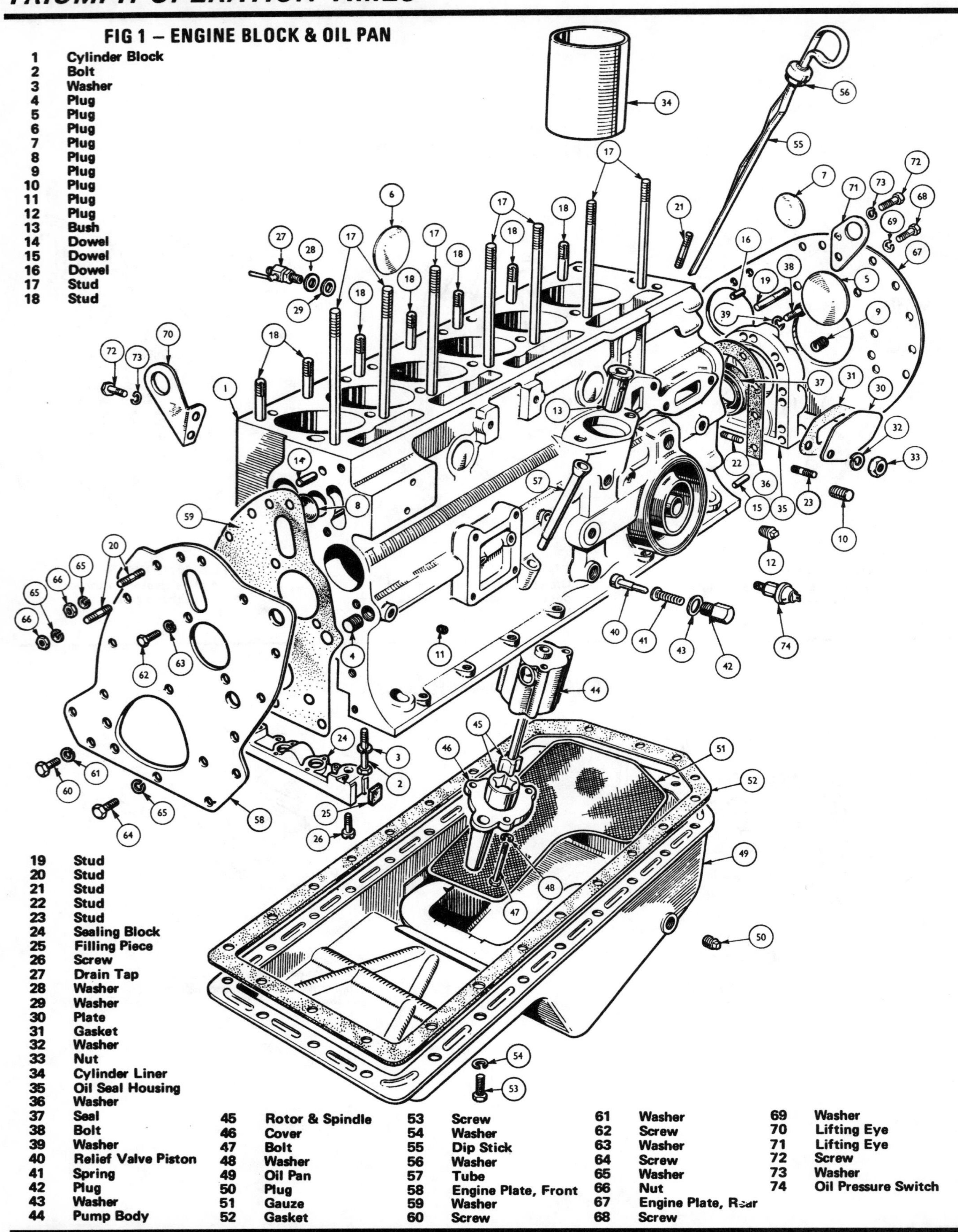

1	Cylinder Block
2	Bolt
3	Washer
4	Plug
5	Plug
6	Plug
7	Plug
8	Plug
9	Plug
10	Plug
11	Plug
12	Plug
13	Bush
14	Dowel
15	Dowel
16	Dowel
17	Stud
18	Stud
19	Stud
20	Stud
21	Stud
22	Stud
23	Stud
24	Sealing Block
25	Filling Piece
26	Screw
27	Drain Tap
28	Washer
29	Washer
30	Plate
31	Gasket
32	Washer
33	Nut
34	Cylinder Liner
35	Oil Seal Housing
36	Washer
37	Seal
38	Bolt
39	Washer
40	Relief Valve Piston
41	Spring
42	Plug
43	Washer
44	Pump Body
45	Rotor & Spindle
46	Cover
47	Bolt
48	Washer
49	Oil Pan
50	Plug
51	Gauze
52	Gasket
53	Screw
54	Washer
55	Dip Stick
56	Washer
57	Tube
58	Engine Plate, Front
59	Washer
60	Screw
61	Washer
62	Screw
63	Washer
64	Screw
65	Washer
66	Nut
67	Engine Plate, Rear
68	Screw
69	Washer
70	Lifting Eye
71	Lifting Eye
72	Screw
73	Washer
74	Oil Pressure Switch

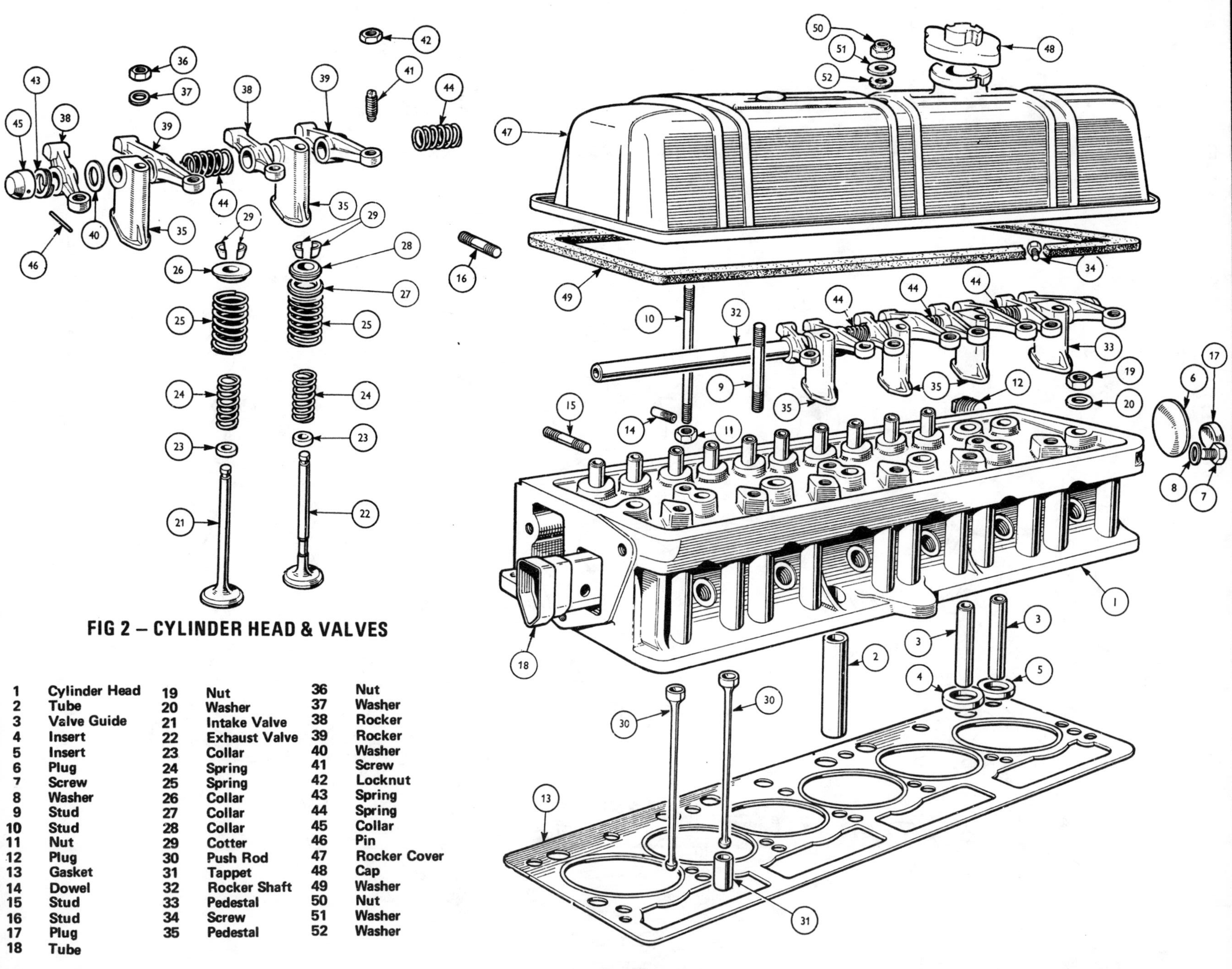

FIG 2 — CYLINDER HEAD & VALVES

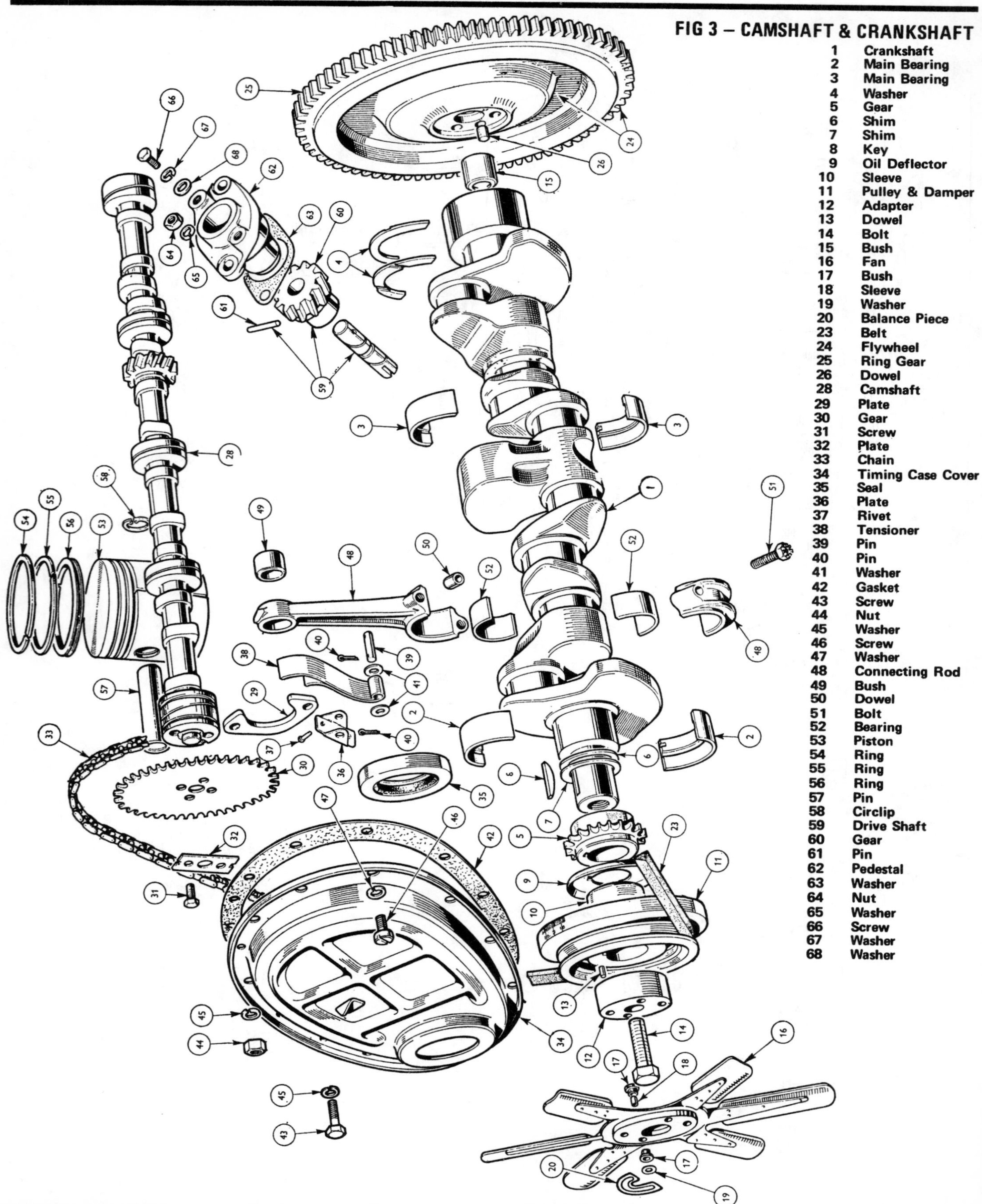

FIG 3 – CAMSHAFT & CRANKSHAFT

1 Crankshaft
2 Main Bearing
3 Main Bearing
4 Washer
5 Gear
6 Shim
7 Shim
8 Key
9 Oil Deflector
10 Sleeve
11 Pulley & Damper
12 Adapter
13 Dowel
14 Bolt
15 Bush
16 Fan
17 Bush
18 Sleeve
19 Washer
20 Balance Piece
23 Belt
24 Flywheel
25 Ring Gear
26 Dowel
28 Camshaft
29 Plate
30 Gear
31 Screw
32 Plate
33 Chain
34 Timing Case Cover
35 Seal
36 Plate
37 Rivet
38 Tensioner
39 Pin
40 Pin
41 Washer
42 Gasket
43 Screw
44 Nut
45 Washer
46 Screw
47 Washer
48 Connecting Rod
49 Bush
50 Dowel
51 Bolt
52 Bearing
53 Piston
54 Ring
55 Ring
56 Ring
57 Pin
58 Circlip
59 Drive Shaft
60 Gear
61 Pin
62 Pedestal
63 Washer
64 Nut
65 Washer
66 Screw
67 Washer
68 Washer

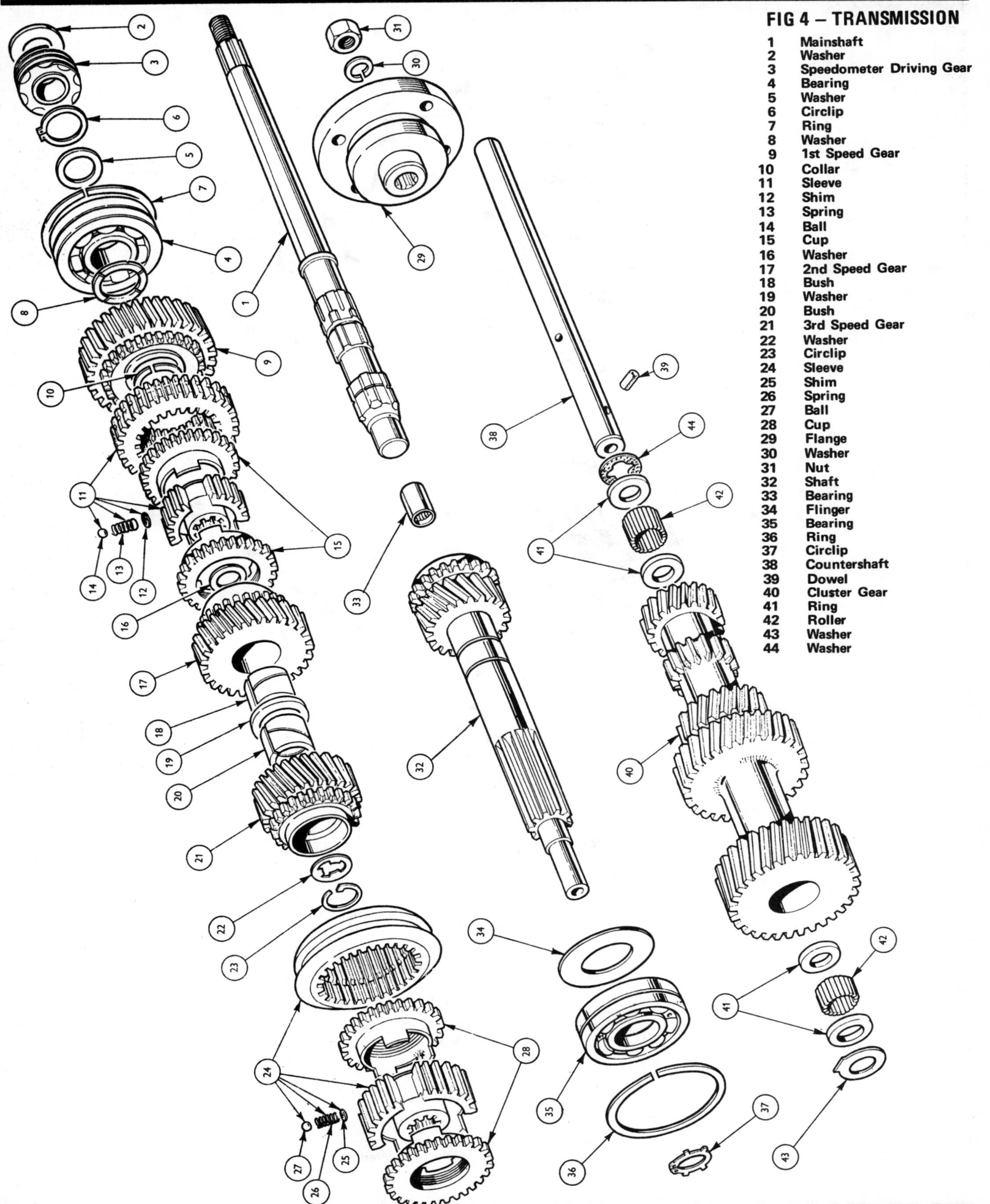

FIG 4 – TRANSMISSION

1 Mainshaft
2 Washer
3 Speedometer Driving Gear
4 Bearing
5 Washer
6 Circlip
7 Ring
8 Washer
9 1st Speed Gear
10 Collar
11 Sleeve
12 Shim
13 Spring
14 Ball
15 Cup
16 Washer
17 2nd Speed Gear
18 Bush
19 Washer
20 Bush
21 3rd Speed Gear
22 Washer
23 Circlip
24 Sleeve
25 Shim
26 Spring
27 Ball
28 Cup
29 Flange
30 Washer
31 Nut
32 Shaft
33 Bearing
34 Flinger
35 Bearing
36 Ring
37 Circlip
38 Countershaft
39 Dowel
40 Cluster Gear
41 Ring
42 Roller
43 Washer
44 Washer

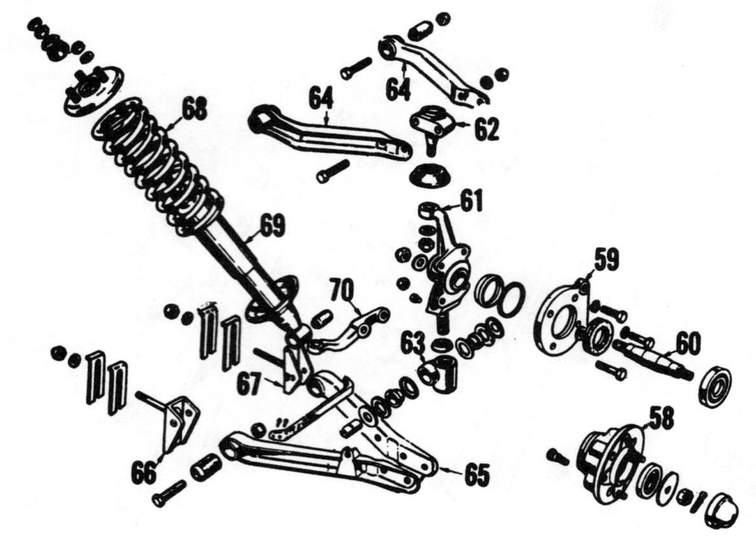

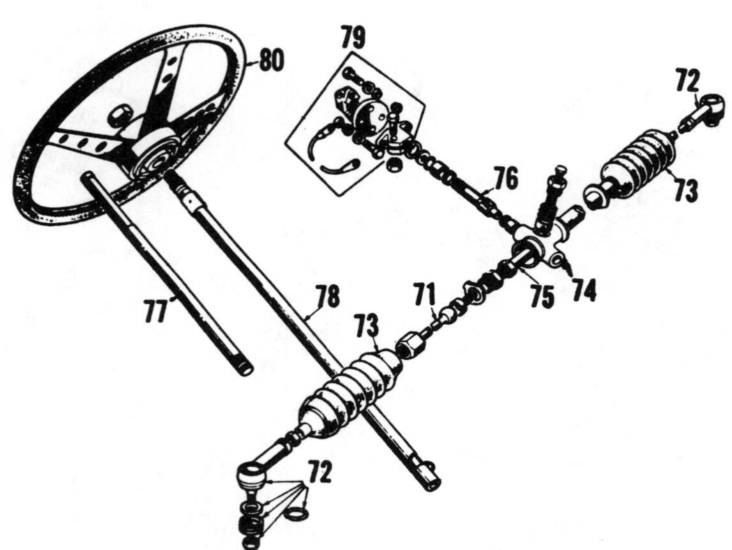

FIG 5 – FRONT SUSPENSION & STEERING

58 Hub
59 Mount Plate
60 Stub Axle
61 Vertical Link Support
62 Ball Joint, Upper
63 Trunnion, Lower
64 Control Arm, Upper
65 Control Arm, Lower
66 Mount Bracket, Front
67 Mount Bracket, Rear
68 Spring
69 Shock Absorber
70 Arm
71 Tie Rod
72 Tie Rod End
73 Boot
74 Gear Assy
75 Rack
76 Pinion
77 Mainshaft, Lower
78 Mainshaft, Upper
79 Joint
80 Wheel

Ignition, Starting & Charging—TIME

OPERATION INDEX

Tune-Up, Minor *1*
Tune-Up, Major *2*
Compression Test *3*
Distributor, R&R Or Renew *4*
Distributor Cap, Renew *5*
Ignition Cable Set, Renew *6*
Vacuum Control Unit Renew *7*
Ignition Coil, Renew *8*
Starter & Ignition Switch, Renew *9*
Starter, R&R Or Renew *10*
Starter Solenoid, Renew *11*
Starter Bendix Drive, Renew *12*
Starter, R&R & Overhaul *13*
Starter Brushes, Renew *14*
Regulator, Renew *15*
Generator, R&R Or Renew *16*
Generator, R&R & Overhaul *17*
Generator Brushes, Renew *18*
Generator Pulley, Renew *19*
Alternator, R&R Or Renew *20*
Alternator, R&R & Overhaul *21*
Alternator Brushes, Renew *22*
Alternator Stator, Renew *23*

1—TUNE-UP, MINOR

Includes: Renew points, condenser and plugs, set spark timing and adjust carburetor idle.

4 Cyl 2.4
6 Cyl 3.0
8 Cyl 3.5

2—TUNE-UP MAJOR

Includes: Check compression, clean or renew and adjust spark plugs. R&R distributor, renew points and condenser adjust ignition timing, carburetor and fan belts. Clean battery terminals and service air cleaner. Check coil and renew fuel filter.

4 Cyl 4.0
6 Cyl 4.5
8 Cyl 5.0

3—COMPRESSION TEST

Exc. Below 0.6
Spitfire 0.5

4—DISTRIBUTOR, R&R OR RENEW

Exc. Below 0.7
TR6-7 .... 0.9

5—DISTRIBUTOR CAP, RENEW

All Models 0.5

6—IGNITION CABLE SET, RENEW

4 Cyl 0.4
6 Cyl 0.5
8 Cyl 0.8

7—VACUUM CONTROL UNIT, RENEW

All Models 0.5

8—IGNITION COIL, RENEW

4 & 6 Cyl 0.3
8 Cyl 0.5

9—STARTER & IGNITION SWITCH, RENEW

Exc Below 0.4
GT6 .... 0.5
Stag 1.0
TR6 .... 2.2
All With Column Lock 1.5

10—STARTER, R&R OR RENEW

Exc Below 0.8
TR6 .... 1.0
Stag Exc 1.5
With Air Cond 2.0

11—STARTER SOLENOID, RENEW

Exc Below 0.3
TR6 .... 1.2
Stag Exc 1.5
With Air Cond 2.0

12—STARTER BENDIX DRIVE, RENEW

Exc Below 0.8
TR6 .... 1.5
Stag Exc 1.9
With Air Cond 2.3

13—STARTER, R&R & OVERHAUL

Exc Below 2.3
TR6 .... 3.3
Stag Exc 3.0
With Air Cond 3.4

14—STARTER BRUSHES, RENEW

Exc Below 1.6
Spitfire 1.3
Stag 2.1

15—REGULATOR, RENEW

All Models 0.3

16—GENERATOR, R&R OR RENEW

Exc Below 0.5
2000 .... 0.7

17—GENERATOR, R&R & OVERHAUL

Exc Below 1.5
2000 .... 2.5

18—GENERATOR BRUSHES, RENEW

Exc Below 1.0
Stag 1.2

19—GENERATOR PULLEY, RENEW

All Models 0.7

20—ALTERNATOR, R&R OR RENEW

Exc Below 0.5
Stag 1.0

21—ALTERNATOR, R&R & OVERHAUL

Exc Below 1.8
Stag 2.3

22—ALTERNATOR BRUSHES, RENEW

Exc Below 1.0
Stag 1.5

23—ALTERNATOR STATOR, RENEW

Exc Below 1.0
Stag 1.5

Fuel, Emission Controls, Intake & Exhaust Systems—TIME

OPERATION INDEX

Carburetor, R&R Or Renew *1*
Carburetor, R&R & Overhaul *2*
Fuel Pump, Renew *3*
Fuel Pump R&R & Overhaul *4*
Fuel Tank, Renew *5*
Choke Control Cable, Renew *6*
Manifold Gasket, Renew *7*
Intake Manifold, Renew *8*
Exhaust Manifold, Renew *9*
Exhaust System Complete, Renew *10*
Auxiliary Muffler Or Tail Pipe, Renew *11*
Exhaust Pipe Front, Renew *12*
Exhaust Pipe Intermediate, Renew *13*
Muffler, Renew *14*

1—CARBURETOR, R&R OR RENEW

TR2,3,3A 0.7
TR4A—
One 1.5
Both 2.0
TR6—
One 0.7
Both 1.2
TR7—
One 1.5
Both 2.0
GT6, Spitfire—
One 0.7
Both 1.2
Stag—
One Exc 0.7
With Automatic Trans 1.0
Both Exc 1.2
With Automatic Trans 1.5
2000—
One 1.5
Both 2.0

2—CARBURETOR, R&R & OVERHAUL

TR2,3,3A 1.9
Spitfire—
One 1.9
Both 3.0
Stag—
One Exc 1.9
With Automatic Trans 2.2
Both Exc 3.0
With Automatic Trans 3.3
All Others—
One 2.5
Both 4.0

3—FUEL PUMP, RENEW

Exc Below 0.4
TR7 .... 0.7
Stag 0.9

4—FUEL PUMP, R&R & OVERHAUL

Exc Below 1.0
TR6 .... 1.2
TR7 .... 1.3
Stag 1.5

5—FUEL TANK, RENEW

Exc Below 1.5
TR7 .... 2.0
Stag 2.0
2000 .... 2.3

6—CHOKE CONTROL CABLE, RENEW

Exc Below 0.7
Stag 1.1

7—MANIFOLD GASKET, RENEW

TR7 .... 1.5
Stag 1.7
TR6 & Gt6 .... 0.9

8—INTAKE MANIFOLD, RENEW

Exc Below 1.7
Spitfire 1.6
Stag Exc 2.0
With Automatic Trans 2.3

9—EXHAUST MANIFOLD, RENEW

Exc Below 1.5
Spitfire 1.6
TR7 .... 1.2
Stag 1.8

10—EXHAUST SYSTEM COMPLETE, RENEW

Exc Below 1.3
GT6 .... 1.1
2000 .... 2.0
Stag 2.2

11—AUXILIARY MUFFLER OR TAIL PIPE, RENEW

All Models 0.5

12—EXHAUST PIPE FRONT, RENEW

Exc Below 1.0
GT6 .... 0.9
Stag, Each 0.8
TR6, TR7 .... 1.2

13—EXHAUST PIPE INTERMEDIATE, RENEW

All Models 0.9

14—MUFFLER, RENEW

Exc Below 0.9
TR6 .... 0.5
GT6 .... 0.6
Stag 1.0
2000 .... 1.5

Engine Cooling & Heater System—TIME

OPERATION INDEX

Radiator, Renew *1*
Radiator Hoses, Renew *2*
Water Pump, Renew *3*
Water Pump, Overhaul *4*
Thermostat, Renew *5*
Heater Unit Ass,Y R&R Or Renew *6*
Heater Blower Motor, Renew *7*
Heater Control Valve, Renew *8*
Heater Control Cable, Renew *9*

1—RADIATOR, RENEW

TR2,3,3A 2.5
Spitfire 1.4
2000 .... 1.5
All Others 1.2

2—RADIATOR HOSES, RENEW

Upper Exc 0.3
Stag 0.4
Lower Exc 0.4
Stag 0.6

3—WATER PUMP, RENEW

TR2,3,3A 1.5
Spitfire 1.0
TR6 .... 1.3
TR7 .... 1.8
TR250, 2000 .... 1.3
GT6 .... 1.3
Stag Exc 2.0
With Air Cond 2.3

4—WATER PUMP, OVERHAUL

After pump is removed.
All Models 1.0

5—THERMOSTAT, RENEW

All Models 0.5

6—HEATER UNIT ASSY, R&R OR RENEW

Exc Below 2.0
TR6, 250 .... 3.1
GT6 .... 3.2
Mark 3 .... 3.3
Spitfire, 2000 .... 3.0
Stag 4.0
TR7 .... 4.5

7—HEATER BLOWER MOTOR, RENEW

TR6 .... 3.5

8—HEATER CONTROL VALVE, RENEW

Exc Below 0.5
Mark 3 .... 0.9

9—HEATER CONTROL CABLE, RENEW

All Models 0.9

Engine—TIME

OPERATION INDEX

Cylinder Head Gasket, Renew *1*
Cylinder Head, Renew *2*
Valves Grind *3*
Rocker Cover Gasket, Renew *4*
Valve Spring Or Rocker Arm, Renew *5*
Rocker Shaft Ass,Y, R&R Or Renew *6*
Tappets Or Cam Followers, Renew *7*
Valve Rocker Clearance, Adjust *8*
Front Sealing Block, Renew *9*
Timing Cover Seal, Renew *10*
Timing Chain Or Gears, Renew *11*
Timing Chain Tensioner, Renew *12*
Camshaft, R&R Or Renew *13*
Oil Sump Gasket, Renew *14*
Oil Pump, R&R Or Renew *15*
Oil Pump, R&R & Overhaul *16*
Piston Ring(S), Renew *17*
Connecting Rod Bearing(S), Renew *18*
Crankshaft, R&R Or Renew *19*
Crankshaft Thrust Washers, Renew *20*
Crankshaft Spigot Bushing, Renew *21*
Rear Main Oil Seal, Renew *22*
Piston(S), Renew *23*
Connecting Rod(S), Renew *24*
Crankshaft Pulley, Renew *25*

1—CYLINDER HEAD GASKET, RENEW

4 Cyl Exc 2.5
TR7 .... 3.5
6 Cyl 3.5
8 Cyl Right Exc 3.5
With Air Cond 4.0
8 Cyl Left Exc 4.0
With Air Cond 4.5

2—CYLINDER HEAD, RENEW

Includes: Minor tune-up.
4 Cyl 7.5
6 Cyl 8.5
8 Cyl Exc 10.0
With Air Cond 11.0

3—VALVES GRIND

Includes: Minor tune-up.
4 Cyl 7.5
6 Cyl 8.5
8 Cyl Exc 10.0
With Air Cond 11.0

4—ROCKER COVER GASKET, RENEW

Exc Below 0.4
8 Cyl 0.5

5—VALVE SPRING OR ROCKER ARM, RENEW

Exc Below, One 1.4
TR6 & Gt6 .... 1.5

6—ROCKER SHAFT ASSY, R&R OR RENEW

Exc Below 1.3
6 Cyl 1.8

7—TAPPETS OR CAM FOLLOWERS, RENEW

4 Cyl 2.7
6 Cyl 3.7
8 Cyl 4.5

8—VALVE ROCKER CLEARANCE, ADJUST

Exc Below 0.5
Spitfire 0.4

9—FRONT SEALING BLOCK, RENEW

Exc Below 5.9
TR6 .... 5.7

10—TIMING COVER SEAL, RENEW

Exc Below 2.4
TR6, TR250 .... 3.3
GT6, Spitfire 2.0
TR2,3,3A 4.0
Stag, Exc 3.5
With Air Cond 4.5

11—TIMING CHAIN, OR GEARS, RENEW

Exc Below 3.4
TR6, TR250 .... 3.8
GT6, Spitfire 3.2
TR2,3,3A 5.0
Stag, Upper Exc 4.5
With Air Cond 5.5
Stag, Lower Exc 4.0
With Air Cond 5.0

12—TIMING CHAIN TENSIONER, RENEW

Exc Below 2.8
TR6 .... 3.3
GT6 .... 2.0

13—CAMSHAFT, R&R OR RENEW

Exc Below 6.5
TR6, TR250 .... 7.9
GT6 .... 6.3
TR7 .... 3.0
Stag 2.5

14—OIL SUMP GASKET, RENEW

Exc Below 1.4
TR6, TR250 .... 0.9
GT6, TR7 .... 2.1
2000, Stag 3.8

15—OIL PUMP, R&R OR RENEW

Exc Below 1.6
TR6, TR250 .... 1.1
GT6 .... 2.4
2000 .... 4.5
Stag 1.3

16—OIL PUMP, OVERHAUL

After pump is removed.
All Models 0.7

17—PISTON RING(S), RENEW

One Piston—
Exc Below 4.8
TR6 .... 5.1
GT6 .... 6.2
All Pistons—
Exc Below 5.6
TR6 .... 7.1
GT6 .... 8.3

—NOTE—
To Renew Conn-Rod Bushings.
Each Add *0.5*
All Add-
Exc Below *1.6*
Spitfire *1.4*

18—CONNECTING ROD BEARING(S), RENEW

One—
Exc Below 1.7
TR6 .... 1.5
GT6 .... 2.4
All—
Exc Below 2.1
TR6 .... 2.0
GT6 .... 3.5

19—CRANKSHAFT, R&R OR RENEW

Exc Below 10.2
TR6 .... 12.1
Spitfire 8.5

20—CRANKSHAFT THRUST WASHERS, RENEW

Exc Below 2.5
TR6 .... 1.5
Spitfire 1.7

21—CRANKSHAFT SPIGOT BUSHING, RENEW

Exc Below 4.8
TR6 .... 5.7

22—REAR MAIN OIL SEAL, RENEW

Exc Below 5.5
TR6 3

23—PISTON(S), RENEW

One—
Exc Below 4.8
TR6 .... 5.1
GT6 .... 6.2
All—
Exc Below 5.6
TR6 .... 7.1
GT6 .... 8.3

—NOTE—
To Renew Conn-Rod Bushings.
Each Add *0.5*
All-
Exc Below *1.6*
Spitfire *1.4*

24—CONNECTING ROD(S), RENEW

One—
Exc Below 4.8
TR6 .... 5.1
GT6 .... 6.2
All—
Exc Below 5.6
TR6 .... 7.1
GT6 .... 8.3

(Continued)

Engine—TIME Cont'd

—NOTE—
To Renew Conn-Rod Bushings.
Each Add *0.5*
All-
Exc Below *1.6*
Spitfire *1.4*

25—CRANKSHAFT PULLEY, RENEW
Exc Below 1.4
TR6 .... 2.5

Clutch, Mounts, Manual Transmission, Overdrive—TIME

OPERATION INDEX

Flywheel, R&R Or Renew *1*
Flywheel Ring Gear, Renew *2*
Clutch Ass,Y, Or Plate, Renew *3*
Clutch Release Bearing, Renew *4*
Clutch Master Cylinder, Renew *5*
Master Cylinder, R&R & Overhaul *6*
Slave Cylinder, Renew *7*
Slave Cylinder, R&R & Overhaul *8*
Clutch Hydraulic System, Bleed *9*
Engine Mounts, Renew *10*
Gearbox, R&R Or Renew *11*
Gearbox, R&R & Overhaul *12*
Gearbox Top Cover, Renew *13*
Gearbox Top Cover, R&R & Overhaul *14*
Gear Lever, Renew *15*
Gearbox Front Cover Oil Seal, Renew *16*
Rear Extension Oil Seal, Renew *17*
Gearbox Companion Flange, Renew *18*
Speedometer Pinion Oil Seal, Renew *19*
Overdrive Unit, Renew *20*
Overdrive Unit, R&R & Overhaul *21*
Overdrive Operating Valve, Renew *22*
Overdrive Solenoid, Renew *23*
Relief Valve, Renew *24*

1—FLYWHEEL, R&R OR RENEW
Exc Below 4.8
TR6, GT6, Spitfire 5.6
Stag 5.8

2—FLYWHEEL RING GEAR, RENEW
Exc Below 5.5
TR6, GT6, Spitfire 6.3
Stag 6.5

3—CLUTCH ASS'Y, OR PLATE RENEW
Exc Below 4.7
GT6 Plus 5.0
TR6, GT6, Stag 5.3
2000, TR250 .... 6.0
Spitfire 5.5
TR4A 6.5

4—CLUTCH RELEASE BEARING, RENEW
Exc Below 4.7
GT6 Plus 5.0
TR6, GT6, Stag 5.3
TR4A 6.5
2000 .... 5.5

5—CLUTCH MASTER CYLINDER, RENEW
Exc Below 0.7
TR6, GT6 .... 0.9

6—MASTER CYLINDER, R&R & OVERHAUL
Exc Below 1.1
TR6, GT6 .... 1.3

7—SLAVE CYLINDER, RENEW
Exc Below 0.6
GT6, TR6 .... 1.5

8—SLAVE CYLINDER, R&R & OVERHAUL
Exc Below 0.9
GT6, TR6 .... 1.8

9—CLUTCH HYDRAULIC SYSTEM, BLEED
All Models 0.3

10—ENGINE MOUNTS, RENEW
Front—
TR2,3,3A 1.7
TR4A, One 1.5
Both 1.9
TR6, TR250, GT6, One 0.7
Both 1.0
Spitfire, One 0.7
Both 1.0
2000 .... 1.0
Stag, One 1.3
Both 2.2
TR7, One 0.9
Both 1.4
Rear—
TR4A, TR6, GT6 .... 2.0
TR7, 2000, STAG 0.8
Spitfire 2.5
TR250 .... 3.2

11—GEARBOX R&R OR RENEW
Exc Below 6.0
GT6 Plus 4.8
TR6, GT6 .... 5.1
TR7, Spitfire 4.5
2000 .... 5.0

12—GEARBOX, R&R & OVERHAUL
Exc Below 9.5
GT6 Plus 8.1
TR6, GT6 .... 9.5
TR7, Spitfire 7.5
2000 .... 9.7

13—GEARBOX TOP COVER, RENEW
Exc Below 2.0
TR6, Spitfire 2.5
TR4A 2.7
2000 .... 5.5
TR250, TR6 .... 3.3
Stag 6.0

14—GEARBOX TOP COVER, R&R & OVERHAUL
Exc Below 2.9
TR6, Spitfire 3.7
TR4A 3.3
2000 .... 7.0
Stag 6.8
TR250, TR6 .... 4.5

15—GEAR LEVER, RENEW
Exc Below 1.6
TR6 .... 0.6

16—GEARBOX FRONT COVER OIL SEAL, RENEW
Exc Below 05.7
TR2,3,3A,6 .... 7.0
TR7 .... 4.5
2000, Stag 6.0
TR250 .... 7.0

17—REAR EXTENSION OIL SEAL, RENEW
Exc Below 2.5
TR6, TR250 .... 3.5
TR4A 3.5
TR7, 2000 .... 1.5
Stag 2.0

18—GEARBOX COMPANION FLANGE, RENEW
Exc Below 2.0
TR6 .... 3.4

19—SPEEDOMETER PINION OIL SEAL, RENEW
Exc Below 0.7
Spitfire 1.5
GT6 .... 2.0

20—OVERDRIVE UNIT, RENEW
Exc Below 4.9
GT6 Plus 5.2
TR6, TR250 .... 5.9
Stag 6.0

21—OVERDRIVE UNIT, R&R & OVERHAUL
Exc Below 8.5
GT6 Plus 8.8
TR6, TR250 .... 9.4
Stag 10.0

22—OVERDRIVE OPERATING VALVE, RENEW
Exc Below 2.0
TR6, TR250 .... 0.9
TR4A 2.5
Stag 1.0

23—OVERDRIVE SOLENOID, RENEW
TR2,3,3A,250 .... 3.0
TR4A 3.5
2000, Stag 1.0
GT6 .... 2.5

24—RELIEF-VALVE, RENEW
Exc Below 2.0
GT6 .... 0.7

Automatic Transmission—TIME

OPERATION INDEX

Transmission, R&R Or Renew *1*
Transmission, R&R & Overhaul *2*
Converter, R&R Or Renew *3*
Oil Pan Or Gasket, Renew *4*
Valve Body, Renew *5*
Governor, Renew *6*
Brake Bands, Adjust *7*
Extension Housing, Renew *8*
Extension Oil Seal, Renew *9*

1—TRANSMISSION, R&R OR RENEW
All Models 6.0

2—TRANSMISSION, R&R & OVERHAUL
All Models 14.0

3—CONVERTER, R&R OR RENEW
All Models 6.5

4—OIL PAN OR GASKET, RENEW
All Models 1.0

5—VALVE BODY, RENEW
All Models 1.7

6—GOVERNOR, RENEW
All Models 3.5

7—BRAKE BANDS, ADJUST
All Models 1.8

8—EXTENSION HOUSING, RENEW
All Models 3.0

9—EXTENSION OIL SEAL, RENEW
All Models 2.8

Brakes, Steering, Suspension, Universals & Rear Axle—TIME

OPERATION INDEX

Brake Shoes Orfriction Pads, Renew *1*
Master Cylinder, R&R Or Renew *2*
Master Cylinder, R&R & Overhaul *3*
Wheel Cylinders, Renew *4*
Wheel Cylinders, R&R & Overhaul *5*
Caliper, R&R Or Renew *6*
Caliper, R&R & Overhaul *7*

(Continued)

Brakes, Steering, Suspension, Universals & Rear Axle—TIME Cont'd

Brakes, Bleed *8*
Brake Hoses, Renew *9*
Disc, Renew *10*
Front Hub Or Bearings, Renew *11*
Brake Drum(S), Renew *12*
Brake Adjuster, Renew *13*
Handbrake Cables, Renew *14*
Handbrake Lever, Renew *15*
Wheel Alignment *16*
Steering Column Flexible Coupling, Renew *17*
Steering Unit, R&R Or Renew *18*
Steering Unit, R&R & Overhaul *19*
Tie-Rod Ball Joints, Renew *20*
Shock Absorbers, Renew *21*
Coil Or Road Springs, Renew *22*
Suspension Sub Ass'y, R&R Or Renew *23*
Wishbone Arms Or Bushings, Renew *24*
Bottom Trunnions, Renew *25*
Vertical Link Ball Joint, Renew *26*
Vertical Link, Renew *27*
Radius Arm Or Bushings, Renew *28*
Stub Axle, Renew *29*
Rear Vertical Link Or Trunnion Housing Bushings, Renew *30*
Anti-Roll Bar, Links Or Bushings, Renew *31*
Univeral Joints, Overhaul *32*
Differential Unit, Renew *33*
Differential Unit Companion Flange, Renew *34*
Differential Unit, R&R & Overhaul *35*
Hub & Outer Shaft Ass'y, R&R Or Renew *36*
Rear Hub & Stub Ass'y, R&R Or Renew *37*
Rear Hub Outer Seal, Renew *38*
Outer Axle Shaft, Inner Hub Ass'y, Bearing Or Seal, Renew *39*
Outer Axle U-Joint, Overhaul *40*
Differential Gear Thrust Washers, Renew *41*
Inner Axle Shaft, Bearing Or Seal, Renew *42*
Pinnion Oil Seal, Renew *43*

1—BRAKE SHOES OR FRICTION PADS, RENEW

All Models, Each Side—
- Drum Type 1.0
- Disc Type 1.3

2—MASTER CYLINDER, R&R OR RENEW

Exc Below 0.9
TR6, Stag 1.1

3—MASTER CYLINDER, R&R & OVERHAUL

Exc Below 1.3
TR6, Stag 1.5

4—WHEEL CYLINDERS, RENEW

All Models—
- Each 1.3
- Both 1.9

5—WHEEL CYLINDERS, R&R & OVERHAUL

All Models—
- Each 1.5
- Both 2.1

6—CALIPER, R&R OR RENEW

All Models 0.9

7—CALIPER, R&R & OVERHAUL

Exc Below 1.4
TR6 .... 1.5

8—BRAKES, BLEED

All Models 0.5

9—BRAKE HOSES, RENEW

All Models—
- Front—
  - Each 0.7
  - Both 0.9
- Rear—
  - Each 0.9
  - Both 1.3

10—DISC, RENEW

All Models, Each 0.9

11—FRONT HUB OR BEARINGS, RENEW

All Models, Each Side Exc 1.1
- Disc Brakes 1.5

12—BRAKE DRUM(S), RENEW

All Models, Each 0.3

13—BRAKE ADJUSTER, RENEW

All Models, One 0.6

14—HANDBRAKE CABLES, RENEW

Exc Below—
- Front 0.9
- Rear 1.0

TR6—
- One 0.9

Both 1.0

15—HAND BRAKE LEVER, RENEW

All Models 0.7

16—WHEEL ALIGNMENT

All Models 1.5

17—STEERING COLUMN FLEXIBLE COUPLING, RENEW

All Models 0.5

18—STEERING UNIT, R&R OR RENEW

Exc Below 1.7
Spitfire 1.3
GT6, TR6, TR250 .... 2.0

19—STEERING UNIT, R&R & OVERHAUL

Exc Below 3.0
Spitfire 2.4
GT6, TR6, TR250 .... 4.5

20—TIE-ROD BALL JOINTS, RENEW

Inner—
- All Models 1.3

Outer—
- All Models 0.9

21—SHOCK ABSORBERS, RENEW

Front—
- Exc Below 0.9
- TR6 .... 0.6
- GT6 .... 0.5

TR7, Stag, 2000 .... 1.3

Rear—
- Exc Below 0.5
- TR6 & Gt6 Plus 0.6

22—COIL OR ROAD SPRINGS, RENEW

Front—
- Exc Below 0.9
- TR6, TR7, Stag 1.4
- GT6 .... 2.5

TR250, TR6, 2000 .... 1.5

Rear—

Coil 1.3
Transverse Exc 3.0
- GT6 .... 2.5

23—SUSPENSION SUB ASS'Y, R&R OR RENEW

Spitfire—
- Left 2.1
- Right 1.9

24—WISHBONE ARMS OR BUSHINGS, RENEW

Upper—
- Exc Below 1.5
- Spitfire, GT6 .... 1.3

Lower—
- Exc Below 2.0
- 2000, Stag 1.7
- Spitfire, GT6, TR7 .... 1.5

25—BOTTOM TRUNNIONS, RENEW

Exc Below 1.0
TR6 .... 2.1
GT6 .... 0.8

26—VERTICAL LINK BALL JOINT, RENEW

Exc Below 0.5
TR6 .... 0.7

27—VERTICAL LINK, RENEW

Exc Below 1.7
TR6 .... 2.0

28—RADIUS ARM OR BUSHINGS, RENEW

Exc Below 0.7
GT6 Plus 0.8

29—STUB AXLE, RENEW

Exc Below 1.5
TR6 .... 2.0

30—REAR VERTICAL LINK OR TRUNNION HOUSING BUSHINGS, RENEW

All Models—
- One Side 1.4
- Both Sides 2.3

31—ANTI-ROLL BAR, LINKS OR BUSHINGS, RENEW

Exc Below 0.6
- GT6 Plus 6

32—UNIVERSAL JOINTS, OVERHAUL

One—
- Exc Below 2.0
- TR6 .... 1.7

Both—
- Exc Below 2.5
- TR6 .... 2.1

33—DIFFERENTIAL UNIT, RENEW

Exc Below 3.7
GT6 Plus 4.5
TR6, TR7 .... 2.1
Stag 2.3

34—DIFFERENTIAL UNIT COMPANION FLANGE, RENEW

Exc Below 1.7
GT6 .... 1.0

35—DIFFERENTIAL UNIT, R&R & OVERHAUL

Exc Below 8.4
GT6 Plus 9.5
TR6, TR7 .... 6.3
Stag 8.0

36—HUB & OUTER SHAFT ASS'Y, R&R OR RENEW

Exc Below 2.0
GT6 Plus 2.2
2000, TR250, TR6 .... 1.5

37—REAR HUB & STUB ASS'Y, R&R OR RENEW

All Models 1.0

38—REAR HUB OUTER SEAL, RENEW

Exc Below 2.0
GT6 Plus 3.6

39—OUTER AXLE SHAFT, INNER HUB, BRG OR SEKL, RENEW

All Models 3.1

40—OUTER AXLE U-JOINT, OVERHAUL

Exc Below 2.5

TR6, TR250, 2000—
- One 1.6
- Both 2.1

41—DIFFERENTIAL GEAR THRUST WASHERS, RENEW

Exc Below 4.5
GT6 Plus 5.3

42—INNER AXLE SHAFT, BEARING OR SEAL, RENEW

Exc Below 1.7
TR6, TR250, Stag, 2000 .... 1.2
GT6 .... 3.5

43—PINNION OIL SEAL, RENEW

Exc Below 1.8
GT6 .... 1.1
TR2,3,3A,4 .... 1.0
Stag 2.5

Speedometer, W/S Wipers, Switches & Instruments—TIME

OPERATION INDEX

Speedometer Drive Cable, Renew *1*
Speedometer Head, Renew *2*
W/S Wiper Motor, Renew *3*
W/S Wiper Cross-Head & Rack, Renew *4*
W/S Wiper Wheel Box, Renew *5*
Fuel Gauge (Dash Unit), Renew *6*
Fuel Tank Gauge, Renew *7*
Oil Gauge (Dash Unit), Renew *8*
Oil Pressure Switch, Renew *9*
Temperature Gauge (Dash Unit), Renew *10*
Temperature Gauge Sending Unit, Renew *11*
Ammeter, Renew *12*
Tachometer, Renew *13*
Instrument Cluster Voltage Limiter, Renew *14*
Headlight Switch, Renew *15*
Light Dip Switch, Renew *16*
Stop Light Switch, Renew *17*
Direction Indicator Switch, Renew *18*
Hazard Flasher Switch, Renew *19*

1—SPEEDOMETER DRIVE CABLE, RENEW

Exc Below 1.6
Mark 3 .... 0.8
TR6 .... 0.9

2—SPEEDOMETER HEAD, RENEW

Exc Below 0.5
GT6, TR6 .... 0.7
Stag 0.9
TR7 .... 1.2

3—W/S WIPER MOTOR, RENEW

Exc Below 0.7
TR6 .... 0.9
TR4A 1.3
Spitfire 1.0
TR250 .... 1.1
TR7 .... 1.1

4—W/S WIPER CROSS-HEAD & RACK, RENEW

Exc Below 0.5
TR6 .... 1.0

5—W/S WIPER WHEEL BOX, RENEW

Left Side—
  Exc Below 1.3
  TR6 .... 1.9
Right Side—
  Exc Below 1.0
  TR6 .... 1.5

6—FUEL GAUGE (DASH UNIT), RENEW

Exc Below 0.4
Mark 3 .... 0.8
TR6, TR250 .... 0.9
GT6, Stag 0.5
2000, TR7 .... 0.7

7—FUEL TANK GAUGE, RENEW

Exc Renew 0.4
TR6, TR4A, TR250 .... 1.3
TR2,3,3A,7 .... 0.7

8—OIL GAUGE (DASH UNIT), RENEW

Exc Below 0.9
TR6, TR250 .... 1.3

9—OIL PRESSURE SWITCH, RENEW

All Models 0.3

10—TEMPERATURE GAUGE (DASH UNIT), RENEW

Exc Below 0.4
Mark 3 .... 0.8
TR6 .... 0.6
GT6, TR4A, Stag 0.5

11—TEMPERATURE GAUGE SENDING UNIT, RENEW

Exc Below 0.3
TR7 .... 0.5

12—AMMETER, RENEW

All Models 0.6

13—TACHOMETER, RENEW

Exc Below 0.4
Mark 3 .... 0.8
TR6, GT6, TR250, 2000 .... 0.5
Stag 0.6

14—INSTRUMENT CLUSTER VOLTAGE LIMITER, RENEW

All Models 0.5

15—HEADLIGHT SWITCH, RENEW

Exc Below 0.4
Mark 3, TR7 .... 0.8
GT6 .... 0.5
2000 .... 1.5

16—LIGHT DIP SWITCH, RENEW

Exc Below 0.9
GT6 .... 0.7
TR4A, TR6, TR250 .... 0.3
2000 .... 0.3

17—STOP LIGHT SWITCH, RENEW

Exc Below 0.3
TR6 .... 0.5

18—DIRECTION INDICATOR SWITCH, RENEW

Exc Below 0.4
GT6 .... 0.5
TR6, TR7, Stag 0.8
2000 .... 1.3

19—HAZARD FLASHER SWITCH, RENEW

Exc Below 0.3
Stag 0.4

IDENTIFICATION

ALL MODELS.......... 439

ILLUSTRATIONS

FIG 1 – ENGINE – AIR COOLED – CYLINDER BLOCK
FIG 2 – ENGINE – AIR COOLED – CRANKSHAFT, FLYWHEEL & PISTONS
FIG 3 – ENGINE – AIR COOLED – CYLINDER HEAD & VALVE DRIVE
FIG 4 – ENGINE – WATER COOLED – CYLINDER BLOCK
FIG 5 – ENGINE – WATER COOLED – CRANKSHAFT, FLYWHEEL & PISTONS
FIG 6 – ENGINE – WATER COOLED – CYLINDER HEAD & VALVE DRIVE
FIG 7 – MANUAL TRANSMISSION CASE & CONTROLS
FIG 8 – MANUAL TRANSMISSION GEARS & SHAFTS
FIG 9 – AUTOMATIC TRANSMISSION CASE & CONTROLS
FIG 10 – AUTOMATIC TRANSMISSION GEARS & SHAFTS
FIG 11 – FRONT SUSPENSION & STEERING – DASHER
FIG 12 – FRONT SUSPENSION & STEERING – RABBIT & SCIROCCO
FIG 13 – FRONT SUSPENSION & STEERING – SUPER BEETLE
FIG 14 – FRONT SUSPENSION & STEERING – BEETLE & GHIA
FIG 15 – FRONT SUSPENSION & STEERING – 411 & 412
FIG 16 – REAR SUSPENSION – DASHER
FIG 17 – REAR SUSPENSION – RABBIT & SCIROCCO
FIG 18 – REAR SUSPENSION – SUPER BEETLE
FIG 19 – REAR SUSPENSION – BEETLE & GHIA
FIG 20 – REAR SUSPENSION – 411 & 412

OPERATION TIMES

A

Air Cooled Engine.......... 453
Air Pump.......... 452
Alternator.......... 451
Automatic Transmission.......... 455
Axle Shaft.......... 457

B

Brake Drums.......... 456
Brakes.......... 455

C

Cables (Ignition).......... 451
Calipers.......... 456
Camshaft Air Cooled.......... 453
-Water Cooled.......... 454
Carburetor.......... 451
Catalytic Converter.......... 452
Clutch.......... 455
Coil, Ignition.......... 451
Compression Test.......... 451
Cooling System.......... 452
Crankshaft Air Cooled.......... 454
-Water Cooled.......... 454
Cylinder Block.......... 454
Cylinder Head, Air Cooled.......... 453
-Water Cooled.......... 454

D

Dash Gauges.......... 457
Differential.......... 457
Disc Brakes.......... 456
Distributor.......... 451

E

Emission Controls.......... 452
Engine Assembly Air Cooled.......... 453
-Water Cooled.......... 454
Engine Mountings.......... 455
Engine Oiling Air Cooled.......... 453
-Water Cooled.......... 454
Engine Tune–Up.......... 451
Exhaust System.......... 452

F

Flywheel.......... 455
Front Suspension.......... 456
Fuel Gauges.......... 457
Fuel Injection.......... 452
Fuel Pump.......... 452
Fuel Tank.......... 452

G

Generator.......... 451

H

Hand Brake.......... 456
Headlight Switch.......... 457
Heater.......... 452
Hose (Brake).......... 456
Hose (Radiator).......... 452
Hydraulic Brakes.......... 455

I

Ignition.......... 451
Ignition Coil.......... 451
Ignition Switch.......... 451
Intake Manifold.......... 452

M

Main Bearings.......... 454
Master Cylinder.......... 455
Muffler.......... 452

O

Oiling, Engine Air Cooled.......... 453
-Water Cooled.......... 454
Oil Pan.......... 454
Oil Pump, Air Cooled.......... 453
-Water Cooled.......... 454

P

Parking Brake.......... 456
Piston Rings Air Cooled.......... 453
-Water Cooled.......... 454
Pistons Air Cooled.......... 453
-Water Cooled.......... 454

R

Radiator.......... 452
Radiator Hose.......... 452
Rear Axle.......... 457
Regulator.......... 451
Rocker Arms.......... 453
Rod Bearings.......... 453

S

Shocks (Front).......... 456
Shocks (Rear).......... 456
Speedometer.......... 457
Springs (Front).......... 456
Springs (Rear).......... 456
Stabilizer Bar.......... 457
Starting Motor.......... 451
Steering Gear.......... 456
Steering Linkage.......... 456
Switches (Light).......... 457
Synchro-Mesh Trans.......... 455

T

Tachometer.......... 457
Temperature Gauge.......... 457
Thermostat.......... 452
Timing Gears.......... 453
Torsion Bar.......... 456
Transmission, Manual.......... 455
Transmission, Automatic.......... 455
Tune-Up, Engine.......... 451

V

Vacuum Control Unit.......... 451
Valve System, Air Cooled.......... 453
-Water Cooled.......... 454

W

Water Cooled Engine.......... 454
Water Pump.......... 452
Wheel Cylinders.......... 455
Windshield Wiper.......... 457

MODEL IDENTIFICATION

Before making an estimate or using any prices listed, it is recommended that the vehicle first be identified by the chassis number. Then, referring to the chart listed below, find the model and chassis number.

CHASSIS NUMBER LOCATION

BEETLE, SUPER BEETLE & THING –
On identification plate and on frame tunnel under rear seat.
GHIA –
On frame tunnel under the emergency seat.
FASTBACK-SQUAREBACK-
On frame tunnel under the rear seat.
411 (TYPE 4) –
On identification plate under rear seat between inner seat belt mountings.
TRUCK & BUS –
On engine cover plate under the air cleaner.
DASHER –
In engine compartment on front partition above windshield washer container.
RABBIT & SCIROCCO –
On the suspension strut mounting at right front wheelhouse.

STARTING CHASSIS NUMBERS

BEETLE (TYPE1)

1968	118000001
1969	119000001
1970	1102000001
1971	1112000001
1972	1122000001
1973	1132000001
1974	1142000001
1975	1152000001
1976	1162000001
1977	1172000001

SUPER BEETLE (TYPE 1)

1971	1112000001
1972	1122000001
1973	1332000001
1974	1342000001

GHIA (TYPE 1)

1968	148000001
1969	149000001
1970	1402000001
1971	1412000001
1972	1422000001
1973	1432000001
1974	1442000001

THING

1971	1812000001
1972	1822000001
1973	1832000001
1974	1842000001
1975	1852000001

TRUCK & BUS (TYPE 2)

1968	218000001
1969	219000001
1970	2102000001
1971	2112000001
1972	2122000001
1973	2132000001
1974	2142000001
1975	2152000001
1976	2162000001
1977	2172000001

FASTBACK-SQUAREBACK (TYPE 3)

1968	318000001
1969	319000001
1970	3102000001
1971	3112000001
1972	3122000001
1973	3132000001

411 & 412 (TYPE 4)

1969	419000001
1970	4102000001
1971	4112000001
1972	4122000001
1973	4132000001
1974	4142000001

DASHER

1974	3242011947
1975	3252000001
1976	3262000001
1977	3272000001

RABBIT

1975	1753025868
1976	1763000001
1977	1773000001

SCIROCCO

1975	5352000001
1976	5362000001
1977	5372000001

ENGINE NUMBER LOCATIONS

BEETLE-SUPER BEETLE-GHIA –
On crankcase at the generator support flange.
FASTBACK-SQUAREBACK-
On the crankcase beside the joint near the oil cooler.
411 (TYPE 4) –
On right hand crankcase half below the breather support.
TRUCK & BUS –
On the crankcase flange under the generator support.
THING –
On crankcase at generator support flange.
DASHER-RABBIT-SCIROCCO –
On left hand side of engine block above fuel pump.

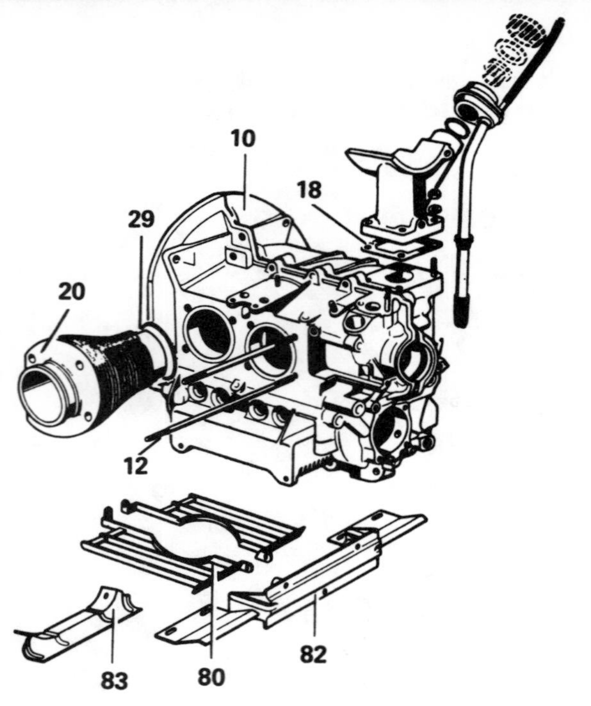

FIG 1 – ENGINE – AIR COOLED – CYLINDER BLOCK

10	Engine Block
12	Stud
18	Gasket
20	Cylinder
29	Gasket
80	Protective Frame
82	Floor Screen Plate
83	Protective Plate

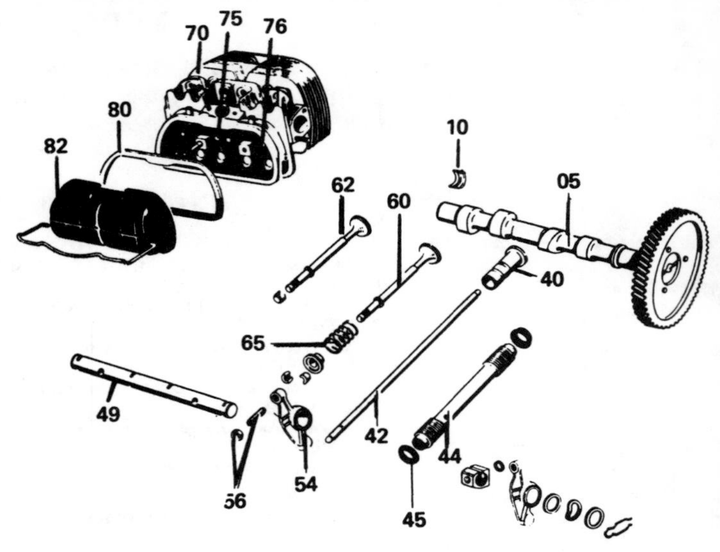

FIG 3 – ENGINE – AIR COOLED – CYLINDER HEAD & VALVE DRIVE

05	Camshaft
10	Bearing
40	Cam Follower
42	Push Rod
44	Push Rod Tube
45	Gasket
49	Rocker Arm Shaft
54	Rocker Arm
56	Adjusting Nut & Screw
60	Intake Valve
62	Exhaust Valve
65	Valve Spring
70	Cylinder Head
75	Intake Valve Guide
76	Exhaust Valve Guide
80	Valve Cover Gasket
82	Valve Cover

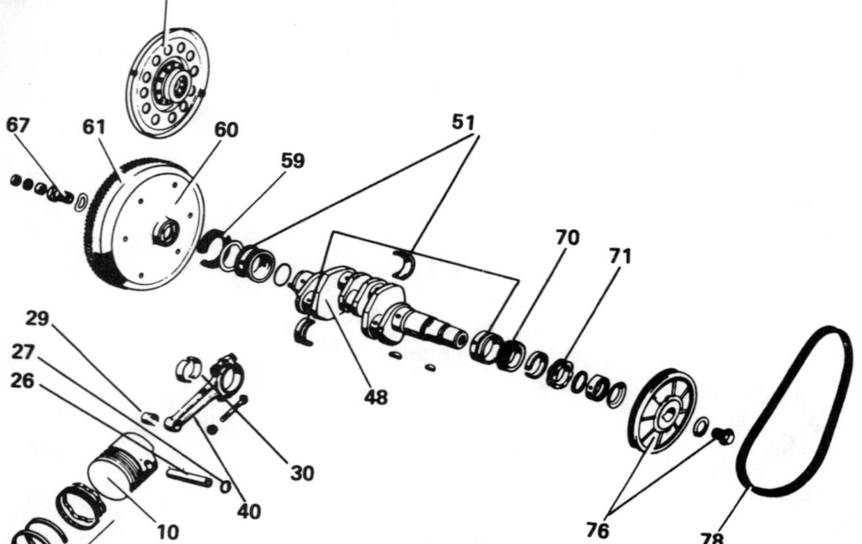

10	Piston
19	Piston Ring Set
26	Piston Pin
27	Lockring
29	Bushing
30	Rod Bearing
40	Connecting Rod
48	Crankshaft
51	Main Bearings
59	Real Oil Seal
60	Flywheel
61	Ring Gear
63	Converter Driving Plate
67	Bearing
70	Crankshaft Gear
71	Distributor Drive Gear
76	Pulley
78	Belt

FIG 2 – ENGINE – AIR COOLED – CRANKSHAFT, FLYWHEEL & PISTONS

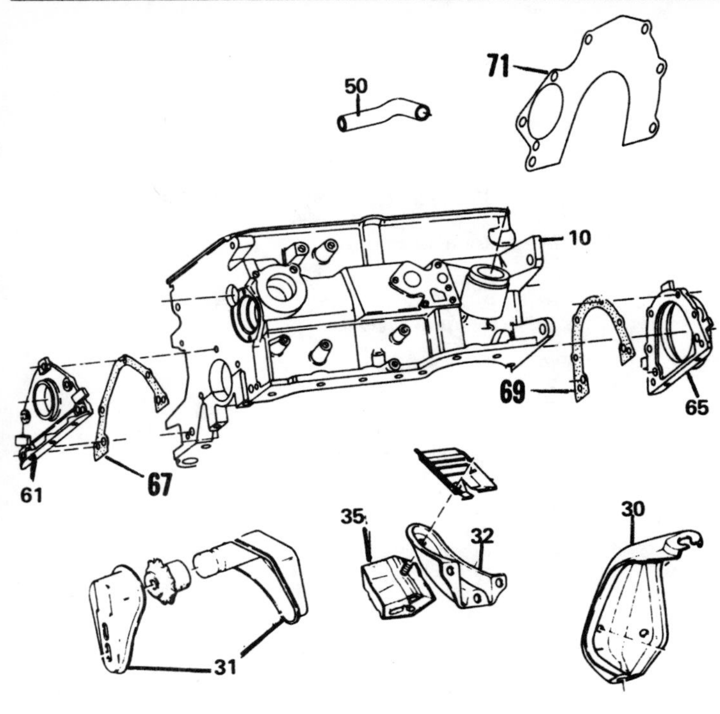

FIG 4 – ENGINE – WATER COOLED – CYLINDER BLOCK

10	Engine Block
30	Engine Support, Left
31	Engine Support, Center
32	Engine Support, Right
35	Rubber Mount
50	Breather Hose
61	Flange, front
65	Flange, rear
67	Gasket
69	Gasket
71	Gasket

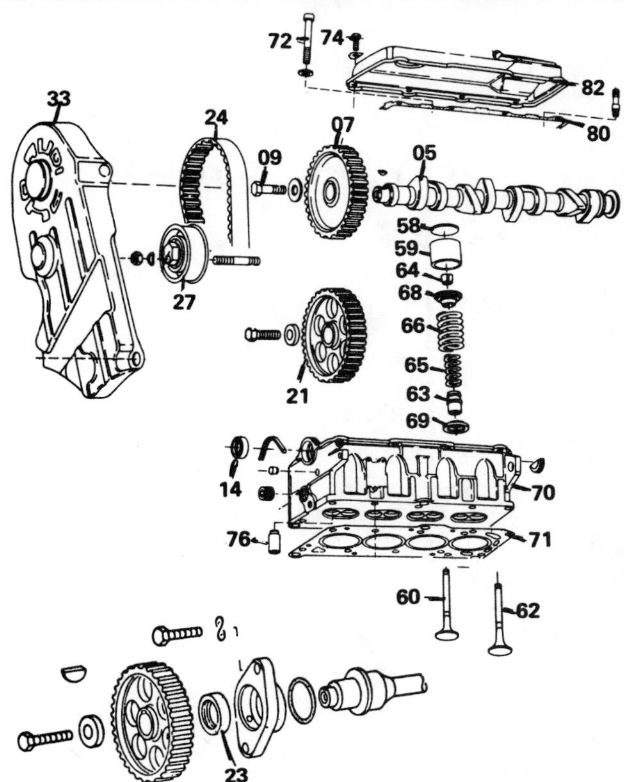

FIG 6 – ENGINE – WATER COOLED – CYLINDER HEAD & VALVE DRIVE

05	Camshaft	63	Valve Stem Seal
07	Camshaft Sprocket	64	Valve Cotter
09	Bolt	65	Valve Spring, Inner
14	Oil Seal	66	Valve Spring, Outer
21	Intermediate Shaft Sprocket	68	Retainer, Top
23	Oil Seal	69	Retainer, Bottom
24	Spur Belt	70	Cylinder Head
27	Pulley	71	Gasket
33	Spur Belt Cover	72	Bolt
58	Cam Follower Disc	74	Bolt
59	Cam Follower	76	Valve Guide
60	Intake Valve	80	Gasket
62	Exhaust Valve	82	Cylinder Head Cover

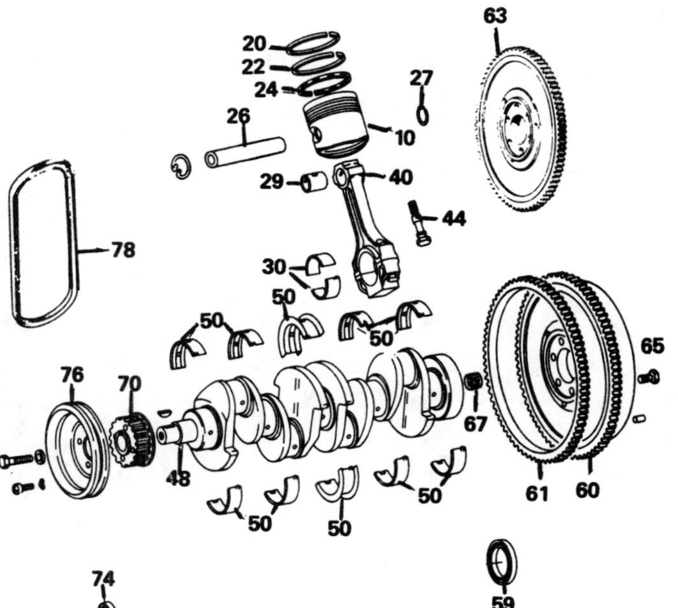

10	Piston	59	Oil Seal
20	Piston Ring 1	60	Flywheel
22	Piston Ring 2	61	Ring Gear
24	Oil Scraper Ring	63	Converter Drive Plate
26	Piston Pin	65	Bolt
29	Connecting Rod Bushing	67	Needle Bearing
30	Connecting Rod Bearing	70	Spur Belt Drive Sprocket
40	Connecting Rod	74	Oil Seal
44	Bolt & Nut	76	Pulley
48	Crankshaft	78	Belt
50	Main Bearings		

FIG 5 – ENGINE – WATER COOLED – CRANKSHAFT, FLYWHEEL & PISTONS

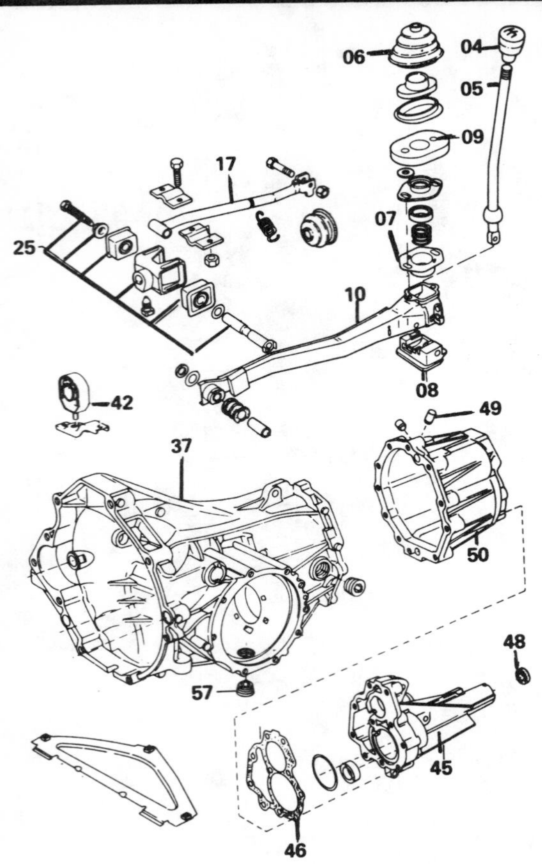

FIG 7 – MANUAL TRANSMISSION CASE & CONTROLS

04	Knob
05	Lever
06	Boot
07	Base Plate
08	Gearshift Plate
09	Gasket
10	Lever Housing
17	Gearshift Tube
25	Tube Coupling
37	Transmission Case
42	Rubber Mount, Center
45	End Cover
46	Gasket
48	Seal
49	Plug
50	Intermediate Housing
57	Drain Plug

FIG 8 – MANUAL TRANSMISSION GEARS & SHAFTS

10	Shift Lever
18	Shift Rod
21	Shift Fork
23	Shift Fork
25	Shift Fork
27	Reverse Gear Lever
30	Shift Rod Plunger
40	Mainshaft
43	Washer
46	Bearing
48	Bearing
50	Oil Seal
60	Pinion Front Bearing
61	Pinion Rear Bearing
65	Speedometer Drive Gear
71	Gear Set – Gear 1
72	Gear Set – Gear 2
73	Gear Set – Gear 3
74	Gear Set – Gear 4
77	Reverse Gear
79	Bushing
80	Bearing
81	Clutch Gear – Gears 1 & 2
82	Clutch Gear – Gears 3 & 4
84	Washer
87	Stop
92	Synchronizing Ring – Gear 2
93	Synchronizing Ring – Gear 3
94	Synchronizing Ring – Gear 4

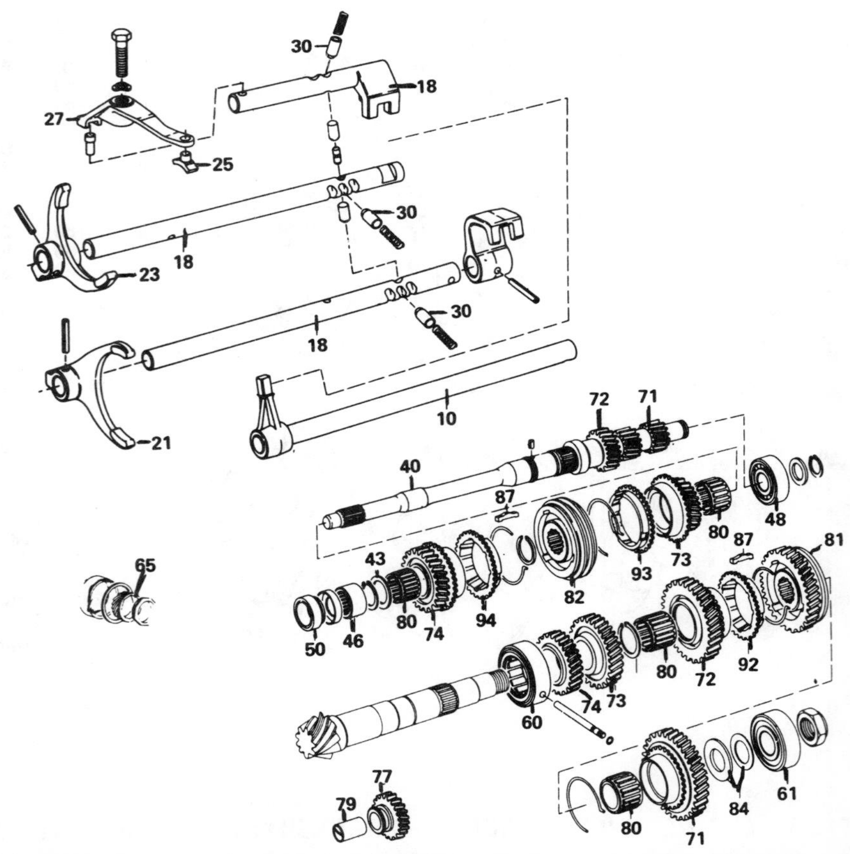

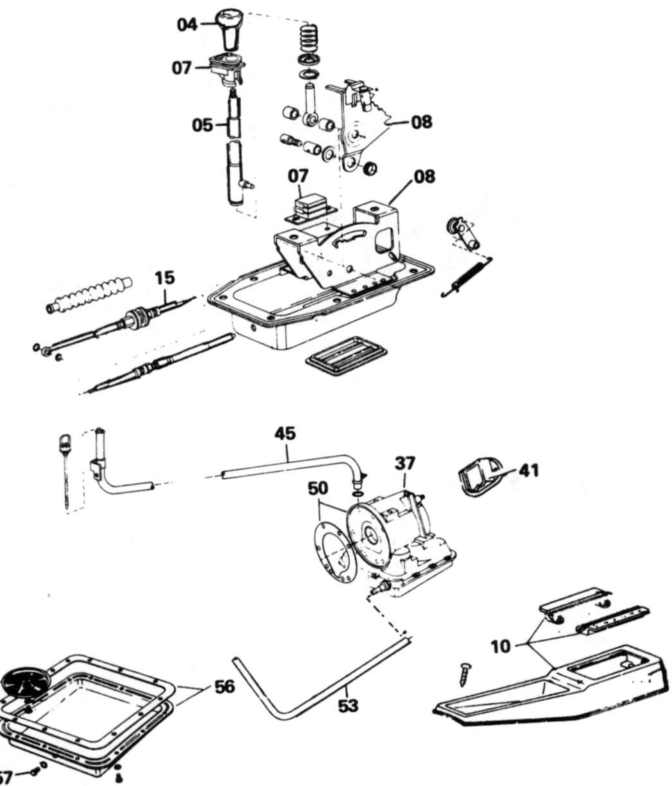

04	Knob
05	Lever
07	Neutral Safety Switch
08	Selector Mechanism
10	Shift Lever Housing
15	Cable
37	Transmission Case
41	Rubber Mount, Rear
45	Filler Pipe
50	Bearing Flange
53	Vacuum Hose
56	Gasket
57	Drain Plug

FIG 9 – AUTOMATIC TRANSMISSION CASE & CONTROLS

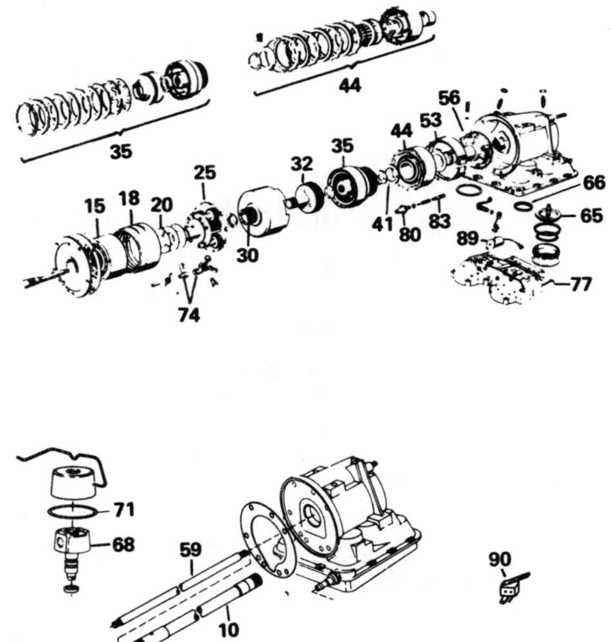

10	Mainshaft
15	Annulus Gear & Clutch
18	Reverse Brake Band
20	Shim
25	Planetary Gear Set
30	Sun Gear
32	Clutch Hub
35	Forward Clutch
41	Washer
44	Direct & Reverse Clutch
53	Brake Band – Gear 2
56	Pump
59	Pump Shaft
65	Servo Piston
66	O Ring
68	Governor
71	O Ring
74	Parking Lock Lever
77	Valve Body
80	Vacuum Unit
83	Primary Pressure Valve
89	Electro Magnet
90	Kickdown Switch

FIG 10 – AUTOMATIC TRANSMISSION GEARS & SHAFTS

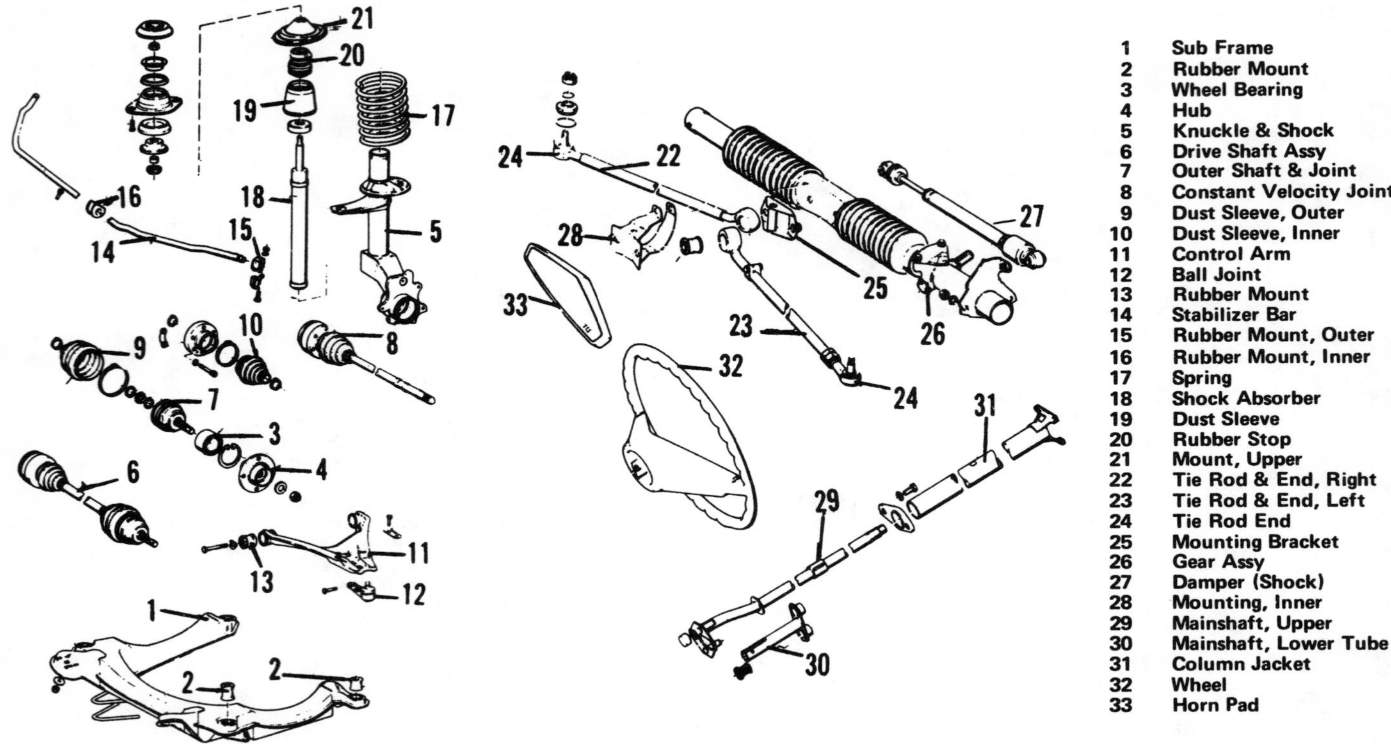

FIG 11 – FRONT SUSPENSION & STEERING – DASHER

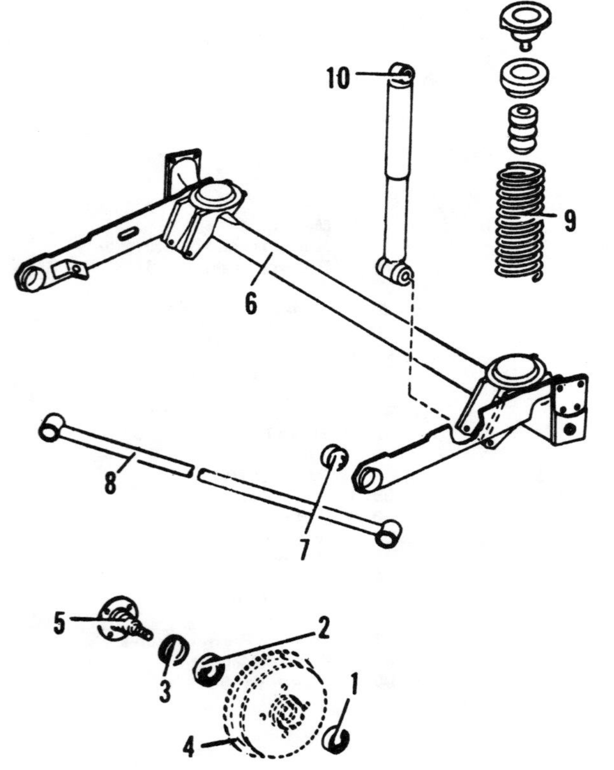

FIG 16 – REAR SUSPENSION – DASHER

1 Wheel Bearing, Outer
2 Wheel Bearing, Inner
3 Oil Seal
4 Hub & Drum
5 Stub Axle
6 Axle Beam
7 Rubber Mount
8 Diagonal Strut
9 Spring
10 Shock Absorber

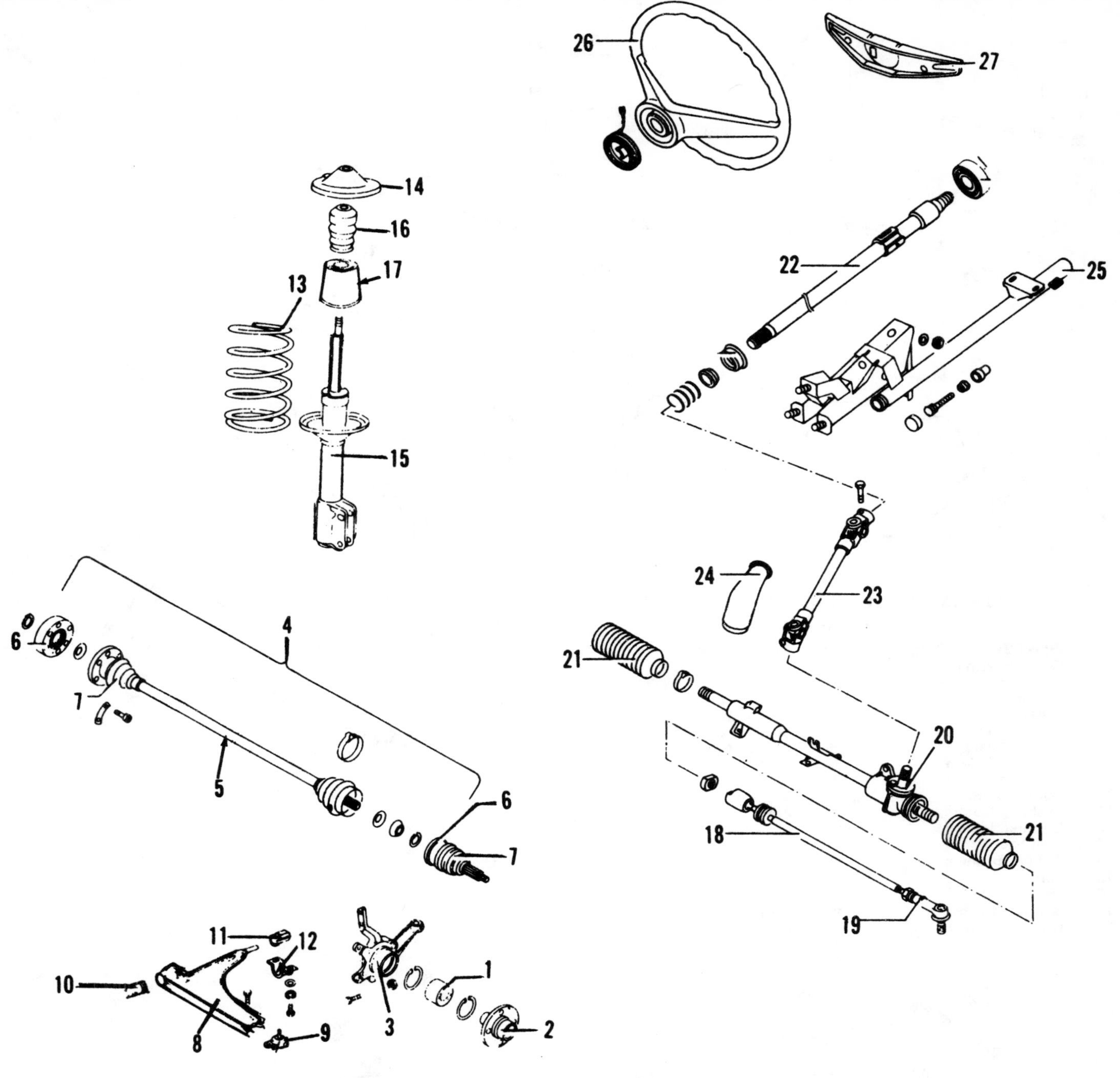

FIG 12 – FRONT SUSPENSION & STEERING – RABBIT & SCIROCCO

1	Wheel Bearing	15	Shock Absorber
2	Hub	16	Stop Pad
3	Knuckle & Arm	17	Dust Sleeve
4	Drive Shaft	18	Tie Rod Assy
5	Shaft & Joint, Outer	19	Tie Rod End
6	Constant Velocity Joint	20	Gear Assy
7	Dust Sleeve	21	Dust Sleeve
8	Control Arm	22	Mainshaft, Upper
9	Ball Joint	23	Mainshaft, Lower
10	Rubber Mount, Front	24	Dust Sleeve
11	Rubber Mount, Rear	25	Column Jacket
12	Clamp	26	Wheel
13	Spring	27	Horn Pad
14	Upper Seat		

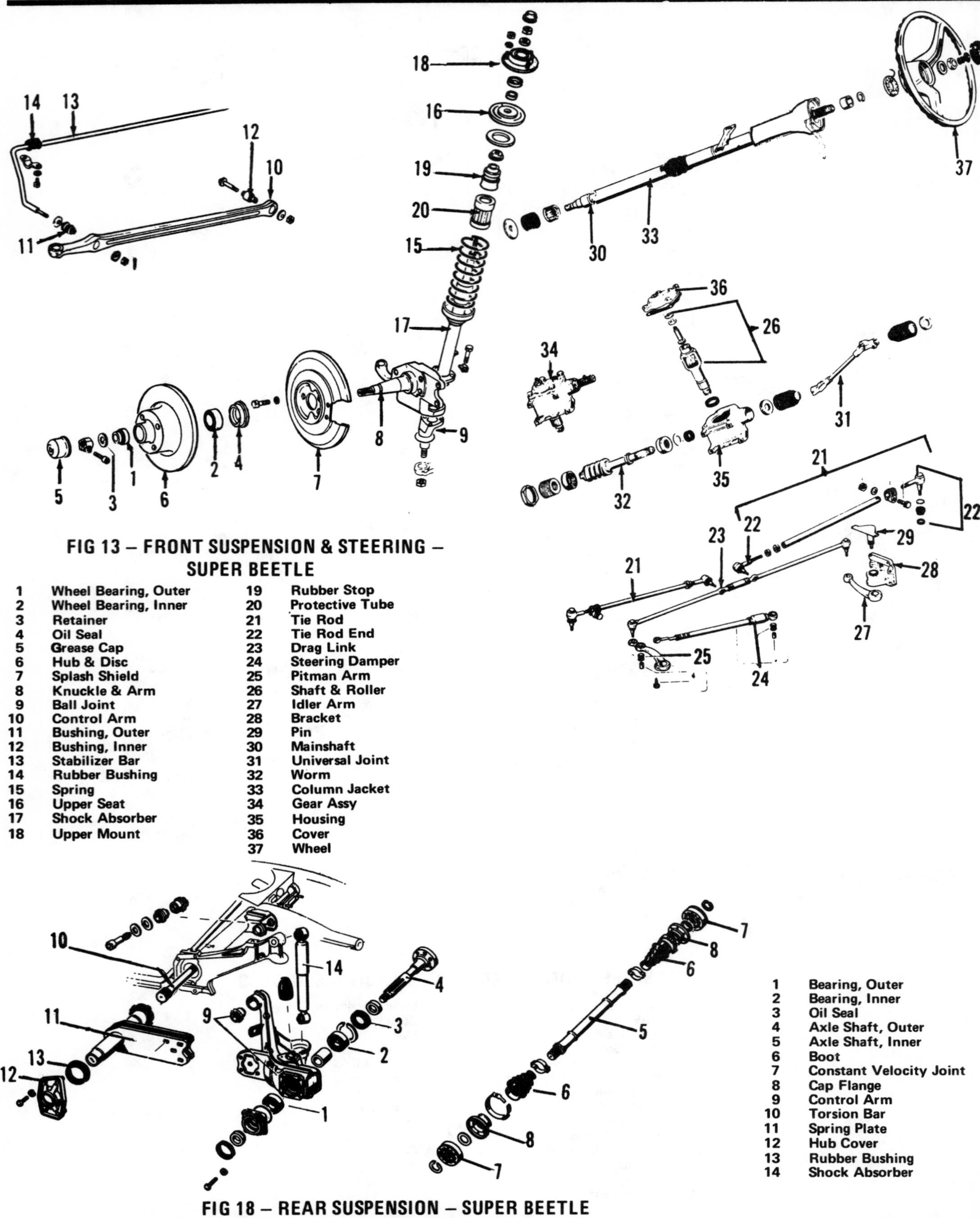

FIG 13 – FRONT SUSPENSION & STEERING – SUPER BEETLE

1	Wheel Bearing, Outer	19	Rubber Stop
2	Wheel Bearing, Inner	20	Protective Tube
3	Retainer	21	Tie Rod
4	Oil Seal	22	Tie Rod End
5	Grease Cap	23	Drag Link
6	Hub & Disc	24	Steering Damper
7	Splash Shield	25	Pitman Arm
8	Knuckle & Arm	26	Shaft & Roller
9	Ball Joint	27	Idler Arm
10	Control Arm	28	Bracket
11	Bushing, Outer	29	Pin
12	Bushing, Inner	30	Mainshaft
13	Stabilizer Bar	31	Universal Joint
14	Rubber Bushing	32	Worm
15	Spring	33	Column Jacket
16	Upper Seat	34	Gear Assy
17	Shock Absorber	35	Housing
18	Upper Mount	36	Cover
		37	Wheel

1	Bearing, Outer
2	Bearing, Inner
3	Oil Seal
4	Axle Shaft, Outer
5	Axle Shaft, Inner
6	Boot
7	Constant Velocity Joint
8	Cap Flange
9	Control Arm
10	Torsion Bar
11	Spring Plate
12	Hub Cover
13	Rubber Bushing
14	Shock Absorber

FIG 18 – REAR SUSPENSION – SUPER BEETLE

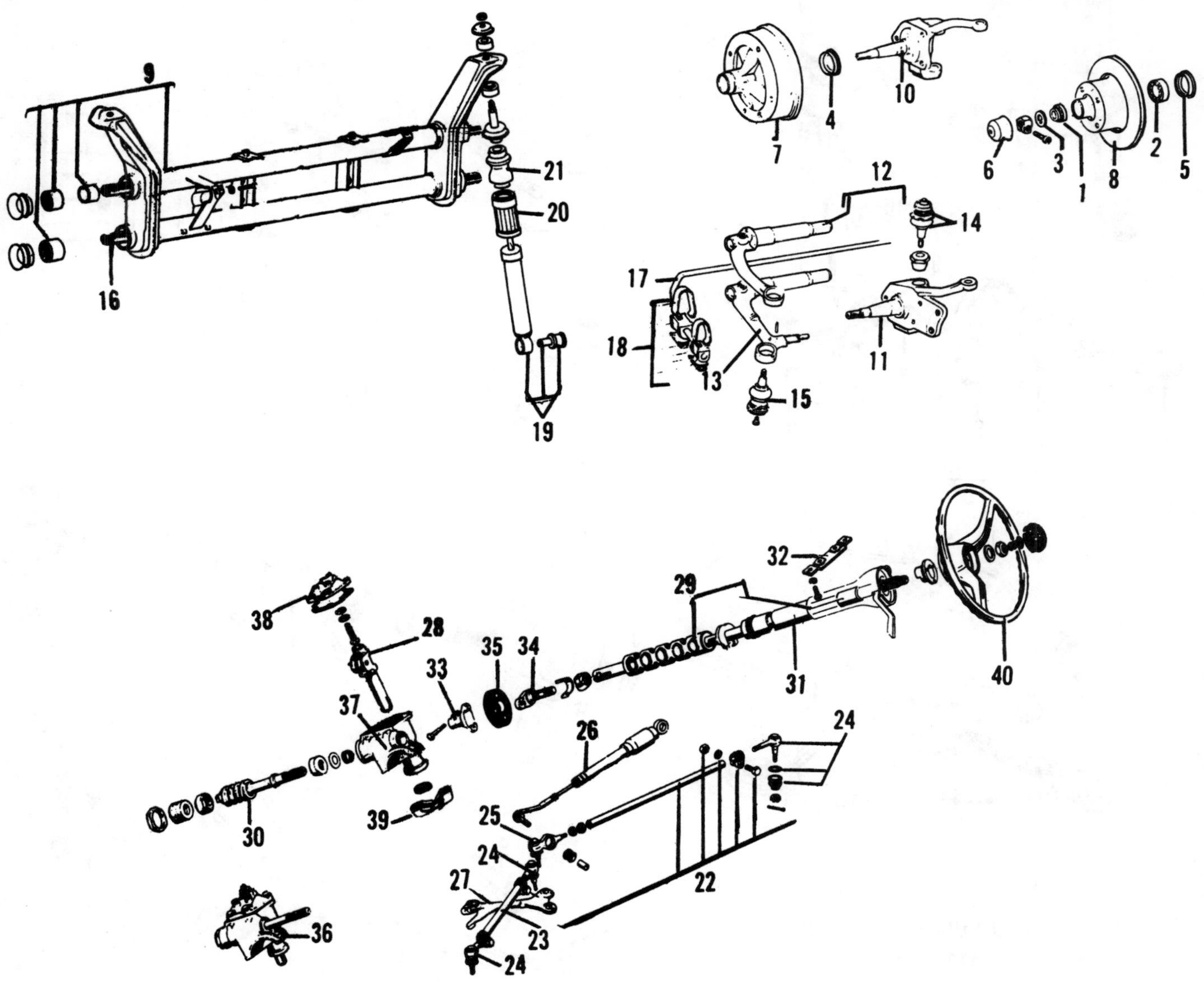

FIG 14 – FRONT SUSPENSION & STEERING – BEETLE & GHIA

1	Bearing, Outer	21	Rubber Stop
2	Bearing, Inner	22	Tie Rod, Right
3	Retainer	23	Tie Rod, Left
4	Oil Seal, Drum Brake	24	Tie Rod End
5	Oil Seal, Disc Brake	25	Strg Damper End
6	Grease Cap	26	Steering Damper
7	Hub & Drum	27	Pitman Arm
8	Hub & Disc	28	Shaft & Roller
9	Axle Beam	29	Mainshaft
10	Knuckle & Arm, Drum Brake	30	Worm
11	Knuckle & Arm, Disc Brake	31	Column Jacket
12	Torsion Arm, Upper	32	Mounting Bracket
13	Torsion Arm, Lower	33	Flange, Lower
14	Ball Joint, Upper	34	Flange, Upper
15	Ball Joint, Lower	35	Coupling (Disc)
16	Spring	36	Gear Assy
17	Stabilizer Bar	37	Housing
18	Stabilizer Mount Kit	38	Cover
19	Shock Absorber	39	Mount Clamp
20	Protection Tube	40	Wheel

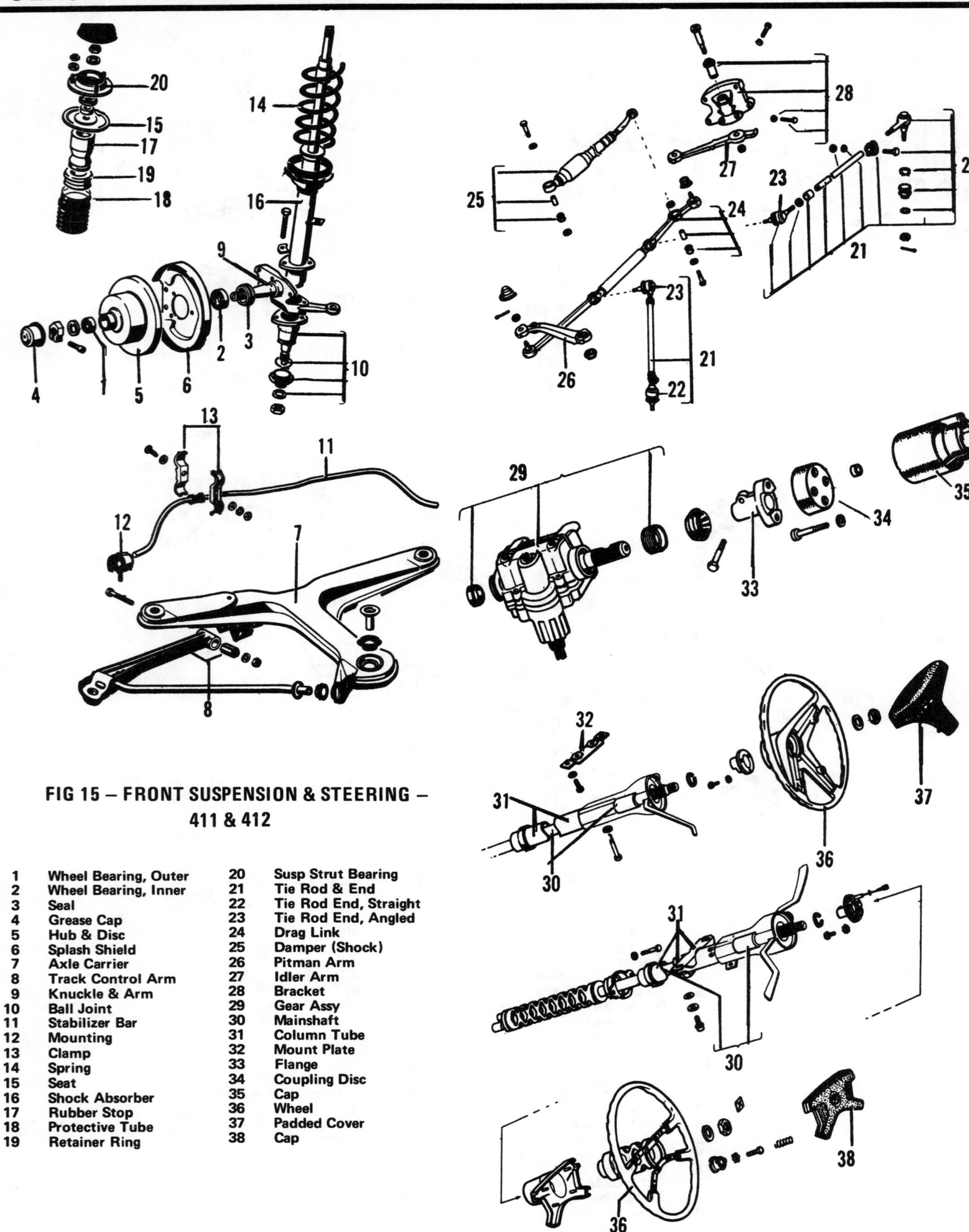

FIG 15 – FRONT SUSPENSION & STEERING – 411 & 412

1	Wheel Bearing, Outer	20	Susp Strut Bearing
2	Wheel Bearing, Inner	21	Tie Rod & End
3	Seal	22	Tie Rod End, Straight
4	Grease Cap	23	Tie Rod End, Angled
5	Hub & Disc	24	Drag Link
6	Splash Shield	25	Damper (Shock)
7	Axle Carrier	26	Pitman Arm
8	Track Control Arm	27	Idler Arm
9	Knuckle & Arm	28	Bracket
10	Ball Joint	29	Gear Assy
11	Stabilizer Bar	30	Mainshaft
12	Mounting	31	Column Tube
13	Clamp	32	Mount Plate
14	Spring	33	Flange
15	Seat	34	Coupling Disc
16	Shock Absorber	35	Cap
17	Rubber Stop	36	Wheel
18	Protective Tube	37	Padded Cover
19	Retainer Ring	38	Cap

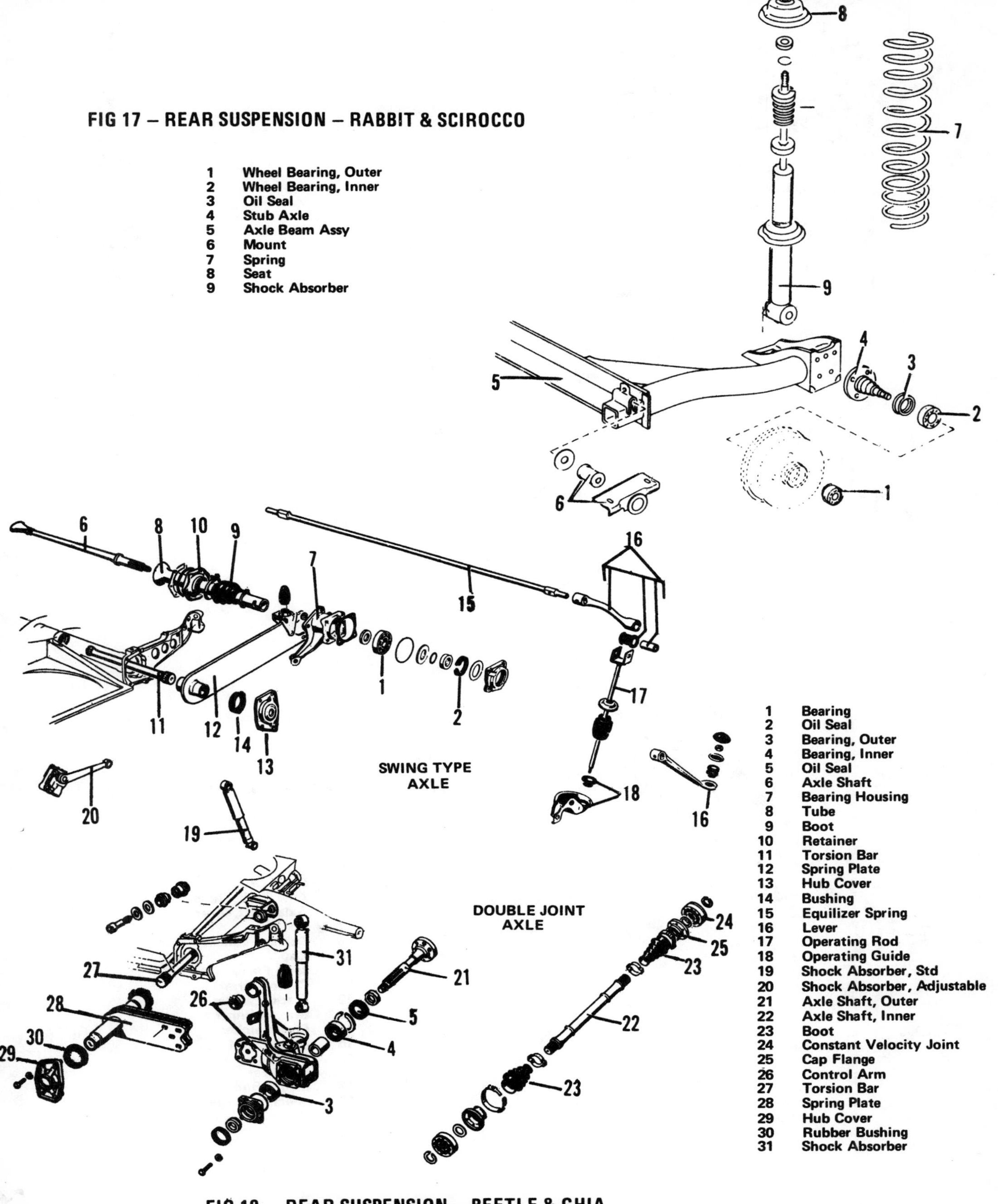
FIG 17 – REAR SUSPENSION – RABBIT & SCIROCCO
1 Wheel Bearing, Outer
2 Wheel Bearing, Inner
3 Oil Seal
4 Stub Axle
5 Axle Beam Assy
6 Mount
7 Spring
8 Seat
9 Shock Absorber
SWING TYPE AXLE
DOUBLE JOINT AXLE
1 Bearing
2 Oil Seal
3 Bearing, Outer
4 Bearing, Inner
5 Oil Seal
6 Axle Shaft
7 Bearing Housing
8 Tube
9 Boot
10 Retainer
11 Torsion Bar
12 Spring Plate
13 Hub Cover
14 Bushing
15 Equilizer Spring
16 Lever
17 Operating Rod
18 Operating Guide
19 Shock Absorber, Std
20 Shock Absorber, Adjustable
21 Axle Shaft, Outer
22 Axle Shaft, Inner
23 Boot
24 Constant Velocity Joint
25 Cap Flange
26 Control Arm
27 Torsion Bar
28 Spring Plate
29 Hub Cover
30 Rubber Bushing
31 Shock Absorber

FIG 19 – REAR SUSPENSION – BEETLE & GHIA

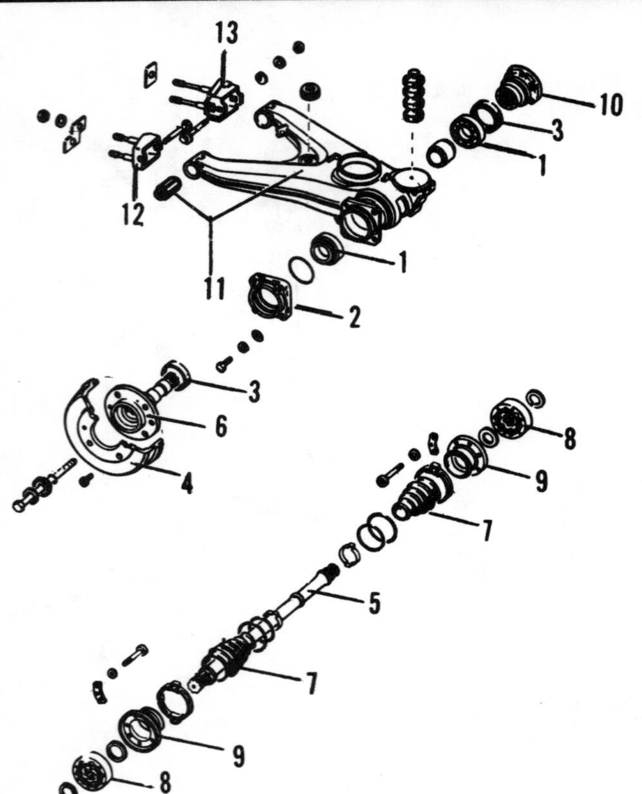

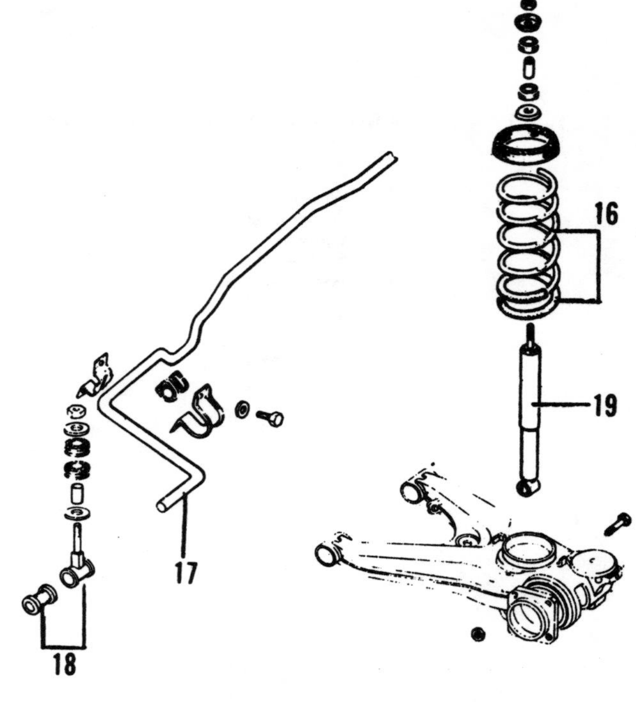

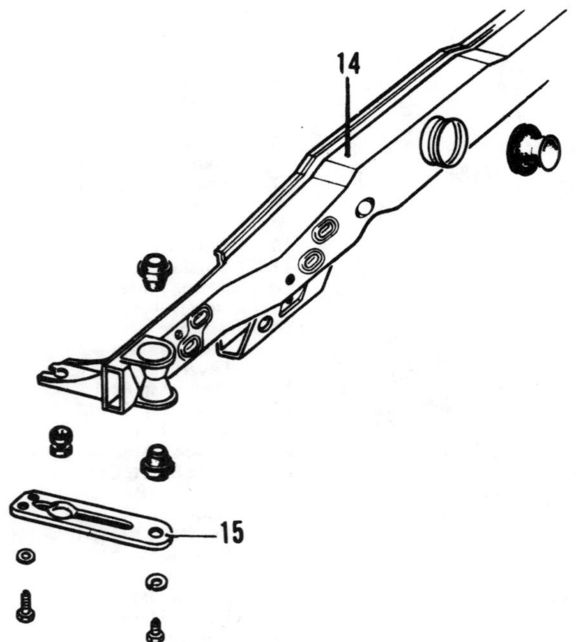

FIG 20 – REAR SUSPENSION – 411 & 412

1	Wheel Bearing
2	Cover
3	Seal
4	Brake Drum
5	Axle Shaft, Outer
6	Axle Shaft, Inner
7	Boot
8	Contant Velocity Joint
9	Cap
10	Joint Flange
11	Control Arm
12	Bracket, Outer
13	Bracket, Inner
14	Crossmember
15	Mount Strut
16	Spring
17	Stabilizer
18	Mount Rod
19	Shock Absorber

Ignition, Starting & Charging—TIME

OPERATION INDEX

Tune-Up, Minor *1*
Tune-Up, Major *2*
Compression Test *3*
Distributor, R&R Or Renew *4*
Distributor Cap, Renew *5*
Distributor, R&R & Overhaul *6*
Ignition Cable Set, Renew *7*
Vacuum Control Unit, Renew *8*
Ignition Coil, Renew *9*
Starter & Ignition Switch, Renew *10*
Starter, R&R Or Renew *11*
Starter Solenoid, Renew *12*
Starter Bendix Drive, Renew *13*
Starter, R&R & Overhaul *14*
Starter Brushes, Renew *15*
Starter Armature, Renew *16*
Voltage Regulator, Renew *17*
Alternator, R&R Or Renew *18*
Alternator, R&R & Overhaul *19*
Alternator Diodes, Renew *20*
Alternator Bearings, Renew *21*
Alternator Brushes, Renew *22*
Alternator Rubber Bushings, Renew *23*
Generator, Renew *24*
Generator, R&R & Overhaul *25*
Generator Regulator, Renew *26*
Generator Armature, Renew *27*
Generator Brushes, Renew *28*

1—TUNE-UP, MINOR
Includes renew points, condenser & plugs, set spark timing and adjust carburetor idle.
Type 1 .... 0.8
Type 3—
W/Carburetors 1.1
W/Fuel Injection 0.8
Type 4 .... 0.8
Dasher 1.5
Rabbit, Scirocco 1.5

2—TUNE-UP, MAJOR
Includes check compression, clean or renew and adjust spark plugs. R&R distributor, renew points and condenser. Adjust ignition timing and adjust or synchronize carburetors. Check fuel injection system. Clean battery terminals and service air cleaner. Check coil & clean fuel pump filter insert.
Type 1 .... 1.3
Type 3—
W/Carburetors 2.0
W/Fuel Injection 1.7
Type 4 .... 1.7
Rabbit 2.5
Dasher, Scirocco 2.5

3—COMPRESSION, TEST
Exc Below 0.5
Dasher 0.3
Rabbit, Scirocco 0.3

4—DISTRIBUTOR, R&R OR RENEW
Includes: Set timing
Type 1 .... 0.4
Types 3 & 4 .... 0.5
Dasher 0.5
Rabbit, Scirocco 0.5

5—DISTRIBUTOR CAP, RENEW
All Models 0.2

6—DISTRIBUTOR, R&R & OVERHAUL
Includes: Set timing
Type 1 .... 1.5
Types 3 & 4 .... 1.6
Dasher 1.5
Rabbit, Scirocco 1.5

7—IGNITION CABLE SET, RENEW
Time allowance covers installation of factory supplied sets only.
Types 1 & 3 .... 0.5
Type 4 .... 0.3
Dasher 0.3
Rabbit, Scirocco 0.3

8—VACUUM CONTROL UNIT, RENEW
After dist is removed.
All Models 0.2

9—IGNITION COIL, RENEW
All Models 0.3

10—STARTER & IGNITION SWITCH, RENEW
Type 1—
Exc Below—
1965-67 .... 0.5
1968 & Later 1.5
Ghia—
1966 .... 0.8
1967 & Later 0.5
Type 3—
1965-67 .... 0.5
1968 & Later 1.8
Type 4 .... 0.7
Dasher 0.3
Rabbit, Scirocco 0.6

11—STARTER, R&R OR RENEW
Exc Below 0.7
Dasher 0.6
Rabbit, Scirocco 0.4

12—STARTER SOLENOID, RENEW
Types 1 & 3 .... 1.1
Type 4 .... 0.9
Dasher 0.9
Rabbit, Scirocco 0.6

13—STARTER BENDIX DRIVE, RENEW
Exc Below 1.6
Dasher 1.1
Rabbit, Scirocco 0.9

14—STARTER, R&R & OVERHAUL
Includes: Replace armature, bendix drive, solenoid switch and bushing in trans case.
Exc Below 3.4
Dasher 1.8
Rabbit, Scirocco 1.6

15—STARTER BRUSHES, RENEW
Exc Below 1.1
Dasher 1.0
Rabbit, Scirocco 0.8

16—STARTER ARMATURE, RENEW
Types 1 & 3 .... 1.9
Type 4 .... 2.1

17—VOLTAGE REGULATOR, RENEW
All Models 0.3

18—ALTERNATOR, R&R OR RENEW
Type 1—
Engine Removed 1.0
Engine In Car ③2.0
Type 4—
Exc Below ①3.5
Square Back ①3.8
Dasher ②0.8
Rabbit, Scirocco ②0.8
①*Includes R&R Engine.*
②*Includes Check Alternator & Regulator Output.*
③*With Air Cond, Add* *0.5*

19—ALTERNATOR, R&R & OVERHAUL
Type 4—
Exc Below ①5.2
Square Back ①5.5
Type 1—
Engine Removed 2.0
Engine In Car ②3.0
Dasher 1.5
Rabbit, Scirocco 1.5
①*Includes R&R Engine*
②*With Air Cond, Add* *0.5*

20—ALTERNATOR DIODES, RENEW
Alternator removed.
Type 4—
One 0.7
All 1.0

21—ALTERNATOR BEARINGS, RENEW
Alternator removed.
Type 4 .... 0.7

22—ALTERNATOR BRUSHES, RENEW
Alternator removed
Type 4 .... 0.5

23—ALTERNATOR RUBBER BUSHINGS, RENEW
Dasher 1.2
Rabbit, Scirocco 1.2

24—GENERATOR, RENEW
Type 1 .... 1.0
Type 3 .... 0.7

25—GENERATOR, R&R & OVERHAUL
Includes: Turn down commutator and replace all necessary parts
Type 1 .... 2.7
Type 3 .... 1.7

26—GENERATOR REGULATOR, RENEW
Includes: Check and adjust
Type 1 .... 0.3
Type 3 .... 0.4

27—GENERATOR ARMATURE, RENEW
Type 1 .... 1.8
Type 3 .... 1.4

28—GENERATOR BRUSHES, RENEW
Type 1 .... 1.5
Type 3 .... 1.0

Fuel, Intake & Exhaust Systems, Emission Controls—TIME

OPERATION INDEX

Carburetor, R&R Or Renew *1*
Carburetor, R&R & Overhaul *2*
Fuel Pump, R&R Or Renew *3*
Fuel Tank, R&R Or Renew *4*
Choke Cable, Renew *5*
Automatic Choke Heater Element, Renew *6*
Fuel Pump Relay, Renew *7*
Pressure Regulator, Renew *8*
Throttle Valve Switch, Renew *9*
Pressure Sensor, Renew *10*
Auxiliary Air Regulator, Renew *11*
Fuel Injectors, Renew *12*
Intake Manifold, Renew *13*
Exhaust Manifold, Renew *14*
Muffler Pipe, Renew *15*
Front Exhaust Pipe, Renew *16*
Tail Pipe, Renew *17*
Muffler, Renew *18*
Catalytic Converter, Renew *19*
Pressure Regulator Valve, Renew *20*
Air Pump, R&R Or Renew *21*
Anti-Backfire Valve, Renew *22*
Pressure Relief Valve, Renew *23*
Temperature Sensor, Renew *24*

1—CARBURETOR, R&R OR RENEW
Type 1 .... 0.6
Type 3—
One 0.7
Both 1.3

(Continued)

Fuel, Intake & Exhaust Systems, Emission Controls—TIME Cont'd

Dasher 0.5
Rabbit, Scirocco 0.5

2—CARBURETOR, R&R & OVERHAUL
Type 1—
Manual Choke 1.2
Automatic Choke 1.5
Type 3—
One 1.7
Both 2.6
Dasher 1.5
Rabbit, Scirocco 1.5

3—FUEL PUMP, R&R OR RENEW
Exc Below 0.5
Elect W/Fuel Injection 0.3
Dasher 0.3
Rabbit, Scirocco 0.3

4—FUEL TANK, R&R OR RENEW
Type 1 ....0.5
Type 3—
Exc Below 0.6
Station Wagon 2.3
Type 4 ....2.6
Dasher 0.8
Rabbit, Scirocco 1.8

5—CHOKE CABLE, RENEW
Type 1—
Exc Below 0.5
Ghia 0.9

6—AUTOMATIC CHOKE HEATER ELEMENT, RENEW
All Models 0.3

7—FUEL PUMP RELAY, RENEW
W/Fuel Injection 0.2

8—PRESSURE REGULATOR, RENEW
Includes: R&R engine cover plate
W/Fuel Injection 0.5

9—THROTTLE VALVE SWITCH, RENEW
Includes: Adjust
W/Fuel Injection 0.3

10—PRESSURE SENSOR, RENEW
W/Fuel Injection 0.3

11—AUXILIARY AIR REGULATOR, RENEW
W/Fuel Injection 0.3

12—FUEL INJECTORS, RENEW
W/Fuel Injection—
Both, One Side 0.5
Both, Both Sides 0.8

13—INTAKE MANIFOLD, RENEW
Type 1 ....1.7
Types 3 & 4 ....1.0
Dasher 0.8
Rabbit, Scirocco 1.2

14—EXHAUST MANIFOLD, RENEW
Dasher ①1.0
Rabbit, Scirocco ①1.2
①*To Drill Out Studs, Add 0.3*

15—MUFFLER PIPE, RENEW
Types 1,3,4 ....0.3

16—FRONT EXHAUST PIPE, RENEW
Dasher 0.5
Rabbit, Scirocco 0.8

17—TAIL PIPE (ONE), RENEW
Types 1,3,4 ....0.3
Dasher 0.2
Rabbit, Scirocco 0.2

18—MUFFLER, RENEW
Types 1 & 3 ....①1.3
Type 4 ....①0.8
Dasher—
Front 0.7
Rear 0.4
Rabbit, Scirocco—
Front 0.5
Rear 0.3
①*With Air Cond, Add 0.5*

19—CATALYTIC CONVERTER, RENEW
Rabbit, Scirocco 0.8

20—PRESSURE REGULATOR VALVE, RENEW
Rabbit, Scirocco 0.2

21—AIR PUMP, R&R OR RENEW
Rabbit, Scirocco 0.4

22—ANTI-BACKFIRE VALVE, RENEW
Rabbit, Scirocco 0.2

23—PRESSURE RELIEF VALVE, RENEW
Rabbit, Scirocco 0.2

24—TEMPERATURE SENSOR, RENEW
Rabbit, Scirocco 0.3

Engine Cooling & Heater System (Air Cooled ENGINE)—TIME

OPERATION INDEX

Cooling Fan, R&R Or Renew 1
Fan Housing, R&R Or Renew 2
Crankshaft Pulley, R&R Or Renew 3
Generator Or Alternator Pulley, Renew 4
Cooling Air Regulator Or Control Cable, Renew 5
Thermostat, Renew 6
Heater Flexible Pipe, Renew 7
Heater Control Cable, Renew 8
Heater Exchanger, Renew 9

1—COOLING FAN, R&R OR RENEW
Type 1 ....1.0
Type 3—
W/Air Condition 4.4
L/Air Condition 3.5
Type 4 ....0.8

2—FAN HOUSING, R&R OR RENEW
Type 1—
W/Air Condition 2.8
L/Air Condition 2.0
Type 3—
W/Air Condition 4.6
L/Air Condition 3.7
Type 4 ....4.4

3—CRANKSHAFT PULLEY, R&R OR RENEW
Type 1—
W/Air Condition 1.0
L/Air Condition 0.5
Type 3—
W/Air Condition 3.4
L/Air Condition 3.0
Type 4 ....0.8

4—GENERATOR OR ALTERNATOR PULLEY, RENEW
Type 1 ....0.3
Type 3 ....0.4
Type 4 ....0.5

5—COOLING AIR REGULATOR OR CONTROL CABLE, RENEW
Type 1 Regulator, Each—
W/Air Condition 3.1
L/Air Condition 2.3
Type 4, Control Cable 0.4

6—THERMOSTAT, RENEW
Type 1 & 4 ....0.4
Type 3 ....0.3

7—HEATER FLEXIBLE PIPE, RENEW
Types 1 & 4, Each 0.2
Type 3, Each 0.4

8—HEATER CONTROL CABLE, RENEW
Type 1 ....0.8
Type 3 ....0.6
Type 4 ....0.5

9—HEAT EXCHANGER, RENEW
Type 1, Each 0.8
Type 3, Each 1.2
Type 4, Each ①1.0
①*Includes R&R Muffler*

Engine Cooling & Heater System (Water Cooled ENGINE)—TIME

OPERATION INDEX

Radiator & Rubber Mounts, R&R Or Renew 1
Coolant Expansion Tank, Renew 2
Radiator Hose, Renew 3
Water Pump, R&R Or Renew 4
Water Pump Pulley, Renew 5
Belt, Renew 6
Thermostat, Renew 7
Fan & Motor, Renew 8
Fan Relay, Renew 9
Fan Thermo Switch, Renew 10
Heater Assy, R&R Or Renew 11
Heater Core, Renew 12
Heater Hose, Renew 13
Heater Control Cable, Renew 14
Heater Valve, Renew 15
Blower Assy, Renew 16

1—RADIATOR & RUBBER MOUNTS, R&R OR RENEW
All Models 1.1

2—COOLANT EXPANSION TANK, RENEW
All Models 0.2

3—RADIATOR HOSE, RENEW
One 0.3
All 0.5

4—WATER PUMP, R&R OR RENEW
All Models 0.9

5—WATER PUMP PULLEY, RENEW
All Models 0.3

6—BELT, RENEW
All Models 0.2

7—THERMOSTAT, RENEW
All Models 0.4

8—FAN & MOTOR, RENEW
All Models 0.2

9—FAN RELAY IN FUSE BOX, RENEW
All Models 0.2

10—FAN THERMO SWITCH, RENEW
All Models 0.2

11—HEATER ASSY, R&R OR RENEW
All Models 1.3

12—HEATER CORE, RENEW
All Models ①0.7
①*For Models With Console, Add Additional Time.*

13—HEATER HOSE, RENEW
One 0.2
Both 0.3

(Continued)

Engine Cooling & Heater System (Water Cooled ENGINE)—TIME Cont'd

14—HEATER CONTROL CABLE, RENEW
Dasher 0.6
Rabbit, Scirocco 0.7

15—HEATER VALVE, RENEW
All Models 0.3

16—BLOWER ASSY, RENEW
All Models 1.2

Engine (Air COOLED)—TIME

OPERATION INDEX

Engine, R&R 1
Engine, R&R & Overhaul 2
Cylinder Head, R&R Or Gasket, Renew 3
Valves, Grind 4
One Valve, Renew & Grind 5
Valve Spring (One), Renew 6
Rocker Arm Cover Gaskets, Renew 7
Push Rod (One Side), Renew 8
Push Rod Tubes And/Or Seals, Renew 9
Rocker Arm & Shaft Assy, Renew Or Overhaul 10
Cam Followers (All), R&R Or Renew 11
Valves, Adjust 12
Camshaft & Timing Gear, Renew 13
Oil Pump, Gasket Or Gears. Renew 14
Oil Cooler, Renew 15
Piston(S), Ring(S) Or Cylinder Unit(S), Renew 16
Rings & Rod Bearings, Renew 17
Rings, Crankshaft Bearings & Rod Bearings, Renew & Grind Valves 18
Connecting Rod Bearings And/ Or Crankshaft Bearings, Renew 19
Crankshaft, Renew 20
Crankshaft Oil Seal (At Flywheel, Renew 21

1—ENGINE, R&R
Type 1—
 1965-66 ....1.5
 1967 & Later—
  Exc Below 1.3
  Auto Stick 1.6
Type 3—
 Exc Below 1.5
 Auto Trans 2.0
Type 4—
 Exc Below 2.7
 Square Back Sedan 3.0

—NOTE—
To Renew Engine, Add *0.7*
With Air Cond, Add *1.3*

2—ENGINE, R&R & OVERHAUL
Includes: Disassemble completely, clean, inspect and replace all worn and damaged parts, plastigage bearings and grind valves.

—NOTE—
For Air Condition, Add *1.3*
Type 1 ....①14.0
Type 3 ....②16.5
Type 4—
 Exc Below 17.3
 Square Back Sedan 17.6
①*For Auto Stick Shift, Add* *0.3*
②*For Auto Trans, Add* *0.5*

3—CYLINDER HEAD R&R OR GASKET, RENEW
Includes: R&R engine.
Type 1—
 1965-66—
  One Side ③4.0
  Both Sides ③5.0
 1967 & Later—
  One Side ①③3.8
  Both Sides ①③4.8
Type 3—
 One Side ②④4.3
 Both Sides ②④5.3
Type 4—
 Exc Below—
  One Side 5.5
  Both Sides 6.5
 Square Back Sedan—
  One Side 5.8
  Both Sides 6.8
①*For Auto Stick Shift, Add* *0.3*
②*For Auto Trans, Add* *0.5*
③*For Air Cond, Add-*
 1965-67 ....*1.3*
 1968 & Later *1.0*
④*For Air Cond, Add* *1.6*

4—VALVES, GRIND
Includes: Minor tune-up
Type 1—
 One Side ①②5.3
 Both Sides ①②7.0
Type 3—
 One Side ③④6.1
 Both Sides ③④7.9
Type 4—
 Exc Below—
  One Side 6.9
  Both Sides 8.6
 Square Back Sedan—
  One Side 7.2
  Both Sides 8.9
①*For Auto Stick Shift, Add* *0.3*
②*For Air Cond, Add*
 1965-67 ....*1.3*
 1968 & Later *1.0*
③*For Auto Trans, Add* *0.5*
④*For Air Cond, Add* *1.6*

5—ONE VALVE, RENEW & GRIND
Type 1 ....①②4.2
Type 3 ....③④4.5
Type 4—
 Exc Below 5.7
 Square Back Sedan 6.0
①*For Auto Stick Shift, Add* *0.3*
②*For Air Cond, Add*
 1965-67 ....*1.3*
 1968 & Later *1.0*
③*For Auto Trans, Add* *0.5*
④*For Air Cond, Add* *1.6*

6—VALVE SPRING (ONE), RENEW
All Models 0.8

7—ROCKER ARM COVER GASKETS, RENEW
All Models—
 One Side 0.2
 Both Sides 0.4

8—PUSH RODS (ONE SIDE), RENEW
Does not include remove engine. Includes adjust valves.
All Models 0.7

9—PUSH ROD TUBES AND/OR SEALS, RENEW
Includes: R&R engine.
Type 1—
 1965-66—
  One Side ③4.0
  Both Sides ③5.0
 1967 & Later—
  One Side ①③3.8
  Both Sides ①③4.8
Type 3—
 One Side ②④4.3
 Both Sides ②④5.3
Type 4
 Exc Below—
  One Side 5.5
  Both Sides 6.5
 Square Back Sedan—
  One Side 5.8
  Both Sides 6.8
①*For Auto Stick Shift, Add* *0.3*
②*For Auto Trans, Add* *0.5*
③*For Air Cond, Add*
 1965-67 ....*1.3*
 1968 & Later *1.0*
④*For Air Cond, Add* *1.6*

10—ROCKER ARM & SHAFT ASS'Y, RENEW OR OVERHAUL
All Models—
 One Side 0.8
 Both Sides 1.6

11—CAM FOLLOWERS (ALL), R&R OR RENEW
Includes: R&R engine

—NOTE—
For Air Cond, Add *1.3*
Type 1—
 1965-66 ....①9.5
 1967 & Later ①9.3
Type 3 ....②10.5
Type 4—
 Exc Below 11.7
 Square Back Sedan 12.0
①*For Auto Stick Shift, Add* *0.3*
②*For Auto Trans, Add* *0.5*

12—VALVES, ADJUST
All Models 0.5

13—CAMSHAFT AND TIMING GEAR, RENEW
—NOTE—
With Air Cond, Add *1.3*
Type 1—
 1965-66 ....①9.5
 1967 & Later ①9.3
Type 3 ....②10.5
Type 4—
 Exc Below 11.7
 Square Back Sedan 12.0
①*For Auto Stick Shift, Add* *0.3*
②*For Auto Trans, Add* *0.5*

14—OIL PUMP, GASKET OR GEARS, RENEW
Type 1 ....1.0
Type 3 ....①②3.7
Type 4 ....③1.8
①*Includes R&R Engine.*
②*For Auto Trans, Add* *0.5*
③*Engine Out.*

15—OIL COOLER, RENEW
—NOTE—
For Air Cond. Add *1.3*
Type 1 ....2.3
Type 3—
 To Ch 0193603 ....①②4.4
 From Ch 0193603 ....1.5
Type 4—
 Exc Below ①4.5
 Square Back Sedan ①4.8
①*Includes R&R Engine, Muffler Intake Manifold And Fan Housing.*
②*For Auto Trans, Add* *0.5*

16—PISTON(S), RING(S) OR CYLINDER UNIT(S), RENEW
Includes: R&R engine

—NOTE—
For Air Cond, Add *1.3*
Type 1—
 1965-66—
  One 4.8
  All 7.9
 1967 & Later—
  One ①4.6
  All ①7.7
Type 3—
 One ②5.1
 All ②8.8
Type 4—
 Exc Below—
  One 6.3
  All 9.5
 Square Back Sedan—
  One 6.6
  All 9.8
①*For Auto Stick Shift, Add* *0.3*
②*For Auto Trans, Add* *0.5*

17—RINGS & ROD BEARINGS, RENEW
Includes: Minor tune-up & plastigage & R&R engine

(Continued)

Engine (Air COOLED)—TIME Cont'd

—NOTE—

For Air Cond, Add *1.3*
Type 1 .... ①12.5
Type 3 .... ②15.0
Type 4—
Exc Below 15.7
Square Back Sedan 16.0
①*For Auto Stick Shift, Add* *0.3*
②*For Auto Trans, Add* *0.5*

18—RINGS, C'SHAFT & ROD BEARINGS, RENEW & GRIND VALVES

Includes: Minor tune-up & plastigage & R&R engine

—NOTE—

For Air Cond, Add *1.3*
Type 1 .... ①14.0
Type 3 .... ②16.5
Type 4—
Exc Below 17.2
Square Back Sedan 17.5
①*For Auto Stick Shift, Add* *0.3*
②*For Auto Trans, Add* *0.5*

19—CONN ROD BEARINGS &/OR C'SHAFT BEARINGS, RENEW

Includes plastigage

—NOTE—

For Air Cond, Add *1.3*
Type 1 .... ①11.0
Type 3 .... ②12.0
Type 4—
Exc Below 13.2
Square Back Sedan 13.5
①*For Auto Stick Shift, Add* *0.3*
②*For Auto Trans, Add* *0.5*

20—CRANKSHAFT, RENEW

—NOTE—

For Air Cond, Add *1.3*
Type 1 .... ①11.0
Type 3 .... ②12.0
Type 4—
Exc Below 13.2
Square Back Sedan 13.5
①*For Auto Stick Shift, Add* *0.3*
②*For Auto Trans, Add* *0.5*

21—CRANKSHAFT OIL SEAL (AT FLYWHEEL), RENEW

All Models ①2.5
①*For Air Cond, Add* *1.3*

Engine (Water COOLED)—TIME

OPERATION INDEX

Engine, R&R *1*
Complete Short Block, Renew *2*
Engine Block, Renew *3*
Exchange Engine, Renew *4*
Cylinder Head, Renew *5*
Cylinder Head, Renew With Exchange Head *6*
Valves, Grind *7*
Cylinder Head Cover Gasket, Renew *8*
Valves, Adjust *9*
Camshaft, Renew *10*
Camshaft Sprocket, Renew *11*
Camshaft Oil Seal, Renew *12*
Intermediate Shaft Sprocket, Renew *13*
Intermediate Shaft, Renew *14*
Intermediate Shaft Guide Oil Seal, Renew *15*
Spur Belt Or Pulley, Renew *16*
Spur Belt Cover, Renew *17*
Cam Followers, Renew *18*
Pistons & Rods, Renew *19*
Piston Rings, Renew *20*
Crankshaft, Renew *21*
Crankshaft Rear Oil Seal, Renew *22*
Crankshaft Front Oil Seal, Renew *23*
Crankshaft Pulley, Renew *24*
Oil Pan, R&R Or Renew *25*
Oil Pump, Renew *26*
Oil Filter, Renew *27*

1—ENGINE, R&R

Includes remove & install radiator, motor mounts, starter motor. Disconnect & reconnect all linkages & cables, coolant hoses, ignition wires & exhaust pipe. Remove & install hood on Dasher.

Dasher 3.0
Rabbit, Scirocco 3.8

2—COMPLETE SHORT BLOCK, RENEW

Includes transfer all necessary engine components and perform minor tune-up.

Includes R & R Engine—
Dasher 9.0
Rabbit, Scirocco 9.5
After Engine Is Removed—
Dasher 6.0
Rabbit & Scirocco 6.5

3—ENGINE BLOCK, RENEW

Includes partially disassemble & reassemble engine, check & adjust valve timing & perform minor tune-up.

Includes R & R Engine—
Dasher 10.0
Rabbit, Scirocco 10.5
After Engine Is Removed—
Dasher 7.0
Rabbit, Scirocco 7.5

4—EXCHANGE ENGINE, RENEW

Includes R&R engine, replace generator, clutch & air cleaner and perform minor tune-up.

Dasher 5.8
Rabbit, Scirocco 6.3

5—CYLINDER HEAD, RENEW

Includes remove & install spur belt, check & adjust valve clearance & timing.

Dasher 3.5
Rabbit, Scirocco 4.0

6—CYLINDER HEAD, RENEW WITH EXCHANGE HEAD

Includes R&R cylinder head & replace all necessary units, check & adjust valve clearance & timing.

Dasher 3.0
Rabbit, Scirocco 3.5

7—VALVES, GRIND

Includes remove & install camshaft, both manifolds, all valves & grind or replace as necessary. Replace valve stem seals

All Models 5.5

8—CYLINDER HEAD COVER GASKET, RENEW

All Models 0.2

9—VALVES, ADJUST

All Models 0.6

10—CAMSHAFT, RENEW

Includes replace cam follower discs if necessary. Check & adjust valve timing.

All Models 1.5

11—CAMSHAFT SPROCKETS, RENEW

Includes remove & install v belt, spur belt and cover, check & adjust valve timing.

All Models 1.0

12—CAMSHAFT OIL SEAL, RENEW

Includes remove & install v belt, spur belt & cover, camshaft sprocket, check & adjust valve timing.

All Models. 1.2

13—INTERMEDIATE SHAFT SPROCKET, RENEW

Includes remove & install v belt, spur belt, crankshaft pulley, water pump pulley, check & adjust valve timing.

All Models. 1.5

14—INTERMEDIATE SHAFT, RENEW

Includes R & R engine, v belt, spur belt & cover, fuel pump, distributor & adjust valve timing.

Dasher 4.2
Rabbit & Scirocco 4.7

15—INTERMEDIATE SHAFT GUIDE OIL SEAL, RENEW

Includes, with engine in car, R&R v belt, spur belt & cover, water pump pulley, intermediate shaft sprocket, adjust valve timing

All Models 1.4

16—SPUR BELT OR PULLEY, RENEW

All Models 0.8

17—SPUR BELT COVER, RENEW

All Models 0.3

18—CAM FOLLOWERS, RENEW

Includes R&R spur belt, camshaft, check & adjust valve clearance & valve timing.

All Models 2.0

19—PISTONS & RODS, RENEW

Includes R&R cylinder head & manifolds, v belt, spur belt, oil pan & oil pump.

All Models 3.9

20—PISTON RINGS, RENEW

All Models 4.5

21—CRANKSHAFT, RENEW

Includes remove & install oil pan, oil pump, spur belt cover, spur belt, crank pulley, front & rear seal flanges, clutch & flywheel

Includes R & R Engine—
Dasher 5.3
Rabbit, Scirocco 5.8
After Engine Is Removed—
Dasher 2.5
Rabbit, Scirocco 2.5

22—CRANKSHAFT REAR OIL SEAL, RENEW

Includes remove & install flywheel & clutch or driving plate.

Includes R & R Engine—
Dasher 3.6
Rabbit, Scirocco 4.1
After Engine Is Removed—
Dasher 0.8
Rabbit, Scirocco 0.8

23—CRANKSHAFT FRONT OIL SEAL, RENEW

Includes remove & install v belt, spur belt & cover, crankshaft pulley, intermediate shaft sprocket, check & adjust valve timing.

All Models 1.1

24—CRANKSHAFT PULLEY, RENEW

All Models 0.3

25—OIL PAN, R&R OR RENEW

Dasher 1.2
Rabbit, Scirocco 1.0

26—OIL PUMP, RENEW

Dasher 1.5
Rabbit, Scirocco 1.3

27—OIL FILTER, RENEW

All Models 0.3

Clutch, Mounts & Transmissions—TIME

OPERATION INDEX

Flywheel, R&R Or Renew *1*
Clutch Or Disc, Renew *2*
Pilot Bearing, Renew (Clutch Out) *3*
Clutch Cross Shaft, R&R Or Renew *4*
Clutch Cable, Renew *5*
Clutch Pedal, Adjust *6*
Engine Mounts, Renew *7*
Rear Axle & Transmission Assy, R&R Or Renew *8*
Transmission, R&R Or Renew *9*
Gear Carrier Gasket, Renew *10*
Manual Trans Case, Renew *11*
Main Drive Shaft Oil Seal, Renew *12*
Gear Shaft Housing, Gasket Or Bushing, Renew *13*

(Continued)

Clutch, Mounts & Transmissions—TIME Cont'd

Oil Pan Gasket, Renew 14
Manual Trans, R&R & Overhaul 15
Selector Fork Or Shaft, Renew 16
Reverse Shift Fork, Renew 17
Gearshift Or Selector Lever, Renew 18
Gearshift Tube, Renew 19

1—FLYWHEEL, R&R OR RENEW

Types 1 & 3 ....2.5
Type 4 ....3.4
Dasher 3.4
Rabbit, Scirocco 3.9

2—CLUTCH OR DISC, RENEW

Includes: R&R engine
Type 1—
1965-66 ....2.0
1967 & Later 1.8
Type 3 ....2.0
Dasher 3.1
Rabbit, Scirocco 3.6

3—PILOT BEARING, RENEW (CLUTCH OUT)

All Models 0.3

4—CLUTCH CROSS SHAFT, R&R OR RENEW

Types 1 & 3 ....①2.3
Rabbit, Scirocco 0.5
①*Includes R&R Engine.*

5—CLUTCH CABLE, RENEW

Dasher 0.3
Rabbit, Scirocco 0.2

6—CLUTCH PEDAL, ADJUST

Type 1 ....0.2
Type 3 ....0.4
Dasher 0.2
Rabbit Scirocco 0.2

7—ENGINE MOUNTS, RENEW

Type 1—
Trans, Front 0.8
Trans, Rear 2.0
Type 3—
Engine—
To July 1968 ....0.2
From July 1968 ....0.7
Transmission 0.6
Type 4—
Engine 2.0
Transmission 0.6
Dasher (Engine)—
Left 0.3
Center 0.2
Right 0.3
Left & Right 0.5
Dasher (Transmission) 1.0
Rabbit, Scirocco (Engine)—
Front Center 0.3
Right 0.4
Rabbit, Scirocco (Trans)—
Left 0.3
Center 0.4

8—REAR AXLE & TRANSMISSION ASSY, R&R OR RENEW

Includes: Bleed rear brakes
Type 1—
Auto Stick Shift—
W/Air Cond 4.2
L/Air Cond 2.9
Std Trans—
W/Air Cond 4.5
L/Air Cond 3.9
Type 3—
Auto Trans 4.6
Std Trans—
W/Air Cond 5.6
L/Air Cond 4.0
Type 4—
Exc Below 5.2
Square Back Sedan 5.5

9—TRANSMISSION, R&R OR RENEW

Dasher—
Manual 2.3
Automatic 3.0
Rabbit, Scirocco
Manual 2.1
Automatic 3.3

10—GEAR CARRIER GASKET, RENEW

Does not include R&R trans.
Type 1—
Exc Below 3.5
Auto Stick Shift 1.5
Type 3—
Std Trans 3.5
Auto Trans 0.9
Type 4 ....0.9

11—MANUAL TRANS CASE, RENEW

Type 1 ....①3.8
Type 3 ....①5.3
Dasher 7.3
Rabbit, Scirocco 5.6
①*With Rear Axle Removed*

12—MAIN DRIVE SHAFT OIL SEAL, RENEW

With engine removed
Types 1 & 3 ....0.3

13—GEAR SHIFT HOUSING, GASKET OR BUSHING, RENEW

With trans removed
Types 1 & 3 ....0.4

14—OIL PAN GASKET, RENEW

Exc Below 0.5
Dasher 0.5
Rabbit, Scirocco 0.4

15—MANUAL TRANS, R&R & OVERHAUL

Types 1 & 3 ....6.7

16—SELECTOR FORK OR SHAFT, RENEW

Includes: R&R trans
Types 1 & 3 ....4.3

17—REVERSE SHIFT FORK, RENEW

Includes: R&R trans.
Types 1 & 3 ....4.0

18—GEARSHIFT OR SELECTOR LEVER, RENEW

Types 1 & 3 ....0.6
Dasher 0.8
Rabbit, Scirocco 0.5

19—GEARSHIFT TUBE, RENEW

Dasher 0.6
Rabbit, Scirocco 0.3

Brakes, Steering, Suspension & Rear Axle—TIME

OPERATION INDEX

Brake Shoes Or Friction Pads, Renew 1
Master Cylinder, Renew 2
Master Cylinder, R&R & Overhaul 3
Wheel Cylinders, Renew 4
Wheel Cylinders, R&R & Overhaul 5
Caliper Assy, Renew 6
Caliper Assy, R&R & Overhaul 7
Bleed System 8
Brake Hose, Renew 9
Brake Disc Or Shield, Renew 10
Brake Drums, Renew 11
Brake Fluid Reservoir, Renew 12
Brake Pedal, Renew 13
Parking Brake Cable, Renew 14
Parking Brake Lever, Renew 15
Coupling Disc (Gear To Shaft), Renew 16
Steering Gear Assy, Renew 17
Steering Gear Assy, R&R & Overhaul 18
Pitman Arm, R&R Or Renew 19
Tie Rods, Renew 20
Idler Arm, R&R Or Renew 21
Steering Arm, R&R Or Renew 22
Steering Damper, Renew 23
Torsion Arm, Bushings (Or Needle Bearings), Renew 24
Torsion Bars, Renew 25
Track Control Arm, R&R Or Renew 26
Front Strut, R&R Or Renew 27
Front Susp Lower Control Arm, Renew 28
Front Suspension Platform, Renew 29
Steering Knuckle, Renew 30
Knuckle, Spring & Shock Assy, Renew 31
Rear Spring Plate, Renew 32
Coil Spring(S), R&R Or Renew 33
Ball Joints, Renew 34
Stub Axle, R&R Or Renew 35
Shock Absorber, Renew 36
Wheel Bearings, Renew 37
Wheel Bearings Oil Seal, Renew 38
Stabilizer Bar, Renew 39
Rear Axle Boot (Spit Type), Renew 40
Rear Axle & Transmission Assy, R&R Or Renew 41
Rear Axle Assy, R&R Or Renew 42
Rear Axle Rubber Bearing, Renew 43
Rear Stub Axle, Renew 44
Rear Strut, Renew 45
Ring Gear & Pinion, Renew 46
Differential Carrier, Renew 47
Differential Carrier Bearings, Renew 48
Pinion Bearings, Renew 49
Axle Shaft Tube, Renew 50
Axle Shaft, Renew 51

1—BRAKE SHOES OR FRICTION PADS, RENEW

Type 1—
Front—
Exc Below 1.6
Ghia W/Disc Brakes 1.0
Rear 1.1
Types 3 & 4 W/Disc Brakes—
Front 1.0
Rear 1.1
Dasher, Rabbit, Scirocco—
Front Pads, Each Wheel 0.4
Both Wheels 0.8
Rear Shoes, Each Wheel 0.9
Both Wheels 1.6

2—MASTER CYLINDER, RENEW

Includes bleed system
Types 1 & 3 ....1.3
Type 4 ....1.0
Dasher 0.8
Rabbit, Scirocco 0.8

3—MASTER CYLINDER, R&R & OVERHAUL

Includes bleed system
Types 1,3,4—
1965-66 ....1.9
1967 & Later 2.0
Dasher 1.1
Rabbit, Scirocco 1.1

4—WHEEL CYLINDERS, RENEW

Does not include bleed system.
Type 1—
Front Or Rear—
One 0.8
Both 1.4
All Four 2.8
Types 3 & 4—
Rear—
One 0.5
Both 1.0
Dasher, Rabbit, Scirocco—
Rear, One 0.7
Both 1.4

5—WHEEL CYLINDERS, R&R & OVERHAUL

Does not include bleed system.
Type 1—
Front Or Rear—
One 1.2
Both 2.1
All Four 4.2
Type 3 & 4—
Rear—
One 0.9
Both 1.7

(Continued)

Brakes, Steering, Suspension & Rear Axle—TIME Cont'd

Dasher, Rabbit, Scirocco—
Rear, One 0.9
Both 1.7

6—CALIPER ASSY, RENEW
Does not include bleed system.
Type 1—
One 0.5
Both 0.9
Types 3 & 4—
One 0.4
Both 0.7
Dasher, Rabbit, Scirocco—
One 0.4
Both 0.6

7—CALIPER ASSY, R&R & OVERHAUL
Does not include bleed system
Type 1—
One 1.2
Both 2.2
Types 3 & 4—
One 1.1
Both 2.0
Dasher, Rabbit, Scirocco—
One 0.8
Both 1.4

8—BLEED SYSTEM
Types 1,3,4—
1965-66 ....0.5
1967 & Later—
Front Or Rear 0.3
Both 0.5
Dasher, Rabbit, Scirocco 0.5

9—BRAKE HOSE, RENEW
Each 0.6

10—BRAKE DISC OR SHIELD, RENEW
All Models—
One 0.9
Both 1.6

—NOTE—
To Renew Shield, Add 0.2

11—BRAKE DRUMS, RENEW
Types 1,2,3—
Front Or Rear, Each 0.4
Dasher, Rabbit, Scirocco—
Rear, One 0.6
Both 1.0

12—BRAKE FLUID RESERVOIR, RENEW
Includes bleed system
Types 1 & 3 ....0.7
Type 4 ....0.8
Dasher 0.7
Rabbit, Scirocco 0.7

13—BRAKE PEDAL, RENEW
Type 1 ....1.5
Type 3—
Std Trans 1.7
Auto Trans 0.7
Type 4 ....1.2
Dasher 0.3
Rabbit, Scirocco 0.4

14—PARKING BRAKE CABLE, RENEW
Types 1 & 3 ....1.0
Type 4 ....0.8
Dasher 1.2
Rabbit, Scirocco 1.5

15—PARKING BRAKE LEVER, RENEW
Type 1 ....0.5
Type 3 ....0.6
Type 4 ....0.4
Dasher 0.6
Rabbit, Scirocco 0.5

16—COUPLING DISC (GEAR TO SHAFT), RENEW
Type 1 ....0.6
Types 3 & 4 ....0.5

17—STEERING GEAR ASSY, RENEW
Includes adjust strg & toe-in.
Type 1—
Exc Below 1.5
Super Beetle 1.2
Type 3 ....1.7
Type 4 ....1.0
Dasher 1.2
Rabbit, Scirocco 1.2

18—STEERING GEAR ASSY, R&R & OVERHAUL
Includes adjust strg & toe-in.
Type 1—
Exc Below 3.2
Super Beetle 2.9
Type 3 ....3.4
Type 4 ....2.7

19—PITMAN ARM, R&R OR RENEW
Includes adjust toe-in
Type 1 ....1.0
Type 3 ....0.9
Type 4 ....0.7

20—TIE RODS, RENEW
Includes adjust toe-in
Types 1 & 3 Except Below—
One 0.9
Both 1.4
Super Beetle—
Outer—
One 0.4
Both 0.7
Inner ....(1)1.0
Type 4—
Outer—
One ....(1)0.8
Both ....(1)1.0
Inner ....(1)1.0
Dasher, Rabbit, Scirocco—
Rod, One ....(2)0.4
Both ....(2)0.6
End ....(2)0.3
(1)*Includes:R&R Steering Linkage*
(2)*Does Not Include Alignment.*

21—IDLER ARM, R&R OR RENEW
Super Beetle 0.2

22—STEERING ARM (ONE), R&R OR RENEW
Includes R&R brake disc & caliper, adjust bearings and toe-in
Type 3 ....0.9

23—STEERING DAMPER, RENEW
Types 1 & 3 Exc 0.5
Super Beetle 0.4
Type 4 ....0.3

24—TORSION ARM BUSHINGS (OR NEEDLE BEARINGS), RENEW
Includes adjust camber & toe-in.
Type 1 ....3.3
Type 3—
1965-67 ....3.4
1968 & Later 3.7

25—TORSION BARS, RENEW
Front—
Type 1, Each ....(1)2.4
Type 3—
1965-67 ....(1)2.5
1968 & Later ....(1)2.8
Rear—
Types 1 & 3, Each 2.4
(1)*Includes Adjust Camber & Toe-In.*

26—TRACK CONTROL ARM, R&R OR RENEW
Includes check camber & toe-in
Super Beetle—
One Side 0.4
Both Sides 0.7
Type 4—
One Side 0.5
Both Sides 0.8

27—FRONT STRUT, R&R OR RENEW
Includes bleed front brakes.
1971—
One Side 1.0
Both Sides 1.4

28—FRONT SUSP LOWER CONTROL ARM, RENEW
Does not include wheel alignment.
Rabbit, Scirocco, Dasher—
One 0.7
Both 1.0

29—FRONT SUSPENSION PLATFORM, RENEW
Dasher 1.7

30—STEERING KNUCKLE, RENEW
Does not include wheel alignment.
Rabbit, Scirocco—
One 1.1
Both 2.1

31—KNUCKLE, SPRING & SHOCK ASSY, RENEW
Dasher—
One 1.2
Both 1.9

32—REAR SPRING PLATE, RENEW
Type 1 ....1.5
Type 3 ....1.9

33—COIL SPRING(S), R&R OR RENEW
Front—
Types 1 & 4—
One 0.5
Both 0.9
Rear—
Type 4—
One 1.0
Both 1.8
Dasher, Rabbit, Scirocco—
One 0.5
Both 0.9

34—BALL JOINTS, RENEW
Type 1 (Exc Super Beetle)—
Upper 0.8
Lower 0.9
Both 1.3
Super Beetle—
One Side 0.9
Both Sides 1.5
Type 3—
Upper Or Lower 0.9
Both 1.3
Type 4—
One Side 0.9
Both Sides 1.5
Rabbit, Scirocco, Dasher—
One Side 0.5
Both Sides 0.9

35—STUB AXLE, R&R OR RENEW
Exc Below—
One Side ....(1)1.3
Both Sides ....(1)2.4
Super Beetle—
One Side ....(2)0.8
Both Sides ....(2)1.4
Type 4—
One Side ....(2)1.1
Both Sides ....(2)1.9
(1)*Includes:Adjust Camber & Toe-In*
(2)*Includes:Check Toe-In*

36—SHOCK ABSORBER (ONE), RENEW
Front—
Exc Below 0.4
Super Beetle ....(1)1.6
Type 4 ....(1)1.6
Dasher 1.5
Rabbit, Scirocco 1.0
Rear—
Exc Below 0.4
Type 4 ....0.5
Dasher, Rabbit, Scirocco 0.5
(1)*Includes:R&R Strut & Bleed Front Brake.*

(Continued)

Brakes, Steering, Suspension & Rear Axle—TIME Cont'd

37—WHEEL BEARINGS (ONE WHEEL), RENEW

Front—
Type 1—
One 0.6
Both 0.8
Types 3 & 4—
One 0.7
Both 0.9
Dasher—
One Side 1.6
Both Sides 2.7
Rabbit, Scirocco—
One Side 1.1
Both Sides 2.1
Rear—
Types 1,3,4 .... 0.8
Dasher, Rabbit, Scirocco—
One Side 0.8
Both Sides 1.3

38—WHEEL BEARINGS OIL SEALS, RENEW

Front—
Type 1—
One Wheel 0.5
Both Wheels 0.9
Types 3 & 4—
One Wheel 0.6
Both Wheels 1.1
Rear—
Types 1,3,4, One Side 0.8
Dasher, Rabbit, Scirocco—
One Side 0.7
Both Sides 1.2

39—STABILIZER BAR, RENEW

Type 1—
Exc Below 0.6
Super Beetle 0.3
Type 3 .... 1.8
Type 4 .... 0.4
Dasher 0.6

40—REAR AXLE BOOT (SPLIT TYPE), RENEW

Types 1,3,4—
One Side 0.6
Both Sides 1.0

41—REAR AXLE & TRANSMISSION ASSY, R&R OR RENEW

Includes bleed rear brakes.
Type 1—
Auto Stick Shift—
W/Air Cond 4.2
L/Air Cond 2.9
Std Trans—
W/Air Cond 4.5
L/Air Cond 3.9
Type 3—
Auto Trans 4.6
Std Trans—
W/Air Cond 5.6
L/Air Cond 4.0
Type 4—
Exc Below 5.2
Square Back Sedan 5.5

42—REAR AXLE ASSY, R&R OR RENEW

Includes remove & install wheels, drums, stub axles, rubber bearings and bleed brakes
Dasher 2.0
Rabbit, Scirocco 2.0

43—REAR AXLE RUBBER BEARING, RENEW

Dasher, Rabbit, Scirocco—
One 0.7
Both 1.2

44—REAR STUB AXLE, RENEW

Dasher, Rabbit, Scirocco—
One 0.7
Both 1.3

45—REAR STRUT, RENEW

Rabbit, Scirocco—
One 0.3
Both 0.5

46—RING GEAR & PINION, RENEW

Types 1 & 3 Exc 10.2
Type 3 Auto Trans 10.7
Type 4—
Exc Below 11.4
Square Back Sedan 11.7
Dasher 6.5
Rabbit, Scirocco—
Manual Trans 6.0
Auto Trans 6.5

47—DIFFERENTIAL CARRIER, RENEW

Includes R&R trans
Type 3 W/Auto Trans 6.2
Type 4 W/Auto Trans 6.7

48—DIFFERENTIAL CARRIER BEARINGS, RENEW

Types 1 & 3 Exc Below 6.7
Type 3 W/Auto Trans 7.2
Type 4—
Exc Below 7.9
Square Back Sedan 8.4

49—PINION BEARINGS, RENEW

Types 1,3,4 .... 8.7
Dasher 6.7
Rabbit, Scirocco 5.5

50—AXLE SHAFT TUBE (ONE), RENEW

Types 1,3,4 .... 2.4

51—AXLE SHAFT (ONE), RENEW

Types 1,3,4 Exc Below 5.5
Double-Jointed Rear Axle—
Exc Type 4 .... 0.7
Type 4 .... 0.9

Speedometer, W/S Wiper & Instruments—TIME

OPERATION INDEX

Speedometer Cable, Renew 1
Speedometer Head, Renew 2
W/S Wiper Motor, Renew 3
W/S Wiper Crank, Renew 4
W/S Wiper Linkage, Renew 5
Fuel Gauge (Dash Unit), Renew 6
Fuel Tank Gauge, Renew 7
Oil Pressure Switch, Renew 8
Tachometer, Renew 9
Temperature Gauge (Dash Unit) Renew 10
Headlight Switch, Renew 11
Headlamp Dimmer Switch, Renew 12
Stop Light Switch, Renew 13
Turn Signal Switch, Renew 14
Hazard Flasher Switch, Renew 15

1—SPEEDOMETER CABLE, RENEW

All Models 0.4

2—SPEEDOMETER HEAD, RENEW

Type 1—
1965-67—
Exc Below 0.4
Ghia 0.9
1968 & Later 0.5
Types 3 & 4 .... 0.4
Dasher 0.7
Rabbit, Scirocco 0.9

3—W/S WIPER MOTOR, RENEW

Type 1—
1965-67 .... 0.6
1968-69 .... 0.7
1970 & Later 0.9
Type 3—
1965-70 .... 1.3
1971 & Later 0.9
Dasher 0.5
Rabbit, Scirocco 0.5

4—W/S WIPER CRANK, RENEW

Type 1 .... 1.0
Type 3 .... 1.5
Type 4 .... 1.2

5—W/S WIPER LINKAGE, RENEW

Dasher 0.5
Rabbit, Scirocco 0.5

6—FUEL GAUGE (DASH UNIT), RENEW

Type 1 .... 0.5
Type 3 .... 0.4
Type 4 .... 1.0
Dasher 0.6
Rabbit, Scirocco 0.9

7—FUEL TANK GAUGE, RENEW

Types 1,3,4 .... 0.3
Dasher 0.3
Rabbit, Scirocco 0.8

8—OIL PRESSURE SWITCH, RENEW

All Models 0.3

9—TACHOMETER, RENEW

Rabbit, Scirocco 0.9

10—TEMPERATURE GAUGE (DASH UNIT), RENEW

Dasher 0.6
Rabbit, Scirocco 0.9

11—HEADLIGHT SWITCH, RENEW

Type 1—
1965-67 .... 0.4
1968 & Later 0.5
Type 3—
Push-Button 1.2
Push-Pull 0.4
Type 4 .... 0.3
Dasher 0.4
Rabbit, Scirocco 0.9

12—HEADLAMP DIMMER SWITCH, RENEW

Type 1 .... (1)0.8
Type 3 .... (1)1.1
Type 4 .... (1)0.4
Dasher, Rabbit, Scirocco—
On Floor 0.4
On Turn Indicator Switch 0.9
(1)*Includes R&R Direction Indicator Switch*

13—STOP LIGHT SWITCH, RENEW

Types 1,3,4 .... 0.5
Dasher 0.6
Rabbit, Scirocco 0.6

14—TURN SIGNAL SWITCH, RENEW

Type 1—
1965-67 .... 0.8
1968 & Later 0.9
Type 3 .... 1.0
Type 4 .... 0.4
Dasher 0.7
Rabbit, Scirocco 0.5

15—HAZARD FLASHER SWITCH, RENEW

Type 1 .... 0.7
Type 3 .... 0.8
Type 4 .... 0.3
Dasher 0.4
Rabbit, Scirocco 0.3

IDENTIFICATION

ALL MODELS.................................. 459

ILLUSTRATIONS

FIG 1 – ENGINE – CYLINDER BLOCK
FIG 2 – ENGINE – CRANKSHAFT, PISTONS & FLYWHEEL
FIG 3 – ENGINE – BELT TRANSMISSION
FIG 4 – ENGINE – CYLINDER HEAD & CAMSHAFT
FIG 5 – TRANSMISSION
FIG 6 – FRONT SUSPENSION & STEERING

OPERATION TIMES

A

Alternator.. 466
Automatic Transmission.................... 467
Axle Shaft.. 469

B

Brakes.. 468

C

Cables (Ignition)................................ 466
Calipers.. 468
Camshaft.. 467
Carburetor.. 466
Catalytic Converter.......................... 466
Clutch.. 467
Coil, Ignition.. 466
Compression Test.......................... 466
Connecting Rods.......................... 467
Cooling System.......................... 466
Cylinder Block.......................... 467
Cylinder Head.......................... 467

D

Dash Gauges.......................... 469
Differential.......................... 469
Disc Brakes.......................... 468
Distributor.......................... 466

E

Emission Controls.......................... 466
Engine Assembly.......................... 467
Engine Mountings.......................... 467
Engine Oiling.......................... 467
Engine Tune-Up.......................... 466
Exhaust System.......................... 466

F

Flywheel.......................... 467
Front Suspension.......................... 468
Fuel Gauges.......................... 469
Fuel Pump.......................... 466
Fuel Tank.......................... 466

G

Generator.......................... 466

H

Hand Brake.......................... 468
Headlight Switch.......................... 469
Heater.......................... 466
Hose (Brake).......................... 468
Hose (Radiator).......................... 466
Hydraulic Brakes.......................... 468

I

Ignition.......................... 466
Ignition Coil.......................... 466
Ignition Switch.......................... 466
Intake Manifold.......................... 466

L

Light Switches.......................... 469

M

Master Cylinder.......................... 468
Muffler.......................... 466

O

Oil Gauge.......................... 469
Oiling, Engine.......................... 467
Oil Pan.......................... 467
Oil Pump.......................... 467
Overdrive.......................... 467

P

Parking Brake.......................... 468
Piston Rings.......................... 467
Pistons.......................... 467
Power Brake.......................... 468

R

Radiator.......................... 466
Radiator Hose.......................... 466
Rear Axle.......................... 469
Regulator.......................... 466
Rocker Arms.......................... 467

S

Shocks (Front).......................... 468
Shocks (Rear).......................... 468
Speedometer.......................... 469
Springs (Front).......................... 468
Springs (Rear).......................... 468
Starting Motor.......................... 466
Steering Gear.......................... 468
Steering Linkage.......................... 468
Switches (Light).......................... 469
Synchro-Mesh Trans.......................... 467

T

Tachometer.......................... 469
Temperature Gauge.......................... 469
Thermostat.......................... 466
Timing Case Cover.......................... 467
Timing Gears.......................... 467
Track Bar.......................... 468
Transmission, Manual.......................... 467
Transmission, Automatic.......................... 467
Tune-Up Engine.......................... 466

U

Universals.......................... 469

V

Vacuum Control Unit.......................... 466
Valve Lifters.......................... 467
Valve System.......................... 467

W

Water Pump.......................... 466
Wheel Cylinders.......................... 468
Windshield Wiper.......................... 469

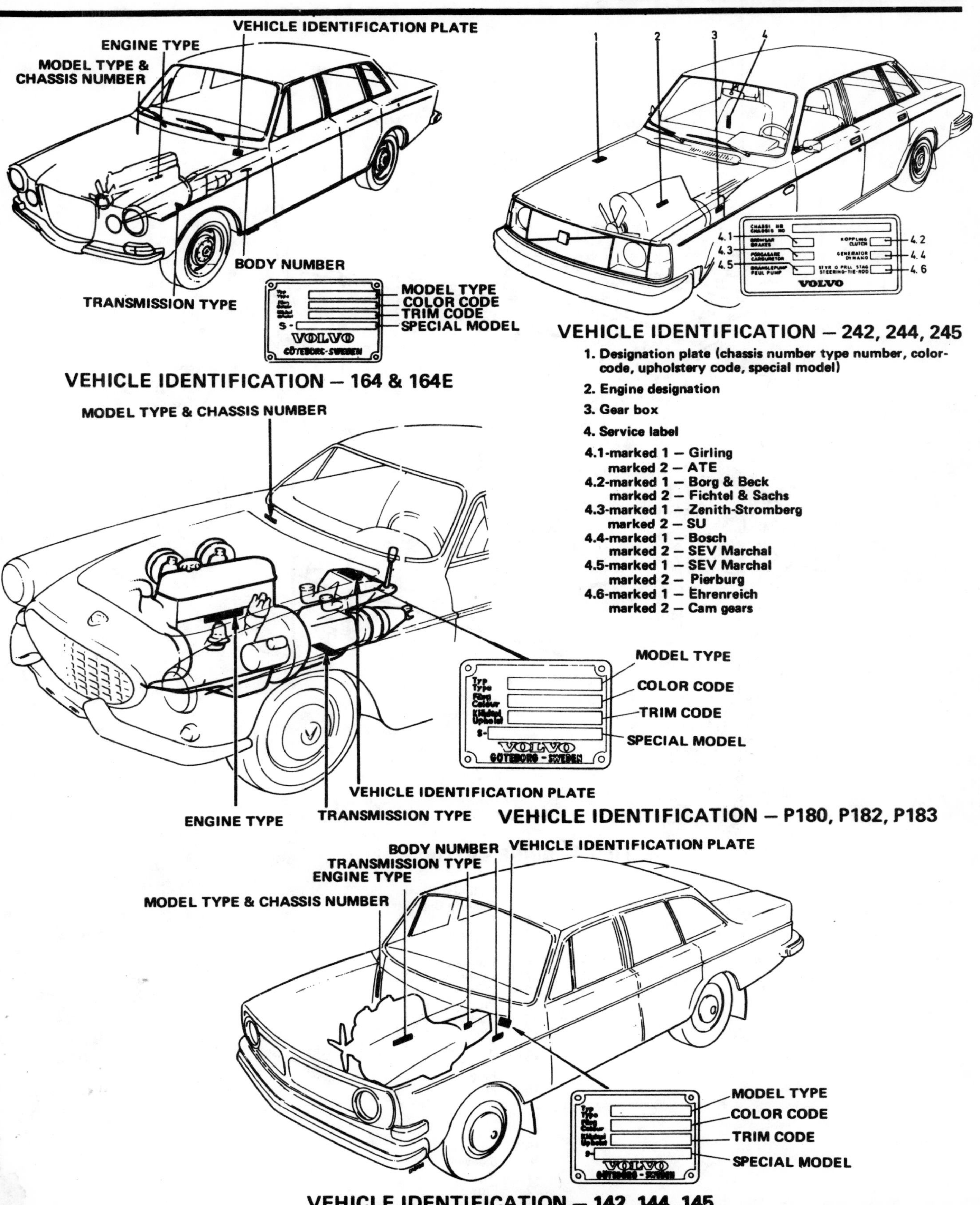

VEHICLE IDENTIFICATION — 164 & 164E

VEHICLE IDENTIFICATION — 242, 244, 245

1. Designation plate (chassis number type number, color-code, upholstery code, special model)
2. Engine designation
3. Gear box
4. Service label

4.1-marked 1 — Girling
marked 2 — ATE
4.2-marked 1 — Borg & Beck
marked 2 — Fichtel & Sachs
4.3-marked 1 — Zenith-Stromberg
marked 2 — SU
4.4-marked 1 — Bosch
marked 2 — SEV Marchal
4.5-marked 1 — SEV Marchal
marked 2 — Pierburg
4.6-marked 1 — Ehrenreich
marked 2 — Cam gears

VEHICLE IDENTIFICATION — P180, P182, P183

VEHICLE IDENTIFICATION — 142, 144, 145

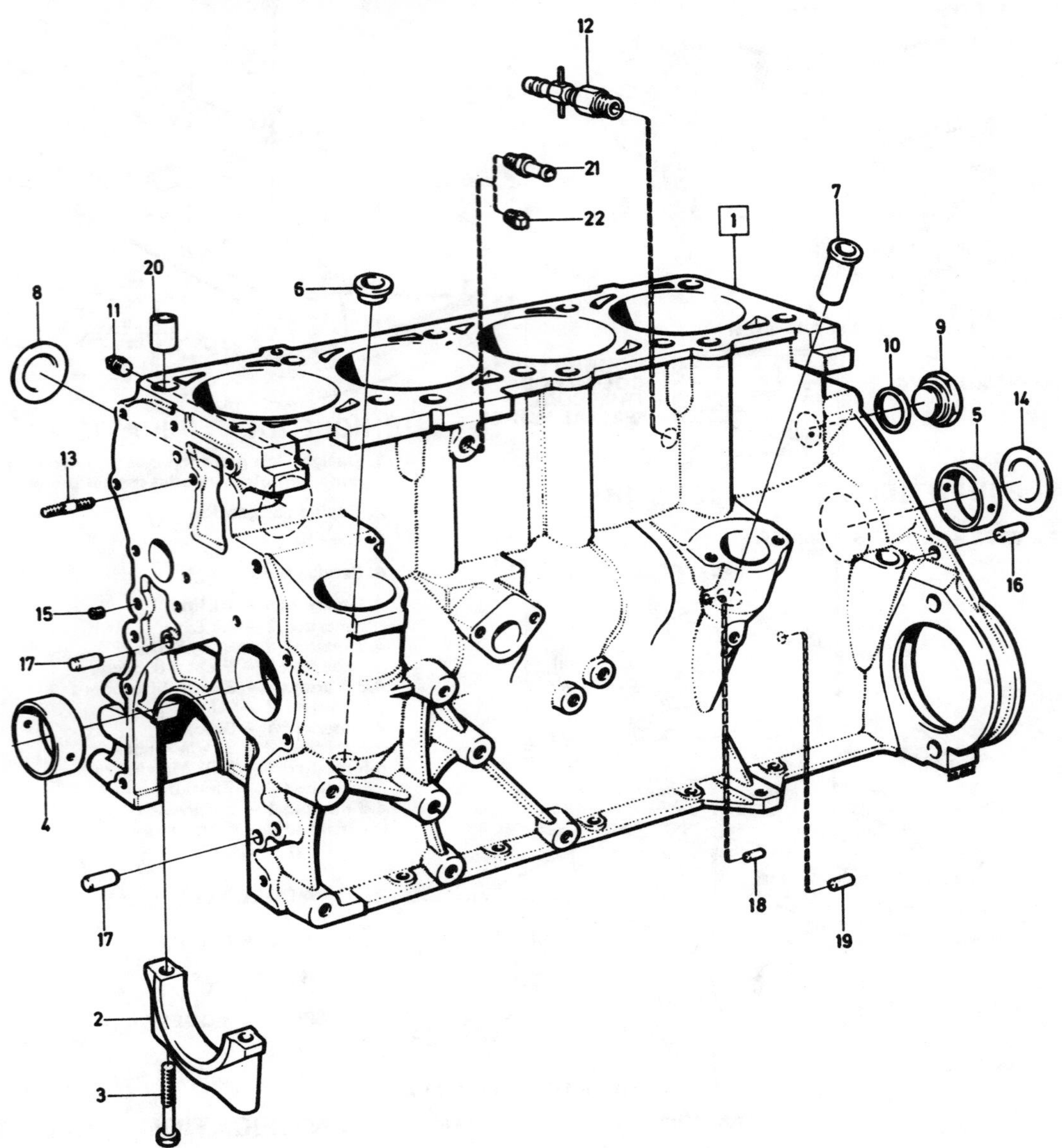

FIG 1 – ENGINE – CYLINDER BLOCK

1	Cylinder Block
2	Bearing Cap
3	Screw
4	Bushing
5	Bushing
6	Bushing
7	Bushing
8	Plug
9	Plug
10	Gasket
11	Plug
12	Drain Cock
13	Screw
14	Plug
15	Plug
16	Pin
17	Pin
18	Pin
19	Pin
20	Sleeve
21	Nipple
22	Plug

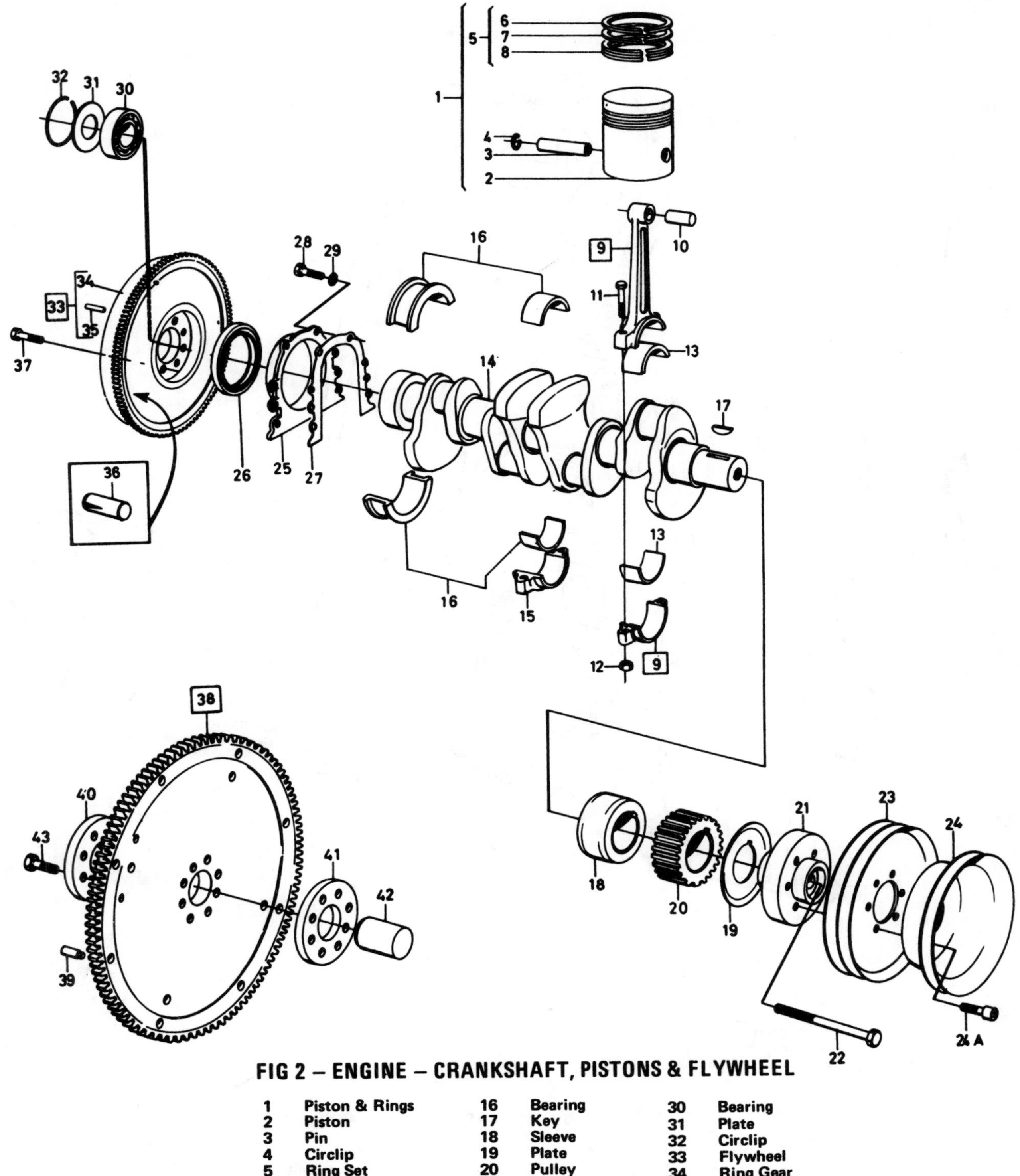

FIG 2 – ENGINE – CRANKSHAFT, PISTONS & FLYWHEEL

1	Piston & Rings	16	Bearing	30	Bearing
2	Piston	17	Key	31	Plate
3	Pin	18	Sleeve	32	Circlip
4	Circlip	19	Plate	33	Flywheel
5	Ring Set	20	Pulley	34	Ring Gear
6	Ring	21	Hub	35	Pin
7	Ring	22	Screw	36	Pin
8	Ring	23	Pulley	37	Screw
9	Connecting Rod	24	Pulley	38	Flywheel
10	Bushing	24A	Screw	39	Pin
11	Bolt	25	Flange	40	Plate
12	Nut	26	Seal	41	Flange
13	Bearing	27	Gasket	42	Bushing
14	Crankshaft	28	Screw	43	Screw
15	Bearing Cap	29	Washer		

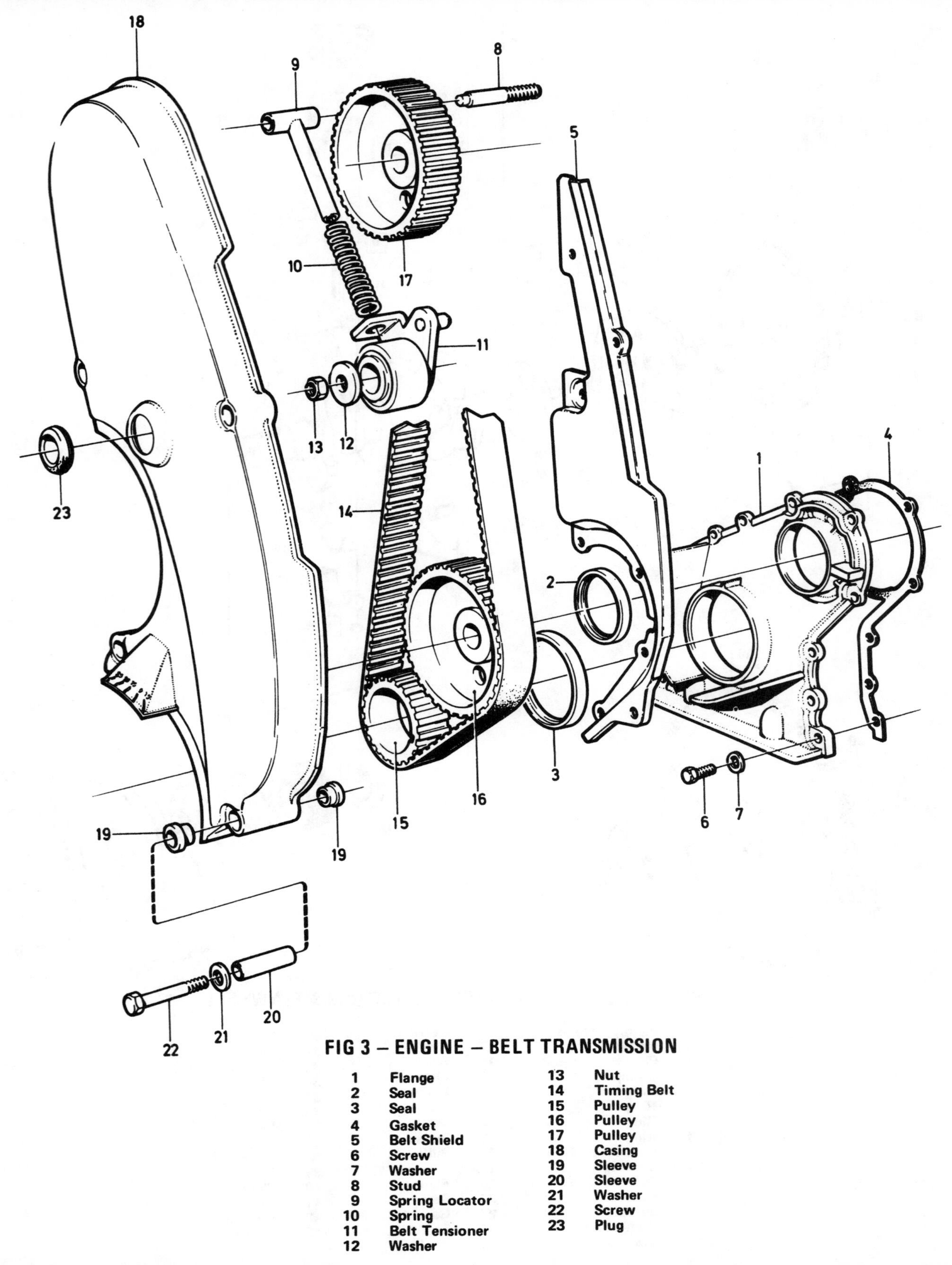

FIG 3 – ENGINE – BELT TRANSMISSION

1	Flange	13	Nut
2	Seal	14	Timing Belt
3	Seal	15	Pulley
4	Gasket	16	Pulley
5	Belt Shield	17	Pulley
6	Screw	18	Casing
7	Washer	19	Sleeve
8	Stud	20	Sleeve
9	Spring Locator	21	Washer
10	Spring	22	Screw
11	Belt Tensioner	23	Plug
12	Washer		

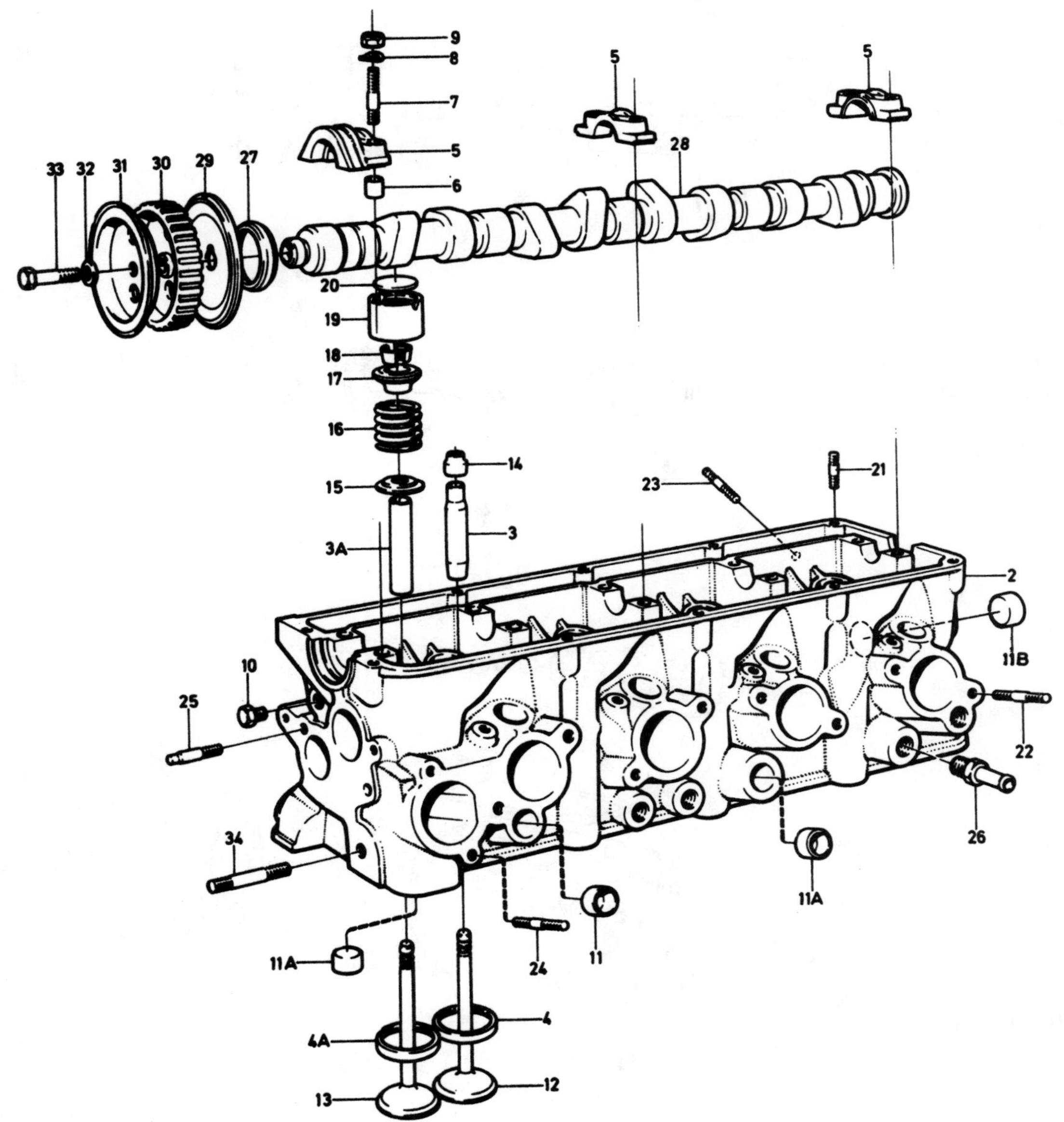

FIG 4 – ENGINE – CYLINDER HEAD & CAMSHAFT

- 2 Cylinder Head
- 3 Intake Valve Guide
- 3A Exhaust Valve Guide
- 4 Intake Valve Seat
- 4A Exhaust Valve Seat
- 5 Bearing Cap
- 6 Sleeve
- 7 Stud
- 8 Washer
- 9 Nut
- 10 Plug
- 11 Plug
- 11A Plug
- 11B Plug
- 12 Intake Valve
- 13 Exhaust Valve
- 14 Intake Valve Seal
- 15 Washer
- 16 Spring
- 17 Washer
- 18 Lock
- 19 Tappet
- 20 Washer
- 21 Stud
- 22 Stud
- 23 Stud
- 24 Stud
- 25 Stud
- 26 Nipple
- 27 Seal
- 28 Camshaft
- 29 Plate
- 30 Pulley
- 31 Plate
- 32 Washer
- 33 Screw
- 34 Stud

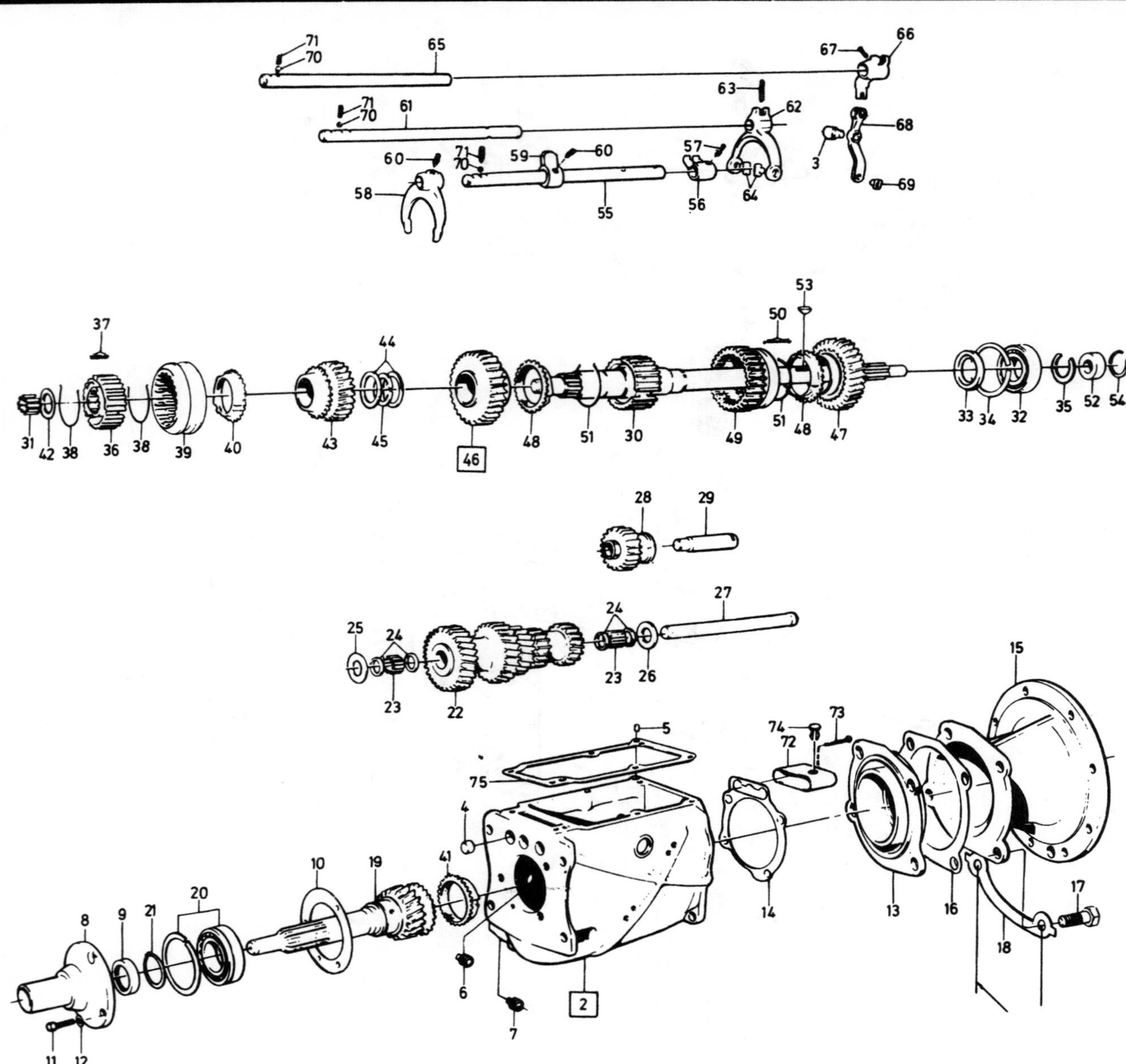

FIG 5 – TRANSMISSION

2	Housing	20	Bearing	39	Sleeve	58	Fork
3	Pin	21	Circlip	40	Cone	59	Dog
4	Plug	22	Gear	41	Cone	60	Screw
5	Pin	23	Roller	42	Circlip	61	Shift Rail
6	Plug	24	Ring	43	3rd Gear	62	Fork
7	Plug	25	Washer	44	Ring	63	Pin
8	Cover	26	Washer	45	Circlip	64	Pin
9	Seal Ring	27	Shaft	46	2nd Gear	65	Shift Rail
10	Gasket	28	Reverse Gear	47	1st Gear	66	Fork
11	Screw	29	Shaft	48	Cone	67	Screw
12	Ring	30	Mainshaft	49	Sleeve	68	Lever
13	Cover	31	Roller	50	Key	69	Pin
14	Gasket	32	Bearing	51	Ring	70	Ball
15	Flange	33	Ring	52	Cam	71	Spring
16	Gasket	34	Circlip	53	Key	72	Casing
17	Screw	35	Circlip	54	Circlip	73	Screw
18	Lockwasher	36	Synchronizer Hub	55	Shif Rail	74	Plug
19	Input Shaft	37	Key	56	Dog	75	Gasket
		38	Ring	57	Screw		

FIG 6 – FRONT SUSPENSION & STEERING

53 Wheel
54 Hub Cap Exc GL
55 Hub Cap, GL
56 Trim Ring
57 Chrome Nut
58 Outer Bearing Cone
59 Outer Bearing Roller
60 Inner Bearing Cone
61 Inner Bearing Roller
62 Oil Seal
63 Grease Cap
64 Knee Mount Crossmember
65 Hub
66 Brake Disc
67 Knuckle & Shock
68 Shock Insert Kit
69 Dust Cover
70 Spring
71 Upper Seat
72 Shock Mount Insulator
73 Control Arm
74 Ball Joint
75 Bushing
76 Bushing
77 Bracket
78 Stabilizer
79 Link
80 Bracket
81 Tie Rod
82 Tie Rod End
83 Boot
84 Gear Assy, Std
85 Gear Assy, Power
86 Rack
87 Pinion
88 Mainshift
89 Universal Joint
90 Coupling
91 Column Jacket
92 Wheel

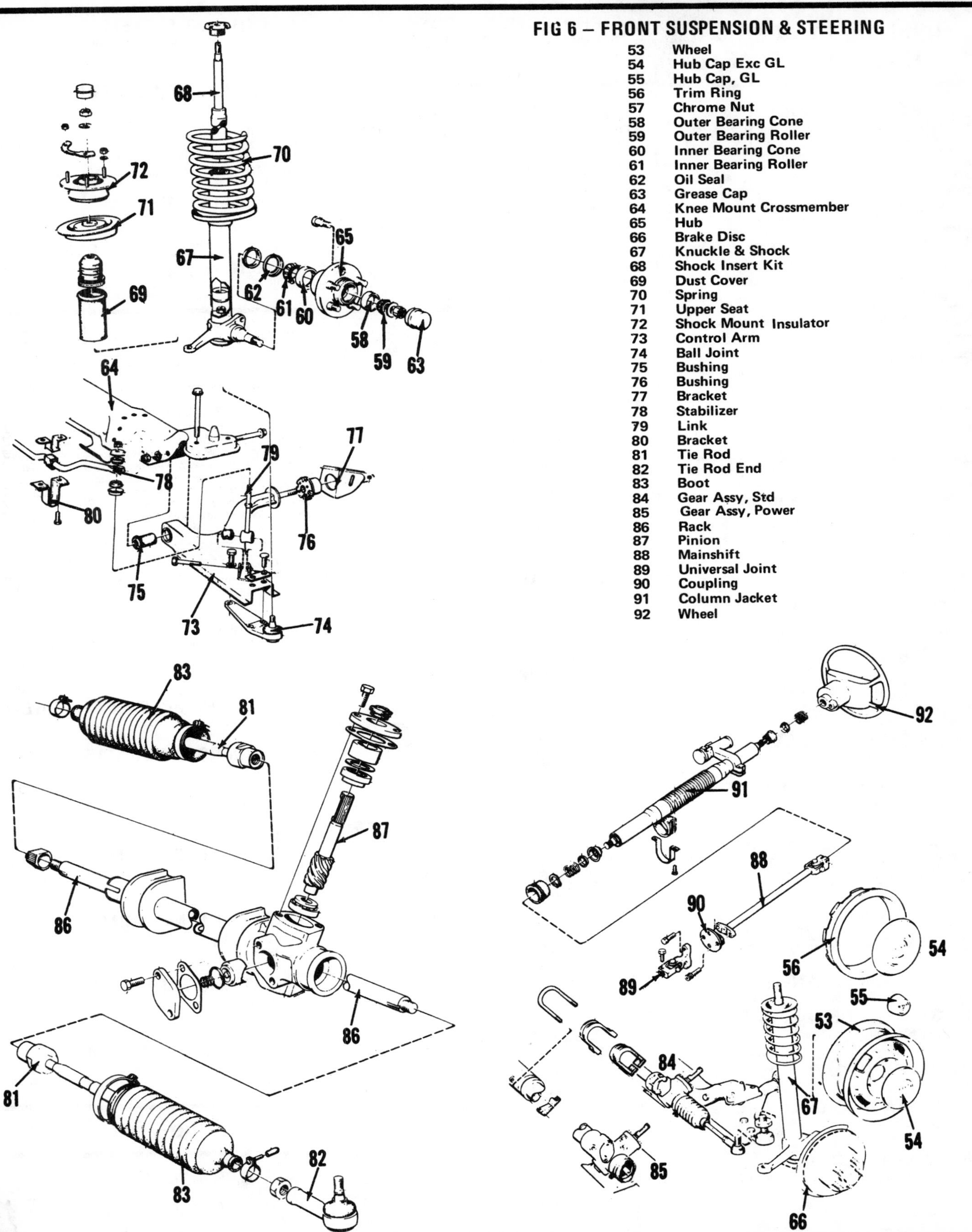

Ignition, Starting & Charging—TIME

OPERATION INDEX

Tune-Up, Minor 1
Tune-Up, Major 2
Compression Test 3
Distributor, R&R Or Renew 4
Distributor Cap, Renew 5
Ignition Cable Set, Renew 6
Vacuum Control Unit, Renew 7
Ignition Coil, Renew 8
Starter & Ignition Switch, Renew 9
Starter, R&R Or Renew 10
Starter Solenoid, Renew 11
Starter Bendix Drive, Renew 12
Starter, R&R & Overhaul 13
Voltage Regulator, Renew 14
Generator Or Alternator, R&R Or Renew 15
Protection Diode (Motorola), Renew 16

1—TUNE-UP, MINOR

Includes renew points, condenser and plugs, set spark timing and adjust carburetor idle.

B18, B20 Eng 1.5
B30 Eng 2.0

2—TUNE-UP, MAJOR

Includes:cHeck compression, clean or renew and adjust spark plugs. R&R distributor, renew points and condenser. Adjust ignition timing, carburetor and fan belts. Clean battery terminals and service air cleaner. Check coil and clean or renew fuel filter.

Exc Below 2.5
B20E Eng ①3.5
B30 Eng 3.5
①*Includes: Test & Adjust Injection System With Bosh Tester.*

3—COMPRESSION TEST

4 Cyl 0.4
6 Cyl 0.6

4—DISTRIBUTOR, R&R OR RENEW

All Models 0.6

5—DISTRIBUTOR CAP, RENEW

4 Cyl 0.2
6 Cyl 0.3

6—IGNITION CABLE SET, RENEW

4 Cyl 0.4
6 Cyl 0.5

7—VACUUM CONTROL UNIT, RENEW

All Models 0.8

8—IGNITION COIL, RENEW

All Models 0.3

9—STARTER & IGNITION SWITCH, RENEW

Exc Below 1.5
180 Series 1.8

10—STARTER, R&R OR RENEW

All Models 0.7

11—STARTER SOLENOID, RENEW

All Models 1.2

12—STARTER BENDIX DRIVE, RENEW

All Models 1.5

13—STARTER, R&R & OVERHAUL

All Models 2.7

14—VOLTAGE REGULATOR, RENEW

All Models 0.3

15—GENERATOR OR ALTERNATOR, R&R OR RENEW

Exc Below 0.5
B18 Eng 0.7

16—PROTECTION DIODE (MOTOROLA) RENEW

All Models 0.3

Fuel, Emission Controls, Intake & Exhaust Systems—TIME

OPERATION INDEX

Carburetor, R&R Or Renew 1
Carburetor, R&R & Overhaul 2
Fuel Pump, R&R Or Renew 3
Fuel Tank, R&R Or Renew 4
Choke Cable Assy, Renew 5
Emission Control Units, Renew 6
Injection System, Test 7
Control Unit, Renew 8
Injector, Renew 9
Pressure Sensor Or Throttle Switch, Renew 10
Fuel Pressure Regulator, Renew 11
Intake Manifold, Renew 12
Exhaust Manifold, Renew 13
Exhaust System Complete, Renew 14
Exhaust Pipe, Renew 15
Muffler, Renew 16
Catalytic Converter, Renew 17

1—CARBURETOR, R&R OR RENEW

All Models, One 1.2

—NOTE—

To R&R Second Carb, Add 0.8

2—CARBURETOR, R&R & OVERHAUL

Exc Below 2.7
Zenith Stromberg 2.0

3—FUEL PUMP, R&R OR RENEW

Exc Below 0.4
Fuel Injection Pump 2.1

4—FUEL TANK, R&R OR RENEW

All Models 1.7

5—CHOKE CABLE ASSY, RENEW

All Models 0.4

6—EMISSION CONTROL UNITS, RENEW

Air Pump 0.5
Diverter Valve 0.4
Canister Filter Exc 0.2
B20E Eng 0.4
E G R Valve 0.5
Anti-Backfire Valve 0.4
Solenoid Valve 0.4

7—INJECTION SYSTEM, TEST

All Models 1.3

8—CONTROL UNIT, RENEW

All Models 1.4

9—INJECTOR, RENEW

All Models, Each 1.7

10—PRESSURE SENSOR OR THROTTLE SWITCH, RENEW

All Models 1.5

11—FUEL PRESSURE REGULATOR, RENEW

All Models 0.2

12—INTAKE MANIFOLD, RENEW

Separate Type 1.9
Intake & Exhaust Assy—
4 Cyl 1.4
6 Cyl 1.6
Fuel Injection 1.5

13—EXHAUST MANIFOLD, RENEW

Separate Type 1.3
Intake & Exhaust Assy—
4 Cyl 1.4
6 Cyl 1.6

14—EXHAUST SYSTEM COMPLETE, RENEW

Exc Below 1.4
164 Series 1.6

15—EXHAUST PIPE, RENEW

Front—
All Models 1.1
Intermediate—
All Models 0.9
Outlet—
Exc Below 0.7
180 Series 0.3

16—MUFFLER, RENEW

All Models—
Front Or Rear 0.9

17—CATALYTIC CONVERTER, RENEW

All Models 0.8

Engine, Cooling & Heater Systems—TIME

OPERATION INDEX

Radiator, R&R Or Renew 1
Radiator Hoses, Renew 2
Water Pump, R&R Or Renew 3
Thermostat Or Gasket, Renew 4
Heater Core, Renew 5
Heater Blower Motor, Renew 6
Heater Temperature Control Valve, Renew 7
Heater Control Cable, Renew 8
Heater Hose, Renew 9

1—RADIATOR, R&R OR RENEW

Exc Below 0.5
B20 Engine Exc 0.6
W/Oil Cooler 0.8
B30 Engine Exc 0.7
W/Oil Cooler 0.9

2—RADIATOR HOSES, RENEW

Upper 0.3
Lower 0.4
Both 0.5

3—WATER PUMP, R&R OR RENEW

Exc Below 1.3
B18 Eng 1.2

4—THERMOSTAT OR GASKET, RENEW

All Models 0.4

5—HEATER CORE, RENEW

Exc Below 2.5
160-180-240-260 ....5.0

6—HEATER BLOWER MOTOR, RENEW

Exc Below 2.4
160-180-240-260 ....4.8

7—HEATER TEMP CONTROL VALVE, RENEW

Exc Below 1.2
180 Series 0.5

8—HEATER CONTROL CABLE, RENEW

Exc Below 0.5
180 Series 0.3

9—HEATER HOSE, RENEW

Each, Exc 0.6
180 Series 0.4

Engine—TIME

OPERATION INDEX

Engine, R&R 1
Engine (Short), Renew & Grind Valves 2
Bare Block Complete, Renew 3

(Continued)

Engine—TIME Cont'd

Cylinder Head Gasket, Renew 4
Cylinder Head, Renew 5
Valves, Grind 6
Rocker Arm Cover Gasket, Renew 7
Valve Rocker Arm Assy, Overhaul 8
Valve Lifters, Renew 9
Valve Lifters, Adjust 10
Oil Pump, R&R Or Renew 11
Oil Pan Or Gasket, R&R Or Renew 12
Timing Cover Or Gasket, Renew 13
Front Crankshaft Seal, Renew 14
Timing Gears Complete, Renew 15
Camshaft, R&R Or Renew 16
Piston Rings, Renew 17
Crankshaft Rear Main Oil Seal, Renew 18
Cylinder, Bore & Hone 19
Pistons, Renew 20
Connecting Rods, Renew 21
Crankshaft Pulley, Renew 22

1—ENGINE, R&R

Does not include transfer of any part of engine or replacement of special equipment.

Exc Below 5.0
B27 Eng 6.5

2—ENGINE (SHORT), RENEW & GRIND VALVES

4 Cyl 12.7
6 Cyl 13.4

3—BARE BLOCK COMPLETE, RENEW

4 Cyl 14.0
6 Cyl 16.0

4—CYLINDER HEAD GASKET, RENEW

4 Cyl 2.6
6 Cyl 3.0

5—CYLINDER HEAD, RENEW

Includes final adjustments & transfer parts

4 Cyl 5.0
6 Cyl 5.4

6—VALVES, GRIND

4 Cyl 5.7
6 Cyl 6.9

7—ROCKER ARM COVER GASKET, RENEW

4 Cyl 0.3
6 Cyl 0.5

8—VALVE ROCKER ARM ASSY, OVERHAUL

4 Cyl 1.7
6 Cyl 2.2

9—VALVE LIFTERS, RENEW

4 Cyl 3.1
6 Cyl 3.5

10—VALVE LIFTERS, ADJUST

4 Cyl 0.4
6 Cyl 0.5

11—OIL PUMP, R&R OR RENEW

4 Cyl 2.5
6 Cyl 2.7

12—OIL PAN OR GASKET, R&R OR RENEW

4 Cyl 2.1
6 Cyl 2.3

13—TIMING COVER OR GASKET, RENEW

4 Cyl 1.3
6 Cyl 1.8

14—FRONT CRANKSHAFT SEAL, RENEW

Exc Below 0.8
B18 Eng 1.3

15—TIMING GEARS COMPLETE, RENEW

4 Cyl 2.5
6 Cyl 3.0

16—CAMSHAFT, R&R OR RENEW

4 Cyl 6.9
6 Cyl 7.3

17—PISTON RINGS, RENEW

4 Cyl 7.0
6 Cyl 8.0

18—CRANKSHAFT REAR MAIN OIL SEAL, RENEW

All Models 4.5

19—CYLINDER BORE & HONE

Engine removed & disassembled.

All Models—
One 0.9
Each Additional 0.2

20—PISTONS, RENEW

4 Cyl 7.3
6 Cyl 8.3

21—CONNECTING RODS, RENEW

4 Cyl 7.3
6 Cyl 8.3

22—CRANKSHAFT PULLEY, RENEW

4 Cyl 0.5
6 Cyl 0.7

Clutch, Mounts & Transmissions—TIME

OPERATION INDEX

Flywheel, R&R Or Renew 1
Flywheel Ring Gear, Renew 2
Clutch Or Disc, Renew 3
Release Bearing, Renew 4
Clutch Pedal, Adjust 5
Clutch Master Cylinder, Renew 6
Slave Cylinder, Renew 7
Clutch Operating Cable, Renew 8
Engine Mounts, Renew 9
Transmission Assy, R&R Or Renew 10
Trans Rear Cover Or Gasket, Renew 11
Trans Oil Seals, Renew 12
Transmission, R&R & Overhaul 13
Overdrive To Trans Flange Gasket, Renew 14
Overdrive Solenoid, R&R Or Renew 15
Overdrive, R&R & Overhaul 16
Oil Pan Gasket, Renew 17
Front & Rear Bands, Adjust 18
Gearshift Or Selector Lever, Renew 19
Neutral Safety Switch, Renew 20
Throttle Cable, Renew 21

1—FLYWHEEL, R&R OR RENEW

Exc Below 2.9
180 Series 3.7
164 Series 3.2

2—FLYWHEEL RING GEAR, RENEW

Exc Below 3.1
180 Series 3.7
164 Series 3.2

3—CLUTCH OR DISC, RENEW

140 Series 2.5
180 Series 3.3
164 Series 2.8
240 Series 2.0

4—RELEASE BEARING, RENEW

Exc Below 2.0
180 Series 2.8
164 Series 2.3

5—CLUTCH PEDAL, ADJUST

All Models 0.4

6—CLUTCH MASTER CYLINDER, RENEW

180 Series 0.5

7—SLAVE CYLINDER, RENEW

180 Series 0.5

8—CLUTCH OPERATING CABLE, RENEW

All Models 1.0

9—ENGINE MOUNTS, RENEW

All Models—
Front, Each 1.0
Front, Both 1.4
Rear 0.6
All 1.8

10—TRANSMISSION ASSY, R&R OR RENEW

Manual—
140 Series 2.4
180 Series Exc 2.7
180E 2.9
164 ....2.6
240 ....2.4
Automatic—
All Models 3.5

11—TRANS REAR COVER OR GASKET, RENEW

All Models 1.4

12—TRANS OIL SEALS, RENEW

Front—
Exc Below 2.8
140 Series 2.6
180E 3.1
164 Series 2.9
Rear—
Manual Trans 1.4
Auto Trans 1.5

13—TRANSMISSION, R&R & OVERHAUL

Manual—
140 Series 4.6
180 Series Exc 4.8
180E 4.9
164 Series 4.6
240 Series 4.0
Automatic 10.0

14—OVERDRIVE TO TRANS FLANGE GASKET, RENEW

All Models 3.1

15—OVERDRIVE SOLENOID, R&R OR RENEW

180 Series 1.0

16—OVERDRIVE, R&R & OVERHAUL

180 Series 6.5

17—OIL PAN GASKET, RENEW

All Models 0.8

18—FRONT & REAR BANDS, ADJUST

All Models 1.2

19—GEARSHIFT OR SELECTOR LEVER, RENEW

Manual Trans—
Exc Below 1.1
140 Series 0.9
Auto Trans 0.6

20—NEUTRAL SAFETY SWITCH, RENEW

All Models 0.7

21—THROTTLE CABLE, RENEW

All Models 1.2

Brakes, Steering, Suspension, Universals & Rear Axle—TIME

OPERATION INDEX

Brake Shoes Or Friction Pads, Renew 1
Master Cylinder, Renew 2
Master Cylinder, R&R & Overhaul 3

(Continued)

Brakes, Steering, Suspension, Universals & Rear Axle—TIME Cont'd

Wheel Cylinders, Renew 4
Caliper Assy, Renew 5
Caliper Assy, R&R & Overhaul 6
Bleed System 7
Brake Hose, Renew 8
Hubs Or Bearings, Renew 9
Front Hub Bearings & Races, Renew 10
Power Brake Unit, Renew 11
Power Brake Unit, R&R & Overhaul 12
Vacuum Check Valve, Renew 13
Warning Light Switch Assy, Renew 14
Brake Pressure Limiting Valve, Renew 15
Hand Brake Cable, Renew 16
Hand Brake Lever, Renew 17
Hand Brake Shoes, Renew 18
Strg Coupling Or U-Moint, Renew 19
Steering Gear, R&R Or Renew 20
Steering Gear, R&R & Overhaul 21
Sector Shaft Seal, Renew 22
Servo Pump Or Bracket, Renew 23
Pitman Arm, Renew 24
Idler Arm Or Bracket Assy, Renew 25
Steering Rod, Renew 26
Tie Rod End(S), Renew 27
Front End Alignment 28
Ball Joints, Renew 29
Spindle, Renew 30
A-Frames, Renew 31
Shaft & Bushings, Renew 32
Crossmember Complete, Renew 33
Coil Spring(S) Or Spacer, Renew 34
Shock Absorbers, Renew 35
Front Sway Bar Or Bushings, Renew 36
Rear Track Bar Or Bushings, Renew 37
Torque Rods Or Bushings, Renew 38
Rear Support Arm Or Bushings, Renew 39
Universal Joint, R&R & Overhaul 40
Rear Axle Assy, R&R Or Renew 41
Rear Axle Assy, R&R & Overhaul 42
Limited Slip Assy, R&R & Overhaul 43
Pinion Oil Seal, Renew 44
Rear Axle Cover Gasket, Renew 45
Axle Shaft(S), R&R Or Renew 46

1—BRAKE SHOES OR FRICTION PADS, RENEW
Disc Type—
Both Front 0.5
Both Rear 0.5
All 0.8
Drum Type Rear—
Both 1.6

2—MASTER CYLINDER, RENEW
Exc Below 1.1
180 Series 0.5
240 Series 1.2

3—MASTER CYLINDER, R&R & OVERHAUL
Exc Below 1.8
180 Series 1.0
240 Series 1.9

4—WHEEL CYLINDERS, RENEW
All Models, Rear—
One 1.1
Both 1.6

5—CALIPER ASSY, RENEW
Front, One—
Exc Below 1.0
180 Series 0.9
Front, Both—
Exc Below 1.5
180 Series 1.2
Rear, One 1.1
Rear, Both 1.6

6—CALIPER ASSY, R&R & OVERHAUL
Front One—
Exc Below 2.0
180 Series 1.6
Front Both—
Exc Below 3.5
180 Series 2.6
Rear, One 1.6
Rear, Both 2.6

7—BLEED SYSTEM
Exc Below 0.7
180 Series 0.5

8—BRAKE HOSE, RENEW
Each 0.6

9—HUBS OR BEARINGS, RENEW
Each Side 1.6

10—FRONT HUB BEARINGS & RACES, RENEW
Both Sides 2.4

11—POWER BRAKE UNIT, RENEW
Exc Below 1.7
180 Series Exc 180E 1.0
180E 1.7
140 Series 1.8

12—POWER BRAKE UNIT, R&R & OVERHAUL
180 Series Exc 180E 1.8

13—VACUUM CHECK VALVE, RENEW
All Models 0.3

14—WARNING LIGHT SWITCH ASSY, RENEW
Exc Below 1.2
180 Series 1.0

15—BRAKE PRESSURE LIMITING VALVE, RENEW
One 0.5

16—HAND BRAKE CABLE, RENEW
Exc Below 1.7
180 Series Exc 180E 1.1
180E 1.7

17—HAND BRAKE LEVER, RENEW
All Models 0.8

18—HAND BRAKE SHOES, RENEW
Includes:bLeed hand brake system.
All Models 2.0

19—STEERING COUPLING OR U-JOINT, RENEW
Rubber Coupling, 180 Ser 0.6
U-Joint, 164 Series 3.0

20—STEERING GEAR, R&R OR RENEW
Manual 1.0
Power Exc 240 Series 1.1
240 Series 1.3

21—STEERING GEAR, R&R & OVERHAUL
Manual 2.1
Power Exc 240 Series 3.8
240 Series 4.0

22—SECTOR SHAFT SEAL, RENEW
All Models 0.9

23—SERVO PUMP OR BRACKET, RENEW
164 Series 0.8

24—PITMAN ARM, RENEW
All Models 0.7

25—IDLER ARM OR BRACKET ASSY, RENEW
All Models 0.7

—NOTE—
To Renew Bracket, Add 0.3

26—STEERING ROD, RENEW
All Models—
Each 0.6
Both 1.0

27—TIE ROD END(S), RENEW
Includes: Toe-in adjustment.
All Models—
Each 0.5
Both 0.8

28—FRONT END ALIGNMENT
All Models 1.1

29—BALL JOINTS, RENEW
Upper—
Each Side—
Exc Below 0.9
180 Series 0.7
Both Sides—
Exc Below 1.3
180 Series 1.0
Lower—
Each Side—
Exc Below 1.0
180 Series 0.7
Both Sides—
Exc Below 1.5
180 Series 1.3
Upper & Lower—
Each Side—
Exc Below 1.2
180 Series 0.9
Both Sides—
Exc Below 1.7
180 Series 1.6

30—SPINDLE, RENEW
One Side—
Exc Below 1.9
180 Series 1.7
Both Sides—
Exc Below 3.4
180 Series 3.0

31—A-FRAMES, RENEW
Upper—
Each Side—
Exc Below 0.9
180 Series 0.7
Both Sides—
Exc Below 1.4
180 Series 1.0
Lower—
Each Side 1.4
Both Sides 2.4
Upper & Lower—
Each Side—
Exc Below 1.9
180 Series 1.7
Both Sides—
Exc Below 3.0
180 Series 2.0

32—SHAFT & BUSHINGS, RENEW
All Models—
Upper—
One Side 1.1
Both Sides 1.8
Lower—
One Side 1.4
Both Sides 2.0

33—CROSSMEBER COMPLETE, RENEW
All Models 4.0

34—COIL SPRING(S) OR SPACER, RENEW
All Models—
Front—
Each 0.9
Both 1.4
Rear—
Each 0.6
Both 0.8

35—SHOCK ABSORBERS, RENEW
All Models—
Front—
Each 0.5
Both 0.8
Rear—
Each 0.6
Both 0.8

36—FRONT SWAY BAR OR BUSHINGS, RENEW
All Models 0.7

37—REAR TRACK BAR OR BUSHINGS, RENEW
All Models 0.5

38—TORQUE RODS OR BUSHINGS, RENEW
All Models—
Each 0.7
Both 1.1

(Continued)

Brakes, Steering, Suspension, Universals & Rear Axle—TIME Cont'd

39—REAR SUPPORT ARM OR BUSHINGS, RENEW

Each Side—
Exc Below 1.3
180 Series 0.8
Both Sides—
Exc Below 1.9
180 Series 1.4

40—UNIVERSAL JOINT, R&R & OVERHAUL

All Models 1.9

41—REAR AXLE ASSY, R&R OR RENEW

All Models 2.9

42—REAR AXLE ASSY, R&R & OVERHAUL

All Models 6.4

43—LIMITED SLIP ASSY, R&R & OVERHAUL

All Models 3.5

44—PINION OIL SEAL, RENEW

All Models 0.9

45—REAR AXLE GASKET, RENEW

All Models 0.6

46—AXLE SHAFTS, R&R OR RENEW

Each 1.5
Both 2.6

—NOTE—

To Renew Bearings, Add 0.3
To Renew Both Seals, Each Axle, Add 0.5

Speedometer, W/S Wipers, Switches & Instruments—TIME

OPERATION INDEX

Speedometer Cable, Renew 1
Speedometer Head, Renew 2
W/S Wiper Motor, Renew 3
W/S Wiper Arm Pivot, Renew 4
W/S Wiper Switchj, Renew 5
Fuel Gauge (Dash Unit, Renew 6
Fuel Tank Sending Unit, Renew 7
Oil Pressure Gauge, Renew 8
Oil Gauge Sending Unit, Renew 9
Temperature Gauge Sending Unit, Renew 10
Oil Temperature Gauge, Renew 11
Water Temperature Gauge, Renew 12
Tachometer, Renew 13
Headlight Switch, Renew 14
Headlamp Dimmer Switch, Renew 15
Stop Light Switch, Renew 16
Overdrive Switch, Renew 17
Direction Signal Switch, Renew 18
Hazard Flasher Switch, Renew 19

1—SPEEDOMETER CABLE, RENEW

Front Exc 0.8
180 Series 1.0
240 Series 0.6
Rear, 140 Series 0.5

2—SPEEDOMETER HEAD, RENEW

Exc Below 1.0
With Air Cond 1.5
Smiths 0.3

3—W/S WIPER MOTOR, RENEW

Front Exc 1.3
W/Air Cond 1.8
Rear, Sta Wgn 0.5

4—W/S WIPER ARM PIVOT ASSY, RENEW

One, Exc 1.6
W/Air Cond 2.1

5—W/S WIPER SWITCH, RENEW

All Models 0.6

6—FUEL GAUGE (DASH UNIT) RENEW

Exc Below 1.0
180 Series (Smiths) 0.3

7—FUEL TANK SENDING UNIT, RENEW

Exc Below 0.4
180 Series (Smiths) 0.6

8—OIL PRESSURE GAUGE, RENEW

180 Series (Smiths) 0.3

9—OIL GAUGE SENDING UNIT, RENEW

All Models 0.4

10—TEMPERATURE GAUGE SENDING UNIT, RENEW

All Models 0.4

11—OIL TEMPERATURE GAUGE, RENEW

180 Series (Smiths)—
Exc Below 1.0
Electrical 0.3

12—WATER TEMPERATURE GAUGE, RENEW

Exc Below 1.0
Smiths Electrical 0.3

13—TACHOMETER, RENEW

180 Series (Smiths) 0.3

14—HEADLIGHT SWITCH, RENEW

All Models 0.6

15—HEADLAMP DIMMER SWITCH, RENEW

All Models 0.4

16—STOP LIGHT SWITCH, RENEW

All Models 0.2

17—OVERDRIVE SWITCH, RENEW

180 Series 0.6

18—DIRECTION INDICATOR (SIGNAL SWITCH) RENEW

All Models 0.4

19—HAZARD FLASHER SWITCH, RENEW

All Models 0.5

Latest Jack & Lift Points for Import Cars

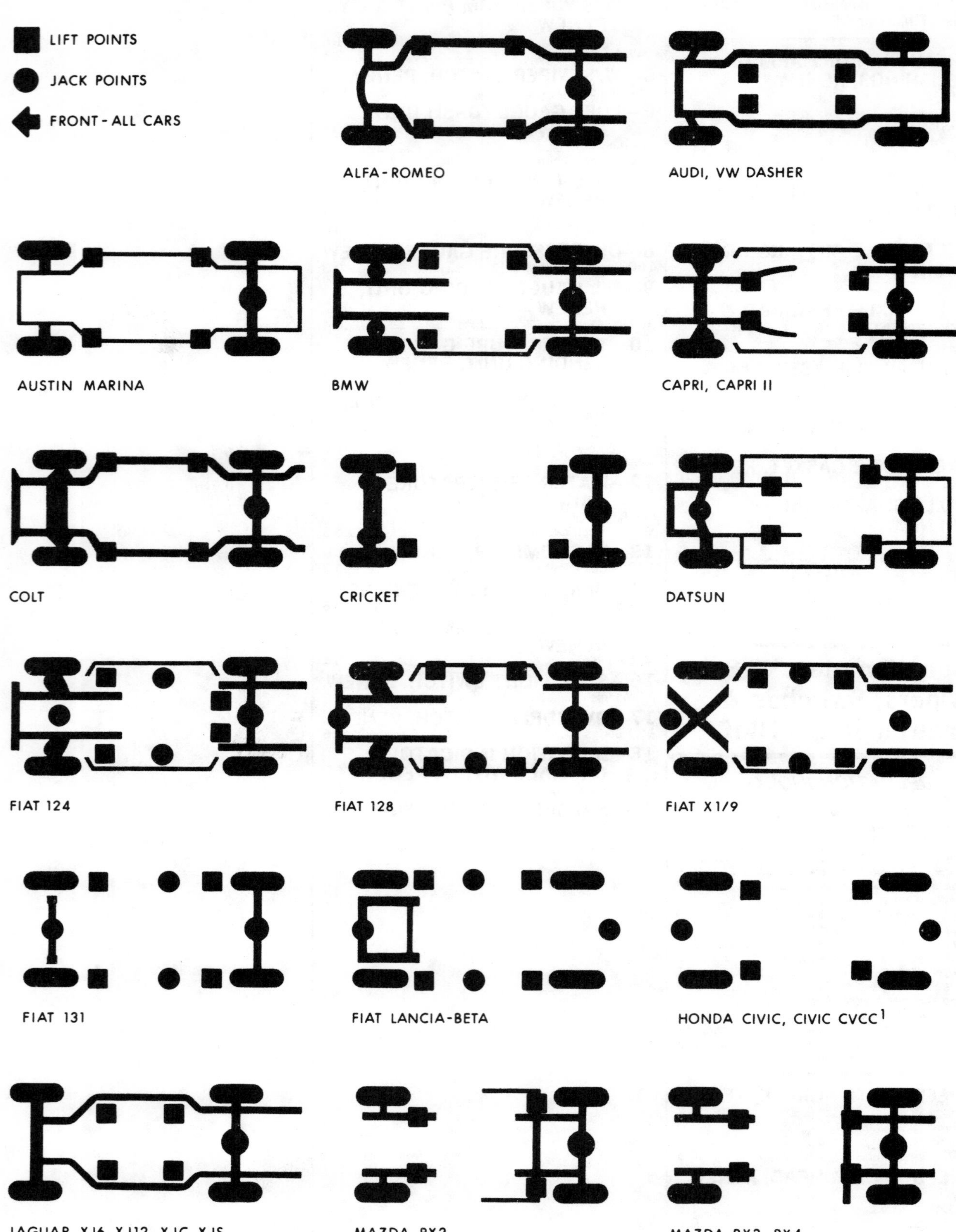

NOTE 1. LIFT PLATFORMS PROVIDED IN FRONT & REAR TO ACCEPT FLOOR JACK.

These diagrams are updated to include most foreign passenger cars currently being imported.

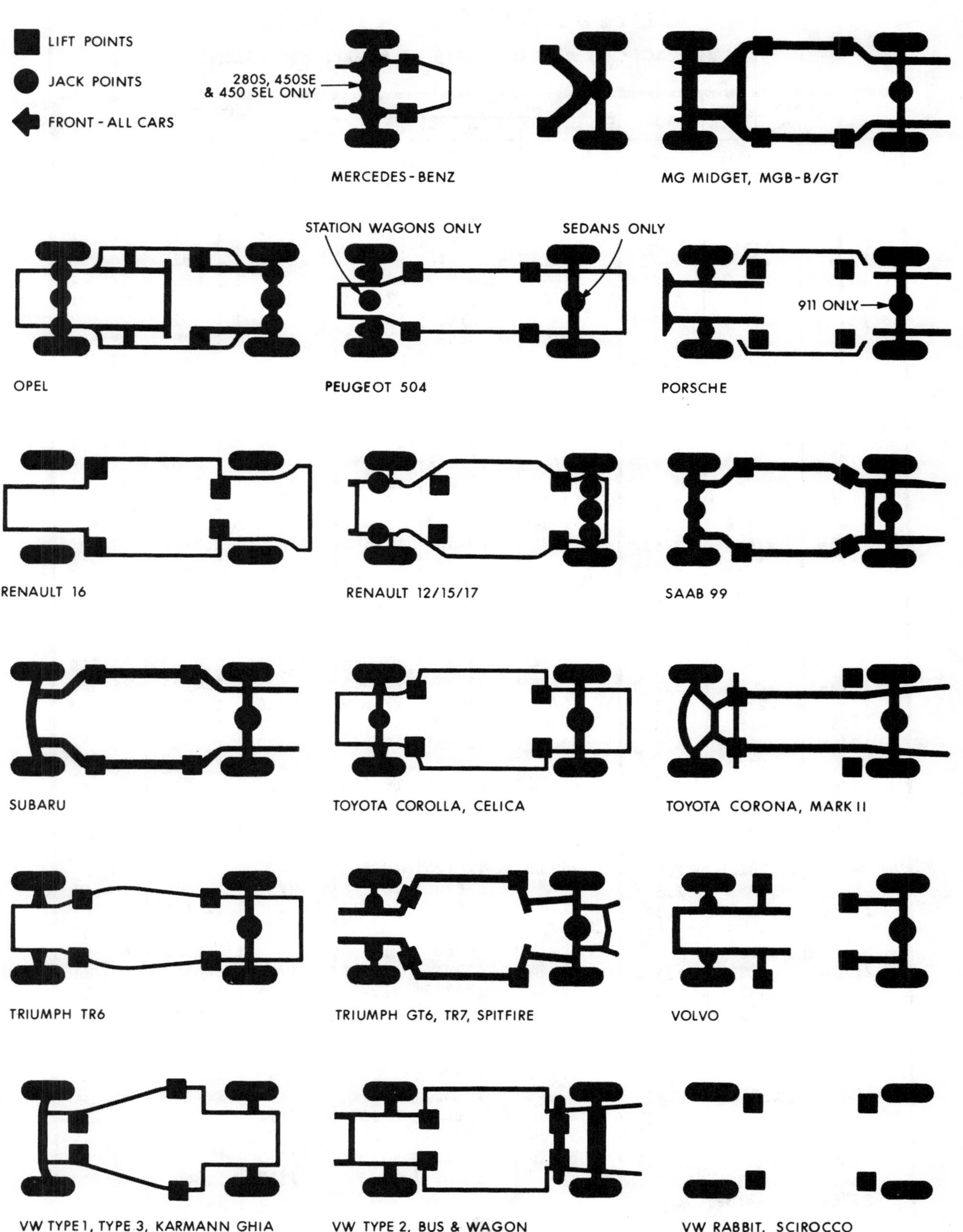

VW DASHER - SAME AS AUDI

CONVERSION TABLE

INCH FRACTIONS AND DECIMALS TO METRIC EQUIVALENTS

INCHES		m m	INCHES		m m	INCHES		m m
Fractions	Decimals		Fractions	Decimals		Fractions	Decimals	
-	.0004	.01	-	.4331	11	31/32	.96875	24.606
-	.004	.10	7/16	.4375	11.113	-	.9843	25
-	.01	.25	29/64	.4531	11.509	1	1.000	25.4
1/64	.0156	.397	15/32	.46875	11.906	-	1.0236	26
-	.0197	.50	-	.4724	12	1 1/32	1.0312	26.194
-	.0295	.75	31/64	.48437	12.303	1 1/16	1.062	26.988
1/32	.03125	.794	-	.492	12.5	-	1.063	27
-	.0394	1	1/2	.500	12.700	1 3/32	1.094	27.781
3/64	.0469	1.191	-	.5118	13	-	1.1024	28
-	.059	1.5	33/64	.5156	13.097	1 1/8	1.125	28.575
1/16	.0625	1.588	17/32	.53125	13.494	-	1.1417	29
5/64	.0781	1.984	35/64	.54687	13.891	1 5/32	1.156	29.369
-	.0787	2	-	.5512	14	-	1.1811	30
3/32	.094	2.381	9/16	.5625	14.288	1 3/16	1.1875	30.163
-	.0984	2.5	-	.571	14.5	1 7/32	1.219	30.956
7/64	.1093	2.776	37/64	.57812	14.684	-	1.2205	31
-	.1181	3	-	.5906	15	1 1/4	1.250	31.750
1/8	.1250	3.175	19/32	.59375	15.081	-	1.2598	32
-	.1378	3.5	39/64	.60937	15.478	1 9/32	1.281	32.544
9/64	.1406	3.572	5/8	.6250	15.875	-	1.2992	33
5/32	.15625	3.969	-	.6299	16	1 5/16	1.312	33.338
-	.1575	4	41/64	.6406	16.272	-	1.3386	34
11/64	.17187	4.366	-	.6496	16.5	1 11/32	1.344	34.131
-	.177	4.5	21/32	.65625	16.669	1 3/8	1.375	34.925
3/16	.1875	4.763	-	.6693	17	-	1.3779	35
-	.1969	5	43/64	.67187	17.066	1 13/32	1.406	35.719
13/64	.2031	5.159	11/16	.6875	17.463	-	1.4173	36
-	.2165	5.5	45/64	.7031	17.859	1 7/16	1.438	36.513
7/32	.21875	5.556	-	.7087	18	-	1.4567	37
15/64	.23437	5.953	23/32	.71875	18.256	1 15/32	1.469	37.306
-	.2362	6	-	.7283	18.5	-	1.4961	38
1/4	.2500	6.350	47/64	.73437	18.653	1 1/2	1.500	38.100
-	.2559	6.5	-	.7480	19	1 17/32	1.531	38.894
17/64	.2656	6.747	3/4	.7500	19.050	-	1.5354	39
-	.2756	7	49/64	.7656	19.447	1 9/16	1.562	39.688
9/32	.28125	7.144	25/32	.78125	19.844	-	1.5748	40
-	.2953	7.5	-	.7874	20	1 19/32	1.594	40.481
19/64	.29687	7.541	51/64	.79687	20.241	-	1.6142	41
5/16	.3125	7.938	13/16	.8125	20.638	1 5/8	1.625	41.275
-	.3150	8	-	.8268	21	-	1.6535	42
21/64	.3281	8.334	53/64	.8281	21.034	1 21/32	1.6562	42.069
-	.335	8.5	27/32	.84375	21.431	1 11/16	1.6875	42.863
11/32	.34375	8.731	55/64	.85937	21.828	-	1.6929	43
-	.3543	9	-	.8662	22	1 23/32	1.719	43.656
23/64	.35937	9.128	7/8	.8750	22.225	-	1.7323	44
-	.374	9.5	57/64	.8906	22.622	1 3/4	1.750	44.450
3/8	.3750	9.525	-	.9055	23	-	1.7717	45
25/64	.3906	9.922	29/32	.90625	23.019	1 25/32	1.781	45.244
-	.3937	10	59/64	.92187	23.416	-	1.8110	46
13/32	.4062	10.319	15/16	.9375	23.813	1 13/16	1.8125	46.038
-	.413	10.5	-	.9449	24	1 27/32	1.844	46.831
27/64	.42187	10.716	61/64	.9531	24.209	-	1.8504	47

CONVERSION TABLE

INCH FRACTIONS AND DECIMALS TO METRIC EQUIVALENTS

INCHES		m m	INCHES		m m	INCHES		m m
Fractions	Decimals		Fractions	Decimals		Fractions	Decimals	
1 7/8	1.875	47.625	-	3.0709	78	-	4.7244	120
-	1.8898	48	-	3.1102	79	4 3/4	4.750	120.650
1 29/32	1.9062	48.419	3 1/8	3.125	79375	4 7/8	4.875	123.825
-	1.9291	49	-	3.1496	80	-	4.9212	125
1 15/16	1.9375	49.213	3 3/16	3.1875	80.963	5	5.000	127
-	1.9685	50	-	3.1890	81	-	5.1181	130
1 31/32	1.969	50.006	-	3.2283	82	5 1/4	5.250	133.350
2	2.000	50.800	3 1/4	3.250	82.550	5 1/2	5.500	139.700
-	2.0079	51	-	3.2677	83	-	5.5118	140
-	2.0472	52	-	3.3071	84	5 3/4	5.750	146.050
2 1/16	2.062	52.388	3 5/16	3.312	84.1377	-	5.9055	150
-	2.0866	53	-	3.3464	85	6	6.000	152.400
2 1/8	2.125	53.975	3 3/8	3.375	85.725	6 1/4	6.250	158.750
-	2.126	54	-	3.3858	86	-	6.2992	160
-	2.165	55	-	3.4252	87	6 1/2	6.500	165.100
2 3/16	2.1875	55.563	3 7/16	3.438	87.313	-	6.6929	170
-	2.2047	56	-	3.4646	88	6 3/4	6.750	171.450
-	2.244	57	3 1/2	3.500	88.900	7	7.000	177.800
2 1/4	2.250	57.150	-	3.5039	89	-	7.0866	180
-	2.2835	58	-	3.5433	90	-	7.4803	190
2 5/16	2.312	58.738	3 9/16	3.562	90.4877	7 1/2	7.500	190.500
-	2.3228	59	-	3.5827	91	-	7.8740	200
-	2.3622	60	-	3.622	92	8	8.000	203.200
2 3/8	2.375	60.325	3 5/8	3.625	92.075	-	8.2677	210
-	2.4016	61	-	3.6614	93	8 1/2	8.500	215.900
2 7/16	2.438	61.913	3 11/16	3.6875	93.663	-	8.6614	220
-	2.4409	62	-	3.7008	94	9	9.000	228.600
-	2.4803	63	-	3.7401	95	-	9.0551	230
2 1/2	2.500	63.500	3 3/4	3.750	95.250	-	9.4488	240
-	2.5197	64	-	3.7795	96	9 1/2	9.500	241.300
-	2.559	65	3 13/16	3.8125	96.838	-	9.8425	250
2 9/16	2.562	65.088	-	3.8189	97	10	10.000	254.000
-	2.5984	66	-	3.8583	98	-	10.2362	260
2 5/8	2.625	66.675	3 7/8	3.875	98.425	-	10.6299	270
-	2.638	67	-	3.8976	99	11	11.000	279.400
-	2.6772	68	-	3.9370	100	-	11.0236	280
2 11/16	2.6875	68.263	3. 15/16	3.9375	100.013	-	11.4173	290
-	2.7165	69	-	3.9764	101	-	11.8110	300
2 3/4	2.750	69.850	4	4.000	101.600	12	12.000	304.800
-	2.7559	70	4 1/16	4.062	103.188	13	13.000	330.200
-	2.7953	71	4 1/8	4.125	104.775	-	13.7795	350
2 13/16	2.8125	71.438	-	4.1338	105	14	14.000	355.600
-	2.8346	72	4 3/16	4.1875	106.363	15	15.000	381
-	2.8740	73	4 1/4	4.250	107.950	-	15.7480	400
2 7/8	2.875	73.025	4 5/16	4.312	109.538	16	16.000	406.400
-	2.9134	74	-	4.3307	110	17	17.000	431.800
2 15/16	2.9375	74.613	4 3/8	4.375	111.125	-	17.7165	450
-	2.9527	75	4 7/16	4.438	112.713	18	18.000	457.200
-	2.9921	76	4 1/2	4.500	114.300	19	19.000	482.600
3	3.000	76.200	-	4.5275	115	-	19.6850	500
-	3.0315	77	4 9/16	4.562	115.888	20	20.000	508
3 1/16	3.062	77.788	4 5/8	4.625	117.475	21	21.000	533.400

NOTES

NOTES

NOTES

NOTES

NOTES

NOTES

Time/Dollar Conversion Table

This conversion table is for your convenience for converting time into dollars to fit local rates per hour. Read across from the time column to the appropriate rate column.

For time or dollar rates not listed, use the combination of columns that total the time or dollar rates.

For dollar rates ending with 50 cents, add the 50 cent column to the appropriate rate column.

	DOLLAR PER HOUR RATES																				
Time	.50	$1.00	$2.00	$3.00	$4.00	$5.00	$6.00	$7.00	$8.00	$9.00	$10.00	$11.00	$12.00	$13.00	$14.00	$15.00	$16.00	$17.00	$18.00	$19.00	$20.00
0.1	.05	.10	.20	.30	.40	.50	.60	.70	.80	.90	1.00	1.10	1.20	1.30	1.40	1.50	1.60	1.70	1.80	1.90	2.00
0.2	.10	.20	.40	.60	.80	1.00	1.20	1.40	1.60	1.80	2.00	2.20	2.40	2.60	2.80	3.00	3.20	3.40	3.60	3.80	4.00
0.3	.15	.30	.60	.90	1.20	1.50	1.80	2.10	2.40	2.70	3.00	3.30	3.60	3.90	4.20	4.50	4.80	5.10	5.40	5.70	6.00
0.4	.20	.40	.80	1.20	1.60	2.00	2.40	2.80	3.20	3.60	4.00	4.40	4.80	5.20	5.60	6.00	6.40	6.80	7.20	7.60	8.00
0.5	.25	.50	1.00	1.50	2.00	2.50	3.00	3.50	4.00	4.50	5.00	5.50	6.00	6.50	7.00	7.50	8.00	8.50	9.00	9.50	10.00
0.6	.30	.60	1.20	1.80	2.40	3.00	3.60	4.20	4.80	5.40	6.00	6.60	7.20	7.80	8.40	9.00	9.60	10.20	10.80	11.40	12.00
0.7	.35	.70	1.40	2.10	2.80	3.50	4.20	4.90	5.60	6.30	7.00	7.70	8.40	9.10	9.80	10.50	11.20	11.90	12.60	13.30	14.00
0.8	.40	.80	1.60	2.40	3.20	4.00	4.80	5.60	6.40	7.20	8.00	8.80	9.60	10.40	11.20	12.00	12.80	13.60	14.40	15.20	16.00
0.9	.45	.90	1.80	2.70	3.60	4.50	5.40	6.30	7.20	8.10	9.00	9.90	10.80	11.70	12.60	13.50	14.40	15.30	16.20	17.10	18.00
1.0	.50	1.00	2.00	3.00	4.00	5.00	6.00	7.00	8.00	9.00	10.00	11.00	12.00	13.00	14.00	15.00	16.00	17.00	18.00	19.00	20.00
1.1	.55	1.10	2.20	3.30	4.40	5.50	6.60	7.70	8.80	9.90	11.00	12.10	13.20	14.30	15.40	16.50	17.60	18.70	19.80	20.90	22.00
1.2	.60	1.20	2.40	3.60	4.80	6.00	7.20	8.40	9.60	10.80	12.00	13.20	14.40	15.60	16.80	18.00	19.20	20.40	21.60	22.80	24.00
1.3	.65	1.30	2.60	3.90	5.20	6.50	7.80	9.10	10.40	11.70	13.00	14.30	15.60	16.90	18.20	19.50	20.80	22.10	23.40	24.70	26.00
1.4	.70	1.40	2.80	4.20	5.60	7.00	8.40	9.80	11.20	12.60	14.00	15.40	16.80	18.20	19.60	21.00	22.40	23.80	25.20	26.60	28.00
1.5	.75	1.50	3.00	4.50	6.00	7.50	9.00	10.50	12.00	13.50	15.00	16.50	18.00	19.50	21.00	22.50	24.00	25.50	27.00	28.50	30.00
1.6	.80	1.60	3.20	4.80	6.40	8.00	9.60	11.20	12.80	14.40	16.00	17.60	19.20	20.80	22.40	24.00	25.60	27.20	28.80	30.40	32.00
1.7	.85	1.70	3.40	5.10	6.80	8.50	10.20	11.90	13.60	15.30	17.00	18.70	20.40	22.10	23.80	25.50	27.20	28.90	30.60	32.30	34.00
1.8	.90	1.80	3.60	5.40	7.20	9.00	10.80	12.60	14.40	16.20	18.00	19.80	21.60	23.40	25.20	27.00	28.80	30.60	32.40	34.20	36.00
1.9	.95	1.90	3.80	5.70	7.60	9.50	11.40	13.30	15.20	17.10	19.00	20.90	22.80	24.70	26.60	28.50	30.40	32.30	34.20	36.10	38.00
2.0	1.00	2.00	4.00	6.00	8.00	10.00	12.00	14.00	16.00	18.00	20.00	22.00	24.00	26.00	28.00	30.00	32.00	34.00	36.00	38.00	40.00
2.1	1.05	2.10	4.20	6.30	8.40	10.50	12.60	14.70	16.80	18.90	21.00	23.10	25.20	27.30	29.40	31.50	33.60	35.70	37.80	39.90	42.00
2.2	1.10	2.20	4.40	6.60	8.80	11.00	13.20	15.40	17.60	19.80	22.00	24.20	26.40	28.60	30.80	33.00	35.20	37.40	39.60	41.80	44.00
2.3	1.15	2.30	4.60	6.90	9.20	11.50	13.80	16.10	18.40	20.70	23.00	25.30	27.60	29.90	32.20	34.50	36.80	39.10	41.40	43.70	46.00
2.4	1.20	2.40	4.80	7.20	9.60	12.00	14.40	16.80	19.20	21.60	24.00	26.40	28.80	31.20	33.60	36.00	38.40	40.80	43.20	45.60	48.00
2.5	1.25	2.50	5.00	7.50	10.00	12.50	15.00	17.50	20.00	22.50	25.00	27.50	30.00	32.50	35.00	37.50	40.00	42.50	45.00	47.50	50.00
2.6	1.30	2.60	5.20	7.80	10.40	13.00	15.60	18.20	20.80	23.40	26.00	28.60	31.20	33.80	36.40	39.00	41.60	44.20	46.80	49.40	52.00
2.7	1.35	2.70	5.40	8.10	10.80	13.50	16.20	18.90	21.60	24.30	27.00	29.70	32.40	35.10	37.80	40.50	43.20	45.90	48.60	51.30	54.00
2.8	1.40	2.80	5.60	8.40	11.20	14.00	16.80	19.60	22.40	25.20	28.00	30.80	33.60	36.40	39.20	42.00	44.80	47.60	50.40	53.20	56.00
2.9	1.45	2.90	5.80	8.70	11.60	14.50	17.40	20.30	23.20	26.10	29.00	31.90	34.80	37.70	40.60	43.50	46.40	49.30	52.20	55.10	58.00
3.0	1.50	3.00	6.00	9.00	12.00	15.00	18.00	21.00	24.00	27.00	30.00	33.00	36.00	39.00	42.00	45.00	48.00	51.00	54.00	57.00	60.00
3.1	1.55	3.10	6.20	9.30	12.40	15.50	18.60	21.70	24.80	27.90	31.00	34.10	37.20	40.30	43.40	46.50	49.60	52.70	55.80	58.90	62.00
3.2	1.60	3.20	6.40	9.60	12.80	16.00	19.20	22.40	25.60	28.80	32.00	35.20	38.40	41.60	44.80	48.00	51.20	54.40	57.60	60.80	64.00
3.3	1.65	3.30	6.60	9.90	13.20	16.50	19.80	23.10	26.40	29.70	33.00	36.30	39.60	42.90	46.20	49.50	52.80	56.10	59.40	62.70	66.00
3.4	1.70	3.40	6.80	10.20	13.60	17.00	20.40	23.80	27.20	30.60	34.00	37.40	40.80	44.20	47.60	51.00	54.40	57.80	61.20	64.60	68.00
3.5	1.75	3.50	7.00	10.50	14.00	17.50	21.00	24.50	28.00	31.50	35.00	38.50	42.00	45.50	49.00	52.50	56.00	59.50	63.00	66.50	70.00
3.6	1.80	3.60	7.20	10.80	14.40	18.00	21.60	25.20	28.80	32.40	36.00	39.60	43.20	46.80	50.40	54.00	57.60	61.20	64.80	68.40	72.00
3.7	1.85	3.70	7.40	11.10	14.80	18.50	22.20	25.90	29.60	33.30	37.00	40.70	44.40	48.10	51.80	55.50	59.20	62.90	66.60	70.30	74.00
3.8	1.90	3.80	7.60	11.40	15.20	19.00	22.80	26.60	30.40	34.20	38.00	41.80	45.60	49.40	53.20	57.00	60.80	64.60	68.40	72.20	76.00
3.9	1.95	3.90	7.80	11.70	15.60	19.50	23.40	27.30	31.20	35.10	39.00	42.90	46.80	50.70	54.60	58.50	62.40	66.30	70.20	74.10	78.00
4.0	2.00	4.00	8.00	12.00	16.00	20.00	24.00	28.00	32.00	36.00	40.00	44.00	48.00	52.00	56.00	60.00	64.00	68.00	72.00	76.00	80.00
4.1	2.05	4.10	8.20	12.30	16.40	20.50	24.60	28.70	32.80	36.90	41.00	45.10	49.20	53.30	57.40	61.50	65.60	69.70	73.80	77.90	82.00
4.2	2.10	4.20	8.40	12.60	16.80	21.00	25.20	29.40	33.60	37.80	42.00	46.20	50.40	54.60	58.80	63.00	67.20	71.40	75.60	79.80	84.00
4.3	2.15	4.30	8.60	12.90	17.20	21.50	25.80	30.10	34.40	38.70	43.00	47.30	51.60	55.90	60.20	64.50	68.80	73.10	77.40	81.70	86.00
4.4	2.20	4.40	8.80	13.20	17.60	22.00	26.40	30.80	35.20	39.60	44.00	48.40	52.80	57.20	61.60	66.00	70.40	74.80	79.20	83.60	88.00
4.5	2.25	4.50	9.00	13.50	18.00	22.50	27.00	31.50	36.00	40.50	45.00	49.50	54.00	58.50	63.00	67.50	72.00	76.50	81.00	85.50	90.00
4.6	2.30	4.60	9.20	13.80	18.40	23.00	27.60	32.20	36.80	41.40	46.00	50.60	55.20	59.80	64.40	69.00	73.60	78.20	82.80	87.40	92.00
4.7	2.35	4.70	9.40	14.10	18.80	23.50	28.20	32.90	37.60	42.30	47.00	51.70	56.40	61.10	65.80	70.50	75.20	79.90	84.60	89.30	94.00
4.8	2.40	4.80	9.60	14.40	19.20	24.00	28.80	33.60	38.40	43.20	48.00	52.80	57.60	62.40	67.20	72.00	76.80	81.60	86.40	91.20	96.00
4.9	2.45	4.90	9.80	14.70	19.60	24.50	29.40	34.30	39.20	44.10	49.00	53.90	58.80	63.70	68.60	73.50	78.40	83.30	88.20	93.10	98.00
5.0	2.50	5.00	10.00	15.00	20.00	25.00	30.00	35.00	40.00	45.00	50.00	55.00	60.00	65.00	70.00	75.00	80.00	85.00	90.00	95.00	100.00
5.1	2.55	5.10	10.20	15.30	20.40	25.50	30.60	35.70	40.80	45.90	51.00	56.10	61.20	66.30	71.40	76.50	81.60	86.70	91.80	96.90	102.00
5.2	2.60	5.20	10.40	15.60	20.80	26.00	31.20	36.40	41.60	46.80	52.00	57.20	62.40	67.60	72.80	78.00	83.20	88.40	93.60	98.80	104.00
5.3	2.65	5.30	10.60	15.90	21.20	26.50	31.80	37.10	42.40	47.70	53.00	58.30	63.60	68.90	74.20	79.50	84.80	90.10	95.40	100.70	106.00
5.4	2.70	5.40	10.80	16.20	21.60	27.00	32.40	37.80	43.20	48.60	54.00	59.40	64.80	70.20	75.60	81.00	86.40	91.80	97.20	102.60	108.00
5.5	2.75	5.50	11.00	16.50	22.00	27.50	33.00	38.50	44.00	49.50	55.00	60.50	66.00	71.50	77.00	82.50	88.00	93.50	99.00	104.50	110.00
5.6	2.80	5.60	11.20	16.80	22.40	28.00	33.60	39.20	44.80	50.40	56.00	61.60	67.20	72.80	78.40	84.00	89.60	95.20	100.80	106.40	112.00
5.7	2.85	5.70	11.40	17.10	22.80	28.50	34.20	39.90	45.60	51.30	57.00	62.70	68.40	74.10	79.80	85.50	91.20	96.90	102.60	108.30	114.00
5.8	2.90	5.80	11.60	17.40	23.20	29.00	34.80	40.60	46.40	52.20	58.00	63.80	69.60	75.40	81.20	87.00	92.80	98.60	104.40	110.20	116.00
5.9	2.95	5.90	11.80	17.70	23.60	29.50	35.40	41.30	47.20	53.10	59.00	64.90	70.80	76.70	82.60	88.50	94.40	100.30	106.20	112.10	118.00